A COMPANION TO THE ARCHAEOLOGY OF THE ANCIENT NEAR EAST

Volume II

BLACKWELL COMPANIONS TO THE ANCIENT WORLD

This series provides sophisticated and authoritative overviews of periods of ancient history, genres of classical literature, and the most important themes in ancient culture. Each volume comprises between 25 and 40 concise essays written by individual scholars within their area of specialization. The essays are written in a clear, provocative, and lively manner, designed for an international audience of scholars, students, and general readers.

ANCIENT HISTORY

Published

A Companion to the Roman Army
Edited by Paul Erdkamp

A Companion to the Roman Republic
Edited by Nathan Rosenstein and Robert Morstein-Marx

A Companion to the Roman Empire
Edited by David S. Potter

A Companion to the Classical Greek World
Edited by Konrad H. Kinzl

A Companion to the Ancient Near East
Edited by Daniel C. Snell

A Companion to the Hellenistic World
Edited by Andrew Erskine

A Companion to Late Antiquity
Edited by Philip Rousseau

A Companion to Ancient History
Edited by Andrew Erskine

A Companion to Archaic Greece
Edited by Kurt A. Raaflaub and Hans van Wees

A Companion to Julius Caesar
Edited by Miriam Griffin

A Companion to Byzantium
Edited by Liz James

A Companion to Ancient Egypt
Edited by Alan B. Lloyd

A Companion to Ancient Macedonia
Edited by Joseph Roisman and Ian Worthington

A Companion to the Punic Wars
Edited by Dexter Hoyos

LITERATURE AND CULTURE

Published

A Companion to Classical Receptions
Edited by Lorna Hardwick and Christopher Stray

A Companion to Greek and Roman Historiography
Edited by John Marincola

A Companion to Catullus
Edited by Marilyn B. Skinner

A Companion to Roman Religion
Edited by Jörg Rüpke

A Companion to Greek Religion
Edited by Daniel Ogden

A Companion to the Classical Tradition
Edited by Craig W. Kallendorf

A Companion to Roman Rhetoric
Edited by William Dominik and Jon Hall

A Companion to Greek Rhetoric
Edited by Ian Worthington

A Companion to Ancient Epic
Edited by John Miles Foley

A Companion to Greek Tragedy
Edited by Justina Gregory

A Companion to Latin Literature
Edited by Stephen Harrison

A Companion to Greek and Roman Political Thought
Edited by Ryan K. Balot

A Companion to Ovid
Edited by Peter E. Knox

A Companion to the Ancient Greek Language
Edited by Egbert Bakker

A Companion to Hellenistic Literature
Edited by Martine Cuypers and James J. Clauss

A Companion to Vergil's *Aeneid* and its Tradition
Edited by Joseph Farrell and Michael C. J. Putnam

A Companion to Horace
Edited by Gregson Davis

A Companion to Families in the Greek and Roman Worlds
Edited by Beryl Rawson

A Companion to Greek Mythology
Edited by Ken Dowden and Niall Livingstone

A Companion to the Latin Language
Edited by James Clackson

A Companion to Tacitus
Edited by Victoria Emma Pagán

A Companion to Women in the Ancient World
Edited by Sharon L. James and Sheila Dillon

A Companion to Sophocles
Edited by Kirk Ormand

A Companion to the Archaeology of the Ancient Near East
Edited by D.T. Potts

A COMPANION TO THE ARCHAEOLOGY OF THE ANCIENT NEAR EAST

Volume II

Edited by

D.T. Potts

A John Wiley & Sons, Ltd., Publication

This edition first published 2012
© 2012 Blackwell Publishing Ltd.

Blackwell Publishing was acquired by John Wiley & Sons in February 2007. Blackwell's publishing program has been merged with Wiley's global Scientific, Technical, and Medical business to form Wiley-Blackwell.

Registered Office
John Wiley & Sons Ltd, The Atrium, Southern Gate, Chichester, West Sussex, PO19 8SQ, UK

Editorial Offices
350 Main Street, Malden, MA 02148-5020, USA
9600 Garsington Road, Oxford, OX4 2DQ, UK
The Atrium, Southern Gate, Chichester, West Sussex, PO19 8SQ, UK

For details of our global editorial offices, for customer services, and for information about how to apply for permission to reuse the copyright material in this book please see our website at www.wiley.com/wiley-blackwell.

The right of D.T. Potts to be identified as the author of the editorial material in this work has been asserted in accordance with the UK Copyright, Designs and Patents Act 1988.

All rights reserved. No part of this publication may be reproduced, stored in a retrieval system, or transmitted, in any form or by any means, electronic, mechanical, photocopying, recording or otherwise, except as permitted by the UK Copyright, Designs and Patents Act 1988, without the prior permission of the publisher.

Wiley also publishes its books in a variety of electronic formats. Some content that appears in print may not be available in electronic books.

Designations used by companies to distinguish their products are often claimed as trademarks. All brand names and product names used in this book are trade names, service marks, trademarks or registered trademarks of their respective owners. The publisher is not associated with any product or vendor mentioned in this book. This publication is designed to provide accurate and authoritative information in regard to the subject matter covered. It is sold on the understanding that the publisher is not engaged in rendering professional services. If professional advice or other expert assistance is required, the services of a competent professional should be sought.

Library of Congress Cataloging-in-Publication Data

A companion to the archaeology of the ancient Near East / edited by D.T. Potts.
    p. cm. – (Blackwell companions to the ancient world)
  Includes bibliographical references and index.
  ISBN 978-1-4051-8988-0 (hardcover : alk. paper) 1. Archaeology–Middle East. 2. Middle East–Antiquities. 3. Middle East–Civilization–To 622. I. Potts, Daniel T.
  DS56.C585 2012
  939'.4–dc23
                            2011034988

A catalogue record for this book is available from the British Library.

Set in 10.5/13 pt Galliard by Toppan Best-set Premedia Limited
Printed and bound in Singapore by Markono Print Media Pte Ltd

1   2012

Contents

VOLUME I

List of Illustrations	x
List of Tables	xvii
Notes on Contributors	xviii
Preface	xxviii
Maps	xxxii

I   The Framework — 1

1. Introduction to Geography, Climate, Topography, and Hydrology — 3
   T.J. Wilkinson

2. Antiquarianism, Copying, Collecting — 27
   Mark B. Garrison

3. Early Excavations (pre-1914) — 48
   Nicole Chevalier

4. The Foundations of Antiquities Departments — 70
   Peter Magee

5. The Political Dimension of Archaeological Practices — 87
   Reinhard Bernbeck

6	The Antiquities Trade and the Destruction of Ancient Near Eastern Cultures *Oscar White Muscarella*	106

II Late Pleistocene and Early Holocene Hunters and Gatherers — 125

7	The Levant *Alan H. Simmons*	127
8	Anatolia *Klaus Schmidt*	144

III Developments in Farming, Animal Husbandry, and Technology — 161

9	The Beginnings of Cereal Cultivation and Domestication in Southwest Asia *George Willcox*	163
10	Fruit-Growing *Margareta Tengberg*	181
11	Animals in the Ancient World *Benjamin S. Arbuckle*	201
12	Fish and Fishing *D.T. Potts*	220
13	Lithic Industries During the Holocene Period *Steven A. Rosen*	236
14	Irrigation *Ariel M. Bagg*	261
15	Ceramic Production *Cameron A. Petrie*	279
16	Metallurgy *Lloyd Weeks*	295
17	Glass *Wendy Reade*	317
18	Textiles *Irene Good*	336

	19	Watercraft R.A. Carter	347

IV Varieties of Early Village and Town Life   373

	20	The Northern Levant Karin Bartl	375
	21	The Southern Levant E.B. Banning	396
	22	Northern Mesopotamia Stuart Campbell	415
	23	The Late Epipaleolithic, Neolithic, and Chalcolithic of the Anatolian Plateau, 13,000–4000 BC Douglas Baird	431
	24	Southern Mesopotamia Joan Oates	466
	25	The Arabian Peninsula Philipp Drechsler	485
	26	The Iranian Plateau Barbara Helwing	501
	27	Southwestern Iran Abbas Moghaddam	512

V Bronze Age Cities of the Plains and the Highlands   531

	28	Southern Mesopotamia Jason Ur	533
	29	Northern Mesopotamia Timothy Matney	556
	30	The Anatolian Plateau Christoph Bachhuber	575
	31	Iran Christopher P. Thornton	596
	32	The Northern Levant Hermann Genz	607
	33	The Southern Levant Timothy P. Harrison	629

VOLUME II

List of Illustrations x

List of Tables xii

Maps xiii

VI The Archaeology of Empire — 647

34 The Akkadian Period: Empire, Environment, and Imagination — 649
    Augusta McMahon

35 The Caucasus and the Near East — 668
    Adam T. Smith

36 Central Asia, the Steppe, and the Near East, 2500–1500 BC — 687
    Michael D. Frachetti and Lynne M. Rouse

37 The Ur III, Old Babylonian, and Kassite Empires — 706
    Marlies Heinz

38 The Hittite Empire — 722
    Trevor Bryce

39 Elam: Iran's First Empire — 740
    Javier Álvarez-Mon

40 India's Relations with Western Empires, 2300–600 BC — 758
    Gregory L. Possehl

41 Levantine Kingdoms of the Late Bronze Age — 770
    Peter Pfälzner

42 Neo-Hittite and Phrygian Kingdoms of North Syria and Anatolia — 797
    Ann C. Gunter

43 North Arabian Kingdoms — 816
    Arnulf Hausleiter

44 Egypt and the Near East — 833
    Thomas Hikade

45 The Assyrian Heartland — 851
    Friedhelm Pedde

46 The Assyrians Abroad — 867
    Bradley J. Parker

47	The Urartian Empire *Alina Ayvazian*	877
48	Iron Age Western Anatolia: The Lydian Empire and Dynastic Lycia *Christopher H. Roosevelt*	896
49	The Neo-Babylonian Empire *Heather D. Baker*	914
50	The Achaemenid Heartland: An Archaeological-Historical Perspective *Wouter F.M. Henkelman*	931
51	The Achaemenid Provinces in Archaeological Perspective *Lori Khatchadourian*	963
52	The Seleucid Kingdom *Lise Hannestad*	984
53	The Arsacid (Parthian) Empire *Stefan R. Hauser*	1001
54	Roman Rule in the Near East *Bettina Fischer-Genz*	1021
55	The Red Sea and Indian Ocean in the Age of the Great Empires *Steven E. Sidebotham*	1041
56	Byzantium in Asia Minor and the Levant *Basema Hamarneh*	1060
57	The Sasanian Empire: An Archaeological Survey, c.220–AD 640 *Ali Mousavi and Touraj Daryaee*	1076
58	Christianity in the Late Antique Near East *Cornelia Horn and Erica C.D. Hunter*	1095

Abbreviations　1113
References　1117
Index　1380

Illustrations

Map 1	Selection of sites and modern placenames mentioned in this volume (western region).	xiii
Map 2	Selection of sites and modern placenames mentioned in this volume (eastern region).	xiv
Map 3	Detail of sites located in the west.	xv
Map 4	Detail of sites located in the east.	xvi
35.1	Physical and political map of the Caucasus showing the major geographical provinces.	670
35.2	Map of sites discussed in the text.	672
36.1	The Bronze Age world of Eurasia and Central Asia in relation to contemporary culture zones.	688
36.2	Sites and regions of Eurasia, Central Asia, and the Near East mentioned in the text.	691
36.3	A gold bowl depicting bull imagery from the Tepe Fullol (Afghanistan) treasure, dating to the Bronze Age in Bactria (courtesy of the Kabul Museum).	694
36.4	Distribution of archaeological sites with published BMAC objects.	700
40.1	Map showing the distribution of the main settlements of the Indus or Harappan civilization.	759
40.2	Coastal settlement during the Early Harappan (A) and Mature Harappan (B) phases.	760

40.3	Representations of Harappan boats.	761
40.4	Some foreign objects in Mesopotamia and the Harappan world.	764
40.5	Harappan seals and seal impressions found in Mesopotamia and at Susa.	765
41.1	Letter from King Rib-Addu of Byblos to the Pharaoh in the Amarna archive.	773
41.2	Map of the historical geography of the Northern Levant with major kingdoms and their capital cities.	775
41.3	Plan of the royal palace at Qatna.	779
41.4	Plan of the royal palace at Ugarit.	785
41.5	Plan of the royal palace of Alalakh, Level IV.	786
41.6	The main chamber of the Royal Hypogeum of Qatna.	788
41.7	Ancestor statues from the Royal Hypogeum of Qatna.	789
41.8	Amber lion's head from the Royal Hypogeum of Qatna.	794
54.1	View of the colonnaded street in Apamea (mod. Qalat-Mudiq, Syria).	1025
54.2	View of the Roman bath, the Bacchus temple, and the Jupiter temple in Heliopolis (mod. Baalbek, Lebanon).	1032

Tables

34.1	Akkadian kings according to the Middle Chronology	650
35.1	Chronological chart of the Caucasus and the northern Near East	671
36.1	Gross comparative chronology of Central Asia and the steppe zone	693
42.1	Comparative chronology of the Iron Age in northern Syria and southeastern Anatolia	805
42.2	Gordion's Iron Age historical and stratigraphic sequence	810
58.1	Synchronic chart of Churches V and XI (al-Hira)	1106

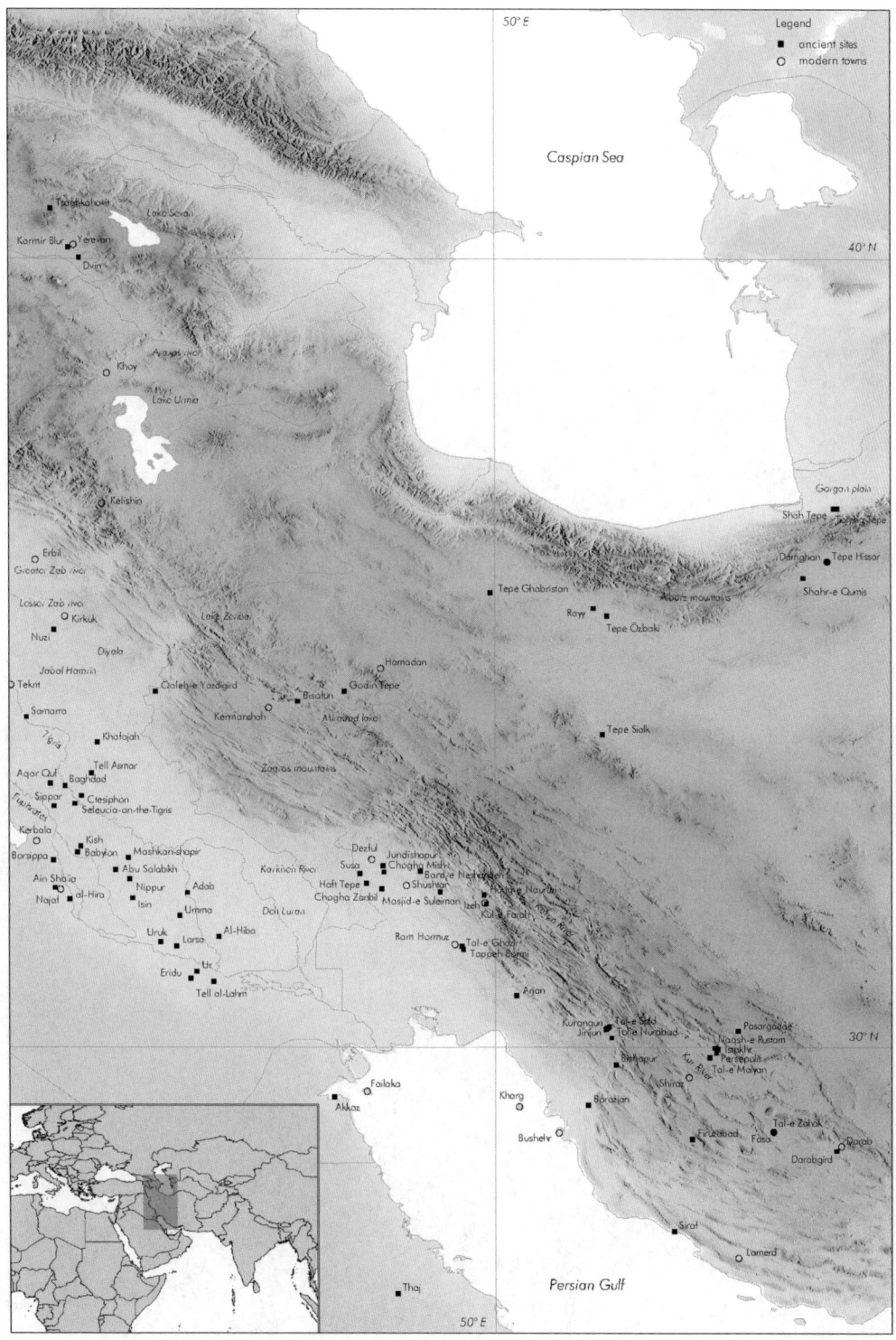

Map 1 Selection of sites and modern placenames mentioned in this volume (western region).

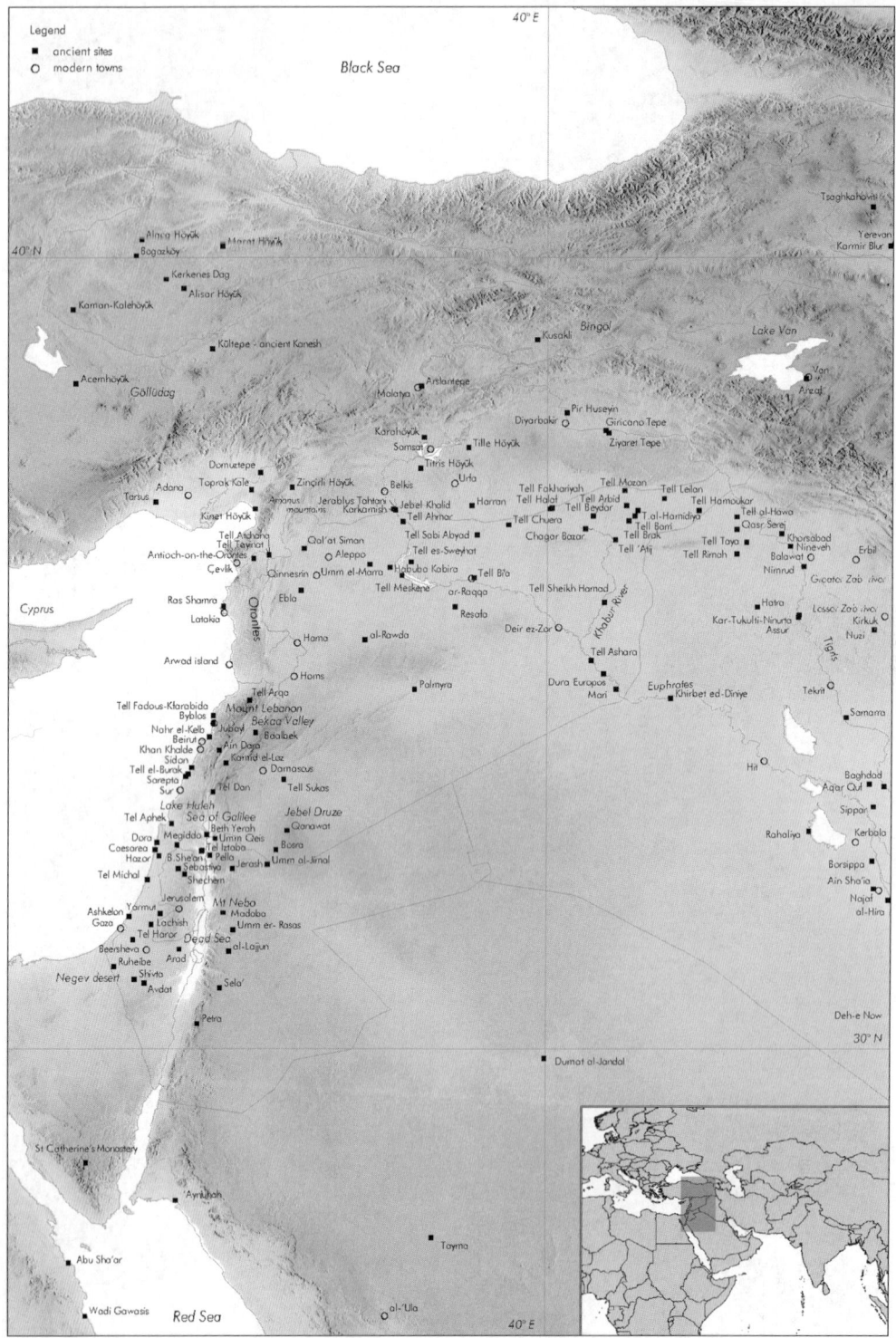

Map 2 Selection of sites and modern placenames mentioned in this volume (eastern region).

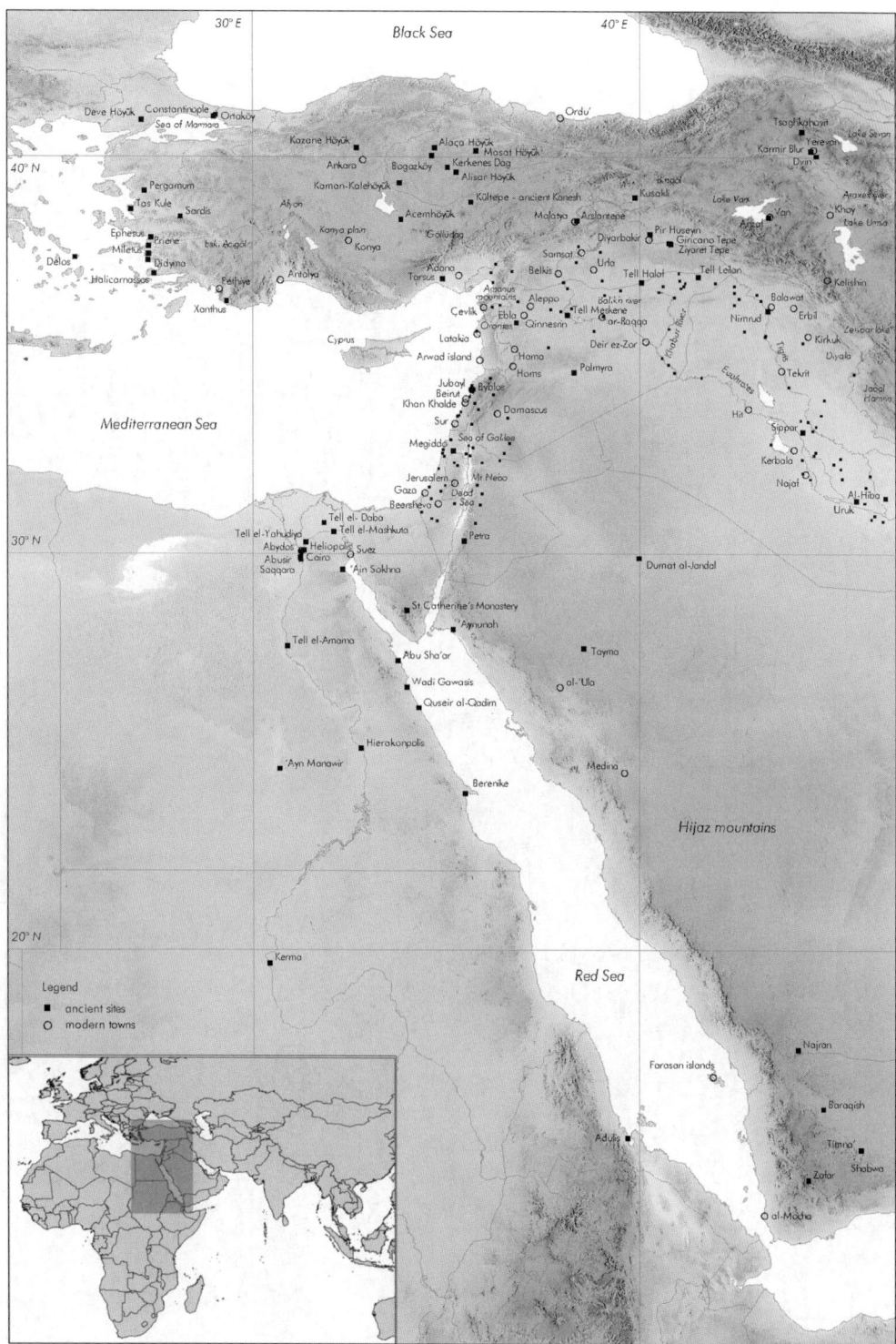

Map 3 Detail of sites located in the west.

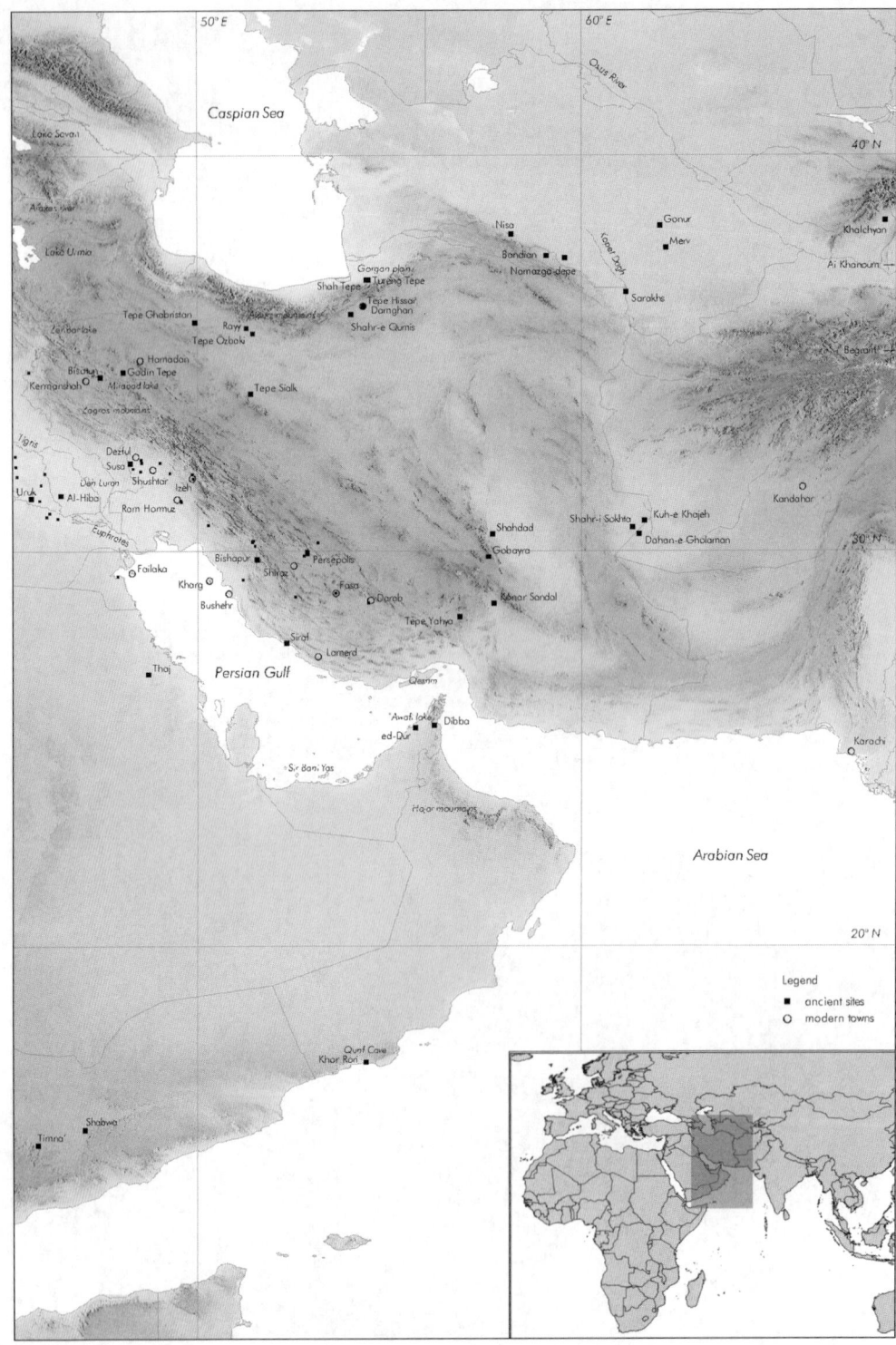

Map 4 Detail of sites located in the east.

PART VI

The Archaeology of Empire

CHAPTER THIRTY-FOUR

The Akkadian Period: Empire, Environment, and Imagination

Augusta McMahon

1 Introduction

The Akkadian period saw a new, unified political structure in southern Mesopotamia, military expansion in all directions, and a dynasty of kings who have proved fascinating to both ancient Mesopotamians and modern scholars. Akkadian artworks are elegant and complicated, with strong ideological statements, and these too cast a spell in past and present. But the dynasty was short-lived and the archaeological record is sparse. However, the Akkadian period provides some of the most vital research questions in Mesopotamian archaeology: What should be considered an empire in this region? How should we use contemporary texts and later literary traditions? When archaeological evidence and texts disagree, which should have primacy? Does political collapse mean social collapse? Can climate change destroy a civilization?

2 Akkadian Political Activities

After the overlapping kings of the late Early Dynastic period (c.2900–2334 BC), the relative clarity of the Akkadian Dynasty and events of their rule provide a distinct contrast. The list of kings and relationships is straightforward (Table 34.1), although the positions of Rimush and Manishtushu are reversed in some texts (Steinkeller 2003) and recorded reign lengths vary. The accumulation of

---

A Companion to the Archaeology of the Ancient Near East, First Edition.
Edited by D.T. Potts.
© 2012 Blackwell Publishing Ltd. Published 2012 by Blackwell Publishing Ltd.

Table 34.1 Akkadian kings according to the Middle Chronology

Sargon	2334–2279 BC
Rimush	2278–2270 BC
Manishtushu	2269–2255 BC
Naram-Sin	2254–2218 BC
Shar-kali-sharri	2217–2193 BC
Igigi	
Nanium	4 kings, 2192–2190 BC
Imi	
Elul-dan	
Dudu	2189–2169 BC
Shu-turul	2168–2154 BC

power and territory from Sargon through Naram-Sin was a gradual process and, although their political control decayed rapidly thereafter, the later Akkadian kings remained among the stronger rulers in the region.

Sargon is traditionally hailed as an innovator, rising from an obscure background to control Kish, then northern Babylonia, the Middle Euphrates, western Iran, and finally the known world from the Upper (Mediterranean) to the Lower (Persian Gulf) Sea. However, his overlap with, and possible "borrowing" from, Lugalzagesi of Uruk, a contemporary ruler of similar strength and scope, is an ongoing issue. If we define Akkadian rulers by their ambition to unify and control the southern plains, then Lugalzagesi (c.2340–2316 BC) might be called the first Akkadian king. Alternatively, Sargon, whose actual hegemony was of limited extent, might be considered the last Early Dynastic ruler.

One of the most noted innovations of the Akkadian kings was the change of official written language from Sumerian to Akkadian. During the late Early Dynastic period, bilingualism and mixed populations were the norm (Cooper 1973) but private and official texts were written in Sumerian. An official language shift was a clever ideological manoeuver that should have interpenetrated society, since even the illiterate would have been affected through records of their labor, taxation, and legal activities. There is even a typical Akkadian tablet shape, with deep line markings and elegant, easily read script that echoes stone reliefs (see below) in the spaces between the signs. However, the persistence of Sumerian in official and private archives (Foster 1982b; Westenholz 1999: 50) reflects significant resistance or indifference to this change. Taxation reached a new level and centralized focus under the Akkadian kings. And standardization of weights and measures, year date formulae based on royal events, and new accounting systems reinforced national ideology through repeated communal practice. However, most of these innovations were not introduced or did not become widespread until the reign of Naram-Sin.

A more dramatic change was the construction of a new capital at Agade. Although not precisely located, it was probably on or near the Tigris in northern Babylonia (Wall-Romana 1990), in contrast to the most powerful, earlier city-states that were associated with the Euphrates river. A new capital city would have symbolized the new political structure and altered the logistics of overland and water transport routes as well as the orientation of mental maps. Finally, as well as an expanded range of heroic epithets, control over increased territory was emphasized in later Akkadian kings' titles, most notably in the new claim to rule over the "four quarters" from the time of Naram-Sin. The self-conferral of divine status by Naram-Sin also represents a dramatic break in the Mesopotamian conception of royalty, although ultimately one that was short-lived.

However, other Akkadian political acts seem to have been designed to have minimal impact and to validate Early Dynastic/Sumerian religious or cultural values. Many city-state leaders were retained as local governors (e.g., Meskigal of Adab under Sargon). Both Sargon and Naram-Sin installed their daughters as priestesses in the temple of the moon god at Ur, and all kings gave offerings in the temples of Sumer, especially Enlil's Ekur at Nippur (rebuilt under Naram-Sin and Shar-kali-sharri).

3 Akkadian Kings: The Legacy

Akkadian rule over Mesopotamia resonates through past and present, the spotlight shining most clearly on Sargon and Naram-Sin, who became the ideal models for Mesopotamian kings (Cooper 1993; Liverani 1993c), beginning in the succeeding Ur III Dynasty. Two Old Assyrian kings of the early 2nd millennium BC revived the names of Sargon and Naram-Sin (the latter also used by a king of Eshnunna); and the Neo-Assyrian king Sargon II chose the name of the first Akkadian ruler to shore up his shaky claim to power. Myths of the Akkadian kings formed parts of royal libraries as far away in place and time as Amarna-period Egypt, the Hittite capital of Boğazköy, and Neo-Assyrian Nineveh.

Sargon has a generally positive reception; he is glorified in texts as the first to unify the independent city-states of southern Mesopotamia and a Moses-like birth story was later ascribed to him. Unusually for a society that embraced hereditary wealth and status, his obscure origins were celebrated. By contrast, the response to his grandson Naram-Sin is ambivalent. He was a powerful, heroic warrior who controlled the known world, but his claim to divinity incited a mixed reaction in later scribal tradition, which invests this behavior with both enviable courage and dangerous arrogance. Statues of Sargon, Manishtushu, and Naram-Sin were placed in temples in southern Mesopotamia and provided with offerings in the Ur III and Old Babylonian periods (Westenholz 1997; Hirsch 1963) and a Neo-Babylonian forger was familiar enough with Manishtushu to create the "autobiographical" Cruciform Monument and attribute it to him (Gelb 1949; Longman 1991).

Akkadian objects, as well as texts and royal identities, had extended biographies. The Naram-Sin Victory Stele, carved c.2150 BC, was still visible in Sippar almost 1,000 years later, until it was taken to Susa when southern Mesopotamia was raided by the Elamites c.1158 BC (Ch. I.2). This is the most famous instance of monument capture, but the Elamite booty included other valued and displayed Akkadian reliefs and statues (Amiet 1976).

4 Texts and Context

Mesopotamian texts describing the actions of the Akkadian kings fall into three groups: contemporary inscriptions on artworks and votive objects, later inscription copies, and later legends, including pseudo-historical records such as the Sumerian King List. These have varying degrees of reliability according to context and audience, but the first two tend to be considered valid, though biased, sources (Tinney 1995). The copies are most commonly texts from the Old Babylonian period purporting to collect inscriptions from dedicatory statues. While we must be skeptical, their stylistic similarities to genuine Akkadian inscriptions and their occasional descriptions of the statues themselves are encouraging (see Buccellati 1993 for a reconstruction of a Rimush statue and base).

Sargon's texts focus on his military activities in the southern plains, in particular against Lugalzagesi of Uruk. Sargon was also the first to claim that the ships of Magan (Oman), Meluhha (Indus Valley), and Dilmun (Bahrain) moored at Agade, hinting that Akkadian political expansion was economically motivated. The inscriptions of Rimush follow the same pattern, recording cities destroyed, mainly in Sumer and Elam (southwestern Iran), with the added details of numbers of captives and dead and weights of booty. Manishtushu's inscriptions add kings and cities further south in the Persian Gulf; but notably, the enumeration of enemies killed and captured abruptly ceased. The apparent absence of battles within the south suggests that his control there may have consolidated, making the implied threat in body counts no longer necessary. The Manishtushu Obelisk records a large land-sale in northern Babylonia that reflects Akkadian reorganization of land ownership, creation of royal estates, and the new practice of giving land as gifts to government and military officials. Although the land was bought and not appropriated, the sale might have been coercive (Westenholz 1999: 44; Van de Mieroop 2007: 66). Government archives from Girsu, Umma, and elsewhere confirm the royal allotment of land to officials (Foster 1982a). Short inscriptions of the first three Akkadian kings appear on stone vessels and maceheads dedicated in the temples of Nippur, Sippar, and Ur, in particular. These kings are identified mainly as "king of the world" (Sumerian LUGAL.KIŠ, in which "Kish" stands for Akkadian *kiššatu*, or "totality").

Descriptions of Naram-Sin's military activities cover a wider geographical area, comprising the Khabur plains (ancient Subartu), Upper Euphrates, Amanus mountains, southeastern Anatolia, and Oman. But the "Great Revolt" of two coalitions of southern city-states meant that Naram-Sin had to reconquer areas supposedly subdued by earlier kings. His titles reflect the expanded map of Akkadian territory, with the innovation of the "king of the four quarters" (LUGAL *kibratim arba'im*) and an emphasis on his going where no king had previously gone (Frayne 1993; Westenholz 1999). His inscriptions also describe temple construction and there are further vases and mace-heads with dedicatory texts. Thereafter, a retraction of territory is visible in the texts of Shar-kali-sharri; he fought Amorites at Mount Bashar (possibly Jebel Bishri) and Elamites and Gutians along his eastern border, but had already lost lands in all directions. His titulary also contracted: he retained the epithet "mighty" (Akkadian *danum*), but was merely king of Agade, not of the four quarters or the totality.

Although many texts were written during the reigns of these kings, it is impossible to verify their claims; for instance, Sargon's destruction of city walls at Uruk, Ur, Umma, and elsewhere is not confirmed by archaeological evidence. The acquisition of materials from Oman (diorite or, more correctly, olivine gabbro) and the Indus valley (carnelian) is supported by archaeological finds, but these may have arrived through trade, booty, or gifting. Destructions at the Syrian cities of Ebla and Mari may be equally attributed to Sargon or Naram-Sin; our temporal control is not fine-grained enough to separate their equal claims.

Later literary texts reveal more about the subsequent millennia and the reception, "social memory," and exploitation of the Akkadian kings than they do about their contemporary impact. These legends compress, select, and transfer events; even texts of the same date are at variance (Tinney 1995). As Westenholz (1999) argued, attempts to extract a "historical kernel" obscure the more important fact that the writers *believed* in the legends. Later texts venerate Sargon, describing his birth, abandonment, and rescue, and his attractiveness to the goddess Ishtar. In the *King of Battle* legend, he assisted traders in Anatolia, more relevant for the Old Assyrian than the Akkadian period. But later texts both venerated and deplored the actions of Naram-Sin: the tales of his favor by Ishtar, suppression of internal rebellion, and foreign conquests (the *Great Revolt*) celebrate his success, while the Ur III and later *Curse of Agade* and *Cuthean Legend of Naram-Sin* blame him for political and religious crisis, as a warning to later kings.

Aside from royal texts describing kings' actions, official archives detail the management of agricultural and pastoral land, labor, and products (Foster 1982a, 1993; Maiocchi 2009). In these archives, the same officials are often responsible for supplying the local governor's palace and city temples; and the detailed, single-event and monthly documentation of raw materials, equipment, processed products, and individuals' rights and obligations leaves no doubt that the bloated bureaucracy of the Ur III period (2100–2000 BC) inherited some systems from Akkadian scribes. Craft production and industry are less well documented, although some administration of these is suggested by "ration" lists and records of commodities and manufactured goods (Foster 1982b, 1993). Non-royal archives indicate a thriving private economy in land sales and trade activities (Foster 1982b).

5   Architecture and Ceramics

Aside from artworks without context and grave goods, southern Mesopotamian archaeological evidence from the Akkadian period is meager. However, there are excavated Akkadian houses at Tell Asmar (Delougaz et al. 1967) and Nippur (McCown and Haines 1967; McMahon 2006) and these houses and neighborhoods match the organic arrangements of Old Babylonian Ur with their meandering streets, variable house plans that may include a courtyard, and tight packing of houses reflecting close social connections. Sub-floor graves were found beneath houses at these sites and Akkadian graves were added in the Royal Cemetery of Ur (Woolley 1934), which became less exclusive in the later 3rd millennium BC. These graves reflect general Mesopotamian traditions of treatment of the dead, containing pottery vessels for the trip to the underworld and status-dependent levels of personal ornamentation as well as seals, weaponry, and bronze vessels. The total ceramic assemblage and specific forms changed only gradually from the late Early Dynastic through the early Akkadian period (McMahon 2006). But there remains debate over the visibility and possible material culture markers of this transition and that between the early and late Akkadian periods (Gibson 1982; Gibson and McMahon 1995, 1997; Matthews 1997a; Roaf 2001; McMahon 2006). The ceramic sequence reconstructed from the Diyala excavations (Delougaz 1952) drew too sharp a distinction between Early Dynastic and Akkadian forms and the use of this sequence for dating other sites both north and south has perpetuated an artificial cultural divide. Distinctive "goddess-handled jars" persisted into the Akkadian period, while the ridged-shoulder jars often attributed to the Akkadian era appeared only late in the period and continued into Ur III times. Similarly, plano-convex bricks, once considered a hallmark of the Early Dynastic period, again on the basis of evidence from the Diyala region (Delougaz et al. 1967), persisted, particularly in domestic architecture, through the Akkadian period (McMahon 2006). Buildings traditionally dated to Early Dynastic, but which may straddle the transition from Early Dynastic to Akkadian, include Palace A and the "Plano-convex" Building at Kish.

Without the capital city of Agade, and with constructions such as the Ekur at Nippur covered by Ur III projects, architectural evidence from northern Mesopotamia is our best evidence of Akkadian architecture of power. Tell Brak (northeastern Syria) has two religious-administrative centers (Areas SS and FS; Oates et al. 2001) and a "palace" (Mallowan 1947). Mudbricks stamped with Naram-Sin's name in the latter leave no doubt it was a southern-imposed and

-commissioned construction. Its square plan, with large courtyards and symmetrical, narrow rooms, resembles a storehouse or military barracks rather than a palace. An administrative building lies adjacent to it (Oates et al. 2001: CH Level 4) and contemporary houses and a scribal school were exposed in Area ER to its east. Area SS, an extensive administrative complex, lies on the opposite side of the southern entrance to the city. At the site's northern edge, Area FS comprises a temple complex dedicated to Shakkan, a deity of steppe animals. The highly visible placement of all these buildings made a power statement both within the city and to the surrounding area. A comparable Akkadian administrative center at nearby Tell Leilan, including massive buildings, a palace, and scribal school, took over the central acropolis (Weiss et al. 2002; Ristvet et al. 2004; De Lillis-Forrest et al. 2007).

Sealings of Akkadian officials in the FS and SS complexes and Area ER houses reinforce the direct connection between southern and northern Mesopotamia (Aruz 2003: No. 156; Oates 2001a; Matthews 1997b). However, a distinctively local variant of seal style and sealing practice is seen in strung clay bullae from SS, impressed with numerical marks and seals bearing rows of frontal bull, lion and/or goat heads (Oates 2001a: 130 ff); other motifs, such as equid chariots, have also been attributed to the "Brak" style rather than being considered southern Mesopotamian (Oates 2001a: 126). Foreign rule did not eliminate local administrative traditions. Thus, the power architecture of these northern sites may also be a local hybrid not representative of southern forms.

6 Settlement Patterns

Rimush's inscriptions record deportations of thousands within the southern plains and, while the veracity of his claim is uncertain, the centralization of taxation and opportunities for new employment in the expanded state bureaucracy and industries should be visible in settlement hierarchies and locations. Exploitation of the northern plains should also have affected the size of both large sites and a number of smaller ones. However, neither a noticeable shift in site size hierarchy nor an increase in the number of smaller villages is apparent (Nissen 1993a). As Mario Liverani said: "If we didn't know from the texts that the Akkad Empire really existed, we would not be able to postulate it from the changes in settlement patterns, nor . . . from the evolution of material culture" (1993a: 7–8).

Reconstruction of the Akkadian settlement pattern of southern Mesopotamia is affected by the difficulty of separating Early Dynastic from Akkadian ceramics, the basis for most survey site dating. Based on the Diyala assemblages, Adams' work in the southern plains provided separate maps for late Early Dynastic and the Akkadian through Old Babylonian periods (for the Uruk area, see Adams and Nissen 1972) or for the late Early Dynastic and Akkadian periods (on the central plains, see Adams 1981). But the late Early Dynastic maps must now be construed as covering not just late Early Dynastic but also the reign of Sargon and possibly his sons. Any Akkadian map covers the era of Naram-Sin, when we expect the densest, economically thriving occupation, as well as the state's decline under subsequent kings.

The problems of separating Early Dynastic from Akkadian material and identifying a distinctive, post-Akkadian assemblage exist in northern Mesopotamia too. Extensive surveys in the Upper Khabur region struggled to subdivide material from the later 3rd millennium BC (Meier 1986; Lyonnet 2000). To the east, the northern Jazirah survey subsumed the complexity between Ninevite 5/late Early Dynastic and the appearance of Khabur Ware around the time of Shamshi-Adad I into a single group (Wilkinson and Tucker 1995). A new regional "Early Jezirah" sequence has been developed, in which the relevant periods are EJ III through V (cf. late ED III through post-Akkadian or Ur III) (Pruß 2004; Koliński 2007 for recent restatements) but it is only just gaining widespread use, at the same time that a number of site-based, intensive surveys are nearing publication (e.g., the Tell Brak Sustaining Area). The continuity of types across the EJ subdivisions remains problematic for settlement pattern reconstructions from surface surveys (Ur 2010a) but the picture so far is of great, subregional variability (Wossink 2009: Fig. 5.14), which cannot wholly be explained by difficulties in establishing chronological markers.

7 Art

In contrast to the continuity seen in ceramics, the style and, to an extent, iconography of formal Akkadian artworks show a definitive change from the Early Dynastic period. Reliefs, statuary, and cylinder seals are distinctive for their elegant appearance. While sometimes characterized as realistic, they are actually highly stylized (and sometimes incorrect) in proportions and representation of hair, fur, and musculature. Mature Akkadian reliefs and seals consciously incorporated empty space that emphasized figures and their active relationships (Nadali and Verderame 2008).

Cylinder seals are dominated by two main themes: combating pairs of humans and animals, and scenes showing the introduction of human figures to deities. The animal and human combat/contest scene was a continuation from the Early Dynastic period but became increasingly heraldic and formalized and, at its best, presents extraordinarily beautiful imagery, both in the fine detail of individual figures and the balanced elegance of pairs. The contest scene became an emblem of Akkadian administration, in contrast to personal seal scenes of introduction (Zettler 1977; Gibson and McMahon 1995; Rakic 2003) which show a procession of deities leading a human figure toward a seated god. Such scenes became the model for the majority of subsequent Ur III and Old Babylonian seals.

Although the scenes were iconic and instantly recognizable, the skill of the Akkadian artists made every example unique through details of individual actors. There are smaller numbers of more complex seal scenes, such as battles among gods or hunting, which may represent myths (Frankfort 1939a; Amiet 1976; Nissen 1993a), mythical themes (Nadali and Verderame 2008), rituals (Barrelet 1970; Frankfort 1939a) or statements of ideology (Bernbeck 1996). During the Akkadian period many of the physical attributes of divinity (e.g., Ishtar's weapons and lion, the shoulder-flames, and gates of Shamash) were canonized.

Although the most skillfully executed and beautiful seals are the focus of many modern scholars, a range of quality is represented in this period, from the highlights of the seal of Shar-kali-sharri's scribe, Ibni-Sharrum, with its water buffalo and kneeling nude heroes with water jars (Aruz 2003: No. 135), through to rapid, sketchy combat scenes on seals in the Ur graves (see Woolley 1934: Pls. 205–15 for a full range). A variety of stones (and shell) was used, from simple limestone and imported lapis lazuli, already seen in the Early Dynastic period, to vibrant, high-visibility serpentine, jasper, rock crystal, and banded agates. The physicality of sealing practice also changed (Rakic 2003) to an emphasis on a centered inscription, flanked by combating pairs (Amiet 1976: 34; Nissen 1993a: 101). Beyond seals, other administrative tools such as weights are rare, although the presence of silver ingots and standard-sized coils in late Akkadian hoards at Tell Brak (Matthews 1994, 2003a; Oates et al. 2001: 45–6) imply the wide diffusion of the new weights and measures system; this is severely underrepresented in the archaeological record, however, due to the recycling of metals.

Reliefs are dominated by representations of military combat. As mentioned above, many Akkadian artworks were still on display in the temples of, e.g., Sippar and Agade in the later 2nd millennium BC and were captured by Elamite forces and removed to Susa. The Susa relief collection documents change across the first half of the Akkadian period, from fairly static, symbolic iconography in organized registers to loosely arranged narrative. The assemblage includes several diorite fragments attributed to a stele or stelae of Sargon, showing registers of marching soldiers, scenes of combat, bound naked prisoners, birds of prey, and a net full of enemies, reminiscent of the slightly more complete Early Dynastic Vulture Stele of Eannatum (Amiet 1976: Pls. 1, 5–6; Nigro 1998; Hansen 2003: Figs. 54–55). A comparison of the Sargon stele and the Vulture Stele underscores the continuity of scene between the periods while emphasizing the Akkadian period's clarity of detail, greater depth of carving, and new focus on the individual and human anatomy. For instance, Sargon has a waist, a feature denied to Eannatum. The Sargon stele has also been interpreted as a complex ideological statement of the new royal order, in that Sargon controls the net holding his enemies, whereas on the Vulture Stele it is the god Ningirsu who does this; it also promotes Ishtar to a larger role and higher status (Nigro 1998). However, the registers still present Sargon's soldiers as an overlapping pattern of figures, something only abandoned in Enheduanna's votive disc (Aruz 2003: No. 128), Rimush's stele from Telloh

(Amiet 1976: Pl. 25; Aruz 2003: No. 129) and a contemporary, green alabaster stele from Nasiriyah (McKeon 1970; Amiet 1976: Pl. 26; Aruz 2003: No. 131). In each of these, there is a new sense of space between individual figures and greater skill in showing human musculature and details of dress and weaponry.

Eventually, the incorporation of natural or landscape features and the abandonment of a horizontal ground line in favor of diagonal, upward trajectories appear on the Victory Stele of Naram-Sin (Amiet 1976: Pl. 27; Benoit 2003: Fig. 114; Winter 1999). The redundant symbolism is easily readable (the broken spear, the nakedness of captives, and the dead) and the foreignness of the enemies (the Lullubi from the Zagros mountains) is strongly indicated by their hair and clothing. Presentation of the king as a young and active warrior with a massive beard and much of his "perfect" body exposed (Winter 1996; Bahrani 2008a) echoes the new royal epithets, including "the mighty" (Akk. *danum*). However, neither the landscape nor the abandonment of registers was a consistent feature of Akkadian art, even within the reign of Naram-Sin, if one compares this with the rather stiff representation on the Pir-Hussein relief (Amiet 1976: Fig. 21; Aruz 2003: No. 130). The early Ur III stele of Ur-Nammu (c.2100 BC) saw a return to the Early Dynastic/early Akkadian register format.

Statues in the round were relatively rare. The "Bismaya head" and other non-royal votive statue fragments from Telloh, Adab, Assur, and Umma (Amiet 1976: Pls. 7–10, 28–30) reveal continuities of form and pose from the Early Dynastic period, but with more "life-like" proportions and details. They retain the Early Dynastic overemphasized eyes, which transfix deities with their devotional gaze. Royal statues are similarly uncommon. The largest number belongs to Manishtushu (Amiet 1972c) and their standardization suggests a program of placement in temples in key southern cities (Eppihimer 2010). The diorite statue, or skirt, of Manishtushu has a deceptively simple, geometric form that, upon inspection, reveals sophisticated skill in the rendering of fringes and shallow ripples in fabric (Amiet 1976: Pl. 13; Benoit 2003: Fig. 111). That the ripples are not structurally possible, a problem shared by the symmetrically clasped hands, detracts only slightly from their impressive technique. Another skirt, in limestone, and fragments of a seated statue have the same ripples and fringe, suggesting they were products of a royal workshop or even a single artist (Amiet 1976: Pls. 11, 15).

A shift in medium from the near-exclusive use of limestone in the Early Dynastic period to mixed diorite/gabbro and limestone in the Akkadian period is visible in the reliefs and statues from Susa, although the non-random nature of their preservation means it is impossible to be certain of this trend. There is a strong symbolic aspect to the "new" stone; diorite/gabbro represents the conquering of an exotic land and the capture of its resources, but also, like hematite, it is extremely hard and has paradoxical qualities of darkness and shine that may elicit complex human reactions.

Recycling means that metal statues are rarely preserved from any period in the Near East. The most famous Akkadian example is a complexly textured, copper head from a later context at Nineveh (Campbell Thompson and Hutchinson

1932; Mallowan 1936). It is attributed stylistically to the Akkadian period and by political history to either Sargon or Naram-Sin (and occasionally to Manishtushu, who may have re-established a temple to Ishtar at Nineveh, according to Samsi-Adad). The hairstyle is similar to that shown on the Early Dynastic, Meskalamdug helmet from the Ur Royal Cemetery, reliefs of both Eannatum and Sargon, and a diorite head of Naram-Sin (Amiet 1976: Pl. 30; Hansen 2003: Cat 137). The abundance of hair and its intricate weaves and curls have been equated with royal masculinity (Hansen 2003: 194). The Bassetki statue from Naram-Sin's reign, a standard base held by a nude hero, is another important work, both for its evidence of metal-casting skill and for its inscription, which describes the deification of Naram-Sin.

All the metal statues in this period were produced through hollow-core, lost-wax techniques, finished by surface engraving (Ch. I.16). The composition of a sample of the statues shows at least 98 percent are copper with traces of minor elements such as arsenic and nickel but no tin (al-Fouadi 1976; Strommenger 1986). Contemporary copper-bronze vessels from south Mesopotamia are occasionally also entirely made of copper, although their tin and other element percentages vary widely and may exceed 10 percent (Müller-Karpe 1993; De Ryck et al. 2005). This might imply a clear separation between workshops, from smelting upwards, in the production of statues as opposed to vessels (although analyses of Akkadian bronze vessels and objects from northern Mesopotamia show a low tin and arsenic content as compared to statues; De Ryck et al. 2005). The source of copper in the Akkadian period is traditionally located in Oman. At 160 kilograms, the weight of the Bassetki statue base is testament to the strength of this Gulf connection.

8 Imperial Power?

Akkadian rule over Mesopotamia is often described as an empire (e.g., Glassner 1986; Foster 1993; Kuhrt 1995; Westenholz 1997, 999; Nissen 1998; Akkermans and Schwartz 2003; Aruz 2003; Hansen 2003; Rakic 2003). And it is tempting to use "empire," since the Uruk and Early Dynastic political arrangements were states and the Akkadian Dynasty represents something quantitatively and qualitatively different (Liverani 1993b). The argument for empire, where expressed, is based on the distinct nature of royal ideology, the unprecedented encompassing and unifying nature of Akkadian rule, and its spread by military means beyond the traditional borders of the southern Mesopotamian plains (e.g. Weiss and Courty 1993; Weiss et al. 2002). While not specifying imperialism, Z. Bahrani has argued for a new concept of kingship under Naram-Sin (2008a: 102 ff.), including a new focus in art on the king's body as physically overwhelming, representing his power over the life and death of others.

But was the Akkadian system of political power an empire? Yoffee characterized it as a "territorial state (or empire)" (1995: 290) and many questions regarding its degree of unification and the nature of its expansion have been raised (Michalowski 1993; Liverani 2005). If it falls short of an imperial definition, what was the nature of the Akkadian kings' control, since it was greater than a city-state? We are hindered in our reconstruction of the political system by a lack of knowledge about the capital city, Agade. Without administrative archives and economic records from the center, as well as contextualized statements of ideology in monumental architecture and art, we are missing key data that could illuminate mechanisms of control over other regions and the integration or non-integration of other peoples and cultures. In addition, the historic glorification of the Akkadian kings has had an impact on our own judgment of their importance, personal charisma, and military skills. The Akkadian period may be simply an "empire of nostalgia" (Barfield 2001: 38), an imagined, glorious past, more important as a myth or memory than an actuality.

Empires should be physically massive, governmentally bureaucratic, economically complex and ethnically, culturally and often linguistically heterogenous (Sinopoli 1994; Barfield 2001; Schreiber 2001). An empire should have an active ideology, an expressed wish for limitless rule and a program of activities to achieve this (Barfield 2001; M.E. Smith 2001; Liverani 2005); empires are usually embodied by a "larger-than-life" individual. An empire should be militarily expansive, with a physical infrastructure that enables centralization and long-distance communication (Barfield 2001; Schreiber 2001; Sinopoli 1994, 2001a). The Akkadian period has the requisite core bureaucracy, ideology, charismatic kings, and military program. But several of these aspects come to us through past inflationary filters, and the extent of control and internal heterogeneity remain questions. A recent material-culture-based approach to empire proposes a set of relevant approaches and data: comparable ceramic assemblages between edge zones and imperial core, visible effect of empire on settlement patterns, "imperial administrative technology" at core and edges, and materialization of ideology through visible landscape monuments (Glatz 2009; cf. Sinopoli 1994). Connections between northern and southern Mesopotamian ceramic assemblages are present, including distinctive angular or ridged jar rim forms and combed decoration seen, e.g., both at Nippur and Tell Brak (McMahon 2006). But these represent slight overlaps rather than a complete borrowing or the import of full sets. We are not yet able to write a narrative of the Akkadian effect on settlement patterns in the north or south, but our limited data do not seem to reflect imperial meddling. There are scattered pockets of administrative artifacts (texts and sealings) at Tell Leilan and Tell Brak, and some highly visible monuments, but the spaces between these are vast. An "empire" should have more than a few, disconnected outposts and stelae, especially when texts describe internal revolts and reveal its unstable core. Is the wish for domination and the assumption of its achievement, over the reality (Liverani 2005), a sufficient trait of empires?

Akkadian internal and external control measures provide ambiguous answers to the question of imperialism. A standing army is often listed as a crucial imperial criterion (e.g., Schreiber 2001). Sargon's claim to have fed 5,400 men every day (Frayne 1993) defies solid interpretation; the number is suspiciously round and these might have been laborers, administrators, and/or soldiers. But a record of 60,000 dried fish from Lagash, to provide for the army, is suggestive that in at least some seasons the army was substantial, while other official texts list troops and military officials (Foster 1993). But an army and warfare are neither sufficient for nor unique to empire. Organized warfare, including mass death, has a prehistory in the region (Late Chalcolithic graves from Tell Brak and destruction at Tell Hamoukar). Organized armies already appear on Early Dynastic artworks (the Ur Standard from the Royal Cemetery, Eannatum of Lagash's Stele of the Vultures). The Akkadian kings raised the value of warriors and war as an agent of change (Forest 2005), but neither war nor armies were new. And violence played both ways; insurrection was common and a startling number of kings met a violent death: Rimush, Manishtushu, Shar-kali-sharri, and probably some of the four obscure kings between him and Dudu.

Other internal features, such as the imposition of language change and new metrology, can be used to flatten variation and to crack city or ethnic allegiance in a nation-state and need not be imperial. Much has been made of the divine ascription of Naram-Sin and his para-mortal right to rule. But royal divinity is not typical of undoubted Mesopotamian empires, such as the Neo-Assyrian, although many kings from the Ur III period onward claimed a close association with gods.

Meanwhile, Akkadian external measures were expressed mainly as control of places but not of people. To the north, boundaries and military goals were labeled after resources (the Cedar Forest or Silver Mountain) or territories and landmarks (the Four Quarters, the sources of the Tigris and Euphrates). Peoples in these regions were viewed as enemies to kill, not subjects to command. And an empire should be about power over people as well as power to annihilate and to exploit things. The south saw more killing, although the Akkadian kings both claimed booty and directed trade from the lands of the Gulf and the Indus. But unquantifiable booty does not make an empire, and there is evidence that Akkadian access to resources was neither secure nor monopolistic. Although diorite/gabbro and exotics such as carnelian flowed in from the southeast, the amounts from southern Mesopotamia, when spread over the years of even one king's reign, are paltry. Gold beads that were solid in the Early Dynastic period are more often copper covered with gold foil in the Akkadian period, an apt analogy for Akkadian control.

The problem of selective and inflated accounts in texts is compounded by sparse archaeological evidence of the relationship between Akkadian kings and bordering lands. Empires should have political and cultural influence over a wider area than that which they directly control (M.E. Smith 2001). Empires are also often associated with reactive political developments in adjacent regions, but no external region became a state or empire because of the reach of Akkadian influence beyond its borders. Elam, in western Iran, provides useful material to test Akkadian influence. From the reign of Sargon, year names refer to the conquest of cities within Elam, while Old Babylonian copies of statue inscriptions describe many as booty from Elamite cities (Gelb and Kienast 1990; Frayne 1993; Potts 1999: 102). Rimush campaigned against many of the same places, and finally under Naram-Sin there is clearer – albeit minimal – evidence of a more permanent Akkadian presence in Elam. Bricks stamped with his name have been found at Susa and, unlike possibly mobile statuary, provide clear evidence of a commissioned building there, possibly comparable to that at Tell Brak. The official language and seal style of Elam conform to Akkadian rules and pottery and metal object types also match Mesopotamian models (Potts 1999: 116). Superficially, the story appears to be one of raiding, booty acquisition, and finally imperial incorporation.

However, contemporary texts include a treaty between Naram-Sin and a king of Awan (possibly Hita; Westenholz 1999: 92), which indicates that some Elamite rulers remained independent allies rather than subjugated vassals. Elamite material culture includes almost as many elements of Gulf or Indus valley origin or influence as of Mesopotamian. In addition, statues, seals, and plaques of the early 3rd millennium BC from sites such as Susa were already similar to those from contemporary southern Mesopotamia; Akkadian period cultural similarity between the regions has a deep history and does not here equate with political control. Rather than imperial control, Akkadianizing material culture in Elam provides a classic example of connection and emulation between elites within a wider region that was already tightly culturally integrated. Finally, a daughter of the king of Marhashi (Elam) was married to Shar-kali-sharri or his son. Dynastic marriage connections may integrate an empire (Sinopoli 2001) but also imply equality or even mutual threat.

Northern Mesopotamia is another area to examine for imperial aspects. The acropolis buildings, sealings, and texts at Tell Leilan imply an Akkadian outpost, matched by similar features at Tell Brak. The Tell Leilan project additionally argued for intensive and directed exploitation of the north's agricultural capacity, reorganization of regional settlement pattern, and, at Leilan itself, a system of ration measurement and imposition of Akkadian bureaucracy and ideology through scribal school training (Senior and Weiss 1992; Weiss and Courty 1993; Weiss et al. 1993; Besonen and Cremaschi 2002). In support of this, at least one state-run grain shipment moved from the north via Tell Brak to Sippar (29 metric tons; Ristvet et al. 2004); but this amount is not as large as it sounds, and there is no evidence for continuous, multiple shipments. The northern Akkadian *sila*-bowl is never seen in the south. A tablet from the Naram-Sin palace at Brak lists men from Nagar (Brak), Shehna (Leilan), Urkesh (Tell Mozan), and other northern cities, suggesting an Akkadian labor levy (Catagnoti and Bonechi 1992) or soldiers (Eidem et al. 2001: 110). But again, the numbers are small and the text describes a single event. It was only under Naram-Sin that we have proof of Akkadian presence in the north (leaving aside the possibly mobile objects of Rimush and Manishtushu at Brak, Nineveh, and Assur). And collapse of the system occurred before it reached its full potential (expressed in the Unfinished Building at Leilan).

The area of northern Mesopotamia that shows Akkadian presence or influence is a strictly bounded triangle within the eastern Upper Khabur, from the Kawkab volcano (near modern Hasseke) to Shehna (modern Tell Leilan) and north to Urkesh (modern Tell Mozan) (Catagnoti and Bonechi 1992). Only the largest sites within that triangle were implicated. Otherwise, there is no evidence of Akkadian presence in the western Upper Khabur; Nabada (modern Tell Beydar) shrank in size during the early Akkadian period, and the buildings and material culture were local in style. A gap exists on the east between Leilan and the ambiguous and minimal Akkadian materials from the upper Tigris (Nineveh, Bassetki). In addition, there are no known outposts on transport routes between this eastern Khabur triangle and southern Mesopotamia, although it must be admitted that the intensity of research in the relevant mid-Euphrates and mid-Tigris area has been relatively low. Empires need not comprise one contiguous territory, but this situation gives the impression of isolated out-stations rather than even a lightly colonized region.

Nearer to the Taurus foothill zone in the Upper Khabur, Akkadian control was minimal, as represented by an equal marriage between Naram-Sin's daughter Taram-Agade and the leader of an independent Urkesh (Buccellati and Kelly-Buccellati 2002, 2003). The massive palace currently under excavation at Mozan expresses significant local power over territory, resources, and people. As in western Iran, the similarity of sealings at Urkesh to south Mesopotamian Akkadian style (Aruz 2003: Nos. 154–155; Buccellati and Kelly-Buccellati 2002) derives from a base layer of cultural connectivity between these regions reaching back to the mid-3rd millennium BC, with an overlay emulation between elites. Our knowledge of the Akkadian relationship with nomadic tribes, both within and beyond its territory, is also an unknown, but the autonomy of these tribes may have been significant.

Was the Akkadian system a "hegemonic state," in contrast to a city-state (Forest 2005)? Many archaeologists and historians of the ancient Near East use the terms "hegemony" and "imperial control" interchangeably. But in modern political thought, hegemony implies a significant element of consent rather than conquest, or leadership rather than oppression, and it is better used to designate political and cultural influence than imperialism. Hegemony may fit the cobwebbed and temporally variable veneer of control that the Akkadians achieved, but their ideology and expressed intent was for more absolute power over place and time.

Can the Akkadian system be called a nation-state? Unlike "hegemony," the relevance of "nation-states" to the past is generally denied. Most postmodern scholars place the innovation of the nation-state in the 18th–19th century AD and reject the application of this term to the more distant past as overly modernizing. This rejection may in part have developed through distaste at the cynical use of archaeological materials and the past have been used cynically in the creation of some modern, oppressive, postcolonial nation-states further tarnished by "ethnic" struggle. But the term "nation-state" may be rehabilitated. Objectively, the Akkadian kings were engaged in overt "nation-building" with their internal, unifying measures, particularly language imposition. They aimed to develop a distinct "national identity" and they did create a distinct leadership identity that combined old and new elements. They had a clear idea of territory, within which variations of material culture, economy, religion, and history were tolerated but limited. They may not have had Benedict Anderson's novel and newspaper to represent and advertise an "imagined community" (1983) but their internal accounting and dating measures and the flexibility of existing Mesopotamian oral tradition were equally rapid modes of communication. Even the resistance of subsumed cities, social classes, and (possibly) nomads to unification may be a characteristic of nations.

9 Collapse

The collapse of the Akkadian political system in southern and especially northern Mesopotamia has been one of the most hotly debated topics in Mesopotamian archaeology and social history over recent decades. The most dramatic cause proposed for collapse is a drought, lasting several centuries, which affected the agricultural carrying capacity of northern Mesopotamia with a domino effect in the south (Weiss and Courty 1993; Weiss et al. 1993; Weiss 2000; deMenocal 2001; Weiss and Bradley 2001; Staubwasser and Weiss 2006). The proposed effects include the near-total abandonment of northern Mesopotamia and the mass movement of economic refugees into the cities of the south. As evidence, an aridity spike in a Gulf of Oman sediment core (Kerr 1998; Cullen et al. 2000), which shows increased aeolian dust for 300 years from c.4025 ± 125 years BP, has been cited. Similar, contemporary evidence of sharply increased aridity comes from the southern Persian Gulf (Aeolian deposits in lake sediments; Parker, Davies, & Wilkinson 2006); the eastern Arabian Sea (oxygen isotope variation in sediment cores; Staubwasser et al. 2003); the Arabian Sea off Oman (foraminifera fluctuations; Gupta et al. 2003); the northern Red Sea (salinity variations; Arz et al. 2006); Soreq Cave, Israel (O- and C-isotope variations in speleothems; Bar-Matthews et al. 2003), the Dead Sea (dropping lake levels; Enzel et al. 2003); the Jableh plain in northwest Syria (pollen core; Kaniewski et al. 2008); and even caves in central Italy (Drysdale et al. 2006) and cores in the Greenland ice sheet (Weiss 2000). Additional, far-flung evidence from the US and Europe and the approximately contemporary collapse of Old Kingdom Egypt, Early Bronze Age cultures around the Mediterranean, and Harappan cultures in the Indus form the basis for the argument that the "4.2 kya Abrupt Climate Change event," within which temporal parameters the historical collapse of the Akkadian state occurred, was a global phenomenon (e.g., Kerr 1998; Staubwasser et al. 2003; Drysdale et al. 2006; Staubwasser and Weiss 2006).

This collapse model has been widely criticized on climatic, historical, and archaeological grounds (see Wossink 2009 for a recent summary). Other climate records from the Arabian Sea indicate not a spike but a long-term, gradual aridity trend, within which an event at 4.2 kya is difficult to isolate (oxygen isotope variation in a Qunf Cave stalagmite, Oman; Fleitmann et al. 2003). The precise dating of climatic events has proven impossible and their relationship to each other and to equally slippery historical events is difficult to reconstruct. Moreover, these climatic records come from places that are far from the northern Mesopotamian plain in which the collapse most visibly occurred; and their reliability as proxies for environmental change within those plains varies greatly, depending upon the interaction of Indian/Asian monsoons, the North Atlantic Oscillation, smaller scale Mediterranean depressions, and Caspian-Black Sea westerlies (Cullen and de Menocal 2000; Gupta et al. 2003; Arz et al. 2006; Staubwasser and Weiss 2006; Magny et al. 2009). Aeolian dust has been recovered in relevant layers at Tell Leilan, sites in its vicinity, and Abu Hjeira south of Tell Beydar (Weiss et al. 1993, 2002), but these discoveries remain in a vacuum. It has also been argued that modern climate change has made "environmental determinism" models for past cultural change plausible again, after they had been written off in the 1970s as too rigid and impersonal (Coombes and Barber 2005). While the argument for total reflexivity of theoretical models may go too far, careful consideration of the enabling and limiting factors inherent in the interaction between culture and climate is needed; synchronicity does not equal causality. More specific data from within archaeological sites in northern and southern Mesopotamia are required, and their precise effects on human behavior must be analyzed before this debate can be concluded.

The archaeological evidence for collapse is mixed. Not all northern Mesopotamian settlements were abandoned: occupation continued at, e.g., Tell Brak and Chagar Bazar, although settlement size in each case was reduced. At Tell Brak, the monumental buildings in Areas SS and FS were filled and capped with ritual donkey burials and "sealing deposits," jars of precious materials and objects (Oates and Oates 1993; Oates et al. 2001: 41ff, 233–6). These sealing deposits are paralleled by hoards of precious metal and lapis objects in house contexts, buried at about the same time but probably with the intent of later retrieval (Mallowan 1947; Matthews 1994; 2003a: 203–9). This implies that the house occupants left rapidly but with the assumption that their absence would be temporary, while the occupants of the administrative buildings left more slowly and with fewer expectations. But the monumental buildings were replaced by houses, and the use (and possibly even construction) of the Naram-Sin palace persisted after this partial abandonment.

A massive administrative building was constructed in the post-Akkadian period on the highest point of Chagar Bazar (Tunca et al. 2007); a similar building was revealed at Tell Arbid (Bielinski 2002). Urkesh remained a large and thriving city (Buccellati and Kelly-Buccellati 2000, 2004). Tell Beydar, further to the southwest, contracted in size but retained a temple at its highest point (Bretschneider et al. 2003). Like the buildings at Chagar Bazar and Arbid, its location was surely intended to achieve high visibility in a nomadized landscape. A shift of populations to increased pastoralism, relocation to smaller sites in pockets of still-viable agricultural land, and decreased hierarchical power (making settlements less archaeologically visible) are plausible alternative models to explain the reduction in size of large sites. Settlement along the Upper Euphrates in Syria and Turkey shifted to an arrangement of more villages and fewer towns (Wilkinson 1998b); but a true picture is still obscured by the abovementioned difficulty of defining northern post-Akkadian (EJ V) ceramics (Koliński 2007). Settlement patterns in the south should show an increase in site size and perhaps numbers, but the picture is murky; due to the difficulties with the menu of material culture, a purported increase in settlement (Weiss 2000: 89) may simply reflect rapid shifts of populations under Naram-Sin and/or under the powerful, early Ur III kings. Specifically collapse-related immigration, if it occurred, is invisible.

Mesopotamian texts do not record reduced rainfall or mass immigration, and their own legends, such as *The Curse of Agade*, ascribe the Akkadian downfall to the Guti, an illiterate mountain tribe (from the Zagros) sent by Enlil as punishment for Naram-Sin's transgressions, which had included, purportedly, the looting of Enlil's temple at Nippur (Cooper 1983b). However, the legend's contrast between civilized Mesopotamians and barbaric surrounding peoples is a generic aspect of the region's "historico-literary" texts that later reappeared in relation to the Amorites; the specifics are therefore questionable. The Sumerian King List does record a Gutian Dynasty with odd names and short regnal lengths; an Uruk Dynasty is listed as intervening between them and Shu-Durul. But both contemporary documentation and the necessary interpolation of the Sumerian King List imply that these Guti and Uruk dynasties overlapped with the later Akkadian period, beginning in the reign of Shar-kali-sharri. Gudea's reign at Lagash also overlaps with the final years of the Akkadian kings. The Guti held minimal control in the central alluvial plains (i.e., Adab, Umma, and Lagash), from which there are royal inscriptions, building inscriptions, and year names, but their power and reach are poorly known. Their presence must be seen as a symptom rather than a cause of collapse. Other external threats include various city-states in Elam, which nibbled at the eastern borders of the Akkadian zone – e.g., in the Nuzi area (near modern Kirkuk).

Internal problems have been less closely scrutinized and are less exciting than the climatic evidence and textual descriptions of barbaric hordes (although see, e.g., Glassner 1986; Yoffee 1995). But internal instability and "overstretch" are important considerations. Even if the Akkadian kings' claims of territorial control are exaggerated, the logistical needs of the larger army and multilayered administration of the Akkadians would have overstretched existing systems. Hyper-centralization of the economy and royal greed have also been cited by Glassner (1986) as causes of collapse. In addition, the simple possibility of social inertia is strong and the independent city-state arrangement that had persisted from the 4th millennium BC Uruk period (if not earlier) through the end of the Early Dynastic period would not have been easily given up. The political arrangements so carefully crafted by the Akkadian kings were an added veneer to extant robust social, civic, and economic systems, and that veneer and its economic and labor demands were a cause of tension (Yoffee 1995). Under Sargon, the governors of many city-states were simply their former kings, and while this may have been intended to minimize change and reduce the chances of revolt, it had the effect of reminding the cities of their past freedom and providing a springboard for rebellion. Rebellions of various city-states occurred throughout the Akkadian period, even under the most powerful and successful kings, such as Naram-Sin.

We can even question the importance of political collapse. While the Akkadian Dynasty certainly declined and vanished, local resilience and adaptation are the opposite face of collapse (McAnany and Yoffee 2010a). And collapse is not visible in the south in quotidian material culture; for many people, the removal of the Akkadian veneer may have meant an economic improvement in their lives. Collapse did not mean disappearance: the Ur III kings inherited the ideology and national ideal of the Akkadian kings, while their seals and iconography are further material expressions of continuity. The social memory (Alcock 2001) of the Akkadian Empire was created during their reign. It evolved and was adapted and reinvented from the late 3rd millennium BC through the present day. From the wider perspective of Mesopotamian history, Akkadian political collapse was a minor blip in a long-term cycle of growth, contraction, and movements of peoples, a minor set-back greatly overwhelmed by cultural continuities.

GUIDE TO FURTHER READING

Surveys of Akkadian political history can be found in Foster and Foster (2009: Ch. 4); Kuhrt (1995: Ch. 1c); Nissen (1988: Ch. 6); van de Mieroop (2004, Ch. 7). Texts and historiography are discussed in the various chapters in Liverani (1993a), with many suggestions for further close text reading. Royal inscriptions of the Akkadian kings are collected in Hirsch (1963), Gelb and Kienast (1990) and Frayne (1993); the later legendary texts can be found in Westenholz (1997). Collected artworks of the Akkadian period are presented in Amiet (1976) (statues, reliefs, and seals), Boehmer (1965) (seals), and Aruz (2003). The Naram-Sin stele is one of the most closely analyzed Mesopotamian artworks; the discussions by Winter (1996, 1999) are among the most intriguing. The archaeological record and settlement pattern data for southern Mesopotamia are quite scattered. The surveys of Adams (Adams and Nissen 1972; Adams 1981) are a useful start, although the dating must be used with caution. Akkermans and Schwartz (2003), Kolinski (2007), and Ur (2010a) give good summary accounts of the archaeological problems and varied evidence from northern Mesopotamia. Many of the publications of the Tell Leilan project that deal with empire, collapse, and climate change are available as PDF downloads from their website: http://leilan.yale.edu/; accessed October 2011). A text-based approach to the Akkadian collapse is presented in Glassner (1986).

CHAPTER THIRTY-FIVE

The Caucasus and the Near East

Adam T. Smith

1 Introduction

In 1887 the French engineer and geologist Jacques de Morgan arrived in the picturesque canyon of the Debed River, near modern Armenia's border with Georgia, to take up a new position as manager of the Alaverdi copper mine. A cosmopolitan polymath, de Morgan was by this time already an experienced archaeologist, having been introduced to the techniques of 19th century excavation as a youth by his father. During his two years in the South Caucasus, de Morgan excavated a staggering 898 burials dating to the Bronze and Iron Ages around the village of Akhtala. The materials that he recovered from the graves were notable, boasting strong parallels to artifacts recovered by earlier antiquarian excavations. But de Morgan's most enduring legacy in the region was his larger theoretical contribution, which bound the prehistory of the Caucasus inextricably to the cultural dynamics and population movements of its neighbors to the south in the greater Near East.

In his expansive scholarly report, *Mission Scientifique au Caucase*, de Morgan mustered the results of his investigations to a wider intellectual agenda staked on principles of cultural diffusion: "As we have seen, the changes in the state of civilization of the various races have almost always been the result the influence of one nation over another, or of the mixing of several ethnic elements; each refining his condition according to his needs or his natural abilities" (1889: 4). De Morgan's diffusionist account of his investigations focused archaeology on a key problematic

---

A Companion to the Archaeology of the Ancient Near East, First Edition.
Edited by D.T. Potts.
© 2012 Blackwell Publishing Ltd. Published 2012 by Blackwell Publishing Ltd.

that continues to frame research to the present day: how are we to understand the relationship between local societies of the Caucasus and their neighbors in the Near East and what explanatory power is this relationship to be accorded in our efforts to account for local historical changes? Since de Morgan, the central axis of dispute has centered on the tension between the explanatory poles of imitation and autochthony, between explanations of historical transformation that rely on intercessions from external forces and accounts that ground historical change exclusively in internal processes of social formation. In this contribution, I provide an overview of the extant archaeological evidence for the shifting relations between the prehistoric Caucasus and the ancient Near East in order to critically assess the social and political dynamics that shaped their interactions.

The first challenge in examining the relationship between the prehistoric Caucasus and the ancient Near East is defining geographically where one ends and the other begins (Figure 35.1). The area between the Terek river and the Great Caucasus ridge is generally referred to as the North Caucasus, a region that incorporates the southernmost provinces of the Russian Federation, including Krasnodar and Stavropol *Krais*, and the Republics of Adygea, Karachy-Cherkessia, Kabardino-Balkaria, North Ossetia, Ingushetia, Chechnya, and Daghestan. The South Caucasus includes the three independent republics of Georgia, Azerbaijan, and Armenia, along with the disputed regions of Abkhazia, South Ossetia, and Nagorno-Karabakh. Although today defined by modern political boundaries established by the Treaty of Lausanne (1923), in topographic terms the South Caucasus flows uninterrupted into the Armenian Highland, the highest of the uplands that make up the northern sectors of the Near East.

It is important to note that chronological systems developed for northwestern Iran, eastern Turkey, Armenia, Georgia, and Azerbaijan all employ slightly different terms and propose distinct temporal phases. The complexities of synthesizing regional chronologies have been discussed extensively elsewhere (Marro and Hauptmann 2000; Rubinson and Sagona 2008). Here, I utilize the system of periodization and chronology recently developed for the South Caucasus by Avetisyan, Badalyan, and Smith (Smith et al. 2009: Ch. 4) as a baseline for exploring the anomalies and regional divergences that make for very complex local histories (Table 35.1).

2 Conflicting Currents: Maikop and the Near East

In 1897, the Russian archaeologist Nikolai Veselovskii excavated a large *kurgan*, or burial tumulus, in the foothills of the Northwest Caucasus, near the town of Maikop (Figure 35.2). The tumulus was more than 10 meters high and almost 200 meters in diameter. The contents of the tomb were sensational: turquoise and carnelian beads, stone tools, bronze weapons and cauldrons, gold animal appliqués, silver drinking vessels with zoomorphic decoration, and six silver rods

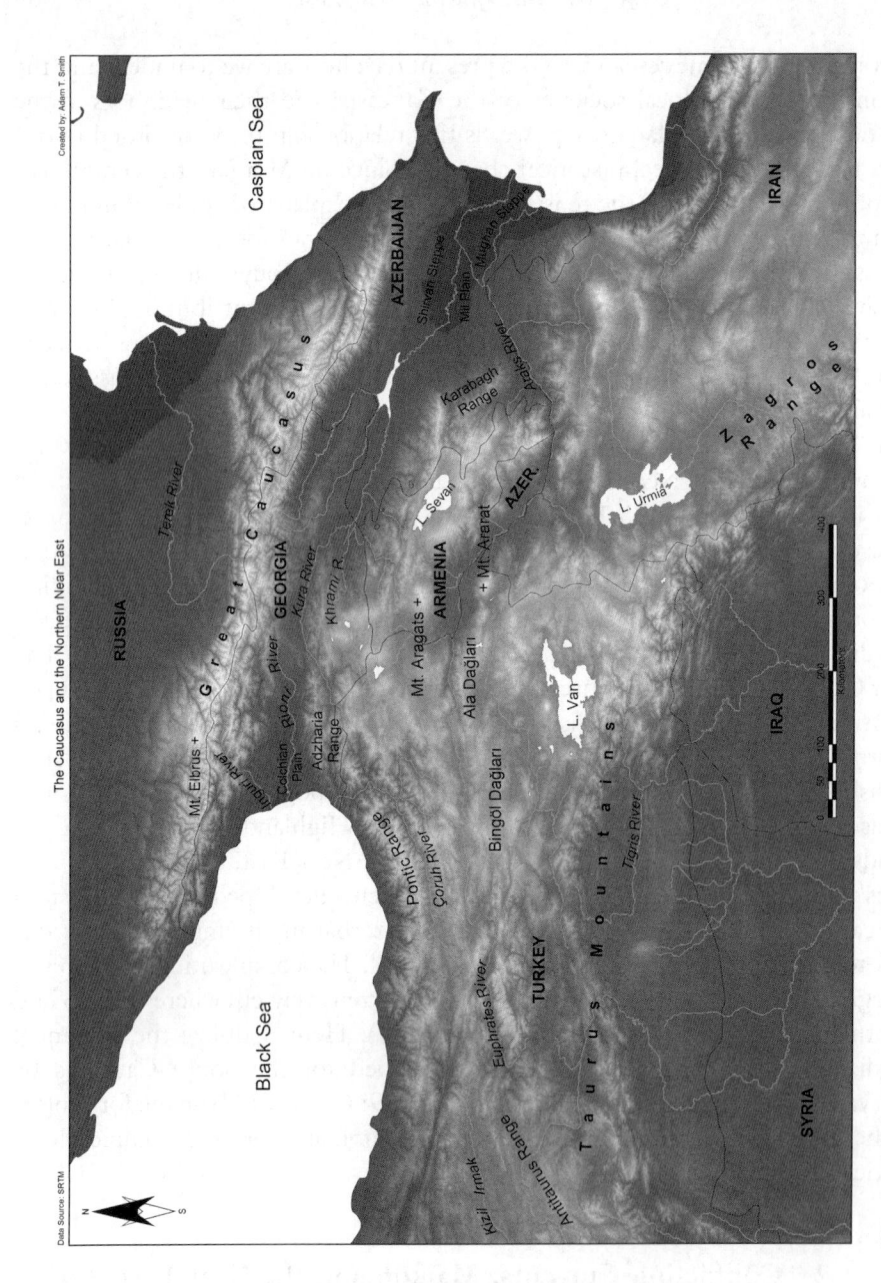

Figure 35.1 Physical and political map of the Caucasus showing the major geographical provinces.

Table 35.1 Chronological chart of the Caucasus and the northern Near East

Date	Archaeological Periodization	Regional Historical Sequences	Horizon Style	Key Sites	Tsaghkahovit Plain Strata Sequence
AD 300					
AD 200		Arsacid / Roman	Artashat-Garni	Garni, Atsavan	
AD 100					
AD 0					
BC 100	Iron IV	Artaxiad / Hellenistic		Artashat	
200					
300	Iron IIIb		Armavir-Tsaghkahovit	Armavir, Benjamin Karchaghpyur, Tsaghkahovit Erebuni, Oshakan	Tsaghkahovit IIIb
400	Iron III	Yervandid / Achaemenid			
500	Iron IIIa				Tsaghkahovit IIIa
600					
700	Iron II	Iron IIb	Urartu / Neo-Assyrian	Lchashen-Metsamor 6 / Urartu	Metsamor, Karmir-Blur Argishtihinili, Erebuni
800		Iron IIa			
900		Iron Ib	Syro-Hittite States	Lchashen-Metsamor 5	Horom, Metsamor
1000	Iron I				
1100		Iron Ia	Middle Assyrian	Lchashen-Metsamor 4	Elar, Artik (group 3) Keti, Dvin (burnt level)
1200	Late Bronze Age	LB III	Hittite Empire	Lchashen-Metsamor 3	Shirakavan, Tsaghkahovit	Tsaghkahovit IIc
1300		LB II		Lchashen-Metsamor 2	Lchashen, Artik	Tsaghkahovit IIb
1400		LB I	Mid. Hittite / Mitanni	Lchashen-Metsamor 1	Karashamb, Gegharot	Tsaghkahovit IIa
1500			Old Hittite			
1600		MB III		Karmir-vank / Karmir-berd / Sevan-Uzerlik	Karmirberd, Lchashen, Horom, Uzerlik 2-3	
1700					
1800			Old Assyrian	Trialeti-Vanadzor Group	Karashamb (kurgan) Vanadzor (Kirovakan) Trialeti (groups 1-3) Lchashen (120, 123) Lori-Berd, Uzerlik 1	
1900	Middle Bronze Age	MB II				
2000						
2100			Ur III			
2200		MB I	Akkadian Empire	Early Kurgans Group	Trialeti ("early group") Berkaber Stepanakert	
2300						
2400						
2500		Kura-Araxes II	Early Dynastic	Karnut-Shengavit Group	Shengavit Karnut, Gegharot	
2600						
2700				Shresh-Mokhrablur Group	Shreshblur, Mokhrablur, Agarak	Tsaghkahovit Ib
2800	Early Bronze Age					
2900						
3000			Jemdet Nasr		Elar, Aragats, Gegharot Frankanots, Djrvezh, Aparan	Tsaghkahovit Ia
3100				Elar-Aragats Group		
3200		Kura-Araxes I				
3300			Late Uruk			
3400						
3500						

Key: Phase out / Phase in

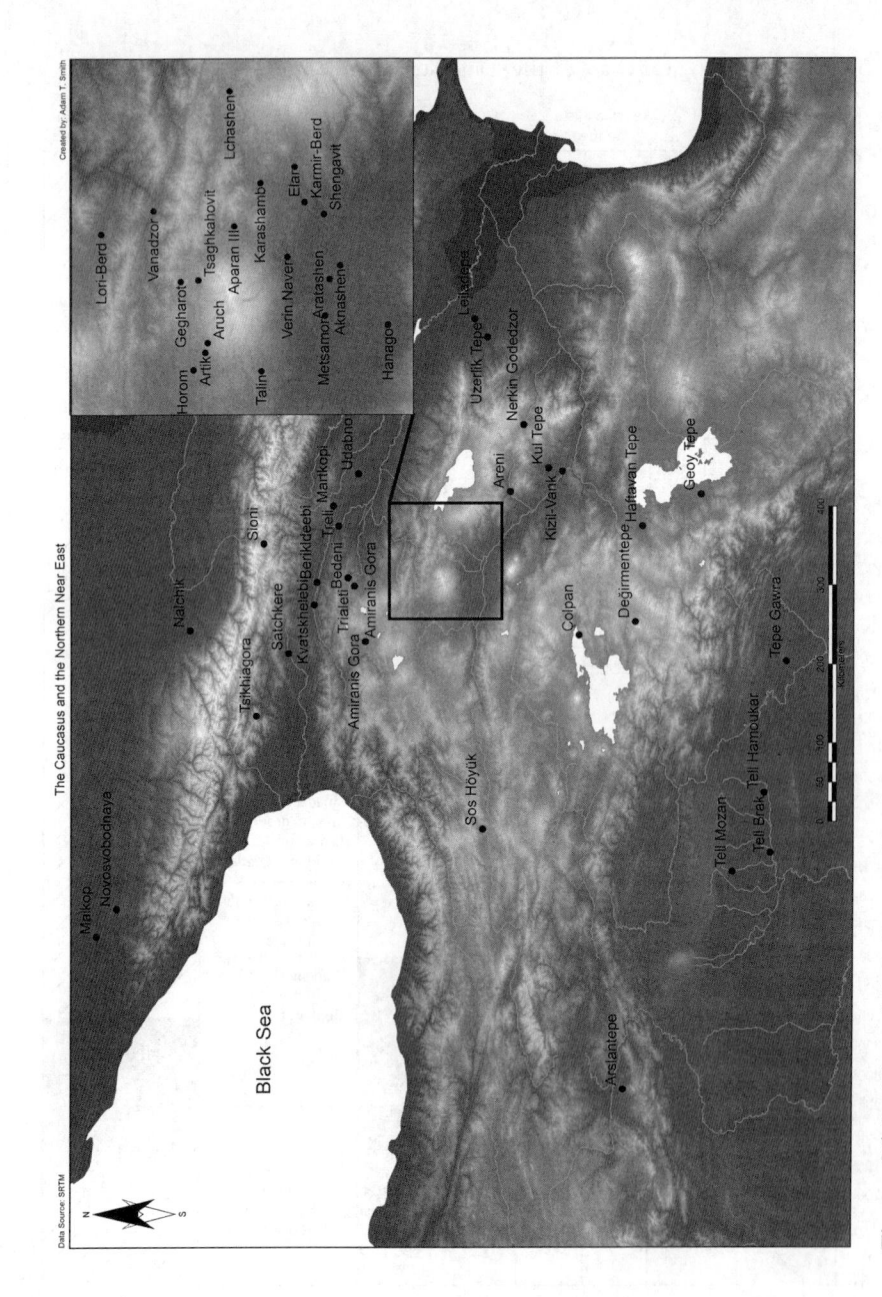

Figure 35.2 Map of sites discussed in the text.

with gold and silver bull terminals (Rostovtzeff 1922: 19–20, Pl. 4). Not surprisingly, the discovery stimulated interest in other large *kurgans* in the North Caucasus, allowing for the subsequent archaeological definition of a broad material repertoire constitutive of a Maikop "cultural community" whose initial appearance has recently been dated to c.3800–3500 BC (Kohl 2007).

Studies of the Maikop "phenomenon" neatly encapsulate the conflicting currents that have shaped archaeological interpretations of the links between the Caucasus and the Near East over the last century. Mikhail Rostovtzeff was the first to set Maikop assemblages within a wider archaeological context, arguing that the finds represented the autochthonous flowering of an independent Caucasian cultural center. For Rostovtzeff (1922: 28), the Maikop materials were products of a broad cultural florescence, part of a wider "artistic movement" of the early metal age:

> The Caucasian bronze age is very peculiar and very original. The only possible connexion is with Mesopotamia and the Asia Minor of the Hittite period. But I do not believe that this connexion came about in the usual way, by influence due to conquest, migration or commercial intercourse; I think that in all these countries the roots of development lay in a great copper age civilization which in each centre arose quite independently and proceeded on different lines, although it presented analogous features in all. (Rostovtzeff 1922: 32)

Rostovtzeff quickly became rather isolated in this view. Just two decades later, the Maikop cultural community had been dramatically reinterpreted as evidence not of regional autochthony but of the transformative impact of Near Eastern influence. "The impact of Mesopotamian civilization on clans living near Caucasian ores must account for the emergence of the chiefs . . . buried in the famous Early Kuban barrows of Maikop, Novosvodobnaya, etc., as well as for their Oriental wealth" (Childe 1942: 132). For V. Gordon Childe, Maikop was a distant effect of processes set in motion in Mesopotamia and it is this perspective that continues to dominate traditions of interpretation to the present day.

For example, in the Soviet tradition, exchange relations between the Caucasus and the Near East were taken not as evidence of economic interdependence amongst peers, but of the north's civilizational deficiency. To cite just one prominent scholar, Boris Piotrovskii argued that "the Maikop burial gives a vivid picture of the interchange between a group of herdsmen and their *more sophisticated* [Near Eastern] neighbors" (Piotrovskii 1973: 12; emphasis mine). Archaeological traditions outside the USSR shared a sense of the North Caucasus' dependency and cultural insufficiency. Årne Tallgren explained the artistic sophistication of the Maikop materials by suggesting that local rulers, bereft of skilled artisans, imported craftsmen from the Near East: "I imagine that at this time there was in Kuban an empire of nomad warriors, who had oriental craftsmen and artists in their service, and who were cattle-keepers and perhaps agriculturists" (1933: 198).

More recently, Andrew Sherratt has argued similarly:

> The picture that emerges, therefore, is of the Caucasus as a peripheral region rather suddenly penetrated by outside influences – most probably motivated by the desire for precious metals – and not thereafter closely involved in the international trading system which grew up . . . among the major urban centres of the Bronze Age world. (1997: 464–6)

The emergence of new sociopolitical forms in the Caucasus, in other words, was driven not by local transformations and innovations, but through the intercession of outside civilizations, particularly those from Mesopotamia.

However, the evidence for Near Eastern "influence" in the North Caucasus at the time of the Maikop phenomenon is at present remarkably thin. The case for the impact of Near Eastern societies on the emergence of the Maikop horizon generally rests on two evidentiary foundations: iconographic parallels between imagery on Maikop metalwork and scenes on seals from northern Mesopotamia (particularly Tepe Gawra) and eastern Anatolia (e.g., Değirmentepe) and perceived similarities between early Maikop ceramic forms and those recovered from sites in Syria and northern Mesopotamia (both Amuq F and Gawra XII–IX; Andreeva 1977). Yet as Kohl (2007: 75) pointed out, an array of arguably more consequential evidence, including residential architecture and subsistence practices, bear little resemblance to Mesopotamian models. Hence we remain uncertain as to whether the transformations in social life in the Northwest Caucasus evidenced by the Maikop assemblages were shaped primarily by encounters with surrounding communities or rather resulted from local innovations in the social mobilization of wealth and mortuary practices that stimulated an original aesthetic, as Rostovtzeff argued. It is important to note that while archaeological interpretations have tended to emphasize either internal or external forces to explain the Maikop phenomenon, these are not necessarily mutually exclusive but rather likely operated in tandem. Yet a significant explanatory burden certainly lies with those arguing for external influence on local transformations to detail the sociology of contact, the processes of interaction, and the local practices that shaped the development of new traditions.

What has long been conspicuously missing from efforts to link the Maikop phenomenon with developments in the Near East has been evidence of interaction in the archaeological records of the intervening spaces of the South Caucasus. That is, arguments for contact between communities in the Near East and North Caucasus must be able to locate the points of contact. Small collections of ceramic materials with stylistic and formal connections to 5th and early 4th millennium BC Mesopotamia have long been known throughout the Caucasus. Halaf ceramics have been reported from Dagestan in the north to Nakhichevan in the south; Ubaid painted wares have been recovered from sites across the South Caucasus, most recently at the site of Nerkin Godedzor in the Arpa valley of southern Armenia (Avetisyan et al. 2006). These finds have traditionally been attributed to interregional exchange. However, a key exception to this tendency has been the work of Narimanov (1985) who has suggested, based on finds from the site of Leiladepe and similar complexes, that a new population arrived in the South Caucasus during the first half of the 4th millennium BC that was "genetically related to the North Ubaid in Mesopotamia and probably emerged through migrations of the Ubaid tribes northwards to South Caucasia" (Museibli 2009: 52).

Catherine Marro (2007) substantially followed Narimanov, arguing that five sites dating to the first half of the 4th millennium BC represent communities of northern Mesopotamians dislocated into the Caucasus: Hanago in the Iğdir plain of northeastern Turkey, Aştepe, and Çolpan along the northeast shore of Lake Van, Berikldeebi in central Georgia, and Leiladepe in central Azerbaijan. The primary basis for Marro's argument is a perceived similarity in chaff-faced wares from these sites with Amuq phase F materials known from northern Syro-Mesopotamia.

Marro is certainly correct to reorient the discussion of Caucasian-Mesopotamian interaction in the 4th millennium BC away from vague claims of "influence" and toward specific locations of encounter and practices of interaction. However, chaff-faced wares are well known in the Caucasus for at least a millennium prior to their appearance within the surface collections of Marro's survey sites or the excavated contexts of Berikldeebi and Leiladepe (e.g., in the Neolithic assemblages from Aknashen, Aratashen, and Areni; Badalyan et al. 2004). These wares constitute an enduring South Caucasian ceramic tradition which can easily accommodate the assemblages cited by Marro, thus obviating the need to take recourse in long-distance migrations. Moreover, it is important to recall the much cited, but regularly forgotten, admonition of Carol Kramer (1977) that pots simply do not equal people. Thus there are risks, both evidentiary and theoretical, in interpreting chaff-faced wares as evidence of Mesopotamians abroad.

Models which detail connections between the Near East and the Northwest Caucasus must eventually come to terms with the territory of the South Caucasus which separated the two, a region caught up in its own dramatic transformations under the chronologically overlapping Kura-Araxes horizon. At present there is very little evidence to suggest the kind of close ties between Maikop and Kura-Araxes communities (Kohl 2007: 84) that might suggest the latter played a role in mediating ties to the Near East. Indeed, in turning to the Kura-Araxes horizon, we find the currents flowing in the opposite direction as the Caucasus takes center stage as a region of intense cultural production that expanded its repertoire of material practices throughout the northern Near East.

3. Out of the Caucasus: The Kura-Araxes

Under the auspices of the Kura-Araxes horizon, communities in the Caucasus became closely tied into an expansive Early Bronze Age (EBA) regional *oikumene* that, at its height, extended from the Northeastern Caucasus to the Levant. In coining the term Kura-Araxes, Boris Kuftin (1940) fixed the homeland of the horizon squarely in the South Caucasus. The discovery of related assemblages across a wide swath of the northern Near East thus constituted compelling evidence for interactions, exchanges, and population movements between the Caucasus and its southern neighbors. Only recently, however, have the specific motivations and mechanisms of these encounters been subject to scrutiny.

While most conspicuously defined by ceramic vessels with black and red-black burnished surfaces, the Kura-Araxes horizon is defined by a complex material assemblage that cuts across a broad array of materials and media, including rectilinear and circular residential architecture, ceramic zoomorphic hearths, and animal figurines, an array of bone implements including spindle whorls and awls, a repertoire of bronze ornaments and weapons, and a lithic toolkit that tends to favor flint for sickle blades and obsidian for scrapers, arrowheads, and other items. The date and location of the initial appearance of the Kura-Araxes horizon is a matter of considerable debate at present, as a series of new radiocarbon determinations have helped to push its earliest appearance back to the third quarter of the 4th millennium BC in northeast Anatolia, the Upper Euphrates, and the South Caucasus (Kavtaradze 1983).

At the site of Sos Höyük in northeastern Anatolia, radiocarbon dates from level VA suggest the appearance of red-black burnished wares sometime around 3500 BC (Kiguradze and Sagona 2003). Similar wares appeared in the Upper Euphrates at roughly the same time, as evidenced by remains from Arslantepe and Tepeçik (Frangipane and Palumbi 2007: 234). In the South Caucasus, calibrated radiocarbon dates from EBA tombs at Horom and Talin (tomb 10), as well as the settlement at Aparan III, all point to the existence of a full-fledged Kura-Araxes material assemblage c.3350 BC (Palumbi 2003), although new evidence from the cave site of Areni in southern Armenia may push the earliest known appearance of Kura-Araxes pottery there back into the second quarter of the 4th millennium BC.

By the last centuries of the 4th millennium BC, Kura-Araxes communities had begun a process of steady geographic expansion that ultimately extended the distribution of related material assemblages in what Palumbi calls the "Kura-Araksization" of eastern Anatolia, the Upper Euphrates, and northwest Iran. The extension of Kura-Araxes communities beyond the Caucasus has been a critical focus of scholarly attention, as it directly challenges traditional models (seen clearly in the case of Maikop above) that privilege Syro-Mesopotamia as a generative location of cultural production. Sherratt (1997: 468), for example, struggled to understand the Kura-Araxes as, like Maikop, a derivative effect of Uruk expansion: "The result of these [Late Uruk] contacts was to transform the Eneolithic cultures of Transcaucasia into a successful and independent bloc of highland peoples, the Kura-Arax culture, which resisted incorporation into lowland polities but absorbed many of the characteristics of contemporary urban civilization."

The suggestion that communities in the late 4th millennium BC Caucasus adopted elements of "urban civilization" is extremely difficult to countenance. Quite the contrary, in the case of the Kura-Araxes, it appears that the South Caucasus not only became an alternative location of cultural production but that the spread of Kura-Araxes communities effectively overturned Mesopotamian hegemony in parts of the northern Near East that had developed during the Late Uruk era. Nevertheless, the practices that drove the Kura-Araxes expansion remain, at present, poorly understood.

One oft-cited explanation for the rapid spread of Kura-Araxes communities is a series of migratory waves resulting from population pressures in the South Caucasus heartland triggered by climate change or overgrazing (Sagona 1984: 138–9). Recent paleoenvironmental studies, however, do not appear to support this suggestion. Palynological studies of sediment cores in the area of the Tsalka plateau indicate that the period c.4000–2000 BC witnessed a rather stable "climatic optimum" (Conner and Sagona 2007: 35). Alternatively, Mitchell Rothman (2003) has suggested that the Kura-Araxes expansion developed out of a series of more quotidian movements and transformations. The primary factor in the expansion of the Kura-Araxes, according to Rothman, was, at least initially, access to new markets in eastern Anatolia and northern Syria (e.g., at Tell Brak or Hamoukar).

Rothman's reconstruction quite rightly emphasized the importance of accounting for both the dynamic geographic spread of the Kura-Araxes horizon out of the Caucasus and into the Near East and the sources of variability within it. However, there is little at present to support the idea of an expansion driven by markets in northern Syria. Some "Transcaucasian"-style metals are indeed found south of the Anti-Taurus range (e.g., Tell Mozan). But there is very little evidence of Kura-Araxes materials in the large sites of northern Syria. And as Kohl (1992: 124) has noted, there is very little to suggest the movement of "materials or peoples" from northern Mesopotamia into the Armenian Highland and the South Caucasus. Indeed, what is most interesting about the relationship between northern Syria and the world of the Kura-Araxes to the north is just how little contact there seems to have been across what appears to have been a tightly regulated social boundary (Smith 2005).

Giulio Palumbi (2008) has offered the most detailed summary to date of the dynamics of Kura-Araxes expansion. Based on the evidence from Anatolia, particularly Arslantepe and Sos Höyük, he cogently argued that red-black burnished ware, a critical element of the Kura-Araxes assemblage, originated in eastern Anatolia yet moved quickly eastwards thanks to intensive interactions along the riverine corridors of the Araks and Kura basins (Palumbi 2003: 104). Communities in the South Caucasus then added these distinctive wares to the larger Kura-Araxes portmanteau which then moved back into Anatolia and beyond as the horizon expanded across the northern Near East. The speed of this movement suggests that the Kura-Araxes expansion was accomplished through multiple social processes including migrations out of the South Caucasus as well as the assimilation of local communities, which adopted the new material traditions and routines.

Of critical importance is how Palumbi's account of the Kura-Araxes expansion reorients our understanding of the relationship between communities in the Caucasus and those in Anatolia. Rather than the Kura-Araxes horizon forming as a result of contact with Mesopotamian traditions, the key dynamic is instead the withdrawal of Uruk influence from eastern Anatolia and the creation of a regional power vacuum. For Palumbi, the spread of Kura-Araxes communities was made possible by the collapse of the Uruk system. Here, the finds from the "royal tomb" at Arslantepe are particularly illuminating.

The tomb is a remarkable mortuary feature built in the wake of the destruction event that razed the earlier (VIA) palatial complex. The lower chamber of the tomb held the skeleton of the principal interred, along with a funerary inventory of extraordinary wealth. But what has attracted the most attention is the geographic and cultural diversity of the offerings, including weapons, jewelry, metal vessels, and ceramic jars with strong parallels to South Caucasian Kura-Araxes assemblages (e.g. Amiranis Gora, Elar, Kvatskhelebi, and Satchkere), Maikop funerary objects from the North Caucasus (such as Klady-Novsvobodnaya cemetery, the Nalchik *kurgans*, and the Maikop tomb itself), Syro-Mesopotamian materials (e.g. tombs from Karkamish and Bireçik), as well as artifacts rooted in local traditions (Palumbi 2008: 111–12).

Palumbi presented two possible interpretations of the tomb, which hinge on varying accounts of the dynamics linking the Caucasus to Anatolia and the wider Near East. In the first, the burial is a tomb of a "chief" from a community in the South Caucasus that periodically migrated to the Upper Euphrates valley (Palumbi 2008: 150). Alternatively, the burial may represent the leader of a local community who maintained strong economic ties with the Caucasus staked particularly in the exchange of metal ores and finished products (Palumbi 2008: 152). Palumbi leaned to the latter interpretation largely because the distances between the Caucasus and Upper Euphrates were simply too great to manage within a routine of seasonal migration.

While interpretations of Maikop assemblages have tended to define the Caucasus as a marginal region caught in the wider transformations reshaping social and political life in the "civilizational centers" of the Near East, investigations of the Kura-Araxes beyond the Caucasus struggle to maintain the integrity of local traditions. Palumbi, for example, was concerned to reassert a local Anatolian presence against the apparent onslaught of Caucasian cultural products. Only by challenging the assumption that red-black ware is a marker of South Caucasian populations, he argued, can we "restore historical depth and regional variability" to the Kura-Araxes phenomenon (Palumbi 2008: 17–18). Palumbi's concern to check the power of historical determination emanating from the South Caucasus during the EBA is in considerable contrast to the contemporary understanding of the articulation of Near Eastern and Caucasian communities during the succeeding Middle Bronze Age.

4 Fragmentation and Fission: The Middle Bronze Age

The beginning of the Middle Bronze Age (MBA) in the South Caucasus heralded the steady eclipse of the Kura-Araxes material tradition, the widespread abandonment of settled villages, and the appearance of tumulus burials known as *kurgans* – archaeological markers which, taken together, testify to considerable upheaval in the social and political order of the region. Currently available radiocarbon determinations suggest that by c.2400 BC, Kura-Araxes villages had been largely abandoned, as a new way of life predicated on increased mobility, social inequality, and a politics of charismatic militarism took hold. To date, only a handful of substantial MBA settlements have been documented in the South Caucasus (e.g., Uzerlik Tepe in western Azerbaijan, Kül Tepe II in Nakhichevan, and Metsamor in Armenia's Ararat Plain), along with a limited number of more ephemeral occupations. The archaeological record of the MBA is thus at present derived largely from excavations of mortuary contexts.

In the North Caucasus, the transition from the EBA to MBA was far less dramatic than in the South. Communities predicated on transhumance, already visible in the funerary assemblages (and limited settlement contexts) of the Maikop era, endured well into the 2nd millennium BC. As a result, while a large number of Middle Bronze Age *kurgans* have been excavated, evidence of settlements continues to be scanty across the central and western segments of the North Caucasus. However, there is a clear moderation in mortuary ritual that resulted in far less extravagant displays of conspicuous consumption. Overall, the region appears to have become increasingly tied to the steppe with grave assemblages suggesting strong links to communities of the Catacomb (Catacombnaya) archaeological horizon. Indeed, as Chernykh (1992: 100) noted, so close are the material parallels between their assemblages that the boundary between the North Caucasian and Steppe Catacomb horizons is extremely vague. The close articulation of the North Caucasus with the steppe during the MBA in large measure overwhelms evidence of interactions with areas to the south, including the South Caucasus and the Near East. As a result, the discussion below focuses on the South Caucasus, which remained in substantive dialog with locations farther south.

Traditionally, the abandonment of EBA communities and the repudiation of their attendant assemblages has also been understood as the end of the sociocultural hegemony of the South Caucasus in the northern Near East: "The evident relationship between eastern Anatolia and Transcaucasia [under the auspices of the Kura-Araxes culture] broke during EB III, and the two regions seem to have had little to do with each other during the Middle Bronze Age" (Edens 1995:

53). It does indeed appear that the end of the EBA initially entailed both an increasing localization of material culture horizons and a reorientation of the more far-flung parts of the Kura-Araxes world toward other regional interlocutors. For example, evidence from the Upper Euphrates area indicates the development of new local traditions during the late 3rd millennium followed by increasingly close relationships with Assyria and, later, the Hittite world of central Anatolia (Özfirat 2006: 160). However, other parts of the Near East, particularly eastern Anatolia, eventually re-established close ties to the South Caucasus during the early 2nd millennium BC, suggesting a continued, close relationship between the two regions.

The initial phase of the South Caucasian MBA (c.2400–2150 BC) is most clearly defined by the appearance of *kurgan*-style burials – pit and stone cist tombs covered by tumuli of earth and/or stone cobbles. We have stratigraphic evidence of a shift between late Kura-Araxes and so-called "Early Kurgans" assemblages from several sites, including Tsikhiagora in Georgia, where settlement layers show a gradual change in the percentages of wares from late Kura-Araxes pottery to mixed levels where post-Kura-Araxes (Martkopi-Bedeni) wares predominate. What is most striking about the initial MBA assemblages are the indications that they provide of significant transformations underway during the third quarter of the 3rd millennium BC.

The dramatic shift in settlement patterns across the South Caucasus during the transition to the MBA is traditionally interpreted as evidence of the advent of increasingly nomadic social groups predicated upon large-scale pastoral economies. Additionally, mortuary assemblages indicate an accelerating process of social differentiation throughout the MBA, overturning the more egalitarian ethos of the preceding era visible in the collective tombs of the Kura-Araxes. A new class of elites entombed in ostentatious *kurgans* filled with an array of grave goods was well established by the end of the 3rd millennium BC. The first appearance of painted ceramic vessels, such as those found in the "Trialeti-Vanadzor" assemblages from the "flourishing stage" *kurgans* at Trialeti, the Great Kurgan at Vanadzor, and tombs excavated at Lori Berd and Karashamb, mark the second phase of the MBA (c.2150–1750 BC; Smith et al. 2009: 62). In addition, it was during this period that mortuary assemblages emphasize growing social stratification and the prominence of pastoral production and equestrian mobility within communities of the South Caucasus. The appearance of carts and wagons, as well as ox and horse sacrifices, in burials from sites such as Trialeti (group II; Gogadze 1972), Lori-Berd (Devedjian 1981), and Aruch (Areshian et al. 1977) attest not only to the technology of mobility during the MBA, but also to its centrality to dimensions of belief and value. The inclusion of large numbers of bronze spearheads, axes, swords, daggers, and arrowheads (also of obsidian) point to the considerable violence of the era, as does the iconography of a silver-plated goblet from the *kurgan* at Karashamb. The Karashamb goblet, in particular, indicates that this violence was politically ordered, undertaken under the auspices of elite competition and framed by a piratical political economy predicated on conquest, raiding, and death (A.T. Smith 2001).

At present, we lack clearly identifiable comparative assemblages of either the Early Kurgans or Trialeti-Vanadzor phase of the MBA in most of eastern Anatolia (an important exception is apparently northeastern Anatolia where ceramic vessels from the cemeteries of Ani, Küçük Çatma [Maly Pergit], and Sos Höyük [IV] include both black burnished and monochrome painted wares of the Trialeti-Vanadzor tradition [Özfırat 2008: 103]). In part, this lacuna in our understanding of eastern Anatolia in the immediate aftermath of the Kura-Araxes may be a result of the restricted scale of archaeological investigations in eastern Turkey dedicated to documenting the region's prehistory after the EBA. However, the lack of assemblages in eastern Anatolia comparable to the Early Kurgans and Trialeti-Vanadzor complexes from the South Caucasus may also indicate a slower pace of sociocultural transformation. Antonio Sagona (et al. 2004: 479, 491–2) has suggested, based on his investigations at Sos Höyük, that Kura-Araxes communities lingered in northeastern Anatolia into the 2nd millennium BC. Furthermore, research by Aynur Özfırat (2001, 2006) has indicated that the final phase of the Kura-Araxes horizon in the Lake Van basin was succeeded by ceramic assemblages with clear parallels to wares attributed to the final phase of the South Caucasian MBA. This would suggest that Kura-Araxes traditions endured in eastern Anatolia for centuries after they were abandoned in the South Caucasus. However, ties between the two regions were re-established during the second quarter of the 2nd millennium BC.

During the final phase of the MBA (c.1700–1500 BC), three distinct, yet geographically overlapping, material culture horizons predominate in the South Caucasus and eastern Anatolia: Karmir-Berd (a.k.a. Tazakend), Karmir-Vank (a.k.a. Kizil Vank, Van-Urmia), and Sevan-Uzerlik (a.k.a. Sevan-Artsakh). The Karmir-Berd horizon, which largely prevails in the highlands of the central South Caucasus, is principally defined by a monochrome painted pottery tradition most iconically represented in the materials from the site of Verin Naver (Simonyan 1984). In contrast, a polychrome painted pottery tradition known as the Karmir-Vank horizon is best known from eastern Anatolia, Nakhichevan, and northwestern Iran (Özfırat 2001). Lastly, the Sevan-Uzerlik horizon tends to predominate in the western steppe of Azerbaijan, the Nagorno-Karabakh highlands, and southeastern Armenia (Kushnareva 1997). Sevan-Uzerlik ceramics are predominantly black polished vessels with incised and punctate decoration.

In detailing relations between eastern Anatolia and the South Caucasus during the last phase of the MBA, it is important to remember that the general regional divisions of the three horizon styles cannot be taken as defining a rigid geographic mosaic. In Georgia, Trialeti-Vanadzor materials persist into the MB III phase at sites such as Treli and Pevrebi; however, it is also possible to detect the influence of Sevan-Uzerlik complexes. Several sites in Armenia boast assemblages composed of Karmir-Berd and Sevan-Uzerlik materials (e.g., Verin Naver) while others combine Karmir-Berd and Karmir-Vank wares (e.g., Aruch, Karashamb, etc.). Sites in the area of Ağrı Dağ (Mount Ararat) principally include Karmir-Berd and Sevan-Uzerlik assemblages (Özfirat 2008: 104) rather than the Karmir-Vank traditions that predominate in nearby Nakhichevan. Finally, numerous sites in northwestern Iran (e.g., Geoy Tepe and Haftavan Tepe) include both monochrome Karmir-Berd and polychrome Karmir-Vank ceramics (Burney 1975).

Hence, we not only face considerable difficulties in understanding the chronology of east Anatolian/South Caucasian interaction during the first half of the 2nd millennium BC, we remain largely in the dark regarding the specific dynamics represented by technically and aesthetically distinct, yet geographically interdigitated, ceramic traditions. Nevertheless, the appearance of MBA assemblages in eastern Anatolia with close ties to South Caucasian traditions suggests the operation of similar socioeconomic transformations across the two regions and the re-establishment of regular interactions amongst local communities. Most notably, the movement toward mobile pastoralism in the South Caucasus was matched by a similar shift in the communities of eastern Anatolia: "[T]here is an obvious reduction in the number of agricultural settlements; cemeteries appear on the high pastures, which are unrelated to any settlement; a new tradition in pottery styles develops; and finally a new type of burial mound (kurgan) occurs" (Özfirat 2006: 162). Furthermore, the appearance of *kurgan*-style burials in eastern Anatolia strongly suggests that the shift in settlement entailed not only similar approaches to subsistence economy but also a wider sense of worldview. Hence the rapid disappearance of MBA traditions from the South Caucasus sometime around 1500 BC effectively reset relations with communities in the northern Near East just a few centuries after they had finally been reestablished following the collapse of the Kura-Araxes horizon.

5 Complex Encounters: The Late Bronze Age and Iron I Period

Beginning around 1500 BC a new sociopolitical apparatus was forged in the South Caucasus, one which welded the social inequality visible in the MBA mortuary landscape to a centralizing administrative apparatus emplaced in variably sized stonemasonry fortresses built atop hills and outcrops. With this fortified landscape came a new pattern of interactions between the Caucasus and the Near East. While exchange relations appear to have become more extensive, political ties became progressively more troubled, culminating in the consolidation and violent expansion of the Urartian Empire during the 8th century BC – the first polity to effectively unite the South Caucasus and portions of the northern Near East under a single authority.

The archaeology of the Late Bronze Age (LBA) in the Caucasus has long languished in relative obscurity – overshadowed by both the imperial grandeur of Urartu and the geographic expansiveness of the Kura-Araxes horizon. However, a number of recent research projects have provided important new views on the initial emergence of complex societies in the South Caucasus during the LBA, including Raffaele Biscione et al.'s (2002) survey in the Lake Sevan region and excavations by Konstantine Pizchelauri (2003) at the fortress of Udabno. At present, it is the combined regional survey and intensive excavations of the joint Armenian/American Project for the Archaeology and Geography of Early Transcaucasian Societies (Project ArAGATS), centered in the Tsaghkahovit plain of central Armenia, that provides the most extensive account of the LBA in the South Caucasus (Badalyan et al. 2003, 2008; Smith et al. 2009). Since 1998, Project ArAGATS has focused on the shifting dynamics of the Tsaghkahovit Plain's LBA occupation and it thus provides a useful case study for grounding the present discussion.

The fortified settlements of the LBA and Iron I period are often associated with large cemeteries, such as Treligorebi located on the outskirts of modern Tbilisi, Georgia, or the vast necropoli documented by Project ArAGATS on the mountain slopes surrounding the Tsaghkahovit plain. The ArAGATS regional survey identified a total of 199 burial clusters with mortuary features broadly describable as typical of the LBA, an overall density of 2.05 cemeteries per square kilometer. While *kurgan* burials do continue into the Late Bronze Age, they are outnumbered by a range of various "cromlech"-style tombs that include earthen pits, or later stone cists, surrounded by a ring of stones (Smith et al. 2009: 106). A conservative estimate of 30 cromlechs per cemetery yields an estimated total of 5970 LBA burials surrounding the Tsaghkahovit plain.

In addition to a radically transformed settlement pattern and new innovations in mortuary architecture, new ceramic and metal material repertoires that are referred to as the Lchashen-Metsamor or Lchashen-Tsitelgori traditions also mark the transition between the MBA and LBA in the South Caucasus. As the painted pottery of the Karmir-Berd and Karmir-Vank horizons disappeared, the Sevan-Uzerlik horizon's punctate designs were folded into, and overshadowed by, new assemblages of black, gray, and buff wares with incised and pressed circumferential decorations (Areshian et al. 1990). In addition, the scale, intensity, and diversity of bronze production increased dramatically during the LBA as manufacturing shifted to employing both open-work and lost-wax casting and the repertoire of artifacts expanded to include new forms such as battle-axes, maceheads, shaft-hole daggers, bits, flanged-hilt weapons, and statuettes. Variations on the Lchashen-Metsamor horizon endured in the South Caucasus through the Iron II period of the 8th–7th centuries BC as a distinct material tradition alongside the better-known palace wares of the Urartian imperial apparatus (Smith et al. 2009).

The beginning of the LBA inaugurated an extended era of political consolidation, centralization, collapse, and reformation. The transition from the mobile communities of the MBA to the complex polities of the LBA is currently most conspicuously visible on the Tsaghkahovit Plain in the assemblages from a single *kurgan* found just below the fortress of Gegharot. The *kurgan* had two main chambers. The west chamber contained a diverse collection of animal bones and a ceramic repertoire that constitutes a perfect transitional MBA to LBA assemblage, including Sevan-Uzerlik wares continuous with earlier traditions, as well as initial iterations of LBA wares. The central chamber, in contrast, contained the skeleton of an adult male laid to rest atop fragments from the body of a young infant. The human skeletons were effectively bracketed by the heads and forelimbs of two horses. Ceramic vessels in the chamber all belong to the emergent traditions of the LBA, as do the obsidian and bronze arrowheads and the single bronze knife. But what harkens back to an earlier era is a mortuary assemblage focused on instruments of mobility and violence.

Within a few years of the *kurgan*'s construction, the new object world of the LBA was emphatically emplaced within a series of fortified hilltop sites constructed along the margins of the Tsaghkahovit Plain. Radiocarbon dates and material assemblages suggest that the fortresses at Gegharot and Tsaghkahovit were built sometime around 1500 BC. Two other major fortified sites, followed no later than the early 14th century. Eight other small fortresses and outposts were in place by the mid-14th century BC. This network of interlinked sites was violently destroyed sometime prior to the beginning of the Iron 1 period in the 12th century BC. But similarly ordered polities appear to have ruled regions of the South Caucasus until its incorporation into the Achaemenid Empire.

While the sequence of material development from the mid-2nd millennium BC through the arrival of significant Urartian forces north of the Araks river around 786 BC has come to be better understood in the Caucasus, far less is currently known about what was happening concurrently in eastern Turkey and northwestern Iran. It does appear that across much of eastern Anatolia, MBA traditions – marked primarily by painted pottery assemblages – endured somewhat longer than in the Caucasus. In the Ağri Dağ region, MBA painted wares were succeeded by Lchashen-Metsamor ceramics, and collections in the Kars museum suggest a similar transformation in parts of northeastern Anatolia (Özfirat 2008: 105). However, in neither location is the timing of this transition well established. Nevertheless, it seems likely based on the chronologies of sites across the Akhourian (Arpaçay) river in the southern Shirak Plain of Armenia that the LBA in Kars began sometime around 1500 BC with the shift in the Ağrı Dağ region coming perhaps a century or two later.

The area from Lake Van west to Erzurum also experienced a more sustained MBA than in the South Caucasus, with polychrome wares continuing until c.1400/1300 BC (Özfirat 2008: 106). The well-dated sequences from sites in Nakhichevan, in contrast, present a somewhat peculiar case. Several sites in the area including Kül Tepe I (levels III–IV), Kül Tepe II (level III), and Kizil Vank (level 1b-2) indicate that polychrome painted pottery continued to be produced in the area through the late 2nd millennium BC, centuries after these wares had disappeared in neighboring regions. This sequence seems to tie the sites of

Nakhichevan more closely to material traditions in the Urmia region of northwestern Iran than to more proximal neighbors in the South Caucasus or eastern Anatolia.

The patchwork nature of the shift from MBA to LBA assemblages between the Caucasus and eastern Anatolia is certainly indicative of a region held together less by formalized relations of power than by informal networks of interaction. Nevertheless, ultimately the two regions again shared similar material horizons and practical regimes. By the beginning of the 1st millennium BC, both regions were ruled by small, rival polities centered in hilltop fortresses that were nevertheless united by a widely shared material culture assemblage. It is significant that once again the communities of the Caucasus served as critical locales of sociopolitical, aesthetic, and material innovation that in large measure drove processes of historical transformation in adjacent sectors of the northern Near East.

The emergent polities of the LBA and Iron 1 period do appear to have gained access to wider Near Eastern exchange networks. Evidence for long distance exchange relations has been recovered from a number of sites across the South Caucasus, including both precious and everyday objects manufactured as far away as northern Mesopotamia and Egypt. To return to our case study, the fortresses of the Tsaghkahovit plain appear to have participated in exchange networks that reached as far as northern Syria. In 2006, two cylinder seals were discovered at the site of Gegharot, traditional items of bureaucratic administration known from across the ancient Near East, but relatively rare in the South Caucasus (Badalyan et al. 2008). Both cylinder seals are of the Mitanni Common Style that gained considerable popularity across southwest Asia and the eastern Mediterranean during the 15th and 14th centuries BC. These seals were generally mass-produced and traded widely. What we do not have anywhere in the LBA South Caucasus, however, are sealings, the clay impressions formed by these items. This leaves open the very real possibility that even though prominent items of material culture testify to interactions between Gegharot and neighbors to the south, the items that came to the site were neither employed nor valued in the same way that they were elsewhere. Archaeological evidence of interaction, these data suggest, does not in itself provide evidence of one region's dependence on another, nor provide proof of one region's causal role in another's historical transformations.

6 Conclusion

Since de Morgan's investigations in the region, archaeological interpretations of the Bronze Age Caucasus have consistently explored the tension between models of autochthony and imitation. Available archaeological evidence suggests that the Caucasus and parts of the northern Near East were repeatedly fused into a coherent ecumene, a zone bound together by shared material practices and thus often lashed to similar historical transformations. The Kura-Araxes communities of the EBA were so tightly bound to one another that, while interactions were intense, sustained, and indeed geographically expansive within the Kura-Araxes world, they were sparse and irregular beyond its limits. The collapse of this EBA ecumene significantly diminished the geographic extent of the Caucasus's material hegemony in the Near East. Yet by the beginning of the 2nd millennium BC eastern Anatolia had re-established its close ties to the South Caucasus, adopting not only new traditions of material production but also a broad repertoire of social institutions and practices. Indeed, the Caucasus became an intensely generative region during this era, as it drove not only the expansion of mobile communities predicated on radical social inequality into eastern Anatolia, but also ultimately elaborated these MBA practices into the fortress-based polities of the LBA. The rise of Urartu and the success of its imperial campaigns ushered in a new era in relations between the Caucasus and the Near East. For the first time, portions of the two regions were formally subsumed to a single unified polity as the formality of sovereign incorporation replaced informal practices of everyday encounters.

Despite the extensive evidence for what archaeologists typically term "interaction," relations between the Caucasus and Near East during the Bronze and initial Iron Age also provide a much-needed caution for our theories of regional articulation. Archaeologies of interaction are consistently plagued by a too easy slippage between the observation of material homologies, the presumption of significant encounters, and the attribution of historical determination. That is, we tend to assume that shared material traits indicate social exchanges that were inherently causal. While there were clearly eras when ties between regions drove critical changes in social life, there are also centuries when the Caucasus and northern Near East explored separate paths. Hence, the continuation of EBA and MBA lifeways in eastern Anatolia long after they were abandoned in the South Caucasus serves as an important reminder that the pace and pathways of historical transformation may be shaped by interaction, but cannot be reduced to simply "le résultat de l'influence d'un peuple sur un autre" (the result of the influence of one people upon another) (de Morgan 1889: 4).

GUIDE TO FURTHER READING

For general orientation, see Kohl (2007) and Smith (2006). The cultures of the Caucasus and their relations with the Near East are treated in Lyonnet (2007) and Palumbi (2008). Recent research in northeastern Turkey is well covered in Sagona et al. (2004). For recent research in the Caucasus, particularly that of the Armenian/American expedition, see Smith et al. (2009).

CHAPTER THIRTY-SIX

Central Asia, the Steppe, and the Near East, 2500–1500 BC

Michael D. Frachetti and Lynne M. Rouse

1 Introduction

Given the geographical focus of this volume and the theme of this section, it might be logical to discuss the societies of Central Asia and the Eurasian steppe as peripheral to the growth of Near Eastern empires from the 3rd to 2nd millennia BC. However, in this chapter we temporarily reorient the focus to investigate tangible ways in which innovations and extensive networks formed by societies of Central Asia and the Eurasian steppe (Figure 36.1) impacted the rapid-pace changes in political economy in the Near East during the late 3rd and 2nd millennium BC. In doing so, this chapter situates our view of Near Eastern empires and states within a wider and more complex arena of economic, political, and social interaction across Asia in the Bronze Age (Possehl 2007).

From roughly 2500 to 1500 BC, proto-urban communities of Central Asia and mobile pastoralists of the Eurasian steppe emerged as integral agents in the growth of a wide network of interactions that bridged the Far East and southwest Asia, millennia before the historically known Silk Road. From the 3rd millennium BC onward, innovations from the Eurasian steppe and Central Asia found their way into the cultures of the greater Near East; whether recognized as equid-drawn war carts depicted on the royal standard of Ur (2600 BC), "intercultural style" vessels at Susa transported by Elamite traders (c.2500 BC), or semi-precious stones and materials extracted from far across Inner Asia and worked into burial adornments of Ur III rulers (2100–2000 BC). To be sure, the city-states and

---

A Companion to the Archaeology of the Ancient Near East, First Edition.
Edited by D.T. Potts.
© 2012 Blackwell Publishing Ltd. Published 2012 by Blackwell Publishing Ltd.

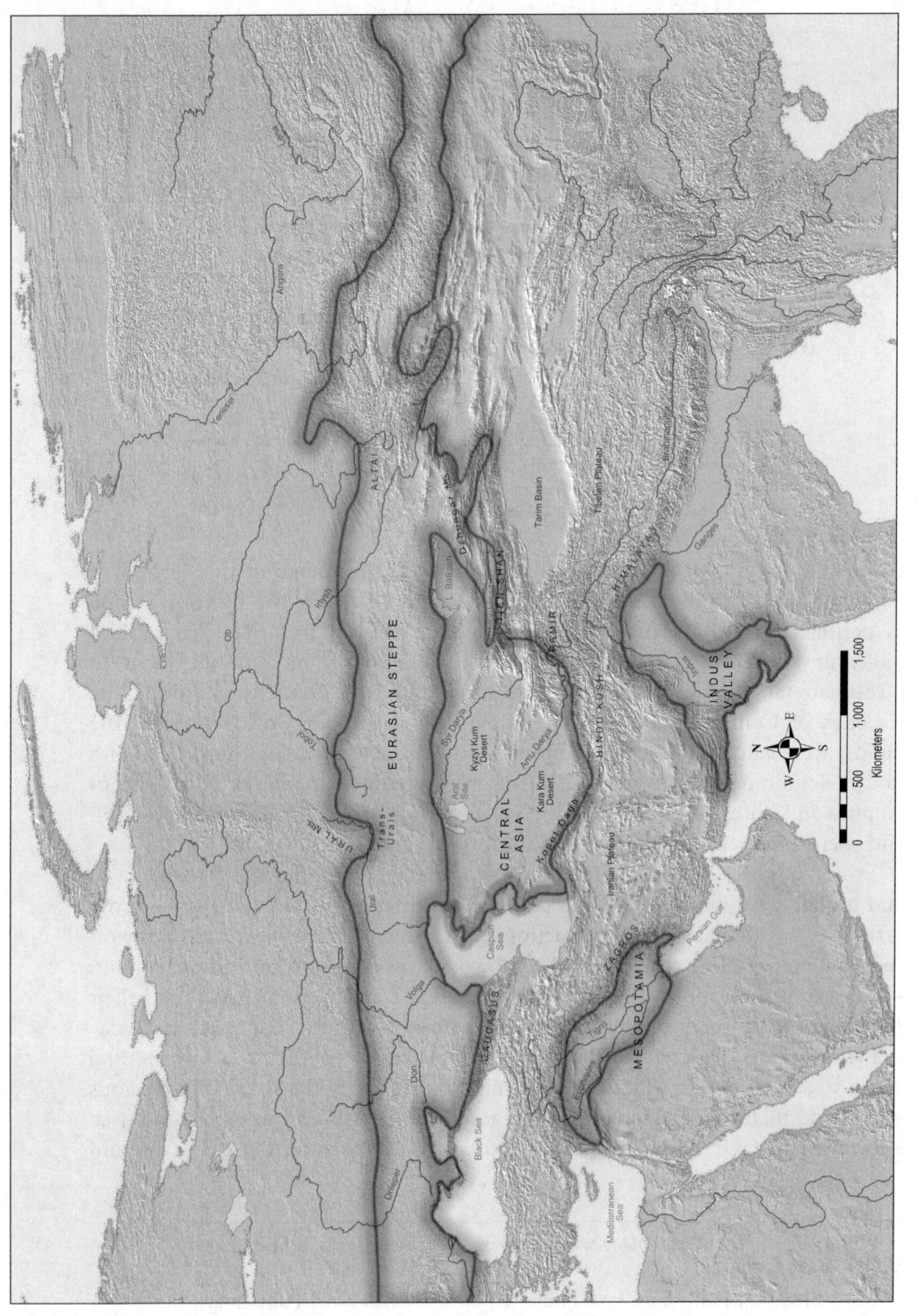

Figure 36.1 The Bronze Age world of Eurasia and Central Asia in relation to contemporary culture zones.

empires of Mesopotamia emerged rich in capital and ideological power by the end of the 3rd millennium BC and were undeniable forces in fostering material relationships that variously benefited and weighed upon their neighbors across southwest Asia. According to current archaeology, it was these neighboring societies – such as the Elamites of the Iranian plateau and the Harappans of the Indus Valley – who were more directly engaged with civilizations native to Central and Inner Asia.

The broad economic arena that took form across Asia in the late 3rd and 2nd millennia BC was not a top-down structure with Near Eastern empires dictating the terms of acquisition from distant subjects. Instead, practically and strategically generated lines of discourse and trade shaped the institutional alignment of groups far beyond the access of Near Eastern rulers, organically gestating independent civilizations in the oases, steppes, and mountains of Central and Inner Asia. For example, late 3rd millennium BC agriculturalists living along the Kopet Dagh mountains of Turkmenistan and foothills of Bactria bred a vital link with the Iranian plateau, connecting sites like Shortugai and Shahr-i Sokhta to resources in the Hindu Kush mountains (Lamberg-Karlovsky and Tosi 1973). Lapis lazuli and other commodities passed over long and diffuse chains of interaction across Central Asia and set the stage for durable economic ties between the Indus and the Near East (Potts 1999). Beyond these well-documented ties between Central and southwest Asia, recent archaeological discoveries in the mountain steppe regions of Kazakhstan now illustrate that similar networks likely extended north into the steppe as well. Mobile mountain pastoralists, like those living in the Dzhungar Mountains (Kazakhstan), were tapped into networks along Inner Asia's mountains and foothills transferring domesticated wheat, millet, and material innovations between southwest Asia and China in the late 3rd millennium BC (Mei and Rehren 2009; Frachetti et al. 2010).

Archaeological discoveries in Central Asia increasingly offer direct and indirect evidence of long-distance contacts in the Bronze Age (Possehl 2002b; Potts 2008a, 2008b; Salvatori 2008a), but our conceptual understanding of the various modes of social interaction that aligned these diverse and disparate societies is only now coming into clearer focus. Prehistoric populations living in the steppe zone and oases of Central Asia together represent a complicated matrix of intra/interregional diversity and overlap, which positions them as elemental players in the formation of Asian political economies more broadly. Here we start our investigation of this interactive arena with a basic geography of both the southern regions of Central Asia and the more northerly Eurasian steppe belt, before shifting attention to the main archaeological characteristics of these regions from 2500 to 1500 BC. This background provides the context to trace the growth of the extensive channels of interaction that emerged across "middle" Asia, both between Central Asian oasis cultures and the Eurasian steppe and further as part of the economic and political developments in the greater Near East during the Bronze Age. By way of a conclusion, some observations are made about the impact of Central Asian networks of exchange on the wide-scale transformations of southwest Asian social landscapes by the end of the 2nd millennium BC. Ultimately, the goal of this chapter is to highlight the contribution of societies which, from the perspective of Near Eastern empires of the 3rd and 2nd millennia BC, lived beyond the periphery of their direct influence, yet which, in concrete ways, fostered the expansion of material and ideological innovations that were important to the growth of civilizations across Asia during the Bronze Age.

2 Geography of Central and Inner Asia

Environmentally, Central Asia represents a series of geographic transitions as one travels north from the Iranian Plateau down the rain-fed piedmont of the Kopet Dagh range to the arid deserts of the Karakum and Kyzylkum, and eventually onward to the desert steppes and grasslands of Central Eurasia (Figure 36.2). Of course these broad environmental zones are carved and variegated by major and minor rivers, oases, and mountain ranges. By mapping these geographic anchors as the core of middle Asia, we can highlight the Eurasian steppes and oasis zones of Central Asia as key interstitial territories between Mesopotamia, Iran, the Indus Valley, and China. The multidirectional access to a wide host of economic and political interactions, as well as a wealth of natural resources, shaped unique strategies of production and interaction in both the Central Eurasian steppe and southern Central Asian oases.

Located to the northeast of what is generally conceived of as the ancient Near East, Central Asia covers the contemporary republics of Uzbekistan, Tajikistan, Turkmenistan, parts of Afghanistan, and the northern fringe of the Iranian plateau. The area is bounded by the Caspian Sea in the west, the Kopet Dagh and Hindu Kush Mountains in the south, the desert steppes of Kazakhstan in the north, and the Pamir Mountains in the east. Many distinct environments are contained within this region, including nearly uninhabitable deserts, oases, rivers and marshy river deltas, clay basins, foothill plains, and mountains.

The dominant deserts of southern Central Asia – the Karakum (Garagum) of Turkmenistan and the Kyzyl kum (Qyzylqum) of Uzbekistan – are characterized by extreme aridity and long, hot summers, where daytime temperatures often exceed 50°C (120°F). Rainfall occurs primarily in winter and spring, but rarely exceeds 150 millimeters per year, while some areas may go without rainfall for up to 10 years. The deserts are shaped by strong winds and cut by high-impact rivers which form marshy, deltaic fans and oases in lowland basins. The result is a variety of landforms which are home to specialized forms of plant and animal life and human adaptations.

Rivers are the lifeblood of southern Central Asia, providing reliable natural water sources and productive agricultural hinterland for numerous ancient and modern cities. Both the Syr Darya (the ancient Jaxartes) and the Amu Darya (the

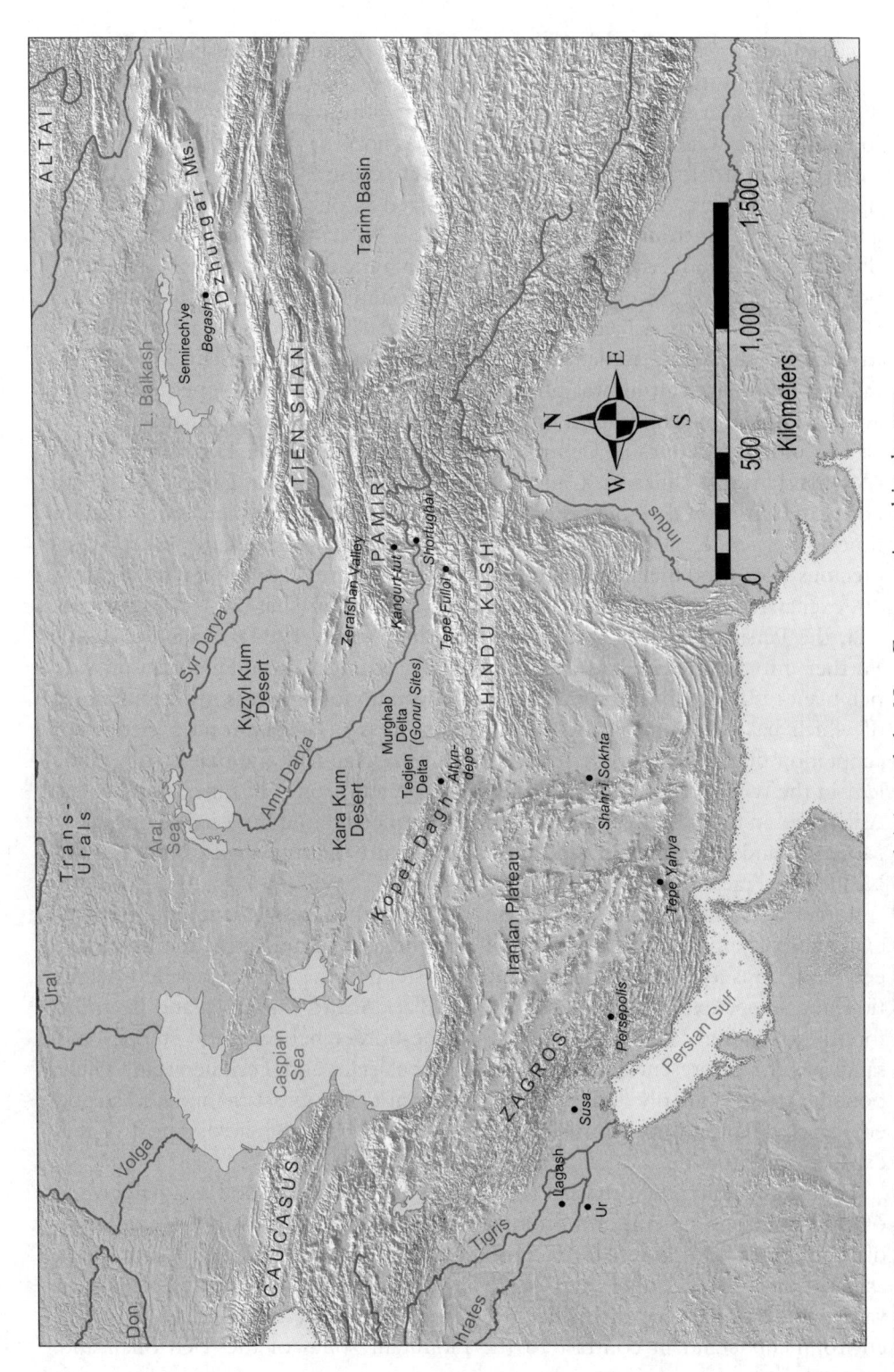

Figure 36.2 Sites and regions of Eurasia, Central Asia, and the Near East mentioned in the text.

ancient Oxus) rivers originate in glacially capped mountain peaks in the east and flow northwest toward the Aral Sea, depositing rich alluvial sediments (silts and clays) and providing water for irrigated agriculture along their courses in the lowlands. The waters of the Amu Darya have been so over-utilized in modern times for industrial-scale cotton production as to cause the nearly complete drying up of the southern Aral Sea, widely recognized as one of the most devastating anthropogenic environmental disasters of the 20th century (Micklin 2007). The diversion of Central Asia's rivers for irrigation agriculture is not a modern phenomenon, however, as evidenced by the exploitation of the Tedjen River delta (Geoksur oasis) in the Chalcolithic period, and the continuous use of canal-based irrigation in the Murghab delta from the Bronze Age to the present day. Stream-fed and runoff agriculture was practiced in the foothills of the Kopet Dagh from at least the 4th millennium BC onward, evidenced at the site of Anau.

The mountain zones of Central Asia, including the Kopet Dagh, the Pamirs (Afghanistan and Tajikistan), and the Hindu Kush (ancient Paropamisus), are zones of rich natural resources that have been regularly exploited since ancient times. Limestone, alabaster, steatite, carnelian, lapis lazuli, and other semi-precious stones and metal ores have been utilized from at least the 3rd millennium BC, exchanged for other raw materials and goods from as far away as Mesopotamia, the Persian Gulf, and the Indian Ocean (Hiebert 1994a; Possehl 2002b). Further into Inner Asia, the Tien Shan and Dzhungar mountains also provide rich plant resources for human and animal consumption, the seasonal exploitation of which has been key to the productive success of agropastoral societies, an adaptation documented from at least the Bronze Age and one that is still prevalent in the region today. Additionally, the mountain zones of Inner and Central Asia make up the traditional trade corridors connecting the Eurasian steppes with Mongolia and western China and Central Asian urban centers with India and the Near East (Frachetti in press).

Intensive strategies based in seasonally patterned movement and pastoral exploitation, known generally as mobile pastoralism, characterize the dominant economic basis for societies of the "Eurasian steppe zone." In its broadest definition, the steppe extends from north of the Black Sea to Mongolia and from the forests of southern Russia and Siberia to the border between arid steppes and sandy deserts of present day Kazakhstan, Uzbekistan, and Turkmenistan. These boundaries are primarily derived from the extent of the grassland and arid steppe ecologies, a typical but inconsistent environmental backdrop across most of this expansive territory.

Environmentally, the Eurasian steppe zone is best understood as a patchwork of localized environments and ecologic niches. Consequently it houses a diverse distribution of natural resources. Lush river valleys carved by such major rivers as the Volga, Ural, Tobol, and Irtysh are complemented by scores of smaller valleys fed by hundreds of smaller rivers and tributaries. These relatively stable environments stand in contrast to the mountain zones of the Tien Shan and

Dzhungar ranges, which experience drastic changes in temperature and precipitation both in a seasonal sense and between different altitudinal zones. Localized ecologic diversity is further highlighted in the Semirech'ye region, south of Lake Balkash in modern Kazakhstan, where the transition from arid, sandy steppe to fertile meadows to glacial peaks occurs over a distance of less than 400 kilometers. Ultimately, the diversity of Semirech'ye stands as a proxy for the geographically uneven distribution of resources and the diversity of ecological and climatic conditions in broader Eurasian and Central Asian contexts. It is precisely these localized conditions, and the sociopolitical and economic strategies they engender, that form the framework over which the social canvas of Bronze Age Asia was stretched.

3 Chronology and Archaeological Communities of Central and Inner Asia (2500–1500 BC)

In parallel with the rise of empires and states in Mesopotamia, Syro-Anatolia, the Persian Gulf, Iran, and the Indus Valley, Central Asia underwent a dramatic shift in social organization, production, and regional integration from the 3rd to the 2nd millennium BC. The Bronze Age of southern Central Asia is outlined chronologically by the Namazga sequence (Table 36.1), named after the type-site in the Kopet Dagh foothills of Turkmenistan. The Namazga I–III (Eneolithic/Chalcolithic) periods witnessed the development of early settlement hierarchies and burgeoning craft industries at sites along Kopet Dagh range (Gupta 1979; Kohl 1984) as well as increased contact and exchange with communities on the Iranian Plateau and in South Asia (Hiebert et al. 2003). By the Namazga IV period (Early Bronze Age) and continuing through Namazga VI (Late Bronze

Table 36.1 Gross comparative chronology of Central Asia and the steppe zone

	Bactria/ Margiana Oases	Central Kopet Dagh	W. Kopet Dagh	Western Eurasia Steppe		Eastern Eurasia Steppe
1500	Molali/ Takhirbai	Late Namazga VI	Anau IVa	Alakul	Andronovo Culture	. . . Karasuk
1700	BMAC	Namazga VI		Alakul		Fedorovo
1900	BMAC	Namazga V		Petrovka		. . . Fedorovo
2200	. . . BMAC	Namazga IV–V		Sintashta		Begash
2700		Namazga III–IV	Anau III	Catacomb/ Yamnaya		Begash (late) Afanasievo

Age), fully fledged urban centers such as Altyn-depe developed specialized craft industries (Masson 1968; Kircho et al. 2008) and clearly participated in inter-regional trade networks, most notably contributing to the crystallization of the Bactria-Margiana Archaeological Complex (BMAC or "Oxus civilization").

The BMAC is represented by large, fortified settlements in the Mughab delta of Turkmenistan and the foothills of northern Afghanistan (ancient Margiana and Bactria, respectively). These urban populations were dependent on irrigation agriculture and domestic animal husbandry (Sarianidi 1984; Hiebert 1994a; Moore et al. 1994; Miller 1999) as well as the importation of exotic raw materials such as metals and semi-precious stones to facilitate craft production (Hiebert 1994b; Salvatori et al. 2008).

Although the demographic and cultural genesis of the BMAC is intensely debated (see Kohl 2002; Sarianidi 2007; and Salvatori et al. 2008 for various viewpoints), it is clear that it participated in a wider theater of interaction. Francfort (1994) and Winkelmann (1997) noted the cross-regional stylistic repertoire underlying BMAC crafts, but emphasized the particular material expression of BMAC ideology in its own right. BMAC crafts display a unique constellation of art and material expression, depicting wild and fantastic animals and anthropomorphic heroes in combat on metal seals and ceremonial weaponry, as well as visually striking contrasts of color and material in worked stone objects and other small items (Hiebert 1994b). The Tepe Fullol treasure, found near ancient lapis lazuli mines in Bactria, one of the most well-known examples of BMAC material, illustrates the blend of local Central Asian craftwork and form mixed with, in this instance, Mesopotamian bull imagery (Tosi and Wardak 1972) (Figure 36.3).

Figure 36.3 A gold bowl depicting bull imagery from the Tepe Fullol (Afghanistan) treasure, dating to the Bronze Age in Bactria (courtesy of the Kabul Museum).

Although unique and readily attributable as BMAC materials, the variety of motifs and the semiotics of trade objects at this time clearly reflect the range of interactions linking south and southwest Asia with the urban centers of Central Asia (Sarianidi 2002; Kohl 2007).

Despite the wide stylistic resonance of BMAC craft production, the only naturally available local raw materials were clay/terracotta and bone, meaning that all other materials – including stone and metals – had to be imported from elsewhere. Evidently, the network for acquiring these raw materials was vast, illustrating contacts with south Asia (various marine shells), mountainous zones of Afghanistan and Tajikistan (semi-precious stone and tin), southern Iran (semi-precious stones) and the Iranian plateau (stone) (Hiebert 1994a, 1994b; Parzinger and Boroffka 2003; Law 2006). Finished BMAC objects have been identified in all these locations, though only a very small number of reciprocal finished items from these territories seem to return to the BMAC core region. Most notable among these cases are stamp seals found at Altyn-depe and carved "stick-devices" resonant of styles and symbols common in Indus civilization assemblages (c.2500–2000 BC) (Possehl 2002a: 230). Thus, the emerging pattern is one in which raw materials were imported to the BMAC region and finished products were exported back to those regions providing the raw material, as well as further afield to the societies of Elam and Mesopotamia.

While BMAC communities were fostering extensive exchange networks with civilizations to the south and west, mobile pastoralist communities dominated the economic and political landscape of the central Eurasian steppe by cultivating extensive networks, in their own right. Traditionally subsumed under the broad culture-historical moniker of the "Andronovo Culture," Bronze Age steppe communities exhibit broadly similar design elements and forms of material culture, burial traditions, and economies, with regional variations such as the Petrovka (c.1900 BC), Alakul (c.1650 BC) and Fedorovo (c.1800 BC) distributed from the Urals to the borders of western Mongolia and as far south as the foothill terraces and oases of eastern Tajikistan, Uzbekistan, Bactria, and Margiana (Turkmenistan) (Vinogradova 1993; Kuz'mina 2007). Material and economic aspects of this complicated mosaic of communities arguably emerged in regionally independent contexts as early as 2500 BC (Frachetti 2008). Recent studies at the site of Begash in southeastern Kazakhstan illustrate the development of a local pastoralist sequence from the mid-3rd to the late 1st millennium BC (Frachetti and Mar'yashev 2007), though documented shifts in ceramic styles and burial rites do indicate a new era of participation in material and technological exchange from 1900 to 1600 BC. As far south as Tajikistan, settlements such as Kangurt-tut and burial sites such as Zardcha Khalifa and Dashti Kozy exhibit ceramics and metallurgy with obvious parallels to late Bronze Age sites in the steppe zone (Bobomulloev 1998). These sites, roughly dated to the late 2nd millennium BC, suggest that the extension of steppe networks was intertwined with exchange vectors of southern Central Asia. It also appears that specialized pastoralists may have been the key to this interaction (Avanesova and Dzhurakulova 2008). In fact, earlier innovations such as two wheeled chariots can also be traced confidently to steppe communities at Sintashta (2300–1900 BC) (Gening et al. 1992), while forms of bronze smelting and casting, and ideological registers innovated in the steppe became part of a wider practical and symbolic lexicon from China to Iran in the Bronze Age (Mei 2003; Peterson 2007; Chernykh 2009; Roberts et al. 2009).

Steppe Bronze Age societies are generally viewed through the lens of their shared designs in ceramics, bronze axes, jewelry, and burial constructions, while the genesis of such wide distributions of steppe material culture and symbolism remains one of the pressing questions in Central Asian archaeology. Some have proposed direct demo/cultural migrations to explain the geographic distribution, originating from the western territories of the steppe and reaching east to China and south to Tajikistan and Turkmenistan by 1500 BC (Kuz'mina 1986; Anthony 2007). Others have proposed a nuanced model of local interactions, whereby regionally entrenched pastoralists generated networks for rapid exchanges of materials and concepts via the normal geographic variation of their limited mobility patterns (Frachetti 2008). Assimilation and diversity of social, political, and even linguistic affiliation may also partly explain the admixture of material elements across the vast Eurasian landmass. As with most models of human behavior, the answer likely lies somewhere between these proposals, as these processes are not, necessarily, mutually exclusive.

4 Links Between the BMAC and the Steppe

The Murghab delta of southern Turkmenistan has been a context for cultural interaction in Central Asia since ancient times (Tashbaeva and Gritsina 2005), as typically sedentary farming communities of the lowlands and mobile agropastoral groups inhabiting the surrounding mountains and mountain steppes formed a complex interrelationship from at least the Early Bronze Age. Material cultural diversity in BMAC contexts is illustrated by the recovery of hand-made ceramic vessels and sherds (known as "steppe ceramics" or "Incised Coarse Ware," ICW) which have been associated with mobile pastoralists (Cerasetti 1998; Pyankova 1994, 2002; Vinogradova 1994; see Cattani 2008b: 143–145 for a concise list of such finds). The first appearance of peripheral, small-scale settlements within the BMAC landscape around 1800 BC and an apparently simultaneous shift in the sociopolitical organization of the BMAC itself may suggest the arrival of outside, pastoralist communities that stood to profit politically and economically through growing social ties and more distant regional access (Sarianidi 1975; Kohl 2002; Pyankova 2002; Salvatori 2008b).

Archaeological investigations aimed specifically at pastoralist strategies in the Murghab delta have been habitually overlooked in favor of large-scale investigations at urban BMAC centers. Two exceptions are the work of Fredrik Hiebert at Gonur-N in 1989–90 and the investigation of Sites 1211 and 1219 by the Joint Italian-Turkmen Archaeological Mission in 2001–2 and 2006. Hiebert's excavation at a discrete scatter of predominantly ICW ceramics, located c.1 kilometer southwest of the fortified BMAC site of Gonur South, recovered pottery belonging to both ICW and BMAC traditions and dated stylistically to the Late Bronze Age (1800–1500 BC). Hiebert considered these forms consistent with the preparation, storage, and consumption of liquids (Hiebert and Moore 2004). On the basis of these observations and the proximity of Gonur-N to Gonur South, Hiebert concluded that Gonur-N represented a short-term, mobile pastoral encampment where members of independent mobile pastoralist and BMAC communities feasted together as part of negotiations over land use (Hiebert and Moore 2004). In this scenario of mobile-sedentary interaction, contact between the two groups was limited to marginal areas, and though interactions may have been formalized (through feasting), they were not necessarily regular or seen as especially essential to the survival of either group.

The only other published archaeological investigation of smaller, peripheral occupation in the Murghab delta was the excavation of Sites 1211 and 1219, which, like Gonur-N, were identified by a surface concentration of ICW ceramics and revealed thinly stratified Bronze Age deposits (Cattani 2004, 2008a; Joint Italian-Turkmen Archaeological Mission 2006). Unlike Gonur-N, these sites represent a more substantial occupation in area, as they are separated only by modern fields and probably represent different areas of the same 1 hectare site complex (Cattani 2004). These sites also probably represent more substantial interaction between different groups, attested by the mix of ICW and BMAC pottery, and the time and energy investment in construction of a semi-subterranean dwelling and storage areas. Additionally, domesticated grains found inside stylistically BMAC vessels may be evidence of trade, though we can only speculate about the bartered product – perhaps textiles, wool, or livestock? The archaeology from this case raises the possibility of physical exchanges of goods as a motivation for pastoralist occupation, rather than the social context proposed at Gonur-N. On the other hand, the data from Sites 1211 and 1219 do not preclude the possibility of occupation by sub-groups of the BMAC population, who moved seasonally for primarily agricultural rather than pastoral activities.

Regular contact between inhabitants of BMAC settlements and nomadic pastoral populations provides a logical explanation of how BMAC craftsmen may have acquired their raw materials, because the semi-precious stones and metals they used had to be imported from outside the core BMAC culture zone. The transformation of these raw materials into finished goods was an important step in the materialization of BMAC ideology, which, together with the construction of massive, carefully planned architecture and the control of a vast delta through irrigation, may have signaled their ability to control nature. The scenes of human figures overpowering animals depicted on BMAC seals may also reflect this "man versus nature" ideology.

Though the exact nature of BMAC ideology can be debated, the undeniable fact is that BMAC ideology and political economy were facilitated by the ability to procure raw materials. As such, mobile pastoralists may have played a foundational role in the development and flourishing of the BMAC by brokering the trade in raw materials that were so essential for the materialization of BMAC ideology. In so doing, the mobile pastoral groups did not sacrifice their own, independent identity (documented archaeologically as a distinct assemblage in both the Bronze Age and Iron Age). Rather, pastoralists may have strengthened and maintained their unique cultural role by constantly renegotiating the social relationships that defined their own sociopolitical structures (Frachetti 2009). From this perspective, mobile pastoralists in the BMAC region were not fringe communities; they were essential to the fabric of Bronze Age urban prosperity and helped drive the system of cultural, economic, and political interaction of the time.

5 Role of Pastoralists as Connectors

Although BMAC populations were successful in establishing a clear sociocultural identity materialized over a wide geographical area, mobile pastoralists directly contributed to the success of urban agricultural settlements and the development of their political economy by physically brokering that materialized ideology. The degree of autonomy of mobile pastoralists within the Central Asian economic arena and the extent of their influence on the BMAC both have theoretical consequences for broader explanations of the social dynamics that shaped interactive channels across southwest Asia (Masimov 1981; Hiebert 1994a; Pyankova 1994; Lamberg-Karlovsky 2002, 2003; Masson 2002; Kohl 2007; Sarianidi 2007).

One hypothesis might consider pastoralist groups in the Murghab delta an outgrowth of the BMAC communities themselves, much like the traditional model of Near Eastern pastoralism (cf. Lees and Bates 1976). However, the currently available archaeological data do not seem to support this, as no material cultural antecedents for this distinct, new, "steppe" assemblage are to be found within the BMAC remains and the appearance of distinct, ephemeral sites and their material began after the establishment of a productive BMAC agricultural system. Rather, the current data is more in line with an alternative model that recognizes groups of mobile pastoralists within the Bronze Age landscape of the Murghab delta as intrusive (Kohl 2002; Anthony 2007). This model rests on the working hypothesis that the ephemeral material remains of the Late and Final Bronze Ages (1800–1300 BC) can be clearly correlated with mobile pastoralists, an idea still under-documented by direct archaeological evidence. Nonetheless, there are strong and even exact parallels between ICW ceramic and architectural remains in the Murghab and archaeological materials of Bronze Age mobile pastoralists in the Tien Shan and Pamir mountains (Pyankova 1994, 2002; Vinogradova 1994; Cattani and Genito 1998; Cerasetti 1998).

In current Eurasian scholarship, economic exchange between mobile and sedentary communities, and especially the role of mobile pastoralists in exchange networks, is often used as a key index for assessing centralized control of resources and power. Koryakova and Epimakhov (2007) have argued for the coalescence of power in agrarian communities in Bronze Age Eurasia, a model that places sedentary communities at the seat of either heterarchically (Epimakhov 2009) or hierarchically (Anthony 2009) organized systems that incorporated peripheral mobile pastoral groups. In Central Asia, Hiebert (1994a), Sarianidi (2007), and Salvatori (2008b) have argued for a model of centralized control in at least a portion of the BMAC period, both in terms of sociopolitical power and manipulation of resources. In contrast, Frachetti (2009) argued that, among mountain mobile pastoral groups of Central Eurasia, social structures were not centrally organized but rather adapted locally to perceived sociopolitical, economic, and environmental conditions. Frachetti's model, termed "non-uniform complexity," roots power in the institutional alignments brought about through dynamic, shifting relationships between agents and communities. Similarly, Honeychurch and Amartuvshin (2007) and Stride et al. (2009) show that in medieval Mongolia and Uzbekistan, respectively, power in mobile pastoral groups was rooted not in any particular place, but in the ability of leaders to negotiate a shifting structure of social relations.

The BMAC craft industry was highly specialized and depended on regular access to metal and stone sources in the mountains of modern Iran, Afghanistan, Tajikistan, and Pakistan. These sources lie within the ranges of coeval mobile pastoralists, and there is strong evidence that these groups mined and possibly controlled the tin ores used in some BMAC craft production (Parzinger and Boroffka 2003; Anthony 2007). Additionally, it is clear the BMAC communities maintained a wide distribution network that reached India and the Persian Gulf (Fig. 36.4) (Hiebert and Lamberg-Karlovsky 1992; Potts 1993c, 2008; Hiebert 1994b; Possehl 2004; Anthony 2007; Salvatori 2008a). The links between these areas cross regions that have historically been utilized by mobile pastoralists (cf. Ratnagar 2004). If these routes were similarly exploited in the Bronze Age, mobile pastoralists would have been ideally placed to broker BMAC trade through a down-the-line exchange network (Vinogradova 1993; Christian 1998). By acting as middlemen, mobile pastoralists could have diversified their income sources without having to sacrifice a pastoral lifestyle or significantly alter their productive strategies, and, importantly, could thus establish themselves as peers rather than subjects of the BMAC communities.

6 Central Asia and the Steppe in Asian Interaction (MAIS Model)

Having outlined the florescence of interactive channels between Central and Inner Asia, we now turn our attention to the nature of interaction as it impacted the Near East. The networks of social interaction feeding diverse political

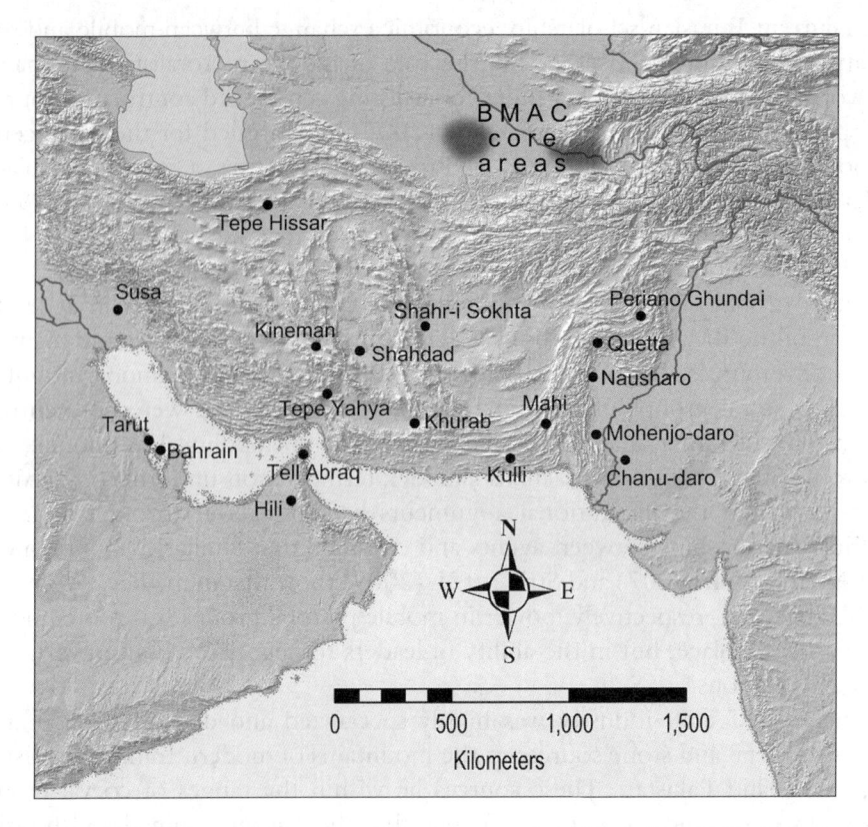

Figure 36.4 Distribution of archaeological sites with published BMAC objects.

economies across Central Asia were well formed by the early 2nd millennium BC, but from where did these networks emerge? In the mid- to late 3rd millennium BC, centuries before the start of the BMAC, the antecedent framework for wide-scale connections between Mesopotamia, Elamite Iran, the Persian Gulf, Oman, Central Asia, and the Indus Valley was taking shape. A pioneer trade network, which Possehl (2007) has called the "Middle Asian Interaction Sphere" (see also Ch. II.40; Tosi and Lamberg-Karlovsky 2003) appears to have fostered the transmission of select innovations and ideologies far across Asia before the more substantial political economic formations of the 2nd millennium BC.

The Middle Asian Interaction Sphere (MAIS) is attested by the exchange of objects sharing particular style and motifs categorized as the "intercultural" style (Kohl 1978). Ideological signifiers within the Intercultural Style are documented at the earliest stages of the MAIS and have led Possehl (2007) to postulate that ideology was key in fomenting the development of the MAIS. The intercultural style, identified on stone objects from Mesopotamia, the Gulf, the Iranian plateau, and the Indus Valley, depicts combatant snakes, bulls, lion-headed birds, rosettes, and other geometric designs. Some of the images are best associated with particular regions, but over the whole of the MAIS the style is coherent. The participants of the MAIS clearly did share a symbology which, as Possehl (2007) has noted, may have formed the lexicon of a more durable belief system at that time.

The MAIS not only provided stylistic precursors to many of the BMAC motifs, but also established awareness of distant cultures and familiarity with administrative systems over a large geographical area. The nature of the MAIS trade relationships insured that exchange operated out of self-interest rather than through direct control. One such self-propelling relationship was the prolonged and direct exchange between Central Asia and the Indus Valley. These regions were in contact across modern Afghanistan from at least the 4th millennium BC, as evidenced through shared Quetta ware (Masson 1988) and developed complex societies at roughly the same time during the 3rd millennium (Kohl 2007). From about 2500–2200 BC, it appears that the trade relationship was facilitated by Indus merchants, documented by an outpost settlement at Shortugai and by Indus seals found at sites in Bactria and the Kopet Dagh foothills (Possehl 2002a). With the emergence of the BMAC, the relationship seems to have reversed, with characteristic BMAC materials appearing at sites in the Indus Valley and little Indus material recovered at BMAC sites. Unlike the earlier Indus system that saw trade moving through outposts, the BMAC finds are attributed to the movement of individual or small groups of merchants, demonstrating different systems of trade organization and administration. However, the use of seals as an administrative tool was common to both regions and throughout the MAIS, where they are documented from excavations at major settlements across the Iranian Plateau in the 3rd millennium BC (Hiebert 1994b).

Mesopotamia was the first southwest Asian region to see the development of an administrative system using writing, and texts have helped archaeologists reconstruct ancient trade and exchange networks from Central and South Asia into the Near East in the 3rd millennium BC (Potts 1999). Although references to the Elamites exist as early as 2600 BC, the Mesopotamians seem to have known little about the people in the far eastern reaches of their exchange networks and there is no demonstrable mention of Central Asia (Tosi and Lamberg-Karlovsky 2003). Nevertheless, sites such as Susa and Tepe Yahya in Iran clearly acted as lynchpins in the MAIS trade network, linking Mesopotamia to the resources and interleaved ideologies circulating across middle Asia in the 3rd millennium BC. More direct material ties between Mesopotamian empires and Central Asia are not completely missing in the record, as a cylinder seal found recently near Togolok in the Murgab delta region (site 1220) illustrates striking iconographic similarity to earlier seals found at Ur (1st Dynasty) and Lagash. Finds such as this suggest that thematic and possibly more direct economic alignments between the Near East and Central Asia might have existed even further into antiquity (Salvatori 2008c).

7 The Inner Asian Mountain Corridor (IAMC)

The benefits of the MAIS network were not restricted to urban agriculturalists; it is simply more research in Iranian and Central Asian urban centers that makes it appear that way. The mid-/late3rd millennium BC also shows some of the earliest archaeological evidence for ties between agricultural communities of southern Central Asia and pastoralists of the vast Central Eurasian steppe belt. Although still fairly isolated at this time, early mobile pastoralists of the steppes and Inner Asian Mountains introduced a number of technologies and materials that impacted upon the ideologies and practices of east Asian and southwest Asian civilizations. A number of vectors of exchange among steppe populations and their neighbors are evident – most notably through the Caucasus (see Ch. II.35) and likely, within the steppe itself, east/west across Eurasia. However, recent archaeology provides mounting evidence to propose more substantial exchange and interaction along the "Inner Asian Mountain Corridor" (IAMC) before the 2nd millennium BC (Frachetti in press). Although still regionally patchy, archaeological evidence from along the foothills and highlands of the Hindu Kush, Pamir, Tian Shan, and Dzhungar Mountains illustrates that mobile upland communities had formed incipient trade networks far earlier than previously thought (Frachetti et al. 2010).

Although steppe and mountain pastoralism likely emerged along different pathways across Central Eurasia, interaction between neighboring pastoralist communities brought about a recognizable shift toward a broadly similar "steppe-type" of pastoralism, based predominantly on mixed herding of sheep/goat and cattle, with limited numbers of horses (Benecke and von den Dreisch 2003; Frachetti and Benecke 2009; but see Outram et al. 2009). From western to eastern Eurasia, this mixed form of mobile pastoralism replaced earlier, more specialized and regionally conscribed strategies found in the western, central, and eastern steppe territories. Variable ecologies across the steppe engendered territorial overlaps of patterned mobility strategies, which may partly explain the punctuated dispersion of technologies and pastoralist regional networks that is evident in the shared materials, technologies, and ideologies across the grasslands at the start of the 2nd millennium BC. Steppe pastoralists of the late 3rd millennium BC also initiated economic transformations that might be considered "globalizing" changes from the perspective of non-pastoralist communities of Central and East Asia as well (Frachetti 2008).

Evidence for 3rd millennium BC trade throughout the IAMC is limited, but the available data are tantalizing. A burial excavated at Sarazm, an agricultural village (3500–1800 BC) located in the lower Zerafshan valley of Tajikistan (see above, Figure 36.2), provided one of the few cases of broadly categorized "steppe" type ceramics dating to the late 4th or early 3rd millennium BC (Lyonnet 1996: 67). The analysts suggest the burial form and vessels recovered at Sarazm are stylistically similar to ceramics of the Afanas'evo culture, material associated with mobile pastoralists living far to the north in the Altai Mountains (Avanesova and Dzhurakulova 2008). N. Avanesova has also recently published a key burial site, Jukov, which illustrates more abundant parallels with Afanas'evo forms in the Zerafshan Valley and provides another well-documented example of contact between (proto-) mountain pastoralists and village agriculturalists in the region (Avanesova and Dzhurakulova 2008). Given that domesticated sheep and goats were heavily exploited at sites like Sarazm, we might expect that some form of mobile pastoralism was practiced by communities of the upper Zerafshan Valley, where rich pastures are abundant (Frachetti in press). A local pastoralist contingent is clearly documented in the 2nd millennium BC throughout the upper and lower Zerafshan Valley (Tajikistan and Uzbekistan respectively), but there is still much work to be done toward establishing an absolute chronology for the growth of relationships with agriculturalists in the Pamir and Zerafshan foothill zones. In the Pamir Mountains, earlier Eneolithic populations have been documented (Ranov and Karimova 2005) but definite pastoralist sites of the 3rd millennium BC are few and the scope and distance of these connections is still a matter for speculation. Whether extensively mobile as pastoralists or not, there is certainly clear archaeological evidence from Indus Valley sites of the 3rd millennium BC for exploitation of economic resources in the Pamir and Hissar mountains, such as metal ores or (semi-)precious stones on the part of mountain communities (Law 2006).

Traveling further north along the mountain corridor, pastoralist settlements in the Dzhungar Mountains of Kazakhstan more clearly demonstrate that mobile pastoralist communities had developed diffuse ties to agricultural communities during the 3rd millennium BC. For example, the Early/Middle Bronze Age levels at Begash provide the earliest direct evidence for emerging exchange networks across the mountains and into western China. Recently published botanical evidence from Begash illustrates the ritual use of domesticated wheat and millet in cremation ceremonies around 2300 BC (Frachetti et al 2010). The archaeological context of the Begash wheat and millet – a cremation burial – does not indicate that the grains were grown locally at this time. Rather, free-threshing wheat, most typical in the southern reaches of Central Asia and the Indus (Fuller 2001), was apparently exchanged northward along the foothills of the IAMC and possibly further east along the Tien Shan range into China through the Hexi corridor (cf. Flad et al. 2010). In the opposite direction it appears that broomcorn millet, most common in China and unknown in southwest Asia until the 2nd millennium BC, was also passing through the hands of steppe pastoralists. Although not the focus here, domesticated broomcorn millet was likely traded westward along the same mountainous corridor out of China, situating sites such as Begash directly at the cross-roads of extremely wide contacts already by the mid-3rd millennium BC.

At the same time as incipient networks were forming along the IAMC, we see other material and economic innovations such as carts (and later chariots), horse domestication, and bronze smelting techniques all stemming from the western Eurasian steppe zones during the 4th and 3rd millennium (Kohl 2007; Ch. II.35). Whether developed first among agriculturalists of the circum-Pontic region or elsewhere in the mid-4th millennium (Kohl 2007; Kenoyer 2009), four-wheeled carts became clearly employed as status items within burial *kurgans* of the so called Yamnaya (Pit-Grave) culture, mobile pastoralists living across the north Caucasus c.3100 BC (Shishlina 2008). As noted above, carts were quickly adopted as high status items at least by the mid-3rd millennium BC, as reflected on the Royal Standard of Ur in the late Early Dynastic III period (Postgate 1992) and appeared in BMAC burials at Gonur in Margiana (c.2000 BC) (Sarianidi 2002; Kohl 2007). The earliest spoked, two-wheeled chariot comes from Sintashta in the Ural steppe region (southern Russia, c.2100–1900 BC) (Gening et al 1992; Anthony 2007). This technology, or at least the idea of it, quickly spread across the Eurasian steppe, as illustrated in petroglyphs depicting spoke-wheeled chariots (c.1800 BC) at Terekty in Kazakhstan, a Bronze Age rock-art sanctuary adjacent to the Bronze Age site of Begash (Mar'yashev and Goryachev 1998). Well known in Mesopotamia by the 2nd millennium BC, chariots became integral to the symbolic power of kings at least by the end of the Akkadian period (Postgate 1992: 246), and ultimately were transmitted across the steppe to the Shang burial sites at Anyang in China by 1200 BC (Cheng 1960).

The likely routes of exchange and passage that fostered the spread of high-status innovations such as the chariot beyond the steppe surely reflect an intricate web of routes with both direct trajectories through the Caucasus into Mesopotamia, as well as northern and southern passages along the IAMC. The trade lines that crossed the Caucasus (Ch. II.35) clearly shaped styles and meanings of metallurgy and other commodities in the Near East from the late 4th millennium BC (Kohl 2007). Mountain/steppe miners on the eastern fringes of Inner Asia – likely nomadic – traded tin bronzes across diverse pathways from the Altai to the Urals and from the tin-mines of the Zerafshan valley to Iran by the Late Bronze Age (Parzinger and Boroffka 2003; Chernykh 2009). The complex process of circulation of raw materials, finished objects, and innovative technologies across Inner Asia in the 3rd millennium BC suggests that steppe and mountain pastoralists contributed significantly to the growth and ideological shape of the urban political economies of the BMAC, the Indus Civilization (Harappans), and the Elamites of the Iranian Plateau – civilizations variously in dialogue with the empires of the Near East throughout the late 3rd and early 2nd millennium BC (Potts 1999).

8 Conclusion

From the 4th millennium BC, societies living throughout the oases of Central Asia and the steppe grasslands of (Inner) Eurasia ushered a "global" expansion in the scale of interregional trade and interaction (Frachetti 2008). Aspects of this expansion gestated for centuries until the middle of the 3rd millennium BC, when political economies across Asia reflect unprecedented alignments of social, political, and economic institutions that recast the interactive landscape of the region (Frachetti 2008, 2009). Here we have focused on the relationships between mobile pastoralist communities of the steppe and urban agriculturalists, where greater evidence for direct interactions with southwest Asia are more evident. In exploring this relationship, it appears that socially and economically pluralistic communities had access to and helped shape the context of trade and material transfer that spawned considerable homologies in symbols and ideology across southwestern and Central Asia in the Bronze Age. Other chapters in this volume devote energy to conceptually and physically illustrating the evidence of these exchanges; here we can propose that the city-states of the Near East, and the empires that they gave rise to, were able to manipulate both economic and political arenas by virtue of their access to exotic commodities. For Near Eastern leaders, these commodities – both raw and finished – were expressions of influence, tribute, deity and globalism, perhaps in the same way that rare or exotic objects are used today. What is remarkable about the agentive role played by Eurasian and Central Asian communities in the passage of metals, technological innovations, stones, grains, and symbols is the apparent lack of a centralized structure of institutions to guide the interchange across incredible territory. Almost inherently, their geographic location at the interstices of eastern and southwestern Asia served them in their own development and enrichment, while cultivating the essential shifts that promoted the success of societies extending from the Near East to the Iranian Plateau, the Indus Valley and East Asia (Kohl 1978; Lamberg-Karlovsky 1996; Kenoyer 1997; Possehl 1997). As these shadowed societies are exposed under more intensive scrutiny, we are compelled to reconceptualize and relocate the essential roots of sociopolitical development of ancient Old World civilizations.

GUIDE TO FURTHER READING

For general orientation on the archaeology of Central Asia in the Bronze Age see Hiebert (1994a). Recent archaeological investigations of the Bactria Margiana Archaeological Complex can be found in Salvatori et al. (2008). Detailed, synthetic studies of the Bronze Age of Central Eurasia include Anthony (2007), Kohl (2007), and Kuz'mina (2007).

CHAPTER THIRTY-SEVEN

The Ur III, Old Babylonian, and Kassite Empires

Marlies Heinz

1 Introduction

One common aspect characterizes Babylonia throughout 900 years of historical, political, economic, and cultural history and thus forms a kind of unifying continuity. This is a certain form of political organization, namely an imperial structure. Three different terms indicate the local origins of the major historical phases between c.2100 and 1200 BC, each of which had its geographical starting point in Babylonia. The term "Ur III" designates an intra-urban political development in the city of Ur itself which was the third dynasty that arose there in antiquity. The term "Old-Babylonian" refers to a chronological and regional development in Babylonia as well as a stage in the development of the Babylonian language. The expression "Kassite" refers above all to a group of people that had migrated from the Zagros region in modern-day Iran into Babylonia. Despite all their differences, these chronological periods and cultural phenomena all share an imperial structure that served as a unifying theme throughout this long period in Babylonian history.

2 The Empire: Characteristics and Implications

The existence of empires illustrates the power as well as the necessity of a ruling elite to secure dominance via supra-regional expansion. The main spatial characteristic of an empire is its supra-regional geographical extent – i.e., its spatial

---

A Companion to the Archaeology of the Ancient Near East, First Edition.
Edited by D.T. Potts.
© 2012 Blackwell Publishing Ltd. Published 2012 by Blackwell Publishing Ltd.

extension beyond a local center or core region in which a ruling elite exercised power. Politically speaking, the empire is expressed through the domination by one political elite of other ruling elites, whether near or far. The forms and scales of domination and control, as well as the degree of political autonomy amongst local elites within dominated areas, varied considerably in this process of empire formation. Above and beyond the establishment of a local and regional rulership, the building of an empire necessitated strong political and ideological signs that made the legitimacy of the ruling order obvious to all concerned – the people who identified with the dynasty as well as, if not even more so, those of the "other" – i.e., the dominated social and cultural entities. Economically, an empire aimed at controlling the resources of the areas and societies that it dominated. Socially and culturally, the creation of an empire thus entailed contact and/or confrontation with people belonging to the "other," and thus to different traditions of social life, political organization, political leadership, religion, value systems, and self- and world-views.

3 Ur III: How the Empire Came Into Being, Developed, Functioned, and Collapsed

The founder of the new Dynasty of Ur and the person who laid the foundations for the Ur III empire was Ur-Nammu. A man of high military rank, Ur-Nammu was installed as governor of Ur by his brother, Utu-hegal, general as well as king of the neighboring city of Uruk and of the land of Sumer. From this military position, Ur-Nammu succeeded in becoming king of Ur. Many of the details of his career are unknown, but it is clear that the rise of Ur-Nammu meant at the same time the disempowerment of his brother at Uruk. Ur-Nammu seems to have had a well-functioning army at his disposal. According to his own inscriptions, Ur-Nammu succeeded in taking over not just Ur and Uruk but also northern Babylonia, particularly the area around Nippur and as far north as the Diyala region, thus assuming rulership over Sumer and Akkad (southern and northern Babylonia) and its eastern neighbor Elam. He extended his rule far beyond the area that his brother, as "king of Uruk and Sumer," had governed, and created a supra-regional sphere of influence beyond the core area of Ur and Uruk, a fact reflected in his title "king of Sumer and Akkad." Notwithstanding the extension of this polity, the most important centers remained in the south, the core of Ur-Nammu's kingdom. Ur became the capital and at the same time one of the major religious centers in Sumer, just as important as Nippur in northern Babylonia. The new king kept close ties with Uruk, even calling himself "brother of Gilgamesh," the legendary king of Uruk.

Unsurprisingly for a dynasty, Ur-Nammu's successor was his son Shulgi. Shulgi's foreign policy built on the aims of his father by enlarging the sphere of Ur's political influence. Campaigns led Shulgi to the north and northwest of his father's territory as far as northern Iraq and western Iran. The advantage of controlling these territories was obvious – these were the areas where the Mesopotamian south, poor in natural resources, could satisfy its needs and safeguard its long-distance trade with adjacent regions. Shulgi's enlargement of the Ur III sphere of influence is reflected in his titles. Whereas his father called himself "king of Sumer and Akkad," Shulgi used both this title and "king of the four quarters (of the world)," signifying that his power extended to Assyria in the north, Mari in the west, and Tell Brak and the Khabur-region to the northwest of Mesopotamia. Shulgi's son Amar-Suena and Amar-Suena'a son Shu-Suen preserved the territorial achievements of their fathers and forefathers, but did not expand the territory of the dynasty. The last king of the Ur III Dynasty, Ibbi-Suen, also tried to preserve the empire, unfortunately enjoying less success than his predecessors. A severe economic crisis during his reign seems to have accelerated a process of decay that eventually led to the demise of the Ur III Dynasty and empire, roughly a century after Ur-Nammu, Ibbi-Suen's great-great-grandfather, had founded it.

When a king established himself by breaking local tradition and acting against the local ruling order – and when he created a new geopolitical order and an empire by breaking the local, regional, and supra-regional traditions of political, religious, and spatial order – he had to think carefully about how to gain acceptance for his (usually militarily-enforced) political acts. How does a king, ruling against the rules, so to speak, represent himself in order to gain the acceptance and authority necessary to establish and stabilize his power at a local, regional, and supra-regional level? Ideally, he must succeed in representing himself as the one who secures the prosperity of the communities affected, creating the image of a king who obeys the gods in taking care of their requests and upholding local traditions, despite the fact he was the one who broke with them. Should the king present himself as the one obedient to the gods and thus conceal the fact that, by changing the local political order, he has, in many ways, interfered in the competences of the local gods? One way around this dilemma is for the king who breaks with local traditions to present himself as the one, who, by expelling the existing king, is re-establishing the "real" local traditions, thus creating the image of a defender, not a destroyer, of local customs. At the same time, a king aiming at creating an empire should offer all those societies under his power the chance to develop an identity that rises above the local "we." To secure its authority throughout the empire, the ruling elite had to do everything in its power to prove to the local populations that their rulers took full responsibility for local, regional, and supra-regional affairs.

When Ur-Nammu developed his rulership and expanded the territory of his power, he paid careful attention to the spatial and political organization of his newly gained territories. Internal frontiers ran along rivers and channels and formed clearly marked administrative districts. These were ruled by administrators under the control of Ur-Nammu and, at the same time, were seen as being protected by local gods. The political advantage of this organization was a clear division of authority, which made it easy to control his subordinates. Moreover, in this way Ur-Nammu recalled the past when the city god was responsible for the territory of an entire city-state, something that no longer applied in an empire.

Ur-Nammu developed and maintained the canal system, thereby securing the water supply for the fields and at the same time enhancing transport routes. He thus built up a local, regional, and supra-regional infrastructure, necessary both for inter-city and long-distance trade, and for securing and maintaining political control throughout the empire. Thus, investment in and maintenance of the canal system went beyond economic needs and was a clever political and ideological ploy. The new political order secured the prosperity of a large part of the population, enabling Ur-Nammu and his successors to control far more than just the economy the empire.

Ur-Nammu created something new while at the same time exploiting ancient local traditions. At Ur, Nippur, Uruk, and Eridu he created the *ziggurat* – an unprecedented, stepped tower of brick on which the temples of the highest gods were erected. At Eridu he looked after the needs of Enki, god of wisdom and sweet water, and thus one of the most important gods for the existence of mankind. Ur-Nammu's concern at Uruk was, in part, connected to his family history. The *ziggurat* of Uruk was dedicated to the city goddess Inanna. At Nippur, among others, cultic buildings set up by Ur-Nammu – the *ziggurat* and another temple – were dedicated to Enlil, who was the city god and also the highest god in the Sumerian pantheon. Unsurprisingly, Ur, the seat of Ur-Nammu's Dynasty, received the greatest attention. The local *ziggurat* had been dedicated to the city god Nanna, the moon-god. Built within a huge courtyard and abutted by a second courtyard, the temple also contained the house of the **en**-priestesses and the cultic building for the goddess Ningal, Nanna's spouse. The religious buildings were surrounded by secular ones. A storage magazine as well as the palace of Ur-Nammu and his successors were part of this architectural ensemble. Nearby stood three buildings, built for the royal funerals.

Ur-Nammu thus made it clear to the public that he and his new administration served the essential needs of the gods and thus of the populace. At the same time, he enhanced his own rule with a comprehensive local, regional, and supra-regional building program. Throughout the empire, architecture and spatial design symbolized the worldview of Ur-Nammu, who developed a visible master plan – a type of religious architecture as a sign and symbol of the new order – that applied everywhere. Standardization characterized the new signature of power – the *ziggurat* – which was placed beside and combined with local architectural monuments and may have served to create a common identity amongst disparate local cultures within the empire. The monumentality of the buildings, the effort behind the building program, the demonstration of power – encompassing the control of resources of all kinds: manpower, time, space, the religious world – and the creation of the new and at the same time the respect for the old: all reveal the astute political thinking of Ur-Nammu. The new ruler projected a view of himself as a religious man, upholding and respecting the old traditions and, at the same time, leaving nobody in doubt that his power and the new order were absolute, without alternative. The new and the old stood side by side, but the new did not threaten the old. Ur-Nammu insured this through his clever placement of new cultic monuments and by according due respect to the gods of each local tradition. Even where local gods were worshipped in new temples, the effort put into building them demonstrated Ur-Nammu's high regard for them. The imperial building program thus contained two messages: the new was both powerful and obviously accepted by the local gods. At the same time, it served as an invitation to local populations to identify with it, as well as an admonition to be aware that there was no alternative.

At Ur, yet another message might be seen in the spatial arrangement of the major monuments there. The gods and the ruler lived side by side. That they belonged together and formed a unit was thus clearly visible to all. The gods were housed in the most monumental building and were accorded the highest esteem. The rulers lived next to them in more modest buildings. At the same time, the life of the living elite and the life of the dead were inextricably intertwined. After death the dead still shared the same space with the living members of the society – as well as with the place of worship created for the gods – clearly shown by the location of the funeral houses.

Standardization was not only used to express the new by means of spatial design. It was also employed to create a visual image of the new order. Royal cylinder seals depicted the kings of the empire in the role in which they obviously wanted to be seen and remembered throughout the empire. Thus, the most important aspect of their rulership as well as the characteristic of the new consisted of the motif of the king as a religious man – not as a warrior, not as a fighter, and rarely as a builder. Ur-Nammu and his successors did not choose a local, traditional story or scenario to represent themselves but, rather, a subject that could be understood widely without presuming a knowledge of local history or tradition. The king was portrayed as a servant of god, introduced to the god by a goddess who led the king to the god. This focus on one subject might be explained by the nature of those who both saw and used the seals. While monumental architecture was visible to many, and this could hardly be controlled – no one could be excluded from seeing a *ziggurat* – images on royal seals were addressed to a different audience. Royal seals served as an instrument of official administration. As such, they were seen and used only in elite circles and by powerful administrators where alternatives to the ruling order would have been considered undesirable. The higher administration had to be loyal to the new order, the success of which depended heavily upon such loyalty. Politically and ideologically, it seems to have been expedient to emphasize this to the administrative elite and thus exclude any alternative to the status quo. It was not so much the subject that was very new, as the exclusion of the variety of subject matter that had previously circulated on cylinder seals.

Another theme that illustrates the overarching authority of Ur-Nammu as the ruler of the empire was his image as a builder. This role was not a result of his own doing, but rather of his Nanna, city god of Ur, who had selected him for this purpose. Ur-Nammu was the architect, simultaneously, of the built environment, the new political order, and the empire. Ur-Nammu was the first ruler to use this image of himself as a means of visualizing his political deeds as founder of the empire.

Ur-Nammu's responsibility for a territory larger than that of a city-state was also expressed in the compilation, and thus the standardization, of laws which were valid for everyone in the empire. The collection of laws known as the Codex Ur-Nammu regulated, among many other things, daily affairs and guaranteed legal uniformity throughout "Sumer and Akkad." This was not the written codification of local traditions but rather the consolidation of an instrument of supra-regional order, and must have been a top priority of the founder of the Ur III empire.

Architecture, pictorial representation, and the codification of laws were all measures to guarantee the success of the new order and its representatives throughout the empire. Mechanisms to enforce each visible act of the king were an important ideological tool in memorializing the good government of the Ur III kings. To do this, Ur-Nammu created a new vehicle, also used by his successors: the royal hymn. In it the royal character and accomplishments in the service of the empire and on behalf of those affected by the new political order were all praised.

How did the successors of Ur-Nammu fare? Shulgi followed on from his father and introduced several organizational innovations. Whereas his father standardized the law, Shulgi added the homogenization of Sumerian cuneiform and weights and measures. The empire encompassed about 40 administrative districts, ruled, as was the case under Ur-Nammu, by civil and military administrators controlled by Shulgi. Marriages between male members of the royal court of Ur and female members of elite families throughout the empire became increasingly important and served to stabilize it. The need for stability was great. The MAR.TU/Amurru nomads (see below) were considered a threat to the political, economical, and cultural achievements of the empire. To keep them out of the heartland and away from cultivated areas, Shulgi began to build a massive wall in the Diyala region (northeastern Iraq). The greatest innovation in Shulgi's lifetime, however, was his deification. Shulgi became not only the ruler of the empire, but its god. He thus positioned himself at the very top of the community, emulating Naram-Sin, the Akkadian king, who was the first Mesopotamian ruler to be deified (Ch. II.34). Deification raises a number of questions. Was this a sign of the king's power? Was it a demonstration that the king's rule was unassailable? Deification was against the tradition throughout the empire and it must have required enormous power to create a new tradition in a domain as conservative and sensitive as religion.

Subsequent rulers of the Ur III Dynasty adopted the custom of deification and at the same time worshipped their predecessor, the late king, as a god. In addition to pursuing a building program and a standardized visual program in the arts, Shu-Suen commissioned statues of himself and had them distributed throughout the empire. God and king were thus united, and this was typified by his drive to build temples for his own worship all over the empire. The best-preserved example is the Shu-Suen temple at Tell Asmar (ancient Eshnunna). The form of the temple type followed accepted tradition, but the dedication of a building to a living, deified king was paralleled only in the Akkadian period, when a temple was built for the worship of the god/king Naram-Sin.

How did the empire collapse? The Ur III Dynasty lost control of its territory mainly due to economic problems that adversely affected a number of cities. More and more cities rose up in rebellion and freed themselves from the grip of Ur. Contact was lost between Ibbi-Suen, the last king, and his administrators in the periphery. A dramatic report survives that informs us about the end of Ur. The gods had left the people of Ur defenseless. As a result, the city was destroyed and Ibbi-Suen was taken away as a captive to Elam (modern southwest Iran).

The economic crisis allowed a high-ranking military officer, Ishbi-Erra of Mari, to extract political concessions from Ibbi-Suen. Promising to neutralize the threat of the MAR.TU nomads in the west, Ishbi-Erra blackmailed Ibbi-Suen into appointing him king of Isin. Once in this position, he proved disloyal, cooperating with other kings against Ur and establishing a powerful position that made him the head of the core territory of the former empire. One decisive move was Ishbi-Erra's support of the Nippur priesthood, some of the empire's most powerful religious elites. For Ibbi-Suen, the loss of Nippur, the spiritual center of Sumer, and, by extension, the loss of the support of Enlil – the god who was alone empowered to bestow kingship – was a disaster. The final blow for Ibbi-Suen came when the army of Elam raided Sumer and destroyed Ur – an event commemorated in the *Lamentation over the destruction of Sumer and Ur*.

In terms of both territory and organization, the reign of Ishbi-Erra can seen as a continuation of the Ur III empire. The decisive change was the end of the dynasty, as power passed from the domination of the Ur-family to the unrelated Ishbi-Erra at Isin. Ishbi-Erra did not enjoy this position for long, however. Although he tried to continue the imperial traditions of Ur, more and more city-states gained their political independence and he progressively lost control of the empire and its resources. Uruk, Babylon, Larsa, Eshnunna, Assur, and Mari – to name only those that stand out in the historical record – became powerful enemies of Isin, but of these it was neighboring Larsa that was most problematic. As it had been between Lagash and Umma in the 3rd millennium, water became a cause of political rivalry and ultimately war. The imperial structure disintegrated, and city-state-based, decentralized polities prevailed for the next two centuries in Babylonia.

4 The Role of the Amorites

The influence of the so-called Amorite tribes, semi-nomads who migrated from the Syrian desert west into Babylonia, became increasingly significant in the post-Ur III period. This was a process that had already begun in the 3rd millennium BC. Like all migrations, that of the Amorites (Sumerian MAR.TU; Akkadian *Amurru*) brought new traditions to Babylonia in terms of lifestyle, world-view, values, economic organization, political habits, and religious views. Increasingly, the ruling elites of the bigger cities had an Amorite background, a sign of successful integration and acculturation on the part of the Amorites and of the fact that the local residents and societies tolerated the new migrants. It is not yet clear how and why nomadic and tribal chiefs decided to abandon their mobile lifestyle and settle permanently in one place, and how they gained their positions and status as urban kings.

5 The Old Babylonian Empire

The founder of the First Dynasty of Babylon, Sumuabum, was an Amorite. It was Hammurabi, however, the sixth king of this dynasty, who first succeeded in extending the power of Babylon, subduing the elites of the neighboring cities and establishing a sphere of influence that resembled, territorially speaking, the empire of the Ur III Dynasty. When Hammurabi came to power, his predecessors had already extended their power beyond the immediate area of Babylon. Unlike Ur-Nammu, however, Hammurabi did not act against the local political tradition in order to obtain his position. Through his own conquests he extended his area of political control from central Babylonia to the north as well as to the Mesopotamian south. He defeated Sippar, Eshnunna, and the Diyala region, conquered Elam in the southeast, and headed south, where he took control of Ur, then the most important Persian Gulf trading station. Hammurabi was not only a successful military officer, he was also capable of forging advantageous alliances with contemporary kings for the purpose of joint military campaigns, using them to build up and solidify the Old Babylonian, or rather the "Hammurabi" Empire (an organization that political science would call a "one-man empire." In the 30th year of his reign, he assumed the title "king of Sumer and Akkad." In reality, however, as we know from his royal inscriptions and from the prologue of his law code, the Codex Hammurabi, he governed a much larger area, stretching from Mari in the west to Elam in the southeast, and from Assur and Nineveh in the north to Ur in the south – in other words, an area roughly the size of the former Ur III empire.

Hammurabi had a strong army and he was a clever strategist. The army worked efficiently under his command and, consequently, Hammurabi represented himself as the conqueror of the world and the pre-eminent military ruler of his time. He drew attention to the fact that it was he who had brought and guaranteed the prosperity of all countries under his power. To emphasize this role as caretaker and protector, he fostered an image as the good shepherd of his subjects – an image that placed Hammurabi squarely in the tradition of Mesopotamian rulers who had used this title since the 3rd millennium BC. Propaganda and the transmission of the ruling ideology were thus manipulated and maintained by an already ancient strategy. Hammurabi enforced the new global political and economical order by waging war, depriving local elites of their power, and legitimating the new order with references to the traditions and values of the past. And in order to assert his entitlement to being seen as the world's ruler and to make his position completely invulnerable, he claimed that Enlil, the god of the world who alone bestowed kingship on men, had given him the title "king of the four quarters (of the world)" and thus legitimated his political deeds.

Nevertheless, in spite of such assertions, there might well have been a gap between his propaganda and the reality of his reign. That this was not the case is due to the fact that the internal administration of the empire was organized under his watchful eye. In every occupied city Hammurabi deployed an administration which stood under his supervision and was decidedly not of local origin. Acts of disloyalty by the conquered cities also obviously occurred. That Hammurabi was not one to hesitate in destroying such rebels is made clear by his use of water, alternately flooding opponent cities or cutting off their supply as the situation demanded.

According to the written tradition, the shaping of the material world followed the clever propagandistic strategy of legitimating the new with the traditional. Hammurabi visibly demonstrated his role as caretaker by looking after temples and irrigation works and by protecting the conquered cities under his rule. According to his own texts of self-praise, he thus took over the duties that in former times had devolved upon local kings. The material evidence of these building activities, however, remains largely undiscovered. At his capital Babylon, for example, buildings from Hammurabi's own time lie buried beneath meters of debris from his later successors, in some cases below the modern water table. Thus, any signs of how Hammurabi may have presented his new world order in architectural terms – in the sense that Ur-Nammu identified himself and his empire with the *ziggurat* – are missing.

Hammurabi's assertion that it was he who took care of the irrigation works throughout the country, created flourishing landscapes and built to the honor the gods, was an important measure in legitimizing the new political order on a local, regional, and supra-regional level. These actions met the material as well as spiritual requirements of people throughout the empire, regardless of their origin or place of residence. Moreover, according to his own political propaganda, Hammurabi controlled the nodal points that guaranteed long-distance trade with the Persian Gulf, the Indus Valley, the Levant, Cyprus, and the Mediterranean.

The building of such trade relationships and communication routes necessarily implies that Hammurabi controlled everything in his empire. His pronouncements to the effect that all his actions served the best interests of the people were also governed by the principle that these actions served first and foremost to secure and expand his power. The guarantee of imports is evidence of this statement. Imports were used to secure royal power, for, as a rule, luxury goods were distributed to the members of the power elite, thus serving mainly as a political tool to keep them loyal to the king.

The royal inscriptions, self-image, and hymns praising Hammurabi give the impression that continuity, not change, characterized his reign – even though the political context had changed considerably. One visible representation that can be attributed directly to Hammurabi is the scene carved on the stele on which the Codex Hammurabi is inscribed. The seated sun god Shamash hands the rope and rod, surveyor's tools that represented kingship as well, to the standing Hammurabi. This is an expression of his mandate to act as the builder – both of houses and of empire. Ur-Nammu was the first to use such imagery to illustrate his political deeds as the founder of an empire. Thus, Hammurabi did not create a new image of kingship but, instead, followed traditional and well-known conceptions of how a king should be seen and remembered. Once again, propaganda and ideology functioned according to the time-honored convention of placing the new beside the old, thus concealing the potentially threatening aspect inherent in all signs of change.

Seals and themes that can be associated directly with Hammurabi and his persona as a "one-man empire" are lacking in the archaeological record. In general, the presentation scene was adopted and modified, according to the needs of the users. In contrast to the Ur III period, however, warrior scenes occurred as well as the depiction of the king as warrior. The representation of Hammurabi as warrior suited both his ideology and his propaganda. The prologue of the Codex Hammurabi explains this imagery. It was the wars, successfully led by Hammurabi, that had brought peace to the empire and justice for all – and it had been the most important gods of this empire who had supported him in his campaigns. The extension of the political influence of cities was, as a rule, connected with the expansion of the influence and competence of the city-gods. With the reign of Hammurabi and his foundation of the empire, the prominence, characteristics, and functions of Marduk, until then only the city god of Babylon, multiplied and began to serve the needs of a supra-regional power in demonstrating and legitimating its world domination.

The territorial achievements of Hammurabi were not of long duration. The so-called Old Babylonian Empire was more a "Hammurabi empire" than the empire of the First Dynasty of Babylon. Hammurabi's son, Samsu-iluna, could not hold on to the territory conquered by his father and, after the reign of four more successors and continual wars, economic and social tensions, the city and Dynasty of Babylon not only lost its leading position among the powers of the south but were conquered by the Hittite king Murshili I in the early 16th century BC.

6 The Kassites: How the Empire Came Into Being, Developed, Functioned, and Collapsed

The Kassites migrated during the 2nd millennium BC from the Zagros region of western Iran into Babylonia. Texts from the reign of Samsu-iluna mention conflicts between Kassites and the Babylonian army. Kassites were called "foreign" and "strangers" in Babylonia and at the same time they are attested in economic texts as farm workers and soldiers in the Babylonian army, where they sometimes gained high rank. It is thought that their knowledge of horse-breeding and chariotry earned them high positions at the Babylonian court. How the jump from such high military positions to absolute political power took place is not yet known in detail. The written sources suggest that the Hittite defeat of the First Dynasty of Babylon and the subsequent withdrawal of the victorious Hittite army in the early 16th century BC created an opportunity for Kassite elites to take control of the city. This implies that the Kassite "strangers" were by then a community within Babylonia that was powerful and well organized, both politically and militarily. By this time, a Kassite kingdom already existed along the Euphrates with its center at the city of Terqa (modern Tell Ashara). Details about the founder of the first Kassite Dynasty and about the installation of this dynasty in Babylon are not yet known. Nevertheless, it is obvious that in a relatively short period of time the Kassites were able to expand their political power to such a degree that we can speak of a Kassite empire.

The Babylonian kinglist mentions 36 Kassite kings, organized according to the dynastic system. Of these Agum (II), whose dates are uncertain, is the first who can be historically verified. Agum II called himself king of Babylon, and claimed to rule at the behest of all of the relevant Babylonian gods – An, Enlil, Ea, Marduk, Sin, and Shamash. At the same time, he emphasized that he was the biological son of Shuqamuna, one of the two Kassite gods having the authority to install kings. Thus, not being a member of a traditional, aristocratic Babylonian family was actually emphasized – a remarkable step for a community that not too long before had been considered "strangers." Besides the honors and legitimate right to be king of Babylon given to him by the local gods, Agum II called himself king of the Kassites and the Akkadians, king of Alman and Padan (located in northeastern Babylonia), and king of Gutium (an area east of the Diyala-region in Iran, presumably stretching as far as Lake Urmia). The Mesopotamian south obviously did not (yet) belong to the Kassites. That the empire was established without war seems unlikely, if we recall the history of early Mesopotamian empire formation. Yet Kassite propaganda emphasized, among other things, that Agum II had brought back the statue of Marduk, deported during a previous period of unrest. The re-establishment of the livelihood of the Babylonians was, according to his propaganda, Agum's outstanding success.

The Kassite Empire continued to develop under a further 26 kings. Ulamburiash, fourth king in the Kassite Dynasty, conquered southernmost Babylonia, proclaimed himself king of the Sealand, and became king of Babylonia as well. For the first time, Kassite rule included the Mesopotamian south and within Mesopotamia extended as far north as Assyria. In the 15th century BC, Karaindash I, who called himself king of the city of Babylon, of Sumer and Akkad, king of the Kassites and the land Karduniash (the name of the Kassite Empire at the time), was the first Babylonian king to meet an Egyptian pharaoh, Thutmose III. The expansion of Kassite political influence was consolidated with the rule of Kurigalzu I. He strengthened the alliance with Egypt through interdynastic marriages, sending his daughter to Egypt to be married to the Egyptian pharaoh. Kurigalzu I called himself "king of the four quarters" and, for the first time since the Ur III period, had himself deified, a logical step for a ruler who strove for world domination and needed maximum legitimacy. While he pretended to have had the support of all the gods within his empire, he still considered the Kassite gods Shuqamuna and Shumaliya to be his personal deities.

In the mid-14th century BC major problems with the Assyrians for the first time threatened the existence of the Kassite Empire. The accession of Karahardash (1333 BC), grandson of the Assyrian king Assuruballit I (1363–1328 BC), and son of the Kassite king Burnaburiash II (1359–1333 BC) by his Assyrian wife Muballitat-Sherua (a daughter of Assuruballit I), provoked a Kassite revolt. The Kassite elite killed him and enthroned their own favorite, Nazi-Bugash (1333 BC). Assuruballit took revenge for the death of his grandson, attacking Babylon, killing Nazi-Bugash, and installing another Kassite on the Babylonian throne who came to be called Kurigalzu II (1332–1308 BC) (Brinkman 1976: 166). This was not a randomly chosen name, but one that harkened back to that of the first global player among the Kassite kings, Kurigalzu I.

Although supported by Assyria, times were tough for the Kassite Empire. After the death of Assuruballit I, wars against Elam and problems with Assyria ensued. Kadashman-Enlil II (1263–1255 BC), however, exploited the rivalries of his enemies. He forged alliances with both the Hittites and the Egyptians, a constellation that constituted a major threat to the growing power of Assyria. For roughly 40 years this alliance protected the Kassite Empire from its northern neighbor. Under the reign of the Assyrian king Tukulti-Ninurta I (1243–1207 BC), however, the situation changed, this time for the worse. According to his royal inscriptions, Tukulti-Ninurta I conquered all of Babylonia and brought the Kassite king Kashtiliashu IV (1232–1225 BC) to Assur as a prisoner. Additionally, he tore down the city wall and fortifications of Babylon, thus stripping the city of protection and any sign of political autonomy. The statue of the god Marduk was again captured and taken to Assyria, the final blow for Babylon and its inhabitants. The city was vandalized, its people killed, but still the Kassite elite were able to rebel against this Assyrian violence.

In effect, "history repeated itself" as the Assyrians again nominated a vice-king to be the local leader, while the Kassite nobles nominated their own Kassite king, Adad-shuma-usur (1216–1187 BC), the son of Kashtiliashu IV. Although details of his rule are unclear, Adad-shuma-usur's 30 years on the throne constitute the longest reign of any Kassite king (Brinkman 1976: 89). Interdynastic marriages with Elam are attested. but when the Elamite king Shutruk-Nahhunte's claim to the Kassite throne, based on the fact that his mother was Kassite, was rejected, he invaded Babylonia, conquering and plundering its cities from the Diyala region to the Persian Gulf. An enormous amount of booty was taken back to Susa, where French archaeologists at the beginning of the 20th century found such objects as the Codex Hammurabi and the victory stele of the Akkadian king Naram-Sin.

Shutruk-Nahhunte's son, Kudur-Nahhunte, became governor of Babylon and Babylonia and the Kassite Empire continued to decline. Renewed Kassite rebellions and repeated attempts to nominate Enlil-naddin-ahhi (1157–1155 BC) as their own king led Kudur-nahhunte to destroy Babylon. Enlil-naddin-ahhi was captured and carried off to Elam, along with the cult statue of Marduk, who became a prisoner of the new Elamite superpower. After nearly 400 years of supremacy over Babylonia and the neighboring regions, the Kassite Empire finally and definitively come to an end.

One of the most important ventures of the Kassite rulers was their self-representation as kings, installed and legitimized by the relevant Mesopotamian gods. Kassite kings thus wanted to be remembered as being obedient to the traditional local gods. The claim that the return of Marduk from captivity happened under Kassite rule must have been an extremely effective piece of propaganda. Kassite adherence to Babylonian religion found its material expression in the care of extant Babylonian temples as well as in the building of new ones, such as the Ishtar temple at Uruk (see below). This temple presented a specific aspect of Kassite acculturation. Like the rulers of earlier empires, Kassite kings understood the importance of connecting the traditional cultural traits with new ones, concealing the fact that they had created a new geopolitical order and thus in reality broken with local traditions. Nominally, the Kassite kings ruled in the name of the Babylonian gods, but the gods who protected and guided them remained Kassite ones. Similarly, the titles of the Kassite kings followed Babylonian norms, but their personal names remained Kassite. Finally, the Kassites cleverly exploited language – Sumerian for building inscriptions and Akkadian for international and political correspondence – in keeping with ancient usage.

Land grants became an important tool of Kassite political patronage. As formerly influential elites lost their power, a new group of landowners developed, one on whom the Kassite kings bestowed their largesse in return for political support. The classical Kassite monument, the so-called *kudurrus* (see below), is a physical embodiment of this phenomenon.

The Kassites established a comprehensive network of control all over the empire. From city to region, administrators stood under the control of the Kassite kings. Economically, the palace dominated the temple, although the temples and priesthood of Nippur, the traditional religious center of Mesopotamia, were taken care of and provided with everything they needed. The Kassites knew how to avoid religiously based upheavals. Enlil, rather than Marduk, became the most important politico-religious authority in the country, the kingmaker and the one who conferred rule over the world. The god with the highest and most extensive authority thus became the most highly esteemed Mesopotamian god under the Kassites. International acceptance of the new world order was demonstrated by the economic and political alliances with the Hittites and especially with the Egyptians, the global power in the Near East.

The principle of combining the old with the new became particularly visible in the built environment. The political propaganda of the Kassite kings announced the caretaking of the traditional temples and reverence for the Babylonian gods. However, this did not deter the Kassites from introducing new elements in Babylonian religion. King Karaindash conducted divine services for Ishtar at Uruk. The temple built for her, its form and especially its external façade decoration – male and female gods placed in niches around the temple – was unparalleled. The temple type as well as its isolated position in the city were likewise unparalleled. Thus, the modification of tradition seems not to have been a problem for the Kassites.

Kurigalzu I took the great step of not only changing but breaking with tradition when he left the religious and political center of Babylon and built Dur-Kurigalzu (modern Aqar Quf), the first and only purely Kassite center of the empire about 200 kilometers north of Babylon. Leaving Babylon, a city with a centuries-old tradition as a cultural center, was an unmistakable sign, but what did it really mean? Were the Kassites expressing their own view of the world and the world order they had created with the building of Dur-Kurigalzu? Certainly, they did not hide the fact that they were not fully acculturated in the Babylonian tradition, but unequivocally emphasized it. While Agum II distinguished himself by returning the cult image of Marduk to Babylon, it was Kurigalzu I who, in his propaganda, explicitly transcended the Babylonian sphere and presented himself as the "king of the four quarters." At the same time, Enlil, the ancestral figure among the Babylonian gods, became increasingly important, while the prominence of Marduk receded. The new world order got a new world center – Dur Kurigalzu – and at the same time the world-view changed and with it the meaning of Babylonian traditions. But as always when a government changes the seat of government, one must ask, was this an expression of power or a sign of weakness? Kurigalzu I demonstrated power in having the manpower and economic resources necessary to build a new city. At the same time, it is possible that the long-established local elites of Babylon might have been obstructing the political and religious goals of the global ruler Kurigalzu I.

The new and most characteristic image-bearer of Kassite culture is the so-called *kudurru*. *Kudurru* is the Kassite term for "border" or "boundary." The term is also used by archaeologists to designate carved stone boulders, up to 1 meter high, that display a variety of divine symbols, objects, architecture, stars, and animal hybridsm as well as text that informs us about the distribution and ownership of land. With the *kudurrus*, the Kassites developed their own visual language. A specific form and system of communication became visible, without the illustration of action that could be easily read and understood. Divine symbols had been used for centuries, but the Kassites were the first to canonize their forms. The reading and understanding of these symbols presupposed some knowledge of their meaning, but whether this knowledge was widespread in Kassite society, representing a kind of standardized shorthand, or whether only a specific group of educated people knew the meaning of the symbols, is unknown. The *kudurrus* were sources of information about land ownership. As noted above, Kassite kings granted land to new owners who thereby become a powerful group of supporters, while old landowners, who lost land, threatened to become a danger for the Kassite kings.

Cylinder seals of the period reflect much more of the religious world than their Ur III and Old Babylonian predecessors. The Kassites used the well-known presentation scene, with some modifications. They truncated the story, so to speak, by depicting a seated god and a prayer (i.e., a prayer incised in cuneiform on the seal itself), a human male or the intercessory goddess, thus a *pars pro toto* of what would earlier have been a scene depicting an intercessory goddess leading a human being to a seating god. The pictorial area was also filled with symbols and other beings, such as dogs, flies, and grasshoppers. As on the *kudurrus*, the text of a prayer, addressing the god, incised on Kassite cylinder seals assumed great importance.

The decline of the Kassite Empire became obvious when the Assyrians begun to intervene in domestic affairs. Instability grew and the attacks by the Elamites army increased political problems in Babylonia. International alliances temporarily eased matters, but could not ultimately halt the erosion and decline of the empire. Marduk was again captured and taken away, this time to Assyria. A war had to be waged on two fronts, against both the Assyrians and the Elamites. In the end the Elamites were successful. After 400 years of Kassite political rule, the empire collapsed and that collapse brought about the end of the Kassites as a political force in Babylonia.

7 Conclusion: 900 Years of Empire and Struggle for Supra-Regional Supremacy

In conclusion, a few aspects seem to have characterized imperial politics between 2100 and 1200 BC. Strong propaganda was necessary to convince the subject social groups that each of the established political orders was *de facto* the best and only order to secure the prosperity of all affected by imperial conquest. Control in both the religious and economical domains and a strong and loyal army were essential to each empire's success. The propaganda deployed, and the messages used to create a common "we" and to foster the acceptance of the new, differed in each case. Yet in each empire a sensitivity was shown to earlier cultural habits and traditions which were mobilized to confer legitimacy upon the new world order of the Ur III, Old Babylonian, and Kassite kings.

GUIDE TO FURTHER READING

On the subject of "empire" generally, see Pomper (2005). For a series of studies concerning empire and change in political orders in times of crisis, see Heinz and Feldman (2007). For theoretical studies related to migration in the ancient world, see Lucassen (2010).

CHAPTER THIRTY-EIGHT

The Hittite Empire

Trevor Bryce

1 Indo-European Origins

Around the middle of the 18th century BC, a king called Pithana led his troops against the city of Nesa and took it by storm. Nesa lay in central Anatolia, just south of the river today called the Kizil Irmak, the Halys of Classical and the Marassantiya of Hittite texts. Also known as Kanesh, Nesa was the seat of one of several Middle Bronze Age kingdoms of central Anatolia, and the headquarters of the network of Assyrian merchant colonies spread through eastern and central Anatolia. It now became the new royal seat of Pithana, whose ancestral city Kussara lay in the anti-Taurus region. From Nesa, Pithana and his son and successor Anitta embarked on a series of military campaigns both east and west of the Kizil Irmak, which culminated in Anitta's conquest of the city of Hattush. This was the capital of the kingdom of Hatti, then ruled by a man called Piyusti. It was located within the Kizil irmak basin on the site of the later Hittite capital Hattusha. Piyusti had been Anitta's most formidable opponent. His defeat marked the end of the kingdom of Hatti. Anitta razed Hattush and declared its site accursed by sowing it with weeds. It was never again to be resettled. But Anitta commemorated his victory by recording it on a stele set up in the city's gateway, and 150 years later, this account of his and his father's triumphs had become firmly entrenched in Hittite historical tradition (Hallo and Younger 2003: 182–4).

A Companion to the Archaeology of the Ancient Near East, First Edition.
Edited by D.T. Potts.
© 2012 Blackwell Publishing Ltd. Published 2012 by Blackwell Publishing Ltd.

Pithana's and Anitta's exploits are generally regarded as a prelude to the history of the Hittite kingdom, whose origins probably date to the early 17th century, early in the Late Bronze Age, half a century or more after the empire built by Anitta had disappeared and the Assyrian colonies had come to an end. The royal dynasty that held sway over the kingdom for virtually the whole of its history, until its collapse early in the 12th century, was of Indo-European origin. Opinion varies widely on when Indo-European speaking groups first appeared in Anatolia. Most scholars favor the theory of Indo-European migrations into the region during the Early Bronze Age (3rd millennium BC), but earlier dates have also been proposed. All we can be certain about is an Indo-European presence in various parts of Anatolia by the early 2nd millennium – on the basis, primarily, of Indo-European names in the texts of the Assyrian merchants. In the Late Bronze Age Hittite texts, three main groups of Indo-Europeans are discernible: one group speaking a language called Palaic, located in the region of later Paphlagonia on the southern shore of the Black Sea; a second group that became widely dispersed though central, southern, and western Anatolia during the 2nd millennium, called the Luwians; and a third group called the speakers of the Nesite language. As a matter of modern convention, we call this language "Hittite." It is from the Nesite-speaking population group that the royal Hittite dynasty emerged.

As its name indicates, Nesite was so called after the city which Pithana adopted as his capital. It is likely that, at the time of Pithana's conquest, the city already had a substantial Indo-European population and that Pithana adopted the language it spoke as his own. But Nesite may in fact have been his native language, if the city from which he came, Kusshara, was primarily an Indo-European foundation. His statement that he made the inhabitants of Nesa "his mothers and fathers" *may* indicate ethnic affinities between the two cities. But other interpretations of this curious expression are possible. At all events, Kusshara was regarded by at least one future Hittite king, Hattushili I, as his ancestral home.

2 The Old Kingdom

Hattushili is in fact the earliest Hittite king with whom written records can be associated. He ascended his throne c.1650 BC (for the dates used throughout this article, see Bryce 2005: 376–80), and from his own and other Hittite records, we know that there was at least one king who preceded him on it. Hattushili reports the exploits of the first clearly attested Hittite king, a man called Labarna, probably his grandfather. In a series of military conquests, reminiscent of those of Pithana and Anitta, Labarna established his sway over many of the small states of eastern Anatolia, from the Marassantiya basin southward to the coast of the Mediterranean (Bryce 2005: 64–8). Later Hittite kings adopted his name as a royal title, much like the title Caesar in Roman imperial titulature. We do not know where the base of his operations was located. Perhaps it was the city

Kusshara, the original home of Pithana. But in any case, his grandson (?) and probable successor Hattushili took a major new step in the consolidation of Hittite power in Anatolia, by resettling the site once declared accursed by Anitta, originally called Hattush and now Hattusha. A large outcrop of rock, today known as Büyükkale ("Big Castle"), provided an excellent location for a citadel, for it was virtually impregnable from the north and could easily be protected by walls built on its eastern, southern, and western sides. The region in which the city lay had abundant water supplies from seven springs, and was at that time thickly forested. Practical considerations such as these clearly outweighed any qualms Hattusili may have had about defying the curse placed upon the site.

Hattushili consolidated and extended Labarna's conquests in central Anatolia, and then carried his arms into Syria. Here he conducted a number of campaigns against the northern Syrian states, like Alalakh in the Amuq plain and Hahhum on the Euphrates (Bryce 2005: 70–3). He crossed the Euphrates and penetrated deep into northern Mesopotamian territory, where he contracted an alliance with a king called Tunip-Teshub (Tuniya), ruler of the land of Tikunani (Salvini 1996).

For all their apparent success, Labarna's and Hattusili's military ventures fell far short of establishing what we might call an empire. Labarna's attempts to hold his conquered territories by sending his sons to govern them proved disastrous. Rebellions broke out in the territories, and Hattushili had to conquer them all over again. Further, Hattushili's Syrian campaigns were little more than raiding expeditions which established the king's credibility as a war-leader and brought rich plunder into his treasuries but failed to make any lasting impact upon the regions thus afflicted. No attempt was made to annex them or subject them in any way to permanent Hittite authority. Indeed, many of them were, and continued to be, vassal states of the northern Syrian kingdom Yamkhad, whose capital was located at Aleppo. Hattushili never succeeding in capturing Aleppo itself. It fell finally to the Hittites during a campaign against it by Hattushili's grandson and successor Murshili I, who followed up his victory by marching south along the Euphrates to the city of Babylon, which he captured, sacked, and destroyed (Bryce 2005: 97–100). This last exploit, dated to c.1595 BC, brought to an end the dynasty of Hammurabi (Ch. II.37).

Murshili too made no attempt to impose his sovereignty upon the lands and cities he had conquered in Syria and Mesopotamia. And within a few years of his military triumphs in these regions, he fell to an assassination plot. The assassin Hantili, Murshili's brother-in-law, now became king. Struggles over the throne in Hattusha persisted through the reigns of five of Murshili's successors, which weakened the kingdom to the point where it not only lost most of its subject territories, but suffered invasion of its core territory, particularly by Hurrian forces from the southeast. This was the first, and would not be the last, time the Hittite kingdom was brought to the brink of annihilation. Order was restored by a king called Telipinu (c.1525–1500 BC) – also a usurper – who drove the enemy occupiers from his homeland, and firmly imposed his authority within it. Most importantly, he established fixed rules for the royal succession, assigning considerable powers to a body of officials called the *panku*. Protection of the reigning sovereign was clearly the prime responsibility of this group, which was authorized to take severe disciplinary action against any subjects, including those of the highest rank, who sought to defy the new succession provisions (Hallo and Younger 2003/I: 196–7). Further afield, Telipinu set about regaining, by force of arms, some of the territories lost by his predecessors. But in one case, he adopted a policy which was to become a lynch-pin of later Hittite influence through much of the Near Eastern world. In southeastern Anatolia a new kingdom had been formed out of the local territories formerly subject to the Hittites. It was called Kizzuwatna. Instead of attempting to regain its territory by military action, Telipinu negotiated a settlement with its ruler Isputakhsu, confirmed by treaty. The treaty was to become an important diplomatic instrument used by many Hittite kings for the maintenance of their control over their subject territories and the establishment of peaceful relations and alliances with foreign rulers.

In the short term, however, Telipinu's reforms and policies had but limited effect. During the next century, the Hittite kingdom made relatively little impact on the international scene. No more campaigns were undertaken into Syria, and squabbles broke out afresh over the royal succession. But Hatti's fortunes rose once more, early in the 14th century, when a man called Tudhaliya occupied the throne in Hattusha. His accession marked the beginning of a new era in Hittite history, the period of the "New Kingdom," which lasted for just over two centuries, until the fall of the Hittite capital Hattusha c.1186 BC. It was in this period that the Hittites built what became for a time the most powerful empire in the Near Eastern world.

3 Language and Scripts

At its greatest extent, in the 14th and 13th centuries BC, the Hittite Empire stretched from the Aegean coast of Turkey across Anatolia through Syria south to the northern frontier of Damascus, and to the western fringes of Mesopotamia. The core region of the empire was what is now commonly referred to as the Hittite homeland, which lay within the region of north-central Anatolia roughly defined by the Marassantiya river. This homeland territory was called the Land of Hatti in Hittite and other ancient sources. "Hittite" is a modern term derived from biblical sources. The Hittites themselves never used any form of ethnic designation. They simply called themselves the people of the land of Hatti – a name which goes back centuries and perhaps even millennia, before Hittite history begins. Hatti was the traditional name of the region, and the term "Hattian" is applied by scholars to the region's indigenous culture, including its art, language, and religion. Remnants of this culture survived in the Hittite period. Indeed, it is possible that the population of the Hittite homeland, including the capital, had a significant Hattian component, at least in the kingdom's earlier years. The Hittite, or more strictly the Nesite, language was certainly the kingdom's official language, used for written communications between the kings and his officials, and in letters and treaties exchanged between the king and his western vassal rulers. It was the language of the elite administrative class of the kingdom, a testimony to the Indo-European origins of the royal dynasty. But we cannot be sure how widely spoken it was outside the highest levels of Hittite society. It was undoubtedly a minority language within the kingdom as a whole, and perhaps even within the Hittite homeland, and the capital itself.

For writing their documents, the Hittites used the cuneiform script, adopted from northern Syria, or from scribes brought back from the region in the wake of Hattushili's campaigns there. The great bulk of our information about the Hittite world is derived from these tablets, first deciphered by a Czech scholar Bedřich Hrozný during World War I. The majority of the tablets have been found in various locations in the Hittite capital, as well as in the kingdom's regional centers. Wood was also used as a writing material. Though no wooden tablets have survived, we know of their existence from references in the clay tablets to "scribes of the wooden tablets." Important documents, like international treaties, were sometimes inscribed on metal, including gold, silver, and bronze. One of the most significant finds made at Hattusha in recent years is a bronze tablet, fully intact, more than 350 lines in length, and containing the text of a treaty between one of the last Hittite kings, Tudhaliya IV (c.1237–1209 BC), and his cousin Kurunta, who had been appointed appanage ruler of the southern Hittite kingdom Tarhuntassa (Hallo and Younger 2003/II: 100–6).

The repertoire of Hittite cuneiform tablets includes international and vassal treaties, a wide range of correspondence, between Hittite kings and their officials, vassal rulers, and foreign peers, festival and ritual texts, mythological texts, lists of duties for royal officials, and a collection of 200 Hittite laws. Seal impressions provide another important category of written information about the Hittite world. The seals of kings, other members of their families, and high officials were impressed on a range of documents, including land-grants, royal gifts, treaties, and records of goods purchased. Many of the seals are digraphic. They contain (for example) the name of a king and his titles in an inner circle, written in a hieroglyphic script (see below), and the king's name and titles and information about his genealogy in (usually) two outer rings, written in the cuneiform script. Only a few hundred of these seals were known prior to 1990, in which year an archive of 3,535 of them came to light during excavations on a rocky outcrop, now known as Nişantepe or Nişantaş, located in the so-called "Lower City" of the Hittite capital (Neve 1992: 48–63). The great majority of the new discoveries were clay *bullae* – i.e., lumps of clay stamped with a seal and attached to a document as a certificate of authentication. There were also a small number of seal impressions on land-grant documents.

The hieroglyphic script used on the seals represent the language used by Hittite kings for their monumental inscriptions. It first appears on a small number of royal seal impressions, dating to the Hittite Old Kingdom and bearing, in hieroglyphic symbols, the Hittite royal title *Labarna*.

The language of the script is not Hittite, but Luwian. This was the language of one of the three Indo-European population groups whose presence is first attested in Anatolia in the early 2nd millennium BC. The Luwians were undoubtedly the most populous and widespread of these groups, and by the Hittite New Kingdom may well have formed a substantial component of the Hittite homeland population. Their language also makes its appearance, in cuneiform script, in a number of ritual passages inserted into Hittite texts. The reading and decipherment of the Luwian hieroglyphic script (the name "hieroglyphic" is adopted from the so-called, but totally unconnected, pictographic script of ancient Egypt) proved an almost impossible task until the discovery, in 1946, of a bilingual text with both Phoenician and Luwian hieroglyphic versions, at Karatepe in eastern Cilicia. Though difficulties still remain, particularly with the reading of a number of the script's symbols, the problems of decipherment have been largely solved, thanks to the work of a number of scholars, primarily J.D. Hawkins, H. Çambel, A. Morpurgo-Davies, and G. Neumann (Hawkins 2000).

Hieroglyphic inscriptions dating to the Hittite Empire include a few graffiti found on the paving stones and orthostats of the Temple of the Storm God at Hattusha as well as a number of bowls and other small metal objects from this period. But the great majority of Late Bronze Age hieroglyphic texts appear as monumental inscriptions on rock faces and built stone surfaces. Of 13th century date, most of these have been found within the Hittite homeland, but they are otherwise widely distributed throughout Anatolia. Some record a king's military exploits and other achievements, or are attached as epigraphs – i.e., identification labels – to the figures of deities or Hittite kings or other members of Hittite royalty. Why did Hittite kings choose the Luwian hieroglyphic script for their public monuments? The usual answer is that it was a much more impressive visual medium than the cuneiform script for the purposes of public display. But T. van den Hout has argued that the main purpose in using this form of communication was to help Hittite kings identify more closely with the Luwian populations in whose regions many of the inscribed monuments were located (van den Hout 2006: 222–37). That may well be so. In any case, the Luwian hieroglyphic script became the standard medium used by Hittite royalty for recording their achievements on stone in many parts of the empire, including Hattusha, during the empire's final century. The longest known inscription in Luwian hieroglyphs appears on the rock face at the site of Nişantaş in the Hittite capital. Though now almost entirely illegible, enough of its first line can be read to identify its author as Shuppiluliuma (II), the last Hittite king (1207–? BC). Also dating to Shuppiluliuma's reign is a recently discovered hieroglyphic text found in one of the rooms of a two-chambered structure on the so-called Südburg ("south hill") at Hattusha, just south of the royal acropolis (Hawkins 1995). This inscription, which is accompanied by reliefs of a deity and the king himself, records a number of the king's military operations in southern Anatolia. It is perhaps a condensed version of the longer Nişantaş inscription. The building in which it appears is believed to be what Hittite texts call a KASKAL.KUR, a symbolic entrance to the Underworld.

4 The Hittite Empire in its Near Eastern Context

Written sources of information provide us with a reasonably comprehensive outline picture of the evolution, development, and fall of the Hittite Empire, though this picture is constantly being adjusted as new information comes to light. Campaigns undertaken by the Hittite king Tudhaliya I as far as the Aegean coast in the west and the Euphrates in the east established the basis for the re-emergence of Hatti, the kingdom of the Hittites, as a major international power (there is some uncertainty as to whether the western and eastern campaigns should be assigned to two different kings called Tudhaliya; hence the convention of referring to the king or kings in question as Tudhaliya I/II.) In the west, Tudhaliya fought several campaigns against enemy coalitions, most notably one commonly known as the Assuwan Confederacy (Bryce 2005: 123–7). Among the leading members of these coalitions were a number of states known collectively as the Arzawa lands, whose populations, most scholars believe, included large Luwian-speaking groups. Despite the victories Tudhaliya claimed to have won during these campaigns, and the thousands of prisoners of war he allegedly brought back from them, the west remained a constant threat to Hittite security, as later events were to demonstrate. In the east and southeast, Tudhaliya claimed crushing victories over Aleppo and the kingdom of Mitanni. He may have paved the way for his operations in the region by annexing the kingdom of Kizzuwatna, which had fluctuated in its external alignments between Hatti and Mitanni.

By the end of the 16th century, the kingdom of Mitanni had been formed from a number of small Hurrian states in Upper Mesopotamia. One of the four great kingdoms of the Near Eastern world during the first half of the Late Bronze Age, it was to become Hatti's greatest rival for political and military supremacy over northern Syria and eastern Anatolia. The other great kingdoms of the age were Egypt, which also sought to expand its territories in Syria, particularly under the pharaoh Thutmose III (1479–1425 BC), and Babylon. The rivalry between Hatti and Mitanni came to a head in the reign of the Hittite king Shuppiluliuma I (c.1350–1322 BC), whose accession to the Hittite throne, by the path of usurpation, followed a period when the Hittite kingdom was, once again, almost obliterated. This happened during the reign of Tudhaliya III, Shuppiluliuma's father and predecessor. In what is commonly called the "concentric invasions," the Hittite homeland was attacked from all around its frontiers and occupied by enemy forces (Bryce 2005: 145–8). Contingents from Arzawa figured prominently among the attackers. Tudhaliya abandoned Hattusha and took refuge in a place called Shamuha, probably located on the upper course of the Marassantiya river, which he used as a base for driving the enemy forces from the homeland. Almost certainly, Shuppiluliuma was the principal architect of the recovery of the homeland, and the restoration of Hatti's status as one of the great powers of the age. No doubt he felt he had the right to succeed his father, in place of his brother Tudhaliya the Younger, the designated successor, who was assassinated in a palace conspiracy.

Once he was firmly seated upon his throne, Shuppiluliuma set his sights on achieving the ultimate ambition of his career, the elimination of the kingdom of Mitanni. Within five or six years of his accession, he had largely realized this ambition. In 1344 BC he conducted a massive campaign of conquest against Mitanni's allies in northern Syria, and followed this up with an invasion deep into Mitanni's homeland in northern Mesopotamia, capturing and plundering its capital Washukkani (Bryce 2005: 161–3). The Mitannian king Tushratta was forced to flee for his life. He was later assassinated by a group of his own subjects, including his son. Shuppiluliuma now became overlord of northern Syria, subjecting to vassalhood the former subject territories and allies of the Mitannian king. But elements of Mitannian resistance lingered on, and it was not until 1326 BC that the final Mitannian stronghold Karkamish on the Euphrates fell to Shuppiluliuma after a six-day siege (Hallo and Younger 2003/I: 190). Shuppiluliuma forthwith placed Karkamish under the rule of his son Sharri-Kushukh (Piyassili) as viceroy. He also appointed another of his sons, Telipinu, as viceroy in the former Syrian kingdom Aleppo. For the first time, large territories outside the Hittite homeland were under direct Hittite rule. Other northern Syrian states retained their own rulers, who were obliged to swear oaths of allegiance to Shuppiluliuma as his vassals. A number of scholars would argue, with some justification, that it was with Shuppiluliuma that the era of the Hittite empire truly began. But there is no doubt that the foundations of empire had been laid several generations earlier, by the first king called Tudhaliya.

Hittite sovereignty was also established in the west, particularly in the reign of Shuppiluliuma's son and second successor, Murshili II (c.1321–1295 BC), who ascended the throne after the premature death of his brother Arnuwanda, Shuppiluliuma's first successor. Military campaigns conducted in the west by Murshili in his third and fourth regnal years were sufficient to bring to heel the recalcitrant Arzawa states in the region (Bryce 2005: 192–7). Their subjection and allegiance to Murshili was formalized in a series of vassal treaties which Murshili drew up with their rulers.

5 How the Empire Was Controlled

The treaties were personal contracts between the king and his vassal ruler (see Beckman 1999b: 11–124). The latter was bound to his overlord by a number of obligations. He swore allegiance to the Great King, and pledged support for his legitimate successors; he undertook to provide the king with troops, particularly when the king or his commanders were campaigning in his region; he promised to inform the king of anti-Hittite activities in his region, to have no dealings with the rulers of foreign states, nor to harbor refugees from Hittite authority, and (in at least some cases) to pay an annual tribute into his overlord's coffers. Provided he fulfilled his treaty obligations, the vassal was allowed, in almost all cases, to rule his state as he saw fit. And, in the event that his kingdom was attacked by outside forces or he was threatened or overthrown in a coup by his own subjects, he was guaranteed the protection of his overlord. Sometimes, Hittite garrisons were stationed in vassal states. But this happened only when the states in question had a history of prolonged instability or were located in frontier territories that were vulnerable to enemy incursions.

The vassal treaty system was one of the most important instruments used by Hittite kings in maintaining their authority over their subject territories. At its height from the mid-14th to the mid-13th century BC, the Hittite Empire consisted essentially of its core homeland territory, the Land of Hatti in the strictest sense, and a large network of subject states, spread over much of Anatolia and northern Syria. As we have noted, Shuppiluliuma I extended direct Hittite rule into Syria with his appointment of his sons as viceroys in Karkamish and Aleppo. Otherwise, Hatti's control over its so-called empire was a relatively loose one, which depended ultimately for its survival on the loyalty and support of treaty-bound vassal rulers. There were periods when the vassal system worked relatively well, particularly during the reign of Murshili II. But there were also many occasions when vassal states rose in rebellion against their overlord, or overthrew a pro-Hittite ruler, necessitating campaigns by the Great King himself or by one of his high-ranking military commanders, to reassert Hittite authority in the region. In the wake of such campaigns, hundreds and sometimes thousands of the populations of the rebel states were brought back to the homeland as deportees, along with large numbers of livestock and other booty. This had the twofold effect of restocking the homeland's workforces and significantly reducing the prospects of further uprisings in the subdued states, since many of the deportees culled from the local populations must have been able-bodied males of military age. In their new homeland, the deportees were given various roles. Some were assigned to the king's officers, to work on their estates as agricultural laborers; some were drafted into the royal militia; some were assigned cultic duties in the Hittite land's numerous religious establishments; and large numbers were settled in regions with low populations near the kingdom's frontiers.

Shortage of manpower seems to have been a chronic problem throughout Hittite history, and the deportation system must have played an extremely important role in replenishing the kingdom's human resources, particularly for agricultural and military purposes. Hittite military expeditions were always costly enterprises, even if ultimately successful, because of the drain they imposed on the kingdom's available manpower. For major campaigns, the king's standing army had to be supplemented by levies drawn from the agricultural workforce. And the absence of large bodies of Hittite troops on campaigns far from their homeland exposed the homeland to attack from the enemies across its frontiers. One of the most formidable and persistent of such enemies consisted of tribal groups from Kashka, a rugged and in parts impenetrable region located in the Pontic mountains south of the Black Sea and north of the Hittites' northern frontiers. Kashkan forces repeatedly raided Hittite territory, particularly in periods when Hittite armies were engaged in expeditions abroad. Though Hittite kings frequently scored victories over Kashkan armies, and destroyed many Kaskhan settlements, the enemy remained an elusive and ultimately unconquerable one.

It is understandable that on many occasions Hittite kings attempted to settle problems that arose in the vassal states, particularly problems associated with rebel movements, by diplomacy rather than military force. A number of their campaigns against the western Arzawa lands, for example, were undertaken only when all attempts at resolution of a crisis by diplomatic means had failed. The western states were particularly prone to rebellion, often, it seems with the prompting and support of a foreign power called Ahhiyawa in Hittite texts. Most scholars believe that Ahhiyawa was the Hittite way of referring to the Greek Mycenaean world, and in some cases to a specific kingdom within this world, perhaps Mycenae itself. The name Ahhiyawa, which also appears in the variant form Ahhiya, is thought to come from the word Akhaioi (Achaeans), one of the names by which the Greeks are known in Homer's epic poems. If the identification is valid, it is clear from Hittite texts that at least one Mycenaean king sought to expand the territories he controlled onto the Anatolian mainland, into what was Hittite vassal territory, and using local anti-Hittite elements as agents for this expansion. For a time, the important city called Milawanda (Milawata) on Anatolia's western coast came under Ahhiyawan or Mycenaean control, and was used by the Mycenaean king as the main base for the extension of his activities through the western Anatolian coastal regions. Milawata was the Bronze Age ancestor of the city later to be called Miletus.

6 Hatti's Relations with Egypt

In the southeast, Hatti's subject territories extended through northern Syria to the frontier of the land of Damascus, which marked the northern limit of Egypt's subject states. Disputes between Hatti and Egypt over control of two local Syrian kingdoms, Amurru and Qadesh, located in the Orontes region to the north of Damascus, had culminated in two military showdowns at Qadesh between Hittite and Egyptian armies. The more famous of these, fought in 1274 BC between the Hittite king Muwattalli II and the pharaoh Ramesses II (Hallo and Younger 2003/II: 32–40), resulted in a stalemate. But the Egyptian forces withdrew to the region of Damascus, and Amurru and Qadesh were gathered firmly within the Hittite fold. A gradual easing of tensions between Hatti and Egypt led finally to the conclusion of a peace treaty in 1259 BC drawn up between Ramesses and Muwattalli's son and second successor Hattushili III. Unlike the Hittite vassal treaties, the Hittite-Egyptian treaty represented a bilateral agreement between its contracting parties. Versions of it were prepared separately in Hattusha and Ramesses' capital Pi-Ramesse, each from the respective treaty partner's viewpoint (Beckman 1999b: 96–100). The Hittite version was originally written in Akkadian, from a first Hittite draft, inscribed on a silver tablet, and then sent to Egypt, where it was translated into Egyptian. The Egyptian version of the treaty was first composed in Egyptian, and then translated into Akkadian on a silver tablet before being sent to Hattusha.

Akkadian was the international language diplomacy of the Late Bronze Age, and many of the tablets found at Hattusha could be read some years before the decipherment of the Hittite language, since they were written in Akkadian. This was the language used by Hittite kings in their communications with their vassal rulers in Syria and in their correspondence with their foreign counterparts. A large number of letters have survived in the Hittite archives from the reigns of Hattushili III and Ramesses II, exchanged between the Hittite and Egyptian kings and also members of their families, in the period leading up to the treaty, and subsequently in the years preceding the first of two marriages which Ramesses contracted with Hattushili's daughters. Each king addressed the other as "my brother," and "Great King." The latter form of address was reserved exclusively for the rulers of the four great kingdoms of the age. The other rulers were the kings of Assyria and Babylon. Assyria had occupied the power vacuum left in northern Mesopotamia by the Hittite destruction of the Mitannian Empire, and became an increasing threat both to its southern neighbor Babylon and to the territories west of the Euphrates. Indeed, fear of a resurgent Assyria, formerly a vassal state of Mitanni, may have been one of the prompts for the treaty concluded between Hattushili and Ramesses.

7 The Duties of Royalty

Like his royal brothers, the Hittite king exercised three major functions: he was the chief priest of the empire, he was its supreme judicial authority, and he was commander-in-chief of its armies (Bryce 2002: 11–31). In all his functions, his role was very much a hands-on one. His appointment as king was divinely sanctioned, but he ruled merely as the servant and chief executive officer of the storm god, the most important deity in the Hittite pantheon. The religious duties which he was expected to fulfill in person were numerous, and in some cases had to take priority over all his other activities. Kings are known to have cut short military campaigns in order to discharge a particular religious responsibility – or else invoke the wrath of the offended gods, which might be unleashed in the form of a plague of devastating proportions. Not least among the king's religious duties was the celebration of certain religious festivals, which often entailed pilgrimages to a number of the kingdom's cult centers. Of the four most important festivals of the religious calendar, two were held in spring – the AN.TAH.ŠUM ("crocus") and the *purulli* ("earth") festivals – and at least one and perhaps two in autumn – the *nuntarriyashas* ("festival of haste") and the KI.LAM ("gatehouse") festival. The AN.TAH.ŠUM festival was performed primarily for the Sun-Goddess of Arinna, consort of the storm god and the second most important deity of the Hittite pantheon.

The Hittite New Year festival way have been celebrated in a natural rock sanctuary located 1 kilometer northeast of Hattusha and now known as Yazilikaya ("Inscribed Rock"). Hattushili III built a gatehouse and temple complex with interior court and inner sanctuary across the front of the site, and his son and successor Tudhaliya IV embellished the complex with relief sculptures. The main group of reliefs in the main chamber (Chamber A) consists of two files of deities, male on the left and female on the right (with one exception in each case). Their depiction and their names, presented in the Luwian hieroglyphic script, show marked Hurrian influence, illustrating the strong impact which Hurrian culture made on the Hittite civilization, especially in Late Bronze Age Hatti's final century. In the second, narrow, rock chamber in the complex (Chamber B), 12 running or marching gods are depicted, with curved swords over their shoulders. They are generally believed to be the 12 gods of the underworld. On the wall opposite them, two human figures are represented. From the royal cartouche above his name, the smaller of the figures can be identified as Tudhaliya IV. He is dressed in priestly garb, with long robe and close-fitting skull-cap, and he carries a curved staff (Latin *lituus*). The larger figure, who extends a protective arm around him and grasps his wrist, is Tudhaliya's patron deity Sharrumma. On the same wall, the relief of a dagger plunged into the ground, its hilt consisting of a human head, with two protomes of lions beneath, is also considered to have underworld associations. A number of scholars have speculated that Yazilikaya may have served as a mortuary chapel in the kingdom's last decades. Chamber B may be Tudhaliya's tomb. If so, it would be the only known royal tomb from the Hittite world.

One of the most powerful figures in the Hittite kingdom was the woman known as Tawannana. In most instances, she was the king's chief consort, and held office for the whole of her life, even if her husband died before her. She was chief priestess of the Hittite world, and by virtue of this and her other roles, she could be a powerful influence within the kingdom. This sometimes proved dangerous for the kingdom's stability, as illustrated by Murshili II's accusations against his stepmother, the Tawannana of the day, wife of his deceased father Shuppiluliuma and a Babylonian princess in origin. Accusing her of stripping the palace of its treasures to lavish on her favorites, introducing undesirable foreign customs into the kingdom, and murdering his wife by witchcraft, Murshili had her banished from the kingdom (see Bryce 2005: 207–10).

But the most powerful of all reigning consorts was the Hurrian priestess Puduhepa, whom Murshili's son Hattushili (III) married on his way home from Syria, following the battle of Qadesh. Apart from her role as chief priestess of the Hittite realm, a role reflected in a number of religious reforms which she made, she closely partnered her husband in many other activities, particularly in the judicial sphere. The king's responsibilities as supreme judge within his realm were far-reaching. Capital offences were referred to him for judgment, and he served as a final court of appeal for all his subjects, as illustrated by an appeal made to him by a priest in Emar on the Euphrates, who was in dispute with a local garrison-commander over property and taxes. Puduhepa's engagement in the administration of justice at a microlevel is illustrated by the judgment she handed down in a case involving a damaged boat in Ugarit. She deputized for the king in this case, and actually used his royal title "My Sun" in authenticating the document recording her decision.

The Hittite collection of 200 laws provide us with many valuable insights into the mores and value systems of Hittite society (Hoffner 1997a; Bryce 2002: 32–55). Though in many instances adopted from earlier Mesopotamian laws, particularly those of the Babylonian king Hammurabi, the Hittite laws generally take a less draconic, more pragmatic approach to the administration of justice. More emphasis is placed on appropriate compensation for the victim of an offence than punishment per se for the offender. The Hammurabic (and biblical) "eye for an eye" principle has no place in Hittite legal provisions. The laws are far from comprehensive in their coverage and consist for the most part of a selection of legal precedents based on earlier court rulings. Property rights figure prominently in the laws, as do marriage provisions – understandably, since marriage regularly involved a transfer of property, in the form of dowries and bride-prices. The status of parties to a dispute had a considerable bearing on the penalties imposed upon the offender and the compensation awarded to the victim. Mutilation was in a number of cases prescribed for a slave offender, whereas such punishments were replaced for offenders of free status by monetary compensation, or compensation in kind. Certain categories of sexual offences were punishable by death, but in general capital punishment was relatively rare.

As commander-in-chief of the Hittite army the king was expected to lead campaigns against rebel or enemy forces in person. Indeed, many kings were engaged in military campaigning for a large part of their reign. On a number of occasions, however, the king delegated command to his highest-ranking officers, generally a close member of his family and often one of his sons, typically the crown prince or one of his brothers. The core element of the Hittite militia was a standing professional army, made up of infantry and chariotry which wintered in military barracks in the capital and could be used as a laborforce for building projects or as a policeforce when not engaged in military duties. For major campaigns, their ranks were supplemented by levies from the homeland population, and also by conscripts provided by various provincial districts. According to Ramesses II, the Hittite king Muwattalli assembled a force of 47,500 infantry and chariotry for the showdown at Qadesh, boosting his own forces with mercenary contingents.

8 Archaeological Sites Within the Homeland

Our knowledge of Hittite history and civilization based on written sources is complemented by archaeological data from various sites within the Hittite world. The largest and most important of these sites is the Hittite capital Hattusha, founded c.2000 BC by an indigenous Hattian population group. It lies adjacent to the modern village Boğazköy (Boğazkale). Excavations have been conducted on the site from 1906 to the present day, primarily as joint operations of the German Archaeological Institute and the Deutsche Orient-Gesellschaft (Neve 1992; Seeher 2002). In its first Hittite phase, beginning around the middle of the 17th century BC, the city was relatively small (c.62 ha). Its two chief features were an acropolis, located on the rocky outcrop now called Büyükkale, where the royal palace and ancillary administrative buildings were located, and to the northwest of it the Temple of the Storm God, a vast, sprawling complex covering an area of more than 20,000 square meters. This first city lacked adequate defenses, until the 15th century BC king Hantili II built an 8 meter thick wall around it. It subsequently fell to invaders and was sacked in the reign of Tudhaliya III (first half of the 14th century BC). The second phase of the city's history began with the restoration of Hittite authority through the Land of Hatti probably late in Tudhaliya's reign. Hattusha underwent a major redevelopment and a expansion of its boundaries to the south. The city now covered an area of c.185 hectares, tripling its original size. It was protected by new walls extending over a distance of 5 kilometers, punctuated by towers at 20 meter intervals along its entire length. The fortifications included an extension to the northeast, spanning a deep gorge and enclosing within the city limits a mountain outcrop now called Büyükkaya. Access to the city was provided by a number of gates in the walls, the most important of which, still to be seen *in situ*, are the Lion, Sphinx, and Warrior Gates. The first of these provided the main ceremonial entrance to the city. The last features on its interior a relief sculpture of a god, equipped for battle. The original city, with the royal acropolis and the Temple of the Storm God walled off within it, is now commonly referred to as the "Lower City," to distinguish it from the great, southern extension, the "Upper City." Excavations conducted in the Upper City by P. Neve brought to light the foundations of 26 temples, increasing to 31 the total number of temples so far unearthed at Hattusha (Neve 1992: 23–43).

Neve believed that Hattusha's substantial redevelopment was due largely to Tudhaliya IV in the late 13th century BC, though allowing that Tudhaliya's father Hattushili may have been the inspiration behind the project. However, Neve's successor J. Seeher has argued, from a range of criteria including radiocarbon dating and pottery analysis, that parts of the Upper City had been occupied and fortified much earlier, in the late 16th or early 15th century BC. We have referred above to a number of comparatively recent finds within Hattusha, including the Südburg structure, with its reliefs and inscriptions, the seal archive unearthed at Nişantaş and the bronze tablet discovered outside the Sphinx Gate. Other recent discoveries include 11 underground grain-pits on Büyükkaya (dated to the 14th–13th century BC) and an above-ground grain-storage complex, consisting of two parallel rows of 16 chambers each (dated to the late 16th/early15th century BC). The granaries, discovered by Seeher, had a total capacity of almost 8,000 tons of grain, mostly barley (Seeher 2000). Seeher also discovered five reservoirs, which he called the "southern ponds," built on the plateau in the Upper City. Up to 8 meters deep, four of these were rectangular in shape, one circular. They have been dated to the 15th century BC. Probably fed from nearby springs, they must have provided a large part of Hattusha's water supply for a short time before silting up and being abandoned by the end of the century.

Forty kilometers northeast of Hattusha lie the remains of the site now known as Alaça Höyük, a fortified Hittite city containing a palace, residential quarters, and several temples (Bryce 2009: 20–2). Well preserved remains of the city's main gateway, flanked by sphinxes, depict in relief a religious festival in progress. The Hittite king and queen are represented standing before an altar of the storm god, represented as a bull. A seated goddess is also depicted – almost certainly the Sun Goddess of Arinna, consort of the storm god. Alaça Höyük may well have been the city Arinna, the goddess's cult-center. Reliefs on the sculptured blocks forming the city's gateway depict other participants in the festival, including acrobats, a sword-swallower, a lute-player, perhaps a bagpiper, cult officials and animals for sacrifice. The city is also well known for its pre-Hittite Early Bronze Age II remains (mid-/late 3rd millennium), which feature 13 "royal" shaft graves, whose most impressive contents, accompanying the burials, include ritual disk and arc standards, incorporating stylized bulls and stags.

Excavations conducted in north-central Anatolia in comparatively recent years have brought to light a number of previously unlocated Hittite sites known from written sources. These include the provincial administrative centers of Shapinuwa, Tapikka, and Sarissa. Shapinuwa is located 60 kilometers northeast of Hattusha, on the site of modern Ortaköy. Covering an area of 9 square kilometers, it is frequently attested in Hittite texts as a religious and administrative center and a base for Hittite military operations. Excavations have been conducted at Ortaköy by A. Süel since 1990 (Süel 2002). Prominent among its architectural remains is a structure designated as Building A, tentatively identified as a palace or administrative building. Three thousand tablets came to light in this building, in widely dispersed fragments. Although not yet published, the majority are apparently Hittite letters with some administrative texts. Other texts are written in Akkadian, and there are a few Hittite-Akkadian, Hittite-Hattian bilingual texts. About 25 percent of the corpus consists of ritual texts written in Hurrian. The tablets have been dated to the first half of the 14th century and probably belong to the reign of Tudhaliya III. Of the other buildings unearthed on the site, one has been identified as the ground floor of a storeroom (Building B) and two are believed to have been part of a ceremonial complex (Buildings C and D).

Tapikka lay a short distance to the east of Shapinuwa, and 116 kilometers northeast of the Hittite capital (near modern Maşat). Though a relatively small site (c.10 hectares), it probably also served as a regional administrative center and military base of the Hittite kingdom. Excavations (1973–84) by T. Özgüç revealed a citadel and lower city (Özgüç 2002). Occupation began in the late 3rd millennium, but the settlement reached its peak in the first half of the 14th century BC, probably during the reign of Tudhaliya III, when its most important feature was a 4,500 square meter building erected on the citadel, clearly the headquarters of the local administration. The remains of the north and east wings of this building, commonly referred to as a palace, are preserved, as well as an inner, colonnaded courtyard. The only significant remains of the lower city are those of part of a temple. Among the small finds from the site, the most important was a tablet archive, consisting of 116 texts. Of these, 96 are letters, mostly exchanges between the king and his local officials. For the most part they deal with matters relating to the security of the region. It is believed that the entire corpus may date to a period of a few months, immediately preceding the city's destruction by enemy forces during Tudhaliya's reign. Texts of a cultic nature were also found. These have been dated to the final phase of Tapikka's existence in the 13th century BC.

The city of Sarissa (modern Kuşakli) was located south of the Marassantiya river, 200 kilometers southeast of Hattusha. It was founded in the 16th and destroyed in the first half of the 14th century BC, no doubt during the massive invasions of the Hittite homeland in this period. Excavated since 1992 by A. Müller-Karpe, the 18 hectare site consists of an acropolis, with settlement spreading over its terraces and slopes and flat areas at the bottom of the hill, and a lower hill lying to its south (Müller-Karpe 2002). The whole area is enclosed within a double casemate wall, with access to the city via four main gates. The largest and most impressive building on the slopes of the acropolis is a rectangular complex of more than 110 rooms, whose focus is a central court. Since its layout is similar to that of the sacred buildings at Hattusha, it is thought to be a temple, perhaps of the storm god. Among its small finds were a number of clay sealings, with the inscription "seal of Tabarna, the Great King. Who changes it will die," and two well-preserved letters of what philologists call the "Middle Hittite" period. Sarissa no doubt played an important role as one of the Hittite kingdom's administrative centers on the outer fringes of the homeland.

9   The End of the Empire

The Hittite kingdom came to an end early in the 12th century BC, within the context of the upheavals associated with the collapse of the Late Bronze Age civilizations and centers of power throughout the Greek and Near Eastern worlds. Many reasons for the collapse have been suggested, including a prolonged drought, food shortages, uprisings of local populations, the collapse of international trading networks, and invasions by outsiders, including the so-called Sea Peoples of Egyptian records. A number of these factors in combination may have been responsible for the end of the Hittite kingdom. Factional rivalries within the royal dynasty may also have played their part in weakening the kingdom to the point of extinction. Some signs of this are evident in the reigns of the last kings of Hatti. The final event which marked the end of the Hittite kingdom was the fall of Hattusha, but there is some question about the circumstances in which this occurred. Earlier excavators of the site, notably K. Bittel and P. Neve, attributed Hattusha's destruction to enemy attack. But Neve's successor, J. Seeher, has argued that this conclusion can no longer be maintained. In his view, and that of his successor A. Schachner, Hattusha was abandoned by a large part of its population, most notably its elite elements including the king and his family, before its destruction. All indications are that many of the city's buildings, including the palace, were systematically cleared of their contents by their occupants, who took these with them on their departure (Seeher 2001). Certainly the destruction by fire of large parts of the city can be attributed to enemy invaders. But according to Seeher, when the invaders entered the city, it was almost deserted.

That of course raises the question of where the city's inhabitants went. A number of scholars assume that many of the peoples of western and central Anatolia moved southeast, following the fall of the Hittite kingdom, and resettled in southeastern Anatolia and northern Syria, where the Iron Age "Neo-Hittite" kingdoms (Ch. II.42) emerged from the late 2nd millennium onwards. "Neo-Hittite" is a term applied by modern scholars to a number of Iron Age kingdoms in these regions (Karkamish, Kummuh, Malatya among them), because they display a degree of cultural continuity with the Late Bronze Age Hittite world, including the retention of the Luwian hieroglyphic script for recording their kings' achievements, the retention of royal Hittite names in their ruling dynasties, and the preservation of a number of Hittite elements in their art and architecture. But conclusions about ethnic and cultural continuity between the Late Bronze Age Hittite Empire and its alleged Neo-Hittite successors raise more questions than they answer. The reasons for the fall of the empire and the subsequent history of its populations remain matters for speculation.

Above all, what happened to the inhabitants of Hattusha after they abandoned their city? Archaeology may one day find us an answer to that question.

GUIDE TO FURTHER READING

O.R. Gurney's 1952 book *The Hittites*, last reprinted in 1990 (with some revisions), is a useful general work on Hittite history, society, and civilization, but it has been superseded in many respects by Collins (1990). Works devoted specifically to Hittite military and political history include Klengel (1999) and Bryce (2005). In the former, aimed more specifically at an academic market, each section is accompanied by a detailed list of the relevant primary written sources. Bryce (2002) covers a range of aspects of Hittite society and civilization, including the role of the king, the laws, marriage provisions, the gods, rituals and festivals, warfare, merchant operations, and myth and literature. Burney (2004) is a comprehensive reference work on Hittite cities, lands, and archaeological sites. Beckman (1999b) provides translations, with accompanying notes, of the majority of extant Hittite treaties, a selection of the correspondence exchanged between Hittite kings and their vassal rulers and foreign counterparts, and a selection of other diplomatic texts. It belongs to a series of publications on the writings of the ancient world published by the Society of Biblical Literature, Atlanta. Other books in the series include Hoffner (1990) on Hittite mythology and Hoffner (2009) on Hittite letters. The latter contains both transliterations and translations of a wide range of Hittite letters, accompanied by extensive notes. Useful general chapters on the history and archaeology of the Hittite Empire and its Iron Age Neo-Hittite successors are contained in Sagona and Zimansky (2009).

CHAPTER THIRTY-NINE

Elam: Iran's First Empire

Javier Álvarez-Mon

1 Introduction: Geographical and Territorial Considerations

The appearance of Elam as a political and cultural notion is deeply entrenched in the unique lowland/highland physical setting provided by the Iranian provinces of Khuzestan and Fars. This setting was responsible for conditioning the material wealth, cultural resiliency and longevity characterizing Elamite civilization. It also determined the political history of Elam as an empire by providing a buffer and retreat zone that allowed for the periodic mustering of expansionistic ambitions upon neighboring political entities. Throughout the centuries, however, the notion and identity of Elam underwent noticeable alterations that forced the reformulation of its territorial, political, social, and cultural character.

The etymology of the name Elam attests to the significance of a ubiquitous geographical presence: the Zagros highlands. The earliest written sources (in Sumerian) speak of the (land) NIM "high, elevated." Akkadian rendered the term *elamtu/elammatum*, possibly related to *elûm* ("high, upper") or, alternatively, derived from the Elamite word *halHa(l)tamti*, meaning conceivably "gracious lord-land" or just "high land." The modern name Elam is a transcription of biblical Hebrew (*'êlam*) from which Greek *Aylam* is derived.

While *stricto sensu* the word Elam acknowledges a physical feature occupied by highland political entities and peoples (highlanders), in time, it came to represent the unique character of a civilization resulting from the interaction of cultures situated in lowland Susiana (broadly the plain of the present-day province

---

A Companion to the Archaeology of the Ancient Near East, First Edition.
Edited by D.T. Potts.
© 2012 Blackwell Publishing Ltd. Published 2012 by Blackwell Publishing Ltd.

of Khuzestan in southwestern Iran) and the Zagros highlands (broadly the present-day province of Fars with its capital Shiraz). In geomorphologic terms, Susiana is an extension of the Mesopotamian plain but with the significant difference that the soil components of this rich alluvial plain were determined by its proximity to the highlands and by numerous river courses (the Karkheh, Karun, Marun or Jarrahi, and Zuhreh or Hindian). Situated between the plain and the highlands, a foothill corridor provided an ecological niche ideal for settlement and pastoralism. Next to the Zagros mountains, the most conspicuous physical boundaries were the Persian Gulf, the main rivers irrigating the Susiana plain and Fars (the Kur with its affluent the Pulvar) and the associated large, dynamic marshland and tidal floodplain located to the south and southwest of the Ahwaz anticline. The single most important overland route was the north/west–south/east plain-foothill-highland corridor connecting the political centers of Susa and Anshan (Potts 1997a: 19–42; 1999: 10–42; Steve et al. 2002: 359–61; Gasche 2004, 2005).

2 Elam Before Elam: Susiana and the Kingdoms of Awan and Shimashki

When Elam emerged and how this term came to embrace various highland Zagros polities, eventually incorporating the Susiana plain, is not entirely apparent in the archaeological and textual sources. Information on the pre-Elamite period – roughly the interval between the foundation of Susa c.4000 BC and the unlocking of the historical door made possible by textual sources around 2700 BC – is largely determined by the study and interpretation of materials unearthed in western Elam, scattered sites in the Elamite highlands, and the better known Mesopotamian archaeological sequences. This evidence provides a picture of great regional diversity, suggesting various models of interaction amongst Mesopotamian city-states and the inhabitants of Susiana and the Zagros highlands. The earliest, unequivocal textual references to Elam around 2675 BC together with Elamite royal inscriptions of the time of Shutruk-Nahunte (12th century BC) link the emergence of Elam to highland polities recognized, most notably, under the banners of Awan and Shimashki. Paradoxically, while much of the genesis and formation of Elamite cultural identity can be presumed to have evolved out of multifaceted patterns of interaction amongst highland regional powers, our earliest sources are heavily biased in favor of "Suso-Mesopotamian" relationships.

In many ways Susiana can be considered boundary territory. From the Mesopotamian perspective, it was the gateway to the eastern Iranian highlands and the plateau beyond, indispensable for access to primary resources such as metals, timber, and stone. From the highland perspective, it was the gateway to a web of flourishing, riverine, Mesopotamian urban-based networks, manufactured luxury goods, and unmatched cultural and social complexity. A significant element in this network and one of the most important settlements in the prehistoric Near East was the city of Susa. Its early chronology has been divided into two periods: Susa I (c.4000–3700 BC) and Susa II (c.3700–3100 BC). Susa I incorporated two distinct areas, both located on top of two natural outcrops c.7–10.5 meters above the level of the surrounding plain. The southern town extended over c.7 hectares (the *alumelu* "high-rising" city, *Acropole* mound) and the northern town extended over c.6.3 hectares (the *Apadana* mound – so named because it was topped by the remains of the columned palace or *apadana* of the Achaemenid Persian king, Darius I). A massive wall c.6 meters wide at the base may have enclosed the Apadana settlement. At a slightly later date this wall included a large, perhaps elite, building with a north–south/east–west orientation and plastered walls. The Acropole mound hosted an enormous solid terrace (*haute terrasse*, or "high terrace") built c.7 meters to the north of a rectangular mudbrick platform (*nécropole/massif-butte funéraire*, or "funerary structure") used as a burial ground for hundreds of bodies associated with eggshell-thin, finely painted wares (Susa I style pottery). The high terrace was a stepped, mudbrick construction with a 2 meter high socle (c.82 × 90 meters), on top of which stood a smaller, monumental platform c.9 meters high. The façade above the socle was decorated with sets of decorative, cylindrical nails or wall cones of baked clay. It has been suggested that this enormous structure must have supported the earliest sanctuaries or most important community buildings of Susa. To the north were additional architectural remains interpreted as grain storage facilities and workshop areas containing potters' kilns. In addition to these sizeable architectural complexes, Susa I was characterized by an advanced metallurgical (copper) industry. This period ended in a massive fire affecting buildings on the Acropole and the Apadana (Dyson 1966; Canal 1978b; Steve and Gasche 1990; Potts 1999: 45–52; Steve et al. 2002: 403–9).

The settlement of Susa II was characterized by changes in the orientation of buildings, brick sizes, and ceramics. The Susa I style pottery was given up in favor of forms with obvious parallels at Uruk in southern Mesopotamia. A major regional, socioeconomic transformation is thought to have taken place. This is indicated by the appearance of an accounting system that evolved from counters (*calculi*) to counters contained in clay balls (*bullae*) and finally to written texts (tablets). Attested in Acropole I Levels 18–17, the earliest cylinder seals at Susa display scenes of daily life such as grain storage in tall granaries topped by cupolas. This period also witnessed an increase in the sheer number and size of sites on the Susiana plain. Susa grew eastwards as the mounded settlement areas called *Ville Royale* ("royal town") and *Donjon* ("dungeon") by the site's French excavators doubled the size of Susa, making it c.25 hectares or more. The Acropole contained residential houses and large numbers of conically shaped, decorative wall nails (as opposed to the cylindrical shapes attested in Susa I, but otherwise similar). The significance of these changes has been interpreted variously (Potts

1999: 52–71; Steve et al. 2002: 409–13). It is generally believed there was a cultural break associated with the arrival of populations from the Mesopotamian plain to the west. Differences of opinion exist, however, with respect to the degree of political influence exercised by the newcomers. The view that Susiana was part of a broader regional process of colonization emanating from Uruk has not gained support, and a more nuanced approach that sees progressive adaptation to Mesopotamian, urban-centered economic models and the reorganization of older exchange networks has more adherents (Wright and Johnson 1975; Potts 1999: 58; Steve et al. 2002: 414).

The nature of settlement during the Susa III (or "Proto-Elamite") period (c.3100–2700 BC) is fraught with many preconceptions and much ambiguity. The final occupation (Level 17) of the Acropole high terrace at the end of Susa II included large ash deposits suggesting destruction by fire; yet the northern part of the terrace contains residential remains in the vicinity of a large city wall, indicating that this part of the city was not affected by fire. A most significant development was the appearance at this time (Acropole I, Level 16; Ville Royale I, Levels 18 B–A) of the first so-called "Proto-Elamite" or "Susa III" tablets, a writing system originally interpreted by V. Scheil (1905: 59) as an archaic form of the later Elamite language (Dahl 2002). This view has generated abundant discussion regarding possible links to the earlier (Susa II) numerical systems, the old Elamite language (c.2300 BC), and the later, so-called "linear" Elamite texts from the reign of Puzur-Inshushinak (c.2100 BC). The fact that Susa III/Proto-Elamite tablets have been found at sites distributed across the Iranian Plateau (Tal-e Ghazir, Tal-e Malyan, Tepe Yahya, Shahr-i Sokhta, Tepe Özbaki, Tepe Sofalin) adds an intriguing aspect to the puzzle. Their spatial distribution has given rise to the notion that a supra-regional economic enterprise (a "Proto-Elamite civilization") centered in Susiana may have existed (Alden 1982; Sumner, 1997: 406; Potts 1999: 71–83; Steve et al. 2002: 414–17; for radiocarbon dates, see Wright and Rupley 2001: 96–7). Despite differences of interpretation, we appear to have a writing system and a technical apparatus of bookkeeping procedures that developed independently from Mesopotamia and were used across a network of Iranian towns. This technological revolution was paralleled by a change in glyptic and ceramics. At the same time, and at the height of the Susa III period, the pace of settlement accelerated in the highlands of Fars. The town of Anshan (Tal-e Malyan) on the Marv Dasht plain, a future eastern Elamite capital, grew to five times the size of Susa in what is known there as the Banesh period (3400–2800 BC). The site covered c.50 hectares within a massive, 5 kilometer long city wall built on a foundation of large stone boulders (Ch. I.31). The interior walls of the large (15 × 25 meter) ABC building there were decorated with polychrome, geometric patterns recalling both eastern and local pottery traditions and perhaps exhibiting associations with textiles (Nickerson 1977; Álvarez-Mon 2005b: 152 n8–10). Malyan appears to have been an impressive political and economic center whose regional, if not interregional, influence is likely to have been significant. This period of settlement expansion has been interpreted as the result of an arrival of migrant populations from the lowlands.

The Early Dynastic period at Susa (Susa IV or Susa D, c.2700–2375) is represented to the north of the high terrace on the Acropole mound by architectural complexes including large jars and grain storage facilities. The Acropole continued to be the religious heart of the city, as attested by the probable existence of a temple ornamented with votive limestone wall plaques exhibiting relief decoration (Pelzel 1977). The ceramics of this period included cream-colored vessels painted with red-orange-black motifs and distinctive iconography such as a chariot pulled by an ox, running horses, and fish. These wares are known as "second" or "Susa II" style and are distributed throughout a broad swathe of the central Zagros as far north as an imaginary line running from Kermanshah to Hamadan (Potts 1999: 85–159; Steve et al. 2002: 418–39). The inhabited extent of the city at this time is difficult to estimate. However, the existence of hundreds of tombs and related material, excavated (albeit poorly and with little attempt at documentation) in the Ville Royale (I) and Donjon by R. de Mecquenem suggests a large urban center whose inhabitants continued to support high levels of metallurgical production represented by weaponry with parallels in Luristan and chariot wheels made of wood with nailed copper tires (Mecquenem 1943: 123, Fig. 89; Amiet 1966: 143, Fig. 103).

At around 2675 BC the first unequivocal reference to Elam appears in the so-called Sumerian King List. The text states that after "kingship was lowered from heaven" (Col. i.1) "the king of Kish (En)Mebaragesi carried away the spoil of the weapons of the land of Elam [Col.ii. 35–37] and [Sumerian] kingship went from Kish to Uruk, from Uruk to Ur, from Ur to Awan, and from Awan back to Kish [Col. ii. 45–iv. 19]" (Jacobsen 1939: 83–97). The inclusion of Elam and Awan here is intriguing. At this stage in history, the extent to which Sumerian scribes distinguished between Awan (the city) and Elam (the highland territory) is uncertain. The fact that they are generally mentioned separately, that two of the earliest kings of Awan bore Elamite names, and that later Elamite kings traced their political (and cultural) identity to Awanite rulers suggests that Awan and Elam may have possibly been coterminous or, more likely, that Awan was a part of the Elamite territory. At the same time, the fact that Awan was mentioned amongst the cities of the Sumerian heartland suggests that it must have been relatively close by, even if its precise location remains unknown. Based on parallels between burial goods from Susa IV, the Pusht-e Kuh region (Luristan), and the Deh Luran plain, Potts (1999: 92) suggested that Awan may have been centered on the Kangavar valley (possibly with the chief settlement at Godin Tepe). Regardless of where Awan was located, the Sumerian King List marks the beginning of a documented pattern of antagonism, trade exchanges, and alliances between Mesopotamia and Zagros-bound polities associated with Elam that lasted for millennia.

Except for the brief interval marked by the reign of the last king of Awan, Puzur-Inshushinak (c.2100), it appears that Susiana was for all practical purposes just one more component of the Mesopotamian socioeconomic and political network. From the Akkadian period (c.2334–2154) to the collapse of the Ur III Dynasty in 2004 BC, a sequence of Mesopotamian kings ruled over Susa, sending their armies on incursions into the highlands and pursuing alliances through interdynastic marriages and, one must assume, treaties of peace and exchange. Eventually, this pattern of asymmetric exchange and hostility seems to have fostered the emergence of highland alliances, eventually culminating in the creation of a multicentric Elamite state.

A most significant document from this period is a fragmentary Elamite text, found at Susa, that records a treaty between Naram-Sin of Akkad (2254–2218 BC) and an Elamite ruler whose name is uncertain (Scheil 1911: 1–11; König 1965: 29–34; Hinz 1967). The content is highly relevant for the history of Elamite language and for the construction of an Elamite religious identity, as it begins with an invocation to more than 30 deities, 26 of whom are of Elamite origin. The "treaty" part of the document states: "the enemy of Naram-Sin is my enemy; the friend of Naram-Sin is my friend." These words suggest an alliance between Akkad and Awan/Elam against a mutual enemy, perhaps the highland Guti, and provides a warning against placing too much emphasis on the often antagonistic rhetoric of Mesopotamian royal inscriptions. Throughout this period, Susa remained under the umbrella of Mesopotamian influence; albeit with evidence of continuing relations with the highlands, the Iranian plateau, and the Persian Gulf. The physical manifestations of this are attested on the Acropole (Levels 1 and 2) in the form of a building interpreted as a granary and in a small area of domestic remains in the Ville Royale I. For the most part, ceramics, metalwork, and glyptic styles follow Mesopotamian norms. Native traditions are most prevalent in clay figurines.

Puzur-Inshushinak (c.2100 BC), the last ruler of Awan, incorporated Susa and Anshan into the Awanite kingdom, conquered more than 70 Iranian towns, and raided northern Babylonian settlements seeking control of the great Khorasan road (the route from southern Babylonia to the Iranian Plateau and on toward Central Asia) and the highland kingdom of Shimashki (Potts 2008b). In addition to these expansionistic activities, his reign was marked by the creation of a unique script known as Linear Elamite (or Proto-Elamite B) that survives in only 19 inscriptions. Of the 103 signs recorded, more than 40 are only attested once. The restricted number of signs and inscriptions has thus far thwarted the decipherment of Linear Elamite. The identity of Puzur-Inshushinak, the political character of Awan, and the characteristics of the "national" language of the kingdom remain matters of scholarly debate. At Susa, the evidence of a decorative votive nail with a text stating "Puzur-Inshushinak **ensí** of Susa *šakkanaku* of Elam, son of Shimbishhuk-Inshushinak, the temple of Shugu he has restored," together with a large statue of the enthroned goddess Narundi, flanked by two lionesses (and bearing a bilingual inscription), and the remains of an alabaster statuette possibly representing Puzur-Inshushinak himself (found in what has been identified as the temple of the goddess Ninhursag), suggest that Puzur-Inshushinak successfully subscribed to a tradition that adopted (and co-opted) the cultural accoutrements of this ancient and vast urban center (Mecquenem 1911: 71; Amiet 1966: 227, Fig. 166; Steve and Gasche 1971: 61 n71 and 73, Pl. 8.4–7).

With Puzur-Inshushinak gone, the Susiana lowlands were reintegrated into the Mesopotamian political orbit under the Ur III Dynasty. Textual information for this period is abundant, but heavily filtered through a Mesopotamian-Susian lens. The Sumerian kings left ample evidence of their religious zeal and administrative practices at Susa through monumental royal constructions and inscriptions (Malbran-Labat 1995). Foundation nails inscribed by Shulgi (2094–2047 BC) suggest he erected temples on the Acropolis to Inshushinak and Ninhursag (apparently above the remains of earlier constructions situated next to the earlier high terrace; Amiet 1966: 238). Another temple probably founded at this time was erected on the southwestern flank of the Ville Royale and included at least three pairs of large, painted terracotta lions guarding the main entrance (Amiet 1966: 292–3). Shulgi's political position was solidified through a series of diplomatic marriages between his daughters and the kings of Anshan, Marhashi, and Bashime. As in earlier times, Sumerian appointees used the titles "governor of Susa" and "viceroy of the land of Elam." During the reign of Shulgi's son, Amar-Suena (2046–2038 BC), the southern Mesopotamian city of Girsu (modern Telloh) became the chief urban entrepôt for trade with the eastern territories, and the governor of Girsu assumed the title *sukkal mah*, or "Grand Regent." The last Ur III rulers, Shu-Suen (2037–2029 BC) and Ibbi-Suen (2028–2004 BC), continued the policy of combining dynastic marriages with military incursions into the highlands. Yet, in 2004 BC a coalition of Elamites and *Su*-people (LÚ.SU^{ki}) from the land of Shimashki captured Ur. King Ibbi-Suen, together with the statues of Nanna and other Sumerian divinities, were taken prisoner to Anshan. In the *Lamentation over the destruction of Sumer and Ur* we read that Ibbi-Suen was taken to the land of Elam in fetters (where he died) and Ur was reduced to "mounds of ruin and ashes" (van Dijk 1978). The Elamite king responsible for the fall of Ur may have been the ruler of Shimashki, Kindattu. Like Awan, it remains unclear where Shimashki was located.

With the unification of Susiana and the highlands by Shimashki, the dual political and territorial structure of the Elamite kingdom was inaugurated. With Susiana secured, the pattern of antagonism appears to have shifted from the Elamite highlands to lower Mesopotamia proper. Politically, the 20th century BC witnessed periods of warfare alternating with diplomatic marriages and peace treaties. Ishbi-Erra of Isin (2017–1985 BC) named his 12th regnal year after a victory over Elam, but in the same year he gave his daughter Libur-nirum to the son of the Elamite *sukkal* Humban-shimti; the following year was again named after the defeat of Elam and the Su-people, and his 23rd year was named after the expulsion of the Elamites from Ur, suggesting an Elamite military presence in the region for some years prior. His descendant, Shu-ilishu of Isin (1984–1975 BC), commemorated the return of the cult statue of Nanna that had been taken by the Elamites from Ur to Anshan. A similar pattern of close Elamite engagement in Mesopotamian affairs emerges from other documented sources. Around 1980 BC the ruler of Eshnunna (modern Tell Asmar, eastern Iraq), Bilalama, gave his daughter Mekubi to Tan-Ruhuratir, the governor of Susa, in marriage. Mekubi marked her presence at Susa by building a temple to Inanna in the religious quarter of the Acropole (Steve et al. 2002: 439). In his first regnal year, Iddin-Dagan of Isin (1974–1954 BC) gave his daughter Matum-niattum in marriage to Imazu, king of Anshan, son of Kindattu. And king Gungunum of Larsa (1932–1906 BC) named his 3rd and 5th regnal years after wars against eastern Elamite territories: first Bashime and then Anshan.

3 The Old Elamite Period: The *Sukkalmahs* (c.1900–1500 BC)

Shilhaha was the first ruler to be called *sukkalmah*, "Grand Regent," and thus is considered the founder of a new dynasty. As the "chosen son of Ebarat," he claimed to be descended from the ninth king of the Shimashki Dynasty and "king of Anshan and Susa." It is unclear, however, what the relationship was between the last rulers of Shimashki (c.1900 BC) and the first *sukkalmahs*. There is no indication of a sharp break between the two, possibly reflecting temporal overlap and dynastic links (Potts 1999: 160–87; Steve et. al. 2002: 440–52).

From the Mesopotamian viewpoint, the early centuries of the 2nd millennium BC were a period dominated by the cities (and dynasties) of Isin and Larsa followed by the empires of Shamshi-Addu of Assyria (1813–1781 BC) and Hammurabi of Babylon (1792–1750 BC). Gradually, textual documentation has led to a modification of this Mesopotamocentric view of international geopolitics. In Elam the early 2nd millennium BC was marked by a political (and territorial?) reorganization under the *sukkalmahs* followed by an expansionistic period that took Elamite political and economic interests beyond their "natural" territorial boundaries – i.e., the area bounded by Mesopotamia in the west, the Persian Gulf in the south, Fars in the east and Kermanshah in the central Zagros mountains to the north. This area, termed "Elam Major" by D.T. Potts (1999), constituted a kingdom whose prestige and influence were unprecedented.

In tandem with Assyria, Babylonia, and Mari, Elam rose to be one of the main political and military powerbrokers of the second millennium BC. The Elamite kingdom of the early 2nd millennium BC was characterized by distinctive systems of government, succession, and titulature. The organization of power followed a tripartite structure along the lines of a "triumvirate" composed of a chief ruler or *sukkalmah*; a senior co-regent, the *sukkal* of Elam (often a brother of the *sukkalmah*); and a junior co-regent, the *sukkal* of Susa (often a son or nephew of the *sukkalmah*). This system may have insulated Elam against disastrous dynastic struggles. Another much discussed singularity of Elamite kingship consists of the use of the royal title "sister's son" (*ruhušak*), originally perhaps indicating royal incest between a king and his sister. Whatever its interpretation, it seems clear that in many cases it assumed a purely symbolic status with the function of providing legitimacy to the royal lineage. This expression, together with terms of family affiliation supported by iconographic evidence, also underscores the singular role played by women in Elamite history.

By the late 19th century BC, the prestige and authority of the "Great King of Elam" (*šarrum rabûm ša Elamtim*) increased to the point where Elam was orchestrating political changes in Mesopotamia. During the reign of Shamshi-Addu the *sukkalmah* Shiruk-tuh and a 12,000-strong force of Elamite soldiers campaigned on the upper course of the Lower Zab in eastern Mesopotamia. The death of Shamshi-Addu brought an end to the early period of Assyrian imperial aspirations and opened the northwestern territories to Elam's expansionist interests. Babylon and Mari joined in an alliance with the *sukkalmah* to conquer Eshnunna, recognizing the leading authority of the Elamite king, probably Siwe-palar-huppak. Letters from the Mari royal archives explicitly document the threats by the Elamite king against Hammurabi of Babylon, telling him to leave the towns of Eshnunna or risk an invasion, and counseling him to break off all correspondence with Zimri-Lim of Mari. A similar tone was used with Zimri-Lim of Mari, Atamrum of Allahad, and Ishme-Dagan of Isin. Elamite influence extended all the way to the Mediterranean, where the prince of Qatna in Syria proposed to submit to the Elamite king if the latter would take up the fight on his behalf against the kingdom of Aleppo. A telling expression of the submissive status of the Amorite kings appears in the correspondence between the Syrian and Babylonian rulers in which they addressed each other as "brother" but considered themselves "sons" of the *sukkalmah* (Durand 1990; Charpin and Durand 1991: 62; Wu 1994: 169; Sasson 1995b: 904; Villard 1995: 881).

The particular treatment of the Elamite king can be explained by the historical status of Elam, the vast resources of the Iranian plateau, and Elamite influence in the commercial network of Anatolia and northern Mesopotamia (perhaps seeking ultimate control over the lucrative interstate commerce in tin which involved commercial links with Central Asia and Afghanistan). Elamite western expansion resulted in the creation of a Mari–Babylon–Aleppo alliance and perhaps in the emergence of a "national" Amorite conscience that shared a common interest against the *sukkalmah*. In three consecutive campaigns, from 1764/3 to 1762/1 BC, Hammurabi confronted the Elamites and attacked their western proxy cities and allies: Eshnunna, Larsa, Subartu, and Gutium (Marhashi and Malgium apparently being out of reach). To complete the victory, Hammurabi put an end to the kingdom of his former Amorite associate Zimri-lim of Mari

(1776–1761 BC). The Mari texts provide an historical snapshot of the influence of the Elamite emperor in the western and northern regions. Together with contemporary inscriptions from Anshan, these documents demonstrate that Elam was one of the largest polities of the early 2nd millennium BC and attest to an ongoing pattern of Elamite involvement in Mesopotamian and, in this case, Assyrian affairs.

The general wealth and politically expansionistic outlook of the *sukkalmah* period is reflected in the material culture of the times by a wealth of archaeological and monumental remains from its western capital (Susa), the Zagros mountains (Kurangun), and the eastern capital of Anshan (Tal-e Malyan), which at this time (Kaftari period, 2200–1600 BC) reached its maximum extent of no less than 130 hectares. On the other side of the kingdom, Susa expanded towards the east with a succession of new constructions in the Ville Royale (chantier A, Levels XV to XII), reaching c.85 hectares in extent. These neighborhoods provide important evidence of Elamite vernacular architecture (Badawy 1958, 1966; Fathy 1986; Kubba 1987; Manzoor 1989). Houses were constructed following the "agglutinative" principle – i.e., different buildings shared common walls along narrow streets to reduce the total surface area exposed to the sun. Characteristic of these houses were large courtyards and associated "reception" halls. Only the courtyards were paved with baked bricks (perhaps for rain collection). The unpaved streets were used as a dumping ground for all sorts of discarded objects, such as broken pottery, animal bones, ashes, and clay figurines. Level XIV of the Ville Royale combined modest houses with large villas belonging to the Susian elite. The well-excavated house of Temti-Wartash, the great chamberlain of the Elamite palace at Susa, was a palace-like, monumental residence with no fewer than six courtyards and 50 ground-floor rooms divided into private and public reception areas. The thickness of the walls around the central courtyard and "reception hall" suggest the existence of a second floor or, possibly, a high, vaulted ceiling. Levels XIII and XII of the Ville Royale contained similar monumental architecture, a substantial city-wall to the north, a building interpreted on the basis of the cuneiform texts found in it as a school, and, in Ville-Royale XII, a building that may have been a tavern or perhaps a brothel with a network of large underground jars, presumed to have been for beer. Building also continued in the religious area of the Acropole. A ramp was added or restored leading to the *Ekikuanna*, a temple of Inshushinak, and to the temple of the goddess Ishmekarab, the escort of the dead to the netherworld.

The material unearthed at Susa is a heterogeneous sample reflecting both Mesopotamian and Elamite traditions combined with materials originating from the borders of the Persian Gulf all the way to Bactria in Central Asia (modern northern Afghanistan and southern Uzbekistan). There is one area of artistic production that can be considered emblematic of a distinctive Elamite highland personality, namely the sculptural art represented in the rock-cut sanctuary of Kurangun and at Naqsh-e Rustam (Miroschedji 1981: 25d; Seidl 1986; Vanden

Berghe 1986). Kurangun is situated in western Fars near the ancient highway linking the Elamite capitals of Susa and Anshan. Here a relief was carved on an outcrop of the Kuh-e Pataweh mountain c.80 meters above the Fahliyan river, which flows through the scenic Mamasani region. Its creation involved cutting deeply into the vertical side of the rock face in order to make a three-dimensional, spatial unit composed of three flights of stairs coming down from the summit of the hill onto a rectangular platform. The platform was carved to represent a basin with three small depressions and the remains of 26 fish. Sculpted on the vertical surface of the rock, above the platform, is a low-relief panel exhibiting a pious religious scene with an enthroned male divinity and his female consort. The god is seated on a throne made of a coiled serpent. In his right hand he holds a ring and rod from which two streams of flowing water emerge, arching forward toward two groups of worshipers framing the divine couple. This scene is an example of an iconic Elamite artistic formula found also on Old and Middle Elamite seals and stelae. The identification of the divine couple has been the subject of scholarly discussion, with the most recent interpretations suggesting a fusion of the main gods of the lowland (Inshushinak) and the highland (Napirisha) Elamite pantheons. Both divinities appear to combine attributes in a synthesis encompassing the primeval, life-giving aspects of flowing water (Potts 2004b).

Additional aspects of Elamite religious beliefs can be teased out of a number of Elamite texts dating to the late Old Elamite period (Ville-Royale, Level XII, c.1500 BC). These documents have no parallels in Mesopotamian literature. They identify Inshushinak as the lord of the underworld and judge in charge of ordaining the destiny of the dead, and illustrate the Elamite belief in the importance of the judgment of the deceased (Bottéro 1982: 394).

4 The Middle Elamite Period: The Golden Age (c.1500–1100)

The interval between the last *sukkalmah* and the kings of Susa and Anshan is not well documented. There is no textual or archaeological indication of a sudden rupture but later royal inscriptions employ a rhetoric of continuity suggesting dynastic links between the two periods. Whatever the true state of affairs, the geopolitical situation of the 15th century BC in Mesopotamia was severely affected by the gradual penetration and ascent to power of the Kassites (probably with links to a homeland in the central Zagros Mountains). The Middle Elamite period has been traditionally divided according to three ruling dynasties or houses: the Kidinuid house (c.1500–1400 BC), the Igihalkid house (c.1400–1200), and the Shutrukid house (c.1200–1100). This division is far from perfect, as the Igihalkids may have been related to the Shutrukids (Potts 1999: 188–258; Steve et al. 2002: 452–70).

An important synchronism has been established between Tepti-ahar and the father of the Kassite king Kurigalzu I, Kadashman-Harbe I (after a new reading for Kadashman ᵈKUR.GAL), who ruled in the late 15th century BC (Potts 1999: 192–3; Cole and De Meyer 1999). Neither genealogical nor political kinship can be demonstrated between Tepti-ahar and the houses of Kidinu or Igihalki. Yet, Tepti-Ahar used the title "king of Susa and Anshan, servant of Kirwashir and Inshushinak," which suggests a conscious reference to the royal ancestry and legacy of Kidinu (who also used the title "king of Susa and Anshan") and to the legitimacy provided by a tradition going back to Ebarat, the last king of Shimashki. Tepti-ahar is associated with the ancient city of Kabnak (modern Haft Tepe), located in the most fertile part of the Khuzestan plain, about 10 kilometers southeast of Susa.

Haft Tepe covers an area of c.1.5 square kilometers and includes 14 major mounds, the largest of which rises about 17 meters above the plain. Only a small percentage of the site has been excavated, revealing massive architectural compounds combining two high terraces (Complexes I and II) and a funerary-temple complex. Most constructions are made of mudbrick, with baked brick used for important buildings and open areas. Gypsum was used to cover baked brick pavements and for plastering the walls and inner surfaces of roofs. Bitumen was used to line basins and water channels. Flat roofs were supported by large palm tree beams covered with reed matting. The halls and ceilings were coated with gypsum plaster painted with polychrome motifs. Terrace Complex I included a scribal school and workshops dedicated to specialized craft and artistic production. A small hall contained the skeletal remains of an elephant and exquisite, life-size, painted terracotta heads possibly representing members of the Elamite elite. Most of the small objects and craft debris recovered suggest relationships with both local and foreign lands from the Persian Gulf in the East to the kingdom of Mitanni in the west. On the other hand, most of the cylinder sealings collected display a thread of local conservatism (Álvarez-Mon 2005a, 2005b).

The funerary temple compound included a royal tomb tentatively ascribed to Tepti-Ahar. The walls of the tomb stood 3.75 meters high and the chamber itself was 3.25 × 10 meters with a massive barrel vault of baked brick. This is one of the largest and oldest standing examples of this type of monumental funerary architecture in the Near East. Parallel to and just to the west of the burial was another vaulted chamber of smaller dimensions containing a mass burial of 23 individuals. Fourteen skeletons had been carefully arranged side by side with their heads oriented to the west, with nine additional skeletons piled over them. Who these individuals were and how they died is not known (Negahban 1991).

The Kassite king Kurigalzu I may have been responsible for the destruction of Kabnak and for placing a new ruling family on the Elamite throne. The family claimed descent from Igihalki and seems to have been based at Deh-e Now (Khuzestan Survey site 120), a high, c.9.5 hectare mound about 20 kilometers east of Haft Tepe and 7.5 kilometers north of Chogha Zanbil (see below). The males of the Igihalkid house engaged in a succession of interdynastic marriages over five generations with a number of Kassite princesses from Mesopotamia. Thus the eldest son of Igihalki, Pahir-ishshan (c.1380–1370 BC), married the eldest daughter of Kurigalzu I; their grandson Humban-numena married a Kassite princess; Humban-numena's son Untash-Napirisha (c.1340–1300 BC) married a daughter of the Kassite king Burnaburiash II; Untash-Napirisha's son Kiddin-Hutran (II) married another Kassite princess; and the founder of the Shutrukid house, Shutruk-Nahhunte (c.1190–1155 BC), married a daughter of the Kassite king Meli-Shipak. The enduring association between Elamite and Kassite royal elites illustrates an endeavor to foster international, blood-related associations amongst the elites of the Near East. This also had the unintended result of establishing an Elamite claim to the Babylonian throne, which eventually led to the downfall of the Kassite Dynasty and the sack of Babylon c.1150 BC (Pintore 1978: 24; Van Dijk 1986; Vallat 1994a, 1999a, 2006a; Goldberg 2004).

Perhaps the most important Elamite king of the Igihalkid house was Untash-Napirisha (c.1340–1300 BC), himself of Kassite heritage by ancestry and maternal lineage and, curiously enough, related by marriage to both the Egyptian pharaoh Amenhotep IV/Akhenaten and the Hittite king Shuppiluliuma. His reign witnessed an artistic golden age and, as some authors have stressed, a religious "revolution" linked to the foundation of a vast religious complex called Al Untash-Napirisha (modern Chogha Zanbil). This complex was built on a high plateau overlooking, to the northeast, the plain drained by the Ab-e Diz River and the (presumed) ancestral city of Deh-e Now. The complex includes three surrounding perimeter walls and was organized around a stepped temple platform, or *ziggurat*, c.53 meters high dedicated to Napirisha and Inshushinak. The *ziggurat* consisted of four levels and, unlike Mesopotamian examples, was scaled internally (and indirectly) via two staircases which were flanked at ground level by pairs of large, glazed bulls and bird-headed griffins. The façade of the high shrine (Elamite *kukunnum*) atop the *ziggurat* was made of brightly glazed, baked bricks decorated with geometric patterns and glazed knob-plaques and nails of different colors. More than 25 temples were built at Chogha Zanbil for the worship of both highland and lowland Elamite deities with a smattering of originally Mesopotamian deities, including Nusku, the god of fire and light (Ghirshman 1968a: 84–7).

The so-called Royal Quarter in the northeastern part of the site had large building complexes arranged along open courtyards and five underground, monumental, vaulted tombs. Tomb II included the remains of eight cremated bodies; Tomb IV had two cremated bodies and a mature female skeleton. It has been suggested that these remains may have belonged to Elamite royalty, including perhaps a queen of Kassite origin. A significant and still poorly understood aspect of the planning of Chogha Zanbil pertains to the function of a sophisticated network of drainpipes, wells, and a massive basin, all part of an intricate hydraulic installation situated at the edge of the city (Auberson 1966: 113–8; Margueron 1991; Corfù 2006; Mofidi Nasrabadi 2007).

Associated with Untash-Napirisha is a corpus of metallurgical and sculptural masterpieces revealing unprecedented levels of skill. Perhaps the most significant piece is the 1.29 meter tall headless statue of queen Napir-Asu, found in the temple of the Ninhursag at Susa. The statue weights 1750 kilograms and was cast in two parts, initially using a clay core that allowed the making of a single shell of copper by the lost-wax technique. Once the core was removed, the shell was filled with solid bronze. The head, which was never found, may have been cast separately. The molded and engraved surface of Napir-Asu's garment was probably once covered with gold and silver leaf (Meyers 2000).

It is uncertain if the Igihalkid Dynasty ended with the arrival of Shutruk-Nahhunte c.1150 BC. The cultural accomplishments of the Shutrukid Dynasty are often overshadowed by their infamous deeds in Mesopotamia. Shutruk-Nahhunte and his sons Kudur-Nahhunte (1155–1150 BC) and Shilhak-Inshushinak (1150–1120 BC) continued a foreign policy of vindication that asserted the claim of the Elamite kings over the Babylonian throne. This claim entailed numerous raids on Mesopotamian cities and eventually led to the collapse of the Kassite Dynasty in 1155 BC, the death of the last Kassite king, the "retirement" to Elam of the statues of Marduk and other deities from Babylon, and the removal to Susa of large amounts of booty. Amongst the most celebrated artifacts dedicated as votive offerings to Inshushinak on the sacred Acropole at Susa were the stele containing Hammurabi's law code from Sippar (Ch. II.37) and the victory stele of Naram-Sin (Ch. II.34). The resources accumulated during this period of Elamite imperial expansion produced a golden age of unprecedented building activity throughout Elamite territory. From Anshan to the shores of the Persian Gulf and the Susiana plain, new temples were constructed and old ones restored. Examples of monumental decorative architecture include the remains of glazed mudbrick panels depicting a royal couple from the façade of a building on the Acropole; and the remains of a molded mudbrick façade showing bull-men grasping date palms and female deities holding their breasts, from a temple located in the Apadana area. This may have represented the "sacred grove" in which the "exterior chapel" of the temple of Inshushinak built by Shilhak-Inshushinak was located.

Around 1120 BC, the Babylonian king Nebuchadnezzar I (1125–1104 BC) entered Elamite territory. He defeated Hutelutush-Inshushinak by the banks of the Ulai (Karkheh) river and the Elamite king retreated to the highlands and the eastern capital of Anshan. Effectively, this marked the end of the Shutrukid Dynasty.

The excavated remains of Anshan (Tal-e Malyan) during the Qaleh-Middle Elamite period (1600–1000 BC) hardly reflect the monumentality expected of a major Middle Elamite urban center. The only exception is a large building (EDD) with a 10×14 meter courtyard. Inside the building were tablets, sealings, and pottery kilns suggesting administrative and storage functions. The building was decorated with glazed ceramic wall knobs, glazed tiles, and painted walls suggestive of a ceremonial role. More importantly, a new pottery tradition characterized by hand-made and wheel-made orange wares appeared at this time, best represented at the nearby sites of Tal-e Shoga, Tal-e Teimuran, and Darvazeh Tepe. Some scholars have suggested that these wares could be an indication of newly arrived Indo-European (speaking) migrant populations, the first "Iranians."

5   The Neo-Elamite Period: Elam and Persia (c.1100–550 BC)

Neo-Elamite chronology is divided into two or three phases, depending on whether one follows textual or archaeological evidence. In both cases, though, the earliest part of the period (c.1000–743 BC) is considered a "dark age" in Elamite history, represented by a gap in textual and archaeological records. This gap has been interpreted as a reflection of the breakdown of the Middle Elamite state, the collapse of urban centers, territorial fragmentation, increasing pastoralism (in line with the presumed arrival of Indo-European groups), and a general contraction of formerly urban populations into the rural highlands (Potts 1999: 259–307; Steve et al. 2002: 470–87). Whatever the virtues of this model, the Elamite Zagros highlands provide evidence of a new sociopolitical authority around the turn of the 9th century BC. This is evident in the region of Izeh/Malamir, which is nestled in a mountain valley about 100 kilometers to the east of Susa. Carved on the sides of cliffs and boulders are a total of 12 Elamite bas-reliefs without parallel in the artistic record of the ancient Near East. Most scholars date the reliefs from Shekaft-e Salman to between 1200–1100 BC, but of the six reliefs carved at Kul-e Farah only one (Kul-e Farah I) has been dated with certainty to the late Neo-Elamite period (Vanden Berghe 1963, 1984). One of the most important carvings is Kul-e Farah IV, a large composition extending over an area c.18 × 6 meters. The relief exhibits a "frozen-in-time" communal banquet centering on a king seated on a throne and surrounded by at least 140 participants partaking of a ritual entailing the consumption of a morsel of food, probably meat. Most participants wear their hair in long braids that are similar, but not identical, to those represented at Kurangun and Kul-e Farah III. The aesthetic choices and organization manifested by these reliefs illustrate a hierarchical order planned along the lines of social status and the existence of a political structure in which communal participation was emphasized (Álvarez-Mon in press).

The archaeological division of the Neo-Elamite period championed by Pierre de Miroschedji favors a bipartite division with a transition from Neo-Elamite I to Neo-Elamite II around 725/700 BC. The tripartite chronological division proposed by philologists relies heavily on the Assyro-Babylonian documentation for an understanding of the Neo-Elamite II period (770/743–653/647 BC), with the year 653 BC represented by the installation by Assurbanipal (668–627 BC) of Humban-nikash II as king of Elam and Tammaritu I as king of Hidalu. The terminal date of 647 BC marks the sack and destruction of Susa by Assurbanipal. Our understanding of the last part of the Neo-Elamite period (Neo-Elamite III; sometimes divided into IIIa and IIIb) is reliant upon local Elamite texts, principally from Susa (Waters 2000). These display a language that had evolved from classic Elamite but was not yet the language of the subsequent Achaemenid period (Vallat 1996: 386). While most scholars agree that these texts post-date the collapse of the Assyrian Empire, there has been a noticeable trend in recent years to shift the date of the Susa tablets, related texts, and seals and sealings to the 6th century BC, perhaps as late as the 520s.

From a political and military standpoint, the 8th and 7th centuries BC were characterized by relentless clashes between the Assyrians and the Elamites. But the political and military history of Assyrian relations with Elam reflects more than patterns of political allegiance and the shifting loyalties of various pretenders to the Elamite throne; it reveals moments of close interaction between Elamite and Assyrian elites (Álvarez-Mon 2009a). Ten years after the campaign against Elam by Assurbanipal and his destruction of Susa in 647 BC, a rapid waning of the Assyrian Empire began, and by 609 BC it had ceased to exist. The standard, monolithic view of the late Neo-Elamite period emphasizes political and military events that led to the assumed destruction of Susa, the ensuing progressive abandonment of urban centers, political fragmentation, and the ultimate disappearance of Elam from the historical record (Miroschedji 2003). In striking contrast to these views, a new model has emerged favoring the notion that Elam played a fundamental role in the genesis of the Persian *ethnos*, the formation of a complex state in Fars and the emergence of the Achaemenid Persian empire (Álvarez-Mon and Garrison 2011a).

The archaeological picture of settlement at the end of the Neo-Elamite period is fragmentary and incomplete (Álvarez-Mon 2010). Much additional survey and archaeological work remains to be undertaken in both Khuzestan and Fars. As it stands, settlement is attested from the Luristan region along a corridor covering the Deh Luran, Susiana, and Ram Hormuz plains, ending in the Mamasani region. New evaluations of the Neo-Elamite archaeological record rely on evidence emerging from a reassessment of Susa's ceramic record, the fortuitous finds from burials in Ram Hormuz and Arjan, and the ongoing Iranian-Australian surveys and excavations in the Mamasani region at Tol-e Spid and Tol-e Nurabad (Potts and Roustaei 2006; Potts, Roustaei et al. 2006, 2009). The Susa-Ram Hormuz-Arjan corridor is characterized by fine polychrome faïence and ceramics as well as metal wares and luxury goods suggesting the existence of a cultural and, most likely, urban political *koine* during the second half of the 7th and the 6th centuries BC (Haerinck in press).

One of the most remarkable finds of recent times resulted from the accidental discovery in 1982 of a stone-walled burial at Arjan near the modern city of

Behbahan (close to the border between the provinces of Khuzestan and Fars). The funerary goods found in the Arjan tomb display considerable artistry and rare craft. A bronze bathtub-style coffin contained the skeletal remains of an adult male lying on his back. Next to the skeleton were 12 pieces of cotton textile with embroidered rosettes and dozens of gold rosettes and disks most likely sewn onto a garment worn by the deceased. These are the earliest and best preserved cotton garments found so far in the Near East. The deceased's right arm was bent in the direction of his chest, resting next to an extraordinary object of gold. This intriguing object has been described as an open "ring" with tubular shaft expanding into flaring disc-shaped finials decorated with identical repoussé and chased design: a palmette tree flanked by two rampant, antithetical, winged, lion-headed griffins. In addition, an iron dagger ornamented with precious stones and gold filigree was found. A lid engraved with registers of floral buds and lotus blossoms was placed over the coffin and secured by ropes to the handles on the sides. Outside the coffin were a number of precious items of a ceremonial and/or functional nature: a bronze bowl (43.5 centimeters in diameter, 8.5 centimeters deep) engraved with a sequence of concentric narratives scenes; a tall (75 centimeter high) bronze candelabrum, the upper part of which consisted of a spool-shaped platform held by six lions and a pedestal combining a triangular frame with three sets of three lions, bulls, and atlas figures; a bronze beaker with an upper register around the neck engraved with six identical running ostriches and a lower bulbous convex section worked in repoussé into the shape of four overlapping lion heads converging on a central rosette; a silver jar; a bronze lamp; and bronze chalices (Álvarez-Mon 2010).

Reflecting the artistic legacy of both Assyria and Elam, the Arjan material provides us with a new frame of reference with which to assess the arts and culture of the late 7th century BC. In it, earlier artistic canons were reformulated into new notions of technical and aesthetic perfection. In addition, the material bespeaks a period of strong Assyrian influence, if not political dominance, in western Elam after the destruction of Susa in 647 BC, resulting in a fertile artistic period combining Assyrian and Elamite traditions. This artistic production exhibits sophisticated intellectual notions of unity, stability and permanence: an orderly worldview which, far from being the manifestation of abrupt change or of a disintegrating culture in the midst of decline, suggests the revitalization of Elamite traditions and an historical nexus where the process of transference and continuity can actually be documented. In the last few years new views have emerged regarding the transition between Elam and Achaemenid Persia that rely on the analysis of autochthonous archaeological and textual evidence (Henkelman 2008a; Álvarez-Mon 2010). It is increasingly apparent that the ancient civilization of Elam provided key cultural accoutrements for the emergent Achaemenid Persian Empire. While we lack information on the exact processes of transmission, this Elamite political and cultural heritage provided the context out of which the House of Teispes and Cyrus I of Anshan (c.610–585 BC) emerged.

GUIDE TO FURTHER READING

For many years the pioneering studies of Cameron (1936), Hinz (1971, 1973), and Labat (1975a, 1975b) remained the standard comprehensive reference works dedicated to Elamite history. They were followed by specialized studies on Elamite art by Porada (1962) and Amiet (1966, and, to a lesser degree, 1986). In 1984, Carter and Stolper combined forces to present separate textual and archaeological accounts of Elamite history; after the Iranian Revolution in 1979, and the almost total freezing of foreign archaeological fieldwork on Iranian soil, there was a period of reassessment leading to Vallat's 1998 entry "Elam" in the *Encyclopaedia Iranica* and, principally, the in-depth, archaeologically based study of Elamite history by Potts (1999). This study is complemented by the extensive entry dedicated to Susa in the *Supplément au Dictionnaire de la Bible* (Steve et al. 2002). There has been a renewal of interest in the late Neo-Elamite period, with the transition between Elam and Persia being the subject of key studies. These concentrate on reviewing key textual evidence (Waters 2000), the religious landscape of the early Achaemenid Persians (Henkelman 2008a); the artistic landscape of later Elam (Álvarez-Mon 2010), and the general reassessment of the period in general (Álvarez-Mon and Garrison 2011a).

CHAPTER FORTY

India's Relations with Western Empires, 2300–600 BC

Gregory L. Possehl

1 Introduction

The ancient peoples of the Indian subcontinent have had interesting and important relationships with the peoples of the Iranian Plateau, Arabia, and the Near East. There seems to be a marked increase in the intensity of these contacts in the mid-3rd millennium BC. These contacts were both maritime and overland. Taken together, including contacts with Central Asia, these activities form what has been called the "Middle Asian Interaction Sphere" (MAIS) (Possehl 2002a, 2007).

2 The Indus Civilization

The story of ancient India's contacts with the Western empires begins with the Indus Civilization (2500–1900 BC). The Indus Civilization covered approximately 1,000,000 square kilometers and was the largest of the Bronze Age civilizations of Asia (Figure 40.1). There appears to have been a period of change that can be called the Early Harappan–Mature Harappan transition at c.2600–2500 BC when the distinctly urban features of the Indus Civilization seem to have been developed.

We know that the Early Harappans were familiar with the sea, since there are marine shells and the occasional marine fishbone found at Early Harappan sites.

A Companion to the Archaeology of the Ancient Near East, First Edition.
Edited by D.T. Potts.
© 2012 Blackwell Publishing Ltd. Published 2012 by Blackwell Publishing Ltd.

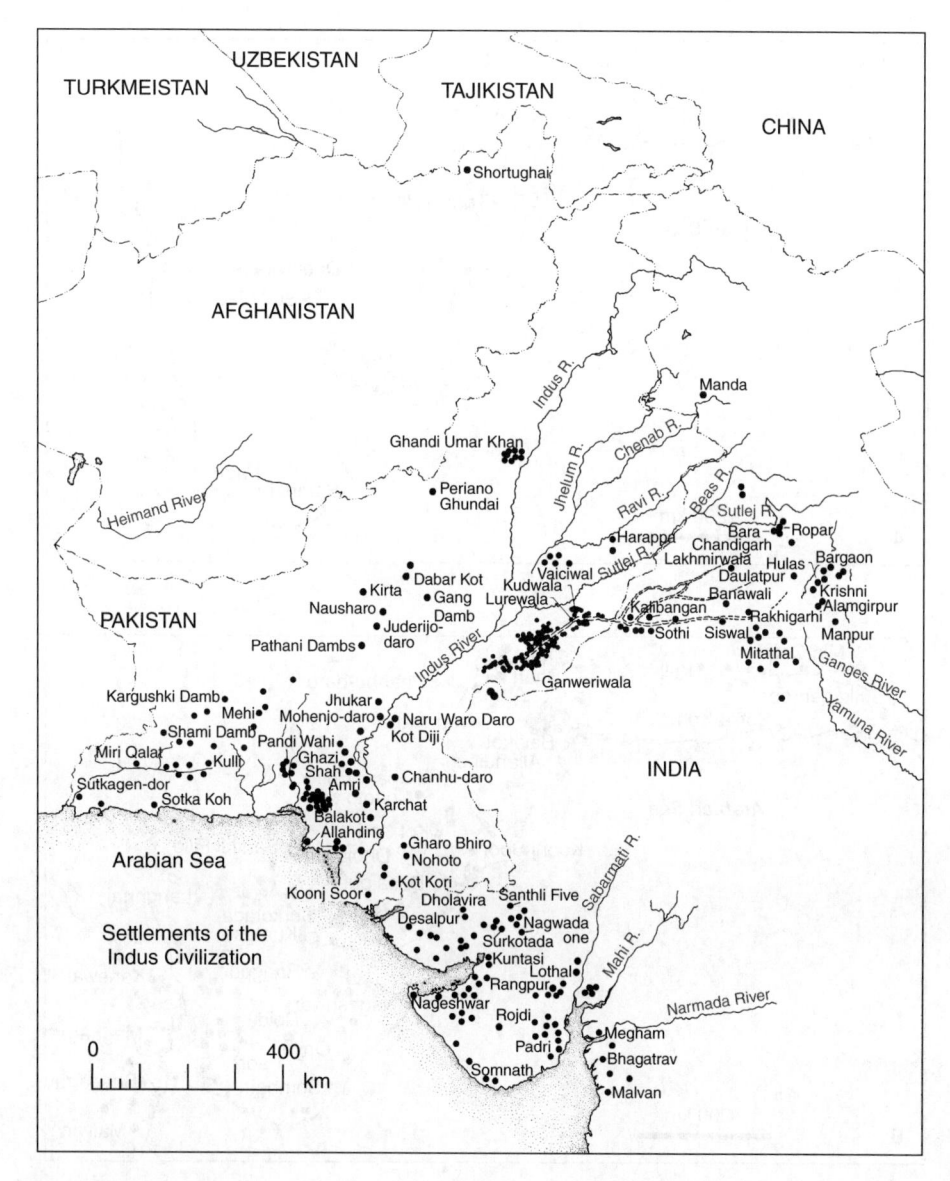

Figure 40.1 Map showing the distribution of the main settlements of the Indus or Harappan civilization.

However, the Early Harappan–Mature Harappan transition saw what has been called the "Indus move to the sea." During the Early Harappan Phase (Figure 40.2A) there were few coastal settlements, but in the Mature Harappan there were many (Figure 40.2B). The Mature Harappan phase is also marked by an increase in the use of sea products (fish, shellfish, and shells) and the beginnings of maritime activity on the Arabian Sea and Persian Gulf.

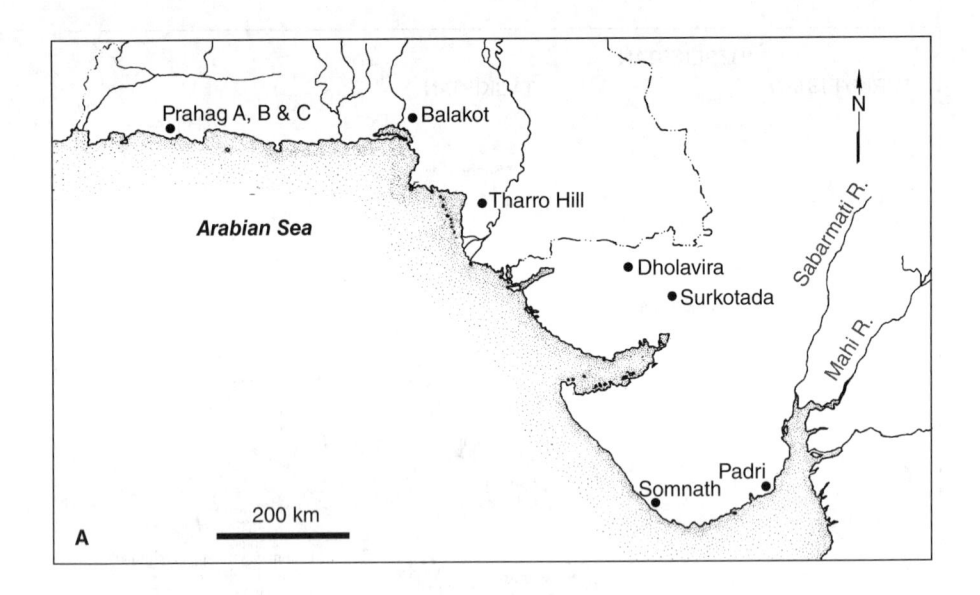

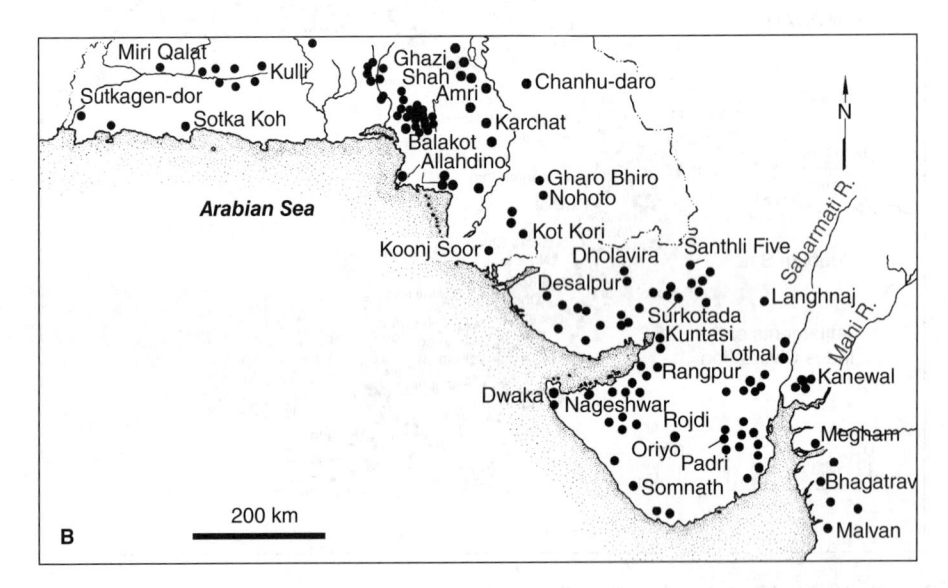

Figure 40.2 Coastal settlement during the Early Harappan (A) and Mature Harappan (B) phases.

Gujarat, especially Saurashtra, had many settlements on or near the sea during Mature Harappan times. There are Early Harappan sites in Kutch; they are found along seacoast and around the *ranns* (salt marshes). It is not known if the *ranns* were open to the sea during the second half of the third millennium, or whether they were much as they are today: shallow arms of the sea during the monsoon, and salt flats during the rest of the year.

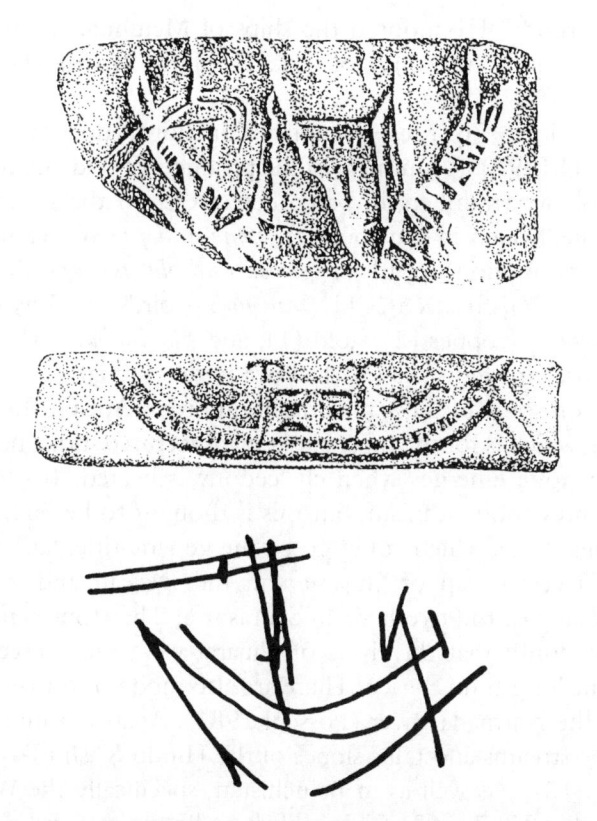

Figure 40.3 Representations of Harappan boats.

Archaeologists have discovered three representations of Indus boats (Figure 40.3). These appear to be fairly small with high prows and sterns. They all have rear steering oars. Two of them could easily have been made of reeds, however, while one (Figure 40.3 bottom) could have been made of wood. On one of them there is a suggestion of a square sail. There are also two or three terracotta models that might be of boats, one of which was found at Lothal at the head of the Gulf of Cambay (see below).

3 Maritime Contacts with Mesopotamia

There is further information about Indus maritime activity that can be gleaned from written records in Mesopotamia. During the reign of Sargon of Akkad (c.2334–2279 BC), the three great lands associated with boats are mentioned – namely Dilmun, Magan, and Meluhha. Dilmun is the island of Bahrain, Magan is principally Oman and the modern United Arab Emirates, and Meluhha is the Indus Civilization. That Indus ships reached Mesopotamia can be inferred from this boast by Sargon: "He moored the ships of Meluhha, the ships of Magan, the ships of Dilmun at the quay of Akkad" (trans. G. Marchesi, 2007, pers. comm.).

There are at least 76 Mesopotamian cuneiform documents mentioning Meluhha (Possehl 1996). A summary of the products of trade mentioned in these records is as follows (numbers in parentheses refer to the number of times a commodity is mentioned in the sources): *stone and pearls* – carnelian (8), lapis lazuli (1, in an incantation), pearls (1); *wood and plants* – **giš-ab-ba-me-luh-ha** (12), **mesu** wood (7), fresh dates (1); *animals* – birds (8, 5 as figurines), dog (1), cat (1); *metals* – copper (2), gold (1); and *"Meluhhan-style" objects* – ships (2), furniture (3), bird figurines (5, as above under animals).

A few words on some of these materials is in order. Ancient India was famous for its carnelian, which is for the most part a manufactured, not a natural, product. The red in the stone emerges when chalcedony is heated. It can be produced through forest fires and volcanism, but this is thought to be rare. Chalcedony is a highly siliceous stone, which could go by the generic title "agate." It is associated with the Deccan trap of Gujarat and the Deccan and is still found in abundance in many of the riverbeds of Saurashtra. The stone tends to be large, and there is no doubt that the rivers of Gujarat were the sources of the stone used to make the long Indus beads. There are also modern sources of large agates at Rajpipla on the Narmada River (Possehl 1981). Agates in much smaller sizes are found in the streams and talus slopes of the Hindu Kush (Tosi 1980; Jarrige and Tosi 1981: 137), as well as in Baluchistan, specifically the Wad Valley and Pab Hills (Minchin 1907: 162). This is likely to be the material used at sites like Mundigak, but it seems an unlikely source for a place like Chanhu-daro, given the size of the beads found there.

Lapis lazuli is mentioned in one text as a product of Meluhha. Lapis lazuli, or properly lazurite (occasionally "lasurite"), is a member of the sodalite group of minerals (Dana 1949: 587–90). Its color ranges through "rich Berlin-blue or azure-blue, violet-blue, greenish blue" and it is easily worked. It comes in many grades, from the deep blue, pure stone to coarser varieties with many inclusions which generally blemish the mineral. There is a significant bibliography on the 3rd millennium trade in and sources of lapis lazuli (e.g. Herrmann 1968; Tosi 1970, 1974; Sarianidi 1971; Piperno and Tosi 1973; Chakrabarti 1978; Herrmann and Moorey 1980–3; Wyart et al. 1981; Majidzadeh 1982; Delmas and Casanova 1990; Casanova 1992, 1994). Another important blue stone was lazulite, in the phosphate group of minerals (Dana 1949: 717–18). Its color is given as "azure-blue, commonly as fine deep blue viewed along one axis, and a pale greenish blue along another."

There were four potential sources of lapis lazuli during the 3rd millennium. The one most frequently cited is in Badakhshan Province, northeastern Afghanistan, where the Sar-i Sangh mines are located (Salah et al. 1977: 281). The area has nine lapis lazuli zones, 20–300 meters long and 1–8 meter thick. There is also lapis lazuli in the Pamir/Lake Baikal region to the east of Badakhshan (Ivanov et al. 1976). Other sources exist in the Chagai Hills of western Baluchistan (Delmas and Casanova 1990), the Pamir mountains, and the Ural mountains of Russia. It was believed for many years that all lapis lazuli in the ancient world came from Badakhshan mines, but analyses of lapis from Shahr-i Sokhta in eastern Iran indicates that the Badakhshan, Pamir, and Chagai Hills sources were all used (Delmas and Casanova 1990: 502). The Ural mountain source does not seem to have come into play. Additional analysis of lapis from Tepe Sialk (central Iran) indicates that another, as yet unidentified, source exists as well (Delmas and Casanova 1990: 502; Casanova 1992: 53).

The botanical identification of the two trees associated with Meluhha in the cuneiform texts are not known. But there are two 19th century identifications of wood from South Asian trees in Mesopotamia: teak (*Tectona grandis*) and deodar, or Indian cedar (*Cedrus deodara*). The teak was mentioned by J.E. Taylor in an 1853 report on his work at Ur and was noted by C.L. Woolley in his report on the *ziggurat*: "it should be remarked that Taylor reports finding '. . . two rough logs of wood, apparently teak, which ran across the entire breadth of the shaft'" (Woolley 1939: 133). P.R.S. Moorey (1994: 352) was justifiably skeptical of this identification and believed that the timbers might have been pine. The deodar was found by Hormuzd Rassam in the course of his excavations at Birs Nimrud (ancient Borsippa) (Kennedy 1898: 266). Once again, there is reason for some skepticism concerning this identification, since there is no evidence that a botanist ever examined the find. We know that Meluhha supplied Mesopotamia with "exotic" woods, and teak and deodar could have been among them, but these identifications remain unconfirmed.

The Meluhha bird mentioned in the texts has not been identified. It was called in Sumerian either **dar-me-luḫ-ḫa** or **dar-me-luḫ-ḫa-mušen**. There are two colorful and important birds associated with the Indus Civilization: the peafowl (*Pavo cristatus*) and the chicken (*Gallus gallus murghi*), the domesticated form of the red Indian junglefowl. They would seem to be good candidates for this identification. The texts speak of the birds themselves as well as ivory models of them. The Akkadian name of the **dar-me-luḫ-ḫa-mušen**, *su-la-mu*, suggests that the bird was black, ruling out the peafowl as a candidate. B. Landsberger (1962: 148) believed that the **dar-me-luḫ-ḫa-mušen** was a "francolin," or the Persian black partridge (*Francolinus francolinus henrici*). This largely jet black bird is found from Sindh, across the Iranian Plateau, into the Near East and Turkey (Ali and Ripley 1983: 99–100); but is also native to Mesopotamia and therefore one can wonder why it would have been called a "Meluhha" bird (see Ratnagar 1981: 69).

We do not have a matching set of products sent from Mesopotamia to India, and Mesopotamian artifacts are relatively rare in the Indus Civilization (Possehl 2002b). The two best examples of "western" material in Indus contexts are the copper/bronze toilet article from Harappa (Figure 40.4[1]) and the Persian Gulf

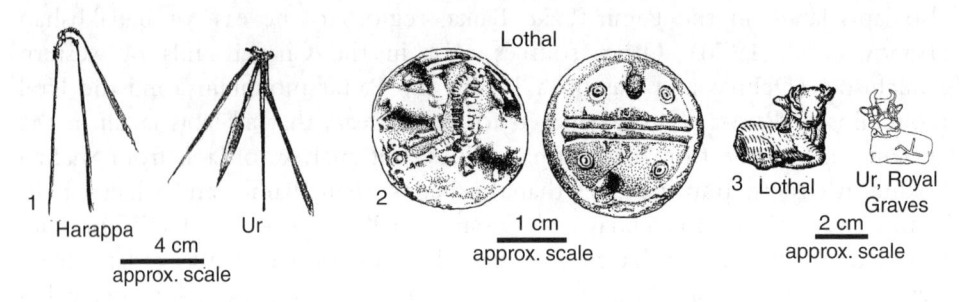

Figure 40.4 Some foreign objects in Mesopotamia and the Harappan world.

seal from Lothal (Figure 40.4[2]). The toilet set, comprising an earscoop, piercer, and tweezers, was found in the AB Mound, c.1 meter below the surface (Vats 1940: 390, Pl. CXXV.1), and probably dates to the late 3rd millennium BC. It has a rather precise parallel in a similar set at Ur (Woolley 1934: Pl. 159b) which dates to the Early Dynastic III period and seems to be quite at home in Mesopotamia. Eleven (or twelve?) toilet sets of this kind were reported from Kish (Mackay 1929: 169, Pl. XLIII, 1–8). The Persian Gulf seal from Lothal was a surface find (Rao 1963, 1985: 318, Pl. CLXI.B–C). A recumbent, Mesopotamian-style bull in copper/bronze (Rao 1985: Figure 117.1), clearly comparable to examples found in the Royal Cemetery at Ur (Woolley 1934: Pls. 141–143), was also found at Lothal (Figure 40.4[3]).

It is interesting that ivory is not mentioned in connection with Meluhha, although it is mentioned in connection with Dilmun. Mesopotamian products sent directly to Meluhha may have been "invisible" (Crawford 1973) – i.e., perishables such as food, cloth, wood, leather, and the like that have not survived in the archaeological record. In later trade with the Roman Empire, there is almost no Indian material in the Mediterranean because the exported Indian goods were largely "invisible" things like spices, and yet we know that there was a strong commercial relationship.

A number of Indus objects in Mesopotamia complement the written sources. There are at least 13 Indus – or Indus-type – seals in Mesopotamia (Possehl 1996: 148–50) (Figure 40.5) as well as etched carnelian beads, pottery, inlays, cubical weights, and other materials of Indus origin (Possehl 1996: 147–76). Queen Pu-abum in the Royal Cemetery at Ur had a cloak of beads, many of which were carnelian and probably Harappan.

There is some evidence that Meluhhans were resident in Mesopotamia. It has often been claimed that, in the Ur III period (2100–2000 BC), there was a Meluhhan village near Lagash (Parpola et al. 1977: 136) and that people called "son of Meluhha" or just "Meluhha" came from the Indus Valley. Care must be exercised in interpreting such names, since they could have been adopted by Mesopotamians who were in some way involved with Meluhha but were not

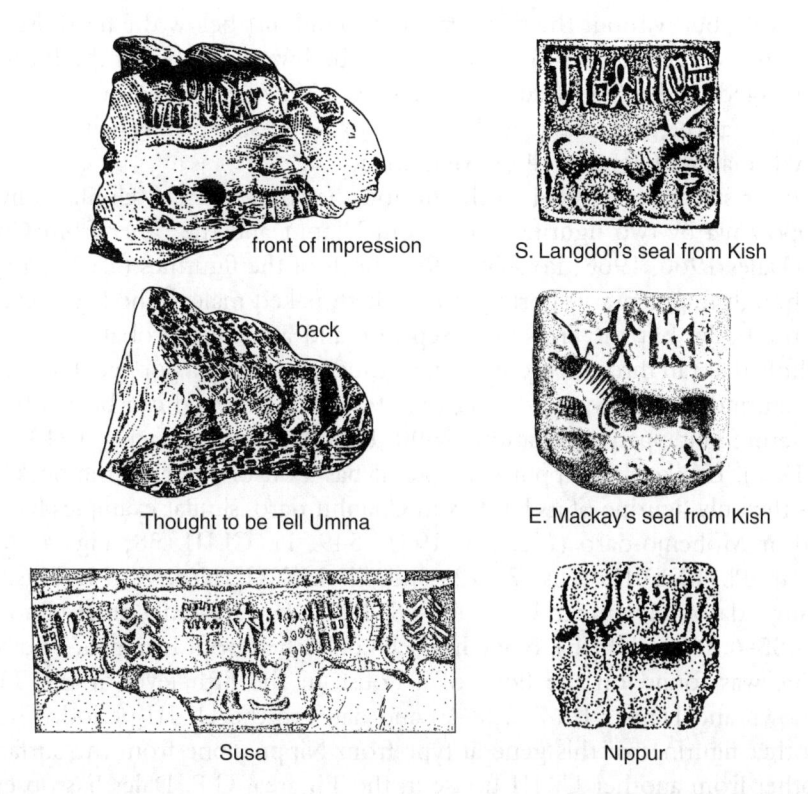

India's Relations with Western Empires, 2300–600 BC 765

Figure 40.5 Harappan seals and seal impressions found in Mesopotamia and at Susa.

Meluhhans themselves, just as "Chinese Gordon" was a British officer, not a person born in China of Chinese parents. One of the most interesting finds is a cylinder seal of unknown provenance in the Louvre bearing the name of Shu-ilishu, identified as a Meluhhan translator (Possehl 2006). As W.G. Lambert noted: "Since the owner bears a typical Old Akkadian name, he was presumably Old Akkadian, and had acquired a command of the language of Meluhha" (1987: 410). As interpreters in ancient Mesopotamia generally had Mesopotamian names, I.J. Gelb felt that the job was of such importance and sensitivity that, generally, natives were picked for this profession (Gelb 1968: 103). Although this makes a great deal of sense, many foreigners in Mesopotamia adopted Sumerian and Akkadian names (Marchesi 2006: 24 n100).

The Meluhhan village and the Shu-ilishu seal make it reasonable to believe that there were Meluhhans – i.e., Harappans – living in Mesopotamia. But there is another interesting, square stamp seal from Ur (Gadd 1932: 5), not classically Indus in style, but nonetheless worth mentioning. The seal is made of grey softstone ("steatite") and is somewhat worn. Unfortunately, it comes from an undated context (Woolley 1928: 26). A cuneiform legend runs across the top of the seal, below which is a short-horned bull, with its head down, as seen on many

Indus seals, but without the manger often found just below the head. M. Vidale (2005) has suggested that the short-horned bull was a symbol of the Indus families engaged in the Gulf trade. G. Marchesi (2007, pers. comm.) has read the inscription as the personal name Ka-lu-lim or Ka-lu-si, which is neither Sumerian nor Akkadian and could well be Meluhhan.

Further strength is added to the notion that there were Meluhhans living in Mesopotamia by two figurines, one from Nippur and the other from Chanhu-daro (Dales 1960, 1968; Possehl 1994). Both of the figurines (c.12 centimeters tall, though fragmentary) portray pot-bellied, naked males. The legs were made with the body, but the arms were separate and attached, probably with string, via a hole that ran through the shoulders, thus resembling a puppet. The Chanhu-daro figurine was excavated during the 1934–5 season and can be attributed to the Mature Harappan occupation (2500–1900 BC) there (Mackay 1943: 166–7, Pl. LIX.2). Unlike the Nippur example, it has a bit of paint on the neck. While this is the only figurine of its kind from Chanhu-daro, similar examples have been found at Mohenjo-daro (Marshall 1931: 549, Pl. CLIII, 38; Fig. 4; Mackay 1937–8: Pl. LXXVII, Nos. 3, 12, and Pl. LXXXI, Nos. 8, 14; Figs. 5–8), Lohumjo-daro (Majumdar 1934: 48–58, Pl. XXII, 38) and Lothal (Rao 1985: 483, 485–6, Pl. CCVIa–b). None has been published from Harappa. The Nippur figurine was found on the floor of a house in the fifth level of the TB area (McCown and Haines 1967: 128–9) and dates to the Ur III period. There are two other figurines of this general type from Nippur, one from the surface and the other from another Ur III house in the TB area. G.F. Dales has observed:

> Hundreds – perhaps thousands – of clay figurines have been excavated from Mesopotamian sites. They are well enough documented so that a reasonably comprehensive classification of them – by type, style and period – has been possible. Figurines of 'foreign' origin or inspiration can be recognized with reasonable assurance. The novel type of nude male figurine under consideration here is emphatically not a characteristic Mesopotamian creation. Neither *male* nudity, male obesity, nor animation are found among Sumero-Akkadian figurines of this date. (1968: 19)

Neutron activation analyses by S. Fleming (Possehl 1994) made it clear that the Chanhu-daro figurine was made in the Indus Valley, while the Nippur figurine was in Mesopotamia, possibly even at Nippur itself. If, as is suggested here, the type is a Harappan one, then the presence of such a figurine at Nippur may be further evidence of the presence of Meluhhans in Mesopotamia or at least of contact between the two regions, as is a typical Harappan stamp seal excavated at Nippur (Gibson 1977).

4 The Land of Magan and the Site of RJ-2

The Mesopotamian "Land of Magan" was located in the area of modern Oman and the United Arab Emirates. This was a place where the Mesopotamians got copper, and a great deal of it. They also made "black boats" that the Mesopotamians took notice of (Cleuziou and Tosi 1994).

The peoples of Meluhha sailed to Magan, as suggested by the abundance of Harappan pottery at Umm an-Nar-period sites (2700–2000 BC) like Ra's al-Hadd, Ra's al-Jins, and Bat (Figs. 16–19). V.D. Gogte undertook the x-ray diffraction (XRD) analysis of some of the ceramics from RJ-2 and Bat in the interior of Oman. Of the 76 "Harappan" sherds analyzed from Ra's al-Jins, 67 were very similar in composition to pottery from Lothal (Gogte 2002: 58–9; cf. Gogte 2000). This is strong evidence that a good portion of the Harappan pottery at Ra's al-Jins was made of clay that came from the delta of the Sabarmati River in Gujarat, possibly Lothal itself. Gogte's findings are in line with analyses of slightly later pottery from Saar on Bahrain (Dilmun) where Sorath and Late Sorath Harappan pottery (c.2000–1600 BC) was recovered in quantity (Carter 2001). These finds demonstrate that Indus trade with the Gulf region continued into the period following the abandonment of Mohenjo-daro at 1900 BC. They also underscore the fact that Gujarat was the focus of Indian maritime activity in the Arabian Sea during the Bronze Age and Lothal, in the Sabarmati delta, emerges as the key site, at least for the moment.

How did Meluhhan sailors reach these sites? During the period from October to March they would have sailed from the mouths of the Indus, westward to the vicinity of the Dasht Valley, and then south to Magan. This route is dictated by the prevailing wind and the sailing technology of the Indus peoples as we know it today. Once in Magan, these sailors could have returned to Meluhha, not by retracing their route, but by sailing directly to the east across the Arabian Sea, landing with little effort on the Indian coast in Gujarat. However, Ra's al-Hadd and Ra's al-Jins seem more like fishing villages than ports, and it is possible that fishermen visiting these places could have been traders as well (Cleuziou and Tosi 2000). The boats that were used at Ra's al-Hadd or Ra's al-Jins seem to have been pulled up on the beach and left there, since there are no docks or port facilities. Many small ports in the subcontinent and the Persian Gulf are noteworthy for not having docking facilities, the boats left to lie on their sides at low tide, or propped-up with wooden timbers when worked on for repairs.

The excavations at Ra's al-Jins 2 (RJ-2) also yielded a copper Indus seal and an ivory Indus comb. Metal seals were very rare in the Harappan world. Two copper seals are known from Chanhu-daro (Mackay 1943: 291, Pl. XLIX.8) and one from Lothal (Rao 1985: 314, Pl. CLIV.C) while two silver seals were found at Mohenjo-daro (Mackay 1937–8: 370, 385, Pls. LXXXIII.16, XCVI.520).

On the other hand, a steatite seal found at Lothal was fashioned from the lid of a rectangular steatite box with dot-and-circle decoration (Rao 1985: Pl. CLXI.D), a diagnostic artifact in the UAE and Oman during the late 3rd and early 2nd millennium BC (Cleuziou and Tosi 2000: 60, Fig.16.3; cf. Frenez and Tosi 2005: 19). This seal has a direct parallel with a seal from RJ-2 and is possibly the earliest Indian import in the land of Magan (Cleuziou and Tosi 2000: 56).

It has already been noted that cubical Indus weights have been found in Mesopotamia. These have also been found in the Persian Gulf on Bahrain (Bibby 1969), and in the northern UAE at Tell Abraq (Potts 1993b: 327) and Shimal (Vogt and Franke-Vogt 1987). The significance of the use of the Harappan weight system on Bahrain is not well understood. Bibby (1970) suggested that it was used because the Harappans were the earliest and/or the most important trading partners for the Dilmun merchants. Given the very early attestations of Dilmun in the Archaic Texts from Uruk, which can be dated to the late 4th millennium (Nissen 1986: 336–7), and early Mesopotamian presence in the Gulf (Frifelt 1975) it would seem unlikely that the Harappans preceded Mesopotamians in this area. A similar qualification would come to bear on this point if one takes the written evidence for economic activity into account. Economic intercourse with Magan and Mesopotamia itself far exceed the attestations for Meluhha. Thus, to propose that the latter as the most important trading partner is problematic.

Nevertheless, it does seem that "Meluhha" had a serious presence in Dilmun. This is documented not only by weights, but by a great deal of Indus pottery, in the form of Sorath and Late Sorath Harappan wares (c.2300–1700 BC), most strikingly at Saar (Carter 2001). The fact that clear Late Sorath Harappan pottery is there would seem to document Indus maritime trade in the Gulf for two or three centuries after the abandonment of the Indus cities as urban spaces, implying that state-level sociocultural complexity was not necessary for it to continue.

5 Indus Material in Iran

There is a scattering of Indus and Indus-related material culture on the Iranian plateau. Most of it is in the form of seals and beads. A seal from Hissar showing a bull, but not a *zebu*, or humped bull (Schmidt 1933: Pl. CXXX, Plate 7; 1937: 198–9; Chakrabarti and Moghadam 1977: 167), may not be Harappan, since it is a cylinder seal. A seal impression on the shoulder of a pot from Tepe Yahya Period IVA (2000–1800 BC) is incomplete, but the characters fit within the corpus of Harappan glyphs (Lamberg-Karlovsky and Tosi 1973: Pl. 137). Etched carnelian beads have been found at a number of sites in Iran, including Tepe Hissar IIIC – Necklaces H 3215 and H 3216 (Schmidt 1937: 229, Pl. XXXV); Tepe Hissar III – H 400 "Little Girl's Grave" (Schmidt 1933: 438, Pl. CXLIVc); Shah Tepe IIA (Arne 1945: Pl. XCII, Fig. 612, II S7, Fig. 28); Kalleh Nisar – Akkadian cist grave (Vanden Berghe 1970: 73); Susa – Akkadian grave (Mecquenem 1943: Fig. 84, 7); Tepe Yahya – one surface find, another in uncertain context, but probably later than 2000 BC (During Caspers 1972: 92); Jalalabad – three beads mid-3rd millennium BC (Chakrabarti and Moghadam 1977: 167, Fig. 10); and Marlik – late 2nd/early 1st millennium BC (Chakrabarti and Moghadam 1977: 167, Fig. 10).

Given its proximity, it is somewhat surprising that there is not more Indus material in Iran. Still, there can be little doubt that the ancient peoples of Iran and those of the Greater Indus Valley were in regular contact, but the form that this took did not leave an appreciable archaeological signature.

After about 1700 BC, Indian westward activity seems to have come to an end for many centuries. Evidence of ancient India's contacts with the West between the end of the "Meluhha trade" and the Achaemenid period is scanty; but the Assyrians knew of India and cotton, and called the fiber *sindhu* (Oppenheim 1964: 94; Talon 1986).

GUIDE TO FURTHER READING

Ratnagar (1981, 2004) provides excellent sources on the ancient sea trade between the Indus Civilization and Mesopotamia, especially for the Mesopotamian data; she also covers the lands of Dilmun and Magan. Potts (1990) and Crawford (1998) are both splendid sources on maritime activity in the Gulf. Potts covers both the prehistoric period and historical ages. Possehl (1999, 2002a) offers a general introduction to the Indus Civilization. Tosi (1991) and Cleuziou and Tosi (2007) do the same for Oman and the United Arab Emirates.

CHAPTER FORTY-ONE

Levantine Kingdoms of the Late Bronze Age

Peter Pfälzner

1 Introduction

This chapter discusses the historical and archaeological data available for the dense cluster of regional states in western Syria, Lebanon, and northernmost Palestine during the Late Bronze Age (LBA). This period began c.1550 and ended c.1200 BC when the regional systems were rather abruptly changed, both politically and culturally, by what is generally termed the invasion of the "Sea peoples." Most of the political entities in the Levant during the LBA were already formed during the preceding Middle Bronze Age (MBA, 2000–1550 BC), in the period of the Amorite state formation. Many of these kingdoms continued to exist throughout the 2nd millennium into the LBA, while gradually – and often only slightly – changing their political, cultural, and partly even ethnic structures. The major force behind the modifications of the Levantine kingdoms from the MBA to the LBA was the growing impact of external political powers such as the Egyptian, Mitanni, and Hittite empires. Nevertheless, the transition from the MBA to LBA in the region was principally characterized by continuity of material culture, settlement, and society. The LBA was a period when interregional contacts and exchange between the eastern Mediterranean and the Near East reached its apex, with the Levant a hub of this communication system. Thus, the LBA can justifiably be termed the "international age" of the Levantine kingdoms.

A Companion to the Archaeology of the Ancient Near East, First Edition.
Edited by D.T. Potts.
© 2012 Blackwell Publishing Ltd. Published 2012 by Blackwell Publishing Ltd.

2 Historical Outline

The first phase of the historical development in LBA Syria has been called the "period of Mitannian and Egyptian domination" (Klengel 1992: 84–99). This period lasted from 1550 to 1350 BC, its final phase corresponding to the so-called "Amarna-period" in Egypt. These dates are based on the Mesopotamian Middle Chronology. If the High Chronology were applied, the beginning of this phase would have to be dated to c.1600 BC (for a discussion of the Mesopotamian Middle, Low, and High Chronologies, see Hrouda 1971: 23; Schwartz 2008). The two external powers – Mitanni with its center in the Khabur headwaters region of northeastern Syria, and Egypt in the Nile Valley – sought constantly to extend their power in the Levant by dominating those kingdoms within their geographical reach. Mitanni exercised overlordship over Halab (mod. Aleppo); Mukish, with its center Alalakh (mod. Tell Atchana); and Kizzuwatna (mod. Cilicia) (Wilhelm 1982: 28–37; 1991: 95ff), all of which are west of the Euphrates, where Mitanni proper ended. Egypt, on the other hand, tried to repel Mitannian influence through military campaigns into Syria. Thutmose III (1479–1425 BC) was initially victorious over a coalition of Syrian and Palestinian kings, led by the king of Qadesh, in the dramatic battle of Megiddo (1457 BC) and, later on (in 1447 BC), reached and crossed the Euphrates at the border of Mitanni, where he erected a stele on the banks of the river as a symbol of Egyptian dominance in the region (Redford 1992, 2003). However, in most cases, Egypt did not establish direct rule over the Syrian kingdoms. Instead, peaceful relations were established, always under Egyptian supremacy. One such case is provided by Qatna, where Thutmose III attended an archery contest together with its king (Redford 2003: 222–6), a conspicuous sign of political understanding. Thanks to a treaty between Artatama I of Mitanni and Thutmose IV (1400–1390 BC) and an interdynastic marriage (Wilhelm 1991: 96–9; Klengel 1989: 271–6), Egypt and Mitanni were on peaceful terms throughout the first half of the 14th century, and particularly during the Amarna Age. This also insured a period of peace (apart from minor local conflicts) and prosperity for the Levantine kingdoms.

A second phase (c.1350–1200 BC), known as the "time of Egyptian and Hittite overlordship" (Klengel 1992: 100–80; 2002; Wilhelm 1991), began with the Hittite conquest of northern Syria under Shuppiluliuma I (c.1350–1320 BC). After the defeat of Mitanni the Hittites conquered the Syrian kingdoms from Alalakh and Ugarit in the north to Qatna in the south. While several of these, such as Ugarit, survived and even prospered under Hittite control (Klengel 1969: 358; 1992: 130–51), others, such as Qatna (Klengel 1992: 156–7; 2000: 249), were destroyed and abandoned. Egyptian influence was thus pushed back to a line south of the kingdom of Qadesh in central-western Syria. The direct conflict of interests between Egypt and the Hittites culminated in the famous battle of Qadesh (1275 BC) where Ramesses II and Muwattalli II clashed – but there was no clear winner. As a result, a peace treaty was concluded between the two superpowers in 1259 BC, one of the first far-reaching international agreements in world history. It concertedly determined Egyptian and Hittite interests in Syria, to the disadvantage of the autonomy and self-determination of the Syrian kingdoms. The period of a *pax* in the Levant enforced by the Hittites and Egyptians lasted for only half a century, until more major disruptions occurred.

The third phase in the LBA history of the Levant is marked by the invasion of the "Sea Peoples" (c.1200–1160 BC) (Klengel 1992: 181–7). This is mainly known from Egyptian sources, particularly from the reign of Ramesses III (1188–1156 BC), according to which the Sea Peoples conquered and destroyed Amurru, a state in western Syria between the Mediterranean and the Orontes Valley and one of the most powerful Levantine kingdoms of the LBA, in order to establish a base from which to launch an attack on Egypt (Bartl 1995: 195ff; Cline and O'Connor 2003: 108–11, 136). The origins, organization, and ethnicity of the Sea Peoples, however, are hotly debated, and it is doubtful that they arrived as a large group of plundering invaders (Ward and Joukowsky 1992; Sherratt 1998; Oren 2000; Cline and O'Connor 2003). Some scholars suggest that they were small, ununified groups of migrants who had been driven – in a cascade effect – out of their home regions because of economic or social crises, eventually forming ad hoc alliances (Cline and O'Connor 2003: 111). Alternatively, it has been suggested that groups of Sea People settled down peacefully and gradually in the southern Levant, particularly in the Jordan Valley, as early as the late 13th century BC (Tubb 1998: 95–106). Destruction layers at settlements are taken as the clearest indicators of these foreign incursions, the most prominent example being at Ugarit (mod. Ras Shamra, Syria), where the destruction, dated to c.1192 BC (Dietrich and Loretz 2003), affected the whole city. Other sites, such as Emar, Alalakh, Ras Ibn Hani, and Ras el-Bassit in the northern Levant and Hazor, Megiddo, Ta'anach, Gezer, Lachish, Ashdod, Beit Mirsim, and Beth Shean in the southern Levant, reveal clear signs of destruction and abandonment as well (Bartl 1995: 197–200; Caubet 1992: 123–31). The Bronze Age Levantine, urban-based political system collapsed, marking the end of a long-lived network of competing kingdoms in the western half of the ancient Near East.

3 Written Sources

Our main source for the political history of the Levantine kingdoms during the LBA is the Amarna archive. Found within the Egyptian royal residence at Achet-Aten (mod. Tell el-Amarna), it consists of correspondence between the pharaohs Amenhotep III and IV (Akhenaten) and various foreign rulers. The letters date to c.1360–1330 BC and shed light on political relations both between the Levantine rulers and Egypt and among the Levantine rulers themselves. One of the best-documented cases concerns the kingdom of Gubla/Byblos on the Lebanese

Figure 41.1 Letter from King Rib-Addu of Byblos to the Pharaoh in the Amarna archive.

coast, whose ruler Rib-Addu was the author of 62 letters to the pharaoh (Figure 41.1). The rulers of Ugarit, Qatna, Nukhashe, Barga, Tunip, Amurru, Qadesh, and Damascus in Syria; the kings of Beruta (Beirut), Sidon, Tyre, and Kumidi (Kamid el-Loz) in Lebanon; and rulers or officials from Hazor, Akko, Megiddo, Gezer, Jerusalem, Ashkelon, and Lachish in Palestine: all these also corresponded with the pharaohs (Moran 1992). These letters provide us with information on the political topography of the Levantine kingdoms in the 14th century, their political leaders, political structures, and internal problems, as well as on international diplomacy expressed through the exchange of gifts between courts

(Liverani 2008; Spar 2008; Feldman 2006). External sources for the history of Syria in the second half of the 2nd millennium BC also include the Hittite archives from Hattusha (Kühne 1982).

In addition, there are internal sources from the Levant which complement the external data. The most abundant corpus of texts comes from Ugarit, and illustrates the international, cosmopolitan character of this trading hub and the economic, political, and cultic activities and structures of this prosperous kingdom (Klengel 1969: 340–407; 1992: 130–51). Texts from Alalakh Level IV shed light on the complex organization of the palace economy of a LBA kingdom (Von Dassow 2008). The archive of Idadda, from the royal palace of Qatna, consists of only 55 tablets, but these include letters to the king of Qatna from other regions in Syria as well as palace inventory texts, administrative documents, and juridical texts, and, as such, they offer a broad insight into the life of the palace at Qatna in the mid-14th century, shortly before its destruction by the Hittites (Richter 2003a, 2003b, 2005; Richter and Lange in press). The texts from Emar reveal the private, social, and commercial activities of LBA households in an urban center belonging to the kingdom of Ashtata on the west bank of the Euphrates (Arnaud 1985a, 1985b, 1986, 1987).

4 Historical and Archaeological Topography of the Northern Levantine Kingdoms

The Amarna archive presents the most detailed picture of the LBA political topography of the entire Levant. The location and distribution of kingdoms in the southern Levant (Palestine) in contact with Egypt has been discussed extensively, though some questions regarding lesser known cities and political entities remain (Finkelstein 1996; Na'aman 1997). The present chapter focuses on the northern Levant (western Syria and Lebanon). On the basis of our knowledge of historical geography, we are able to identify a number of the capitals of the Levantine kingdoms and to roughly locate the territories of others (Figure 41.2).

Surri, Siduna, Beruta, and Gubla

There were four major kingdoms on the coast of Lebanon. From south to north these were Tyre/Surri (mod. Sur), Sidon/Siduna (mod. Saida), Beruta (mod. Beirut), and Byblos/Gubla (mod. Jbeil). Important Phoenician harbor cities during the Iron Age, they shared a regional, pre-Phoenician culture during the LBA, generally labeled Canaanite (Klengel 1970: 15–22). Most of these sites were built over so extensively by later occupations that hardly any traces of their LBA levels can be detected. Byblos, despite being the only one of these sites that is not covered by a modern city and being comparatively large (5 hectares),

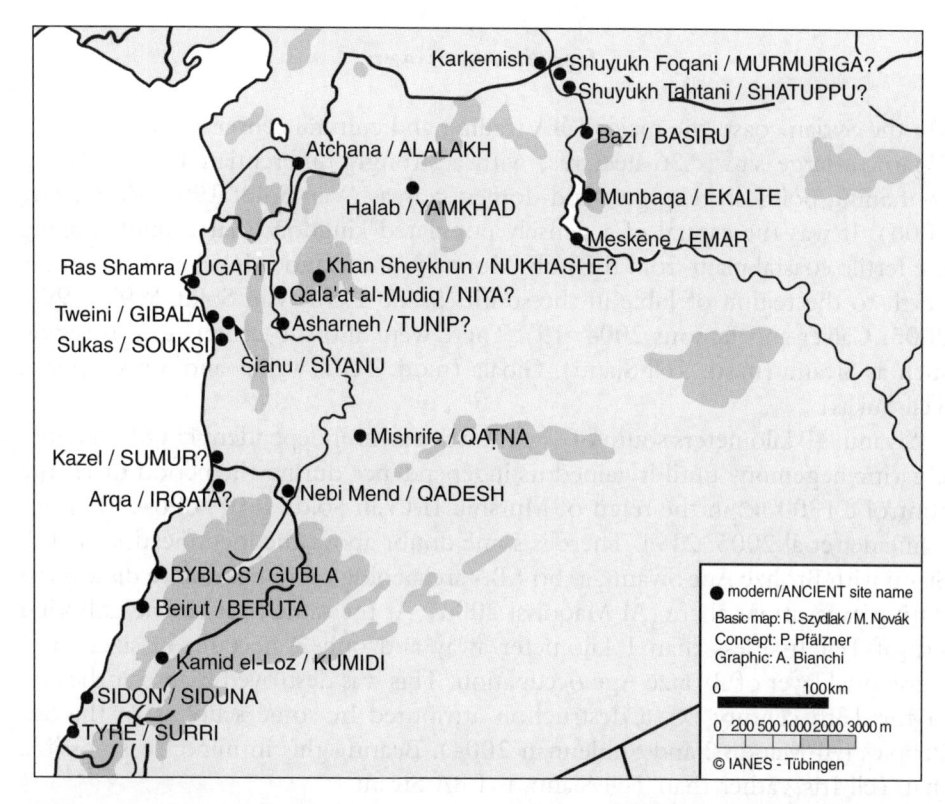

Figure 41.2 Map of the historical geography of the Northern Levant with major kingdoms and their capital cities.

yielded, apart from some grave material, no LBA remains (Salles 1980; Merrillees 1983). Rescue excavations in central Beirut brought to light a LBA city wall revetment and glacis, demonstrating that Beruta at that time was a strongly fortified, moderate sized (2 hectares) city (Badre and Thalmann 1996: 91–3, Fig. 3; Badre 1998). At Sidon new excavations at the "College site" proved that LBA monumental religious architecture existed in the city. Aegean and Egyptian imports and objects showing influences from those regions testify to close contact, and probably also gift exchange, with neighboring regions (Doumet-Serhal 2010: 125–8). Sarepta (mod. Sarafand), 13 kilometer south of Sidon (Pritchard 1978), has extensive LBA remains including one of the rare Near Eastern examples of an extensive pottery production area with 24 kilns (Anderson 1987). This important city probably belonged to the kingdom of Sidon (Klengel 1970: 18–19). As the pottery production area was active from LBA II (1450/1400 BC) until the Iron Age (Anderson 1987: 42), Sarepta provides a good example of social and economic continuity from a LBA urban center to a Phoenician settlement of the Iron Age (Anderson 1988: 433).

Ugarit and Siyanu

On the Syrian coast, the major LBA trading and cultural center was indisputably Ugarit, a large site (c.26 hectares) with a strongly differentiated urban layout containing political, religious, and domestic areas (Van Soldt 1995; Yon 1997, 2006). It was the capital of a densely populated kingdom that extended along the fertile coastal plain from the holy Mount Saphon (mod. Jebel el-Aqra) in the north to the region of Jable in the south (Saadé 1990; Van Soldt 1997, 1998, 2005; Calvet and Jamous 2004: 19). There were also sub-centers in this region such as Siyanu (mod. Tell Sianu), Gibala (mod. Tell Tweini) and Souksi (mod. Tell Sukas).

Siyanu, 40 kilometers south of Ugarit, was a semi-independent kingdom under Ugaritic hegemony until it gained its independence during the period of Hittite control c.1300 BC in the reign of Murshili II (Van Soldt 1997: 696–701; Bretschneider et al 2005: 219). There is some doubt about the identification of Tell Sianu with Bronze Age Siyanu, as no LBA archaeological remains were discovered during excavations there (Al-Maqdissi 2006). At the same time the neighboring site of Tell Iris, less than 1 kilometer away and only 2 hectares in size, has a substantial layer of Bronze Age occupation. This was destroyed by fire at the end of the 13th century BC, a destruction attributed by some scholars to the Sea Peoples (Al-Maqdissi and Souleiman 2004). Bearing this in mind, it is possible that Tell Iris, rather than Tell Sianu, is LBA Siyanu.

The large site of Tell Tweini (12 hectares), possibly ancient Gibala, has evidence of LBA occupation and an impressive Middle to Late Bronze Age stone fortification system (Bretschneider et al. 2005; Bretschneider and Van Lerberghe 2008). Like Ugarit, Gibala lies 2 kilometers inland from its harbor. The site shows traces of destruction by fire c.1200 BC or shortly after, an event which the excavators have linked to the invasion of the Sea Peoples (Bretschneider and Van Lerberghe 2008: 32–3).

Nearby Tell Sukas, 6 kilometers south of Tell Tweini, was intensively inhabited during the LBA and controlled two harbors. As a minor center, Souksi/Shuksu (Tell Sukas) seems to have belonged to Siyanu (Lund 2004: 63). In addition, there must have been villages and hamlets in the coastal plain and foothills of the coastal mountains. With a pattern of centers, sub-centers, minor centers and villages, a complex, four-tiered political hierarchy of settlement becomes evident in the wider Ugarit region. Tell Sukas was destroyed after 1200 BC, supposedly by the Sea Peoples according to some scholars (Lund 2004; Riis et al. 2004).

The Ugaritic palatial dependencies at Ras Ibn Hani (probably ancient Biruti), only 5 kilometers from Ugarit, were part of the district controlled by it. Thus, Ugarit presents the clearest picture of the geographical outline of a Levantine kingdom and it is the part of Syria with the largest number of excavated sites belonging to one and the same kingdom.

Amurru

The territory of the Kingdom of Amurru must have been located south of Ugarit and the kingdom of Siyanu. Its capital is unknown, so its location remains difficult to pinpoint. It is generally assumed that Amurru extended from the Mediterranean coast around the Akkar plain far into the coastal hinterland up to the Middle Orontes valley in central Syria (Klengel 1969: 178–325; 1992:160–74; Goren et al. 2003). The important route from inner Syria to the Mediterranean through the Homs Gap, a wide passage between the Lebanon Mountains in the south and the Syrian coastal mountain (Jebel Ansariyeh) to the north, seems to have been controlled by Amurru. The control of traffic between coastal and inland Syria was thus key to its prominence in the LBA. Two sites are known to have belonged to the kingdom of Amurru: Tell Kazel and Tell Arqa. Tell Kazel is situated in the northern part of the Akkar plain and has been tentatively identified with Sumur (the later Phoenician Simyra) (Klengel 1984). From the reign of Thutmose III (mid–15th century BC) onward, Sumur was an Egyptian garrison and administrative seat. Later it became one of the most prominent places in the kingdom of Amurru. Excavations have revealed an important and extensive LBA settlement, including a LB II (14/13th century BC) temple complex (Badre 2006; Badre and Gubel 1999–2000). Tell Arqa is located in the southern part of the Akkar plain (in modern Lebanon). It has been tentatively identified with the city of Irqata (Hawkins 1976–80a), known from the Amarna letters, and has signs of an important MBA occupation. However, during the LBA, Tell Arqa fell into gradual decline and was reduced to a minor village, especially in comparison to Tell Kazel, which was the major center on the Akkar plain (Thalmann 2006, 2010).

Tunip and Niya

In the middle Orontes valley of inland western Syria were two urban centers: Tunip and Niya. Tunip can be regarded as a kingdom (Dietrich and Loretz 1997) but it seems to have been organized differently from the other kingdoms, perhaps a sort of oligarchic political system. A letter from the Amarna archive (Amarna letter EA 59) shows that its inhabitants had the right to petition the Pharaoh directly (Moran 1992: 130ff). In the reign of king Aziru of Amurru (13th century BC) Tunip was incorporated into the domain of Amurru (Alt 1944–5; Klengel 1969: 75–95; 1992: 165). It has been tentatively identified with Tell Asharneh, one of the largest mounds in the southern part of the Ghab plain, the wide rift valley drained by the Orontes, west of Hama (Courtois 1973; Helck 1973; Klengel 1995). However, excavations there have not yielded any traces of LBA occupation, casting doubt on this identification (Fortin 2006: 101ff, 117, 136; Cooper 2006b).

Niya is famous because of the episode of the elephant hunt of Thutmose III near the lake of Niya, during which he killed 120 animals (Redford 2003). Niya also figures prominently in the Hittite sources on the Syrian campaigns of Shuppiluliuma I (Klengel 1969: 58–74; 1992: 151–6). This small kingdom maintained connections with Qatna during the 14th century BC, as demonstrated by three letters found in the Idadda archive from King Takuwa of Niya to the king of Qatna, whom he calls "brother" – hinting at a position of political equality (Richter 2003b: 178–80). Richter has argued for the development of a special dialect in the region of the two cities, "Niya/Qatna-Hurrian," a hybrid based on Akkadian with a large dose of Hurrian components (Richter 2003b: 171–7; Richter and Lange in press). Besides political and cultural relations, there is another plausible motive for close cooperation between Niya and Qatna: the damp rift valley of the Ghab near Niya was a preferred habitat of the Syrian elephant, which was hunted not only by the Egyptians but also by the kings of Qatna, as demonstrated by the discovery of huge elephant bones carefully deposited in the Royal Palace there (Dohmann-Pfälzner and Pfälzner 2008: 35–42; Pfälzner 2009c; Pfälzner and Dohmann-Pfälzner 2010: 77). Niya is generally identified with Qalat Mudiq in the central Ghab plain, the site of Hellenistic Apamea (Klengel 1969: 58ff; 1970: 54; Röllig 1999: 314a; Otto 2006a), but the presence of a medieval castle on the *tell* has to date precluded archaeological excavations there.

Qatna

Qatna is located in a fertile agricultural zone with abundant springs in western Syria, to the east of and within the Orontes drainage system. It stands at the crossroads of important trade routes leading east–west from Mesopotamia to the Mediterranean and north–south from Anatolia toward Palestine. Surrounded by 20 meter high ramparts, the nearly square site covers 100 hectares and is the largest LBA site in the Levant (Du Mesnil du Buisson 1935; Novák and Pfälzner 2000; Morandi Bonacossi 2007a; Pfälzner 2006; Al-Maqdissi et al. 2009). With its advantageous geographical and ecological setting, Qatna became, along with Halab (Aleppo), the most powerful Syrian kingdom of the MBA (Klengel 2000). However, its political and commercial importance declined rapidly during the LBA because of the growing influence of Egypt and Mitanni, of which Qatna and other Syrian regions became dependencies. This enabled the growth of numerous other competing political units in western Syria, purposely supported by the foreign powers with the aim of dividing and weakening the local Syrian polities.

The large Royal Palace of Qatna (Figure 41.3) was built in MB IIA (Novák and Pfälzner 2000, 2001, 2002a, 2002b, 2003, 2005; Dohmann-Pfälzner and Pfälzner 2006, 2007, 2008, 2010; Pfälzner 2006, 2007b, 2008a, 2009a) and was used as a royal residence continuously for c.400 years until its final destruc-

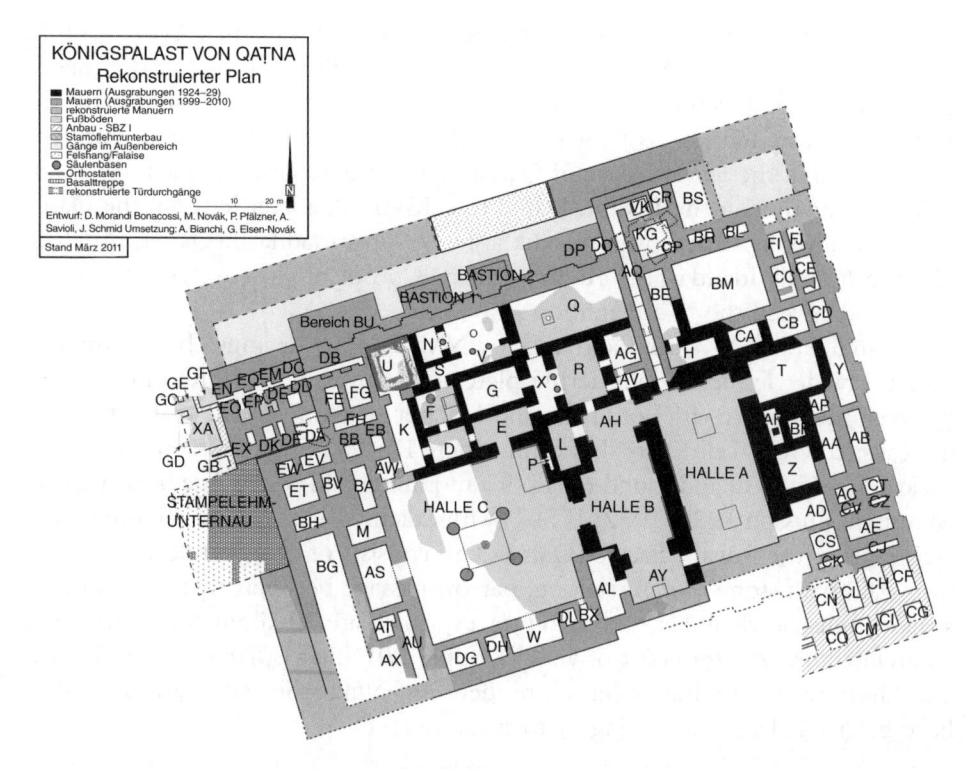

Figure 41.3 Plan of the royal palace at Qatna.

tion in the LBA by the Hittite king Shuppiluliuma I in c.1340 BC. Throughout this long period, only minor changes were made to the layout of the palace, a clear indication of continuity in the Syrian kingdoms from the MBA to the LBA, both in political and cultural terms. As shown by the rich inventory of objects from the destruction phase of the palace (Level G 7b), particularly the Royal Hypogeum, and the cuneiform tablets listing the inventory of treasures belonging to the goddess of the palace, Belet-ekallim, and the "gods of the kings" (Bottéro 1949; Fales 2004b; Rossberger in press), the kingdom was, despite its political decline, still very prosperous during the final phase of its existence in the 14th century BC. Excavations in other parts of the large, heavily fortified city have exposed minor palaces and private houses, demonstrating that Qatna was a flourishing metropolis during the LBA (Morandi Bonacossi 2007b: 76–82; 2009a; Pfälzner 2006: 164–9).

Nukhashe

North of Qatna was the large kingdom of Nukhashe (Klengel 1999–2001), with which Qatna maintained close ties. During the reign of Adad-nirari of Nukhashe

(14th century BC) it even seems to have been united with Qatna (Richter 2003a: 608–10; 2005: 123ff.). A juridical text of Adad-nirari's was found in the Idadda archive at Qatna (Richter and Lange in press) and his name also appears in the Qatna inventory tablets. As joint king of Qatna and Nukhashe, Adad-nirari may have resided in the Royal Palace of Qatna, one of the largest and most luxurious palaces of its time in the Levant. Dated to c.1340 BC, a later letter in the Qatna archive from king Sharrupshe of Nukhashe to king Idadda of Qatna, in which Sharrupshe calls Idadda his lord and father, is proof of close, ongoing political relations between the two neighbors.

Located north of Qatna and east of Niya, Nukhashe must have extended into the wide, fertile to semi-fertile plateau to the east of the Orontes valley, between the modern cities of Hama and Ma'aret en-Numan. The major archaeological site here is Tell Khan Sheykhun, where Du Mesnil du Buisson carried out excavations in 1930 and found traces of a monumental Bronze Age building (Du Mesnil du Buisson 1930; 1932: 175–7) with exactly the same unusual foundation technique as the Royal Palace of Qatna. This consists of deep, mudbrick foundation walls with stone *couloirs* (a long, narrow passage between separate rooms or spaces), thus clearly linking the two palaces, which are 70 kilometers apart, from an architectural design point of view (Döpper 2010). It is likely that Tell Khan Sheykhun was the capital or central residence of Nukhashe. Alternatively, it may have been Ugulzat, where king Sharrupshe resided.

Qadesh/Kinza

The southern neighbor of Qatna was the kingdom of Qadesh or Kinza. Qadesh's key role stemmed from its geographical position. Situated at the northern entrance to the Beqaa valley, which separates the Lebanon and Anti-Lebanon mountains, Qadesh controlled access to this important corridor of communication between Syria and Palestine, and between the Hittite Empire and Egypt. While the identification of Qadesh with Tell Nebi Mend, south of Homs (Klengel 1969: 139–77; 1970: 56; Ahrens 2005), is accepted, excavations at this huge *tell* (10 hectares) have not yet produced clear architectural or material evidence of the outstanding importance of Qadesh during the LBA (Pézard 1931; Parr 1983, 1991). LBA levels (Phases B–F) have only been exposed on a limited scale and no complete buildings or contexts have been recorded (Bourke 1993: 158–64). Nevertheless, five cuneiform tablets from Tell Nebi Mend, dating to the last quarter of the 14th century BC, include a letter from the king of Aleppo to Niqmaddu, king of Qadesh, the son of the powerful king Aitakama (Millard 2010), confirming the site's identification with Qadesh. Previously, Qadesh had been a buffer state between Egypt and the Hittite territory in Syria with shifting loyalties. The fact that the king of Qadesh led the Syrian coalition against Egypt in the battle of Megiddo (1457 BC) demonstrates its strategic importance.

Kumidi

Further south, in the Beqaa valley, Kumidi (mod. Kamid el-Loz) was the major LBA center. Here, Egypt installed another military and administrative hub in the 15th century BC, the purpose of which was to control the conquered territories in the area without dismantling the local polities. This hints at a more stable Egyptian presence at Kumidi compared to its less reliable vassal Qadesh further north. Kamid el-Loz has extensive LBA remains, including a temple area (Metzger 1991, 1993) and part of a palace (Hachmann 1982, 1983) with a royal tomb containing luxury goods and imported objects (Miron 1990; Adler 1994; Hachmann 1996). Amongst nine cuneiform tablets discovered at the site is a letter from the Egyptian Pharaoh to Zalaja, a ruler of Damascus. The fact that this tablet was archived at Kumidi hints at the central role of the city in the administration of Egyptian territories in the central Levant (Edzard 1970: 55–8; 1982) and clearly underlines the site's political importance at the time.

Alalakh

Close to the Orontes River, Alalakh (mod. Tell Atchana, Turkey) was the northern neighbor of Ugarit and the center of the kingdom of Mukish, a vassal polity of Halab (Aleppo) from which it became independent in the second quarter of the 15th century BC when king Idrimi, after seven years of exile, restored his royal dynasty – formerly located at Halab – at Alalakh. Thus, Alalakh became an independent kingdom, albeit under Mitanni suzerainty (Klengel 1965: 203–57; Kühne 1982: 210ff; Wilhelm 1991: 95ff). The central area of Mukish was the wide and fertile Amuq plain, east of the Amanus mountains (Casana 2009). At Alalakh, C.L. Woolley excavated a palace and a temple of the 15th century BC in Level IV, one of five main levels (Alalakh V–I) dating to the LBA (Woolley 1955b).

Yamkhad/Halab

The kingdom of Yamkhad/Halab (Aleppo), a major power in Syria during the MBA, was of minor political importance during the LBA (Klengel 1965: 175–202). It seems to have been particularly reduced in significance by its mighty neighbor Mitanni, who dislodged Alalakh from Yamhad's control (Kühne 1982: 210 n68). Later, under Hittite hegemony (probably mid-14th century BC), Halab was further reduced by being forced to hand over territories to its southern neighbor Nukhashe and to its eastern neighbor Ashtata (Na'aman 1980).

Archaeological excavations on the citadel of Aleppo have brought to light a Temple of the Storm God, the only structure yet known from ancient Halab (Kohlmeyer 2000; Gonnella, Khayyata and Kohlmeyer 2005). Built sometime in the MBA, it was destroyed by fire at the end of the period, probably in the wake of the Hittite attack. In the LBA (14th/13th century BC) it was rebuilt and equipped with relief orthostats before being modified in the 11th century BC, at the beginning of the Iron Age (Kohlmeyer 2008: 121–3; 2009: 194–7). As in previous periods, the LBA temple must have been one of the most prominent religious centers in Syria, proving that the religious importance of Halab persisted despite its political decline.

Ashtata and Karkamish

In the LBA, the area around the bend of the Syrian Middle Euphrates was dominated by two important kingdoms: Karkamish and Ashtata. Karkamish controlled the northern strip of the valley and its importance increased under Hittite hegemony, beginning in the reign of Shuppiluliuma I (c.1350–1320 BC) when the Hittite crown prince was installed as its ruler. His task was to control the Syrian territories in collaboration with another son of the Hittite king installed at Halab (Klengel 1965: 15–101; 1992: 120–8; Wilhelm 1991: 104ff). Because of the important Iron Age architecture which covered the older levels, Woolley's excavations at Karkamish did not yield many remains of the LBA (Hogarth 1914; Woolley 1921; Woolley and Barnett 1952; Hawkins 1976–80b: 435). Elaborate gold and lapis lazuli jewelry dating to the LBA, but discovered in the so-called "gold tomb" of Iron Age date, indirectly illustrates the wealth of the city during the LBA (Woolley and Barnett 1952: 250–7, Pls. 63–64).

A number of cities, such as Murmuriga and Shatuppu, are said in Egyptian and Hittite texts to have been south of Karkamish. In the LBA these must have belonged to the kingdom of Karkamish. Murmuriga has been tentatively identified with Tell Shiyukh Fawqani and Shatuppu with Tell Shuyukh Tahtani (Boese 2009). Both sites are situated only a few kilometers south of Karkamish and excavations at each have revealed LBA occupation (Bachelot 1999: 146–8; Falsone 1998: 35–7; 1999: 139).

The southern part of the big bend of the Syrian Euphrates was the location of Ashtata, which emerged as a regional power in the 15th century BC, especially as a buffer between Mitanni and the Hittites (Klengel 1970: 89ff; Na'aman 1980: 37–40; Adamthwaite 2001: 219–23). It is not known to have been a kingdom, but rather seems to have consisted of several large towns, each with a town council or a council of elders (Sallaberger et al. 2006: 92–3; Otto 2008). Emar was the most prominent center in Ashtata and was politically decentralized, with a powerful council of elders and an institution of limited kingship (Fleming 1992; Adamthwaite 2001: xx–xxi). Excavations at Meskene (ancient Emar) revealed extensive LBA remains, including two temples, a large residence, and so-called "Emar type" houses (Beyer 1982; Margueron 1995; Finkbeiner 2001, 2002; Finkbeiner and Sakal 2003).

To the north, Tell Munbaqa, ancient Ekalte, was another major LBA center in the land of Ashtata. The urban layout of this large city has been traced extensively, with streets, living quarters, and four temples exposed (Machule et al. 1996; Werner and Busch 1998; Mayer 2001; Blocher et al. 2009). A similar insight into urban structure is provided by Tell Bazi, ancient Basiru, further north along the Euphrates, where LBA houses were exposed on a large scale in the lower city and an LBA temple was revealed on the citadel hill (Einwag and Otto 2001–3; Otto 2006b; Otto and Einwag 2007). Two royal Mitanni tablets found at Tell Bazi clearly show that Basiru was under Mitanni rule in the late 15th/early 14th century (Sallaberger et al. 2006). Whether Basiru belonged to the northern territory of Karkamish or the southern country of Ashtata is unclear.

5 Courts and Palaces

LBA palaces were loci of intense political activity and cultural development. They were, furthermore, the focal points of the accumulation of wealth and prestige objects. The economic organization of the LBA kingdoms was based on the palace economy. This consisted of a combination of central redistributive mechanisms, entrepreneurial commercial activities, and reciprocal gift exchange between courts (Pfälzner 2009b). The importance of the palace's redistributive functions should not be overestimated, however. It was not an all-encompassing system, but seems to have been rather limited in extent, with the palace extracting a certain amount of surplus, village-based, agricultural production (Liverani 1974, 1975, 1989; Klengel 1974, 1979b; Heltzer 1979; Schloen 2001; Von Dassow 2008). The restricted nature of the palace economy is demonstrated by the parallel existence of palace-owned and independent villages within these kingdoms and by the fact that the palace could purchase or exchange individual villages (Klengel 1974: 278–80; Liverani 1975: 146–7). Palaces could commission private traders or private craftsmen with an order for production, purchase, or sales. Courts also owned and managed workshops, as demonstrated by the inventory of a palace textile workshop in the Idadda archive at Qatna (Richter in press). These workshops were not necessarily located within the palace compound, but might be located in the city or its environs. The internal organization of the courts seems to have been complex, as illustrated by the Idadda archive, which contains two lists enumerating the considerable possessions of individual members of the court (Richter in press), indicating individual property rights. Thus, a LBA palace can be understood – to use a modern analogy – as a kind of large, differentiated, internationally active enterprise.

The Royal Palace of Qatna is one of the most impressive archaeological examples of a LBA palatial complex (Pfälzner 2007a, 2008a, 2009a). With a total size of 16,000 square meters, it is the largest palace of this period in the Levant. In addition, the building is a clear illustration of strong continuity between the MBA and LBA. Constructed during the MBA IIA period, it remained in continuous use into the LBA IIA period, when it was destroyed c.1340 BC during the Hittite wars in Syria. There were no major changes in the layout of the building over this long time and its plan is typically MBA, with the main, tripartite representative unit consisting of a large courtyard, throne room, and ceremonial hall (*Festsaal*) (Novák and Pfälzner 2000: 260–4; Pfälzner 2007b: 43–51). The courtyard took the form of a square, covered hall (Hall C), with four huge, internal, wooden columns supporting the roof. In its center was a large, circular hearth. This architectural model is the oldest known example of its kind and, thus, probably the Syrian prototype of the four-columned representative hall which became widely diffused over the eastern Mediterranean, especially in the Aegean world (Driessen 1989–90, 1999; Preziosi and Hitchcock 1999: 155–65) in the mid-/late 2nd millennium BC. Measuring 1,300 square meters, it is the largest known roofed space in the Near East of Bronze Age date. The two adjoining rooms are impressive as well, and in size exceed all other contemporary palaces. Although built in the MBA, the palace of Qatna was the most monumental LBA palace in the Levant. Furthermore, it was decorated with wall paintings at the beginning of the LBA (Pfälzner 2008b; Pfälzner and von Rüden 2008a, 2008b; von Rüden 2009, 2011). While only one room contained enough remains to allow the reconstruction of ornamental patterns and landscape scenes with plants and water animals (see below), the other rooms yielded small, individual fragments indicating that most rooms in the palace were colorfully painted.

Also of particular importance is the huge palace well, with a rectangular shaft measuring 9 x 9 meters that was equipped with a winding, monumental staircase of basalt steps (Pfälzner 2007b: 51–5; 2009d). This well is unique in Bronze Age Syria. Moreover, due to the wet soil conditions, large quantities of wooden beams and planks were found in a perfect state of preservation at the bottom of the well. This wood must have belonged to the roof of the well-house and probably to a construction for drawing water (Dohmann-Pfälzner and Pfälzner 2007: 157–63; 2008: 65–71). Most of it was cedar. Cedar beams once probably covered most of the palace rooms and were available in the nearby Lebanon and Syrian coastal mountains in sufficient quantities to abundantly furnish the palace. This precious, high-value timber was also traded to foreign regions (Pfälzner 2009e).

The Royal Palace was surrounded by smaller, official buildings and was not the only palatial structure in LBA Qatna. The so-called Lower City Palace, in use between the 16th and 14th centuries BC, was located in the northern lower city (Luciani 2003; Morandi Bonacossi 2009b). It contains a small representative suite, as well as service, storage, and other rooms in which an administrative cuneiform archive and ivory inlays were found, both hinting at the elite, governmental function of the building. South of the Royal Palace was a smaller, well-constructed residential building comparable in many ways to the larger, official structures (al-Maqdissi 2003: 235–8). Clearly, this cluster of palaces and elite residences formed the political and administrative core of Qatna. The large

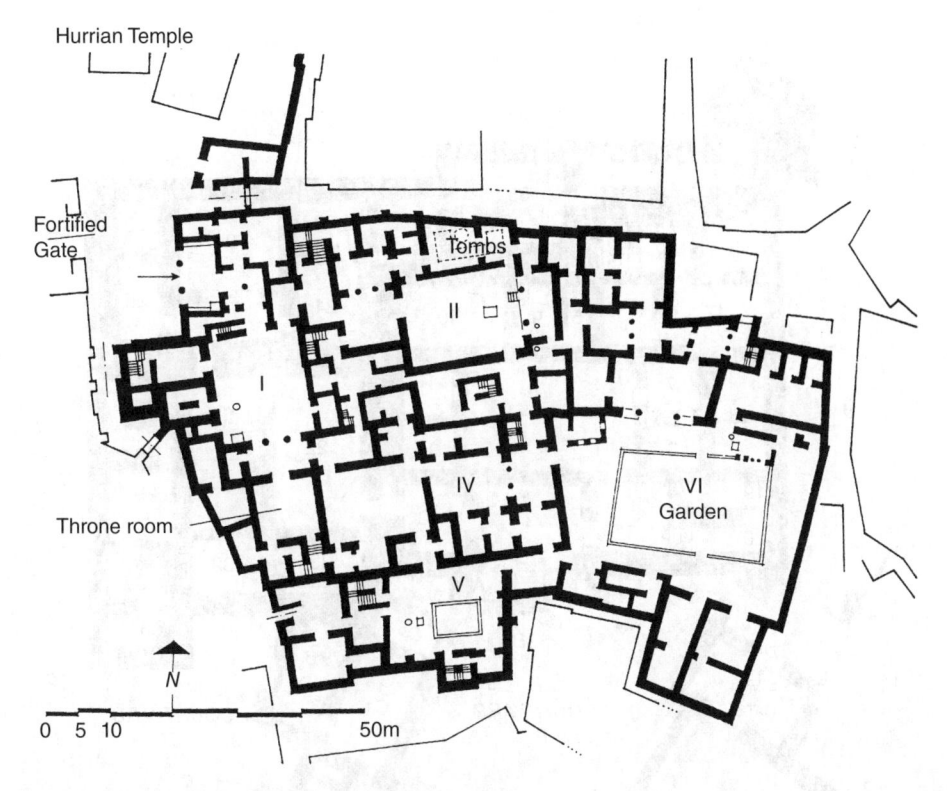

Figure 41.4 Plan of the royal palace at Ugarit.

Eastern Palace, located in the area immediately to the east of the Royal Palace, was, like the Royal Palace, built during the MBA but already abandoned by the LBA (Morandi Bonacossi et al. 2009). This suggests that the administrative core of Qatna had already started to disintegrate in the LBA.

The huge (6,500 square meter) Royal Palace at Ugarit (Figure 41.4; Schaeffer 1962; Yon 2006: 36–45) differs in its architectural layout from that of Qatna. It was not built as a cohesive unit, but consists of several independent parts. This could be explained by the fact that the palace was erected, step-by-step, in an additive process (Schaeffer 1962: 9–15; Yon 2006: 36) or by the fact that parts of it were reconstructed or remodeled at different times (Margueron 2004: 145). The palace consists of six units, four with a central courtyard and two with a central, covered hall. The square throne room is completely unlike the one at Qatna, not only because of its smaller, more intimate size, but also because of its accessibility from a courtyard via a vestibule with two columns in front. The main entrance to the palace took the form of a wide, double-columned vestibule, typical of LBA architecture. Another principal difference between the palaces of Ugarit and Qatna is their relative location: the palace of Ugarit was located close to the western city gate, on one side of the site, whereas the palace at Qatna was

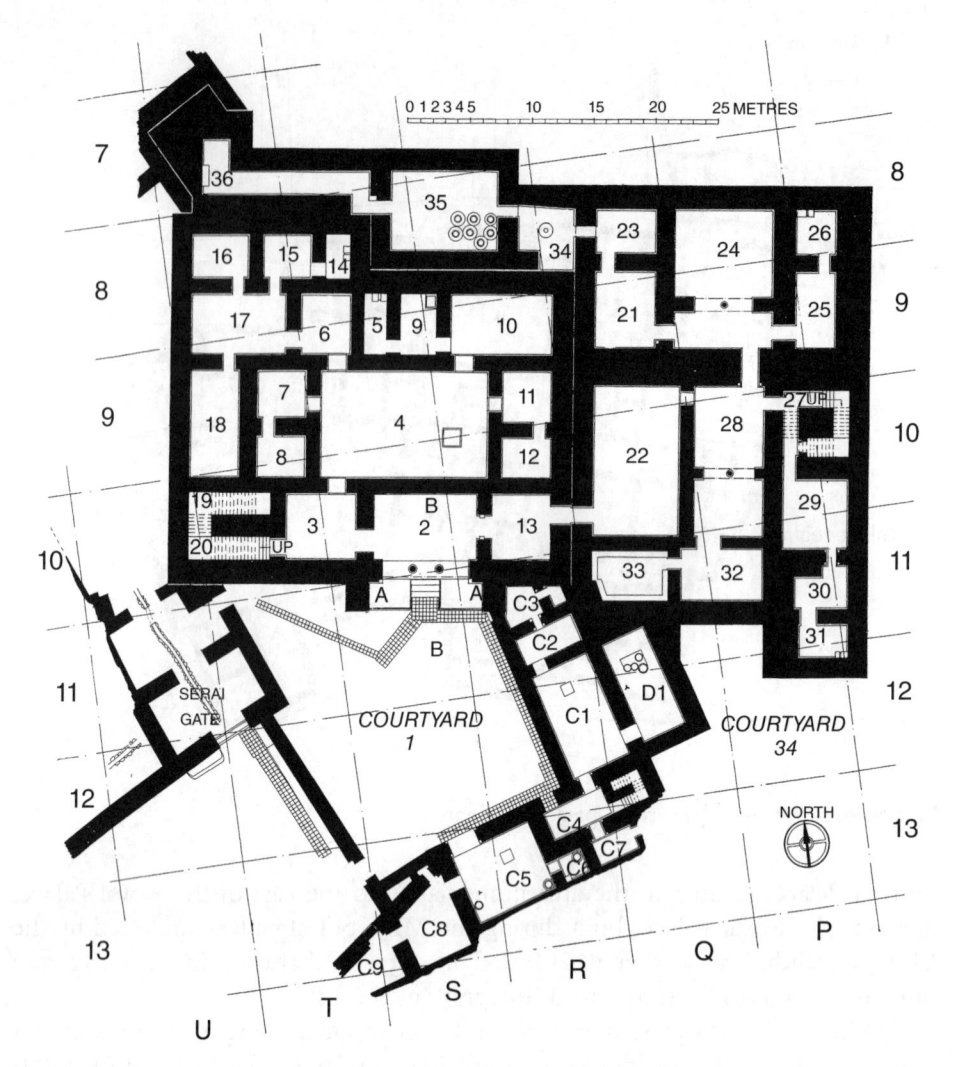

Figure 41.5 Plan of the royal palace of Alalakh, Level IV.

in the center of the city. When the palace of Ugarit was destroyed by fire at the beginning of the 12th century, it contained a very rich inventory, including several archives with thousands of cuneiform tablets. As at Qatna, the palace at Ugarit was surrounded by a series of public buildings, probably used as residences for palace dependents and officials (Margueron 2004). Two palaces with similar structural elements have also been excavated at the coastal site of Ras Ibn Hani, a satellite of Ugarit's (Bounni et al. 1998).

Like the palace at Ugarit, the Level IV palace at Alalakh (Figure 41.5; Woolley 1955b: 110–31) is also located in the periphery of the city, near the northern city gate. Another point of similarity to Ugarit is the double-columned entrance hall of the so-called palace of Niqmepa which was flanked by two smaller rooms giving access to the interior of the building, an arrangement clearly reminiscent of the later Iron-Age *ḫilani*-type of architecture, for which the Alalakh IV palace is often considered a prototype. The official rooms are arranged around a central court or hall, much like a so-called *Mittelsaal*-house ("central hall house"). A second unit, including typically LBA single-columned, double rooms, is attached to the east side of the building, again reminiscent of Ugarit.

The LBA palace at Kamid el-Loz has only been partly exposed (Hachmann 1982; Adler and Penner 2001). It has a long entrance corridor with multiple buttresses giving access to the interior rooms of the building, which surround an irregular courtyard. Regrettably, the central rooms of the palace could not be excavated.

A palace showing Syrian architectural traditions was found as far south as Hazor in northern Palestine. The LBA "Ceremonial Palace" in the center of the Acropolis of Hazor consists of a large throne room wing labeled the "Black Building." This is situated to the west of a spacious central courtyard, and a long-room unit, the "White Building," to the north of the courtyard (Bonfil and Zarzecki-Peleg 2007). The "Black Building" resembles the throne-room unit of the Royal Palace of Ugarit, lending support to the interpretation of this structure as a palace. The function of the "White Building," whether sacral or palatial, is unclear. The layout of the building has no direct parallels in Syrian palatial architecture, but rather resembles the Levantine long-room temple type. Therefore, from a northern Levantine point of view, its identification as a sanctuary seems more likely than as a palace. As such, the Hazor "Ceremonial Palace" may have combined both palatial and religious functions, thus representing an architectural type unknown in the north.

6 Dying in the LBA Kingdoms

The most abundant set of data on mortuary practices in the Levantine Bronze Age comes from the Royal Hypogeum of Qatna discovered in 2002 (Al-Maqdissi et al. 2003; Pfälzner 2002/3, 2005, 2009i, 2011b). This is an impressive architectural complex consisting of a 40 meter long corridor, a 5 meter deep antechamber, and four spacious, rock-hewn grave chambers. The inventory of this tomb complex (Figure 41.6) was perfectly preserved in the state of its last use, shortly before the destruction of the palace c.1340 BC when access to the tomb was blocked suddenly and definitively, so that no looting could take place. The rich inventory of over 2000 individual items is instructive for two reasons. First, it contains an array of luxury objects from jewellery to stone vessels, made of imported materials and executed in various hybrid styles, which offers a vivid picture of the international exchange of art, objects and ideas in the LBA. Second, it enables us to reconstruct in detail the funerary rites practiced in LBA royal

Figure 41.6 The main chamber of the Royal Hypogeum of Qatna.

burials and distributed across different activity areas within the tomb chambers (Pfälzner 2002/2003, 2007b, 2009f, 2011a, in press a).

The primary burial consisted of the anointment, followed by an intentional heating of the corpse to desiccate it. The body was placed on numerous layers of valuable textiles within a wooden burial container inside the tomb. In addition, there is ample evidence of secondary burial inside the tomb chambers. These were accompanied by repetitive *kispu*-rituals intended to feed and tend the dead over time. Decomposed skeletons were re-deposited during these rituals. After this a tertiary burial took place, in which the bones were transferred to a special chamber within the tomb, the ossuary, for final deposition. Eventually, there might even be a quaternary burial, when the bones were taken out of the royal tomb – for space reasons or other concerns – for reburial in a secondary tomb (Pfälzner in press a).

In 2009 a second, unlooted tomb was found below the Royal Palace of Qatna. It contained possibly up to 100 skeletons, deposited in a number of wooden coffins accompanied by a wide range of grave goods (Pfälzner and Dohmann-Pfälzner 2010). This, most probably, can be understood as a subsidiary tomb,

Figure 41.7 Ancestor statues from the Royal Hypogeum of Qatna.

into which royal burials were transferred in order to create space for new burials in the main tomb.

Ancestor worship was important in the LBA Levantine kingdoms. This is amply attested in the Qatna Royal Hypogeum (Pfälzner 2005, 2009g) where the antechamber was specifically used as a place for ancestor veneration. There, two identical basalt ancestor statues (Figure 41.7) stood. These represent sitting kings holding a bowl in one hand (Novák and Pfälzner 2003: 155–62; Pfälzner 2009h). As shown by the discovery of offering bowls at their feet, offerings to the ancestors were made in front of them. The Qatna statues were sculpted in the MBA and still venerated in the LBA. This type of ancestor statue was common from the 2nd to the 1st millennium in the Levant, forming part of a continuous tradition that can be traced from the MBA statues at Ebla (Matthiae 2006) to the Iron Age statues at Tell Halaf (Bonatz 2000a). The most well-known ancestor statue of LBA date is that of Idrimi of Alalakh, dating to the 15th century BC (Smith 1949; Fink 2007). It is not only characterized by the conventional sitting position and the typical style of Middle Syrian sculpture, but also by the accompanying inscription that demanded the veneration of the image of Idrimi as part of the royal ancestor cult at Alalakh.

Many tombs have been discovered at Ugarit, both in the Royal Palace and in private houses (Salles 1995; Marchegay 2008), presenting ample evidence of the treatment of the dead there. Despite the fact that the royal tombs of Ugarit, which were situated in a special funerary unit of the Royal Palace, were completely looted in antiquity, some interesting hints regarding royal burial can be gleaned from architectural observations (Niehr 2006b). The royal ancestor cult of Ugarit was probably located in the funerary unit of the palace. Funerary rituals and royal ancestor veneration at Ugarit can be reconstructed from tombs, texts (Cornelius and Niehr 2004: 79–86; Niehr 2006a, 2006b), and stelae relating to funerary banquets held close to the temples (Lange in press).

At Kamid el-Loz, the remains of a royal burial were found in a semi-subterranean room complex of the LBA palace (Miron 1990; Adler 1994; Hachmann 1996) that contained a rich inventory of imported calcite-alabaster vessels, jewelry, ivory, and metal objects, much like those found in the Royal Hypogeum at Qatna and also dating to the 14th century BC. This suggests that funerary rituals at both sites were similar.

7 The Topography of Cult in LBA Levantine Kingdoms

One of the most important sanctuaries in Syria was the Temple of the Storm God on the citadel of Aleppo (Durand 2002). When this temple was found in 1996 and subsequently excavated, it was possible to demonstrate archaeologically that it was built during the MBA, above an Early Bronze Age predecessor, and remained in use throughout the LBA and into the Iron Age. The huge (c.27 × 17 meter) MBA temple building is a "broad-room-type" cella which was accessed via an entrance chamber with two side rooms. After its destruction by fire, the temple was restored during the Hittite period when the ground plan was principally left unchanged, but orthostat reliefs, featuring false windows, bull-men, and composite animals, were added. These included a large relief of the storm god erected on the side wall. This probably indicates a change to a bent-axis type of cella, reflecting a typically Hittite religious principle. The entrance was formed by a portal guarded by basalt statues of a sphinx and a lion and the relief of a fish-man in Babylonian tradition. The temple decoration clearly shows a blend of local Syrian, Hittite, and Mesopotamian styles and cultural concepts (Kohlmeyer 2009: 194–6).

The main decorations of the temple of Ain Dara, in the Afrin valley to the northwest of Aleppo, date to the Early Iron Age, but some of the sculptures seem to go back to the LBA as well (Abu Assaf 1990). Thus, the sphinxes at the entrance clearly resemble those at Aleppo and can be attributed to the Hittite period of the 13th century BC (Kohlmeyer 2008).

A sequence of LBA temples was excavated at Alalakh in Levels V–I. These are located in close proximity to the palace with which they seem to have been functionally connected. Perpetuating the royal ancestor cult, attested by the statue of Idrimi (see above) that stood in a side chamber of the temple of Level I (Fink 2007), was at least one function of these temples. The ground plan is similar to that of the temple of Aleppo which, given its religious importance, must have been an influential archetype for Syrian sacral architecture. The Level IV temple consisted of a "broad-room" cella with a similarly shaped antechamber. The Level I temple is even closer to the Aleppo archetype. It contains a "broad-room" cella in front of which were an entrance chamber and two smaller, lateral rooms. The extremely wide rear wall of the cella is also comparable to the Alalakh Level I and Aleppo temples.

A different type of temple, said to have been devoted to Baal and Astarte (Margueron 1982; Faist and Finkbeiner 2002; Finkbeiner 2001: 46–51; 2002: 110–15; Finkbeiner and Sakal 2003: 12–17), is attested at Emar. Situated next to each other and, as with most temples in the Levant, at the highest point of the city is a pair of temples *in antis* (a temple longer than it was broad, with a front, columned porch), which contains a "long-room" cella. These were accessible via a long flight of stairs. In the lower town of Emar was a third *antis*-type temple (Temple M2) (Margueron 1982).

The temples of Munbaqa differ from those at Emar, both in their larger dimensions and their massive stone substructures, for which they have been called "Steinbauten" (literally, stone-buildings). Four stone-buildings (I–IV) can be distinguished (Werner 1994: 102–6; Werner and Busch 1998), all of which belong to the *antis*-type. Three were built in a row on the highest point of the city. The fourth (Steinbau IV), discovered more recently (Blocher et al. 2007, 2009), is situated in the lower part of the inner city. The combination of temples that were exposed (I–III) and embedded (IV) in the city is similar to Emar.

A peculiar type of religious building is represented by Temple 1 on the citadel of Tell Bazi, located further north in the Syrian Euphrates valley. This is a monumental, two-room temple with a square, stone-paved, antechamber (Room A) and a larger, rectangular cella of the long-room type (Room B). The temple was entered through a door in the long wall giving access to Room A and from there, at right angles, to the larger Room B. The plan differs in layout from both the *antis*-type of the Middle Euphrates region and the broad-room-type of northwestern Syria. This might be explained by its possible additional use as a meeting place for the "council of elders" of Basiru, as suggested by two cuneiform texts found in Room A (Otto and Einwag 2005; Otto 2008: 722–4).

The temples of Baal and Dagan (or more probably El; see Cornelius and Niehr 2004: 63ff) at Ugarit are located on the highest point of the Acropolis. They are oriented parallel to each other and overlook the city, as is typical in the Levant. Both have a peculiar plan, consisting of a square antechamber in the front of a broad-room cella (Yon 1997; 2006: 106–15). As the antechamber is narrower than the cella, the temples appear T-shaped. The main parts to have survived are the massive foundations, suggesting that the buildings might have been very tall or even tower-like.

Another LBA temple on the Syrian coast was excavated at Tell Kazel. Located in the western half of the flat *tell*, it was embedded in a dense cluster of domestic buildings. The temple is a single-room building with a long-room cella and two internal columns (Level 6). It was later (Level 5) replaced by a larger, long-room-cella temple with an *adyton* (an inaccessible area restricted to the priests) in the rear (Badre 2006). The LBA temple area of Kamid el-Loz consists of two adjacent sanctuaries. These differ in layout from other known, northern Levantine temples, as they center on an open courtyard with cultic installations and a series of rooms surrounding it (Metzger 1991, 1993). The reconstruction of an open courtyard in the two sanctuaries, however, is not entirely convincing and it is possible that these large areas were roofed.

At Qatna, the only sanctuary identified to date is the shrine of the palace goddess Belet-Ekallim in the Royal Palace. Adjoining the audience Hall C is a tiny (c.4 × 1 meter) chamber (Room P). It has a larger rectangular area in front of it, which lies within the huge Hall C and is offset from the rest of Hall C by a wooden threshold in the floor (Novák and Pfälzner 2001: 168ff; 2002a: 214–17; Pfälzner 2007b: 45). Here, most probably, the cult image and the treasury of the palace goddess were kept, as indicated by the Belet-Ekallim inventory tablets found in this room (Fales 2004b).

At Hazor, in northern Palestine, is a LBA temple of the long-room type, very similar to contemporary northern Levantine temples such as those at Tell Kazel and on the Syrian Euphrates. The temple is situated immediately to the north of the so-called "Ceremonial palace" on top of the Acropolis of Hazor (Bonfil and Zarzecki-Peleg 2007). Located only a short distance to the south is the so-called "White Building," which is part of the "Ceremonial palace complex." It has a similar ground plan as the aforementioned temple, and therefore could possibly also be interpreted as a temple structure. This contradicts existing assumptions that the "White Building" might have had palatial functions (see above).

8 Exchange and Interregional Contacts in the LBA Levant

The LBA was a time of intensive trade and international exchange. Economic exchange was accompanied by cultural exchange and communication. Hence, the LBA has often been described as an "International Age." The harbors along the Levantine coast, real "ports of trade" in Karl Polanyi's (1971a) sense, were the nodal points of international exchange. Minet el-Beidha, ancient Mahadu, the harbor of Ugarit, is one of the most prominent examples (Yon 2006: 8–10). This is a rounded, perfectly protected natural bay, which served as the import–export hub of Ugarit, connecting the eastern Mediterranean with the Levantine hinterland. Very limited excavations around the harbor have yielded parts of a storage structure filled with "Canaanite jars," typical LBA storage and transport vessels (Killebrew 2007). Further excavations at Minet el-Beidha would have the potential to add invaluable information to our knowledge of international exchange. However, because of a modern military presence, the site is currently inaccessible. Favorable harbors also existed at Byblos and on the island of Arwad, but, because of modern housing, excavations are practically impossible at these sites too.

There has been a long-standing debate concerning the organizational nature of LBA trade. Polanyi (1957, 1975) was convinced that trade – e.g., at Ugarit and other Near Eastern trade centers – was conducted exclusively by palace agents and was not profit-oriented but followed fixed rules and agreements between elites. Our knowledge base has improved since his day and this thesis needs to be modified. LBA exchange was a complex system of various interrelated economic principles, comprising reciprocity, redistribution, and the free market system (Polanyi 1971b, 1971c, 1971d). Reciprocity was an essential principle of LBA exchange, as demonstrated by the intensive practice of gift exchange between courts and elites which not only sustained and strengthened sociopolitical relations, but was also a significant factor of economic exchange (Liverani 1990; Zaccagnini 1987; Cochavi-Rainey 1999; Pfälzner 2007a). Market principles were another important aspect of LBA trade. This is shown by the often independent position of individual merchants, their concern for profit, and their tendency to combine private and official business ventures (Heltzer 1978; Silver 1983). In addition, the redistributive principle functioned at the level of internal exchange within the Levantine kingdoms, when a surplus of agricultural products was obtained, stored, and administered by the palace (Schloen 2001: 221–54). This, however, did not encompass the totality of the economy of Levantine kingdoms, but left room for independent economic activities by villages, farmers, and landlords (Klengel 1974, 1979b; Liverani 1974, 1975, 1989). Thus, the three major principles of economic exchange did not operate independently of each other in different historical periods, as assumed by Polanyi, but coexisted within the complex economic systems of the Levantine kingdoms.

An important element of the LBA economy was long-distance trade by specialized merchants (Renfrew 1972: 455–71; Sherratt and Sherratt 1991). The best illustration of this is afforded by the Uluburun shipwreck. This vessel sank in the late 14th century BC off the coast of southwestern Turkey. It must have come from the Levantine coast, possibly even Ugarit, laden with goods destined for the Aegean regions or even the Mycenaean heartland (Yalçin et al. 2005). These include ox-hide-shaped copper ingots, tin ingots, glass ingots, pieces of ebony, an elephant tusk and hippopotamus tusks, Cypriote, Mycenaean and other pottery, faience beads, amber beads, a bronze weight, and individual luxury items, such as gold vessels, gold and silver jewelry, an ivory box, a bronze and gold figurine, seals, and amulets (Pulak 2005). This extraordinary discovery presents a kaleidoscopic collection of LBA international trade goods.

Long-distance exchange is typified by the variety of raw materials involved. One very precious import was lapis lazuli from the northeastern Afghan mountains of Badakhshan. It was mainly used for jewelry, often in combination with carnelian, as illustrated by a large gold rosette from the Royal Tomb of Qatna which was richly inlaid with both stones (Pfälzner 2008c; Rossberger 2009). It was also used to make cylinder seals (Dohmann-Pfälzner and Pfälzner 2009; Pfälzner and Dohmann-Pfälzner 2011).

Another material that traveled huge distances in the LBA was amber. Originating in the Baltic region, it arrived in Mycenaean Greece and from there was traded to the Levant. The largest and most spectacular amber object discovered in the Near East is the lion head vessel (Figure 41.8) from the Royal Hypogeum of Qatna (Mukherjee et al. 2008). Made of a large piece of Baltic amber, it was carved by skilled Levantine craftsmen into a fine and detailed lion head somewhere in LBA Syria, probably at Qatna itself (Al-Maqdissi et al. 2003: 211–13; Pfälzner and Rossberger 2009).

Close contacts with Cyprus are evident in the quantities of Cypriote pottery in the Levant, such as white ware I and II, white shaved and base ring wares (Yon 2001; Bergoffen 2003). Exchange with the Aegean world is also attested

Figure 41.8 Amber lion's head from the Royal Hypogeum of Qatna.

by imported Minoan and Mycenaean pottery, found in large quantities at Byblos, Ugarit, and Tell Kazel (Yon et al. 2000; Van Wijngaarden 2002; Badre 2006), and even as far inland as Qatna (Du Mesnil du Buisson 1928: 13, 21, Pls. XVII.3, XVIII). In addition, Aegean influence is clear in palace wall paintings, such as those found at Alalakh Level VII during the late MBA and at Tell Kabri and Qatna during the LBA (Niemeier 1991; Niemeier and Niemeier 1998, 2000; Bietak 2007; Feldman 2007). The wall paintings of the Royal Palace of Qatna display typical Minoan motifs, such as palm trees, river landscapes, spiral bands, and a dolphin. In addition, typical Aegean colors and techniques, such as fresco, were used (Pfälzner 2008b; Pfälzner and von Rüden 2008a, 2008b; von Rüden 2009, 2011) and it is possible that, in collaboration with local Syrian craftsmen, Aegean artists were involved in the execution of the wall paintings at Qatna. A "craftsmanship interaction model" has been proposed to explain the hybrid Aegean-Syrian style and technique of the Qatna wall paintings (Pfälzner 2008: 106–9). The exchange of artists between different parts of the Levant, Anatolia, and Mesopotamia is well known, especially during the LBA (Zaccagnini 1983; Bonatz 2002), and can be understood as another dimension of the "reciprocal" exchange of goods, persons, and ideas between courts.

Exchange between the Levant and Egypt is attested by imported Egyptian calcite alabaster, granite, and serpentine vessels – e.g. at Ugarit, Kamid el-Loz, and Qatna (Caubet 1991; Miron 1990: 91–7; Ahrens 2009, 2011). Some of these bear Egyptian inscriptions, clearly indicating their place of origin. One such example is the fine calcite alabaster vessel with an inscription of the queen mother Ahmes Nefertari of the early 18th dynasty (c.1550 BC) found in the Qatna Royal Tomb (Ahrens 2007). Other calcite vessels might have been produced in the Levant in Egyptian style, a reflection of the high esteem in which exotic stone vessels were held throughout the Levant. They were particularly popular as grave goods in the Levant, and no fewer than 56 Egyptian and Egyptianizing stone vessels were found in the Qatna Royal Hypogeum.

The main vehicle for the exchange of such luxurious objects might have been gift exchange between male and female court members in different kingdoms and regions, as clearly shown in the Amarna letters. The constant reciprocal flow of goods resulted in the evolution of an international art style, in which motifs and styles from different cultural spheres were combined (Caubet 1998; Feldman 2006). Feldman (2006) has argued that this international style was intentionally created in order to craft luxury items for interregional gift exchange which could not be traced to a specific region, but were recognizable as belonging to an artistic *koiné* encompassing the entire eastern Mediterranean and the western Near East. In constrast to this view, however, it must be said that of all known objects of international exchange found in Egypt, the Mediterranean, the Levant, or Mesopotamia, there is hardly a single piece which does not bear the stylistic traits that are characteristic of a specific region or cultural sphere. Rather, one can isolate "hybrid regional styles" in the Levant and beyond, into which "international motifs" were adopted, but rendered in a specific stylistic manner characteristic of their region of origin (Pfälzner in press b). They would thus have gained even more value within the international exchange of gifts and goods.

GUIDE TO FURTHER READING

For an introduction to the political history of the LBA kingdoms, see Klengel (1965, 1969, 1970, 1992). International politics and interregional exchange of art in the Late Bronze Age are well described in Liverani (1990) and Feldman (2006). For the economic system of LBA kingdoms, the reader is referred to Schloen (2001) and Von Dassow (2008). For the recent excavations at Qatna, see Pfälzner (2008a) and Al-Maqdissi et al. (2009).

CHAPTER FORTY-TWO

Neo-Hittite and Phrygian Kingdoms of North Syria and Anatolia

Ann C. Gunter

1 Introduction

During the Late Bronze Age (LBA, c.1400–1200 BC), central and southeastern Anatolia and northern Syria belonged to the Hittite Empire, ruled by a dynasty at the capital city of Hattusha (modern Boğazköy) in north-central Turkey. This multiethnic, multilingual state consisted of the Hittite heartland, provinces administered by governors and vassal kingdoms bound in loyalty to the king of Hatti. Its inhabitants, who included speakers of Hittite (Nesite), Luwian, Hattian, and Hurrian, shared many elements of material culture, perhaps most visibly in the remarkably homogeneous ceramic repertoire now attested from west-central to southeastern Anatolia (Gates 2001: 137–8, 141; Gunter 2006; Postgate 2007: 144–5).

Following the dissolution of the Hittite Empire shortly after 1200 BC, a new political and social landscape obtained in the Anatolian and North Syrian domains formerly under its hegemony. With the empire's demise, provinces and kingdoms dissolved into smaller sociopolitical units and new population groups entered northern Syria and perhaps also west-central and southeastern Turkey. Across the southeastern reaches of the former Hittite Empire emerged smaller kingdoms or city-states today designated "Neo-Hittite" (also Late Hittite, Syro-Hittite, and Luwian-Aramaean) because they preserve Hittite features: in their monumental stone architecture and accompanying sculptural decoration, sometimes in their rulers' names, and above all in their inscriptions written in the language and

---

A Companion to the Archaeology of the Ancient Near East, First Edition.
Edited by D.T. Potts.
© 2012 Blackwell Publishing Ltd. Published 2012 by Blackwell Publishing Ltd.

hieroglyphic script of Anatolia known as Hieroglyphic Luwian (Ch. II.38). These states coexisted with new polities established by large numbers of Aramaeans, beginning c.1100 BC, in the formerly Hittite upper Euphrates region (Lipiński 2000: 45–50, 77–407; Sader 2000; Akkermans and Schwartz 2003: 367–8). In their inscriptions, the rulers of these Aramaean states employed a variant of Northwest Semitic (Aramaic, Phoenician), written in an alphabetic script borrowed from the Phoenicians of the eastern Mediterranean coast. Beginning in the 9th century, Assyrians increasingly moved into the area from their rapidly expanding empire to the east, creating new pressures on local kingdoms and exploiting rivalry among them. Through conquest or accommodation, the Neo-Hittite states were gradually absorbed into the Neo-Assyrian Empire as client kingdoms or provinces by about 700 BC. Written records from the Neo-Hittite kingdoms themselves consist almost exclusively of commemorative inscriptions carved in stone, most of which celebrate building activities and other royal accomplishments (Hawkins 2000: 19–22; 2003: 147–51). Assyrian cuneiform sources, chiefly accounts of military campaigns carried out against their neighbors to the west by Tiglath-pileser I (1114–1076 BC) and later kings (9th century BC onward) provide additional information on local political and economic circumstances as well as providing correlations with Mesopotamian absolute chronologies (Hawkins 2000; Collins 2007: 82–5; Giusfredi 2010: 35–63).

In west-central Anatolia, on or beyond the Hittite empire's western frontier, a Phrygian state emerged in the 10th and 9th centuries BC with its chief urban center at Gordion (modern Yassıhöyük), southwest of Ankara. According to Herodotus (*Hist.* 7.73) and Strabo (*Geog.* 14.5.29), the Phrygians migrated to central Anatolia from their homeland in the Balkan region of Thrace during or after the widespread disruptions of the early 12th century BC. Inscriptions on stone, metalwork, and ceramics document their language, which was Indo-European and closely related to Greek (Brixhe and Lejeune 1984; Brixhe 2002, 2004a). Phrygian was written in an alphabetic script, perhaps adopted through contact with Phoenicians in the Cilician Plain (Brixhe 1991, 2004b; Mellink 1998). In the 7th and early 6th centuries BC, Phrygia seems to have come under the domination of Lydia, a kingdom in far western Anatolia centered on Sardis (Ch. II.48). The Achaemenid Persian conquest of Anatolia in the mid-6th century BC brought an end to the Phrygian kingdom and other independent states in central Anatolia. Written sources for the Phrygians are comparatively few, consisting chiefly of votive inscriptions on rock-cut monuments and small objects, along with graffiti on ceramic and metal vessels. Texts are short, often consisting of only a few words or a personal name (Brixhe and Lejeune 1984; Roller 1987). As a result, we rely heavily on archaeological evidence to assist in reconstructing historical developments.

Biblical, Assyriological, and Classical frameworks have shaped modern interest in and exploration of the Neo-Hittite and Phrygian states. Modern scholarly investigation began in the late 19th century when these regions formed part of the Ottoman Empire, and was prompted by interest in the Hittites mentioned in the Bible and in newly deciphered texts from Mesopotamia and Egypt. The recovery of inscribed monuments in southeastern Anatolia and northern Syria preceded excavations begun in 1906 in the extensive ruins of Boğazköy, northeast of Ankara (Collins 2007: 1–20). Exploration of the western Anatolian plateau, the Phrygian heartland, began around 1900 with excavations at Gordion, followed by exploration at Midas City and other monuments in the Phrygian highlands near modern Eskişehir and Afyon (Körte and Körte 1904; Haspels 1971; Berndt 2002; Sams 2005; Berndt-Ersöz 2006: xxii–xxiv). Gordion's Classical past, both legendary and historical, initially guided the modern investigation of Phrygia and emphasized its ties to western Anatolia and the Greeks, among whom a memory of the Phrygians survived in the legend of King Midas and his fabulous wealth (Roller 1983). Farther east, within the former Hittite heartland, Phrygian-related material culture came to light chiefly as a by-product of research into the region's Bronze Age past. At sites such as Boğazköy, Alaca Höyük, and Alişar Höyük, Iron Age levels with Phrygian affiliations overlay cultural deposits of the Hittite Empire. Over the past few decades, exploration of Iron Age occupation in the central and west-central plateau has continued at well-established centers such as Boğazköy and Gordion, but has also expanded to many new sites, including Kaman-Kalehöyük and Kerkenes Dağ. Encouraged by a Classical framework that regarded the Phrygians as new arrivals from southeastern Europe, traditional reconstructions of Iron Age developments in both central and west-central Anatolia have emphasized the role of migrations and invasions. Current perspectives acknowledge significant continuity with LBA and even earlier traditions, and recognize greater interaction between central Anatolia and regions to the east and southeast, including the Neo-Hittite states.

Archaeological investigations of these Iron Age kingdoms, which initially targeted monumental buildings, inscriptions, and sculptures at select urban centers, have increasingly encompassed broader surveys in recent decades as well as the elaboration of ceramic sequences and the reconstruction of local and regional economies. Advances in philology and paleography, along with radiocarbon dating and dendrochronology, have contributed significantly to tighter chronological control. Key areas of ongoing research include the formation or regeneration of polities and complex society following the end of the LBA empires, the development of new urban centers and associated expressions of political and social identity, and the elaboration of regional diversity.

2 The Transition from Late Bronze to Early Iron Age: Continuity, Change, and Revival

Recent discoveries of inscriptions and the reinvestigation of long-familiar monuments and sites have shed dramatic new light on the last period of Hittite imperial rule, a period of crucial significance for understanding subsequent Iron Age developments. As central authority in the Hittite heartland declined, the appanage kingdoms of Karkamish (in the southeast) and Tarhuntassa (in the south) gained in importance, positioning these regions to withstand the demise of control from the imperial center.

A trading center probably from the mid-3rd millennium BC onward, Karkamish acquired new prominence following the Hittite conquest of Syria and the capture of the city shortly after 1350 BC. Instead of delegating provincial administration to a local vassal ruler, the Hittite king Shuppiluliuma I established a kingdom at Karkamish and installed his son in the new office. Another son was appointed king of Aleppo, inaugurating a dynasty that administered this major center for the worship of the storm god. But, as the archives of Ugarit (Ras Shamra) and Emar (Tell Meskene) show (Hawkins 2000: 388; Bryce 2005: 187–8), the kings of Karkamish effectively governed as Hittite viceroys in Syria. This no doubt reflects the city's strategic significance from both a commercial and a security point of view. The dynasty at Karkamish lasted for at least five generations and survived the empire's dissolution, adopting the title "Great King" and founding at least one vice-kingdom at Melid (Malatya). Two kings of Malatya claimed descent from the king of Karkamish (Hawkins 1988; 2000: 73, 282–3). Throughout southeastern Anatolia and northern Syria, the subsequent success of appealing to the authority and legitimacy of the imperial Hittite past surely rested in large measure on the model and pan-regional importance of Karkamish.

South of the Hittite heartland, recent epigraphical discoveries substantiate Tarhuntassa's increased importance following the appointment of Kuruntiya as a ruler with privileges similar to those of the Karkamish viceroys. When and under what circumstances Kuruntiya claimed the title "Great King," as in his inscription at Hatip near Konya, is unclear (Singer 2000; van den Hout 2001; Bryce 2007). The kingdom features prominently in the latest inscriptions from the Hittite capital, in which Shuppiluliuma II declared the conquest and annexation of Tarhuntassa (Hawkins 1995: 61–3; cf. Melchert 2002). A trio of inscriptions composed by a "Great King" Hartapu, son of the "Great King" Murshili, at Kizildağ and Karadağ in the Konya Plain and at Burunkaya near Aksaray, attest to a dynasty that assumed the royal titles soon after the empire's dissolution and formed a kind of successor state to Tarhuntassa in the southeastern plateau (Hawkins 2000: 429, 433–42; 2002: 148; Bryce 2003: 93–7). While the date and dynastic affiliations of these rulers and the extent of their domains remain under debate, many scholars believe that an organized polity claiming descent from imperial predecessors emerged in the southeastern Anatolian plateau – the region of the later kingdom of Tabal – soon after the fall of Hattusha.

The decline of unified power in north-central Anatolia must have also allowed or encouraged the mobility of peoples along the frontiers. Within the bend of the Kizilirmak (modern Red river, classical Halys), in the Hittite heartland, new evidence for the Early Iron Age has emerged from recent excavations at Boğazköy. Soon after the capital's abandonment and partial destruction, settlers using ceramics altogether different in manufacture and decoration, hand-made and now often painted or incised, occupied the area of the site known as Büyükkale (Genz 2004). Some of the ceramics exhibit similarities with much earlier ceramic traditions attested in central Anatolia in the Early and Middle Bronze Ages, and may suggest their continued production outside the standardized, mass-produced (and possibly centralized) Hittite ceramic industry (Genz 2005). The new arrivals may have included the Kashka, northern neighbors of the Hittites who had periodically threatened the capital and at this time moved into the interior of the plateau and the former capital.

At Gordion (Yassihöyük), near the empire's western frontier, recent stratigraphic soundings have provided new information on the LBA–Early Iron Age transition. The LBA settlement (YHSS 8), whose ceramics, metalwork, and sealings with Hieroglyphic Luwian legends confirm its generally Hittite character, was abandoned without destruction around 1100 BC. New houses were soon built above (and partly into) its ruins, documenting two phases of Early Iron Age settlement (7B and 7A, c.1100–950 BC). Both architecture and ceramics differed significantly from those of Gordion's LBA occupation. On the floors of the Phase 7B houses were hand-made, low-fired ceramic vessels, unevenly formed and suggesting household production; in the subsequent Phase 7A, a buff ware assemblage quite distinct both technically and typologically from the hand-made ware appeared alongside it. The later, wheel-made gray wares that characterize the Early Phrygian ceramic assemblage at Gordion appear to have developed directly out of the Early Iron Age buff ware tradition, suggesting that the Early Iron Age settlers should be identified as Phrygians. Gordion's excavators recognized similarities between the Early Iron Age hand-made ware and possibly related traditions from northwestern Anatolia and even farther afield in southeastern Europe (Sams 1994: 19–29; Henrickson and Voigt 1998; Voigt and Henrickson 2000a: 332–56, 2000b: 40–6). Such a link with the material culture of southeastern Europe would seem to bolster or confirm the opinion of classical authors that the Phrygians migrated to central Anatolia from Thrace. Other scholars find the parallels between the ceramics of these regions too general to support such inferences (Genz 2003: 185–6; Tsetskhladze 2007: 289–95). As noted above, hand-made pottery likewise representing a major break with Hittite ceramics and suggestive of household-level production has also been recovered in the Early Iron Age settlement at Boğazköy, where it is plausibly interpreted as a continuation of much older ceramic traditions in central Anatolia. Whenever the Phrygians arrived and whatever their geographical source, however, newcomers apparently did not altogether replace the local inhabitants. Gordion's population in later Phrygian times must have included survivals from the LBA, as indicated by continuity in some of the marks incised on ceramic vessels, for example (Roller 1987: 1, 71–3).

At some Cilician sites (including Kilise Tepe, Tarsus, and Soli Höyük) Hittite or "sub-Hittite" (post-imperial) levels were followed by a reoccupation, or a new occupation, that introduced Mycenaean/Late Helladic IIIC-style pottery in considerable quantities (Yağci 2003; Mountjoy 2005; Ünlü 2005; Postgate and Thomas 2007: 148–9, 373–8; Postgate 2008: 170–1). By contrast, at Tell Tayinat near Alalakh (Tell Atchana) in the Amuq plain, an occupation containing an assemblage with Aegean-style traits represents a new foundation, established on a mound abandoned since the Early Bronze Age (Harrison 2009b: 180–3; 2010: 87–90). Locally made Aegean-style pottery, Aegean (or Cypriot)-style cooking ware, and spool-shaped loom weights at these sites have been associated with the movements of the Philistines as part of widespread migrations from the Aegean to the Levant at the end of the LBA, via a southern coastal or perhaps an inland route through the Taurus mountains north of Cilicia.

New epigraphic finds have contributed to these discussions. In a bilingual, Phoenician-Hieroglyphic Luwian inscription carved on the base of a colossal statue found at Çineköy near Adana, Warika (Awariku), king of Adana, styles himself grandson of Muksas, king of Hiyawa, the Neo-Hittite state known in Assyrian sources as Que. Scholars have connected the name Hiyawa with Ahhiyawa, a state generally located in southwestern Anatolia that is attested in Hittite sources and associated with the Mycenaean Greeks. Muksas has been identified with Mopsos, the legendary seer from Colophon, credited in Classical and later sources with founding cities in Lycia, Pamphylia, and Cilicia (Tekoğlu and Lemaire 2000; Jasink and Marino 2007: 407–15; Hawkins 2009: 165–6). Another recent find is a relief inscribed in Hieroglyphic Luwian from the Temple of the Storm God at Aleppo (c.1100–1000 BC), which records a dedication by Taita, king of Palistin (Walistin) – i.e. Philistia (Palestine) (Hawkins 2009: 169–72; Kohlmeyer 2009: 194–200). Previously known from inscriptions found near Hama in northern Syria, Taita seems to have ruled a kingdom extending from the coast to Aleppo, with its capital perhaps at Tell Tayinat (later probably Kunulua, capital of Unqi). Together, these sources seem to support the hypothesis that in the 12th century newcomers from the Aegean (perhaps specifically the west Anatolian coast) settled in Cilicia, the Amuq region, and northern Syria, coexisting with local communities that continued many of their older traditions (Yasur-Landau 2010: 154–63, 186–93). Yet not all sites in this region have yielded comparable quantities of Aegean-style material culture, and individual site histories demonstrate regional complexity. At Kinet Höyük in eastern Cilicia, for example, a "sub-Hittite" period of occupation was followed in the 12th century BC by a settlement of newcomers, perhaps from inland Syria. Here, altered subsistence strategies favoring herding accompanied marked changes in settlement layout and the introduction of previously unattested ceramic features, including hand-made vessels and painted decoration (Ikram 2003; Gates 2010: 70–1; in press).

3 The Neo-Hittite Kingdoms

The Neo-Hittite kingdoms lay in a region extending from the southeastern Anatolian plateau across the Taurus mountains and eastwards to the Euphrates river and northern Syria. South of the Kizilirmak, on the plateau's southeastern edge, were a number of city-states collectively known to the Assyrians as Tabal. Assyrian sources demonstrate that in the 9th century Tabal's kings numbered more than 20; by the end of the 8th century the region comprised the two kingdoms of Tabal in the north (encompassing modern Kululu and Sultanhan) and Tuwana/Tyana in the south (in the vicinity of Niğde, Kemerhisar, and Bor). Although the Iron Age remains of this region have not been extensively explored archaeologically, a number of isolated inscribed monuments and rock reliefs have been recorded (Hawkins 2000: 425–33). Excavations begun in 1969 at Porsuk (Zeyve Höyük), south of Niğde, have uncovered Iron Age deposits (Dupré 1983; Crespin 1999; Beyer 2008). Across the Taurus mountains, in Hilakku (Rough Cilicia) and Que (the Cilician Plain) along the Mediterranean coast, was a similarly fragmented group of polities. At remote Azatiwataya (modern Karatepe), northeast of Adana, a lengthy bilingual Phoenician-Hieroglyphic Luwian inscription of the late 8th or early 7th century was discovered in 1946, providing the key to the decipherment of Hieroglyphic Luwian. Its citadel gate and reliefs have been extensively investigated for their subjects, date and style (Çambel 1999; Hawkins 2000: 40–1, 44–70; Çambel and Özyar 2003).

The most important of the Neo-Hittite kingdoms was Karkamish, located on the west bank of the Euphrates river at a key crossing-point, at what is now the border between Turkey and Syria. Among the first of the Neo-Hittite sites to be investigated archaeologically, its Iron Age buildings and inscribed monuments were uncovered and recorded between 1911 and 1914 (Hawkins 2000: 74, with bibliog.). A short distance to the south, on the river's opposite bank, lay Masuwari, also know as Til Barsip (modern Tell Ahmar), where excavations have yielded significant remains of architecture and sculpture (Bunnens 1990, 2006; Hawkins 2000: 224–6). On the upper Euphrates, north of the Amanus mountains, a kingdom developed around Melid (modern Malatya), whose Iron Age remains were explored at Arslantepe in the 1930s (Delaporte 1940). South of Melid lay Kummuh (classical Commagene), a region illuminated archaeologically through salvage excavations at Tille Höyük (Blaylock 1999, 2009) and Lidar Höyük (Müller 1999a, 1999b, 2003, 2005). West of Kummuh was Gurgum, with its capital at Marqas (modern Kahramanmaraş), where recent surveys have contributed substantially to understanding its Late Bronze and Iron Age history and material culture (Dodd 2003, 2005a, 2007). Sam'al (modern Zincirli), located west of Karkamish and east of the Amanus mountains separating the Cilician Plain from inland Syria, was one of the first centers to be explored in modern times (1888–1902) and is again the focus of a new expedition launched in 2006 (Schloen and Fink 2009b; Casana and Herrmann 2010). Some of its rulers bore Luwian names, and its architecture and sculptural decoration clearly drew on Neo-Hittite practices, but its inscriptions were written in a dialect of Aramaic and its city gate reliefs primarily depict Aramaean deities (Wartke 2005). The kingdom of Unqi (Patina) occupied the northern Orontes river valley and included the site of Ain Dara, northwest of modern Aleppo, where a Late Bronze and Early Iron Age temple and settlement have been investigated (Stone and Zimansky 1999; Zimansky 2002). New excavations in Aleppo itself have yielded remains of the Temple of the Storm God and associated reliefs and inscriptions (Gonnella et al. 2005). Tell Tayinat, a large site in the Amuq plain excavated from 1933 to 1938 and under renewed investigation since 2004, is generally identified as Kunulua, capital of the kingdom of Unqi, which also included Ain Dara (Haines 1971; Harrison 2009a). The southernmost Neo-Hittite state was Hamath (modern Hama), on the Orontes in central Syria, whose Iron Age citadel and cemetery were excavated in the 1930s. Hamath controlled the land of Luhuti and its capital Hatarikka (Tell Afis) in the middle Orontes Valley (Hawkins 2000: 398–403). Excavations at Tell Afis have furnished an important sequence from the Late Bronze and Iron Ages (Cecchini and Mazzoni 1998; Mazzoni 2000; Venturi 2007).

Recent excavations have begun to elaborate foundational sequences established during the 1930s in regions such as Cilicia and the Amuq plain, and link them with newly documented ceramic chronologies in northern Syria and southeastern Anatolia (Table 42.1). In the Amuq, the appearance of red-slipped burnished ware, chiefly as shallow bowls, signaled the beginning of Phase O around 950 BC, following without stratigraphic break Phase N with its Aegean-style painted wares (Swift 1958: 124–41). The ceramic diversity apparent throughout the region in Iron I gradually contracted, and by Iron II (c.900–700 BC) red-slipped burnished bowls and kraters appeared at a number of sites in southeastern Turkey and northern Syria, including Karkamish (citadel mound and Yunus Cemetery burials) and Hama (Period IV cremation cemetery and Phase E on the citadel mound). Iron II assemblages also included hole-mouth cooking pots, Cypriot painted imported pottery, and Greek imported wares (Mazzoni 2000: 41–53; Akkermans and Schwartz 2003: 361–6).

The use of Hieroglyphic Luwian prevailed among the Neo-Hittite city-states even though their populations were certainly mixed, as evidenced by the use of Hurrian, Hattian, and Aramaean names. An Indo-European language closely related to Hittite (Nesite), Luwian was written in both cuneiform and hieroglyphic scripts in Hittite imperial times. Whereas in the Hittite empire Hieroglyphic Luwian seems to have been employed exclusively for monumental inscriptions and seals, the Iron Age kingdoms apparently used this language and writing system not only for commemorative inscriptions but also for commonplace purposes such as letters and contracts. The survival of correspondence and

Table 42.1 Comparative chronology of the Iron Age in northern Syria and southeastern Anatolia

Iron Age sequence	Karkamish	Amuq	Tell Tayinat	Hama	Tell Afis
IA		Phase N			Afis VII (E:9b)
1150 BC					
1100 BC	Ini-Teshub (Water Gate)			Cim. I F2	E:9a–8
IB					
1050 BC					E:7abc–6
1000 BC	Herald's Wall (Suhi II)				
IC					
950 BC	Long Wall (Katuwa)	Phase Oa (950–900 BC)		Cim. II F1 Gate 1	E:5–3 Afis VIII
900 BC	King's Gate	Phase Ob (900–800 BC)	BP I	Cim. III E2	E:2–1
IIA	Processional Entry			Bldgs. II–III	
850 BC					
800 BC		Phase Oc (800–725 BC)	BP II		D:7–6
IIB	(Astiruwa)			Cim. IV	
750 BC	(Yariri) Royal Buttress			E4	D:5–4
700 BC		Phase Od (725–550 BC)	BP III BP IV		G:8b–a Afis IX D:3–1
III					

economic transactions on lead strips suggests the possibility that other documents were written on perishable materials (Hawkins 2000: 433; Giusfredi 2010: 185–233, 236–9). The use of Hieroglyphic Luwian for everyday transactions also implies that knowledge of the language extended beyond a small elite. In addition to their urban contexts of display, Hieroglyphic Luwian inscriptions were also carved on the natural rock face, often together with figures, creating monuments that may have functioned as cult centers. Arguably one of the more stable regions following the abandonment of Hattusha, southeastern Anatolia and northern Syria may have become favored destinations for peoples migrating from collapsed centers of power, perhaps especially from the former Hittite capital (Bryce 2005: 350). Yet the use of this language and script for monumental inscriptions, accompanying architectural reliefs of a type closely associated with Hittite imperial traditions, indicates a cultural choice by rulers of these clearly mixed populations. The predominance of Hieroglyphic Luwian may also reflect its suitability for programs of visual propaganda, as it became "a part of the monumental architectural decoration, and so was easily integrated into the new urban ideology" (Collins 2007: 87). That no hieroglyphic inscriptions have yet come to light farther west in southern Turkey, in Hilakku (later Rough Cilicia) and Lycia, despite clear evidence for the continuity of their Luwian-speaking populations, suggests that the script's adoption manifests, at least in part, a deliberate effort to create a political and cultural continuity and establish authority by appeal to imperial traditions. Rulers' self-identification with the Hittite imperial past thus reflects both continuity and choice. As territorial encroachment and political pressures by Assyrians and Aramaeans in southeastern Anatolia and northern Syria increased during the 9th century, so too did invocation of the Hittite past as a model of kingship and legitimacy (Bunnens 2000b: 17; 2006: 97–9, 104; Dodd 2005a, 2007).

Some of the Neo-Hittite states, such as Karkamish, correlate with centers and provinces of the Hittite Empire, and they must have inherited an urban layout. Similarly, centers in northern Syria such as Aleppo, itself the seat of a Hittite viceroy, and Ain Dara, whose LBA temple continued in use well into the Iron Age, were perhaps ruled by descendants of imperial times or by individuals who chose to present themselves as "Hittite" kings. Excavations at Lidar Höyük in the kingdom of Kummuh have demonstrated considerable ceramic continuity with LBA traditions (Müller 2003). Continuity with Hittite Empire-period patterns of settlement, and presumably other strategies of resource exploitation, also seems evident in Gurgum, where recent surveys in the Kahramanmaraş valley reveal that nearly all early Iron Age settlements were founded on existing LBA sites (Dodd 2003: 131–2). Other states were new foundations, or were re-founded in the Iron Age. Following the abandonment of nearby Alalakh (Tell Atchana), Tell Tayinat was resettled in the Early Iron Age and to the north, Zincirli Höyük was also re-founded. Yet whether old or new, the urban centers of these states – modern expeditions have thus far focused primarily on monumental buildings, architectural decoration, and inscriptions – exhibit many shared notions of layout, royal ideology, and elite identity.

While limited to relatively few excavations, current evidence suggests that the Neo-Hittite states consisted of sizeable urban centers that served as seats of power and economic activities, presumably sustained by an agricultural hinterland and in certain locations, as at Karkamish, surely also by trade. Their rulers typically commanded a fortified town with a citadel, or upper mound, enclosing monumental buildings such as palaces and temples, while the lower town housed domestic architecture and presumably workshops and other production areas. Common to several urban centers, including Tayinat, Karkamish, and Zincirli, is the organization of the settlement into two or three zones, individually fortified, with double walls and multiple gates (Pucci 2008: 166–72). Fortifications were an early feature of the Iron Age urban foundations at several sites, indicating the need for security. In addition, the series of walls and gates both around and within the city at Karkamish, Zincirli, and Tayinat restricted access to particular areas and constructed boundaries demarcating ceremonial spaces and procession routes (Denel 2007; Pucci 2008: 170–1).

Along with the use of Hieroglyphic Luwian, Hittite traditions of representational art and architectural decoration, distinctly associated with imperial authority and royal ideology and luxury craft production, became the characteristic features of the Neo-Hittite states (Mellink 1974; Mazzoni 1997). Recent advances in clarifying dynastic sequences, along with detailed and comprehensive studies of style and iconography, have placed the chronology of the carved reliefs on firm ground (Mazzoni 2000: 32–52; Orthmann 2002; Bunnens 2006: 49–53). Gate figures in the form of lions guarded the city walls at Ain Dara, Malatya, and Karkamish. Orthostats, upright stone slabs placed along the lower parts of walls and left plain or carved with narrative scenes, have Middle and LBA antecedents in North Syrian and imperial Hittite architecture (Harmanşah 2007: 72–85). In the Iron Age, however, the Neo-Hittite centers richly developed "their symbolic function as bearers of images and sacred materials with no practical function" (Pucci 2008: 174). These programs of decoration closely associate individual rulers with particular deities such as the storm god and most often convey the ruler's unique access to divine realms. The Lion Gate at Malatya, for example, depicts the king pouring a libation in the presence of deities. Whereas religious subjects dominated Hittite imperial art, Neo-Hittite representations also display a rich repertoire of political and historical themes. The Long Wall of Sculptures at Karkamish, an extensive series of decorated orthostats, depicts deities followed by chariots and foot soldiers victorious over the defeated enemy, perpetuating the ruler's exclusive abilities to ensure divine protection and maintain or restore order (Denel 2007: 188–9). The widespread adoption of these features probably also suggests emulation of the model of Karkamish, which has yielded the most extensive series of orthostat reliefs, including reused blocks originally carved in Hittite imperial times (Özyar 1998). Although the city gate reliefs at Zincirli chiefly depict Aramaean deities, their iconography drew on the orthostat reliefs at Karkamish.

Other shared architectural features include palaces of the so-called *bit-hilani* type. This term refers to a columned entryway or entrance portico consisting of two or three columns, reached by a flight of stairs, which leads to one or more rectangular central rooms that presumably served as audience rooms (Aro 2003: 302–3; Pucci 2008: 176). Examples have been identified at Zincirli, Tayinat, Göllüdağ in Tabal, and perhaps Karkamish.

Comparatively few buildings devoted to religious functions have been discovered thus far, perhaps reflecting the worship of many deities in open-air sanctuaries near springs and on mountain peaks. The earliest temples, at Aleppo and Ain Dara, were founded in the Bronze Age and continuously remodeled into the Iron Age. At Aleppo, the massive Middle Bronze Age Temple of the Storm God was continuously rebuilt. Its LBA carved orthostats depict the storm god driving his chariot and other deities, including the tutelary god Runtiya and the winged goddess Ishtar-Shaushka. In another series of reliefs, the storm god appears in a smiting pose opposite Taita, king of the land of Palistin (Palasatini) (Kohlmeyer 2009). Originally constructed in the LBA, the Ain Dara temple in its final phase (900–740 BC) consisted of a recessed porch with two columns, a wide ante-cella, a main square cella, and a surrounding corridor (ambulatory) built around the cella. On the exterior, lion and sphinx orthostats and protomes decorated the lowest parts of the ambulatory walls and flanked the doorways to the cella and ante-cella (Zimansky 2002).

The deity most frequently depicted in the Neo-Hittite centers was the Luwian storm god Tarhunza, shown holding a hammer or axe and his distinctive trident thunderbolt (Long Wall of Sculpture at Karkamish; stelae from Tell Ahmar, Maraş, and Domuztepe), and sometimes standing on a bull (Tell Ahmar, Gölpinar, and Adiyaman). In the Tabal region the storm god was associated with grapes and grain, Tarhunza of the vineyard (rock reliefs at Ivriz, stelae from Ivriz and Niğde) (Aro 2003: 317–320; Bunnens 2006: 58–9, 121–2; Bonatz 2007: 11–13). Karkamish worshiped a divine triad of the storm god, the city goddess Kubaba, and the protective deity Karhuha. The worship of Kubaba was introduced in Tabal and at Karatepe in Cilicia, along with worship of the sun and moon. In general, however, relatively few deities of the Luwian pantheon were represented. Only the orthostat reliefs at Azatiwataya (Karatepe), dating to the late 8th or early 7th century, depict the pantheon of a single city, and few of the deities can be individually identified (Çambel and Özyar 2003; Bonatz 2007: 13–14).

Burial practices, documented at several sites, suggest that extramural cremation cemeteries were the most common and continued LBA traditions in northern Syria, but that multiple modes of commemorating the deceased coexisted, reflecting social differentiation. At Hama (Riis 1948) a cremation cemetery was in use from the Iron IA through Iron IIB period (c.1100–700 BC), and cremation cemeteries of Iron II date have been excavated near Karkamish (Yunus and Merj Khamis), at Deve Höyük, and at nearby Tell Shiyukh Fawqani (Woolley 1939–40; Moorey 1980; Tenu and Bachelot 2005; Tenu et al. 2005). Their burial urns typically contained ceramic vessels and other modest grave goods. New to the Iron Age is a category of private funerary monument consisting of stone sculptures or stelae, which almost always depict the deceased seated at a funerary meal. Introduced in the 9th century, they depict both royal and non-royal figures, and males and females, individually and as couples. More than 100 such monuments have been recovered in southeastern Turkey and northern Syria, many bearing inscriptions in Hieroglyphic Luwian or Aramaic. Their imagery and emphasis on the family as a symbol of social order reflect developing notions of memory and collective identity in the Iron Age kingdoms (Bonatz 2000a, 2000b). A newly unearthed, inscribed stele from Zincirli, exceptionally found in its original context, furnishes evidence for the placement of some of these monuments in mortuary chapels, perhaps associated with temples or the residence of the deceased (Struble and Herrmann 2009: 33–43). Unlike the more common extramural burials, the stelae and sculptures were apparently sometimes set up within the city walls, reflecting their owners' privileged status with respect to rituals of commemoration and memorialization.

The production and consumption of prestige goods, such as decorated ivory cosmetic containers and panels for furniture inlay, provide additional evidence for the material expression of elite identity and document emerging individuality among the Neo-Hittite city-states in workshop specialization and artistic styles. Many of these goods, including multicolored garments and textiles, finished ivories, and unworked tusks, are enumerated in Neo-Assyrian records of tribute collected from these centers, beginning in the 9th century BC, and some are preserved archaeologically. In particular, large quantities of furniture panels, containers, and other carved ivories have been recovered from the Assyrian imperial cities, especially the royal center Kalhu (modern Nimrud). In recent decades, scholars have extensively catalogued and analyzed these objects, with significant results for documenting types of furniture and other luxury goods, manufacturing techniques, subjects, styles of decoration, and patterns of interregional exchange (Symington 1996; Cecchini et al. 2009, with bibliog.). The production of carved ivories in the Neo-Hittite centers is generally thought to have ceased around 700 BC, when the last independent states had been incorporated into the Neo-Assyrian Empire.

4 The Kingdom of Phrygia and its Iron Age Neighbors

In addition to stories of a legendary King Midas, famous for his insatiable greed, Classical sources document more than one historical ruler of the Phrygians named Midas, the first of whose activities date to the later 8th and early 7th centuries BC (Berndt-Ersöz 2008). Neo-Assyrian texts from the reign of Sargon II (721–705 BC) refer to a figure named Mita of Mushki, ruler of a tribe the Assyrians located in northern and eastern Anatolia. Since these records were discovered, most scholars have identified Mita with the Midas of Greek tradition and the Mushki with the Phrygians. Sargon's intervention in the kingdom of Tabal led to his encounter with Mita, whom the Assyrians considered the instigator of a rebellion against their rule by several Neo-Hittite states, including Tabal, Tuwana/Tyana, Que, and Karkamish. After about a decade of organizing and aiding anti-Assyrian coalitions, as recorded in Assyrian royal inscriptions and correspondence, Mita allied himself with Assyria (Mellink 1991: 622–4; Hawkins 2000: 426–8; Vassileva 2008). Greek sources associate Midas, a dynastic name, only with the Phrygians and western Anatolia. The names *Phrygia* and *Phrygians* are not found in the cuneiform or Hieroglyphic Luwian inscriptions, and it is not known what the Phrygians called themselves.

Table 42.2 Gordion's Iron Age historical and stratigraphic sequence

Period	YHSS Phase	Dates (approximate)
Early Iron Age	7	1100–950 BC
Initial Early Phrygian	6B	950–900 BC
Early Phrygian	6A	900–800 BC
Early Phrygian Destruction		800 BC
Middle Phrygian	5	800–540 BC
Late Phrygian	4	540–330 BC

Located about 100 kilometers southwest of Ankara near the confluence of the Sakarya and Porsuk rivers, Gordion is by far the best-known Phrygian site. Today called Yassıhöyük ("flat" or "flat-topped mound"), it was initially explored in 1900 by the Classicist Alfred Körte and his brother Gustav (Körte and Körte 1904). The site was identified as Gordion because its location corresponded to ancient authors' descriptions, and subsequent archaeological investigations have indeed yielded extensive remains of Iron Age date on an impressive scale, along with inscriptions in the Old Phrygian language. The University of Pennsylvania Museum of Archaeology and Anthropology has conducted excavations at Gordion over a period of more than 30 years, beginning with R.S. Young's campaigns (1950–73), which concentrated on the large habitation mound, or citadel, and tumulus burials in its vicinity (Sams 2005). A later, multifaceted series of investigations (1988–2002), directed by G.K. Sams and M.M. Voigt, has furnished crucial new evidence for Iron Age stratigraphy and chronology (Table 42.2), along with a regional survey (Voigt 2005).

Inhabited from the Early Bronze Age (c.2300 BC) onward, Gordion's Iron Age remains constituted the most impressive structures on the citadel (c.500 × 350 meters) and among the large burial mounds, or tumuli, constructed nearby. Young's excavations uncovered two major levels of monumental architecture, an old and a new fortified citadel, separated by a thick clay fill 4–5 meters deep. The Old Citadel, or Early Phrygian level (YHSS 6A), was destroyed in a great conflagration that preserved the lower parts of many buildings along with their rich contents. By contrast, the New Citadel, or Middle and Late Phrygian settlement (YHSS 5–4), had been largely robbed by later inhabitants in search of building materials in the Middle Phrygian structures. In both cases, the citadel plan consisted of a substantial defensive wall enclosing monumental buildings constructed of stone, mudbrick, and timber in three distinct areas and pierced by a monumental gate complex in the southeast. In the northeast, the palace area consisted of two large courts flanked by buildings of *megaron* plan (a rectangular structure composed of anteroom and main hall, entered on one of the short sides). In the southwest, two long buildings identical in plan faced each other across a wide street, occupying an extensive terrace. The "Terrace Building" consists of eight parallel *megaron* units forming a total length of more than 100 meters, housing workshop units that produced food and textiles for the local elite (Burke 2005). In the northwest a multi-roomed structure occupied a third area. In addition to this walled palace area on the eastern part of the citadel mound, the recent excavations have shown that in the western part of the Middle Phrygian citadel (YHSS 5) the buildings are chiefly of a domestic character. The Middle Phrygian city also expanded to include a walled lower town south of the citadel mound and an outer town to the north (Voigt 2007: 317–32). Gordion's Iron Age economy was based primarily on agriculture and herding, while textiles were produced both as a medium of exchange and a prestige commodity.

Young associated the burned buildings of the Old Citadel with an invasion by marauding Cimmerians from the north (followed by the alleged suicide of Midas) referred to in Classical sources, and accordingly dated to c.700 BC. Until a few years ago, this century, this event and its date were chronological points firmly fixed in the site's history and, consequently, in Phrygian history and Iron Age Anatolian archaeology more broadly. A series of discoveries and analyses carried out in conjunction with the recent campaigns has convincingly challenged this chronology and interpretation. In the light of new stratigraphic observations, the evidence of independently dated artifacts, radiocarbon determinations and dendrochronology, the excavators have re-dated the Early Phrygian Destruction Level (YHSS 6A) to c.800 BC, approximately 100 years earlier than previously thought (Voigt 2005: 28–31; DeVries 2007: 79–80; 2008: 30–3; cf. Muscarella 2003b; Keenan 2004). The correlation of the Early Phrygian citadel with the Mita of Mushki, mentioned in records from the reign of Sargon II and the historical Midas of approximately contemporaneous date, can thus no longer be maintained. The "age of Midas" would belong instead to the Middle Phrygian period (YHSS 5) when Gordion attained its maximum extent and the regional population reached its peak (Voigt 2007: 331–2). While the profound and far-reaching consequences of this revised chronology are still being worked out with respect to specific categories of material, new sequences in the typological development of several groups of artifacts, including fine ceramic wares, bronze omphalos bowls, and bronze fibulae, can already be established (DeVries 2007' 2008: 34–43). A fragmentary group of porous limestone orthostats carved in low relief with figural scenes, recovered from a reused context and initially dated to before 800 BC, exhibit similarities in subject and style with orthostat sculptures from Neo-Hittite centers such as Karkamish and Zincirli (Sams 1989; 1994: 194–5). Manufacturing debris recently excavated from buildings of the Initial Phrygian Period (YHSS 6B) included similar carved blocks which could be joined with some of the examples found earlier, thus establishing their date in the first half of the 9th century, much closer in time to their Neo-Hittite models in northern Syria from the 10th and 9th centuries BC (Voigt and Henrickson 2000b: 50; Kelp 2004: 285–98).

Gray wares constitute the overwhelming majority of Gordion's Early Phrygian ceramic assemblage and continued to dominate both utilitarian and fine wares throughout the Middle and Late Phrygian periods (YHSS 5–4). Vessels were typically wheel-made, with larger containers built by hand and finished on a slow wheel or tournette. Occasionally embellished with incised or impressed decoration, the gray ware repertory of relatively standardized shapes and dimensions includes bowls, goblets, basins, jars of various sizes, and storage jars (Sams 1994: 33–6, 41–133; Henrickson 2005). A few distinct groups of painted ceramics, represented in much smaller quantities at Gordion, bear witness to more elaborately decorated styles and also help to establish correlations with Iron Age sites in central and south-central Anatolia. Alişar IV pottery, named for the site in central Turkey where it was first recognized, is chiefly found within the bend of the Kizilirmak, but Gordion's Early Phrygian settlement yielded a few imports and imitations. It features figural decoration in silhouette technique; typical are jars with stag friezes painted in brown on a light ground filled with concentric circles (Sams 1994: 163–4). A group of vessels painted with simple geometric patterns links Gordion to a wider tradition of painted ceramics of the Neo-Hittite sphere, well represented at Karkamish, Malatya, and Hama (Sams 1994: 135–6). Brown-on-buff ware, a fine class exhibiting elaborate figural and geometric decoration and highly distinctive shapes such as jugs with elongated spouts, is best known from the burial tumuli of the 9th and 8th centuries BC. Like other developments in the Early Phrygian visual idiom, such as programs of architectural sculpture, its linear animal style was indebted to Neo-Hittite models in media other than vase-painting (Sams 1974, 1994; Sievertsen 2004; Roller 2009a).

Beginning with the Körtes' explorations in 1900, about 35 of the approximately 85 burial tumuli near Gordion have been scientifically excavated. Most of the excavated tumuli date to the Phrygian period (9th and especially 8th–6th centuries BC), although some are Hellenistic. Initially, the Phrygian-period examples were inhumations placed in wooden tombs, followed in the late 7th century by the introduction of cremation burials without wooden tombs (Kohler 1980; Kohler 1995). Tumulus MM (Midas Mound), which measures more than 50 meters in height and 300 meters in diameter, is the largest and most spectacularly furnished of the burial mounds. Constructed of pine and juniper and surrounded by a massive stone wall, the tomb chamber contained a single male inhumation accompanied by quantities of elaborately carved wooden furniture and metal belts, textiles, and bronze and ceramic vessels (Young et al. 1981: 79–190). Often identified as the tomb of King Midas because of its monumental dimensions and opulent furnishings, Tumulus MM has recently been re-dated to around 740 BC on the basis of dendrochronology and artifact style, and is therefore too early for the Mita of Neo-Assyrian records and the historical Midas of the late 8th century (DeVries 2008: 33–8). The tumulus contents also provide unique evidence of media rarely preserved in Anatolia, such as the intricately decorated wooden furniture recovered from several burials (E. Simpson 1996, 2010; Simpson and Spirydowicz 1999). Given their comparatively small number and rich furnishings, the tumuli as a group must represent the burials of a small elite, presumably Gordion's ruling dynasty. Large cemeteries for the majority of the population must be located elsewhere.

Recent investigations employing both archaeological and textual sources have considerably advanced the understanding of Phrygian religion and cult practices. The only Phrygian deity known to us, and the only one represented in anthropomorphic form, is the goddess the Phrygians called Matar, "mother," who is occasionally given the epithet *kubileya* (from which derives her classical name, Cybele). By the 8th century BC a sculptural tradition of representing this important deity had been established which clearly drew on the iconography of Kubaba, the city goddess of Karkamish (Roller 1999: 46–53; Collins 2004: 91–2). The presence at Gordion of cult objects of varying dimensions throughout the city suggests that the cult of Matar was practiced in both public and private domestic shrines from the 8th to the mid-6th centuries BC (Roller 1999: 77–9). Her sanctuaries were typically located not within urban centers, however, but on the boundaries of human and natural landscapes, near city gates (Boğazköy, Gordion, Midas City, Kerkenes Dağ) or funerary monuments (Ankara, Gordion, Arslan Tash). Phrygian cult installations, many of which were dedicated to Matar, consisted almost exclusively of rock-cut shrines and monuments, of which more than 100 examples have been documented; freestanding, built shrines are known only at Boğazköy and Kerkenes Dağ (Berndt-Ersöz 2006; Draycott and Summers 2008; Roller 2009b). Two major categories of rock-cut monuments are distinguished, which can also be differentiated chronologically and which are most abundantly represented in the Phrygian highlands near modern Afyon and Eskişehir. Step monuments, the earlier group, consist of a seat (or throne) atop several steps; most often, the seatback is topped by a semicircular block or idol. Façades and niches form a second group, ranging in size from tiny niches to representations of a building or architectural façade measuring several meters in height, where the niche represents the entrance and typically frames an image of the mother goddess (Berndt-Ersöz 2009). While the architectural façades are often understood to refer to the deity's temple, it appears increasingly likely that the reliefs depict instead the façade of a palace or elite residence in which cult ceremonies were enacted, and thus emphasize a close relationship between the cult of the mother goddess and the local ruler (Roller 2006; Roller 2009b). As a group, the rock-cut monuments seem to have originated in the vicinity of Gordion itself. Dümrek, a sanctuary located north of Gordion, houses multiple step monuments. Its predominantly Early Phrygian ceramics indicate that it was established in the 9th century BC, but it continued to be used in Middle and, in part, also in Late Phrygian times. While its proximity to Gordion suggests that it was probably established and most often visited by nearby inhabitants, the presence of ceramics from other regions of central and west central Anatolia indicate its wider regional importance as a center of worship and place of pilgrimage (Grave et al. 2005; Berndt-Ersöz 2009).

The nature and extent of the Phrygian state ruled from Gordion are difficult to define because so few other sites of this period have been investigated in any detail and because the presence of Old Phrygian inscriptions and Phrygian-style material culture, such as ceramics or metalwork, may not necessarily reflect centralized or unified Phrygian political control. Drawing in part on the Greek tradition concerning Phrygia, earlier reconstructions tended to emphasize Phrygian hegemony and Gordion's status as its political center. Recent excavations at several sites in central Anatolia, including Boğazköy, Kaman-Kalehöyük, and Kerkenes Dağ, have furnished new information on settlement, architecture, economy, and material culture in the Middle and Late Iron Ages (Kealhofer et al. 2009; Summers 2006, 2007, 2008). The results of these investigations do not unambiguously confirm a territorially extensive Phrygian state with its capital at Gordion, although both the city and the nearby sanctuary at Dümrek were clearly of pan-regional importance. At Boğazköy, the Middle and Late Iron Age inhabitants shared elements of Phrygian material culture, including architecture, painted ceramic styles, and graffiti, with the "nuclear" Phrygian zone of west central Anatolia (Bossert 2000; Genz 2003, 2007; Kealhofer et al. 2009). Tumulus burials similar to those at Gordion, containing closely comparable Phrygian-style ceramics and metalwork, cluster in several distinct regions of central and southern Anatolia: to the northeast, at Ankara; at Kaynarca, near the Neo-Hittite kingdom of Tuwana/Tyana; and in the southwest at Bayindir, west of modern Antalya (Akkaya 1991; Börker-Klähn 2003; DeVries 2008: 42–3). A close association between a male ruler and the Phrygian goddess is attested at Gordion, Boğazköy, and Kerkenes Dağ. Some scholars interpret these settlements as Phrygian "outposts" or emporia, with Gordion as the center of a Phrygian oligarchy; others, while acknowledging Gordion's pan-regional importance, reconstruct a political landscape of multiple independent polities whose ruling elites shared certain forms of material culture and dynastic funerary practices (Wittke 2007). Whatever the precise configuration of the Iron Age states of central and west-central Anatolia, the Achaemenid Persian conquest of the mid-6th century BC brought an end to their independence.

GUIDE TO FURTHER READING

For the Neo-Hittite kingdoms, recent surveys with helpful bibliographies include Akkermans and Schwartz (2003), Bryce (2005), and Collins (2007). *Near Eastern Archaeology* 72/4 (December 2009) features accessible articles on the recent archaeological and epigraphical finds from Cilicia, the Amuq region, and Aleppo, with additional bibliography.

Hawkins (2000) is the magisterial scholarly corpus of original Hieroglyphic Luwian texts, with extensive commentary and bibliography.

A recent exhibition catalogue devoted to the Phrygians presents a number of introductory essays intended for a broad readership, treating individual sites as well as religion, language, and other topics (Sivas and Tüfekçi Sivas 2007). A collection of essays elaborating recent work at the site of Gordion and in its environs offers a more detailed introduction to multiple categories of archaeological remains, with extensive bibliography (Kealhofer 2005). Two monograph series, Gordion Excavations Final Reports and Gordion Special Studies, publish detailed scholarly studies (bibliography to date in Kealhofer 2005; cf. Dusinberre 2005a; Roller 2009a). Studies of material from Gordion and other Iron Age Anatolian sites are regularly included in the proceedings of the ongoing Anatolian Iron Ages Symposia (Çilingiroğlu and French 1994; Çilingiroğlu and Darbyshire 2005; Çilingiroğlu and Sagona 2007).

Reports on investigations at Boğazköy are published in several series, including *Boğazköy-Hattuša*, *Studien zu den Boğazköy-Texten*, and *Boğazköy-Berichte*; preliminary reports are regularly published in *Archäologischer Anzeiger* and *Istanbuler Mitteilungen*. The *Reallexikon der Assyriologie* (Berlin, 1928–), a major reference work that is updated on an ongoing basis, includes entries on many sites, regions, personal and place names.

Websites devoted to ongoing excavations and research at several key sites provide current information on each new season and additional bibliography. For some of the sites highlighted in this discussion, see: Gordion/Yassihöyük (http://sites.museum.upenn.edu/gordion/), Boğazköy (http://www.dainst.org/index.php?id=643&sessionLanguage=en), Kerkenes Dağ (http://www.kerkenes.metu.edu.tr/kerk1/index.html), Tell Tayinat (http://www.utoronto.ca/tap/), and Zincirli (http://ochre.lib.uchicago.edu/zincirli/).

CHAPTER FORTY-THREE

North Arabian Kingdoms

Arnulf Hausleiter

1 Sources

The image of the history of Northern Arabia has long been influenced by a variety of written non-autochthonous sources: mainly cuneiform texts from Mesopotamia and, to a lesser but not entirely insignificant extent, biblical texts of the Old Testament. Additionally, there are testimonies from Egypt and Classical authors. Finally, there are writings by medieval Arab historians and geographers. There is a large amount of local epigraphic evidence, mainly early northwest Arabian (Jaussen and Savignac 1909, 1914; Winnett and Reed 1970; Macdonald 2004) or Aramaic inscriptions, but these still await systematic investigation and study. Complementary to these written sources, new and significant data have emerged from a number of recent archaeological excavations and surveys in the region, considerably extending our knowledge of environmental changes, subsistence strategies, social life and political organization in 1st millennium BC northern Arabia. Compared to other regions in the Near East, excavations in the region are still limited to a small number of sites, although in the 19th century a number of travelers were already publishing informative accounts of ancient settlements.

Most of the epigraphic and archaeological sources illuminate the role of northern Arabia as a region of contacts, and cultural and economic transfer. One of the most important trade routes in the Arabian peninsula, the so-called frankincense road, crossed the western part of the Arabian peninsula from south to

---

A Companion to the Archaeology of the Ancient Near East, First Edition.
Edited by D.T. Potts.
© 2012 Blackwell Publishing Ltd. Published 2012 by Blackwell Publishing Ltd.

north (Maigret 1997; Macdonald 1997; Potts 1988b). The image of northern Arabia as solely a transit region of lesser interest, therefore, is not entirely unexpected, at least with regard to mainstream ancient Near Eastern studies. However, it is by no means justified. A systematic recording of the thousands of rock inscriptions in northern Arabia may alter current ideas of ancient concepts of political and social organization. A north Arabian history exclusively considering the sources from within the region still remains to be written. Attempts to frame the historical narrative using terminology borrowed from tribal- and placenames mentioned in religious texts, such as the Bible or the Qur'an, appear outdated in this context and, by associating ancient names with certain classes of artifacts, such as pottery, also neglect more recent methodologies (cf. Chan in press).

2 General Framework

Geographically speaking, northern Arabia constitutes the bridge between the central and southern parts of the peninsula, including South Arabia, and an area reaching from Egypt in the west to the Levant and Syria in the northwest, the Syrian Desert in the north and Babylonia (and Assyria) to the northeast (the regions next to the Gulf belong to eastern Arabia). Since all these areas, with the exception of the southern parts of Egypt divided from the peninsula by the Red Sea, are connected to each other by land, there were excellent possibilities for direct contacts, both hostile and peaceful, between the different political, social, and cultural entities in the region. The existence of a land bridge between Africa and Asia was of prime importance for the history of humankind, since it is considered a factor that enabled the spread of hominids all over the world (Rose 2010; Armitage et al. 2011). Investigations in eastern Egypt, Saudi Arabia, and Ethiopia show that similarly intense cultural and economic contacts were established and maintained by maritime connections across the Red Sea.

As to the internal organization of landscape and environment, "Arabia is by no means all desert" (Macdonald 1995: 1355) and there is a great variety of different landscapes in the peninsula (Wilkinson 2003a; see Ch. I.1). Nevertheless, from a long-term perspective, the ability to easily move about and survive in this environmentally hostile region lay, without doubt, with mobile, nomadic groups rather than with representatives of foreign, mainly sedentary, societies. Therefore, efforts by foreign powers to gain permanent territorial control, as attempted in the 6th century BC by the Babylonian King Nabû-na'id (Nabonidus, 555–539 BC), did not last very long.

According to present knowledge, trade relations between Arabia and Syro-Mesopotamia may have started at the turn of the 2nd to the 1st millennium BC, and subsequently long-distance trade between South Arabia and the eastern Mediterranean developed, using camels as pack-animals for the large-scale export of high-quality luxury goods, particularly aromatics (incense and myrrh) from South Arabia and northeast Africa. In addition, other export items, such as precious metals and stones, were traded, especially during the initial phase of trade. Consequently, the intensity of cultural and economic exchange between the Arabian peninsula and its neighbors reached a previously unparalleled degree of intensity, embedded in the general economic growth of the early Iron Age.

On the other hand, it must not be overlooked that there is also growing evidence of international contacts with this region during earlier periods. To what extent was northern Arabia touched by the achievements of the sedentary civilizations of the 3rd millennium BC such as Egypt, Syro-Mesopotamia, the South Arabian highlands, the Oman peninsula, or the Gulf (Edens et al. 2000)? There are in fact, a number of archaeological indications of a common cultural background, at least in the western part of the peninsula (Schiettecatte 2010), which suggest that the northwest Arabian oases may have played a leading role in the development of the South Semitic alphabet (Robin 2008).

It seems clear that the political and economic organization of northern Arabia was divided between a number of powerful oases, situated at a considerable distance from each other. These were characterized by their sedentary lifestyle and regionally active, mobile groups, mainly involved in camel-breeding and the provisioning of meat to the oases as well as safeguarding the trade, while, at the same time, benefiting from it. There is now a consensus about these two economic units cooperating with each other. Outside the large oases, water was available at many watering holes in the desert area, many of them not yet recognized or systematically investigated, but all important in providing this life-giving resource for nomadic groups and their animals. Large-scale, systematic investigation of water resources would probably lead to changes in scholarly perceptions of land use, as was the case in the 1980s and 1990s in the north Syrian and Iraqi Jazirah (Bernbeck 1993; Wilkinson and Tucker 1995).

As a form of sociopolitical organization, kingdoms in this region are normally thought to have been territorially less extensive than those in contemporary northern Mesopotamia, Babylonia, or Egypt, areas with largely sedentary societies that were both more densely populated and located in climatically more favorable parts of the Near East. Interactions between sedentary and mobile groups, many of them organized as tribes, may not have been dominated by sedentarist norms of behavior. This is relevant to the perception of the role of a king or queen as *primus inter pares* in the hierarchical organization of groups or societies headed by tribal leaders or *sheikhs* (Macdonald 1995: 1364). From an Assyrian perspective, Qedar was the most influential tribe, at least in the reign of the 7th century BC Assyrian king Assurbanipal (668–627 BC), and one also involved in the aromatics trade. Before this time, the Aramaean tribes of southern Syria were essential for establishing contacts between the inhabitants of northern Arabia and the populations of Syro-Mesopotamia (Retsö 2003). Other politically and economically active north Arabian tribes were the Nebayot and Massa (probably located between the northwestern and northern parts of Arabia), and for over two centuries the Assyrian records illuminate the changing alliances of tribes, in search of good relationships with their powerful Mesopotamian neighbors.

Apart from this general outline, several important aspects remain to be discussed in detail, once additional evidence is available. These relate particularly to the establishment, development, survival, and decline of the north Arabian kingdoms and, to a lesser extent, the dynamics of power – i.e., the implementation of rule, also in terms of territory and political space. The 8th and 7th century BC Assyrian sources mainly provide insights into one foreign power's (Assyria's) dealings with the regional political players and thus offer a one-sided perspective, which is nevertheless of importance for an understanding of the situation. Sources from the later 1st millennium BC are more heterogeneous and reflect increasingly multi-layered historical traditions.

In the 1st millennium BC, three north Arabian oases can be identified on the basis of both epigraphic and archaeological evidence as outstandingly powerful political centers: Duma (mod. Dumat al-Jandal), Dedan (mod. al-Khuraybah), and Tema (mod. Tayma). Numerous other oases are known as well, but at present it appears as if their importance was restricted to a local or sub-regional level, except for Yathrib (mod. Medina), a major oasis located at a southern bifurcation of the so-called "frankincense road."

As to the indigenous image of rulers, there is some information on royal representation during the last centuries of the 1st millennium BC, but little is known about the earlier periods. Apart from city walls, public building activities by royal decree, resulting in secular architecture, seems virtually absent, interestingly also from the texts. Recent excavations have not provided any evidence for residences or seats of rulers, kings or queens. Unless these remains have been overlooked by excavators, it seems that different types of royal residences, probably including those of a temporary nature, such as tents, must be taken in consideration. On the other hand, buildings with a religious character are recorded epigraphically and archaeologically, in some cases with parts of their inventory still in place.

3 Settlement Before the 1st Millennium BC

According to recent geoarchaeological studies in the oasis of Tayma (see below), it seems probable that mid-Holocene climatic changes forced mobile groups to become sedentary during the 4th millennium BC, when different strategies for water control had to be adopted because of an aridization process which resulted in the disappearance of a number of ancient lakes. Based on this model, a number of oases, located in the most favorable zones of an increasingly hostile environment, were established in northern Arabia (Ch. I.25; Drechsler 2009).

Little is known about the history of the centuries predating the 1st millennium BC, but this by no means implies that the oases were not occupied. On the contrary, there is growing evidence of substantial 2nd millennium BC occupation in some of them, such as Qurayyah, Tayma, and al-Khuraybah, although no large-scale excavations of relevant occupational remains have been carried out yet. At least at Tayma, certain parts of the c.10 kilometer long city wall were constructed of mudbrick during the 2nd millennium BC (i.e., before the Early Iron Age, 12th–9th century BC), implying the social and political need for such a construction, not to speak of the organizational skill and manpower necessary. P.J. Parr (1988) suggested a foreign, Egyptian impetus for the foundation of some of these oasis settlements, but this has not been accepted unanimously. Whether the presence of Late Early Bronze/Early Middle Bronze Age bronze weapons, including a fenestrated axe and a ribbed dagger (information kindly provided by M. al-Hajjari, 2003), in Middle Iron Age graves indicates the presence of such objects at Tayma already in the early 2nd millennium BC, as in Syria and the Levant ("warrior graves"), cannot yet be said with certainty.

New light has recently been shed on the relationship between north Arabia and Egypt. A number of Egyptian and Egyptianizing objects (Sperveslage in press a) have been recovered together with prestige goods of Syro-Levantine type from an apparently isolated structure at Tayma, and a recently discovered cartouche of Pharaoh Ramesses III in the vicinity of Tayma may indicate a stronger political connection between Egypt and northwest Arabia than previously assumed. Slightly earlier, the presence of Qurayyah painted ware (Parr, Harding and Dayton 1970) already strongly indicated links between northwestern Arabia and the Levant during the Late Bronze Age, thus underlining the northwestern orientation of cultural contacts. Although evidence is scarce, it appears plausible that some time after the reign of the Assyrian king Tiglath-pileser I (1114–1076 BC), commercial contacts with Mesopotamia began, as indicated by Assyrian cuneiform sources (Bagg in press). These contacts endured throughout the remainder of the 1st millennium BC. Thus, by the end of the 2nd millennium BC, the Arabian peninsula started to make its appearance on the mental, political, and economic maps of the neighboring Near Eastern powers.

4 The Neo-Assyrian Empire and North Arabia: 8th–7th Centuries BC

Assyrian interest in aromatics in Arabia (*māt aribi*) features in the cuneiform sources from the 9th century BC onwards. Camels, the only suitable means for crossing desert areas (probably apart from donkeys), were mentioned amongst the booty collected by the Assyrian king Tukulti-Ninurta II (890–884 BC) from tribes along the Euphrates; Arabs (in the person of a certain Gindibu) were mentioned for the first time by Shalmaneser III (858–824 BC) as members of a coalition of Syrian cities against the Assyrian army in 853 BC (Eph'al 1982; Retsö 2003; Bagg in press).

More detailed information on political organization in Northern Arabia appeared a century later, during the reign of Tiglath-pileser III (744–727 BC). Before that time, a text from Sur Jar'a (Iraq), written by Ninurta-kudurri-usur, governor of the land Suhu and Mari, sheds light on the perils faced by caravans traveling between Assyria and Arabia (Cavigneaux and Khalil Ismail 1990; Macdonald 1997: 339–40). In 738 BC, Tiglath-pileser III collected tribute from queen Zabibe – the first time that Arabs paid tribute to an Assyrian king – and also from Damascus and Palestinian cities. Subsequently, he defeated queen Samsi from the Arab land at Mount Shaqurri (location uncertain) and collected, among other things, 30,000 camels from her. Samsi is presently the best known of a number of 8th–7th century BC female rulers or princesses in northern Arabia (all of them called "queens" by the Assyrians, using the Akkadian term *šarratu*; in the case of male rulers, the term "king," *šarru*, was used). She is probably also depicted on one of Tiglath-pileser III's sculptures at Nimrud. After her defeat and the conquest of Gaza, Tiglath-pileser III installed an Arab official who controlled the trade route toward Egypt (Macdonald 1995: 1365). In the context of the conflict between Assyria and the Arabs, a number of tribes, including Massa, Tema, and Saba'a, are said to have paid tribute to the Assyrian king, probably because they may have been worried about safeguarding their own commercial interests (Retsö 2003: 135–6). The mention of "Sabaeans" by Tiglath-pileser III in connection with tribes in the area of Dedan has been interpreted as evidence of the aromatics trade in the 8th century BC, even though aromatics are not mentioned in the textual sources of this period.

In the last two centuries of Assyrian rule a number of Arabian queens were mentioned in Assyrian royal documents, such as Zabibe (Tiglath-pileser III); Samsi (Tiglath-pileser III and Sargon II); Yathi'e and Te'elhunu (Sennacherib); Apkallatu, Baslu, Yapa', and Tabu'a (Esarhaddon); and Atiya (Assurbanipal). Apart from the remarkable presence of female rulers, as late as the reign of Sargon II (721–705 BC) the Arabs were described as having no leaders and having paid no tribute to any king (Bagg in press). Sargon II took several steps in the region between Lebanon, Palestine, Egypt, and north Arabia in order to guarantee the functioning of commerce (in particular the opening of a harbor and the establishment of a mercantile settlement composed of Egyptians and Assyrians), and he "receives gifts, which he describes as tribute" (Macdonald 1995: 1365) from the king of Egypt, Samsi, and It'amra of Saba'a, each of whom was interested in maintaining trade relations. Some Arabs even successfully conducted raids in the northern parts of the Syro-Arabian desert and were apparently involved in commercial activities not much liked by the ruling Assyrians. During the reign of Sargon II, Arabs may have settled in northwestern Iran (for the purpose of camel breeding?), Assyria, and Syria (Retsö 2003: 150–2).

Assyrian rulers entered the Arabian peninsula on only two occasions. Otherwise deeply involved in Babylonian affairs, in which Arab tribes sided with the Babylonians, Sennacherib (704–681 BC) successfully attacked Haza'il, king of Qedar, and queen Te'elhunu and chased them to the city of Adummatu. There he captured a number of statues of local gods which he transported to the Assyrian capital Nineveh. Sennacherib also collected thousands of camels from Te'elhunu. He named one of the city gates of Nineveh "the gifts of the people of Sumu'il and Tema enter here," indicating perhaps the end of hostilities between Assyria and Arabia. There is good evidence that Assyro-Arabian commerce continued (as evidenced, e.g., by the delivery of gifts from the people of Tema to Nineveh and from Karib'il of Saba to Assur).

In the reign of Sennacherib relations between Arabia and Babylonia were quite close. Textual evidence and individual artifacts of Arabian origin attest to the presence of Arabians in Babylonia and the existence of settlements that probably functioned as trading posts. Settlements with an Arabian population appear to have existed in Babylonia until the Achaemenid period (Retsö 2003).

The main site of Assyrian concern, Adummatu, was described as the "fortress of the Arabs" by Sennacherib's successor, Esarhaddon (680–669 BC), who, on his way to eastern Arabia and the land of *Bazu*, conquered six fortified cities (Leichty 2011). During this campaign, six kings and two queens were defeated and killed. Since one of the Arab queens' names was reportedly (according to Esarhaddon) *Apkallātu* (Leichty 2011: 341 with references), they may have fulfilled priestly functions (cf. Akkadian *apkallu*, "priest"). Upon receiving a request from Haza'il, Esarhaddon returned to the Arabs the divine statues of Atarsamayin, Daya, Nuhaya, Rulda'u, Abir'ilu, and Atarquruma that had been seized by Sennacherib during his conquest of Adummatu. Esarhaddon installed the Arab princess Tabu'a, educated at Nineveh, as queen, and after the death of Haza'il, he made his son Yautha' king. A local attempt to replace the latter was thwarted by Assyrian intervention. Eventually, when Yautha' rebelled, the divine images were deported for a second time to Nineveh. The king fled from Adummatu, and not until the reign of Assurbanipal were the divine images, at least that of Atarsamayin, returned to Adummatu.

Along the southwestern flank of the Assyrian empire, the king fully depended on the cooperation of the local Arab tribes for the supply of resources, such as camels and water, when traveling to Egypt. "The Arabs of this region thus acquired a dual importance to the rulers of Mesopotamia, the smooth passage of the incense trade to its Mediterranean and Egyptian outlets, but they held the key to any invasion to Egypt" (Macdonald 1995: 1366; cf. Retsö 2003: 159).

Like Esarhaddon before him, Assurbanipal initially faced problems with the local ruler Yautha', King of Qidru (Qedar), resulting in the latter's defeat and his removal to Nineveh. Yautha' was replaced by a puppet king, Abiyate. The textual evidence (Retsö 2003) further reports on the dynamics of conflicts between Assyrians and Arabs at this time (including the participation of Arabs in the revolt of Assurbanipal's brother, Shamash-shum-ukin, in Babylonia in 651 BC), culminating in the second war against the Arab tribes between 641 and 638

BC and the defeat of the Qedarites and a number of their leaders (according to Retsö 2003 the Qedarites and Arabs may not necessarily be identical). In this conflict, the Assyrians were backed by the Nebayaot who clearly benefited from this alliance.

Apart from the hostile relationship between Assyria and Arabia, there is evidence of a mutual interest in maintaining commercial relations (Eph'al 1982; Macdonald 1997), especially after the conquest of Damascus by Tiglath-pileser III in 733 BC. However, since no Assyrian trading itineraries survive, only a few placenames can be identified, such as Tayma (Tema), Duma (Adummatu), and Kaf (Kapannu). Although little is known about traded goods, the Sur Jar'a text gives us an idea of what an 8th century BC camel caravan consisted of: namely, camels, purple-dyed wool and other textiles, stones, metal, etc.

As mentioned above, trade between Arabia and Assyria may have begun as early as the late 2nd millennium BC. Assyrian kings list the import of goods originating from the Arabian peninsula in the area of Hindanu (Bagg in press; Liverani 1992: 113–14; Maigret 1999) which may have had an important role in their distribution (Edens and Bawden 1989). However, in the reign of Tiglath-pileser I, Hindanu was part of Suhu and apparently did not yet provide any foreign trade goods (Bagg in press).

5 Babylon and the Achaemenids: North Arabia in the 6th–4th Centuries BC

In 601 BC, Nebuchadnezzar II (604–562 BC) conducted raids against nomads in the Syrian steppe, probably as a preamble to his attacks on Judah, Ammon, Moab, Edom, Sidon, Tyre, and the Arabs in the subsequent year. These campaigns were probably sparked by his strategic and economic interests in the region and yielded considerable booty. At this time, Edom may have become "the bastion of Babylonia in Arabia" (Retsö 2003: 182). It was probably the geographical proximity of Arabia to Babylonia that led the last Babylonian king, Nabonidus, to adopt a strategy different from that of the Assyrians in dealing with northern and especially northwestern Arabia. Nabonidus was the first Mesopotamian ruler to gain territorial control of large areas in the Hijaz in order to establish de facto control of the trading network of the Arabian peninsula. He came and went between the most important oases of the region, including Tema (Tayma), Dadanu (Dedan), Padakku (al-Huwayit?), Hibra (Khaybar), and Iadihu (al-Hayit?) and reached Iatribu (Medina), essential for controlling both the northwestern and northeastern branches of the frankincense road. The decision to establish his residence at Tayma clearly reflects its importance. Sickness, mentioned by the king himself (Beaulieu 1995), and the fall of Edom may have influenced his decision to remain in Arabia (Retsö 2003). Nabonidus' powerful intervention, at least according to his own writings, prompted a number of his neighbors, including the kings of Egypt, Media, and the Arabs of the Syrian desert, to pay him tribute and seek to cooperate with him (Macdonald 1995: 1367). In addition to the religious conflicts he faced in his hometown Babylon, however, a glance at the map supports the hypothesis that it was the king's manifest economic interests that led him to stay for 10 years in Arabia, away from his capital, forcing him to neglect his religious duties as king of Babylon.

In his inscriptions, Nabonidus mentions his stay in northwest Arabia, but it is the propagandistic Verse Account, a text compiled during the Achaemenid period – i.e., after the death of Nabonidus – that explicitly mentions a king (*malku*) of Tema, whom Nabonidus killed, along with the cattle and flocks of its inhabitants. It also claims that Nabonidus built a palace "as in Babylon" (Schaudig 2001). Although, the "large Neo-Babylonian style building, that is likely to be Nabonidus' palace" (Beaulieu 1995: 974) still awaits confirmation by archaeological excavations, the discovery of a Babylonian stele with a royal inscription in cuneiform mentioning Nabonidus on a possible pedestal for the stele (Hausleiter and Schaudig 2010a, 2010b) are clear signs of a Babylonian presence at Tayma. A number of Taymanite graffiti on rock formations around the site also mention Nabonidus (al-Said 2009; Müller and al-Said 2002), a thus far unparalleled phenomenon in the history of northern Arabia, giving important clues to the contemporary perception of the Babylonian occupation by parts of the local population. Although its chronological relationship with the Late Babylonian period is not entirely clear, the important oasis of Dedan was at this time a place of undoubted significance ("kingdom"), since it was mentioned by Nabonidus.

While the political situation in northern Arabia during the early Achaemenid period (reigns of Cyrus and Cambyses) is poorly documented in written sources (Graf 1990; Knauf 1990; Retsö 2003; Stein in press), important monuments from Tayma, among them the "Tayma Stone," date to this period, and indicate the influence of Near Eastern textual tradition and iconography on northwestern Arabia (Hausleiter 2010a: 220; Jacobs and Macdonald 2009; Potts 1991b). An Achaemenid governor, probably responsible for the Hijaz region (Graf 1990), is mentioned at Dedan (Anderson 2010: 450) but the alleged presence of one at Tayma (Retsö 2003: 239) is a phantom.

Achaemenid domination, partly described by Herodotus (Macdonald 1995: 1367), apparently allowed for the subsequent development of regional powers, at least in northwest Arabia, such as the Lihyanite dynasty at Dedan. Political changes (Retsö 2003: 275–7) led to the decline of Sabaean influence over the aromatics trade c.400 BC. They were replaced by the kingdom of Qataban and the Minaeans. The latter established a merchant colony at Dedan, and it was probably at this time that Achaemenid influence in northern Arabia ended (Ch. II.51). An Arabian kingdom between Egypt and Palestine, centered on the Qedar tribe, lasted until the time of Alexander the Great, who conquered the port of Gaza in 332 BC (Retsö 2003).

6 The Lihyanite Dynasty of Dedan: 5th–1st Centuries BC

Following the kingdom of Dedan (al-Said in press), the Lihyanite dynasty may have ruled the Hijaz between the 5th and 1st centuries BC. Historical reconstructions of this dynasty began with the first exhaustive report on Dedan (al-Khuraybah) by A. Jaussen and R. Savignac (1909, 1914). The name Lihyan is taken from that of a tribe in the Hijaz (Abu al-Hassan 2010) and the Lihyanite script is one of several so-called North Arabian Oasis Scripts (Macdonald 2004). The absolute dates of this dynasty are still under discussion, and, recently, new epigraphic evidence from Khuraybah and Tayma has provided additional information on the Lihyanite king list (Stein in press; Farès-Drappeau 2005; Abu al-Hassan 2010). The Lihyanite dynasty ruled for more than 200 years at Khuraybah, following, for the most part, a dynastic principle of passing on rule to the following generation.

Based on inscriptions from Tayma (see below), it appears that Dedan controlled Tayma for several generations and installed a governor there, probably putting an end to the long-lasting rivalry between these oases, reflected, e.g., in Taymanite rock inscriptions mentioning a war between them. According to a recently proposed chronology of Lihyanite inscriptions at Tayma (Stein in press), a new king has to be added to the existing list of at least 14 kings. In addition, the transition from Achaemenid rule to the dynasty of Lihyan can now be traced, at least at Tayma. Contrary to the so-called Tayma Stone, which should be dated, most probably, to c.380 BC, in the reign of Artaxerxes II (404–359/8 BC), no Persian date appears on the al-Hamra stele, which would have to postdate the former monument. Rather, the al-Hamra stele mentions, for the first time, a certain PSGW of Lihyan, without title. On a newly discovered fragment of a sphinx, PSGW's son is called "king of Lihyan," thus probably indicating the dynastic rise of the PSGW family at Tayma and Dedan. Other Lihyanite rulers at Tayma included 'Ulaym/Gulaym Shahru; Lawdhan (I), in charge of the Lihyanite governor Natir-Il at Tayma; and Tulmay, son of Han-'Aws, mentioned in four inscriptions (years 4, 20, 30, and 40) from the temple of Tayma. References to regnal years spanning five decades (except for the second decade, years 11–20), may indicate that the Lihyanite king repeatedly and regularly visited Tayma to commemorate his rule, but there is no evidence that a Lihyanite king resided at Tayma itself. There were at least three, over-lifesize, royal statues in the temple at Tayma. These may have served to remind the population of the king during his absence. Together with their counterparts at Dedan, they attest to the emergence of a standardized, regional style in the representation of rulers in connection with certain architectonic structures (Hausleiter 2010d, 2010e; al-Said 2010), thus suggesting the leading role of Dedan as a regional power.

Interestingly, contemporary foreign sources, from the Seleucid and Parthian empires, offer no details on internal political affairs in northern Arabia.

Apparently, the fringes of the peninsula were more important than the interior. The increasing significance of maritime trade in the 1st century BC may have been one contributing factor in the shrinking importance of the overland trade for the export of South Arabian aromatics to other parts of the world. Although the end date of the Lihyanite dynasty is uncertain, the growth of Nabataean influence in the region may have been assisted by a weakened Lihyanite dynasty.

7 Archaeological Data From Significant Oases

There are three major oases with 1st millennium BC occupational remains and rich epigraphic references in north Arabia: Duma, Dedan, and Tema. In most of them, recent fieldwork and study of inscribed material has provided new evidence, allowing for a better reconstruction of the history of the north Arabian kingdoms.

Duma (Dumat al-Jandal) can be considered one of the "gateways" of Mesopotamia/Babylonia leading toward Arabia. Located at the eastern end of the Wadi Sirhan, where routes leading toward Syria and the Levant in the west and Assyria to the north intersected, Duma must have played an important role in the trading activities and contacts between these regions and the north and northwest of the Arabian peninsula. Most probably identical with *Adummatu* of the Assyrian sources (see above), the oasis was known from the Neo-Assyrian period onward, and for many years the Assyrians tried to obtain control over it and the tribes in the area. Nabonidus, on the other hand, did not mention Duma in describing his attempted conquest of northwest Arabia. Although "in order to reach Mesopotamia it was necessary to go north and then east to Dumâ, modern al-Jawf" (Macdonald 1997: 335), an undated rock relief of Nabonidus at the Jordanian site of Sela' (Dalley and Goguel 1997) may indicate that the king preferred a westerly route to enter Arabia.

Information on the political and religious significance of Duma for both the region and its tribes, the most important of which was Qedar, is provided by Assyrian sources. In the reign of Assurbanipal, the Qedarite tribes were part of the confederation of Atarsamayin, the equivalent of Ishtar/Astarte/Athtar and chief god of Duma which remained the religious center of the tribes for centuries. The close ties between Babylonia and the Duma region in the 1st millennium BC have been explained by their geographical proximity.

When Duma was investigated archaeologically in the 1980s the architectural remains recovered were mainly attributed to the Nabataean or later periods (al-Muaikel 1994). Recently, a Saudi-Italian and French cooperative project has resumed work at the site, one of the aims of which is to examine the site's development in the earlier 1st millennium BC.

Located in the Wadi al-Qura in modern al-'Ula, the site of al-Khuraybah has been identified with the seat of the kingdom of Dedan and the later Lihyanite dynasty. Dedan/Dadanu was mentioned by Nabonidus on the Harran Stele. Although it is not entirely clear whether the king actually visited there (Schaudig 2001), it has been suggested from the context that he may have defeated its king (Macdonald 1997: 335; Retsö 2003). A number of sites around al-Khuraybah reflect the importance of the settlement at Dedan (Abu al-Hassan 2010; al-Said 2010), although a systematic archaeological and epigraphic reconnaissance has yet to be conducted in the area. Favorable hydrological conditions led to the construction of an elaborate system of water management and irrigation, but it is often difficult to date the elements of it with any degree of chronological precision (Nasif 1988).

The importance of Dedan is reflected in biblical sources indicating, according to some authors, the existence of a "well-organized state" there before the mid-1st millennium BC (al-Said 2010). Like Tayma, Dedan is mentioned together with Saba, but more often it is connected with Qedar. At the very least one can speak of a kingdom of Dedan during the reign of Nabonidus (Macdonald 1995). A king of Dedan, called Kabar'il son of Mati"il, is known from a funerary inscription at the site. A governor 'Abd may date to the Neo-Babylonian period. Apart from some pottery at Tell el-Katheeb (al-Zahrani 2007) similar to Middle Iron Age painted pottery at Tayma, archaeological evidence dating to this period is still absent at al-Khuraybah.

Dedan was well connected to the Levant, the eastern Mediterranean (including the Greek islands, e.g. Delos), and Syria, as well as to South Arabia. A colony of Minaean merchants was established at Dedan from the time of the Dedanite rule until the Lihyanite dynasty and a number of rock-cut Minaean tombs, some of them decorated with lion sculptures and bearing inscriptions, are located around the site. Edomite sources refer to Dedan as the southernmost part of their kingdom, and the name of the Edomite god Qos appears as a theophoric element in one of the Lihyanite king's names. The marriage lists of Qarnaw (ancient Ma'in, in Yemen) listing Dedanite women to be married to merchants [?] from Ma'in, attest to strong ties between Dedan and South Arabia. Better known than the Dedanite kings are the representatives of the dynasty of Lihyan who ruled Dedan in the late 1st millennium BC.

Since 2004, archaeological excavations by the King Saud University (Riyadh, Saudi Arabia) have revealed architectural remains, interpreted as temples or shrines on the basis of their plans and contents, at al-Khuraybah, Tell al-Katheeb, Jabal Umm Daraj, and Danan (Abu al-Hassan 2010). Located next to a famous monolithic water basin in the central part of the site, the most significant building is a temple. It was equipped with a number of over-lifesize human statues, which may have been either royal figures (one of them bears the inscription MLK LYHN, "king of Liyhan") or gods (al-Said 2010).

The main god of Lihyanite Dedan was Dhu Ghabat. In addition, numerous deities from neighboring regions, including Han-'Uzza (morning star), Han-'Aktab (equivalent of Nabu), Qos (chief god of Edom), Ba'al Shamin (southern

Syria), and Wadd (chief god of the Minaeans), belonged to a "cosmopolitan pantheon" (Macdonald 1995: 1362).

As at Tayma, ceramic evidence indicates settlement at Khuraybah began in the 2nd millennium BC (al-Said 2010) and some 13th–12th century BC Qurayyah painted ware sherds have been identified at nearby Tell al-Katheeb, immediately north of al-Khuraybah (al-Zahrani 2007: 184, nos. 77–79, 186, no. 82), where a temple of the goddess al-Kutba was uncovered. At al-Khuraybah, there was a local painted pottery tradition (al-'Ula painted ware; Parr et al. 1970) which probably developed out of the Qurayyah painted ware, although distinctively different from it. The former has been dated to the 6th–1st centuries BC, roughly corresponding to the period of the Lihyanite rule at Dedan.

Tayma is a c.950 hectare oasis located south of an extended former lake (playa, Arab. *sabkha*) which forms the deepest point of a large hydrological catchment area. The presence of groundwater there allowed for irrigation agriculture, and numerous wells and other irrigation installations have been identified. New archaeological excavations have provided substantial evidence of occupation pre-dating the mid-1st millennium, and settlement may have begun as early as the 4th millennium BC, when mid-Holocene climatic changes caused increasing aridity in northern Arabia (Engel et al., in press). Tayma is mainly known as a 1st millennium BC site on the easternmost branch of the incense road, and, especially, as the residence of Nabonidus. It often appears together with Saba in Mesopotamian and biblical sources, a reflection of either specifically South Arabian or generally southerly contacts.

Active at the site since 2004, a Saudi-German cooperative project (Eichmann et al. 2006, 2010, in press a, in press b; cf. Bawden et al. 1980) has defined six occupational periods on the basis of stratigraphic excavations (Hausleiter 2010a). The overwhelming majority of the archaeological remains date to the Early Iron Age (12th–9th century BC), Middle and Late Iron Ages, Late Antiquity/Pre-Islamic period (2nd century BC to 4th century AD) and Islamic period (9th–10th centuries AD).

Apart from two bronze weapons of late 3rd/early 2nd millennium BC Syro-Levantine type found in secondary contexts, only the large city wall dates to the 2nd millennium BC. Other public buildings associated with the probable administrative or religious center of the early to mid-2nd millennium BC have not yet been found. However, sherds of Late Bronze Age Qurayyah painted ware occur in secondary contexts throughout the site.

Early Iron Age contexts occur in scattered locations in the oasis. An isolated but almost complete building complex, surrounded by a c.2 meter thick enclosure of considerable size (c.35 × 38 meters), between the inner and outer walls of the central part of the settlement, contained a number of prestige goods such as faience figurines, painted bowls with representations of lotus flowers, and a scaraboid (Sperveslage in press b) pointing to substantial Egyptian connections, while a faience mask pendant, incised gaming pieces of stone and ivory, and bone combs indicated Syro-Levantine connections at the turn of the 1st millennium BC. Painted pottery with representations of birds and geometric patterns is characteristic of the Early Iron Age at Tayma. It bears only a general similarity to the abovementioned 13th–12th century BC Qurayyah painted ware (Hausleiter 2010b). It remains unclear whether this complex is related to the events leading to the engraving of Pharaoh Ramesses III's cartouche in the vicinity of Tayma. The occurrence of large amounts of small, standardized ceramic beakers may indicate the repeated consumption of liquids, probably in connection with rituals. The presence of faience figurines of Egyptian gods and goddesses, together with the separation of the complex from its surroundings, may point to the religious use of the building, which was destroyed by fire. The area was reused as graveyard at the time of the Lihyanite dynasty. Further traces of limited Early Iron Age occupational remains have been found along the outer wall of Tayma but, so far, not in the (later) center of the settlement. This spatially discrete evidence raises questions about the internal organization of the settlement during the Early Iron Age, although sherds of Early Iron Age pottery with birds have now been found at many other locations of the site in secondary contexts.

The period between the Early Iron Age and Late Iron Age occupations is bridged by the cemetery of Tal'a located southeast of Tayma (outside the walls), from which a series of 9th–5th century BC radiocarbon dates have been obtained (Eichmann 2009; Lora et al. 2010). Since there are large quantities of painted pottery in these graves, some of it still in situ, a similar date has been given to this group of pottery, otherwise known as Sana'iye ceramics (Hausleiter 2010c), which differs from the Early Iron Age painted pottery in both technology and a total lack of figural representation. Based on this data, occupational remains with Sana'iye pottery have been assigned to the Middle Iron Age or even later. Sherds of Sana'iye pottery have been recognized at Tell al-Katheeb (al-Zahrani 2007: 224–5) and in Palestine (Hausleiter 2010a: 233). Middle Iron Age layers have been identified on the outer city wall. However, extensive architectural evidence from the Neo-Assyrian and Late Babylonian periods is still lacking. Nonetheless, the discovery of several monumental, cuneiform-inscribed monuments, chief among them a stele attributed to Nabonidus, as well as further ceramic evidence of the Middle Iron Age period, indicate that this picture may change in the future.

The temple shrine of Qasr al-Hamra (Abu Duruk 1988; Hausleiter in press) and probable remains of one or two of its precursors in the northeastern-central part of the site (Building E-b1) are most probably of Achaemenid date (6th–4th century BC). The same goes for the al-Hamra stele and the "Tayma Stone." A recently discovered funerary stele was used in different periods by three females, each indicated, respectively, by an Imperial Aramaic, a Taymanite Aramaic, and a Nabataean inscription. The texts are written beneath a presentation or drinking scene similar to one seen on a fragment discovered by C. Huber and J. Euting in the late 19th century (Potts 1991b) which can be dated to the 5th–4th centuries BC.

Most of the available information on religion at Tayma dates to this period. The main gods of Tayma were SLM (Salm), Ashima, and Shingalla, all thought to be of Syro-Aramaic origin (Maraqten 1996; Hausleiter in press). Although positive evidence is still lacking, it can be hypothesized that Salm Mahram was venerated in Qasr al-Hamra and Salm HGM in the predecessor of the Hellenistic temple E-b1 (Hausleiter in press).

Substantial occupational remains are only attested in the center of the site after the 4th century BC. The two sanctuaries continued in use during the period of Lihyanite rule. Statues of the type found at Dedan and the Aramaic inscriptions of four Lihyanite kings were found in and around the temple E-b1. Two Imperial Aramaic inscriptions mention governors of Tayma. One of them, dated to the reign of Lawdhan (I), provides evidence of the actual organization of power at Tayma in the late 1st millennium BC. The governor was apparently entrusted with construction works near the inner city wall. Since this reduced the former size of the central area of Tayma (until then c.20 hectares), it could be suggested that this shrinkage may have been a consequence of the shift of regional power toward Dedan. Public royal or administrative buildings of this period have not been identified.

Several funerary stelae, with a stylized representation of a face and a short Aramaic inscription, from a cemetery of the Lihyanite period seem to reflect south Arabian traditions. Based on new archaeological evidence, it has recently been argued, against diffusionist models explaining the origin of southern Arabian cultures, that there was a common, western Arabian cultural background facilitating contacts and exchange between north and south (Schiettecatte 2010).

Nabataean building elements and an inscription of Aretas IV (8 BC–AD 40) have been found in temple E-b1. Additionally, some inscribed sherds and a number of coins have been found in a residential quarter of Nabataean date. A Nabataean inscription on a funerary stele (see above) mentions the 24th year of Aretas IV's reign. The role of the site as part of the Nabataean empire with its regional capital at Mada'in Salih are illuminated by two *strategoi*-inscriptions from the vicinity of Tayma (Nehmé 2009).

8 Conclusions

During the 1st millennium BC, northern Arabia was well connected with its neighbors from Egypt in the west to Mesopotamia in the east. Rather than having a ruling elite concentrated in one capital that functioned as both a political and a religious center (as in Assyria and Babylonia), the political organization and control of the vast and environmentally often hostile territory was distributed amongst a number of powerful oases. These served as economic, religious, and, to a lesser extent, political reference points for mobile nomadic groups possessing the essential means of transport – i.e., the camel – as well as a deep knowledge of the territory, its dangers, and the location of water sources, all essential for survival. This rather decentralized or multicentric model of settlement and local power, combined with the possibility of very flexible reactions, another consequence of the complex geography of the region, severely limited the success of potential foreign conquerors right up until the time of the Ottoman Empire and the establishment of the Kingdom of Saudi Arabia. On the other hand, as a result of the immense demands of the Mesopotamian and Mediterranean elites for luxury goods (particularly aromatics), the populations of northern Arabia and their male and female leaders were able to thrive and develop their interests against the foreign powers, benefiting economically from trade. Even during the Nabataean period, the cooperative way of life forged by sedentary, agriculturally active, oasis populations and nomadic, camel-breeding groups was a sufficient and stable model, apparently never exceeding a regional concentration of power. Dispersed oases, even 150 kilometers apart from each other, were not isolated entities and there were several attempts at broadening the scale of territorial/economic control at a sub-regional scale, as the cases of Dedan and Tayma show.

Since the general outline of the political behavior of the northern Arabian kingdoms during the 1st millennium BC toward foreign powers seems clear, it is hoped that future research will lead to more insight into the inner workings of the region – e.g., on the resolution of social and political conflicts and economic crises, demographic developments, and religion in this ancient contact zone.

GUIDE TO FURTHER READING

A concise historical summary of 1st millennium BC northern Arabia was published by M.C.A. Macdonald (1995), with reference to original textual sources; the same author has written an excellent overview of ancient northwest Arabian languages and scripts (2004). Fundamental studies on the history and culture of the Arabs include Eph'al (1982) and Retsö (2003), the latter exhaustively discussing the available textual evidence up to the Umayyad period. Avanzini (1997) unites important contributions on trade and trade relations in the Arabian peninsula, mostly with reference to textual sources. Archaeological survey and excavation reports from northern Arabia have been published in the Saudi Arabian journal *Atlal* since 1977. Many relevant studies can also be found in the journal *Arabian Archaeology and Epigraphy*. The monumental exhibition catalogue *Roads of Arabia* (al-Ghabban et al. 2010) summarizes the current state of archaeological research in Saudi Arabia. Excavation reports and studies on rock inscriptions have been published as monographs (in Arabic) by the Antiquities Sector of the Saudi Commission for Tourism and Antiquities. Several brief reports have also been published in the *PSAS*. Based on their investigations at Tayma in 1979, Edens and Bawden (1989) discussed the history and trade relations of the Hijaz as well as the pottery chronology of Tayma (Bawden and

Edens 1988), mainly contrasting the views of P.J. Parr (1988). The publication of the north Arabian survey by Parr et al. (1970, 1972) in the late 1960s is still essential for an understanding of regional aspects of material culture, especially pottery. As to the history of research and the first publication of inscriptions, the studies of Jaussen and Savignac (1909, 1914), Euting (1914), and Winnett and Reed (1970) are among the most significant contributions concerning 1st millennium BC inscriptions from the region.

CHAPTER FORTY-FOUR

Egypt and the Near East

Thomas Hikade

1 Egypt and the Near East in Prehistoric Times

At the onset of the Lower Pleistocene, *Homo erectus* evolved in Africa and was well adapted to migrate through changing vegetational zones. The mobile and highly adaptable *Homo erectus* radiated out of Africa more than 1,000,000 years ago, one possible route leading via the Sahara toward the west into Europe and a second eastern movement via northeast Africa into Asia (Fagan 2007: 71–8). At this time, we also see the first use of stone as a raw material to manufacture tools. Finds from Ubeidiya (Israel), dated to around 1.4 million years ago (mya), are some of the few finds of this early radiation into southwest Asia (Bar-Yosef 1999). Given the distribution of the hand-axe, the multipurpose tool most closely linked with *Homo erectus*, from England in the west to the India–Bangladesh border in the east, and throughout Africa, including Egypt, it seems obvious that the mobile hunter-gatherers of the Lower Paleolithic may have moved back and forth from Egypt into the Near East. Such movements also occurred during the Middle Paleolithic, which saw the widespread use of the so-called Levallois technique, from Europe to southwest Asia and northern Africa. This method, associated with Neanderthals, archaic and modern humans, allowed for the production of predetermined stone flakes, blades, and even stone spearheads. Then another migration wave brought people from Africa to the Near East. Using mitochondrial DNA to trace maternal ancestry, it has been shown that modern humans moved into the Levant from Africa around 100,000 years ago (Rose and Petraglia

---

A Companion to the Archaeology of the Ancient Near East, First Edition.
Edited by D.T. Potts.
© 2012 Blackwell Publishing Ltd. Published 2012 by Blackwell Publishing Ltd.

2009: 9, with refs), thus confirming the out-of-Africa model proposed by Lewin (1987).

Later, during the Epipaleolthic, hunter-gatherers crossed, apparently back and forth, from the Sinai to the Nile Valley, where they stayed in seasonal camps. Several of these campsites were discovered in the 19th century at Helwan, just south of modern Cairo (Schmidt 1996). The type-fossils of the toolkit used by these hunter-gatherers were the "Helwan lunate" and the notched "Helwan point," which show similarities with stone tool traditions of the Sinai. One similar arrowhead was also discovered in Layer I at the Neolithic site of Merimde-Benisalâme in the western Nile Delta (Eiwanger 1984: Pl. 57.I.1106). Pottery from the same layer also seems to have affinities with material from southwest Asia and might be an indication of contact or migration between this region and the Nile Delta (Eiwanger 1984: 59–63).

The important site of Maadi, near Cairo, gives us a good insight into Egypt's place in the wider trading network of the Near East and northern Africa in the early 4th millennium BC. Commodities that reached Maadi ranged from asphalt and resin, cedar wood and ceramics, to tabular flint scrapers, large "Canaanean blades" used as harvesting tools, copper objects, and copper ore (Rizkana and Seeher 1987, 1988, 1989, 1990). Analyses of copper objects and ore suggest that they possibly originated at Timna and Feinan in the Wadi Arabah (Pernicka and Hauptmann 1989). Specialized metallurgical sites just north of Aqaba in Jordan may have supplied copper objects and ore to Maadi as well (Khalil and Schmidt 2009). It has even been suggested that some of the stone tools from Aqaba were Egyptian and are an indication of a possible Egyptian presence there (Hikade 2009). At the same time, underground dwellings have been linked to immigrants coming to Egypt from the southern Levant to settle at Maadi (Hartung 2004), a situation similar to that found at Buto in the western Nile Delta (Faltings 2002). It has been suggested that these immigrants brought with them the Near Eastern technique of building with mudbrick (Wilkinson 2010) as well as the idea of writing (Wilkinson 2003). This hypothesis requires additional archaeological evidence, however, as there are very early hieroglyphs at Abydos in Upper Egypt (Dreyer 1998).

Various Egyptian finds also point to the adoption and adaptation of Mesopotamian motifs in artwork. On an ivory knife handle, said to be from Gebel el-Arak in Upper Egypt, we see on one side a man depicted between two lions (Asselberghs 1961: Pl. 39). In clear Mesopotamian fashion the bearded man wears a cap and a long skirt. In the Painted Tomb 100 at Hierakonpolis, we see a similar figure amongst other scenes of combat (Quibell and Green 1902: Pl. 76). There, however, the execution of the painting is rather simplistic and, while the lions are easy to identify, the man is not shown wearing the garment seen on the Gebel el-Arak knife. The so-called "lion tamer" or "master of the animals" seems to be the classic iconography of humans controlling the wilderness – i.e., a *topos* of "order vs chaos" and obviously an idea shared by the elites of Egypt and the

Near East (Boehmer 1974). Further shared motifs highlighting the transfer of ideas between Mesopotamia and Egypt include the rosette, intertwined snakes, and the griffin. However, contacts between Egypt and Mesopotamia remained small scale and were most likely effected via the northern Levant through sites like Byblos, and from there onward by sea or overland by caravan.

Later, during the Levantine Early Bronze Age Ia, when interregional trade picked up pace, foreigners from the Levant, probably merchants, stayed for some time at Maadi making use of underground dwellings (Hartung 2004). At this time Levantine pottery also appeared at other sites in the Delta such as Tell el-Farkha (Mączyńska 2004: Fig. 10) and more and more sites in Egypt had copper, turquoise, and lapis lazuli (Hartung 2001: Figs. 54–55; Hendrickx and Bavay 2002). Cylinder seals and seal impressions were initially imports or copies of seals from Mesopotamia and Susa in Iran (Boehmer 1975; Hill 2004). The appearance of lapis lazuli in Egypt highlights the fact that Egypt was an active partner in a long-distance trade network that extended as far east as Afghanistan, where the major source of lapis lazuli used in the Near East is located.

One of the major finds documenting the long-distance trade and exchange of luxury goods is tomb U-j, in Predynastic Cemetery U at Abydos in Upper Egypt, dated to c.3300 BC. Not only did it contain a large obsidian bowl, manufactured in an Egyptian style (Dreyer 1992), and some of the earliest hieroglyphs (Dreyer 1998), but it also yielded about 360 imported vessels (Hartung 2001, 2002). These once held wine and, with a volume of 6–7 liters each, this represents about 4,500 liters of wine for the afterlife. Based on archaeological and chemical analyses, the containers came from a wide area in greater Palestine (Hartung 2001: 53–66) and represent a perfect example of long-distance trade between Egypt and the Levant. Finds of "spiral reserved slip" pottery at Buto provide further evidence that this contact also extended to northern Syria, where this pottery originated (Köhler 1998: 37–9, Pls. 68, 74).

The relationship between Egypt and the southern Levant was characterized by a variety of interactions (Braun 2004, 2009). There were sites in the southern Levant that were only populated by Egyptians and appear to have been permanent way stations. At some sites large quantities of Egyptian pottery and stone tools indicate an Egyptian presence, while at others a few Egyptian finds indicate that these places were hardly in contact with Egyptians at all. The absence of Egyptian finds at places in the hill country suggests that it was beyond the Egyptian sphere of interest.

2 Egypt and the Near East from the Early Dynastic to the End of the First Intermediate Period (c.3100–2055 BC)

Egypt emerged as a unified state at the end of the 4th millennium BC and was governed in the Early Dynastic period by kings of the 1st and 2nd Dynasties, c.3100–2686 BC (Bard 2000). It was clearly the demand for cedar that led the Egyptian kings to focus on the important harbor site of Byblos in Lebanon. By the end of the 2nd Dynasty, Byblos had become so important that the Egyptian king Khasekhemwy sent a diorite vessel with his name on it to the ruler of Byblos (Dunand 1937: Pl. 39, no. 1115; 1939: 26). Other foreign products, such as oil and wine, were also imported. Ceramic containers for these Levantine commodities have been found at several sites in Egypt, including the Royal Tombs of the 1st Dynasty at Abydos (Braun 2009: 27–8). Stone vessel fragments inscribed with the names of Old Kingdom Egyptian kings (c.2680–2160 BC) show that this type of gift exchange continued throughout the 3rd millennium BC (Dunand 1928: 68–75; 1937: Pls. 36–38; 1939: 27).

King Sneferu of the 4th Dynasty mentioned in an inscription on the Palermo Stone that he commissioned the building of c.50 meter long ships made of cedar (Breasted 2001: 66). The remains of one such cedar ship belonging to his son and successor Khufu (Cheops) have survived, as the boat was disassembled and buried next to the king's pyramid (Jenkins 1980). One expedition returning from the Levant during the early 5th Dynasty with people from that region, including sailors and their families, often referred to as Asiatics in Egyptological literature, was depicted in the pyramid complex of King Sahure at Abusir (Borchardt 1913: Pls. 12–13) and a similar scene can be found in the causeway of the pyramid of King Unas at Saqqara from the end of the 5th Dynasty (Bietak 1998: 36). The Asiatic men are shown with long hair, sometimes with a hairband, wearing either short kilts or long cloaks. Interestingly, the commanding officers in both cases were Egyptian, while the crew consisted of people from the Levant (Bietak 1998). Some of the Asiatics obviously settled permanently in Egypt. This is indicated by the fact that non-Egyptian, bent-axis, and broad-room temples were established at sites such as Tell Ibrahim Awad in the eastern Nile Delta (Bietak 2003a).

Sources from tombs and literature, however, also hint at a hostile relationship between Egypt and the Levant. Two scenes in Egyptian tombs depict the Egyptian siege of a fortified town somewhere in the Levant (Schulz 2002). In both instances the Levantine men are again shown in a stereotypical fashion similar to that seen on the royal monuments. The women also have long hair and wear a long overcoat. In the tomb of Inti at Deshasheh they are even shown joining in the fight. In the autobiography of Weni, a high official during the 6th Dynasty, we hear of a raid against the Levant with his troops sent by land and by sea (Lichtheim 1975: 20). Slightly closer to home, the Egyptian kings began, during the 3rd Dynasty under King Sekhemkhet, to send out expeditions to the turquoise mines in the western Sinai Peninsula (Gardiner et al. 1952, 1955; Eichler 1993).

At the end of the Old Kingdom, Egypt became a fragmented country with no supreme ruler governing the land, a time that is commonly known as the First Intermediate Period (c.2160–2055 BC). The so-called "Instruction addressed to King Merikare" (Lichtheim 1975: 9–109), a text set in the First Intermediate

Period but only preserved on papyri from the New Kingdom, hints at an ambivalent relationship between Egypt and the Levant at that time. The text mentions the import of cedar wood, seemingly confirming a long-standing, peaceful trading tradition. On the other hand, Asiatics are also described as having infiltrated Egypt and having had to be pushed out. No matter how historical this text is, the fractured political nature of the Egyptian state would not have allowed for intense and wide-ranging economic and diplomatic exchanges between Egypt and her neighbors to the northeast and the south during the First Intermediate Period.

Looking further afield, while various contacts with the Levant and Syria are clearly in evidence from Early Dynastic times and onward throughout the Old Kingdom, it seems that there were no direct contacts between Egypt and Mesopotamia during the 3rd millennium BC.

3 Egypt and the Near East During Middle Kingdom and the Second Intermediate Period (c.2055–1550 BC)

Around 2055 BC, one of the regional rulers of the First Intermediate Period, Mentuhotep II of Thebes, succeeded in once again uniting the country, becoming the first king of the 11th Dynasty (c.2055–1985 BC) and founding father of the Middle Kingdom (c.2055–1650 BC). This dynasty was followed by the very stable government of the 12th Dynasty (c.1985–1795 BC). Although evidence for contacts between Egypt and the Levant during the Middle Kingdom comes from various Egyptian texts, wall paintings, and temple reliefs, as well as from the archaeological record of Egyptian finds in the Levant and Syro-Palestinian objects in Egypt, the relationship between Egypt and her northeastern neighbors and the history of this period remain enigmatic (Redford 1992: 71–97; Cohen 2001).

The experiences of an Egyptian actually living in the Levant are described in the *Tale of Sinuhe* (Lichtheim 1975: 222–35), a story set in the reign of King Senwosret (Sesostris) I. It tells how Sinuhe, a middle-ranking courtier, fled to Byblos after the assassination of Amenemhet I. He ended up in Upper Retenu, in modern Lebanon, where he was welcomed by the benevolent ruler Ammunenshi, whose court hosted other Egyptians too. Sinuhe moved throughout the southern Levant with his tribes, fighting other tribes and plundering their food and livestock (cattle, sheep, and goats). He spent many years living in this way, as a kind of Bedouin *sheikh*, before finally returning to Egypt. His story gives us a window onto the tribal, semi-nomadic societies of the Levant during the Middle Bronze Age.

People from the Levant, on the other hand, participated as small contingents in Egyptian expeditions to the mining regions in the western Sinai Peninsula led by Khebded, brother of the ruler of Retenu (Bietak 1996: 10–21, Figs. 13–15;

Hikade 2007: 12–18). During the early Middle Kingdom, Asiatic men were still shown with yellow skin, long hair, and beards, similar to those of the Old Kingdom. During the later 12th Dynasty, however, depictions of Asiatics show a change to a "mushroom" hairstyle. In the tomb of the mayor Khnumhotep at Beni Hasan in Middle Egypt, we see a small caravan of eight Asiatic men together with four women and three children approaching the tomb owner and handing him galena (lead sulfide, PbS) from the eastern desert (Newberry 1893: Pl. 31). The Asiatics are dressed in multicolored, woolen dresses, knee-length kilts, and sometimes an overcoat. Some of the men wear sandals, while the women and one boy wear shoe-like coverings on their feet. The women have long hair, with a hairband, and wear long, colored, woolen dresses, exposing one shoulder. The men bear a variety of arms, including spears, bows, and axes. In this case, the accompanying text speaks of 37 *aamu*, meaning Asiatics. Highlighting the ambivalent feelings that ancient Egyptians had toward foreigners, the determinative glyph for Asiatics takes the form of a bound captive. Asiatics, however, were also employed as normal workers by the Egyptians, given Egyptian names and apparently assimilated into Egyptian society during the Middle Kingdom (T. Schneider 2003).

At the beginning of the 2nd millennium BC, Egypt's 12th Dynasty kings initiated an aggressive policy toward the regions beyond Egypt's borders. To the south they erected a string of fortresses to ward off the rising power of Kerma in the Third Cataract Region, while to the north fortifications were built along the Way of Horus, a route that led from the eastern Nile Delta to the Levant (Vogel 2004, 2008, 2010) which was mostly home to semi-nomadic pastoralists. Yet some sites in the Levant, especially Byblos, were again of particular interest to the Egyptian crown.

The general attitude toward foreigners becomes quite clear in some of the texts that we have from ancient Egypt. In one case, King Amenemhet I expressed his distaste by making Asiatics do the "dog walk" (Lichtheim 1975: 135–9). This submissive tone was also picked up by Khnumhotep, who served under Amenemhet I, in the autobiography in his tomb at Beni Hasan where he states that Asiatics were defeated (Breasted 2001: section 465). A similar attitude is evident in the so-called "Execration Texts" from the late 12th Dynasty (Posener 1940). These texts were written in hieratic (cursive) script on figurines and pots that were smashed in order to magically destroy those named. They list the names of places and regions in the Levant, as well as tribes, like those living around Ullaza and Byblos. Interestingly, the fact that the ruler of Byblos is never named in the Execration Texts indicates Egypt's appreciation of and continued good relations with the city. Other texts, however, confirm a generally hostile attitude toward the Levant and Cyprus. A text of Amememet II mentions aggressive, targeted attacks against Cyprus, Ura in southeastern Anatolia, a site near Ugarit (Altenmüller and Moussa 1991), and later Shechem, as documented on the stele of Khu-Sobek, a soldier who served under Senwosret III (Raedler 2008). In the first text, the number of prisoners is given as 1,554 Asiatics. As the text mentions c.150 kilograms of silver booty, one might link the famous "Tod Treasure," discovered in a temple in Upper Egypt, with this event. The treasure, in fact a ritual temple deposit, contained four bronze chests bearing the name of Amenemhet II (Bisson de la Roque 1937). These were filled with more than 100 silver objects (ingots, chains, and small bowls, flattened and folded in order to reduce their volume) weighing almost 10 kilograms. In addition, cylinder seals and several thousand beads of lapis lazuli provide evidence of the wider trade and diplomatic networks linking Egypt and the Near East at this time (Pierrat-Bonnefois 1999).

In spite of this seeming hostility, Egypt also helped to ease tension amongst the city-states of Syria-Palestine. For instance, a conflict between Byblos and Ullaza was resolved under Senwosret III with Egypt's involvement (Allen 2009).

Egypt's influence on and contacts with Byblos were manifold and relatively well documented. The rulers of Byblos actually took on the Egyptian title of mayor or count (*h3ty-c*), as did the rulers of Kumidi (modern Kamid el-Loz; Ch. II.41) (Edel 1983), as well as the title of hereditary prince (*iry-pct*) (Montet 1928: 155–61). One of the rulers of Byblos, Ip-shemu-abi, son of Abi-Shemu, who was buried in Tomb II in the Royal Cemetery at Byblos, even wrote his name in an Egyptian cartouche on a pendant made of gold and semi-precious stones (Montet 1928, 1929: 165–6, Pl. 97). This "prince of Byblos" also possessed a sickle-sword featuring hieroglyphics and Egyptian uraei (Montet 1928; 1929: 174–7, Pl. 99), the stylized, upright, spitting cobra. Antin, one of the rulers of Byblos, even took on the title "ruler of rulers" according to an Egyptian text found at Byblos (Dunand 1937: Pl. 30). Furthermore, the ruling elite at Byblos developed a pseudo-hieroglyphic script (Dunand 1978; Hoch 1995). The close connection and cultural interplay between Egypt and Byblos is also visible in the so-called "Temple of the Obelisks" at Byblos and its deposits (Dunand 1950, 1954, 1958). The temple is so named because of its many standing stones with a pyramid-shaped top resembling Egyptian obelisks. For many years priests buried votive offerings in jars under the floor of the temple after removing them from their original place in the temple. The most prominent group of offerings consists of a large number of copper or bronze figurines, c.40 centimeters tall and gilded, in the form of a standing male with a tall, conical cap (Dunand 1950: Pl. 115). Both their posture and headgear bear a clear resemblance to the striding figures of Egyptian kings wearing the White Crown of Upper Egypt, and are evidence of Egyptian influence. Yet they were mass-produced at Byblos and are not simply efforts to copy an Egyptian style, but rather to incorporate it into a local tradition (Hansen 1969). This blending of Levantine and Egyptian style marks the beginning of a synthesis of artistic modes that ultimately resulted in an "international style" across the Near East, Egypt, and the eastern Mediterranean. A second notable group of votive offerings was made up of hundreds of locally made, faïence figurines with obvious parallels in Middle Kingdom Egypt

(Dunand 1950: Pls. 96–108). Finally, the famous Montet Jar contained many Egyptianizing objects such as seals, amulets, and figures of animals that were worshipped in Egypt, such as the ibis and baboon (Montet 1928: 111–25 and Pls. 61–64, 68; Tufnell and Ward 1966).

The Egyptian kings of the Middle Kingdom clearly had contact with the rulers of Levantine coastal centers such as Ugarit, Beruta (Beirut), and Byblos. These contacts were embedded in a system of diplomatic gift exchange among ruling elites. Some of these gifts have actually been found during excavation, although their archaeological context is not always clear and some might have found their way into the Levant and Syria after the Middle Kingdom. Finds from intact tombs in the Royal Cemetery at Byblos include an obsidian jar (Tomb III) and a golden pectoral (Tomb I) with the name of Amenemhet III, as well as a box (Tomb II) inscribed with the name of Amenemhet IV (Montet 1928: nos. 610, 611, 614), confirming gift exchange during the late 12th Dynasty. Other precious finds include an Egyptian-made mace of silver, gold, ivory, and marble that was sent by the 13th Dynasty Egyptian king Hetepibre to Immeya, a king of the Syrian city of Ebla, in whose tomb it was found, along with an Egyptian golden ring inlaid with a scarab (Scandone Matthiae 1988: 71–3).

Egyptian scarabs also appeared in the southern Levant during the Middle Kingdom. They became so popular that many were later locally produced and, while used as seals of administration in the Egyptian context, they often functioned as funerary amulets in the Levant (Ben-Tor 2007). Finally, a very fragmentary text from the Papyrus Lythgoe mentions a merchant loading his ship for a journey to Byblos (Simpson 1960). As the inscription of a "scribe of the army" found at Byblos indicates (Dunand 1937: Pl. 129, no. 3594), such trips may have served to transport military personnel between Egypt and Byblos.

At the beginning of the 18th century BC, the 13th Dynasty (c.1795–1650 BC) initially continued the foreign policies of its predecessor. Growing internal political divisions, however, again created a fragmented country with a volatile ruling house (Quirke 1990). More and more people from the Levant entered the Nile Delta where they increasingly gained political and economic control. This process is best illustrated at Tell el-Dab'a (ancient Avaris), one of the most important excavations in Egypt of the past few decades (Bietak 1996, 2001, 2008). Founded in the early Middle Kingdom and completely resettled by Canaanites in the 12th Dynasty, Avaris grew into an administrative center and developed over time into a large, cosmopolitan trading city and harbor with a mixed population made up of Egyptians, partially Egyptianized people from the Levant, and people from the Aegean. Based on the analysis of pottery from Tell el-Dab'a, it has been shown that an initial trading interest in the southern Levant shifted northward to the area around Byblos and Syria. Imported pottery at Tell el-Dab'a, including Levantine painted ware, mostly jugs with red-banded zones for serving wine and luxurious bichrome jugs (Bagh 2003), first appeared in the reign of Amenemhet II. Later, this was increasingly replaced by so-called Syro-Cilician pottery that originated further north and may be taken as a sign of increasing political and economical interest in the region. It is very likely that many of the foreign residents of Tell el-Dabʻa originated there.

During the 12th Dynasty it seems that the Asiatics in Egypt were predominantly male, working as soldiers for the Egyptian administration. Around half of their tombs contained weapons such as javelins, battle axes, and daggers (Schiestl 2008, 2009). Of particular interest is the fenestrated, so-called "duckbill axe" that was used throughout the Middle Bronze Age by warriors in the Levant (Schiestl 2008: Fig. 1). A fine example with a golden blade and shaft comes from the Temple of the Obelisks at Byblos (Dunand 1950: Pl. 134). One of the tombs at Tell el-Dabʻa also contained the broken statue of an Asiatic with a typical, mushroom-shaped hairstyle (Bietak 1996: Pl. 4), resembling what we see depicted in the tomb of the mayor Khnumhotep at Beni Hasan, noted above.

At the beginning of the 13th Dynasty a large palace was built at Tell el-Dabʻa which was inhabited by Asiatic governors (Bietak 1996: 21–30, Figs. 18–19). A hematite cylinder seal found in its northern wing has the earliest depiction of the Syrian weather-god Baal Zephon portrayed as protector of sailors and overlord of the sea (Porada 1984). The seal displays Syrian glyptic traits but was cut in Egypt under Egyptian influence. Thee foreign governors were buried in a small cemetery right next to the palace. These were built in Egyptian mudbrick style, but the funerary rituals were un-Egyptian. One clearly Asiatic burial custom was the interment of a pair of donkeys and sheep/goat in an adjacent burial pit (Bietak 1996: Figs. 20–21, Pls. 9–10). By this time the town had widespread contacts not only with the Levant but also the Aegean, as finds of Kamares ware and an Aegean gold pendant from the palace reveal (Bietak 1996: Pl. 1).

By the 13th Dynasty the Asiatics also had their own sacred precinct at Tell el-Dabʻa (Bietak 1996: 36–48, Figs. 30–32). Remains of acorn point to a kind of tree cult, and the "absence of pig bones in the offerings suggests that the consumption of pork was taboo. In one cemetery surrounding Temple III the tomb of a deputy treasurer named ʻAmu (lit. "the Asiatic") was found. His grave goods consisted of eapons of late Middle Bronze Age IIA type, some Egyptian pottery, early Tell el-Yahudiya ware, a scarab, and six sacrificed donkeys (Bietak 1996: 41, Fig. 35). Tell el-Yahudiya is thought to have originated near Byblos, eventually becoming so popular that it was mass-produced in pottery workshops in the Levant, Cyprus, and Egypt (Bietak 1996: 5–59, Figs. 46–49). The Tell el-Yahudiya ware at Tell el-Dabʻa consists of small, ovoid, or piriform jugs with handles, polished surface, and impressed decoration, often in triangles, and bands covering almost all the body of the vessel. The jugs were possibly for oil and, along with so-called Canaanite amphorae, used for wine and olive oil, are among the most recognizable pottery forms of this genre. Their vast quantity highlights the substantial scale of trade in these commodities (Bietak 1996: Fig. 50).

A short-lived 14th Dynasty in the eastern Nile Delta was followed by the Hyksos rulers (15th Dynasty) who had their capital at Avaris. Hyksos, the Greek form of the Egyptian *heqa-khasut*, essentially meaning "foreign ruler," were, however, neither invaders nor a people, but they rose to power from the Asiatic elite and warrior class that had probably lived at Avaris for generations. They adopted the royal Egyptian titulary, including the title *heqa-khasut* (Bietak 1996: Fig. 52). We may also assume that they wore all the other royal regalia of an Egyptian king. Their rule, however, did not encompass the entirety of Egypt. At Thebes, in the south, another line of Egyptian kings known as the 17th Dynasty reigned. After initially cooperating with the Hyksos rulers, the Theban kings Seqenenra and Kamose rose up against them. As we learn from the autobiography of the military officer Ahmose in his tomb (Lichtheim 1976: 12–15), it was King Ahmose, founder of the 18th Dynasty, who ultimately marched and sailed north with his troops, besieged the Hyksos capital Avaris, and finally drove out the Hyksos rulers and their supporters. Yet, parts of the Asiatic population in Egypt remained in the country and continued to live within Egyptian society.

4 Egypt and the Near East During the New Kingdom (c.1550–1069 BC)

After the violent expulsion of the Hyksos, we see the rise of the Late Bronze Age New Kingdom (Bryan 2000). This empire extended its power far beyond Egypt's borders and controlled the Levant. Its armies marched to the Euphrates, and up the Nile to the 4th Cataract, almost 1,000 kilometers south of the traditional Egyptian border at the 1st Cataract, near modern Aswan. Egyptian texts on papyri, stelae, and temple walls, as well as autobiographies of military leaders found in Egyptian tombs, are a major source for the history of the New Kingdom and its relations with the Near East.

The 18th Dynasty (1550–1295 BC) undertook a series of aggressive campaigns of conquest in order to gain economic and political control over the Levant and southern Syria. At the same time, Egyptian armies sailed south to gain control over Nubia. This aggressive expansion of Egypt beyond its borders, in a manner of pay-back, was most likely triggered by the traumatic experience of rule by the Hyksos and the attack of the Kushites from Nubia at the end of the Second Intermediate Period.

Egypt's major competitors in the Near East around 1500 BC were Babylon (then ruled by the Kassites), the Hittites in Anatolia, and the Hurrian-speaking kingdom of Mitanni in the northern Levant, Syria, and Assyria. According to Egyptian sources, the first king to mount a large-scale and wide-ranging campaign northward was Thutmose I (c.1504–1492 BC) (Redford 1992: 153–5). His troops reached the Euphrates in an area the Egyptians called Nahrin and on the way back the king indulged in hunting Syrian elephants in Niya (Ch. II.41), probably along the Orontes River. In the absence of any archaeological material from the Levant and Syria to confirm such a military show of force, it is possible that the impact of the campaign was not very great. However, during the 15th century BC Thutmose III (c.1479–1425 BC) campaigned relentlessly in the Levant to gain Egyptian control (Redford 2003, 2005). According to Egyptian sources, this militaristic strategy faced its first major crisis in the first year of Thutmose III's sole reign, just after the death of his co-regent Queen Hatshepsut, at the famous battle of Megiddo, an account of which is inscribed on the temple walls at Karnak and was recounted decades later on a stele erected in Nubia (Redford 2003: 7–34; Spalinger 2005: 83–100). At Megiddo, the king of Qadesh had gathered a coalition of hundreds of city-states. Intent on meeting this challenge to his regional control, the pharaoh mustered his troops, marching quickly north from Egypt along the coast road. In a surprising and bold move, Thutmose III led his troops trough the narrow Aruna Pass and caught the enemy off guard. The ensuing battle was won and, after a seven-month siege, the defeated enemies had to swear an oath of allegiance to the Egyptian king. Yet Thutmose III's major opponent, the king of Qadesh, managed to escape.

A good insight into how the nobility of the Levant and Syria, and thus Thutmose III's enemies, were dressed when they were not in combat is provided by the wall painting in western Thebes of the Vizier Rehkmire, who served under Thutmose III and his successor and co-regent Amenhotep II. In this tomb, men from the Levant and Syria bring various precious objects as tribute, such as a chariot, metal vessels, and copper ingots, as well as horses, a bear, and a Syrian elephant (Davies 1944: Pls. 21–23). Some of the men have long hair, others short hair, and most are bearded. They wear long cloaks with tassels in front. The women wear a cape over a folded, tri-partite dress which is tightened around the waist, and several are accompanied by children.

A more humorous insight comes from the Ramesside tale of the taking of the city of ancient Joppe, near modern Tel Aviv, set in the time of Thutmose III. In this tale the Egyptians tricked the locals by having 200 Egyptian soldiers, under the command of General Djehuti, enter the town hidden in sacks on the backs of donkeys, in a kind of Ali Baba and the 40 thieves motif, to take the town (Petrie 1895).

The climax of Thutmose III's campaigns was his attack on the kingdom of Mitanni. Once again his army reached the Euphrates (c.1472 BC). The account of this victory can be found in the annals of Thutmose III and, with Mitanni's defeat, Egypt's empire extended further into the Near East than ever before (Redford 2003: 220–32). Thutmose III had established Egypt as a major international power in the Near East, an achievement soon acknowledged by Babylon, Assyria, and the Hittites. Yet Mitanni later regained its power and Amenhotep II (c.1427–1400 BC) ended hostilities by signing a peace treaty with the kingdom of Mitanni (Redford 1992: 163–6).

During the long reign of Amenhotep III (c.1390–1352 BC) and his successor Amenhotep IV (c.1352–1336 BC), Egyptian military and diplomatic activities are well documented in the correspondence known as the Amarna letters, found in the capital of Amenhotep IV, modern Tell el-Amarna in Middle Egypt (Cohen and Westbrook 2000; Moran 1992). The archive comprises around 350 cuneiform tablets inscribed in Akkadian, the *lingua franca* of the age, and spans roughly four decades during the latter part of the reign of Amenhotep III, the reign of Amenhotep IV (Akhenaten), and the early years of the reign of Tutankhamun (c.1336–1327 BC). About 50 of the tablets deal with diplomatic ties between the Great Powers, a "band of brothers" of the time: Babylon, Assyria, the Hittites, Cyprus, and Egypt. This corpus deals mainly with imperial concerns including dynastic succession, interdynastic marriage, gift exchange, and matters of allegiance. We read, for instance, of princesses from Mitanni and Babylon taken by the Egyptian kings as wives while, surprisingly, Egypt refused to send any princesses away, deeming it apparently inappropriate (Meier 2000). The bulk of the archive consists of letters sent to the Egyptian court by Egypt's vassal states in the Levant (Na'aman 2000). Imperial documents of this sort provide insight into the quarrels between the city-states in the Levant. They also touch upon tribute and economics and clearly reveal the attempts of the local Levantine rulers to balance their alliances within Egypt's empire there.

Egypt's Near Eastern domains were organized in three provinces. Closest to Egypt was the region of Canaan with its capital at Gaza. Then came the province of Upe around Damascus and the Beqaa valley with its center at Kumidi (modern Kamid el-Loz). Finally, to the north lay the province of Amurru, including Byblos, with its Egyptian headquarters at Sumur. Each of the territories was governed by an official titled *rabisu* which might be the equivalent of the Egyptian title "overseer of the northern foreign countries," who had to liaise with the local rulers. The tone of the vassals' letters is very subservient and the local rulers stress at length that they will obey Egypt's rule through a special controller of the north, and always be on guard for Egypt. Amongst the many letters from Egyptian vassals the correspondence from Byblos assumes a prominent position. Suffering a barrage of attacks and plots instigated by its northern neighbor Amurru under its king Abdi-Ashirta, Rib-Addu of Byblos, a true and loyal ally of Egypt, sent dozens of letters to Egypt requesting support. Egypt stepped in, Abdi-Ashirta was executed, and his son Aziru replaced him, swearing allegiance to Egypt (Moran 1992: 137–225).

Archaeologically, the cosmopolitan flair, as well as the scale and variety of economic and diplomatic exchanges between Africa, the Near East, and the Aegean in the Late Bronze Age (Liverani 1990) is perfectly illustrated at Uluburun, off the southern coast of Anatolia, where a ship sank at the end of the 14th century BC (Pulak 2001, 2008). The armed merchants and crew were most likely Canaanites, while two men came from the Mycenaean elite and a third individual from the northern Balkans (Pulak 1998: 216–18). The ship was carrying 10 tons of copper ingots from Cyprus, more than one ton of tin (possibly from Central Asia), blue and turquoise glass ingots from the Near East and Egypt, ebony from tropical Africa, half a ton of resin (possibly from the area around the Sea of

Galilee), and many other sorts of herbs, spices, nuts, and fruits. Oil was traded in large storage jars from Cyprus. A most astonishing find from Egypt is a small gold scarab with the name of Queen Nefertiti on it found among the scrap gold and silver jewelry (Weinstein 1989).

From an Egyptian point of view, the cultural symbiosis with the Near East is best exemplified in the person of a man called Aper-al, who was Asiatic by origin, yet rose to the Egyptian office of vizier under the pharaohs Amenhotep III and IV (Zivie 1990).

After the long period of relative diplomatic and military calm enjoyed by Egypt during the 14th century BC, the picture changed dramatically during the 19th Dynasty (c.1295–1186 BC) with the appearance of the Hittite empire as a major power in Anatolia, parts of Syria, and the northern Levant. Seti I (c.1294–1279 BC) had to intervene to maintain Egyptian control and influence in the Levant and Syria (Spalinger 2005: 187–208), but it was his son Ramesses II (c.1279–1213 BC) who faced the Hittite army in the famous battle at Qadesh (Spalinger 2005: 209–34). This encounter is described and illustrated on many temple walls in Egypt, and it seems that it was as crucial for Ramesses II's reign as the battle of Megiddo had been for Thutmose III. In his fifth regnal year, Ramesses II mustered four divisions and marched north. With only his first division, called Amun, he set up his camp west of Qadesh. Due to a lack of intelligence, the second division, Ra, was ambushed by the Hittite chariotry and almost completely destroyed. The Hittite chariotry then attacked Ramesses II's camp, but the Egyptian Pharaoh and his troops were saved by auxiliary troops who entered the battle at the rear of the Hittite chariots. Surprisingly, the Hittite king Muwattalli never deployed his large force of infantry to win the day and so the battle ended at best in a stalemate. Ramesses II had to withdraw and a peace treaty was reached between the pharaoh and the Hittite king Hatushilli 16 years later, strengthened by the marriage of a Hittite princess to Ramesses II.

The late 13th and 12th centuries BC brought about dramatic changes in the eastern Mediterranean and the Near East. Attacks by the so-called "Sea Peoples" against countries and people in Anatolia, the Levant, and ultimately Egypt were characterized by urban destruction and the displacement of people (Sandars 1985; Oren 2000). From the so-called Israel Stele and inscriptions at Heliopolis and Karnak, we learn that Egypt already faced an enemy, said to come from the sea, under Pharaoh Merenptah (c.1213–1203 BC), son and successor of Ramesses II (Spalinger 2005: 235–48; O'Connor 2000). The Sea Peoples comprised the Akywash, Lukki, Sherden, Shekelesh, and Teresh. Later, in the reign of Ramesses III (c.1184–113 BC), these groups were joined by the Danuna, Peleset, and Washosh (O'Connor 2000; Spalinger 2005: 249–63). According to Egyptian sources, the Sea Peoples were ultimately defeated in a land and a sea battle, and at least one group of them, the Peleset or Philistines, settled in the southern Levant in a territory known in the Bible as the Pentapolis (Oren 1973; Bietak 1991; Redford 1992: 289–297; Dothan 1995; Barako 2006).

Ramesses III maintained some control over Palestine and southern Syria and had some strongholds such as Beth Shean (Mazar 2003). The Egyptian crown also continued to send out expeditions to the area around Timna in the Wadi Arabah to procure copper ore, but after Ramesses III these missions began to be phased out (Hikade 1998; 2001: 24–30). Despite Ramesses III's relatively successful foreign policy, he nevertheless faced major economic problems at home. In a drastic economic downturn (Janssen 1975), the pharaoh was apparently not even able to feed and supply the very workforce that built his tomb in the Valley of the Kings. Tomb robbery in the main cemeteries at Thebes also became rampant, as did corruption at all levels of society, eloquently revealed in court documents (Peet 1930). By the end of the 12th century BC, Egypt's political control over the Levant had evaporated and Egypt had to withdraw completely from the region (Bietak 1991).

With Ramesses XI (c.1099–1069 BC), the last king of the Ramesside era and the 20th Dynasty, we see a domestic breakdown of the empire. The north was nominally ruled by the pharaoh, residing at Tanis in the eastern Nile Delta, while the south was governed by the general and high priest of Amun, Herihor, who also claimed to be King of Egypt (Thjis 2005). The impact on foreign affairs is most vividly described in the *Story of Wenamun*, a priest of Amun at Thebes (Lichtheim 1976: 224–30). He was supposed to sail to Byblos in order to acquire cedar wood in the 19th year of Ramesses XI, a time which already saw a new ruler called Smendes I, founder of the 21st Dynasty (1069–945 BC), in control of the north. Wenamun was not only robbed on his way, but later received a rather hostile reception at his final destination when Zaker-Baal, king of Byblos, denied him a free supply of cedar wood and instead demanded payment for the logs. Wenamun had to send a message back to Smendes asking for the payment. This clearly reveals the waning power and influence of the Egyptian crown in the Levant. Wenamun finally left for Egypt, but the ship encountered a storm and he ended up on Cyprus, where he was almost killed by the locals. Unfortunately, the end of the story is lost. Although a fictional history, the text describes the domestic division in Egypt and the fading influence of Egypt over the rulers of the Levant and southern Syria (Egberts 2001; Schipper 2005).

5 Egypt and the Near East During the Third Intermediate Period and the Late Period (1069–332 BC)

At the onset of the 1st millennium BC Egypt witnessed the growing power and influence of the Philistines on the coastal plains of the southern Levant. At the same time, the Aramaeans, a West Semitic group already present in the Late Bronze Age, increased their influence in southern Syria and the mountains of Palestine, while farther to the north the Neo-Hittite kingdoms (Ch. II.42) emerged in northern Syria (Redford 1992: 297–9). Several Libyan tribes infiltrated the Nile Valley and the Delta and reigned as the 21st to 24th Dynasties from the mid-11th to the late 8th century BC, at times controlling only parts of the Nile Delta or Middle Egypt (Taylor 2000; Broekman et al. 2009).

According to the Bible, however, bonds between 21st Dynasty Egypt and the newly founded state of Israel were strengthened when, in the 10th century BC, King Solomon made a marriage alliance with Egypt by taking one of the pharaoh's daughters to his court in Jerusalem (1 Kings 3:1, 7:8, 9:16, 24). If this alliance between Israel and the 21st Dynasty was indeed forged, it was not long-lasting. As soon as the united monarchy of Israel broke apart, the Egyptian king Shishak marched against Jerusalem and the Kingdom of Judah with 1,200 chariots and 60,000 horsemen (1 Kings 14:25–26; 2 Chronicles 12:2–3). King Rehoboam of Judah surrendered and Shishak took away all the treasures from the temple at Jerusalem, including the Ark of the Covenant (2 Chronicles 12:9). As there is evidence from the temple at Karnak of a military campaign led by Sheshonq I, founder of the 22nd Dynasty (945–715 BC), it is possible that Shishak was Sheshonq I and a campaign against Judah may have taken place around 925 BC (Kitchen 1996: 293–302, 432–47; Redford 1992: 312–15). The inscription of Sheshonq I at Karnak contains a list of 154 towns in the Levant, essentially an itinerary of warfare, that were all destroyed by Egyptian forces. Although there is no mention of Israel or Judah, a military expansion and revival of the Egyptian empire may be inferred from this text. Given that parts of the inscription have been destroyed, a march against the kingdom of Judah under Sheshonq I is possible. Contacts with Byblos were certainly restored, as evidenced by votive statues with the names of Sheshonq I, Osorkon I, and Osorkon II that were found at Byblos, where they had been dedicated to the god Ba'alat (Montet 1928: 49–57, Figs. 17–18, Pls. 36–38). Apart from the obvious cedar that the Egyptians wanted, it seems that oils were also traded from the Levant to Egypt (Hosea 12:1). It is also possible that people in the Levant were well aware of the unstable political situation in Egypt, as the Bible speaks of turmoil in Egypt and uncertainty in the capital of Tanis over how to govern the country (Isaiah 19:1–15). The Bible makes it clear that in the 8th century BC the Kingdom of Judah aspired to being a major political player in the Levant alongside Egypt and Assyria (cf. Isaiah 19:21).

The might of Assyria was already evident a century earlier when Shalmaneser III (858–824 BC) marched into northern Syria, where he met a coalition of local city-states and Egyptian forces under King Osorkon II in battle at Qarqar on the Orontes River in around 853 BC (Pritchard 1969: 278–9). However, all resistance to Assyria was crushed by Tiglath-pileser III (744–727 BC), who subdued the entirety of Syria and the Levant during the second half of the 8th century BC (Pritchard 1969: 282–3). As this danger appeared on Egypt's northeast horizon, her southern neighbor, Kush, witnessed the rise of a new dynasty that would ultimately conquer Egypt and rule as the 25th Dynasty (747–656 BC) (Welsby and Anderson 2004). Thus, at a time when Egypt suffered a political vacuum, two predatory foreign powers vied for her control. The first move was made by Kush invading Egypt in 711 BC (Redford 1985) before moving north to take on the Assyrian forces under Sennacherib (704–681 BC) on the plains of Eltekeh in 701 BC, where the Assyrian king had just laid siege to the city of Ekron (Pritchard 1969: 287). This battle ended inconclusively, as the Assyrian troops did not continue onward toward Egypt's borders when the Egyptian army was apparently in retreat. Later, the Kushite king Taharqa opted for a more active Egyptian role in the Levant, and we learn of friendly relations, for instance, between Egypt and the city-states of Tyre and Sidon (Pritchard 1969: 290). It was this kind of cordial interaction and alliance between Egypt and cities in the Levant that later caused Esarhaddon of Assyria (680–669 BC) to campaign against Egypt's allies (Pritchard 1969: 290, 302) and finally triggered the complete Assyrian conquest of the Levant (Pritchard 1969: 291). Although the first Assyrian attempt to conquer Egypt in 674 BC was unsuccessful (Pritchard 1969: 303), Assyrian troops entered Egypt and ultimately conquered it three years later (Pritchard 1969: 292–3). This assault came as such a surprise to the Kushite king Taharqa that he at first struggled to muster his troops and later, when Memphis fell, he fled, leaving his queen and family to be captured by the Assyrians. Yet Taharqa fought back and one year later regained control over Egypt. This was short-lived, however, and when Assurbanipal (668–627 BC) returned to Egypt, he drove out Taharqa. The Assyrian campaign ended with the defeat of Taharqa's successor, Tanwentamun (664–656 BC), and the sacking of Thebes in 663 BC (Pritchard 1969: 295). The Assyrians chose one of the Libyan leaders in the Delta, Psametik I (664–610 BC) of Sais, as the new Egyptian pharaoh (Lloyd 2000: 364–74). With the help of Carian and Ionian soldiers, he defeated his rivals and consolidated his authority over all of Egypt. Psametik I then took advantage of Assyria's preoccupation with the Babylonians and Medes, and succeeded in making Egypt independent once more around 650 BC. The weakness of Assyria even led Psametik I to campaign further afield in the Near East than his predecessors Thutmose I and Thutmose III had done during the 18th Dynasty. Psametik I's successor, Nekau II (610–595 BC), defeated Josiah of Judah at Megiddo and even fought the Chaldaeans east of the Euphrates as an ally of the late Assyrian king Assur-uballit II. However, in 604 BC he suffered a major defeat at the hands of the Babylonian king Nebuchadnezzar II (604–562 BC) at Karkamish. Hostilities with Babylon over the control of the Levant continued until Pharaoh Amasis (570–526 BC) ultimately became an ally of Nabonidus of Babylon (555–539 BC) and Croesus of Lydia (560–546 BC) in 547 BC against the rising empire of the Persians. Yet this was all in vain, as Psametik III of Egypt was defeated by the Persian troops under Cambyses (529–522 BC) at the battle of Pelusion in 525 BC.

For the next 120 years Egypt was a satrapy of the Persian Empire (Lloyd 2000: 374–7). Persian garrisons were established, but the local administration continued to function. Cambyses defined himself in Egypt as a pharaoh, showed respect for Egyptian religion and promoting Egyptians in his administration. After a brief uprising in Egypt following the death of Cambyses, a similar policy was continued by Darius I (521–486 BC). At several sites, such as the Kharga Oasis and Saqqara, Darius either began the construction of temples or continued existing works. An Egyptian-made statue of Darius of greywacke was found in 1972 in the royal palace at Susa (Kervran et al. 1972; Razmjou 2002). The statue is missing its upper part and head, but, including its base, would have originally stood to a height of c.3.5 meters. It is an interesting hybrid of Egyptian sculptural canon, inscription, and royal symbols, and Near Eastern writing and royal iconography. While the striding posture of the king is typically Egyptian, the royal dress and shoes of Darius are Persian, and he carries the so-called Elamite dagger. The sides of the statue base name 24 countries under Persian rule, among them Arabia, India, Nubia, Libya, and, of course, Egypt. Carved Egyptian fecundity figures symbolically unify the country by binding a lotus and papyrus representing Upper and Lower Egypt. The quadrilingual inscription on the statue basis and royal robe is written in Egyptian hieroglyphs, Old Persian, Elamite, and Babylonian cuneiform. It records that Darius conquered Egypt and refers also to the Egyptian god Atum of Heliopolis, probably the original home of the statue. In Iran itself a blending of artistic and iconographic traditions is exemplified by several buildings at Persepolis which display certain Egyptian traits.

By around 404 BC, Persian troops had left Egypt and the last independent native dynasties, the 28th–30th (404–343 BC), governed the country under constant threat from Persia. The break-up of the Persian Empire gave Pharaoh Teos (362–360 BC) a last chance to conquer the Levant. After several unsuccessful Persian counter-attacks on Egypt, the Persian king Artaxerxes III (358–338 BC) reconquered the land along the Nile in 343 BC. Little more than a decade later, however, the conquest of Egypt by Alexander the Great in 332 BC brought about the definitive end of the long line of native Egyptian kings extending back almost 3,000 years.

GUIDE TO FURTHER READING

An essential study of the foreign contacts of ancient Egypt from prehistoric times to the 1st millennium BC was published by Redford (1992). Van den Brink and Levy (2002) brings together the expertise of various scholars discussing the 4th and early 3rd millennium BC. A wealth of illustrations with short chapters of archaeological sites of the 2nd millennium BC and various aspects of contacts can be found in Aruz et al. 2008. Foreign contacts during the Middle Kingdom are discussed in Cohen (2001) while Bietak's publications on Avaris (1996, 2008) give an insightful discussion of the following Second Intermediate Period when the Asiatic Hyksos ruled large parts of Egypt from their capital in the Eastern Nile Delta. For 2nd millennium chronology and its implications in the eastern Mediterranean and Egypt, see Bietak and Czerny (2006) and Bietak (2003a). International relations during the Late Bronze Age are discussed in a broader frame in

Liverani (1990). Thutmose III was constantly on military campaigns in Nubia and the Levant and the detailed study by Redford (2003) concentrates on the wars of this king in Syria. Moran (1992) presents in translation the invaluable corpus of the Amarna letters, the correspondence of the Egyptian crown with its vassal states in the Levant and the large empires of the Near East during the middle to end of the 14th century BC, while Cohen and Westbrook (2000) offers a series of papers that look into the similarities and differences between modern diplomacy and that of the Late Bronze Age, as evidenced in the Amarna letters. The intriguing history of the Sea Peoples and their impact on the ancient Near East were the topics of Sandars 1985 and the conference papers edited by Oren (2000). An overview of history of Egypt during the Third Intermediate Period was published by Kitchen (1996), while Lloyd (2000) provides a very good summary for the Late Period.

CHAPTER FORTY-FIVE

The Assyrian Heartland

Friedhelm Pedde

1 Introduction

The Assyrian heartland extends along the river Tigris, from the region of the modern town of Eski Mosul and the site of Khorsabad (ancient Dur-Sharrukin) in the north to the Lesser Zab river and the site of Assur in the south. The border in the east may be drawn somewhere around the modern town of Erbil, whereas there is no clear boundary in the steppe to the west. Today the center of this ancient landscape is Mosul. Because of its geographical position and favorable climate, with sufficient rainfall for rain-fed agriculture, large parts of Assyria consist of rich farmland. Other parts are covered with grass and offer good conditions for breeding livestock. In antiquity the hills were covered with trees. These favorable conditions explain why Assyria was settled from the Neolithic period onwards, as the evidence from Nineveh clearly shows. Assur was already occupied by the mid-3rd millennium BC (Early Dynastic III period) when a temple of the goddess Ishtar is attested. During the Akkadian period in the late 3rd millennium BC, the name of the settlement Assur is recorded for the first time. The ancestors of the Assyrians were nomads who came from the steppe in the west and settled first at Assur. It is unclear when this happened, but in the early 2nd millennium BC Assur was the home of Assyrian-speaking merchants who developed a network of business establishments extending from Babylonia and the Iranian mountains to northern Syria and central Anatolia, trading in metals and textiles. Assur's

---

A Companion to the Archaeology of the Ancient Near East, First Edition.
Edited by D.T. Potts.
© 2012 Blackwell Publishing Ltd. Published 2012 by Blackwell Publishing Ltd.

location enabled the town to control the trade routes in all directions, and the fertile plains in the north and east supplied its inhabitants with their basic needs.

It was not until the Middle Assyrian period, in the 14th century BC, that the heartland of Assyria became a united realm with its capital at Assur. Apart from the reign of Tukulti-Ninurta I (1243–1207 BC), who tried to establish a new residence at Kar-Tukulti-Ninurta (modern Tulul al-'Aqir), Assur remained the capital of Assyria until the 9th century BC. Assurnasirpal II (883–859 BC) built new palaces at Assur, Nineveh, and several other cities, but moved to Nimrud, where a new, much larger residence was erected. Still, Assur remained the seat of the national god Assur, visited on occasion by all Assyrian kings. The palace at Nimrud was the king's domicile until Sargon II (721–705 BC) decided to build a palace at Dur-Sharrukin (modern Khorsabad). After his violent death his son Sennacherib (704–681 BC) moved to Nineveh and built his own "palace without rival." In these centuries the Assyrians controlled the Fertile Crescent – the Levantine coast, northern Syria, the southern regions of the Anatolian mountains – as well as the western regions of the Iranian highlands and Mesopotamia. In the 7th century BC even Egypt was conquered (Ch. II.44).

The Assyrian heartland was poor in mineral resources. Material and labor shortages in Assyria were the main motivations for the many military campaigns of the Assyrian kings in all directions. These constant campaigns and their cruelties against the inhabitants of the subjugated countries were part of a military strategy and the basis of the Assyrian economic system, which functioned for as long as resources in the surrounding countries could be exploited. This system of war and tribute is the main topic of the pictorial representations on the Assyrian reliefs, obelisks, wall paintings, and decorated gates. The second main topic is the king as hunter. In all cases the political intention was to demonstrate the power of the Assyrian king.

All Assyrian capitals were located in the Assyrian heartland. For military and economic reasons, the Assyrian towns in the heartland were well connected by roads. The towns were surrounded by a network of smaller towns and villages and it is assumed that many settlements must have existed – e.g., around the little modern town of Mahmur in the hinterland of Assur and Kar-Tukulti-Ninurta. Though there have been some archaeological surveys and excavations in different regions – e.g., around Makhmur and in the Eski-Mosul district – the extent of Middle and Neo-Assyrian settlement has never been fully investigated. Furthermore, distortions in our understanding of Assyrian settlement have been introduced with respect to excavated as opposed to unexcavated areas at Assyrian sites. In the Assyrian capitals, those areas with official buildings have been examined to a much greater extent than those with residential quarters, and comparing capitals with smaller settlements is difficult because the latter have barely been investigated.

Nineveh remained the capital until 612 BC when, after endless revolts, the empire was destroyed by a coalition of Medes and Babylonians. Traces of destruction are found not only in the capitals, but also at smaller sites in Assyria. However, in most cases there are signs of continuity over the subsequent few generations. The immediately post-Assyrian period is the subject of ongoing investigations.

2 Assur

Assur (Aššur/Ashur, modern Qalat Sherqat), the first capital of the Assyrian empire, is situated on the west bank of the Tigris, about 110 kilometers south of Mosul. Brief excavations were conducted in 1847 and 1850 by A.H. Layard and H. Rassam, who did not realize that Qalat Sherqat was ancient Assur. Systematic excavations were carried out by a German expedition under W. Andrae (in 1903–14) and later by R. Dittmann (in 1988–9), B. Hrouda (in 1990) and P.A. Miglus (in 2000–1). In addition, the Department of Antiquities of Iraq has worked there intermittently since 1979.

Andrae was able to open large areas, especially in the northern part of the site, exposing the temples of Anu and Adad, Sin and Shamash, and Ishtar and Nabu, as well as the Old Palace, the Assur/Enlil *ziggurat* (stepped temple tower), and the Assur temple. Living quarters were found to the northwest and south of the temple area (Miglus 1996), as well as a double city wall with bastions and gates. In contrast to the separated, official areas of the later capitals in Assyria, there were no fortifications dividing domestic from public quarters at Assur.

Deep soundings in the Ishtar temple and the Old Palace reached layers of the Early Dynastic (2900–2350 BC), Akkadian (2350–2150 BC), and Ur III (2100–2000 BC) periods. In the Old Assyrian period Assur became the capital of the Assyrian state and the religious center with the temple of the "national" god Assur. The town is characterized by large structures: the "*Schotterhofbau*" (lit. "gravel courtyard building") under the Old Palace seems to have been a prestigious building (Miglus 1989; Pedde and Lundström 2008: 28–9), probably of the ruler Erishum I (1974–1935 BC). Later, the "*Ur-Plan*" (Pedde and Lundström 2008: 29–30) was laid out on this location: a large system of foundation trenches filled with mudbricks, probably the remains of the palace of Shamshi-Adad I (1813–1781 BC), who also built the Assur temple and the Enlil *ziggurat*. Because of the limited deep soundings, not very much is known about the living quarters, most of which were small houses with incomplete ground plans. Exceptions are two large buildings, one from the Akkadian and one from the Ur III period. Graves and tombs were found, some of which had rich finds (Hockmann 2010).

In the 16th century BC the systematic construction of the city's fortification wall (Miglus 2010) was a sign of political independence. At the end of the century Assur-nirari I built the temple of Sin and Shamash (Werner 2009) and the Old Palace. After a period of Mitanni rule, the Middle Assyrian king Assur-nadin-ahhe

II (1400–1391 BC) rebuilt the palace. This and the fact that he received gold from the Egyptian pharaoh shows that Assur had regained its power. Between c.1400 and 1200 BC the Middle Assyrian kings conquered vast regions in northern Mesopotamia and northern Syria and Assur was one of the most important capitals in the Near East. The Old Palace was later renovated (Pedde and Lundström 2008: 32–7), especially under Adad-nirari I (1305–1274 BC). Tukulti-Ninurta I built his own palace (the New Palace) on a terrace in the northwestern part of the site and rebuilt the Ishtar temple. Tiglath-pileser I (1114–1076 BC) erected the temple of Anu and Adad with a double *ziggurat*.

An unusual find consisted of two rows with stelae – an Assyrian calendar system – mentioning the names of the Assyrian kings and officials of the Assyrian state, beginning in the Middle Assyrian period with Eriba-Adad I (1390–1364 BC) and ending in the Neo-Assyrian period with the wife of Assurbanipal (668–627 BC). At least one king, Assur-bel-kala (1073–1056 BC), was buried in a tomb under the Old Palace. It is not known, however, where all the other kings from the earlier periods were entombed (Lundström 2009).

In the Neo-Assyrian period Tukulti-Ninurta II (890–884 BC) decorated the Old Palace with glazed and painted brick orthostats, obviously the predecessors of the stone reliefs that are so typical of the later capitals. His son, Assurnasirpal II, moved to his new residence in Nimrud, and also completely renovated the Old Palace in Assur (Pedde and Lundström 2008: 37–58, 179–81), as well as building or renovating palaces throughout the country – e.g., at Nineveh and Imgur-Enlil (modern Balawat). He did not decorate the Old Palace with stone reliefs as he did at Nimrud, but clay hands and knob tiles were found in situ in the walls. The room layout seems to have been the model for all later Assyrian palaces, with an official part (Akkadian *bābanu*) and a more private part (Akk. *bītanu*) separated by a wing, with the throne room and one or two rooms behind.

Though no longer the center of the realm, the city of Assur remained the religious center of Assyria until the fall of the empire because it housed the temple of the god Assur, and some of the Neo-Assyrian kings, including Assurnasirpal, Shamshi-Adad V (823–811 BC) and Esarhaddon (680–669 BC), were buried underneath the Old Palace (Lundström 2009). As the town expanded to the southeast alongside the Tigris, a new city wall beyond the old one was erected in this period, first following the old city wall before turning to the south. South of the Assur temple, Assurnasirpal's son Shalmaneser III (858–824 BC) built a new palace, the East Palace. He renovated Assur's official buildings and fortifications, as did Sennacherib, Esarhaddon, and Assurbanipal after him. Sennacherib erected a building for the New Year's celebration outside the city wall toward the northwest and a Prince's Palace for his son Assur-ili-bullit-su toward the southeast, near the river.

In 614 BC Assur was conquered by the Medes under king Cyaxares (625–585 BC). Official buildings were demolished and the tombs of the kings systematically destroyed. Some of the surviving inhabitants still lived in the ruins for one or two more generations, leaving behind only a few traces. Because of the collapse of Assyrian infrastructure, the town never recovered. In the following centuries Assur seems to have been an unimportant village, though it was mentioned by Cyrus the Great (559–530 BC), founder of the Persian empire. Apart from some pottery and Achaemenid and Seleucid coins, there is little trace of post-Assyrian occupation, although new excavations could change this.

Not until the Parthian era (c.250 BC–AD 224) did the town experience a period of new period of prosperity (Andrae and Lenzen 1933). Six hundred years after the fall of Assyria, a new temple for Assur-Sherua was built in the traditional religious precinct in the northeastern part of the site, along with several other temples and official buildings. Assur became the seat of a governor, whose large palace was situated in the south. Destroyed by the Sasanians under Shapur I (241–272 AD), Assur was resettled in the 12th century AD, when it was called al-'Aqr.

In the 11 years of Andrae's work, 44,000 objects were registered. After the end of the excavation, the finds were divided between the Ottoman Empire and Germany and taken to the Vorderasiatisches (Pergamon) Museum in Berlin and the Eski Sark Müzesi in Istanbul. Though the architecture and a remarkable number of texts were published in the following years, few of the objects were examined. More recently, the Assur Projects in Berlin and Heidelberg have been studying and publishing the finds, texts, and architecture in a series published by the Deutsche Orient-Gesellschaft (German Oriental Society). These volumes cover cuneiform inscriptions on clay (Pedersén 1985, 1986; Faist 2005, 2007; Freydank and Feller 2004, 2005, 2008; Freydank 2006; Frahm 2009; Maul and Heeßel 2010) and stone (Pedersén 1997); the architecture of the palaces and temples (Pedde and Lundström 2008; Werner 2009, Schmitt in press); tombs and graves (Lundström 2009; Hockmann 2010; Pedde 2010, in press a); and objects, like pottery (Hausleiter 2010f), obelisk fragments (Orlamünde 2011), orthostats (Orlamünde and Lundström 2011), doorkeeper figures, knob tiles (Nunn 2006), alabaster vessels (Onasch 2010), objects of ivory and bone (Wicke 2010), mace heads (Muhle in press), terracotta and lead, and seals and sealings.

3 Kar-Tukulti-Ninurta (Tulul al-'Aqar)

Kar-Tukulti-Ninurta lies 3 kilometers north of Assur, on the east bank of the Tigris. Excavations were conducted in 1913–14 by W. Bachmann, a member of the Assur expedition. Although Bachmann never published his results in full, the results of the old excavations have been summarized (see Eickhoff 1985). Renewed excavations took place under R. Dittmann in 1986 and 1989 (Dittmann et al. 1988, 1989–90; Dittmann 1992).

Kar-Tukulti-Ninurta was founded by the Middle Assyrian king Tukulti-Ninurta I as his new residence, but abandoned shortly after his violent death. The city consisted of different quarters. The official, fortified part was divided by a wall into an eastern and a western section. Two modern villages cover the eastern quarter, which remains largely uninvestigated as a result. In the western section several public buildings were found. In the northern area, close to the city wall and the river, parts of a large building, called the "North Palace" and "South Palace," were excavated. The North Palace is an entrance complex of three main rooms, each one behind the other, and some more rooms. The gate of the main outer room is flanked by bastions, while the inner room leads to a courtyard. The walls of this building stood 7–8 meters high. This seems to be part of the "South Palace" on a high terrace with large rooms. Both complexes had plaster decorated with colored geometric, vegetal, and figural motifs. Inscribed bricks identify this building as the palace of Tukulti-Ninurta I. A temple of Assur with a *ziggurat* is situated to the southeast of the terrace. The *ziggurat* was erected first and the temple was added on its northeastern (front) side. The cella was built directly adjacent to the *ziggurat* and its niche even projects into it. Several niches in the large room at the front were interpreted as places of worship for other gods. Dittmann excavated a small temple north of the North Palace (Tell O), but the identity of the god worshipped there remains unknown. Cuneiform texts, pottery, and clay hands indicate that the site was resettled in the Neo-Assyrian period.

4 Nimrud (Kalhu, Biblical Calah)

In the 9th and 8th centuries BC, Nimrud was the capital of the Assyrian empire. Located 35 kilometers south of Mosul, on the east bank of the Tigris close to the Greater Zab, it sits halfway between Assur and Nineveh. Nimrud was visited in 1820 by C.J. Rich, and the first excavations were carried out there in 1845–7 and 1849–51 by A.H. Layard and H. Rassam, who thought they had found Nineveh (Layard 1849a, 1849b). They excavated in several palaces (the Northwest, Southwest, Southeast and Central Palaces) as well as in the temples of Sharrat-niphi and Ninurta. In 1854–5 W.K. Loftus reinvestigated most of these palaces, along with the Burnt Palace and the Nabu temple. Between 1877 and 1879 Rassam again investigated the Southeast Palace, the Central Palace and the Nabu temple (Rassam 1897). These early excavations all recovered spectacular finds, including stone slabs (orthostats) with reliefs and over-lifesize, standing winged bulls, some of which can be seen in the British Museum. Moreover, Layard, Rassam, and Loftus all wrote popular books for the public about their work. Layard's *Nineveh and Its Remains* became an international bestseller and was translated into many languages, sparking interest in the general public in the Ancient Near East. On the other hand, the excavators did not document their results very well, from today's point of view.

Some 70 years later a British team began systematic excavations (1949–63) under the direction of M.E.L. Mallowan, D. Oates, and J. Orchard (Mallowan

1966). Later excavations were undertaken by a Polish team under J. Meuszynski (1974–6), an Italian team under P. Fiorina (1987–9) and again by a British team under J. Curtis and D. Collon (1989). The Department of Antiquities of Iraq has also worked at Nimrud since 1956 (Oates 2001).

Although traces of prehistoric settlement dating to the Halaf period and Middle Assyrian construction by Shalmaneser I (1273–1244 BC) are attested, it was not until Assurnasirpal II moved his residence from Assur to Nimrud that the site became one of the most important capitals in the ancient Near East. Assurnasirpal II ordered work on a new city wall, about 8 kilometers long, as well as a new palace (the Northwest Palace) on the citadel mound of the old settlement. This was inaugurated in 864 BC, only a few years before the king died. The arrangement of the courtyards and rooms resembles the Old Palace at Assur and both palaces were the prototypes of many of the later Assyrian palaces.

The Northwest Palace consists of three parts. The first part is a large courtyard (c.90 × 60 m) with a row of rooms in the north. The main gate in the east, the court itself and the western side have been destroyed by erosion. The throne room is located on the south side, beyond which comes the second part of the palace. In the center of this part lies a courtyard, surrounded by official rooms and chambers. The doorways of the large rooms were flanked by pairs of *lamassus*, human-headed winged figures with the body of a lion or a bull. The throne room, the courtyard, and all the state apartments were decorated inside and outside with many hundreds of large, originally colored relief orthostats depicting the king, his attendants, winged genii, and scenes of war and hunting. Most of the reliefs are inscribed in the center with the so-called "standard inscription" mentioning the king's titles and achievements (Meuszynski 1981; Paley and Sobolewski 1987, 1992). South of this official area lies the private domestic quarter, excavated by British and later Iraqi archaeologists. There Mallowan found the grave of a royal woman and the Iraqi team discovered three partly reused tombs containing a further 16 individuals and very rich grave goods (Damerji 1999). As some of the inscribed finds reveal, four Neo-Assyrian queens – the wives of Assurnasirpal II, Tiglath-pileser III (744–727 BC), Shalmaneser V (726–722 BC) and Sargon II – were buried here. All these burials were hidden under the floors of unpretentious-looking rooms.

The Northwest Palace continued in use during the reigns of Shalmaneser III and Shamshi-Adad V. Later, when Adad-nirari III (810–783 BC) and Tiglath-pileser III built their own palaces at Nimrud, and even after Sargon II moved his residence to Khorsabad, the Northwest Palace continued to be a very important building, as the royal burials demonstrate. Sargon filled its storerooms with tribute and treasure, and from there he prepared his removal to Khorsabad. Under Sennacherib and his successors, the palace lost its importance; Esarhaddon took away some of its orthostats to decorate his own new palace, the Southwest Palace. But the palace remained in use until 612 BC, when Nimrud was sacked and, afterwards, parts of it were inhabited by squatters.

In addition to the Northwest Palace, Assurnasirpal II founded and renovated several temples. In the northwestern corner of the citadel he and his son Shalmaneser III (858–824 BC) erected a *ziggurat*, and between this and the palace he built a temple for Ninurta. This suggests that the *ziggurat* was dedicated to Ninurta as well. The entrances of the temple were flanked by a pair of 5 meter high *lamassus*, comparable in size only to those at the main entrance to the Northwest Palace. A magazine with rows of large jars was discovered, as well as a vaulted, blocked corridor containing hundreds of beads and many cylinder seals which had been deposited under the floor and date to the middle of the 2nd millennium BC. East of the Ninurta temple a temple for the goddess Ishtar was rebuilt by Assurnasirpal. Its entrance was flanked by two lions and its interior was decorated with glazed knob tiles.

Another building erected by Assurnasirpal II – probably a temple – was the so-called Central Building, excavated in the 19th century. Some relief slabs and parts of four doorkeeper figures were found, but only a small part of the building was documented. South of this, a statue and two obelisks were discovered: the Black Obelisk of Shalmaneser III and fragments of an obelisk of Assurnasirpal II known as the Rassam Obelisk.

Situated in the southeastern part of the site, the Burnt Palace has a trapezoidal ground plan. Built in the Middle Assyrian period, it was completely renovated under Assurnasirpal or Shalmaneser, rebuilt again by Adad-nirari III, and later used by Sargon II. In the reign of Adad-nirari III, mudbrick boxes containing small, protective figures were deposited under the doors and at the corners of the building. A great number of high-quality ivory objects were found here, predating the destruction in 612 BC.

The wing of another palace of Shalmaneser III, the Southeast Palace, was preserved in the southeastern corner of the citadel. Two large rooms and some adjacent chambers represent a further throne room module, comparable to that found in the Northwest Palace and in the Old Palace in Assur. Another vast, unusual structure built by Shalmaneser and later renovated by Esarhaddon lies at the southeastern edge of the outer town. It is an arsenal incorporating a palace, and was called "Fort Shalmaneser" by the British team that began work there in 1957 (Mallowan 1966). Because no orthostats were found at Fort Shalmaneser, the building was of no interest to 19th century excavators and later archaeologists were therefore fortunate in discovering untouched structures and a great number of objects. The building was something like a military headquarters with an empty space in the north and the west, which may have been a training ground for troops. Fort Shalmaneser consists of three large courtyards, separated by a double row of rooms, including residential suites, workshops for chariots and many other objects, and storage magazines. In the southeastern corner a royal palace was erected with the standard large throne room suite plus two additional courtyards. The throne base in the throne room deserves particular mention. It consists of two slabs of limestone, the sides of which are decorated in relief, showing Shalmaneser three times. The front relief presents a unique gesture: Shalmaneser (right) "shakes" the hand of the Babylonian king Marduk-zakir-shumi (left). The text above the relief reports that Shalmaneser restored the Babylonian king to the throne after a revolt. On the left and right side of the throne base, Shalmaneser is shown receiving tribute from a Syrian ruler and from Chaldaean tribes. These scenes are best compared with the reliefs on the Assyrian obelisks and the Balawat gates. The wing behind the audience room consists of three large reception rooms and might have been the prototype of similar arrangements in Sargon's palace at Khorsabad. West of the state apartments was a residential quarter, consisting of several courtyards surrounded by a single or double row of rooms, recalling the Northwest Palace and the Old Palace at Assur.

Adad-nirari III built a palace very close to the walls of the southern edge of the Northwest Palace. In 1993 this was discovered by an Iraqi team under the direction of Muzahim Mahmud Hussein in the area where Layard had found a structure decorated with elaborated frescoes called the "Upper Chambers." Although these chambers cannot be located today, they were probably part of Adad-nirari's palace. North of the Burnt Palace, a large, partly excavated building called the Governor's Palace might have been built by the same king. It consists of an almost square courtyard, surrounded by a double row of rooms decorated with frescoes. This building may have been an important administrative office or residence. To the south of it and east of the Burnt Palace lies the temple of the scribal god Nabu, originally erected in the 9th century, but completely rebuilt under Adad-nirari.

The largest building in the southeastern part of the citadel mound was excavated by Loftus and Rassam and later investigated by the British and Iraqi teams. The entrance on the northern side is called the Fish Gate because of the flanking fishmen figures. The courtyard behind the gate leads to a building on the right for the king. Behind the entrance to this complex lies a smaller court with access to a throne room and some chambers in the usual pattern, as well as two rooms which seem to be a smaller version of the sanctuaries reserved for the king. Carved ivories of extraordinary quality were found here. These had decorated the throne room, the throne itself, and other furniture. Some show tribute scenes comparable to those on the orthostats and obelisks. The main court has another gate in the south, flanked by 4 meter high attendants, leading to a second court of the same size and a double sanctuary for the god Nabu and his wife Tashmetum (?) with antechambers and slightly raised, stepped podiums. In one of the rooms on the eastern side of the court a library, as well as indications that cuneiform tablets were written there, were found. The library contained literary texts and royal inscriptions, including the so-called "vassal" treaties of Esarhaddon.

Tiglath-pileser III built a palace in the central part of the citadel, the so-called Central Palace (Barnett and Falkner 1962). It is likely that the older buildings here, like the Central Building, were pulled down at this time. According to the king's own inscriptions, this palace must have been huge, but little of it remains.

Originally it had been decorated with relief slabs, but about 50 years after it was built Esarhaddon, building his own palace at the time, began to remove not only the orthostats from the Northwest and Central Palaces – Layard found about 100 orthostats stacked up and ready for transportation – but even the pavement

Esarhaddon's palace was erected on the southwest corner of the mound and is therefore known as the Southwest Palace. Although planned on a grand scale, it was never completed. The only parts preserved are traces of a large courtyard and a huge complex of state apartments on the southern side of the court, consisting of two large halls with rooms on the short sides. The three main entrances were flanked by *lamassus*, facing north. The use of a pair of crouching sphinxes as column bases in two of the doorways is unique. In addition, pairs of round column bases stood on the short sides.

Another official building, named "Town Wall Palace of Assurbanipal," was excavated between the citadel and Fort Shalmaneser. It consists of a typical reception suite with adjacent rooms, and a probable domestic wing in which an inscription with Assurbanipal's name was found.

Traces of destruction everywhere in the town show that Nimrud was attacked once and, before repair work could be completed, a second time. This probably occurred in 614 and 612 BC when the Assyrian empire was destroyed.

5 Balawat (Imgur-Enlil)

Balawat is located 15 kilometers northeast of Nimrud and 27 kilometers southeast of Nineveh on the road between Kirkuk and Nineveh. It was excavated by H. Rassam in 1878, M.E.L. Mallowan in 1956, and J. Curtis in 1989. The site is enclosed by a fortification wall 800 meters on a side. Excavations took place on the citadel mound (c.250 × 150 meters) in the northern part of the site. Surface sherds suggest the area was settled in the Ubaid and Northern Uruk periods, and perhaps again in the Middle Assyrian period. The main occupation dates to the Neo-Assyrian period, when Assurnasirpal II and his son Shalmaneser III (859–824 BC) erected small palaces and a temple. As the pottery and cuneiform tablets show, Balawat seems to have been inhabited until the end of the Assyrian empire in 614/612 BC with traces of reoccupation in the Hellenistic period.

At the southwestern edge of the citadel, Rassam found parts of a palace. Although the area could not be excavated thoroughly, Rassam discovered two gates decorated with embossed bronze bands built by Assurnasirpal II (Gate A) (Curtis and Tallis 2008: 23–46, Figs. 5–43) and Shalmaneser III (Gate C) (Schachner 2007) Another prominent building in the northeastern part of the site was the temple of Mamu, the god of dreams, built by Assurnasirpal. This consisted of a row of rooms with a courtyard in the center. At the gate leading from the court to the antechamber (Gate B), Mallowan excavated another pair of bronze bands (Curtis and Tallis 2008: 47–71, Figs. 46–90). Decorative bronze bands are also attested in Assurnasirpal II's Northwest Palace at Nimrud (earlier than Balawat); the Anu Adad temple at Assur (Shalmaneser III); the temples of Adad, Nabu, and Shamash at Khorsabad (Sargon); and the Nergal temple at Tell Hadad/Hamrin (Assurbanipal). The Balawat bronze bands, however, are by far the best preserved. The three Balawat gates were all decorated with eight bands on each door showing scenes of hunting, war, and tribute, comparable to scenes on Assyrian reliefs and obelisks. The bands of the two palace gates are exhibited in the British Museum, whereas the bands of the Mamu temple, in the Mosul Museum, were partially looted in 2003.

6 Khorsabad (Dur-Sharrukin)

Located 20 kilometers northeast of Nineveh, Khorsabad was the new capital of Sargon II. The first excavations there were conducted by the French consul in Mosul, P.É. Botta (1843–4), who thought he had discovered Nineveh. The recovery of large stone orthostats decorated with Assyrian reliefs, their exhibition in the Louvre beginning in 1847, and the publication of the stone slabs and architecture by Botta and his draftsman E. Flandin (Botta and Flandin 1849–50; Albenda 1986) marked the beginnings of European interest in ancient Assyrian antiquities, and the French and British search for artifacts in that area. Botta's work was continued in 1852–4 by his successor as French consul, V. Place, who also found a large number of reliefs and statues. Fortunately these were drawn by the draftsman F. Thomas and photographed by G. Tranchard, for, in 1855, as the finds were being transported on rafts down the Tigris for eventual shipment to Paris, local Bedouin launched a raid during a sandstorm, the rafts sank, and all the slabs were lost. It took more than 70 years before new excavations were started. From 1929 to 1935 the Oriental Institute of Chicago, mainly under the direction of G. Loud, investigated three areas in the palace (Loud et al. 1936; Loud and Altman 1938). After 1957, shorter campaigns were conducted by the Iraqi Department of Antiquities under B. Abu al-Soof.

It is not known why Sargon II decided to build a new residence. In the fifth year of his reign (717 BC), after choosing the location and compensating the local inhabitants, Sargon began construction. The work was carried out by the Assyrian army and civilians, as well as by prisoners-of-war and deportees who were afterwards forced to settle in the new city (Blocher 1997). Though the city still was under construction, Dur-Sharrukin was inaugurated in 706 BC.

A massive city wall of mudbrick on stone foundations c.12 meters high, 14 meters thick, and equipped with seven gates enclosed a rectangular area measuring 1,750 × 1,683 meters. On top of the wall two palaces were erected, one in the northwest and one in the southwest. The Northwest Palace is the kings's palace. It was built on a 12 meter high, irregularly shaped, trapezoidal terrace protruding beyond both sides of the wall and accessed by a ramp. The palace is a complex building measuring 290 meters on a side with two very large courtyards, a couple of smaller courtyards, and 207 rooms. The large courtyard XV is situated directly behind the main gate with one main and two minor entrances and some small apartments placed around it. In the southwest a small entrance leads to a complex of six temples (interpreted as a harem by Place) of the gods Sin, Shamash, Ningal, Ninurta, Ea, and Adad. Fragments of bronze bands with narrative scenes, comparable to those of the Balawat Gates, were found here. A narrow corridor led to a platform with a *ziggurat* (interpreted by Place as an observatory). On the northeast side of courtyard XV are four entrances to a large complex with many courtyards and rooms. In court XVIII and in the adjacent rooms 126–9 stone rings were fixed in the floor, perhaps for tying up horses. If this were the case, then the entire wing may have been stables and the other rooms storage magazines. On the northwest side, a gate with a double room led to the next large courtyard VIII. On its northeastern side, a single doorway led to a building which was originally planned as a temple but later changed to a wine cellar. At the front (southwest side) of courtyard VIII a triple entrance to the throne room was located, consisting of two minor doors and a main entrance, flanked by two enormous towers and decorated with *lamassus*, winged bulls with human faces that functioned as doorkeeper figures. The throne room measured 47 × 10.5 meters and the throne stood on a monolithic stone base (4 × 4.6 meters) on one of the short sides. Behind the throne room was a parallel room, followed by the square courtyard VI, which was flanked by a system of double rooms on each side. As in the Northwest Palace of Nimrud, these rooms have an official character and only those in the southeast seem to represent private quarters. Between this official part and the main courtyard XV lies a large complex of private rooms, probably the king's residential apartments, whereas on the opposite side in the northwest another official building with remarkable large rooms is located, surrounded by a huge terrace. These rooms were used for audiences and festivities. West of this large building complex stood a separate, badly preserved building with column bases. Most of the stone orthostats and statues found by the French archaeologists came from the official areas in the northern part of the terrace. The narrative scenes of the reliefs differ from wing to wing, depending on the function of the room. Mainly, they show scenes of war and tribute, a few feasts and hunting scenes and the transport of timber on a river.

On the inner side of the city wall, beneath the terrace, were several very large buildings (H–M) separated from the town by an enclosing wall with two gates flanked by *lamassu* figures. This area has the same level as the area outside the wall, but was called a "citadel" by the excavators. The buildings in question were the residences of Assyrian notables. Between these buildings a temple for the god Nabu was erected on a separate terrace, accessible from the palace terrace by a bridge. This was the most important temple complex built by Sargon.

The second building on the city wall, so-called "Palace F," was only partly excavated. It was believed to be the crown prince's palace, but has also been interpreted as an arsenal. Like Sargon's palace, the building stands on a terrace protruding beyond the inner and outer sides of the city wall. A large, central court is surrounded by different wings. A triple entrance with a gate in the center flanked by towers led to a throne room of similar size to that in the Northwest Palace. The throne room is integrated in a wing with two rows of parallel rooms. Close to the western corner of the Central Court, a gate led to a pillared portico, opening onto a large terrace (140 × 63 meters). Here a building with four banquet halls was erected. Its main entrance, also flanked by towers, corresponds with a similar entrance to the room behind the throne room. At the corners of this wing are two separate apartments, one of which has the same kind of triple entrance as the throne room and might be the king's private living quarters.

Only a few buildings in the city have been discovered. This may be because only limited excavations has been conducted outside the main palaces, or perhaps because only a small number of houses were ever built there in antiquity, because Sargon II's died while on military campaign shortly after the inauguration of the city. Although Sargon's son Sennacherib abandoned his father's ambitious building program and moved to Nineveh, Dur-Sharrukin remained a provincial capital until the end of the Assyrian empire.

7 Nineveh

In the 7th century BC Nineveh was the capital of the Neo-Assyrian empire. Situated on the east bank of the Tigris across from Mosul, knowledge of Nineveh's existence lived on in Europe thanks to the Bible. The first known Western visitor there was Benjamin of Tudela, who wrote an account of it in 1178, though this was not published until 1543 in Constantinople. One of the many later travelers to mention Nineveh was Ibn Battuta (1327). The travels of C.J. Rich in 1820, published only in 1836, were a prelude to French and British excavations. P.E. Botta began work there in 1842, and between 1846 and 1852 the British Museum excavated under the direction of A.H. Layard and H. Rassam. They were succeeded by W.K. Loftus, and later, in 1931 and 1932, by R. Campbell Thompson and M.E.L. Mallowan, who resumed work there. In the 1960s the Iraqi Department of Antiquities excavated at Nineveh, while in the 1980s a team from the University of California (Berkeley) worked there briefly (Scott and Macginnis 1990; Matthiae 1998). Most of the excavations at Nineveh have taken place on the mound of Küyünjik. The smaller mound of Nebi Yunus contains the *ziggurat* and Esarhaddon's arsenal, but has not been extensively investigated because, according to Islamic tradition, this is the site of the tomb of the prophet Jonah.

Mallowan's excavations reached virgin soil. The pre-Assyrian levels were called Ninevite 1 (6th millennium BC, Hassuna period) to 5 (early 3rd millennium BC). Campbell Thompson and Hutchinson worked in the temple of the goddess Ishtar (Campbell Thompson and Hutchinson 1932), where they discovered an inscription of the Old Assyrian king Shamshi-Adad I, who not only renovated the temple, but identified the Akkadian king Manishtushu (2269–2255 BC) as its founder. Though no architecture of the Akkadian period was identified, the bronze head of an Akkadian king, perhaps Naram-Sin (2254–2218 BC), was found. Later, the Middle Assyrian kings Assur-uballit I (1363–1328 BC), Shalmaneser I, and Assur-resh-ishi I (1132–1115 BC) rebuilt the temple as well as the *ziggurat*. In the Neo-Assyrian period, the temple was rebuilt by Assurnasirpal II and Assurbanipal. In the area of the Ishtar temple, Rassam found two obelisks: the Broken Obelisk, dated to the reign of Assur-bel-kala, and the White Obelisk, showing scenes of war and tribute and ascribed to Assurnasirpal I or II.

Campbell Thompson and Hutchinson excavated a small palace in the center of Küyünjik on the citadel mound. Because inscriptions of Assurnasirpal II were discovered everywhere in the palace, the building was assigned to his reign (Campbell Thompson and Hutchinson 1931). The architecture was badly preserved. The walls were made of baked brick, with painted decoration showing rosettes, figures, and the king. Fragments of two obelisks with tribute scenes were found, as well as many painted terracotta orthostats, probably the precursors of marble orthostats. These show scenes of war and tribute and the king with mural crown (representing a city wall). This was likely one of the palaces where Assurnasirpal lived before his palace at Assur was renovated and long before he moved to Nimrud in the 19th year of reign. The building was restored by his successors Shalmaneser III, Shamshi-Adad V, and Adad-nirari III.

The Nabu temple was founded by Adad-nirari III (Campbell Thompson 1929). The architecture of the Ishtar and Nabu temples is poorly documented. The latter stood on a high terrace and had the shape of an irregular quadrangle. It was extended and rebuilt by Sargon II and Assurbanipal. Until the reign of Sennacherib these two temples were the most important buildings on the citadel.

After Sennacherib moved to Nineveh from his father's capital Khorsabad, he began a major building program. The circuit of the city wall was extended from 5 to 12 kilometers, 15 gates were built or renovated, and the city was given new infrastructure in the form of new roads, a canal system, and a park. Besides a palace in the eastern part of the citadel, the most important building was the large new palace, the so-called Southwest Palace covering the southern part of the citadel. According to Sennacherib himself, the building measured 503 × 242 meters and was the largest palace in Assyrian history. Named in Assyrian the "Palace without Rival" (Russell 1991), it was inaugurated in 694 BC. To date, however, the northern and northwestern areas of the palace are completely unknown. The architecture is reminiscent of Sargon's palace at Khorsabad, but there is a new element of symmetry and visual permeability. The throne room lies in the northeast and the courtyards are surrounded by state apartments, in a double or triple row of rooms. The outer walls on the southwestern and southeastern sides seem to have disappeared. A second large gate was found in the southwestern side, but the access route from there to the center of the palace is unclear. The wing in the northwest has gone, but there are indications of at least one further courtyard. The excavated architecture of the palace belongs to the official part, whereas the domestic quarters were not found.

The gates of the state apartments were flanked by *lamassus* and the rooms were decorated with relief stone slabs of extraordinary quality, showing narrative scenes, mainly of war, now in the British Museum (Barnett et al. 1998; Nadali 2006). The orthostats are systematically arranged. In the throne room and the adjacent courts and rooms, Sennacherib's first military operations to the east, west, and south (Babylonia) are shown. These are repeated in detail in the wings beyond. Early in his reign, Sennacherib's grandson Assurbanipal lived in this palace. Half of his library, found in rooms XL and XLI, was probably originally stored in the floor above.

Another important complex built by Sennacherib was the arsenal on the east side of Nebi Yunus. Because of the presence of a later Islamic cemetery, this building complex has not been excavated and its plan is unknown, but, according to Sennacherib's reports, the arsenal consisted of one palace built in Assyrian style and another in Syrian style. Like Fort Shalmaneser at Nimrud, the complex was used as a military headquarters. It was extended by Sennacherib's son, Esarhaddon, whose own palace may be identified with a building about 100 meters east of the arsenal.

Another large building complex at Nineveh is the so-called North Palace of Assurbanipal, excavated by Rassam and Loftus (Barnett 1976; Nadali 2006). Here they found a great number of excellent wall reliefs as well as the second half of Assurbanipal's library, altogether more than 25,000 cuneiform tablets, but the architecture is poorly preserved and the northeastern area is effectively unknown. The outer wall of the palace, the throne room with courtyard and some state apartments behind it, and a long corridor leading to a gate in the western corner are all preserved. This gate seems to be an entrance to a park, which is mentioned in several texts. The gates were not flanked by human headed winged colossi, the *lamassu*, and, although the palace is large, the size of the state apartments seems to be more modest than in the palaces of Assurbanipal's forefathers. On the other hand, the orthostats found here are amongst the best surviving works of art from the ancient Near East. The slabs in the throne room and the state apartments depict vivid scenes of war against the Egyptians, Elamites, Babylonians, and Arabs. The rooms beyond are decorated with orthostats showing the king in the park with servants and musicians, and in a series of scenes the king is shown hunting lions, gazelles, and onager. It is probable that these hunts took place in the park to the west of the palace. In 612 BC Nineveh was conquered by a coalition of Medes and Babylonians. This marked the end of the Assyrian empire, but the site was reoccupied in the Hellenistic, Arsacid, and Roman periods.

8 Other Assyrian Sites in the Heartland

Besides the Assyrian capitals and the other large, well-known Assyrian sites, there are many other settlements containing Middle and Neo-Assyrian material (Green 1999; Altaweel 2008; Hausleiter 2010f: 183–7, 192–201). Most of these are small and excavations have been limited, so that only a few preliminary findings have been published. These include sites like Tell as-Sidr (Shakir 2005–6), Kaula Kandal (El Amin and Mallowan 1949, 1950), Qasr Shamamuk (Anastasio 2005), Khirbet Khatuniya (Curtis and Green 1997), Qasrij Cliff and Khirbet Qasrij (Curtis 1989b), Khirbet Hatara (Fiorina 1997), Tell Jigan (Fujii 1987), and Tell Rijm (Green 1999: 97–9). Northwest of Tell Rijim are some sites along the western bank of the Tigris with Assyrian material like Khirbet Karhasan, Tell Abu Dhahir, and Khirbet Shireena, and west of the Assyrian heartland Tell Taya and Tell al-Rimah have evidence of Neo-Assyrian occupation as well. Toward the eastern border of Assyria the town of Erbil (ancient Arbela), where a Neo-Assyrian tomb was found, must be noted. A Neo-Assyrian tomb dating to the 7th century BC (Hausleiter 2010f: 192–3), with a rich inventory of pottery and bronze vessels, was also found c.25 kilometers northwest of Nineveh on the west bank of the Tigris (Ibrahim and Amin Agha 1983).

GUIDE TO FURTHER READING

For an overview of 11 years of constant excavations (1903–14) at Assur, see Andrae (1977[1938]). The catalogue of a major exhibition on Assur at the Vorderasiatisches Museum (Pergamon) Berlin also provides a good overview of the work at Assur (Marzahn and Salje 2003). For a detailed overview of the German excavations in Kar-Tukulti-Ninurta, see Eickhoff (1985). Mallowan (1966) presents the most important results of the British excavations at Nimrud, and for a survey of 150 years of work at the site, see Oates and Oates (2001). The well-known bronze bands of the Balawat palace gates of Shalmaneser III are described systematically in Schachner (2007). Curtis and Tallis (2008) fills a gap, because there the bronze bands of a palace and a temple at Balawat, erected by Assurnasirpal II, are published the first time in detail with excellent drawings. Albenda (1986) investigates the relief slabs of Sargon's palace in Khorsabad, in particular their placement at the walls and the different topics of the scenes. The book includes many of the original drawings of Botta and Flandin. Caubet (1995) is a collection of interesting studies on the French investigations at Khorsabad. Matthiae (1998) is a very good résumé of the history of the Assyrian capitals with a focus on Nineveh, describing all the important buildings, with many good plans and photographs. Russell (1991) is a detailed study of Sennacherib's "Palace without Rival" at Nineveh.

CHAPTER FORTY-SIX

The Assyrians Abroad

Bradley J. Parker

1 Introduction

The Assyrian state that emerged from northern Iraq during the Mesopotamian Iron Age was indeed of imperial proportions. At the height of their power, the Assyrians claimed dominion over almost the entire Middle East, from the Persian Gulf to the Taurus mountains and from the Zagros mountains to the Mediterranean Sea. For a short period during the 7th century BC, the Assyrians even captured Egypt. In almost any textbook, one can read that the Neo-Assyrian Empire was the largest and most complex polity in Mesopotamian history up to this point. It was a large, expansionist state that extended its control over less powerful polities through conquest, coercion, and/or diplomacy (Parker 2001: 12; Sinopoli 2001b: 444; Wilkinson et al. 2005: 24). In doing so, it formed incorporative political and economic systems that transcended local political, social, and ethnic boundaries, thus claiming hegemony over a large and culturally diverse area. However, the success of Neo-Assyrian imperialism was not dependent solely upon Assyria's ability to expand but, more importantly, upon its ability to incorporate conquered regions into the imperial superstructure. In spite of the fact that there is a vast body of textual and archaeological evidence pertaining to the Neo-Assyrian imperial period (c.900–600 BC), evaluating how the Assyrians expanded, consolidated, and maintained their vast empire is still a difficult proposition.

A Companion to the Archaeology of the Ancient Near East, First Edition.
Edited by D.T. Potts.
© 2012 Blackwell Publishing Ltd. Published 2012 by Blackwell Publishing Ltd.

This chapter will begin to address this issue by examining a number of topics pertinent to the construction and maintenance of the Assyrian imperial power outside Assyrian's core area in what is today Iraqi Kurdistan. Obviously, the specifics of where, when, and why the Assyrian imperial infrastructure was constructed and maintained varied dramatically over the period in question. In many cases, states that began as autonomous neighbors became vassals of the empire only to be eventually annexed as provinces; provinces or vassal states occasionally threw off the Assyrian yoke; and some areas that were overrun by the Assyrian military were never successfully brought into the Assyrian administrative system. The following pages are not meant to document the ebb and flow of this history. Instead, they should be seen as a starting point for understanding some of the larger trends underlying Assyrian imperialism. The goal of this chapter is, therefore, to present an overview of the topic by creating a synthesis that allows a generalized understanding of various ways in which the Assyrians acquired and controlled territory outside the their own heartland.

2 Modes of Expansion

A fairly complete picture of Neo-Assyrian military history can be reconstructed by combining the annals of the Assyrian kings with Assyrian and Babylonian chronographic texts (e.g., Grayson 1982, 1991b). Further information about the administration of the Assyrian provinces can be gained from the corpus of Neo-Assyrian letters (Parpola 1981). What is less often discussed is how these documents combined with archaeological data reflect Assyrian military strategy and the implementation of Assyrian imperialism. Viewing the data in this light, a number of general observations are immediately apparent. First, military force was used both to defeat Assyria's enemies and to maximize Assyria's opportunities for expansion through coercive diplomacy. And, second, military action did not create a territorially contiguous political unit. Instead, the degree of control exercised by the empire outside the imperial heartland varied greatly.

The use of military force was the primary means of expanding Assyria's imperial domain. Since virtually all the young men in the empire could be called up for military service if need be, the full complement of the Assyrian military could be exceedingly large. Assyriologists have long argued that some Assyrian provinces were able to raise large contingents of cavalry and thousands of infantry. Relief carvings from the Assyrian palaces also show that Assyrian military officials effectively incorporated contingents of foreign soldiers into their own military (Dalley 1985). Although the full potential of the Assyrian army was rarely, if ever, gathered together for a single campaign, the army was, nevertheless, an extremely large and very well-organized fighting force. It also employed the latest military technology, including state-of-the-art weaponry such as siege machines, battering rams, and war chariots, and had considerable logistical support in the form of corps of engineers, a complement of priests and diviners, and a vast network of spies (Dubovský 2006; and see below).

Military expansion began with an ideologically charged military campaign. Such campaigns were, at least in theory, led by the king and were recorded by the royal chroniclers in the Assyrian annals. Data contained in the Assyrian annals suggest that royal campaigns were aimed at specific targets which are said to have committed some sort of affront against the empire, such as failure to recognize Assyrian authority, an offense against a god or gods, or an attack on an Assyrian ally. Whatever the offense was, it provided the ideological justification for an initial military expedition and paved the way for imperial expansion into peripheral regions. A key characteristic of military expansion was that royal campaigns involved the use of overwhelming force. Specific targets were chosen for attack, while the interceding towns and villages in a given area were often left unscathed. Thus, the purpose of initial forays into peripheral regions was not to conquer contiguous tracts of territory; instead, these campaigns were meant to neutralize the centers of opposition, while leaving most of the surrounding area and its inhabitants available for incorporation and exploitation (Parker 2001).

Not all military gains were followed by an attempt to consolidate those gains. However, in areas where annexation was the goal, Assyrian campaigns were only the first step in the larger process of imperial expansion (Sinopoli 1994). The initial step toward the consolidation of conquered areas was the establishment of a centrally or strategically located administrative and military center. The Assyrians usually chose a previously existing settlement to fill this role. We learn from the textual record that soon after an initial conquest, sites chosen to serve as administrative and military centers in a newly conquered region were the object of large construction projects (e.g., Grayson 1991a: 202). Labor and materials for such construction projects were gathered from all over the empire. A letter concerning the construction of a remote fort on the Assyrian frontier, for example, shows that laborers from at least four cities participated in the construction (B.J. Parker 1997). Such projects often included the construction of fortification walls, fortified citadels, and sophisticated water systems. There is also evidence that provincial centers contained factories and storage facilities where military hardware and luxury goods were manufactured and where the more mundane produce of the land, such as wool and grain, were processed and stored.

Once Assyrian military and administrative centers were established in newly conquered regions, the area around and between these centers was colonized either through land grants to Assyrian officials or through Assyria's policy of deportation and resettlement. A high official named Nabu-sharru-usur, for example, owned more than 1,700 hectares of land in at least seven locations throughout the empire (Kataja and Whiting 1995: no. 27). Granting estates to high officials in various parts of the empire worked both to limit the power of provincial authorities, since it "established a network of interlocking economic interests," and, at the same time, to tie the personal interests of the Assyrian elite to the well being of the empire (Mattila 2000: 141). Other areas were colonized by persons deported from various parts of the empire (Oded 1979). Although the purpose of deportation was first and foremost to break up nationalistic tendencies among rebellious populations, it also acted as a means to incorporate such groups into Assyrian provincial society (Parker 2001). This policy is vividly recorded in the Old Testament. When standing at the gates of Jerusalem, an Assyrian general promised the inhabitants of the city that if they surrendered peacefully they would live in "a land of grain and wine, a land of bread and vineyards" (Isaiah 36:17; cf. Fales 2008; Machinist 1983). Assyrian sources augment this picture by showing, first, that families were not split up when deported but, rather, family groups were allowed to stay together and settle in the same area. Second, provincial officials were obliged to provide provisions and equipment to deportees traveling through their area. Third, upon arriving at their destination, deportees were given land, which often consisted of fields and garden plots, a dwelling, and in some cases one or more animals. And fourth, provincial governors were responsible for protecting deportees resettled in their provinces.

Assyrian military actions may be interpreted not just as a means of achieving victory over Assyria's enemies, but also as a way of creating and spreading Assyrian power to potential imperial subjects (Matthews 2003b: 149). As mentioned above, campaign itineraries suggest that when moving through a sensitive region, Assyrian forces were not arrayed across the landscape. Instead, the military traveled in a straight line from one destination to the next. In utilizing this strategy, the full force of the Assyrian military was brought to bear on specific singular targets (Parker 2001: 259–63), which were then completely obliterated. This strategy accomplished several things. First and foremost, it made the Assyrian army seem invincible. The magnitude of the destruction wrought by the onslaught was awe-inspiring, and news of the might of the Assyrian military machine surely traveled far and wide. Once victory was achieved, the Assyrians employed another gruesome but effective military tactic, one that H.W.F. Saggs (1963) called "psychological warfare" (see also Dubovský 2006: 161–88). This tactic, described by the Assyrians in their annals and depicted on the walls of their palaces, included such atrocities as flaying rebel leaders and hanging their skins from the walls of the captured city, burning the children of rebel families, piling the heads of enemy soldiers in great pyramids along roadways, and impaling rebel captives on high stakes around captured enemy cities. Such acts were clearly meant to spread fear among the surviving population. Assyrian military campaigns were thus not only a means by which the Assyrians defeated their enemies and increased the imperial dominion; they were also a means of actualizing the king's power and, in doing so, increasing Assyria's potential for expansion though coercive diplomacy.

Assyrian victories were recorded by scribes and artists and were later translated into both written and visual media for propagandistic purposes. The Assyrian annals were initially composed as a means of recording royal campaigns, but these texts were constantly re-edited for display in the palaces, burial in foundation deposits, as messages to the gods, and surely as texts to be read aloud in temple festivals (Oppenheim 1960; Liverani 1981). The heroic deeds of the Assyrian kings were also displayed in visual form on the walls of their palaces. These representations were not merely for posterity but were meant to perpetuate the power created in past battles. Visiting dignitaries and Assyrian officials alike were reminded of the heroic deeds of the king whenever they visited rooms in the palace where such reliefs were displayed (Reade 1979a; Winter 1983; Russell 1991).

The power generated by the Assyrian military set the stage for expansion through coercive diplomacy. In many cases the Assyrian authorities could impose hegemonic rule over peripheral regions by binding exiting states to the empire as vassals. Vassalage was a compromise between degree of control and cost. On the one hand, the Assyrians obviously retained far more political and economic control over a province than over a vassal. On the other hand, manipulating a vassal was much more cost-effective than annexing a province. The decision to incorporate peripheral regions into the empire's vassal state system required the existence of a state-level political structure in a location where the threat of Assyrian force made submission by the local government an attractive option and geographic and logistical constraints would not diminish the strength of an Assyrian strike if the use of force became necessary.

3 Administrative Systems

The above discussion of Assyrian modes of expansion shows that Assyrian imperial administrators maintained a flexible policy toward the peripheral regions of the empire. When the Assyrians expanded into a new area, they had a variety of options by which to exercise their authority. They could establish territorial control through the military conquest and annexation of a region and its integration into the Assyrian provincial system; they could establish hegemonic rule by binding existing political structures to the empire through loyalty oaths, effectively converting autonomous polities into vassal states; or they could leave existing states or regions intact to act as neutral buffer states or zones between their frontier provinces and their enemies.

The Assyrians maintained territorial control inside provinces through a hierarchical system of provincial officials (see below) who administered authority from the provincial capital. These capital cities contained a palace and the offices of the various governmental departments as well as industrial installations and storage facilities. The provincial capital was at the top of a hierarchy of settlements that usually included several smaller towns and villages integrated into the empire from the previously existing settlement system, as well as many agricultural villages, road stations, outposts, and garrisons established as part of the process of imperial consolidation (Wilkinson 1995; Parker 2003; Wilkinson et al. 2005).

The Assyrians exercised hegemonic control over peripheral regions by imposing vassal obligations on existing polities. Where the Assyrians found viable political structures in the imperial periphery, they often attempted to force those polities into a subordinate status through either the threat or the show of military force. If the polity in question submitted peacefully to Assyrian demands, the ruling elite were allowed to remain in power and retain control over their subjects and territory and therefore maintain a relatively autonomous status. However, if the polity opposed Assyrian rule or allied itself with an Assyrian enemy, it could be the object of a military campaign. In this case, the Assyrians would not hesitate to set up a puppet government.

Vassal status involved varying degrees of obligations on the part of both the vassal state and the empire. The most basic demand made by the Assyrians upon their vassals involved the flow of information. The Assyrian authorities were extremely concerned with gathering military intelligence and for this reason vassal states were required to send regular reports about political and military matters in their area to the imperial authorities. Vassals were also obligated to give tribute, not only in material goods, but also in labor, both for military operations and construction projects. In some cases, the Assyrians were allowed full military freedom in vassal territory and they often exploited the natural resources in and around vassal territory. They also imposed political and economic restrictions on vassals by regulating, or attempting to regulate, their interaction with other states. Vassal obligations were monitored by an Assyrian official who was stationed in the subject state. This official had a garrison of cavalry at his immediate disposal. He reported on the daily activities of himself and his hosts to the provincial governor in charge of his region, but, on more urgent matters, he wrote directly to the king or the crown prince.

In return for their loyalty, the empire promised to protect vassal states from foreign aggression. This protection pact applied first to the threat of invasion from rival states. How seriously the Assyrians abided by this obligation is difficult to say. In some cases, vassals were left to fend for themselves when disaster loomed, and, in others, it appears that the Assyrians used the protection clause as an excuse to invade states that might threaten a loyal vassal. In any case, it is clear that the Assyrians used this agreement to their own advantage. Promises of protection also applied to hostile forces from within the vassal state itself, and for this reason threatened or weakened regimes often sought help from the empire as a means of propping up a dynasty that was otherwise destined to collapse.

The Assyrians made every effort to win control over existing states in their periphery. However, when the geopolitical or geographic situation made military logistics difficult or impractical, and/or when no state-level polities existed in such a region, some areas were left intact to act as buffers between Assyria and its enemies. Geographers generally agree that a buffer state is a polity that lies between two or more rival states or their spheres of influence. The continued existence of the buffer state as an autonomous polity is tolerated, or even encouraged, by its neighbors because it serves to spatially separate rival states and, therefore, as long as the buffer state remains neutral, it provides a degree of security for both sides (Chay and Ross 1986). Buffer zones are similar to buffer states in that they consist of neutral areas that lie between two or more rival states or their spheres of influence. However, buffer zones are substantially different from buffer states because they contain no viable political structures and they are not controlled by any outside political force. Instead, the rival states between which these zones lie consider them to be largely empty spaces, or no-man's land, and, since they physically separate the rival states, they too provide a degree of security for all sides.

4 Provincial Administration

The nature of the Assyrian royal correspondence, which is largely made up of letters sent from the provincial capitals to the palace, means that we have far more information about Assyrian provincial governors and other high officials than we do about their subordinates (Parpola 1981). Most of the information that we have about lower-ranking provincial officials comes in the form of short references to such persons within these texts. The exception is the small number of texts that have been excavated in the Assyrian provinces.

The provincial governor stood at the top of a hierarchy of officials and administrators. The second in command was probably the "deputy," since his title (Akk. *shaniu*) literally means "second" (Parpola 1987: 227). At the bottom of the hierarchy was the "village manager" (Akk. *rab alani*), who was in charge of a small area including one or more villages or hamlets. References to "village managers" reveal that their primary duty was to collect taxes in the form of goods and labor. This aspect of the work is exemplified by a letter that mentions mudbricks supplied by village managers for the construction of Sargon II's (721–705 BC) new capital at Dur-Sharrukin (Lanfranchi and Parpola 1990: no. 291) and a letter from Nimrud in which we learn that "the silver dues of the prefects and the village managers imposed on the local population have been handed over (to the central government)" (Parpola 1987: no. 176). In addition to having a small number of troops at their disposal, village managers were also expected to aid the imperial administration in the exploitation of the natural resources of the land. One letter relates how a village manager has led troops into the forest to protect his men as they attempted to transport felled trees through a dangerous area (Lanfranchi and Parpola 1990: no. 3). A letter from a governor named Duri-Assur mentions an official called the ^{LÚ}ša bīt kūdini. This term literally means "mule stable attendant," but in fact this official was in charge of implementing the empire's system of corvée labor (Postgate 1974). Corvée officers kept careful track of the people in their jurisdiction, presumably by recording census lists and tallies of time served and time owed (B.J. Parker 1997). Since this official's duties included retrieving fugitives fleeing their corvée labor obligations to the empire, these officers must also have had access to cohorts of soldiers or police.

Assyrian provincial governors were concerned with various aspects of the administration of their realm. Broadly speaking, their activities can be grouped into three categories: development (discussed above), security, and taxation. Security concerns were particularly acute in frontier provinces. One of the main preoccupations of officials on the northern frontier of the empire, for example, was gathering military information about Urartu. To this end, Assyrian administrators had access to a vast network of spies or informants (Akk. *daiālu*) who kept provincial officials apprised of events both within and beyond the empire (Dubovský 2006). The correspondence of the governors of the northern provinces contains numerous references to "news of the Urartians" (e.g., Lanfranchi and Parpola 1990: nos. 32 and 41; see also Deller 1984), including two fragments that possibly refer to Urartian governors (Lanfranchi and Parpola 1990: nos. 23 and 41) and one letter that describes Urartian troop movements (Lanfranchi and Parpola 1990: no. 21). The central administration in the Assyrian capital expected to be constantly updated about developments in the provinces. The anxiety of officials about this topic, as well as the vagaries of the Assyrian mail system, are exemplified by a letter in which a governor (Sha-Assur-dubbu) responds to an inquiry from the palace saying: "I have (already) sent [a detailed report to] the king, my lord, […]! Let me now send it a second time" (Lanfranchi and Parpola 1990: no. 34) and a fragmentary text from an unidentified author that reports, "I have sent out (spies) to go and inquire; (when) they return with a detailed report, I shall write to the king, my lord" (Lanfranchi and Parpola 1990: no. 40). Another method of gathering intelligence was to kidnap enemy soldiers or officials and transfer them under armed escort to the capital where they would be interrogated. However, we learn in a letter that reports on the capture of Urartian spies that this was not solely an Assyrian activity (Lanfranchi and Parpola 1991: no. 55). Not only did Urartian spies infiltrate Assyria's provincial administration, but the Urartians also captured Assyrian operatives and even tried to influence Assyrian vassals.

Numerous letters in the Assyrian royal correspondence speak of the extraction of revenues from Assyrian provinces and vassal states. A royal delegate named Assur-resuwa, for example, extracted barley, wine, sheep, bronze objects, lumber, and carnelian from the vassal state of Kumme (Parker 2001: 93–4). Provincial governors were responsible for supplying offerings to temples, especially the Ashur temple, in the Assyrian heartland. Channeling revenues from the far-flung provinces to religious institutions in the imperial core was not only a method of underwriting state religious cults; it was also a means of connecting provincial elites to Assyria's religious institutions.

5 Territoriality

On most maps of the Ancient Near East, the Neo-Assyrian Empire is shown as a territorial polity separated from its periphery by a thick black line or the intersection of two contrasting colors (e.g., Saggs 1984: 110; Miller and Hayes 1986: 368; Roaf 1990a: 164; Hunt 2004: 92). This image is echoed in much of the literature, especially in introductory textbooks, where the Assyrian Empire is described as a "territorial unit" (Van De Mieroop 2007: 247), "divided into provinces" (Kuhrt 1995: 531) that stretched "from Egypt on one side to Persia (Iran) on the other" (Saggs 1984: 2). Such representations, in text or image, carry with them deep-seated meaning for the modern reader: they imply that the Assyrians held firm, homogenous control within a territory bounded by impervious borders (Smith 2005; Wilk 2004).

This vision of ancient states and empires is clearly at odds with the available data from the Mesopotamian Iron Age. These data show that the Neo-Assyrian Empire was not made up of contiguous stretches of land. Instead, much of the empire consisted of a patchwork of provinces, vassal states, and buffer areas linked to the imperial core by a network of fortified transportation and communication corridors. Although the imperial core almost certainly consisted of a series of adjoining provinces (Postgate 1995), as the empire expanded into its periphery, transportation costs and logistic constraints increased dramatically (Ekholm and Friedman 1979; cf. Hassig 1985). Flexibility was a key factor in forming imperial policy (Morris 1998). The Assyrian administration carefully weighed the potential military, political, and economic benefits of expansion into new regions, and chose a specific policy for each region that would maximize imperial gains. The further the empire expanded, the greater the economic, ideological, or strategic benefit had to be to make territorial control tenable and thus the areas that were suitable for annexation become more restricted. The sociopolitical landscape beyond the imperial core was, therefore, dotted with "islands" of imperial control (Liverani 1988). Some of the area between the "islands" that made up the outlying regions of the empire were filled in by establishing hegemonic control over existing states. This strategy was economical, since it provided income, in the form of vassal obligations, at a low cost; but, more importantly, it limited the possibility of rebellion in regions that may lie around or between Assyrian provinces. Other areas around and between imperial holdings consisted of neutral buffer states or buffer zones, and still others can contain hostile enemies.

GUIDE TO FURTHER READING

On Neo-Assyrian history, see Grayson (1982 and 1991a); Kuhrt (1995); and Saggs (1984). For Assyrian administration and officialdom, see, e.g., Larsen (1979), Grayson

(1993), Deller (1999), Mattila (2000), Parker (2001), and Dubovský (2006). Many original Assyrian letters from the state archives of Assyria are now easily accessible in the volumes of the University of Helsinki's Neo-Assyrian Text Corpus Project. On the Assyrian royal annals, recounting campaigns and actions undertaken across the empire, see, e.g., Fales (1981) and Tadmor (1997). For helpful discussions of ancient imperialism, see Doyle (1986), Sinopoli (1994 and 2001b), D'Altroy and Hastorf (2001), and Alcock et al. (2001).

CHAPTER FORTY-SEVEN

The Urartian Empire

Alina Ayvazian

1 Introduction

The roots of Urartu can be traced as far back as the 13th century BC when the land of *uruatri* was first mentioned in the annals of the Assyrian king Shalmaneser I (1273–1244 BC). At that time, according to B. Piotrovskii, *uruatri* denoted a tribal coalition located to the south and southeast of Lake Van (Piotrovskii 1959: 44). In 1271 BC Shalmaneser undertook the first of a series of five campaigns against *uruatri*. From this time onward, and for two more generations of Assyrian rulers, the term *uruatri* was replaced in Assyrian texts by "the lands of Nairi." Beginning in the 12th century, the Assyrians began a series of increasingly regular forays into the Anatolian highlands, the main purpose of which was the extraction of booty and tribute, particularly timber and horses (Saggs 1984: 48; Zimansky 1985: 50). The area's geography and climatic factors prevented the Assyrians from conquering these territories outright, but the tribes started the process of consolidation to counter the Assyrian threat. By the early 1st millennium BC, *uruatri* began to denote not only the land, but also the inhabitants of the area around Lake Van (Piotrovskii 1969: 43), and by the 9th century, Urartu arose as a political unit centered on its capital Tushpa, on the shores of Lake Van. Thus, in the words of P. Zimansky, "the Urartian state . . . seems ultimately, if unwittingly, to have been a creation of the Assyrians" (1985: 48). Throughout Urartu's history, Assyria remained its greatest adversary as well as one of its greatest sources of inspiration. The Urartians borrowed Assyrian cuneiform writing, making it conform to their own language; military and diplomatic practices;

A Companion to the Archaeology of the Ancient Near East, First Edition.
Edited by D.T. Potts.
© 2012 Blackwell Publishing Ltd. Published 2012 by Blackwell Publishing Ltd.

literary forms; artistic motifs and styles; and more. The two empires lived in a state of continuous mutual influence and uneasy respect.

The core of Urartu was located around the Sevan, Van, and Urmia lakes, in present-day Armenia, eastern Turkey, and northwestern Iran. The kingdom was separated from the areas to the north and the south by mountain chains, creating a sort of natural fortress. The Urartians themselves called their country "Biainili" – a term echoed in the modern name Van. Power belonged to a small, "ethnically Urartian" elite (Zimansky 1995a: 103ff; 1995b; Grekyan 2006: 150 n3) who imposed their beliefs and, possibly, their language on the diverse population of the kingdom. Throughout its history, Urartu remained a multiethnic and multicultural coalition. Two major efforts to centralize the kingdom occurred early in Urartu's existence during the reigns of kings Ishpuini (c.830–810 BC) and Menua (c.810–785 BC), and again during the reign of Rusa II (c.685–639 BC), shortly before Urartu's decline. Nevertheless, the goal of true centralization remained elusive, because in times of trouble people quickly and naturally reverted to the old-fashioned way of living within localized clans.

2 Kings and Reigns

Aramu was the first Urartian king attested in the cuneiform sources. He was mentioned in connection with campaigns by Shalmaneser III (858–824 BC) undertaken in the king's accession year (859/8 BC), in his 10th year (849 BC), and in his 15th year (844 BC) recorded in the Annals (Grayson 1996: 8, 14), and in three epigraphs on the bronze bands of the "Balawat Gates" found at Imgur-Enlil (modern Balawat) southeast of Nineveh (Grayson 1996: 140, 143, 146; cf. Gunter 1982). According to these texts, Shalmaneser captured three of Aramu's cities: Sugunia, Arne, and Bit-(A)gusi. The Balawat Gates show the Assyrian army marching over three mountain passes to Lake Van, while Shalmaneser performed sacrifices to the gods at the shores of the lake. Another set of bronze sheets shows the graphic aftermath of the battle with the Urartians, a deserted fortress and the cruel punishment of prisoners, illustrating the account given in the Annals where Shalmaneser says: "I besieged the city, captured [it], massacred many of their [people], [and] carried off booty from them. I erected a tower of heads in front of his city. I burned fourteen cities in their environs" (Grayson 1996: 14). The Assyrian sources show that the reign of Aramu, though largely unknown to scholarship, was rather eventful and lasted for at least 15 years.

The earliest known Urartian monument dates to the reign of Sarduri I (c.840–830 BC). It is a wall of colossal boulders (0.75 × 6 meters) in the western piedmont of the Rock of Van, which served as the citadel of the Urartian capital city Tushpa. The wall was inscribed with three identical inscriptions in Assyrian:

> The inscription of Sarduri, son of Lutipri, great king, mighty king, king of the Universe, king of the land of Nairi, who knows of no equal, a pastor worthy of

admiration, fearless in battle . . . Sarduri, son of Lutipri, king of kings; I received tribute from all kings. Thus speaks Sarduri, son of Lutipri: I brought this limestone from the city of Alniunu, I erected this wall. (Arutiunian 2001: 9, no. 1)

The fact that Sarduri calls himself "son of Lutipri" and not "son of Aramu" may point to significant shifts in the internal politics of the Urartian kingdom in the 9th century. It is possible that during Aramu's reign the kingdom's center was located to the north of Lake Van. G.A. Melikishvili suggested that Aramu and Sarduri may have belonged to different Urartian tribes which came to the fore at different times (Piotrovskii 1959: 59–60). Sarduri's accession to the Urartian throne might represent the beginning of a new dynasty, one that possibly ruled Urartu for the next 200 years.

Sarduri was succeeded by his son, Ishpuini (c.838–810 BC) who, in many ways, was the first true monarch of the land of Biainili. Ishpuini ruled out of his father's capital city, Tushpa, and from there campaigned to the south, southeast, and north of his kingdom. The first inscriptions in the Urartian language date to Ishpuini's reign. These consist of short formulae carved into column bases, mentioning only the name of Ishpuini, son of Sarduri. Later, more extended inscriptions named both Ishpuini and his son and successor, Menua (c.810–786 BC).

Ishpuini and Menua were the great architects of the Urartian state. Their policies and reforms shaped Urartu into a strong, centralized polity. In addition to introducing written Urartian, they built roads and canals, extended the kingdom's borders, and introduced a centralized religion built around the worship of a new supreme god, Haldi. The extent of Urartu during the reigns of Ishpuini and Menua can be estimated from the widespread distribution of inscriptions extending from the lower Murat River basin (around Elazig, eastern Turkey) in the west to the Araks River in the north, and the southern shore of Lake Urmia in the southeast. The seat of the god Haldi was Ardini (its Urartian name) or Musasir (its Assyrian name). Conquered by Tiglath-pileser I (1114–1076 BC) of Assyria c.1100 BC, it fell within the Urartian sphere of influence during the 9th century BC.

At the end of the 9th century, Ishpuini and Menua erected a bilingual, Urartian/Assyrian stele near the Kelishin pass, on the border of Iran and Iraq. This important document, which provided clues for the decipherment of the Urartian language, testifies to the Urartian conquest of the city called Musasir, the site most closely associated with the cult of Haldi and the Urartians' main, official sanctuary. It may also have been the site of royal coronations. M. Salvini has suggested that the erection of the Kelishin stele established a *via sacra*, a processional way that connected the twin centers of Urartian political power (near Lake Van) and religion (at Musasir) (Salvini 1989: 81).

The introduction of an official pantheon was an important step in Ishpuini's campaign to secure the identity of his kingdom and the health of his dynasty. He placed a relatively new god – Haldi – at the head of the kindgom's pantheon to preside not only over the plethora of ancient local gods, but also over the high-ranking gods of Hurro-Hittite descent, Teisheba and Shiwini. During Ishpuini's reign, the worship of god Haldi spread to newly conquered territories, mainly to the southeast of Tushpa, to the southern shores of Lake Urmia, and north into Transcaucasia. Ishpuini's policy was continued by his son and successor Menua.

The accession of Menua (c.810–785) signaled the beginning of the greatest period in Urartian history, one that lasted nearly 70 years. Menua started a rigorous building campaign, amply attested in more than 100 cuneiform inscriptions, one of which may testify to the completion, at this time, of the walls of the Urartian capital Tushpa (Piotrovskii 1959: 63). Menua expanded both westward and eastward, securing vital mineral resources around Malatya (Saggs 1984: 81–2) in eastern Anatolia. He extended the boundaries of Urartu both north and southeast, in the directions of Lakes Sevan and Urmia. Among the goals of this expansion were the control of rich agricultural lands for the cultivation of staples like wheat and barley, ill-suited to the cold climate of the highlands, as well as access to valuable commercial trade routes. Menua then conquered the north Syrian corridor, which gave the Urartians access to the markets and products of the Mediterranean. Eventually, Urartu came to dominate the export of Anatolian resources and controlled the shipment of tin and luxury goods that came overland from Central Asia, which, in turn, allowed it to profit from their distribution to the greater Mediterranean area.

Menua continued his father's policy of northern expansion, reaching the wealthy country of Diauehi across the Araks. To facilitate his operations in this area, he built an administrative center on the right bank of the Araks, and called it Menuahinili. Access to the Araks valley opened the way for Menua's heirs to the fertile Ararat valley, further north.

The approaches to the Urartian capital were protected by a chain of forts that followed an ancient route connecting Lake Van to the site of Khoy and Urartu's more easterly regions (Lehmann-Haupt 1926: 38; Piotrovskii 1959: 63). Approximately 10 kilometers to the northeast of Van, Menua erected a massive fortress near the modern village of Anzaf. More fortifications were erected in the northern parts of the country, around modern Malazgirt. According to extant inscriptions, other fortresses and "gates of Haldi" were established in the newly acquired territories.

At the beginning of the 8th century Urartu reached the height of its power and territorial extent. However, the westward expansion initiated by Menua, especially in northern Syria, was at odds with Assyrian interests in Asia Minor. The Assyrian king Shalmaneser IV (782–773 BC) therefore launched a series of energetic campaigns against Urartu in the years 781–778, 776, and 774 BC. In this challenging political climate, Menua was succeeded by his son Argishti I (c.785–760 BC). Argishti was probably not Menua's eldest son, nor his first choice as heir. Another name – Inushpua – follows Menua's in one of the inscriptions from Van. There is no firm evidence to show that Inushpua ever reigned Urartu, however. Instead, Argishti acceded to the throne to face the challenges that a confrontation with Urartu's mighty neighbor Assyria would bring.

Argishti I left behind an extensive cuneiform record of his reign. His annals, known as the Horhor inscription, were carved into the southwestern wall of the Rock of Van. The second part of this inscription was carved on two stones – originally parts of a stele that was reused in the Armenian church of Surb Sahak in Van. The Horhor inscription consists of more than 295 lines in seven columns and describes 13 years of Argishti's reign. The similarities between parts of the Horhor inscription and the text of the stele fragments from Surb Sahak has allowed scholars to restore the missing parts of the inscription and thus obtain a rather complete picture of Argishti's campaigns. An energetic ruler, Argishti expanded the borders of Urartu in almost every direction. One of his first campaigns was directed north, to Transcaucasia. He crossed the Ararat valley, subdued the rich country of Diauehi, and laid upon it an annual tribute of gold, copper, horses, and cattle. Two years later he led his troops into northern Syria, returning with scores of prisoners whom he resettled in his new administrative center in Transcaucasia, the fortress of Erebuni (modern Yerevan, Armenia).

According to his annals, six years after the construction of Erebuni, Argishti built another large administrative center in Transcaucasia, and named it Argishtihinili. This new city replaced the earlier administrative center of Menuahinili, built by Menua to the south of Araks River. Argishti's own inscriptions describe the construction of four canals that supplied Argishtihinili with water from the Araks (Melikishvili 1960: nos. 136–137). During Argishti's reign, southern Transcaucasia firmly became a part of the Urartian state, and Urartu gained access to the fertile Ararat valley and the regions around Lake Urmia, further south. Urartu now monopolized all the principal trade routes to the west, replacing Assyria as the dominant power in the Near East.

The reign of Sarduri II (c.760–730 BC), son of Argishti, began auspiciously with victorious campaigns in the west, from which the Urartian troops brought back large quantities of gold, silver, and cattle, as well as a number of battle chariots (Melikishvili 1960: no. 158). Sarduri then proceeded to reaffirm his power in Transcaucasia, after which he marched south and won several seemingly effortless victories over Assyria, extending Urartian influence southward to the upper reaches of the Tigris and northern Syria (Piotrovskii 1959: 76) and northwards to the land of Qulha (legendary Colchis, in modern western Georgia). From this time onward, we see more and more north Syrian motifs in Urartian art. The representations of female goddesses, enthroned and tended by a female figure, so abundant on Urartian medallions, pectorals, and arrow quivers, may be dated to this period. Even though the goddesses are shown holding not a mirror but a leaf or a branch in their hand – recalling representations of the branch or a leaf of an aspen tree, sacred in later Armenian legends – such figures are reminiscent of earlier Hittite representations.

Sarduri's victories are described in his annals, partially preserved near Argishti's, on the Rock of Van, and partially on a stele that was incorporated into the construction of the church of Surb Sahak in Van. In the sixth year of his reign, he marched to the south of Lake Urmia, and to the north of Mount Aragats, to the land of Eriahi. The following year he cruelly punished the land of Qulha, which had continued to resist Urartian encroachment, and erected victory stelae there on the ashes of the defeated city (Arutiunian 2001: 238, no. 241D; Piotrovskii 1959: 80). In his eighth year Sarduri returned to the region of Lake Sevan, where he reaffirmed his control over all the districts of the rich land of Etiuni. Territories around Lake Sevan, especially its western and southern shores, thus became a part of Urartu. The territory of Urartu increased, and, after several victorious marches into northern Syria, the Euphrates became the kingdom's western border.

During Sarduri's reign, Erebuni and Argishtihinili continued as centers of Urartian royal administration in Transcaucasia. Argishtihinili seems to have been especially favored by Sarduri, who continued the construction and expansion of its fortresses, temples, and vineyards. Some of his inscriptions describe the establishment of stelae and gates of Haldi, as well as sacrifices made before them. Sarduri also continued to explore the center of his kingdom. A few of Sarduri's inscriptions describe the planting of vineyards and construction activity near Van (Melikishvili 1960: nos. 163, 167). By the mid-8th century, Urartu was at the height of its power. However, the political situation in the Near East soon changed.

After the uprising in Kalhu (Nimrud) in 745 BC, the Assyrian throne was occupied by Tiglath-pileser III (744–727 BC), who swiftly launched an aggressive campaign focused on breaking the Urartu/north Syrian alliance which stood in the way of Assyria's imperial aspirations. In 743 BC, he decisively defeated the Urartians at the battle of Arpad and proceeded to reassert Assyrian political control of the area, thus re-establishing Assyrian commercial links with the Mediterranean world. Seeking access to the sources of tin in the east, the Assyrians then turned to regaining control of the Zagros region. Between the reign of Tiglath-pileser III and Sargon II (721–705 BC), the Assyrians entered the Zagros eight times. These campaigns were aimed at robbing the Urartians of their commercial economic base. None of these campaigns was aimed directly at Urartu. Instead, the Assyrians concentrated on reopening the southern pass across the Zagros, the Khorasan road, in order to redirect the east–west trade through Assyria as an alternative to the northern route that was dominated by Urartu (Levine 1977b: 148–9).

The end of Sarduri's reign is not very clear. Various districts in Urartu started to rebel against centralized control, and Sarduri's descendant, Rusa I (c.730–714/713 BC), was faced with the challenge of putting his kingdom back together. By the time of Rusa I's accession c.730 BC, the kingdom had been weakened economically by Assyria and even more so by the raids of the Cimmerians on

Urartu's borders. The accession and reign of Rusa I have been discussed extensively (Lanfranchi 1983: 132 with earlier bibliography). Sargon II's boast that, "[w]ith my two horses and my charioteer I took over the kingdom of Urartu," has caused many to doubt the legitimacy of Rusa's reign. Moreover, Rusa adopted new royal titles to replace formulae that had been more or less standardized prior to his reign. From this point on, the Urartian archaeological record changes in nature.

In the very first years of his reign, Rusa had to take measures to protect his kingdom against Assyria. A bilingual inscription carved on the road to Musasir describes his installation of Urzana on the throne of Musasir. With the help of Urzana's troops, Rusa conducted raids on Assyrian territories. Nevertheless, Rusa avoided open confrontation with Assyria, focusing instead on strengthening the borders of his kingdom and fostering useful alliances. The Assyrian annals preserve a detailed description of Sargon II's eighth campaign of 714 BC. This was a punitive expedition against the countries to the northeast of Assyria. The expedition against Musasir and Urartu is described with special care, in 430 lines of cuneiform text in the form of a letter to the god Assur. According to the Assyrian annals, as Sargon approached the land of Mannea, its ruler came out to greet the Assyrian army with rich presents. Rulers of other smaller states around Lake Urmia followed suit, begging Sargon to rid them of Rusa's presence there. However, as Sargon continued his campaign to the east, he was informed that Rusa had gathered his army and allies at his rear, at Mount Uaush. Having learned this, Sargon changed course and turned back to the country of Uishdish to confront Rusa. Sargon personally led the attack. He overwhelmed the Urartian camp without warning, in the middle of the night, thus ensuring a swift and easy victory. After defeating the Urartian army, Sargon continued his advance into Urartian territory, around the eastern shore of Lake Urmia. His "Letter to Assur" describes in great detail the prosperous Urartian lands – gardens, canals, and luxurious palaces – in order to powerfully drive home the detailed picture of doom and destruction wrought by the Assyrian troops.

For most of his Urartian campaign Sargon remained on the outskirts of the kingdom. However, on his return journey home he decided to take a detour and headed for Musasir. Having sent the rest of his troops on their way, he led a small battalion of 1,000 cavalry through treacherous mountain passages and thick forests. At Musasir Sargon's army looted the city, carrying off tons of gold, silver, copper, lead, and semi-precious stones. The list contains a detailed description of objects of special interest, including bronze statues of Urartian kings. Sargon annexed Musasir, and laid upon it the conscription and building tax.

The loss of Musasir was a blow for Urartu. Not only did it signify the loss of a buffer state, but it also meant the loss of Urartu's identity, exemplified by the worship of Haldi. Sargon's annals state that having learned about the capture of Musasir and the cult image of Haldi, Rusa took his own life. At this juncture, the kingdom of Van came very close to its demise.

Rusa I was succeeded by his son, Argishti II (c.713–685 BC). We possess only a handful of inscriptions from his reign (Melikishvili 1960: nos. 275–277). Extant sources shed little light on Urartu at this time. Sargon's attention was demanded elsewhere and his successor Sennacherib (704–681 BC) was preoccupied with wars in Babylonia, Syria, and Palestine. Assyrian sources from this period are silent about the activities of their northern neighbor. Argishti II was involved in rebuilding his kingdom. Two stelae, found near Ardjesh, talk about the construction of a city, an artificial lake, and a canal in the center of the kingdom (Piotrovskii 1959: 112; Arutiunian 2001: 312, no. 406).

In 681 BC, Sennacherib was killed during a palace revolt by his two sons (see, e.g., 2 Kings 19:37; Isaiah 37:38). According to the Armenian historian Moses of Khoren, the murderers fled to Armenia and settled there, founding two of Armenia's most prominent clans – the Artsruni and the Gnuni. Argishti II's rule probably lasted as long as Sennacherib's. However, in the annals of the next Assyrian king – Esarhaddon (680–669 BC) – we encounter the name of a different king, Rusa II (c.685–640/639 BC). From this time until the end of Urartu, Assyria worked to support the status quo within the uneasy political climate of the day. The 7th century BC may be truly considered a period of flux. It was the time when, against the background of shifting events and the emergence of new powers, both Assyria and Urartu tried to find ways to survive rather than expand. This was Urartu's last great period, inaugurated by the accession to the throne of the extraordinary Rusa II.

Rusa II's reign manifested the arrival of a new, albeit short-lived, order in the kingdom of Van. The leitmotif of his efforts was not expansion but sensible consolidation. Learning from the mistakes of earlier rulers, Rusa reformed the kingdom's administration, replacing local governors with viceroys responsible directly to him. Rusa II seems to have been the last Urartian king to have left significant archaeological evidence of his rule. He founded at least five new cities: Teishebaini (modern Karmir Blur), Rusahinili on Mount Qilbanu (modern Toprak Kale), Rusahinili on Mount Eiduru (modern Ayanis), Bastam, and Kef Kalesi (by Adilcevaz). He also enlarged the fortresses of Argishtihinili (Armavir), originally founded by Argishti I, and Çavuştepe, founded by Sarduri II.

Building campaigns, sculpture, and artistic revival testify to Urartu's resurgence at this time. However, Rusa's consolidation efforts are best illustrated by his efforts to reinforce the importance of royal religion and ritual, and by his complete restructuring of the kingdom's administration. Under Rusa II, the "message" of Urartian kingship changed. Whereas Argishti I, for example, sought to portray himself as a great warrior, Rusa II presented himself as a pious builder. Faith and ceremony seemed to be of paramount importance during his reign. In place of Musasir, the Urartian holy city ravaged by Sargon II's troops in 714 BC, Rusa II established a new religious center at Kef Kalesi (Zimansky 1998: 36). The Urartian pantheon was broadened to include new deities, reflecting the shifting ethnic composition of the kingdom, and may have, for the first time, included the royal ancestors (Ayvazian 2006: 14).

For the first time, the Urartian administrative system was reorganized to facilitate the centralized control of the provinces. Not only did Urartian records include practical administrative documents, comparable to those introduced later by the Achaemenid monarchs, but they also displayed active bilingual elements, such as inscriptions in Urartian cuneiform and "Urartian" and Luwian hieroglyphs side by side (Zimansky 1998: 60). The bilingual nature of Urartian rule reflected changing ethnic realities in the kingdom. Urartu was becoming increasingly diverse, with migrant workers from Syria (Azarpay 1968: 62 n227) and deportees from Phrygia, Cappadocia, and territories mostly to the west and north of the Urartian core adding to its already diverse population.

3 The Kingdom's Demise

Like the date of its origin, the date of Urartu's demise is uncertain. A confusing series of successors followed Rusa II and a dearth of written records prevents us from being able to create a coherent picture of events. Based on a biblical reference (Jeremiah 51:27) and the Neo-Babylonian chronicles, the traditional date of Urartu's destruction was thought to have been c.590 BC. In the 1980s. this view was challenged by Stephan Kroll (1984: 170), who argued that the kingdom was essentially gone after the end of Rusa II's rule, c.640 BC.

Certainly, there is some evidence to support this view. Rusa II's inscriptions are the last known Urartian lapidary inscriptions. After his reign we have only cuneiform documents on clay tablets and brief texts inscribed on bronze objects. Rusa II's name occurs for the last time in the annals of the Assyrian king Assurbanipal, in connection with events in 654 BC. The names of up to five kings who may have occupied the Urartian throne after Rusa II's death are mentioned on various inscribed objects. In 639 BC, Rusa's son Sarduri III is said to have gone to Assyria, after which the Assyrian sources are silent on Urartu. Sarduri III is also attested on a clay tablet and a seal impression found at Karmir Blur. After Sarduri III, the next king of Urartu is thought to have been Sarduri, son of Sarduri, whose royal inscription appears on a bronze shield from Teishebaini (Piotrovskii 1969: 195). He was possibly followed by Rusa III, son of Erimena, whose father's name was preserved in the legend of a seal impression on a text from Teishebaini. Rusa III is attested in a dedicatory inscription carved on a highly artistic shield from Toprak Kale. Finally, the name "Rusa, son of Rusa" – possibly Rusa IV – appears on seal impressions on a clay tablet and bulla from Karmir Blur. Practically nothing can be said about these rulers with any certainty.

Virtually all the major Urartian sites show signs of violent destruction. Scythian-type arrowheads were found lodged in the walls and floors of buildings. Family treasures were discovered millennia later, tucked inside mudbrick walls or under the clothes of their owners or looters who were trying to escape the burning buildings. It has been suggested that arrows tipped with Scythian-type arrowheads may have been used not only by the Scythians themselves, but also by the Medes, who are thought to have passed through Urartu on their victorious march to Lydia in 585 BC (Piotrovskii 1969: 197ff). A. Çilingiroğlu (2002), however, proposed a different scenario, suggesting that the kingdom may have fallen victim to internecine strife, rather than foreign invaders, some time in the 7th century BC.

Following the tumultuous events of the mid-7th century BC, Urartu may have broken up into a number of independent or semi-independent principalities. This idea receives some support from the apparent emergence of new political units – "houses" (Akk. *bīt*) – in Urartu during the reign of Rusa II (Grekyan 2006: 176–7 n207).The disparate princedoms (*nakharar*-doms) of later Armenian history may have their roots in this period. By the time historical Armenia comes into focus, the *nakharars* were strong enough at times to defy the power of a supreme ruler.

In the Bisotun inscription of Darius the Great (c.520 BC), the Babylonian toponym "Urashtu" appears in Old Persian as "Armina," and in Elamite as "Harminuia," corresponding to modern "Armenia." "Urashtu" was still mentioned in the inscriptions of Xerxes in the early 5th century BC, but by the time Xenophon passed through Armenia in 401 BC, the great kingdom of Van seems to have been thoroughly forgotten. An echo of it was preserved in the art and languages of its former territories, yet neither the religion nor the memory of Urartu survived until it was discovered once again more than 2,000 years later.

4 Religion

Rock-cut niches, one of the key features of Urartian religion, made their first appearance during the late 9th century BC, in the reign of Ishpuini. A niche was seen as a door, a symbolic gateway between worlds. Urartian rock-cut funerary monuments usually contain stepped niches, possibly to indicate the presence of several "gateways," or sacred passages, between spaces. The most important Urartian rock-cut niche is Mheri Dur, or Meher Kapisi ("the Door of Mithra"), just above modern Van. It is covered with an inscription that names all the major and minor Urartian gods, along with the sacrifices ordained for each deity. The Mheri Dur inscription continues to serve as the basic document for the study of the Urartian pantheon. The pantheon described in the Mheri Dur inscription consists of 70 deities – 48 gods of various ranks and 22 aspects or attributes of the god Haldi. The male and female deities in the Urartian pantheon may have formed couples, though it is possible that the supreme god Haldi, like Assur, did not originally have a spouse (Grekyan 2006: 155). "Minor" gods mentioned in the inscription were most likely those worshipped by the individual tribes of Urartu. They were headed by the supreme trinity of Haldi, Teisheba, and Shiwini. The worship of Teisheba, god of thunder, and Shiwini, the sun god, harkened back to the Hurro-Hittite traditions that formed an important part of the composite Urartian identity. Haldi, on the other hand, seems to have been a newcomer, introduced by the Urartian monarchs with the aim of distinguishing, or even separating, their kingdom's identity from any ancestral associations. The supreme god further acted as a protector of the Urartian dynastic line and a unifying element for Urartu's many ethnic groups (Ayvazian 2004: 29ff).

While the Mheri Dur inscription is our most important source for understanding the structure of the Urartian pantheon, knowledge of Urartian religion was recently supplemented by an important bronze shield excavated in the fortress (?) of Anzaf (Belli 1999). Dated to the time of Ishpuini and/or Menua, the shield depicts a dozen Urartian gods who may have been the native deities of the Urartians and of the royal house. It is possible that these gods – including Teisheba, Shiwini, Hutuini, Shebitu, Quera, Elip(u)ri, Ua, Ura, and Nalaini – were introduced by Menua along with the worship of Haldi and may be the gods referred to as "all gods" on dozens of stelae from the reign of Menua and in many later Urartian inscriptions (Grekyan 2006: 157).

Haldi was the supreme god, the sun, the fertility god, the warrior and the god of war (Hmayakian 1990: 33ff). The center of Haldi's worship was Musasir. Even though it was never under direct Urartian control, Musasir served as an important symbolic locus of Urartian religion, the seat of the supreme god who came to signify Urartu itself. The original center of Haldi worship may have been near Yeşilaliç, where the monument called the "Gate of Haldi" and an open-air sanctuary, possibly pre-dating Mheri Dur, are located (Sevin and Belli 1976–7: 378ff). Haldi's rise to prominence was accompanied by the appearance of typically Urartian tower temples and rock-cut niches. The kings of Urartu probably served as the state's chief priests (Tarhan 1983: 300; Hmayakian 1990: 73).

With Urartu's demise, the cult of Haldi quickly disappeared, suggesting that the deity was never deeply embraced by the Urartian population. With him, the traditional tower temple disappeared as well, although the worship of niches and gateways remained strong and continued into recent, maybe even into modern, times.

Haldi's consort Arubaini was possibly the mother goddess as well as the goddess of fertility and flora (Loseva 1962: 307ff) and the patroness of arts and crafts (Hmayakian 1990: 38). Teisheba was the god of thunder and natural elements. Etymologically, his name is connected to the Hurrian supreme god Teshub. Finally, Shiwini was the god of the sun. Tushpuea, the goddess of the Urartian capital city Tushpa, was Shiwini's consort and the goddess of dawn (Hmayakian 1990: 46). Some historians have associated her with "siren" figures that often appear on Urartian bronze work, notably as attachments for ritual cauldrons (Piotrovskii 1959: 226). Amongst the multitude of Urartian gods, we may also mention Hutuini (fate), Shebitu (possibly the Pleiades), Melardi (the moon), Quera (god of soil and fertility, connected to the worship of water streams), and Elip(u)ri, a god of Hurrian origin connected to the worship of the

Taurus mountains (Grekyan 2006: 159–60). The worship of the moon god is not attested at Mheri Dur, but is referred to in the inscription from the *susi-*temple at Ayanis (Salvini 2001: 254).

5 Art

Urartian art went through an especially rich, formative period during the reigns of the early Urartian monarchs Menua and Argishti I. Long considered little more than a conglomerate of features and themes borrowed from its neighbors and predecessors, it remained understudied and misunderstood. In general, it reflects the artistic traditions of many different ethnic and cultural groups within the kingdom. Nevertheless, it emerged as both unique and highly distinctive. As the kingdom expanded and contracted over the course of two and a half centuries, its art continued to develop as well. Assyrianizing motifs gave way to more indigenous expressions and, over time, stylistic elements which originated in the far west made their way into local arts and fashions.

The goal of early Urartian art was to promote the idea of the divine nature of the Urartian state. Nature was perceived as being alive, divine, and filled with magical creatures. The king was a divinely guided defender and shepherd of his land and people. This idea is expressed over and over again in both minor and monumental Urartian art, from the early frescoes of Argishti I's fortress of Erebuni to Urartian seals. The king is always shown dressed simply, in a long tunic, usually wearing a conical helmet and carrying a shepherd's crook – an ancient Near Eastern symbol of royal power. He is shown among nature and animals, and in mystical contexts, entering realms inaccessible to simple humans. These "mystical" realms are easy to recognize through the presence of one or a combination of the following three elements: an animal (most often a lion, bull, or horse), a star, or a composite creature (i.e., one consisting of different parts of two or more animals). The choice of animals probably reflects early totemic beliefs in this geographic area, and by Urartian times may be symbolic representations of nature deities. Through comparison with Mesopotamian and Anatolian antecedents, Urartian scholars have suggested that the lion may have represented the chief god Haldi; the bull, the thunder god Teisheba; and the horse, the sun god Shiwini. Other animals and composite creatures may have stood for Urartian deities of lower rank.

6 Bronzes

Of all Urartian bronzes, military gear is best represented. Urartian armor is illustrated in detail on the Balawat gates of Shalmaneser III. Urartian warriors wore short tunics and wide belts. They carried short lances and bows as well as small, round shields. Early Urartian helmets appear to be similar to Hittite ones. Later, in the 8th century BC, Urartian armor began to resemble Assyrian gear. It is to this later group that the objects found at Karmir Blur (ancient Teishebaini) belong.

A number of Urartian bronze helmets were found at Karmir Blur. Symbols of the god Teisheba – the storm god, depicted either as a bolt of lightning, or as snakes that mimic its motion by rushing down the center in an arched movement originating at the temples – are typically represented on these helmets. Another group of helmets shows standing deities flanking sacred trees. Both beardless and bearded deities, carrying pollination buckets in left hands and a cone in the right hand, are shown. The sacred trees in the center are framed by eight lion-headed snakes. The backs of these helmets are decorated with depictions of eight war chariots and ten horsemen. These helmets bore inscriptions by Argishti I and Sarduri II.

Other typically Urartian bronzes include large shields with dedicatory inscriptions of Argishti I, Sarduri II, Rusa, son of Argishti, and Rusa, son of Erimena (Piotrovskii 1959: 168). Such shields were described in Sargon II's "Letter to Assur," amongst the booty from the Urartian temple of Haldi in Musasir, and illustrated on the lost relief from Dur-Sharrukin (modern Khorsabad), known to us from Flandin's detailed drawing (Botta and Flandin 1848–50/II: Pls. 141). The drawing of the relief shows that these large shields were placed by the Urartians on the walls and columns of the Haldi temple. The Letter to Assur (ll. 370–371) claims that Assyrian soldiers removed "six golden shields" from the Haldi temple at Musasir, the centers of which were decorated with the heads of snarling dogs.

The Urartian shields found at Karmir Blur were decorated with lions and bulls arranged within concentric bands that ran around the shields' perimeter. The animals were shown in such a way as to always remain upright – that is, the artist inverted them halfway around the shield, instead of continuing in the same fashion, which would have made the animals in the lower half appear upside down. This suggests that such shields were votive offerings, like the ones illustrated on Sargon's relief from Dur-Sharrukin, rather than functional battle gear. Urartian bronze shields have been excavated at Karmir Blur, Toprak Kale, and Anzaf (Belli 2000).

Sargon's text also describes large bronze statues in prayer that functioned as temple "guardians of the gates," as well as statues of Urartian kings – specifically those of "Sarduri, son of Ishpuini," "Argishti, king of Urartu, in a starry tiara of the gods, blessing with the right hand, within its own niche," and that of Rusa with his horses and a chariot driver (ll. 400–403). The production of these, possibly life-size, statues would have required a high level of technical expertise. We can only regret not being able to see these objects today.

The Louvre (Paris), Hermitage (St Petersburg), and the British Museum contain examples of possible Urartian throne decorations. These include recumbent bulls with human faces, ornately adorned with detailed incisions and inlays; divine statuettes in elaborate dress standing atop bulls; lions; and mixed beings. However, like so many bronze objects designated "Urartian," regrettably, they lack secure archaeological information and need to be used with caution (Muscarella 2006). An exception to these unprovenanced objects is a bronze candelabrum discovered during the German excavation of Toprak Kale in 1898–9. The candelabrum is c.1.36 meters tall, its shaft decorated with pendant leaves and supported by three legs terminating in bulls' hooves issuing from lions' jaws. The upper portions of the legs were adorned with statuettes of recumbent, winged bulls with human heads. The candelabrum was crowned with a simple lamp-bowl with tall sides. The shaft is inscribed with the name of the Urartian king Rusa.

Other well-known objects traditionally associated with Urartu are mounts for large bronze cauldrons in the form of sirens – birds with human faces and spread wings that rest against the cauldrons' outer surface, as well as bulls' heads with wing-like protrusions at the base. It has been suggested that the disc placed between the sirens' wings may indicate a connection between these creatures and the sun god's consort, Tushpuea (Piotrovskii 1969: 32). Most of these objects derive from illicit excavations.

In attempting to classify Urartian art stylistically and chronologically, many scholars (e.g. Azarpay 1968; Piotroskii 1969; Kellner 1976) have relied on bronze belts and votive plaques with lavish depictions of hunting and military scenes, religious motifs, and purely decorative designs. Unfortunately, as P. Zimansky (1995a: 108) has pointed out, many of these objects come from a single plundered site at Giyimly, rather than from controlled excavations. Although of great interest and technical and artistic ingenuity, they cannot match excavated material in determining the stylistic developments that took place in Urartu.

In the mid-7th century, Urartian art was greatly influenced by Scytho-Cimmerian groups in Transcaucasia. The discovery of an unfinished Scythian bird's head in the craftsmen's quarters at Karmir Blur may serve as an illustration for the process of cultural transfer, as well as explaining the appearance of purely Urartian indications of musculature in later Scythian finds from Melgunov and Kelermes, and in the treasure of Ziwiye.

7 Pottery

Urartian pottery is very varied. It ranges from miniature jars no more than a few centimeters tall to huge storage jars (*pithoi*) with a 1,200 liter capacity that could easily hold a human being inside them. According to S. Kroll (1976b), approximately 85 percent of all Urartian pottery consists of rough, hand-made grey ware found throughout the kingdom. However, the hallmark of the Urartian ceramic assemblage is the highly burnished red pottery called "Toprak Kale ware" by Charles Burney (1957: 432) because its production was traditionally associated with the central part of the kingdom. Most often found at large fortresses and rarely seen in the smaller ones, such vessels may have been linked to the royal economy (Zimansky 1995a: 107), particularly storage and royal consumption. Especially fine vessels were often stamped or incised with potter's marks. Many stamped sherds of red burnished ware and one stamped sherd of black burnished ware were discovered during recent (2000–7) excavations at Erebuni (Ayvazian 2006; Ter-Martirosov 2009).

Urartian ceramic decoration consisted of incisions, indentations, and painted designs. Some vessels appear to imitate metal objects (Piotrovskii 1959: 189–91). Piotrovskii distinguished three groups in his excavations at Karmir Blur: red burnished ware, either manufactured at the kingdom's center or imitated locally; coarse, black vessels, often in the form of wide-mouth jars with incised chevron, wave, or dot decoration; and, finally, dark-colored vessels with pattern burnishing and deeply impressed, connected triangles. Pottery of this latter group finds analogies in Transcaucasian burials dating to the 7th–6th centuries BC (Piotrovskii 1959: 193).

Ceramic figurines of minor deities were found during excavations at Karmir Blur in 1949 and 1950. Three examples discovered in a storage room during the 1949 season take the form of bearded human figures in a "fish dress," with the head of a fish acting as a hood, and the body and tail as the back of the figures' outfits. The figurine found in 1950 in a different storage room is that of a scorpion-man whose face is painted white, eyes black, beard and hair maroon, and headgear bright blue, like the cloak of the figurines wearing fish garb.

8 Seals and Seal Impressions

Urartian seals came in a wide variety of shapes and sizes, including cylinders, stamp-cylinders, faceted stamps (bell-shaped, conical, cylindrical, cube-shaped, zoomorphic, ring, even phallic), flat bi-faced (rectangular and discoid) and scaraboid (Ayvazian 2006: 340ff). Excavated seals are known in a variety of materials, including ceramic, black amber, bone, onyx, lapis lazuli, bronze, ceramic, frit, jasper, faience, and many other simple, precious, or semi-precious stones. Based on design, workmanship, and shape, Urartian seals have been subdivided into several categories, from royal household and administrative seals to those of petty officials, ritual practitioners, and others (van Loon 1966; Seidl 1979, 1988; Abay 2001; Ayvazian 2006). Urartian officials seem to have preferred the cylinder or stamp-cylinder seal. Seals used by high officials are further distinguished by a balanced, "Assyrianizing" sense of composition. Their subject matter consists of pollination motifs, which differ from their Assyrian prototypes. All these seals were inscribed in cuneiform, sometimes supplemented with hieroglyphic notations. An analysis of currently known material shows that only royal seals and seals of royal officials were inscribed with a person's name, though it is impossible to tell whether this happened by royal decree or because of general illiteracy amongst the population.

Stamp seal impressions exhibited a much greater variety of motifs – for example, mythical animals, including winged horses, winged lions, gazelles, dogs, birds, snakes, even hedgehogs (Museum of Erebuni, unpublished); composite beings, such as fish-goats, bird-men, sirens, etc.; ritual or symbolic scenes, including goddesses, stelae, altars, trees or branches, and astral bodies; dancers; and figures such as the "tree man" that may have come from Urartian folk tales and myths. Since these seals did not need to reflect official ideology, it is assumed that they depicted objects that the general population found auspicious, thus providing a glimpse of Urartian myth and oral tradition.

Faceted seals had four or more lateral sides and sometimes a bottom stamp. Formally speaking, these seals appear to be intermediate between a stamp and a cylinder seal. On the one hand, rolling the seal would produce a visual story, often in a sequential order. On the other hand, each facet stood on its own and had its own significance. All the seals and seal impressions of this type appear to have been used for ritual purposes, since they all carry designs that seem to have been either sacred or related to ritual activity. Additionally, when impressed on clay, each facet formed an indentation around the image, possibly alluding to the sanctity of niches for the Urartians. Common motifs on such seals were deities riding mythical animals; seven stars, possibly representing the Pleiades; symbolic objects; and drooping or blossoming trees or branches to indicate the season or the mood of the scene.

9 Architecture

The most well-known examples of Urartian architecture are the imposing fortresses perched upon high hills and gorges in the vicinity of drinking water. Their building blocks and walls sometimes preserve the name of the Urartian kings who ordered their construction. Urartian citadels were usually well protected and able to withstand lengthy sieges. The minimal amount of pottery found in these fortresses suggests that they were used as administrative, cultic, and defensive installations, rather than residential centers (Piotrovskii 1959: 197; Kroll 1976a: 12–13; Zimansky 1995a: 105). Fortresses represent the pinnacle of the building hierarchy, followed by habitation sites and small, unfortified settlements or farmsteads in the countryside where the majority of the Urartian population presumably lived (Zimansky 1995a: 106). In times of war, royal fortresses served as places of refuge for the population.

Urartian construction techniques were standardized throughout the kingdom. Before starting construction, Urartian builders strengthened the hillside by constructing a series of terraces. This not only prevented landslides, but also created extra space. Foundations consisted of footings carved into the bedrock. Walls usually consisted of unbaked mudbrick on a stone socle c.1 meter high. No mortar was used, but the stone foundations were very solid due to the care apparent in the selection and working of the stones used. Some sort of level appears to have been used during construction to ensure horizontality (Zimansky 1995a: 106).

Most important buildings, such as temples, were constructed of high-quality ashlar masonry. Fortress walls were punctuated with regular buttresses – alternately large and small in the 8th century, and of uniform size in the 7th century (Kleiss 1976: 35–6; Zimansky 1995a: 106). B. Piotrovskii observed a decrease in the size of the stones used for socles over time. Earlier fortresses boasted huge, cyclopean masonry, while later ones were built of relatively smaller stones (Piotrovskii 1959: 199).

A signal feature of Urartian religious architecture is the square tower temple with reinforced corner buttresses. In accordance with ancient Near Eastern tradition, Urartian temples were placed at the highest point of a site. Temples consisted of a single cella, the substantial height of which is suggested by the quantity of thick mudbrick debris. Both excavations and glyptic evidence confirm the use of open-air platforms as shrines.

10 Burial Practices

The diversity of Urartian funerary practices enforces the belief that the kingdom of Van was culturally and ethnically diverse (Zimansky 1995a: 109). Both inhumation and cremation were practiced in the central part of the kingdom. In addition, jar burials, cremation urns, and multi-chambered, rock-cut tombs are attested. Several rock-cut tombs bear the inscriptions of Urartian kings. The annals of Argishti I were carved outside the entrance to the Horhor chambers at Van; an inscription of Rusa II was carved into the rock outside a tomb chamber at Kale Köyü/Mazgert (Öğün 1978: 642); and an inscription mentioning Argishti II was found in a subterranean tomb at Altin tepe (Özgüç 1969: 70; Zimansky 1995a: 109). This may indicate that such burials were associated with Urartian aristocracy, or state officials.

11 Language

In the past, the kingdom of Urartu was often considered backward and illiterate, a "pale reflection of Assyria" (Burney and Lang 1971: 28). The Urartians adapted Assyrian cuneiform to their language and used some common formulaic expressions from the Assyrian literary tradition. However, it is possible that before the kingdom was formed, the *uruatri* employed a more cumbersome, hieroglyphic script that continued in use in Urartian administration and cult practices (Piotrovski 1969: 65). It has also been suggested that the dearth of evidence for the early use of Urartian hieroglyphic system is due to the fact that it was written on perishable materials (Klein 1974: 77ff). The discoveries at Altintepe, near Erzincan in eastern Turkey, illustrate the use of a syllabic hieroglyphic script to record the Urartian language. There, inscriptions written in Neo-Hittite hieroglyphic signs on large storage vessels record the contents in the usual Urartian measures. Cuneiform was reserved for more monumental messages that were meant to endure the test of time.

The Urartians recorded the contents of storage jars, usually liquids, in *aqarqi* and *terusi*. These terms are used in their full form at Toprak Kale, Shushantsa, and Arin-berd, while in other instances they are shortened to *a* and *te*. In both cases, simple cuneiform numbers were used to indicate quantity. Sometimes, different types of pictorial or hieroglyphic signs were used in combination with cuneiform, in which case numbers were indicated on the surface of a vessel by means of small holes drilled into its surface.

All the above-mentioned examples date to the early 8th century BC. Later, the needs of the growing kingdom could no longer be met by the rather cumbersome hieroglyphic script. Thus, the Urartians borrowed the Assyrian cuneiform system and adapted it to their own language. However, Urartian cuneiform script was used quite differently from other examples of cuneiform writing such as Elamite, Hurrian, Hittite, and Akkadian. As far as we know, Urartian was not used for the creation of literary works. It was reserved exclusively for monumental inscriptions on stone, and, to a lesser extent, dedicatory inscriptions on various other objects. The oldest inscriptions, produced under Sarduri I, were in Assyrian. Urartian-Assyrian bilinguals appeared during the reign of Ishpuini, and later rulers exclusively used Urartian for their annals and dedicatory inscriptions.

Urartian was an agglutinate ergative language. An affinity between Urartian and Hurrian has long been noted (Diakonoff 1971; Khačikyan 1995). This was expressed in vocabulary as well as grammatical forms. Both Diakonoff and Khachikian attempted to demonstrate a connection between Hurrian-Urartian and northeastern Caucasian languages, spoken today in the former Checheno-Ingushetiya, Daghestan, Georgia, and parts of Turkey (Diakonoff 1978: 24–42). The study of the Urartian language is far from complete. There is still no comprehensive grammar of Urartian and no unanimity on details of phonology, morphology, and syntax. We are yet to discover any Urartian law codes, myths, or rituals of any kind, even though a detailed study of the glyptic evidence may provide some understanding of common themes in the Urartians' worldview (Ayvazian 2006).

GUIDE TO FURTHER READING

Urartian studies are ever-evolving. With each excavation report, we have come to expect new, surprising discoveries. B.B. Piotrovskii, the former Director of the Hermitage

Museum, was a pioneer of Urartian studies. Despite the use of unprovenanced material, normal for his time, the breadth of his historical knowledge and unexpected perspectives was unprecedented (Piotrovksii 1967, 1969). The most comprehensive study of Urartian art to date is Van Loon (1966). For a thorough analysis of Urartian seals, see Ayvazian (2006, with extended bibliography), Seidl (1979 and 1988), Calmeyer (1974) and Calmeyer and Seidl (1983). Melikishvili (1960) remains the classic work on Urartian cuneiform inscriptions, but also see Arutiunian (2001) for an updated corpus (both in Russian). The work of Salvini (1989, 1994, 1995) is highly recommended for newer Urartian epigraphic material, as well as refreshing historical insights. For the comprehensive corpus of all known Urartian inscriptions, see Salvini et al. (2008). *Aramazd: Armenian Journal of Near Eastern Studies* presents the work of many young scholars and contains many thought-provoking ideas.

CHAPTER FORTY-EIGHT

Iron Age Western Anatolia: The Lydian Empire and Dynastic Lycia

Christopher H. Roosevelt

1 Introduction

Two Iron Age cultures of western Anatolia that emerged in the aftermath of the collapse of Late Bronze Age (LBA) systems merit special discussion because of their importance both as cultures with indigenous traditions and languages and as geographical, political, and cultural intermediaries between the Near Eastern and Aegean worlds: the Lydians in central western Anatolia and the Lycians in southwestern Anatolia. The LBA histories of Lydia and Lycia were presumably related in as much as the two regions were likely the heartlands of western Anatolian groups identified in Hittite archives – the Seha River Land and Mira, on the one hand, and the Lukka Lands, on the other – and they featured significantly in Hittite territorial campaigns in the west. They are related also in their unfortunate dearth of evidence pertaining to the transition from the LBA to the Early Iron Age. Yet, despite the clear and common impacts of interactions with other Anatolian, Greek, and later Achaemenid Persian cultures, the Iron Age histories of Lydia and Lycia remain almost entirely distinct.

The history and archaeology of early 1st millennium BC Lydia is illuminated by a combination of pseudo-historical, historical, epigraphic, and archaeological evidence, providing a rich synthesis of the sociopolitical, economic, and religious traditions of this indigenous and territorially unified kingdom down to the Persian conquest in the mid-6th century BC. While much of the material record in 6th century Lydia cannot be sorted according to specifically Lydian versus

Achaemenid features – a result of a strong degree of cultural continuity – a clear picture of the pre-Achaemenid Lydians can be drawn. The Iron Age history and archaeology of Lycia before its mid-6th century BC conquest by the Persians, however, remain almost entirely unknown. Yet, Lycian traditions attested in and after the 6th century presumably owe at least as much to the continuity of older, local traditions as they do to the introduction of foreign features. Furthermore, while Lydia remained politically and geographically cohesive throughout both Lydian and Achaemenid hegemony, at no point in its early history can Lycia be defined as imperial, or even federal, and its dynastic history under the Achaemenids displays a territorial and, perhaps, political fragmentation that may have resembled its LBA configuration.

Our knowledge of Lydia and Lycia derive from a long tradition of scholarship beginning with early travelers in the 17th through 19th centuries who relied heavily on histories and rich anecdotes relating to these areas in Classical literature, and whose "archaeological" activities consisted primarily of collecting and/ or cataloguing sculptural, architectural, numismatic, and epigraphic evidence for Western audiences. Early pictures of Lydia and Lycia were thus painted from the perspective of Classical Greek and Roman understandings of the local cultures of Asia Minor, as Anatolia was commonly known in Classical sources. Such sources directed scholarly interest toward the primary urban sites of the regions: Sardis, the capital of Lydia, and Xanthus, the capital of Lycia, at least during certain periods. More recently, archaeological excavations, regional surveys, and linguistic studies have highlighted the indigenous, Anatolian character of these cultures, and expanded research foci beyond primary centers to hinterlands and rural settlements. With reference to all such sources, this chapter aims to provide overviews of the Lydians and Lycians in western Anatolia from their earliest archaeological attestation to the Persian conquest in Lydia and to the loss of local administrative control during the Achaemenid period in Lycia.

2 Early Lydia

The obscurity of early Lydia, among its Aegean and western Anatolian neighbors in the Early Iron Age, is demonstrated by a lack of secure answers to seemingly basic questions regarding the origins of the Lydians and the extent of their territory. From where and when did Lydian-speaking populations arrive in Lydia? What was the territorial definition of Lydian culture at this time? Primary obstacles to answering such questions include a dearth of historical and archaeological evidence. Nevertheless, while Lydian origins remain debated, the probable core of early Lydia was the area surrounding its eventual capital and only known urban settlement of the Iron Age: Sardis, where over half a century of excavations have uncovered stratified occupation sequences beginning in the LBA. Located at the southern edge of the valley of the Hermus (Gediz) River, along the middle stretch of its course from Mount Dindymus (Murat Daği) to the Aegean Sea, Sardis and its immediate environs were undoubtedly the heartland of Lydia from its early days through the establishment of the Lydian Kingdom and later Empire. According to later Classical sources, the Lydian Kingdom included at least the valleys of the Hermus and Cayster (Küçük Menderes) rivers and their tributaries, separated by the Tmolus (Boz Daği) range. A string of peaks and ranges separated inland Lydia from coastal Ionia and Aeolis to the west, while mountainous uplands to the north and east shared borders with Mysia and Phrygia, respectively. Ancient accounts vary as to whether parts of the Caicus (Bakir) and Maeander (Büyük Menderes) river valleys, on the northwest and south, respectively, were part of Lydian territory. This core region, then, contained diverse topography – rivers and lakes, broad and fertile valley floors, rolling and forested uplands, and lofty peaks reaching more than 2,000 meters above sea level – as well as varied resources – abundant water, wood and stone, richly arable land and precious metals, most notably gold. The discovery of gold, or rather the natural alloy of gold and silver called electrum (Ch. I.16), in the Pactolus (Sart) river at Sardis may, in fact, have been a primary attraction in the early settlement of the site in the LBA. But who were the first settlers of Sardis?

Toward the end of the LBA the region described above belonged to two vassal kingdoms of the Hittites, according to texts found at Hattusha (Chs. I.30, II.38). Mira, the better known of the two, had its capital at Apasa (Classical Ephesus) and controlled an elongated swathe of territory stretching from the Aegean toward the interior along the Maeander and Cayster river valleys. North of Mira and probably separated from it by the Tmolus range was the Seha River Land, with its capital probably in central Lydia and coinciding territorially with most of northern Lydia and perhaps the Caicus river valley as well (Hawkins 1998). The unnamed capital of the Seha River Land may have been located recently in central Lydia, not at Sardis but near the shore of the Gygaean Lake (Marmara Gölü) at Kaymakçi, the size and monumental remains of which suggest its probable regional significance (Luke and Roosevelt 2009; Roosevelt 2009, 2010). It was during the LBA when Kaymakçi was a regional capital, then, that Sardis, 18 kilometers to the southeast, appears to have been first settled.

The inhabitants of these western Anatolian vassal kingdoms of the LBA are usually thought to have spoken Luwian, an Indo-European dialect related to Hittite (Nesite) and Palaic, among other languages, all descending from Common Anatolian, the speakers of which are thought to have entered Anatolia by or sometime in the 3rd millennium BC. By the 7th century BC, at the very latest, however, it is clear that the inhabitants of Iron Age Lydia were speaking and recording things in their native tongue, Lydian. Known from around 115 inscriptions of the 6th–4th centuries, most of which are funerary in nature, Lydian is a dialectical descendant of Common Anatolian and is thus a member of the larger Indo-European language group. It had developed from its common Anatolian roots over a long time before its appearance in written form. If the Seha River

Land was primarily Luwian-speaking in the LBA, then, Lydian speakers must have entered Lydia some time after the collapse of LBA society in the 12th century, but before the appearance of written Lydian in the 7th century. Those who adhere to this view usually cite a Bronze Age origin for the Lydians somewhere in northwestern Anatolia, from where they later migrated south to Lydia (Melchert 2010). Citing the paucity of evidence for Luwian speakers in Bronze Age central-western Anatolia, however, other scholars think it likely that Lydian speakers inhabited the area already in the Bronze Age (Yakubovich 2008a). Thus, the first settlers of Sardis would have been Lydian speakers, as would the inhabitants of Bronze Age political centers in the area, notably Kaymakçi. Although both the pseudo-historical evidence of Greek accounts and archaeological data have been brought to bear on this problem, no firm resolution has emerged.

Greek accounts written well after the fact, yet perhaps containing kernels of truth, name many early kings of Lydia. Yet the earliest Greek account we have for this area, Homer's *Iliad*, written down some time around 700 BC, mentions nothing at all of a place called Lydia, referring to the same area, rather, as Maeonia. For later Greek authors, such as Herodotus and Strabo, writing in the 5th and 1st centuries BC, respectively, Maeonia was an early name for Lydia – and this may have been the case, since Maeonia appears to have roots in a LBA toponym of the Seha River Land (van den Hout 2003). At any rate, while Homer mentions neither Lydia per se nor its kings, others give accounts of numerous Lydian kings that appear to be irreconcilable, and the existence of none of these kings can be substantiated before the rise of the Mermnad Dynasty in the early 7th century, for which we have firm historical evidence.

The clearest account of early Lydian successions is by Herodotus (1.7), who reports that two dynasties ruled in Lydia before the Mermnads. The first of these was the Atyad Dynasty, with an eponymous founder named Atys, whose son, Lydus, gave his name to the region and people. Little else is revealed of this earliest Lydian dynasty, yet it is probably apocryphal given the nature with which it provides a neat history for the name of the Lydians. Herodotus knew the second dynasty of Lydia as the Heraclids, and he reports that Heraclid kings ruled for 22 generations, a total of 505 years, before the usurpation of Candaules by the first Mermnad king, Gyges. While the rule of Gyges is historically corroborated by the Assyrian archives of Assurbanipal (668–627 BC), which help to date his accession to c.680 BC and refer to him as Gugu of Luddi, the reigns of his predecessors have no external historical support. Nevertheless, it may be more than an interesting coincidence that the Heraclid Dynasty dawned, according to Herodotus, around 1185 BC, or 505 years before the reign of Gyges (c.680 BC). This would place the beginning of Heraclid rule in Lydia (and the end of Atyad rule, if historical) to just the time when LBA society in western Anatolia had fallen into turmoil. Unfortunately, archaeological evidence for this period of transition neither confirms nor denies such circumstances.

Limited excavations at Sardis have exposed levels extending well into the LBA and indicate the occupation of the site at least by this time. A burnt level is attested at some point toward the end of the LBA, but neither the date, the circumstances, nor the extent of this burning are firmly established. The exposure is too small to warrant any far-reaching conclusions about conflagrations at Sardis during a time when many sites in the eastern Mediterranean were destroyed and/or abandoned.

Abandonment, and possibly destruction as well, are attested, however, at Kaymakçi and other LBA citadels in central Lydia. In the Iron Age, such citadels remained abandoned in favor of settlement in other locations with both upland and lowland situations. Aside from this shift in settlement patterns, certain production technologies in central Lydia, including those for mudbrick and ceramics, also seem to change between the Late Bronze and Iron Ages. As for the burning level at Sardis, however, the timing and nature of such changes are too poorly understood to determine whether they derive from external or internal developments or from a combination of the two. Thus the archaeological record at Sardis and in central Lydia in general cannot yet distinguish between changes in population and changes in local, socioeconomic conditions during the transition from the LBA to the Iron Age.

The archaeological record at Sardis as it progressed into the Iron Age, however, especially ceramic evidence, bespeaks the general cultural affinities of Sardians during these times. Just as in the LBA, when the Seha River Land and Mira were intermediaries between the Hittites and their Aegean adversaries, to the east and west, respectively, and their material culture featured both Anatolian and Aegean characteristics, the evidence of the Early Iron Age shows shifting affinities from inland to coast among Anatolian, especially Phrygian and Aegean Greek features (Ramage 1994). By the late 8th century, just before the advent of the Mermnad Dynasty, Lydian material culture continued to show similarities with these two broad cultural regions. By this time, though, some classes of evidence, especially ceramics, appear to show a significant increase in Greek features that can be correlated with historically documented interactions between the Mermnad kings and the Greek city-states of coastal western Anatolia during the 7th century.

3   The Lydian Kingdom and Empire

Lydian interactions with coastal Anatolian Greek city-states naturally dominate the primarily Greek written sources that document the period of the Mermnad Dynasty, dating from c.680 to the mid-540s BC. Yet interactions with central Anatolian and Near Eastern powers are illustrated historically as well as archaeologically. The intermediary nature of Lydian territories between East and West, along with the Mermnads' eagerness to interact in both directions, helped produce a capital city, Sardis, a kingdom, and later an empire suffused with cosmopolitan internationalism. The dynasty is defined by five kings reigning in hereditary succession, from Gyges (c.680–644 BC) to Ardys (c.644 to the late 7th century BC) and Sadyattes (late 7th century to c.610 BC), followed by Alyattes (c.610–560 BC) and Croesus (c.560 to the mid-540s BC). The military campaigns of each of these kings are chronicled by Herodotus and others, but the reigns of Gyges, Alyattes, and Croesus are known best.

Herodotus tells a romantic tale about Gyges' usurpation of Candaules' Heraclid throne involving superlative beauty, hubris, and honor (1.8–12), yet Gyges' rise appears to have been enabled by external support from Caria and external sanction from the Greek oracle at Delphi, just as it may ultimately have resulted from internal revolt or feuding (Ramage 1987). Shadowy as his beginnings may be, by c.664 BC Gyges was embroiled in territorial defenses against Cimmerian invaders who were laying waste to much of the Anatolian peninsula. We know of these invaders from Greek accounts, but more explicitly from the Assyrian archives of Assurbanipal that mention Gyges' requests for military assistance (Cogan and Tadmor 1977; Spalinger 1978). Specific confrontations between the Lydians and Cimmerians are noted in c.664 and 657, and again in c.644 BC, when Gyges was allegedly killed in battle. The Cimmerian problem long-outlasted Gyges' reign, however, causing difficulties throughout the 7th century for his immediate successors, one of whom, Ardys, also requested Assyrian assistance. According to Greek sources, the threat was at last put down by Gyges' great-grandson, Alyattes. Even then, remnant Cimmerian populations near coastal Adramytteion, just northwest of Lydia proper, may have prompted Alyattes to install his son Croesus there as governor.

Even while occupied with the Cimmerian threat to their immediate east, however, Gyges maintained diplomatic and military activities in other areas of the eastern Mediterranean, notably sending mercenaries to Egypt to assist Psammetichus I between c.662 and 658 BC. At the same time, Gyges attacked Ionian and Aiolian Greek city-states, including Smyrna, Colophon, and Miletus, to the west, and his successors Ardys and Sadyattes kept up similar campaigns. Ardys even captured Priene. There is little evidence that Priene or any other coastal areas were held for long, however, as the territorial bounds of the Lydian Kingdom appear never to have encompassed the Aegean coast. Lydian control probably stretched inland by the late 7th century, with the Phrygian capital of Gordion (Ch. II.42) serving as an important symbolic, if not also strategic, conquest. The real expansion of Lydian territories, however, came later during the reigns of Alyattes and Croesus, when the eastern border of Lydia was established at the central Anatolian Halys (Kizilirmak) river and Croesus began to exact annual tribute from all conquered states to its west.

The eastern border of Lydia was set at the Halys river as a compromise between the Lydian king Alyattes and the Median king Cyaxares, whose armies had previously fought to a standstill over some years. Herodotus (1.74) reports that a total eclipse of the sun (dated astronomically to May 28, 585 BC) interrupted the inconclusive battles and helped precipitate the negotiation of a boundary between Lydian and Median territories at this river. He also says the treaty was witnessed by the kings of Babylon and Cilicia and was further cemented by a Lydian–Median royal marriage alliance. Alyattes' daughter, Aryenis, was wed to Astyages, son of Cyaxares, and it is likely that Alyattes or his kin reciprocated by taking a Median wife of royal blood. Such marriage alliances were by no means limited to Lydian diplomacy in the Near East, and seem to have been a defining feature of Lydian interactions with Greek polities. Carian and Ionian Greek wives bore children to Alyattes and a daughter of Alyattes was wed to Melas, the tyrant of Ephesus. Croesus, whose mother was Alyattes' Carian wife, thus had an Ionian half-brother and both Ephesian and Median brothers-in-law. The trend extends back even further to the founder of the dynasty, Gyges, whose mother was said to be Phrygian and whose wife was Mysian. This long tradition of royal intermarriage between Lydians and other western Anatolian cultures is only one example of interactions between such territories on many cultural levels. Increasingly strong ties with Greek cultures were notable in the spheres of religious practice and artistic production, among others, and are well documented in Greek sources.

Lydian kings, for example, appear to have regularly patronized Greek sanctuaries, as has been established for Gyges, Alyattes, and Croesus. All three of these kings made rich offerings to Apollo at his oracle at Delphi, and Alyattes rebuilt one temple and founded a second temple dedicated to Athena at Assessos. Croesus made dedications at a wider array of sanctuaries, including those at Thebes, the Amphiaraion, Sparta, Didyma, and Ephesus, and he commissioned precious works of fine craftsmanship from Greek artisans of Chios and Samos. Furthermore, inscriptions in Lydian and Greek attest Lydian technical and financial contributions to the construction of the monumental temples of Athena at Smyrna and Artemis at Ephesus, respectively. These two cities may have had particularly close connections to Lydia, perhaps because they would have served as its most important maritime ports of trade, at least under the reign of Croesus (Kerschner 2010).

The richness of Lydian interactions with other western Anatolian and Aegean Greek peoples and polities, however, never seemed to have limited, nor to have been limited by, Lydian attacks and eventual territorial conquest. Alyattes followed in the footsteps of his forebears by attacking Miletus and Smyrna, besieging Priene and invading Clazomenae. Croesus attacked all these again, yet significantly altered Lydian diplomacy in the area by imposing annual tribute on each of the places he conquered. Thus Croesus transformed the Lydian kingdom into an empire, with territories spread across most of Anatolia west of the Halys river, including the coastal Aegean region, but excluding, for reasons unexplained by Herodotus (1.28), the coastal Mediterranean areas of Lycia and Cilicia. Just as it had been the capital of the Lydian Kingdom, Sardis became the capital of the Lydian Empire, and its imperial status was reflected in new monuments built throughout the city and in its immediate environs.

Sardis, the only known urban settlement in all Lydia during these times, flourished during the 7th and 6th centuries BC under Mermnad rule, primarily that of Alyattes and Croesus. Located among the northern foothills of the Tmolus Range, along the southern margin of the Hermus River valley, Sardis likely gained importance from its strategic location: it sat along major routes of communication, had an extremely defensible acropolis and could exploit an abundance of nearby resources, including wood and stone in the mountains, arable land in the plain, and fresh water from springs and rivers. The topography of the site was shaped by rivers flowing north from the mountains that defined between them residual hills of local conglomerate bedrock. The most important of these was the Pactolus, the river that bore the silver-gold alloy electrum extracted in abundance by the Lydians. To its east lay the most intensively inhabited areas of Sardis, atop and covering the foothills of its acropolis, a naturally well-fortified citadel. West of the Pactolus was another precipice known today as the Necropolis because of the rock-cut chamber tombs and other burials of Lydian and later periods that cover its lower foothills.

By the late 7th or early 6th century, and perhaps earlier, the urban area of Sardis was defined by a monumental fortification wall that enclosed c.108 hectares of the northern foothills of the acropolis. Built atop stone foundations c.20 meters wide, on average, and with its varying mudbrick and stone-faced superstructure preserved in places up to 10–13 meters high (Cahill 2010b), the wall appears to have been built to impress on an imperial scale. Its functionality is demonstrated by the additional 20 meter wide sloping glacis that abutted its exterior in places, probably intended to waylay the likes of siege engines, chariots, and sappers. Below the strong citadel on the acropolis and within the area defined by the fortification wall, then, the city of Alyattes and Croesus took form. Prior to this centralization of the urban space, settlement remains including domestic workshop complexes and perhaps even public structures suggest that the focus of activities was along the eastern bank of the Pactolus. Yet, scattered remains from earlier periods have been recovered on the acropolis and in its northern foothills, too. During the mid-6th century, natural terraces on the acropolis and its northern foothills were transformed by a large-scale terracing project, with finely worked stone walls reveting natural spurs. The building technology and monumentality of such constructions, and of parts of the fortification wall as well, may have derived from Near Eastern traditions and they seem to have been pioneered in western Anatolia by Lydians and Ionians at around the same time (Ratté 1993). Terrace construction at Sardis was undoubtedly of royal sponsorship, yet its exact purpose has yet to be clarified. Palaces and temples at Sardis are attested in Greek sources, and, despite a lack of archaeological confirmation, it is likely that the terraces of central Sardis supported these types of buildings.

Textually attested sanctuaries at Sardis include only those of Artemis of Sardis and Cybele, locally known as *Kuvava* and, more generally, the "mother." Although remains of these sanctuaries do not survive, a modest altar of Kuvava and small-scale models of her monumental temple were recovered during excavations. The latter seem to depict temples of Ionic Greek form, perhaps similar in design to those that Alyattes and Croesus sponsored at Miletus and Ephesus. Other sanctuaries, shrines and small cult places must have been quite common at the site, for several other deities of Anatolian and Greek origin are known from Lydian inscriptions and later textual sources. In addition to the above goddesses, who seem to have been especially important at Sardis, with Cybele probably serving as a protector of the royal house, Artemis appears to have been worshiped in the city in two other guises: Artemis of Ephesus, attesting to the special relationship between Sardis and that city, and Artemis Coloëne, or of Lake Coloë, another name for the Gygaean Lake, located some 12 kilometers north of the city. Other local deities include *Leus,* or Lydian Zeus; *Qldans,* perhaps the moon god or a sun god equivalent to Greek Apollo; *Baki,* the Lydian Dionysus; and *Sandas,* a warrior god with Luwian roots sometimes equated with Heracles. Deities originating in the Greek world yet who worshiped at Sardis include Apollo, Hera, Demeter, Kore, and possibly Aphrodite. In addition to these identifiable gods and goddesses, deities of unclear nature (perhaps Lydian or Carian) were probably the recipients of so-called ritual-dinner offerings, 26 examples of which have been excavated across the site. Each was remarkably consistent in content, including a place-setting (cup and plate), a small pitcher, a cooking pot, a knife, and the bones of a young canine (Greenewalt 1978). Obscure though they may be, each was deposited in what may be classed best as a form of household cult practice.

Spread across the spurs and terraces of the acropolis in and around more monumental constructions were the main residential areas of the mid-6th century city. Most houses were probably built with rubble foundations, mudbrick walls, and thatch roofs. Finely molded and painted terracotta tiles and architectural revetments have been recovered in excavations in some areas of the site, but these must have been associated with high-status buildings, such as elite or royal houses and cult buildings. More common houses or house complexes appear to have been composed of several single-room units arrayed within a courtyard space. Kitchen spaces attest to a variety of food processing and preparation activities as well as a diversity of foodstuffs, including cereals, pulses, garlic, and grapes, and the remains of meaty meals with bone scraps from bovines, fowl, pig, sheep, and goat (Cahill 2002). Other spaces within house complexes appear to have seen mixed use for both domestic purposes and cottage industry, with households producing small, rock-crystal and glass items and textiles, for example. Larger-scale workshops – e.g., for ceramics and stonework, including sculpture – have yet to be located within the city and may have been situated outside the fortifications, as in the case of a 6th century metal refinery located in the Pactolus river valley where the two-stage separation of electrum into its component parts of gold and silver was carried out. Earlier, during the 7th century, it was probably at a similar workshop that electrum was first hammered into lumps of regular size and stamped with a royal insignia, a lion's head, thereby guaranteeing its value and inventing coinage, a particular claim in Lydian history. The separation technique that allowed Croesus to issue coins of pure gold and pure silver may have been hit upon at this very refinery, but, to date, minting facilities and paraphernalia have eluded discovery.

Also confined to areas outside the city walls were burials of the Lydian period. These include burial forms of three main types attested both at Sardis and throughout greater Lydia: pit burials, some lined and covered with stone slabs; sarcophagi of terracotta or stone; and chamber tombs, either hewn from bedrock or covered with mounds of rubble and earth and, in that form, commonly known as "tumuli" (sing. tumulus). Rock-cut chamber tombs, pits, and sarcophagi were used most frequently in the urban cemeteries of Sardis along the Pactolus river, especially in the foothills of the Necropolis, where more than 1,100 were excavated in the early 20th century. While these types of burials are found elsewhere in Lydia, too, the conspicuous monumentality of tumuli has resulted in a clearer understanding of their distribution and significance.

The largest Lydian tumuli are those containing the tombs of Alyattes and other members of Sardian royalty and elite found roughly 7 kilometers north of Sardis in the largest known tumulus cemetery of Anatolia, known locally as Bin Tepe (Turkish for "thousand mounds"). With its 70 meter height and 361 meter diameter, the tumulus covering the tomb of Alyattes is the largest example in western Anatolia and, as Herodotus first noted (1.93), vies with the Egyptian pyramids of Giza in its monumentality. While none of the royal tumuli of Bin Tepe have yet been found intact by archaeologists – having been looted some time ago, some already in antiquity – smaller tumuli located elsewhere in Lydia give pale hints of the grandeur of these royal burials. Tumuli at Güre, near Uşak (eastern Lydia), for example, had wall paintings decorating the interiors of finely built stone tomb chambers (Özgen and Öztürk 1996). The deceased were laid out on stone funeral couches (Greek *klinai*), adorned in fine jewelry of precious metals and stones, and covered with shrouds. Abundant grave goods included items of personal care and adornment, such as cosmetic boxes, perfumes, and combs, in addition to what may be interpreted as the remains of funerary feasts, including plates, bowls, cups, and incense burners made of ceramic, glass, stone, silver, and gold.

These tombs belonged to high-status individuals living in the early years of Achaemenid rule in the area, yet the quality and quantity of their finds reflect ultimately Lydian traditions concerning the dead, just as their locations reflect Lydian traditions concerning the living. More than 600 tumuli spread throughout Lydia are clustered into fewer than 100 groups that were sited with reference to subsistence, communication, territorial, and resource control (Roosevelt 2006) and probably mark the locations of elite family estates tasked by the Lydian court at Sardis to attend to such concerns. As such, they can serve as proxies for understanding the organization of regional settlement. While elite family members may have spent much of their time at the Lydian court, slaves and/or commoner inhabitants living in small hamlets or villages near to or within estate lands would have farmed their holdings. In addition to slaves and commoners, Lydian society at Sardis was defined by at least three other broad social strata attested textually: a very broad middle class, including merchants, shopkeepers, craftsmen, artisans, etc.; high-status or elite groups, including noble families and religious officials; and royalty (Roosevelt 2009). A lack of evidence prevents further elucidation of Lydian social structure or differentiation along age or gender lines, yet it is clear that Lydian society was ethnically diverse, at least by the 6th century. Phrygian, Mysian, and, especially, Carian immigrants and influences are common among Anatolian sources and are attested at Sardis in material production as well as by historical texts and personal names. Further afield, similar types of evidence reflect possible interactions with, if not the local presence of, Phoenicians, Assyrians, and Scythians. Yet Greeks from the mainland and the east Aegean coast, as well as their cultural traditions, most permeated Lydian society. Lydian–Greek affinity was probably a result of long-term interaction on military, religious, commercial, and artistic levels and reached a crescendo in reign of Croesus, when several Greek leaders visited his court.

It was perhaps because of his close connection to Greece and its sanctuaries that Croesus made the fateful mistake attributed to him by Herodotus (1.46–81) that put an end to both his reign and the Mermnad Dynasty. According to this romantic tale, Croesus was unnerved upon learning that an upstart king of Persia named Cyrus had conquered the Medes under their king Astyages c.550 BC. Perhaps because of a familial obligation to avenge his brother-in-law, perhaps in an attempt to protect or even expand his rule in Anatolia west of the Halys River, Croesus planned to confront Cyrus and his army. Before doing so, however, he sought sanction from what he considered the best of the Greek oracular sanctuaries, the oracles of Apollo at Delphi and of Amphiaraus in Thebes. When asked whether Croesus should attack, both oracles answered that were he to do so "he would destroy a mighty empire." Fatefully misunderstanding the answer, Croesus led his armies east, having sent embassies of alliance to Sparta, Egypt, and Babylon. After an inconclusive battle near Pteria in Cappadocia, and outnumbered by Cyrus' vast army, Croesus retreated to Sardis, released his mercenaries, and awaited his allies' reinforcements. Cyrus and his army followed too closely upon Croesus' heels for his plans of reinforcement to come to fruition, however. Cyrus surprised the Lydians and engaged in open battle in front of Sardis, besting their cavalry with the strategic aid of a Mede named Harpagus. After a brief siege, Cyrus overcame Sardis' defenses, laying waste to its urban landscape, monumental and residential alike. This mid-540s BC Persian sack of Sardis has been attested archaeologically and impressively in numerous contexts across the site, vividly illustrating the destructive end of Croesus' Lydian rule. While Cyrus quickly sent his armies beyond Sardis to continue his territorial conquests, Sardis only gradually recovered from its violent sack. By the end of the 6th century, and after a brief Lydian resistance, the city was transformed into the satrapal capital of an imperial Achaemenid province, with its administrative operations continuing much as they had under Lydian rule.

4 Pre-Achaemenid and Dynastic Lycia

Following the sack of Sardis and the successful conquest of rebellious contingents in Ionia and Caria, Cyrus' troops under Harpagus made their way south to Lycia. Importantly, while Herodotus refers to Harpagus' suppression of several peoples and places in Ionia and Caria (1.162–176), he reports that Harpagus took only Xanthus in Lycia, suggesting that, like Sardis, it may have been the only centralized seat of power in Lycia at that time. Here, the Lycians met the Persians in the Xanthus river valley and retreated to the acropolis of Xanthus after suffering defeat in open battle. Besieged by the Persians, the Lycian troops gathered their women, children, servants, and possessions in the acropolis and burnt it down completely in a final suicidal sally against the invading forces. We learn also from Herodotus that the city was later reinhabited by "foreigners" as well as 80 Xanthian families who had been absent during Harpagus' siege. Contrary to the earlier and longer thread of evidence available for Lydia, this account is the earliest historical testimony we have on Lycia, yet it clearly indicates the presence of a Lycian culture, if not a political entity, that was well established before the mid-6th century. What else can be said of pre-Achaemenid Lycia, its territory and people?

By the later 5th or 4th century BC, Lycia could be defined as the mountainous coastal area of southwestern Anatolia stretching between Caria, to the west, and Pamphylia, to the east, roughly between modern Fethiye and Antalya. The courses of several major rivers divided the mountainous terrain, and the largest of them, the ancient Xanthus (Eşen) River, achieved a width of 20 kilometers in places and was likely the political core of Lycia in the early 1st millennium BC and perhaps earlier. Other rivers created a dissected, circumscribed coastal terrain that encouraged both landed isolation (and the eventual establishment of more than 30 independent cities) and maritime communication. To the northwest of Lycia lay the territory of the Cibyratis and to the north-northeast that of Milyas, both separated from the coastal strip by mountain ranges. While Milyas displayed markedly Phrygian characteristics in material culture during the 7th century, as known from the Bayindir tumuli in Elmali, the area seems not to have been brought under Lycian political control until the 4th century BC (Keen 1998: 13–20).

The archaeological evidence of 2nd and early 1st millennium BC Lycia includes rare Bronze Age pottery from a handful of Lycian sites and early tombs and sparse pottery of the late 8th/early 7th and 6th centuries from sites such as Pinara, Xanthus, the Letoön, and Patara, in the Xanthus river valley, and Phellus,

Antiphellus, and Limyra, further east (Keen 1998: 28, 214–20). The 7th century remains at Xanthus also include architectural remains that resemble Near Eastern *bīt ḫilāni* (Ch. II.41) structures (Marksteiner 2005: 39). Little else can be said about pre-Achaemenid Lycia from a material perspective. Accordingly, one must speculate about the early history and geographical definition of Lycia on the basis of LBA historical, Iron Age pseudo-historical and linguistic evidence. That "Lycians" were associated with the area described above at least since the LBA is suggested by continuity in placenames between Iron Age Lycia, as it was known to the Greeks, and the Bronze Age Lukka Lands in Hittite sources (Bryce 1986: 1–10; Keen 1998: 214–20). The people of the Lukka Lands appear to have been politically unconsolidated groups dwelling in areas stretching from southern Caria into western Lycia, perhaps practicing transhumant pastoralism. Their maritime activities and coastal situation are indicated as well by their description as sea-borne marauders in the royal correspondence between Cyprus and Ugarit, and by their identity among the "Sea Peoples" plaguing the eastern Mediterranean during the reign of Merneptah in the late 13th century BC. Furthermore, the territorial affinity between the Lukka Lands and later Lycia, at least western Lycia, has been confirmed by an itinerary of the Hittite king Tudhaliya IV recorded in the Yalburt inscription (Poetto 1993) which names *inter alia* several places that can be identified with Tlos, Xanthus, and Patara, and that align well with the topography of the Xanthus river valley.

References to Lycia and the Lycians in the *Iliad*, too, though pseudo-historical, seem to confirm the importance of the Xanthus river valley and its population by the time of its composition around 700 BC. The Lycian contingent is taken to be Troy's most important ally, with their leaders Sarpedon and Glaucus playing important roles in the Trojan War's final year (e.g., *Iliad* 2.816–877, 5.471–492). "Lycia" and "Xanthus" even seem to be used interchangeably in Homeric epic, suggesting that, from a Greek perspective, the two were inseparable. The Bellerophon saga, and its location in Lycia, also, draws attention to the area and suggests a general familiarity with the region and its people amongst Homer's intended audience.

The troubling paucity of corresponding archaeological evidence of the 2nd and early 1st millennium BC for either the people of the Lukka Lands or for Homer's Lycians has been explained most commonly by assuming that the people of Iron Age Lycia lived elsewhere during the LBA and migrated into Lycia only later (Bryce 1986: 24–40), or that heavy alluvial sedimentation, the relative archaeological invisibility of transhumant pastoralist ways of life, and a lack of intensive surveys in the area have collectively failed to identify pre-7th century remains (Keen 1998: 27–8). Until richer remains of the LBA and Early Iron Age are located, and these can be associated with the Lukka or Lycians, this question will remain unanswered. Further confounding the story of 1st millennium Lycia is Herodotus' testimony that Lycians were earlier called "Termilae" (1.173) and that they migrated to Lycia from Crete. This and other Greek tales of Lycian origins were probably literary inventions written to suit contemporary purposes and we need not rely on tales of foreign migrations today. Yet, Herodotus' account may have a kernel of truth, as "Termilae" resembles *Trmmili*, the term used by the Lycians in their native language in referring to themselves and the name by which they were known to the Persians and Babylonians (Keen 1998: 30).

Like Lydian, Lycian is attested in a relatively small corpus of texts, most of which date to the late 5th and 4th centuries BC. The earliest examples found in Lycia date to the 6th century, however, presumably well after the language had reached maturity. A corpus of around 200 inscriptions in stone is dominated by funerary dedications and burial instructions, though a few decrees and religious dedications are known as well. Bilingual (e.g., Lycian-Greek) and trilingual (e.g., Lycian-Greek-Aramaic) texts are also known, the longer of which aided the decipherment of the language (Bryce 1986: 42). Lycian is an Anatolian language, dialectically descendant from Common Anatolian like Lydian, but much closer to Luwian. Aside from indicating what the Lycians called themselves – *Trmmili* – Lycian inscriptions are among the richest evidence available for understanding family composition, burial traditions, bureaucratic and religious offices, and local political history.

Lycian sociopolitical, religious, and economic traditions have been partially reconstructed on the basis of epigraphic evidence in combination with analyses of numerous sculptural monuments, thousands of coins, settlement patterns, and burial traditions. Such sources are of great importance given the comparative dearth of reliable contemporary testimony pertaining to Lycian ways of life. It is difficult to judge the accuracy of reports (e.g., Herodotus 1.173) referring to Lycian men wearing long hair, practicing a matronymic pattern of self-identification, or donning feminine dress during mourning (Bryce 1986: 128, 139, 212). Equally unclear is how early and how widespread such customs may have been. Did they pre-date or post-date the Achaemenid conquest? Were they limited to the Xanthus river valley or not? That such evidence derives almost entirely from Greek authors writing for Greek audiences encourages caution in its acceptance.

Lycian tomb inscriptions provide the fullest evidence of family composition, showing that tomb owners, usually males, provided for the burial of their spouses and offspring, and sometimes for extended family members also, especially nieces and nephews (Pembroke 1965; Bryce 1979; 1986: 116). The inscriptions also provide the names, but rarely the associated responsibilities, of a variety of religious and secular titles and professions, including priest, seer, military commander, and even "king" or "dynast" (Bryce 1986: 129–35). Administrative institutions are named in inscriptions as well, and include a council known as the *minti*, which provided now obscure mortuary services, and a group of people or deities, the *itlehi*, that could be invoked to punish those who mistreated particular tombs. Other common invocations of tomb protection and/or retribution were made directly to a variety of deities of Lycian, Carian, and Greek origin. These included *Eni Mahanahi*, the Lycian mother goddess later syncretized with the Greek Leto; *Trqqas*, the Anatolian storm god later equated with Zeus; *Maliya*, later equated with Athena; the *Teseti*, a set of oath gods; and the *Eliyana*, apparently akin to Greek nymphs. Greek deities adopted later included Artemis, Aphrodite, and Apollo (Bryce 1986: 172–82). No pre-Achaemenid cult places have been identified for any of these deities except, perhaps, at the Letöon near Xanthus. The early 7th century remains there were probably associated with a cult of the mother goddess and/or nymphs before it became something of a national sanctuary dedicated to Leto and her offspring in and after the late 5th or early 4th century.

Post-dating the sparse pottery and other remains that date the earliest Iron Age activities in Lycia to the late 8th/early 7th centuries BC, the first substantive archaeological evidence of settlement dates to the later 6th century and includes settlement and tomb remains at Xanthus and a number of rich tombs from other sites in central Lycia. Structures on the so-called Lycian Acropolis at Xanthus, usually described as a series of dynastic residences, were preserved beneath a destruction layer dated to c.540 BC. We know from Herodotus' account of Harpagus' conquest of Lycia that Xanthus must already have been an important center at that time – hence Harpagus' decision to conquer it – and these finds support that view. A particular class of monumental tomb known from Xanthus and sites in central Lycia also serves as evidence of pre-Achaemenid Lycian traditions and settlement distribution (Draycott 2007, following Marksteiner 2002b). These are the so-called pillar tombs, consisting of stone pillars that supported squared chambers decorated with relief sculpture on their exterior façades. The sculpture of these tombs not only reveals an openness to the ultimately Greek tradition of sculpted tomb embellishments, consonant with the adoption of Greek deities mentioned above, but also, through comparison with better known monuments in the Aegean, provides dates for the monuments, the earliest group of which was carved in the later 6th century. The distribution of the earliest group, with one each at five sites in central Lycia and two at Xanthus, indicates not only shared cultural traditions that encouraged prominent displays articulated in funerary architecture, but also the likely nodes of personages and/or families that had been important before and/or quickly rose to power during the early years of Achaemenid rule.

Already by the end of the 6th century, then, we can talk of a number of centers in Lycia where prominent families likely served in leadership roles and expressed their positions in society through common cultural signifiers. The commonality of Lycian cultural traditions in this and earlier periods may not have extended to political unification, however, and there is little evidence of regional political organization at this time. In addition to settlement patterns, tomb types, and sculptural styles, coinage also bears on such issues because the issuers and guarantors of coins of standard value were probably politically as well as economically important. The earliest coinage in Lycia appeared by the last decade of the 6th century and had a limited range of decorative motifs and standard weights that, despite the invention of coinage in Lydia, suggest an introduction from Greece (Zahle 1991). Their uniformity implies a single mint, probably at Xanthus. The uniformity of the early coinage, however, gave way, by the end of the first quarter of the 5th century, to a confusing variety of coin weights, decorative motifs, and legends, which endures into the last decades of the 5th century (Zahle 1991).

The number of coin issues in circulation during the mid-5th century is paralleled by an increase in the number of prominent centers (usually referred to as "dynastic centers") that appear contemporaneously and persisted into later times. The prominence of such sites is suggested by the remains of sometimes fortified spaces called "dynastic residences" at Xanthus, Sura, Limyra, and Avşar Tepesi, among others (Işik and Yilmaz 1996; Marksteiner 2002a, 2002b). Additionally, new types of monumental tombs appeared by the mid-5th century at Xanthus, Phellus, Apollonia, Trysa, and Limyra, and these, too, are commonly thought to mark the locations of dynastic centers (Kjeldsen and Zahle 1975; Zahle 1983; Keen 1998: 182–6). Just who these "dynasts" were, however, and whether such sites were truly political centers, is unclear (Zimmermann 1992; Marksteiner 2002b). Equally unknown is whether and how they functioned within the overarching framework of Achaemenid governance. That at least some of these centers issued coinage throughout the mid-5th century suggests a degree of regional administrative fragmentation uncharacteristic of other Achaemenid satrapies and it is likely that at least some parts of Lycia were relatively autonomous in this period.

The administrative fragmentation of Lycia during the mid-5th century BC and later should be considered together with the broader military and political narratives of the time. In the first two decades of the century, the armies of Darius and Xerxes campaigned against mainland Greece. Greek and Persian naval conflicts persisted through the middle of the century as the Athenians continuously pressed to forge broad alliances (Childs 1981). Because of their strategic control of protected harbors, and thus maritime routes between the Aegean and the eastern Mediterranean, Lycian centers were likely pulled between Persian and Athenian allegiances and not all centers may have responded similarly. Thus the "Lycians" contributed 50 ships to Xerxes' fleet c.480 BC (Herodotus 7.92); Cimon gained "Lycian" allegiance to Athens before c.468 (Diodorus Siculus, *Hist.* 11.60.4); Telmessus and the "Lycians" are listed as paying tribute to Athens in the late 450s and 440s (Bryce 1986: 105); and the Athenian Melesander was killed in a "Lycian" conflict c.430/29 (Thucydides 2.69). The pendulum of support seems to have swung back and forth, yet a clearer understanding of the period and its local political developments is hindered by our inability to determine to which Lycia or Lycians – that is to which Lycian centers – such historical testimony refers. Nevertheless, continuous political interactions with Greek city-states during the 5th century foreshadowed the relatively thorough Hellenization of such centers in later centuries.

At least one of the many centers of Lycia, Xanthus, appears to have been the seat of a hereditary dynasty that remained relatively faithful to its Achaemenid overlords throughout the 5th century BC. Inscriptions at Xanthus provide the names of five or six rulers of the Harpagid Dynasty, whose founder, one Harpagus, may or may not have been the same as Cyrus' general of the same name (Keen 2002). Beginning with Kybernis and his successor Kuprlli, who reigned from the late 6th into the mid-5th century, the allegiance of Xanthus to the Achaemenid Empire is displayed in part by features of sculpture and coinage appearing first around 480 BC. The so-called Harpy Tomb (c.480–470 BC) and the later Heroön G (c.460 BC) show pronounced Persian influences (Draycott 2007). Coins probably minted at Xanthus show similar affinities in their decorative motifs, suggesting that the dynasts of Xanthus wished to highlight their close connections to the Achaemenid administration at this time (Zahle 1991: 153).

Later pronounced Persian affinities may have also resulted from the personal ambitions of particular regents. Thus, in the late 5th/early 4th century, Erbbina, the ruler of Xanthus, decorated his clearly Greek-inspired tomb, the well-known Nereid Monument, with Persian motifs. Following Erbbina's death and the end of the Harpagid Dynasty c.380–370 BC, two western Lycian dynasts named Arttumpara and Mithrapata claimed power simultaneously. We know little of their activities, but their Achaemenid sympathies are suggested by their Persian names. Despite such examples, there seems to have been no pervasive Persianization of Lycia, or at least Xanthus. Persian personal names appear in inscriptions, yet this may reflect only a desire on the part of some families for close ties to Achaemenid sources of power rather than the presence of ethnic Iranians in the area. The balance of inscriptional evidence, in fact, seems to suggest a continuity of local traditions, especially in burial and religious practices, mixed with a gradual and broad Hellenization (Bryce 1986: 158–71). Thus, while Achaemenid features appeared again on coin issues circulating around Xanthus in western Lycia during the very late 5th/early 4th century BC, contemporary with Erbbina's reign and the Persian stylization of his tomb, the light monetary standard used for these issues was adopted directly from Athenian coinage (Zahle 1991: 152). Erbbina and his contemporaries appear to have embraced certain aspects of the Greek world while striving to maintain their own power and giving the appearance of being effective servants of Achaemenid hegemony, even if that hegemony was not uniform throughout Lycia.

Achaemenid rule in Lycia was soon challenged again, however, by a certain Pericles, who came to power at Limyra in c.380 BC. The extent of his growing power is paralleled by coin issues circulating in central and eastern Lycia at this time, struck on a single, regular standard, heavier than the Athenian one used in the west (Zahle 1991: 150–2). Whether or not he ever claimed allegiance to the Achaemenids, by c.360 BC, Pericles had briefly united a previously fragmented

Lycia under his autonomous rule, from Telmessus in the west, to Phaselis in the east, and to the Elmali Plain in the north (Keen 1998: 13).

Following broader crises in Achaemenid provincial control in western Anatolia, known collectively as the "Great Satraps' Revolt," it was untenable for the Achaemenids to allow such autonomy in Lycia and the area was soon brought back within the fold. At this point the region was put under the protectorship of the greatly Hellenophile, yet pro-Achaemenid Hecatomnid satraps of Mylasa and Halicarnassus, and thus the regional administration of Lycia left Lycian hands. The area remained this way through the end of the Achaemenid period and, because of its strategic location, was regularly contested among the powers of the Mediterranean throughout the Hellenistic period. Nevertheless, the region's persistent trend of political disunity was reflected again in the 2nd century BC, with the federalization of Lycia's many polities into a "Lycian League." Enduring for more than half a millennium, this league provided the first and only long-lasting and cooperative local administration of the area in its history, and serves well to contrast its earlier political fragmentation. However, by the time firm Roman rule took hold in the 1st century AD, most traces of indigenous Lycian culture had been supplanted by broader Greek and Roman cultural traditions.

GUIDE TO FURTHER READING

In addition to the sources cited in the chapter, further detailed reading on Sardis and Lydia should begin with Sardis excavation reports, published regularly in *BASOR* and *AJA*, and the numerous *Report* and *Monograph* volumes of the Harvard and Cornell University-sponsored Archaeological Exploration of Sardis, which present the ongoing work of that expedition at Sardis begun in 1958. For broader syntheses on Sardis and Lydia, see Hanfmann (1983) and, more recently, Dusinberre (2003), (Roosevelt 2009), and the papers in Cahill (2010a) Further reading on Xanthus and Lycia should begin with the series of volumes in the *Fouilles de Xanthos* series (Paris) published by the French team responsible for ongoing excavations at Xanthus and the Letöon begun in 1951. Regular reports of ongoing work at these sites can be found in *Anatolia Antiqua*. For a selection of other recent work at the many sites and areas in Lycia recently and currently being investigated, see Borchardt and Dobesch (1993); *Lykia*, the annual of Akdeniz University's Archaeology Department edited by Işik and others (Anatlya, 1994–); and the *Lykische Studien* volumes (Bonn, 1995–), an important series on work in central Lycia around Kyaneai edited by Frank Kolb. Other useful collections of articles on various Lycian subjects include Borchardt et al. (1990), French (1994), and Giorgieri et al. (2003).

CHAPTER FORTY-NINE

The Neo-Babylonian Empire

Heather D. Baker

1 Introduction

The Neo-Babylonian empire spanned the period from the accession of Nabopolassar in 626 BC to the conquest of Babylonia and the defeat of its last native ruler, Nabonidus (555–539 BC), by the Persian king Cyrus in 539 BC. During the century preceding the rise of the Neo-Babylonian (or "Chaldean") dynasty, Babylonia had been involved in a long-standing struggle for independence from its more powerful neighbor to the north, Assyria. When Nabopolassar finally defeated Assyria with the aid of his Median allies in 612 BC, Babylonia gained control over the Assyrian heartland and what remained of its subject territories.

In terms of its material culture assemblage, the Neo-Babylonian empire, which lasted less than 100 years, forms a continuum with what went before: it is difficult to distinguish it from that of the long period from c.1150 to 626 BC which has been variously termed "Middle Babylonian" or "Post-Kassite" (Brinkman 1984a: 3). Sometimes the latter part of this long period has been referred to as "Assyrian" – for example, Woolley (1965) wrote of "the period of the Assyrian kings" at Ur. However, Assyrian control over the region was by no means stable and continuous; moreover, the material culture of the time was Babylonian rather than Assyrian, so the term is of purely historical application.

It is difficult to distinguish not only the beginning of the Neo-Babylonian period proper in material culture terms, but also its end. Historians have repeatedly stressed the continuity in administration and daily life which marked the

---

A Companion to the Archaeology of the Ancient Near East, First Edition.
Edited by D.T. Potts.
© 2012 Blackwell Publishing Ltd. Published 2012 by Blackwell Publishing Ltd.

transition to Achaemenid rule over Babylonia. From a material culture perspective, Zettler (1979: 268), for example, noted that typical Neo-Babylonian seal types remained in common use until at least the reign of Darius I (521–486 BC), a quarter of a century after the Persian conquest in 539 BC. As Zettler also noted (1979: 269), we have to consider the possibility that some items of material culture were more easily affected than others by political change. Moreover, when old pottery forms are only gradually superseded by new ones, decisions about dating may rest on the relative proportions of certain types within the overall assemblage. This in turn requires an overview of entire assemblages – something often lacking because most of the relevant sites were excavated before the development of modern techniques of excavation and analysis, and selective publication of ceramic types was the norm.

Our knowledge of the archaeology of this period in Babylonia itself is dominated by monumental buildings located at the heart of the major cities. In large degree this reflects the preoccupations of earlier excavators, who were primarily interested in these impressive structures to the neglect of the other (to them) less prepossessing urban features such as residential areas and the margins of settlements. This bias of interest has resulted not only in an incomplete picture of the makeup of urban sites; it has also seriously affected our understanding of the settlement hierarchy, since smaller sites, especially villages, remain unexplored. Further investigation is clearly needed in order to make good these gaps in our knowledge, but in the meantime we have to work with what is available; nevertheless, this state of affairs should be kept in mind when reading the overview that follows.

For a number of reasons, relatively little is known about the immediate precursors of the Neo-Babylonian cities. Royal building inscriptions, which were typically buried in the foundations of the structures which they commemorated, are an approximate indicator of the level of such activity in a particular period. When found in situ, they serve to date the building level with which they are associated and often to identify a structure by name. The dearth of building inscriptions for the period between the reign of king Adad-apla-iddina (1068–1047 BC) and the mid-8th century BC therefore reflects, in all likelihood, the actual situation: the absence of a powerful central authority with the means and motivation to implement construction projects on any significant scale. During this period, which has been termed a "Dark Age," the material culture associated with the Babylonian rulers is dominated by inscribed artifacts, often of bronze, such as arrowheads, generally of uncertain or unknown provenience (on the so-called "Luristan bronzes," see Frame 1995: 3–4). Even when monumental building activity resumed, the first projects documented after this long interval were those carried out in Borsippa and Uruk by local inhabitants rather than by rulers, during the reigns of Nabu-shuma-ishkun (c.760–748 BC) and Nabu-nasir (747–734 BC), respectively. We should note also that the inscribed monuments generally known as *kudurru*s, especially associated with the Kassite dynasty and the

Middle-Babylonian era (Ch. II.37), are known also from the earlier 1st millennium, with dated examples spanning the 10th–7th centuries BC. Yet these artifacts are frequently of unknown or uncertain provenance (Slanski 2003).

The first Babylonian ruler whose works have been recovered through excavation is Marduk-apla-iddin II (721–710 and 703 BC), who was responsible for restoration work on the Eanna temple at Uruk, including the shrine of Ningizzida located within the precinct wall. He was followed by a succession of Assyrian kings who sponsored reconstruction works in Babylonia: Sargon II (the Eanna temple at Uruk; the city walls of Babylon); Sennacherib (the Processional Way at Babylon); Esarhaddon (work on the Marduk temple Esagila, the *ziggurat* Etemenanki, and the Processional Way at Babylon; the Gula temple at Borsippa; the Enlil and Ishtar temples at Nippur; Eanna at Uruk); Assurbanipal (the city wall at Babylon and the shrines of Ea, Ishtar-of-Babylon, and Ninmah, as well as Esagila and Etemenanki; the Ebabbar temple at Sippar; the city wall and Nabu temple at Borsippa; the *ziggurat* and Enlil temple at Nippur, and the Eanna temple at Uruk). During the reign of Assurbanipal (668–627 BC) one governor of Ur, Sin-balassu-iqbi, exercised a considerable degree of autonomy and carried out building projects in his own name. These included work on a number of shrines and a well, which have been excavated (Woolley 1965: 4). Also during the reign of Assurbanipal, the Assyrian king's brother Shamash-shum-ukin, who served as king of Babylon until he revolted in 652 BC, performed work on the city wall and the Ebabbar temple at Sippar and on the Nabu temple in Borsippa. Finally, Assur-etel-ilani, whose precise dates are unknown but who ruled in the 630s BC, carried out work on the Urash temple at Dilbat and the Enlil temple at Nippur. Most of the aforementioned projects are known from excavation as well as written sources. However, building levels attributable to the period of Neo-Assyrian rule are in general much less well known than the Neo-Babylonian (re)buildings that overlay them.

2 Settlement Patterns

Settlement survey has identified sites datable to the Neo-Babylonian period in several regions of southern and central Mesopotamia: the Diyala region (Adams 1965); the "heartland" region between Nippur and Uruk (Adams 1981); the Uruk region (Adams and Nissen 1972); the Kish region (Gibson 1972); and the Sippar region (Gasche and De Meyer 1980). It should be noted that the periodization of surface collections based on ceramic typology is necessarily imprecise, and the dating criteria used to define the period vary between different surveys, making it difficult to compare results. Moreover, the most densely settled area may by now have lain somewhat to the west of the most intensively surveyed "heartland" region (Brinkman 1984b: 175–6), a difficulty which may now be partly surmounted using advanced techniques for the study of high-resolution satellite imagery (Hritz 2004). By this time, fairly broad expanses of land had been brought under continuous cultivation and the Neo-Babylonian (NB) and Achaemenid (Ach) settlement systems were connected to "an interlocking, much more 'artificial' grid of watercourses that broke large, contiguous areas of cultivation into polygons of fairly uniform size and shape" (Adams 1981: 188).

Survey evidence indicates a period of sustained population growth, beginning in the 8th century BC. According to this evidence, the Neo-Babylonian period saw a substantial increase in the number of settlements, with 182 sites identified in the "heartland" area, compared with 134 of Middle Babylonian (MB) date (Adams 1981: 177). Moreover, average site size increased, to 6.88 hectares (NB/Ach) compared with 4.6 hectares (MB) (Adams 1981: 178). While the numbers of sites in all size categories increased, the increase was proportionally greater for sites in the larger size brackets. For NB/Ach, 51 percent of the total occupied area was composed of settlements classified as urban – i.e., larger than 10 hectares, as compared with only 36 percent of MB sites (Adams 1981: 178). Of the 30 NB/Ach urban settlements identified, some two-thirds had no earlier MB occupation and thus represent new settlements. Survey in the Diyala region revealed similar long-term trends, though with some variation in matters of detail: new sites tended to be rather small and the total area occupied by sites classified as urban was relatively low (Adams 1965: 58–9).

Various reasons have been put forward for this steady and sustained increase of population, the most significant of which were most likely the relatively stable political conditions and a general increase in prosperity. The population of Babylonia may have been boosted also by the return of groups exiled by the Assyrians and by immigrants resettled there by the Babylonian kings, such as the Judeans and Cilicians (Adams 1981: 177–8).

3 Babylonian Urbanism

The Babylonian cities at this time typically combined both planned elements (generally monumental structures of various kinds – see below) and quarters that developed without much (if any) intervention from the central authorities. Among the relatively small areas of street network that have been excavated, we find nothing remotely approaching an orthogonal grid, most likely because streets conformed to centuries-old patterns, bearing in mind that we are dealing with long settled *tells* whose topography helped to shape subsequent urban development.

The best-known city layout in this period is that of Babylon. However, it cannot be taken as typical: as the seat of kingship and the capital (both actual and cosmic), it received special treatment at the hands of successive rulers. Nevertheless, certain key elements were common to most Babylonian cities of this period: a main temple precinct housing the city's patron deity, and a *ziggurat*, with other temples and shrines scattered around the settlement; city walls with gates; and residential areas whose integration into the wider city was articulated by a three-tier hierarchy of major public streets, minor public streets, and blind alleys. Some city walls of this period enclosed not only areas of occupation proper, but also unbuilt areas, especially around the lower-lying margins of the *tell*, which might be used for intramural gardens and orchards. Within the residential areas, such unbuilt plots as existed were generally part of residential house complexes.

According to Van de Mieroop (1999: 82), residential areas mixed with industrial sectors were a key element of the Mesopotamian city. However, while this observation certainly applies to some cities of the earlier 2nd millennium, from 1st millennium Babylonia evidence of such discrete areas of industrial activity within the city is scarce, for several reasons. First, within the residential areas, craft activity in the private sphere very likely took place at the level of the household rather than in separate areas dedicated to it; archaeological evidence of such activities within the Neo-Babylonian house has not yet been recovered. Second, the urban margins, where some industrial activities such as pottery manufacture are likely to have been located, remain under explored. Third, judging from the written evidence, a significant amount of production took place within the institutional sphere; for example, the temple precincts housed workshops and storerooms where personnel carried out the various activities related to supplying the divine meals and looking after the cultic paraphernalia. Like the residential areas, these too have yet to be investigated with a view to identifying different activity zones.

4 The Babylonian Cities and Towns

In this section I shall focus only on those sites that have yielded a certain amount of information about their urban structure as a result of controlled excavation. These include Babylon, Borsippa, Kish, and Sippar in northern Babylonia; Isin and Nippur in central Babylonia; and Larsa, Tell al-Lahm, Ur, and Uruk in the south.

The main double city wall of Babylon enclosed a rectangular area of c.450 hectares, bisected by the north–south course of the Arahtu (i.e., Euphrates) river. The center of settlement, as evidenced by the concentration of occupation mounds, was on the eastern bank of the river; the western site of the city remains unexplored. Within the city walls on the east side, the principal excavated features include the South Palace of Nebuchadnezzar II (604–562 BC), to its south the religious precinct comprising the *ziggurat* Etemenanki and its enclosure, and, still further to the south, the Esagila or temple of Marduk. The Processional Street separated the palatial and religious sectors from a substantial residential district to the west, known today as the Merkes quarter. The excavated part of

Merkes represents an area of high-status housing; beyond it to the south the excavators traced the street network for several further blocks. In addition to these three key areas within the city, several other temples were excavated which were integrated into the local residential areas, although – with the exception of the temple of Ishtar-of-Akkad in Merkes – their immediate surroundings have not been explored.

The city wall of Borsippa can still be traced for much of its course; it encloses a roughly rectangular area measuring c.220 hectares, with its long axis oriented roughly northeast–southwest. Within the walls are two main mounds separated by an ancient watercourse. Off the mounds are ample lower lying areas enclosed by the city wall, especially on the southeastern side of the site. The smaller mound, Birs Nimrud, is the site of the *ziggurat* and the Ezida, temple of the city god Nabu. The larger mound to its northeast, Tell Ibrahim al-Khalil, remains unexplored. Investigations at the site have focused almost entirely on the main temple precinct and *ziggurat*, and very little is known about the remainder of the city. The impressive, vitrified remains of the *ziggurat* were long identified by early travelers and archaeologists with the Tower of Babel (e.g., Peters 1921), and Borsippa was thought to be a mere suburb of Babylon. The results of the soundings made by Hormuzd Rassam in the Ezida on behalf of the British Museum between 1879 and 1882 have been summarized and evaluated by Reade (1986b). An additional, brief campaign of excavation was carried out on Ezida by German archaeologists in 1901–2 (Koldewey 1911: 50–9, Taf. XII; further details in Jakob-Rost 1989, especially regarding the excavated objects and inscriptions). In recent decades excavations have been carried out on the *ziggurat* and Ezida by an Austrian team (Allinger-Csollich 1991, 1998; Trenkwalder-Piesl 1981; Trenkwalder 1997–8, 1999–2000). Their work has shown that the Ezida temple uncovered in earlier excavations is not actually Neo-Babylonian, as previously thought, but, rather, a later rebuilding (Allinger-Csollich et al. 2010: 32–3). Thanks to a foundation cylinder found in situ, the *ziggurat* is known to have been rebuilt by Nebuchadnezzar (Allinger-Csollich 1991: 494–8). Its destruction was attributed by Boehmer (1980) to Xerxes' suppression of revolts which took place early in his reign (484 BC), but it is now known to have happened more than a millennium later (Allinger-Csollich et al. 2010: 32).

Kish is made up of an extensive area of at least 40 discrete mounds. Excavations were carried out by H. de Genouillac in 1912–14, and then again in 1923–33 by a joint expedition from Oxford University and the Field Museum (Chicago). The results of these later seasons have been re-evaluated by Gibson (1972) and Moorey (1978), focusing on the finds and records housed in Chicago and Oxford, respectively. A new project aiming at the complete publication of all the relevant material from these excavations is currently being conducted by the Field Museum in collaboration with the Ashmolean Museum (Oxford). Japanese archaeologists have also worked at the site, uncovering part of what may be a Neo-Babylonian house (Matsumoto 1991: 276–80). At the western end of the site, on the mound known as Tell Uhaimir, one of the *ziggurats* of Kish was located. This is traditionally identified as that of the main city god, Zababa, and associated with his temple Edubba; the latter is known to have been rebuilt by Nabopolassar and his son Nebuchadnezzar II. Investigation of the *ziggurat* revealed a phase attributable to Nebuchadnezzar II (Moorey 1978: 25–6, and plan facing p. 24). Within the rooms flanking the *ziggurat* to the southeast, as well as in the temple area to the northeast, Neo-Babylonian remains were scarce, perhaps owing to erosion; the extant plan dates to the Old Babylonian period. Aside from the *ziggurat* and temple precinct, Uhaimir seems to have been unoccupied in the 1st millennium (Moorey 1978: 28–9), though one wonders whether here too erosion might have affected preservation.

The main center of Neo-Babylonian occupation at Kish was in the part of the city known as Hursagkalamma, identified with Tell Ingharra in the eastern part of the site. A Neo-Babylonian temple partly excavated by de Genouillac was investigated further by the Oxford/Chicago team; it turned out to be a double temple, built by either Nebuchadnezzar or Nabonidus. The temple itself cut into the fabric of two *ziggurats* made of plano-convex bricks; these were probably ruined by this time, though they may have been intended to be rebuilt (Moorey 1978: 85). It seems likely that these can be identified with the two *ziggurats* of Hursagkalamma named in temple lists of the later 2nd millennium – namely, those of Ninlil and Enlil (George 1993: 45–56) – and that the temple itself is that of Ninlil/Ishtar, called Ehursagkalamma (despite Jursa 2005: 103, who considered its identification as the Zababa temple to be "virtually certain").

The site of Sippar is rectangular in shape, enclosed on three sides by the city wall and on the fourth (southwest) side by a watercourse. The wall comprises a continuous earthen rampart with no evident breaks for gates; access to the interior was probably via ramps. The mound itself stretches along the site's long axis from the canal on the southwest to the city wall on the northeast side. The wall also enclosed lower-lying areas, along the northwestern side of the *tell* and at the eastern corner of the site. In the Neo-Babylonian era, much of the *tell*'s southwestern end was occupied by the great Ebabbar temple, dedicated to the city god Shamash. Elsewhere, excavations on the mound have mostly encountered Old Babylonian (or earlier) occupation immediately below the surface, thus tending to support what the written sources also suggest, namely that the walled city was rather sparsely occupied during the Neo-Babylonian period and that settlement was concentrated in an area known as the Quay of Sippar. This quay has yet to be located, but it must have lain outside of the city walls on a major watercourse, probably the King's Canal to the north. Early excavators at Sippar (Rassam in 1881–2, Scheil in 1894) concentrated on the Ebabbar temple (see Walker and Collon 1980 for details of Rassam's work and the finds, without precise provenance, from the temple). In 1972–3 a sounding was dug into the city wall on the northeastern side, on the basis of which Belgian excavators determined that the earthen rampart had served as a flood barrier. Their report includes a contour plan of the site, plus a plan of the Ebabbar temple (De Meyer 1980: Plan 2). Among the episodes of heightening the wall which the excavators identified in the city wall sounding, the penultimate one may be identified with work known to have been carried out by Shamash-shum-ukin, while the latest may be late Neo-Babylonian in date (Baker forthcoming). Iraqi archaeologists working in the northwestern part of the Ebabbar precinct in 1985–6 discovered a library with cuneiform tablets lying in situ in niches built into the walls of the room (Pedersén 1998: 194–7 for details and further refs.). In 2002 further excavations by Iraqi archaeologists revealed fragmentary building remains dated to the Neo-Babylonian era, as well as a couple of graves of the same period or possibly later (Fadhil and Alsamarraee 2005).

The site of Isin was excavated between 1973 and 1989 by archaeologists from Munich University. Near the Gula temple they found a dog cemetery dated to the early 1st millennium BC (the dog was a symbol of the goddess Gula) (Hrouda 1977: 18–19; Livingstone 1988). The Gula temple itself is known to have been restored by Nebuchadnezzar II, whose stamped bricks were found in and around the building (Hrouda 1987: 151). In other soundings, remains of this period were too poorly preserved to shed much light on the Neo-Babylonian settlement, although a near-complete house was excavated in Nordabschnitt III (Ayoub 1981).

Nippur consists of two areas of high mounds bisected by an ancient northwest–southeast watercourse, once a branch of the Euphrates. On the northeastern side are the temples of Enlil (the Ekur) and Inanna and the North Temple, as well as soundings TA, TB, and TC. To the southwest of the ancient watercourse soundings WA and WB were excavated on the high mound, while the WC soundings were located at the low-lying, southernmost extremity of the site. Excavations at Nippur by a team from the University of Pennsylvania began in the late 19th century. In the mid-20th century work was undertaken jointly by archaeologists from the universities of Pennsylvania and Chicago, and subsequently (1972 onward) by a team led by McG. Gibson of the Oriental Institute (Chicago). According to his account of the settlement's history, Nippur was a mere village from the 11th to the 8th century BC, but then underwent a revival during the 8th and especially the 7th century BC (Gibson 1992: 46–9). The Assyrian kings Esarhaddon and Assurbanipal (and his brother, the Babylonian regent Shamash-shum-ukin) implemented major construction projects, including the rebuilding of the city wall and the restoration of several temples. The construction of the wall was similar to that of Babylon, with an inner and outer wall surrounded by a moat, in this case apparently a dry one (Gibson et al. 1998: 26–7). Though none of the city gates has been excavated, the names of several which are known from everyday documents of the mid-1st millennium BC feature on the so-called "Kassite city map" of Nippur (Ch. I.28 and Fig. 28.8), suggesting that the general layout of the city at this time resembled that of the later 2nd millennium. In contrast to the attention it received at the hands of the

Neo-Assyrian kings, Nippur appears to have been neglected by the Neo-Babylonian rulers, who left scarcely any trace of major works at the site. This may well have been a matter of deliberate policy whose background lay in the downgrading of the city's major deity, Enlil, in favor of the god Marduk, now head of the Babylonian pantheon, with his seat in Babylon (Baker forthcoming). In spite of this royal neglect, the city remained occupied and remains of housing dated to the 7th and 6th centuries, such as the houses (Buildings A and B) excavated in the WC-2 area (Gibson et al. 1983; Baker 2010: 190–3), have been uncovered. Housing was also excavated in the TA sounding. Armstrong's (1989) re-evaluation of its stratigraphy has made a vital contribution to clarifying the ceramic sequence for the earlier 1st millennium.

Neo-Babylonian remains at Larsa have been mainly uncovered in the area of the Shamash temple, Ebabbar, and the *ziggurat*. When Nabonidus rebuilt the *ziggurat*, he was the first ruler to carry out work on it since the Old Babylonian period (Bachelot and Castel 1989: 75). In the 2nd millennium the *ziggurat* precinct was separated from the mound on which the Ebabbar temple was situated by two substantial courtyards, but these seem not to have been rebuilt in Neo-Babylonian times. The Ebabbar was the focus of building activity by Nebuchadnezzar, who, in addition to rebuilding it, constructed an oval enclosure wall around the small mound on which it was situated (Huot 1985; Huot et al. 1987). Nabonidus also carried out some work on the temple.

Tell al-Lahm (ancient Kissik) was excavated by Iraqi archaeologists in the 1940s (Safar 1949). Of the two mounds which make up the site (Wright 1981a: 345, nos. 172 and 173), the more northerly one was found to contain significant remains of the 1st millennium BC. On the basis of seven soundings there, three levels were identified: the lowest was dated to the late Neo-Assyrian period, the middle to the Neo-Babylonian era, and the latest to the Achaemenid period. The Neo-Babylonian level yielded a cylinder of Nabonidus commemorating his reconstruction of a temple of Ningal, presumably located at the site (though not excavated). An area of Neo-Babylonian housing was uncovered comprising partial plans of two adjacent structures, together with some graves of this period, but beyond this little is known about the character of the urban settlement.

The extent of Neo-Babylonian occupation at Ur has been estimated at c.40 hectares (Wright 1981a: 338, no. 10). During the period of Neo-Assyrian domination, a substantial amount of rebuilding work was carried out by Sin-balassu-iqbi, a governor during the reign of Assurbanipal (Woolley 1965: 4). Both Nebuchadnezzar II and Nabonidus also carried out various construction projects at Ur (Woolley and Mallowan 1962). However, the remains of this period were badly eroded, to the extent that their poor state of preservation has hampered understanding of the excavated levels. Nebuchadnezzar rebuilt a number of major shrines within the religious center dedicated to the moon-god, which he surrounded with a massive *temenos* wall. Nabonidus rebuilt the *ziggurat* of Sin and the Ningal temple Enunmah, and constructed the Egipar for the newly installed Entu-priestess (his daughter). He is also credited with having built the palace next to the North Harbor. A small area of private housing crossed by streets was excavated in the AH area southeast of the *temenos*; House 1, with a triple courtyard layout, is one of the largest houses known from this period. Evidence has also been found for the rebuilding of the city wall during this period; its rather insubstantial remains have been ascribed to Nebuchadnezzar (Woolley 1974: 63).

The vast site of Uruk, with its city wall originally enclosing an area of 550 hectares, has been the subject of many seasons of investigation by German archaeologists, beginning in 1912. The Neo-Babylonian levels are scheduled for publication by A. Kose; in the meantime, a series of preliminary reports is available (UVB), as well as the final reports, such as the one on graves (Boehmer at al. 1995), which include discussion of Neo-Babylonian material. At the center of Neo-Babylonian Uruk lay the great Eanna temple precinct, including its *ziggurat*, dedicated to the goddess Ishtar. Within Eanna, various building operations were carried out by Merodach-baladan II, Sargon II, Esarhaddon, and Nebuchadnezzar. Areas of residential housing have been excavated immediately to the west and southwest of the main temple precinct; these were, in turn, located within a greater walled enclosure associated with the temple complex. Judging from the contents of the tablets in archives excavated in this housing area, it was occupied by mid-level temple personnel. Another *ziggurat*, that of the god Anu, located some distance west of Eanna, was rebuilt by Esarhaddon (Kose 1998: 133). Beyond this central area of the city occupied by the temple and associated housing, little is known of the settlement of this period. An *akitu* house (where the New Year's festival was celebrated) located outside of the city wall is known to have been rebuilt by Nabonidus. The city wall seems to have lain in ruins by this time, though it survived as a monument and the written sources show that it was still used by the inhabitants to distinguish urban space from the steppe beyond. Aerial photography has revealed the presence of intramural canals at Uruk; these are difficult to date, but textual sources confirm that some canals in the city were certainly in use at this time.

5 Monumental Architecture

Monumental architecture clearly encompasses palaces, temples and *ziggurats*, city walls, and processional streets, but we should also take into account other large-scale construction projects which involved a significant investment of labor, resources, and planning, such as artificial waterways (canals, whether urban or rural, and their associated features such as embankments) and cross-country defensive structures. The building (or rebuilding) of monumental structures was essentially the prerogative of the ruler. Rare exceptions to this involve the (re)construction of temples by local officials, generally at times when central government was relatively weak.

The only royal palaces to have been excavated are those located in Babylon (Kuhrt 2001a; Miglus 2004). Heinrich (1984: 198–231) discussed the Neo-Babylonian palaces in the context of the Mesopotamian architectural tradition of palace building. Several palaces situated in other cities are mentioned in cuneiform sources (Jursa 2004a), though with one exception (see below) none has yet been identified and excavated. Nothing is known of any palace in the capital Babylon prior to the reign of Nabopolassar, first builder of the South Palace (*Südburg*) in the area of the later *Westhof*. Nabopolassar's work was continued by his son Nebuchadnezzar, who extended the South Palace as far east as the Processional Street. The building comprised a linear arrangement of five units, each with its own central courtyard. The functions of these courtyard units encompassed administration and storage at the eastern end of the palace, with the central unit housing the throne room suite and residential suites situated in the units to the west. The South Palace occupied a corner formed by the Euphrates river to the west, and the city wall to the north; it was heavily fortified at its western end where it adjoined the river. On the other side of the city wall Nebuchadnezzar built another palace, the so-called North Palace (*Hauptburg*). The remains of this building were badly preserved and the plan of the palace is poorly understood. It too adjoined the Processional Street to the east, where its course extended northward beyond the Ishtar Gate. A third Summer Palace was built some distance to the north of the main city walls, in the corner formed by the defensive wall which Nebuchadnezzar built to the east of the city.

The only building which can be identified with some certainty as a local governor's palace is the so-called "Palace of the Entu-priestesses" or "Palace of Bel-shalti-Nannar" at Ur (Woolley and Mallowan 1962: 41–3, Pl. 70) which shares certain design features with the South Palace at Babylon, though it was built on a considerably smaller scale (c.5,743 square meters, compared with more than 43,000 square meters for the South Palace). The building occupied a roughly trapezoidal plot by the North Harbor of Ur, and was surrounded by a substantial outer wall with a corridor running around much of its internal face, except for on the north side and at the southeast corner, where a number of rooms were built up against the wall's inner face. The corridor in turn enclosed the palace building proper, comprising four courtyard suites, the largest of which occupied the southwest sector of the building. The surviving floor of the building was paved with bricks of Nabonidus, but these came from another building.

The temples of this era fall into two categories: the main temple of a city's patron deity which lay within its own walled enclosure (and which might well incorporate the shrines of a good many other deities), and other freestanding temples which were scattered around the city, often in residential quarters, and which had no precinct of their own. This distinction is important not merely from the point of view of the typology of cultic structures, but also for the spatial organization of the cultic activities associated with the care and feeding of the gods. The great temple precincts housed substantial working areas where such activities were performed, whereas the free-standing temples were relatively restricted as to the facilities they could accommodate.

The *ziggurat*, comprising a massive stepped tower with a shrine on top, was normally located within the precinct of the city's major temple, though at Babylon the *ziggurat* Etemenanki had its own enclosure, which was separated from that of the great Marduk temple, Esagila, by the east–west stretch of the Processional Street leading to the east bank of the river. Some cities are known to have had two *ziggurats*. Cultic pedestals and daises were also located in the streets (Baker 2009: 96–7).

The layout of the Neo-Babylonian temple consisted of the same basic elements as the palace at one end of the scale and the typical residential house at the other: a central courtyard enclosed on all sides, with the principal room(s) – in this case the cella(s) – normally situated on the south side. Some temples contained smaller, subsidiary courtyards (e.g., the Ishhara temple, Babylon), while others were single-courtyard affairs (e.g., the Ninurta temple, Babylon). The main entrance was often located on the side opposite the cella(s) and its exterior was marked by projecting towers decorated with pilasters.

A number of ceremonial streets are known from Neo-Babylonian textual sources (Miglus 2006), but only one of these has so far been excavated, namely the Processional Way at Babylon. It ran along the eastern side of Nebuchadnezzar's South Palace and exited the city wall via the Ishtar Gate, continuing northward past the North Palace (*Hauptburg*) and beyond. To the south of the South Palace, it continued past the *ziggurat* precinct, turning to the west at its southeast corner and running as far as the bridge over the Euphrates built by Nabopolassar (or possibly his son). The excavated levels of the Processional Way were built by Nebuchadnezzar, but some of the limestone blocks with which its surface was paved were reused: they bore inscriptions of Nebuchadnezzar on the upper side, but inscriptions of Sennacherib (704–681 BC) on their underside; the Assyrian king was probably responsible for an earlier phase of construction.

Turning to the question of defensive structures, among the great monuments planned and constructed by Nebuchadnezzar II were two cross-country walls aimed at strengthening the defenses of the realm. One of these, running some distance to the north of Sippar, stretched between the Euphrates and Tigris rivers at around the point where their courses ran closest together. Part of this massive baked brick structure, known as Habl as-Sahr, has recently been excavated (Black et al. 1987). The other cross-country wall, situated to the east of Babylon in the vicinity of Kish, is known from textual sources but has not been located for certain on the ground (see Reade 2010 for a discussion of various landscape features in this vicinity and their possible identification with projects described in Nebuchadnezzar's inscriptions).

Nebuchadnezzar's strategy in focusing on the defense of Babylonia's northern borders – presumably perceived as the most likely direction from which an external threat might come – is evident not only in the construction of these massive cross-country walls, but also in the treatment of the walls of the Babylonian cities: those of the key cities of northern Babylonia (Babylon, Borsippa, Kish, Kutha) were rebuilt and kept in good order, while archaeological evidence indicates that those of the south (Ur, Uruk) were not (Baker forthcoming). This seems to reflect a considered policy of concentrating resources on fortifying the northern part of the Babylonian heartland, near to its point of entry, while neglecting the south.

Royal construction projects involving watercourses may be divided into two groups: canals in the rural hinterland, and watercourses and related structures in and around cities. The former have generally not yet been the subject of detailed archaeological research (see Cole and Gasche 1998 for the current state of knowledge, and Reade 2010 on Nebuchadnezzar's lagoons to the east of Babylon). Nabopolassar canalized an old branch of the Euphrates just north of Sippar, the so-called King's Canal (Brinkman 1998–2001: 15). In an urban context, water-related structures include river embankments, bridges, intramural canals, and moats; examples of all of these have been excavated at Babylon (see the references given above).

6 Domestic Architecture

Houses of this period typically comprised a single, unroofed central courtyard enclosed on all four sides by suites of rooms; occasionally they might contain two courtyards, and more rarely even three, in the case of exceptionally large houses. Each side of the courtyard had a centrally placed doorway by which the main room on that side of the house was accessed. Often these main rooms gave access to further, smaller rooms, the whole forming a self-contained suite. Houses were generally orientated southeast–northwest, and the largest room/suite – presumably the main living area – was typically the one situated at the southeast side of the courtyard, while the second-largest room/suite was the one facing it on the northern side of the house. The exterior wall presented a blank, unadorned façade to the outside world, without windows and normally with a single entrance located at the farthest end of the house from the main living room. Sometimes adjacent houses shared a party wall; this seems to be connected with status, since the larger, better appointed houses tended to be free-standing, even when they were situated right next to another house.

Neo-Babylonian houses were constructed of sundried mudbrick; baked brick was reserved for certain features such as the paving of the courtyard and of rooms which were exposed to water, and for built drains, toilet installations, and the like. The roofs were made using locally available timbers, which could span rooms of up to c.3.5–4 meters in width. These beams were overlain with reeds or reed matting, which was in turn overlain by a slab of straw-tempered mud (Baker 2007: 70–2; 2010, 2011, forthcoming).

7 Material Culture and Long-Distance Trade

The written sources attest to a wide variety of commodities imported into Babylonia over a long distance, including metals (Cypriot copper, Cilician iron); alum (Egypt); dyes, mordants, and colored textiles (the Levant); wines and aromatics (Syria); timber for construction (Lebanon); and aromatics (Arabia and the east) (Jursa 2004b: 129–132). Many of these were, of course, perishable, and actual finds of imported goods tend to be restricted to the kinds of precious items found in graves, such as items of jewelry made of gemstones and/or precious metals. Other products of skilled craftsmanship include the inlaid wood and ivory box found in Grave 423 at Uruk (Boehmer et al. 1995: Taf. 158–159). Cylinder seals and stamp seals were also, of necessity, usually made of imported materials (on their iconography, see Collon 1987: 80–3, with further discussion in Collon 2001). The few rare cylinder seals that are provenienced come mostly from Ur and Uruk (Collon 2001: 1; note also M. Sax's summary of the materials identified on p. 19, and the discussion of the provenience of the materials used in Babylonian seals on pp. 33–4). Locally made artifacts include anthropomorphic terracotta figurines such as those excavated at Babylon (Klengel-Brandt and Cholidis 2006).

8 Beyond Babylonia

Outside Babylonia itself, the effects of Babylonian imperialism can be seen more in the destruction levels that can occasionally be related to the conquests of its rulers than in any evidence for a governmental infrastructure imposed from the center. Evidence of the process of post-conquest integration is conspicuous by its absence, thus it is extremely difficult to develop anything approaching a model for the archaeology of empire at this period, since Babylonian rule left so few material culture traces in the areas under its control.

After the fall of Assyria at the end of the 7th century BC, it seems clear that Babylonia (rather than Media) exercised control over northern Mesopotamia, as well as over the northern Levant, and in recent years increasing attention has been paid to the Neo-Babylonian presence in the former Assyrian heartland. The evidence remains scanty because of the more or less complete collapse of urban life at this time, which means that no substantial, post-Assyrian occupation levels have been detected at any of the former major urban sites. Moreover, potentially relevant finds are difficult to evaluate because it is rarely possible to distinguish remains datable to the period of Neo-Babylonian control from those of the Achaemenid period which followed, hence the catch-all label "post-Assyrian" that has been applied to the material culture, especially the ceramics, of northern

Mesopotamia at this time. Beyond the heartland this problem is being addressed by study of the ceramic material found in situ at Dur-Katlimmu (mod. Tell Sheikh Hamad) in the Khabur valley, where the so-called "Red House" continued in use throughout the 6th century BC. Kreppner (2008) determined that there was continuity in ceramic production at the site from the mid-7th to the early 5th century BC, although he detected a decline in general living standards over the course of the 6th century. Thus, he concluded that the term "post-Assyrian" is of merely historical significance and has no application in the sphere of ceramics.

The northern Mesopotamian evidence for the presence of, or contact with, Babylonians is rather limited. It includes sparse finds of tablets, such as the Assyrian tablets found at Dur-Katlimmu which were dated to the reign of Nebuchadnezzar II according to the Babylonian convention. Babylonian tablets written after the fall of Assyria were also found at Guzana (Tell Halaf). In the case of other items identified (however tentatively) as Neo-Babylonian, in the absence of an unequivocal, well-stratified context it cannot necessarily be assumed that they reflect a post-612 BC Babylonian presence, since they could equally well represent either imports or the personal effects of Babylonian immigrants or visitors during the later decades of the Assyrian empire. Remains which might be indicative of Babylonian infrastructure are lacking. Two small, post-Assyrian temples at Assur have been assigned to the Neo-Babylonian period, with a Parthian-period rebuilding (Andrae 1977[1938]: 164–6). This has generally been followed by subsequent authors (e.g., Haider 2008: 194–5), while Czichon (1998–2001: 205) attributes them specifically to Nebuchadnezzar II, without adducing any evidence. However, there are no grounds for dating the construction of these shrines to the Neo-Babylonian period. Curtis (2003: 161) cited a suggestion by M. Roaf that they may have been founded in the Parthian era, though an Achaemenid or Seleucid date seems equally possible.

Harran was the last refuge of the Assyrians following the conquest of their heartland. However, remains of this era (late 7th century BC) have not been excavated, except for monuments of the last Neo-Babylonian ruler. Four stelae dating from the reign of Nabonidus were found, unfortunately not in their original contexts but reused as part of the fabric of the Great Mosque (Gadd 1958). Two bore the well-known inscription of Nabonidus's mother, Adda-guppi, in which it is claimed that she lived for 104 years until her death in the ninth year of her son's reign; the other two were inscribed with a text of Nabonidus himself. Additional fragments of inscriptions found by D.S. Rice in deep soundings in the area of the Great Mosque suggest that it was indeed the site of the earlier Sin temple which Nabonidus rebuilt and which is where the stelae may originally have stood (Saggs 1969).

Turning to the Levant, rock inscriptions of Nebuchadnezzar II have been found in Lebanon, at Nahr el-Kelb and Wadi Brissa (new studies are being prepared by R. da Riva). In Jordan, a poorly preserved Neo-Babylonian rock relief and inscription recently discovered at Sela' near Buseirah has been tentatively attributed to Nabonidus and perhaps reflects the route taken by that king on his way to Tayma (Ch. II.43) (Dalley and Goguel 1997). Dalley goes on to suggest that the destruction levels found at Buseira, Tawilan and Tall al-Khalayfi may be related to Nabonidus's subjection of Edom (Dalley and Goguel 1997: 175).

These monuments are clearly testimony to Neo-Babylonian political domination of the region. However, apart from the destruction levels found at a number of sites which have been attributed to the actions of Nebuchadnezzar's army, other material traces of a Babylonian presence are remarkably scarce. In this respect it is difficult to reconcile the archaeological remains with the historical record, which suggests rather a firm grip on the region (Katzenstein 1997: 335). It is often assumed that Neo-Babylonian rulers simply took over the previously existing Neo-Assyrian governmental infrastructure, though Vanderhooft (2003: 236–7) noted that by 605 BC direct Assyrian control over Judah had been defunct for two, if not three, decades. Stern (2001: 348–50) wrote of a vacuum during the Neo-Babylonian period, with settlements that were destroyed during the Neo-Babylonian conquest being rebuilt only in the Persian period. He concluded that in the archaeology of Palestine "there is virtually no clearly defined period that may be called "Babylonian," for it was a time from which almost no material finds remain" (Stern 2001: 350; cf. Vanderhooft 2003: 253).

Nabonidus, the last Neo-Babylonian king (556–539 BC), is known to have stayed for 10 years in the oasis city of Tayma (Ch. II.43) in northwestern Arabia (Dandamayev 1998–2001: 8). Recent excavations at the site have uncovered evidence for the Neo-Babylonian presence there, including a fragment of a stele of Nabonidus (Eichmann et al. 2006). However, the palace which the king is known from written sources to have built there has not yet been found. In the vicinity of Tayma a handful of rock inscriptions bear the names of members of Nabonidus' military entourage; these particular individuals seem not to have been of Babylonian extraction, judging from their personal names (Müller and al-Said 2002).

As for the Persian Gulf region, a votive inscription on a bronze vessel found on Failaka (part of ancient Dilmun) indicates that the local temple Ekarra, known from earlier periods, was in use during the reign of Nebuchadnezzar; it was very likely dedicated to the god Shamash of Larsa. A stone slab with an inscription identifying it as belonging to the palace of Nebuchadnezzar, king of Babylon, has also been found on Failaka; however, it was probably en route to Babylon when it was deposited and does not reflect the presence of a royal palace on Dilmun itself (Ferrara 1975; cf. Potts 1990: 348–9; Glassner 2008: 190–1, 193). Burials of Neo-Babylonian type have also been found on Bahrain (Potts 1985: 702 with refs.).

GUIDE TO FURTHER READING

This chapter draws heavily on the author's forthcoming study of Babylonian cities of the 1st millennium BC, where a more detailed treatment of the archaeological and written evidence for each site can be found (Baker forthcoming). To date, no general account of Neo-Babylonian material culture has been written; for a recent introduction to the art of the period, see Hrouda (1998–2001). On *kudurrus,* see Slanski (2003; with additional comments and corrections by Charpin 2002 and Brinkman 2006). On burial practices, see Baker (1995) and especially the detailed publication of Neo-Babylonian graves from Uruk in Boehmer et al. (1995). For a general discussion of the factors influencing the physical form of the Babylonian city, see Baker (2007), and for a discussion of the various categories of unbuilt urban land at this period, see Baker (2009). For a detailed overview of Neo-Babylonian temple architecture, see Heinrich (1982: 243–82). The same author discusses the Neo-Babylonian palaces in the context of the Mesopotamian architectural tradition of palace building (Heinrich 1984: 198–231). A comprehensive overview of Babylonian housing in early 1st millennium BC, with numerous illustrations, can be found in Miglus (1999: 177–213). On Neo-Babylonian settlement patterns, see the invaluable critique of Brinkman (1984b), who examines the survey data in the light of the written documentation for the period 1150–625 BC. See also Cole and Gasche (1998) on the watercourses of northern Babylonia. For a summary of the results of the German excavations at Babylon, see Koldewey (1990); Oates (1988) is also a good general introduction. In addition, several recent volumes have been devoted to the archaeology and history of Babylon, including Renger (1999) and the well-illustrated books accompanying the major exhibitions held in Berlin, Paris, and London (Marzahn 2008; André-Salvini 2008; and Finkel and Seymour 2008, respectively). The Neo-Babylonian presence in Assyria is treated in detail by Curtis (2003), with further relevant discussion in Curtis (2005b).

CHAPTER FIFTY

The Achaemenid Heartland: An Archaeological-Historical Perspective

Wouter F.M. Henkelman

1 Geographical, Climatic, and Chronological Setting

Though the Achaemenid heartland in a strict sense corresponds roughly to the modern Iranian province of Fārs (ancient Pārsa, Περσίς), its immediate cultural and historical context comprised parts of the provinces of Esfahān, Yāzd, Kermān and Būšehr, as well as Khūzestān, where a Neo-Elamite kingdom existed until c.540 or 520 BC. An Iranian presence was noticeable on Elam's northern and eastern borders from the 7th century BC onward and Elamite culture provided a critical impulse for the early Persians (Henkelman 2008a). When Darius I (522–486 BC) transformed Susa into a principal Achaemenid residence (c.520 BC), he confirmed Elam's special status and de facto made it part of the empire's core. In fact, the bipolarity of lowland Khūzestān and highland Fārs had characterized successive Elamite states from the 3rd millennium onward (Amiet 1979; Potts 1999; Miroschedji 2003; for other parts of Achaemenid Iran, see Boucharlat 2005).

In physical terms, the area comprises the southern Zagros range of northwest–southeast-oriented valleys, ending in larger intermontane plains (the Kūr River basin, including the Marv Dašt with Persepolis); the Būšehr province coastal plains (and further east?); and the Khūzestān alluvial plain. As the ancient coastline extended further northwestward than it does today, only higher Khūzestān is relevant here, roughly the area north of Ahwāz (Gasche 2004, 2005, 2007; Heyvaert and Baeteman 2007). A range of foothills, a crucial transition zone

---

A Companion to the Archaeology of the Ancient Near East, First Edition.
Edited by D.T. Potts.
© 2012 Blackwell Publishing Ltd. Published 2012 by Blackwell Publishing Ltd.

(c.50–75 kilometers wide), intervenes between Khūzestān and the higher Zagros valleys and is approximately defined by the Masğed-e Soleymān, Rām Hormoz, and Behbahān plains. Natural boundaries include the Persian Gulf (though the Achaemenids were by no means "land-locked"), the actual Iranian plateau in the northwest, and the western Tigris/al-Hawīza marshes.

The Achaemenid heartland comprised a great variety of climatic zones (Carter and Stolper 1984: 103–7; Potts 1999: 10–42). The Khūzestān plain alone has three – arid, semi-arid, and dry – divided by ranges of low hills (Carter and Stolper 1984: 103–7; Alizadeh 1992: 15–17; Steve et al. 2002/3: 360). Susa is on the 300 mm isohyet, at the southern edge of the upper zone stretching from the northwestern Deh Lorān plain to the Izeh valley in the east. As for the southern Zagros, contemporary tribal terminology sometimes distinguishes four altitudinal climate zones, between which conditions may differ radically: dry and warm coastal lowlands and foothills well suited for date culture (*garmsir*, up to 900–1300 meters); a fertile and populous moderate zone with grape, fruit, and vegetable cultivation (*moʿtadel*); higher and colder lands suited for summer pasture and cereal cultivation (*sardsīr*, starting at 2,000–2200 meters); and an alpine zone (*sarhadd*) with summits rising to 4000 meters, fit only for summer pasture (Bobek 1968; Planhol 2000; Alizadeh 2006: 30–31). A similar "vertical" categorization is preserved in Strabo (*Geography* 15.3.1) and Arrian (*Indica* 40.2–4), who drew on descriptions of Pārsa from the late Achaemenid period. Classical sources also preserve reports of the lush scenery of the Persepolis region, attesting to the massive projects undertaken by the Achaemenids to exploit their lands (Q. Curtius, *Hist.* V.4.5–9, Diodorus 17.67.3; cf. Briant 2002: 443, 943).

In contrast to such seemingly straightforward images, quantifiable data on 1st millennium climatic conditions are scarce and contradictory (Potts 1999: 19–22; McCall 2009: 36–7). Whereas sediment samples from Lake Mīrābād (Lorestān) registered no conspicuous variations for the period (Van Zeist 1967; Stevens et al. 2006), recent pollen analysis of a core from Lake Mahārlū near Šīrāz identified drastic vegetation change c.2800 BP, probably related to intensified grazing and possibly coinciding with a period of increased drought (Djamali et al. 2009: 131–2; cf. McCall 2009: 43–4, 239–43).

The existence of the Achaemenid empire (c.550–330 BC) is not reflected sharply in the archaeological record. Ceramic horizons from the early, late and post-Achaemenid periods remain imperfectly defined. Historians and archaeologists are increasingly aware that Herodotus' reductive image of Cyrus' appearance from a cultural and historical void has lost all relevance as a leading (if often implicit) paradigm. A longer incubation period necessarily preceded the rise of empire. Likewise, the fall of the Achaemenids did not constitute the complete rupture that Alexander historians (ancient and modern) like it to be, but should be seen against the backdrop of a longer transition period, with continuities reaching far into the Seleucid period (Ch. II.54). Our chronological scope here is therefore broader, c.750–300 BC, and comprises the Neo-Elamite II (in

Khūzestān, c.725–520 BC)/Iron Age III (in Fārs, c.800–550 BC), Achaemenid and early post-Achaemenid periods (the last two sometimes labeled "Iron IV").

2 Neo-Elamite Beginnings

Although the old diffusionist theory that made the Achaemenids direct heirs of a fully-formed Indo-Iranian culture still lingers, a new perspective has become firmly established in recent decades. Instead of the unhelpful and undesirable image of a take-over by culturally advanced Indo-Iranian migrants, Achaemenid or Persian culture is increasingly seen as a product of southwestern Iran. There, the "ethnogenèse des Perses" (ethnogenesis of the Persians) took shape, resulting from centuries of cohabitation, acculturation, and integration by Indo-Iranians and Elamites (Miroschedji 1985, 1990, 2003).

Persian identity, as it emerged in the 8th and 7th centuries BC (or earlier), was *inclusive* and far from limited to inherited Indo-Iranian traditions. Examples of this circumstance range from the Persepolis pantheon, in which gods of Indo-Iranian and Elamite ancestry were treated indiscriminately (Henkelman 2008a, 2011), to the extensive use of Elamite in inscriptions and as the main administrative language in the heartland (exported even to Kandahār; Henkelman 2008a: 78–9; 2010: 714 n174). In fact, from the standpoint of linguistic typology, Achaemenid Elamite presents a restructured variety of Elamite, resulting from considerable imposition of Old Iranian morphology and syntax, and attests to the widespread usage of Elamite by Iranophones (Henkelman in press a). As such, it provides a reverse parallel to the contact varieties of Indo-Iranian languages of central India, which resulted from prolonged cohabitation of speakers of Indo-Iranian and speakers of Dravidian languages and a shift of the latter to Indo-Iranian (Gumperz and Wilson 1971; Southworth 1971).

In material culture, the Arğān hoard (Behbahān region) and what is left of the Kalmākarra hoard (Saimarreh region, southern Lorestān), from the late 7th or early 6th century, unmistakably attest to Iranian-Elamite acculturation (Ch. II.39), signifying transition rather than rupture (Curtis 2005c: 125–6; Boucharlat 2005: 246–8; Henkelman 2003a; 2008a: 28–32; Álvarez-Mon 2010). A major factor must have been the persistence of the Elamite state in the post-Assyrian period, which has been argued on philological and archaeological grounds (Miroschedji 1981b, 1981c; Boucharlat 1990a; Vallat 1996; Tavernier 2004, 2006; Henkelman 2008a: 1–57). In fact, the brutal Assyrian campaigns of the 640s BC did not leave clear markers in either the stratigraphy or the material culture of Susa and central Khūzestān, hence Miroschedji's chronological definition of Neo-Elamite II as c.725–520 (Miroschedji 1981a; cf. Henkelman 2003a: 183, 2003b: 253).

Despite a great deal of scholarly attention, the earliest Indo-Iranians, presumably agropastoralist tribes, remain elusive in the archaeological record of Iron III southwestern Iran (c.800–550 BC). The predominantly painted Šogā and Taymūrān A wares have tentatively been linked to them (Sumner 1994, following M.B. Nicol), as has a distinctive grey ware found at Čogā Miš (northeastern Khūzestān) and about 20 sites in valleys northwest of the Marv Dašt (Alizadeh 2003b: 88, 93–97; 2006: 54, 159; 2008: 48). Apart from the problems involved in linking ethnic identities with ceramic traditions, chronological difficulties arise, however. The first two wares do not seem to post-date c.900/800 BC (or perhaps c.700); the third at least partially dates to the early Achaemenid period (Jacobs 1994; Delougaz and Kantor 1996: 10–18; Overlaet 1997: 20, 48–9; 2007: 73–75; Boucharlat 2005: 226–8, 239). The gap, perhaps more apparent than real, between the end of the Iron II horizon in Fārs (Qal'eh, Šogā, Taymūrān) c.1000–800/700 BC, and the appearance of Achaemenid "Late Plain Ware" at 550/520 BC (or even later), is one of the gravest problems in the study of 1st millennium Iran (cf. Boucharlat 2003a; Young 2003). It is now partially being bridged by survey and excavations in the Mamasanī region in western Fārs, where Neo-Elamite wares have tentatively been identified at 11 sites, at least four of which were occupied during the Neo-Elamite II (roughly equivalent to Iron Age III) *and* the ensuing Achaemenid period (McCall 2009: 202–203, 235–238, 248; cf. 188 on Čalābād wares). Excavations at Tol-e Nūrābād revealed Neo-Elamite levels directly below the Achaemenid settlement (McCall 2009: 237; Weeks et al. 2006a). Similar continuity can be observed in the Rām Hormoz plain, at Tappeh Bormī (ancient Huhnur), Tall-e Ǧazīr and perhaps other sites (Carter 1994; Carter and Wright 2003). Other surveys have not always made a distinction between Neo-Elamite I and II ceramics, but continued settlement of a dozen sites in the Miān Āb plain and the corridor between Rām Hormoz and Šuštar (Moghaddam and Miri 2003, 2007) and six sites in the Būšehr hinterland (Carter et al. 2006) from the later Elamite through the (post-)Achaemenid periods is plausible. In lowland Khūzestān, continuous occupation in the Neo-Elamite II and Achaemenid periods is attested at Susa and a limited number of other sites though, in contrast to Tol-e Nūrābād, the transition is not yet documented stratigraphically (Miroschedji 1981a, 1981b, 1981c, 1987a; cf. Boucharlat 1994).

Though historical conditions in the three regions just mentioned are likely to have differed from central Fārs (notably the Kūr River basin), it is significant that the dearth of Iron Age III horizons in that area emerges as an isolated phenomenon. Only the establishment of a more definitive chronology of 1st millennium ceramic sequences will determine whether it is reflective of divergent circumstances or is simply an artifact of insufficient exploration.

Whereas the spread of various Iron Age I–II grey wares in northwestern and central Iran in the later 2nd and early 1st millennium (Young 1985, 1988: 8–9) is nowadays disputed as an indicator of Indo-Iranian migrations, as is the very concept of (mass) migration (Dittmann 1990: 134–5; 2001; Azarnoush and Helwing 2005: 232–3), it is still tempting to situate the hypothetical appearance, or rather formation, of Indo-Iranian groups in southwestern Iran at least some centuries before the emergence of the Achaemenid empire. This would conform with Neo-Assyrian and Neo-Elamite cuneiform sources (Waters 1999; Henkelman in press a) indicating that certain groups in Fārs from the late 8th to the early 6th centuries BC already referred to themselves as *Pārsa-*. This is not to say that such groups can be readily identified as "early Persians" any more than they can be equated with the elusive Indo-Iranian migrants, but rather that we are dealing with various proto-Persian formations which, when first mentioned, already appear to be integrated into a larger cultural and political matrix. At the very minimum, this suggests a period of prolonged exposure to the Elamite and other resident cultures, if not an entirely local development indeed, best described as the Persian ethnogenesis.

3 Surveys

Survey results are beginning to yield comprehensive occupation patterns for the period(s) and region under discussion. Unfortunately, they cannot be readily compared, since various (Neo-)Elamite horizons have not always been recorded separately and the definition of Achaemenid pottery has varied considerably. The excavators of Persepolis and Pasargadae dated Late Plain Ware to the late and post-Achaemenid periods (Schmidt 1957: 96, Pls. 71–74; Stronach 1974b: 243–5; 1978: 183–5), which left the early Achaemenid period basically undocumented. Sumner, Miroschedji, and others subsequently re-dated the beginning of Late Plain Ware to the later 6th century (Sumner 1986b, 1994; Miroschedji 1987a: 32–35; cf. Boucharlat and Haerinck 1991), which would accord with continuities with Iron Age III horizons from the (central and northern) Zagros. The excavations at Tol-e Nūrābād and especially Tol-e Spīd seem to confirm the new dating, though additional radiocarbon dates are required to establish it with certainty (Potts et al. 2006: 12; Weeks et al. 2006a: 77–78; Petrie, Asgari Chaverdi, and Seyedin 2006: 132; Petrie, Weeks et al. 2006: 181–2; Asgari Chaverdi et al. 2010).

Contemporary with the Fārs tradition, there is a related yet different tradition (with a stronger emphasis on glazed and so-called eggshell wares), known at Susa, some sites in the surrounding plain, and central and southern Mesopotamia (Miroschedji 1981a, 1981b, 1981c, 1987a: 32–5; Stronach 1987b: 293–4; Boucharlat 1987b: 192–4; 2003a). Sites on the fringes of lowland Khūzestān – the northern plains of Deh Lorān and Patak (Miroschedji 1981c), Čoḡā Miš in the northeast, the eastern Zagros foothills – generally adhere to the highland tradition (see Alizadeh 2008: 48 on Čoḡā Miš; but cf. Boucharlat 2005: 239 on parallels with Susa). Both wares seem to persist into the post-Achaemenid period, although a well-dated stratigraphy is not yet available (cf. Boucharlat 2005, 2006).

Starting with Jacques de Morgan in the late 19th entury, numerous surveys have been and are being undertaken in southwestern Iran (Sumner 1990b; McCall 2009: 7–17). Before World War II, a campaign of aerial photography initiated by Erich F. Schmidt in 1935–7 covered vast stretches of Lorestān and Fārs (Schmidt 1940). Around the same time, Sir Marc Aurel Stein made four extensive journeys through southern and western Iran, surveying, among other areas, the Mamasanī region, the Behbahān plain, and the Īzeh valley, the districts of Fasā and Dārāb, and the entire coast from Bandar Abbās to Būšehr (Stein 1934, 1936, 1937, 1940; cf. Kerner 1993). Although concentrating on earlier periods, Stein recorded a number of Achaemenid sites such as Qalēh-ye Kalī (also known as Ǧīnğīn or Tappeh Sūrūvān) and conducted soundings at Tall-e Zohāk and Pasargadae. After the war, Louis Vanden Berghe surveyed the Marv Dašt (the Persepolis plain) and did test excavations at seven sites, resulting in a pioneering chronology of the region's ceramic horizons (Vanden Berghe 1952, 1954; 1959: 37–45; cf. Overlaet 1997, 2007; Haerinck and Overlaet 2003).

Central Khūzestān has been surveyed more extensively than other areas (Boucharlat 1990a: 157–66; Kouchoukos and Hole 2003). Miroschedji (1981c) tentatively identified 23 sites with possible Achaemenid occupation (out of 102), whereas Wenke, working with different ceramic diagnostics over a larger area, recorded dozens of larger and smaller sites (often in clusters), covering a total of 108.2 hectares (Wenke 1975/76; see Boucharlat 2005: 239 n.14, 245–6). Interestingly, the area between the Karkheh and Dez rivers, *viz* the immediate surroundings of Susa, had few settlements. Achaemenid sites are concentrated east of the Dez (Wenke 1975/76: maps 14, 16; Miroschedji 1981c: Fig. 56). The southernmost Achaemenid site is Tall-e Tendī, not far from the Rāmšir foothills and perhaps identical with Šullaggi in the Persepolis Fortification archive (Hansman 1978; Alizadeh 1985b; Gasche 2005; Henkelman 2008a: 43, 426; in press d).

Surveys in the Deh Lorān plain identified a few smaller Achaemenid sites and two larger towns, Tappeh Patak and Tappeh Gārān, both of which seem to have been occupied in the Neo-Elamite period and were served by a system of canals and perhaps *qanāt*s (underground water channels bringing water from an aquifer). These may have been stops on the Achaemenid Royal Road (Carter 1971: 229, 231–5; Neely and Wright 2010; Miroschedji 1981c) linking Susa and Babylon (and ultimately Sardis). Patak has tentatively been identified as ancient Madaktu, an important Neo-Elamite strategic center (Miroschedji 1986; Neely and Wright 2010; but see Potts 2001c: 20–2). The survey of the Mīān Āb plain south of Šūštar has identified 11 "Neo-Elamite" (no distinction between I and II is made) and as many as 29 Achaemenid sites (Moghaddam and Miri 2003: 102–3, 105). Some of these must have been stops on the Royal Road, as seems likely for some sites in the "eastern corridor" – between the Mīān Āb and Rām Hormoz plains – where seven or eight sites with "Achaemenid-Seleucid-Parthian" occupation were identified (Moghaddam and Miri 2007). As for the Rām Hormoz plain, Achaemenid presence was documented at Tappeh Bormī, Tall-e Ǧazīr, and a few other sites, all also occupied during the Neo-Elamite II period (Carter 1971: 256–71, 274–82; 1994; Carter and Wright 2003). Tappeh Bormī, now identified as ancient Huhnur (Mofidi Nasrabadi 2005), appears in the Persepolis Fortification archive as Hunar (Henkelman 2007; Potts 2008c: 293). Survey in the Īzeh plain yielded few signs of (early) Achaemenid (or Neo-Elamite) settlement, though this could be a problem of classification (Eqbal 1979; Bayani 1979). Sites recorded in the Behbahān plain and the adjacent lower Zohreh valley include 32 (out of 102) with 1st millennium habitation, but as the survey concentrated on earlier periods, the report does not distinguish between Elamite, Achaemenid, and post-Achaemenid wares (Dittmann 1984). A survey of the Būšehr hinterland identified no fewer than 32 (post-)Achaemenid sites, including a huge, fortified area. Many of the sites cluster around Borāzğān (Carter et al. 2006).

Moving into Fārs, surveyed areas include the the Īzeh plain, the Bakhtīārī mountains, and the Mamasanī region. The first yielded few signs of (early) Achaemenid (or Neo-Elamite) settlement, though this could be a problem of classification (Eqbal 1979; Bayani 1979). Zagarell's surveys in the Bakhtīārī mountains (1982) focused on the Chalcolithic sites and yielded little evidence of Iron III and Achaemenid settlements. A more recent survey in the Fārsān plain, also in the Bakhtīārī area, identified 24 possible Achaemenid sites, including cemeteries. The occurrence of Iron Age III and Neo-Elamite wares in adjacent zones renders the region potentially important for Elamite-Iranian encounters (Khosrowzadeh 2010). The Mamasanī survey identified 15–17 (out of 51) sites with (post-)Achaemenid occupation, including two or three "pavilions" (cf. below). Most of these seem to continue Elamite settlements (McCall 2009: 250–63; Zeidi et al. 2009; Asgari Chaverdi et al. 2010). Apart from Tol-e Nūrābād, Tol-e Spīd, and Qalēh-ye Kalī, all three subject to recent excavations, notable Achaemenid sites are Tol-e Sorna and Tappeh Pahnū (cf. below).

Vanden Berghe's surveys and test soundings in the Marv Dašt were followed by a program, initiated by William Sumner in the late 1960s, that covered the entire Kūr River basin (Sumner 1972: 263–9). In a paper on the Achaemenid settlement system in this vast area, Sumner sought to establish links between archaeological sites and toponyms attested in the Persepolis Fortification archive. He listed 39 secure Achaemenid habitation sites, alongside features such a bridges, weirs, canals, and parts of the Royal Road (Sumner 1986b, 1990b; but cf. Callieri 2007: 43–4) and estimated aggregate Achaemenid settlement of 675 hectares a sedentary population of 44,000 (or less). This should be weighed against much higher figures for the early 2nd millennium (cf. Miroschedji 1990: 53–4; Boucharlat 2003a: 264; 2005: 226–8). Some sites have been described anew recently, while others, particularly in the Marv Dašt piedmont zone, have been added (Boucharlat and Feizkhah 2007; Hartnell 2010; Hartnell and Asadi 2010). Recent surveys at Pasargadae and the nearby Tang-e Bolāği are discussed below. The final report on Alizadeh's 1995 northern Marv Dašt survey is not yet published (cf. Alizadeh 2003b).

Southern Fārs and Lārestān remain relatively unexplored, certainly with regard to signs of Achaemenid presence (cf. Boucharlat 2005: 233–4). After Stein, the valleys of Fasā and Dārāb were resurveyed by Miroschedji, but no extensive report was published (Miroschedji 1972; 1990: 52). Achaemenid material, if any, from Andrew Williamson's survey also remains unpublished (Priestman 2003). Tal-e Zohāk (Zahhāk), near Fasā, is the most impressive Achaemenid site in the region. Achaemenid sherds and two (possibly more) column bases were found there; the mudbrick platform on top of the mound may be Achaemenid, too (Hansman 1975, 1999; Pohanka 1983; Kerner 1993: 122–5; Callieri 2007: 88–96). (Post-)Achaemenid pottery and a column base were found near Dārābgird (Morgan 2003: 333–5; Callieri 2007); ceramics were also found at Tall-e Pol-e Bīzdān, also in the Dārāb district (Miroschedji 1987a: 34). Achaemenid sherds have also been reported from sites near Lake Mahārlū and Sarvestān (Kleiss 1973: 69; Stein 1936: 182; Callieri 2007: 45).

As for the coastal regions, a recent survey identified (post-)Achaemenid occupation at Tol-e Pīr (c.125 kilometers south-southwest of Fīrūzābād) and three other sites (Asgari Chaverdi and Azarnoush 2004; Asgari Chaverdi et al. 2008: 29). Architectural elements (capitals, zoomorphic capitals, a human bust) of Achaemenid inspiration have been found at Tomb-e Bot, also in the Lāmerd district. These date to the post-Achaemenid or even early Sasanian period (Asgari Chaverdi 1999/2000, 2002; Boucharlat 2005: 234–235; Callieri 2007: 138–141). An alleged Achaemenid port on the island of Qešm has been reported but never verified (Boucharlat and Salles 1981: 68).

Finally, the excavations at Tepe (Tappeh) Yahyā in Kermān should be mentioned, not only for the pottery indicating an Achaemenid occupation level, but also for the mudbrick platforms that were, presumably, constructed between 650 and 500 BC (Lamberg-Karlovsky and Magee 1999; Magee 2004: 73–5, 79–81; cf. Boucharlat 2005: 266–7).

The Achaemenid heartland emerges from all this as a region dotted with smaller and larger sites, yet significantly less densely populated than it had been in the early and middle 2nd millennium BC (Sumner 1972: 193; Miroschedji 2003: 31; Boucharlat 2005: 276–7). One area, notably the Zagros foothills east of Khūzestān proper, appears to have had a higher population density and was of crucial importance to the Neo-Elamite state, as it is here that Hidali, Huhnur, Šullaggi, and Dašer were all situated. Formerly within the administrative purview of the Elamite crown, these towns reappeared by the end of the 6th century as centers controlled from Persepolis, suggestive of a progressive, westward "Persianization" (Henkelman in press a, d). In other areas, the survival of fewer but centrally located towns may indicate a clustering of the sedentary population. In some cases, large-scale planning is obvious. This is the case around Susa, which appears to have had few settlements in the Achaemenid period (and in the preceding and following periods). With irrigation, the vast stretches of land around Susa could have fed a population of 40,000 (Adams 1962: 115). As such, what appears to archaeology as an "empty" zone may have been a function of the regular (yet temporary) presence of the Achaemenid court (Boucharlat 1985b, 1990a).

The total number of sites recognized thus far is likely to be on the low side given the varying definitions of Achaemenid pottery and the focus of some surveys on earlier periods. The Fortification archive, which oversaw only part of the region under discussion, indicates the existence of hundreds of smaller and larger settlements. Some of the most important, such as Hidali, are yet to be located (Stolper 2004; Potts 2008c: 291; Henkelman 2008a: 499–501 and index s.v. Hidali). Tirazziš was another major town, but, despite the continuity of its name in modern Šīrāz, no unequivocal signs of Achaemenid settlement have been found at Qaṣr-e Abu Naṣr, the site of old Šīrāz (Tilia 1972: 54–55; Whitcomb 1985; Henkelman et al. 2006; Henkelman in press c).

4 Royal Residences

Strabo's *Geography* preserves a remarkable summary on the royal residences:

> They adorned the royal residence at Susa more than the others, but held in no less honour those at Persepolis and Pasargadae. The treasure, storehouses, and funeral monuments of the Persians were there, in places more strongly fortified and at the same time ancestral. And there were also other royal residences – the one in Gabae somewhere in the upper parts of Persis, and the one on the coast, near Taoce, as it is called. (Strabo, *Geogr.* 15.3.3; cf. 3.6–10, 21)

The selection of residences listed here is not fortuitous. Susa-Persepolis and Gabae-Taoce were cardinal points on the major royal roads that crossed the Achaemenid heartland: one that ran from Babylon *via* Susa and Persepolis to the east, and one that descended from Ecbatana *via* Gabae, to Taoce on the Persian Gulf. These roads and their intersection(s) define the layout and subdivision of the territory under the purview of the administration based at Persepolis (Henkelman 2008b).

Gabae (Old Persian *Gaba-*) appears in the Fortification texts as Kabaš and seems to denote both a region and town in the area of modern Esfahān (Henkelman 2008b). The remains of ancient Gabae have not been identified (Schmitt 2000b; Hansman 2006: 635–6; Planhol 2006: 618). The region and town of Taoce (mediaeval Tawwāğ/Tawwāz) are known as Tamukkan in the Fortification archive and Taḫ(u)makka in Neo-Babylonian documents. They correspond to a cluster of Achaemenid sites at and near modern Borāzğān, inland from Būšehr. Best known is a site immediately south of Borāzğān, where a hypostyle hall, reminiscent of the Pasargadae palaces, and a number of other constructions were excavated by Ali Akbar Sarfaraz (Sarfaraz 1971; Boucharlat 2005: 236). Another hypostyle hall (24.40 × 20.50 meters) was found c.12 kilometers north of Borāzğān, at Sang-e Sīāh. Here too, black and white column bases were excavated, as were capitals and mudbrick walls covered with green plaster. A third such structure is being excavated at Bardak-e Sīāh, northwest of Borāzğān, where bas-reliefs and a cuneiform inscription have been reported (Yaghmaee 2010). Achaemenid structures have also been found at Tall-e Kandaq near Borāzğān (Rahbar 1999c: 228). As for the Būšehr peninsula, no Achaemenid remains were discovered in Pézard's brief excavations at Tappeh Sabzābād (ancient Liyan) (Pézard 1914: 1) and Achaemenid occupation at Rešahr is uncertain (Callieri 2007: 46–48).

Classical sources sometimes mention additional βασίλεια, royal residences, such as the one in Gedrosia, in the district of Pura (Arrian, *Anab.* 6.24.1; cf. Henkelman 2010: 705–6) but none of these has been discovered yet.

Pasargadae and the Tang-e Bolāği

Pasargadae, Greek Πασαργάδαι (modern Mašhad-e Morğāb), renders Old Persian *Pāθragadā- (Tavernier 2007: 392), the name of the oldest Achaemenid residence (Stronach 1985a; Boucharlat 2004; Stronach and Gopnik 2009). Founded by Cyrus (c.550–530 BC), it retained special, dynastic significance for the later Achaemenids. Funerary sacrifices at Cyrus' tomb were still performed in the later 4th century (Arrian, *Anab.* 6.29.4, 7; Strabo, *Geog.* 15.3.7; Henkelman 2003c) and the royal investiture took place at a local temple (Plutarch, *Artaxerxes* 3.2, cf. Sancisi-Weerdenburg 1983; Briant 2002: 523–4, 667, 998; Brosius 2006; Henkelman 2011: 109, 111). The Persepolis Fortification tablets regularly refer to *Batrakataš* and suggest the presence of an extensive treasury (depot and craft center; Henkelman 2008a: 431; cf. Arrian, *Anab.* 3.18.10). Pasargadae sits at 1,900 meters above sea level in the southern Dašt-e Morğāb plain, close to the Pulvār river. It is connected to Persepolis via the defiles of the Tang-e Bolāği (c.50 kilometers). After Ker Porter, Flandin and Coste, Lord Curzon, the Dieulafoys and Ernst Herzfeld, among others, had documented the visible remains and identified the site as ancient Pasargadae (Stronach 1978: 1–5; 2005; Boucharlat 2004: 352–3), soundings and small-scale excavations were initiated by Herzfeld in 1923 and 1928 (Herzfeld 1926: 241–3; 1929–30a; Krefter 1979). Subsequent soundings by Ali Sami followed in 1949–55 (Sami 1956), and major excavations were undertaken by David Stronach in 1961–3 (Stronach 1963, 1964, 1965, 1978). More recently, Rémy Boucharlat has directed a geomagnetic survey of the site (Boucharlat 2002, 2003b; Boucharlat and Benech 2002), which revealed more extensive occupation of the c.300 hectare site than was previously assumed. The results of Pierfrancesco Callieri's soundings on the Tall-e Takht have not yet been published (2007: 38–9, 100–1).

Most construction at Pasargadae appears to have started before the introduction of the toothed chisel in Iran (presumably from mainland Greece). Where toothed chisel marks are present, a date late in the reign of Cyrus, or later, is assumed (Nylander 1966b, 1991). Pasargadaean architecture and sculpture adapt, transform and synthesize western Iranian, Elamite, Assyrian, Ionian, and other cultural traditions. Pasargadaean art is therefore no less truly "Persian" than that of Persepolis or Susa. Stone working and construction techniques (masons' marks, anathyrosis joints, dovetail clamps) are a different point and betray the presence of Ionian and Lydian workmen (Nylander 1970, 2006; Boardman 2000). The involvement of these craftsmen in the realization of a Persian design reflects, in both a territorial and cultural sense, the imperial leap taken by Cyrus. An eye-catching characteristic of early Achaemenid architecture at Pasargadae (and elsewhere) is the contrast of black and white elements, especially in the column plinths. Blocks of both colors were quarried at Tunb-e Karam near Sīvand (Sami 1956: 42–6).

Pasargadae can be divided in four sectors. In the northeast, an imposing stone platform (c.80 × 100 meters), with two monumental staircases and an outer wall built of fine ashlar blocks, crowns the Tall-e Takht ("throne hill"). Construction remained in its initial phase under Cyrus; mudbrick superstructures (courtyards, storerooms, a columned hall) were erected under Darius I and remained partly in use in the post-Achaemenid period, until c.280 BC. Judging from the structures and small finds, the Takht's functions may have included that of "treasury" or storehouse (Stronach 1978: 8–23, 146–59, 178–86, 208–75; 1985a: 853–4; Root 1999). Directly north of the Takht lay a vast mudbrick enclosure with towers covering c.20 hectares, the "Outer Fortification." Geomagnetic survey revealed a series of small mudbrick buildings, making it "the most densely built area on the site" (Boucharlat 2001: 118; Boucharlat and Benech 2002: 26–9).

The buildings in Pasargadae's official, central area combine stone architectural elements with mudbrick walls. They are set, with parallel orientation, in extensive, landscaped surroundings (Boucharlat and Benech 2002: 16–24). A free-standing gate (Gate R) with eight columns, up to 16 meters high, controlled the main access (Stronach 1978: 44–55). Of its eight door-jamb reliefs, one remains; it depicts a four-winged figure with an Egyptianizing crown and Elamite royal robe (see Root 1979: 46–9; 2011; Henkelman 2003a: 192–3; Garrison 2009: 11–12; Álvarez-Mon 2009b; cf. Canal 1976, Caubet 2007: 110 no. 46). The northern and southern doors may have been flanked by human-headed, winged bulls (Calmeyer 1981).

From Gate R, one crossed the bridge over a canal deriving from the Pulvār river and reached Palace S. This structure, probably not a real residence, comprised a columned hall (c.32 × 22 meters) with doors opening onto four columned porticoes. Double zoomorphic (lion, bull, horse) column capitals (Calmeyer 1981; Krefter 1979: 15–16), a characteristic feature of Achaemenid architecture, probably faced inward and outward (Seidl 2003). The composite creatures on the partly preserved door-jamb reliefs betray (indirect) Assyrian influence (Kawami 1972; Stronach 1978: 56–77; cf. Calmeyer 1994b).

In the area northeast of Palace S a system of stone water channels, sluices, and basins irrigated what Stronach considered a precursor of the traditional Persian *čahārbāḡ*, or fourfold garden (Stronach 1989, 1990, 1994; but see Boucharlat and Benech 2002: 16). Along with two smaller "pavilions" (A and B), a third structure, Palace P, bordered the garden (Stronach 1978: 78–106). This comprised a hall (c.31 × 22 meters) with 30 columns opening onto two porticoes of unequal width, the southernmost of which overlooked the garden and had a platform presumably intended for a throne. Door-jamb reliefs (with metal inlays) in Palace P are of uncertain date (late Cyrus or early Darius?); they depict the king with a follower (Root 1979: 49–58; Calmeyer 1981). Only fragments remain of the bright wall and column frescoes in the hall (Herzfeld 1929/30a: 13; Sami 1956: 58; Stronach 1978: 85–87). A jar hoard comprising spoons and jewelry was found buried near pavilion B (Stronach 1978: 168–77, 200–7).

The "Zendān-e Soleymān," a 12 meter high tower at the northern edge of the central sector, has an exterior staircase giving access to a single, elevated room, and may have been enclosed by a wall. Among many interpretations, a connection with royal investiture is plausible though difficult to corroborate (Stronach 1978: 117–37; 1985a: 848–52; Sancisi-Weerdenburg 1983; Seidl 1994; Boucharlat 2003b; Potts 2007). Directly behind the tower, geomagnetic survey revealed a 45 × 40 meter, buttressed and probably stone-built structure (Boucharlat 2003b). A better preserved twin tower is located at Naqš-e Rustam (cf. below).

The third sector (the "sacred precinct") in the north is adjacent to a small stream that drains into the Pulvār. Two monumental limestone plinths, one with a staircase, are generally dated to the early Achaemenid period and may be related to sacrificial feasts held at the site (Stronach 1978: 138–45; Henkelman 2008a: 385–92, 427–34; 2011). A low, stepped terrace, is probably late or post-Achaemenid (Stronach 1978: 138–145), rather than the base of an Achaemenid temple (Herzfeld 1929–30a: 8–10). The antiquity of a low stone enclosure is doubtful (Boucharlat and Benech 2002: 30–33).

At the southwestern end of the site, in the fourth sector, a gable-roofed "house" set on a 13 × 12 meter stepped platform is generally identified as Cyrus' tomb (Stronach 1978: 24–43). A large stone rosette was carved at the apex of the roof front (Stronach 1971; von Gall 1979). In the 13th century the tomb became an Islamic sanctuary (Qabr-e Mādar-e Soleymān), reusing columns from the palaces; it was drastically restored to its former state in 1971 (Kleiss 1979b; Calmeyer 1994a: 15).

Various inscriptions on reliefs, pillars, and a stone tablet were found at Pasargadae; most mention Cyrus (Schmitt 2009: 35–6), one Xerxes (Stronach 1978: 152), and one perhaps Darius (Borger and Hinz 1959; Schmitt 2009: 99–100). The Cyrus inscriptions introduce the king as an Achaemenid; most scholars assume that Darius commissioned them to create a connection between the empire's founder and his own dynastic line (Briant 2002: 90–2, 111, 889; Stronach 1997b, 2001).

In 2004–7 dam construction occasioned a survey and salvage excavations in the gorge and valley of Tang-e Bolāģi, southwest of Pasargadae (Fazeli [Nashli] 2009; Atai and Boucharlat 2009). Achaemenid and post-Achaemenid remains are attested at seven sites, including a cave (Adachi and Zeidi 2009), a small rural settlement (Asgari Chaverdi and Callieri 2006; 2009: 3–27), a buttressed building (farmstead? Helwing and Seyedin 2009), a complex surrounded by a massive wall (way station? Asadi and Kaim 2009), a fortified structure (Asgari Chaverdi and Callieri 2009: 27–32), and a small (25 × 19 meter) stone "pavilion" (Atai and Boucharlat 2009). Also investigated was a system of partially rock-cut, canals (Atai and Boucharlat 2009). Most sites yielded Achaemenid pottery, especially fragments of large storage jars and "pilgrim" flasks. The Tang-e Bolāģi project brought to light unique evidence for the development of rural areas by the Achaemenid administration; as such, it provides a tantalizing complement to the information on regional economic structures from the Persepolis Fortification archive.

Persepolis and the Marv Dašt

Persepolis (modern Takht-e Ğamšīd or Čehel Minār; Περσέπολις, Old Persian Pārsa) has been regularly visited since antiquity (Shahbazi 1977; Arndt 1984; Drijvers et al. 1991; Mousavi 2002; Invernizzi 2005). Among the first European travelers to see it was the Franciscan Odoric de Pordenone, in 1382 (Le Long et al. 2010). Views of the ruins were drawn by Cornelis de Bruijn in 1704/5 (1711; Drijvers and MacDonald 1995; Jurriaans-Helle 1998), Carsten Niebuhr in 1765 (1772), and Eugène Flandin and Pascal-Xavier Coste in 1851–4 (Maupoix and Coulon 1998; Calmard 2001). In 1878 they were photographed by Franz Stolze (Stolze and Andreas 1882; cf. Dieulafoy 1884–9). While many visitors left their names on the Gate of All Nations (Simpson 2005), some also took away sculpture fragments. At least 110 pieces of Persepolitan sculpture are currently in museums outside Iran (Roaf 1987; Mitchell 2000; Curtis and Tallis 2005: 68–85; Nagel 2010: 237–51).

Stolze and Andreas (1882) and Herbert Weld Blundell (1893) did small-scale soundings at Persepolis, but major excavations only started in 1931, under Ernst E. Herzfeld (Mousavi 2002; Dusinberre 2005b). While no comprehensive report on the 1931–5 excavations exists (see Herzfeld 1929–30b, 1934; 1941: 221–74), Herzfeld's successor, Erich F. Schmidt, produced three monumental volumes on the 1935–9 campaigns (1953, 1957, 1970; also 1939; cf. Balcer 1991). Subsequent excavations were conducted by Ali Sami (1941–61) and Akbar Tadjvidi (1968–73) (Sami 1967; cf. Mousavi 1990, 2002; Tadjvidi 1970,

1973, 1976). Extensive restoration, limited excavation, and detailed studies were undertaken by Cesare Carbone and Giuseppe and Ann Britt Tilia between 1964 and 1972 (Zander 1968: 1–127; Tilia 1968, 1969, 1972, 1978). Friedrich Krefter, Herzfeld's deputy, drew reconstructions of all the main buildings (Krefter 1971; Trümpelmann 1988). New research after 2002 included geomagnetic surveys to the north and south of the platform, revealing additional stone structures. Some 600 meters of water channels under the platform were mapped, an operation that produced great numbers of (post-)Achaemenid sherds (Asgari Chaverdi 2008; Talebian 2010). Like Pasargadae, Persepolis is a UNESCO World Heritage site.

Persepolis can be divided into three sectors: the mountain fortification, the terrace (or Takht) and the plain surrounding the terrace (Roaf 2004; Shahbazi 2004, 2009). The c.450 × 300 meter terrace was created partly by leveling the natural rocky outcrop known as Šāhi Kūh ("Mt. Royal," part of the Kūh-e Rahmat range), and partly by construction using tightly fitting blocks, in polygonal or "cyclopaean" technique, to erect massive walls rising up to 18 meters above the plain (Tilia 1978: 3–27; quarries: Pugliese Carratelli 1966; Tilia 1968; Calmeyer 1990a; Kleiss 1993a). On the west side, a monumental double staircase with a crenelated parapet provides the main access. This leads to the "Gate of All Nations," so identified in an inscription of Xerxes. Flanked in front by colossal bulls (perhaps referred to by Diodorus 17.71.6) and at the rear by human-headed winged bulls, the gate was set back from the terrace edge, perhaps between mudbrick walls. Its interior, secured by giant wooden doors with gilt decoration, was supported by four columns almost 17 meters high. The exterior was decorated with glazed bricks (Schmidt 1953: 64–8; Krefter 1968; Tilia 1972: 37–40).

In the original layout, one approached the throne hall from a southern staircase, via a terrace flanked by Darius' Palace and the Central Building. After this access had been closed and a new, northwestern one, just described, constructed under Darius or Xerxes (486–465 BC), the southwestern sector remained recognizable as all its buildings stand on separate socles (with sculptured staircases), raising them above the remainder of the terrace (Kleiss 2000; Roaf 1983: 150–9; Jacobs 1997).

The throne or audience hall is, perhaps erroneously, referred to by the Old Persian term *apadāna* on analogy with its counterpart at Susa (cf. below). Traces of an earlier floor plan indicate a building of smaller proportions begun early in Darius' reign. The decision to enlarge the interior to a 60 × 60 meter rectangular hall necessitated an extension of the terrace 18 meters to the west (Tilia 1972: 127–65; 1978: 11–27; Jacobs 1997; Kleiss 2000). In two corners of this building Krefter found foundation deposits containing inscribed, gold and silver "tablets"; Cypriot, Lydian, and Greek coins; and pieces of amber (Krefter 1971: 52–4; cf. Root 1988; Jacobs 1997: 287–91; Nimchuk 2010). Inscriptions on the building's exterior confirm its completion under Xerxes.

The interior throne hall, with its six rows of six columns crowned with double bull capitals, standing 19 meters high, must have overwhelmed any visitor. The four mudbrick corner towers had interior staircases, sometimes believed to have led to private royal quarters; they were decorated on the outside with friezes of glazed tiles. The tower entrances were flanked by statues of mastiffs and ibexes. Between the towers, three giant, columned porticoes opened to the west, north, and east. The doors between the porticoes and the interior (two on the north, one on the west and east) were decorated with gold overlay. In the south, storage rooms and a columned porch connecting Darius' palace intervene between the corner towers. Rainwater from the roof drained through bitumen-coated conduits in the towers into a network of canals cut into the bedrock. The entire building is set on the same 3 meter high socle, accessible by two double staircases with the same (yet stylistically slightly different) sculptures in mirror image (Schmidt 1953: 69–106; 1957: 69–70; Sami 1967: 95; Krefter 1971: 45–54; Stronach 1987a; Huff 2010).

Other buildings begun under Darius include the Central Building, the Treasury. and the king's palace (Old Persian *tačara*). The palace has a rectangular floor plan (40 × 30 meters) comprising a central hall with adjoining smaller rooms. The southern portico overlooks a courtyard and was accessed via a sculptured staircase. Another staircase was added by Artaxerxes III (359/8–338 BC) on the west side. Like most Persepolitan buildings, the doorframes, windows, niches, column bases, and other structural elements of the palace were made of stone and mostly sculpted. Columns were made of plastered wood and walls of mudbrick. As in the Treasury, lime plaster with a red ochre coating covered the floors (Schmidt 1953: 217–29; Root 1979: 76–86).

The Central Building (also called the Tripylon or Council Hall) had an estimated height of 11–12 meters (Krefter 1971: 39) and comprised a four-columned interior with three, 9 meter high sculpted doorways, two columned porticoes, subsidiary rooms, and passages. All its columns were crowned by human-headed bulls. An elaborately sculpted staircase gave access to the northern portico; a smaller staircase led from the courtyard abutting the southern portico to subsidiary rooms. The building was finished under Xerxes or Artaxerxes I (Schmidt 1953: 107–22; Root 1979: 95–100).

The Treasury was built, without a socle, on the southeastern terrace. It was altered and expanded twice, finally measuring 134 × 78 meters. The building consists of four large columned halls, two courtyards, and a great number of passages and subsidiary rooms; it had only two entrances and no windows. Much evidence for the use of color was found: red, blue, and white plaster on the wooden columns, greenish-grey plaster on most walls, painted decorations on some doorways, and durable lime plaster with red ocher coating on all floors. Arrow-shaped slots and niches with multiple rabbet frames decorated the exterior walls (later lowered by the excavators to a uniform height). Part of the building had a second story (Schmidt 1953: 138–200, 285–7; Matson 1953: 285–7; Roaf

1998). Two audience reliefs – originally from the throne hall staircases – and (animal) statues adorned the smaller courtyard; elsewhere in the building a Greek statue was found. Small finds included inscribed wall pegs; items of Elamite, Hittite, Egyptian, Assyrian, and Babylonian origin; personal ornaments; inscribed tableware; coins; weaponry (thousands of spearheads); tools; and an archive of clay tablets (Schmidt 1957; see below).

The Hall of 100 Columns, Xerxes' palace, and the "Harem" are among the buildings added at a later date. The first was begun by Xerxes and finished by Artaxerxes I (465–425/4 BC). Covering 68 × 68 meters, one is tempted to see it as the throne hall's counterpart. Yet, the building was lower (by 13 meters), not set on a socle, and its interior hall is surrounded by passages on three sides; the eight sculpted entrances from the passages and the northern portico did not have doors. A ceremonial gate on the northern courtyard remained unfinished (Schmidt 1953: 124–37; Krefter 1971: 57–9; Tilia 1972: 46–52; Root 1979: 105–8). Of the functions proposed for the building (e.g., Schmidt 1953; Trümpelmann 1983), an interpretation of the courtyard and hall as dining spaces for the royal guards would link the complex to the "Table of the King," an institution that fed thousands dependent on the royal household (Henkelman 2010).

Already as crown prince, Xerxes may have begun constructing his own palace, referred to in inscriptions by the Old Persian term *hadiš*. A novel element is that the socle extends in front of the building, adding a large raised courtyard accessed by two sculpted staircases. The eastern staircase had a small gate building, the western one was flanked by bull sculptures. The *hadiš* comprised a columned hall flanked by smaller rooms, a northern portico, and a southern, panoramic terrace (Schmidt 1953: 77, 230–44; 1957: 70; Calmeyer 1995–6). It is clear that, along with the throne hall, the Hall of 100 Columns, and the Treasury, the *hadiš* suffered most from the targeted burning of Persepolis ordered by Alexander (Sancisi-Weerdenburg 1993).

An L-shaped building divided into 22 units, each one a small columned hall with one or two subsidiary rooms, is known, on dubious grounds, as the "Harem." It was partly rebuilt by Krefter, served as a dig house and now houses the Persepolis museum. It includes a large hall with sculpted doorframes. All columned halls seem to have had three-stepped niches constructed in the green-plastered walls (Schmidt 1953: 3, 245–64; Krefter 1971: 22–8, 77–8; Tilia 1972: 58–9). In the "Harem" (as in Darius' palace), a number of Achaemenid and later graffiti are preserved (Razmjou 2005c; Callieri 2007: 133–5).

In the southwestern corner of the terrace, a palace begun under Xerxes and finished by Artaxerxes I replaced an older building. Though mostly destroyed by post-Achaemenid construction, a stairway façade depicting delegations of subject nations could be reconstructed (Tilia 1972: 243–316; Calmeyer 1990b: 15–16). In the same section (and further northward), the terrace wall was crowned by a horned parapet (Tilia 1969), perhaps an echo of the importance of horns in Elamite (religious) architecture, and possibly echoed in post-Achaemenid iconography (Callieri 2007: 115–24). Artaxerxes III built a palace directly north of Xerxes' palace (Schmidt 1953: 274–5; Calmeyer 1990b: 12–13).

Xerxes is to be credited with the expansion and development of the vast sculptural program initiated under Darius. Staircases and socle façades, doorways, and other stone elements were covered with thousands of figures, illustrating a vision of royalty and empire. The repertoire includes the royal audience, the king either with attendants or enthroned, the royal hero combating mythical beasts, royal guards, Persian nobles, the lion and bull motif (the supposed meaning of which has been discussed *ad nauseam*), and a panorama of distinctively dressed, subject peoples carrying gifts that may have inspired the Parthenon frieze (Root 1985). The imperial panorama is notably depicted on the throne hall staircases (Walser 1966; Roaf 1974; 1983: 47–64, 114–20; Root 1979: 86–95, 227–84; Calmeyer 1982, 1983, 1987a). Later Achaemenids, notably Artaxerxes I and III, continued the sculptural program. Persepolitan sculpture offers an unmatched opportunity for the study of the creative process and historical development of Achaemenid art (Root 1990; Calmeyer 1987b, 1990b), as well as sculpting techniques and the organization of labor (Roaf 1980, 1983, 1990; but cf. Root 1986; Sancisi-Weerdenburg 1992). Together with the royal inscriptions, it is the basis of discussions of Achaemenid kingship, also in comparison to its manifestations outside the empire's core (Root 1979; Jacobs 2002).

Achaemenid art tends to represent a timeless and unchanging state of affairs, an idealized *pax achaemenidica* (Root 1979; cf. Sancisi-Weerdenburg 1999; Briant 2002: 204–25; Kuhrt 2010). There are no portraits, just images of *the* king of kings (Root 1979: 117–18, 310; Calmeyer 1988; cf. Sancisi-Weerdenburg 1989). The replacement of the audience scenes (showing king and crown prince) from the throne hall staircases by images of royal guards (Tilia 1972: 175–208; Root 1979: 91–5; Roaf 1983: 144–5) is therefore unlikely to have been occasioned by dynastic unrest or other historical circumstances. Also, the reliefs appear to be unfinished (Tilia 1978: 57; Porada 1979; Henkelman 1995–6: 280–1).

Reflecting the empire of many tongues and nations extoled in the royal inscriptions, Persepolitan art is willfully synthetic. As at Pasargadae, it transcends its eclectic origins by subtly appropriating and transforming motifs and forms into a coherent vision (Root 1979; Nylander 1979). An additional aspect may be illustrated by the motif of a ruler carried on a platform. Whereas such processions existed in Elam (and perhaps in the Achaemenid heartland) and the motif was known in Elamite art, it gained a new dimension in Achaemenid art. The platform is now carried by delegates of the empire's nations, stressing collaboration and unity. Or, in Peter Calmeyer's arresting words, "Es entstand, scheinbar mühelos, das Kennzeichen aller großen Kunst: symbolische Form" ("What emerged, seemingly without effort, was the hallmark of all great art: symbolic form") (Calmeyer 1973: 147).

In the 1930s Herzfeld could still observe bright colors on newly excavated reliefs (Herzfeld 1941: 255; Krefter 1979: 19; 1989; cf. Weld Blundell 1893:

556–8). Today, only traces (and finely incised sketch patterns) of pigment remain on most reliefs and on the façade of Darius' tomb. The colors used included light and dark blue, red, green, white, and perhaps gold. Wooden columns were plastered with painted gypsum (Schmidt 1939: 54; 1953: 160–1; 1970: 83–4; Roos 1970; Tilia 1972: 245–6; 1978: 31–69; Nagel 2010). Inlays and appliqué of gold and Egyptian blue adorned many reliefs (Herzfeld 1941: 255–6; Sami 1967: 95; Tilia 1978: 58–66; Henkelman 1995–6). Glazed brick, ubiquitous at Susa, was less important at Persepolis, though it was notably used on the corner towers of the throne hall, for friezes with some of Xerxes' inscriptions.

Numerous display and foundation inscriptions, often in multiple copies, in Elamite, Akkadian, and Old Persian, have been found at Persepolis (Roaf 2004: 400–1; Shahbazi 1985; Lecoq 1997; Schmitt 2000a). These were commissioned by Darius I, Xerxes, and Artaxerxes I and III, and tend to present a timeless state of affairs. They are of prime importance for revealing royal ideology but are a feeble basis for historical reconstruction. Variation largely depended on the choice of medium and location. Among the architectural terms, the description of the residence as a fortress on a throne/podium is noteworthy (Grillot 1987: 67–9).

A strong fortification wall (with arrow slots, vaulted interior rooms, and corridors, with stairs to a second floor), where the Fortification archive was discovered (cf. below), protected the terrace on its northern side, where the mountain slope had not (yet) been leveled (Krefter 1971: 85–89; Kleiss 1992b). It was an extension of the mountain fortification, Persepolis' second sector. This defensive system, with 25 towers (reaching 15 meters in height) connected by walls with vaulted corridors, enclosed a lozenge-shaped area (500 × 400 meters), divided in two, on the slope of the Kūh-e Rahmat. The lower part included two royal tombs. Where the fortification runs parallel to the eastern terrace it incorporates a moat (which diverted rain water from the mountain) and garrison quarters. In the higher part of the citadel, great amounts of surface ceramics were found (Weld Blundell 1893: 552–5; Schmidt 1953: 199–213; Tadjvidi 1970; Huff 1990: 148; Kleiss 1992b).

The third sector is that of the plain surrounding the terrace. In the west, two additional defensive walls were previously visible (Weld Blundell 1893: 547–56; Schmidt 1939: 7–15; 1953: 202–11; Sami 1967: 14; Krefter 1971: 85–9; Tadjvidi 1973, 1976; Kleiss 1992b; Mousavi 1992; cf. Diodorus 17.71.3–6). In the south and southwest various constructions were excavated, including a hypostyle building similar to the throne hall. Remains of plastered wooden columns were found in situ. Walls surrounding a courtyard were crowned with crenelated parapets, access staircases flanked by animal statues. As a whole, the southern complex almost doubles the surface of representative constructions on the terrace (Herzfeld 1929–30b: 32; Schmidt 1953: 48–9, 55; Sami 1967: 89–91; Vanden Berghe 1959: Pl. 45b; Tadjvidi 1976; Mousavi 1999b: 148–151; 2002: 237; Callieri 2007: 17). North of the terrace, the *fratarakā* (the title used by a post-

Achaemenid dynasty in Fārs) complex is generally dated to the early Seleucid period, but may continue an Achaemenid layout (Schmidt 1953: 50–1, 55–6; Boucharlat 1984: 130–2; Stronach 1985b: 613–17; Wiesehöfer 1994: 70–9; Roaf 1998: 70–2; Boucharlat 2006: 452–3; Callieri 2007: 51–64). Geomagnetic survey there has not revealed additional buildings (Boucharlat and Gondet in press).

At Naqš-e Rustam, c.6 kilometers northwest of Persepolis, the rock-cut tombs of four Achaemenids are found (see below) as well as the *Ka'ba-ye Zardošt*, a twin of the Pasargadae tower. Soundings indicated that this tower too was surrounded by several structures (Schmidt 1970: 18–65; Boucharlat 2003b: 92–8). Although the fortifications in front of the tombs seem to be Arsacid or Sasanian in date, an Achaemenid citadel may have been located on the mountain of Naqš-e Rustam (Schmidt 1970: 58; Kleiss 1976).

Between Naqš-e Rustam and the Persepolis terrace lies a site known as Dašt-e Gohar. It includes the stepped basis of a "house" tomb (cf. below) and, probably associated with this, a porticoed hypostyle hall of Pasargadaean inspiration but probably later date (Tilia 1974; 1978: 73–80; Kleiss 1980; Bessac and Boucharlat 2010).

Two sites located 1 and 5 kilometers west of Persepolis are known as "Persepolis West" and Bāḡ-e Fīrūzī. The former is a 25 hectare site with a dense covering of Achaemenid ceramics on the surface; the second is a cluster of mounds with Achaemenid pottery, glazed brick fragments, and architectural and sculptural remains (Sumner 1986b: 8–9; Tilia 1974: 203–4, 1978: 80–5; Boucharlat 2007; Boucharlat and Feizkhah 2007; Asgari Chaverdi and Callieri forthcoming). Sumner tentatively suggested that the two sites should be seen as parts of the same agglomeration. Some 20 other Achaemenid sites have been recorded in the Marv Dašt, but at greater distance from Persepolis, leaving empty a zone of 15–20 kilometers around Persepolis itself (Tilia 1978: 85–7; Sumner 1986b; Boucharlat 2003a: 263–5).

Two important archives were found at Persepolis (Briant et al. 2008; Henkelman 2008a: 65–179; Azzoni et al. in press). One, consisting of 747 clay tablets and fragments and 199 sealings, was found in the Treasury (Room 33; Schmidt 1939: 33–43; 1957: 4–41). Most tablets are sealed and inscribed in Elamite, though one is written in Babylonian. The Fortification archive, found in two bricked-up spaces in the northeastern terrace fortification, comprises at least 7,000 legible Elamite tablets, 5,000 anepigraphic but sealed tablets, some 1,000 Aramaic texts on clay tablets, and a handful of texts in other languages. The seal impressions constitute a rich iconographic corpus (Root 1996, 1997, 2008; Garrison 2000, 2008, 2009, 2010; Garrison and Root 2001, forthcoming a, b; Dusinberre 2008). In addition, 52 sealed bullae and anepigraphic tablets and three cylinder seals were found in the mountain fortifications (Tadjvidi 1970, 1973, 1976; Rahimifar 2005; cf. Schmidt 1953: 209). In the Treasury, 269 green chert mortars, pestles, and plates were also found, about two-thirds of which bore Aramaic inscriptions in ink (Schmidt 1957: 53–6). The texts are probably not ritual texts (*pace* Bowman 1970), but inventory notes (Bernard 1972b; Naveh and Shaked 1973; Delaunay 1974; Hinz 1975; Stolper 2001; Briant 2002: 428–33, 940–1).

The Fortification and Treasury archives help to elucidate the function of Persepolis. They document a large institutional economy in Achaemenid Fārs, with Persepolis as its bureaucratic and administrative center. They also show the regular presence of the king and court at Persepolis, apparently mainly in the autumn (Henkelman 2011: 110–12). The old and often repeated thesis (found as early as Bruijn 1711: 217, probably from local legend; cf. Shahbazi 1977; Sancisi-Weerdenburg 1991) that Persepolis was built for the celebration of *Nō Rūz* (Iranian New Year, on March 21, the vernal equinox and first day of spring) is contradicted by evidence suggesting that the king was usually in Susa at that time (Waerzeggers 2010: 801–4). In general, the idea that Persepolis was a "ritual city" remains unsupported; the tablets document funerary sacrifices and sacrificial feasts near Persepolis, but not sacrifices taking place on the terrace.

Susa

Exploration of Susa (modern Šūš-e Dānīāl; Σοῦσα, ancient *Šušan*) began in 1850–4 under William Kennett Loftus, who identified the site, mapped it, opened trenches on the Acropole, Apadana, and Ville Royale mounds, and uncovered parts of the throne hall (Loftus 1856; 1857: 314–433; Curtis 1993). Two campaigns by Marcel and Jane Dieulafoy in 1885–6 marked the beginning of nearly a century of French explorations at Susa. The finds included a first complete series of glazed brick reliefs (Dieulafoy 1890–2), displayed in the Louvre since 1888. In 1895 the Iranian Imperial government sold exclusive excavation rights to France. Although the monopoly was abolished in 1927, the Délégation en Perse (later Délégation Archéologique Française en Iran) continued its activities in Susa and Khūzestān until 1979 (Mecquenem 1980; Mousavi 1996; Chevalier 1997, 2010; Steve et al. 2002/3: 375–403; Gasche 2009; Perrot 2010a). Most finds (including epigraphic and numismatic materials) are published in *Mémoires de la Délégation en Perse* (1900–) and *Cahiers de la Délégation Archéologique Française en Iran* (1971–87; cf. Vanden Berghe 1959: 91–8).

The mission's first director, Jacques de Morgan (1897–1912), concentrated on the Acropole Mound (Morgan 1898, 1900c, 1905a, 1905c) and constructed the "Château" (a fort used as an excavation house) as a defense against attacks from belligerent tribes. Roland (le comte) de Mecquenem followed suit (1912–14, 1920–39) with the excavation of the Donjon ("dungeon") and much of the palace of Darius (Pillet 1914; Mecquenem 1943, 1947; Chevalier 2010: 94–110). From 1946 to 1967, Roman Ghirshman opened trenches on the northwestern Ville Royale, Apadana, Ville des Artisans, and parts of the fortifications (Ghirshman 1947, 1954, 1968b; Steve and Gasche 1990). The last French director (1968–79), Jean Perrot, conducted and supervised excavations and geomagnetic surveys in all sectors, with particular attention to the throne hall and palace of Darius (Perrot 1981, 2010c; Hesse 2010). Despite extensive (and sometimes excessive) earlier work, the Perrot campaigns are the prime source of knowledge about Achaemenid Susa.

The Iranian Cultural Heritage Organization commissioned new excavations at Susa in 1982; from 1994 onward they were directed by Mir-Abedin Kaboli, whose prime focus was the western side of the Apadana mound (Kaboli 2000; Razmjou 2002: 103).

Unlike Pasargadae and Persepolis, Susa was not a new foundation of the Persian kings, but an old Elamite city. Pre-Achaemenid Persians from Fārs were already in contact with Susa, but actual Achaemenid presence is not evident at the site before 521 BC (Darius I). It cannot be excluded that a Neo-Elamite (vassal) king ruled Susa and its surroundings until that date (*pace* Vallat 2006b; cf. Waters 2000: 85; Tavernier 2004: 22–9; Henkelman 2008a: 13–14, 56–7, 362–3). At any rate, the city was completely redesigned after the ascent of Darius (Steve et al. 2002/3: 485–95; Boucharlat 2009). Susa's recognition as official Achaemenid residence in Babylonian and Elamite documents provides an approximate *terminus ante quem* of 500 BC for the most important Achaemenid constructions there (Briant 2010: 28–9).

Early in Darius' reign, a residential palace (3.8 hectares) and monumental throne hall (109 × 109 meters) were erected on the Apadana Mound (Ladiray 2010; Perrot 2010d), perhaps on the location of the Neo-Elamite palace (Vallat 1999b). After leveling and transforming the Elamite mound into a regular platform, gravel foundations were laid to a depth of 10 meters, a technique of possible Elamite origin (Boucharlat 1994: 225; Ladiray 2010: 161–3).

The palatial complex is centered on three courtyards, interconnected by gated passages. Each was surrounded by series of spaces, including a columned room (added by Artaxerxes II), rooms for guards and official purposes, and two suites of spaces intended for storage or the chancellery. A hypothesized second floor (Amiet 1994, 2010b) is considered unlikely by the excavator (Perrot 2010d: 231). Notable spaces are two sets of twin, oblong halls which may have been vaulted (Gasche 2010; Perrot 2010d: 224–8); those south of the western court functioned as monumental ante-chambers to the royal apartments. The larger, eastern courtyard (and possibly the other courtyards too) had walls adorned with glazed brick reliefs and perhaps painted decoration (Ghirshman 1947: 446; Perrot 2010d). Red ocher flooring, also known at Persepolis and Achaemenid Babylon, is attested in most rooms in the residence (Haerinck 1973: 112–14; Schmidt 1953: 31–2). An intricate drainage system was constructed underneath the complex (Ladiray 2010: 164–6).

Though the term *apadāna* occurs in Achaemenid inscriptions at Susa, its etymology and identification with square hypostyle throne halls are uncertain (Schmitt 1987; Lecoq 1997: 115–16; Razmjou 2010: 231–3) and the term is best avoided. Like its Persepolitan equivalent, the throne hall had 36 (6 × 6), 19 meter high columns covering a space measuring 58 × 58 meters; three grand porticoes were flanked by corner towers. Whereas the palace area is variously considered to be of Assyro-Babylonian or Elamite inspiration (Ghirshman 1965b; Roaf 1973; Amiet 1973, 2010b; Gasche 2010), hypostyle throne halls have long been linked to an architectural tradition attested in the Iron Age II–III central and northern Zagros (e.g. at Ḥasanlū, Bābā Ǧān, Nūš-e Ǧān, Godīn). Discoveries on the eastern Arabian peninsula (Muweilah, Rumeilah, and elsewhere), seem to suggest a broader tradition, existing by the 8th century BC or earlier (Boucharlat and Lombard 2001; Magee et al. 2002; Magee 2003, 2008; Stronach and Roaf 2007: 188–90; Muscarella 2008b; Gopnik 2010). The extensive use of round and square baked-brick columns on Susa's southwestern Acropole in the later 2nd millennium BC should also be considered – even though there is a woeful lack of published material on this – especially given their size (up to 70 centimeters in diameter), foundation footings (0.54 meters deep), placement in a paved space, and inscriptions mentioning the *hiyan*, "palace, court" (Morgan 1898: 46–51; 1905b; Mecquenem 1911: 73; cf. Heim 1992: 124–5; Malbran-Labat 1995: 79–81).

The Apadana complex was completed by Xerxes, damaged by fire under Artaxerxes I and restored by Artaxerxes II (Nylander 1975; Perrot 2010b: 222–322). Unlike its counterpart at Persepolis, the Susa throne hall (and residence) was not destroyed during the Macedonian invasion, but decayed slowly. Darius' statue (below) even remained visible until the Islamic period (Ghirshman 1947: 446; Boucharlat 1990b, 2006).

A free-standing "propylaeum" (porch, gatehouse) on the northwestern edge of the Ville Royale, built by Darius I and Xerxes (Perrot et al. 1999), marked the principal access route from the east. After the Propylaeum the road turned left, crossed a ravine by a broad causeway, and reached the Gate of Darius. This gate gave access to the eastern esplanade of the Apadana mound (Perrot and Ladiray 1974; Boucharlat 1987: 145–52; Ladiray 2010: 184–95). A headless, 2.5 meter tall granite statue of Darius, originally made to be set up in Egypt (presumably at Heliopolis), was found on its west side (Ch. II.44). The statue has inscriptions in Egyptian, Elamite, Old Persian, and Akkadian, and images of subject peoples (Kervran 1972; Yoyotte 1972, 2010; Stronach 1974a; Roaf 1974; Vallat 1974; Trichet and Vallat 1990; Calmeyer 1991; Razmjou 2002). Additional sculptural fragments belong to two or three statues of the king, and possibly one of the royal hero (Root 1979: 68–72, 110–16; Luschey 1983; Muscarella 1992). The existence of a second gate has been postulated at the foot of the western slope of the Apadana mound; it would be connected to a staircase decorated with friezes of glazed bricks similar to some Persepolis reliefs (Kaboli 2000; cf. Perrot 2010c: 141, 143 n18).

The Apadana Mound, Ville Royale, and Acropole (total c.400 hectares), were surrounded by a plastered mudbrick *glacis* (artificial earthen slope) with salients (projections), but apparently not by a wall (Ghirshman 1965a: 6; 1968b: 14–17; Perrot 1981: 80–1; 2010c: 135–7; Steve and Gasche 1990: 28–31; Boucharlat 1997a: 57, 67). The 10–12 meter high *glacis*, built over an Elamite wall (Ghirshman 1965a: 6, Figs. 22–23), may be the older "fortification" that Darius says he restored (Steve 1987: 56–63; Schmitt 2009: 123–7).

Apart from the Apadana complex and the *glacis*, indications of Achaemenid presence are scarce within the enclosed area of c.100 hectares (Boucharlat 1997a, 2001). No residential quarters were found in the Ville Royale excavations and geophysical survey. Nevertheless, this mound was leveled in the Achaemenid period and undoubtedly formed part of Darius' urban design. Notably, its central part may have been purposely emptied (Perrot 1981: 90–91; Miroschedji 1987a: 40; Boucharlat 1990a: 150, 153). The only architectural remains are a ramp and gate at the eastern edge (Perrot 1981: 81–2; Ladiray 2010: 178–9), and the foundation of, perhaps, another causeway (Steve and Gasche 1990: 30–1).

The Donjon in the southern Ville Royale yielded Achaemenid stone reliefs, column bases, ivories, and other finds (Allotte de la Fuÿe et al. 1934: 222–36; Mecquenem 1943: 70–137; Amiet 1972a, 2010a), apparently in secondary, Seleucid, or later context. The presence of Achaemenid structures here remains debated (Martinez-Sève 1996: 174–5; Boucharlat 2000: 145–7; 2006: 447–8; 2010: 380–3; Amiet 2001: 241–4; Steve et al. 2002/3: 486–7).

The Acropole is the probable location of the Achaemenid citadel (Morgan 1898, 1900a; Perrot 1981: 81, 91; Boucharlat 2001: 119–20; 2010: 374–7). Early excavations revealed parts of the citadel's outer walls, column bases, a bronze lion weight (121 kilograms), and other objects. On the south side of the Acropole, near a Neo-Elamite temple, Morgan found two Achaemenid bronze "bath-tub" coffins. The first was empty, but the second, originally located in a vaulted tomb (hence continuing a Neo-Elamite tradition), contained a silver bowl with lotus decoration, gold bracelets, necklaces, and earrings with inlays of (semi-)precious stones, and alabaster vessels. The find is dated by coins to the late 5th century (Morgan 1905a; Amiet 1988: 134–7; Elayi and Elayi 1992; Tallon 1992; Razmjou 2005b; Frank 2010; cf. Boucharlat 1994: 219, 226). Fragments of inscribed royal tableware, made of stone and (in Elamite fashion) hardened bitumen, were found on the Acropole and elsewhere (Amiet 1990, 2010a; vitreous materials: Caubet and Daucé 2010: 343–6).

East of the enclosed area, the vast Ville des Artisans has yielded few Achaemenid remains. Ghirshman excavated a "village perse-achéménide" (1954), which, however, largely pre-dates the Achaemenid period. The small settlement was (re-)occupied in the late Achaemenid period (Steve 1986: 8–9; Miroschedji 1987a: 38–9; 1987b: 149–50).

Almost 13,000 glazed and molded (un)glazed bricks were recovered on the Apadana mound and elsewhere. They once formed decorative friezes of floral designs, archers (the "Susian" guards), lions, lion-griffins, winged bulls, sphinxes, lion-and-bull, and servants/tribute-bearers bringing food. The highly siliceous mixture of bricks and glazing materials continues an Elamite tradition (Dieulafoy 1890–2: 263–321; Mecquenem 1947: 47–86; Haerinck 1973: 118–27; Caubet and Muscarella 1992; Caubet 2007: 130–7; 2010; Maras 2010; Caubet and Daucé 2010). Though glazed reliefs were known at Persepolis (and stone reliefs in Susa), it is clear that vitreous materials were more important at Susa.

Building inscriptions from Susa, inscribed (and stamped) on a wide range of media, mention various constructions, not all of which can be identified. Few are found in situ. The texts date to the reigns of Darius I, Xerxes, Darius II (425/4–405/4 BC), and Artaxerxes II and III (Steve 1987; Lecoq 1997; Schmitt 2009; Vallat 2010; cf. Steve et al. 2002/3: 493–4; Boucharlat 2000: 142–4). The best known of these is Darius' "Susa Charter," actually a family of inscriptions describing the materials assembled in the palatial complex and the nations that collaborated in its construction. Minor variations have often been used as the basis for a reconstruction of building history, but this seems ill-advised (Grillot 1990; Henkelman 2003d).

The apparent emptiness of major parts of Susa (and other residences) does not necessarily indicate a reduced population. Apart from the possible incompleteness of the archaeological record (cf. Briant 2002: 257–8), a crucial point is that the Achaemenid court was itinerant (Briant 1988; 2002: 186–92; Henkelman 2010). Classical sources describe the spectacular royal tent, set up amidst a vast camp wherever the court halted. The leveling of the Ville Royale Mound and its inclusion within the protected area could suggest a royal residence conceived as combination of representative stone buildings and extensive residential camp (Boucharlat 1997b, 2001, 2007).

One or two of three Elamite tablets found in Ghirshman's Ville des Artisans excavations may be early Achaemenid (Ghirshman 1954: 79–82; Paper 1954; a Babylonian business document dates to an Artaxerxes (Ghirshman 1954: 83–5; Rutten 1954). Two more tablets from unknown locations at Susa are in the format of the Persepolis Fortification tablets (Scheil 1911: 89, 101; 1939: 109 [no. 468]; Jones and Stolper 1986: 247–53). There are also a few Achaemenid sealed bullae or dockets (Amiet 1972b/I: 284–7). Occasional doubts about Susa's administrative status are unwarranted: the few surviving tablets and bullae unquestionably reflect an extensive bureaucracy, like that of Persepolis (Stolper and André-Salvini 1992: 273; Garrison 1996; Henkelman 2008a: 78–79, 111–15; Briant 2010), that probably controlled an extensive agricultural zone around Susa, treasuries and storehouses built by successive Achaemenid kings (Strabo, *Geogr.* 15.3.21) and teams of workers sent to "Elam" from other parts of the empire. Also, Susa was an important destination for traveling officials and Babylonian businessmen (Joannès 1990; 2005: 193–6; Stolper 1992; Briant 2010; Waerzeggers 2010). Note also the Aramaic (votive?) graffiti from the Donjon (Amiet 2001: 243–4).

About 350 meters west of the main site, across the Šāhūr/Šāvūr River, Artaxerxes II constructed a 3 hectare palatial complex, perhaps as an additional palace in a landscaped environment or "paradise" (cf. Schmitt 1999: 80–5) rather than a temporary replacement of the damaged throne hall. The enclosed complex comprises several buildings flanking a vast, empty space (garden?). Most prominent is a hypostyle hall with four porticoes and an interior measuring 37 × 35 meters, reminiscent of the larger Susa throne hall. Some of its bricks had inclusions of mercury, perhaps a foundation deposit. A smaller building on a socle may have been a palace. Original flooring, figurative wall and column painting, sculptured orthostats, and glazed bricks were excavated at various locations (Labrousse and Boucharlat 1972; Boucharlat and Labrousse 1979; Hesse 1979; Boucharlat 1997a: 61–2, Figs. 14–15; 2010: 384–409). An Achaemenid stone staircase was found, in secondary context, about 800 meters north of the Šāhūr complex (Boucharlat and Shahidi 1987; Boucharlat 2000: 148–9).

The so-called *āyadana* building – now largely lost – was found by Dieulafoy (Dieulafoy 1890–2: 410–19) about 4 kilometers northeast of Susa. It included Achaemenid column bases in secondary (Seleucid or Parthian) context. Even if there was an older building at the site, the religious function implied in Dieulafoy's designation (*āyadana*, "place of worship") remains unfounded (Boucharlat 1984: 127–30; 2010: 410–22; Stronach 1985b: 619–22; Steve et al. 2002/3: 500). An isolated column base was found between Susa and Haft Tappeh (Kleiss 1975).

5 Tombs, Burials

Deceased Achaemenids were probably embalmed and put to rest in stone sarcophagi, either in house-shaped monuments or in rock-cut tombs (Jacobs 2010). Both varieties persisted throughout the Achaemenid period. Foremost in the first category is Cyrus' gable-roofed "house" tomb at Pasargadae. The dimensions of its stepped substructure are repeated in a stepped platform located 5 kilometers north of Persepolis, known as the Takht-e Rustam (Kleiss 1971). Recent investigations suggest that this monument was (provisionally) finished, may have carried a superstructure, and probably dates to Darius' reign. The common attribution to Cambyses lacks substance; reported finds of bones and jewelry remain unpublished (Bessac and Boucharlat 2010; Henkelman in press e). A smaller, gable-roofed "house" tomb on a stepped platform, known as Gūr-e Dokhtar, at Bozpār (c.50 kilometers east-southeast of Borāzğān), may date to the late or post-Achaemenid period (Nylander 1966a: 144–5; Stronach 1978: 300–2; von Gall 1979: 277–8; Vanden Berghe 1990; Boucharlat 2005: 236). The design of the "house" superstructure is sometimes connected to Lydian and Phrygian tombs (Stronach 1978: 40–3; Hanfmann 1983: 57; Ratté 1992: 158), the stepped platform to Elamite ziggurats (Herzfeld 1941: 215; Ghirshman 1963: 135; Stronach 1997a: 41–2).

Darius I was the first Achaemenid king to order a rock-cut tomb in the cliff of Naqš-e Rustam; the choice of location may have been informed by an Elamite relief there and open-air sanctuary (Henkelman 2008a: 44, 58). The tomb façade is cruciform: the upper section depicts the king carried on a platform, the central section a palace façade (inspired by Darius' *tačara*) with stone doors, while the lower part is empty (Calmeyer 2009; Krefter 1968; Seidl 1999, 2003). This design was repeated three times at Naqš-e Rustam and twice on the mountain east of the Persepolis terrace, where stepped terraces replace the lower façade section (Schmidt 1970). Tomb I has an inscription of Darius I (Schmitt 2000a: 23–49; later Aramaic inscription, Frye 1982); Tomb V at Persepolis has one by an Artaxerxes, perhaps Artaxerxes III (R. Schmitt cited in Calmeyer 2009: 35–41). The assignment of the remaining tombs is debated. The same is true for an eighth, unfinished tomb south of Persepolis, previously assigned to the last Achaemenid, Darius III (Calmeyer and Kleiss 1975; Briant 2003: 39–52, 510–13). The number of rock-hewn sarcophagi inside the tombs varies from two to nine (total: 26).

The dynastic monuments of Naqš-e Rustam and Persepolis may have inspired a number of (private) rock-cut tombs in the region, including those at Akhūr-e Rustam and Kūh-e Ayyūb. Their date is debated (Vanden Berghe 1953; 1959: 45, Pls. 61b–d, 62a–f; von Gall 1974: 143; Kleiss 1976: 136–9; Huff 1988: 155–9, 1991; Wiesehöfer 1994: 86–9). At Qadamgāh (50 kilometers southeast of Persepolis), a three-layered terrace approaching a rock façade is cut into the mountain slope. Tentatively dated, by the stone masonry techniques used, to the Achaemenid period, the monument shares some traits with the royal tombs at Persepolis. The façade, with two series of (unfinished) shallow niches, is very different, however. Qadamgāh is variously interpreted as a funerary monument or open-air sanctuary (Boucharlat 1979; Kleiss 1993b; Wiesehöfer 1994: 82–3; Bessac 2007).

Other Achaemenid or later rock tombs are found in western Fārs, such as those 14 kilometers southeast of Behbahān (Kleiss 1978) or that of Dā o Dokhtar, near Fahliyān. The façade of the latter is inspired by Achaemenid funerary monuments, but may be post-Achaemenid (von Gall 1993; Stronach 1978: 304; Huff 1988: 155; Wiesehöfer 1994: 85–6; Callieri 2007: 142–4). Most (but not all) cairns in Fārs and Kermān also post-date the Achaemenid period (Boucharlat 1989).

Some of the 31 burials (in earthenware coffins and in simple pits; orientation: north-northwest) in the Persepolis spring cemetery may date to the later Achaemenid period (Schmidt 1957: 117–23; Haerinck 1984: 304; Wiesehöfer 1994: 83–4). Otherwise, no cemeteries of possible Achaemenid date have been excavated. An oval pit grave in the Tang-e Bolāḡi is radiocarbon dated to c.370–350 BC (Asgari Chaverdi and Callieri 2009). Single jar burials and simple graves of uncertain date were recorded in the southern Ville Royale (Mecquenem 1930: 86–7; 1938: 326; Miroschedji 1987a: 15; Boucharlat 1990a: 155). The bathtub coffins from the Susa Acropole continue a tradition attested in Neo-Elamite Iran at Arğān, Rām Hormoz, and elsewhere (Álvarez-Mon 2010: 23–9; Henkelman in press a).

Achaemenid religious beliefs are much debated. Reports in classical sources are often taken to reflect Zoroastrianism, including the practice of exposure of the dead, commonly understood as Zoroastrian funerary orthodoxy. Archaeological evidence is limited to a few inhumations. There are no well-dated *dakhma*s, *astōdān*s, or other material indications of the practice of excarnation (Boucharlat 2005: 279–81). Rather, secondary inhumation may already have been practiced at Susa in the 5th millennium BC, pre-dating Zoroastrianism by at least three millennia (Hole 1990 [assuming fractional inhumation]; Potts 1999: 47).

Strictly religious monuments are rare in Achaemenid southwestern Iran (Boucharlat 2005: 281–2; for Dahan-e Ḡolāmān in Sīstān, see Gnoli 1993; Genito 2010). Apart from the stone plinths in the Pasargadae "sacred precinct," the tomb of Cyrus is the only place where religious activity may confidently be assumed to have occurred, given the funerary sacrifices mentioned in Classical sources. The Fortification archive mentions funerary sacrifices at the tombs of Cambyses, Hystaspes, and others (Henkelman 2003c); other such sacrifices may be assumed to have taken place at the Takht-e Rustam tomb and the funerary complexes of Naqš-e Rustam and Persepolis. A stone terrace at Zargaran (Kūh-e Ayyūb) may or may not have had a cultic purpose (Kleiss 1993c); a stone "shrine" on top of the Naqš-e Rustam cliff is of uncertain date and may be part of a fortification (Schmidt 1970: 10; Kleiss 1976: 145–6). The function of the towers of Pasargadae and Naqš-e Rustam is unknown. Despite all this, *āyadanā*, "places of cult/veneration," mentioned in Darius' Bisotun inscription, refers to concrete structures (temples or open-air sanctuaries), as appears from the Elamite and Akkadian versions. Temples or sanctuaries (Elamite *ziyan*) are occasionally mentioned in the Fortification tablets, as they are in the Greek sources (Henkelman 2008a: 469–73, 547–9; see above on the so-called *āyadana* complex near Susa). A post-Achaemenid (Elymaean?) date is preferable for the terraces of Masǧed-e Solaymān and Bard-e Nešānda (see Haerinck 1984: 302; Schippmann 1988; Boucharlat 2005: 238).

6 "Pavilion" Sites

A number of smaller sites defined by Achaemenid column bases and sometimes other structural stone elements have come to light in recent decades. On analogy with Pavilions A–B at Pasargadae, such structures are commonly known as "pavilions." Simultaneously, they are often interpreted as way stations. These characterizations are certainly too limited, if only because some of the pavilions are not situated along a royal road (Boucharlat 2005: 272–4).

The best-known pavilions are those of Tang-e Bolāǧi and Qalēh-ye Kalī. Both structures have gravel foundations, a technique attested at Achaemenid Susa. The first structure, located on the banks of the Pulvār river, is relatively small. It has two porticoes and a number of irregular spaces; interior walls were covered with green plaster (Atai and Boucharlat 2009). A concentration of Achaemenid pottery, an oven, rectangular platforms made from fragments of large storage jars, and small finds including arrow heads, ivory fragments, and a pair of frit eyes are all indications of a workshop area near the structure. The pavilion of Qalēh-ye Kalī (also Ğınğın or Tappeh Sūrūvān), in the Mamasanī region, was briefly investigated in 1959 (Atarachi and Horiuchi 1963; cf. Boucharlat 2005: 235–6) and excavated in 2007–9 (Potts et al. 2007, 2009; Potts 2008c: 276–280, 295). A stone-paved portico bordered by a stone parapet was accessible via three stone staircases; three monumental, bell-shaped column-bases, found in situ, are nearly comparable in size (basal diameter: 1.25 meters) to those in the Hall of 100 Columns at Persepolis. A large, rectangular mudbrick structure stood north of the portico; it may have been crowned by stepped stone merlons. There are indications of other buildings, perhaps one with another, smaller portico. Small finds include fragments of stone tableware comparable to that found at Persepolis, and a glass bowl. The site also yielded numerous fragments of large storage jars and three millstones. The small finds thus suggest elite contexts as well as local food production and storage. A second occupation phase occurred in the post-Achaemenid period.

Four plain column bases were discovered at Tappeh Pahnū (Mamasanī); in the same ploughed field, Achaemenid sherds were found (Asgari Chaverdi et al. 2010: 292–3). A third Mamasanī pavilion site may be Tol-e Gachgāran-e Ka Khodada, near Nūrābād, where Achaemenid column bases and capitals were found (Asgari Chaverdi et al. 2010: 293, 295; Potts et al. 2006: 4; 2009: 212, 215). At Tall-e Malyān (ancient Anshan) in central Fārs two probable Achaemenid column bases have been reported (Boucharlat 2005: 231; Abdi 2001a: 93 [cf. 97 n7 on another site]). More Achaemenid column bases have been found at sites in the Persepolis plain (Sumner 1986b). In none of these cases can a floor plan be reconstructed.

More pavilions are located in southern Fārs and the coastal regions. Best known are the abovementioned columned halls at Borāzğān, Sang-e Siāh, and Bardak-e Siāh. To these, Tall-e Hakavān in the Farmeškān district north of Fīrūzābād should be added. The site, briefly excavated in the late 1950s, yielded distinctive black and white limestone architectural elements, a sculptured lion and relief fragments of (early-)Achaemenid date (Razmjou 2005a). Stone courses on the surface indicate a series of buildings, also of Achaemenid date, the largest of which measured 9.40 × 8.32 meters.

At the Sasanian city of Fīrūzābād a number of different column drums, presumably Achaemenid, were found in secondary context. They may have belonged to structures at or near the site, but could have been brought there from further afield (Mostafavi 1967; Huff 1999: 634). The column bases found at Tall-e Zohāk and nearby Dārābgird may also stem from secondary context, but could originate from local structures, given the presence of Achaemenid pottery. The structural elements found at Tomb-e Bot near Lāmerd are probably post-Achaemenid. Outside Fārs, Achaemenid column bases have been found in the vicinity of Susa (cf. above) and further away, in northwestern Iran (see Boucharlat 2005: 252–4).

The Persepolis Fortification archive provides evidence for the development of Tamukkan/Taoce, where Strabo located a royal residence (Henkelman 2008b). This should already cast some doubt on the reductive label "pavilion." The monumental structures found in the Borāzğān region served as markers of royal control and prestige, but were doubtless also part of an administrative network controlling the strategically important coastal region.

Also documented in the Fortification archive are the movements of the courts of the king and the royal women Irdabama and Irtaštuna through the Achaemenid heartland (Henkelman 2010: 727–31). Periodic "local" tours served to make Achaemenid kingship tangible (just as the movements throughout the empire did on a larger scale), but probably also had more practical purposes, such as the settlement of disputes, confirmation of rights, etc. (Briant 2002: 191–5). Similarly, the tours undertaken by Darius' highest representative in Fārs and director of the Persepolis economy, Parnakka, obviously served administrative purposes. Elite structures like the one at Qalēh-ye Kalī may well have played a role in the royal and official itineraries. The large storage jars found there and at the Tang-e Bolāğī site may be connected with the large quantities of food and drink stored at royal halting places in preparation for the "table of the king." At the same time, as in Borāzğān, the pavilion sites may be seen as nuclei in the administrative and political grid.

7 Other Remains of Achaemenid Infrastructure

Kleiss' surveys north of Pasargadae revealed an impressive network of dams and sluices designed to protect the residence (Kleiss 1992a; Boucharlat and Feizkhah 2007: 19). The micro-region provides ample testimony to Achaemenid agricultural policy and efforts to manage available surface water. Other such remains include the two-arched sluice of Band-e Dokhtar near Dorūdzan (60 kilometers northwest of Persepolis), at the head of a canal that can be traced for c.50 kilometers (Nicol 1970: 249–65; Tilia 1972: 69–70, 1997; Sumner 1986b: 13–14). A causeway dam, again with sluice gates, at Bard Burīdeh (II), controlled a reservoir and a canal (Berger 1937; Nicol 1970: 269–81; Kleiss 1983: 106–7; Sumner 1986b: 14–16). Partially rock-cut canals in the Tang-e Bolāğī are part of yet another irrigation system (Kleiss 1991; Atai and Boucharlat 2009). Canals, dams, reservoirs, and associated constructions have also been documented in the surroundings of Persepolis (Kleiss 1976, 1992a, 1994; Boucharlat and Feizkhah 2007; Boucharlat and Gondet in press). Thanks to such irrigation efforts, vast territories could be claimed for cultivation – a circumstance reflected by the enormous harvests documented in the Fortification archive. One important clarification is in place here, however: although the *qanāt* technique appears to have been known and used by the Achaemenid rulers, there is as yet no unequivocal archaeological evidence for it in southwestern Iran (Briant 2001a).

The road system was a second major infrastructural element, not only as a communication network, but also as an artery opening up the hinterlands of the Persepolis economy. Whereas the courses of the various roads remain disputed (Potts 2008c), the Fortification archive in tandem with other written evidence and physical remains help to reconstruct their functioning. A stretch of the Royal Road west of Naqš-e Rustam, including two way stations 26 kilometers apart, was described by Kleiss (1981; Sumner 1986b: 17) and another such structure may be recognized among the Tang-e Bolāḡi structures (Asadi and Kaim 2009). More way stations, though perhaps not all of Achaemenid date, have been identified in western Fārs and Khūzestān (Yaghmaee 2006). Stone-paved sections of the Royal Road are found at various locations (Nicol 1970: 278; Sumner 1986b: 17; Callieri 1995).

Boucharlat (2005: 245–6) has made the interesting suggestion that the (unexcavated) "fortified sites" recorded during R.J. Wenke's survey in central Khūzestān (1975–6) may in fact be part of the state infrastructure relating to transport routes and centralized agricultural activities. The Fortification tablets indeed document numerous granaries, storage and administrative centers, plantations, bird farms, and livestock stations. Archaeological correlates are still rare: apart from the farmstead (?) and other structures in the Tang-e Bolāḡi, the Circular Structure at Čoḡā Miš (interior diameter: 7.5 meters) is the most important find. Plausibly dated to, and certainly used in, the Achaemenid period, it may have served as a central granary; it is comparable in shape to Persian-period granaries in southern Palestine (Delougaz and Kantor 1996: 11–12). An Achaemenid-Elamite clay tablet, a cylinder seal, and a sealing (on what seems to be a Persepolis-type, anepigraphic tablet) from Čoḡā Miš are additional glimpses of a local branch of the Achaemenid administration in the heartland (Jones and Stolper 1986: 248; Delougaz and Kantor 1996: 10, 17–18).

The fortified structure excavated in the Tang-e Bolāḡi (Asgari Chaverdi and Callieri 2009: 27–32) may perhaps be compared to what the Fortification tablets call a *halmarraš*, a "fortress" that simultaneously functioned as storage center. A second type of fortified structure is represented by the fortifications and citadels of Pasargadae, Persepolis, and Susa. Yet other strongholds may have guarded stretches of the Royal Road, such as, perhaps, a site at the foot of the Kūh-e Ayyūb (30 kilometers northwest of Persepolis; Kleiss 1993c). Tall-e Zohāk (see above) is likely to have been an important regional stronghold. It would be a good candidate for the location of Paišiyāuvādā/Naširma, documented in the Bisotun inscription and the Fortification archive. At the modern towns of Fūrg and Tarūm (southeast of Dārāb), thought to continue the early Achaemenid strongholds of Parga and Tāravā, no signs of Achaemenid occupation have thus far been found (Henkelman 2010: 704–13; in press b).

8 Transition

Like its beginning, the end of the Achaemenid period is not reflected sharply in the archaeological record. Overall, the little we know of the period of transition (c.350–300 BC) suggests continuity and gradual change, rather than rupture (Boucharlat 2006; Callieri 2007). Emblematic of this phenomenon is painted festoon ware, which seems to start in the late Achaemenid and continue into the Parthian period (Stronach 1974b: 241–3; Haerinck 1984: 303–4; Dyson 1999). Parts of the palatial complexes of Susa and Persepolis were used and modified in the Seleucid period. At Pasargadae, the Tall-e Takht has yielded relatively abundant Seleucid (and later) material; an early Hellenistic or Roman sculpture was found near Borāzğān (Rahbar 1999c; Callieri 2007: 105–8). The beginning of the Seleucid period rarely manifests itself clearly at any of these sites, however (Miroschedji 1987a: 35–43; Boucharlat 1987b: 195, 233–4; 1990b; Wiesehöfer 1994: 64–100). At Susa, an exception could be a rare dark glazed ware, also known in Mesopotamia, which may imitate Greek examples (Boucharlat 1987b: 187; 2006: 445–6). At Persepolis, a series of five Greek inscriptions on stone slabs found north of the terrace, mentioning the names of five divinities, are sometimes dated to the late 4th century. If they are indeed connected to the sacrificial banquet organized by Peucestes in 316 BC (Wiesehöfer 1994: 72–3; Callieri 2007: 50–67), they would, however, also be part of a continued Achaemenid (and Elamite) tradition (Henkelman 2011).

In the past decades two other transitions have taken place. The first involves intensified agriculture and land use, which pose a serious threat to smaller sites in the Achaemenid heartland. This could obliterate the least investigated aspect of Achaemenid archaeology: life beyond the residences, where the realities of continuity and transformation may have left a much clearer footprint. At the same time, Achaemenid archaeology has experienced a period of renewal, as the number of recent Iranian and foreign surveys and excavations amply testifies. Current work on the comprehensive publication of the Fortification archive happily coincides with new excavations like those in the Mamasanī and Tang-e Bolāği areas. The future of the Achaemenid heartland could be bright.

GUIDE TO FURTHER READING

The rich survey by Boucharlat (2005) is currently the most up-to-date overview of the archaeology of Achaemenid Iran. For the preceding Iron III and earlier periods see the important report by Azarnoush and Helwing (2005). Synopses of current excavations are regularly published in the journal *Iran*. Entries on ancient Iran are found in *Encyclopaedia Iranica* (also online) and the *Reallexikon der Assyriologie*, including surveys on Pasargadae, Persepolis, and Susa. Among site-oriented publications, the recent volume on Darius' palace at Susa should be mentioned (Perrot 2010b).

The standard reference for the history and culture of the Achaemenid Empire is Pierre Briant's 1996 synthesis (English translation: Briant 2002). Concise overviews are given in Wiesehöfer (1996) and Kuhrt (1995: 647–701). Kuhrt (2007) also includes a very helpful sourcebook. Allen's (2005) introduction to the Achaemenid Empire stands out among publications aimed at a wider audience. Among recent exhibitions catalogues, those from Vienna (Seipel 2000), London (Curtis and Tallis 2005), and Bochum (Stöllner et al. 2004) may be mentioned. A virtual "Achaemenid Museum" (MAVI), a sub-site of www.achemenet.com, aims to digitize Achaemenid monuments and objects in museum collections. Scholarly literature on pre-Islamic Iran and the Achaemenid Empire (archaeological and historical) is vast but well inventoried in a range of bibliographies. See the annual "Archäologische Bibliographie" by Peter Calmeyer in *Archäologische Mitteilungen aus Iran* (1974–2004) and the review abstracts in *Abstracta Iranica* (1978–; also online). Periodic archaeological bibliographic surveys have been published by Louis Vanden Berghe and his successors (Vanden Berghe 1979; Vanden Berghe and Haerinck 1981, 1987; Haerinck and Stevens 1996, 2005). More than 14,000 titles (up to 1991) on the Achaemenid Empire are listed in the vast bibliography Weber and Wiesehöfer (1996). Briant's synthesis (see above) includes notes with critical biography; updates are found in Briant (1997 and 2001a).

CHAPTER FIFTY-ONE

The Achaemenid Provinces in Archaeological Perspective

Lori Khatchadourian

1 Introduction

In the 1990s, at a time when the study of the Achaemenid Persian Empire was beginning to coalesce as a self-conscious field of inquiry, Margaret C. Root (1991) lamented that a "politics of meagerness" dominated the archaeology of this unprecedented experiment in world empire. Root had in mind a troubling tendency on the part of commentators to underscore *absences* when addressing the material impact of Achaemenid art and institutions in the western reaches of the empire. This discourse of feebleness betrayed, in Root's assessment, a modern predisposition to underrate the efficacy of the Achaemenid imperial project. It both fueled and was fueled by a deeply entrenched scholarly perspective that privileged the cultural production and world-views of the Greeks, through whose literary works much of Achaemenid history is compiled. As many before and since have noted, when it comes to the Persians we moderns have long been beguiled by the tropes of those to whom we credit the origins of Western civilization – tropes that emphasize Persian barbarism and weakness (Sancisi-Weerdenburg 1987; Briant 2005). These and other disciplinary origin myths account for the liminal status of Achaemenid studies, long marginalized by both Classical and Near Eastern archaeology. Contesting traditional "Hellenocentric" approaches to the Persians and their empire (and a clarion call for a corrective to this particular manifestation of Eurocentrism) has become a central element of the subfield's "process of self-legitimation" (Giddens 1995: 5).

A Companion to the Archaeology of the Ancient Near East, First Edition.
Edited by D.T. Potts.
© 2012 Blackwell Publishing Ltd. Published 2012 by Blackwell Publishing Ltd.

Two decades after Root's defiant dictum, it may be said that the politics of meagerness in the archaeology of the Achaemenid Empire is on the wane. A growing community of scholars is now studying the empire on its own terms, no longer refracted solely through the lens of Greek cultural production. Archaeologically, this is well attested by a recent edited volume, *L'Archéologie de l'empire achéménide*, that provides a much-needed, candid assessment of the state of the field. Bygone narratives staked upon a Greek civilizational prerogative have been rendered, if not obsolete, then at least irrelevant. What remains, however, are preambles and asides about insufficient evidence that still permeate an (ironically) expanding body of work. What are we to make of the current talk of meagerness that still prevails? In part it emerges from a rather banal fact: the evidentiary record of a little-investigated imperial phenomenon that is over two millennia past – indeed, one that has scarcely been the object of targeted archaeological research – is limited, sometimes even threadbare. But there may be more at work in the concern to underscore the dearth of evidence. The grievance over scanty material remains emanates in part from the misplaced expectation that "normal" imperialisms express themselves in the form of abrupt material ruptures and the diffusion of canonical artistic styles of a dominant group – an expectation encoded in the abused term "impact" – and that deviations from this must constitute imperialism's aberrant forms. But imperialisms both ancient and modern are rarely so straightforward and unimodal in their manipulations of the object world. As we shall see, the evidentiary record appears far less meager when this expectation is relinquished, when formal style is no longer the barometer of imperial efficacy, but more subtle forms of social re-engineering within materially constituted sociopolitical worlds.

The intended or unintended effect of the qualifications and forewarnings about limited evidence is to dampen expectations with respect to the interpretation of what data there are. The unfortunate need simply to demonstrate that the Achaemenid Empire *existed* – to conjure the spaces and things within it into the field of vision of Classical and Near Eastern archaeology – has led to an understandable commitment to description as an end in itself. This, in turn, has diminished Achaemenid archaeology's epistemological prerogative vis-à-vis ancient history. Despite work theorizing the relation between text and artifact within historical archaeologies (Andrén 1998; Moreland 2001), one still encounters the perspective that archaeology's capacity to inform the Achaemenid past resides in its ability to play "un rôle correcteur" against partial interpretations of Greek literary sources (Briant and Boucharlat 2005b: 22). Briant and Boucharlat have acknowledged archaeology's role in contributing to socioeconomic history and the study of material techniques, even if they place political and cultural analysis beyond its ambit. Other historians hold an even less sanguine view. Tuplin (2007a: 297) has opined that "there is little point in pretending that [literary] texts do not (or should not) provide a framework with which purely material evidence has to interact."

This is neither the place, nor any longer the era, to mount a defense of archaeology's capacity to extend the study of past and present into domains of knowledge production where history is relatively impotent. However, it is an opportunity to begin to recalibrate the archaeology of the Achaemenid provinces, opening it up to contemporary anthropological perspectives that probe the profoundly spatial and material constitution, and conditions, of social and political life. As a starting point, in place of the more customary region-by-region approach to the archaeology of the Achaemenid Empire (cf. Briant and Boucharlat 2005b; Curtis 2005a, 2005b), this contribution adopts a thematic organization, highlighting a selection of sites that best illuminate a given problematic. In forsaking aspirations for comprehensive coverage and the useful catalogues that such coverage can generate, it is hoped that a comparative account can bring into greater relief the degree to which agents of the Achaemenid Empire pursued material strategies toward imperial integration. In addition, although the present contribution is intended primarily to provide a broad overview of the archaeology of the Achaemenid provinces, thus hovering at a general register that prohibits in-depth analysis, where appropriate I draw upon my own research on the Achaemenid province of Armenia in order to provide a small window onto an archaeology of the empire that forwards the spatiality and materiality of social life.

Reasons more prosaic also dictate the economy of data sources and themes chosen for these pages. The proliferation of research on this empire in recent decades has given rise to the entirely felicitous need to delimit inquiry. Thus, little will be said about entire artifact classes customarily researched through art historical approaches (e.g., glyptic, coins, sculpture, toreutics). I steer clear of the minefield of "Greco-Persian" style and related questions of "cultural" influence that, by their very nature, reify normative ethnic positions. Also set to one side is the growing body of landscape and settlement pattern studies in places like Arabia (Anderson 2010), Armenia (Khatchadourian 2008), Judah (Milevski 1996–7), Lydia (Roosevelt 2009), Paphlagonia (Johnson 2010), Phoenicia (Tal 2000), and Samaria (Zertal 1990). So much, then, for meagerness.

2 History at a Glance

At the time of its ascendancy, the Achaemenid Empire (c.550–330 BC) was, by all accounts, the largest polity the ancient world had ever known. From the imperial heartland in southwestern Iran, the Achaemenid Dynasty maintained ever shifting degrees of sovereignty over an enormous domain, stretching from the Aegean Sea to the Indus River, and from Egypt and Arabia to the Caucasus mountains and Central Asia. Some of this realm was conquered during the reign of the founder king Cyrus, who took control of Media (in 550 BC), conquered Babylonia (in 539 BC), possibly reduced areas along the Aegean coastline, as well as Lydia or Armenia (in 547 BC), and campaigned in Central Asia. His immediate successor, Cambyses, continued this expansionary phase of the empire's development with his conquest of Egypt. A period of severe dynastic and provincial unrest followed Cambyses' death in 522 BC, but it was brought to an end by the charismatic king, Darius I (522-486 BC), who, in addition to adding more territory to the empire, inaugurated a period of consolidation. Both before and after Darius, much of what ancient Classical authors wrote about the Achaemenid empire is a story of revolts and military campaigns as various kings faced uprisings from recalcitrant subalterns, for instance in Ionia (Asia Minor), Egypt, and Babylonia. The events of the reigns of Darius' successors up until the empire's demise at the hands of Alexander of Macedon are less well known, but recent attention to these long-dismissed periods suggests that the later kings focused primarily on internal administrative concerns.

What is meant by a "province" of this enormous macropolity? Strictly speaking, the Persians themselves had no such word. They appear to have envisioned their empire as constituted by a number of countries or peoples. In each such realm they appointed privileged Persian individuals known as *xšaθrapāvan*, or protectors of dominion. Greek authors called these individuals "satraps" and, from this, coined the word "satrapy" to designate a province of the Achaemenid Empire (Klinkott 2005). By and large, these satraps were based in the locations of the satrapies' earlier political centers (e.g., Babylon in Babylonia, Sardis in Lydia, Memphis in Egypt), from which they conducted administrative duties such as collecting taxes and tribute, maintaining military forces, and carrying out royal decrees. Beneath the level of the satrapy, the imperial establishment appears to have relied heavily on pre-existing institutions and local ruling families, inevitably creating conditions of tremendous diversity across the empire. This raises one of the prevailing questions in Achaemenid studies: to what extent should we speak of local autonomy as a function of ineffective governance, or to what extent was a policy of indirect rule and the use of pre-existing institutions a deliberate strategy of hegemonic control? Recent trends favor the latter interpretation.

3   The Armor of Coercion: In Defense of Empire

On his tomb at Naqsh-e Rustam, Darius underscored his ability to extend the empire's military might into the outermost reaches of his realm through the poetic metaphor of a singular warrior: "the spear of a Persian man has gone forth far." Archaeologists of the Achaemenid Empire have long been attuned to that most elemental dimension of imperial power – the capacity to act on the threat of organized political violence in order to forge and maintain sovereignty. Although often indirect, scattered across the empire is tantalizing evidence for the deployment of the instruments of violence. At Gordion, for example, a major stronghold in Phrygia strategically located on the Royal Road from Sardis to Susa, archaeologists have associated the presence of arrowheads embedded in fortification walls, the destruction of a nearby pre-Achaemenid fortress abutted by what appears to be a monumental siege mound, and the abandonment of a pre-Achaemenid Lower Town, with the historically attested Persian capture of Gordion in 546 BC (Voigt and Young 1999). And amidst the debris surrounding a fortification wall at Sardis, unsettling remains of battle – weaponry, armor, and skeletons – have been associated with Cyrus's capture of the Lydian city (Cahill and Kroll 2005). Apart from initial conquest, material traces of the many rebellions known to have flared up over the course of the empire's long history – in Ionia, Egypt, Babylon, to name a few – are rare but extant. Some have attributed the destruction levels and renovations of several sites in Persian-period Palestine – Megiddo, Dor, Nebi Yunis, Mikhmoret – to the Tennes Revolt of the mid-4th century BC although debate surrounding such claims continues (Barag 1966; Stern 1990, 2001; Betlyon 2005). And as at Gordion, the extensive remains of a siege mound at Palaipaphos on the island of Cyprus, coupled with hundreds of sling stones, arrowheads, and javelin points, have been taken as telltale signs of the Achaemenids' aggressive response to the Cypriot revolt at the turn of the 5th century BC (Briant 1994; Maier 1996).

Such examples may serve to illustrate specific events of Achaemenid military history and, however faintly, render palpable the devastating force of political violence, otherwise easily obscured by the remove of textual representation. But insofar as the defense of empire hinges more critically upon the deterrence of instability rather than solely its brutal suppression, we must look elsewhere as well for its archaeological correlates. Our immediate concerns are not the social institutions of persuasion and consensus that are so critical to the project of maintaining political order, but the "armour of coercion" that ultimately protects hegemony (Gramsci 1971: 263). In the archaeology of the Achaemenid provinces, an infrastructure of military preparedness, marked most conspicuously by fortresses and garrisons, attests to the empire's coercive capabilities.

This is particularly visible in Persian-period Palestine, where numerous military outposts protected the strategic routes that traversed the region both north–south, along the Mediterranean coast, and west–east, from the coast to inland territories (Tal 2005). In addition to building new military installations, in many cases local or imperial leaders renovated existing facilities first built in the age of Assyrian ascendancy (Stern 2001). Though their sizes varied, many of these forts shared a highly standardized architectural form. The strongholds of Hazor in the north, Nahal Tut on the Phoenician coast, and Ashdod, Tell Jemmeh, Tel Sera', Tell el-Far'ah (S), and Tel Qatif in Philistia, for example, all exhibit a characteristic quadrangular courtyard structure (Stern 2001; Betlyon 2005; Tal 2005). The presence of silos, granaries, storage pits, and storehouses at some of these sites further suggests that many of the forts may have served as way stations for army garrisons, just as did Tell el-Hesi in Philistia, Tel Michal on the Sharon Plain, and Tel Halif in Idumaea, where evidence for provisioning is also present. Yet the material remains of daily life – pottery, figurines, agricultural tools –

caution against a solely martial interpretation that precludes the multifunctionality of these sites as lived places. Indeed, across this region we find several towns and administrative centers, such as Megiddo, Dor, Lachish, and Tel Haror, that also project a concern for defense, billeting, and provisioning. That said, special-purposes installations like the observation tower at Tel Qatif and the fortified encampment at el-Qaʿadeh also existed (Zertal 1990; Stern 2001).

Some of the abovementioned sites likely functioned to safeguard agricultural production and commerce along busy thoroughfares, but the relatively dense concentration of logistical depots in southern Palestine may more directly represent an apparatus of political violence. The region was at times a border zone between the empire and the recalcitrant province of Egypt, which attained a period of independence from c.400 to 342 BC (Fantalkin and Tal 2006). Not surprisingly, then, we find signs of military preparedness on the other side of this frontier. In the northern Sinai, investigations at the imposing fortified site of Tell Kedoua, for instance, have revealed bastions, access ramps, and a system of casements. Encampments may have surrounded this fortress, possibly a satrapal center or fortified royal pavilion. Religious, civic, and administrative activities likely also took place at the nearby fortresses at Tell el-Herr, whose saw-toothed fortification walls recall earlier, Egyptian defensive architecture (Valbelle and Deferenz 1994). Together with Tell el-Maskhuta in the eastern Delta – a Saite-period site that was expanded subsequent to its attack by the Persian army in 525 BC – these fortresses guarded access into Egypt from the north (Bard 2008). To extend and protect Egypt's southern frontier, the Persians garrisoned troops within a network of fortresses, most notably Elephantine and Dorginarti, at the First and Second Cataracts (Heidorn 1991).

The twin need to secure crucial transit routes and provide bases for military engagement in the face of actual or potential political unrest appears also to have been particularly pronounced in western Anatolia. Surface survey suggests that the Mediterranean coastal regions of Aiolis and Ionia, for example, hosted a system of strategically placed fortifications that protected routes leading to and from major inland centers, such as Sardis. The nature of these sites range from fortified towns to garrisons and lookout stations, all seemingly integrated into a single defensive network (Gezgin 2001). The immediate hinterlands of Sardis itself exhibit a similar investment in an infrastructure of defense, in the form of dispersed rural garrisons, some of which were situated at high elevations and heavily defended, such as Şahankaya and Kel Dağ. These likely functioned not only to insure tax collection and safeguard agricultural productivity, but also as military bases in the frequent skirmishes that threatened imperial authority in the Lydian countryside (Roosevelt 2009). Elsewhere in Asia Minor, as in Lycia, we see a pattern of fortified settlement marked by towering strongholds that guarded residential areas clustered around their slopes (Marksteiner 2005). Forts and fortified settlements also regulated transit routes along the Black Sea (Johnson 2010).

Hilltop fortresses dotted the landscape in more easterly regions of the empire as well, possibly serving as both defensive locations and provincial centers. Included among them is the monumental fortified town of Meydancikkale in Cilicia (Gates 2005). In Central Asia, of particular note are the massive walled sites (not exclusively forts) of Old Kandahar in Arachosia, Kiuzeli-g'ir and of Kalal'i-g'ir in Chorasmia, Erk Qala, and other fortresses in Margiana, possibly Koj Tepa in Sogdiana, and numerous fortresses surrounding undefended settlements in Bactria (Vogelsang 1992; Genito 1996; Helms 1997; Francfort 2005a; Khozhaniyazov 2006; Gricina and Genito 2010).

Two important caveats conclude this cursory discussion on the archaeological correlates of the empire's armor of coercion. First, we must allow for some fluidity when ascribing social roles to the actors who occupied the empire's fortified spaces. While at some times, and in some places, such strongholds may have buttressed directly the long and heavy arm of the imperial apparatus, they also likely worked to satisfy local concerns for defense and stability in the face of threats (real or imagined) that were outside the purview of the imperial gaze. Second, the tendency to narrowly associate monumental fortifications and lofty perches with an anxiety over security can obscure the intra-communal social divisions and power disparities that such spatial dividers can engender, reproduce, or reflect. In the satrapy of Armenia, for example, it appears that fortified sites such as the possible satrapal centers of Erebuni and Altintepe (see below), as well as more modest citadels like that at Tsaghkahovit, were linked not exclusively to defense in the narrow sense of resistance from violent attack, but more fundamentally to the defense of a longstanding sociopolitical arrangement that had staked inequality upon topographic distance and the further symbolic and practical segmentation of political community through massive stone enclosure walls (Khatchadourian 2008). Comparative survey data from across the Armenian highlands hints at a movement of settlements in the Achaemenid period downward from the commanding heights of mountain citadels, and outward from walled spaces into unfortified locales. Though possibly attributable to a *pax Persica* in this region, the probable shift away from fortified living in some regions of the Armenian satrapy may be more immediately linked to a transformation in the material constitution of social difference in the Achaemenid era. The separation of the archaeological dimensions of coercion from those of political life is a heuristic gesture whose limitations are clearly exposed when the sociopolitical work of the armor of coercion is taken into account.

4 The Armature of Authority

Agents of empire have well understood the work of built spaces in appropriating and maintaining authority within conquered territories. From the "other Cuzcos" of the Inka, to the far-flung cities of the Roman Empire and modern Europe's

Gothic colonial architecture, many imperial projects have relied in part on the perceptive and experiential dimensions of somewhat standardized political landscapes (A.T. Smith 2003). Understood in only its broadest contours, the Achaemenid Empire presents an early and, on current evidence, tantalizingly minimalist iteration of this materially constituted strategy of expansive rule. That is, in place of a stock architectonic of provincial governance, in most cases the Achaemenid establishment (by which I mean both central and local authorities) incorporated and adapted existing spatial logics.

Thus, dotting the full breadth of the empire from Syro-Palestine to Central Asia was a myriad of privileged places that have come to be called "palaces," "residences," or "administrative centers." Such locales stand out as sites of local officialdom on account of several of the following factors, in terms of the built spaces that constituted them: relatively monumental scale; agglomerations of integrated, functionally differentiated rooms; supra-household storage facilities; and architectural elements of canonical Achaemenid (formal) style. In the eastern reaches of the empire, attention has turned to such palaces or administrative centers at Dahan-e Golaman in Drangiana (eastern Iran) (Scerrato 1966), Old Kandahar (Helms 1997), and Kalal'i-g'ir (Vogelsang 1992). In Arabia and Mesopotamia, there is Qalat al-Bahrain in the Persian Gulf (Potts 2010) and Tell ed-Daim in northern Iraq (Curtis 2005b). Recently published sites like Tille Höyük on the Upper Euphrates (Blaylock 2009) and Meydancikkale (Gates 2005) are filling in the picture for Anatolia, a region where the accretions and erasures of subsequent occupations at known satrapal centers such as Daskyleion and Sardis have limited our understanding of civic architecture (Ateşlier 2001; Bakir 2001a; Dusinberre 2003; Erdoğan 2007). Such built spaces of political authority have been uncovered with particular density in Syro-Palestine (coastal Syria, Jordan) and Cyprus: Vouni, Lachish, Ashkelon, Ashdod, Dor, Tel Michal, Tell Qasile, Tell es-Sa'idiyeh, Tell el-'Umeri, Akko, Tall Jalul, al-Dreijat, Buseirah, Tell Mardikh – the list could go on (Mazzoni 1990; Bienkowski 2001; Stern 2001; Zournatzi 2003, 2011; Betlyon 2005; Tal 2005; Fantalkin and Tal 2006). A cluster of "palaces," so described on account of the presence of stone column bases distinctly Persepolitan in their formal style, have recently been uncovered in the South Caucasus, at sites like Gumbati, Sari Tepe, Beniamin, and Karacamirli (Gagošidze and Kipiani 2000; Knauss 2005, 2006; Knauss et al. 2010).

Though listed here with little elaboration, these sites should by no means be conflated as a singular homogenous phenomenon. Among other things, these "palaces" or centers differ in the timing of their emergence, the scale of their operations, the details of their built plans, and their histories of occupation before and after Achaemenid takeover. That said, a shared research approach certainly provides a common ground for our understanding of these provincial centers. Scholars of these major and minor centers have attended carefully to matters of chronology and periodization, architectural description, and, in some cases, the specific historical circumstances – both eventful and structural – that can account for their emergence and functioning. Where the density of such "palaces" is particularly high – namely, in Syro-Palestine – efforts at typology are underway (relevant here is the prevalent open courtyard house whose closest parallels are to be found in Neo-Assyrian architecture; see Tal 2005). And where architectural elements invoke forms of the imperial heartland, as in the Caucasus, there has been a concern to define the ethnic identities of the occupants and workmen (Knauss 2005, 2006). What the current approaches offer is an effective antidote to the discourse on meagerness, by providing a rich dataset for querying the spatiality of local power in the Achaemenid Empire.

New findings will continue to thicken the descriptions of these sites and there can be little doubt that additional examples will emerge. But the time is ripe to begin considering the symbolic efficacy of such sites within local regimes of rule and their practical operation in promulgating local authority. As they are currently deployed, the terms in circulation are elusive. "Palace," "residence," "administrative center," though useful as shorthand, can lend a false sense of understanding to spaces whose practical affordances and affective capacities in the production of political community and the everyday making of empire remain underexamined. In the remainder of this section, I illustrate an approach to the armature of Achaemenid authority that fixes its gaze on such unaddressed concerns, using as examples two sites from the highland satrapy of Armenia: Altintepe (Turkey) and Erebuni (Armenia) (Khatchadourian 2008, in press). It is often emphasized that the Achaemenids, like a great many imperialists, largely co-opted the major centers of their conquered communities, insinuating themselves into well-entrenched structures of political authority. But in some of their building programs, agents of the empire also appreciated the need to deploy a distinctive architectonic vocabulary that extended and signified the institutions of Achaemenid power. In the case of Altintepe and Erebuni, reappropriation and rebranding appear to have gone hand in hand. It should be said that the analysis that follows is preliminary; the findings from recently revived excavations at Erebuni may alter the chronology of its construction and occupation.

Once counted among the iconic hilltop fortresses of the earlier Urartian Empire, based on current understandings of these sites, it appears that Achaemenid authorities reconfigured fortresses by building hypostyles halls within their walls – spacious, internally undivided chambers with roofs supported by multiple rows of pillars. As an architectural form, the columned hall signals a departure from the local past of the Armenian highlands. This building type finds no direct counterpart in the earlier architecture of the region (even as similar columned halls are known from pre-Achaemenid sites in Iran). By and large, Urartian fortresses were labyrinthine spaces premised on the segmentation of activities and the regulation of movement through the use of densely compacted rooms (A.T. Smith 2003). As a new kind of built space, the highland halls articulate most immediately with an Achaemenid tradition of configuring places of authority with strictly rectilinear colonnaded structures (other full-fledged hypostyle halls outside of the imperial centers of Pasargadae, Persepolis, Susa, and Babylon have only been postulated on the basis of isolated archaeological elements, such as column bases and capitals fashioned in distinctive Achaemenid formal style). I have argued elsewhere that the halls of Altintepe and Erebuni may have served metaphorically as extensions of the empire's struggle for cosmic and political order into the provinces (Khatchadourian in press). They can thus be seen to evoke the aspirations that underlay an Achaemenid world-view.

At the same time, by building the halls within the buttressed walls of Urartian fortresses these satrapal centers of Achaemenid control were effectively anchored to a familiar and enduring local political landscape. The new users of these sites appear to have vested their authority in part on the potentially diverse affective responses such reoccupations might have created for those both within and beyond the walls of the fortresses. They were citing a distinctly highland conception of the proper constitution of authority, as vested in topographic difference, augmented by formidable defensive constructions that accentuated the distance between rulers and ruled. In other words, on view in the conjoining of hilltop fortress and hypostyle hall at Erebuni and Altintepe is a complex assimilation of old places into new traditions of political practice.

Apart from the perceptive dimension of these spaces, considerations of the halls' architectonics (scale, circulation, and orientation) open a window onto the kinds of everyday activities that may have taken place within them. I have argued on the basis of such architectonic analysis that they were multifunctional places in which group council among highland elites periodically took place (Khatchadourian 2008, in press). Assembly halls would have facilitated the production of cadres versed in the norms of Achaemenid social practice through face-to-face interaction. If so, the halls would have served as critical mediating locations between local leaders from across the highlands and representatives of imperial authority. The highland halls likely inculcated local leaders, thus binding the communities from which they came to a larger collective and sustaining the empire's rules and conventions. The spaces at Erebuni and Altintepe not only mediated certain kinds of Achaemenid practices that sustained hegemony, but in the process these spaces enabled the preservation, albeit in altered form, of deeply engrained highland political values that became implicated in imperial reproduction.

5 Living Under Empire: Households Beyond Palaces

The archaeology of households is now widely recognized as a research focus uniquely positioned to inform the everyday practices that reproduce relations of power, yet it has made few inroads in the archaeology of the Achaemenid Empire. The tendency to seek the "impact" of the empire in only the most privileged locales of social life has given rise to a rather restrained view of imperialism as a contained phenomenon that extends no further than the rarified spheres of elite activity. This is not to say that ordinary residential contexts have gone entirely unnoticed in the archaeology of the Achaemenid provinces, as we shall see, but that such contexts have not been traditionally understood as constitutive of the social and political reproduction of empire. Yet, as archaeologists of other empires have demonstrated, domestic contexts and quotidian routines are key arenas for the imposition, adoption or rejection of imperial institutions at the microscale (Brumfiel 1997; Voss 2008).

A rather different set of preoccupations surrounds the study of household contexts in the Achaemenid Empire. In Palestine, for instance, a concern to trace the emergence and development of Hippodamian (or gridded) town planning looms large, such that the residential quarters at sites like Tel Dor, Akko, Shiqmona, Megiddo, Tel Megadim, and Tel Michal are examined less as spaces of social production than as models that more or less conform to an urban ideal predicated upon regularly gridded streets that intersect at right angles (Stern 1990, 2001; Betlyon 2005). The social world of everyday life under empire is equally absent from efforts to develop typologies of domestic architecture in this region (Stern 2001; Tal 2005). Elsewhere across the empire, the limited attention given to domestic contexts has focused on the grounds for their identification, the description of their architecture, and the cataloguing of the objects they contained. In Jordan, for example, domestic contexts have been identified at Tall al-Mazar and Tall el-'Umeri, among other sites, on the basis of evidence for everyday activities requiring storage pits, groundstones, spindle whorls, oven fragments, etc. (Bienkowski 2001). In Egypt, houses at Ayn Manwir have attracted interest for the dated documents (ostraca) found within them (Wuttmann et al. 1996), much as Aramaic papyri from the site of Elephantine dating to the 27th Dynasty have overshadowed interpretive analysis of the houses excavated there. However, variability among domestic contexts at the site of Tell el-Muqdam in the central Delta invites further investigation into the everyday making of social difference in one town under empire (Redmount and Friedman 1997). At the Anatolian site of Gordion, questions of continuity and change in domestic architecture before and after Achaemenid conquest surround the study of a relatively large sample of excavated houses (Voigt and Young 1999). In this same region, a large residential complex at Tille Höyük may illustrate the intermingling of domestic and official activities among privileged landholders or local administrators (Blaylock 2009). And in the eastern Iranian province of Sistan, a substantial residential quarter at Dahan-e Golaman preserves local traditions of domestic architecture even as public buildings at the site reveal the long hand of empire (Gnoli 1993; Scerrato 1966).

Research currently underway at Tsaghkahovit, a remote mountain town in the satrapy of Armenia, was designed with the express purpose of investigating the material making of Achaemenid hegemony in the everyday (Khatchadourian

2008). The daily lives of Tsaghkahovit's denizens revolved largely around a subsistence economy of mixed agropastoralism supplemented by craft production involving bone and stone tools, ceramics, textiles, and iron implements and adornments. In a semi-subterranean residential complex of more than 20 interconnected rooms, tantalizing evidence is emerging for specific routines linked to the reproduction of certain imperial institutions. Faunal analysis hints at the rearing of horses, perhaps consistent with the satrapy's tribute obligation, as described in historical sources. More importantly, excavations across several sectors of the site are opening the possibility to gauge the social segregation of subsistence and tribute economies. In addition, the faunal remains, coupled with morphological, quantitative, and qualitative characteristics of ceramic assemblages in select rooms of the complex, point to forms of commensal consumption that, in various ways, reference conventions of the imperial heartland. Similarly, Dusinberrre's (2003) analysis of ceramics from Sardis also indicates new patterns of consumption attendant upon Achaemenid imperialism, offering important insights into the practices that extended the empire's reach into the everyday lives of ordinary subjects.

6 Dying Under Empire: Archaeology of Mortuary Practice

In the middle of the 4th century BC, the satrap Maussollos and his wife (and sister) Artemisia designed a tomb of such scale and ostentation that the monument would later join the ranks of the Seven Wonders of the Ancient World. Maussollos' tomb at Halicarnassus, in Caria (southwestern Anatolia), was set atop a high, rectangular podium perched by an Ionic peripteral upper stage that was roofed with a stepped pyramid, which was in turn crowned with a statue of a four-horse chariot. Though scarcely extant today, written descriptions, sculptures, and fragmentary building remains suggest a massive and elaborate construction that harnessed a diverse architectural and iconographic vocabulary drawn from Mediterranean and Near Eastern traditions.

The Mausoleum of Halicarnassus represents the culmination of an Achaemenid phenomenon that is strikingly unique in the archaeology of archaic empires: provincial authorities who were either granted, or appropriated, the prerogative to build immense tombs that displayed their status and materialized their claims to authority. The existence of such tombs in various regions of the empire and across the two centuries of Achaemenid hegemony suggests that they signal less the inability of central imperial authorities to reign in ambitious provincial leaders than a strategy of rule that capitalized upon the local sources of legitimacy enjoyed by regional collaborators. Given the nature of the evidence, this discussion primarily focuses on the upper echelons of Achaemenid society, suggesting that more work remains to be done on lower-status burials that might articulate with the archaeology of the everyday described in the previous section.

The available data point to two broad patterns. First, a limited but notable pattern comprises funerary practices that appear to conform either overtly or obliquely to the mortuary traditions and material practices of the Achaemenid Persians themselves. For instance, reconstructions of the Pyramid Tomb in the Lydian capital of Sardis, with its built chamber placed atop a stepped base, closely resemble the tomb of king Cyrus at Pasargadae (Ratté 1992), as does a freestanding, rectangular, two-story monument hewn from a single bedrock outcrop at Taş Kule, near the Ionian city of Phokaia (Cahill 1988). So confidently do these tombs appear to cite an iconic symbol of the Achaemenid founder king that the question of the ethnic identity of the deceased (some have suggested they may have been Persian) recedes in importance relative to the bold declarations of authority that such monuments represent. Later free-standing stone tombs of the 4th century BC, such as Maussolos' tomb and the "heroa" or "ruler-tombs" of Lycia, distantly echo the Cyrus monument, but apart from their elevated podia the designers looked principally to the architectural and iconographic traditions of Greece rather than Persia. The precise funerary rites enacted in association with these tombs remain obscure. Cahill posits that the stone hollow in front of Taş Kule recalls the fire bowls used in Zoroastrian ritual. Others have also identified archaeological evidence for mortuary rites that may have adhered to funerary laws proscribed by Zoroastrianism, such as ossuaries and possible fire installations in Lycia, Lydia, and Caria (L'vov-Basirov 2001). Yet interpretation of mortuary remains as locales for the disposal of the dead in accordance with a putative Achaemenid proto-Zoroastrian code sits uncomfortably alongside ongoing scholarly debate concerning the relationship between Achaemenid religion and codified Zoroastrianism.

In addition, evidence for mortuary rituals in the mountainous zones of inland Palestine and Jordan suggest the deliberate, if selective, reproduction of Achaemenid practical (as distinct from iconographic) conventions. The coffin burials in the cemeteries of Shechem and Tell al-Mazar, for example, contained assemblages of ceramic and metal vessels that morphologically replicate Achaemenid royal tableware and finewares. Some have assigned such burials to Persian soldiers serving in provincial garrisons (Stern 2001; Wolff 2002), but rather than viewing them as passive reflections of normative ethnic positions, we might instead consider such assemblages for their role in funerary ritual activities that to some degree reproduced Achaemenid conventions of ritual consumption. A particularly complex mortuary dataset survives in Paphlagonia (northern Anatolia). Here, columnar, rock-cut tombs hewn from sheer cliff faces amalgamate Aegean, Achaemenid, and Anatolian architectural and iconographic elements whose social efficacy, Johnson has argued, can only be understood when situated within their local landscapes (Johnson 2010; cf. Dönmez 2007; Summerer and von Kienlin 2010). Such rock-cut cliff tombs occur elsewhere in Anatolia (see below), in some cases pre-dating the Persian conquest. While the Paphlagonian tombs are unique, resisting neat attribution to the predominant Greek and Persian sculptural traditions of the day, they articulate in subtle ways with Achaemenid ritual practices (Johnson 2010).

Across the provinces of the empire, individuals and families of varying social status drew upon and reimagined mortuary and material practices of the Achaemenid heartland as expressions of Persian identity, strategic gestures of political allegiance, or cynical appropriations of hegemonic symbols. However, the far more widespread pattern in the Achaemenid provinces entails either the persistence of old or the emergence of new local funerary traditions that exhibit limited, if any, association with the mortuary and material practices of imperial Persia. At the highest echelons of Achaemenid society, we may look to the elaborate shaft tombs of Egyptian elites, like the senior official and Persian supporter Udjahorresnet and the priest and administrator of palaces, Iufaa (and his family), who embedded themselves within ancient sacred and royal landscapes by aligning their tombs with the pyramids of the 5th dynasty at Abusir, the Step Pyramid at Saqqara, the Giza pyramids, and the Sun Temple at Heliopolis. More modest shaft tombs appeared later in the Persian period around Memphis, perhaps as new imperial overlords imposed limits on excesses of affluence and stature among regional elites (Stammers 2009). But the overall conception of elite Persian-period burials of the 27th Dynasty remained decidedly Egyptian, so much so that they can be difficult to assign narrowly to the period of Achaemenid hegemony (Aston 1999). In nearby Phoenicia, stone anthropoid sarcophagi redolent of Egyptian prototypes in overall form, yet inflected in the Achaemenid period with Greek modes of facial representation, likewise perpetuate earlier traditions (Moscati 1988b).

Available evidence suggests a thoroughgoing commitment to local burial traditions among several privileged families of western Anatolia as well, although the work of tomb robbers has left us with a woefully partial basis for reconstructing mortuary practice. Most widespread are the region's tumuli burials – large earthen mounds built atop chamber tomb complexes that dot the landscapes of several regions of Asia Minor (e.g. Phrygia, Lydia, Paphlagonia). In some cases, such tumuli contained elaborately carved sarcophagi, such as those from Kizöldün and Çan (in northwestern Anatolia). Both draw upon the iconographic traditions of the Aegean. Yet they evince a possible shift over time in elite conceptions of the themes appropriate to funerary art, with the earlier sarcophagus calling up Greek mythology and the later one deploying subject matters more prevalent in the artistic circles of the Achaemenid establishment (Kaptan 2003; Rose 2007). In the case of the Lydian tumuli, the presence of ceramic assemblages associated with drinking, of couches possibly symbolic of (eternal) banqueting, and of charcoal deposits that hint at a ceremony involving fire provide a sense of the broad contours of a funerary rite (Dusinberre 2003). The tumuli burials derive from Anatolian antecedents that predate Achaemenid conquest, and they appear to have been reserved for the region's political and social elites. The more than 600 known tumuli in Lydia alone point to a funerary strategy premised on individual and kin-based status display and ostentation (Roosevelt 2009). Though highly conspicuous on account of their strategic placement and monumental scale, in some cases phallic stones, stelae, and lion statues further marked the locations of the mounds, and perhaps variously symbolized rebirth and passage, or functioned apotropaically. Such Lydian tumuli likely both reflected and encouraged a strong sense of autonomy rooted in pre-Achaemenid local traditions of imperial hegemony. The phenomenon of secondary burials in the form of pits and sarcophagi dug into pre-existing tumuli in Lydia may attest to the ideological efficacy of these monuments in reaffirming commitments to a local past.

Also common to several regions of Anatolia (e.g. Lydia, Lycia) are rock-cut chamber tombs hewn from cliffs and hillsides that differ from the Paphlagonian variants in that their origins and forms reside primarily in the pre-Achaemenid traditions of the region. Roosevelt (2009: 140) has assigned the rock-cut chamber tombs of Sardis to the city's "large and affluent middle classes" (cf. Ch. II.48). Zahle (1983) has posited that the "house-tombs" of Lycia, whose stone architectural features are thought to reproduce the region's wooden houses, belonged to individuals of more modest social standing relative to Lycia's sarcophagi and "pillar tombs" (Keen 1995). Reigning dynasts or leading personages of Lycia built large, rectilinear, upright shafts of stone that taper slightly toward the top, out of which a burial chamber was hewn. Perhaps the most distinctive burial form in Achaemenid Anatolia, the Lydian pillar tombs, confidently (and perhaps at times insubordinately) asserted local authority through an entirely unique mortuary monument whose inscriptions and artistic motifs emphasize themes of wealth, public fame, personal achievement and aggression (Draycott 2007).

For the vast majority of subjects in the imperial provinces, below the highest echelons of society, burial traditions varied widely. Some communities buried their dead much as they had before the Achaemenid takeover, while others introduced new forms and incorporated grave goods of distinctive Achaemenid style. Commoner burials have received the least attention in the archaeology of Achaemenid mortuary practices. But those that have been exposed – like the humble pit burials of Tall al-Mazar and Tall es-Sa'idiyeh (Jordan) (Bienkowski 2001), Tell Shiyukh Fawqani (Syria) (Luciani 2000), Kamid el-Loz (Lebanon), or the terracotta and limestone "bathtub" sarcophagi of Lydia (Roosevelt 2009) – adopt forms that point to the continuity of local material practices. Other, modest burials, such as the shaft tombs, cists, and pits of Phoenicia and the Palestinian coastal plain (e.g., Tel Michal, Akhziv, Atlit, etc.) contain inventories, in many cases quite limited, that derive from traditions not of Persia but of the Mediterranean (e.g., Phoenecia, Greece, Egypt) (Stern 2001; Wolff 2002). The humble pit and stone-lined cist graves of Deve Höyük introduce a new mortuary practice to this region of ancient Syria (inhumation rather than cremation) and contain eclectic assemblages that combine Mediterranean ceramic traditions with metal weapons and jewelry associated with the material culture of the empire's eastern lands (Moorey 1980). Amidst similarly eclectic assemblages, the jewelry recovered from the stone-lined cist and ceramic "bathtub" burials of Haçinebi suggest related associations to Achaemenid material repertoires (McMahon in Stein et al. 1997). As at Haçinebi, humble pit, cist, coffin, or "bathtub" sarcophagus burials excavated at sites of past grandeur, such as Ur, Babylon, and Tushpa (modern Van, Turkey) are embedded within or above the ruins of earlier structures (Woolley 1962; Haerinck 1995; Tarhan 2007), inviting analysis into the commemorative acts that transform houses of the living into houses of the dead (Khatchadourian 2007).

This discussion has remained largely silent on the myriad artistic representations deployed in Achaemenid-era burials of particularly privileged individuals in the provinces. The implied distinction between, on the one hand, the practices linked directly to the disposal of the deceased and, on the other, the ways in which funerary imagery provided an opportunity for the broader expression of identities, political and social aspirations, and personal aesthetics may be largely heuristic. For example, in Achaemenid Anatolia, in particular, many elites clearly deemed visual representation as a desirable, if not essential, element of proper burial practice and they favored imagery that engaged with a wide range of concerns, such as banquets and battles, hunts and mythological accounts, scenes of audience, procession, and gift-bearing, and the symbolism of the vegetal and animal kingdoms. These are encountered across media, but attention has focused especially on free-standing stone stelae, relief fragments, sculptures, architectural façades, wall-paintings from tombs, and sarcophagi. The scholarly approaches to these representations have become increasingly refined in recent years, such that efforts to segregate putatively fixed Persian, East Greek, and Anatolian iconographic traditions are giving way to a subtler mode of analysis that recognizes complex processes of hybridization and the strategies entailed therein. Suffice it to say that few themes appear to relate directly to funerary rituals (banquets and processions may, but the contextual meaning of these are also debated), constituting instead representational contemplations upon the concerns and identities of the deceased during their lifetimes. They are thus beyond the scope of the above discussion.

7 Divine Disjuncture

Whether seeking to incorporate compatible structures of cosmological meaning or to eradicate and replace putatively idolatrous beliefs, agents of empire often turn to material tactics in the religious integration of conquered communities (Jennings 2003; Wernke 2007). The archaeology of religious life in incorporated provinces of empire becomes a particularly challenging enterprise, however, when religious integration itself is not an aspiration of imperial authorities. Such appears to have been the case in the Achaemenid Empire, where religious heterodoxy was, if not cultivated, strategically tolerated across the empire. The thorny question of the Achaemenid Dynasty's religious practices lies beyond the limits of this inquiry. But what is clear from an assessment across the provinces is that there is little evidence for the promulgation, materially or otherwise, of a state religion or imperial cult deployed as an instrument of imperial integration. Claims of a systematic policy of religious syncretism that amalgamated local deities with the pre-eminent Achaemenid gods also rest on shaky ground (Bedford 1996).

Instead, the written record points to what Allen (2005: 125–6) has succinctly described as the crown's "positive but removed relationship" to local religions, whose "Civic sanctuaries and regional pantheons, when relevant and convenient, could be cultivated and drafted into a recognition of Achaemenid rule." This is most vividly apparent in Babylon and Egypt, where early Achaemenid kings co-opted the mantle of indigenous kingship by fashioning themselves as upholders of local cults (Bedford 1996). The temple of Hibis in the Kharga oasis, completed under Darius I and dedicated to Amun, provides archaeological evidence for this phenomenon (Winlock 1941). Cooperative communities met with religious tolerance and sometimes even beneficence toward their cults and temples, but tolerance was, as Allen (2005: 131) contends, "a tactic of domination": the sanctuaries of the uncooperative or rebellious could be subject to religious repression. In this section we explore the kinds of material evidence of sacred practices that register efforts on the part of imperial authorities to reckon with the tremendous diversity of pantheons and pieties within their realm. The discussion here focuses mainly on built sacred spaces, setting aside the ways in which natural features, cultic objects, ritual deposits, and iconographic representations of sacred activity were also constitutive of religious practice.

Material evidence of religious rituals in the Achaemenid provinces thought to derive from the imperial heartland centers primarily on an enigmatic construction known as a "fire altar" – an installation, typically consisting of a stand with stepped top and base, used to hold fire for the purpose of veneration (and sometimes, not uncontroversially, with Zoroastrianism) (Houtkamp 1992; Garrison 1999). Depictions of fire altars on the tombs of the Achaemenid kings and on sealings associated with the imperial court establish their sacral and political significance in the constitution of Achaemenid ideology. Material remains of presumed fire altars from the heartland (cf. Ch. II.50) are at present restricted to stepped stone fragments and a podium that may have hosted such an altar from Pasargadae (Stronach 1978).

In the provinces, the appearance of such features and, more broadly, evidence for extensive usage of fire are customarily associated with Achaemenid religious ritual. Stepped pyramids of clay often interpreted as fire altars were found at the sites of Dahan-e Golaman in eastern Iran (QN6 and QN16) and Altyn-10 in Bactria (Structure II) within apparently residential ("palatial") and public contexts (Sarianidi 1977; Scerrato 1979). Scerrato regarded the large sacred enclosure of QN3 at Dahan-e Golaman, with its multiple altars and oven-like installations, as not necessarily a centrally imposed ritual space intended for the veneration of fire or the worship of Achaemenid deities (Ahuramazda, Mithra, and Anahita), as others have suggested (although for a more recent assessment, see Sajjadi 2007). Instead, he contended that, prior to the Achaemenid takeover of this region, religious practices were reserved for the "private" sphere, suggesting that the large-scale ritual space may be the result of a centrally mandated institutionalization of religious practices.

Installations that may have been used in rites involving sacred fire also appear in western Anatolia. In addition to the presumed fire bowl at Taş Kule discussed above, a limestone feature with a two-stepped plinth and top recovered from Bünyan in central Anatolia may represent one such altar, as may the rock-cut stepped feature with platform from Lycian Limyra (Wurster 1974; Houtkamp 1992; Işik 1996). Excavations of a free-standing rectangular platform in the refinery area at Sardis revealed traces of burning episodes that some have taken as evidence that this edifice, originally built before the Achaemenid conquest as an altar to Cybele, was converted into a fire altar (Ramage and Craddock 2000). The structure does not conform morphologically with the altar types known from the imperial heartland. Dusinberre (2003: 68) has cogently argued that this instance of religious rehabilitation provides evidence of Achaemenid religious "cooptation and conversion." In contrast, Roosevelt (2009) regards the fire altar near the fortress of Şahankaya in greater Lydia as a sanctuary intended for Persian troops stationed in the nearby garrison (see above). Dusinberre's and Roosevelt's differing interpretations of these two installations highlight a key struggle in the effort to make sense of the "fire altar" phenomenon: if the notable occurrence of such features is attributed to a deliberate policy of imperial intervention in religious life, then the infrequency of the phenomenon demands explanation. On the other hand, interpreting the altars as places of worship for Persian colonists, soldiers, or adherents to a pan-Iranian Mazdean religion risks stripping these sites of their potential political significance as institutions of domination.

A different set of challenges is presented by sites of enduring religious significance that underwent some transformation upon or during the imposition of Achaemenid control, but where the correlation between such transformations and the imperial hand remains obscure. For example, in Phoenicia, the longstanding temple of Eshmun and Astarte, near Sidon, was renovated in the Achaemenid period to include a massive podium that recalls Achaemenid architectural elements (Ciasca 1988), but for what new ritual purpose remains uncertain. Perhaps most striking is the open-air temple complex, a rock-cut stepped altar with stepped crenellations enclosed by a colonnaded portico, dedicated to Melqart-Heracles near Amrit. The structure arguably incorporates architectural elements drawn from Phoenicia, Egypt, Greece, and Persia. While much debate has surrounded the stylistic analysis of the site (Jigoulov 2010: 184), it remains to be considered how such eclecticism in built form might have forged hybrid ritual practices and to what social ends. Lastly, we might include in this category a second altar at Sardis – a rectangular stepped platform built in the Achaemenid period possibly in a place of earlier religious significance, whose built form merged East Greek and Persian architectural traditions for the veneration of a local instantiation of Artemis. If Dusinberre (2003: 63) was correct in ascribing the stepped component to Achaemenid influence, we have yet to understand what practical significance this would have had in the worship of a local deity. In all these examples, the agents, motivations, and meanings behind the observed changes in spatial practices demand further elaboration that admits for direct, indirect, or even absent involvement on the part of imperial authorities.

Further investigation needs to undertaken into the archaeological evidence of religious practices in the Achaemenid provinces that suggest a thorough disinclination on the part of imperial agents to intervene in local cults. Such evidence is particularly abundant in Phoenicia. The sanctuary of Tanit-Astarte at Sarepta, for instance, underwent little change from its Late Bronze Age predecessor. Likewise, the conversion of the temple of Tell Sukas from a Greek to a Phoenician religious site, dedicated to the worship of Astarte and Melqart, betrays no indication of imperial intervention, though it may have been an indirect consequence of social transformations brought about by Achaemenid hegemony. Newer temple sites at Tel Michal and Mizpe Yammim point to the viability of a diverse and pluralistic sacred landscape that embraced Phoenician and Egyptian deities, but the Achaemenid/Iranian pantheon is virtually absent. Smaller shrines or chapels at several sites of Palestine (Dan, Tel Michal, Achzib) represent an enduring Iron Age tradition of cultic practice that was unhindered in the Persian period (Betlyon 2005; Stern 2001). At present, we lack a sufficient sociopolitical explanation for the conspicuous homogenization of some dimensions of ritual practice across this region, marked by a newfound uniformity of cult objects such as figurines associated with the worship of Phoenician, Egyptian, and Greek deities. But, by and large, local religious traditions prevailed without disruption in much of Phoenicia and Palestine.

This observation holds in other regions of the empire as well. In Mesopotamia, Woolley (1962) suggested that a late complex associated with the *ziggurat* at Ur might indicate the continued maintenance of the Nanna priesthood under Achaemenid occupation. In Egypt, the temple of Amun at Hibis and the temple to Osiris at Ayn Manawir attest to the strength of indigenous cults, in the case of the former, with direct royal benefaction. Yet the absence of such direct intervention should not be taken as an indication of imperial irrelevance. As Zahle (1994) remarked with respect to the "Ionian Renaissance" and the lavish, sacred building projects of the Carian Hecatomnid satraps, the wealth and authority needed to undertake initiatives such as the temple of Zeus Labraynda at Halicarnassus were privileges largely conferred by the crown.

8 Conclusions and New Beginnings

This chapter began with a critical discussion on the rhetoric of meagerness that has long pervaded the archaeology of the Achaemenid provinces. In that context, an encouraging statistic concludes this account of the materiality of coercion, authority, households, death, and religion in the archaeology of the Achaemenid provinces: more than half the relevant publications cited in these pages have appeared since the turn of the new millennium and as many as a third have been published since 2005. The accelerated pace of recent archaeological research begs the unconfronted question: What is the measure against which paltry and plenty are to be gauged? Archaeology offers no such yardstick, but recent decades of archaeological thought have productively resisted the notion that processes of data collection and analysis are either strictly sequential or independent. Future fieldwork and methodological advances are critical, to be sure, and we can be generally confident that they will occur. It can also be hoped that, with the abundance of new evidence coming into view, mutterings over insufficient datasets will subside as the work of robust interpretation begins.

Several potential new directions of research may enrich that project. As Sinopoli (1994, 2001b) has noted, the tremendous scale of most empires makes the task of comparative archaeological analysis within them (let alone amongst them) incredibly daunting. Yet integrative analysis offers an important complement to tightly focused research, providing a window onto "the extent to which the impact of empire on households, communities, and local economies was uniform across diverse regions or whether imperial hegemony differentially affected imperial subjects and imperial territories, and how this changed over time" (Sinopoli 2001). More broadly, as it strives to refine higher levels of abstraction on the materiality of imperialism, the comparative archaeology of empires stands to gain from more active interventions on the part of those who study one of the earliest experiments in expansionary macropolity. Students of the Achaemenid Empire will likely continue to struggle over the relationship between the different epistemologies engaged in their enterprise. But some resolution may be found in the comparative social archaeology of provinces under empire that allows the archaeological to collaborate with the historical and the art historical, without dissolving the distinctions among them.

GUIDE TO FURTHER READING

For a brief, general introduction to Achaemenid history, students may consult Kuhrt (2001b) while for a lengthier treatment, see Allen (2005). For a comprehensive, primarily historical work, see Briant (2002). A number of edited works touch on the key themes in Achaemenid studies. Most important among these are the *Achaemenid History* series published between 1987 and 2003. See also the studies published in Tuplin (2007b) and Curtis and Simpson (2010). Works dedicated to material culture that bring together multiple regions of the Achaemenid Empire include Briant and Boucharlat (2005a) and Curtis (2005a). For full-length archaeological works devoted to particular regions, see, e.g., Stern (2001) on Palestine; Dusinberre (2003) and Roosevelt (2009) on Sardis and Lydia; Khatchadourian (2008) on Armenia; and Johnson (2010) on Paphlagonia.

CHAPTER FIFTY-TWO

The Seleucid Kingdom

Lise Hannestad

1 Introduction

The death of Alexander in Babylon in 323 BC left a vacuum not only in the leadership of his huge army, but also in the leadership of Macedonia, since he had no obvious successor, his still unborn son by his Iranian wife and his mentally handicapped half-brother being the only blood-related options. In this situation, more than a handful of talented and ambitious generals made "agreements," but actually began to fight each other for territorial gains and, in the end, also for the royal title as the successor of Alexander. It was in these tumultuous circumstances that the Seleucid kingdom was born. One of those generals was Seleucus who in 321/320 BC came to rule Babylonia. Fifteen years later, in 304 BC, after continued fighting, he was able to assume the title of king. In 303 BC he took possession of the regions east of Babylonia, the so-called "upper satrapies," including Iran and present-day Afghanistan. After the battle of Ipsus in 301 BC and the defeat of Antigonus the One-Eyed, Seleucus' main rival in Asia, northern Syria fell to him. The Seleucid kingdom, which for periods also included extensive parts of Asia Minor, was by far the largest of the Hellenistic kingdoms. By the mid–3rd century BC, however, Bactria, the easternmost satrapy, had broken away and become an independent Greek kingdom. This was to some extent compensated for in the late 3rd century when one of Seleucus' successors, Antiochus III (the Great), conquered and took Phoenicia and Palestine from the Ptolemies based in Egypt. From the 2nd century onwards the kingdom gradually shrank in

---

A Companion to the Archaeology of the Ancient Near East, First Edition.
Edited by D.T. Potts.
© 2012 Blackwell Publishing Ltd. Published 2012 by Blackwell Publishing Ltd.

size, most notably when the Parthians conquered Mesopotamia. In 64 BC the last Seleucid king, Antiochus XIII, lost his kingdom, at the time comprising only Syria, to the Romans, and a few years later the area became a Roman province.

2 Administration and Royal Economy

The nature of the Seleucid kingdom has been the subject of a large number of scholarly discussions. The traditional view of it as a "Western" kingdom, based on a continuation of Macedonian kingship and firmly rooted in the Greek way of life, was challenged in the late 1980s and 1990s by, e.g., E. Will (1979–82), P. Briant (1990), and A. Kuhrt and S. Sherwin-White (Sherwin-White and Kuhrt 1993) who claimed that it was an "Eastern" kingdom centered in the Middle East – to a large extent a successor of the Achaemenid empire. A more recent approach argues that this is not an either/or issue. It is now accepted by most scholars that the kingdom cannot be classified as one or the other, for in reality the situation was much more complex (Austin 2003; Hannestad 2004, in press a).

As in the other Hellenistic kingdoms, the administration of the Seleucid kingdom was centered on the king's court. The highest-ranking group of administrators and officials, the so-called "friends" (*philoi*), was the heart of the power structure in all of the kingdoms. The court was normally located in the palace (or palaces) of the capitals in the kingdom. To the "friends" also belonged the governors of the various provinces. The structure of governance with satrapies as the main units was inherited from the Achaemenids. We have a wealth of royal correspondence from the Seleucid kingdom from which we learn of the administrative procedures involved as decisions taken by the king were executed through a chain of higher- to lower-ranking officials. The central issue, as in all the Hellenistic kingdoms, both for the central administration and local bureaucracy, was clearly to maximize income for the royal treasury.

Rich evidence of the fiscal system has been found in several cities in the kingdom, both ancient ones and new foundations. This consists mainly of sealed bullae (clay dockets) that were originally affixed to parchment or papyrus documents or, in Mesopotamia, cuneiform texts with seal impressions. Among the taxes attested is a tax on land and its produce – undoubtedly the largest source of royal income (Aperghis 2004). The salt tax, evidence of which is provided by bullae found, e.g., at Seleucia-on-the-Tigris and Uruk, was also important. From Uruk we also have evidence of a tax on sales of slaves, probably also other types of goods, and on transport on the Euphrates. At Ai Khanoum in northern Afghanistan (ancient Bactria), excavations in the royal or satrapal palace (see below) have revealed part of the treasury where jars containing "drachms," "silver of high quality," "olive oil," and "incense," to mention some of the best attested products, were stored. On the jars we find Greek inscriptions in ink with information on their contents and volume or weight (Rapin 1983).

Economic transactions, although based on the tax-collecting system of the Achaemenid Empire, saw a move towards monetization, undoubtedly brought about by the Greek and Macedonian conquerors. During the lifetime of Alexander, only one mint, at Babylon, was established east of the Euphrates, immediately after the conquest. There huge quantities of Alexander coins were produced. With a few exceptions, the Greek coinage tradition became completely dominant. Alexander coins continued to be produced in the early decades of Seleucid reign, but later the Seleucids used the portrait of the reigning king on the obverse of coins, while the reverse shows an incredible wealth of motifs, among them Apollo or Zeus, the tutelary deities of the Seleucids (Mørkholm 1991; Houghton and Lorber 2002). Coins in gold, silver, and bronze were produced at mints scattered across the kingdom. Seleucus established a mint at his first capital, Seleucia-on-the-Tigris, and others at Ecbatana (modern Hamadan) and Susa in Iran, all of them very productive. Other important mints included the one at Ai Khanoum in Bactria. After the conquests in the west, mints were established at, e.g., Antioch-on-the-Orontes in Syria and later at Sardis in Lydia (western Turkey). From the 2nd century onward, Antioch was by far the largest mint in the gradually diminishing kingdom. Large emissions of coins were often connected with the kings' military campaigns.

The impact of the Alexander coinage on economic life is reflected in Babylonian administration, where we find cuneiform texts stating prices in "x shekels of silver in staters of Alexander." A text from 321 BC records the wages of workers restoring a temple as "1/3 mina of silver, the weight of 10 staters" (van der Spek 2007). In cuneiform texts from Uruk dated to shortly after 295 BC, prices were given in "Alexander staters in good condition." The impact of the Alexander coinage outside the empire is perhaps best witnessed by the imitations produced in Arabia (Potts 1990, 1991a; Callot 2010; van Alfen 2011), a region in close trading contact with Mesopotamia as well as Egypt and the Mediterranean, reflecting how sociopolitical circumstances influenced old trading networks. Alexander types became the recognized international means of exchange.

3 Cities and Settlements in the Kingdom: A Program of Colonization

Alexander founded a large number of new cities in the territories he conquered, the most famous of which was undoubtedly Alexandria in Egypt. Like Alexander's other successors, Seleucus continued this tradition, founding his first capital in Babylonia and naming it Seleucia-on-the-Tigris after himself. Following the conquest of Syria, Seleucus founded a number of cities there, the most important being the so-called "Tetrapolis," the four cities of Antioch (mod. Antakya, Turkey), Laodikeia (mod. Latakia, Syria), Seleucia-in-Pieria (mod. Çevlik, Turkey) and Apamea (mod. Afamia, Syria), all named after close family members or himself and situated in the coastal region of northern Syria and the hinterland along the Orontes River. Smaller cities were founded on the main routes heading east (e.g., Kyrrhos and Gindaros) and along the Euphrates (Cohen 2006). This ambitious program, which clearly shows that Seleucus saw the newly won territories as the future center of his kingdom where he wished to make an unprecedented display of wealth and power, changed the physical landscape significantly and represented one of the most impressive and lasting displays of Hellenistic royal power on a landscape (Hannestad in press b). Seleucia-in-Pieria was undoubtedly intended as his western capital, since it was given his own name. Later, Antioch-on-the-Orontes became the capital and would grow to become one of the largest cities in the Hellenistic and Roman world. Many foundations mentioned in the literary sources remain unknown to us, whereas excavations have brought to light other cities of Seleucid origin, the ancient names of which are lost, such as Jebel Khalid in Syria (see below) and Ai Khanoum in Bactria (see below).

Who were the inhabitants of these new cities and how did they interact with the existing populations? That ex-soldiers in the Seleucid armies were settled here cannot be doubted. The conquered territories were to a large extent classified as royal land, and the king had the power to distribute the land as he saw fit. Land allotments (Greek *kleroi*) in and around the new cities were given to soldiers and their families. North and northeast of Damascus, rectangular (96 × 144 meters) Hellenistic land plots have been identified that are closely connected with the Hippodamian layout of the street grid of the city. It is uncertain, however, whether this land division dates to Ptolemaic or Seleucid times (Dodinet et al. 1990).

As Chaniotis (2005) has stressed, the foundation of new cities and military settlements in the Hellenistic world provided opportunities for large numbers of immigrants from mainland Greece, the islands, and the coast of Asia Minor.

Seleucia-in-Pieria

Seleucia-in-Pieria was undoubtedly intended to be Seleucus's western capital, since, like his capital in Mesopotamia, it was given the king's own name. The fact that Seleucus was buried there after being murdered in 280 BC is yet another argument favoring its identification as his capital. Based on the standing remains of its city wall, Seleucia-in-Pieria may have covered c.300 hectares. In his account of its re-conquest by Antiochus III in 219 BC (at the beginning of the Fourth Syrian War), Polybius described the city thus (*Histories* 5.59.3):

> The town descends in a series of broken terraces to the sea, and is surrounded on most sides by cliffs and precipitous rocks. On the level ground at the foot of the slope which descends towards the sea lies the business quarters [*emporia*] and a suburb defended by very strong walls. The whole of the main city is similarly fortified by walls of very costly construction and is splendidly adorned with temples and other fine buildings. (Trans. W.R. Paton, Loeb Classical Library)

Excavations have revealed Hellenistic fortification walls preserved for c.5 kilometers with at least nine towers (McNicoll 1997). The foundations and remains of a Doric temple (possibly Seleucus' burial monument (Hannestad and Potts 1990) were discovered, as well as one of the characteristic traits in the townscape mentioned by Polybius – i.e., the staircase connecting the lower and the upper city.

Antioch-on-the-Orontes

Antioch is a case where contradictions between archaeological and literary evidence (Cohen 2006: 80–4) have caused confusion, the main problem being how to relate the wealth of literary evidence available from late Antiquity to the scarce archaeological evidence of the Hellenistic period. Among the earlier literary sources, Strabo informs us (*Geography* 16.2.4) that the city in itself was a Tetrapolis,

> since it consists of four parts: and each of the four settlements is fortified both by a common wall and by a wall of its own. Now Nikator [i.e., Seleucus I] founded the first of the settlements, transferring thither the settlers from Antigoneia, which had been built near it a short time before by Antigonus; the second was founded by the multitude of settlers; the third [the palace area] by Seleucus Callinicus; and the fourth by Antiochus Epiphanes. (Trans. H.L. Jones, Loeb Classical Library)

The layout and the development of Antioch during the Seleucid period have been studied and discussed by many scholars since the 19th century (Lassus 1972b; Hoepfner 1999a; Leblanc and Poccardi 1999; Hannestad in press a), but archaeological excavations have been severely hampered by the fact that the modern city of Antakya is situated on top of the ancient city, which today lies c.10 meters below the surface. Trial excavations along the modern main street have revealed several strata, the oldest of which date to the Hellenistic period and confirm the hypothesis that the main street of modern Antakya is identical to part of the ancient central street of the city. The city may have covered no less than 600 hectares by the time of Antiochus IV. Two issues in particular, however, still cause disagreement among scholars. One is the size of the city in the period after its foundation; and the other is the location of Strabo's fourth quarter, the so-called Epiphania, which was built during the reign of Antiochus IV.

Apamea

Despite the fact that Apamea has been excavated by a Belgian team since 1965, Hellenistic Apamea raises as many open questions as Antioch. The main reason is probably the severe earthquake of 115 AD and the intensive building activity that followed in its wake. Recent studies, however, have confirmed that, apart from a short stretch near the theater, elements of the Hellenistic city wall can be traced everywhere in the preserved Roman wall (Leriche 1987; Balty 2003). That the wall has two Hellenistic phases is shown by the reuse of earlier blocks in a second phase, which has been dated by the discovery of a well-preserved didrachm of Alexander Balas, struck in 146/145 BC (Leriche 1987; Balty 2003). The earlier phase probably dates to the foundation of the city. Lamps – probably Attic imports – of Howland's type 25A–D (Howland 1958) and some pottery bear witness to very early Hellenistic layers in most parts of the city (Balty 2003). The layout was probably very similar to that of Antioch, with a broad, central street. The Hellenistic (and the Roman) wall enclosed an area of c.255 hectares (Balty 2000).

Laodikeia

Laodikeia, the fourth city of the Tetrapolis, was described by Strabo (*Geography* 16.2.9) as a beautifully built city with a good harbor and hinterland producing, among other things, huge quantities of wine. It was laid out according to a grid system still reflected in modern-day Latakia. A street running north–south, about 2 kilometers long, seems to have been the central street of the city (Bejor 1999: 49). Laodikeia was probably about the same size as Apamea. Its importance in the scheme of Seleucus I is suggested by the fact that, during his lifetime, Laodikeia had the largest mint in Syria, possibly targeted particularly at the international market (Houghton and Lorber 2002).

Apamea-on-the-Euphrates

The fairly meager evidence of how these four large cities in Syria looked in the Hellenistic period has in recent years been supplemented by material from two sites on the Euphrates, where a number of fortified settlements were founded to control and protect river transport, river crossings, and the fertile Euphrates river valley. At Apamea-on-the-Euphrates, on the east bank of the river (now flooded by the Bireçik dam), geophysical surveys and excavations (1996–9) offered detailed insight into the history and layout of the city (Abadie-Reynal and Gaborit 2003). The city wall, which could be traced over a length of 2,200 meters, surrounded a triangular area of c.40 hectares. That strong defensive measures were considered necessary is attested by the use of massive towers. The wall was built using a polygonal technique with the upper part made of mudbrick and the entrances to the towers made in an isodomic technique (Desreumaux et al.1999).

The orthogonal city plan is clear. Streets were of varying width. Those leading to the gates were c.10 meters wide. Two houses and a row of shops have been partly excavated. Pottery from the latest floors (including black-glazed and early shapes of Eastern Sigillata A) suggest that the settlement was abandoned in the middle or late 2nd century BC. A burnt destruction layer covers the site, reflecting no doubt the coming of the Parthians.

Jebel Khalid

Jebel Khalid is the most spectacular Seleucid site excavated in Syria in recent years. It is located just below the new Tishrin Dam and about 300 kilometers upriver from Dura Europos (see below). Since the mid–1980s, an Australian team has worked at the site, which is located on a rock outcrop extending for c.1.5 kilometers alongside the Euphrates (*Jebel Khalid 1*) and covering c.50 hectares, about 30 hectares of which show signs of occupation. Jebel Khalid is protected on the inland side and along the southern river frontage by a wall, and the acropolis was further protected by a separate inner wall. The outer wall had some 30 towers and bastions and a massive gate complex protected by towers built in the 3rd century BC. No traces of pre-Hellenistic occupation have been found, and finds from later periods, including those of a Late Roman camp, are rare. Thus the site offers the best possible conditions for the study of a Seleucid foundation. So far, the best dating evidence from the site is provided by the coins. The earliest are two posthumous Alexander silver issues and two bronzes of Seleucus I; the latest dates to the late 70s BC (Nixon 2002). Coin frequencies peak under the two first Seleucids and, as everywhere in the kingdom, under Antiochus III and again in the late 2nd/early 1st century BC.

A large building on the acropolis identified by the excavators as the governor's palace has been excavated (Clarke et al. 2002: 25–48; Clarke 2003). The building centers on a peristyle court (c.17 meters on a side) with a Doric colonnade. On the south side of the peristyle is an *andron* complex (area reserved for men) with two columns *in antis* at the entrance, clearly for audiences and other such occasions. The north wing also seems to have had an official function consisting of a large room surrounded by kitchens and storerooms. The entrance to the main room, situated directly opposite the *andron* complex, was flanked by two attached columns; the roof was supported by a column in the middle of the room, and the floor was covered with marble slabs and decorated with wall paintings in the so-called Pompeian First Style, imitating marble slabs, and also a kind of floral decoration. One unusual element in the building when considered in a Greek context is the two corridors that close off the peristyle from the suite of rooms on the south and the north side. This is undoubtedly a result of the influence of local Oriental traditions. The palace dates broadly to the 3rd century BC, or, more specifically, to the first half of the 3rd century.

Part of a domestic quarter has been identified in the northern part of the site (Jackson 2003, 2005, 2009). One *insula* (an "island" between four streets, consisting of residential buildings) has been completely excavated. The houses were mainly built of rubble, but mudbrick was used for the upper parts of the houses. A common feature is a courtyard. Most rooms contained two floor levels, the lower built directly on bedrock and the upper reflecting a time of radical renovations. The second floor levels can be dated by the appearance of early Eastern Sigillata A pottery to c.150 BC. The coins found in the *insula* date from the reign of Antiochus I (281–261 BC) to the first quarter of the 1st century BC, the majority dating to the 2nd century BC. Remains of painted wall stucco were recorded here. The remains of a small figured frieze with *erotes* in chariots drawn by goats – clearly attesting the continued close connection with the Mediterranean world – are particularly interesting.

In the saddle between the Acropolis to the south and the Domestic Quarter to the north, excavations have revealed remains of a Doric temple (Clarke 2005). Close to the temple a small fragment of a marble sculpture was found, probably from the cult statue (Harrison 2000). In front of the temple stood five altars of unusual shape, one of which was found in situ. The temple was so situated that it would have been visible from the main gate. In the same area are also remains of houses and what may have been a civic structure including a peristyle court or a *pi*-shaped stoa of Doric order.

The faunal material from Jebel Khalid allows us some insight into the diet and animal economy of the people living at the site (Steele 2002: 125–45). Animal husbandry was mainly based on sheep and goat, sheep being far more common than goat. Equids (ass/onager) and cattle apparently served a dual purpose, for transport and labor (as draft animals) and for food. In these groups the animals seem only to have been slaughtered at a late stage of their lives. Camel is also present. Pigs were quite common, whereas fishbones were comparatively rare. Since the condition of the bones is generally very good, the absence of fishbones is surprising at a site on the Euphrates, and may reflect the recovery techniques employed (cf. Ch. I.12). Hunted animals included young gazelles and deer.

Dura Europos

Dura Europos (or more correctly Europos Dura, since Europos was the Greek name taken from a city in Macedonia and Dura was the later Parthian name) was founded during the reign of Seleucus I (305–281 BC) on a rock plateau on the west bank of the Euphrates (Cohen 2006: 156–69). Only the west side offered natural and easy entry to the city, a fact reflected in the defensive measures on this side, including numerous towers. The walled area covered c.63 hectares. Since its excavation, Dura has often served as the model of a Seleucid colony, though the remains are mainly of the Parthian/Roman period. In particular, the city walls and the general layout, with an orthogonal street plan and a main street running southwest–northeast through the city from the river to the main gate, have been considered part of the earliest settlement on the site.

The Citadel was situated on a separate plateau formed by the *wadis* and strongly fortified with a solid stone wall (McNicoll 1997: 93). It included a palace, the earliest parts of which are very scanty, whereas the second phase probably dating to the 2nd century BC is better preserved. A sounding (Leriche and Mahmoud 1994: 403; Leriche et al. 1997) behind the northern façade of the other palace at Dura (the Redoubt Palace), often identified as the Strategeion (originally, the meeting room of the generals, *strategoi*, in Athens), has yielded numismatic evidence that this façade, which belongs to a second phase of the building, cannot predate the early 2nd century BC (Leriche and Mahmoud 1994). Among the coins found there on the lowest floor level of room W is a small bronze denomination from the reign of Antiochus III, probably from 223 to 200 BC, struck at a western Seleucid mint (Augé 1988). The first phase of the building probably dates to the foundation of the settlement. The Strategeion is situated beside the Parthian temple of Zeus Megistos and it is possible that, already in the earliest phase of the settlement, the main temple of the city – probably also dedicated to Zeus – was situated there.

The city walls represent two different types: toward the west and the desert a type completely built of stone, and on the northern and southern sides a type constructed of mudbrick over a socle of stone and gypsum and/or mud-mortar.

In recent years our traditional understanding of the development of Hellenistic Dura Europos has been challenged by P. Leriche (2003, 2004, 2007), who interprets the result of his test trenches across the main street and along the inside of the western wall together with the fact that the archive building on the agora (Block G3) contained seal impressions dating to no earlier than year 184 of the Seleucid era – i.e., 129/8 BC – as proof that it was only at this time that the street grid was laid out. He assumes that before this date the site consisted only of a garrison in the citadel and some habitation in the adjacent area to the south and west of the citadel where the main street descends into the *wadi*. However, the evidence from the test trenches does not seem entirely convincing for such a radical re-dating of the layout of the city. It is also difficult to see why the settlement should then have had, from an early period, two palaces indicating the existence of an administration including two high-ranking officials. It is perfectly possible that during the early phase of the city's existence not all of the walled area and *insulae* within the street grid were inhabited.

From at least 141 BC, with the fall of Seleucia-on-the-Tigris to the Arsacids, the Seleucids must have invested massive resources in the defensive line that the Euphrates provided, concentrating their efforts on the west bank of the river. It is thus very likely that repairs and improvements – if not a completely new circuit, as suggested by Leriche – date to these years. Leriche considered Antiochus VII

Sidetes (138–129 BC) the possible "founder" of the new Dura Europos. Against Leriche's hypothesis, however, is the fact that most of the coins found at Dura date to the reign of Antiochus III (223–187 BC), with large numbers also from the reigns of Antiochus I (281–261 BC, 89 coins) and Seleucus III (225–223 BC, 80 coins). A smaller peak dates from the time of Antiochus VII (138–129 BC, 62 coins). This pattern is somewhat surprising if Leriche's re-dating of the layout of the city and of the city wall is correct. One would instead expect a stronger reflection of the economic activity connected with a completely new layout of the city and of the building of the walls. Thus, the coins clearly suggest major activities during the reigns of Antiochus I and Seleucus II (246–225 BC), culminating in the late 3rd and early 2nd centuries (for similar reflections, see Yon 2003).

Seleucia-on-the-Tigris

Seleucia-on-the-Tigris is still poorly known. Despite two long excavation programs, one in 1927–36 by an American expedition (Hopkins 1972) and one from 1964 onward by an Italian team, our knowledge of Seleucus I's eastern capital is still sadly meager. Situated on the Tigris, the city replaced Babylon on the Euphrates as the power center of Mesopotamia and was probably founded c.305/304 BC when Seleucus I assumed the royal title. It seems to have covered c.550 hectares. The Seleucid layers are overlain by thick deposits of the Parthian period. From ancient sources (e.g. Strabo, *Geography* 16.5.1) we know that the city was surrounded by strong walls, no traces of which remain today. The building material seems mainly to have been mudbrick on stone foundations. The layout of the city was the usual grid system found in most other new foundations (Invernizzi 1993; Messina 2007). The house blocks (*insulae*) were usually large (144.70 × 72.35 meters), and one such block (G6), dating to the Parthian period, was excavated by the American expedition.

A significant element was a canal running through the city from east to west. The Italian team uncovered a large building which was undoubtedly an official archive situated on what seems to have been the main square (Greek *agora*) of the city, opposite which the remains of a *stoa* (a covered, columned portico, often around a marketplace) were excavated. The American expedition concentrated part of their efforts on Tell Umar, where remains identified originally as a Parthian house were later dated to the Sasanian period. These may have been built on top of a theater dating to the Seleucid and Parthian periods. The most interesting finds made at Seleucia are probably the c.25,000 stamp seal impressions from bullae in the archive building (Invernizzi 2004), about 10,000 of which show the enormous variety of Hellenistic inconography in mainly Greek style, but often with a Mesopotamian flavor, e.g. in depictions of syncretistic gods such as Apollo-Nabu.

Ai Khanoum

Ai Khanoum is located in Bactria (northern Afghanistan) on the bank of the Oxus river. It was founded by Seleucus I in c.300 BC in what was then the easternmost part of his kingdom (Bernard 2008). A main feature of the layout of the city is a long, central street similar to the main streets at Antioch, Laodikeia, and Apamea in Syria. The street divided the city into a lower and an upper town, the upper part running up to the acropolis and citadel of the city. The natural stronghold of the site was further strengthened by a number of defensive mudbrick walls. Like Seleucia-on-the-Tigris, Ai Khanoum was founded on a previously uninhabited site. It was excavated by French archaeologists from 1964 until the Soviet invasion of Afghanistan in 1979, and the impressive results have contributed decisively to our understanding of a Seleucid royal city founded thousands of kilometers from the homeland of its Macedonian and Greek colonists. Excavations have revealed two of the most characteristic elements of Greek culture: a gymnasium (Veuve 1987) and a theater. A large palace and a number of sanctuaries, a single private house, and a mausoleum outside the city walls have also been excavated.

The palace was situated in the center of the lower city. Macedonians were familiar with their own type of royal palaces, but the plan of the Ai Khanoum palace was Achaemenid, consisting of a number of building blocks with long corridors and courtyards. The forecourt, at more than 100 × 100 meters, was surrounded by four colonnades with Corinthian capitals, typical of Greek architecture. The inner courtyard used columns of another Greek architectural order, the Doric. All the walls were built of sun-dried mudbrick. The roofs were flat, typical of the Oriental building tradition, but along the edges of the roofs Greek antefixes were erected.

The mixture of Oriental and Greek elements which the palace presents permeates the whole city. Thus the main sanctuary inside the city, the "temple with niches," has a layout quite unlike a Greek temple (Francfort 1984). Even if the niches belong to a later phase of the temple (the earliest phase had no niches and just one cella), the plan still differs significantly from that of a traditional Greek temple with its oblong shape and use of columns. Additionally, the fact that an altar with ash still in situ stood in the cella suggests a ritual far removed from normal Greek practice, where one would expect the altar to have stood outside the temple. The cella of the late phase (IV), with a corridor on each side, is clearly related to the Mesopotamian tradition. On the other hand, a fragmentary foot with thunderbolt on the sandal, and a left hand, both from a colossal acrolithic statue (a wooden statue with marble hands, feet, and head), are purely Greek in style and suggest that the cult was dedicated to Zeus, possibly fused with a local god. What is striking is the combination of the temple and some rituals reflecting an Oriental tradition with a purely Greek cult statue. Bernard has dated the initial phase of the temple (phase V) to around 300 BC, and phase IV to the early 3rd century. In this later phase, two wooden columns placed on Attic Ionic bases of stone stood in the interior of the cella. Thus a trend toward more and more local elements is not obvious. Rather, hybridization characterized the temple from beginning to end (Hannestad and Potts 1990: 98).

Among the earliest buildings in the city is the so-called *heröon* of Kineas, a sanctuary built of mudbrick and dedicated to the city's founder (Bernard 1973: 85–102). Here the Greek elements are stronger. The *heröon* underwent four building phases, the earliest of which resembles Greek *heroa* in plan, such as those at Kalydon or the tomb of Lefkadia in Macedonia (Hannestad and Potts 1990). A sarcophagus, probably that of Kineas, was interred below the building in a pit lined with mudbrick antedating the building itself. This is thus a Greek type of sanctuary, but built mainly in the local style. In phase 2 the plan was changed to a more traditional Greek temple with two columns *in antis*, but the three-stepped *crepis* (the solid base of a structure) was transformed into a podium. Another burial was interred at this time and later two more followed.

The gymnasium, also built of mudbrick, underwent at least two construction phases, the earlier of which seems to have involved two large courtyards (pre-175 BC) while the later one dated to the reign of Eucratides (175–145 BC), when Bactria had become an independent Greco-Macedonian kingdom. The enormous building (388.5 × 99.9 meters) with a southern courtyard and a northern one with *exedras* (semi-circular recesses, semi-domed) is easily recognizable as a gymnasium for anyone coming from the Mediterranean world, despite differences due to the local building tradition and materials, and the apparent lack of a *loutron* (bath). Among the Greek traits are the *herm* (sculpture with a head on top of a rectangular lower portion) in the niche in the middle northern *exedra* with the dedicatory inscription of Triballos and Straton, sons of Straton, to Hermes and Heracles (the traditional protectors of the Greek gymnasium). The date of the inscription is uncertain, but is thought to be either mid-3rd (Robert 1968) or 2nd century BC (Bernard in Veuve 1987: 111–12), corresponding to phase 2 of the gymnasium.

In accordance with Greek tradition the necropolis was situated outside the city walls. Excavations have brought to light a mausoleum used over several generations (Bernard 1972a). Inscriptions on three of the jars where bones were collected for reburial are in Greek, as are two very fragmentary inscriptions found in connection with the mausoleum. One relief-decorated tombstone was found there, not intact but in fragments, which had been used to block the entrance to the mausoleum. The relief depicts a naked young man with a long cloak which clearly enhances the ideal of Greek male nudity, and a *petasos* (traveling hat) hanging on his shoulder. His distinctly non-Greek, long hair provides an interesting contrast to the use of Greek (language and names) in the inscriptions from the mausoleum. Greek was the most common language attested in inscriptions at Ai Khanoum, whether on stone, clay, parchment, or papyrus (Robert 1968; Rapin 1983; Bernard 2008) and Greek names were by far the most common as well.

The problem when analyzing the material culture of Ai Khanoum is that one very easily tends to stress either the Greek or the local elements. But what the city really represents is a true hybrid of the Hellenistic period. It is neither Greek nor Oriental/local, but a unique blend. What is perhaps the most interesting element in this hybrid city is the evidence of continued links to and mobility from the Mediterranean across thousands of kilometers. People traveled and so did ideas.

4 On the Borders of the Kingdom and Beyond

For a while the Seleucids had a keen interest in the Arabian coast of the Persian Gulf. They may have had at least one, possible more, naval bases in the area. As mentioned above, trade with Arabia was important. Here just one settlement, clearly built on the command of a Seleucid king, will be mentioned, a "fortified sanctuary" on the island of Failaka (ancient Ikaros) in the bay of Kuwait excavated in the late 1950s and early 1960s by Danish archaeologists. In its early phase the Failaka fortification seems to have protected a sanctuary with a temple very much in Greek style both architecturally and with respect to the rituals connected with it (Jeppesen 1960, 1989). Among the finds was one of the very rare stone stelae with a long Greek inscription found outside of Asia Minor. The inscription contains two letters, the first of which is from an official named Anaxarchos, probably a local administrator, who forwarded a letter from another high-ranking official, Ikadion. Ikadion instructed Anaxarchos about the King's wishes respecting the island of Ikaros (i.e. Failaka). This letter and stele, which was originally set up in front of the temple, mentions a sanctuary of Soteira, which must have been the temple excavated by the Danish expedition. The date of the letter is damaged and has been much debated by modern scholars (e.g., Jeppesen 1960, 1989; Sherwin-White and Kuhrt 1993; Hannestad 1994). Most probably the king in question was Seleucus II (246–226/5 BC) and the letter probably dates to either 243 or 241/240 BC. In a later period another temple was added, the fortress extended and a moat laid out around it. Gradually the sanctuary filled up with private houses. From that period, if not earlier, the fortress probably housed a Seleucid garrison. The finds, including coins, terracotta,s and pottery, all suggest that the settlement came to an end in the late 2nd or early 1st century BC, although some pottery in the larger temple may relate to either a squatter habitation or continued cultic practice in the late 1st century BC or 1st century AD. Many of the finds suggest close contact with southern Mesopotamia and Susiana.

5 Continuity vs Change: Tradition in a Changing World

The many new Seleucid foundations should not obscure the fact that across the empire many areas and already existing cities remained little affected by changing political circumstances and the immigration of probably quite a large number of foreigners. An interesting example of this phenomenon can be seen at Uruk, an ancient city and religious center in Mesopotamia. More than 100 years of German excavations there allow us to study in detail the theme of continuity and change in material culture (Falkenstein 1941; Finkbeiner 1993b; Boehmer et al. 1995; Kose 1998; Lindström 2003). The period between c.300 and 125 BC actually seems to have been the most intense building period in the long history of the city, which then covered about 300 hectares. An ongoing discussion concerns the extent to which Greco-Macedonian settlers lived at Uruk (Sherwin-White and Kuhrt 1993: 149ff). Only a single Greek inscription – dating from after the region had been conquered by the Arsacids in 141 BC – has been found. The Greek names recorded on cuneiform tablets have often been taken as evidence of the presence of Greeks in the city, but in fact the situation was more complicated.

If we consider other cultural markers, it is striking that the material culture speaks strongly of a continued local tradition in most aspects of life and death. As an important Babylonian religious center, Uruk surely was the object of royal interest, not only for tax purposes but also with respect to royal propaganda and the display of power and wealth, as attested by the impressive building activity at the site. Two enormous temple complexes were built during Seleucid period, the Bit Resh sanctuary and the Irigal, as well as the largest *ziggurat* in Babylonia (Falkenstein 1941; Kose 1998). Building techniques are traditional Babylonian – without the use of stones or columns, but with mudbrick, glazed brick, and typically Babylonian plans. The enormous Bit Resh complex (217 × 167 meters) seems to have had an earlier, pre-Hellenistic phase, but most of the complex was built under the Seleucids (Kose 1998: 93ff). The construction was carried out under Anu-uballit Nikarchos (a characteristic double name – the Greek name being given to him by the king himself) (Doty 1988: 96) and was dedicated in 244 BC to the divine couple Anu-Antum. The king's direct involvement is attested by an inscribed clay cylinder (Clay 1915: no. 52) which states that the king gave the Greek name Nikarchos to Anu-uballit and that Anu-uballit built the temple for the sake of the lives of Antiochus and Seleucus, the kings. In a later phase, the main temple of the two deities was built of baked brick. Several of the bricks on the façade were stamped with a building inscription in Aramaic mentioning Anu-uballit Kephalon and the phrase "for the sake of the life of Antiochus, king (of the lands), my lord." This part of the complex dates from 201 BC. Anu-uballit Kephalon was also responsible for the building or rebuilding of parts of the Irigal, a sanctuary dedicated to Ishtar. The main cella there was decorated with glazed bricks above the cult niche bearing an Aramaic inscription which reads "Annu-uballit, whose other name is Kephalon" (Falkenstein 1941: 30–9; Doty 1988: 97ff).

The archives found in the Bit Resh included two types of records: clay tablets with cuneiform texts, a medium that was still alive in the city during the Hellenistic period, and texts written in Greek or Aramaic on parchment or papyrus and sealed with bullae (Lindström 2003). The seal types used were new. Instead of Babylonian-style cylinder or stamp seals, elliptical seals in metal – usually mounted in finger rings – were now the rule. The ratio of bullae to tablets seems to have been 10:1 (640 bullae and 61 tablets). The iconography of the seal impressions points to various sources of inspiration: a significant number are in Greek style, among them all the official seals showing royal portraits, royal symbols or Greek gods and heroes. Among the private seal impressions the prevailing iconography is Mesopotamian, with winged bulls and mythological animals. However, they also include Greek motifs. A third and particularly interesting group is a new creation of the Hellenistic period which shows, for instance, motifs from the zodiac reflecting the continued role of the city as a center for astronomy and astrology.

Moving to more modest artifacts such as pottery, we note that Greek imported pottery was rare in the city. The most common type of fine ware was alkaline-glazed ware. Greek shapes, such as the fish plate, the bowl with angular profile and outturned rim, and the plate with thickened interior rim, were attested. Of closed shapes, the so-called West Slope Ware (named after a site opposite the Acropolis in Athens) amphora was popular. But in this type of ware and in other classes of pottery there remained a strong element of Babylonian tradition in the shapes used (Finkbeiner 1993b: 3–16).

Uruk also offers us the possibility of examining cross-cultural relations as evinced in burial practices. In this aspect apparently little changed: the burials found inside the city walls of Uruk from the Seleucid and Early Parthian periods continued the old local tradition of sub-floor burial under houses. Also the few grave gifts including the pottery show a strong link to older Babylonian practices (Boehmer et al. 1995: 152 ff). However, a very different picture emerges at two tumuli (at Frehat en-Nufegi) north of Uruk (Boehmer et al. 1995: 141–52). In the burial chamber of the western tumulus four vessels in traditional Babylonian style were discovered. Otherwise, the finds in the chamber point distinctly to some of the most characteristic traits of Greek culture, such as the golden wreath of olive leaves. The wreath was probably originally placed on the funerary urn of a male. Closest to this urn were also found four *strigils* (a curved metal tool used to scrape grease and dirt off the body), reflecting the Greek gymnasium tradition. The eastern tumulus shows a stronger Greek tradition with the body laid out on a *kline* (Greek funerary bed) and a golden wreath around its head, suggesting a symbolic representation of the Greek symposium. Among the grave gifts was a Greek wine amphora, possibly of eastern Mediterranean origin. The two tumuli and their burial customs raise the question of the identity of the deceased. Bearing in mind the names recorded at Uruk, were they of Greek descent or members of the local elite with Greek names or double names such as Anu-uballit Nikarchos or Anu-uballit Kephalon? Whatever the case, the tumuli themselves and the grave goods point to quite a strong hybridization of material culture amongst the city's elite. It must remain an open question, however, whether the *strigil*s point to the existence of a gymnasium in the city, no traces of which have been found so far, or whether they should simply be taken as a symbol of "Greekness."

6 Conclusion

Our insight into the archaeology of the Near East during the reign of the Seleucids has grown exponentially in recent decades. We no longer depend solely on literary sources, coins, or assumptions based mainly on sites heavily overlain with Roman and later buildings. It is now possible to see in the material culture of the period that the Seleucid kingdom was characterized by strong regionalism with few overarching elements, such as coins, characterizing the entire empire.

The period under the first Seleucids, not least the years under Seleucus I, witnessed a large number of new settlements and an influx of new settlers bringing with them their own customs, but apparently also adapting to new ecological and cultural environments. Enormous investments were made by the early kings in the organization of their kingdom. The resources to some extent probably derived from Alexander's conquest and the seizure of the treasures accumulated by the Achaemenid kings. Continued warfare among the Hellenistic kingdoms was costly, but could of course – if won – also bring substantial gain. The running of the kingdom depended on an extensive taxation system and tributes.

The archaeological evidence collected so far suggests that the division of the kingdom into an eastern and a western part, which is clear from the two capitals (Seleucia and Antioch) and from Seleucus I making his son Antiochos I co-regent of the east, is also reflected to some extent in the material culture. Thus, from the very beginning, settlements as far east as the banks of the Euphrates have their strongest ties with the west. This is clearly attested by coins, most of which were minted at Antioch, even at Dura and Jebel Khalid. Pottery and lamps also show strong affinities to the west and thus to the Greek Hellenistic pottery tradition – a picture totally different from what is found in Mesopotamia. Western imports, such as Rhodian wine, seem to have been more common west of the Euphrates than in Mesopotamia. The overall pattern strongly suggests that the Euphrates may have formed a tax barrier between Syria (the western part of the kingdom) and Mesopotamia and the east (cf. Bikermann 1938: 115–18; Lindström 2003: 54) which drastically reduced the amount of trade in items of daily life. Alternatively, or in addition, the number of immigrants from Greek areas and from coastal Syria was comparatively small in regions east of the Euphrates from the early 3rd century onwards. The archaeological evidence also suggests that the western part of the empire experienced a peak in wealth by the mid–2nd century BC, as seen at Antioch, Jebel Khalid, and Dura. The political disasters that befell Antiochus III in his wars with the Romans and the rivalry for the throne that later ensued still left the western core area of the earlier empire in a state of comparative wealth (Hannestad in press b).

GUIDE TO FURTHER READING

For general orientation on the subject of the Seleucids in the Near East, see, e.g., Shipley (2000) and Austin (2003). On Seleucid colonies and earlier settlements that continued to be settled, see Cohen (2006). The economy of the Seleucids is dealt with comprehensively in Aperghis (2004). For a more Near Eastern/Central Asian perspective on the Seleucids see, e.g., Sherwin-White and Kuhrt (1993) and Hansen and Lindström (in press). A comparison of a new foundation (Ai Khanoum) and an ancient city (Uruk) can be found in Hannestad (in press a).

CHAPTER FIFTY-THREE

The Arsacid (Parthian) Empire

Stefan R. Hauser

1 Introduction: Perception and Neglect

The Arsacid Empire was founded in the mid-3rd century BC and lasted until c.AD 226. Although the Arsacid family ruled over one of the most extensive and long-lasting political entities in Near and Middle Eastern history, this period is one of the least known in the region's history and archaeology. The traditionally used term "Parthian" is derived from the former Achaemenid province Parthyene, east of the Caspian Sea, where the eponymous Arsaces I assumed independence from Seleucid authority. "Parthia" thus refers to a geographical area and "Parthian" was used as an ethnic label in Roman sources. Nevertheless, there are no indications that ethnic "Parthians" ever settled throughout or controlled the empire, or that the multiethnic, multilingual population of the empire was "Parthianized" in language, customs, or behavior. Increasingly, therefore, "Parthian" is being replaced by the ruling dynasty's name "Arsacid" in historical and archaeological literature (Wolski 1993; Hauser 2005).

There are several reasons why the Arsacids have aroused comparatively little interest amongst historians and archaeologists. The first reason is the privileged role of cuneiform in Near Eastern studies, which has limited interest in the post-Alexandrian East. In many (not only early) excavations, these levels have been marginalized. On the periphery of the Greco-Roman world, the Arsacids were relegated to the margins of ancient (Western) history (Hauser 2001).

A Companion to the Archaeology of the Ancient Near East, First Edition.
Edited by D.T. Potts.
© 2012 Blackwell Publishing Ltd. Published 2012 by Blackwell Publishing Ltd.

Conceptualized as superficially Hellenized barbarians, they attracted little interest among Classical scholars.

A second reason for neglect is the limited number of written sources. Indigenous historical narratives and administrative archives have not survived. Notable exceptions are the astronomical diaries from Babylon and some archives from Babylon, Nippur, and Uruk, which offer succinct information on the early years of Arsacid rule in Babylonia (Oelsner 1986; van der Spek 1997–8, 1998). Approximately 2,500 ostraca found at Nisa mostly concern the distribution of wine during the 1st century BC, coincidentally providing information on Arsacid genealogy (Schmitt 1998: 168–170). A number of contemporary Greek inscriptions are known from Susa and Babylon, while Parthian Aramaic texts accompany rock reliefs at various sites in Iran (Vanden Berghe and Schippmann 1985). Finally, more than 500 building and honorary inscriptions in Hatrean Aramaic have been found at Hatra, Assur, and the vicinity (Ibrahim 1986; Beyer 1998). In addition, a multitude of coins provides the basis for the list of rulers.

Due to the scarcity of indigenous written sources, reconstructions of Arsacid history depend on Roman authors, although only a minor part of the extensive ancient literature known through secondary references has survived (Debevoise 1938; Wiesehöfer 1998). Important sources for the first three centuries of Arsacid history are Justin's *Epitome* of Pompeius Trogus' lost *Philippic History*, Tacitus' *Annals*, Strabo's *Geography*, and the geographical descriptions in Pliny the Elder's *Natural History*. Additional information can be gained from Plutarch's biographies of Crassus and Antonius and anecdotes reported by Flavius Josephus. For the last two centuries of Arsacid history, our sources are even more limited. The framework is provided by Dio Cassius, whose report is supplemented by references to Arrian's lost *Parthica*, the *Historia Augusta*, and Herodian's *Roman History*.

Sasanian and Islamic sources are limited in their value. Attempts to infer the state of affairs from the Sasanian example encounter the problem of incongruity and the Sasanian tendency to denounce their predecessors as petty kings. Only recently have the various sources, including reports by Chinese embassies to the west, been conveniently collected for the first time (Hackl et al. 2010).

Finally, the necessary reliance on Roman sources creates an awkward situation. While the accuracy of geographical information is by and large admirable, descriptions of the administrative or social organization of the empire are lacking. Sources report on events of interest to Romans and thus overemphasize military actions and periods of internal differences which invoked Roman (diplomatic) reactions. As a result, even the basic features of the structure of the Arsacid Empire remain a matter of debate.

This has resulted in the often uncritical acceptance of and generalization from the available information. Consequently, the Arsacid Empire has been treated as a barbarian foil of the superior Roman, western civilization. In connection with essentializing ideas about the (successively or conflated) nomadic, Oriental, or

Iranian character of "the Parthians," this view has created a negative image of the Arsacid Empire as a loosely or rather poorly organized entity with a weak central government which, even after centuries of being based in Mesopotamian and other metropolises, still adhered to ancient nomadic traditions (cf. Wolski 1993; Keall 1994; Koshelenko and Pilipko 1994; Olbrycht 2003). Only recently has the dubiousness of these often unstated biases been fundamentally challenged (Boyce 1994; Hauser 2005, 2006a). In the necessary re-evaluation of the Arsacid Empire archaeology gains specific importance, for, without it, it would be impossible to properly understand variations and changes within an empire that lasted 470 years and encompassed huge areas with different climates, lifestyles, social organization, and identities.

2 Arsacid Political History: A Brief Outline

Arsacid history can be divided into three phases. The early phase covers the beginnings of Arsacid rule from the mid–3rd century BC to the transition to empire in the mid- to late 2nd century BC. The middle Arsacid phase covers its development up to the mid-1st century AD. The later Arsacid period encompasses the years from the consolidation of Arsacid family rule in the 1st century, through the wars with Rome in the 2nd century and the replacement of the Arsacids by the Sasanians (Ch. II.57; cf. Debevoise 1938; Ziegler 1964; Schippmann 1980, 1987; Wolski 1993).

The beginnings of the "Parthian Empire" are connected with the successful secession of several Central Asian provinces, namely Bactria under its governor Diodotus, and Parthia, either under its satrap Andragoras or already under Arsaces, from the Seleucid Empire in the mid-3rd century BC (Wolski 1993: 37–65; Lerner 1999: 13–31). Arrian, Strabo, and Justin offer four conflicting versions of the ethnic and social origins of Arsaces, the events and their respective chronology. Despite many attempts to either reconcile these stories or to establish one as "the truth," it seems preferable to understand them as literary works which employ the typical rhetorical figures and *topoi* of foundation myths (Hauser 2005: 175–8). We can only conclude that shortly after the mid-3rd century BC the Seleucids lost control of their former province Parthia (Parthyene). According to Justin (41.5.1–2), Arsaces hastened to strengthen existing places and founded new cities in the previously settled areas of northern Iran and southern Turkmenistan, and to build fortresses against the nomads in the north. Despite several Seleucid attempts to reclaim these territories, Arsaces and his successors ruled over Parthia, Hyckania, and neighboring areas from their capital at Nisa (in Turkmenistan) for nearly 100 years until their kingdom was transformed into an empire.

The transition to empire was mainly connected to internal turmoil and the demise of Seleucid power following the death of Antiochus IV (175–164 BC). A number of satraps in Media (central and western Iran), Elymais (southwestern Iran), and Mesene (southern Iraq) attempted to gain independence. The Arsacid Mithridates I (171–138 BC) took the opportunity and successively conquered the former Seleucid provinces of Media (148 BC), Babylonia (141 BC), and Elymais (139/8 BC). About the same time the Macedonian dynasty in Bactria was replaced by western Chinese tribal confederations called Yüechi. A common border was established in the reign of the Arsacid Phraates II (138–127 BC), who extended his territory eastwards into Margiana. This territorial division by and large remained stable even after the Kushan clan seized power in the east in the 1st century AD and lasted until the Sasanian conquests.

Arsacid rule between the Euphrates and eastern Iran was consolidated by Phraates II (138–127 BC) and Mithridates II (123–88 BC). Fighting with Elamite armies continued until 132 BC (Potts 1999: 387–91). The last battles with Seleucid armies occurred in 129 BC when the recapture of Media by Antiochus VII Sidetes was thwarted. The Arsacid conquests were completed, probably during the earlier reign of Mithridates II, when Assyria (now called Adiabene) and neighboring areas up to the Syrian Euphrates were incorporated. Probably in 109/8 BC, Mithridates II introduced the title "King of Kings" for the Arsacid ruler.

The empire's center shifted to the densely settled, economically strong areas of Media, Elymais, and, especially, Babylonia. The capital was moved from Nisa to Ecbatana (modern Hamadan, in western Iran) and finally to Ctesiphon, which originated as a royal winter residence across the Tigris from the populous, former Seleucid capital, Seleucia-on-the-Tigris. Even if there had been any specific nomadic residue in social practices or organization at this time, which is doubtful, it became overshadowed by the urbanized imperial setting.

In 96 BC Arsacid and Roman envoys met for the first time on the Euphrates, which was agreed on as the border between their respective spheres of interest. The first open hostilities between the Arsacids and Rome ensued with the invasion of Crassus, which ended with a devastating defeat of the Roman troops near Harran (Carrhae) in 53 BC. This initiated a period of nearly 100 years of repeated intervention in civil wars or contested successions by both sides, as well as occasional military incursions. Despite all the official rhetoric of a Roman *imperium sine fine* (empire without borders), it was well understood already in the Augustan age that the Arsacid Empire was the equal of Rome (Sonnabend 1986: 202–3, 214–15).

For the later 1st century BC and early 1st century AD, Roman sources (esp. Tacitus) repeatedly report on the internal struggle for the throne between members of the Arsacid family supported by different factions of nobles. In the absence of written Arsacid sources, such conflicts have also been reconstructed from the often poorly understood coinage of the later Arsacid period (1st–3rd century AD). In fact, with the exception of the inner-Arsacid conflict between the king of kings Vologases IV and Meredates, king of Mesene, in AD 150/1, there are very few indications of continued turmoil.

On the contrary, a long period of stability seems to have begun with the reign of Vologases I (AD 51–78). Following an earlier, inconsistently applied pattern, local dynasts were replaced by Arsacid family members. During the last two centuries of the Arsacid Empire all the important provinces were probably ruled by Arsacids carrying the title "king." But neither the title "king" nor the right to mint coins necessarily implied independence. Rather, they entailed submission with certain rights and duties under the aptly titled "king of kings" (Hauser 2005: 185–99). This was precisely the system taken over by the Sasanians after Ardashir's defeat of the last Arsacid ruler (AD 224–8).

Up to this time, despite a number of nomadic incursions in the north (by the Alans) and several wars with Rome, the Arsacid Empire remained more or less intact. Avidius Cassius (Dio Cass. 71.2.3) in AD 165 and Septimius Severus (Dio Cass. 75.9.2–5) in 197 or 198 AD led their forces to Ctesiphon. In 116 AD Trajan even conquered the whole of Mesopotamia for a few months before he was forced to retreat. But apart from the loss of Osrhoene to Rome in AD 165, the Arsacid Empire's borders with Rome in the west and the Kushans in the east remained stable.

The Arsacid family was brought down by the insurrection of a minor noble of the province of Fars. Quarrels between the Arsacid brothers Vologases VI and Artabanus IV might have paved the way for Ardashir I, grandson of Sasan. The reasons for his revolt and its success, leading to him being crowned king of kings at Ctesiphon in AD 226, are difficult to ascertain (Schippmann 1990: 10–19). But it seems important to note that, contrary to older research which followed Sasanian and early Islamic sources in emphasizing the differences between the Arsacids and their Sasanian successors, one could argue that in replacing kings from the Arsacid family with Sasanian family members, Ardashir perpetuated the Arsacid administrative structure. Resistance to the Sasanians continued until AD 240/1 when, after a siege lasting two years, they finally managed to conquer Hatra (in northern Iraq), the last Arsacid standhold.

3 Major Sites of the Arsacid Period

Arsacid-period architecture at Hatra and Nineveh, stucco and slipper-shaped glazed coffins at Uruk and Susa, as well as rock reliefs in Iran, were among the first archaeological remains documented in the Near and Middle East (Ross 1839; Loftus 1857; Flandin and Costa, 1843–54). Until World War II, extensive excavations in Arsacid levels were limited to a handful of sites in Iraq (Nippur, Assur, Hatra, Dura Europos, Seleucia-on-the-Tigris) (Andrae 1908, 1912; Cumont 1926; Baur and Rostovtzeff 1929–52; Andrae and Lenzen 1933; Hopkins 1972; 1979) and the former USSR (Nisa, Merv). Work in Turkmenistan and Chorasmia (Uzbekistan) intensified after World War II (cf. the summaries in Pugachenkova 1988; Baimatowa 2008: 3–14) and resumed at Hatra in 1951 (Safar and Mustafa 1974).

From the 1960s to the 1980s research at Arsacid sites multiplied and diversified in connection with surveys, rescue work in dam areas, and the resumption of excavations at major sites like Seleucia-on-the-Tigris, Nippur, Uruk, and Susa. This period was further characterized by the extension of research into the Gulf area (Potts 1990, 1996). In what follows, I attempt to identify essential chronological traits discernable at major excavated sites.

The earliest known capital was at Nisa in Turkmenistan. This consists of two independently fortified parts, a large settlement area (New Nisa) and Old Nisa (renamed Mithradatkert in the 1st century BC), which probably served as a royal citadel and possibly a ceremonial center for Arsacid royalty (Invernizzi 2001, 2007; Pilipko 2008). Large-scale excavations at Old Nisa since the 1930s have facilitated our understanding of early Arsacid culture as largely influenced by Hellenistic art and central Asian architecture. The monumental "Square House" furnished a splendid collection of c.40 ivory rhyta which display Greek mythological scenes and deities (Masson and Pugachenkova 1982). Likewise, a group of small metal figurines in gilded silver or bronze, including Athena, Eros, griffins, and eagles, displays Greek as well as Central Asian elements (Invernizzi 1999). Marble statues of Aphrodite (possibly identified with Anahita), Artemis, and Dionysus are purely Hellenistic in style.

References to Central Asian architecture are found in the "Round Hall," part of a complex structure of several buildings grouped around a central courtyard. The walls of a circular hall (dia. 17 meters) inside a 30 meter wide square building were standing to a height of 4 meters when excavated. Slightly incurving walls and comparisons with nearby monuments led the excavators to reconstruct a hyperbolic dome of a local style. On the floor multiple fragments of the architectural decoration and of painted, over life-sized clay sculptures were found. The latter certainly remind one of the Yüechi palatial structure at Khalchyan in Uzbekistan (Pugachenkova 1971; Nehru 1999–2000) from the late 2nd century BC. But the male and female statues at Nisa were probably placed on plinths on the floor, not on the walls. The monumentality of the "Round Hall" and the findings inside, including a clay portrait of Mithridates, has led to the hypothesis that it had a sacral nature (Invernizzi 2007). The unusual character of the complex is also suggested by the "Red Building" (42 × 42 meters), which displays a large central hall with four wooden columns bearing traces of gold leaf and stone bases surrounded on three sides by rooms and corridors and preceded, on the north, by a portico, 17 meters wide (Invernizzi and Lippolis 2007).

The taste for Hellenic-inspired sculpture recalls contemporary sites in Bactria, where cities like Ai Khanoum, which was already destroyed in the mid-2nd century BC, display the impact of Greek settlers with its theater, gymnasium, and Greek inscriptions. The local heritage is visible in the temple form and the huge palace with a room of many columns reminiscent of Achaemenid palatial architecture (Bernard 2007 with bibliography). At both Ai Khanoum and Nisa, sculpture and architectural decoration (antefixes, capitals) in Hellenic style were produced locally in clay and limestone. The early Arsacid period at Nisa is thus characterized by architecture in a regional tradition showing Hellenistic influences in fittings and sculpture.

Another important early Arsacid capital was Hecatompylos. Mentioned by Strabo, Pliny, and Ptolemy, it has been identified with Shahr-e Qumis on the important east–west route south of the Alburz mountains. In the preliminary excavations of this enormous site, only a few structures, including a palace-like building (also interpreted as a temple) and a fortified complex with several towers were cleared (Hansman 1968; Hansman and Stronach 1974). The general layout of the city is unclear. The same applies to most cities mentioned in ancient texts as important (sometimes newly founded) places in Media and Media Atropatene – e.g., Rhagae (Rayy) and Aganzana (Zanjan). An exception is found at the Arsacid summer residence of Ecbatana. Excavations by the Iranian Center for Archaeological Research unearthed a perfectly regular city plan, of probable Arsacid foundation, with large building units (Sarraf 2003; Azarnoush 2007).

Impact on conquered regions

Following its incorporation into the empire in the 2nd century BC, Babylonia became the economic and political nexus of the Arsacid Empire. The large urban centers of Babylonia, Seleucia-on-the-Tigris, Babylon, Nippur, and Uruk provide ample evidence of Arsacid material culture. At first, the change in government found no immediately recognizable visual expression. Earlier differences observed between sites in northern Babylonia and those in the south continued as the main buildings of the earlier periods remained in use. According to the intensive survey of Uruk (Finkbeiner 1991), the Seleucid and early Arsacid periods there were among the most prosperous in its history. Nearly all of Uruk's 300 hectare area was densely settled. The enormous Babylonian-style temples build in the later 3rd century BC, the Bit Resh (Anu-Antum-temple; 213 × 167 meters) and the Irigal (205 × 198 meters), were maintained well into the 1st century BC (Kose 1998). Huge industrial areas in the north, hundreds of coins, and sarcophagi, which once had been below the floors of private houses, but now appeared on the surface of the site due to erosion, attest to the vitality of this metropolis (cf. Finkbeiner 1991: 211–13 with Beilage 32).

In the later Arsacid period, Uruk began to shrink in size. In the 1st century AD, private houses seem to have occupied much of the no longer functioning temple complexes, although smaller temples were still maintained. An entirely different architectonic character is displayed by the new Gareus temple which combines a small two-room cella and anteroom in the middle of a large, square courtyard framed by rooms with a western-style façade of half columns with Ionic capitals, niches, and a frieze with mythical creatures (Kose 1998: 291–335). Simultaneously with the decline of Uruk itself, the landscape in the south suffered from the appearance of new swamps and marshy areas necessitating the relocation of settlements.

Nippur, on the contrary, expanded greatly in the 1st century AD. A large fortress with round towers was built around the Enlil *ziggurat* and a new Inanna temple was erected above the Ur III temple in the same architectural tradition. Nearly the entire city area was in use again, and nowadays it is littered with Arsacid period pottery and the fragments of thousands of glazed, slipper-shaped coffins (Keall 1970).

Changes probably starting in the 1st century AD also affected Seleucia-on-the-Tigris and Babylon. The traditional capital Babylon was long thought to have been in a state of decline and virtual abandonment after the foundation of Seleucia. The reanalysis of earlier excavations, however, revealed a city of c.120 hectares in the earlier Arsacid period with an interesting mixture of cultural traits (Hauser 1999). Texts confirm regular offerings by the Arsacid rulers at the temple of Marduk until at least 77 BC. Although the later Arsacid Bel temple has not been found, cuneiform texts probably originating in its offices are attested until AD 75. Private houses spread over the site of the former royal palace and continued north of the old city center. The presence of a Greek community is confirmed by inscriptions. The Seleucid theater was renovated in the 1st and 2nd centuries AD. Although the settlement's size had sharply declined by this time, Babylon was still marked as an important town on the late Roman map known as the *Tabula Peutingeriana* and by Cassius Dio (75.9.3).

The former Seleucid capital, Seleucia-on-the-Tigris, is one of the best-known Arsacid period sites (Hopkins 1972; Anonymous 1985a). The city encompasses c.550 hectares, and although Pliny's claim of a population of more than 600,000 (*Nat. Hist.* 6.122) seems grossly exaggerated, it was certainly one of the biggest cities in antiquity. The blocks of its Hippodamian urban layout, measuring 144.70 × 72.35 meters, are the largest known anywhere in antiquity.

At the site's northwestern limit the mound called Tell Umar was identified as a theater later transformed into a massive Sasanian tower. Several excavated house blocks provide a stratigraphy and pottery chronology for the entire Arsacid period (Debevoise 1934; Valtz 1984, 1991). South of Tell Umar, the ruins of a Seleucid archive building (Ch. II.52), destroyed in the last quarter of the 2nd century BC, yielded more than 25,000 clay sealings (Level V). The archive was discontinued after its destruction. Throughout most of the Arsacid period (Levels III–I) the area was converted into dwellings with intramural burials beneath the floors and some shops. Street Block B6, unearthed in the 1930s, is particularly interesting for the changes in architectural ideas that it illustrates. Level III (dated 143 BC to mid-1st century AD) displays some Hellenistic features in its open courts connected in the south to large halls fronted by *antae* (columns flanking the entrance to a temple). In Level II, which was probably destroyed by Trajan, the columns are replaced by a large opening. At least one of these might already be an *iwan*, a barrel-vault that was a hallmark of Arsacid architecture. In the less well-preserved 2nd century AD Level I, the whole block was transformed into one building complex, the main court of which featured a huge *iwan*. Major changes are also visible in architectural decoration. Generally speaking, Hellenistic vine scrolls and *cyma* (molding with a double curvature), terracotta lion-headed spouts (*sima*), and palmette *antefixes* (vertical blocks concealing the joint between a row of tiles) in the earlier levels were replaced by locally inspired (Iran/Mesopotamia) stucco pattern-friezes on walls and *iwans* (Hopkins 1972: 127–48).

Despite the repeated description of Seleucia as a "Greek city," its population must have been mostly indigenous. The local descent of the inhabitants is suggested, for example, by the traditional, Mesopotamian pattern of intramural burial, something that would have been unfamiliar to Greek settlers. Nevertheless, the material culture displays an unusual closeness to the eastern Mediterranean, not only in Seleucid, but also in Arsacid times. In later Arsacid times many people might have moved to the new capital Ctesiphon, across the Tigris. Unfortunately, this city, called *al-'Atīqa* in Arab sources, has not yet been explored (cf. Negro Ponzi 2005; Hauser 2007a for the topographical situation).

A striking intensity of settlement connects northern Babylonia and Khuzestan, the most intensively researched part of Iran (Potts 1999: 384–409). Seleucid coins were minted at its capital Susa until the reign of Demetrius II (146–140 BC), thus overlapping with those of local dynasts (Le Rider 1965). From c.25 BC until AD 224 an Elymaean Arsacid dynasty was in power (van't Haaff 2007). The long-term, large-scale excavations at Susa have demonstrated that the Arsacid period was marked by substantial expansion and prosperity. Greek inscriptions and sculptures attest to the preservation of Hellenic traditions. While Arsacid material was rather poorly attested in the early campaigns, later excavations in Ville Royale A, the Apadana East/Ville Royale (Levels 4/3; Boucharlat 1987b) and Ville Royale II (Levels 3c–A, 2C–B; Miroschedji 1987a) offer an important starting point for the pottery chronology of the wider area (Haerinck 1983; Boucharlat 1993). No fewer than three levels of large private houses with interior courtyards and fragments of Greek architectural decoration were unearthed in Ville Royale A.

Further evidence for the later Arsacid period has been found at two temple complexes with numerous reliefs and life-sized sculpture in the round in the mountains east of the plain. At Bard-e Neshanda a four-pillared room (1st–2nd century AD) has been identified as a temple for Anahita and Mithra, who might be represented on pillars at the entrance of the building (Ghirshman 1976; for the coins, cf. Augé et al. 1979). Probably built in the 2nd century AD, the 2 hectare large stone terrace at Masged-i Solayman supported a centrally placed "great temple" and another temple possible dedicated to Heracles. The sculpted male figures are usually fully bearded and clad in richly decorated tunics, trousers, and shoes. Several heads with a tiara from Masged-i Solayman, dating to the 2nd–3rd centuries AD, have been identified as Elymaean kings (Ghirshman 1976;

Mathiesen 1992: 151–64). Rock reliefs at Tang-e Sarvak, halfway between Susa and Persepolis in the Bakhtiari mountains, depict rulers worshipping at a fire altar, enthroned, hunting animals or in combat (Vanden Berghe and Schippmann 1985: 40–80; Kawami 1987; Mathiesen 1992: 119–51).

Outside Elymais, evidence of the Arsacid period in Iran is surprisingly rare and uneven. In contrast to the rich evidence for early Sasanian architecture with stucco decoration and figurative capitals, the Arsacid period in Fars is mainly represented by coins issued by the local dynasts under Arsacid sovereignty (Wiesehöfer 2009). Recent rescue excavations in the Bolagi Gorge, near Persepolis, and numerous graffiti on the walls at Persepolis, including portraits of Arsacid rulers and popular Sasanian motifs (equestrian combat and hunting scenes) have shed new light on this period (Callieri 2003; Razmjou 2005c).

Further evidence for the later Arsacid period is found in western Iran at Qaleh Zohak (in Azerbaijan) and Qaleh Yazdigird (near Qasr-e Shirin), and especially in northern Iraq at Assur and Hatra. At Qaleh Zohak, a square room supported by four massive corner pillars, with four arches covered by a high barrel vault, still stands (Kleiss 1973). Dated to the 2nd century AD, this pavilion was built with alternating vertical and horizontal courses of brick, covered with plaster. This building technique, also employed at Assur, Qaleh Yazdigird, and other sites, is characteristic of the period.

One of the most impressive Arsacid sites known is Qaleh Yazdigird, situated on a hill overlooking the main route from Babylonia to the Iranian plateau on the western flanks of the Zagros Mountains. A huge enclosure surrounds the site. Residential units and a well-preserved palace have been partly cleared. More than 300 stucco panels, reliefs, and figurative capitals, dating to the late 2nd–3rd century AD, were recovered from the walls and columns of the palace. These have bands of repeated designs of interlocking meanders suggestive of textile ornament and stylized leaves, as well as brightly colored patterns of repetitive figural compositions in varying scales. The figural repertoire includes images interpreted as Dionysus and Aphrodite and their followers, humans – e.g., a frontal male bust, standing males in "Parthian" costume, and naked dancers – and animals and mythological creatures resembling the *sen-murw*, a mythological dog-headed bird (Keall et al. 1980; Keall 1982, 2002). The Qaleh Yazdigird stuccos foreshadow Sasanian décor, but the suggestion that the site was the stronghold of a rebel warlord is purely speculative.

The various regions of Arsacid Iran offer no uniform picture of Arsacid/Parthian material culture. On the contrary, in architecture as in tombs and burial practices, reliefs, and pottery, local traditions are clearly present and differences between strongly Hellenized city centers such as Susa and sites in the countryside are marked.

Further west the province of Adiabene shows its own distinct material culture. Excavations in the former Assyrian heartland remain limited, and the provincial capital Arbela (Erbil) is unexplored. No detailed surveys have been carried out east of the Tigris. The early excavations at Nineveh provided plenty of local and imported Roman pottery and sculpture, but from undocumented contexts (Eiland 1998). At Kilizu (Kakzu) a number of burials were excavated. Ceramic sarcophagi with blue-green glaze and relief decoration, e.g. grapes alternating with a frontal nude female figure in an arched niche, find comparisons at Assur (Anastasio 2008), where the evidence is compelling. Two-thirds of the Assyrian city was covered with private houses. Settlement lasted from the 1st century BC until a fatal destruction around AD 230. These buildings uniformly include a southern *iwan* and show liberal use of plaster. A large complex around a court framed by four *iwans* which also features a *peristyle* was called the "Parthian palace" and considered the seat of local administrators. Such lords (*marja*) are attested by several inscribed reliefs in the city's main temple, which was devoted to Assur and his consort Seru'a. The temple was placed atop the older Assyrian Assur temple and represents remarkable continuity of cult (Andrae and Lenzen 1933; Hauser 2011). The temple's layout consisted of three large parallel *iwans* within a large *temenos* area covering 4 hectares that included a number of other temples – e.g., for Heracles-Nergal – and one in western Greek peripteral style. The whole assemble is thus architectonically closely related to the 14 hectare *temenos* area of Hatra.

A traditional meeting point for nomads in the steppe, Hatra was founded in the 1st century AD. In the 2nd century the city of the sun-god was enlarged to 310 hectares and served as economic, political, and religious center of the steppe. After the Arsacids lost Osrhoene to the Romans in 164 BC, the lord of Hatra was awarded the title "king of the Arabs" (Hauser 1998). Excavations since 1951 have concentrated on the centrally placed *temenos* with multiple temples constructed as parallel *iwans* and 15 smaller, probably tribal temples outside the *temenos*. Some 300 sculptures, most of them offerings devoted for the life of a ruler or noble, were excavated in these shrines (Safar and Mustafa 1974; Dirven 2008). The strong fortification walls resisted several Roman and Sasanian attacks before Ardashir I conquered the city after a two-year siege. The siege walls, the largest known in Near Eastern history, were recently rediscovered (Hauser and Tucker 2009). The siege of AD 238/9–40/41 was the final battle between the Sasanians and the last stand of the once glorious Arsacid Empire.

4 The Administration of Empire in Light of its Material Culture

Archaeological research has contributed in various ways to a re-evaluation of the Arsacid Empire's internal structure and diversity as well as its external contacts. Its internal structure is reflected in coinage, settlement systems, representations of officials, and military installations. Its diversity is illustrated by the various languages, economies, and religions practiced within this huge state. Finally, Arsacid material culture reflects external contacts, trade relations, local traditions, and Hellenistic influences.

Administration and power

Although awareness of Arsacid coinage dates to the early 18th century (Foy Vaillant 1728), the system and its implications are still not fully understood. The current reference system has been criticized for its unconvincing typology, dubious assignation of coins, and insufficient illustrations (Sellwood 1980; de Callataÿ 1994; Alram 1998). A long-awaited *Sylloge Nummorum Parthicorum* in nine volumes is currently in preparation. Coinage in the Arsacid Empire by and large followed the Seleucid system. In greater Mesopotamia and Elymais, silver tetradrachms predominated, while drachms were used in Iran. Various mints issued coins, most importantly the royal mints at Seleucia-on-the-Tigris and Ecbatana. Drachms and tetradrachms were also struck by the local rulers of Mesene, Elymais, Persis, and the eastern Indo-Parthian areas. Until recently, this was seen as evidence of their independence. Alternatively, it could be judged as an expression of a system comparable to medieval Europe, where the issuing of coins was one the rights and duties of certain noblemen without implying independence. While early central and regional Arsacid coins followed Seleucid models in their obverse portraits, from the first century AD onward these became less detailed and the traditional Greek legend was replaced in Iran by Parthian Middle Persian. In addition, silver content decreased, and provincial coinage, which in general followed the issues minted at Seleucia-on-the-Tigris, became debased.

Apart from coins, only a few rock reliefs preserve images of the king of kings. Three of these were carved at Bisotun. One badly damaged relief shows Mithridates II (in profile) receiving the obeisance of four dignitaries. A rather crude, life-sized, frontal image of a man making an offering at a small altar is identified in an accompanying inscription as "Vologases, king of kings, son of Vologases, king of kings, son of P. . . ." A third relief shows an equestrian combat between a victorious king accompanied by Nike carrying a diadem and his fatally wounded enemy. Because of a short inscription that reads "Gotarzes Geopothros" above the central figure, the scene has usually been interpreted as a depiction of the king of kings Gotarzes II defeating Meherdates in 49 BC, but no consensus has been reached (Mathiesen 1992: 174–5). Images of local rulers accompanied by inscriptions were also carved at Tang-e Sarvak and at Hung-e Nauruzi. Life-sized statues of rulers in finely embroidered tunics, trousers and shoes have been excavated at Masged-i Solayman and Hatra.

Settlement development

The workings of administration are visible in grandiose irrigation projects. As surveys have conclusively demonstrated, settlement and irrigation reached unprecedented levels in Babylonia during the Arsacid period (Adams 1965, 1981;

Adams and Nissen 1972; Gibson 1972; Gasche and De Meyer 1980). A mayor break in this development can be inferred for the mid-1st century AD. At this time Babylon was partly replaced as the economic center of Iraq by the yet to be identified site of Vologesias, which was probably on a different arm of the Euphrates. Likewise, Seleucia started to be no longer situated "on-the-Tigris" and ceded population and economic importance to Ctesiphon and a new city (later Sabat) further south.

Clearly, both rivers changed their courses. In the south this led to increased areas of swamp, which prompted new irrigation systems and a relocation of settlement. While Nippur witnessed considerable growth, in the long run Uruk and its hinterland were victims of this development and diminished in size (Adams and Nissen 1972; Finkbeiner 1991). Larger parts of the population must have moved north or east toward Elymais and its capital Susa. Settlement in Elymais expanded threefold. Almost the entirety of Khuzestan was brought under cultivation and wet rice cultivation and sugar cane were introduced (Wenke 1975–6, 1987). Weirs on all major rivers, provisionally described as "Roman," could be from the Arsacid period (Adams 1962). Study of the lower Diyala river shows very similar patterns to those in Khuzestan. The capital Ctesiphon became the center of a complex irrigation system (Adams 1965: 61–82). The enormous size of the artificially dug main arteries and the complex networks of smaller canals greatly exceeded all earlier systems.

These observations receive confirmation wherever surveys have taken place, in northern Mesopotamia and Osrhoene (Wilkinson and Tucker 1995; Ball 1996; Yardimci 2004) as well as in the upper Atrek valley (Venco Ricciardi 1980). In the steppe south of Hatra, a high number of settlements reflects the sedentarization of nomads ruled by the king at Hatra (Ibrahim 1986; Hauser 1998, 2000). Because of an expansion of the irrigated territory and the building of fortifications as protection against nomadic incursions, the Arsacid period has been called the golden age of Margiana (Gaibov and Koshelenko 2002: 51; Koshelenko 2007).

The military

It has long been noted that the Roman army in the east was reorganized, especially by the introduction of heavy cavalry, in response to the tactics of the Arsacid forces which were renowned for their mounted archers and their iron-clad *cataphracti* (Mielczarek 1993; James 2006). Contrary to older opinions it has been demonstrated that the empire possessed standing armies in garrisons and specifically on the borders under the control of the local kings. Only in times of crisis were territorial armies of reservists raised (Hauser 2006b).

While it has been shown that the famous Gorgan wall was a late Sasanian construction (Omrani Rekavandi et al. 2007, 2008), many fortresses in the region beyond this wall are probably Arsacid. This goes for sites like Toprak-Kale in Chorasmia and Durnali in Margiana (Kiani 1982; Bader et al. 1998) which often show the same architectural features, especially the outlying corner towers, as examples in Babylonia (Bergamini 1987). While *castella* in present-day northern Iraq and Syria have generally been identified as Roman, dated inscriptions in Hatrean Aramaic at several such structures prove the existence of fortresses built against the Romans by the mid-2nd century AD, as indicated by Cassius Dio (79.26.3) (Hauser 1998: 517–19).

The impressive irrigation systems of Babylonia, Elymais, and elsewhere, as well as the fortifications, clearly indicate comprehensive, abstract planning. The design, organization, and maintenance of these large systems must have depended on strong supra-local administration. This view is in stark conflict with older ideas about the weak internal organization of the empire and represents a shift of research paradigm.

5 Trade

The Arsacid period witnessed an enormous surge in the intensity of the trade that connected Mesopotamia and the Mediterranean with China via the steppes and with India along the coast and across the Indian Ocean. Exchange along the Central Asian caravan routes, the "silk road," was supported by a favorable climate and the military protection of routes by Han China, as shown by research in Xinjiang (Wieczorek and Lind 2007 with bibliog.). The intense cultural exchange of the period is most impressively demonstrated at Begram, 60 kilometers north of Kabul. The site controls the main north–south route to Central Asia. Excavations in a small, 35 × 60 meter "palace" furnished a spectacular collection of artifacts. Ivories from India and lacquer work from China were found alongside painted and millefiori glass from the Mediterranean as well as finely executed gypsum *tondi* representing gods, humans, and animals from Alexandria in Egypt. While probably produced from the 3rd century BC onward, the objects are prime examples of long-distance cultural contact in the 1st and 2nd centuries AD (Hackin 1939; Ghirshman 1946; Mehendale 2005; Cambon 2007a).

At the same time, the long established sea trade with India along the Persian Gulf (Mare Erythraeum) also intensified (cf. Raschke 1978; Young 2001). The main port, "where the merchants of the east meet" (Acts of Thomas) was Spasinou Charax, capital of Mesene, which, although identified c.50 kilometers north of Basra, has never been excavated (Hansman 1967; Schuol 2000: 379–97). Thus, the various trading establishments established there, catering, e.g., for Ctesiphon, remain elusive. Only in the case of the Palmyrenes, who transported goods from the east to the Roman Empire, do we possess sources indicating the intensity and enormous profits of the trade (Schuol 2000: 47–90; Hauser 2007b).

Once the Arsacids had conquered Fars and Mesene, their influence in the Gulf area was felt (cf. Potts 1990, 1996). Like its predecessor, the Seleucid "satrapy of the Erythrean Sea," the province of Mesene included part of the coast and islands in the Gulf. In the mid-2nd century AD, Mithridates of Mesene called himself "king of (the) Oman(i)" and established a governor on Bahrain (Potts 1997b), where archaeological evidence for the settlement currently ends with the 1st century AD (Hannestad 1983; Callot 1991; Gachet and Salles 1993). Trade across the Gulf in the later Arsacid period is reflected by finds of Roman glass, pottery from Baluchistan, India, and plenty of Babylonian glazed wares at ed-Dur on the coast of the United Arab Emirates. Excavations in this sprawling site revealed private houses, a temple, a small fortress, and burials (cf. Potts 2001b). The fortress with round corner towers and the subterranean tombs with barrel vaults show strong connections with contemporary Mesopotamian architecture. Further evidence of intense contacts and the securing of trade by military posts along the coast is provided by the city of Thaj (Potts 1993a) as well as burials and the fortress at Bahrain (Thiloua) (Herling and Salles 1993; Lombard and Kervran 1993). Despite these constant contacts, the areas of modern Oman and the UAE seem not to have been under direct Arsacid control.

6 Religion

Earlier periods in the Ancient Near East bear witness to the importance of local gods and their cults for civic identity. In Mesopotamia multiple efforts were made to merge them into a united pantheon. The situation in the Arsacid Empire was much more diverse and fragmented. In several Mesopotamian cities the traditional gods were revered. Theophoric elements in personal names attest to the continued importance of Bel, Nabu, Assur, Inanna, and Anu (Müller-Kessler and Kessler 1999). At Assur the ancient *akitu*-festival (New Year's celebration), entailing a procession from the Assur temple to the *akitu* house, was still celebrated and temples for traditional gods were renovated or rebuilt in various styles in the 3rd century AD (Hauser 2011). At Nippur the Inanna temple of the 1st century was modeled on the Ur III (2100–2000 BC) example, while the 1st–3rd century AD Assur temple displayed the new form of three parallel *iwans* (Downey 1988). Along with the sun god Shamash (Hatra) and the moon god Sin (Harran), Nabu and Nanaya gained particular importance. Nanaya became prominent from about the 2nd century BC in many parts of the Arsacid realm, most notably in Assyria and Elymais (Susa). Her cult is attested from Bactria to Greece and Egypt (Ambos 2003). Although not originally a moon goddess, Nanaya was transformed into a lunar deity. This may have been due to her identification by the Hellenized with Artemis, who was transformed into a moon goddess equal to Roman Selene.

The syncretism between local and Western gods was already attested in the Seleucid period when Nabu became identified with Apollo – e.g., in an inscription on a column in the Nabu temple at Nineveh, or at Borsippa, where Nabu and Tashmetum are identified with Apollo and Artemis in 268 BC (Dirven 1999:

128–56). The most popular god was Heracles/Nergal, also revered as Iranian Verethragna. His temples have been found at Assur, Dura Europos, Hatra, and Masged-e Solayman, and sculptural representations of him are numerous (Downey 1969; Safar and Mustafa 1974: 350–67; Tubach 1986, 256–68; Invernizzi 1989; Kaizer 2000). Like Heracles/Nergal, many traditional gods were now depicted in Mediterranean attire and style.

In the Arsacid period monotheistic religions steadily gained ground. The Babylonian Talmud attests to the existence of a large, flourishing Jewish community in the region with an *exilarch* living at Ctesiphon (Oppenheimer 1983). The ruling family of Adiabene converted to Judaism in the mid-1st century AD. Coincidentally, from about this time on Christianity spread in Mesopotamia. Allegedly, the first Christian bishop was ordained at Seleucia/Ctesiphon in the late 1st century (Jullien and Jullien 2002: 230–1). In the far east of the empire, Buddhism increasingly found followers.

The Arsacids themselves were probably Zoroastrians, but the role of Zoroastrianism is difficult to ascertain. It is commonly assumed that the *Avesta* was widely spread all over Iran and beyond during this time. The first collection of all written or oral testimonies of the *Avesta* and *Zand* was probably ordered by Vologases I (Hintze 1998). The immediate impact of this in religious life is nevertheless rarely traceable, since temples for Iranian gods like the supposed Anahita temple at Bard-e Neshanda (Vanden Berghe and Schippmann 1985: 20), are rare.

There is neither proof of the Arsacid rulers' religious orientation nor any indication that the kings of kings interfered with the various cults. The simultaneous reverence of such a diversity of traditional Mesopotamian, Greek, Arab, and Iranian, as well as monotheistic gods which is mirrored in the diversity of local temple architecture (Downey 1988), makes the Arsacid period a most interesting field for research.

7 Architecture, Regionalism, and "Parthian Art"

The material culture of the Arsacid Empire shows strong regional tendencies in pottery and burial customs (cf. Negro Ponzi 1968–9), while architecture and sculpture, although incorporating to various degrees influences of different heritages, show common trends. Encounters, mixtures, and coexistence between the earlier Seleucid Greek culture and local traditions form an overarching theme.

Architecture

The early to middle Arsacid period is mostly represented at Nisa and in former Seleucid Greek colonies. The intensity of Hellenization is visible in buildings foreign to the area, especially theaters with *palaestra* at Babylon and Seleucia-on-the-Tigris. Nevertheless, even in these cities most of the population must have been indigenous, and the Hellenistic style might not be representative of the poorly researched areas outside these settlements. A typical, western feature is the use of columns. The only examples of columned streets occur at Babylon (Wetzel et al. 1957: 33). Peristyle buildings, a typical element of Mediterranean private architecture, have been found at various sites including Seleucia-on-the-Tigris (Block G6), Babylon (House I) and the manor house at Khorkhe, in Iran, which displays Ionic capitals (Hakemi 1990; Rahbar 1999a). Architectural elements such as flat tiles, palmetto roofings, or lion-headed *simas* are known from Susa and Uruk. The so-called "Parthian palaces" of Nippur and Assur, both built in the 1st century AD, show the persistence of peristyle architecture. On the other hand (pseudo-)peripteral temples with Greek *peristasis* are only known from the late Arsacid period at Uruk, Assur, and Hatra. They indicate the reception and integration of contemporary or earlier western influences. Other temples in Babylonia, Elymais, and Central Asia – e.g., Takht-i Sangin – seem to follow local traditions.

The hallmark of later Arsacid architecture is a parlor in the form of a barrel-vaulted hall open on one side, the *iwan*. If it opens to the north, it provides shade and admits cool breezes in the summer. South-facing *iwans* were built for use in winter to keep out cold winds, while allowing sunshine to enter. Although usually considered an Iranian feature, the earliest *iwans*, except for Khorkhe, appear in the early 1st century AD Mesopotamian "palaces" at Nippur, Abu Qubur, and Assur (Wright 1991; Lecuyot 1993). At Assur every house had at least one *iwan* in the south. The main court of the "Parthian palace" was framed by four complexes with a central *iwan*. At Assur and Hatra even the temples used this open form. The construction of *iwans* was made possible by another hallmark of Arsacid architecture, the generous use of gypsum mortar. The fast-setting mortar enabled the rapid building of large vaults. A third typical aspect of the later Arsacid period was the lavish use of stucco in rich residences (Assur, Seleucia-on-the-Tigris, Uruk, Susa, Qaleh Yazdigird).

Regionalism in commodity crafts

To a surprising degree many crafts are still poorly known. Glass vessels, found especially in graves at Kilizu, Assur, Hatra, Abu Skheir, and ed-Dur (Negro Ponzi 1972; Dorna Metzger 2000), were often considered Roman imports or assigned a Sasanian date. Only recently has the existence of a differentiated production of cast (especially ribbed bowls) and blown glass (bowls, balsamaria, jars, and ewers), some of them with mold-blown or appliqué decoration, been demonstrated for Seleucia-on-the-Tigris (Negro Ponzi 2002).

A comparable problem exists for Arsacid period seals which are difficult to distinguish from Seleucid or Sasanian examples. Phraates II bullae from

Göbekly-Depe in Margiana and sealings from Shahr-e Qumis allow rare insights into Arsacid seal-cutting and use (Gaibov 1996, 2007; Bivar 1982).

The development of pottery also reveals many regional variants (Haerinck 1983; Finkbeiner 1993b; Hauser 1994; Adachi 2005). At Susa, Seleucia, and other Babylonian cities, Seleucid trends continued. Many types of Hellenistic models, especially two-handled amphorae and fish plates, were produced in large numbers with green to blue glaze, a trademark of western Arsacid pottery. A second ceramic hallmark in Babylonia and beyond is the extremely thin eggshell ware used for small jars or amphorae. But even in Adiabene this ware is unknown and glazed wares appear less often. Instead, wavy lines and stamped impressions are common decorations. Connections to Roman forms are very rare. These differences confirm Haerinck's (1983) observation of strong regional trends in pottery production during this period.

"Parthian art"

Our understanding of representational arts in the Arsacid Empire is still limited. Often, sculptures and even minor arts like silver bowls have been considered a provincial offshoot of Greco-Roman art, dependent on the constant influx of new inspirations from the West (Mathiesen 1992: 13; Pfrommer 1993). Unfortunately, this view hinders an understanding of artistic expression as an act of communication and as part of societal and discursive practices within the Arsacid realm, as it constructs a continuous dependence upon the West and presupposes a common ideal in art. In fact, the use and production of representational objects was much more diverse.

Clearly imported marble statues of Venus, Hermes and other Greek deities have been found at Hatra, Nineveh, and Susa. Others were locally produced according to western norms – e.g., the Heracles from Mesene after Lysippus (Invernizzi 1989; Bernard 1990) or the city *tyche* from Susa. Alongside these Hellenic sculptures many statues of men were found, typically clad in long tunic, mantle, trousers, and shoes, often richly embroidered. They appear comparatively stiff and look frontally at the viewer. This frontal view is also found in reliefs where it is even used in scenes of communication between the persons depicted, who, nevertheless, gaze at the observer. This frontality is considered the most typical, formal aspect of so-called "Parthian art" as defined by Rostovtzeff (1938) in his attempt to understand Arsacid visual language in its own right. His definition was criticized for its inappropriate ethnic connotation "Parthian," as well as for being based largely on pieces from Dura Europos in Syria, a site just on the western fringes and after AD 166 even outside the empire's borders. Still, as a specific formal and symbolic quality which expresses immediacy, direct contact between the person or god depicted and the viewer was obviously considered more important than a naturalistic rendering of interaction and is characteristic of the less-Hellenized Arsacid period art. Nevertheless, it is neither ethnically "Parthian art," nor official "Arsacid art," but just the most commonly used from of representation within the empire and in its vicinity.

Later Arsacid period reliefs and statues of the 2nd and 3rd centuries in Khuzestan as well as Hatra adhere to this form (Safar and Mustafa 1974; Vanden Berghe and Schippmann 1985; Dirven forthcoming). In contrast, the earlier and middle Arsacid sculpture represented by the life-sized terracottas at Nisa, reliefs of lords at Assur, or rock reliefs by Mithridates II at Bisotun or at Hung-e Nauruzi present the figures in profile (Mathiesen 1992).

The same difference between Hellenistic and local styles can been seen in terracotta. The locally produced terracottas at Seleucia-on-the-Tigris and Babylon attest to the continued intensity of Greek cultural influence into the late Arsacid period. Women and men appear draped in Greek dress. The traditional local subjects, such as nude females with their arms at their sides, were adopted to Hellenistic style and produced in a new technique using two molds (van Ingen 1939; Karvonen-Kannas 1995; Klengel-Brandt and Cholidis 2006). At Uruk and Susa, the new subjects and production methods are well attested, but the iconographic program remained much more tied to traditional topics – e.g., nude females and horsemen (Martinez-Sève 2002). At Assur, on the contrary, double mold and composite cast techniques were not employed, and the subjects remained traditional (Klengel-Brandt 1968).

The important conclusion is that, especially in the major cities of Arsacid Babylonia and Elymais, Hellenistic culture had become part of the local heritage. This is attested in terracottas and in commodities like pottery. The Arsacid period is thus a phase which shows a profound process of acculturation in which elements of Mediterranean, Mesopotamian, and Iranian material culture were fused into innovative and distinctive regional as well as context-specific, visual, and material forms of expression. These processes of cultural exchange and adoption, the diversity of religions, languages, and material expressions, as well as the intensification of long-distance trade and irrigation systems, make the Arsacid period a most intriguing subject for study. Particularly in view of the comparatively poor textual evidence available, archaeological research on the Arsacids contributes to a more differentiated picture of one of the most undervalued but successful empires of the ancient Near East.

GUIDE TO FURTHER READING

Literature on the Arsacid Empire is widely dispersed. A useful, but dated introduction into the material evidence is Herrmann (1977). More recent scholarship is reflected in Herrmann (2000), and in the short, but well illustrated volume 271 of *Dossiers d' archéologie* (March 2002). The latter provides some easy accessible synopses for research in Iran,

Margiana, and Northern Mesopotamia. History and archaeology of Elymais are best approached with the compendium by Potts (1999). Schuol (2000) provides résumés and bibliographies on the results from excavations in southern Mesopotamia and the Gulf. For a concise summary on the Gulf area, Potts 2009b should be consulted.

Particularly strong on the written sources for Arsacid history is the volume edited by Wiesehöfer (1998). Various Roman, Chinese, Armenian, and other authors and their contributions are discussed. The sources are now assembled and translated in the three volumes edited by Hackl et al. (2010).

Traditional prejudices created the idea of a weak king of kings barely able to rule. This image is explicit in Wolski (1993), less so in Debevoise (1938) or Schippmann (1980.) A nomadic heritage, an important question concerning the northern and western frontier areas, has been championed in eastern European research; cf. Koshelenko and Pilipko (1994) and Olbrycht (2003). Recently these concepts were summarized and critically evaluated by Hauser (2005 and 2006a). Still the best historical analysis of Romano-Arsacid relations is provided by Ziegler (1964).

Important resources are also available on the web. First of all, the *Encyclopaedia Iranica* (www.iranica.com) offers (sometimes outdated, but mostly reliable) discussions of persons, places, and events. A constantly growing bibliography is provided by E.C.D Hopkins at www.parthia.com. This website provides the best images of Parthian coins available today.

CHAPTER FIFTY-FOUR

Roman Rule in the Near East

Bettina Fischer-Genz

1 Introduction

The geographical boundaries of this study extend from the city of Seleucia-Zeugma (modern Belkis, Turkey) on the Euphrates in the north to the port of Aila (mod. Aqaba, Jordan) in the south. In the east, the boundary follows the military and political struggle for supremacy over Armenia and Mesopotamia between the Roman armies and the Parthian and later Sasanian Empire along the line of the Euphrates as far as Dura Europos (mod. Qalat es-Salihiye, Syria).

Generally, the geography of the Near East can be divided into five zones, differentiated by geology as well as the accessibility of water. In the west this includes the coastal strip with rainfall and melting snow from the adjacent Amanus, Jebel Ansariyeh, and Lebanon mountain ranges; and the Rift valley running from north to south with carstic groundwater and springs, as well as two rivers emerging in the Beqaa close to Baalbek, the Orontes running north and the Litani running south. The southern continuation of the Rift valley is the Jordan river, the Dead Sea, and the Wadi Araba down to the port of Aila (mod. Aqaba, Jordan). Another mountain range, the Jebel Zawiyah and the Anti-Lebanon, delimit the rift valley to the east, beyond which, to the east and south, the more arid steppe and desert zones of southeastern Syria and eastern Jordan appear. Transportation networks followed, on the one hand, the north–south coastal plains as well as the Rift valley, while, on the other, transversal routes connected the caravan routes from the eastern desert zones to the Euphrates and the Red Sea ports, and the inland

---

A Companion to the Archaeology of the Ancient Near East, First Edition.
Edited by D.T. Potts.
© 2012 Blackwell Publishing Ltd. Published 2012 by Blackwell Publishing Ltd.

regions to the Mediterranean ports along the coast, for example through the Homs Gap and various mountain passes.

Chronologically, this chapter examines the period between the annexation of the Near Eastern provinces by Pompey in 64/63 BC and the death of Constantine in AD 337, which marked the appearance of a new administrative structure in the eastern provinces. The political history of the Near East in the Hellenistic and Roman periods has been studied intensively through textual sources (Millar 1993; Butcher 2003; Sartre 2005) and provides a solid framework for archaeological research in the area. But when investigating the effects of political decisions and events on people, communities, and landscapes through material remains, archaeologists are frequently confronted with the contrasting narratives of Braudel's *longue durée* and the accounts of historical sources. The impact of Roman rule on the Hellenized cities and rural population of the Near East is difficult to trace in the archaeological record, since initially Roman rule did not entail a specific mode of political organization, language, or cult (Sartre 2005: 365). The archaeological record gives us building remains, funerary monuments, and stone sculpture, as well as the more mundane objects of everyday life such as pottery, glass, and metalwork. In addition, a growing number of inscriptions by individuals as well as officials can provide valuable information on different aspects of Roman rule and influence. Thus, archaeological research continues to yield new information on this vast region, but in addition to fieldwork and surveys a number of more general questions have also come into the focus of research. However, it must be stressed that the archaeology of the Roman Near East is highly complex and in the following only some of the more important issues and key examples will be touched upon.

The Eastern provinces were already part of the Hellenistic *koiné* before entering the Roman empire, and thus recent studies aim at understanding how the processes of Roman imperialism and the construction of provincial identity there might differ from the situation in the western provinces and North Africa, and whether, in some respects, the Near East might even be regarded as occupying a peripheral position within the empire. There is also a lively debate on the different concepts of identities of the local populations, opposing "Hellenizers" and "indigenizers" in defining ethnicity, culture, and identity (Butcher 2003: 63; Ball 2000: 3). It is not surprising that populations subject to different political structures such as the city-state, colony, or province probably employed different identities simultaneously, according to the context of social relations on a communal, regional, or provincial level. In light of these questions, a new assessment of the role of the Greek-style *polis* and city-state is also warranted: while it was certainly decisive in the formation of the political and cultural networks of the Near East during the Hellenistic period (Sartre 2005: 365), the diversity of systems used to govern the various regions of the Near East as well as their lack of uniformity demands more research on the relationship and interaction between cities and their rural hinterlands, and between sedentary and nomadic societies.

The foundation of cities continued throughout the region in the Roman period, particularly in Palestine and Arabia, thus providing us with comparisons between the already existing "Greek" cities and either newly founded cities or rural centers that achieved city status.

Finally, ever since the influential studies of Antoine Poidebard using aerial photography to map ancient structures in Syria (Poidebard 1934; Mouterde and Poidebard 1945), research has been undertaken on the question of what effect the military frontier situation of the Near East had on settlement structure, especially in the arid zones (Isaac 1992).

2 Political Framework and Provincial Administration

The different forms of political organization in kingdoms, tribes or city-states provided the framework for Roman provincial governance. While some parts of the Near East, such as the former Seleucid kingdom, were directly controlled by Rome, others were left in the hands of client kings. Generally it seems that centralized and strongly hierarchical political entities were favored (Butcher 2003: 79). Gaining the support of local elites through honors and privileges was crucial in the early Roman Empire, as the bureaucracy of the government was not yet as well established as the military administration. Client kings, especially in the province of Syria and Judaea, were left in power in the first century of Roman rule, and only when local disputes or internal problems arose did the Roman administration impose direct rule. These client kings had personal ties with the emperor and enjoyed a certain independence in taxation and their relationships in the dynastic networks of the region. It can be argued that indirect rule was an expedient way of administering the peripheries and rural areas (Butcher 2003: 89), and that only gradually was more direct control imposed on client kings and tribal states, often because of open belligerence or the failure of dynastic rule. This was not a linear development, for, in some cases, such as the kingdoms of Emesa (mod. Homs, Syria) or Commagene (in Turkey), dynasts were deposed and after a period of direct rule new ones nominated.

After the victory at Actium in 31 BC by Octavian (later honored with the name Augustus by the senate), the Near Eastern provinces became imperial provinces due to the four legions stationed there and the military significance of the Parthian border. Therefore the governors of Syria were usually highly experienced politicians and competent senators rather than just military men, and Augustus assigned as governor of Syria a legate with consular rank residing in Antioch-on-the-Orontes (mod. Antakya, Turkey). In the 1st century AD, the Syrian government, with its large number of wealthy cities, was far from being a peripheral position in the senatorial *cursus honorum* (Rey-Coquais 1978: 61; Sartre 2005: 56–7). Due to the mosaic of diverse and often independent political entities and the resulting geographical fragmentation of the province in the early

Imperial period, additional prefects under the authority of the provincial governor sometimes had to be delegated, e.g. in the administration of Judaea and the Decapolis.

For the creation of an effective provincial administration, new communication infrastructure had to be built, and a number of port installations, roads, bridges, and milestones are attested, including the coastal road through Berytus (mod. Beirut, Lebanon) to Ptolemais (mod. Akko, Israel) and the *via nova Traiana* (Goodchild 1949; Galliazzo 1994: nos. 813–815). These road networks were primarily built to facilitate communications as well as the movement of troops, and they served to connect forts, water sources, cities, and ports: the archaeological evidence for these dates mostly to the 2nd and 3rd centuries AD (see below).

A census of people and possessions as well as land had to be implemented for the collection of the two main taxes, the *tributum soli* (land tax) and the *tributum capitis* (poll tax). The land tax was probably restricted to agricultural lands and not extended to desert or steppe regions. Due to the many different monetary systems in the Near East (Butcher 2003: 212–23), money taxes were problematic and thus payment in agricultural goods or a mixed payment is probable. The best known census is certainly the one mentioned in the Gospel of Luke for Palestine (Luke 2:1–2), which actually took place in AD 6 under the authority of P. Sulpicius Quirinius (Millar 1993: 35, 46–8; Kennedy 2006: 112). An inscription of Aemilius Secundus puts the population of Apamea (mod. Qalat-Mudiq, Syria; Figure 54.1) in AD 6 at 117,000 citizens, which must include the city's hinterland, but presumably does not include non-citizens, slaves, and nomads (Kennedy 2006: 113–17). Archaeologically, this data can be compared to the actual space enclosed by the city walls of Apamea, which comprises 250 hectares. Although the density of housing inside the city area in the 1st century AD is unknown, a population density of 100–200/hectare would imply 25,000–50,000 inhabitants (Balty 1988: 96; 2003: 227–9; Kennedy 2006: 118). In order to explain the total figure of 117,000 citizens, rural settlements in the territory of Apamea need to be taken into account across an area measuring c.100 kilometers between Antioch and Palmyra (mod. Tadmur, Syria). On analogy with the Roman villages of the Jebel Ansariyeh, one can assume two-story houses and land holdings of 2–7 square kilometers in and around Apamea (Tchalenko 1953–8; Tate 1992; Kennedy 2006: 121). Another census for the province of Arabia is documented in the Babatha archive of AD 127 found in the Cave of the Letters at the Dead Sea, but many more censuses must have been carried out on a regular basis (Isaac 1991; Kennedy 2006: 112). The Babatha archive, like the Mesopotamian papyri and other archives from Dura Europos and Petra (mod. al-Batra, Jordan), contain mainly legal documents attesting to a very complex financial system for the cities and for the rural settlements as well (Butcher 2003: 143–4). Inscriptions also mention a number of senatorial legates employed in military and civil administration and a procurator nominated by the emperor who was in charge of managing the finances. Multiple administrators were probably in charge of specific taxes

Figure 54.1 View of the colonnaded street in Apamea (mod. Qalat-Mudiq, Syria).

and custom duties such as the *portorium* (a tax on traded goods) and other taxes mentioned in the tax law and caravan trade inscriptions of Palmyra from the 3rd century AD (Matthews 1984; Young 2001). After the administrative reforms of Diocletian (284–305) in the late 3rd century, governors continued to exercise primarily administrative and judicial functions, but were subordinate to vicars who were in charge of groups of provinces, in our case the diocese *Oriens*. The tax reforms of Diocletian also entailed important cadastral changes in Syria (Millar 1993: 535–44), again attested in inscriptions on border stones (Tchalenko 1958/III: 6–7).

3 The Geographical Expansion of Roman Rule

From historical sources it can be deduced that, following the campaigns of Pompey and his legates, the annexation of the large territory comprising the Near Eastern provinces was motivated by the need to prevent piracy and brigandage from re-establishing itself. Administration through different forms of direct and indirect government, from the established *provincia* structure to client kings, indigenous chiefdoms, and city-states, was expedient. Thus, while the Seleucid rulers reinstated shortly before by Lucullus were deposed, most of the client kings and chiefs were confirmed in their positions. To name only a few examples, the Ituraean dynasty received the central Beqaa valley and the north of Mount Lebanon, while Sampsigeramos was confirmed further north in his realm around Emesa and Arethusa. Best known is certainly the case of the Herodian dynasty in Judaea, confirmed in their kingdom after Actium, which managed to enlarge their territory considerably to encompass the Hauran as well as the Beqaa. As such, the Herodians were intermittently in territorial conflict with the neighboring Nabataean kingdom that also remained independent until its annexation in AD 106.

During the ensuing 30 years of civil war, what with Parthian invasions and different Roman factions warring and pillaging, the region had to supply funds as well as war equipment to the different factions. Under Marc Antony, with the exception of a few years of direct rule from Egypt when Cleopatra VII was given Phoenicia, Coele Syria, and part of Cilicia in 37/36 BC, client kings continued to be favored. Although many cities were ruled by client-kings, the independent city-states were also consolidated and strengthened. Most were in the former Seleucid kingdom and Phoenicia, with groups in the Transjordan region and on the coast (Sartre 2005: 42). Pompey restored some destroyed cities and, after the reduction of the Jewish Hasmonaean kingdom, gave independence to a number of new city-states in order to ensure the continuous support of the "Greek" population, i.e. the descendants of colonists as well as Hellenized natives, probably to compensate for a lack of provincial administration.

After the victory of Actium, Augustus retained these different forms of government, and added the eastern part of Cilicia as well as Seleucia-Zeugma on the Euphrates to the province of Syria. Most of the client kingdoms were gradually annexed by the end of the 1st century AD, one of the last being the Nabataean kingdom in AD 106. The Decapolis cities were divided between the newly founded provinces of Arabia and Judaea, and after the Bar Kokhba revolt (AD 132–5) the latter was renamed Syria Palaestina. Under Septimius Severus there was a further subdivision between Syria Coele and Syria Phoenicia, and by the end of the 3rd century it was divided into three parts called Palaestina Prima, Secunda, and Tertia. In the east, Lucius Verus exploited a period of Parthian weakness to push the imperial border to the Tigris, and in AD 195 the new provinces of Mesopotamia and Osrhoene were created.

These reorganizations often entailed shifts in the number of legions stationed in the individual provinces, which led in turn to changes in the rank of the governor: under Trajan or Hadrian Judaea got a second legion and thus had to be governed by a former consul, while under Septimius Severus Syria Phoenicia had only one legion and was only governed by a former praetor. By the end of the 2nd century this system had started to change, as the province of Mesopotamia was governed by an equestrian prefect despite its two legions, and during the 3rd century more and more formerly senatorial appointments were held by equestrians (Butcher 2003: 85).

In AD 224 the Arsacid dynasty of Parthia was toppled by one of its vassal rulers, Ardashir of Fars, thus creating the Sasanian dynasty. During the 3rd century, incursions by the newly founded Sasanian Empire as well as the threat of Germanic tribes to the Rhine and Danube provinces, created a period of political instability and economic strain, necessitating the profound administrative reforms undertaken by Diocletian. He created a collegiate system with two senior emperors (*augusti*) and two junior successors (*caesars*) who shared the responsibilities and military interventions of the vast empire with the assistance of praetorian prefects. The provinces were divided into smaller units, and a new imperial official, the vicar, was appointed to supervise a diocese comprising a group of provinces. The number of legions was augmented and they were now put under the command of a *dux* and *magister militum*, effectively dividing administrative and military power in the provinces. Finally, a new taxation system (*capitatio-iugatio*) was introduced, which took into consideration livestock and agricultural land.

4 The Roman Military

The transformation of the eastern Roman frontier into a territorial border was a slow and gradual process. Until Lucius Verus managed to push it to the Tigris in the late 2nd century AD, the Roman and the Parthian empires were in direct confrontation. The *limes* (chain of frontier forts) facing Parthian territory ran along the Euphrates and branched south at the legionary camp of Sura (mod. Suriya, Syria), down through the Syrian desert along the old caravan route to Palmyra. In addition to legionary camps, there were numerous smaller *castellae* for *equites* or cohorts such as Callinicum (mod. ar-Raqqa, Syria) as well as fortified military posts such as Tetrapyrgium (mod. Qusair as-Saila, Syria), the plan of which (60 × 60 meters with a 2 meter high foundation of fieldstones and mudbrick walls) follows Mesopotamian-Parthian building traditions of the same type (Konrad 2001: 21–46). A typical plan can also be seen in the fort of Ayyas (mod. Qreiye, Syria) on the Euphrates near Deir ez-Zor. The outer fortifications had intermittent as well as corner towers, while the interior held a headquarters building (*principia*), rooms housing the archive, storage areas (*horrea*), and, most importantly, numerous barracks for the soldiers (Gschwind-Hasan 2008). As recent excavations along the *limes* have shown, this line of fortifications with different types of *castellae* and encampments seems to have been established as early as the Parthian wars of 61/62 (Konrad 2001: 114), and was enhanced with the establishment of the *via nova Traiana*, which ran through the new province of Arabia down to the Red Sea, in the early 2nd century AD (Parker 2007, 351). In periods of peace the *limes* lost some of its importance, but after the Sasanian incursions and the rebellion of Zenobia (AD 270–72) it was again fortified. Both milestones and building inscriptions date most of the constructions to the reign of Diocletian. A series of fortresses and military camps formed the *limes Arabicus*, the most important one being the legionary fortress of Betthorus (mod. al-Lajjun, Jordan) established under Diocletian at the site of the key water source in the region.

Most of the *castellae* in this later phase seem to have been surrounded by fortified *vici* consisting of courtyard houses, 40–60 meters in width, which were planned according to an orthogonal system inside a rectangular outer fortification (Konrad 2001: 110–11; Parker 2007: 352). Military camps such as Raphanaea, located 35 kilometers northwest of Homs on the Orontes, were probably established in connection with the *strata Diocletiana*.

In the steppe and desert regions Roman military camps were established near waterholes or *wadis*. Large cisterns provided water for daily use and, when possible, for irrigation, enabling permanent agricultural settlements to thrive in their vicinity. But military tombstones indicate that the soldiers were not closely integrated into civilian society. Rather, they generally stayed apart, often not even speaking the same language (Butcher 2003: 399). Veterans who were given land in less Hellenized areas might have had an influence on local communities, as seen in Latin inscriptions and specific cults, and it can be assumed that they had some impact on agricultural production in remote marginal areas such as the Hauran or Jebel al-Arab (Butcher 2003: 402; Clauss-Balty 2008b: 43).

Especially after the Jewish revolt in AD 70, there was a good deal of shifting in the camps of the different legions in the 1st century AD. Originally, the Legio III Gallica was stationed in the north, the VI Ferrata near Laodikeia (mod. Latakia, Syria) and the X Fretensis in Cyrrhus (mod. Nebi Huri, Syria). In AD 56 the IV Scythica was sent to Seleucia-Zeugma at a crossing point on the Euphrates, and after AD 75 the XVI Flavia Firma arrived in Samosata (mod. Samsat, Turkey), capital of the annexed kingdom of Commagene (Sartre 2005: 61). At the end of the Jewish war, the X Fretensis was sent to Judaea, and after the division of the province under Septimius Severus the III Gallica stayed in Phoenicia, the IV Scythica and the XVI Flavia Firma in Syria Coele (the latter had replaced the VI Ferrata sent to Arabia under Trajan). The X Fretensis in Cyrrhus was sent in AD 18 to Seleucia-Zeugma in order to watch the Euphrates crossing, and was replaced under Vespasian by the IV Sythica. In AD 72 Commagene was occupied by the VI Ferrata, then under Trajan by the XVI Flavia Firma with its garrison at Samosata. Three different legions used Raphanaea as their camp, the last one being the III Gallica until the reign of Elagabal (AD 218–22). During the Parthian wars other legions, such as the XV Apollinaris with its camp on Arados/Antiochia-in-Pieria (mod. Arwad, Syria) under Trajan, and the II Parthica, which stayed repeatedly in Apamea under the Severans, were temporarily stationed in Syria. The numerous auxiliary units such as *alae* and *cohortes* are much more difficult to identify and trace, but may have numbered c.20,000 men in the 1st century AD.

Already in the 1st century AD, on the right bank of the Euphrates, a military zone divided in two sectors had been created under the command of a prefect or curator (Rey-Coquais 1978: 69). In the 3rd century the Euphrates was placed under the command of a *dux* residing in Dura Europos. In general, the northwestern legions served to protect Antioch-on-the-Orontes and the Syrian provinces against an attack from the east, while the desert zone from the Euphrates to the Hauran was defended by auxiliary troops as well as the troops of the vassal kings, and later the militias of Palmyra. Some reinforcements were sent to the Hauran under Marcus Aurelius (AD 161–80) and Commodus (AD 180–92). Finally, under Aurelian (AD 270–5) and Diocletian the defenses and military organization of the Near East as a whole were reorganized, with the legio I Illyricorum newly established at Palmyra.

Thus the locations of military installations and legions were determined as much by availability of water and supplies as by their strategic position against an enemy attack, and the legions were distributed among the provinces in order to minimize the risk of concentrating too much military power under one single governor who might challenge the power of the emperor (Butcher 2003: 406).

5 The Development of the Cities Under Roman Rule

Weakened by the internal power struggles of the Seleucid dynasty, the political landscape of the Near East in the 1st century BC was anarchic and marked by the establishment of several Arab tribal kingdoms, such as the Ituraeans in Phoenicia and the Rhambeans along the Euphrates, as well as local tyrants in some of the cities. Thus in 64 BC Pompey was received by many cities as a liberator, but soon the Roman civil war created new conflicts that lasted until the victory of Octavian Augustus at Actium. These political upheavals can be traced in the different eras adopted after consecutive "liberations," such as the Pompeian era used in Antioch, Apamea, Byblos, Tripoli, and other cities along the coast, but especially in the cities of the Decapolis (Rey-Coquais 1978: 45). The coming of Caesar, Antony, Cleopatra, and finally Augustus' armies led to new eras in many cities. In general, however, city-eras were kept or reverted to after a period of using an era tied to a specific event, and they can be seen as a marker of civic identity (Butcher 2003: 123).

In the north, the most important cities constituted the Syrian Tetrapolis: Antioch-on-the-Orontes, Seleucia-in-Pieria (mod. Çevlik, Turkey), Apamea-on-the-Orontes and Laodikeia-on-the-Sea (Jones 1971). Apamea had been the former military base of the Seleucid dynasty and, along with Antioch, was one of the largest cities in the Roman Near East. In the 1st and 2nd centuries AD the imperial mint at Antioch was the most important one in entire the Near East.

A number of smaller cities such as Seleucia-Zeugma and Cyrrhus were important regional centers. The old Phoenician coastal cities from Arados/Antiochia-in-Pieria to Ptolemais adapted to the Hellenistic city model, as did the newly founded cities of the Decapolis, despite their mainly indigenous population

(Sartre 2005: 152). But the network of cities was rather sparse in central and southern Syria as well as in Transjordan and Palestine, and at the beginning of Roman rule most urbanization efforts by client princes were concentrated in this area, with cities such as Caesarea Maritima (mod. Caesarea, Israel), Samaria-Sebaste (mod. Sebastiya, West Bank), and Antipatris (mod. Tel Aphek, Israel) founded by Herod the Great, or Arca-Caesarea (mod. Arqa, Lebanon) established by the Ituraean client kings. At the beginning of the 2nd century AD, new cities were primarily founded in the Hauran, Transjordan, and Palestine. A network of cities was also established along the Hauran and the Transjordan plateau down to the Gulf of Aila. Except for Bostra (mod. Bosra, Syria), Petra, and Aila, the Nabataean kingdom had no real cities, and after its annexation inscriptions point to the establishment of civic institutions in Bostra and Petra (Sartre 2005: 445 n22). Aila was identified as a *polis* by Strabo in the 1st century AD (*Geog.* 16.2.30), and the archaeological evidence shows that it was not only a center of trade, but also of several industries such as pottery manufacture and copper-processing (Parker 2006: 228).

In general, the classical Greek *polis* was the model for the administrative institutions and infrastructure of the Roman cities in the Near East. Before the extension of citizenship to every free person in the empire in AD 212, only the leading families and veterans were given that privilege. Citizenship was not given to the rural population, freed slaves, or foreigners, and was considered an honor as well as an obligation. At the beginning of Roman rule, the cities generally retained their autonomy, as shown by their right to issue silver coinage. Taxes that had been paid to local dynasts since Hellenistic times now had to be paid to the Roman provincial government. Private benefactors therefore became essential for financing festivals and building programs, as in Asia Minor and elsewhere. Magistrates, elected by the city council (*boule*) or by popular vote, came mostly from the same wealthy families and were expected to cover major expenses. Although far fewer decrees and honorific dedications of civic institutions are preserved than for the Aegean world, municipal life was probably just as active, especially in the constant contest between leading families for recognition and advancement through the imperial administration. Monumental construction programs were financed by municipal elites, as in the case of Apamea and Gerasa; by direct sponsorship of the emperors, as at Antioch-on-the-Orontes; or by client kings, as Josephus reports for the donations of Agrippa I and Agrippa II to Berytus (Josephus, *Jewish Antiquities* 19.335–7, 20.211–12).

Competition between cities prompted the construction of imposing buildings, sometimes planned on such a monumental scale that they were often unfinished due to a lack of funds, rather than essential infrastructure such as aqueducts or streets. By the beginning of the 2nd century AD, civic finances had reached an alarming state as many cities had accumulated large debts, necessitating the appointment of curators (*logistai*) and requiring imperial approval for permission to erect public buildings using civic funds (Butcher 2003: 227).

Although there is much continuity in urban layout between the Hellenistic and Roman periods, rebuilding and shifts in settlement occurred as a result of demolition and the requirements of specific building programs. The Roman city of Palmyra seems to have been built north of the Hellenistic remains, reusing an already existing axis (Millar 1993: 319–36). Dura Europos is a special case, as it was partly transformed into a military camp and the area inside the city walls was later filled with private houses rather than additional public buildings (Butcher 2003: 259–61).

In general, the larger cities have a planned, axial layout, while smaller cities often have a more irregular plan of streets and buildings, but there is no standardized urban plan. Whereas, in the Hellenistic period, only a few large public buildings, such as the colonnaded portico at Apamea, were erected, in the larger cities the first two centuries of the Roman period were marked by the construction of baths, theaters, hippodromes, temples, and other monumental public buildings. In the 3rd century AD there seems to have been a shift toward the endowment of new civic festivals as a means of elite representation, rather than larger public buildings, either because most cities already had the required "set" of public buildings, or to reduce the financial risks involved in large building projects (Butcher 2003: 227–8; Sartre 1991: 343).

While there were many new city foundations throughout the first two centuries of Roman rule, true colonies of military veterans were established only in four instances. The first was the *Colonia Iulia Felix Berytus* established in the reign of Augustus for the veterans of the legio V Macedonica and the legio VIII Gallica, with a large territory that probably encompassed Heliopolis (mod. Baalbek, Lebanon; Figure 54.2) (Rey-Coquais 1978: 51). Under Claudius, Ptolemais was transformed into a colony with veterans from four legions. Veterans were settled in Caesarea Maritima under Vespasian, and at the beginning of the Bar Kokhba revolt Aelia Capitolina was founded on the ruins of Jerusalem. From the Severan period onward, no true veteran settlements are attested, while the promotions of existing cities to colonial status became more frequent. Especially early in their history, veteran colonies such as Berytus seem to have used more Latin inscriptions throughout their territory, as in the case of the *pagus Augustus* in the rural sanctuary of Niha or in Heliopolis, where at least some of the veterans must have lived (Rey-Coquais 1978: 52; Butcher 2003: 230). According to coins minted at Heliopolis under Septimius Severus, the city became an independent colony with *ius italicum* (an honorific title, suggesting in name that a colony was on Italic soil) in AD 193 and was called *Colonia Iulia Augusta Felix Heliopolis*, thus making it problematic to distinguish it in inscriptions from Berytus. It appears that the building program of the Jupiter sanctuary in Heliopolis was aimed at transforming the city into a cultural model of Romanization in the Beqaa valley already in the 2nd century AD. The urban development of Berytus experienced at least two phases, which are difficult to date at the moment (Rey-Coquais 1978: 51; Curvers and Stuart 2004). With several monumental baths and a

Figure 54.2 View of the Roman bath, the Bacchus temple, and the Jupiter temple in Heliopolis (mod. Baalbek, Lebanon).

Hippodrome (Butcher 2003: 230) comparable to those found at other coastal cities, Roman Berytus saw an extension of the Achaemenid-Hellenistic urban layout to the northwest, closer to the seashore. Its Latin character was later preserved in the famous center for the study of Latin literature and law. Under Septimius Severus, the title *colonia* became an epithet like *metropolis*, a mark of distinction and imperial patronage in the hierarchy of cities (Millar 1990: 8). In addition to Heliopolis, colonial status was granted to Laodikeia, Antioch, Seleucia-Zeugma, Emesa, Arca-Caesarea, Sidon (mod. Saida, Lebanon), Tyre (mod. Sur, Lebanon), Damascus, Palmyra, Samaria-Sebaste, Bostra, Petra, and Dura Europos, but the *ius italicum* was not given in all cases. Tyre is a good example of imperial strategies of reward and punishment: it was destroyed in the conflict between Septimius Severus and Pescennius Niger in AD 194 and reconstructed as a *metropolis* as well as colony with *ius italicum* after 197. But it lost these titles to Sidon after having sided with an enemy of Elagabal. Later, Neapolis (mod. Nablus, West Bank) and Philippopolis (mod. Shahba, Syria) as well as Gaza (mod. Gaza, Palestine), Ascalon (mod. Ashkelon, Israel), Gerasa (mod. Jerash, Jordan), and possibly Gadara (mod. Umm Qeis, Jordan) also became *coloniae* (Millar 1990). Philippopolis was founded by Philip the Arab in AD 244 and seems to conform more or less with the rectangular plan of the "ideal" Greco-Roman city, but a closer look reveals definite regional influences from the choice of building material to specific monuments (Ball 2000: 204–6). Generally speaking, it seems that, after Severan times, neither the original veteran colonies nor the honorific *coloniae* differed in their monuments or culture significantly from the earlier Greek cities.

Some of the most vital engineering works were the aqueducts that provided cities with water. Their construction was connected to the establishment of public baths as well as fountains and latrines, but, as in the case of Heliopolis, water basins inside the courtyard of the Jupiter sanctuary were also supplied.

Large, unfortified cities seem to have been rare, but it is often difficult to date fortification walls (Sartre 2005: 168). In general, the main element was a monumental city gate or some other entrance monument, such as those at Gadara, Gerasa, and Heliopolis. City walls were costly and not always approved of by the imperial administration. Hence, ramparts such as those at Apamea and Palmyra might be interpreted as a prestigious symbol of independence.

The urban plan of the Roman period was by no means standardized, although two axial, main streets are a frequent feature in what is considered the Greco-Roman city. But a single main street, as at Gadara, appears to be just as common, and in the case of Bostra and Petra that single street did not cross the city, but led to its main sanctuary (Dentzer-Feydy et al. 2007; Freyberger and Joukowsky 1997). Long, colonnaded streets, serving as a processional way for religious festivals and delimiting a public area in front of shops and private businesses, were a prominent feature. Also common was a central, open space, the *agora* or *forum*, as for example at Palmyra, but oval spaces like the ones at Bostra and Gerasa served the same function.

6 Rural Areas and Communication Networks

Since Max Weber and Moses Finley the traditional dichotomy between the rural countryside as a place of agricultural production and the city as consumer has been at the heart of most economic models of the ancient world. But rural areas present a variety of settlements, from isolated farmsteads to hamlets and villages, some of them acting as regional religious and economic centers in their own right. The difference between a small city and a large village is a legal and constitutional one, but archaeologically only the presence of monumental public buildings and a civic center might indicate the category to which a settlement belongs. On the other hand, funerary inscriptions and archaeological remains demonstrate that the processing of marine and agricultural products, as well as the production of pottery, glass, and metal objects, were also done in urban centers. Thus, cities were consumers and producers, as well as being instrumental in the economic organization of their territory.

There are only a few examples of villa estates known from the Near Eastern countryside, and the main productive unit was the village (Sodini et al. 1980; MacAdam 1984: 51; Tate 1992; Anderson 2003: 452–3; Butcher 2003: 137).

Imperial estates were a common feature, but their exact location is difficult to determine on the basis of inscriptions alone. Whether, in general, land was owned by its inhabitants or by city elites cannot be determined on the basis of our sources (Villeneuve 1985: 82). There were also imperial domains and probably land owned by sanctuaries, as in Asia Minor. Surveys in the limestone massif and the Hauran, around Emesa and in the Beqaa valley indicate that there was a growth of settled population and a spread of rural settlements in the Roman period (Tchalenko 1953–8; Marfoe 1982; Fischer-Genz and Ehrig 2005; Newson et al. 2008–9). As the fertile lowlands, such as the Amuq plain, were intensively cultivated in close connection to the cities (Yener 2005) expansion was only possible into marginal regions such as steppe and mountain areas. It is not clear to what extent there was indeed demographic growth or if some of the nomadic population became sedentary. This may also be the reason why regular field systems can be observed in the limestone massif of northern Syria as well as the Orontes valley, for, according to Roman law, farmers were allowed to own and plant previously uncultivated land (Tate 1997: 57–8; Butcher 2003: 141). In the 4th century AD the *Codex Theodosianus* (7.20.3) granted privileges to veterans who were willing to farm deserted lands, and in the earlier periods centuriation was also connected to land plots for veterans. Some areas around cities are known to have been cadastrated already in the Hellenistic Period, but whenever they are regular and aligned with roads they were probably created by Roman surveyors.

The so called "Dead Cities" of the limestone massif in northwestern Syria, roughly between Antioch-on-the-Orontes, Apamea, and Beroea (mod. Aleppo, Syria), are the best preserved of more than 700 rural hamlets and settlements. The ceramic material from surface surveys indicates a first phase of development between AD 100–250, while the main remains are from the 4th–6th centuries AD (Butcher 2003: 146). Contrary to earlier beliefs, their economy was probably varied, with crops such as olive and grapes (for wine) supplemented by other fruit trees, grain, and livestock (Tate 1992: 254; Butcher 2003: 148). Olive and grape presses are the most common indicator of these kinds of crops, and are frequently found in marginal areas unsuitable for cereals, such as the Anti-Lebanon foothills (Fischer-Genz 2008). In the plains grain was the most important crop, since both the cities and the army consumed large quantities. Surpluses of olive oil and other crops were sold in city markets, and the distribution of storage containers such as the Late Roman I amphorae indicates that they might also have been exported overseas.

Rural buildings were mostly one-story structures built of undressed field stones. Often high towers, which might have served to supervise the fields as well as being defensive structures, are found integrated into buildings or free-standing in villages.

The area toward the Euphrates, called Chalcidice after the city of Chalcis-ad-Belum (mod. Qinnesrin, Syria), was viewed by Antoine Poidebard and René Mouterde as a frontier zone, the settlements and military installations of which formed part of the Syrian *limes* (Mouterde-Poidebard 1945; Butcher 2003: 153). But this change seems only to have taken place in the late Roman period, while in the 2nd and 3rd centuries the evidence points to the presence of a semi-nomadic population raising livestock, as in the area of the Dead Cities. Archaeological markers for these would be stone water troughs or mangers, either in the settlement or in the countryside. Caves were also frequently used as shelters and may show some of these features. Water installations such as the *qanat* tunnels, as well as large reservoirs and cisterns, made farming possible, while further east crops could at least be grown alongside the *wadis*. Communal works such as dams at Emesa and Palmyra as well as the well system of Canatha (mod. Qanawat, Syria) in the Hauran are seen as measures aimed at providing the rural villages with a sufficient water supply for their agricultural needs, supplementing the cisterns common in all settlements (Tate 1997: 62–4; Butcher 2003: 140; Freyberger 2004).

In the basalt region of the Hauran, villages, often situated on rocky outcrops, were abundant. These were located so as to maximize the use of agricultural soils for viticulture and fruit trees, often in areas where the altitude prohibited the cultivation of olives. The same situation has been observed in the Anti-Lebanon foothills around Heliopolis (Fischer-Genz 2008) and in both cases there are indications of a close relationship between sedentary and nomadic populations.

Roman roads known in the Near East were visible markers of imperial presence and technological achievement, and the milestones on them usually recorded distances as well as giving the name of the emperor under whom the construction or repair of the road was done (Roll 1999; Butcher 2003: 127). These were constructed to facilitate the rapid movement of troops as well as for the *cursus publicus*, the imperial postal system. The network of Roman roads is not completely established yet, but the main ones connected the ports along the coast; another ran through the Rift valley all the way to Aila on the Gulf of Aqaba; and two lateral roads joined the Euphrates with the Mediterranean coast via Antioch-on-the-Orontes, and crossed the steppe from Emesa via Damascus or Palmyra. Only in cities or in difficult terrain were the roads paved with large stone slabs, and thus the main archaeological evidence of them consists of milestones, but unfortunately these are rarely found in their original location. Otherwise, the official roads with the legal status of *via publica* were packed dirt surfaces or covered with gravel on a foundation of densely packed stones with a width of 4–7 meters that required frequent repair (Roll 1999: 109; Butcher 2003: 128). The *strata Diocletiana*, although only a dirt road, is easily visible from the air due to the fact that stones from the surface were cleared to either side in order to create it. Construction dates, although difficult to determine, are crucial for an understanding of the motives and strategies involved in the construction of specific road segments. According to the epigraphy of the milestones, there seem to be peaks in construction activity related to the Parthian and Sasanian campaigns during the 2nd and 3rd centuries AD.

While a lack of sources makes the importance of riverine transport difficult to assess, seaports were of major importance for trade, and also used by the military. Under Vespasian (AD 69–79) Seleucia-in-Pieria seems to have been the main military port in Syria, and several ports such as Tel Dor (mod. Dora, Israel), Tyre, Sidon, Tripolis (mod. Trablus, Lebanon), and Laodikeia were probably used as ports of call and are connected to inscriptions mentioning a *nauarchos* (Rey-Coquais 1978: 71). The harbor built by Herod for the newly founded city of Caesarea Maritima consisted of three basins protected by two large breakwaters. All of the Mediterranean ports needed frequent maintenance and repair to protect them from silting up and from the damage of wave action.

7 Material Culture and Economic Development

Agricultural goods were often processed in stone installations such as water mills, basalt querns, or presses, all of which are abundant in the archaeological record both inside and outside settlements. At Chhim (a village on the slopes of Mount Lebanon), multiple olive presses were found inside one building, while simple lever or screw presses are scattered along roads in the rural countryside (Frankel et al. 1994; Waliszewski and Ortali Tarazi 2002: 53–6). The trade in olive oil and wine can be partially traced through the distribution of amphorae and other pottery containers, although wood or leather containers may have been used as well. According to the literary sources, some regions, such as the coastal areas around Gaza and Berytus, or the Orontes valley near Apamea, were famed for the quality of their wine.

While resin, papyrus, and balsam do not leave a lot of archaeological evidence, the extraction of purple dye from murex shells was a profitable and labor-intensive industry which left huge shell middens, such as the one near Sidon, as visual testimony. Important raw materials, for example timber for shipbuilding, were taken from the Amanus, Bargylus, and Lebanon mountains. Numerous rock-cut inscriptions in the Lebanon mountains, carved under Hadrian, reserved four types of wood for the emperor, probably cedar, juniper, oak, and spruce (Breton 1970; Abdul-Nour 2001). Unfortunately, we do not have enough evidence to determine to what extent deforestation was advancing during the Roman period, but the baths and industries of the cities as well as naval and architectural construction certainly required large amounts of timber. Some limestone quarries, such as the ones found near Heliopolis, have MER inscribed in large letters hewn into the rock. The meaning of this is unclear, but it was probably connected to them being under imperial administration. Traditional ashlar building techniques with dry masonry consumed resources in abundance. Mudbrick was less commonly used in the coastal regions, except for the construction of baths, but it was the normal building material in the steppe. Although mineral resources are not abundant in the region, iron deposits are attested and important copper mines, complete with good archaeological evidence of slag from primary and secondary smelting (Hauptmann 2007), exist in the Feinan region (Jordan).

In northern Syria an intensification of olive culture is attested in the 2nd century AD between Antioch-on-the-Orontes and Apamea. This also led to a reorganization of the rural communities as recorded in G. Tchalenko's important study (1953–8). Under Trajan, many cities in that area received the right to mint coins, probably in reaction to the increase in trade and production (Rey-Coquais 1978: 54). The income of cities often came from fines and the collection of municipal tolls, such as those described in the famous tax law of Palmyra (Sartre 2005: 161).

Glass and pottery production was widespread, although in both cases the identification of workshops is often impossible. Textile production can mainly be deduced from the written sources, for almost no evidence is preserved in the archaeological record. According to the *Descriptio Totius Orbis*, the cities of Scythopolis (mod. Beth Shean, Israel), Tyre, Berytus, Byblos (mod. Jbeil, Lebanon), and Laodikeia exported linen (Jones 1974: 147).

The annexation of Arabia allowed direct access to the Red Sea ports, but caravan trade with the east had still to be negotiated with the Parthian Empire after the defeat of Trajan. Before the annexation of the Nabataean kingdom, the decline of Petra in the 1st century AD had led the last king Rabel II to transfer his capital to Bostra (Bowersock 1983: 72–5). But by favoring other trade routes Palmyra saw an increase in wealth and trade in the 2nd century AD, and may even have achieved a de facto monopoly of the spice and silk trade. It has been assumed that Emesa, Arca-Caesarea, and Tripolis were involved in this alternate trade route to the Mediterranean.

The crisis of the 3rd century AD was linked to political instability caused by conflict with the Sasanian Empire. Three consecutive Persian invasions, as well as the revolt of the Palmyrene queen Zenobia, caused severe destruction, especially in northern Syria, which seems to have been disconnected from the main economic networks from the middle of the 2nd century to the victory of Aurelian over Zenobia in AD 272. The eastern trade with Persia was taken over from the destroyed cities of Dura Europos and Palmyra by Nisibis (mod. Nusaybin, Turkey), and desert tribes arose as new political forces in the region.

Long-distance trade was in evidence long before the Roman period, as attested by the close connection between Byblos and Egypt. In the Roman period, the coastal sites in particular benefited from intensive sea trade and routinely received imported tablewares as well as fish sauce and wine from abroad. Some of the imported pottery types might reflect changes in culinary practices, more commonly amongst the soldiers, but possibly also amongst the inhabitants of the coastal cities who adapted to new culinary fashions. The secondary cargoes of pottery not used as containers increased the trade in perishable agricultural goods and display a distribution pattern, particularly of imported cooking pots, even at remote rural sites. The standardizing tendency observable in the material culture of the Roman period was due to the mass-production of specific goods such as Eastern Sigillata tableware, and reflects close commercial interchange between the provinces. But also at a regional level amphorae or Nabataean fine wares provide evidence of widespread local exchange. All marble and granite had to be imported from Egypt, North Africa, or Italy, but brick and tile were imported from overseas as well, thus indicating that the costs of long-distance trade were not prohibitive (Butcher 2003: 183). Half-finished stone sarcophagi were imported from Asia Minor, and local imitations in limestone show very distinctive decoration analogies (van Ess and Petersen 2003).

Caravan trade in exotic goods is not easy to pinpoint in the archaeological record, although clearly spices, cloth, and other goods were imported from China, India, and Sri Lanka via the Persian Gulf and up the Euphrates or from Arabia and the Red Sea via Petra and Bostra. The conflict with Sasanian Persia led to several trade embargos and certainly affected the caravan trade. It is difficult to quantify this trade in luxury goods in comparison to the Mediterranean sea trade, but it was probably less important to the economy of the cities than the latter (Butcher 2003: 184). Palmyrene inscriptions reveal a close connection between the merchants and nomadic tribes, whose cooperation was essential for the safe passage of caravans.

8 The Impact of Roman Rule on Cults and Religion

The most important impact of Roman rule is certainly to be seen in the introduction of the imperial cult in the Near East. This is first attested in an inscription from Apamea dating to the reign of Augustus (27 BC–AD 14) that refers to a certain Dexandros as the first high priest of the Imperial cult in Syria (Rey-Coquais 1978: 47–8). This points to its widespread introduction as an expression of unity and loyalism early on. In the Julio-Claudian era (AD 14–70) three eparchies were created for the imperial cult, one in the south with its center in Tyre, one in the north with its seat in Antioch-on-the-Orontes, and one in Cilicia. A fourth one was created under Hadrian (AD 117–38) in Coele Syria (Rey-Coquais 1978: 53). Geographically speaking, this was an unusual division and was not retained in AD 134 when the new province of Arabia was created and Judaea became Syria Palaestina. The title of *metropolis* held by Antioch and Tyre was linked to the imperial cult and thus was also a source of revenue and prestige, but it remains unclear whether the metropolis title of Petra implied this as well. The residence of the "high priest of the four eparchies," or head of the imperial cult for the whole province, was located at Antioch (Sartre 2005: 58).

Some local cults gained wide recognition far beyond their areas of origin, such as the cult of Jupiter Heliopolitanus or Jupiter Dolichenus, who was especially favored by Roman soldiers (Butcher 2003: 337). Soldiers were probably also responsible for the introduction of some Egyptian cults into Bostra and the spread of the Mithras cult, although eastern in origin. Research on the famous sanctuary of Jupiter Heliopolitanus at Heliopolis has revealed, on the one hand, clear western influences in architectural decoration, while the cultic infrastructure, including the raised altars and the interior layout of the *cella*, reflect Near Eastern influences. The monumental size of the building project as well as representative features such as the Trilithon podium were beyond the financial scope of the local or even regional economy, and invite speculation about direct imperial sponsorship. When looking at the numerous Roman temples in the Beqaa valley, it appears that Heliopolis might have been used in the rural areas to showcase Roman influence through monumental religious representation (Aliquot 2009).

Religious syncretism was a common feature in the Roman Empire, and is widely attested in the iconographic association of Atargatis with Cybele and Astarte with Aphrodite, to name just a few deities (Butcher 2003: 344). Other deities such as Bel were imported from the Babylonian pantheon and were given major cults in Apamea and Palmyra. The architecture of new sanctuaries generally followed the Roman podium temple type, but a great variety of architectural types, such as the "Nabataean"-style temple of Baalshamin at Sia (in the Hauran, Syria) or the Great Temple in Petra, occur as well.

9 Conclusion

From a military and economic point of view, the Near East certainly does not merit being regarded as occupying a peripheral position in the Roman Empire. The cities, whether founded in the Hellenistic or in the Roman period, were instrumental in organizing and distributing the agricultural revenues of their rural territories, and the striking expansion of rural settlements in the Roman period attests their economic success. The archaeological record does not give a lot of information on the origin of the expanding rural population, but it seems logical to assume that nomadic or semi-nomadic societies formed part of it, and were otherwise closely connected to the sedentary population in a mutually beneficial symbiotic relationship.

Some of these developments were only possible through the infrastructural engineering works such as the building of roads, dams, and aqueducts initiated by the Roman provincial administration and the military. The culture and identity of the populations in the Near East under Roman rule differ according to the context of social relations on a communal, regional, or provincial level. Religion certainly formed an important part of Roman influence and was showcased in some monumental as well as numerous rural sanctuaries, and especially in the spread of the imperial cult.

GUIDE TO FURTHER READING

A valuable introduction is given in Millar's influential volume (1993). Butcher's thorough study of Roman Syria and the Near East (2003) incorporates numismatic evidence and Sartre (2005) is the English translation of parts of his excellent source book published originally in French (Sartre 2001). For the south, Bowersock (1983) remains a useful starting point in terms of historical data. For Palestine, Anderson (2003) is quite useful. The role of the military is approached in Isaac (1992). Jones (1971) remains a good general introduction to the cities, while Alcock (1997) contains articles on the rural settlements.

CHAPTER FIFTY-FIVE

The Red Sea and Indian Ocean in the Age of the Great Empires

Steven E. Sidebotham

1 Introduction

Since the 1970s and 1980s, we have seen a quantitative and qualitative leap in knowledge about states and peoples bordering the Red Sea and northwestern Indian Ocean littorals between the end of the 4th century BC and the early 7th century AD: from Alexander the Great to the advent of Islam. Archaeological explorations have added significantly to our understanding of these polities, their *modus operandi*, their cultures, peoples, and interactions with others. Re-examination of ancient textual sources in light of newly documented archaeological evidence addresses issues of state and empire formation, especially in South Asia, Southern Arabia, and the Red Sea coast of Africa south of Egypt, and commercial, diplomatic, military, and cultural contacts among the disparate governments and peoples located along these littorals.

2 The Political Situation: The Ptolemies, the Seleucids, the Nabataeans, and Other African and Arab States

The oldest state within our parameters was Egypt, unified as a relatively sophisticated polity by c.3000 BC. From the Old through the New Kingdom Egypt had maritime and overland (via the Nile) contacts with other points in the Red Sea, especially Punt (location undetermined), via ports/roadsteads at Ayn Sokhna

---

A Companion to the Archaeology of the Ancient Near East, First Edition.
Edited by D.T. Potts.
© 2012 Blackwell Publishing Ltd. Published 2012 by Blackwell Publishing Ltd.

and Wadi Gawasis (Abd el-Raziq et al. 2006; Bard and Fattovich 2007; Bard et al. 2007).

Alexander the Great briefly unified much of the Near East, northwestern parts of South Asia, portions of Central Asia, and northeastern Africa during the 330s–320s BC, but by the end of the 4th and early 3rd centuries BC his empire had fragmented into a number of major and lesser Hellenistic states. The most relevant here was the Ptolemaic Egyptian Empire which, at its height, included, in addition to Egypt, parts of Libya, Cyprus, coastal Asia Minor, the Levantine coast, and some of the Aegean islands (Bagnall 1976). Diplomatic and military wrangling among the Ptolemies, their Seleucid adversaries (in Asia Minor, Syria, portions of the Levantine coast, and areas to the east), and the kingdom of Nabataea (in Jordan, southern Syria, sections of the Sinai, Negev, and northwestern Saudi Arabia) were frequent.

Although the Seleucids exercised no control over the Red Sea, they held sway over portions of the Persian Gulf and viewed much of it as within their sphere of influence. Via the Persian Gulf and overland routes, they engaged in commercial, cultural, and diplomatic exchanges with states along the shores of the Gulf itself and in South Asia (Salles 1988, 1992, 1993; 1996: 260–3; 2005; Potts 1990: 10–22; Sherwin-White and Kuhrt 1993: 91–113).

The Ptolemies dominated the northern end of the Red Sea and intermittently battled Nabataean "pirates," privateers or the Nabataean navy there (see below) (Tarn 1929: 13, 15–16, 21, 22; *OGIS* 132 (130 BC); Diodorus Siculus 3.43.4–5; Strabo, *Geog.* 16.4.18 on piracy), undoubtedly for control of maritime routes. The Ptolemies maintained commercial and diplomatic contacts with the African coast of the Red Sea where Ptolemaic government-sponsored expeditions founded ports on the coast of Sudan and Eritrea to transport elephants and ivory by ship to emporia in Egypt, especially Berenike (Scullard 1974: 126–33; Casson 1993; Burstein 1996; Sidebotham 2011). None of these Ptolemaic Red Sea ports outside of Egypt, however, has ever been precisely located or excavated (Cohen 2006: 305–343).

The Ptolemaic government acquired gold from the central and southern portions of the Eastern Deserts of Egypt and northern Sudan (Castiglioni et al. 1998; Klemm et al. 2001, 2002; Gates 2005). There were also Ptolemaic contacts with southern Arabia and, likely, the Horn of Africa to obtain aromatics (Wilhelm 1937: 148–50; Wilcken 1963: 92–4; Fraser 1972/I: 175; 1972/II: 295 n334; Préaux 1978: 377–8; 1979: 364 and n4). By the 2nd century BC these relations were important enough that the Ptolemaic government created several offices specifically to deal with them (*Papyrus Cairo Zenon* 59001, 59009 and *PSI* 628; Otto and Bengtson 1938: 1–22; Bernand 1969: 306–11, no. 352; 311–14, no. 353; 319–21, no. 356; Fraser 1972/I: 182; Thomas 1975: 121–2; Mooren 1972: 127, 132; Sidebotham 1986: 6 and n31; *SB* 2264 and 8036). Ptolemaic contacts with South Asia, however, were sporadic and mainly diplomatic rather than commercial. The 3rd century BC Mauryan King Aśoka's Thirteenth Rock

Edict (Thapar 1997: 166–8), a dearth of literary references and the few "western" Hellenistic coins, including Ptolemaic ones, found in India (Krishnamurthy 2000: 1–56) all combine to suggest that these connections were of no great significance, either for the Ptolemies or their South Asian contemporaries.

The most important state bordering the northern end of the Arabian Red Sea coast in the 1st century BC-first and very early 2nd centuries AD was the kingdom of Nabataea. Although there are references in the annals of Assurbanipal (668–627 BC) to the north Arabian "Nebayot" (Retsö 2003: 168–9), the Nabataeans first appear in a Classical, "western" literary source in the 1st century BC (Diodorus Siculus 2.48.1–5; 19.94.1–95.2), in presenting, however, a context datable to the 4th century BC. Agriculture and animal husbandry were both important for the Nabataean economy (Gawlikowski 1997; Markoe 2003). During the 1st century BC/1st century AD Nabataean power, exercised from the capital at Petra, reached its zenith due to wealth generated by overland caravan traffic from South Arabia to Gaza and other southeastern Mediterranean ports and onward to Syria that necessarily passed through Nabataean territory (Groom 1981: 165–213; Crone 1987: 3–50; Gatier and Salles 1988; Salles 1988; Macdonald 1994: 134 and n18; al-Saud 1996; Maigret 1997, 2004; Wiesehöfer 1998: 16, 18; Goren 2000; Kitchen 2001; Beeston 2005: 53, 54, 59, Fig. 2; Jasmin 2005). The Nabataeans often led or protected and taxed overland caravans, as well as operating ships in the Red Sea, Indian Ocean, and Persian Gulf (Tarn 1929: 13, 15–16, 21, 22; *OGIS* 132 [of 130 BC]; Diodorus Siculus 3.43.4–5; Strabo, *Geog.* 16.4.18). Despite having a port on the Red Sea at Leuke Kome (see below) and indications of naval clashes with the Ptolemies (noted above), we cannot, however, determine how important maritime commerce was overall to the Nabataean economy.

Evidence is also inconclusive about how deep into the northwestern portion of the Arabian peninsula Nabataean political hegemony reached, and the same goes for that of the Roman province of Arabia (Provincia Arabia) that supplanted it in AD 106 (Sartre 1981; Bowersock 1983: 90–9; Gatier and Salles 1988). Nabataean inscriptions (which mention diplomatic exchanges) and pottery found along routes to southern Arabia, in South Arabia itself, and along the Persian Gulf littoral attest to commercial interests in these regions (Groom 1981: 165–88; al-Ansary 1982: 22, 63, nos. 2–6; al-Kabawi et al. 1989: 43, 47–8; Macdonald 1994: 134; Mildenberg 1995, 1996; Gerlach 2005: 39, Fig. 8 for a bilingual Sabaean-Nabataean inscription, but note the 7th–6th century BC date in the caption is incorrect; Sartre 2005: 268; Hashim 2007: 102–22; Schmid 2007: 62–5; Salles and Sedov 2010: 201, 204–5 [nos. 855–859], 525 [Pl. 97].)

The Nabataeans also traded throughout the Roman world. Inscriptions, graffiti, and pottery confirm their activities in Egypt along the Nile, in the Delta, in the Eastern Desert, and on the Red Sea coast (Clermont-Ganneau 1919; Winkler 1938: 4 [site nos. 1 and 6], 5 [site no. 12D], 7 [site nos. 24B and 24N], 10; Tregenza and Walker 1949; Littmann and Meredith 1953, 1954; Jomier 1954;

Hammond 1979; Fiema and Jones 1990; Zayadine 1990: 151–3; Toll 1994; Briquel-Chatonnet and Nehmé 1998; Ruffing 2002: 373–4; Cuvigny 2003a: 276; Fournet 2003: 428; Reddé and Brun 2003: 80; Sartre 2005: 268; Schmid 2007: 66). Epigraphic evidence indicates their presence throughout the eastern Mediterranean and Near East at Gaza, Sidon, Beirut, Salamis in Cyprus, Rhodes, Kos, Miletus, Priene, Delos, Rhene Island near Delos, Tinos, Athens, Kourion (Cyprus), and Dura Europos in Syria (Graf and Sidebotham 2003: 71; Schmid 2007: 71–3, 74). Nabataean inscriptions and artifacts also appear in Italy at Puteoli, Ostia, and Rome as well as Aventicum (modern Avenches, Switzerland), and Carnuntum (mod. Petronell, Austria). Possible Nabataean sherds have been recorded on Sri Lanka. The Nabataeans were also in contact with Palmyra, a caravan trading state in Syria (Teixidor 1984; De Romanis 1993: 64–5; Roche 1996: 86–95 [nos. 15–23]; Zayadine 1996; Bowersock 1997; Graf and Sidebotham 2003: 71; Schmid 2007: 66, 72–5). We have little information about which political powers exerted control over long strips of the Arabian coastline of the Red Sea in this period.

3 Early to Late Roman Activities in the Red Sea and Indian Ocean

The Roman Empire acquired portions of the Near East especially during the 1st century BC and 1st and early 2nd centuries AD. With the annexation of Ptolemaic Egypt in 30 BC and the kingdom of Nabataea in AD 106, the Roman Empire came into direct contact with, and held political-military control over, much of the northern end of the Red Sea, which was maintained, at least in Egypt and in Provincia Arabia (later known as Palaestina Tertia), until the AD 630s–40s. For a very brief interlude, toward the end of the reign of the Emperor Trajan (AD 98–117), the Romans also occupied the northernmost end of the Persian Gulf; this, however, played no role in Rome's relations with states bordering that body of water or beyond.

Rome's commercial, cultural, diplomatic, and military contacts with other polities and peoples along the Red Sea and northwestern Indian Ocean littorals – including much of East Africa, Southern Arabia, southern and western India, and Sri Lanka – were more extensive, intensive, and enduring than those of the Ptolemies. Roman-era activity in the Red Sea and Indian Ocean was more commercially driven by private entrepreneurs, promoted by the Roman government and its proxies. In addition to private businessmen and some government officials, the Roman provincial and imperial governments and their representatives also profited handsomely by levying taxes and tolls on the commerce. The Roman military protected, monitored, and promoted these economic exchanges by stationing garrisons on some Red Sea islands at least as far south as the Farasan Archipelago (Villeneuve et al. 2004a, 2004b) and along roads in Provincia Arabia and the Eastern Desert of Egypt (Bowersock 1983; Sidebotham 1986, 2011). In addition to private entrepreneurs, states in southern Arabia and South Asia also profited from this trade (Palmer 1951; Doe 1971: 215 and Pls. 112–113; Groom 1981: 181–2; Casson 1989: 271–7; Seland 2005). Less is known, however, about Axumite government involvement in this commerce.

Reasons for heightened, Mediterranean-wide interest in acquiring primarily civilian consumer goods beginning in the late 1st century BC/1st century AD included greater demand for commodities by denizens of the wider Mediterranean basin and Western Europe, obtained from regions beyond the eastern and southern limits of the Roman world. Successful exploitation of the monsoon winds in the northwestern Indian Ocean, which facilitated more rapid sea voyages, was also important. Optimal use of the monsoons, long known to Indian Ocean mariners, but only "discovered" by a Ptolemaic helmsman or sea captain, probably in the late 2nd century BC and only first exploited on a substantial scale after the Roman annexation of Egypt, increased the speed and volume of commercial contacts and resulted in some moderation of prices, which further stoked consumer demand (Raschke 1978; Sidebotham 1986, 2011; Young 2001; Tomber 2008; McLaughlin 2010).

Roman activity waxed and waned in the Red Sea and Indian Ocean, primarily due to political and economic conditions throughout the Mediterranean basin and secondarily as a result of the relative power of Axumite, South Arabian, and South Asian states and entrepreneurs in contact with the Roman world. Roman commercial, cultural, diplomatic, and, less often, military relations with these other polities peaked between the late 1st century BC and the 2nd century AD, again from about the middle of the 4th into the 5th centuries, and finally in the 6th century – especially during the reigns of Justin I (518–27) and Justinian I (527–65). At other times (3rd–4th centuries, and after the 6th) Roman activity, power and prestige in the region declined. Some of the South Arabian kingdoms and the African kingdom of Axum exercised varying degrees of political and economic influence throughout the first six and a half centuries AD. Both the later Roman Empire, from the early 4th century onwards, and the kingdom of Axum had important Christian religious, diplomatic, and commercial ties, and both states flourished in the 4th and 5th centuries (Munro-Hay 1996; Peacock and Blue 2007). This bond was especially evident when Rome and Axum united in a war against the South Arabian kingdom of Himyar in the AD 520s (*Martyrium Sancti Arethae* 27, 28, 29; Cosmas Indicopleustes, *Christian Topography* 2.56 in Wolska-Conus 1968: 368–9; Kobishchanov 1979: 91–108 in general for the 517–37 wars; Rubin 1989; Eide et al. 1998: 1185–8 [no. 327]; Desanges 1978: 272–307). Though ostensibly religiously driven (the Jewish king of Himyar had martyred Christians at Najran), there were certainly economic and political motivations behind the proposed, joint Roman-Axumite expedition: expelling or at least containing Sasanian Persian (Ch. II.57) political and economic interests in the region.

4 Kingdoms of Southern Arabia

During peak periods of "international" contacts in the 1st–2nd and mid-4th–6th centuries, the most important kingdoms of southern Arabia were Saba, Hadramaut, and Himyar. These and other South Arabian states lay on or near the Red Sea and Indian Ocean in the southwestern part of the peninsula (modern Yemen). Other South Arabian kingdoms of less importance during the zenith of international contacts considered here include Ma'in. The kingdom of Awsan dates to c.800–500 BC, thus prior to our period of interest. The histories of Saba, Hadramaut, Himyar, and Ma'in, as well as their interactions with one another and with other polities and peoples both in and beyond the Arabian peninsula, are not well understood (de Maigret 1996).

The diplomatic and commercial contacts of South Arabian kingdoms with northern Arabia, the Persian Gulf, the Mediterranean, the Red Sea, the northern Indian Ocean coasts of Africa, and South Asia were primarily due to trade in aromatics (especially frankincense and myrrh) or the trans-shipment of products between the Red Sea and the Indian Ocean coast of Africa, on the one hand, and south Asia, on the other. Some products of Mediterranean, Red Sea, and African provenance found in the Persian Gulf region were trans-shipped via major ports on the Indian Ocean coast of Arabia, especially Kané (Qani') in Yemen and Sumhuram/Moscha Limen (Khor Rori) in Dhofar (southwestern Oman); other items of Mediterranean origin likely arrived in the Persian Gulf via overland caravan routes.

Sabaean inscriptions first mention the kingdom of Ma'in in northwestern Yemen with its capital at Qarnaw. Although not a producer of frankincense or myrrh, important overland caravan routes linking southern Arabia and the Horn of Africa to the wider Mediterranean world passed though Ma'in between the 4th and 2nd centuries BC. Ma'in became part of the kingdom of Saba in the 2nd century BC, before the zenith of commerce in the region beginning in the late 1st century BC and early centuries AD. Minaean inscriptions indicate a transit trade until the 2nd century BC. Minaean texts have been documented at Dedan (al-'Ula) in northwestern Saudi Arabia, on the Aegean island of Delos, and on a sarcophagus in Egypt (Beeston 1984; Sayed 1984; Seipel 1998: 293, 295 n164; Groom 2005: 108). At least one, likely 2nd century BC, Minaean graffito has been recorded in Egypt's Eastern Desert (Luft 2010: 178–9). In the mid-3rd century BC the Ptolemies used both Minaean and Gerrhaean (Gerrha was a trading emporium in northeastern Arabia) weights, which suggests the influential role that the aromatics' trade played in their realm at that time (Beeston 2005: 55).

Along with Qataban and Hadramaut, Saba was one of the important states in southwestern Arabia in this period (Robin 2005). Biblical, Assyrian, and Classical Greek and Roman literary sources, as well as archaeological evidence from the c.8th century BC to the 5th century AD attest to Saba's importance; traces of Sabaean civilization date back to the 12th/10th centuries BC. Saba's best-known city and capital was Marib. The Sabaean kingdom, alternately, had alliances and fought wars with other states in the region, most notably Qataban and Hadramaut, both of which it dominated during the course of the 3rd century AD.

The Sabaeans engaged in both terrestrial caravan and maritime trade. For centuries they controlled the Bab el-Mandeb, the strait separating the Arabian peninsula from Africa and the Red Sea from the Indian Ocean; they also colonized portions of the Horn of Africa (modern Eritrea and Ethiopia). By the end of the 3rd century AD, Saba had become the dominant power in the southwestern Arabian peninsula. Although the kingdom of Axum seems to have held political sway over Saba in the mid-4th century AD, by the end of that century Saba had regained its autonomy. In the early 6th century Sasanian Persia briefly controlled the region, and during the course of the 7th century it was conquered by the Muslim Arabs (Crone 1987).

The earliest references to the kingdom of Qataban, with its capital at Timna, appear in Sabaean inscriptions (Avanzini 2005). Qataban existed from the 4th century BC until the early 3rd century AD and seems to have been independent until at least the 2nd century AD. Like Ma'in, Qataban does not appear to have been a major producer of frankincense or myrrh, though overland trade routes through the kingdom supplemented the government's revenues and enriched some of its entrepreneurs.

The kingdom of Himyar, with its capital at Zafar, operated from the 2nd century BC until about AD 525. At its zenith Himyar controlled southwestern Arabia, the southern reaches of the Red Sea and the Gulf of Aden, as far east as the Persian Gulf, and north to the Arabian desert. References to the kingdom of the Himyarites – *Homeritai* in Greek, *Homeritae* in Latin – appear in Greek and Latin authors (cf. Casson 1989: 149–51) including Pliny the Elder (*Nat. Hist.* 6.32.161) in the mid- to third quarter of the 1st century AD and in the contemporary, but anonymously authored, *Periplus Maris Erythraei* or Periplus of the Erythraean Sea (hereafter *PME*) §23.

The earliest references to the kingdom of Hadramaut, with its capital at Shabwa, appear in inscriptions of the 8th century BC. Hadramaut occupied southern and southeastern Yemen and Dhofar (southwestern Oman) and was politically independent until conquered by the kingdom of Saba in the late 3rd century AD. During the mid-1st century AD, at the least, Hadramaut also controlled the Indian Ocean island of Soqotra (ancient Dioscurida/Dioscurides: *PME* §§30–31), which lies about 350–400 kilometers south of Ras Fartak (southern Arabia) and approximately 240 kilometers east–northeast of Cape Guardafui (in the Horn of Africa). Soqotra exported frankincense to the mainland, especially to the port at Kané where there was a warehouse (*PME* §27), presumably belonging to the king. In addition to Kané (Salles and Sedov 2010) the kingdom of Hadramaut also possessed the Indian Ocean port of Moscha Limen/Sumhuram (mod. Khor Rori, Oman) (Avanzini 2002, 2007, 2008). Through these Indian Ocean emporia and by overland caravan routes Hadramaut maintained contacts with the Mediterranean and Red Seas, the Persian Gulf, the northern Indian Ocean coast of Africa, and western and southwestern India.

During the 3rd century AD, the South Arabian kingdoms were in frequent conflict with one another and with the kingdom of Axum, a political and military dissonance mirrored in the contemporary Roman world. This turmoil resulted in a decline in commercial and cultural contacts throughout the Red Sea and Indian Ocean at that time.

6. The Red Sea: Northern End Outside Egypt – Ancient Sites

Emporia in the Red Sea played varying roles in commercial, diplomatic, and cultural exchanges in the Ptolemaic and Roman periods. Ampelome (or Ampelone) was probably founded by Ptolemy II Philadelphus (285/282–246 BC) as part of a broader initiative to establish ports throughout the Red Sea, especially along the African coast. Though Ampelome has never been located, it likely lay somewhere along the eastern (Arabian) coast of the Red Sea or, possibly, on one of the Red Sea islands. Pliny the Elder (*Nat. Hist.* 6.32.159) noted that colonists from the Aegean city of Miletus, while under Ptolemaic control, founded Ampelome (cf. Tarn 1929: 21–2; Fraser 1972/I: 177; 1972//II: 301–2 n352; Cohen 2006: 44–5, 307, 329 n3, 400). There is no record of Ampelome's role in Ptolemaic exchanges with Arabia.

Leuke Kome/Albus Portus ("white village" in Greek and Latin, respectively) – another port still unlocated, but possibly around Khuraybah/Aynunah near the Straits of Tiran, on the Arabian coast of the Red Sea (Cohen 2006: 329–330) or al-Wadj (Nappo 2010) – was initially under Nabataean control. Strabo (*Geog.* 16.4.23–24) and the *PME* (§19) indicate that the Leuke Kome was active in Nabataean/early Roman times both as a terminal and transit point for caravans connecting southern Arabia to the Mediterranean and also as a port for smaller ships sailing to and from Egypt and along the Arabian coast of the Red Sea, though not, apparently, into the Indian Ocean.

It may have been from Leuke Kome that the Nabataeans engaged in naval activities (noted above) that adversely affected the Ptolemies. The Roman Emperor Augustus ordered a military expedition against Arabia Felix in 26/25 BC that passed through Leuke Kome (*Res Gestae Divi Augusti* 5.26; Strabo, *Geog.* 16.4.22ff; Pliny the Elder, *Nat. Hist.* 6.32.160; Josephus, *Jewish Antiquities* 15.317; Dio Cassius, *Roman History* 53.29.3–8). Though a military failure, Augustus clearly viewed the foray as a political-diplomatic success (Jameson 1968; von Wissmann 1978; Sidebotham 1986: 120–30; Buschmann 1991; Marek 1993; Luther 1999). The fragment of a bilingual Greek-Latin inscription from Baraqish (ancient Yathil) may be the tombstone of a Roman soldier who perished during this operation (Costa 1977; Marek 1994). This is the only example of a Roman attack beyond imperial boundaries with overtly commercial objectives.

Strabo (*Geog.* 16.4.23) and the *PME* (§19) report that a heavily used caravan route linked Leuke Kome to Petra (cf. al-Ghabbān 2007). The *PME* says that freight arrived at Leuke Kome from Arabia in small ships and that a customs officer collected a 25 percent (*tetarte*) duty on imports (Millar 1998: 124–5; Young 2001: 95–6; also Bowsher 1989 on the Nabataean army in general). In the 6th century Cosmas Indicopleustes (*Christian Topography* 2.62 in Wolska-Conus 1968: 376–7) suggested that Leuke Kome continued to operate in his day.

A settlement at Iotabe, which remains unidentified and unlocated but was likely in the area of the Straits of Tiran, seems to have operated, perhaps as a customs house, for only about 60 years in the 5th century AD before being abandoned (Mayerson 1994b).

Aila/Aela/Aelana (modern Aqaba) lay at the northeastern-most point on the Red Sea in the Gulf of Aqaba. Despite literary evidence for a port here or in the vicinity in Hellenistic times and the 1st century AD (Josephus, *Jew. Ant.* 8.163; Strabo, *Geog.* 16.2.30, cf. 16.4.18; Pliny the Elder, *Nat. Hist.* 5.12.65), archaeological evidence does not suggest much activity prior to the Roman annexation of the kingdom of Nabataea in AD 106 or the early Roman occupation as Provincia Arabia (cf. Claudius Ptolemy, *Geography* 5.16.1). Excavations have uncovered late Roman and Islamic settlements including evidence of contact with other ports in the Red Sea, especially Berenike and Adulis, between the 4th and 6th centuries (Eusebius, *Onomasticon* 6.17–20 and 8.1; *Martyrium Sancti Arethae* 27–29; Procopius, *History of the Wars* 1.19.3, 1.19.24; Antonius of Placentia: cf. Vasiliev 1950: 364–5; Wilkinson 1977: 88 [40.v186]).

Axumite/Adulis-made pottery and Axumite coins found at Aila indicate contacts with that African kingdom (Tomber 2005: 42–7 for pottery; Whitcomb 1994: 16–18 for coins). Yet, little or nothing of Indian origin has been documented in excavation at Aila. Parts of a city wall, a possible church, an amphora kiln, and other structures have been excavated; no harbor has yet been found (Parker 1996, 1997, 1998a, 2000, 2002), but areas of early Islamic Aqaba have been excavated (Whitcomb 1989a, 1989b, 1994, 1995, – and 1990 for the debate on the date of the fort as Diocletianic/Tetrarchic or early Islamic).

7 The Red Sea: Egyptian Ports

Expanded archaeological investigations over the last few decades – especially in the Eastern Desert and Red Sea coast of Egypt (Sidebotham et al. 2008; Sidebotham 2011); South Arabia (Avanzini 2002, 2005, 2007, 2008; Sedov 2007; Salles and Sedov 2010); the kingdom of Axum, especially at the eponymous capital city (Phillipson 2009) and the port of Adulis (see below) (Peacock and Blue 2007); India, especially, but not exclusively along the Coromandel (southeastern) (Begley 1996; Begley et al. 2004) and Kerala/Malabar (southwestern) coasts (Cherian et al. 2007); and Sri Lanka (Hannibal-Deraniyagala 2000; Schenk 2000; Weisshaar and Wijeyapala 2000; for urbanization of the island, see Coningham and Allchin 1995) – have yielded abundant data on the explosion of commercial, cultural, and diplomatic contacts among these regions during the first six centuries of the Christian era.

The Ptolemaic era was one during which Egypt had expanded contacts with other areas on the African coast of the Red Sea, especially, as noted above, for the acquisition of elephants used in warfare and ivory (Sidebotham 2011). The acquisition of frankincense and myrrh either directly from southern Arabia or trans-shipped via southern Arabia from the Horn of Africa was the main commercial interest. During the early Ptolemaic period, especially the reigns of Ptolemy II Philadelphus (285/283–246 BC) and Ptolemy III Euergetes (246–222 BC), the creation of infrastructure in both Egypt between the Nile and the Red Sea coast (roads, caravanserai, a canal) and along the Red Sea shore of Egypt itself indicate a concerted and sustained policy not previously seen in the region (Gates 2005; Sidebotham 2011). Based on literary, etymological, and archaeological evidence, the ports founded along the Red Sea coast at this time included Arsinoë/Cleopatris/Clysma (near and under modern Suez); Philoteras (location unknown); Myos Hormos (Quseir al-Qadim); Nechesia (at Marsa Nakari?); and Berenike. A late Roman fort built in the early 4th century lay on the coast between Arsinoë and Myos Hormos at Abu Sha'ar. Foundation of ports along the Red Sea coast of Africa south of Egypt also reflects expanded Ptolemaic interest in the region (Cohen 2006: 313–16, 341–3). While there is some evidence that contacts in the Ptolemaic era were not solely government-driven and involved some private entrepreneurs, most interaction between Egypt and the rest of the Red Sea/Indian Ocean littorals was state sponsored or under some degree of state control.

French excavations in the 1930s identified Arsinoë/Cleopatris/Clysma as a significant emporium in late Roman and Islamic times, but documented little from the Ptolemaic and early Roman periods. The terminus of a canal linking the Red Sea with the Nile (at various locations throughout its history) contributed to Arsinoë's importance (Cooper 2005; Cohen 2006: 308–9; Sheehan 2010: 35–53; Cooper 2009).

A Latin inscription excavated at Abu Sha'ar indicates the foundation of a fort there in the early 4th century. Created as part of the *limes* (Roman administered frontier area) and housing a mounted cavalry or dromedary unit, the inscription also mentions merchants. The army abandoned the installation in the late 4th/early 5th century and a Christian monastery replaced the military garrison. The fort lay close to the junction of the *via nova Hadriana* and the road leading from the fort, past the quarries at Mons Porphyrites, to the Nile at Qena (Kainepolis/Maximianopolis) (Sidebotham et al. 1989; 2008: 53–60, 145–6, 241–2; Sidebotham 1993, 1994a, 1994b). Philotera(s), however, has never been identified or located (Cohen 2006: 339–41), it probably lay somewhere between Abu Sha'ar and Myos Hormos.

Myos Hormos and the more southerly emporium at Berenike were the largest of the Ptolemaic-Roman Red Sea emporia in Egypt. They have been more extensively excavated than any other Hellenistic-Roman-era ports in the Red Sea and, as a result, are the best known. Myos Hormos was excavated by both American (1978–82; Whitcomb and Johnson 1979, 1982) and British (1999–2003; Peacock and Blue 2006) expeditions. There is a hint of Ptolemaic activity here, but the zenith of the emporium was in the 1st and 2nd centuries; by the mid-3rd century AD the port lay abandoned. During the Roman era, Myos Hormos had contacts with the Nile valley and the wider Mediterranean basin as well as with other areas of the Red Sea (Aila and Axum, via Adulis), southern Arabia, and southern and western India. Myos Hormos revived as Quseir (al-Qadim) in the medieval Islamic period. In Roman times, if not earlier, a trans-desert route lined with forts (*praesidia*) provided with wells (*hydreumata*) and watchtowers (*skopeloi*) linked Myos Hormos to its Nile counterpart at Coptus/Koptos (Cuvigny 2003a; 2003b).

Nechesia has never been located and identified (Cohen 2006: 338–9). Nevertheless, limited American excavations in 1999, 2000, and 2002 documented a small, walled settlement at Marsa Nakari, the location of which corresponds approximately with that given for Nechesia by Claudius Ptolemy (*Geog.* 4.5.8). Excavations recorded early and late Roman activity and some indication of a Ptolemaic presence as well (Seeger 2001; Seeger and Sidebotham 2005; Sidebotham et al. 2008: 166–7). There was, however, no evidence that the settlement engaged in extensive long-distance maritime commerce on a regular basis. A road linked Marsa Nakari with mines and quarries along or near the route to the Nile at Contrapollonopolis Magna/Apollonopolis Magna (modern Edfu) (Sidebotham 1997: 388–90; 1999: 364–8).

Berenike was the southernmost Ptolemaic-Roman Red Sea port in Egyptian territory. Excavations, begun by an American-Dutch consortium (1994–2001) and continued under the aegis of an American-Polish team (2008–10), have recorded much about this emporium. Founded before the mid-3rd century BC and abandoned by the mid-6th century AD, Berenike played a pivotal role in contacts between the Mediterranean basin, Egypt, and the Red Sea and Indian Ocean for about 800 years. Artifacts indicate a trade network extending as far west as Spain and Gaul, as far north as Europe and Asia Minor/Syria, and as far east as Java. Excavations have documented 12 written European, African, and Asian languages. Berenike was also a local and regional economic hub (Sidebotham 2011).

8 Trog(l)odytes/Ichthyophagoi

Other groups dwelling along the African coast of the Red Sea included the *Trog(l)odites* (cave-dwellers) and *Ichthyophagoi* (fish-eaters). We have some information about these peoples from Agatharchides, Diodorus Siculus, Strabo, Pliny the Elder, and the *PME* (cf. Casson 1989: 97–100; Thomas 2007; Burstein 2008; Winnicki 2009: 373–8). The Classical Greek and Roman sources written between the 2nd century BC and the 1st century AD report on the passive, feral nature of these people, their physical appearance, and various aspects of their lives. The sources, however, provide little or no indication that they – or other contemporary groups living, apparently, slightly away from the coast (including the *Agriophagoi*, "wild animal eaters," or the *Moschophagoi*, "eaters of shoots and stalks") – formed coherent polities and little indication of the type or extent of commercial or cultural exchanges maintained by the Ptolemies, Romans, Axumites, or others with these groups. There must have been some contact, even if fleeting, with these peoples, but they did not form an important component in the political-diplomatic-economic network of the Red Sea/Indian Ocean regions.

9 The Red Sea: Kingdom of Axum

The other major state in this period along the Red Sea coast of Africa was the kingdom of Axum (centered in modern Ethiopia and Eritrea). Cosmas Indicopleustes (*Christian Topography* 2.58 in Wolska-Conus 1968: 370–3) remarked on a throne and inscription of Ptolemaic date from Adulis (Fauvelle-Aymar 2009). Certainly in existence by the 1st century AD, Axum's rise to prominence and zenith occurred during the late 3rd/early 4th to the 7th century. Through its major Red Sea emporium of Adulis (Gabaza) the eponymous capital city of Axum was an 8 (*PME* §4) to 12–15 day overland trip (Procopius, *History of the Wars* 1.19.22; Nonnosos section 2b). There were two separate sites in the region of Adulis, one from the early centuries AD (cf. *PME* 4, 17, 24) and another from approximately the 4th–7th centuries (Peacock and Blue 2007). Axum had diplomatic and commercial-cultural contacts with Egypt and southern Arabia (Pliny the Elder, *Nat. Hist.* 6.34.173; *PME* 4, 6, 17, 24; Cosmas Indicopleustes, *Christian Topography* 2.49, 2.54–56, 11.15, 11.17, 11.19 in Wolska-Conus 1968: 358–9, 364–9; Wolska-Conus 1973: 346–51; Stephen of Byzantium in Billerbeck 2006: 56–7) both of which were especially significant, and also with India and areas of the Indian Ocean coast of Africa. The latter, however, seem to have been less important. Axum's rise to political and commercial prominence in the late 3rd/early 4th century coincided with the appearance of the earliest coins minted by the kingdom, suggesting that commerce played a key role; Christianity also arrived in Axum from Egypt in the 4th century.

A military expedition launched in 524–5 AD by Axum against the Himyarite Jewish king Dhu Nuwas had the support of the Roman emperor Justin I (518–27). The pretext was Dhu Nuwas' persecution of Christians, but there were also political and commercial considerations involving the Sasanians, Axumites, and Romans (*Martyrium Sancti Arethae* 27, 28, 29; Cosmas Indicopleustes, *Chris-*

tian Topography 2.56 in Wolska-Conus 1968: 368–9; Rubin 1989; Eide et al. 1998: 1185–8 [no. 327]; for Axumite-South Arabian Wars in AD 517–37 and the 524/525 campaign, see Kobishchanov 1979: 91–108; for dates, see Fauvelle-Aymar 2009: 135).

Justinian I (527–65) proposed an alliance with the kingdoms of Axum and Himyar to fight the Sasanians; we are unsure, however, what became of his initiative (McCrindle 1897: vi–vii with notes; Kobishchanov 1979: 78–9; Munro-Hay 1982: 116–17). Procopius and Cosmas Indicopleustes record – and the recovery of Roman artifacts at Adulis and of Axumite finds at Berenike and Aila, and to a lesser extent at Myos Hormos, confirm – trade contacts, in early Roman times and increasing in the later period, between the Roman world and this African state. Cosmas Indicopleustes spent time in Axum and was apparently there in 524/525 when the expedition against Himyar was launched. A 4th–7th century shipwreck has been identified and partially excavated near Adulis (Pedersen 2000).

10 Indian Ocean: Kingdoms of South Arabia

Several polities dominated southern portions of the Arabian peninsula in this period. The South Arabian kingdoms most in contact with India and the Red Sea, either directly or as intermediary stops between India and the Red Sea (by sea and overland caravan routes), included Saba (capital Marib), the oldest and most important of the South Arabian kingdoms; Qataban (capital Timna); Ma'in (capital Qarnaw); Hadramaut (capital Shabwa); and Himyar (capital Zafar). At the southern end of the Red Sea the Himyarites dominated through their Red Sea ports of Mouza (*PME* §§7, 16, 17, 21, 22, 28, 31) and Ocelis (*PME* §§7, 25), both of which remain unlocated, though the former may be beneath the modern port of al-Mocha (Yemen) and the latter on the Arabian side of the Bab al-Mandeb). Both maritime and overland caravan routes linked these states, though the latter seem to have been more important.

The Hadrami-controlled island of Soqotra (noted above) had cemeteries and settlements (Shinnie 1960; Raschke 1978: 645, 853 n839; Doe 1992: 41–112; Naumkin and Sedov 1993; Beyhl 1998; Weeks et al. 2002; Biedermann 2006; Cohen 2006: 325–6; Tomber 2008: 108–9). A cave at Hoq, on the northeastern coast, produced ancient documents, including one written on a wooden tablet in Palmyrene, likely from the 3rd century AD. Other texts from this cave indicate the presence of Nabataeans, Indians, Ethiopians, and other "foreigners" (Dridi 2002; Dridi and Gorea 2003; Lévêque 2002; Robin and Gorea 2002; Villeneuve 2002, 2003; Strauch and Bukharin 2004). In antiquity, Soqotra was a crossroads for traffic between the Red Sea, India, and coastal sub-Saharan Africa south of the Horn of Africa. These multilingual texts are, therefore, a reflection of Soqotra's position on the trade routes.

Though Pliny the Elder (*Nat.l Hist.* 6.32.153) and Claudius Ptolemy (*Geog.* 6.7) mention Soqotra, the *PME* (§§30–31) provides the most information about it, reporting that the few inhabitants dwelt on the northern side of the island and that comprised Arabs, Indians, and Greeks engaged in maritime commerce. The island was poor, barren (no farm products, vines, or grain) and damp with rivers, crocodiles, vipers, and huge lizards. It exported tortoise shell and Indian cinnabar. At the time of the *PME* Soqotra was under the control of Hadramaut, whose main port was at Qani'. Shippers from Mouza, Limyrikê (Kerala, the southwestern coast of India), and Barygaza (Broach, in western India) traded with the island sporadically bringing rice, grain, cotton cloth, and female slaves.

Early Roman authors, including Dioscorides, who penned his *Materia Medica* c.AD 65, noted that the best-quality aloe came from Soqotra. Aloe had a number of medical applications, one of which was as a laxative for both humans and animals (Scarborough 1982: 138–41; Groom 2005: 110). In the 4th century Ammianus Marcellinus (23.6.47) referred to the island as Dioscurida and considered it, erroneously, a city on the Arabian coast. The latest ancient Classical reference to Soqotra was in the 6th century when Cosmas Indicopleustes (*Christian Topography* 3.65 in Wolska-Conus 1968: 502–5) mentioned that Christian clergy from Persia inhabited the island and that some of its residents, who were descendants of Ptolemaic colonists, spoke Greek (Bengtson 1955: 155–6).

Undoubtedly the two most important and best-known South Arabian emporia lay on the Indian Ocean. They were Kané (modern Qani'), near Bir 'Ali in Yemen and, about 800 kilometers farther east along the coast, Sumhuram/Moscha Limen (modern Khor Rori) in the Dhofar Province of Oman. According to the *PME* (§§27–28), Kané and Moscha Limen (32) were ports of the kingdom of Hadramaut in the 1st century AD. They were trans-shipment points for domestic products, particularly frankincense coming from Soqotra, conveyed by overland caravan routes to points north in the Mediterranean and Persian Gulf. Sea routes linking Kané and Moscha Limen to emporia in the Persian Gulf, the Red Sea in Egypt and Adulis, as well as to entrepôts in the Horn of Africa and on India's west coast also bore frankincense, as well as products in transit between India and the Red Sea. Both Qani' and Khor Rori also moved Roman products, including glass and fine ceramics, from the Red Sea to the Persian Gulf, especially ed-Dur (in modern Umm al-Qaiwain, United Arab Emirates), in the late 1st century BC/1st century AD.

Roman merchandise, particularly glass and fine pottery excavated at ed-Dur and from a high-status, collective grave excavated at Dibba (Sharjah, UAE), arrived either by sea via one of the southern Arabian ports on the Indian Ocean (cf. Rutten 2007) or overland from the Middle East via Mesopotamia (cf. Bukharin 2007). Possibly, too, some of these items and other objects (such as intaglios) of Mediterranean provenance may have come via Indian ports such as Barygaza (Broach) (*PME* §§14, 27, 31, 32, 36, 40–48, 50–52, 56–57, 64) and Barbarikon (near Karachi) (*PME* §§38, 39) in the Gulf of Cambay and mouth of Indus Delta, respectively.

At the time of the *PME*, Qani' traded with Barygaza, Scythia, Omana, and Persis. Ships sailing between the Red Sea and India often stopped at Qani'; epigraphic evidence indicates the presence of a royal Hadrami shipyard there (Beeston 2005: 58, 62 n11). Frankincense, an imperial monopoly, was brought to Qani' from Soqotra, which was also under Hadramaut control, for storage in a warehouse there. This was the port's major export. Aloe, as noted above, was also exported and may have been transshipped to Qani' from Soqotra. Qani' imported wheat from Egypt, and also wine, copper, tin, coral, and embossed silverware, a great deal of money (coins?), horses, statuary, and fine clothing. Pliny (*Nat. Hist.* 6.26.104) and Claudius Ptolemy (*Geog.* 6.7) also knew the port. There have been both land excavations (Sedov 1992, 1996, 1997, 2007; Mouton et al. 2006; Salles and Sedov 2010) and underwater surveys of the harbor (Davidde 1997a: 354–5; 1997b: 86–7; 1998: 8; Davidde et al. 2004). Excavations unearthed storage magazines, a temple, likely dedicated to the god Sayin, and a synagogue (for temple, see Sedov 2005: 162–5; for synagogue, see 165, 166 [Fig. 77], 169–71; cf. Bowersock 1994b; for temple and synagogue, see Sedov 2007: 74, 88 [Fig. 4.15], 92, 99 [Fig. 4.24], 103; Salles and Sedov 2010: 87–122). Also recovered were numerous Egyptian, Nubian, Black Sea, and Mediterranean-made amphoras, especially from Campania (Bay of Naples region of Italy) and from Kos, Laodikeia (Syria), Spain, and Gaul; excavations also documented Eastern Sigillata wares made in the Roman Near East and fine pottery made in Aswan (Egypt), attesting a lively commerce with various Red Sea ports in Egypt in the 1st century AD (for Mediterranean amphoras at Qani', see Ballet 1998: 47–50; Sedov 2007: 77–8; for Roman fine wares, see Davidde et al. 2004; Rutten 2007: 12, 13 [Fig. 5], 14, 18, 20; also see Salles and Sedov 2010). Indian and Nabataean ceramics were also recorded (Sedov 2007: 78; Salles and Sedov 2010: 201, 204–25, nos. 855–859). There were three main phases of occupation with the most significant being the 2nd–5th/6th centuries (Davidde et al. 2004; Sedov 2007). In later times Qani' had little or no contact with India (Sedov 1996; Mango 1996: 154–155).

About 800 kilometers by sea east of Qani' along the southern coast of Arabia is Moscha Limen (*PME* §32; Claudius Ptolemy, *Geog.* 6.7), the South Arabian name of which was Sumhuram (mod. Khor Rori, Oman). Excavations (Avanzini 2002, 2007, 2008; Avanzini and Sedov 2005) in this fortified settlement have unearthed residential areas, temples, and palaces (Sedov 2005: 171–84; Avanzini 2007: 25). Moscha Limen was founded in the 3rd century BC and functioned until at least the 5th century AD (Avanzini 2007: 23, 25–6). The harbor itself has not yet been found. The city flourished in the 1st century AD; finds include Roman amphoras and fine ceramic wares, some perhaps destined for onward shipment to the Persian Gulf (Rutten 2007: 12, 13 [Fig. 5], 14, 18, 20). A graffito carved on wall plaster depicts a two-masted sailing ship (Avanzini 2007: 27,

28, Fig. 4) similar to those on coins minted by the Sātavāhanas/Andhras between the 2nd/1st century BC and 2nd century AD. This doodling may represent one of the ships that put into Sumhuram.

11 Indian Ocean: Parthian and Sasanian Persia

A spin-off from the Hellenistic kingdom of the Seleucids was the Persian-centered polity of Parthia. The Parthians (247 BC–AD 228) at times in their history controlled sections of the coastline adjacent to the northwest Indian Ocean (Potts 1990: 197–348; 1996). They were major political and military competitors of the Romans straddling important land routes between the eastern Mediterranean, Central Asia, and India. By the mid-1st century BC, the Parthians and Romans had completely absorbed the former Seleucid empire. Another Persian dynasty, the Sasanians, supplanted the Parthians, ruling the Iranian plateau and adjacent areas until the Islamic conquest in the mid-7th century. The Sasanians were more aggressive toward the Romans than the Parthians had been. Both the Parthians and Sasanians had substantial levels of military, diplomatic, and commercial interaction with neighbors. Their maritime commercial outlets were primarily through the Persian Gulf to the northwestern Indian Ocean, especially with states in the Persian Gulf, kingdoms in southern Arabia, polities along the western coast of India, and, to a much lesser extent, the Red Sea (Potts 1990: 197–348; Whitehouse 1996). There is debate about the level of Sasanian hegemony over the Persian Gulf. A recent re-evaluation of the extant archaeological evidence from the region suggests that Persian control over eastern Arabia had slipped badly during the Sasanian era (Whitehouse 1996; Kennet 2002, 2007).

12 Indian Ocean: States in Western and Southern India

The Mauryan Dynasty (c.321–185 BC) of India, with its capital at Pataliputra, chronologically parallels the period of Alexander the Great and the Hellenistic period in the West. The Thirteenth Rock Edict of Aśoka (Thapar 1997: 255–7), third monarch of that dynasty (c.273–232 BC), records diplomatic contacts between this large Indian kingdom and at least five Greco-Macedonian, Hellenistic-era kings to the west, including the Seleucid Antiochus II (261–246 BC), Ptolemy II Philadelphus, Antigonus Gonatas of Macedonia (276–239 BC), Magas of Cyrene (c.258–250 BC), and an unidentified Alexander – either Alexander of Corinth (252–244 BC) or Alexander of Epirus (272–255 BC). Pliny the Elder (*Nat. Hist.* 6.21.58) said that a man named Dionysus was Ptolemy II's ambassador to the Mauryan court; the Seleucid ambassador was Megasthenes, fragments of whose description of India survive in later sources. Unfortunately, we cannot gauge the nature and frequency of these exchanges or who initiated them (Rostovtzeff 1932: 743; Cunningham 1961: 84–8, 125–6; Gokhale 1966: 34, 52, 79; Fraser 1972/I: 180–181; Raschke 1975; McEvilley 2002: 368–9). In any event, these contacts seem to have been of little practical importance to any of the parties concerned; their significance was, most likely, in enhancing the prestige of the monarchs involved.

Mauryan hegemony never seems to have extended south of the Narmada River and it was in those southernmost reaches of the subcontinent that contemporary and later polities developed. The earliest references to those groups (Cholas, Cheras, Pandayas, and Satiyaputras) appear in Aśokan inscriptions. These later developed into the Tamil kingdoms of the Cholas, Cheras, and Pandyas. The histories of these chieftains, later kingdoms, can be partially reconstructed from megalithic burials in the region, Tamil inscriptions written initially in Brahmi script, Tamil poems in S(h)angam literature (mainly dating c.300 BC–AD 300) and authors writing in Greek and Latin from the 1st century BC on.

These Tamil states had extensive commercial, cultural, and, likely, diplomatic contacts with West Asia and the Indian Ocean coast of Africa, especially at the turn of the Christian era and in the early centuries AD. The Cholas ruled the eastern (Coromandel) coast and the Pandyas the southernmost tip of the subcontinent, while the Cheras dominated much of the Malabar (southwestern) littoral, bordering the Pandyas to the south and the Cholas to the east. Chera rulers engaged in frequent warfare with the Pandyas and Cholas. The Cholas undoubtedly also had commercial, cultural, and diplomatic contacts with parts of southeast Asia. There has been scholarly debate about the role regional and "international" commerce and religious establishments (especially monasteries) may have played in the formation of some of these smaller states in southern India (cf. Ray 1986). Much debate has focused on the role local, regional, and "international" contacts between these south Indian and Sri Lankan states, on the one hand, and "Western" kingdoms and empires, on the other (Parthian, South Arabian, Roman, and later Axumite) had in the formation and consolidation of the Cholas, Cheras, and Pandyas in southern India (cf. Turner 1989; Turner and Cribb 1996; McLaughlin 2010: 48–57) and the kingdom of Anuradhapura in Sri Lanka (Thapar 2002: 245–53).

After the demise of the Mauryan Empire, several states appeared. Aśokan documents mention the Satavahanas (Andhras), an empire that ruled over southern and central India from about 230 BC with administrative centers at Junnar (Pune), Prathisthan (Paithan) in Maharashtra, and later Dharanikota or Amaravati and Kotilingala (Karimnagar) in Andhra Pradesh. Sātavāhana rule lasted perhaps as long as 450 years until it finally ended in c.220 AD. The Satavahanas were thus contemporary with the Parthians (Pahlavas). There are depictions of single and two-masted ships in India Sātavāhanas/Andhra coins of the early centuries AD as well as representations in paintings in the Ajanta caves of about the 6th century. The appearance of ships on Sātavāhanan/Andhran coins suggests that maritime contacts may have been of some significance to them.

The Kushan Empire arose in the 1st century AD in ancient Bactria around the middle course of the Oxus River (Amu Darya) in northern Afghanistan, southern Tajikistan, and Uzbekistan. The port of Barbaricum/Barbarikon, at the mouth of the Indus River (on the Indian Ocean) was their major maritime outlet. The *PME* (§39) notes that Barbarikon imported glassware and other commodities of Mediterranean provenance from the Red Sea ports and similar items have been documented at sites in Afghanistan (Hiebert and Cambon 2008: 168–75 for imported glass), Central Asia, and China (Brill 1991–2; Kinoshita 2009 for 4th–12th centuries AD) along the "Silk Road".

The last of the important states in India in the period considered here was the Gupta Empire, with its early capital city at Pataliputra and later one at Ujaini (Thapar 2002: 281–7). Controlling much of the Indian subcontinent, the Gupta Empire lasted from c.AD 320 to 550. The period of peace and prosperity that this engendered led to important intellectual contributions in the scientific and artistic literary fields. The Guptas had commercial-cultural contacts with southeast Asia and East Africa, but evidence of links between the Mediterranean world and the Guptas is not as strong. The government seems to have been laissez-faire, with respect to the economy, and there is little evidence of government interference.

Periodic excavations at Arikamedu (ancient "Poduca emporium"/Podukê) on the southeastern (Coromandel) coast of India (Begley 1996; Begley et al. 2004; *PME* §60; Claudius Ptolemy, *Geog.* 7.1) and other emporia (e.g., Alagankulam) along the Coromandel coast and at Pattanam (likely ancient Muziris) (Cherian et al. 2007; cf. *PME* §§53, 56; Pliny the Elder, *Nat. Hist.* 6.24.104; Claudius Ptolemy, *Geog.* 7.1; *Peutinger Table*) on the Malabar/Kerala coast have revealed substantial material remains, mainly in the form of thousands of Mediterranean-made amphora fragments, documenting Red Sea/India contacts. According to the *PME* (§§53–55) another important emporium was located south of Muziris at Nelkynda (unlocated). Clearly, well-organized and regular interaction at many levels reflects a sophisticated land and sea communication network linking these disparate regions of India together.

13 Indian Ocean: States in Sri Lanka

Western sources from the 1st to 6th century AD, including Strabo (*Geog.* 2.1.14; 15.1.14–15), Pomponius Mela (*De Chorographia* 3.70), Pliny the Elder (*Nat. Hist.* 6.24.81 and 6.24.84–85), the *PME* (§§59, 61), Claudius Ptolemy (*Geog.* 7.4.11), and Cosmas Indicopleustes (*Christian Topography* throughout his Book 11 in Wolska-Conus 1973: 314–57), among others, write about Taprobane/Serendip (modern Sri Lanka) (De Romanis 1988; Rosenberger 1996; Bopearachchi 1996; Faller 2000: 135–88). The most significant state in this era was the kingdom of Anuradhapura, whose capital of the same name lay in the northwestern part of the island.

The results of excavations at Mantai at the extreme northern end of Sri Lanka have not been fully published. Settled initially in the Mesolithic period and then abandoned, the site was reoccupied sometime during the second half of the 1st millennium BC and continued in use until the 10th century AD (cf. Begley 1967; Silva 1985; Carswell 1991: 198). Ancient authors allude to the region around Mantai while Claudius Ptolemy (*Geog.* 7.4) calls the site Modutti/Modurgi Emporium. Mantai was a major glass bead manufacturing center exporting as far afield as East Africa and Korea; pearls were also a major export (Carswell 1991: 200).

Another important emporium in the Indian Ocean/Red Sea nexus lay in southern Sri Lanka at Tissamaharama, which functioned between the 4th/3rd century BC and the 9th century AD. Excavations there have produced considerable evidence of contact with the Mediterranean basin, likely via the Red Sea and Persian Gulf, in the Roman period (Weisshaar and Wijeyapala 2000; Hannibal-Deraniyagala 2000; Schenk 2000; for urbanization of the island, see Coningham and Allchin 1995).

GUIDE TO FURTHER READING

A good overview of "international" contacts within the Mediterranean/Red Sea/Indian Ocean region and beyond is the now dated Raschke (1978), who also discusses land routes through Asia. For a more recent treatment emphasizing pottery as an indicator of Mediterranean trade via Egypt and the Persian Gulf with India, see Tomber (2008). McLaughlin (2010) discusses the sea routes between the Mediterranean world and India as well as the Central Asian Silk Road. Sidebotham (2011) focuses on the port of Berenike in the ancient commercial-cultural network and its relationship with partners in Egypt, the Red Sea, and Indian Ocean in Ptolemaic and Roman times.

CHAPTER FIFTY-SIX

Byzantium in Asia Minor and the Levant

Basema Hamarneh

1 Byzantine Archaeology: Subject and Main Tools

Owing to growing interest in the Late Antiquity of Asia Minor (Anatolia) and the Levant (modern Syria, Lebanon, Israel, the Palestinian Territories, and Jordan), a wide range of subjects has recently been brought to scholarly attention, enriched by an increasing number of excavated and surveyed sites. In chronological terms, it is widely accepted that the term "Byzantine archaeology" applies to the post-Constantinian epoch, or, more appropriately, to lands ruled by the Byzantine emperors, from Constantine (307–37) to Heraclius (610–41). In some cases, "Byzantine archaeology" equals "Christian archaeology". The official recognition of Christianity by Emperor Constantine (307–37) transformed what had been formerly remote lands of the Empire into an area of prime importance. This was due initially to the establishment of a new capital at Constantinople, the New Rome, and secondly to the force of attraction of the Holy Land, the place where the events of the life and passion of Christ had taken place.

There were sharp contrasts within the Byzantine Empire, but the cultural basis was common: the gradual withdrawal of paganism in the face of the new Christian religion imposed by the new ruling dynasties caused significant changes in the organization of urban space. Temples were gradually replaced by churches, thanks to the generous endowments of the imperial court and local donors (*evergetes*) and, leaving aside the maintenance of defensive systems, public spaces were reorganized to meet new demands. Moreover, provincial and local administration

---

A Companion to the Archaeology of the Ancient Near East, First Edition.
Edited by D.T. Potts.
© 2012 Blackwell Publishing Ltd. Published 2012 by Blackwell Publishing Ltd.

was completely reorganized, church officials emerging as the new holders of ecclesiastical and civic power (Saradi 2006: 151–60). During the Roman period, cities had attracted the local aristocracy by offering social and political advantages; the elite reciprocated by lending financial support and patronage. This relationship was mutually advantageous, as the cities' prosperity reflected that of the local elites (Fiema 2002: 218). The stagnation and decline of the Later Roman Empire was characterized by the gradual diminishing in importance of central government and the redirection of power toward ecclesiastical institutions. As episcopal dioceses were created in the 4th–5th centuries, civic administration was taken over by church officials. The bishop's authority in urban administration was formalized by a law promulgated in 505 for the East: the *defensor civitatis* (a judicial official) was to be appointed by the bishop, the clergy, the *honorati* (those with municipal honors), the *possessores* (landlords), and the *curiales* (hereditary members of the assembly, *curia*, often charged with duties like tax-collection). This power to protect the weak and to ensure the food supply of the city was granted to the bishop in view of his spiritual authority. During the reign of Emperor Justinian (527–65), numerous laws recognized the bishop's authority in civic administration, along with his fiscal responsibilities over cities and their districts. Bishops in fact assessed taxes from land owned by the church and promoted the construction of churches in urban and rural centers as well as civic structures. In addition, particularly under Justinian, the 6th century witnessed a gradual growth of the economic potential of the area both in agriculture and trade. Oil, wine, and cereal crops circulated from the hinterland to the ports on the Mediterranean shore. Economic prosperity reached its peak at this time, as evidenced by a densely populated landscape with a large number of cities, towns, villages, and farmsteads that overshadowed in number their Roman predecessors (Jones 1964: 713; Russell 1986; Cameron 1993: 180; Millar 1993: 251–3; Morrisson and Sodini 2002: 219–20). The gradual and catastrophic decline that hit some regions prior to the Arab conquest was due to earthquakes, Persian attacks, and the Great Plague that struck Constantinople in 542 and spread to Gaza, Antioch, Syria, and Asia Minor. When the Arab conquerors finally overran large areas of the Byzantine East in 636, the combined effect of these factors was a recession, and the abandonment or contraction of urban and rural life over the whole area.

2   Byzantine Archaeology of Palaestina I, II, III (Israel and Palestinian Authorities)

When Christianity prevailed, the territory of Palestine received primary attention, becoming the cultural focus of the new Empire. The major transformations included the building of churches within the street grid of the old Roman towns. In this way, the established centers retained many of their Classical features even though temples were replaced by churches. From the 4th century onward the

The Holy Sepulcher

newly embellished holy shrines represented a major attraction for large groups of pilgrims, causing the development of auxiliary structures such as hospices and monasteries as well as devotional art objects (*eulogiae*) that exhibited, impressed upon them, representations of sanctuaries and saints (Vikan 1982).

The Holy Sepulcher

The discovery of the True Cross by Helen, the mother of Emperor Constantine, caused fundamental changes to Jerusalem, starting with the site of the death, burial, and resurrection of Christ to the north of the Roman forum. According to Eusebius, Bishop of Caesarea, Hadrian covered the site with an embankment so as to erase from view the *loca sancta* of the passion and tomb of Christ. A temple of Aphrodite-Venus was erected over the Golgotha, while the Capitolium, dedicated to the triad Jupiter, Juno, and Minerva, was erected over the holy tomb (Bagatti and Testa 1978: 31–4). Constantine ordered the destruction of all pagan buildings, while an excavation revealed the exact position of the tomb. A few months later, he ordered the erection of a monumental complex consisting of five buildings accessible from the *cardo maximus* (major north–south street and axis of commercial activity in Roman cities), which was dedicated on September 14, 335. The entrance was through a *propylea-atrium* (monumental gateway leading to a courtyard surrounded by columned porticoes) on the western side of the *cardo maximus*, with stairs leading east decorated with marble and embellished by an exedra (semi-circular recess, often set into the façade of a building and sometimes covered with a semi-dome) (Brenk 2007: 113–14). These led to the main church – the *martyrium* – with three doors giving access to an apsed, five-aisled basilica with galleries. In the presbytery (that part of a church reserved for clergy), 12 columns were arranged in a silver ring around the altar. Beyond the basilica, a large triportico-courtyard linked the *martyrium* to the Anastasis (resurrection) Rotunda, allowing the spur of the Golgotha topped by a cross to be visible. According to the pilgrim Egeria, who visited the complex in the 4th century, the name *martyrium* was given to the church in memory of the Lord's suffering in his Passion. To the west stood the tomb of Christ, the Anastasis (resurrection). The monument had 8 portals and 8 elongated windows, 12 columns inside and 3 sets of alternating pilasters which supported a tunnel topped by a dome with an *oculus* (circular window). From this opening, daylight illuminated the shrine of the resurrection (Piccirillo 2008: 57–8). The Holy Sepulcher was visited by many pilgrims, who gave detailed accounts of the aspect of the original church and of the liturgy, besides mentioning that the complex also included the bishop's palace and a baptismal font (Egeria in the 4th century; the Bordeaux pilgrim in 333; the Anonymous Piacenza pilgrim in 570; see Hunt 1982: 28–49; Peters 1985: 131–9; and the Madaba Mosaic map, Piccirillo 1993). Destroyed by the Persians in 614, the Constantinian basilica was restored by

Patriarch Modestus, who had been the abbot of the Monastery of St Theodosius on the edge of the Judean Desert. Reconstruction work was completed by Patriarch Theodore when the relic of the Holy Cross was triumphantly reinstated in Jerusalem in 630 by the Byzantine Emperor Heraclius (610–41).

Constantine also built two other basilicas: that of the Nativity in Bethlehem in 339, consisting of a central nave and four aisles, with stairs to the east leading downward to the sacred grotto identified as the birthplace of Christ (Bagatti 1971b: 175–84; Walker 1990: 171–98); and the Eleona Church on the Mount of Olives, erected over the cave believed to be the site of the Ascension (Bagatti 1971b: 184–90; Walker 1990: 199–209). Two more churches were added in Gethsemane and Bethany at the end of the 4th century (Bagatti 1971b: 192–206; Piccirillo 2008: 62–3).

In the first half of the 6th century, Palestine reached an acme in terms of population and number of settlements all over the country, including the Negev Desert (Dauphin 1998/I: 77–121). This expansion reflected relative stability with intense territorial occupation and extraordinary technological quality of building. The 5th–6th centuries were characterized by fervent and feverish building activity, since most of the pagan temples were demolished or replaced by churches, causing a physical change in the urban structure of many cities. Imperial endowment also played a crucial role: Empress Eudoxia built a church over the Marneion in Gaza around 400, while Emperor Justinian rebuilt the Church of the Nativity in Bethlehem and founded the Nea Ekklesia with two pilgrim hospices in Jerusalem as well as the Katholikon of the Monastery of St Catherine in Sinai (Piccirillo 2008: 103–7). In the reign of Emperor Justinian, the Church of St Sergius in Gaza was decorated with outstanding mosaics celebrated by the rhetor Choricius of Gaza (*Laudatio Marciani* I.17–76; Saliou 2005). Most urban centers expanded beyond their city limits in the Roman period, showing that the Byzantine quarters were built within and outside the core of the former Roman centers. Houses literally spilled out of the defensive walls, notably in Scythopolis (modern Bet Shean), capital of Palaestina II (Tsafrir and Foerster 1997: 100–2; Patrich 2011), where a monastery was dedicated to Lady Mary in the mid-6th century within the city and close to the walls, while a large circular church, erected on the summit of the *tell*, eradicated the memory of the former temple of Zeus Akraius (Piccirillo 1989b: 465–468; Tsafrir and Foerster 1997: 111). Two other churches in Tel Iztaba were dedicated, respectively, to a martyr and to the metropolitan Andreas (Tsafrir and Foerster 1997: 104). The city of Hippos (mod. Sussita, Israel), on the eastern shore of the Sea of Galilee, also afforded a well-organized Roman city grid, with three churches to the north of the *cardo* and one to the south dedicated to St Cosmas and Damian (Piccirillo 1989b: 477–8). Recent excavations to the northwest of the city have brought to light a basilical complex, richly adorned with imported marble and mosaics, dated to the 6th century (Młynarczyk and Burdajewicz 2005: 40–7; Burdajewicz and Młynarczyk 2006). Caesarea, the capital of Palaestina I, had at least 10 churches, including an elaborate, hexagonal one dated to the 5th–6th centuries which replaced a Roman temple (Tsafrir and Foerster 1997: 111; Patrich 2011), and a basilical *martyrium* dedicated to Procopius that was erected over the ruins of Herod's temple (Holum and Hohfelder 1988: 176–9). Several large, suburban villae were discovered near Caesarea and at Ascalon (mod. Ashkelon, Israel), while numerous well-organized farmsteads and villages developed in the Golan Heights (Dauphin 1995: 667–73; Dauphin et al. 1996: 305–40; Urman 2006), in Judea, along the coast between Dor and Gaza, in the Samaria hills, and in the Negev (Hirschfeld 1997). Some, like those at Horvat Zikhrin and Horvat Migdal in Western Samaria, Gelilot on the coastal plain, and Capernaum on the shore of the Sea of Galilee, included small bathhouses (Hirschfeld 1997: 65). In the Negev desert, several cities and large settlements developed, notably Mampsis (Kurnub), Oboda (Avdat), Subaita (Shivta), Nessana (Nizzana), and Rohoba (Ruheibe). Monasteries flourished, particularly in the hinterland of Jerusalem – the Judean Desert – and in southern Sinai along the main pilgrim routes from Sinai to Jerusalem. In addition, a large number of monasteries were founded near rural villages (Hirschfeld 1990; Patrich 2004: 426–33; Bar 2005).

3 Byzantine Archaeology in Anatolia/Asia Minor

Constantinople

Some months after he had defeated his rival Licinius, Constantine embarked on an ambitious project: the establishment on May 11, 330 of a new capital for his Empire on the site of ancient Byzantium. New city walls were erected about 3 kilometers to the west of the Roman ramparts, enclosing c.700 hectares (Strube 1973: 131–47; Dagron 1974: 401–8; Mango 1980). The eastern promontory, sloping sharply to the shores of the Propontius, was chosen to host the main buildings: the Senate, the Imperial Palace, and the Hippodrome with an imperial loggia (Dagron 1974: 329; Mango 1985: 24). These projects required great feats of engineering because of the geological conditions of the area. In particular, the Hippodrome was erected on a massive substructure (Dagron 1974: 312; Barsanti 1992: 119). The Imperial Palace consisted of an articulated complex enclosed within a boundary wall and raised on terraces formed by containment walls and vaulted structures on several levels. It included the Palace of Daphne, the Augustus (or boardroom), and the guard Scholae, only a monumental portico of which today survives east of the Agora (Miranda 1983: 41–9, 196–204). The Agora, the Roman Tetrastoos, was named Augustaeum after the column erected by Constantine in honor of his mother Helen. It was a colonnaded square adorned with statues of the Emperor, his children, and other imperial personages. The second Senate house was built on the eastern side; it included a large basilica, its stoa adorned with the most representative works of Classical antiquity (Barsanti

1992: 121). On its southern side, the public baths of Zeuxippus were restored and embellished by Constantine. Subsequently, the maintenance of these baths was regulated by Honorius and Theodosius in 424 (Saradi 2006: 334). The structure was severely damaged by fire during the Nika riots of 532. To the west of the Augustaeum ran the city's monumental avenue: the Mese, which led to the Thracian Gate. It was bounded by Constantine's Forum, the Forum Tauri (Barsanti 1995), the Forum Bovis, and the Forum of Arcadius. At the point of convergence of the Roman Stoa, stood the Milion/*miliarium aureum* (lit. "golden milestone"). The forum was located in front of the Senate house, with a *nymphaeum* (shrine dedicated to the water nymphs with a fountain, reservoir, flowers, sculpture, and wall paintings, used for weddings) on the opposite side. It was circular, adorned with the emperor's statue on a porphyry column dedicated in 328, perhaps on the occasion of the consecration of New Rome. The forum porticoes were damaged by the fires of 465, 498, and 532 during the Nika riots. Constantine also built the Church of the Holy Apostles where he deposited in 356–7 the relics of Saints Andrew, Timothy, and Lucas.

Theodosius II (408–50) contributed to the transformation of Constantinople into a magnificent capital. He first turned his attention to improving its defensive capacity by building a new, double land wall that included towers of various shapes (Meyer-Plath and Schneider 1943; Tsangadas 1980; Foss and Winfield 1986: 41–77; Ahunbay and Ahunbay 2000: 227–39). This was probably linked to the already existing Constantinian wall with 10 main gates. The latter were repaired by Emperor Justin II (565–78). The most important landmarks of the city were erected under Emperor Theodosius: the Great Palace and the Church of St Sophia. The Great Palace dominated a large terrace overlooking the Sea of Marmara (Brett et al. 1947; Talbot Rice 1956). This consisted of a labyrinth of halls, courts, gardens, and porticoes, each with its own function: halls of audience, private apartments, chapels, churches, and administrative buildings (Dark 2007). To the north stood the Chalke, a rectangular building communicating with St Sophia through a bronze door; in its domed, central hall were exhibited many works of art brought from all over the empire (Mango 1959). Through the Chalke, a passage led to the guard Scholae, and then through halls to the Palace of Daphne in which the Imperial Throne stood. Emperors Justin II and Tiberius I (578–82) completed the construction and decoration of a domed, octagonal aula that hosted the main symbols of imperial power. The Great Palace included several churches dedicated to the Holy Virgin, St Demetrius, and St Elias. Official delegations and foreign ambassadors were received in the Magnaura, to the northeast, also lavishly decorated. Little of this palace survives today except for the extraordinary mosaic pavement of the peristyle, set around a rectangular court. Though the exact date of this pavement is still debated, it has been ascribed to the 6th century (Bardill 1999, 2006; Barsanti 2009). The church of St Sophia, built over a Roman necropolis, originally had a basilical plan and was dedicated in 360 in the reign of Emperor

Constans. It was destroyed by fire in 404 and reconstructed by Theodosius II in 415. Other churches were founded in the 5th century, such as St John Studios to the southeast (Mango 1974: 61) and the Theotokos Chalkoprateia to the west of St Sophia.

The city's commercial potential was improved by the construction of port facilities and harbors on the Propontid coast (Mango 1985: 37–40). Theodosius II built a harbor south of the mouth of the River Lykos, in the IXth region, well equipped with warehouses, such as the *horrea Alexandrina* and *horrea Theodosiana*, where cereals and other crops brought from Egypt were stored (Mango 1985: 40; Asal 2010: 152–5). Recent archaeological excavations at Yenikapi in the western part of the inner harbor have uncovered the land walls made of large stone blocks and the beginning of a pier on the west but reaching out to the east and northeast. The masonry of the north–south quay included well-dressed blocks used to anchor boats. The Port of Theodosius was protected by the tower of Belisarius, which stood on the sea, near the harbor entrance, and probably served as a lighthouse. The excavations also revealed a shipwreck, dated to the 9th century, which has contributed valuable information on naval construction in the Byzantine period. Moreover, it has provided a variety of traded items and naval equipment, such as amphorae, baskets, pulleys, hoists, ropes, rope loop, stone, and iron anchors; and, personal items, such as combs, leather sandals, wicker baskets, wooden bowls, and other objects of organic or inorganic matter (Kocabaş and Özasait-Kocabaş 2010: 143–7).

A crucial issue concerned the maintenance of the water supply system: the aqueduct of Valens provided running water for the baths and the fountains, while a system of water storage with huge cisterns was the main source of drinking water for the population. Responsibility over these as well as over other public works, such as harbors, streets, bridges, and walls, was entrusted, according to Justinian's Novellae, to bishops, governors, and community leaders (Saradi 2006: 344–5).

In the 6th century, Anastasius I (491–518) and Justinian I (518–27) did not alter the aspect of their capital, but contributed in improving its structures. Justinian made great efforts to maintain existing structures, such as the vestibule of the Great Palace, the Senate, and civic complexes, in addition to the founding of new churches. In the central part of the city, the Church of St Polyeuctos was built, probably around 524–7 (Harrison 1985; Hayes 1992); it communicated with the adjacent church of SS Peter and Paul and was connected to the Hormisdas Palace, Justinian's private residence. As the result of the Nika riots, the church of SS Sergius and Bacchus required restoration, and again in 558 after the original dome had collapsed (Mango 1974: 106–23). Similar was the situation of St Irene, burnt down in 532 and then rebuilt. Two other churches, St Euphemia and Basilica A, were discovered during excavations in the Beyazit quarter of Istanbul. One of the major churches was a cross-shaped building dedicated to the Apostles.

4 Anatolia

Set geographically on the cross routes that connected Europe to Asia and to the countries of the Mediterranean shore and the Black Sea, the Province of Asia was, from its early development, one of the richest and most populated of the Roman Empire (Foss 1996; Zah 2003). There, two different cultural traditions met: the Oriental or Asiatic that flourished inland, and the Graeco-Roman that dominated the coast. This duality conditioned and left its mark on settlement patterns, which remained of urban character in the coastal areas and near the main trade routes, while inland, agricultural and rural settlements prevailed, particularly along the Eastern *limes* (the line of defensive forts on the Roman frontier). The archaeological record indicates a great number of Byzantine sites: surveys conducted in the central part of Lycia around Kyaneani have brought to light farmsteads, villages, and traces of farmed terraces (Foss 1994: 1–52). In the territory of the Meander River, a network of economic exchange linked the cities to their hinterland characterized by villages of independent farmers or small landowners (Morrisson and Sodini 2002).

The strategic value and the position of the southern Oriental cities in frontier areas necessitated the construction of massive fortifications in the reigns of Anastasius, and later of Justinian. The walls of several urban centers were reinforced: Sardis (Foss 1996), Dara (Zanini 1990; Forlan 1995), Amida (mod. Diyarbakir), Edessa (mod. Urfa) (Guidetti 2009), Martyropolis, Theodosiopolis (mod. Erzerum), Melitene (mod. Eski Malatya), and Carrhae (mod. Harran). The maintenance of public services was increased under Justinian, primarily the land communication network; bridges in Tarsus, Misis and Amida, aqueducts in Nicaea, and Trebizond; and public baths in Nicomedia, Nicaea, and Pithiae/Bithyinia. Imperial munificence was also directed toward the re-edification of entire cities damaged by earthquakes, such as Anazarba, as well as the foundation of churches and sanctuaries. Several churches were built, such as the Panagia in Antalya, the episcopal basilica of Hierapolis (mod. Pammukale), and that of Alaşehir in Phrygia (Buchwald 1981), and many others in Lyconia, Caria, Bithynia, Tur Abdin, and the Pontus. Several other churches in Cappadocia and Nicaea are dated to the second half of the 6th century. Offering an important variety of shrines, the most prominent of which were probably in Ephesus, Asia Minor had long been also the destination of pilgrimage.

The gradual decline of urban structures started in 615 as the result of the Persian invasion, which was followed by the Arab Conquest. During this period, several towns were sacked and destroyed (Vryonis 1971). Those that survived these catastrophic events were forced to limit the habitat to the fortified summits of their acropolis, as at Cesarea of Cappadocia (Kayseri) and Ancyra/Ankara (Foss 1977), while Sardis Pergamum, Miletus, Priene, and Magnesia became small fortresses (Foss 1996). Constantine II (641–68) added new fortifications to

Sardis (Foss 1977), Ankara, Ephesus (Foss 1979), and Miletus, paying particular attention to those cities near major crossroads.

Ephesus

Before the Byzantine period, Ephesus was already one of the greatest cities of Asia Minor. Its nucleus had developed on a small plain near its harbor around important public buildings dominated by the shrine of Artemis, which was considered one of the wonders of the ancient world (Foss 1979). In the Byzantine period, the city underwent important transformations: its main colonnaded street, the Arkadiana, which connected the city to the harbor, was repaved, subsequently four columns were added by Justinian, and it was adorned with the statues of the Evangelists. In the 4th century, the Museion, which rose to the north of the colonnaded street and had been damaged by fire, made way for a large elongated cathedral dedicated to the Virgin, with a baptismal domed chapel, and the bishop's residential quarter to the west. The cathedral hosted two important Church Councils in 431 and 449. Though the exact date of its construction is debated, epigraphic evidence indicates that the building was renovated under Justinian. According to tradition, the tomb of St John the Evangelist was located on a hill to the north of the city and was one of the holiest sites of Asia Minor. Under Emperor Constantine, the tomb was in a simple quadrangular building. In the 5th century, the *martyrium* assumed the aspect of a cruciform building covered by a wooden roof (Verzone 1982) and to which was attached a baptismal font (Castelfranchi 1981). It was rebuilt under Anastasius, and again under Justinian in 548, who donated to the sanctuary precious marble adornments brought directly from Constantinople. Thus the *martyrium* developed into the new cathedral of the city. Amongst the Christian shrines of the city, pride of place should be given to the Cave of the Seven Sleepers, built in the Panayr Dağ mountain range probably under Theodosius I (379–95), but which reached its greatest development with the edification of the mausoleum of Abradas. Pilgrims also visited the tombs of Mary Magdalene, St Timothy, and St Hermione (Foss 2002: 130–1). The archaeological record shows that after the Persian attack of 614, several areas of the city were abandoned, notably the agora and the embolus, and many dwellings were leveled, this triggering the city's decline (Foss 1990).

Edessa

Bisected by the river Skirtos/Kara Koyun, Edessa in southeastern Turkey was dominated by a fortress built to the south on a hilltop, the fortifications being connected to the city wall which was rebuilt under Justinian after the river had overrun its bed in 525, causing major destruction and alluvial silting. In the 6th century, its name was changed to Iustinianopolis. Dedicated to St Thomas, the most ancient church of the city was described by the pilgrim Egeria in the 4th century. The cathedral, probably cross-shaped and including a baptistery, held the relic of the sacred Mandilion on which were imprinted Christ's facial features. It was rebuilt by Justinian after the 525 disaster (Grabar 1947). Another 6 churches rose in the city and a further 30 in the Edessa countryside are mentioned in the historical sources (Segal 1970).

Amida (mod. Diyarbakir)

An outpost on the southeastern edge of the Empire, the late Antique city of Amida experienced continuous political instability. The city fell to the Persians in 359, was reconquered by the Byzantines in 363, taken again by the Persians in 502, and two years later was back in Byzantine hands. In 602, the Persian ruler Chosroes took the city; Heraclius recaptured it in 628, but nearly 11 years later it fell definitively to the Arabs. The original core of the Late Antique city of Amida was enclosed by a "chain" of fortification walls under Constans II between 324 and 327 (Gabriel 1940; Van Berchem 1954). These often needed repairs, especially after each military campaign. Massive repairs were undertaken by Anastasius, while to Justinian may only be attributed restoration and maintenance work (Maffei 1985). In the 5th–6th centuries, the city had a well-defined Christian character which included auxiliary and charitable structures, such as a xenodochion built in the 5th century, several churches, and five monasteries (Mango 1982; Guidetti 2009).

5   Byzantine Archaeology in Syria

A rich and important province, Syria experienced major development in the 4th century thanks to the endowment of the imperial house that gave impetus to the transformation of the urban and rural topography. Eusebius mentions an octagonal church covered by a golden dome built by Constantine near the imperial palace in Antioch and dedicated to Christ in 341 by Constans II. In Damascus, Emperors Theodosius and Arcadius built the Church of St John the Baptist inside the *temenos* of the pagan sanctuary of Zeus (now the Umayyad mosque), while a second basilica was erected within the temple of Zeus in Heliopolis-Emesa/Homs. Likewise, the temple of Apollo in Daphne (a suburb of Antioch) became the church of the Archangel Michael. Further importance was given to churches as a result of holy relics and bodies of saints being deposited in them. Thus, the body of St Babila was laid to rest in a cruciform church in Qaousiyah-Daphne in 351/4 (Levi 1947: 283–5, 423–6). Theodosius II (405–50) transformed the Tychaion (the temple to the city's Tyche or goddess of fortune) into the Church of St Ignatius by translating the saint's relics from the cemetery near Daphne. Similar is the case of the shrine of St Sergius in Rusafa/Sergiopolis, which became an episcopal see in the first half of the 5th century and the main center for the Ghassanid tribes allied to the Emperor. Great was the influence of local saints believed to be invested by God with the power of healing and foreseeing the future, as St Simeon the Elder (386–459) who spent much of his life atop a column, and St Simeon the Younger, native of Antioch, who dedicated his life to an analogous form of asceticism on Mons Admirabilis (521–92).

West of the Euphrates were the following administrative provinces: Syria I, with its capital Antioch (later called also Theopolis), Syria Salutaris (Apamea), Theodorias (Loadikeia/Latakia), Euphratensis (Ierapolis/Menbij), Phoenicia I (Tyr), and Phoenicia Libanensis (Emesa/Homs). Urban centers continued to flourish during the Byzantine period, some being rebuilt, such as Leontopolis (Callinicum/ar-Raqqa) and Justinianopolis (Burqush), while others displayed a remarkable continuity, in particular those in the Orontes valley, such as Antioch, Apamea, Epiphanea, as well as Bosra in the Hauran. One of the major undertakings of Anastasius and Justinian in Syria was the reorganization of the defense of the northern frontier along the Euphrates, which was largely exposed to Persian attack (Ulbert 1989: 283–96). The cities of Rusafa (Karnapp 1976), Halabiye (Lauffray 1991: 15–26), Dara (Zanini 1990), Chalchis (Fourdrin and Feissel 1994), Barbalissos (Meskene), Neocaesaria (Dibsi Faraj), and Antioch were literally transformed into strongholds.

Antioch

Antioch was one of the most fascinating cities of the Eastern empire, a patriarchal see and the capital of a district. The city boasted 15 churches and 20 temples. Besides being the home of wealthy landowners, it was chosen as imperial residence during the eastern campaigns against the Persians led by Constans II from 337 to 350, Valens from 371 to 378, and Julian in 362. Gradual decline set in during the 6th century as a result of a series of disastrous events: a fire in 525, followed in the next year by an earthquake that destroyed all major churches (Downey 1961: 521–6). A second quake in 528 literally demolished the city, calling for the urgent rebuilding of cultural and private edifices. This restoration, however, was unable to replace the city's earlier splendor. Valuable proof of this restoration was unearthed in the excavation of the great villa at Yakto, which yielded important stratigraphic evidence of both reconstruction and definitive abandonment (Foss 1997: 194). This recovery did not last long. In 540, Antioch was captured and put to the torch; its population was deported by the Persians. An extensive second restoration, under Justinian, encompassed the walls, public porticoes, markets, water conduits, fountains, theaters, and baths in an attempt to resurrect the city's splendor (Saradi 2006: 252–3). Two years later the plague, and another earthquake in 551, followed by further pandemics, heralded the city's final collapse as it fell to the Arab conquerors.

Apamea

The city of Apamea was endowed with an extensive circuit of walls and maintained its Roman plan in the Byzantine period. There, in the 6th century, resided most of the great landowners, forming an aristocratic caste (Le Strange 1890: 384). The city was privileged to own one of the most sacred relics: a fragment of the Holy Cross (Procopius, *Historia Ecclesiastica* 4.26). Under Justinian, major reconstruction work was undertaken: the main streets were paved anew, a tetrastylon (a monument with four columns crowned by capitals) was added, and new shops built along the decumanus (Foss 1997: 208–10). To the south of the main artery, three large churches were constructed under Justinian: the Rotunda, the Atrium church with several reliquary chapels (Lassus 1972a; Foss 1997: 212), and the cathedral.

Epiphanea

Epiphanea's role was different: it was a road station and a bishopric. The city's main acropolis was encircled by walls under Justinian, while the building of residential quarters was followed by that of a monumental cathedral beneath the acropolis in the first half of the 5th century (Piccirillo 2007a: 599–607). In the suburbs of modern Hama, the Church of the Holy Martyrs at Tayyibat al-Imam was built in 442 and paved with mosaics of extraordinarily high quality of workmanship (Zaqzuq and Piccirillo 1999: 443–64).

Bostra

In Bostra (Bosra), capital of Provincia Arabia, the cathedral was erected in the eastern part of the city probably in the 6th century (Dentzer 1989: 229), while the church of SS Sergius, Bacchus, and Leontius was an important center of pilgrimage (Farioli Campanati 1992: 173–8).

The landscape of Byzantine Syria was predominantly one of rural settlements. Most of these were on the limestone plateau of Northern Syria, in the fertile plains, particularly around the cities of Antioch (Haines 1971: 10–13), Apamea, Beroea (Aleppo), and Chalcis, and in the mountains – Jabal Samn, Jabal Halaqa, Jabal Berisha, Jabal Ala, Jabal Dueili, Jabal Wastani, and Jabal Zawiye (Foss 1997: 232–7). Archaeological excavations have demonstrated that these villages developed in close proximity to each other, had well-marked and well-evidenced territorial limits, and predominantly practiced dry-farming. The local economy was based on the production of olive oil, fruit, cereal crops, and vegetables (Tate 1992: 191–271). These settlements, with well-preserved structures of well-dressed masonry, were mostly inhabited without interruption from 350 to 550 (Tchalenko 1953–8; Foss 1997: 200; Gatier 2005). Some villages were particularly wealthy, as may be surmised from the hoard of 56 extraordinary silver objects discovered in Kaper Koraon. The silver objects were the gift of local notable to the village church and to its saint, Sergius between 540 and 640 (Mango 1986).

6 Byzantine Archaeology in Phoenicia (Lebanon)

In the cities of Phoenicia, churches were integrated into the Roman urban centers, especially along the coast as in Berytus/Beirut, Byblos/Gibelet, Sidon, and Tyre, as well as in Baalbek in the Beqaa. These centers were connected to the Roman road network that led from the coast to the Beqaa and on to Aleppo, Homs, and Damascus and beyond (Walmsley 1996; Morrisson and Sodini 2002). In the 6th century, several churches were built, as in Ma'ad (near Batrun). On the coast, Byzantine Khan Khalde was a large city with many churches paved with mosaics. Similar elaborate mosaic pavements were unearthed in Khalde, 'Awza'i, Jenah, and Zahrani (Donceel-Voûte 1988). Near Tyre, the church of Qabr Hiram exhibits a spectacular mosaic floor. In Baalbek, the temple of Zeus was converted into a church dedicated to St Peter.

7 Byzantine Archaeology in Arabia and Palaestina III (Jordan)

The undeniable prosperity and the outstanding development of the territory of Provincia Arabia and of the three Palaestinae, within the ecclesiastical jurisdiction of the Patriarchate of Antioch and Jerusalem (Devreesse 1945: 213–14; Piccirillo 1989b: 461), with their large urban and multitudinous rural centers, is well evidenced by recent field studies (Walmsley 2005). Excavations have shown an intensive exploitation of the landscape, which reflects the favorable political and economic conditions of development of that area in that particular period. The roots of this remodeling may be traced back to the 4th century, as imperial policy encouraged private ownership of land by promulgating laws that remained in force at least until the end of the Byzantine period. The demographic expansion, due probably to increased security experienced in marginal areas or as a result of climatic improvement, resulted in a large number of villages concentrating around major urban centers (Hamarneh 2003). The gradual transformation of the modes of territorial occupation was twofold and probably began in the second half of the 5th century, as local tribes shifted from a nomadic to a sedentary lifestyle, either reoccupying abandoned Roman military structures or establishing new settlements in the fertile areas in the hinterland of cities (Hamarneh 2003). Nomadic populations provided a reliable agricultural workforce, besides militarily policing the *limes* frontier zone. Thus, the new settlement policy was correlated to a process of Christianization and may have started under Emperor Constans 337–61 and his successors: Sozomenos, in his *Historia Ecclesiastica*, mentions the conversion of large groups of *foederati* represented by their own Bishop of the Arabs at the Church Councils of Seleucia in 359 and Antioch in 363 (Devreesse 1945; Shahid 1989). The formation of the episcopal dioceses attested in the 4th–5th centuries was also due to the decline of provincial administration (Liebeschuetz 1997: 113–25; Saradi 2006: 181). The formal recognition of the bishop's authority in urban administration was sanctified by several Justinianic laws. The bishop thus procured both ecclesiastical and civic functions that persisted into the 7th century (Dagron 1979: 44–47; Walmsley 1996: 129). In Provincia Arabia, such involvement is attested by a lintel inscription discovered in Gerasa (mod. Jerash) which mentions the building of a prison for the accused by Bishop Paul of the same city in 539–40 (Gatier 1985; Piccirillo 2002: 133–5). Urban centers, as in other provinces, maintained their regular Classical plan, which, however, was rapidly modified owing to the ascendancy of Christianity (Whittow 1990). It must be stressed that the process of Christianization in the area is well documented by mosaic dedicatory inscriptions on church pavements that attest the continuity of the local Christian tradition long after the Arab Conquest (Di Segni 1999; Hamarneh 1996). Most churches exhibit a basilical plan, some an octagonal (Gerasa/Jerash and Gadara), centralized (Gerasa and Madaba), or cruciform plan, as in Gerasa (Duval 1994; Michel 2001). Christian churches were erected either in vacant lots over ruined pagan temples, or on land plots donated to the church, as was the case of the Hippolytus Hall in Madaba, which was subsequently converted into the entrance vestibule of the Church of the Virgin in the 8th century (Piccirillo 2007b). In Madaba, the cathedral and its baptistery were built in the 5th century, the main *cardo* was flanked in the 6th–8th centuries by several churches and houses, reusing building materials from adjacent pagan temples (Piccirillo 2002; Piccirillo 1989a). Dated to the second half of the 6th century, the church to the north of the *cardo* displayed a mosaic representing the biblical lands to the east and west of the Jordan river, from the Lebanon to Egypt (Piccirillo 1993). Gerasa, Pella, Abila, and Gadara also kept their original urban plan, although it was modified by Christian monuments constructed between the 5th and the 7th centuries (Piccirillo 1981; Piccirillo 2002).

From an archaeological standpoint, excavations have demonstrated that agricultural settlements in Arabia and Palaestina Tertia were mainly villages that rose within *castrum* enclosures (Haldon 1999; Fiema 2002: 211; Hamarneh 2003). Most of these settlements illustrate an important building policy which reflects the key position of the church. The cases of Umm el-Quttein, Umm el-Jimal, Khirbet es-Samra/Haditha, Rihab (in the bishopric of Bosra), Jiza/Zizia/Zizium, Dhiban/Libona, Nitl and Umm er-Rasas/Mefaa (in the bishopric of Madaba), Khirbet al-Mureigha, Zodocatha/Kastron, Zadakathon/Sadaqa, Kastron Ammatha (mod. al-Hammam), Khirbet Nahas, Arindela/Gharandal, and Huana/Humaima show the habitat expanding outside the enclosure walls, this presuming that no military actions were taking place at the time. Not only is the number of ecclesiastical foundations in each locality – up to 15 – impressive, but most are dated by inscriptions which bear witness to the patronage of local bishops and lay donors (Hamarneh 2003). In the 6th century, the gradual shift in social and economic importance toward villages, which is traceable in the structure of the Byzantine tax system, confirms the strength of the local rural economy and implies the decrease of international trade in Arabia, the population relying increasingly on local resources.

Archaeology has shown that Arabia was not targeted by the Persian invasion of 614. Several dated church inscriptions prove that intense building activity occurred under Polyeuctos (594–623) and Theodoros (634–37), archbishops of Bosra, before and after the Arab Conquest, in the villages of Rihab, Khirbet es-Samra, Sama, and Yasilah, alongside other rebuilding or restoration projects (Piccirillo 1981, 2007b). Some churches were rebuilt on a smaller scale, as in Khilda, in the vicinity of Amman, in 687. Similar remodeling is attested in al-Quweismeh (Amman) and Khirbet Daria (Pella). Fervent activity was also present at Rihab: a church dedicated to the Martyr Philemon was rebuilt in 663, followed in 691 by the construction of the basilica of St Sergius. At any rate, construction activity is attested in the countryside under the Umayyads in the bishoprics of Madaba and Pella. As in Umm er-Rasas, where the Church of St Stephen was built in 718 and a new pavement was added in the presbytery in 756 (Piccirillo and Alliata 1994), a church was built in 719–720 in Ma'in/Belemounta (Piccirillo 1989a). The mosaic floors at Umm er-Rasas and Ma'in/Belemounta displayed a series of towns flanked by donors; in the frame of the pavement of the central nave, cities in the Nile delta, Arabia, and Palaestina were depicted probably to emphasize the Christian identity and prosperity of the settlements under the new Umayyad rule. The lower Church of al-Quweismeh was erected in 717, the monastery of the Theotokos near Ain al-Kanisah was decorated in 762, and a mosaic-paved room was added to the south wing of the large cenobitic Monastery of Mar Liyas near Ajlun in 775–6 thanks to the generosity of the pulse merchant John and his family (Piccirillo 2007b). On the other hand, urban churches dated to the same period are extremely rare; the only case so far is the Theotokos Church, built in Madaba in 767 (Piccirillo 1989a).

Important information is contributed by the papyri recently discovered in the Church of Petra, which cover property rights, tax responsibilities, several types of negotiated contracts, and methods of settling disputes. Though the texts discuss mainly family business, one may surmise that the higher classes of 6th century Petra were not very different from their contemporaries in other cities of

Palaestina and Arabia (Fiema 2002). The papyri show evidence of a vital economy that included farmhouses, gardens, vineyards, orchards, and several agricultural installations, such as cisterns, threshing floors, stables, and water channels. Produce included wine, grain (mostly wheat), and fruit, while farming methods include the intensive use of terracing and *wadi* cultivation. The territories of Arabia and Palaestina Tertia had important cenobitic monasteries connected to holy sites and located along pilgrim routes. Such were the monasteries of Mar Liyas dedicated to the Prophet Elijah (Piccirillo 2007b), the Memorial of Moses on Mount Nebo (Piccirillo 1992, 1998), and the monastery of St John the Baptist at Ainon-Saphsaphas (Hamarneh and Roncalli 2009), St Aaron near Petra (Fiema and Frösén 2008), and the Sanctuary of Lot at Deir Ain Abbata (Politis 2010). The earliest of the above-mentioned monasteries is probably that of Ainon-Sphsaphas, built on the eastern shore of the Jordan river and connected with the traditional site of Christ's baptism. According to the pilgrim Theodosius, who visited it in 530, a church was erected there by Emperor Anastasius I (491–518).The care of the shrine and of the needs of pilgrims were assured by a monastic community that had received from the imperial treasury five golden *solidi* (Roman and Byzantine gold coin weighing c.4.5 grams) as an endowment (Piccirillo 2000: 84–85; Hamarneh and Roncalli 2009: 199).

GUIDE TO FURTHER READING

For general orientation on late Roman history, see Jones (1964). Kaplan (1992) is a general overview of economy and society in Byzantium from the 6th through the 11th century, while Mango (1986) and Saradi (2006) present surveys of Byzantine architecture and cities, respectively. More specific regional studies include Foss (1990) on the history and archaeology of Byzantine Asia Minor, Sivan (2008) on Byzantine Palestine, and Piccirillo (2002) on the Christian population of the Roman province of Provincia Arabia. Bowersock (2006) provides an excellent review of the use of mosaics as historical sources.

CHAPTER FIFTY-SEVEN

The Sasanian Empire: An Archaeological Survey, c.220–AD 640

Ali Mousavi and Touraj Daryaee

1 Introduction

A large number of monuments, buildings, rock reliefs, inscriptions, and collections of coins and manuscripts have shaped our present image of Sasanian archaeology. The systematic study of material remains of the Sasanian period began in the 17th century with the exploration of monuments, rock reliefs and sites by European travelers (Huff 1986: 302) but it was not until the 1920s that the first archaeological excavation of a Sasanian site began at Ctesiphon in central Iraq (Reuther 1929a, 1929b). More fieldwork was carried out in Iran during the 20th century, resulting in a better understanding and interpretation of Sasanian material culture. Regional survey in southwestern Iran was initiated by Robert McC. Adams of the Oriental Institute (Chicago) in the 1960s and was later continued by Robert Wenke (1975–6). Archaeological explorations and surveys in Fars and northeastern Iran significantly enriched the body of evidence available on the archaeology of the late pre-Islamic Iranian empires.

Except for major monumental remains such as royal cities, palatial and religious buildings, and rock reliefs, the archeological evidence indicates regional diversity in material culture across the Sasanian Empire. This regionalism can be observed in pottery, building techniques, and settlement patterns, making the identification of Sasanian remains difficult. Only in southwestern Iran and central Iraq, thanks to the excavations at Susa, Ctesiphon, and other sites in Mesopotamia, is there a well-stratified corpus of artifacts that can be safely attributed to

---

A Companion to the Archaeology of the Ancient Near East, First Edition.
Edited by D.T. Potts.
© 2012 Blackwell Publishing Ltd. Published 2012 by Blackwell Publishing Ltd.

the Sasanian period. Despite the fact that the study of spectacular monuments has always dominated archaeological research programs, the major Sasanian sites have not all been fully explored and published. The first capital of the empire, Firuzabad, has been the object of limited archaeological investigations (Huff 1971, 1972, 1974); other large sites in southern Iran such as Darabgird and Istakhr are inadequately known (Morgan 2003; Whitcomb 1979). The destruction of important Sasanian sites in southwestern and western Iran, due to agricultural and urban activities, continues today. The sites of Eyvan-e Karkheh and Qasr-e Shirin were severely damaged in the 1980s during the Iran–Iraq war and the celebrated site of Jundishapur has been extensively destroyed by agricultural activities. Similarly, the waterworks at Shushtar suffer from the urban development of the modern town there. Most of the archaeological surveys concentrated in southwestern Iran and southern Mesopotamia have been surface reconnaissances for collecting potsherds, the study of which is based largely on the excavated materials from Susa and sites in the Deh Luran plain (Adams 1962: 116–19; 1965: 71–80; Neely 1974; Wenke 1975–6, 1987). Whereas these surveys provide an important body of information on settlement patterns, the utility of the data depends largely on the excavated ceramic sequence from Susa (the only site that has been extensively excavated), which had already lost its importance by the 4th century – i.e. early in the Sasanian period.

To date, the difficulty of presenting a satisfying picture of the archaeological remains of the Sasanian period has been addressed in two ways. Early attempts to tackle the problem were largely art historical, as illustrated by the pioneering works of L. Vanden Berghe (1959: 235–48), R. Ghirshman (1962), and A. Godard (1965), which emphasize architecture and minor arts, often at the expense of other types of evidence (e.g. ceramics, coins, and settlement patterns). The second approach consists of a regional study of the remains. This is reflected in the only comprehensive survey of the archaeology of the Sasanian period, by D. Huff (1986), and is probably the best way to handle the considerable quantity of archaeological evidence. With an emphasis on more recent research, surveys, and excavations, this chapter attempts to highlight some key aspects and recurrent patterns in the art and archaeology of the Sasanian empire as reflected in excavation reports and general syntheses.

2 Settlement Patterns and Cities

The bulk of our archaeological evidence on urbanization and settlement patterns in the Sasanian empire comes from the western and southern parts of the empire – i.e., Iran and Mesopotamia. In these regions, archaeological surveys and textual records bear witness to a series of intense urbanization efforts combined with the expansion of irrigation and large-scale exploitation of arable land. The urbanization project under the Sasanians brought about an influx of population from other parts of the empire. Both Middle Persian and later Islamic sources attest to intense interest in city-building projects on the part of Sasanian rulers. The *Shahrestaniha-ye Iranshahr* (*Provincial Capitals of Iran*), a Middle Persian geographical text completed in the late 8th or early 9th century, names cities across Central Asia, the Iranian plateau, and Mesopotamia, many of which were named after the king who built or rebuilt them – e.g., Weh-Ardashir, Adashir-Khurrah, Bishapur, Weh-Andiog-Shapur, etc. (Markwart 1931: 14, 19; Daryaee 2002: 20).

The urbanization project in southwestern Iran and Mesopotamia brought about a decline in rural settlement and migration to the cities, phenomena attested by archaeological evidence (Adams 1962: 115–116; Wenke 1987: 259; Neely 1974: 30). Population increase and urbanization were a direct result of planned expansion and economic growth promoted by the Sasanian government (Morony 1994: 227). As surveys around Damghan in northeastern Iran show (Maurer-Trinkaus 1983: 134–5, 1989: 135–41), the urbanization process does not seem to have dramatically affected other parts of Iran. Archaeological evidence suggests that the Sasanians continued to occupy earlier settlements, although settlement was more widespread and more uniform than in the preceding Parthian period. Shahr-e Qumis, the major Parthian settlement in the Damghan area, continued to be occupied throughout the Sasanian period (Maurer-Trinkaus 1983: 130–2, Figs. 2–3). Damghan's city wall was probably built in the late Sasanain period (Adle 1993) and the existence of a palace or manor house at Tepe Hissar shows that the area was densely occupied during the 6th and 7th centuries (Schmidt 1937: 327–350; Kimbal 1964). The Bronze Age site of Tureng Tepe was reoccupied and fortified in the Sasanian period. French excavations there uncovered a mudbrick fort, on the ruins of which a fire temple was later erected (Boucharlat 1985a; Boucharlat and Lecomte 1987: 25–30, 52–5). Excavations have been undertaken at royal and monumental sites in Fars and southeastern Iran, but there is a corresponding scarcity of archaeological surveys. Remains of the Sasanian period have been excavated at Qasr-e Abu Nasr, Shiraz, Tal-e Malyan, and Siraf on the coast of the Persian Gulf. Further east, at Tepe Yahya in the Soghun Valley (Kerman province), substantial Sasanian levels were excavated and a number of Sasanian settlements have been found between there and the Straits of Hormuz. At Gobayra the remains of a Sasanian settlement and a nearby Sasanian city have been identified (for a complete listing of sites, see Huff 1986: 303).

The Sasanian Empire also required a large urban workforce in order to develop textile, glass, metalworking, and other industries. The capture of Roman engineers, skilled workers, and craftsmen, and their deportation to newly built or older cities by Shapur I (mid-3rd century AD) brought a much-needed workforce into Iran and helped to alleviate a shortage of skilled workers (Wenke 1987: 259). The use of the suffix *Eran* or *xwarrah* ("glory") in the names of many cities suggests the ideological tendencies of the Sasanians as well, and reflects their concept of kingship (Gnoli 1989: 131). Thus, for the Sasanians, urbanization had both economic and political significance.

3 Cities of the Highlands

In Fars, a series of large, royal cities at Firuzabad, Bishapur, and Darabgird provide most of our archaeological evidence for settlement patterns in the heart of the empire. The layout of these sites consists of either a circular plan around a few central monuments (Firuzabad and Darabgird) or a geometric plan introduced by east Roman engineers (Bishapur). It should be noted that very few vernacular architectural remains of the Sasanian period are known. Surveys have been limited to the Marv Dasht and Mamasani regions. The extensive ruins of Istakhr, 5 kilometers north of Persepolis, were excavated in the 1930s without yielding any satisfying archaeological material from the Sasanian period. Small finds consist of pottery, fragments of sculpture and architectural decoration, and coins (Schmidt 1939: 105–125; Whitcomb 1979).

The castle of Ardahshir Papakan, founder of the Sasanian dynasty, at Firuzabad is probably the earliest building of the Sasanian period. Known as Qaleh Dokhtar, the structure is a well-defended fortress on a plateau 150 meters above a bend in the Firuzabad river. It controls the main access to the plain of Firuzabad, which Ardashir had chosen as the nucleus of his emerging empire. The main structure stands on the highest point of the plateau and consists of a square, domed hall with side rooms and an *eyvan* (or *iwan*, barrel vault). The structure, the first known of its kind in Iran, is not the residence of an undisputed great king, but the splendid and powerful castle of an ambitious usurper, still fighting for supremacy in Iran (Huff 2008: 42; 2009: 83–4). The new king had two large reliefs carved on the opposite bank of the river Tangab: one depicts his investiture, while the other is a long panel representing a victorious combat against the last Parthian king, Artaban, in which Ardashir's son and successor, Shapur, is also shown along with another Sasanian knight (Vanden Berghe 1983: 62–6, figs. 8–9).

The first true Sasanian city is Adashir-Khurrah ("divine glory of Ardashir"), modern Firuzabad, the former Shahr-e Gur, founded in the very early years of Ardashir's reign, c.220. The site is located in the northern part of the plain near the eastern bank of the Firuzabad river, about 5 kilometers from the exit of the gorge that controls access to the plain. The circular city, 8 kilometers in diameter, was laid out on a concentric master plan and is a masterpiece of ancient surveying skills (Huff 2008: 45). The walls of the city form a perfect circle 1.85 kilometers in diameter, within which is a circular inner area that included, among other buildings, a central tower (known as the *tarbal*) and a square structure, the Takht Neshin, probably a fire temple. The outer area was divided by radiating streets, with two main axes, into 20 sectors. The city was encircled by a wide ditch (Huff 1974: 157–8), still visible today, that was fed by a deep canal. The radiating sectors and main axes extended beyond the city walls into the countryside, resulting in an intricate pattern of paths with the city as its center. The standing remains of Firuzabad show that Ardashir not only built a city, but that he carried out a program of hydraulic works and land division all over the plain (Huff 1974: 160), confirming later literary tradition. According to the 10th century historian Istakhri, the Firuzabad plain had been a swamp or lake, which Ardashir had to drain before he could build his new city (Le Strange 1905: 255; Mostafavi 1978: 66). The question of water is also addressed in both the *Karnamak-e Ardashir-e Babakan* and *Farsnama* of Ibn Balkhi (Huff 1974: 161; Le Strange and Nicholson 1921: 137–8).

Ardashir's palace was built close to the city, next to a spring rising in the center of a pool, and has been studied many times (e.g. Flandin and Coste 1843–54/I: Pls. 39–43; Herzfeld 1936: 96; Reuther 1964: 534–5; Godard 1965: 191–3). In the 1970s Huff carried out the most recent study of the monument (Huff 1972, 1974, 1978a). The palace covers an area measuring 103 × 54 meters and is divided into two main parts: a reception hall and a residential sector. The entrance is in the form of a great *eyvan*, a typical monumental gate with its opening in the center of the main façade, which gives access to three large, domed halls arranged side by side. Beyond the reception halls lies the residential sector arranged around an internal courtyard. The walls were all plastered. Stucco cavetto cornices above doors and niches decorated the main halls of the palace (Godard 1965: 190–1). The palatial complexes at Firuzabad reveal the earliest examples of domed constructions on squinches above a square hall. The buildings also show a widespread use of barrel vaults (*eyvans*) which became a diagnostic feature of Sasanian architecture (Godard 1965: 191; Huff 1993: 49). A reminiscence of this type of vault is particularly reflected in the building at Sarvestan. The date and function of this "Sasanian palace" are debated. Its layout does not correspond to that of a palace, and its advanced architectural forms and decoration suggest a post-Sasanian date (Bier 1986: 28–50).

In 2005 the Cultural Heritage Organization of Iran undertook brief excavations at Firuzabad (www.chn.ir: 5/2/2006) aimed at exploring the area within the city's circular enclosure. Three areas were selected for fieldwork: the area of the high tower (*tarbal*), the Takht Neshin or fire temple (*chahar taq*), and the palace. Research at the foot of the *tarbal* revealed traces of steps belonging to a staircase that once led to the upper levels of the tower. The most outstanding discovery was a series of wall and floor paintings depicting royal figures. Paintings, apparently found on coffins in a subterranean tomb near the *tarbal*, show the busts of two young women, a young man, and a boy. The style and treatment of these paintings reflects the influence of Parthian art still in force in the early years of the Sasanian Empire. It has been suggested that the figures are Sasanian princes or dignitaries.

After the overthrow of the Parthians, Ardashir transferred his capital to Ctesiphon on the Tigris, in central Iraq, where the Parthians and Seleucids before them had their capital city. Little is known of Parthian and early Sasanian

Ctesiphon. The locality is known in Arab sources as Al-Mada'in ("the cities"). The oldest part was the walled city on the east bank of the Tigris, which the Arabs called the Old City (*al-madina al-atiq*). Here the royal residence or White Palace (*al-qasr al-abyaz*) was located (Kröger 1993: 447; Morony 2009). To the south of Ctesiphon lay the sprawling, unwalled residential district of Aspanbar, where the great *eyvan*, baths, treasury, game preserve, and stables were located (Fiey 1967: 28). Excavations in Choche on the west bank of the Tigris revealed the remains of Ardashir's new capital, Veh-Ardashir ("the beautiful city of Ardashir"), which occupied c.700 hectares (Gullini 1966: 26; Negro Ponzi 2005: 150–2, 157–8). During the Sasanian period Ctesiphon developed into a sprawling metropolis consisting of a series of cities and suburbs along both banks of the Tigris, hence the name Al-Madai'n (the cities). In 1616 the Italian traveler Pietro Della Valle correctly identified these ruins with Ctesiphon, describing them in some detail and measuring them by pacing out the remains (Invernizzi 2005: 196–7). Excavations by German and Italian teams have revealed part of the fortifications, artisans' quarters, and residential areas.

In the mid-5th century the course of the Tigris shifted, dividing Veh-Ardashir in two (Gullini 1966: 36; Negro Ponzi 2005: 151–2). Owing to a series of repeated floods that disrupted the city's life, a new Ctesiphon developed on the east bank of the river, south of Parthian Ctesiphon, where the famous Sasanian royal palace with its enormous audience hall, known as Taq-e Kesra, stands. The French art historian Marcel Dieulafoy took the first photographs of this monument in 1883. These show the two lateral façades flanking the great *eyvan* (today only the central *eyvan* stands). The structure was part of a larger complex that included a corresponding building on the east side of a large courtyard. The standing monument consists of a large *eyvan* 43.5 meters deep and 25.5 meters wide, penetrating a blind façade that stretches 46 meters in either direction from the center line of the *eyvan* and was originally 35 meters tall (Keall 1986: 156). The floors and walls of the palace were decorated with marble, *opus sectile*, mosaics, and stucco sculptures. It has been suggested that the complex was built by Khosrow I Anushirvan (531–79), who decorated it with mosaics commemorating his conquest of Antioch (modern Antakya, Turkey) in 540. It is also possible that Byzantine craftsmen sent by the emperor Justinian I (527–65) were employed in its construction (Keall 1986: 157). Medieval historians and geographers described the monument as the most beautiful ever built of brick and plaster (see, e.g., the description by Ibn Faqih Hamadani in Invernizzi 2005: 9–10). In the 10th century, Tabari mentioned details of the throne hall and its amazing treasures that the Arabs captured at the time of the Islamic conquest, in particular a fine "winter carpet" with gold embroidery (Invernizzi 2005: 14–15).

Sasanian Ctesiphon was protected by an enormous city wall, 10 meters thick, the ruins of which, called Al-Sur, rise from the plain as mounds of various heights (Reuther 1929b: 451). Italians excavations at the site revealed the residential and commercial areas of the city as well (Invernizzi and Venco Ricciardi 1999:

42). The discovery of iron and glass slag, and a number of plaster molds, indicates the presence of workshops within the city. According to an early 7th century source prepared for the Chinese court, the population of Sasanian Ctesiphon numbered more than 100,000 households (Simpson 2000: 61). The city was conquered by the Arabs in 639, and gradually lost its importance to the benefit of the newly founded Abbasid capital Baghdad.

The circular urban plan seen at Firuzabad was later abandoned for a geometric layout or Hippodamian plan. Shapur I, whose victorious battles against the Romans were described and illustrated at Naqsh-e Rustam, intended to found a new capital city, this time in southwestern Fars. Bishapur or Veh-Shapur is another *ex nihilo* foundation in the western foothills of Fars. The city – as described in Shapur's inscriptions – was built by Roman engineers captured after the defeat of Valerian in 260 (Ghirshman 1971b: 11; Daryaee 2009: 7). Indeed, some of the architectural remains at Bishapur reflect the influence of these Roman prisoners, particularly the celebrated *eyvan* of Roman-style mosaics excavated before and during World War II by Roman Ghirshman (1962: 141–7, Figs. 180–6). Other architectural components excavated by the French include a fire temple and a spacious, cruciform palace with a huge cupola, the walls of which were probably decorated with mosaics and stucco. Half a kilometer to the south of the fire temple lies another building in which two votive columns stand. The inscription on one of the columns bears the name of Shapur and dates the building to 266 (Ghirshman 1962: 151). The city was well protected by a fortress named Qaleh Dokhtar (not to be confused with the fortress of the same name near Firuzabad) on its eastern side, giving access to a gorge (Sarab-e Qandil) where an important Sasanian rock relief of Bahram II was carved (Hermann 1983: Pls. 33–40). The northern edge of the city was protected by the Shapur river, while a thick city wall enclosed its southern and western sides. An Iranian team, under A.-A. Sarfaraz, excavated portions of the northern city wall where the river imposed an irregular boundary on the otherwise rectangular city plan (Sarfaraz 1970). The wall was punctuated by an evenly spaced series of rounded towers at intervals of less than 1 meter, a technique that may have been derived from an ancient model known in the Roman Empire, but whether this reflects the work of Roman prisoners or not is unknown. Recent excavations of the Governor's Palace, dated to the late 7th century, and an early Islamic bath (Mehryar 2000: 58–60, 70–81) suggest that Bishapur continued to be occupied after the fall of the Sasanian Empire.

4 The Lowland Settlements: Shushtar, Jundishapur, Eyvan-e Karkheh, Susa, and Mesopotamia

The Sasanians, whose economy depended largely on agriculture, developed large irrigation systems in Iran and southern Mesopotamia. Waterworks from this period, especially bridges and dams, can be seen in Khuzestan and Fars. Bridges were necessary for crossing the major rivers in Khuzestan (Karun, Karkheh, and Ab-e Diz) and it is here, too, that most of the known canals, tunnels, and mills are located. The focal point of this activity was at Shushtar, where a number of waterworks built in the Sasanian period, such as the Shadorvan weir (see below), still function. Road construction was also related to the improvement and exploitation of watercourses in the region.

Besides putting them to work on the construction of Bishapur, a number of Roman prisoners were employed by Shapur I (c.240–72) in the construction of waterworks, dikes, and weirs at Jundishapur, Shushtar, and Dezful. Some of these were described by medieval Arab and Persian historians and geographers (Le Strange 1905: 235–6), but none has yet been the object of thorough investigation save for the pioneering survey by Graadt van Roggen (1905), the Dutch engineer of the French Delegation at Susa, who explored the hydraulic structures of Susiana in the early 1900s. The World Heritage nomination file of the Shushtar waterworks presented to UNESCO in 2009 provides a complete list of the Sasanian-era hydraulic structures (bridges, dams, canals, watermills, etc.) in the region.

Shushstar is situated on a cliff at the northern extremity of an island formed by the Karun River to the west and the Ab-e Gargar canal on the east (Curzon 1882: 371–87). Its position offers considerable commercial and strategic advantages. The town has long been celebrated for a number of major waterworks there. The Ab-e Gargar canal (the Mashreqan of medieval sources) ran from the left bank of the river (about 500 meters north of the town) southward along the east side of the Shushtar cliffs, before rejoining the Karun at Band-e Qir. The great barrage called Band-e Qaysar or Band-e Valerian (the "dike of Caesar/ Valerian"), also known as Band-e Mizan, runs across the principal arm of the river, which is here called the Shuteit. It is located east of the town and is about 350 meters long. This barrage supports a bridge that connected the town with the west bank. It is still extant, although there is now a considerable gap in it. The Mian Ab canal begins above the barrage in the form of a tunnel cut out of the rock on the western side of the town. It turns southwards and irrigates the land south of the town. In Shushtar, part of the riverbed was leveled and paved with stones by order of Shapur, and called in consequence Shadorvan (Curzon 1882: 374; Kramers and Bosworth 1996: 512). Aside from its roles in irrigation and flood control, the Shadorvan bridge-dam also functioned as a city gate in the road from Shushtar to other towns like Dezful. In order for the dam to be built, the riverbed was emptied, its water diverted into a diversion canal. Afterwards, construction progressed in a multi-staged procedure with the building of temporary dams (Roggen 1905: 183–4).

Jundishapur is a site of extensive ruins c.14 kilometers southeast of Dezful. Both it and Eyvan-e Karkheh (see below) have a similar plan. Today the site consists of a series of mounds in a vast quadrilateral measuring 3,400 × 1,500 meters. In the 1930s Ghirshman studied the remains of the city and noted that it had been built like a Roman military fort: a rectangular walled city, with the longer northern and southern sides c.2 kilometers long and the shorter eastern side 1 kilometer long, and streets arranged in a grid system, just as Hamza Esfahani (894–970) described it (Ghirshman 1971b: 138; Shahbazi 2002). In 1963, on behalf of the Oriental Institute (Univ. of Chicago), Robert McC. Adams and Donald P. Hansen undertook soundings in the ruins, recognizing the "rectangular outline of the city" and "a grid pattern suggesting regularly placed intersecting streets" on aerial photographs (Adams and Hansen 1968: 55–62). None of the soundings produced "positive findings of inherent importance" in that they did not yield any significant Sasanian remains, other than pottery (Adams and Hansen 1968: 55).

The vast city of Eyvan-e Karkheh was founded to the northwest of Susa by Shapur I. With its rectangular shape (4 × 1 kilometers) and its impressive remains of a monumental *eyvan*, the site soon attracted the attention of French archaeologists working at Susa. Dieulafoy took the first and still best published photographs of the ruined *eyvan* in 1884 (Dieulafoy 1884–9/V: Pls. 7–9). Ghirshman undertook soundings at the site in the fall of 1950 and published a succinct report on his work (Ghirshman 1951: 296–7). Excavations in the southeastern part of the palatial complex uncovered two of four halls, each 30 meters long and 6 meters high. Other trenches near the city walls revealed semi-circular towers reinforcing a massive, 8 meter thick wall. Another trench in the central mound revealed the remains of a triple *eyvan* of baked brick, the walls of which must have supported a vault 12 meters high and 8 meters wide. The walls were probably decorated with painted frescoes over plaster (Ghirshman 1951: 294; Gyselen and Gasche 1994). Illustrations of the finds have never been published in full. Adams' survey of the region in the early 1960s confirmed that these new foundations, Jundishapur and Eyvan-e Karkheh, both depended heavily on intensive irrigation and water management for their livelihood. In addition, a series of vented tunnels were dug specifically for Jundishpur as an alternative source of water. Adams suggested that their construction may have been related either to an increasing need for water in the summer, or to the need for assuring winter irrigation during periods when the weirs near Dezful were inoperative due to washouts (Adams 1962: 118). Adams also produced a map of Jundishapur from aerial photographs (Adams 1962: Fig. 7). This is particularly valuable given the regrettable fact that the site was largely destroyed in the early 1980s during the Iran–Iraq War. Wenke surveyed these sites and their environs in the 1970s, concluding that an increase in population density accompanied the rebuilding of Eyvan-e Karkha around 525 by the late Sasanian king Kavad I (Wenke 1975–6: 137–8).

Ghirshman also explored the Sasanian remains at Susa in his large trench A in the Ville Royale (Boucharlat 1987a: 359–60; 1993: 44–5; Vallat 2002: 516–17). Sasanian remains were found in three levels. Level V contained destruction layers corresponding to the Partho-Sasanian conflict in the early 3rd century. Level IV dated to 341 when Shapur II (309–79) captured the city and persecuted its inhabitants. This was capped by an important destruction layer containing a number of graves, jar burials for infants, and bronze crosses, attesting to the Nestorian Christian presence in the city so well attested in literary sources. For the excavator, this was clear evidence of the massacre and destruction ordered by Shapur II. Level III, dated to the 5th–6th centuries, including a dozen inscribed bullae mentioning the name of the city and province. Coins were rare at Susa. Most were found in hoards, but unfortunately almost all (96 percent) date to the reign of one king, Khosrow II (591–628).

Excavations in the 1970s in the Ville Royale, *chantier* II, provided an almost continuous sequence of occupation from the 2nd millennium BC to the late Parthian period, followed by a hiatus until the Islamic era (Boucharlat 1987a: 359). Archaeological evidence and textual records point to a city in decline as early as the 3rd/4th century and a revival in the late Sasanian period. As Boucharlat noted, with the foundation of new, competing settlements such as Jundishapur and Eyvan-e Karkheh, Susa was marginalized. Moreover, Susa's decline was also exacerbated by the deliberate actions of some kings, like Shapur II, who destroyed Susa in 341 (Boucharlat 1987a: 363). The use of adjacent areas to boost agricultural production was also prominent in the late Sasanian period, as can be seen by the evidence of agricultural intensification in the Deh Luran plain to the north of Susa (Neely 1974).

Sasanian levels have been reported at Mesopotamian sites such as Babylon and Uruk, but the best-known architectural remains were found at Kish, where five domestic structures were excavated, three of which were well-preserved buildings with abundant stucco decoration, including a bust of king Peroz (457–84). These buildings have very distinctive layouts with columned halls, *eyvans*, and rooms arranged around a central courtyard and basin. They have been dated to the 5th century AD or later (Watelin 1964; Moorey 1978: 122–4, 141–2).

5 Fire Temples and Sanctuaries: Takht-e Suleiman, Bandian, Mele Hairam, and Kuh-e Khajah

Sasanian religious remains and cult buildings consist mostly of fire temples, a large number of which are still visible in Iran; fire altars; *dakhmas* (circular "towers of silence" for the exposure of corpses and their excarnation); and ossuaries. The most significant of these remains is the *chahar taq* – a building with a central domed square and four arches. Fars is dotted with numerous *chahar taqs* from Darab and Bishapur in the south to Yazd-e Khast in the north. These monuments have been frequently explored (Godard 1938; Vanden Berghe 1961, 1965, 1984; Schippmann 1971; Huff 1998; Boucharlat 1985a, 1999).

The most distinguished of all fire temples is the religious complex at the World Heritage site of Takht-e Suleiman in Azarbaijan. This impressive site lies 30 kilometers north-northeast of Takab, at an elevation of c.2,200 meters above sea level, on top of a 60 meter high natural hill situated in a broad mountain valley. The hill was built up by the sedimentation of calcium-rich water, the overflow of a thermal spring-lake located on the site. Its growth was only interrupted when the overflow was conducted away from the hill by artificial canals. Occupied sporadically between the 4th century BC and the 4th century AD, Takht-e Suleiman became the site of monumental structures in the second half of the 5th century. Literary sources and archaeological finds identify these buildings as the ruins of the fire temple of Atur Gushnasp ("fire of the stallion"), one of the three most revered Zoroastrian fire sanctuaries in the Sasanian empire (Naumann 1965: 25; 1977: 70–1, Fig. 47; Huff 1978b: 778). Medieval geographers and travelers such as Abu Dalaf, who left a detailed description of the site in the 10th century, knew it by the name of Shiz (Naumann 1965: 23; Huff 2004: 462). Sir Robert Ker Porter published the first modern description of the site following his visit there in 1818 (Ker Porter 1822: 556–62). In the account of his journey from Tabriz to Takht-e Suleiman, Henry C. Rawlinson described the ruins in detail, but erroneously identified them with the Median capital Hagmatana/Ecbatana (Rawlinson 1840: 47–54). In the early 20th century, A.V. Williams Jackson published a thorough description of the ruins, collecting all medieval sources describing the site (Williams Jackson 1906: 124–43). In 1937 Arthur Upham Pope and members of the American Institute for Iranian Arts and Archaeology briefly surveyed Takht-e Suleiman (Pope et al. 1937). Their report served as the basis for V. Minorsky's fascinating, but now refuted, thesis that Takht-e Suleiman may have been the Parthian site of Phraaspa captured by the Romans in 36 BC (Minorsky 1944). Between 1959 and 1978 the German Archaeological Institute in Tehran carried out several seasons of meticulous excavations, resulting in the correct identification of the site as Sasanian Ganzak, with its fire temple Atur Gushnasp.

Takht-e Suleiman consists of an oval platform, c.350 × 550 meters, rising c.60 meters above the surrounding valley. It has a small, calcareous artesian well that has formed a lake 120 meters deep. From here, small streams bring water to the surrounding lands. The temperature of this deep, mysterious lake is 21°C. It is the focal point of the site and its existence was without doubt the reason for the construction of the Sasanian fire temple and palaces there (Naumann 1965: 24; Huff 2004: 462). The lake is also an integral part of the layout of the monumental complex and was surrounded by a rectangular "fence." To the north are the Sasanian sanctuary and its components, flanked originally by two monumental *eyans* (only a single wall of which remains today). The sanctuary was enclosed by a massive, 13 meter high stone wall with 38 towers and two entrances (north and south). This wall was apparently of mainly symbolic significance, as no gate has been discovered. The main buildings are on the north side of the lake, forming a square around a square, baked brick Zoroastrian fire temple in the center. To the east of the temple is another square hall reserved for the "everlasting fire." The royal residences are situated to the west of the temples. In the northwest corner of this once enclosed area are the ruins of the Western *eyvan*. In front of the southern entrance of the temple (southern *eyvan* of the temple complex) is a rostrum with a monolithic stair at the eastern side. The blocks of hewn stone are worked in a careful manner which is not found in any of the other buildings, suggesting that it is most probably the king's *takht* or throne, reminiscent of Khosrow II Parviz's (590–628) celebrated Takht-e Taqdis (Naumann 1977: 42–3, Figs. 20–21; Huff 1978b: 786).

Takht-e Suleiman was destroyed by the Byzantine army in 627 as a countermeasure to a Sasanian attack on Byzantine territory (Naumann 1977: 69). The site was revived in 1256 when it became the summer palace of the Mongol ruler, Abaqa. In the past decade, limited excavations were undertaken by the Cultural Heritage Organization of Iran, but no substantial report has yet been published. Dozens of seal impressions and bullae were reported to have been found near the northern city gate (Moradi 2003). Some 8 kilometers northeast of Takht-e Suleiman, on top of the Belqeys mountain, are the remains of a fort known as Takht-e Belqeys. Measuring 60 × 50 meters and built of yellow sandstone, the fort was explored by the German team working at Takht-e Suleiman. It may have been an outpost associated with the defense of the fire temple situated 1,000 meters below (Naumann 1977: 115–18).

Probably the most outstanding Sasanian discovery of recent times is the site of Bandian, 2 kilometers northeast of Dargaz in northern Khorasan, where archaeological remains were revealed by agricultural activities in 1990. Excavations carried out by M. Rahbar (1994–9) under the auspices of the Iranian Cultural Heritage Organization resulted in the discovery of an important architectural ensemble with a number of highly interesting stucco reliefs that decorated the interior walls of the main building (Rahbar 1997, 1998, 1999b). The Sasanians' desire to protect the northeastern frontiers of their empire from invasion provides the main justification for the presence of monumental and defensive buildings in this region. Such invasions are reflected in the written and visual records of the time, as the archaeological remains at Bandian have shown. The excavations uncovered three levels of Sasanian occupation, the second of which is the most important. Here a building was excavated measuring 20 × 21 meters, which included a columned hall, a fire temple with altar, and an ossuary. The main construction material used was *pisé* (packed mud). Mudbrick was also used to reinforce some of the structures and foundations. The stucco decoration on the interior walls of the columned hall is remarkably varied both in theme and treatment. The 33 meter long decorated panels cover the walls of much of the hall. The upper parts of the panels were not preserved, but it is possible to reconstruct the scenes depicted at Bandian through comparison with the decorated walls found further north at Panjikent in Turkmenistan (Rahbar 1999b: 64). On the northeast panel a standing individual is represented holding an incense burner, above which there is an inscription in Pahlavi. According to this text, the name of the person is Weh-Mihr Shabur who was apparently a high ranked official (Bashash Kanzag 1997; Gignoux 1998). On the central wall the decoration shows a fire altar placed on a platform; on each side of the altar there is an individual holding incense burners and sticks – another inscription was found here. The southwest wall shows a man holding a horse ornamented with necklace of pearls. A third inscription is placed on the body of the horse. There is also an investiture scene represented on the northern wall of the columned hall with four figures. To the right of this scene is a seated figure, which might be the representation of the king himself.

A layout similar to that of the Bandian complex was previously observed in a manor house at Hajiabad, near Darab in Fars, where M. Azarnoush's excavations in 1978 revealed an especially rich figural program. The stuccos of ladies in niches were interpreted by the excavator as evidence of a cult of Anahita. Busts attributable to Shapur II and Bahram Kushanshah led the excavator to date the building to c.359 (Azarnoush 1994). The house included a residential and a religious area. According to Azarnoush (1994: 50–1), the religious part of the building was meant to be decorated with stuccos, a project that was never completed. Other sites with rich, decorative stucco remains include Chal-Tarkhan near Rayy and Tepe Hissar near Damghan (Kröger 1982).

A building like that at Bandian was also discovered at Mele Hairam, near Sarakhs in Turkmenistan. Excavations carried out by a Polish team in 1997 revealed installations and a fire temple (Kaim 2004, 2006). The earliest phase of the building is Parthian and may be tentatively dated to the 2nd century. It consists of a main building, the access to which is through a large *eyvan* (7.5 × 5.2 meters). Two layers of wall paintings were found in the vaulted entrance, depicting a series of floral and geometric motifs. Inside the building were several small mudbrick platforms. The fire temple is a square room (5 × 5 m) with an altar in the center.

The monumental complex at Kuh-e Khajeh, 30 kilometers southwest of Zabol on an island in the middle of Hamun Lake, is the easternmost Sasanian building ever found. The mountain of Kuh-e Khajeh, situated 600 meters above sea level, has a diameter of 2–2.5 kilometers. The ruins, first reported by Beresford Lovett, a British army officer, were explored in 1915 by Sir Marc Aurel Stein, who claimed that "the extensive and well-known ruins situated on its eastern slope proved to be the remains of a large Buddhist sanctuary," a view that has not been entirely shared by other scholars (Stein 1916: 221; Kawami 1987: 20–5). The site was later excavated by Ernst Herzfeld who discovered a number of magnificent wall paintings. Further investigations were carried out by Giorgio Gullini in 1960 (Gullini 1964). Mahmoud Mousavi resumed excavations (1990–2) at Kuh-e Khajeh (Mousavi 1999a) with a view to restoration and the preservation of the mudbrick structures at the site. The complex consists of a large esplanade, access to which may have been by a steep path. Access to the Central Courtyard was via a monumental gate composed of a vestibule and an elongated hall, decorated with wall painting and covered originally with a mudbrick cupola c.8 meters high. Unusually, the lower part of the hall was made of baked brick, indicating its importance. The Central Courtyard (20 × 20 meters) is flanked by painted galleries, two *eyvans* and vaulted halls. To the north is the Painted Gallery that leads to the highest point of the site, where Herzfeld found frescoes depicting human figures as well as geometric and floral motifs. It is clear that the area underwent a number of changes. In view of the fact that there are two small mounds at each end of the gallery, Herzfeld reconstructed a double staircase, giving access to the gallery in the first phase; he then thought that in the second phase the front of the gallery had been changed, and envisaged a simple staircase in that phase. The new excavations uncovered only traces of a single, axial staircase perpendicular to the gallery. The mounded areas located on either side of the gallery may have been buttresses to strengthen the fragile mudbrick buildings. The excavations also revealed painted stucco in this area. Radiocarbon dates confirm Herzfeld's proposal of two phases, the earlier dated to c.80–240 and the later to c.540–650 (Ghanimati 2000: 145). Thus, the foundation of the monumental complexes dates to late Parthian or very early Sasanian times. The site was occupied until the late Sasanian period (Mousavi 1999a: 84).

6 Sasanian Fortifications and Castles: Gorgan Wall and Qaleh Zohak

Stretching from the Kopet Dagh mountains to the shores of the Caspian Sea, the mudbrick structure known as Sadd-e Eskandar ("Alexander's Wall") or Divar-e Gorgan ("Gorgan Wall") is at least 200 kilometers long and can be clearly seen in the northern part of the Gorgan plain, bordering the Turkoman steppe. This structure consists of a thick, mudbrick wall or embankment with some 33 forts of varying shape and size (120 × 120 to 300 × 200 meters) along it. The wall was built as a bulwark against invaders from the north, much like the Roman *limes* in Europe. As far as is known, the eastern end of the wall joins the mountain range at Pishkamar, 58 kilometers northeast of Gonbad-e Qabus. Any further prolongation to the east is doubtful (Adle 1992). The wall is at present 2–5 meters high and about 10 meters wide. A 3 meter deep, up to 30 meter wide ditch runs along the outer (northern) side of sections of the wall. The wall is constructed of both unbaked mudbricks (50 × 50 × 10 centimeters) and baked bricks (40 × 40 × 10 centimeters). In 1978, M.Y. Kiani excavated parts of the wall and one of the forts. He attributed its foundation to the early Parthian period, specifically the reign of Mithridates II (123–88 BC) (Kiani 1982: 38). A joint team from the Cultural Heritage Organization of Iran and the University of Edinburgh carried out three seasons of exploration and excavation under the direction of Eberhard Sauer, with the aim of clarifying the chronology of the wall. Radiocarbon dating suggests that it was constructed and expanded in the 5th century during the reign of Peroz (457–83) in the context of his wars against the White Huns or Hephthalites (Nokandeh et al. 2006; Omrani Rekavandi et al. 2007).

Qaleh Zohak is located 50 kilometers east of Mianeh in Azerbaijan. The castle sits on top of a high mountain surrounded by two rivers and is one of the largest fortresses in the region. First visited by Colonoel Monteith in 1830, Qaleh Zohak was later explored by M.T. Mostafavi, K. Schippmann (1967), and W. Kleiss (1973). It was excavated (2000–4) by a team from the local office of the Iranian Cultural Heritage Organization based in Tabriz. The complex is made up of two areas: a fort on the south side of the mountain and a palace on the north side. The most prominent remains are those of a *chahar taq* of baked brick measuring 8.5 × 8.5 meters and standing 9 meters high. The original height of the monument is estimated at 12 meters, including the crenelated upper part of the façade. The building was decorated with stucco and molded brick, fragments of which litter the foot of the monument. The existence of a columned hall is also indicated by fragmentary column bases that have often been compared with those from the Parthian site of Khorkhe in central Iran (Kleiss 1973: 172–8). Excavations have revealed stucco fragments and a series of wall paintings (Qandgar et al. 2004: 202–3). The finds tend to date the main period of the fortress of Qaleh Zohak to the late Parthian/early Sasanian period, although it continued in use during the Buyid and Saljuq periods (10th–11th century).

7 Rock-Reliefs

To date, a total of 39 Sasanian rock-reliefs have been discovered, most of which are located in Fars apart from one at Salmas, northwest of Lake Urmia (Vanden Berghe 1983: 67); six at Taq-e Bustan, near Kermanshah (Vanden Berghe 1983: 92–5, Pls. 36–40); and one at Rag-e Bibi in northern Afghanisatn (Grenet 2005). A relief of Shapur I at Rayy was destroyed in the early 19th century (Ouseley 1823: Pl. 65). The reliefs in Fars include nine carved below the Achaemenid rock-cut tombs at Naqsh-e Rustam (Schmidt 1970: 122–37, Pls. 80–95), two at Naqsh-e Rajab, 2 kilometers north of Persepolis (Schmidt 1970: 123–7, Pls. 96–101), two at Barm-Delak, near Shiraz (Vanden Berghe 1983: 80–1, 136–7), one at Guyum, also near Shiraz (Vanden Berghe 1983: 77, 137), six in Tang-e Chowgan, near Bishapur (Vanden Berghe 1983: 72–4, 131–4), one at Tang-e Qandil, 15 kilometers northwest of Bishapur (Vanden Berghe 1983: 80), one at Sarab-e Bahram, near Nurabad-e Mamasani (Venden Berghe 1983: 78–80, Fig. 10), two at Tangab, Firuzabad (Vanden Berghe 1983: 62–6, Figs. 8–9), one at Sar-Mashad, between Kazerun and Bushehr (Vanden Berghe 1983: 80, Pl. 29), and two at Darabgird in southeastern Fars (Vanden Berghe 1983: 72, 108). Most of these reliefs, placed high up on cliffs, were meant to be viewed from below, not frontally. This explains why individuals and animals are represented with their bust and head larger than the lower parts of their bodies (Haerinck

1999: 57). Some reliefs, such as the victory scenes of Shapur I, bear inscriptions in Middle Persian, but a large number are devoid of any text, and in this case the identification of royal figures is based on the crowns and other royal attributes of specific kings as represented on their coins (Vanden Berghe 1983: 60–1; Herrmann and Curtis 2002). Sasanian reliefs were highly personalized and their locations were significant. Locations such as the lower part of the cliff at Naqsh-e Rustam, the gorge at Naqsh-e Rajab, or the cliffs on the rivers banks of Tangab and Bishapur were favored because of their symbolic value (Canepa 2010: 114–16). No Sasanian relief is ever associated with the buildings of that period. As Herzfeld rightly pointed out some 70 years ago, painting was the source of inspiration for Sasanian rock sculpture. This is why the bas-reliefs stand independent of Sasanian architecture.

Most of the Sasanian rock-reliefs belong to the first 75 years of the period. After a gap of some 70 years, Shapur III (383–8) placed the panel depicting the image of his father and himself at Taq-e Bustan, near Kermanshah. The last rock-reliefs were carved more than 200 years later at Taq-e Bustan by Khosrow II (610–28). The reasons for this hiatus are unclear, but it seems that crucial political events such as royal investiture and military victories occasioned the realization of rock reliefs (Vanden Berghe 1983: 57–8). No major relief was carved after Shapur II, whose reign was marked by a number of military triumphs. Surprisingly enough, no reliefs are known from the reigns of Kavad or Khosrow I, whose reigns were also full of military exploits.

8 Ceramics

The pottery of the Sasanian period poses a number of problems owing to its diversity and lack of formal and decorative motifs. In the excavation of large settlements such as Ctesiphon and Bishapur, there has been a tendency to concentrate more on luxury objects and fine art (mosaics, stucco, glass, coins) than evidence for everyday crafts such as pottery. As a result, pottery assemblages from the excavations of important centers have been inadequately examined and published. The problem is exacerbated by the fact that Sasanian ceramics were mass-produced. There are fewer distinctive types and the lifespan of different vessel types varies from region to region (Trinkaus 1986: 49). There are also considerable differences in ceramic tradition across the Sasanian Empire, dividing Mesopotamia from the Iranian plateau and the northeastern frontier of the empire. R. Boucharlat and E. Haerinck published the first comprehensive regional study of Sasanian pottery (Boucharlat and Haerinck 1991). Their study shows a neat difference between the regions. In the lowlands, excavations at Susa provide the only stratified assemblage that is linked with the corpus of ceramics in Mesopotamia (Boucharlat and Haerinck 1991: 306). These assemblages are important for the dating of sherds picked up on surface surveys in Khuzestan.

The best-known type is a blue/green-glazed pottery, very common in Sasanian Mesopotamia but scarce on the Iranian Plateau (Huff 1986: 307). In Fars, a recent surface collection at Darab is said to include Sasanian ceramics, but these remain unpublished (Morgan 2003: 333, and n35). In some cases, as at Qasr-e Abu Nasr, in Fars, a meticulous re-examination of finds and excavation reports has produced interesting information with regard to ceramics (Whitcomb 1985: 47–40). The most distinctive Sasanian type in Iran and Mesopotamia combines simple decorative patterns, including raised bands, horizontal grooves, and wavy and cross-hatched incision, often from combs (so-called "comb-incised" technique) (Huff 1986: 307; Adams 1965: 131; Venco Ricciardi 1967: 93–4). Excavations at Khirbet Deir Situn in northern Mesopotamia yielded an assemblage of late Sasanian stamped ceramics, but this seems to be only a regional variant (Simpson 1996: 99–101).

The lack of a reliable ceramic typology for the Sasanian core areas creates difficulties in the identification of Sasanian sites throughout the empire and has led to detailed studies in the periphery of the Sasanian world. For example, in the Oman peninsula a thorough examination of excavated ceramics resulted in a primary classification of the ceramic assemblages from the Sasanian period (Kennet 2002). In the Merv Oasis, an analysis of the ceramics from various excavations enabled G. Puschnigg to distinguish three pottery groups which are representative of different phases in the development of Sasanian Merv (Puschnigg 2006).

9 Bullae and Coins

The Sasanians used stamp seals. Bullae (clay balls) were used to seal packages destined for caravan or maritime trade (Frye 1970b: 79, 84). Bullae with seal impressions provide insights into Sasanian administrative institutions and imperial organization both in the cities and in the provinces (Göbl 1971). This evidence throws light on the involvement of the priesthood in administration (Frye 1970a: 240; 1974a: 68; Gyselen 1989); the scope and degree of economic activity; who was in charge of these activities; and where they took place (Gignoux 1980: 299–314; Gignoux and Gyselen 1982, 1987). In terms of economic activity, we can tell that there was a vibrant domestic exchange, since bullae and seals often carry the names of cities, districts, or provinces. While there have been many publications of bullae acquired on the antiquities market, and hence of unknown provenance, at least four major storehouses of bullae have been excavated, including those at Takht-e Suleiman, Qasr-e Abu Nasr, Aq Tepe (Afghanistan), and Dvin (Armenia). Sasanian bullae have even been found at the coastal site of Mantai in Sri Lanka (Bopearachi 2002: 110).

Literary sources suggested that, administratively, four chanceries (*diwan*s) were created for the empire, a fact confirmed by the numismatic evidence (Gurnet 1994: 36–7). G. Gnoli suggested that there certainly was a military quadripartition as well, in which the entire empire (*Eranshahr*) was placed under the control of four generals (*spahbed*s) as a reaction to foreign incursions from the four corners of the Sasanian Empire (Gnoli 1985: 265–70). R. Gyselen (2001) corroborates the literary evidence on the military division of the Sasanian Empire in the 6th century and provides a wealth of information about administrative and military offices throughout the empire (Gyselen 2007).

The Sasanian imperial administration imposed standardization in weights and in the minting of coinage. The units and types of coins struck by the Sasanian government were the gold *denar* (from Latin *denarius*), the silver *drahm* (from Greek *drachma*), the silver *dang*, and the copper *pashiz* used in local, daily transactions. The use of copper coinage certainly indicates that during the Sasanian period, especially in its later stages, there was a move toward a monetary economy. While the increase in the use of copper and bronze coinage in certain parts of the empire attests to an increase in trade and governmental control, silver coinage was much more common. Among the coins, the most widely minted and attested in documents is the silver *drahm* weighing about 4.25 grams. From the time of Ardashir I we find coins with this uniform weight, which vary typologically. On the obverse, we find the portrait of the *shahanshah* ("King of Kings") along with a name and title, such as "Ardashir King of Kings of Eran whose race (is) from the Gods." On the reverse of the coinage is a fire alter, either alone or flanked by two attendants.

Until the late 5th century mint names were not put on Sasanian coins, making it difficult to gauge the activity and output of mints across the empire. While more than 100 mint marks are known, fewer than 20 mints produced the majority of coins that circulated in the Sasanian empire (Göbl 1983: 332). The situation prior to the advent of mint names on coins is unclear, but there may have been as few as three different mints in operation, mainly in Fars and in the capital Ctesiphon (Reider 1996: 10–11).

With the introduction of mint marks on the reverse and the regnal year of the king in which a coin was struck, we begin to have an idea of the periodicity of minting and of which mints were the most productive and stable. Certainly, those that were close to economic centers like Fars had a huge output which supported the Persian Gulf trade (Daryaee 2003: 1–16), while the mints of Media had much smaller outputs. In times of war, however, mint productivity increased enormously. Thus, during the reign of Khusrow II (590–628) a huge quantity of coins was minted, largely to finance the long war with Byzantium.

Sasanian silver *drahm*s were so well known that they were imitated in places as far away as India, clearly attesting to the economic power and/or prestige of the Sasanian Empire in the eyes of its neighbors. The purity of Sasanian coinage also gives us indications about mines and where coins were minted. For example, we know that coins produced in the northeastern part of the empire were purer than those from other regions and thus, even when coins lack mint marks, it can be assumed that those of particularly pure silver were minted from silver mined in this region. In fact, Islamic sources confirm that the silver mines of the northeast were heavily worked by the earlier Islamic dynasties which came after the Sasanians. Of these, none produced silver as pure as Panjshir in modern-day northeastern Afghanistan.

GUIDE TO FURTHER READING

A number of good works exist which provide general orientation on Sasanian history and archaeology. See, e.g., Schippmann (1990) and Daryaee (2008 and 2009). Sasanian political history is reviewed concisely in Frye (1983).

CHAPTER FIFTY-EIGHT

Christianity in the Late Antique Near East

Cornelia Horn and Erica C.D. Hunter

1 West of the Euphrates

Introduction

Ancient Christian archaeology in the Near East is a fascinating and challenging subdiscipline. In general histories of the field it does not readily receive the attention it deserves (Frend 1996). Both biblical archaeology and early Christian archaeology are in the process of overcoming misleading assumptions that have impeded the reception of data, one of which is that data derived from archaeological work supplements and supports historical reconstructions that derive from reading sacred or otherwise authoritative texts, primarily the Bible and writings of patristic authors. Yet such literature does not necessarily or intentionally present the historical situation. Not infrequently it offers interpretative constructions that may be idealized and tendentious. Therefore, Christian archaeology has to strive to take into consideration the widest possible network of ancient textual sources, Christian and non-Christian, to overcome the limitations inherent in the phenomenon of the (attempted) erasure of alternative voices ("orthodox" vs "heretical") and the tensions between literature and religious practice (Wharton 1995: Ch. 1; Snyder 2003: 15). The best approach to Christian archaeology is one of constant, inclusive, and comprehensive dialogue between material data, ancient texts, and methodological developments in the constituent fields (MacDonald 2001: 663; Humphries 2008; Jensen 2008: 104–7).

A Companion to the Archaeology of the Ancient Near East, First Edition.
Edited by D.T. Potts.
© 2012 Blackwell Publishing Ltd. Published 2012 by Blackwell Publishing Ltd.

Christian archaeology of ancient Syria

Ancient Christian Syria was home to numerous churches and monasteries throughout its villages and towns, both along the Mediterranean coast and in the interior, many of which have been surveyed and studied (Butler 1929; Lassus 1947; Tchalenko 1953–8; Tchalenko and Baccache 1979; Baccache 1980; Donceel-Voûte 1988; Tate 1992). Valuable insights for the history of the ancient Christian community, its liturgical practices, and its social context are to be gained from diverse evidence ranging from church architecture to floor mosaics and liturgical inventory. Liturgical objects like the 6th century silver "Antioch Chalice," possibly a lamp used in worship in the Church of St Sergius in Kaper Koraon, southeast of Antioch, have been singled out repeatedly for study (Jerphanion 1926; Strzygowski et al. 1936; Rorimer 1954; Milburn 1988: 263; Metropolitan Museum of Art 2006). The debris found in excavated churches in Syria frequently includes glass lamps, bottles, and goblets of such high quality that it is likely that this fine ware was used in church services. Glass lamps shaped in the form of goblets, either with handles or with a stem, were very popular (Watson 2001: 477).

Initially, Christian congregations gathered for liturgies, commemorations, and communal events in gardens, other open spaces, and congregational spaces, at times of a more confined nature, as for instance in the catacombs or in private homes, referred to in Latin as *domus ecclesiae* and in Greek as *oikos tes ekklesias* (Milburn 1988: 9–18; White 1996; Osiek et al. 2006). Recent study of villa churches demonstrates that this practice continued at least into the 5th century (Bowes 2007). The oldest excavated example of such a house church is at Dura Europos (Ch. II.52), a garrison town at the border between the Roman and Persian empires on the Syrian Euphrates (Rostovtzeff 1934; Kraeling 1967; Hopkins 1979; Matheson 1982). There, the Jewish synagogue and the Christian house church, which evidences a differentiated arrangement and formation of rooms on the first floor, can both be dated to 256, the year in which the Sasanians conquered Dura and permanently dispersed its population (Wharton 1995: Ch. 2; Piltz 2007: 4). Elaborate wall paintings, both in the synagogue and in the Christian building, point to an awareness of the power of attraction as well as revelation exercised by visual art, and both congregations, perhaps in competition with one another or by way of exchange with one another, availed themselves of this (cf. Wharton 1995: 59–63; Elsner 2003: 118–19). Wall paintings of New Testament scenes on the north wall of the Christian baptistery at Dura include the earliest known depiction of Christ, who is shown as a beardless youth, healing the paralytic (Milburn 1988: 11–12 and Fig. 4). The architectural style of the baptistery of the Christian house at Dura Europos antedates the square baptisteries that continued to be constructed at Dar Qita and elsewhere in Syria throughout the 5th and 6th centuries (Milburn 1988: 10).

The cult of martyrs and saints attracted flocks of pilgrims to sites throughout the Near East. In Syria, relatively small-sized martyr shrines could be found virtually everywhere (Butler 1929; Lassus 1947; Tchalenko 1953–8; Peña et al. 1987, 1990, 2003). In some instances the remains of reliquary ossuaries or badly deteriorated inscriptions on the wall of a tomb chamber are all that is left of these shrines (Hunter 1989b, 1991, 1993). The archaeology of sites related to the veneration of soldier martyrs (e.g. Sergiopolis, modern Rusafa) and pillar saints (Qalat Siman, near Aleppo) captures aspects of the hardships characteristic of Christian life in Syria.

Located southwest of modern ar-Raqqah near the Euphrates, Rusafa was a desert outpost of the Roman army on the caravan routes connecting Aleppo, Dura Europos, and Palmyra. When the Roman soldier Sergius was brought to the city for his execution, the Christians there quickly capitalized on his martyrdom and developed it into a significant pilgrimage site (Ulbert 1986; Fowden 1999). Of the city's two basilicas, one was erected around c.520 as a *martyrium* over St Sergius' grave (Dussaud et al. 1931: Pl. 75–7; Loosley 2003: 277–80). The change of the city's name to Sergiopolis illustrates the importance of Christian pilgrimage for the development of the city's identity. In a frontier town marked by the daily realities of trade and defense, the *martyrium* of St Sergius invited the meeting and exchange of cultures. Thanks to Justinian I's (527–65) building program the whole area was enclosed behind a c.12 meter high wall. Thus the complex also offered protection against invaders (Krautheimer 1986: 274; Bowes 2008: 593).

The Syrian landscape was home to a fascinating and manifold tradition of ascetic life. Both within and in close proximity to well-populated towns and villages, monastic sites flourished. G. Tchalenko (1953–8) found evidence of monasteries as manifestations of communal ascetic life in close association with churches located in towns. In the countryside, his surveys identified towers that were built or restored for the use of ascetics living in greater isolation. On the upper level, an anchorite would take up residence, while one or two assistants dwelt in a room on the lower level of the tower (Peña et al. 1980, 1983; Bowes 2008: 602). Christian Syria became especially famous for its pillar saints (Brown 1971) who lived primarily in the hinterland. Most prominent among them was Simeon the Stylite. At Qalat Siman in northern Syria, about 32 kilometers northwest of Aleppo, hosts of pilgrims could gather at his pillar. In 470 architects surrounded the pillar with a cross-shaped building, centering on an octagon with the pillar in its middle. The central octagon appears to have been left without a roof, leaving both the saint on his pillar and the pilgrims who approached him without immediate protection against sun and rain (Evagrius Scholasticus, *Church History* I.14 in Migne 1865: Col. 2459). Each of the four arms of the cross-shaped main church featured a basilica-style building with three naves, displaying three apses in the eastern basilica and narthices in the arms to the west and south (Krencker 1939: 13; Piltz 2007: 6–7). The pilgrimage complex at Qalat Siman also contained a monastery and a baptistery (Tchalenko 1953–8/II: Pl. 182;

Milburn 1988: 128; Wharton 1995: 79). Metal objects found in the area contribute to the reconstruction of the cultural and social profile of visitors to the site (Kazanski 2003).

The central Limestone Massif, east of Antioch, is particularly rich in remains of ancient churches featuring the *bema*. Within the Syriac-speaking architectural realm, the term *bema* refers to a raised platform, often horseshoe-shaped and located in the nave of the church (Loosley 2003: 29), that served predominantly for liturgical practices centering on the reading and exposition of scripture. Among the essential elements of the Syrian *bema*, Tchalenko identified the platform, base, chancel, access paths, bench, throne, and a kind of shelf for liturgical objects (Tchalenko 1990: 259). Many of these churches date to the 5th and 6th centuries, while the earliest examples belong to the late 4th century. Their remains have been the subject of intensive, interdisciplinary research (Taft 1968; Tchalenko 1990; Renhart 1995; Loosley 2003). Of particular interest for further study is the character of the *bema* as an archaeological, architectural, and liturgical monument of both continuity and difference across monotheistic religions in the Near East (Renhart 1995; Habas 2000; Loosley 2003: 30–2, 44–7, 86–8; Milson 2007: 102ff).

The Limestone Massif separated the Syrian littoral from the towns of inner Syria. Visual, formal, and spatial analyses of standing remains of secular and ecclesiastical buildings there point to a complex exchange between the architectures of domestic dwellings and churches as well as between architectural manifestations in urban and rural settings. Similarities as well as discontinuities and breaks can be readily discerned (Kidner 2001: 350). Archaeological data illuminate aspects of the process of Christianization of the region that are not readily apparent in texts.

Christian archaeology of Byzantine/Late Antique Palestine

Studies of Christian archaeology in Roman and Byzantine Palestine have primarily emphasized pilgrimage, asceticism, and the architecture and functionality of churches, chapels, and baptistries. The remains of more than 350 churches have been discovered and many scholars have attempted to present the evidence systematically and in an integrated fashion (Crowfoot 1941; Ovadiah 1970; Bagatti 1971b; Ovadiah and De Silva 1981, 1982, 1984; Bottini et al. 1990; Tsafrir 1993; Hoppe 1994; Patrich 1995: 477–9; 2003, 2006). Palestine featured various types of churches, ranging from memorial churches erected at sacred sites, to monastic churches attached to monastery complexes, and, most of all, regular parish churches, serving the worship needs of the general Christian population (Patrich 2006: 361). Of particular interest are excavations of ancient Christian churches in the Negev at Shivta, Rehovot-in-the-Negev, Nessana, Avdat, Elusa, and Mamshit (Negev 1974, 1989; Rosenthal-Heginbottom 1982; Margalit 1987). By uncovering several churches each at individual villages and small towns, the archaeological evidence has revealed that church construction throughout this region and elsewhere in Palestine was especially intensive in the 6th century (Patrich 2006: 361).

Surveys of archaeological evidence of ancient Christianity in villages have been conducted in a number of regions, including Galilee, Samaria, Judea, and the Negev (Bagatti 1971a, 1979, 1983; Aviam 1999). K. Bieberstein and H.Bloedhorn (1994) published an exceptionally useful guide to archaeological data for the city of Jerusalem up to the Islamic era. In a monumental work, R. Schick (1995) has assembled and analyzed the archaeological record for the history of the Christian communities in Palestine during the transition from Byzantine to Islamic rule in the 7th through early 9th centuries.

Pilgrimage was one of the prevalent phenomena of life in Byzantine Palestine. While not originally intended for pilgrim traffic, the monumental Constantinian churches in Bethlehem (Church of the Nativity) and Jerusalem (Church of the Holy Sepulchre/Anastasis) were host to many a pilgrim from the West, like Egeria, and the East, like Peter the Iberian (Horn 2006: 248–51). Other 4th century Constantinian churches include those found on the Mount of Olives (Eleona Church) and at Mamre (Church of Abraham) (Patrich 2006: 368–70). In the 6th century Justinian I's significant construction efforts added the "New Church of St Mary, Mother of God" to Jerusalem's sacred and ecclesiastical landscape (Avigad 1993).

Especially at the churches in the orbit of Jerusalem, archaeologists regularly unearth clay lamps, often with decorations and/or inscriptions that confirm their use by pilgrims in processions held at night at the holy sites or churches (Loffreda 1990). Archaeological evidence of the widespread popularity of pilgrimage to Palestine is plentiful across the Mediterranean world. It can be detected, for instance, in the form of *ampullae*. These small flasks, round in shape and flattened, were produced to hold oil or dust that had been brought into contact either with a holy place or with the relics of a saint (Milburn 1988: 263–4; Ousterhout 1990). On their return home, pilgrims took *ampullae* along as physical objects for commemoration. A valuable collection of 35 such flasks is now preserved in Monza and Bobbio, Italy (Grabar 1958).

A good number of pilgrims never returned home but instead stayed on at the holy places. They joined already existing monasteries or set up their own ascetic dwellings. The habitations used by such ascetics were diverse. The archaeological exploration of desert monasticism in the Judaean Desert is especially well advanced (Hirschfeld 1992, 2006; Patrich 1994). Structures based on caves or cliff formations are very common. Ascetics contented themselves with rudimentary dwellings of relatively small size. They used caves to construct churches, setting aside space for worship. Cliffs offered useful structures for *lavras*, a form of monastery that combined elements of temporary individual isolation with community-focused worship at regular intervals. Some *lavras* were constructed on a plain or in a hilly area. The Great Lavra of Saint Sabas, to the southeast of

Jerusalem, is probably the best-known example of this type of monastic establishment. In it, a network of paths connected the cells and communal buildings with each other and integrated these individual components into a closed, architectural entity (Patrich 1995: 487). Coenobitic (communal) monasteries in Palestine tended to be erected on flat ground, yet varied in their layout from planned, orthogonal layouts, found for example at the Monastery of Martyrius, east of the Mount of Olives (Patrich 1995: 487), to the more irregular floor plans of the Judean desert monasteries (Bowes 2008: 602). Archaeologists have explored or excavated at least 65 monasteries and monastic settlements in the Judean Desert and its fringes (Corbo 1955; Hirschfeld 1992; Patrich 1995). Evidence of monasteries elsewhere in Palestine is likewise plentiful. For example, new documentation has become available for the early presence of monks of international background at Gaza (Elter and Hassoune 2005) and at a Byzantine monastery in Umm Leisan, a Palestinian neighborhood southeast of Jerusalem (Horn 2006: 72; Mgaloblishvili 2007). It is challenging and difficult to determine the precise doctrinal allegiance of the worshipers who used a given church or chapel or of the monks who inhabited a particular monastery (Patrich 2006: 359–60). Some believe, for instance, that the remains of a 6th/7th century monastery at Tel Masos, east of Beersheva and southeast of Gaza, belonged to a so-called ante-Ephesian or "Church of the East" coenobium. Yet whether there is sufficient evidence to determine the anti-Chalcedonian/"Monophysite" or the "Church of the East" identity of particular monasteries or cemeteries in Jerusalem, Gaza, Eleutheropolis, the regions in between those cities, or around Jericho remains a matter of scholarly debate (Figueras 1995: 445; Dauphin 1998: 145, 259, 268; Sadeq 1999; Sadeq et al. 1999; Horn 2003: 124–6; 2006: 196–214; Hirschfeld 2004: 75, 85; Hoyland 2009). At other sites, such as Jericho in the Jordan valley, archaeologists were able to discover the remains of a so-called "Church of the East" hermitage.

Christian archaeology of Jordan/Arabia

The arrival of Christianity constitutes a significant phenomenon in the archaeology of Roman Jordan. Churches, cemeteries, and changes in iconographic representation during the Roman period bespeak the spread of Christianity into the area. Archaeologists feel comfortable in generalizing that many of the ancient churches in Jordan were erected on the sites of earlier Roman structures, which were reused or transformed (Freeman 2001: 451). In 365, for example, the Christians at Gerasa (modern Jerash) conducted a dedication ceremony for their Great Cathedral. For the building of this church, they had made use of a Roman temple that seems to have been built in the 1st century and dedicated to an unnamed deity (Freeman 2001: 450). Excavations at Tell Abila have brought to light the remains of a sizeable 6th century basilica, which appears to have been built on top of an earlier temple or church (Freeman 2001: 450–1). In other instances, Christians availed themselves of building materials taken from secular sites or from the worship sites of other cults, incorporating them into their own churches. This practice continued throughout the centuries. The 6th/7th century church on Jabal al-Luweibdeh, which seems to have reused materials from a secular or religious Roman building, is a good example (Bikai et al. 1994: 410–12). Quite likely, the church was dedicated to St George, a saint whose veneration is known in some cases to have replaced that of Heracles/Hercules (Freeman 2001: 450).

At some sites, archaeological evidence of Christian churches is plentiful (Michel 2001). At Gerasa, for instance, at least 15 churches, all dating to the late 4th–5th centuries, have been documented archaeologically (Kraeling 1938). The complementarity between archaeological and textual evidence at some of these sites is noteworthy. The Great Cathedral at Gerasa features a fountain that dates to the 1st or 2nd century. Some scholars do not exclude the possibility that this fountain was the point of reference for Bishop Epiphanius's comments on a spring at Gerasa that miraculously ran with wine once a year on the commemoration of the miracle at the Wedding Feast at Cana in Galilee (John 2:1–11; Wharton 1995: 73; Freeman 2001: 451). At Khirbet Faynan (ancient Phaeno), located further inland to the east of the Dead Sea, the discovery of the extensive remains of five ancient churches, three of which date to the Roman period, may be a witness to the importance attached by local Christians to the commemoration of Christian martyrs who suffered in their regions. Writing about Phaeno, Eusebius of Caesarea said (*On the Martyrs in Palestine*) that Christians (among others, the confessors Paulus, Nilus, Patrimytheas, and Elias) had been condemned to work in its copper mines (Cureton 1861; Freeman 2001: 452; Watson 2001: 470–1). This suggests that the construction of shrines for the veneration of local saints was an important part of Christian praxis and material culture, even if these sites, which are off the beaten path, were not patronized by pilgrims from abroad.

The full development of Christian archaeology in the regions of modern Jordan and northern Arabia is evidenced during the Byzantine period. The 5th and 6th centuries saw the construction of a multitude of churches that dominated the monumental architecture, especially in the cities of the Decapolis (Watson 2001: 467). Many settlements acquired churches of their own. In the area of Amman (ancient Philadelphia) numerous sites came to be noted only when the archaeological remains of ancient churches were discovered. About 56 kilometers northeast of Amman, the town of Umm al-Jimal once boasted 15 churches, roughly one for every 200 inhabitants. According to the Arabic sources, this part of the Hauran was well connected by trade with the Hijaz (northwestern Arabia) and Mecca in the 6th and early 7th centuries (Sartre 1987: 160–2; Watson 2001: 472).

The wealth of early Christians manifested itself in the lavish decoration of their churches. In Jordan, excavations have brought to light magnificent floor mosaics (Piccirillo 1993, 2001, 2003; Piccirillo and Alliata 1994). Particularly well known among them is the Madaba Map mosaic, decorating part of the floor of the city's basilica (Avi-Yonah 1954; Piccirillo and Alliata 1988). Floor mosaics have also been discovered in churches dating to the Umayyad period (661–750). Prominent among these is the floor mosaic of the Church of St Stephen in Umm ar-Rasas which, in a manner similar to the Madaba Map mosaic, focuses on geography, showing vignettes of villages and cities between Jordan and Egypt (Piccirillo and Alliata 1994; Piccirillo 2001: 674–5). In a good number of these mosaics in ancient churches, as well as in some synagogues, seemingly intentional and carefully executed disfigurations of living beings can be dated to the early 8th century (Piccirillo 2001: 675; Bowersock 2006: 91–111). The question of who was responsible for the erasure of recognizable features of animals and human beings on such mosaics is still debated. Quite clearly, however, the phenomenon points to discrepancies of opinion either among Christian co-religionists or between Jews and Christians, on the one hand, and early Muslims, on the other. This is one clear indication that mosaics are not merely archaeological raw material but serve as valuable documents of history (Bowersock 2006; on the comparative study of mosaics, see also Talgam 2000).

Sites east of the Jordan river were significant destinations of Christian pilgrims and excavations there have unearthed the remains of important pilgrimage sites (MacDonald 2009). The monastery and church complex commemorating Moses at Mount Nebo, as well as the related town of Khirbet al-Mukhayyat, represent only one set of such sites. Further sanctuaries, chapels, and monasteries in the region, like Ayn Musa, Ma'in, Massuh, and Abu Sarbut, have all yielded valuable treasures in the form of mosaics and ruins (Piccirillo 1993; Watson 2001: 468). Thermal springs, such as those at Livias, Ayn az-Zara (ancient Callirhoe), and Ba'ar (ancient Baarou) in the mountainous region along the eastern shores of the Dead Sea (*Life of Peter the Iberian* 118, 123–5 [Horn and Phenix 2008: 170–3, 180–7]; Clamer 1997; Watson 2001: 468; Horn 2006: 252–3;), were popular with pilgrims visiting the area.

Located about halfway between the southern end of the Dead Sea and the city of Aila (modern al-Aqaba) at the northern head of the Gulf of Aqaba, Petra is most famous as the capital of the Nabataean kingdom. By the end of the 4th century it was the capital of the Roman province of Palaestina Tertia. Given the limited textual information available, and based on assumptions about a lasting economic and political depression following the destruction of the city in the earthquake of 363, scholars once suggested that Petra was permanently abandoned by the mid-6th century. Excavations conducted in the 1990s, however, challenged this picture. At least three churches and chapels once offered Christians at Petra space for worship (Bikai 1996; Fiema et al. 2001: xii). American archaeologists have uncovered a church complex with magnificent floor mosaics that was erected in the late 5th century (Fiema et al. 2001: 218–332). Despite destruction by fire in the late 6th century, usage of this space, even if no longer as a church, continued well into the 7th century, if not beyond (Fiema 2001:

113; Fiema et al. 2001: 94–105). In the Petra church complex archaeologists discovered a large archive of carbonized Greek papyri documenting aspects of the economic and personal affairs of an extended family from 528 (or 513) to 592 (Fiema 2001: 114; Fiema et al. 2001: 139–51, 445–6). The attention of the members of that family focused less on urban business than on land holdings, farms, and residences in the countryside. Not long after the Islamic conquest, the metropolitan see was transferred from Petra to al-Rabba (Zayadine 1971: 75–6; Fiema 2001: 121; Fiema et al. 2001: 2). This was but one further indication that Petra's character as an urban center was in decline. Recent Finnish excavations have concentrated on Jebel Haroun, about 5 kilometers southwest of Petra. At this site, associated with the death of Moses' brother, evidence was detected for a large 5th century church that was possibly connected to the presence of ascetics or monks and pilgrims (Peterman and Schick 1996; Fiema 2001: 114; Fiema et al. 2001: 3; Fiema and Frösén 2008, 2009).

Excavations at Aila have unearthed a mudbrick building, tentatively identified as a church and possibly founded in the late 3rd or early 4th century. The excavated remains date to the later 4th century, when the building seems to have been destroyed by an earthquake. The identification of the structure as a church relies on the building's orientation toward the east, its layout, finds (glass oil lamp fragments) frequently associated with rituals, and the presence of a cemetery immediately west of the building (Parker 1998b). If the evaluation of the data is correct, the building would constitute the earliest building erected explicitly as a church anywhere in the world (Parker 1998a, 1999a: 151, 1999b; Watson 2001: 496).

Christian archaeology of the Sinai Peninsula

Beginning with Julian Saba in the 4th century ascetics settled in the southern Sinai (Theodoret of Cyrrhus, *Religious History* II.13 [Price 1985: 29]). A rich collection of textual sources combined with material remains forms the basis for the reconstruction of the history of ancient Christianity through the Byzantine period in the region (Caner, Brock, Price and van Bladel 2010; Finkelstein and Ovadiah 1985). Archaeologists have identified 72 sites on Mount Sinai, at Raithou, and in more remote locations that were inhabited by hermits or monks (Dahari 2000: 28–146, 167). Pilgrims to St Catherine's Monastery in the Sinai left behind lapidary inscriptions, primarily in Greek, Armenian, Georgian, and Latin (Stone 1982a, 1982b). The heyday of pilgrimage to the Sinai dates to the 6th and 7th centuries, when groups of hundreds of pilgrims visited at a time, continuing even after the Arab conquest (Dahari 2000: 164). Papyrological evidence has identified the Darb Ghaza ("road to Gaza"), starting at Nessana in the Negev, as one of the roads that took pilgrims to their destination in Byzantine times (Kraemer 1958: Nos. 47, 72, 73, 89; Meshel 2000: 110–11).

2   East of the Euphrates

Material evidence of Christianity in Mesopotamia

Oscar Reuther wrote in Arthur Upham Pope's magisterial survey of Persian art, "[f]ar fewer Christian churches built during the Sāsānian period have so far been found in the territory that was then Sāsānian than in the neighboring countries" (Reuther 1977: 560). In contrast to the "western" regions of Syria and the Levant, the earliest evidence is late, dating from the 6th and 7th centuries. This stems both from the dislocation and disruption that Christians experienced and from fact that the building materials used, particularly in southern Mesopotamia – mudbrick and baked brick – were less durable than stone, hence earlier structures have not survived. Excavations and surveys have identified churches and monasteries on the basis of diagnostic features and supporting small finds, such as crosses. These have led to a focus on the official presence of Christianity, over and above an appreciation of Christian domestic settlement and collateral questions relating to the participation of Christians within Sasanian society. Jewish and Mandaean vernacular clusters in the late Sasanian/early Islamic era have been pinpointed through provenanced discoveries of incantation bowls, principally written in Jewish Babylonian Aramaic and Mandaic, especially at Nippur (Montgomery 1913; Hunter 1997–8). A handful of incantation bowls include Christian formulae, especially the name of Jesus, but they are unprovenanced.

Seals and seal impressions are the most common personal items, indicating Christian ownership by specific formulae – e.g., "protection of Jesus" or "trust in Jesus" as well as proper names (Lerner 1977; Shaked 1977; Gyselen 2006b). However, many Christians bore Pahlavi (Middle Persian) names and are thus indistinguishable within mainstream Sasanian society. The cross, often in combination with other symbols, was commonly used, even though, on occasion, it may have had other, non-Christian meanings (Shaked 1977: 20–1). Apart from crosses, other symbols or subjects drawn from the Old and New Testaments were used (Lerner 1977; Gyselen 2006b: 30–9, 42–51; Gyselen 2007: 78–80, 83). Most seals and seal impressions are unprovenanced. However, at al-Hira stamped sherds with crosses and other motifs were found on the surface (Talbot-Rice 1932a: 69 and Fig. 22). A fragment of a plaster cross was excavated in an area of housing on Mound III (Hunter 2008: 50 and Pl. 4). A "small bronze cross with a loop at the top for suspension," possibly of Byzantine workmanship, was excavated at the mansion on Mound I (Talbot-Rice 1932b: 266). At Tulul al-Ukhaidir, 2.5 kilometers northwest of the Abbasid fortress of the same name in southern Iraq, a gypsum fragment with a four-line Syriac inscription was discovered (Finster and Schmidt 1976: 139–41; Hunter 1998: 635–8, Pl. 4) amongst Arabic *graffiti* and large quantities of Sasanian/early Islamic stucco, ceramic and glass fragments (Finster and Schmidt 1976: 80–150). The site also yielded a glass fragment with a cross enclosed in a circle (Finster and Schmidt 1976: 129 and Pl. 63g), similar in design to a pottery sherd bearing two stamp impressions (3 centimeters in diameter) of a cross with circles in the four quarters between the cross arms. This resembles a cross on a stamped sherd found at Thaj in northeastern Saudi Arabia (Langfeldt 1994: 47–8, Fig. 20).

Christian archaeology in Mesopotamia

The following discussion summarizes data on some of the main sites with Christian remains in Mesopotamia. Situated 60 kilometers northwest of Mosul, near the hamlet of Jebel Qusair, the church (23 × 14 meters) at Qasr Serej was gazetted by Seton Lloyd, noted by Gerald Reitlinger, and described by David Oates (Lloyd 1938: 136; Reitlinger 1938: 148–9; Oates 1968: 107–17; Lerner 1992: 529). The "small basilica of North Syrian type" there was constructed of carefully dressed limestone blocks (Oates 1968: 107). A central nave arcade consisting of wide arches springing from rectangular piers, flanked by aisles, terminated in the sanctuary, featuring an intact, half-domed apse and flanked by a *diakonikon* (Greek, "appertaining to the deacon" – the chamber south of the sanctuary where the sacred vessels were kept and cleansed and where the service books, vestments, and other necessaries of the Divine Service were held, corresponding to the sacristy in the western church) and a *prothesis* (the chamber north of the sanctuary, i.e. on the side opposite the *diakonikon*) which often functioned as a *martyrium* (a chapel housing the grave or relics of a martyr) on the north and south sides, respectively (Oates 1968: 107, plan 108). Entered by an archway that spanned almost the full width of the south aisle, the *martyrium* had rectangular niches in the east and north walls, as well as tapering windows, one above the east niche and one in the south wall. Another entrance in the west wall connected directly with a portico enclosing the north, south, and west sides of the church. Three windows pierced the west wall of the narthex, the largest intact one of which was located over the central doorway. A mid-6th century date is proposed on the basis of the hagiography of Ahudemmeh, which states that he had the church constructed as a copy of the famous shrine to the warrior-saint St Sergius at Sergiopolis (modern Rusafa, Syria), in a bid to curb pilgrimages into Byzantine territories by the Arab tribes who had recently become Monophysite (Fiey 1958: 126; Nau 1909: 6–52).

In 1928, the Deutsche Orient-Gesellschaft (German Oriental Society), directed by Oscar Reuther, excavated a church at the mound of Qasr bint al-Qadi on the western side of Ctesiphon (Meyer 1929: 23–4; Reuther 1929a: 11–15; 1929b: 449–451, Figs. 1–2; 1977: 560–1; Awad 1947: 105–7; Lerner 1992: 529). Built of baked brick set in gypsum mortar, the earliest phase was distinguished by thick, rounded columns on square bases standing close to the side walls, while a later phase had rectangular columned walls (Reuther 1929b: 450). No destruction

Table 58.1 Synchronic chart of Churches V and XI (al-Hira)

	Church V	Church XI
Dating	Late 7th to early 8th century	
Orientation	43° south from due east	41° south from due east
Layout	Tripartite, separated from main body of the church by massive piers	Tripartite, divided into 3 aisles by burnt brick arches standing on brick piers
Roof	Single span	Barrel-vaults
Floor	Burnt brick (26 × 26 × 5 cm) laid diagonally	Burnt brick (20 × 20 × 4 cm) laid diagonally
	Bema?	Bema surrounded by raised benches
Walls	Brick (replastered with lime-plaster) Undecorated.	Brick (5 layers white lime-plaster) Undecorated
Sanctuary	No apse	No apse
	Decorated: 2 levels: figurative, geometric	Decorated: geometric
Narthex	None, multiple doorways on northern side	None, two doorways on northern side

levels were found, suggesting that rebuilding might have been a result of financial endowment. The east end of the church culminated in three chambers: a *diaconikon* and a *prothesis*, flanking the sanctuary that had a straight, eastern wall instead of an apse. Four round holes in front of the steps leading into the sanctuary suggest that the church originally had a *ciborium* (a canopy resting on four pillars over the altar of a basilica; termed a *baldachino* in western churches) (Reuther 1929b: 450). An ostracon with a Syriac inscription was discovered under the floor of the sanctuary in the second phase (Kröger 1982: 48). The six-line text was possibly a scribal exercise. Written in black ink, it mentions the God of Abraham, Isaac, and Jacob (Kröger 1982: 48; Hunter 1997: 361–7 and Figs. 1–2; 1998: 618–26). Nearby were fragments of a three-quarter life-size statue of a garbed male, possibly a patron saint, made of painted stucco in high relief, demonstrating that the Church of the East embraced figurative art (Meyer 1929: 25 and Fig. 13; Reuther 1929a: 12 and Pl. 6; Kröger 1982: 48; Baumer 2006: 75). Pieces of painted and gilded ornamental stucco, some decorated with palmettes and zigzag patterns, were also found (Reuther 1929b: 450; Kröger 1982: 48). The patron saint of this church is unclear although Ctesiphon is known to have had several churches, including one dedicated to Mar Narkos, and a monastery of Mar Pethion, martyred in 447 (Streck 1917: 45).

Financed by Gerald Reitlinger and directed by David Talbot-Rice (Talbot-Rice 1932a, 1932b, 1932c; Awad 1947: 107–11; Fiey 1968/III: 206–7; Lerner 1992: 529; Hunter 2008: 41–56), the 1931 Oxford Expedition to al-Hira investigated

12 mounds in the northeastern corner of the site, nearest to the most ancient part of Kufa (Talbot-Rice 1932a: 51). On Mounds V and XI, two churches (designated V and XI, respectively) described as "long basilicas with three rectangular chambers at the eastern end," which were almost identical to the church at Ctesiphon, were excavated (Table 58.1). These dated to the late Sasanian/ early Islamic era (Talbot-Rice 1932b: 265). Only the northern side of Church XI was excavated, but both churches were similar in plan, oriented south of due east. Talbot-Rice surmised that small barrel vaults covered each of the three aisles of Church XI (Talbot-Rice 1932a: 57–8 and Fig.6; 1932b: 265 and Fig. 1). In each case, the sanctuaries had straight, eastern walls flanked by a *diakonikon* and a *prothesis*.

The sanctuary of Church V (Talbot-Rice 1932b: 279–81 and Fig. 2) was decorated with murals dating to two different periods: the upper portraying fragments of crosses and the lower depicting a bird and colored circles as well as a decorative floral pattern which Talbot-Rice dated to the 7th century, describing it as "more Sasanian in character, both in appearance and style" (1932a: 57). Small finds included "icons" or fragments of plasterwork crosses of East Syrian design. These belonged to two types: incised, with the incisions picked out in red pigment; and molded, with designs in high-relief (Talbot-Rice 1932a: 58 and Fig. 24; 1932c: 282 and Figs. 3–4; Okada 1990). Fragments of glass lamps "shaped like champagne glasses" and having "close relationships with Byzantine glass from Jerash" were also found (Talbot-Rice 1932b: 266; 1932c: 290). The floor and side chambers of Church V were made of baked bricks set diagonally. The walls were plastered with white lime-plaster.

The mudbrick walls of Church XI were coated with five layers of white plaster. In the sanctuary area a painted red cross was found in situ on the wall (now in the Ashmolean Museum, Oxford, where many of the finds were deposited; see Talbot-Rice 1932a: 58; 1932c: 280 and Pl. 2). As in Church V, the floor was paved with baked bricks, set diagonally. In the middle of it was a plastered mudbrick *bema* (Greek, "platform"), the raised platform in the nave of the church from which the lessons and scriptures were read and the sermon delivered (Talbot-Rice 1932b: 280; Fiey 1959: 76–8; Taft 1968; Cassis 2002). Benches were arranged on each side in an arc with a screen behind. A *sheqaqona* (a processional way) connected the *bema* to the sanctuary and featured 12 arches that may have originally contained statues of the Apostles (Maniyattu 1995: 333–4; Hunter 2008: 36 and Pl. 3). Plasterwork crosses or "icons" were also found at various points in Church XI (Talbot-Rice 1932a: 58).

A survey at Rahaliya oasis, 110 kilometers southwest of Baghdad, by Barbara Finster and Jürgen Schmidt on behalf of the German Archaeological Institute, documented a church (15.5 × 23 meters) (Finster and Schmidt 1976: 13, 40–3 and Fig. 13; Lerner 1992: 529). Built of stone and clay, it featured a triple nave punctuated by two rows of columns composed of three, free-standing columns and two half-columns attached to the western and eastern walls, respectively

(Finster and Schmidt 1976: 40). A stone barrier connecting the final pair of free-standing columns with the two half-columns attached to the sanctuary wall may be interpreted as a *sheqaqona*. Columns in the each of the four corners of the sanctuary suggest that it was originally domed (Finster and Schmidt 1976: 41). The sanctuary, which had a straight eastern wall, was flanked by a *diakonikon* and *prothesis*. The southern chamber had a mudbrick tub, "reminiscent of a terracotta sarcophagus," suggesting a *martyrium* rather than a baptistery, as Finster and Schmidt suggested (1976: 42). Associated buildings indicate that the site was a monastery, perhaps dedicated to a martyr or holy man. Judging by the late Sasanian sherds that were found, the church at Rahaliya probably dates to the 6th century (Finster and Schmidt 1976: 43; Lerner 1992: 529).

Finster and Schmidt also documented two churches of similar dimensions and layout at Qusair, 7 kilometers northwest of the Umayyad fortress of Ukhaidir, near Kerbala (Finster and Schmidt 1976: 27–39). Church A is identical to Church B, 1 kilometer away, that was partially destroyed when the nearby *wadi* shifted its course (Finster and Schmidt 1976: 35). These churches are distinguished by their long naves, in excess of 30 meters, a feature also seen in the Kharoba Koshuk church at Merv (Turkmenistan), dated to the 6th century (Finster and Schmidt 1976: 35: Pugachenkova 1967: 87; Puschnigg 1999). Church A culminated in a domed sanctuary (5.8 square meters) with an apse (3.23 × 1.35 meters) that had a small window (Finster and Schmidt 1976: 28 and Fig. 8). As at Qasr Serej, the sanctuary was entered via a triumphal arch "reminiscent of western, early Christian churches" (Finster and Schmidt 1976: 27). The north and south walls of the sanctuary featured two small windows and two small entrances, the latter possibly connecting to a *diakonikon* and *prothesis* (Finster and Schmidt 1976: 28). At the western end of the church a single doorway, flanked by columns, may have led to the narthex. The location of Church A, in the center of a walled compound, with various other structures, suggests a monastery site (Finster and Schmidt 1976: 37). A gate on the eastern side provided entry, the wall acting as a barrier against raids by nomadic tribes and future changes in the *wadi*. A late Sasanian date may be inferred from the architectural parallels with Qasr Serej as well as the surge of Monophysite activity in the region. Syrian Orthodox monks settled at the nearby oasis of Ain al-Tamr (Finster and Schmidt 1976: 35).

The University of Mosul excavated a church at Tell Museifneh at Imsefnu during the Saddam Dam Basin Salvage project. Oriented east–west, it was constructed of dressed stone blocks (Abbu 1987: 133–55 and Fig. 2; Okada 1992: 77 and Fig. 2). Set within a large courtyard complex, arcades, each with two arches sprung from a square column and pilasters on the eastern and western walls, divided the church into three aisles (Abbu 1987: 136, Fig. 4). The sanctuary, typically situated in the east, featured an apse, and was flanked in the north by a *diakonikon* and in the south by a large *martyrium* that extended beyond the south wall of the church. Entrances in the southern courtyard provided access, through a columned porch, to the church and the *martyrium*. Dated to the 7th century (Abbu 1987: 217; Okada 1991: 77), the architectural features of this church suggest that, like Qasr Serej, it was affiliated with the Monophysite tradition.

In 1972 the Japanese Archaeological Expedition to Iraq, directed by Hideo Fujii, located the site of Ain Sha'ia at the foot of the Kerbala escarpment, 15 kilometers west of Najaf. Preliminary soundings in 1986 were followed by two seasons of excavation (1987–8, 1988–9) (Fujii et al. 1989). Centrally located earthen ramparts enclosed a church built of mudbrick coated with gypsum plaster that had plastered floors (Fujii et al. 1989: 35–61 and Fig. 5). The nave was divided by pier-walls into three aisles that were punctuated by three openings aligned with the entrances/exits to the church in the north and south walls. The south wall opened onto a courtyard paved with baked bricks. The west wall of the church culminated in a narthex (Okada 1991: 73, Fig. 1). The church's orientation was not due east–west but was "deflected as much as 60 degrees to the north" (Okada 1992: 91). Painted gypsum fragments, with red, blue, and black geometric designs, were found in the sanctuary, the layout of which resembles that of the churches at al-Hira, Rahaliya and Ctesiphon (Fujii et al. 1989: 38). Gypsum plaques or "icons", similar to those at al-Hira, were recovered in various parts of the church (Fujii et al. 1989: 58–9, Okada 1990). At the southwest end of the central nave were 48 pieces of decorated or inscribed gypsum (Hunter 1989a: 95–105; 1998: 626–30). Two Syriac inscriptions on gypsum discovered near two chests or boxes, one within the other, built into the north pier wall, suggest the burial place of an ecclesiastical dignitary (Hunter 1989a: 92–5; 1998: 628–30; Fujii et al. 1989: 38–9). These were filled with mudbricks and crushed mud-stone (Fujii et al. 1989: 39). Their contents were possibly exhumed when the monastery complex declined. Similar boxes were built into the walls of Church XI at Hira, but Talbot-Rice's unpublished field-notes do not disclose whether they contained anything.

Plaster "icons," similar to those at al-Hira, were found at buildings 200–400 meters northwest of the church, suggesting that these were cells occupied by monks or pilgrims (Fujii et al. 1989: 72–3 and Figs. 34–5). The monastery complex was served by a *qanat* system (underground water galleries) that conducted water from the nearby spring, from which Ain Sha'ia derives its name (Fujii et al. 1989: 70–2). The Dukakin caves, 500 meters to the north, housed anchorites, indicating both eremitic and coenobitic activity at Ain Sha'ia. The hewn marlstone walls and ceiling of one of the caves were coated with chaff-tempered mud plaster (Fujii et al. 1989: 84). The floor of marlstone chips and baked bricks had a fireplace in the center and was littered with sherds. An ostracon with a Syriac inscription on both sides in black ink had quotations for the season of Epiphany from the *Hudra*, the liturgical cycle of the Church of the East (Hunter 1989a: 105–8; 1998: 630–5; Brock 2004). The posited identification of Ain Sha'ia and Dukakin with Deir Allaj, one of the most famous monasteries at al-Hira, remains speculative (Hamid 1988: 9; Hunter 1996: 80).

The wider context of Christian archaeology

The 1928 excavations of a church at Ctesiphon opened a new vista in the Christian archaeology of Mesopotamia and, to date, nine churches have been investigated in Iraq. Six of these are located near Kerbala and Najaf, revealing a singular concentration in an area that is now staunchly Shia. The sanctuaries of the churches at Ctesiphon, al-Hira, Ain Shai'a, and Rahaliya are all distinctly Mesopotamian (Finster and Schmidt 1976: 36) with postulated origins in Babylonian temple architecture (Talbot-Rice 1932a: 58; Awad 1947: 111). The affiliation of the churches with the Church of the East is confirmed by both epigraphic evidence and the iconography of the plaster "icons" at various sites. By contrast, the apsidal sanctuaries at Qasr Serej, Museifneh, and Qusair belonging to the Monophysite tradition affirm that the two branches of Syriac Christianity adopted distinctive architectural norms, just as they adopted different scripts. The physical evidence from Qusair supports textual accounts that the Monophysite church was a growing power in southwestern Mesopotamia in the 6th century.

Although bishoprics had already been established in eastern Arabia (Beth Qatraye and Beth Mazunaye) and Bahrain by 410, the Church of the East's expansion into the Persian Gulf may have been spurred by Khosrow II's support for the Monophysites. In 1989 a typical East Syrian church was excavated on Failaka island in the bay of Kuwait (Bernard and Salles 1991; Bernard et al. 1991). Another church, part of a monastery complex, was accidentally discovered at Jubayl, on the Saudi Arabian coast, in 1986 (Langfeldt 1994). A further Church of the East monastery complex, on the Iranian island of Kharg (Ghirshman 1971a; Bowman 1974, 1974–5; Steve 2003), displays almost exact parallels with Ain Sha'ia (Okada 1992) and another complex on Sir Bani Yas island in Abu Dhabi (King 1997). This was originally dated to the 6th or 7th century (King 1997: 228–31; Elders 2003: 231), but a detailed study of the ceramics recovered there suggests a late 7th or early 8th century date (Carter 2008).

Additional sites in the Persian Gulf belonging to the Church of the East have been identified by iconographic evidence. A stucco fragment with a cross in the East Syrian style as well as a poorly preserved church were found on the island of Akkaz, in the bay of Kuwait (Gachet 1998: 73–6 and Fig. 14). Three crosses, two made of bronze and one of mother-of-pearl, were discovered at Jabal Berri, c.10 kilometers southwest of Jubayl in northeastern Saudi Arabia (Potts 1994: 61–5 and Figs. 2–7). A post–500 date has been suggested on the basis of two glazed pottery vessels of Sasanian type that were found in the general vicinity (Potts 1994: 63). At Thaj, 90 kilometers inland from Jubayl, two East Syrian crosses were roughly incised on stones flanking a doorway of a building with ashlar stone foundations and mudbrick upper layers (Langfeldt 1994: 44–7). Five or six tombstones at al-Hinnah, 10 kilometers from Thaj, incised with East Syrian crosses, indicate a cemetery (Langfeldt 1994: 49).

Concluding remarks

Excavation and surveys conducted since the early 20th century have opened new perspectives in the Christian archaeology of Sasanian Mesopotamia. First, the considerable Christian presence in the southwestern "flank" of Mesopotamia near modern Najaf and Kerbala has been exposed, the material evidence highlighting an area that Syriac writers only mentioned sporadically. Second, distinct architectural traditions of the Diophysite Church of the East and the Monophysite Syrian Orthodox Church have emerged, complementing the theological and paleographic hallmarks that differentiated these branches of Syriac Christianity. Third, the discovery of decorated stucco-work and plastic arts has shed light on the decoration of churches, placing them within the larger context of Sasanian decorative arts and also challenging the so-called aniconic nature of the Church of the East. Fourth, small finds and inscriptions give rare glimpses of Christian activity, the latter supplying some of the earliest evidence of the liturgy of the Church of the East, pre-dating extant manuscripts by several centuries. Finally, the material evidence confirms the Church of the East's vigorous expansion in the Persian Gulf and the tangible links that were maintained with the Mesopotamian motherland.

The dimensions that Christianity achieved under the Sasanians did not die out with the dynasty but continued for several centuries after the coming of the new Islamic order. British Museum excavations in 1983 and 1986 at Khirbet Deir Situn revealed Sasanian pottery under a much later, 13th century monastery (Curtis 1989a). At Tekrit, major works by the Iraqi Department of Antiquities in the 1990s exposed a variety of churches that functioned for several centuries after the Arab conquest (Harrak 2001a, 2001b). As shown by the Monophysite churches at Qasr Serej and Tell Museifneh, dated to the 6th and 7th centuries, respectively, the architecture of both the West Syrian and East Syrian traditions spanned the transition from the late Sasanian dynasty to the early Islamic era, making change difficult to pinpoint chronologically from architectural plans alone.

Ceramic, epigraphic, numismatic, and iconographic analyses provide important adjuncts. In recent years, lively debate has emerged surrounding the dating of many sites, based on the results of ceramic studies. The monastic complexes in Mesopotamia and the Persian Gulf are now thought to date to the 8th or 9th centuries, rather than the 6th or 7th centuries (Carter 2008: 97–8). This shift does "not reflect the introduction of Christianity but simply a change in the quantity or disposition of resources, evident as a burst of building activity" (Carter 2008: 103). Surviving well into the Islamic era, these churches and monasteries may tie in with the remarkable florescence of East Syrian mystical activity that took place at this time in the Gulf region, epitomized by the writings of Isaac of Nineveh and Dadisho' of Qatar (Wensinck 1923; Brock 1999–2000, 2006).

GUIDE TO FURTHER READING

For a general discussion of Christianity in Mesopotamia, see Hunter (2009. Lacking a monograph devoted to the topic, the Christian archaeology of Late Antique Mesopotamia is best approached through articles. Finster and Schmidt (1976), Fujii et al. (1989), and Okada (1992) are useful studies of churches in southwestern Iraq. For al-Hira and Ctesiphon, see the articles by Talbot-Rice (1932a, 1932b, 1932c) and Reuther (1929b, 1964, 1977). Okada (1990) is an important, comparative analysis of East Syrian iconography, focusing on plaster "icons." For Christian archaeology in the Persian Gulf, see, e.g., Bernard and Salles (1991), Bernard et al. (1991), Langfeldt (1994), Potts (1994), King (1997), Elders (2003), and Carter (2008). For the history of Christianity in the Gulf, see Potts (1990).

Christian Syria has to be assessed through Tchalenko and Baccache (1979), Baccache (1980), and Tchalenko (1990), helpfully revisited and supplemented by Lassus (1947), Tchalenko (1953–8), Donceel-Voûte (1988), Tate (1992), Renhart (1995), and Loosley (2003). Price (1985) is the classic text on asceticism in Syria to be read alongside Peña et al. (1980, 1987). Bowersock (2006) offers an engaging, well-illustrated perspective on the value of mosaics as a source of history. In Piccirillo (1993, 2001) the reader gains authoritative access to the mosaics of ancient Jordan. For Jordan, MacDonald (2009) and, more broadly and thematically, Ousterhoot (1990), open up fruitful avenues for engaging the phenomenon of pilgrimage in the ancient Christian east. Freeman (2001) and Watson (2001) provide the reader with a useful orientation on Christian archaeology in Jordan. Piccirillo and Alliata (1988) provide attractive visuals and allow entry to Madaba research in a concentrated manner. A wealth of documentation on population groups in Palestine from the Byzantine to the early Islamic period can be found in Dauphin (1998) in combination with Schick (1995). Bieberstein and Bloedhorn (1994) is a very useful, well-documented reference work on the archaeology of Jerusalem proper. Tsafrir (1993) provides a useful introduction to the archaeology of selected, representative churches and other religious buildings in Palestine. Ovadiah (1970) and subsequent supplements in Bitton-Askhelony and Kofsky (2004), combined with Saliou (2005), provide an up-to-date entry point to studies of intellectual and material aspects of Gaza during the late ancient Christian period. Patrich (1994) offers a balanced approach to one of the most important, individual monastic sites in ancient Palestine. A wider perspective on Palestininan monasticism is to be gained from Hirschfeld (1992, 2004, 2006). Excellent access to textual traditions relevant for the ancient Christian history of Sinai is to be found in Caner et al. (2010). The material aspects of monasticism can be accessed through Dahari et al. (2000). Krautheimer (1986) provides an art-historical framework for a good number of sites and monuments relevant for the present discussion.

Abbreviations

AA	*American Anthropologist*
AAA	*Liverpool Annals of Archaeology and Anthropology*
AAAS	*Annales Archéologiques Arabes Syriennes*
AAE	*Arabian Archaeology and Epigraphy*
AAL	*Acta Archaeologica Lovaniensia*
AAnz	*Archäologischer Anzeiger*
AAS	*Anatolian Archaeological Studies*
ACSS	*Ancient Civilizations from Scythia to Siberia*
ADAJ	*Annual of the Department of Antiquities of Jordan*
AfO	*Archiv für Orientforschung*
AIUON	*Annali dell'Istituto Universitario Orientale di Napoli*
AJA	*American Journal of Archaeology*
AJPA	*American Journal of Physical Anthropology*
ÄL	*Ägypten und Levante*
AmAnt	*American Antiquity*
AMI	*Archäologische Mitteilungen aus Iran*
AMIT	*Archäologische Mitteilungen aus Iran und Turan*
ANES	*Ancient Near Eastern Studies*
ANET	Pritchard, J.B., ed. (1969), *Ancient Near Eastern Text Relating to the Old Testament*. Princeton.
ANRW	Temporini, H. and Haase, W., eds. (1972–), *Aufstieg und Niedergang der römischen Welt*. Berlin/New York.

A Companion to the Archaeology of the Ancient Near East, First Edition.
Edited by D.T. Potts.
© 2012 Blackwell Publishing Ltd. Published 2012 by Blackwell Publishing Ltd.

AnSt	Anatolian Studies
AO	Ars Orientalis
AoF	Altorientalische Forschungen
ARA	Annual Review of Anthropology
AWE	Ancient West & East
BA	Biblical Archaeologist
BAAL	Bulletin d'archéologie et d'architecture Libanaises
BAI	Bulletin of the Asia Institute
BaM	Baghdader Mitteilungen
BASOR	Bulletin of the American Schools of Oriental Research
BIFAO	Bulletin de l'Institut français d'archéologie orientale
BiOr	Bibliotheca Orientalis
BSA	Bulletin on Sumerian Agriculture
BSOAS	Bulletin of the School of Oriental and African Studies
CA	Current Anthropology
CAH	Cambridge Ancient History
CAJ	Cambridge Archaeological Journal
CHI	Cambridge History of Iran
CRAIBL	Comptes-rendus de l'Académie des inscriptions et belles lettres
CT	Cuneiform Texts from Babylonian Tablets in the British Museum
CQ	Classical Quarterly
CY	Chroniques Yéménites
DA	Dossiers d'archéologie
DAFI	Cahiers de la Délégation archéologique française en Iran
DaM	Damaszener Mitteilungen
DOP	Dumbarton Oaks Papers
EnIr	Encyclopaedia Iranica
EVO	Egitto e Vicino Oriente
EW	East and West
GJ	The Geographical Journal
IEJ	Israel Exploration Journal
IJAH	Iranian Journal of Archaeology and History
IJNA	The International Journal of Nautical Archaeology
ILN	Illustrated London News
IM	Iraq Museum
IrAnt	Iranica Antiqua
IstMitt	Istanbuler Mitteilungen
JA	Journal Asiatique
JAA	Journal of Anthropological Archaeology
JAE	Journal of Arid Environments
JAOS	Journal of the American Oriental Society
JAMT	Journal of Archaeological Method and Theory
JAR	Journal of Archaeological Research

JARCE	*Journal of the American Research Center in Egypt*
JAS	*Journal of Archaeological Science*
JCS	*Journal of Cuneiform Studies*
JEA	*Journal of Egyptian Archaeology*
JEOL	*Jaarbericht Ex Oriente Lux*
JESHO	*Journal of the Economic and Social History of the Orient*
JFA	*Journal of Field Archaeology*
JGS	*Journal of Glass Studies*
JIAAA	*Journal of Inner Asian Art and Archaeology*
JIES	*Journal of Indo-European Studies*
JIPS	*Journal of the Israel Prehistoric Society*
JMA	*Journal of Mediterranean Archaeology*
JNES	*Journal of Near Eastern Studies*
JOS	*Journal of Oman Studies*
JQS	*Journal of Quaternary Science*
JRA	*Journal of Roman Archaeology*
JRAS	*Journal of the Royal Asiatic Society of Great Britain and Ireland*
JRGS	*Journal of the Royal Geographical Society of London*
JRGZM	*Jahrbuch des Römisch-Germanischen Zentralmuseums, Mainz*
JRS	*Journal of Roman Studies*
JSGT	*Journal of the Society of Glass Technology*
JSS	*Journal of Semitic Studies*
JWP	*Journal of World Prehistory*
LA	*Liber Annuus*
MDOG	*Mitteilungen der Deutschen Orient-Gesellschaft*
MDP	*Mémoires de la délégation en Perse, Mémoires de la mission archéologique de Susiane, Mémoires de la mission archéologique de Perse, Mémoires de la délégation archéologique en Iran*
MeditArch	*Mediterranean Archaeology*
MUSJ	*Mélanges de l'Université Saint-Joseph*
N.A.B.U.	*Nouvelles Assyriologiques brèves et utilitaires*
NAPR	*Northern Akkad Project Reports*
NEA	*Near Eastern Archaeology*
OCP	*Orientalia Christiana Periodica*
OGIS	Dittenberger, W., ed. (1903–5), *Orientis Graecae Inscriptiones Selectae*. Leipzig.
OJA	*Oxford Journal of Archaeology*
Or	*Orientalia*
PBA	*Proceedings of the British Academy*
PEQ	*Palestine Exploration Quarterly*
PG	private grave, designation used in the Royal Cemetery at Ur
PNAS	*Proceedings of the National Academy of Sciences*
PPS	*Proceedings of the Prehistoric Society*

PSAS	*Proceedings of the Seminar for Arabian Studies*
PSI	*Pubblicazioni della Società Italiana per la ricerca del papiri greci e latini*
QI	*Quaternary International*
QR	*Quaternary Research*
QSR	*Quaternary Science Reviews*
RA	*Revue d'Assyriologie*
RB	*Revue biblique*
RDAC	*Report of the Department of Antiquities, Cyprus*
RlA	*Reallexikon der Assyriologie und Vorderasiatischen Archäologie*
SB	*Sammelbuch griechischer Urkunden aus Ägypten*
SCCNH	*Studies on the Civilization and Culture of Nuzi and the Hurrians*
SDB	*Supplément au dictionnaire de la Bible*
SEL	*Studi Epigrafici e Linguistici sul Vicino Oriente Antico*
SMEA	*Studi Micenei ed Egeo-Anatolici*
SRAA	*Silk Road Art and Archaeology*
StIr	*Studia Iranica*
SWJA	*Southwestern Journal of Anthropology*
TCL	*Textes cuneiforms du Louvre*
TÜBA-AR	*Turkish Academy of Sciences Journal of Archaeology*
UF	*Ugarit-Forschungen*
UVB	*Vorläufige Bericht über die von dem Deutschen Archäologischen Institut aus Mitteln der Deutschen Forschungsgemeinschaft unternommenen Ausgrabungen in Uruk-Warka*
VHA	*Vegetation History and Archaeobotany*
WA	*World Archaeology*
WMAH	Sauren, H. (1969), *Wirtschaftsurkunden aus der Zeit der III. Dynastie von Ur im Besitz des Musée d'Art et d'Histoire in Genf.* Naples.
WO	*Die Welt des Orients*
WZKM	*Wiener Zeitschrift für die Kunde des Morgenlandes*
YOS	*Yale Oriental Series*
ZA	*Zeitschrift für Assyriologie*
ZDMG	*Zeitschrift der Deutschen Morgenländischen Gesellschaft*
ZDPV	*Zeitschrift des Deutschen Palästina-Vereins*
ZOA	*Zeitschrift für Orient-Archäologie*

References

Anonymous, ed. (1965), *Comptes Rendus; VIIe Congrès International du Verre, Bruxelles, 28 juin–3 juillet 1965, Section B.* Brussels.

Anonymous, ed. (1968), *The Memorial Volume of the Vth International Congress of Iranian Art & Archaeology, Tehran-Isfahan-Shiraz, 11th–18th April 1968.* Tehran.

Anonymous, ed. (1974a), *Commémoration Cyrus: Actes du congrès de Shiraz 1971 et autres études rédigées à l'occasion du 2500e anniversaire de la fondation de l'Empire perse.* Leiden.

Anonymous, ed. (1974b), *Gururājamañjarikā: Studi in onore di Guiseppe Tucci.* Naples.

Anonymous, ed. (1975), *Proceedings of the XIV International Congress of Papyrologists, Oxford, 24–31 July, 1974,* 241–246. London.

Anonymous, ed. (1979), *Akten des VII. internationalen Kongresses für iranische Kunst und Archäologie, München, 7.–10. September 1976.* Berlin.

Anonymous, ed. (1981), *Actes du XVe Congrès international d'études byzantines.* Athens.

Anonymous, ed. (1985a), *La terra tra i due fiumi. Venti anni di archeologia italiana in Medio Oriente. La Mesopotamia dei tesori.* Alessandria.

Anonymous, ed. (1985b), *Vsesoyuznaya Arkheologicheskaya Konferentsiya "Dostizheniya Sovetskoj Arkheologii v XI Pyatiletke".* Baku.

Anonymous, ed. (1986), *The 17th International Byzantine Congress, Washington DC: Major Papers.* New York.

Anonymous, ed. (1987), *Researches on the Antiquities of Saddam Dam Basin Salvage and Other Antiquities.* Mosul.

Anonymous, ed. (1996a), *Annales du 13e Congrès de l'Association Internationale pour l'Histoire du Verre.* Lochem.

Anonymous, ed. (1996b), *La Persia e l'Asia Centrale da Alessandro al X secolo.* Rome.

A Companion to the Archaeology of the Ancient Near East, First Edition.
Edited by D.T. Potts.
© 2012 Blackwell Publishing Ltd. Published 2012 by Blackwell Publishing Ltd.

Anonymous, ed. (1997), *Atti del convegno nazionale di archeologia subacquea: Anzio, 30–31 maggio e 1° giugno 1996*. Bari.

Anonymous, ed. (1998), *Liban. L'autre rive*. Paris.

Anonymous, ed. (1999), *International Symposium on Settlement and Housing in Anatolia Through the Ages*. Istanbul.

Anonymous, ed. (2000), *Dovvomin Kongre-ye Tārikh-e Me'māri va Shahrsāzi-ye Irān, Bam, Kermān, 25–29 farvardīn 1378*, vol. 3. Tehran.

Anonymous, ed. (2002a), *Glass Technology 43C, Proceedings XIX International Congress on Glass, Edinburgh, 1–6 July 2001*. Sheffield.

Anonymous, ed. (2002b), *Die Hethiter und ihr Reich. Das Volk der 1000 Götter*. Stuttgart.

Anonymous, ed. (2003), *The Date Palm: From Traditional Resource to Green Wealth*. Abu Dhabi.

Anonymous, ed. (2005), *Annales du 16e Congrès de l'Association Internationale pour l'Histoire du Verre*. London.

Anonymous, ed. (2007a), *Vor 12000 Jahren in Anatolien. Die ältesten Monumente der Menschheit*. Stuttgart.

Anonymous, ed. (2007b), *The 9th Annual Symposium on Iranian Archaeology*. Tehran.

Anonymous, ed. (2009a), *Annales du 17e Congrès de l'Association Internationale pour l'Histoire du Verre*. Antwerp.

Anonymous, ed. (2009b), *De Méditerranée et d'ailleurs: Mélanges offerts à J. Guilaine*. Toulouse.

Anonymous, ed. (2009c), *30. Kazı sonuçları toplantısı*. Ankara.

Anonymous, ed. (2009d), *Varusschlacht*. Mainz.

Anonymous, ed. (2009e), *Interconnections in the Eastern Mediterranean. Lebanon in the Bronze and Iron Ages*. Beirut.

Anonymous, ed. (2010), *De Byzance à Istanbul: Un port pour deux continents*. Paris.

Abadie-Reynal, C. and Gaborit, J. (2003), "Le développement urbain en Syrie du Nord: étude des cas de Séleucie et d'Apamée de l'Euphrate", in Sartre et al., eds., 149–169.

Abay, E. (2001), "Seals and sealings", in Çilingiroğlu and Salvini, eds., 322–353.

Abbès, F. (2003), *Les Outillages néolithiques en Syrie du Nord: Méthode de débitage et gestion laminaire durant le PPNB*. Oxford/Lyon.

Abbès, F. (2008), "Analyse technologique", in Ibáñez, ed., 236–280.

Abbo, S., Shtienberg, D., Lichtenzveig, J., Lev-Yadun, S. and Gopher, A. (2003), "The chickpea, summer cropping, and a new model for pulse domestication in the ancient Near East", *Quarterly Review of Biology* 78/4: 435–448.

Abbot, N. (1968), "Jundī Shāhpūr: a preliminary historical sketch", *AO* 7: 71–73.

Abbu, A.N. (1987), "The excavations of the Mosul University at Imsefna", in Demerji, ed., 133–155 (in Arabic).

Abd el-Raziq, M., Castel, G. and Tallet, P. (2006), "Ayn Soukhna et la Mer Rouge", *Égypte, Afrique et Orient* 41: 3–6.

Abdi, K. (2001a), "Malyan 1999", *Iran* 39: 73–98.

Abdi, K. (2001b), "Nationalism, politics and the development of archaeology in Iran", *AJA* 105: 51–76.

Abdi, K. (2002), *Strategies of Herding: Pastoralism in the Middle Chalcolithic Period of the West Central Zagros Mountains*. Ann Arbor.

Abdi, K. (2008), "From pan-Arabism to Saddam Hussein's cult of personality", *Social Archaeology* 8/1: 3–36.

Abdi, K. and Miller, N., eds. (2003), *Yeki bud, Yeki nabud: Essays on the Archaeology of Iran in Honor of William M. Sumner*. Los Angeles.

Abdul-Nour, H. (2001), "Les inscriptions forestières d'Hadrien: mise au point et nouvelles découvertes", *Archaeology and History of Lebanon* 14: 64–95.

Abu al-Hassan, H. (2010), "The kingdom of Lihyan", in al-Ghabban et al., eds., 270–275.

Abu Assaf, A. (1990), *Der Tempel von 'Ain Dara*. Mainz.

Abu Duruk, H.I. (1988), *Introduction to the archaeology of Tayma*. Riyadh.

Abu El-Haj, N. (2001), *Facts on the Ground: Archaeological Practice and Territorial Self-Fashioning in Israeli Society*. Chicago.

Abusch, T., Huehnergard, J. and Steinkeller, P., eds. (1990), *Lingering Over Words: Studies in Near Eastern Literature in Honor of William L. Moran*. Atlanta.

Ackerman, P. (1938), "Textiles through the Sasanian period", in Pope, ed., 681–715.

Adachi, T. (2005), "Considering the regional differences in the Parthian fine pottery", *al-Rāfidān* 26: 25–36.

Adachi, T. and Zeidi, M. (2009), "Achaemenid and post-Achaemenid remains from TB 75 and the general survey of the Tang-i Bulaghi", *ARTA* 2009.002.

Adams, R.B., ed. (2008a), *Jordan: An Archaeological Reader*. London.

Adams, R.B. (2008b), "Archaeology in Jordan: a brief history", in Adams, ed., 1–6.

Adams, R.McC. (1962), "Agriculture and urban life in early southwestern Iran", *Science* 136: 109–122.

Adams, R.McC. (1965), *Land Behind Baghdad*. Chicago.

Adams, R.McC. (1972), "Patterns of urbanism in early southern Mesopotamia", in Ucko et al., eds., 735–749.

Adams, R.McC. (1974), "The Mesopotamian social landscape: a view from the frontier", in Moore, ed., 1–22.

Adams, R.McC. (1981), *Heartland of Cities*. Chicago.

Adams, R.McC. (1983), "The Jarmo stone and pottery vessel industries", in Braidwood et al., eds., 209–232.

Adams, R.McC. and Hansen, D.P. (1968), "Archaeological reconnaissance and soundings in Jundī Shāpūr", *AO* 7: 53–70.

Adams, R.McC. and Nissen, H.J. (1972), *The Uruk countryside*. Chicago and London.

Adams, R.McC., Parr, P.J., Ibrahim, M. and al-Mughannum, A.S. (1977), "Saudi Arabian Archaeological Reconnaissance 1976: The preliminary report on the first phase of the Comprehensive Archaeological Survey Program", *Atlal* 1: 21–40.

Adamthwaite, M.R. (2001), *Late Hittite Emar: The Chronology, Synchronisms, and Socio-Political Aspects of a Late Bronze Age Fortress Town*. Louvain.

Adle, C. (1992), "Investigations archéologiques dans le Gorgan: au pays Turcoman et aux confins Irano-Afghans (notes)", in Bacqué-Grammont and Dor, eds., 177–205.

Adle, C. (1993), "Damghan", *EnIr* 6: 632–638.

Adler, W. (1994), *Kamid el-Loz 11. Das "Schatzhaus" im Palastbereich. Die Befunde des Königsgrabes*. Bonn.

Adler, W. and Penner, S. (2001), *Kamid el-Loz.18. Die spätbronzezeitlichen Palastanlagen*. Bonn.

Adriaens, A., Veny, P., Adams, F., Sporken, R., Louette, P., Earl, B., Özbal, H. and Yener, K.A. (1999), "Analytical investigation of archaeological powders from Göltepe, Turkey", *Archaeometry* 41: 81–89.
Afanas'ev, G., Cleuziou, S., Lukacs, J. and Tosi, M., eds. (1996), *The Prehistory of Asia and Oceania*. Forli.
Agelarakis, A. (2004), "The Shanidar Cave Proto-Neolithic human condition as reflected through osteology and palaeopathology", in Solecki et al., 159–184.
Agius, D. (2002), *In the Wake of the Dhow: The Arabian Gulf and Oman*. Reading.
Aharoni, Y. (1979), *The Land of the Bible: A Historical Geography*. London.
Ahlström, G.W. (1993), *The History of Ancient Palestine*. Minneapolis.
Ahrens, A. (2005), "Eine Stadt zwischen den Fronten. Der Tell Nebi Mend – Kadesch (Syrien): Eine Siedlung im Grenzbereich der Großmächte Vorderasiens", *Antike Welt* 3: 62–64.
Ahrens, A. (2007), "A journey's end – two Egyptian stone vessels with hieroglyphic inscriptions from the Royal Tomb at Tell Mišrife/Qatna", *ÄL* 16: 15–36.
Ahrens, A. (2009), "Alabastren und Amphoren – Die Steingefäße", in Landesmuseum Württemberg, ed., 236–239.
Ahrens, A. (2011), "Die Steingefäße aus der Königsgruft von Tall Mišrife/Qatna: Verteilung, Typenspektrum und Funktion", in Pfälzner, ed., 259–74.
Ahunbay, M. and Ahunbay Z. (2000), "Recent work on the land walls of Istanbul: Tower 2 to Tower 5", *DOP* 54: 227–239.
Akkaya, M. (1991), "Objets phrygiens en bronze du tumulus de Kaynarca", in Le Guen-Pollet and Pelon, eds., 25–27.
Akkermans, P.A., Boerma, J.A.K., Clason, A.T., Hill, S.G., Lohof, E., Meiklejohn, C., Le Mière, M., Molgat, G.M.F., Roodenberg, J., Waterbolk-van Rooijen, W. and van Zeist, W. (1983), "Bouqras revisited", *PPS* 49: 335–372.
Akkermans, P.A., Fokkens, H. and Waterbolk, H.T. (1981), "Stratigraphy, architecture and layout of Bouqras", in Cauvin and Sanlaville, eds., 485–502.
Akkermans, P.M.M.G., ed. (1989a), *Excavations at Tell Sabi Abyad: Prehistoric Investigations in the Balikh Valley, Northern Syria*. Oxford.
Akkermans, P.M.M.G. (1989b), "Halaf mortuary practices: a survey", in Haex, Curvers and Akkermans, eds., 75–88.
Akkermans, P.M.M.G. (1993), *Villages in the Steppe: Late Neolithic Settlement and Subsistence in the Balikh Valley, Northern Syria*. Ann Arbor.
Akkermans, P.M.M.G. (1995), "An image of complexity: the Burnt Village at late Neolithic Sabi Abyad, Syria", *AJA* 99: 5–32.
Akkermans, P.M.M.G., ed. (1996), *Tell Sabi Abyad: The Late Neolithic Settlement*. Istanbul and Leiden.
Akkermans, P.M.M.G. (2010), "Late Neolithic architectural renewal: the emergence of round houses in the northern Levant, c.6500–6000 BC", in Bolger and Maguire, eds., 22–28.
Akkermans, P.M.M.G., Cappers, R., Cavallo, C., Nieuwenhuyse, P., Nilhamn, B. and Otte, I. (2006), "Investigating the Early Pottery Neolithic of northern Syria: new evidence from Tell Sabi Abyad", *AJA* 110: 123–156.
Akkermans, P.M.M.G. and Duistermaat, K. (1997), "Of storage and nomads: the sealings of Late Neolithic Sabi Abyad, Syria", *Paléorient* 22: 17–44.

Akkermans, P.M.M.G. and Duistermaat, K. (2004), "More seals and sealings from Neolithic Tell Sabi Abyad, Syria", *Levant* 36: 1–11.

Akkermans, P.M.M.G. and Schwartz, G. (2003), *The Archaeology of Syria: From Complex Hunter-Gatherers to Early Urban Societies (ca.16,000–300 BC)*. Cambridge.

Akkermans, P.M.M.G., van der Plicht, J., Nieuwenhuyse, O.P., Russell, A., Kaneda, A. and Buitenhuis, H. (2010), "Weathering climate change in the Near East: dating and Neolithic adaptations 8200 years ago", *Antiquity* 84: 71–85.

Akkermans, P.M.M.G. and Verhoeven, M. (1995), "An image of complexity: the Burnt Village at Late Neolithic Sabi Abyad, Syria", *AJA* 99: 5–32.

Akkermans, P.M.M.G. and Wittmann, B. (1993), "Khirbet esh-Shenef 1991: Eine späthalafzeitliche Siedlung im Balikhtal, Nordsyrien", *MDOG* 125: 143–166.

Aksu, A.E., Hiscott, R.N., Mudie, P.J., Rochon, A., Kaminski, M.A., Abrajano, T. and Yaar, D. (2002), "Persistent Holocene outflow from the Black Sea to the Eastern Mediterranean contradicts Noah's flood hypothesis", *GSA Today* (May): 4–10.

Al Abed, E.I. and Hellyer, P., eds. (2001), *United Arab Emirates: A New Perspective*. London.

Al-A'dami, K. (1968), "Excavations at Tell es-Sawwan", *Sumer* 24: 57–94.

al-Ansary, A.R. (1982), *Qaryat al-Faw: A Portrait of pre-Islamic Civilization in Saudi Arabia*. Riyadh and New York.

Albenda, P. (1986), *The Palace of Sargon King of Assyria*. Paris.

Alberti, M.E., Ascalone, E. and Peyronel, L., eds. (2006), *Weights in Context: Bronze Age Weighing Systems of the Eastern Mediterranean: Chronology, Typology, Material and Archaeological Contexts*. Rome.

Alcock, S., ed. (1997), *The Early Roman Empire in the East*. Oxford.

Alcock, S. (2001), "The reconfiguration of memory in the eastern Roman empire", in Alcock et al., eds., 323–350.

Alcock, S., d'Altroy, T., Morrison, K. and Sinopoli, C., eds. (2001), *Empires*. Cambridge.

Alden, J.R. (1979), *Regional Economic Organization in Banesh Period Iran*. Ann Arbor.

Alden, J.R. (1982), "Trade and politics in Proto-Elamite Iran", *CA* 23: 613–640.

Alden, J.R. (1987), "The Susa III period", in Hole, ed., 157–170.

Alden, J.R. (in press), "The Kur River Basin in the late 4th and 3rd millennia BC: ceramics, settlement, and socio-political organization", in Petrie, ed.

Alden, J.R., Abdi, K., Azadi, A., Beckman, G. and Pittman, H. (2005), "Fars Archaeological Project 2004: Excavation at Tal-e Malyan", *Iran* 43: 39–47.

Alden, J.R., Abdi, K., Azadi, A., Biglari, F. and Heydari, S. (2004), "Kushk-e Hezar: a Mushki/Jari period site in the Kur River basin, Fars, Iran", *Iran* 42: 25–45.

Alex, M. (1984), *Middle East. Mean Annual Rainfall and Variability, Map A IV 4*. Wiesbaden.

Alex, M. (1985), *Middle East. Rainfall Reliability, Map A IV 5*. Wiesbaden.

al-Fouadi, A.-H. (1976), "Bassetki statue with an Old Akkadian royal inscription of Naram-Sin of Agade (2291–2255 BC)", *Sumer* 32: 63–77.

al-Gailani Werr, L. (1988), *Studies on the Chronology and Regional Style of Old Babylonian Cylinder Seals*. Malibu.

al-Gailani Werr, L. (2008), "The story of the Iraq Museum", in Stone and Bajjaly, eds., 25–30.

al-Gailani Werr, L., Curtis, J., Martin, H., McMahon, A., Oates, J. and Reade, J., eds. (2002), *Of Pots and Plans: Papers on the Archaeology and History of Mesopotamia and Syria Presented to David Oates in Honour of his 75th Birthday*. London.

Algaze, G. (1989), "The Uruk expansion: cross cultural exchange in early Mesopotamian civilization", *CA* 30: 571–591.

Algaze, G. (1993), *The Uruk World System: The Dynamics of Expansion of Early Mesopotamian Civilization*. Chicago.

Algaze, G. (2001a), "Initial social complexity in southwestern Asia: the Mesopotamian advantage", *CA* 42: 199–233.

Algaze, G. (2001b), "The prehistory of imperialism: the case of Uruk period Mesopotamia", in Rothman, ed., 27–84.

Algaze, G. (2005a), *The Uruk World System: The Dynamics of Expansion of Early Mesopotamian Civilization*, 2nd ed. Chicago.

Algaze, G. (2005b), "The Sumerian takeoff", *Structure and Dynamics* 1/1: 5–48.

Algaze, G. (2008), *Ancient Mesopotamia at the Dawn of Civilization: The Evolution of an Urban Landscape*. Chicago.

Algaze, G., Breuninger, R. and Knudstad, J. (1994), "The Tigris-Euphrates Archaeological Reconnaissance Project: final report of the Bireçik and Carchemish Dam Survey Areas", *Anatolica* 20: 1–96.

Algaze, G., Dinckan, G., Hartenberger, B., Matney, T., Pournelle, J., Rainville, L., Rosen, S., Rupley, E., Schlee, D. and Vallet, R. (2001), "Research at Titriş Höyük in southeastern Turkey: The 1999 season", *Anatolica* 27: 23–106.

Algaze, G. and Pournelle, J. (2004), "Climatic change, environmental change, and social change at Early Bronze Age Titriş Höyük: can correlation and causation be untangled?", in Özdoğan et al., eds., 103–128.

Algaze, G. and Pournelle, J. (in press), "Travels in Edin: deltaic resilience and early urbanism in Greater Mesopotamia", in Crawford et al., eds.

al-Ghabban, A., André-Salvini, B., Demange, F., Juvin, C. and Cotty, M., eds. (2010), *Roads of Arabia: Archaeology and History of the Kingdom of Saudi Arabia*. Paris.

al-Ghabbān, M.A.B.I. (2007), "Le Darb al-Bakra. Decouverté d'une nouvelle branche sur la route commerciale antique, entre al-Hijr (Arabie sa'udite) et Pétra (Jordanie)", *CRAIBL* 2007: 9–24.

Al-Ghazzi, A.S. (2010), "The kingdom of Midian", in al-Ghabban et al., eds., 211–217.

Alhaique, F. and Gopher, A. (2005), "Animal resource exploitation at Qumran Cave 24 (Dead Sea, Israel) from the Pre-Pottery Neolithic to the Chalcolithic", in Buitenhuis et al., eds., 139–149.

Ali, S. and Ripley, S.D. (1983), *Handbook of the Birds of India and Pakistan: Compact Edition*. Delhi.

Alimov, K., Boroffka, N., Bubnova, M., Burjakov, J., Cierny, J., Jakubov, J., Lutz, J., Parzinger, H., Pernicka, E., Radililovskij, V., Ruzanov, V., Širinov, T., Staršinin, D. and Weisgerber, G. (1998), "Prähistorischer Zinnbergbau in Mittelasien: Vorbericht der ersten Kampagne 1997", *Eurasia Antiqua* 4: 137–199.

Aliquot, J. (2009), *La Vie religieuse au Liban sous l'Empire romain*. Beirut.

Alizadeh, A. (1985a), "A Protoliterate pottery kiln from Choga Mish", *Iran* 23: 39–50.

Alizadeh, A. (1985b), "Elymaean occupation of lower Khuzestan during the Seleucid and Parthian periods: A proposal", *IrAnt* 20: 175–195.

Alizadeh, A. (1992), *Prehistoric Settlement Patterns and Cultures in Susiana, Southwestern Iran*. Ann Arbor.

Alizadeh, A. (2003a), "Letter from the field, Oriental Institute returns to Iran", *Oriental Institute News and Notes* 177.

Alizadeh, A. (2003b), "Some observations based on the nomadic character of Fars prehistoric cultural development", in Miller and Abdi, eds., 82–97.

Alizadeh, A. (2004), "Recent archaeological investigations on the Persepolis plain", *The Oriental Institute News and Notes* 183: 1–7.

Alizadeh, A., ed. (2006), *The Origins of State Organization in Prehistoric Highland Fars, Southern Iran: Excavations at Tall-e Bakun*. Chicago.

Alizadeh, A., ed. (2008), *Chogha Mish, Volume II. The Development of a Prehistoric Regional Center in Lowland Susiana, Southwestern Iran: Final Report on the Last Six Seasons of Excavations, 1972–1978*. Chicago.

Alizadeh, A. (2010), "The rise of the highland Elamite state in southwestern Iran", *CA* 51/3: 353- 383.

Alizadeh, A., Kouchoukos, N., Wilkinson, T.J., Bauer, A.M. and Mashkour, M. (2004), "Human-environment interactions on the Upper Khuzestan Plains, Southwest Iran: recent investigations", *Paléorient* 30/1: 69–88.

Alizadeh, A., Majidzadeh, Y. and Shahmirzadi, S.M., eds. (1999), *The Iranian World: Essays on Iranian Art and Archaeology Presented to Ezat O. Negahban*. Tehran.

Alizadeh, A., Zeidi, M., Askari, A., Niakan, L. and Atabaki, A. (2004), "Iranian Prehistoric Project", *The Annual Report of the Oriental Institute of the University of Chicago for 2003–2004*: 94–106.

al-Kabawi, A., Khan, M., al-Mubarak, A., al-Tamai, M., al-Ubaid, S. and al-Subhan, I. (1989), "Preliminary report on the fourth season of Comprehensive Rock Art and Epigraphic Survey of northern Saudi Arabia 1408 AH/1987 AD", *Atlal* 12/2: 41–51.

al-Khalifa, H.A. and Rice, M., eds. (1986), *Bahrain Through the Ages: The Archaeology*. London.

Allchin, B., ed. (1984), *South Asian Archaeology 1981*. Cambridge.

Allchin, R., ed. (1995), *The Archaeology of Early Historic South Asia: The Emergence of Cities and States*. Cambridge.

Allchin, R. and Allchin, B., eds. (1997), *South Asian Archaeology 1995*. Cambridge.

Allen, J.P. (2008), "The historical inscription of Khnumhotep at Dhashur: preliminary report", *BASOR* 352: 29–39.

Allen, J.P. (2009), "L'inscription historique de Khnoumhotep à Dahchour", *Bulletin de la Société française d'Égyptologie* 173: 13–31.

Allen, L. (2005), *The Persian Empire: A History*. Chicago and London.

Alley, R.B. (2000), *The Two-Mile Time Machine: Ice Cores, Abrupt Climate Change, and Our Future*. Princeton.

Allinger-Csollich, W. (1991), "Birs Nimrud I. Die Baukörper der Ziqqurrat von Borsippa", *BaM* 22: 383–499.

Allinger-Csollich, W. (1998), "Birs Nimrud II: 'Tieftempel' – 'Hochtempel' (Vergleichende Studien: Borsippa – Babylon)", *BaM* 29: 95–330.

Allinger-Csollich, W., Kuntner, W. and Heinsch, S. (2010), "Babylon: past, present, future. The project 'Comparative Studies Babylon-Borsippa', a synopsis", in Matthiae et al., eds., 29–38.

Allotte de la Fuÿe, F.M., Belaiew, N.T., Mecquenem, R. de and Unvala, J-M. (1934), *Archéologie, métrologie et numismatique susiennes*. Paris.

al-Maqdissi, M. (2003), "Ergebnisse der siebten und achten syrischen Grabungskampagne 2001 und 2002 in Mišrife/Qatna", *MDOG* 135: 219–245.

al-Maqdissi, M. (2006), "Notes d'archéologie levantine VIII. Stratigraphie du Chantier B de Tell Sianu (plaine de Jablé)", *Syria* 83: 229–246.

al-Maqdissi, M. (2007), "Notes d'archéologie levantine X. Introduction aux travaux archéologiques syriens à Mishrifeh/Qatna au nord-est de Homs (Émèse)", in Morandi Bonacossi, ed., 19–27.

al-Maqdissi, M., Dohmann-Pfälzner, H., Pfälzner, P. and Suleiman, A. (2003), "Das königliche Hypogäum von Qatna", *MDOG* 135: 189–218.

al-Maqdissi, M., Luciani, M., Morandi Bonacossi, D., Novák, M. and Pfälzner, P., eds. (2002), *Excavating Qatna*, vol. 1. Damascus.

al-Maqdissi, M., Matoïan, V. and Nicolle, C., eds. (2002), *Céramique de l'Âge du Bronze en Syrie, I. La Syrie du Nord et la vallée de l'Oronte*. Beirut.

al-Maqdissi, M., Matoïan, V. and Nicolle, C., eds. (2007), *Céramique de l'Âge du Bronze en Syrie, II. L'Euphrate et la région de Jézireh*. Beirut.

al-Maqdissi, M., Morandi Bonacossi, D. and Pfälzner, P., eds. (2009), *Schätze des Alten Syrien – Die Entdeckung des Königreichs Qatna*. Stuttgart.

al-Maqdissi, M. and Souleiman, A. (2004), "Tell Iris", in Galliano and Calvet, eds., 64.

Al-Muaikel, K. (1994), *Study of the Archaeology of the al-Jawf Region*. Riyadh.

Alon, D. and Levy, T.E. (1990), "The Gilat sanctuary: its centrality and influence in the Southern Levant during the late 5th–early 4th millennium BCE", *Eretz-Israel* 21: 23–36 (in Hebrew).

Alp, S. (1968), *Zylinder- und Stempelsiegel aus Karahöyük bei Konya*. Ankara.

Alp, S. (1991), *Hethitische Briefe aus Maşat Höyük*. Ankara.

Alperson-Afil, N., Sharon, G., Kislev, M., Melamed, Y., Zohar, I., Ashkenazi, S., Rabinovich, R., Biton, R., Werker, E., Hartman, G., Feibel, C. and Goren-Inbar, N. (2009), "Spatial organization of hominin activities at Gesher Benot Ya'aqov, Israel", *Science* 326/4960: 1677–1680.

Alram, M. (1986), *Nomina propria Iranica in nummis. Materialgrundlagen zu den iranischen Personennnamen auf antiken Münzen*. Wien.

Alram, M. (1998), "Stand und Aufgaben der arsakidischen Numismatik", in Wiesehöfer, ed., 365–387.

al-Said, S.F. (2009), "Eine neu entdeckte Erwähnung des Königs Nabonid in den thamudischen Inschriften", *ZOA* 2: 358–363.

al-Said, S.F. (2010), "Dedan (al-Ula)", in al-Ghabban et al., eds., 262–269.

al-Said, S.F. (in press), "A recent epigraphic evidence from the excavations at Al-'Ula reveals a new king of Dadan", *AAE* 22.

al-Saud, S.A. (1996), "The domestication of the camel and inland trading routes in Arabia", *Atlal* 14: 129–136.

al-Sayari, S.S. and Zötl, J.G., eds. (1978), *The Quaternary Period in Saudi Arabia*, vol. 1. New York.

Al-Sindi, K. (1999), *Dilmun Seals*. Manama.

Alt, A. (1944–5), "Zur Geschichte von Tunip", *ZDPV* 67: 159–162.

Altaweel, M. (2008), *The Imperial Landscape of Ashur: Settlement and Land Use in the Assyrian Heartland*. Berlin.

Altekamp, S., Hofter, M. and Krumme, M., eds. (2001), *Posthumanistische Klassische Archäologie. Historizität und Wissenschaftlichkeit von Interessen und Methoden*. Munich.

Altenhain, C., Danilina, A., Hildebrandt, E., Kausch, S., Müller, A. and Roscher, T., eds. (2008), *Von "Neuer Unterschicht" und Prekariat: Gesellschaftliche Verhältnisse und Kategorien im Umbruch*. Bielefeld.

Altenmüller, H. and Moussa, A. (1991), "Die Inschrift Amenemhet II aus dem Ptah Tempel von Memphis. Ein Vorbericht", *Studien zur Altägyptischen Kultur* 18: 1–48.

Althusser, L. (1971), *Lenin and philosophy*. New York.

Álvarez-Mon, J. (2005a), "Elamite funerary clay heads", *NEA* 68/3: 114–122.

Álvarez-Mon, J. (2005b), "Aspects of Elamite wall painting: new evidence from Kabnak (Haft Tepe)", *IrAnt* 40: 149–164.

Álvarez-Mon, J. (2009a), "Ashurbanipal's feast: a view from Elam", *IrAnt* 44: 131–180.

Alvarez-Mon, J. (2009b), "Notes on the 'Elamite' garment of Cyrus the Great", *Antiquaries Journal* 89: 21–33.

Álvarez-Mon, J. (2010), *The Arjan Tomb, at the Crossroads of the Elamite and the Persian Empires*. Leiden.

Álvarez-Mon, J. (in press), "Braids of glory: Elamite sculptural reliefs from the highlands, Kūl-e Farah IV", in De Graef and Tavernier, eds.

Álvarez-Mon, J. and Garrison, M.B., eds. (2011a), *Elam and Persia*. Winona Lake.

Álvarez-Mon, J. and Garrison, M.B. (2011b), "Postscript", in Álvarez-Mon and Garrison, eds., 489–493.

al-Zahrani, A. (2007), *Tall al-Kathib bi-alʿUla, dirasiya athariyya maqarniyya*. Riyadh.

al-Zeebari, A. (1982), "Die Ausgrabungen der Universität Baghdad in Tell Aswad", in Hirsch, ed., 189–191.

Ambos, C. (2003), "Nanaja – eine ikonographische Studie zur Darstellung einer altorientalischen Göttin in hellenistisch-parthischer Zeit", *ZA* 93: 231–272.

Ambrose, S.H. (1993), "Isotopic analysis of palaeodiets: methodological and interpretive considerations", in Sandford, ed., 59–130.

Amiet, P. (1966), *Elam*. Auvers-sur-l'Oise.

Amiet, P. (1972a), "Les ivoires achéménides de Suse", *Syria* 49: 167–191, 319–337.

Amiet, P. (1972b), *Glyptique susienne: Des origines à l'époque des Perses achéménides. Cachets, sceaux-cylindres et empreintes antiques découverts à Suse de 1913 à 1967*, 2 vols. Paris.

Amiet, P. (1972c), "Les statues de Manishtusu, roi d'Agadé", *RA* 66/2: 97–109.

Amiet, P. (1973), "Quelques observations sur le palais de Darius à Suse", *Syria* 51: 65–73.

Amiet, P. (1976), *L'Art d'Agadé au Musée du Louvre*. Paris.

Amiet, P. (1979), "Alternance et dualité: essai d'interprétation de l'histoire élamite", *Akkadica* 15: 2–24.

Amiet, P. (1980), *La Glyptique mésopotamienne archaïque*, 2nd ed. Paris.

Amiet, P. (1983), "Iconographie de la Bactriane proto-historique", *AnSt* 23: 19–27.

Amiet, P. (1986), *L'Âge des échanges inter-iraniens, 3500–1700 avant J.-C.* Paris.

Amiet, P. (1988), *Suse, 6000 ans d'histoire*. Paris.

Amiet, P. (1990), "Quelques épaves de la vaisselle royale perse de Suse", in Vallat, ed., 213–224.
Amiet, P.(1994), "Un étage au Palais de Darius à Suse?", in Dietrich and Loretz, eds., 1–5.
Amiet, P. (2001), "La sculpture susienne à l'époque de l'Empire parthe", *IrAnt* 36: 238–291.
Amiet, P. (2010a), "L'art mobilier à Suse à l'époque perse", in Perrot, ed., 350–363.
Amiet, P. (2010b), "Le palais de Darius à Suse: problèmes et hypothèses", *ARTA* 2010.001.
Amin, S. (1976), *Unequal Development: An Essay on the Social Formations of Peripheral Capitalism*. New York.
Amiran, R. (1970a), *Ancient Pottery of the Holy Land: From its Beginnings in the Neolithic Period to the End of the Iron Age*. New Brunswick.
Amiran, R. (1970b), "The beginnings of urbanization in Canaan", in Sanders, ed., 83–100.
Amiran, R. and Gophna, R. (1989), "Urban Canaan in the Early Bronze II and III periods -Emergence and structure", in de Miroschedji, ed., 109–116.
Ammerman, A.J. (2010), "The first Argonauts: towards the study of the earliest seafaring in the Mediterranean", in Anderson et al., eds., 81–92.
Ammerman, A.J., Flourentzos, P., Gabrielli, R., Higham, T., McCartney, T. and Turnbull, T. (2008), "Third report on early sites on Cyprus", *RDAC*: 1–32.
Amr, K., Zayadine, F. and Zaghloul, M., eds. (1995), *Studies in the History and Archaeology of Jordan*. Amman.
An, Z. (1992), "The Bronze Age in eastern parts of Central Asia", in Dani and Masson, eds., 319–336.
Anastasio, S. (2008), "La missione archeologica italiana in Mesopotamia del 1933 e lo scavo di Kilizu (Qasr Shamamuk, Iraq): I materiali conservati a Firenze", *Annuario della scuola archeologica di Atene e dell missioni italiane in oriente* 83: 197–234.
Anastasio, S., Lebeau, M. and Sauvage, M. (2004), *Atlas of preclassical Upper Mesopotamia*. Brussels.
Anati, E. (1968), "Anatolia's earliest art", *Archaeology* 21: 22–35.
Anbar, M. (1991), *Les tribus amurrites de Mari*. Fribourg.
Andersen, E. and Nosch, M-L., eds. (2011), *Textile Production in the Ancient Near East*. Copenhagen.
Andersen, H.H. and Højlund, eds. (2003), *The Barbar Temples*, 2 vols. Aarhus.
Anderson, A., Barrett, J. and Boyle, K., eds. (2010), *The Global Origins and Development of Seafaring*. Cambridge.
Anderson, B. (1983), *Imagined Communities: Reflections on the Origin and Spread of Nationalism*. London.
Anderson, B. (2010), "Achaemenid Arabia: a landscape-oriented model of cultural interaction", in Curtis and Simpson, eds., 445–455.
Anderson, D.E., Goudie, A.S. and Parker, A.G. (2007), *Global Environments Through the Quaternary: Exploring Environmental Change*. Oxford.
Anderson, D.G., Maasch, K.A. and Sandweiss, D.H., eds. (2007), *Climate Change and Cultural Dynamics: A Global Perspective on Mid-Holocene Transitions*. New York.
Anderson, J.D. (2003), "The impact of Rome on the periphery: the case of Palestina – Roman Period (63 BCE–324 CE)", in Levy, ed., 446–469.

Anderson, P. (1991), "Harvesting of wild cereals during the Natufian as seen from the experimental cultivation and harvest of wild einkorn wheat and microwear analysis of stone tools", in Bar-Yosef and Valla, eds., 521–556.

Anderson, P., Chabot, J. and van Gijn, A. (2004), "The functional riddle of 'glossy' Canaanean blades and the Near Eastern threshing sledge", *JMA* 17: 87–130.

Anderson, W.P. (1987), "The kilns and workshops of Sarepta (Sarafand, Lebanon): remnants of a Phoenician ceramic industry", *Berytus* 35: 41–66.

Anderson, W.P. (1988), *Sarepta I. The Late Bronze and Iron Age Strata of Area II,4*. Beirut.

Andrae, W. (1908), *Hatra. Teil 1: Allgemeine Beschreibung der Ruinen*. Leipzig.

Andrae, W. (1909), *Der Anu-Adad-Tempel*. Leipzig.

Andrae, W. (1912), *Hatra. Teil 2: Einzelbeschreibung der Ruinen*. Leipzig.

Andrae, W. (1913), *Die Festungswerke von Assur*. Leipzig.

Andrae, W. (1922), *Die archaischen Ischtar-Tempel in Assur*. Leipzig.

Andrae, W. (1935), *Die jüngeren Ischtar-Tempel in Assur*. Leipzig.

Andrae, W. (1977[1938]), *Das wiedererstandene Assur*. Munich.

Andrae, W. and Bachmann, W. (1914), "Aus den Berichten über die Grabungen in Tulul Akir (Kar Tukulti-Ninib)", *MDOG* 53: 41–57.

Andrae, W. and Lenzen, H. (1933), *Die Partherstadt Assur*. Leipzig.

Andrássy, P., Budka, J. and Kammerzell, F., eds. (2009), *Non-textual Marking Systems, Writing and Pseudo Script from Prehistory to Modern Times*. Göttingen.

Andreeva, M.V. (1977), "K Voprosu o Yuzhnykh Svyazakh Maikopskoi Kul'tury", *Sovetskaya Arkheologiya* 1: 39–56.

Andrefsky, W., Jr. (1998), *Lithics: Macroscopic Approaches to Analysis*. Cambridge.

Andrén, A. (1998), *Between Artifacts and Texts: Historical Archaeology in Global Perspective*. New York.

André-Salvini, B., ed. (2008), *Babylone*. Paris.

Andrews, P. (1973), "The White House of Khurasan: the felt tents of the Iranian Yomut and Göklen", *Iran* 11: 93–110.

Anreiter, P., Bartosiewicz, L., Jerem, E. and Meids, W., eds. (1998), *Man and the Animal World: Studies in Memoriam Sándor Bökönyi*. Budapest.

Anthes, R.J. (1954), *The Head of Queen Nofretete*. Berlin.

Anthony, D.W. (1991), "The domestication of the horse", in Meadow and Uerpmann, eds., 250–277.

Anthony, D.W. (2007), *The Horse, the Wheel, and Language: How Bronze-Age Riders from the Eurasian Steppes Shaped the Modern World*. Princeton.

Anthony, D.W. and Vinogradov, N. (1995), "Birth of the chariot", *Archaeology* 48/2: 36–41.

Aperghis, G.G. (2004), *The Seleukid Royal Economy: The Finances and Financial Administration of the Seleukid Empire*. Cambridge.

Appadurai, A. (2006), *Fear of Small Numbers. An Essay on the Geography of Anger*. Durham.

Aqrawi, A.A.M. (2001), "Stratigraphic signatures of climatic change during the Holocene evolution of the Tigris-Euphrates delta, lower Mesopotamia", *Global and Planetary Change* 28: 267–283.

Arbuckle, B.S. (2008a), "Revisiting Neolithic caprine exploitation at Suberde, Turkey", *JFA* 32: 219–236.

Arbuckle, B.S. (2008b), "Zooarchaeology at Koşk Höyük", *Kazi Sonuçlari Toplantisi* 27: 124–136.
Arbuckle, B.S. (2009), "Chalcolithic caprines, Dark Age dairy and Byzantine beef", *Anatolica* 35: 179–224.
Arbuckle, B.S. and Makarewicz, C.A. (2009), "The early management of cattle (*Bos taurus*) in Neolithic central Anatolia", *Antiquity* 83: 669–686.
Arbuckle, B.S. and Özkaya, V. (2007), "Animal exploitation at Körtik Tepe: an early Aceramic Neolithic site in southeastern Turkey", *Paléorient* 32: 198–211.
ArchaeNova, ed. (2009), *Erste Tempel – frühe Siedlungen. 12000 Jahre Kunst und Kultur. Ausgrabungen und Forschungen zwischen Donau und Euphrat*. Oldenburg.
Archi, A. (1991), "Culture de l'olivier et production de l'huile à Ebla", in Charpin and Joannès, eds., 211–222.
Archi, A. (1993), "Bronze alloys in Ebla", in Frangipane et al., eds., 615–625.
Archi, A. and Biga, M.G. (2003), "A victory over Mari and the fall of Ebla", *JCS* 55: 1–44.
Archibald, Z.H., Davies, J., Gabrielsen, V. and Oliver, G.J., eds. (2001), *Ancient Economies*. London/New York.
Areshian, G., ed. (in press), *Empires and Complexity: On the Crossroads of Archaeology, History, and Anthropology*. Los Angeles.
Areshian, G., Kafadarian, K., Simonian, A., Tiratsian, G. and Kalantarian, A. (1977), "Arkheologicheskie Issledovaniya v Ashtarakskom i Nairiskom Raionakh Armyanskoi SSR", *Vestnik Obshchesvennikh Nauk* 4: 77–93.
Areshian, G., Oganesyan, V.E., Muradyan, F.M., Avetisyan, P.S. and Petrosyan, L.A. (1990), "Konets Srednego Bronzovogo Veka v Mezhdurech'e Araksa i Kury", *Istoriko-Filologicheskij Zhurnal* 128/1: 53–74.
Arimura, M. (1999), "The lithic industry of the Final Pottery Neolithic: new evidence from Tell Ain el-Kerkh, Northwest Syria", *Neo-Lithics* 3: 7–10.
Armitage, S.J., Jasim, S.A., Marks, A.E., Parker, A.G., Usik, V.I. and Uerpmann, H.-P. (2011), "The southern route 'out of Africa': evidence for an early expansion of modern humans into Arabia", *Science* 331: 453–456.
Armstrong, J.A. (1989), *The Archaeology of Nippur from the Decline of the Kassite Kingdom until the Rise of the Neo-Babylonian Empire*. Chicago.
Arnaud, D. (1985a), *Recherches au Pays d'Aštata. Emar VI.1. Textes sumériens et accadiens. Planches*. Paris.
Arnaud, D. (1985b), *Recherches au Pays d'Aštata. Emar VI.2. Textes sumériens et accadiens. Planches*. Paris.
Arnaud, D. (1986), *Recherches au Pays d'Aštata. Emar VI.3. Textes sumériens et accadiens. Texte*. Paris.
Arnaud, D. (1987), *Recherches au Pays d'Aštata. Emar VI.4. Textes de la bibliothèque. Transcriptions et Traductions*. Paris.
Arndt, A., Van Neer, W., Hellemans, B., Robben, J., Volckaert, F. and Waelkens, M. (2003), "Roman trade relationships at Sagalassos (Turkey) elucidated by ancient DNA of fish remains", *JAS* 30/9: 1095–1105.
Arndt, H. (1984), *Persepolis*. Stuttgart.
Arne, T.J. (1935), *The Swedish Archaeological Expedition to Iran, 1932–1933*. Copenhagen.
Arne, T.J. (1945), *Excavations at Shah Tepe, Iran*. Stockholm.

Arnold, D.E. (1985), *Ceramic Theory and Cultural Process*. Cambridge.
Aro, S. (2003), "Art and architecture", in Melchert, ed., 281–337.
Arsebük, G. (1998), "A review of the current status of Pleistocene archaeology in Turkey", in Arsebük et al., eds., 71–76.
Arsebük, A., Mellink, M.J. and Schirmer, W.J., eds. (1998), *Light on Top of the Black Hill: Studies Presented to Halet Çambel*. Istanbul.
Artin, G. (2010), "The necropolis and dwellings of Byblos during the Chalcolithic period: new interpretations", *NEA* 73/2–3: 74–84.
Artzi, P., Cohen, C., Eichler, B.L. and Hurowitz, V.A., eds. (2005), *An Experienced Scribe Who Neglects Nothing: Ancient Near Eastern Studies in Honor of Jacob Klein*. Bethesda.
Arutiunian, N. (2001), *Korpus Urartskih Klinoobraznih Nadpisei*. Erevan.
Aruz, J., ed. (2003), *Art of the First Cities: The Third millennium BC from the Mediterranean to the Indus*. New York.
Aruz, J., Benzel, K. and Evans, J.M., eds. (2008), *Beyond Babylon: Art, Trade, and Diplomacy in the Second Millennium BC*. New Haven and London.
Arz, H.W., Lamy, F. and Pätzold, J. (2006), "A pronounced dry event recorded around 4.2 ka in brine sediments from the northern Red Sea", *QR* 66: 432–444.
Asadi, A. and Kaim, B. (2009), "The Achaemenid building at site 64 in Tang-e Bulaghi", *ARTA* 2009.003.
Asal, R. (2010), "Les ports byzantins au quotidien", in Anonymous, ed., 152–155.
Asgari Chaverdi, A. (1999/2000 [2001]), "Fārs after Darius III: discoveries at an ancient site in Lāmerd, Fārs", *IJAH* 13/2–14/1: 66–72, 6.
Asgari Chaverdi, A. (2002), "Recent post-Achaemenid finds from southern Fars, Iran", *Iran* 40: 277–278.
Asgari Chaverdi, A. (2008), "Excavations at the Persepolis drainage system", *IJAH* 21/1: 65–72.
Asgari Chaverdi, A. and Azarnoush, M. (2004), "Archaeological survey in the hinterland of the Persian Gulf: Lamerd and Mohr districts, Fars", *IJAH* 18/2: 3–18.
Asgari Chaverdi, A., and Callieri, P. (2006), "A rural settlement of the Achaemenid period in Fars", *JIAAA* 1: 65–70.
Asgari Chaverdi, A. and Callieri, P. (2009), "Achaemenid and post-Achaemenid remains at TB 76 and TB 77", *ARTA* 2009.004.
Asgari Chaverdi, A. and Callieri, P. (forthcoming), "The activities of the Irano-Italian Joint Archaeological Mission at Persepolis West (Fars, Iran). First results of the studies on the pottery of Achaemenid and Post-Achaemenid age", in *Proceedings of the Workshop "Territorial System and Ideology in the Achaemenid State: Persepolis and its Settlements"*.
Asgari Chaverdi, A., Khosrowzadeh, A., McCall, B., Petrie, C.A., Potts, D.T., Roustaei, K., Seyedin, M., Weeks, L. and Zaidi, M. (2010), "Archaeological evidence for Achaemenid settlement within the Mamasani Valleys, western Fars, Iran", in Curtis and Simpson, eds., 287–297.
Asgari Chaverdi, A., Petrie, C.A. and Taylor, H. (2008), "Early villages on the Persian Gulf littoral: revisiting Tol-e Pir in the Galehdār Valley", *Iran* 46: 21–42.
Aslan, R., Blum, S., Kastl, G., Schweizer, F. and Thumm, D., eds. (2002), *Festschrift für Manfred Korfmann*. Grunbach.
Asouti, E. (2006), "Beyond the Pre-Pottery Neolithic B interaction sphere", *JWP* 20: 87–126.

Asouti, E. and Hather, J. (2001), "Charcoal analysis and the reconstruction of ancient woodland vegetation in the Konya basin, south-central Anatolia, Turkey: results from the Neolithic site of Çatalhöyük East", *VHA* 10: 23–32.

Asselberghs, H. (1961), *Chaos en beheersing*. Leiden.

Aston, D.A. (1999), "Dynasty 26, Dynasty 30, or Dynasty 27? In search of the funerary archaeology of the Persian period", in Leahy and Tait, eds., 17–22.

Aston, D.A. (2008), "A history of Tell el-Yahudiyeh typology", in Bietak and Czerny, eds., 165–194.

Astruc, L., Binder, D. and Briois, F., eds. (2007), *Technical Systems and Near Eastern PPN Communities*. Antibes.

Astruc, L., Gaulon, A. and Salanova, L. eds. (2009), *Méthodes d'approche des premières productions céramiques: Étude de cas dans les Balkans et au Levant*. Rahden.

Atai, M.T. and Boucharlat, R. (2009), "An Achaemenid pavilion and other remains in Tang-i Bulaghi", *ARTA* 2009.005.

Atalay, S., and Hastorf, C. (2006), "Foodways at Çatalhöyük", in Hodder ed., 109–124.

Atarachi, K. and Horiuchi, K. (1963), *Fahlian I. Excavations at Tepe Suruvan, 1959*. Tokyo.

Ateşlier, S. (2001), "Observations on an early Classical building of the satrapal period at Daskyleion", in Bakir, ed., 147–168.

Athanassopoulis, E. and Wandsnider, L-A., eds. (2004), *Mediterranean Archaeological Landscapes: Current Issues*. Philadelphia.

Atici, L. (2009), "Implications of age structures for Epipaleolithic hunting strategies in the western Taurus mountains, southwest Turkey", *Anthropozoologica* 44: 13–40.

Attinger, P. and Wäfler, M., eds. (1998), *Mesopotamien: Späturuk-Zeit und frühdynastische Zeit*. Fribourg/Göttingen.

Attinger, P. and Wäfler, M., eds. (1999), *Mesopotamien: Akkade-Zeit und Ur III-Zeit*. Fribourg and Göttingen.

Atwood, R. (2004), *Stealing History: Tomb Raiders, Smugglers, and the Looting of the Ancient World*. New York.

Auberson, P. (1966), "Étude des gouttières (Annexe 2)", in Ghirshman, 113–118.

Augé, C. (1988), "Note sur les monnaies découvertes en 1986 et 1987", *Syria* 65: 283–284.

Augé, C., Curiel, R. and Le Rider, G. (1979), *Terrasses sacrées de Bard-è Néchandeh et Masjid-e Solaiman. Les trouvailles monétaires*. Paris.

Aurenche, O. (1982), "À l'origine du temple et du palais dans les civilisations de la Mésopotamie ancienne", *Ktema* 7: 237–261.

Aurenche, O., Evin, J. and Hours, F., eds. (1987), *Chronologies in the Near East: Relative Chronologies and Absolute Chronology, 16,000–4,000 B.P.* Oxford.

Aurenche, O. and Kozłowski, S.K. (1999), *La Naissance du Néolithique au Proche Orient*. Paris.

Aurenche, O. and Kosłowski, S.K. (2000), "Continuité, convergances, influences et innovations dans la préhistoire récente de Mésopotamie", in Guilaine, ed, 83–95.

Austin, M.M. (2003), "The Seleukids and Asia", in Erskine, ed., 128–129.

Austin, M.M., Harries, J. and Smith, C., eds. (1998), *Modus Operandi: Essays in Honour of Geoffrey Rickman*. London.

Avanesova, N.A. and Dzhurakulova, D.M. (2008), "Drevneishchei Nomady Zeravshana", in Pidaev, ed., 13–33.

Avanzini, A., ed. (1997), *Profumi d'Arabia*. Rome.
Avanzini, A. (2002), *Khor Rori Report I*. Pisa.
Avanzini, A. (2005), "The hegemony of Qataban", in Gunter, ed., 20–24.
Avanzini, A. (2007), "Sumhuram: a Hadrami port on the Indian Ocean", in Seland, ed., 21–31.
Avanzini, A. (2008), *A Port in Arabia Between Rome and the Indian Ocean (3rd C. BC – 5th C. AD). Khor Rori Report 2*. Rome.
Avanzini, A. and Sedov, A. (2005), "The stratigraphy of Sumhuram: new evidence", *PSAS* 35: 11–17.
Avery, D.H. (1982), "The iron bloomery", in Wertime and Wertime, eds., 205–214.
Avetisian, P., Badaljan, R., Hmayakian, S. and Piliposian, A. (1996), "Regarding the problem of periodization and chronology of Bronze and Iron Age Armenia", in Kalantarian, ed., 8–10.
Avetisyan, P., Chataigner, C. and Palumbi, G. (2006), "The results of the excavations of Nerkin Godedzor (2005–2006): preliminary report", *Aramazd* 1: 6–18.
Avi-Yonah, M. (1954), *The Madaba Map*. Jerusalem.
Aviam, M. (1999), "Christian Galilee in the Byzantine period", in Meyers, ed., 281–300.
Avigad, N. (1993), "The Nea: Justinian's church of St Mary, mother of God, discovered in the Old City of Jerusalem", in Tsafrir, ed., 128–135.
Awad, G. (1947), "Ancient church architecture in Iraq belonging to the Eastern Syrians", *Sumer* 3: 100–116 (in Arabic).
Ayoub, S. (1981), "Nordabschnitt III., 1977 (5. Kampagne)", in Hrouda, 51–53.
Ayvazian, A. (2004), "The god Haldi and Urartian statehood", in Hutter and Hutter-Braunsar, eds., 27–30.
Ayvazian, A. (2006), *Urartian Glyptic: New Perspectives*. Berkeley, or online: http://gradworks.umi.com/32/54/3254256.html.
Azarnoush, M. (1994), *The Sasanian Manor House at Hajiabad, Iran*. Florence.
Azarnoush, M., ed., (2004), *Proceedings of the international symposium on Iranian archaeology: Northwestern Region*. Tehran.
Azarnoush, M. (2007), "Gozāreš-e kavousha-ye layešenakhti-e Tapeh Hagmatāne, Hamadān", in Anonymous (2007b), ed., 20–37.
Azarnoush, M. and Helwing, B. (2005), "Recent archaeological research in Iran: prehistory to Iron Age", *AMIT* 37: 189–246.
Azarpay, G. (1968), *Urartian Art and Artifacts: A Chronological Study*. Berkeley/London.
Azize, J. and Weeks, N., eds. (2007), *Gilgameš and the World of Assyria*. Leuven/Paris/Dudley.
Azzara, V.M. (2009), "Domestic architecture at the Early Bronze Age sites HD-6 and RJ-2 (Ja'alan, Sultanate of Oman)", *PSAS* 39: 1–15.
Azzoni, A., Dusinberre, E., Garrison, M.B., Henkelman, W.F.M., Jones, C.E. and Stolper, M.W. (in press), "Persepolis Administrative Archives", *EnIr* online.
Baadsgaard, A., Boutin, A.T. and Buikstra, J.E., eds. (2011), *Breathing new life into the evidence of death: New approaches to bioarchaeology*. Santa Fe.
Baccache, E. (1980), *Églises de village de la Syrie du Nord. Album*. Paris.
Bachelot, L. (1999), "Tell Shioukh Faouqâni (1994–1998)", in del Olmo Lete and Fenollós, eds., 143–162.

Bachelot, L. and Castel, C. (1989), "Recherches sur la ziggourat de Larsa", in Huot, ed., 53–77.
Bachhuber, C. (2006), "Aegean interest on the Uluburun ship", *AJA* 110: 345–63.
Bachhuber, C. (2009), "The treasure deposits of Troy: rethinking crisis and agency on the Early Bronze Age citadel", *AnSt* 59: 1–18.
Bachhuber, C. (2011), "Negotiating metal and the metal form in the Royal Tombs of Alaçahöyük in north-central Anatolia", in Wilkinson et al., eds., 158–174.
Bachhuber, C. (in press), "The Anatolian context of Philia material culture on Cyprus", in Knapp and van Dommelen, eds.
Bachhuber, C. (in preparation), *Material and Landscape in Early Bronze Age Anatolia: Citadels, Cemeteries and Their Interpretation*. London.
Bachmann, H-G. (1980), "Early copper smelting techniques in Sinai and in the Negev as deduced from slag investigations", in Craddock, ed., 103–134.
Bacon, E. (1954), "Types of pastoral nomadism in Central and Southwest Asia", *SWJA* 10: 44–68.
Bacqué-Grammont, J.-L. and Dor, L. eds. (1992), *Mélanges offerts à Louis Bazin*. Paris.
Badalyan, R. and Avetisyan, P. (2007), *Bronze and Early Iron Age Archaeological Sites in Armenia I: Mt Aragats and Its Surrounding Region*. Oxford.
Badalyan, R., Lombard, P., Chataigner, C. and Avetisyan, P. (2004), "The Neolithic and Chalcolithic phases in the Ararat Plain (Armenia): the view from Aratashen", in Sagona, ed. 399–420.
Badalyan, R., Smith, A.T. and Avetisyan, P.. (2003), "The emergence of socio-political complexity in southern Caucasia", in Smith and Rubinson, eds., 144–166.
Badalyan, R., Smith, A.T., Lindsay, I., Khatchadourian, L. and Avetisyan, P. (2008), "Village, fortress, and town in Bronze and Iron Age southern Caucasia: a preliminary report on the 2003–2006 investigations of Project ArAGATS on the Tsaghkahovit Plain, Republic of Armenia", *AMIT* 40: 45–105.
Badawy, A. (1958), "Architectural provision against heat in the Orient", *JNES* 17/2: 122–128.
Badawy, A. (1966), *Architecture in Ancient Egypt and the Near East*. Cambridge/London.
Bader, A., Callieri, P. and Khodzhaniyazov, T. (1998), "Survey of the 'Antiochus' wall. Preliminary report on the 1993–1994 campaigns", in Gubaev et al., eds., 159–186.
Bader, N.O. (1989), *Earliest Cultivators in Northern Mesopotamia: The Investigations of the Soviet Archaeological Expedition in Iraq at Settlements Tell Magzaliya, Tell Sotto, Kültepe*. Moscow (in Russian with English summary).
Bader, N.O. (1993), "Tell Maghzaliyah: an early Neolithic site in Northern Iraq", in Yoffee and Clark, eds., 7–40.
Badre, L. (1998), "Beyrouth: découverte d'une cité fortifié", in Anonymous, ed., 76–78.
Badre, L. (2006), "Tell Kazel-Simyra: a contribution to a relative chronological history in the Eastern Mediterranean during the Late Bronze Age", *BASOR* 343: 65–95.
Badre, L. and Gubel, E. (1999–2000), "Tell Kazel (Syria): excavations of the AUB Museum, 1993–1998. Third preliminary report", *Berytus* 44: 123–203.
Badre, L. and Thalmann, J.-P. (1996), "Les découvertes archéologiques du centre-ville de Beyrouth", *CRAIBL* 996: 87–97.

Baeteman, C., Dupin, L. and Heyvaert, V. (2004), "Geo-environmental investigations", in Gasche, ed., 155–205.
Bagatti, B. (1971a), *Antichi villaggi Cristiani di Galilea*. Jerusalem.
Bagatti, B. (1971b), *The Church from the Gentiles in Palestine: History and Archaeology*. Jerusalem.
Bagatti, B. (1979), *Antichi villaggi Cristiani di Samaria*. Jerusalem.
Bagatti, B. (1983), *Antichi villaggi Cristiani della Giudea e del Neghev*. Jerusalem.
Bagatti, B. and Testa, E. (1978), *Il Golgota e la Croce*. Jerusalem.
Bagg, A.M. (2000), *Assyrische Wasserbauten*. Wiesbaden.
Bagg, A.M. (2001), "Wasserhebevorrichtungen im Alten Mesopotamien", *Wasser & Boden* 53/6: 40–7.
Bagg, A.M. (2003), "2000 Jahre Wasserbau im Alten Mesopotamien: Ein Überblick", in Ohlig, ed., 107–117.
Bagg, A.M. (in press), "Untersuchungen zu den arabischen Toponymen und zur Rezeption der Araber in den historischen Quellen der Assyrer", in Eichmann and Hausleiter, eds.
Bagh, T. (2003), "The relationship between Levantine Painted Ware, Syro/Cilician Ware and Khabur Ware and the chronology implications", in Bietak, ed., 219–237.
Bagherzadeh, F., ed. (1972), *Proceedings of the Ist Annual Symposium of Archaeological Research in Iran 1972*. Tehran.
Bagherzadeh, F., ed. (1974), *Proceedings of the IInd Annual Symposium on Archaeological Research in Iran, 29th October–1st November 1973*. Tehran.
Bagherzadeh, F., ed. (1975), *Proceedings of the IIIrd Annual Symposium on Archaeological Research in Iran, 1974*. Tehran.
Bagherzadeh, F., ed. (1976), *Proceedings of the IVth Annual Symposium on Archaeological Research in Iran 1975*. Tehran.
Baginski, A. and Tidhar, A. (1980), *Textiles from Egypt: 4th–13th Centuries CE*. Jerusalem.
Bagnall, R.S. (1976), *The Administration of the Ptolemaic Possessions Outside Egypt*. Leiden.
Bahrani, Z. (2008a), *Rituals of War*. New York.
Bahrani, Z. (2008b), "The battle for Babylon", in Stone and Bajjaly, eds., pp. 165–172.
Bailey, G., al-Sharekh, A., Flemming, N., Lambeck, K., Momber, G., Sinclair, A. and Vita-Finzi, C. (2007), "Coastal prehistory in the southern Red Sea Basin, underwater archaeology and the Farasan Islands", *PSAS* 37: 1–16.
Bailey, H.W., Bivar, A.D.H., Duchesne-Guillemin, J. and Hinnells, J.R., eds. (1985), *Papers in Honour of Professor Mary Boyce*, 2 vols. Leiden.
Baimatowa, N.S. (2008), *5000 Jahre Architektur in Mittelasien. Lehmziegelgewölbe vom 4./3. Jt. V. Chr. bis zum Ende des 8. Jhs. n. Chr.* Mainz.
Baines, J. (2007), *Visual and Written Culture in Ancient Egypt*. Oxford.
Baines, J., James, T.G.H. and Leahy, A., eds. (1998), *Pyramid Studies and Other Essays Presented to I.E.S. Edwards*. London.
Baird, D. (2006), "The history of settlement and social landscapes in the Early Holocene in the Çatalhöyük area", in Hodder I ed., 55–74.
Baird, D. (2007), "Pinarbaşi Orta Anadolu'da Epi-Paleolitik Konak Yerinden Yerlesik Köy Yaşamina", in Özdoğan and Başgelen eds., 285–311.

Baird, D. (2010), "Was Çatalhöyük a centre: the implications of a late Aceramic Neolithic assemblage from the neighbourhood of Çatalhöyük", in Bolger and Maguire eds., 207–216.

Baird, D. (in press), "Pinarbaşi: From Epipalaeolithic campsite to sedentarising village in central Anatolia", in Özdoğan and Başgelen eds.

Baird, D., Carruthers, D., Fairbairn, A., and Pearson, J., (2011), "Ritual in the landscape: evidence from Pinarbaşi in the 7th millennium BC cal Konya Plain", *Antiquity* 85: 380–394.

Baird, D., Fairbairn, A., Martin L. and Middleton, C. (in press), "The Boncuklu Project: the origins of sedentism, cultivation and herding in central Anatolia", in Özdoğan and Başgelen eds.

Baker, H.D. (1995), "Neo-Babylonian burials revisited", in Campbell and Green, eds., 209–220.

Baker, H.D. (2007), "Urban form in the first millennium BC", in Leick, ed., 66–77.

Baker, H.D. (2009), "A waste of space? Unbuilt land in the Babylonian cities of the first millennium BC", *Iraq* 71: 89–98.

Baker, H.D. (2010), "The social dimensions of Babylonian domestic architecture in the Neo-Babylonian and Achaemenid periods", in Curtis and Simpson, eds., 179–194.

Baker, H.D. (2011), "From street altar to palace: reading the built environment of urban Babylonia", in Radner and Robson, eds., 533–552.

Baker, H.D. (forthcoming), *The Urban Landscape in First Millennium BC Babylonia*.

Baker, H.D. and Jursa, M., eds. (2005), *Approaching the Babylonian Economy: Proceedings of the START Project Symposium Held in Vienna, 1–3 July 2004*. Münster.

Baker, H.D., Robson, E. and Zólyomi, G., eds. (2010), *Your Praise Is Sweet: A Memorial Volume for Jeremy Black from Students, Colleagues and Friends*. London.

Baker, P. (2008), "Economy, environment and society at Kilise Tepe, southern central Turkey. Faunal remains from the 1994–1998 excavations", in Vila et al., eds., 407–430.

Bakhit, M.A., ed. (1987), *Proceedings of the Second Symposium on the history of Bilād al-Shām during the Early Islamic Period up to 40 A.H./640 AD.*, vol. 1. Amman.

Bakhit, M.A. and Schick, R., eds. (1989), *The Fourth International Conference on the History of Bilād al Shām during the Umayyad Period. Proceedings of the Third Symposium 2–7 Rabī' 1408 A.H./24–29 October 1987. English Section*, vol. 2. Amman.

Bakir, T., ed. (2001a), *Achaemenid Anatolia: Proceedings of the First International Symposium on Anatolia in the Achaemenid period, Bandirma 15–18 August, 1997*. Leiden.

Bakir, T. (2001b), "Die Satrapie in Daskyleion", in Bakir, ed., 169–180.

Bakker, E.J., de Jong, I.J.F and van Wees, H., eds. (2002), *Brill's Companion to Herodotus*. Leiden.

Balcer, J.M. (1991), "Erich Friedrich Schmidt, 13 September 1897–3 October 1964", in Sancisi-Weerdenburg and Drijvers, eds., 147–172.

Balfet, H. (1980), "A propos du métier de l'argile: exemple de dialogue entre ethnologie et archéologie", in Barrelet, ed., 71–92.

Balkan-Atli, N. (1994), "The typological characteristics of the Aşikli Höyük chipped stone industry", in Gebel and Kozlowski, eds., 209–222.

Balkan-Atli, N., Kayacan,N., Özbaşaran, M. and Yildirim, S. (2001), "Variability in the Neolithic arrowheads of Central Anatolia (typological, technological and chronological aspect)", in Caneva et al., eds. 27–43.

Ball, W. (1996), "The Upper Tigris area: new evidence from the Eski Mosul and North Jazira projects", in Bartl and Hauser, eds., 415–427.

Ball, W. (2000), *Rome in the East: The Transformation of an Empire*. London.

Ball, W., Tucker, D. and Wilkinson, T.J. (1989), "The Tell al-Hawa Project: archaeological investigations in the North Jazira 1986–87", *Iraq* 51: 1–66.

Ballet, P. (1998), "Cultures matérielles des déserts d'Égypte sous le Haut et le Bas-Empire. Productions et échanges", in Kaper, ed., 31–54.

Balon, E.K. (1995), "Origin and domestication of the wild carp, *Cyprinus carpio*: from Roman gourmets to the swimming flowers", *Aquaculture* 129: 3–48.

Balossi, F. (2004), "New data for the definition of the DFBW horizon and its internal developments: the earliest phases of the Amuq sequence revisited", *Anatolica* 30: 109–149.

Balout, L. and Roubet, C., eds. (1985), *La Momie de Ramses II: Contribution scientifique à l'Égyptologie*. Paris.

Balter, M. (2010), "Hodder cleans house at famed Çatalhöyük dig", *Science Insider*, 9/3/2010. http://news.sciencemag.org/scienceinsider/2010/09/hodder-cleans-house-at-famed-ata.html. Last accessed on 17/12/2010.

Balty, J.-C. (1988), "Apamea in Syria in the second and third centuries AD", *JRS* 78: 91–104.

Balty, J.-C. (2000), "*Claudia Apamea*. Données nouvelles sur la topographie et l'histoire d'Apamée, *CRAIBL* 2000: 459–495.

Balty, J.-C. (2003), "À la recherche de l'Apamée hellénistique: les témoignages archéologiques", in Sartre et al., eds., 223–252.

Bangsgaard, P. (2003), "Appendix 1. Animal bones from the Barbar temple", in Andersen and Højlund, eds., 7–16.

Banning, E.B. (1996), "Houses, compounds, and mansions in the prehistoric Near East", in Coupland and Banning, eds., 165–185.

Banning, E.B. (1998), "The Neolithic period: triumphs of architecture, agriculture, and art", *NEA* 61/4: 188–237.

Banning, E.B. (2002), "Spatial and architectural aspects of Neolithization", in Hausleiter et al., eds., 307–312.

Banning, E.B. (2003), "Housing Neolithic farmers", *NEA* 66: 4–21.

Banning, E.B. (2004), "Changes in the spatial organization of Transjordanian settlements from Middle PPNB to Late Neolithic", in Bienert et al., eds., 215–232.

Banning, E.B. (2007), "Wadi Rabah and related assemblages in the Southern Levant: interpreting the radiocarbon evidence", *Paléorient* 33: 77–101.

Banning, E.B. (2009), "From out of left field: excavations in the South Field, 'Ain Ghazal", in Gebel et al., 18–23.

Banning, E.B. (2010), "Houses, households, and changing society in the Late Neolithic and Chalcolithic of the Southern Levant", *Paléorient* 36/1: 49–87.

Banning, E.B. and Byrd, B.F. (1987), "Houses and the changing residential unit: domestic architecture at PPNB 'Ain Ghazal, Jordan", *PPS* 53: 309–325.

Banning, E.B. and Chazan, M., eds. (2006), *Domesticating Space: Construction, Community, and Cosmology in the Late Prehistoric Near East*. Berlin.

Banning, E.B., Dods, R.D., Field, J.J., Maltby, S.L., McCorriston, J., Monckton, S., Rubenstein, R. and Sheppard, P. (1989), "Wadi Ziqlab Project 1987. A preliminary report", *ADAJ* 33: 43–58, 370.

Banning, E.B., Rahimi, D. and Siggers, J. (1994), "The Late Neolithic of the Southern Levant: Hiatus, settlement shift, or observer bias?", *Paléorient* 20: 151–164.

Baqir, T. (1944), "Iraq Government excavations at 'Aqar Quf. First interim report, 1942–43", *Iraq* Supplement: 3–16.

Baqir, T. (1945), "Iraq Government excavations at 'Aqar Quf. Second interim report, 1943–44", *Iraq* Supplement:1–15.

Baqir, T. (1946), "Tell Harmal. A preliminary report", *Sumer* 2: 22–30.

Baqir, T. (1948), "Excavations at Harmal", *Sumer* 4: 137–139.

Bar, D. (2005), "Rural monasticism as a key element in the Christianization of Byzantine Palestine", *Harvard Theological Review* 98/1: 49–65.

Bär, J. (2003), *Die älteren Ischtar-Tempel in Assur*. Saarbrücken.

Bar-Adon, P. (1980), *The Cave of the Treasure: The Finds from the Caves in Nahal Mishmar*. Jerusalem.

Barag, D. (1962), "Mesopotamian glass vessels of the second millennium BC", *JGS* 4: 9–27.

Barag, D. (1966), "The effects of the Tennes rebellion on Palestine", *BASOR* 183: 6–12.

Barag, D. (1970), "Mesopotamian core-formed glass vessels (1500–500 BC)", in Oppenheim et al., eds., 131–200.

Barag, D. (1985), *Catalogue of Western Asiatic Glass in the British Museum*. London.

Barako, T.J. (2006), "Coexistence and impermeability: Egyptians and Philistines in Southern Canaan during the twelfth century BCE", in Bietak and Czerny, eds., 509–516.

Baram, A. (1994), "A case of imported identity: the modernizing secular ruling elites of Iraq and the concept of Mesopotamian-inspired territorial nationalism, 1922–1992", *Poetics Today* 15: 279–319.

Barber, E.J. (1975), "The proto-European notion of cloth and clothing", *JIES* 3: 294–320.

Barber, E.J. (1987), "Problems and methods of reconstructing steppeland cloth and clothing", in Seaman, ed., 134–142.

Barber, E.J. (1991), *Prehistoric Textiles: The Development of Cloth in the Neolithic and Bronze Ages with Special Reference to the Aegean*. Princeton.

Bard, K.A. (2000), "The emergence of the Egyptian state", in Shaw, ed., 57–82.

Bard, K.A. (2008), *An introduction to the archaeology of Ancient Egypt*. Malden.

Bard, K.A. and Fattovich, R., eds. (2007), *Harbor of the Pharaohs to the Land of Punt: Archaeological investigations at Mersa/Wadi Gawasis, Egypt, 2001–2005*. Naples.

Bard, K., Fattovich, R. and Ward, C. (2007), "Sea port to Punt: new evidence from Marsa Gawasis, Red Sea, Egypt", in Starkey et al., eds., 143–8.

Bardill, J. (1999), "The Great Palace of the Byzantine emperors and the Walker Trust excavations", *JRA* 12: 216–230.

Bardill, J. (2006), "Visualizing the Great Palace of the Byzantine emperors at Constantinople: archaeology, text and topography", in Bauer, ed., 5–45.

Barfield, T. (2001), "The shadow empires: imperial state formation along the Chinese-nomad frontier", in Alcock et al., eds., 10–41.

Bar-Gal, K., Khalaily, H., Marder, O., Ducos, P. and Horwitz, K. (2002), "Ancient DNA evidence for the transition from wild to domestic status in Neolithic goats: a case study from the site of Abu Gosh, Israel", *Ancient Biomolecules* 4/1: 9–17.

Barkai, R. (2005), *Flint and Stone Axes as Cultural Markers*. Berlin.

Barker, G. (2000), "Farmers, herders and miners in the Wadi Feynan, southern Jordan: a 10,000 year landscape archaeology", in Barker and Gilbertson, eds., 63–85.

Barker, G. and Gilbertson, D., eds. (2000), *The Archaeology of Arid Lands*. London.

Barkoudah, Y. and Henderson, J. (2006), "Plant ashes from Syria and the manufacture of ancient glass: ethnographic and scientific aspects", *JGS* 48: 297–321.

Bar-Matthews, M. and Ayalon, A. (2011), "Mid-Holocene climate variations revealed by high-resolution speleothem records from Soreq Cave, Israel and their correlation with cultural changes", *The Holocene* 21/1: 163–171.

Bar-Matthews, M., Ayalon, A., Gilmour, M., Matthews, A. and Hawkesworth, C.J. (2003), "Sea-land oxygen isotopic relationships from planktonic foraminifera and speleothems in the Eastern Mediterranean region and their implication for paleorainfall during interglacial intervals", *Geochimica et Cosmochimica Acta* 67: 3181–3199.

Bar-Matthews, M., Ayalon, A. and Kaufman, A. (1997), "Late Quaternary paleoclimate in the Eastern Mediterranean region from stable isotope analysis of speleothems at Soreq Cave, Israel", *QR* 47: 155–68.

Barnard, H., Dooley, A.N., Areshian, G., Gasparyan, B. and Faull, K.F. (2011), "Chemical evidence for wine production around 4000 BCE in the Late Chalcolithic Near Eastern highlands", *JAS* 38: 977–984.

Barnard, H. and Wendrich, W., eds. (2008), *The Archaeology of Mobility: Old World and New World Nomadism*. Los Angeles.

Barnes, R. and Parkin, D., eds. (2002), *Ships and the Development of Maritime Technology in the Indian Ocean*. London.

Barnett, R.D. (1956), "Ancient Oriental influences on Archaic Greece", in Weinberg, ed., 218–238.

Barnett, R.D. (1976), *Sculptures from the North Palace of Ashurbanipal at Nineveh (668–627 BC)*. London.

Barnett, R.D., Bleibtreu, E. and Turner, G. (1998), *Sculptures from the Southwest Palace of Sennacherib at Nineveh*. London.

Barnett, R.D. and Falkner, M. (1962), *The Sculptures of Aššur-nasir-apli II (883–859 BC), Tiglath-Pileser III (745–727 BC), Esarhaddon (681–669 BC) from the Central and South-west Palaces at Nimrud*. London.

Barrelet, M.-L. (1970), "Étude de glyptique akkadienne", *Or* 38: 213–251.

Barrelet, M.-L., ed. (1980), *L'Archéologie de l'Iraq du début de l'époque néolithique à 333 avant notre ère*. Paris.

Barrow, S.C. (1998), "A monograph of *Phoenix* L. (*Palmae: Coryphoideae*)", *Kew Bulletin* 53: 513–575.

Barsanti, C. (1992), "Costantinopoli: testimonianze archeologiche di età costantiniana", in Bonamente and Fusco, eds., 115–150.

Barsanti, C. (1995), "Il foro di Teodosio I a Costantinopoli", in Iacobini and Zanini, eds., 9–50.

Barsanti, C. (2009), "I mosaici del grande palazzo imperiale di Costantinopoli: alcune riflessioni", in Lentini, ed., 55–73.

Barth, M.M. (2006), "The lithic artifacts from Baaz Rockshelter", in Conard, ed., 25–109.

Bartl, K. (1995), "Das Ende der Spätbronzezeit und das 'dunkle Zeitalter' im westlichen Vorderasien", in Bartl et al., eds., 193–208.

Bartl, K. (2002), "Archäologische Untersuchungen in der südlichen Akkar-Ebene, Nordlibanon: Vorläufige Ergebnisse einer Oberflächenprospektion", in Eichmann, ed., 23–48.

Bartl, K. (in press), "Shir/West Syria: the settlement and its surroundings in the 7th millennium BC", in Nieuwenhuyse et al., eds.

Bartl, K. and al-Maqdissi, M. (2007), "Ancient settlements in the Middle Orontes region between ar-Rastan and Qal'at Shayzar: first results of archaeological surface investigations 2003–2004", in Morandi Bonacossi, ed., 243–252.

Bartl, K., Bernbeck, R. and Heinz, M., eds. (1995), *Zwischen Euphrat und Indus. Aktuelle Forschungsprobleme in der Vorderasiatischen Archäologie*. Hildesheim, Zürich and New York.

Bartl, K. and Haidar, A. (2008), "Šīr – Ein neolithischer Fundplatz am mittleren Orontes. Vorläufiger Bericht über die Ergebnisse der Testkampagne Herbst 2005 und Grabungskampagne Frühjahr 2006", *ZOA* 1: 54–88.

Bartl, K. and Hauser, S., eds. (1996), *Continuity and Change in Northern Mesopotamia from the Hellenistic to the Early Islamic Period*. Berlin.

Bartl, K., Hijazi, M. and Ramadan, J. (2009), "Die spätneolithische Siedlung Shir/ Westsyrien. Vorläufiger Bericht über die Ergebnisse der Grabungskampagnen Herbst 2006 und Frühjahr 2007", *ZOA* 2: 140–161.

Bartoloni, G. and Benedettini, M.G., eds. (2007–8), *Sepolti tra i vivi. Evidenza ed interpretazione di contesti funerari in abitato*. Rome.

Bartosiewicz, L., van Neer, W. and Lentacker, A. (1997), *Draught Cattle: Their Osteological Identification and History*. Tervuren.

Baruch, U. (1986), "The late Holocene vegetational history of Lake Kinneret (Sea of Galilee), Israel", *Paléorient* 12/2: 37–48.

Baruch, U. and Bottema, S. (1999), "A new pollen diagram from Lake Hula: vegetational, climatic and anthropogenic implications", in Kawanabe et al., eds., 75–86.

Bar-Yosef, O. (1981), "The 'Pre-Pottery Neolithic' period in the southern Levant", in Cauvin and Sanlaville, eds., 555–569.

Bar-Yosef, O. (1986), "The walls of Jericho: an alternative interpretation", *CA* 27/2: 157–162.

Bar-Yosef, O. (1998a), "The Natufian culture in the Levant, threshold to the origins of agriculture", *Evolutionary Anthropology* 6: 159–177.

Bar-Yosef, O. (1998b), "Öküzini: comparisons with the Levant", in Otte, ed., 501–507.

Bar-Yosef, O. (1999), "Lower Palaeolithic sites in Southwestern Asia: evidence for 'out of Africa' movements", *Anthropologie* 37: 51–69.

Bar-Yosef, O. (2001), "From sedentary foragers to village hierarchies: the emergence of social institutions", in Runciman, ed., 1–38.

Bar-Yosef, O. (2002a), "Natufian: a complex society of foragers", in Fitzhugh and Habu, eds., 91–147.

Bar-Yosef, O., (2002b), "The Natufian culture and the early Neolithic: social and economic trends in Southwest Asia", in Bellwood and Renfrew, eds., 113–126.

Bar-Yosef, O. (2006), "Defining the Aurignacian", in Bar-Yosef and Zilhão, eds., 11–18.

Bar-Yosef, O. (2010), "Warfare in Levantine Early Neolithic: a hypothesis to be considered", *Neo-Lithics* 1/10: 6–10.

Bar-Yosef, O. and Alon, D., eds., (1988), *Nahal Hemar Cave*. Jerusalem.

Bar-Yosef, O. and Belfer-Cohen, A. (1989), "The Levantine 'PPNB' interaction sphere", in Hershkovitz, ed., 59–72.

Bar-Yosef, O. and Belfer-Cohen, A. (1999), "Encoding information: unique Natufian objects from Hayonim Cave, Western Galilee, Israel", *Antiquity* 73: 402–410.

Bar-Yosef, O. and Gopher, A., eds. (1997), *An Early Neolithic village in the Jordan Valley, Part I: The Archaeology of Netiv Hagdud*. Cambridge.

Bar-Yosef, O., Gopher, A., and Nadel, D. (1987), "The 'Hagdud Trunction' – a new tool type from the Sultanian industry at Netiv Hagdud in the Jordan Valley", *JIPS* 20: 151–157.

Bar-Yosef, O., Gopher, A., Tchernov, E. and Kislev, M.E. (1991), "Netiv Hagdud: an Early Neolithic village site in the Jordan Valley", *JFA* 18/4: 405–424.

Bar-Yosef, O. and Khazanov, A., eds. (1992), *Pastoralism in the Levant: Archaeological Materials in Anthropological Perspective*. Madison.

Bar-Yosef, O. and Meadow, R.H. (1995), "The origins of agriculture in the Near East", in Price and Gebauer, eds., 39–94.

Bar-Yosef, O. and Valla, F., eds. (1991), *The Natufian Culture in the Levant*. Madison.

Bar-Yosef, O. and Zilhão, J., eds. (2006), *Towards a Definition of the Aurignacian*. Lisbon.

Bar-Yosef Mayer, D.E. and Porat, N. (2008), "Green stone beads at the dawn of agriculture", *PNAS* 105/25: 8548–8551.

Bar-Yosef Mayer, D.E., Porat, N., Gal, Z., Shalem, D. and Smithline, H. (2004), "Steatite beads at Peqi'in: long-distance trade and pyro-technology during the Chalcolithic of the Levant", *JAS* 31/4: 493–502.

Barzilai, O. (2009), *Social Complexity in the Southern Levantine PPNB as Reflected Through Lithic Studies: The Bidirectional Blade Industries*. Jerusalem.

Başgelen, N., Çelgin, G. and Vedat Çelgin, A., eds. (2000), *Anatolian and Thracian Studies in Honour of Zafer Taşlıkoğlu*, vol. 1. Istanbul.

Basham, A.L. 1967. *The Wonder That Was India*, 3rd edn. London.

Bashash Kanzag, R. (1997), "Translation of inscriptions discovered at Bandiyān, Darreh Gaz (Dastkard-e Yazd Shāpourān)", *Archaeological Reports of Iran* 1: 33–38 (in Persian with English abstract).

Bass, G.F. (1986), "A Bronze Age shipwreck at Ulu Burun (Kaş): 1984 campaign", *AJA* 90: 269–296.

Bass, G.F., Pulak, C., Collon, D. and Weinstein, J. (1989), "The Bronze Age shipwreck at Ulu Burun: 1986 campaign", *AJA* 93: 1–29.

Batiuk, S. and Rothman, M.S. (2007), "Early Transcaucasian cultures and their neighbors: unraveling migration, trade, and assimilation", *Expedition* 49/1: 7–17.

Bator, P.M. (1982), "An essay on the international trade in art", *Stanford Law Review* 34/2: 275–384.

Bauer, F.A., ed. (2006), *Visualisierung von Herrschaft. Frühmittelalterliche Residenzen – Gestalt und Zeremoniell*. Istanbul.

Bauer, J. (1998), "Die vorsargonische Abschnitt der mesopotamischen Geschichte", in Attinger and Wäfler, eds., 431–585.

Baumer, C. (2006), *The Church of the East: An Illustrated History of Assyrian Christianity*. London.

Baur, P. and Rostovtzeff, M. et al., eds., (1929–52), *The Excavations at Dura-Europos Conducted by Yale University and the French Academy of Inscriptions and Letters. Preliminary Reports I-IX*. New Haven.

Bawden, G. and Edens, C. (1988), "Tayma Painted Ware and the Hejaz Iron Age ceramic tradition", *Levant* 20: 197–213.

Bawden, G., Edens, C. and Miller, R. (1980), "The archaeological resources of ancient Taymā: Preliminary investigations at Taymā", *Atlal* 4: 69–106.

Bawden, G. and Reycraft, R.M., eds. (2000), *Environmental Disaster and the Archaeology of Human Response*. Albuquerque.

Baxter, M.J., Cool, H.E.M., Heyworth, M.P. and Jackson, C.M. (1995), "Compositional variability in colourless Roman vessel glass", *Archaeometry* 37: 129–141.

Bayani, M.I. (1979), "The Elamite periods on the Izeh Plain", in Wright, ed., 99–105.

Beach T.P., and Luzzadder-Beach S. (2008), "Geoarchaeology and aggradation around Kinet Höyük, an archaeological mound in the eastern Mediterranean, Turkey", *Geomorphology* 101: 416–428.

Beal, R. (2009), "Schiff und Boot. C. Bei den Hethitern", *RlA* 12: 171–174.

Beale, T.W. (1978), "Bevelled-rim bowls and their implications for change and economic organization in the later 4th millennium BC", *JNES* 37: 289–313.

Beale, T.W. (1986), *Excavations at Tepe Yahya, Iran. 1967–1975: The Early Periods*. Cambridge.

Beaulieu, P.-A. (1989), *The Reign of Nabonidus, King of Babylon 556–539 BC*. New Haven.

Beaulieu, P.-A. (1994), "Antiquarianism and the concern for the past in the Neo-Babylonian period", *Bulletin of the Canadian Society for Mesopotamian Studies* 28: 37–42.

Beaulieu, P.-A. (1995), "King Nabonidus and the Neo-Babylonian Empire", in Sasson, ed. 969–979.

Beaulieu, P.-A. (2003), "Nabopolassar and the antiquity of Babylon", in Eph'al et al., eds., 1–9.

Beaulieu, P.-A. (2007), "Nabonidus the mad king: a reconsideration of his steles from Harran and Babylon", in Heinz and Feldman, eds., 137–168.

Beaumont, P., Blake, G.H. and Wagstaff, J.M. (1976), *The Middle East: A Geographical Study*. London.

Beazley, E. and Harverson, M., eds. (1982), *Living with the Desert: Working Buildings of the Iranian Plateau*. Warminster.

Beck, H.C. (1934), "Glass before 1500 BC", *Ancient Egypt and the East* 2/2: 7–21.

Becker, C. (2008), "The faunal remains from Dur-Katlimmu: insights into the diet of the Assyrians", in Vila et al., eds., 561–580.

Beckman, G. (1988), "Herding and herdsmen in Hittite culture", in Neu and Rüster, eds., 33–44.

Beckman, G. (1999a), "The city and the country in Ḫatti", in Klengel and Renger, eds., 161–169.

Beckman, G. (1999b), *Hittite Diplomatic Texts*, 2nd edn. Atlanta.

Beckman, G. and Hoffner, H., eds. (1996), *Hittite Diplomatic Texts*. Atlanta.

Bedford, P.R. (1996), "Early Achaemenid monarchs and indigenous cults: toward the definition of imperial policy", in Dillon, ed., 17–39.

Beech, M.J. (2003a), "The development of fishing in the UAE: a zooarchaeological perspective", in Potts, Al Naboodah & Hellyer, eds., 290–308.

Beech, M.J. (2003b), "Archaeobotanical evidence for early date consumption in the Arabian Gulf", in Anonymous, ed., 11–31.

Beech, M.J. (2004), *In the Land of the Icthyophagi: Modelling Fish Exploitation in the Arabian Gulf and Gulf of Oman from the 5th millennium BC to the Late Islamic period.* Oxford.

Beech, M.J. and Al-Husaini, M. (2005), "Preliminary report on the vertebrate fauna from site H3, Sabiyah: an Arabian Neolithic/'Ubaid site in Kuwait", in Buitenhuis et al., eds., 124–138.

Beech, M.J., Cuttler, R., Moscrop, D., Kallweit, H. and Martin, J. (2005), "New evidence for the Neolithic settlement of Marawah Island, Abu Dhabi, United Arab Emirates", *PSAS* 35: 37–56.

Beech, M.J. and Elders, J. (1999), "An 'Ubaid-related settlement on Dalma Island, Abu Dhabi Emirate, United Arab Emirates", *Bulletin of the Society for Arabian Studies* 4: 17–21.

Beech, M.J., Elders, J. and Shepherd, E. (2000), "Reconsidering the 'Ubaid of the Southern Gulf: New results from excavations on Dalma Island, UAE", *PSAS* 30: 41–47.

Beech, M.J., Kallweit, H., Cuttler, R. and Al-Tikriti, W.Y. (2006), "Neolithic sites in Umm az-Zamul, SE desert of Abu Dhabi, UAE", *Bulletin of the Society for Arabian Studies* 11: 17–26.

Beeston, A.F.L. (1984), "Further remarks on the Zaydil sarcophagus text", *PSAS* 14: 100–102.

Beeston, A.F.L. (2005), "The Arabian aromatics trade in Antiquity", in Macdonald and Phillips, eds., 53–64.

Begemann, F., Schmitt-Strecker, S. and Pernicka, E. (1992), "The metal finds from Thermi III-V: a chemical and lead-isotope study", *Studia Troica* 2: 219–239.

Begley, V. (1967), "Archaeological exploration in Northern Ceylon", *Expedition* 9/4: 21–29.

Begley, V. (1996), *The Ancient Port of Arikamedu: New Excavations and Researches 1989–1992,* vol. 1. Pondicherry.

Begley, V., Francis, P., Jr., Mahadevan, I., Raman, K.V., Sidebotham, S.E., Slane, K.W. and Will, E.L. (2004), *The Ancient Port of Arikamedu: New Excavations and Researches 1989–1992,* vol. 2. Paris.

Begley, V. and de Puma, R.D., eds. (1991), *Rome and India: The Ancient Sea Trade.* Delhi.

Behm-Blancke, M.R., ed. (1991), *Hassek Höyük. Naturwissenshaftlichte Untersuchungen und lithische Industrie.* Tubingen.

Beja-Pereira, A., Caramelli, D., Lalueza-Fox, C., Vernesi, C., Ferrand, N., Casoli, A., Goyache, F., Royo, L.J., Lari, M., Martini, A., Ouragh, L., Magid, A., Atash, A., Zsolnai, A., Boscato, P., Triantaphylidis, C., Ploumi, K., Sineo, L., Mallegni, F., Taberlet, P., Erhardt, G., Sampietro, L., Bertranpetit, J., Barbujani, G., Luikart, G. and Bertorelle, G. (2006), "The origin of European cattle: evidence from modern and ancient DNA", *PNAS* 103: 8113–8118.

Beja-Pereira, A., England, P.R., Ferrand, N., Jordan, S., Bakhiet, A.O., Abdalla, M.A., Mashkour, M., Jordana, J., Taberlet, P. and Luikart, G. (2004), "African origins of the domestic donkey", *Science* 304: 1781.

Bejor, G. (1999), *Vie Colonnate. Paesaggi Urbani del Mondo Antico.* Rome.

Bekker-Nielsen, T., ed. (2005a), *Ancient Fishing and Fish Processing in the Black Sea Region*. Aarhus.
Bekker-Nielsen, T. (2005b), "The technology and productivity of ancient sea fishing", in Bekker-Nielsen, ed., 83–95.
Belfer-Cohen, A. (1991), "Art items from Layer B, Hayonim Cave: a case study of art in a Natufian context", in Bar-Yosef and Valla, eds., 569–588.
Belfer-Cohen, A. (1995), "Rethinking social stratification in the Natufian culture: the evidence from burials", in Campbell and Green, eds., 9–16.
Belfer-Cohen, A. and Goring-Morris, A.N. (2002), "Why microliths? Microlithization in the Levant", in Elston and Kuhn, eds., 57–68.
Bell, G.L., ed. (1982), *The Churches and Monasteries of the Tur 'Abdin*. London.
Bell, G.L. (no date), Gertrude Bell Archive (http://www.gerty.ncl.ac.uk/).
Belli, O. (1999), *The Anzaf Fortresses and the Gods of Urartu*. Istanbul.
Belli, O. (2000), "Metallgegenstände und Waffen im Urartäischen Königreich", in Başgelen et al., eds., 271–287.
Bellwood, P. (2005), *First Farmers: The Origins of Agricultural Societies*. Oxford.
Bellwood, P. (2009), "The dispersals of established food-producing populations", *CA* 50/5: 621–626.
Bellwood, P. and Renfrew, C., eds. (2002), *Examining the Farming/Language Dispersal Hypothesis*. Cambridge.
Benecke, N. (2011), "Faunal remains of Arismān", in Vatandoust et al., eds., 376–382.
Benecke, N. and Neef, R. (2005), "Faunal and plant remains from Sohr Damb/Nal: a prehistoric site (c. 3500–2000 BC) in central Balochistan (Pakistan)", in Franke-Vogt and Weisshaar, eds., 81–93.
Benecke, N. and von den Driesch, A. (2003), "Horse exploitation in the Kazakh steppes during the Eneolithic and Bronze Age", in Levine et al., eds., 69–82.
Bengtson, H. (1955), "Kosmas Indikopleustes und die Ptolemäer", *Historia* 4/2–3: 151–156.
Benitom, G., Baker, V.R. and Gregory, K., eds. (1998), *Palaeohydrology and Environmental Change*. Chichester.
Benoit, A. (2003), *Art et archéologie: Les civilisations du Proche-Orient ancien*. Paris.
Benoit, A. (2004), "Susa", in Stöllner et al., eds., 178–193.
Ben-Tor, A. (1978), *Cylinder Seals of Third-Millennium Palestine*. Cambridge.
Ben-Tor, D. (2003), "Egyptian–Levantine relations and chronology in the Middle Bronze Age: Scarab research", in Bietak, ed., 239–248.
Ben-Tor, D (2007), *Scarabs, chronology, and interconnections: Egypt and Palestine in the Second Intermediate Period*. Fribourg.
Bentwich, N. (1924), "The antiquities law of Palestine", *Journal of Comparative Legislation and International Law* 6: 251–254.
Berardi, F. (2001), *La fabbrica dell'infelicità: New Economy e movimento del cognitariato*. Rome.
Bergamini, G. (1987), "Parthian fortifications in Mesopotamia", *Mesopotamia* 22: 195–214.
Berger, K. (1937), "Bericht über unbekannte achaemenidische Ruinen in der Ebene von Persepolis", *AMI* 8: 1–3.
Berger, P.-R. (1973), *Die neubabylonischen Königsinschriften*. Neukirchen-Vluyn.

Bergoffen, C.J. (2003), "The Cypriote pottery from Alalakh: chronological considerations", in Bietak, ed., 395–410.
Berman, J. (1986), *Ceramic Production and the Development of Complex Polities in Late Prehistoric Southwest Iran*. New York.
Berman, J. (1987), "Ceramic production and its implications for the sociopolitical organization of the Suse Phase Susiana", *Paléorient* 18: 47–60.
Berman, J. (1994), "The ceramic evidence for sociopolitical organization in Ubaid southwestern Iran", in Stein and Rothman, eds., 23–34.
Bernand, A. (1969), *Les Inscriptions grecques de Philae. Époque ptolémaique*. Paris.
Bernard, P. (1972a), "Campagne de fouilles d'Aï Khanoum", *CRAIBL* 1972: 605–632.
Bernard, P. (1972b), "Les mortiers et pilons inscrits de Persépolis", *StIr* 1: 165–176.
Bernard, P. (1973), *Fouilles d'Aï Khanoum I (campagnes 1965, 1966, 1967, 1968), rapport préliminaire*. Paris.
Bernard, P. (1990), "Vicissitudes au gré de l'histoire d'une statue en bronze d'Héraclès entre Séleucie du Tigre et la Mésène", *Journal des Savants*: 3–68.
Bernard, P. (2007), "La colonie grecque d'Aï Khanoum et l'hellénisme en Asie centrale", in Cambon, ed., 55–68.
Bernard, P. (2008), "The Greek colony at Aï Khanoum and Hellenism in Central Asia", in Hiebert and Cambon, eds., 81–129.
Bernard, V. and Salles, J.-F. (1991), "Discovery of a Christian church at al-Qusur, Failaka (Kuwait)", *PSAS* 21: 7–13.
Bernard, V., Callot, O. and Salles, J.F. (1991), "L'église d'al-Qousour Failaka, État de Koweit", *AAE* 2: 145–181.
Bernbeck, R. (1993), *Steppe als Kulturlandschaft*. Berlin.
Bernbeck, R. (1996), "Siegel, Mythen, Riten: Etana und die Ideologie der Akkad-Zeit", *BaM* 27: 159–213.
Bernbeck, R. (2005), "The past as fact and fiction: from historical novels to novel histories", in Pollock and Bernbeck, eds., 97–122.
Bernbeck, R. (2008a), "An archaeology of multisited communities", in Barnard and Wendrich, eds., 43–77.
Bernbeck, R. (2008b), "Structural violence in archaeology", *Archaeologies* 4/3: 390–413.
Bernbeck, R. (2008c), "Archaeology and English as an imperial lingua franca", *Archaeologies* 4/1: 168–170.
Bernbeck, R. (2010a), "Heritage politics: learning from Mullah Omar?", in Boytner et al., eds., 27–54.
Bernbeck, R. (2010b), "Imperialist networks: Ancient Assyria and the United States", *Present Pasts* 2/1: 142–168. doi:10.5334/pp.30.
Bernbeck, R. (2011), "Arbeitsteilung beim Erzählen von Geschichte? Zum Verhältnis von Archäologie und Philologie in Studien Altvorderasiens", in Burmeister and Müller-Scheeßel, eds., 227–246.
Bernbeck, R., Fazeli, H. and Pollock, S. (2005), "Life in a fifth-millennium BCE village: excavations at Rahmatabad, Iran", *NEA* 68: 94–105.
Bernbeck, R. and Pollock, S. (2004), "The political economy of archaeological practice and the production of heritage in the Middle East", in Meskell and Preucel, eds., 335–352.

Bernbeck, R., Pollock, S. and Coursey, C. (1999), "The Halaf settlement at Kazane Höyük: Preliminary report on the 1996 and 1997 seasons", *Anatolica* 25: 109–147.

Berndt, D. (2002), *Midasstadt in Phrygien: Eine sagenumwobene Statte im anatolischen Hochland*. Mainz.

Berndt-Ersöz, S. (2006), *Phrygian Rock-Cut Shrines: Structure, Function, and Cult Practice*. Leiden.

Berndt-Ersöz, S. (2008), "The chronology and historical context of Midas", *Historia* 57: 1–37.

Berndt-Ersöz, S. (2009), "Sacred space in Iron Age Phrygia", in Gates et al., eds., 11–19.

Bernhardsson, M.T. (2005), *Reclaiming a Plundered Past: Archaeology and Nation Building in Modern Iraq*. Austin.

Berton, R. and Mashkour, M. (2008), "Animal remains from Tilbeşar excavations, southeast Anatolia, Turkey", *Anatolica Antiqua* 16: 23–51.

Besonen, M. and Cremaschi, M. (2002), "Geomorphological field survey report: Tell Leilan, June 2002" (http://leilan.yale.edu/works/geo_report/index.html).

Bessac, J.C. (2007), "Étude technique et interprétations du monument rupestre de Qadamgah (Fars)", *IrAnt* 42: 185–206.

Bessac, J.C. and Boucharlat, R. (2010), "Le monument de Takht-e Rustam, près de Persépolis dit 'tombeau inachevé de Cambyse.' Note technique et reconsidérations", *ARTA* 2010.003.

Betancourt, P., Karageorghis, V., Laffineur, R. and Niemeier, W-D., eds. (1999), *Meletemata: Studies in Aegean Archaeology Presented to Malcolm H. Wiener as he Enters his 65th year*. Liège.

Betlyon, J.W. (2005), "A people transformed: Palestine in the Persian Period", *NEA* 68: 4–58.

Betts, A.V.G., ed., (1998), *The Harra and the Hamad: Excavations and Surveys in Eastern Jordan*, vol. 1. Sheffield.

Beuger, C. (in press), *Keramik der spätfrühdynastischen bis spätassyrischen Zeit aus Assur*. Berlin.

Bevan, R. (2006), *The Destruction of Memory: Architecture at War*. London.

Beyer, D., ed. (1982), *Meskéné-Emar: Dix ans de travaux 1972–1982*. Paris.

Beyer, D. et al. (2008), "Zeyve Höyük (Porsuk): rapport sommaire sur la campagne de 2007", *Anatolia Antiqua* 16: 313–44.

Beyer, K. (1998), *Die aramäischen Inschriften aus Assur, Hatra und dem übrigen Ostmesopotamien (datiert 44 v.Chr. bis 238 n.Chr.)*. Göttingen.

Beyhl, F.E. (1998), "Anmerkungen zum Drachenblut und zu den Namen der Insel Soqotra", *ZDMG* 148: 35–82.

Bezborodov, M.A. (1975), *Chemie und Technologie der antiken und mittelalterlichen Gläser*. Mainz.

Biagi, P. and Nisbet, R. (1989), "Some aspects of the 1982–1985 excavations at the aceramic coastal settlement of RH5 at Qurum (Muscat-Sultanate of Oman)", in Costa and Tosi, eds., 31–46.

Biagi, P. and Nisbet, R. (1992), "Environmental history and plant exploitation at the aceramic sites of RH5 and RH6 near the mangrove swamp of Qurum (Muscat – Oman)", *Bulletin de la Société Botanique Française* 139/2–4: 571–578.

Biagi, P. and Nisbet, R. (2006), "The prehistoric fisher-gatherers of the western coast of the Arabian Sea: a case of seasonal sedentarization?", *WA* 38/2: 220–238.

Bianchi, R.S., Schlick-Nolte, B., Bernheimer, G.M. and Barag, D., eds. (2002), *Reflections on Ancient Glass in the Borowski Collection*. Mainz.

Bibby, T.G. (1969), *Looking for Dilmun*. New York.

Bieberstein, K. and Bloedhorn, H. (1994), *Jerusalem: Grundzüge der Baugeschichte vom Chalkolithikum bis zur Frühzeit der osmanischen Herrschaft*. Wiesbaden.

Biedermann, Z. (2006), *Soqotra: Geschichte einer christlichen Insel im Indischen Ozean vom Altertum bis zur frühen Neuzeit*. Wiesbaden.

Biek, L. and Bayley, J. (1979), "Glass and other vitreous materials", *WA* 11: 1–25.

Bielinski, P. (2002), "The sixth campaign of excavations. Preliminary report", *Polish Archaeology in the Mediterranean* 13: 279–294.

Bienert, H.-D., Gebel, H.-G., and Neef, R., eds. (2004), *Central Settlements in Neolithic Jordan*. Berlin.

Bienert, H.-D. and Häser, J., eds. (2004), *Men of Dikes and Canals. The Archaeology of Water in the Middle East*. Rahden.

Bienkowski, P. (2001), "The Persian period", in MacDonald et al., eds., 347–365.

Bienkowski, P. and Galor, K., eds. (2006), *Crossing the Rift: Resources, Routes, Settlement Patterns and Interaction in the Wadi Arabah*. Oxford.

Bier, C. (1978), "Textiles", in Harper, 119–140.

Bier, L. (1986), *Sarvistan: A Study in Early Iranian Architecture*. University Park.

Bietak, M. (1993), "The Sea Peoples and the end of the Egyptian administration in Canaan", in Biram and Aviram, eds. 292–306.

Bietak, M. (1996), *Avaris: The Capital of the Hyksos – Recent Excavations at Tell el-Daba*. London.

Bietak, M. (1998), "Zur Marine des Alten Reichs", in Baines et al., eds., 35–40.

Bietak, M. (2001), "Daba, Tell ed-", in Redford, ed., vol. 1, 351–354.

Bietak, M. (2002), "Relative and absolute chronology of the Middle Bronze Age: comments on the present state of research", in Bietak, ed., 29–42.

Bietak, M., ed. (2002), *The Levant in the Middle Bronze Age*. Vienna.

Bietak, M., ed. (2003a), *The Synchronisation of Civilisations in the Eastern Mediterranean in the Second Millennium BC*, vol. 2. Vienna.

Bietak, M. (2003b), "Two Near Eastern temples with bent axis in the eastern Nile Delta", *ÄL* 13: 13–38.

Bietak, M. (2008), "Bronze Age paintings in the Levant: Chronological and cultural considerations", in Bietak and Czerny, eds., 269–300.

Bietak, M. (2008), "Tell-el-Dab'a", in Aruz, Benzel and Evans, eds., 110–112.

Bietak, M. and Czerny, E., eds. (2006), *The Synchronisation of Civilisations in the Eastern Mediterranean in the Second Millennium BC*, vol. 3. Vienna.

Bietak, M. and Czerny, E., eds. (2008), *The Bronze Age in the Lebanon: Studies on the Archaeology and Chronology of Lebanon, Syria and Egypt*. Vienna.

Bietak, M. and Schwarz, M., eds. (2002), *Krieg und Sieg: Narrative Wanddarstellungen von Altägypten bis ins Mittelalter*. Vienna.

Biggs, R.D., Myers, J. and Roth, M.T., eds. (2008), *Proceedings of the 51st Rencontre Assyriologique Internationale held at the Oriental Institute of the University of Chicago, July 18–22, 2005*. Chicago.

Bikai, P.M., Sha'er, M. and Fitzgerald, B. (1994), "The Byzantine church at Darat Al-Funun", *ADAJ* 38: 401–415.
Bikai, P.M. (1996), "The ridge church at Petra", *ADAJ* 40: 481–486.
Bikermann, E. (1938), *Institutions des Séleucides*. Paris.
Bilde, P., Engberg-Pedersen, T., Hannestad, L. and Zahle, J., eds. (1990), *Religion and Religious Practice in the Seleucid Kingdom*. Aarhus.
Bilde, P., Engberg-Pedersen, T., Hannestad, L., Zahle, J. and Randsborg, K., eds. (1993), *Centre and Periphery in the Hellenistic World*. Oakville.
Billerbeck, M. (2006), *Stephani Byzantii Ethnica Volumen I: Α-Γ*. Berlin/New York.
Bimson, M. and Freestone, I.C. (1983), "An analytical study of the relationship between the Portland vase and other Roman cameo glasses", *JGS* 25: 55–64.
Bimson, M. and Freestone, I.C., eds. (1987), *Early Vitreous Materials*. London.
Binder, D. (2002), "Stones making sense: what obsidian could tell about the origins of the central Anatolian Neolithic", in Gérard and Thissen, eds., 79–90.
Binford, L. (1964), "A consideration of archaeological research design", *AA* 29: 425–441.
Biram, A. and Aviram, J., eds. (1993), *Biblical Archaeology Today, 1990*. Jerusalem.
Biscione, R., Hmayakyan, S. and Parmegiani, N. (2002), *The North-Eastern Frontier: Urartians and Non-Urartians in the Sevan Lake Basin*. Rome.
Biscione, R., Salvatori, S. and Tosi, M. (1977), "Shahr-i Sokhta: l'abitato protostorico e la sequenza cronologica", in Tucci, ed. 77–113.
Bishay, A., ed. (1974), *Recent Advances in Science and Technology of Materials*. New York.
Bishop, R.L. and Lange, F.W., eds. (1991), *The Ceramic Legacy of Anna Shepard*. Boulder.
Bishop, R.L., Rands, R.L. and Holley, G.R. (1982), "Ceramic composition analysis in archaeological perspective", in Schiffer, ed., 275–330.
Bisson de la Roque, F. (1937), *Tod*. Cairo.
Bittel, K. (1969a), "Bemerkungen über die prähistorische Ansiedlung auf dem Fikirtepe bei Kadiköy, (Istanbul)", *IstMitt* 19: 1–19.
Bittel, K., ed. (1969b), *Boğazköy IV: Funde aus den Grabungen 1967 und 1968*. Berlin.
Bittel, K. (1983), *Hattuscha: Hauptstadt der Hethiter*. Cologne.
Bittel, K., Houwink ten Cate, P.H.J. and Reiner, E., eds. (1974), *Anatolian Studies Presented to H.G. Güterbock on the Occasion of his 65th Birthday*. Istanbul.
Bitton-Ashkelony, B. and Kofsky, A., eds. (2004), *Christian Gaza in Late Antiquity*. Leiden/Boston.
Bivar, A.D.H. (1982), "Seal-impressions of Parthian Qūmis", *Iran* 20: 161–176.
Black, J.A. (2008), "The libraries of Kalhu", in Curtis et al., eds., 261–265.
Black, J.A., Cunningham, G., Robson, E. and Zólyomi, G. (2004), *The Literature of Ancient Sumer*. Oxford.
Black, J.A., Gasche, H. and Killick, R.G. (1987), "Habl aṣ-Ṣaḫr 1983–85: Nebuchadnezzar II's cross-country wall north of Sippar", *NAPR* 1: 1–46.
Black, J.A. and Green, A. (1992), *Gods, Demons and Symbols of Ancient Mesopotamia: An Illustrated Dictionary*. London.
Black, J.A. and Tait, W.J. (1995), "Archives and libraries in the Ancient Near East", in Sasson, ed., 2197–2209.
Blackman, M.J. (1984), "Provenance studies of Middle Eastern obsidian from sites in highland Iran", *Advances in Chemistry Series* 205: 19–50.

Blackman, M.J., Stein, G.J. and Vandiver, P. (1993), "The standardization hypothesis and ceramic mass production: technological, compositional, and metric indices of craft specialisation at Tell Leilan, Syria", *AmAnt* 58: 60–81.

Blakolmer, F., Krierer, K.R., Krinzinger, F., Landskron-Dinstl, A., Szemethy, H.D. and Zhuber-Okrog, K., eds. (1996), *Fremde Zeiten: Festschrift für Jürgen Borchhardt zum sechzigsten Geburtstag am 25. Februar 1996, dargebracht von Kollegen, Schülern und Freunden*. Vienna.

Blaylock, S. (1999), "Iron Age pottery from Tille Höyük, south-eastern Turkey", in Hausleiter and Reiche, eds., 263–286.

Blaylock, S. (2009), *Tille Höyük 3: The Iron Age*. London.

Bliss, F. (1898), *A Mound of Many Cities*. London.

Blocher, F. (1997), "Eine Hauptstadt zieht um", *Das Altertum* 43: 21–43.

Blocher, F., Kara, H.-C., Machule, D. and Werner, P. (2007), "Bericht über die Ausgrabungen in Tall Munbāqa/Ekalte 2005–2007", *MDOG* 139: 83–130.

Blocher, F., Kara, H.-C., Machule, D. and Werner, P. (2009), "Bericht über die Ausgrabungen in Tall Munbāqa/Ekalte 2008", *MDOG* 141: 85–95.

Blot, J. and de Contenson, H. (1992), "Les vertèbres de poisson de Ras Shamra", in de Contenson et al., 207–208.

Blue, L.K., Cooper, J.P., Thomas, R.I. and Whitewright, R.J., eds. (2009), *Connected Hinterlands: Proceedings of the Fourth International Conference on the Peoples of the Red Sea Region*. Oxford.

Blum, H., Faist, B., Pfälzner, P. and Wittke, A-M., eds. (2002), *Brückenland Anatolien? Ursachen, Extensität und Modi des Kulturaustausches zwischen Anatolien und seinen Nachbarn*. Tübingen.

Boardman, J. (2000), *Persia and the West: An Archaeological Investigation of the Genesis of Achaemenid Art*. London.

Bobek, H. (1968), "Vegetation", in Fisher, ed., 280–293.

Bobomulloev, S. (1998), *Verkhov'ya Zarafshana*. Dushanbe.

Bocherens, H., Billiou, D., Charpentier, V. and Mashkour, M. (2000), "Palaeoenvironmental and archaeological implications of bone and tooth isotopic biogeochemistry (13C, 15N) in southwestern Asia", in Mashkour et al., eds., 104–115.

Bocherens, H., Mashkour, M., Drucker, D.G., Moussa, I. and Billiou, D. (2006), "Stable isotope evidence for palaeodiets in southern Turkmenistan during Historical period and Iron Age", *JAS* 33/2: 253–264.

Bocquentin, F. and Bar-Yosef, O. (2004), "Early Natufian remains: evidence for physical conflict from Mt. Carmel, Israel", *Journal of Human Evolution* 47: 19–23.

Boehmer, R.M. (1965), *Die Entwicklung der Glyptik während der Akkad-Zeit*. Berlin.

Boehmer, R.M. (1974), "Orientalische Einflüsse auf verzierten Messergriffen aus dem prädynastischen Ägypten", *AMI* 7: 15–40.

Boehmer, R.M. (1975), "Das Rollsiegel im prädynastischen Ägypten", *AAnz 1975*: 495–514.

Boehmer, R.M. (1980), "Zur Zerstörung der Zikkurrat von Borsippa", *BaM* 11: 88–89.

Boehmer, R.M. (1999), *Uruk. Früheste Siegelabrollungen*. Mainz.

Boehmer, R.M, Pedde, F. and Salje, B. (1995), *Uruk. Die Gräber*. Mainz.

Boese, J. (1995), *Ausgrabungen in Tell Sheikh Hassan I*. Saarbrücken.

Boese, J. (2009), "Murmuriga und Nappigu: Zur historischen Topographie am nördlichen syrischen Euphrat vom 15. bis zum 7. Jahrhundert v. Chr.", *MDOG* 141: 65–84.

Boessneck, J. (1978), "Tierknochenfunde aus Nippur", in Gibson et al., 153–187.

Boessneck, J. and von den Driesch, A. (1976), "Die Wildfauna der Altinova in vorgeschichtlichler Zeit, wie sie die Tierknochenfunde vom Norsuntepe und anderen Siedlungshülgeln erschliessen", *Middle East Technical University, Keban Project Publications Series/Keban Projesi 1972 Çalismalari'ndan Ayribasim*, 91–100. Ankara.

Boessneck, J. and von den Driesch, A. (1979), *Die Tierknochenfunde aus der neolithische Siedlung auf dem Fikirtepe bei Kadiköy am Marmarameer*. Munich.

Boessneck, J., von den Driesch, A. and Steger, U. (1984), "Tierknochenfunde der Ausgrabungen des Deutschen Archäologischen Instituts Baghdad in Uruk-Warka, Iraq", *BaM* 15: 149–189.

Bogaard, A. (2005), "'Garden agriculture' and the nature of early farming in Europe and the Near East", *WA* 37: 177–196.

Bogaard, A., Charles, M., Twiss, K., Fairbairn, A., Yalman, N., Filipović, D., Arzu Demirergi, G., Ertuğ, F., Russell, N. and Henecke, J. (2009), "Private pantries and celebrated surplus: Storing and sharing food at Neolithic Çatalhöyük, Central Anatolia", *Antiquity* 83: 649–668.

Bogdanos, M. (2005), "The casualties of war: the truth about the Iraq Museum", *AJA* 109: 477–526.

Bogdanos, M. (2008a), "See no evil: Museums, art collectors and the black markets they adore", in Rothfield, ed., 57–61.

Bogdanos, M. (2008b), "Thieves of Baghdad", in Stone and Bajjaly, eds., 109–134.

Bogdanos, M. with Patrick, W. (2005), *Thieves of Baghdad: One Marine's Passion to Recover the World's Greatest Stolen Treasures*. New York.

Bogucki, P. (1993), "Animal traction and household economies in Neolithic Europe", *Antiquity* 67: 492–503.

Bökönyi, S. (1973), "The fauna of Umm Dabaghiyah: a preliminary report", *Iraq* 35: 9–11.

Bökönyi, S. (1977), *Animal Remains from the Kermanshah Valley, Iran*. Oxford.

Bökönyi, S. (1986), "The equids of Umm Dabaghiyah, Iraq", in Meadow and Uerpmann, eds., 302–317.

Bökönyi, S. (1991), "Late Chalcolithic horses in Anatolia", in Meadow and Uerpmann, eds., 123–131.

Bökönyi, S. and Bartosiewicz, L. (2000), "A review of animal remains from Shahr-i Sokhta (eastern Iran)", in Mashkour et al., eds., 116–152.

Bolger, D. and Maguire, L.C., eds. (2010), *The Development of Pre-State Societies in the Ancient Near East: Studies in Honour of Edgar Peltenburg*. Oxford.

Bollati, A., Messina, V. and Mollo, P. (2004), *Seleucia al Tigri. Le impronte di sigillo dagli Archivi*, 3 vols. Alessandria.

Bonamente, G. and Fusco, F., eds. (1992), *Costantino il Grande*. Macerata.

Bonatz, D. (2000a), *Das syro-hethitische Grabdenkmal: Untersuchungen zur Entstehung einer neuen Bildgattung in der Eisenzeit im nordsyrisch-südostanatolischen Raum*. Mainz.

Bonatz, D. (2000b), "Syro-Hittite funerary monuments: A phenomenon of tradition or innovation?", in Bunnens, ed., 189–210.

Bonatz, D. (2002), "Fremde 'Künstler' in Hattuša: Zur Rolle des Individuums beim Austausch materieller Kultur in der Späten Bronzezeit", in Blum et al., eds., 69–83.

Bonatz, D. (2007), "The iconography of religion in the Hittite, Luwian, and Aramaean kingdoms", *Iconography of Deities and Demons* (http://www.religionswissenschaft.unizh.ch/idd).

Bonatz, D., Czichon, R.M. and Kreppner, F.J., eds. (2008), *Fundstellen: Gesammelte Schriften zur Archäologie und Geschichte Altvorderasiens ad honorem Hartmut Kühne*. Wiesbaden.

Bonfante, L. and Karageorghis, V., eds. (2001), *Italy and Cyprus in Antiquity, 1500–450 BC*. Nicosia.

Bonfil, R. and Zarzecki-Peleg, A (2007), "The palace in the Upper City of Hazor as an expression of a Syrian architectural paradigm", *BASOR* 348: 25–47.

Bonogofsky, M. (2002), "Reassessing 'dental evulsion' in Neolithic plastered skulls from the Levant through the use of computed tomography, direct observation, and photographs", *JAS* 29: 959–964.

Bonogofsky, M. (2003), "Neolithic plastered skulls and railroading epistemologies", *BASOR* 331: 1–10.

Bonogofsky, M. (2004), "Including women and children: Neolithic modeled skulls from Jordan, Israel, Syria and Turkey", *NEA* 67: 118–119.

Booher, L.J. (1974), *Surface irrigation*. Rome.

Bopearachchi, O. (1996), "Seafaring in the Indian Ocean: archaeological evidence from Sri Lanka", in Ray and Salles, eds., 59–77.

Bopearachchi, O. (2002), "Archaeological evidence on shipping communities of Sri Lanka", in Barnes and Parkin, eds., 92–127.

Bopearachchi, O. and Boussac, M.-F., eds. (2005), *Afghanistan, ancien carrefour entre l'Est et l'Ouest*. Turnhout.

Borchardt, J. and Dobesch, G., eds. (1993), *Akten des II. internationalen Lykien-Symposions, 6–12 Mai 1990*. Vienna.

Borchardt, J., Jacobek, R. and Dinstl, A., eds. (1990), *Götter, Heroen, Herrscher in Lykien*. Vienna.

Borchardt, L. (1913), *Das Grabdenkmal des Königs Sahure*, vol. 2. Leipzig.

Bordaz, J. (1965), "The threshing sledge: ancient Turkish grain separating method still proves efficient", *Natural History* 74/4: 216–229.

Borgard, P., Brun, J.-P. and Picon, M., eds. (2005), *L'Alun de Méditerranée*. Naples and Aix-en-Provence.

Borger, R. and Hinz, W. (1959), "Eine Dareios-Inschrift aus Pasargadae", *ZDMG* 109: 117–127.

Börker-Klähn, J. (2003), "Tumulus D von Bayindir bei Elmali als historischer Spiegel", in Giorgieri et al., eds., 69–105.

Boroffka, N., Cierny, J., Lutz, J., Parzinger, H., Pernicka, E. and Weisgerber, G. (2002), "Bronze Age tin from Central Asia: preliminary notes", in Boyle et al., eds., 135–160.

Boroffka, R. and Parzinger, H. (2011), "Pottery of the Sialk III period", in Vatandoust et al., eds., 100–195.

Borrell, F. (2011), "Bi-directional blade technology in the Northern Levant during the 7th–8th millennia CAL BC: new insights from Mamarrul Nasr 2, Syria", *JFA* 36: 132–150.

Bossert, E-M. (2000), *Phrygische Keramik aus Boğazköy*. Mainz.

Bostanci, E. (1971), "A research on the Solutrean and Adiyamanian Cultures surrounding of Adiyaman – Adiyaman Çevresinde Proto-Solutreen ve Adiyamaniyen Paleolitik Kültürler Üzerinde Bir Araştirma", *Antropolji* 5 (1969–1970): 47–82.

Bostanci, E. (1973), "A new research on the palaeoanthropological prehistory and Quarternary problems of the Adiyaman Province in the Southeast Anatolia – Güney-doğu Anadoluda Adiyaman Çevresinde Yapilan Paleoantropolojik Prehistorik ve Quarterner Problemleri Üzerinde Bir Araştirma", *Antropolji* 6 (1971–1972): 89–170.

Botsch, F. (1986), *Hydraulik und Nutzungspotentiale der antiken Ḥaburkanäle in Nordost-Syrien*. Berlin.

Botta, P.-E. and Flandin, E. (1849–1850), *Monuments de Ninive*, 5 vols. Paris.

Bottema, S., Entjes-Nieborg, G. and Van Zeist, W., eds. (1990), *Man's Role in the Shaping of the Eastern Mediterranean Environment*. Rotterdam.

Bottema, S. and Woldring, H. (1990), "Anthropogenic indicators in the pollen record of the eastern Mediterranean", in Bottema et al., eds., 231–264.

Bottéro, J. (1949), "Les inventaires de Qatna", *RA* 43: 1–40, 137–215.

Bottéro, J. (1982), "Les inscriptions cunéiformes funéraires", in Gnoli and Vernant, eds., 373–404.

Bottéro, J. (1995), *Textes culinaires mésopotamienes/Mesopotamian Culinary Texts*. Winona Lake.

Bottini, G.C., Di Segni, L. and Alliata, E., eds. (1990), *Christian Archaeology in the Holy Land: New Discoveries. Essays in Honour of Virgilio C. Corbo*. Jerusalem.

Boucharlat, R. (1979), "Le monument rupestre de Qadamgah (Fars): essai d'interprétation", *IrAnt* 14: 153–166.

Boucharlat, R. (1984), "Monuments religieux de la Perse achéménide. État de questions", in Roux, ed., 119–135.

Bouchalat, R. (1985a), "Chahar taq et temple du feu sassanide: quelques remarques", in Huot et al., eds., 461–478.

Bouchalat, R. (1985b), "Suse, marché agricole ou relais du grand commerce. Suse et la Susiane à l'époque des grands empires", *Paléorient* 11: 71–81.

Bouchalat, R. (1987a), "Suse à l'époque sassanide", *Mesopotamia* 22: 357–366.

Bouchalat, R. (1987b), "Les niveaux post-achéménides à Suse, secteur nord. Fouilles de l'Apadana-Est et de la Ville Royale-Ouest (1973–1978)", *DAFI* 15: 145–312.

Bouchalat, R. (1989), "Cairns and pseudo-cairns du Fars: l'utilisation des tombes de surface au Ier millénaire de notre ère", in De Meyer and Haerinck, eds., 675–712.

Bouchalat, R. (1990a), "Suse et la Susiane à l'époque achéménide: données archéologiques", in Sancisi-Weerdenburg and Kuhrt, eds., 149–175.

Bouchalat, R. (1990b), "La fin des palais achéménides de Suse: une mort naturelle", in Vallat, ed., 225–233.

Bouchalat, R. (1993), "Pottery in Susa during the Seleucid, Parthian and early Sasanian period", in Finkbeiner, ed., 41–57.

Bouchalat, R. (1994), "Continuités à Suse au Ier millénaire av. J.-C.", in Sancisi-Weerdenburg et al., eds., 217–228.

Bouchalat, R. (1997a), "Susa under Achaemenid rule", in Curtis, ed., 54–67.

Bouchalat, R. (1997b), "Camp royal et résidences achéménides", in Boussac, ed., 217–228.

Bouchalat, R., (1999), "Temples du feu sassanides", *DA* 243: 68–70.

Boucharlat, R. (2000), "Les autres palais achéménides de Suse", in Dittmann et al., eds., 141–154.
Boucharlat, R. (2001), "The palace and the royal Achaemenid city: two case studies – Pasargadae and Susa", in Nielsen, ed., 113–123.
Boucharlat, R. (2002), "Pasargadae", *Iran* 40: 279–282.
Boucharlat, R. (2003a), "The Persepolis area in the Achaemenid period: some reconsiderations", in Miller and Abdi, eds., 260–265.
Boucharlat, R. (2003b), "Le Zendan de Pasargades: de la tour 'solitaire' à un ensemble architectural. Données archéologiques récentes", in Henkelman and Kuhrt, eds., 79–99.
Boucharlat, R. (2004), "Pasargadai", *RlA* 10: 351–363.
Boucharlat, R. (2005), "Iran", in Briant and Boucharlat, eds., 221–292.
Boucharlat, R. (2006), "Le destin des résidences et sites perses d'Iran dans la seconde moitié du IVe siècle avant J.-C.", in Briant and Joannès, eds., 443–470.
Boucharlat, R. (2007), "Achaemenid residences and elusive imperial cities", in Rollinger et al., eds., 454–471.
Boucharlat, R. (2009), "Susa, III. The Achaemenid period", *EnIr* online.
Boucharlat, R. (2010), "Autres travaux de Darius et successeurs", in Perrot, ed., 374–419.
Boucharlat, R. and Benech, C. (2002), "Organisation et aménagement de l'espace à Pasargades: Reconnaissances archéologiques de surface, 1999–2002", *ARTA* 2002.001.
Boucharlat, R. and Feizkhah, M. (2007), "Joint Iranian-French expedition in Marvdasht plain, Fars. A report of the autumn 2005–spring 2006 seasons", in Anonymous (2007b), ed., 7–25.
Boucharlat, R. and Gondet, S. (in press), "Parsa and the Persepolis Plain: field research 2005–2008."
Boucharlat, R. and Haerinck, H. (1991), "Ceramics xii. The Parthian and Sasanian periods", *EnIr* 5: 304–307.
Boucharlat, R., Haerinck, E., Phillips, C. and Potts, D.T. (1991), "Note on an Ubaid-pottery sites in the Emirate of Umm al-Qaiwain", *AAE* 2: 65–71.
Boucharlat, R. and Labrousse, A. (1979), "Le palais d'Artaxerxès II sur la rive droite du Chaour à Suse, *DAFI* 10: 21–136.
Boucharlat, R. and Lecomte, O., eds. (1987), *Fouilles de Tureng Tepe 1: Les périodes sassanides et islamiques.* Paris.
Boucharlat, R. and Lombard, P. (2001), "Le bâtiment de Rumeilah (oasis d'al Ain). Remarques sur les salles à poteaux de l'âge du Fer en Péninsule d'Oman", *IrAnt* 36: 213–238.
Boucharlat, R. and Salles, J.-F. (1981), "The history and archaeology of the Gulf from the fifth century BC to the seventh century AD. A review of the evidence, *PSAS* 11: 65–94.
Boucharlat, R., and Salles, J.-F., eds. (1984), *Arabie orientale, Mésopotamie et Iran méridional de l'age du fer au début de la période islamique.* Paris.
Boucharlat, R. and Shahidi, H. (1987), "Fragments architecturaux de type achéménide: découvertes fortuites dans la ville de Shoush 1976–1979", *DAFI* 15: 313–327.
Bounni, A., Lagarce, E. and Lagarce, J. (1998), *Ras Ibn Hani I: Le palais nord du Bronze récent, fouilles 1979–1995, synthèse préliminaire.* Beirut.
Bourdieu, P. (1988), *Homo Academicus.* Cambridge.

Bourdieu, P. (1997), *Pascalian meditations*. Stanford.

Bourguet, P. du (1964), *Catalogue des étoffes coptes*, vol. 1. Paris.

Bourke, S.J. (1993), "The transition from the Middle to the Late Bronze Age in Syria: the evidence from Tell Nebi Mend", *Levant* 25: 155–195.

Bourke, S.J. (2001), "The Chalcolithic period", in MacDonald et al., 107–162.

Bourriau, J. and Oates, J. (1997), "Spinning or sailing? The boat models from Eridu", *Antiquity* 71: 719–721.

Boussac, M.-F., ed. (1997), *Recherches récentes sur l'Empire achéménide*. Lyon.

Boussac, M.-F. and Invernizzi, A., eds. (1996), *Archives et sceaux du monde hellénistique*. Paris.

Boussac, M.-F. and Salles, J.-F., eds. (2005), *Athens, Aden, Arikamedu: Essays on the Interrelations Between India, Arabia and the Eastern Mediterranean*. New Delhi.

Bowden, W., Lavan, A. and Machado, C., eds. (2004), *Recent Research on the Late Antique Countryside*. Leiden and Boston.

Bowden, W., Gotteridge, A. and Machado, C., eds. (2006), *Social and Political Life in Late Antiquity*. Leiden and Boston.

Bowersock, G.W. (1983), *Roman Arabia*. Cambridge/London.

Bowersock, G.W. (1994a), *Studies on the Eastern Roman Empire. Social, Economic and Administrative History, Religion, Historiography*. Goldbach.

Bowersock, G.W. (1994b), "The new Greek inscription from South Yemen", in Bowersock, 285–290.

Bowersock, G.W. (1997), "Comentarii Breviores: Nabataeans on the Capitoline", *Hyperboreus* 3/2: 347–352.

Bowersock, G.W. (2006), *Mosaics as History: The Near East from Late Antiquity to Islam*. Cambridge.

Bowes, K. (2007), "'Christianization' and the rural home", *Journal of Early Christian Studies* 15/2: 143–170.

Bowes, K. (2008), "Early Christian archaeology: a state of the field", *Religion Compass* 2/4: 575–619.

Bowie, F. (2006), *The Anthropology of Religion*. Oxford.

Bowman, J. (1974–5), "The Christian monastery on the island of Kharg", *The Australian Journal of Biblical Archaeology* 2: 49–64.

Bowman, J. (1974), "The Sasanian church in the Kharg Island", in Anonymous (1974a), ed., 217–220.

Bowman, R.A. (1970), *Aramaic Ritual Texts from Persepolis*. Chicago.

Bowsher, J.M.C. (1989), "The Nabataean army", in French and Lightfoot, eds., 19–30.

Boyce, M. (1994), "The sedentary Arsacids", *IrAnt* 29: 241–251.

Boyd, B. and Cook, J. (1993), "A reconsideration of the 'Ain Sakhri figurine'", *PPS* 59: 399–405.

Boyer, P., Roberts, N. and Baird D. (2006), "Holocene environment and settlement in the Konya Plain, Turkey: integrating geoarchaeology and field survey", *Geoarchaeology* 21/7: 675–698.

Boyle, K., Renfrew, C. and Levine, M., eds. (2002), *Ancient Interactions: East and West in Eurasia*. Cambridge.

Boytner, R., Dodd, L.S. and Parker, B., eds. (2010), *Controlling the Past, Owning the Future*. Tucson.

Braden, M. (2006), "Trafficking in treasures", in Vitelli and Colwell-Chanthaphonh, eds., 27–33.
Bradley, D.G. and Magee, D.A. (2006), "Genetics and origins of domestic cattle", in Zeder et al., eds., 317–328.
Braemer, F., Cleuziou, S. and Coudart, A., eds. (1999), *Habitat et Société*. Antibes.
Braemer, F., Échallier, J-C. and Taraqji, A. (2004), *Khirbet el Umbashi: Villages et campements de pasteurs dans le «désert noir» (Syrie) à l'âge du Bronze*. Beirut.
Braemer, F., Genequand D., Dumond Maridat, C., Blanc, P-M., Dentzner, J-M., Gazagne D. and Wech P. (2009), "Long-term management of water in the Central Levant: the Hawran case (Syria)", *WA* 41/1: 36–57.
Braemer, F., Nicolle, C., Steimer Herbet, T., Broutin, P. and Flambaux, A. (2008), "Atlas archéologique des sites pré- et protohistoriques de Syrie du Sud. Études préliminaire du site de Qarassa", *Chronique Archéologique en Syrie* 3: 87–101.
Braidwood, L.S. and Braidwood, R.J. (1982), *Prehistoric Village Archaeology in Southeast Turkey*. Oxford.
Braidwood, L.S., Braidwood, R.J., Howe, B., Reed, C.A. and Watson, P.J., eds. (1983), *Prehistoric Archaeology Along the Zagro Flanks*. Chicago.
Braidwood, R.J. (1960), "The agricultural revolution", *Scientific American* 203: 130–148.
Braidwood, R.J. (1961), "The Iranian Prehistoric Project, 1959–1960", *IrAnt* 1: 3–7.
Braidwood, R.J. and Braidwood, L., eds. (1960), *Excavations in the Plain of Antioch: The Earlier Assemblages Phases A–J*. Chicago.
Braidwood, R.J., Braidwood, L., Smith, J. and Leslie, C. (1952), "Matarrah: A southern variant of the Hassunan assemblage, excavated in 1948", *JNES* 11: 1–75.
Braidwood, R.J., Braidwood, L.S., Tulane E. and Perkins, A. (1944), "New Chalcolithic material of Samarran type", *JNES* 3: 48–72.
Braidwood, R.J. and Reed, C.A. (1957), "The achievement and early consequences of food-production: a consideration of the archaeological and natural-historical evidence", *Cold Spring Harbor Symposium on Quantitative Biology* 22: 19–31.
Brain, C.K. (1981), *The Hunters or the Hunted? An Introduction to African Cave Taphonomy*. Chicago.
Braun, E. (1989), "The problem of the apsidal house: new aspects of Early Bronze domestic architecture in Israel, Jordan and Lebanon", *PEQ* 121: 1–43.
Braun, E. (2004), "Egypt and the southern Levant in the late 4th millennium BCE: shifting patterns of interaction", in Hendrickx et al., eds., 507–517.
Braun, E. (2009), "South Levantine Early Bronze Age chronological correlations with Egypt in the light of Narmer serekhs from Tel Erani and Arad: New interpretations", *British Museum Studies in Ancient Egypt and Sudan* 13: 25–48.
Braun, T. (1993), *The Earliest Silk in Europe*. Oxford.
Braun-Holzinger, E.A. (1984), *Figürliche Bronzen aus Mesopotamien*. Stuttgart.
Braun-Holzinger, E.A. and Matthäus, H. eds. (2002), *Die nahöstlichen Kulturen und Griechenland an der Wende vom 2. zum 1. Jahrtausend v. Chr. Kontinuität und Wandel von Strukturen und Mechanismen kultureller Interaktion*. Möhnesee.
Breasted, J.H. (2001), *Ancient Records of Egypt*, vol. 1. Chicago (orig. 1906).
Breniquet, C. (1987a), "Les petits objets de la fouille de Tell el 'Oueili'", in Huot (1987b), ed., 141–158.

Breniquet, C. (1987b), "Nouvelle hypothese sur la disparition de la culture de Halaf", in Huot (1987a), ed., 231–242.
Breniquet, C. (1991), "Tell es-Sawwan – Réalités et problèmes", *Iraq* 53: 75–90.
Breniquet, C. (2000), "De Bouqras à Tell es-Sawwan. Les premiers avatars des plans tripartites du Nord mésopotamien", in Rouault and Wäfler, eds., 55–70.
Brenk, B. (2007), "Chiesa e strada in epoca paleocristiana", in Quintavalle, ed., 112–126.
Breton, J-F. (1970), *Les Inscriptions forestières d'Hadrien dans le Mont-Liban*. Paris.
Bretschneider, J., al-Maqdissi, M., Vansteenhuyse, K., Driessen, J. and Van Lerberghe, K. (2005), "Tell Tweini, ancient Gabala, in the Bronze Age", *ÄL* 14: 215–230.
Bretschneider, J., Jans, G. and Suleiman, A. (2003), "Die akkadzeitlichen Tempel auf der Akropolis von Tell Beydar: die Bauschichten Früh Ğezira IV-Zeit", in Lebeau and Suleiman, eds., 149–168.
Bretschneider, J. and Van Lerberghe, K., eds. (2008), *In Search of Gibala: An Archaeological and Historical Study Based on Eight Seasons of Excavations at Tell Tweini (1999–2007) in the A and C Fields*. Barcelona.
Brett, G., Macauly, W.S. and Stevenson, R.B.K. (1947), *The Great Palace of the Byzantine Emperors: First Report*. Oxford and London.
Brewer, D. (2002), "Hunting, animal husbandry and diet in ancient Egypt", in Collins, ed., 427–456.
Briant, P. (1988), "Le nomadisme du Grand Roi", *IrAnt* 23: 253–273.
Briant, P. (1990), "The Seleucid Kingdom, the Achaemenid Empire and the history of the Near East in the first millennium BC", in Bilde et al., eds., 40–65.
Briant, P. (1994), "À propos du boulet de Phocée", *Revue des Études Anciennes* 96: 111–114.
Briant, P. (1997), "Bulletin d'histoire achéménide", in Boussac, ed., 5–127.
Briant, P. (2001a), *Bulletin d'histoire achéménide*, vol. 2: *1997–2000*. Paris.
Briant, P., ed. (2001b), *Irrigation et drainage dans l'antiquité: Qanāts et canalisations souterraines en Iran, en Égypte et en Grèce*. Paris.
Briant, P. (2002), *From Cyrus to Alexander: A History of the Persian Empire*. Trans. P.T. Daniels. Winona Lake.
Briant, P. (2003), *Darius dans l'ombre d'Alexandre*. Paris.
Briant, P. (2005), "Milestones in the development of Achaemenid historiography in the era of Ernst Herzfeld", in Gunter and Hauser, eds., 263–280.
Briant, P. (2010), "Suse et l'Élam dans l'empire achéménide", in Perrot, ed., 22–48.
Briant, P. and Boucharlat, R., eds. (2005a), *L'Archéologie de l'Empire achéménide: Nouvelles recherches*. Paris.
Briant, P. and Boucharlat, R. (2005b), "Introduction", in Briant and Boucharlat, eds., 17–25.
Briant, P., Henkelman, W.F.M. and Stolper, M.W., eds. (2008), *L'archive des Fortifications de Persépolis. État des questions et perspectives de recherches*. Paris.
Briant, P. and Joannès, F. (2006), *La Transition entre l'empire achéménide et les royaumes hellénistiques*. Paris.
Brice, W.C., ed. (1978), *The Environmental History of the Near and Middle East Since the Last Ice Age*. London.
Brichambaut, G.P. de and Wallen, C.C. (1963), *A Study of Agroclimatology in Semi-Arid and Arid Zones of the Near East*. Rome.

Brill, R.H. (1967), "A great glass slab from ancient Galilee", *Archaeology* 20: 89–95.
Brill, R.H. (1970), "The chemical interpretation of the texts", in Oppenheim et al., eds., 105–128.
Brill, R.H., ed. (1971), *Science and Archaeology*. Cambridge.
Brill, R.H. (1991–2), "Some thoughts on the origin of the Chinese word 'BOLI' ", *SRAA* 2: 129–136.
Brill, R.H. (1999a), *Chemical Analyses of Early Glasses*. Vol. I: *Catalogue of Samples*. Corning.
Brill, R.H. (1999b), *Chemical Analyses of Early Glasses*. Vol. II: *Tables of Analyses*. Corning.
Brill, R.H. and Moll, S. (1963), "The electron-beam probe microanalysis of ancient glass", in Matson and Rindone, eds., 293–302.
Brill, R.H. and Shirahata, H. (1997), "Laboratory analyses of some glasses and metals from Tell Brak", in Oates et al., eds., 89–94.
Brill, R.H. and Wosinski, J.F. (1965), "A huge slab of glass in the ancient necropolis of Beth She'arim", in Anonymous, ed., 219.1–11.
Brinkhuizen, D.C. and Clason, A.T., eds. (1986), *Fish and Archaeology: Studies in Osteometry, Taphonomy, Seasonality and Fishing Methods*. Oxford.
Brinkman, J.A. (1976), *Materials and Studies for Kassite History*. Vol. 1: *A Catalogue of Cuneiform Sources Pertaining to Specific Monarchs of the Kassite Dynasty*. Chicago.
Brinkman, J.A. (1977), "Appendix: Mesopotamian chronology of the historical period", in Oppenheim, 335–348.
Brinkman, J.A. (1984a), *Prelude to Empire. Babylonian Society and Politics, 747–626 BC*. Philadelphia.
Brinkman, J.A. (1984b), "Settlement surveys and documentary evidence: regional variation and secular trend in Mesopotamian demography", *JNES* 43: 169–180.
Brinkman, J.A. (1998–2001), "Nabopolassar", *RlA* 9: 12–16.
Brinkman, J.A. (2006), "Babylonian royal land grants, memorials of financial interest, and invocation of the divine", *JESHO* 49: 1–47.
Briquel-Chatonnet F. and Nehmé, L. (1998), "Graffitti nabatéens d'al-Muwayah et de Bi'r al-Hammâmât (Égypte)", *Semitica* 47: 81–88.
Brixhe, C. (1991), "Les inscriptions paléo-phrygiennes de Tyane: leur interêt linguistique et historique", in Le Guen-Pollet and Pelon, eds., 37–46.
Brixhe, C. (2002), "Corpus des inscriptions paléo-phrygiennes. Supplément I", *Kadmos* 41: 1–102.
Brixhe, C. (2004a), "Corpus des inscriptions paléo-phrygiennes. Supplément II", *Kadmos* 43: 1–130.
Brixhe, C. (2004b), "Nouvelle chronologie anatolienne et date d'élaboration des alphabets grec et phrygien", *CRAIBL* 2004: 271–89.
Brixhe, C. and M. Lejeune. (1984), *Corpus des inscriptions paléo-phrygiennes*, 2 vols. Paris.
Brock, R. and Hodkinson, S., eds. (2000), *Alternatives to Athens: Varieties of Political Organization and Community in Ancient Greece*. Oxford.
Brock, S.P. (1999–2000), "Syriac writers from Beth Qaṭraye", *ARAM* 11–12: 85–96.
Brock, S.P. (2004), "Some early witnesses to the East Syriac liturgical tradition", *Journal of Assyrian Academic Studies* 18: 11–13.
Brock, S.P. (2006), *The Wisdom of Isaac the Syrian*. Piscataway.

Brodie, N. (2008), "The Western market in Iraqi antiquities", in Rothfield, ed., 63–74.
Brodie, N., Doole, J. and Renfrew, C., eds. (2001), *Trade in Illicit Antiquities: The Destruction of the World's Archaeological Heritage*. Cambridge.
Brodie, N., Doole, J. and Watson, P., eds. (2000), *Stealing History: The Illicit Trade in Cultural Material*. Cambridge.
Brodie, N., Kersel, M.M., Luke, C. and Tubb, K.W., eds. (2006), *Archaeology, Cultural Heritage and the Antiquities Trade*. Gainesville.
Brodie, N. and Renfrew, C. (2005), "Looting and the world's archeological heritage: the inadequate response", *ARA* 34: 343–361.
Brodie, N. and Tubb, K.W., eds. (2002), *Illicit Antiquities: The Theft of Culture and the Extinction of Archaeology*. London.
Broekman, G.P.F., Demarrée, R.J. and Kaper, O.E., eds. (2009), *The Libyan Period in Egypt: Historical and Cultural Studies into the 21st–24th Dynasties*. Leuven.
Brogiolo, G.P. and Ward-Perkins, B., eds. (1999), *The Idea and Ideal of the Town Between Late Antiquity and the Early Middle Ages*. Leiden.
Bronk Ramsey, C., Dee, M.W., Rowland, J.M., Higham, T.F.G., Harris, S.A., Brock, F., Quiles, A., Wild, E.M., Marcus, E.S. and Shortland, A.J. (2010), "Radiocarbon-based chronology for Dynastic Egypt", *Science* 328: 1554–1557.
Broodbank, C. (2010), "'Ships a-sail over the rim of the sea': voyaging, sailing and the making of Mediterrean societies, ca.3500–800 BC", in Anderson et al., eds., 249–264.
Brookes, I.A., Levine, L.D. and Dennell, R.W. (1982), "Alluvial sequence in central west Iran and implications for archaeological survey", *JFA* 9: 285–299.
Brooks, N. (2006), "Cultural responses to aridity in the Middle Holocene and increased social complexity", *QI* 151: 29–49.
Brosius, M., ed. (2003), *Ancient Archives and Archival Traditions: Concepts of Record-Keeping in the Ancient World*. Oxford.
Brosius, M. (2006), "Investiture", *EnIr* 13: 180–182.
Broudy, E. (1979), *The Book of Looms: A History of the Handloom from Ancient Times to the Present*. Hanover.
Browicz, K. and Zohary, D. (1996), "The genus Amygdalus L. (Rosaceae): Species relationships, distribution and evolution under domestication", *Genetic Resources and Crop Evolution* 43: 229–247.
Brown, L.D. and Heron, C.P. (2005), "Presence or absence: a preliminary study into the detection of fish oils in ceramics", in Mulville and Outram, eds., 67–76.
Brown, P.R. (1971), "The rise and function of the Holy Man in Late Antiquity", *JRS* 61: 80–101.
Brückner, H. (1986), "Man's impact on the evolution of the physical environment in the Mediterranean region in historical times", *GJ* 13: 7–17.
Bruford, M.W. and Townsend, S.J. (2006), "Mitochondrial DNA diversity in modern sheep: Implications for domestication", in Zeder et al., eds., 306–316.
Bruijn, C. de (1711), *Cornelis de Bruins Reizen over Moskovie, door Persie en Indie*, etc. Amsterdam [English edition C. le Brun (1720), *Voyage to the Levant and Travels into Moscovy, Persia, and the East Indies*, 3 vols. London].
Brumfiel, E.M. (1997), "Tribute cloth production and compliance in Aztec and colonial Mexico", *Museum Anthropology* 21: 55–71.

Brun, J.-P. (2004a), *Archéologie du vin et de l'huile de la préhistoire à l'époque hellénistique*. Paris.
Brun, J.-P. (2004b), *Archéologie du vin et de l'huile dans l'Empire romain*. Paris.
Brun, J.-P. (2005), *Le Vin et l'huile dans la Méditerranée antique: Viticulture, oléiculture et procédés de transformation*. Paris.
Bryan, B.M. (2000), "The 18th Dynasty before the Amarna Period (c. 1550–1352)", in Shaw, ed., 207–264.
Bryce, T.R. (1979), "Lycian tomb families and their social implications", *JESHO* 22: 296–313.
Bryce, T.R. (1986), *The Lycians in Literary and Epigraphic Sources*. Copenhagen.
Bryce, T.R. (1998), *The Kingdom of the Hittites*. Oxford.
Bryce, T.R. (2002), *Life and Society in the Hittite world*. Oxford.
Bryce, T.R. (2003), "History", in Melchert, ed., 27–127.
Bryce, T.R. (2005), *The Kingdom of the Hittites*, rev. edn. Oxford.
Bryce, T.R. (2007), "The secession of Tarḫuntašša", in Groddek and Zorman, eds., 119–129.
Bryce, T.R. (2009), *The Routledge Handbook of the Peoples and Places of Ancient Western Asia*. Abingdon.
Bucak, E. and Schmidt, K. (2003), "Dünyanin en eski heykeli", *Atlas* 127: 36–40.
Buccellati, G. (1993), "Through a tablet darkly: a reconstruction of Old Akkadian monuments described in Old Babylonian copies", in Cohen et al., eds., 58–71.
Buccellati, G. and Kelly-Buccellati, M., eds. (1998), *Urkesh and the Hurrians: Studies in Honor of Lloyd Cotsen*. Malibu.
Buccellati, G. and Kelly-Buccellati, M. (2000), "The royal palace of Urkesh: report on the 12th season at Tell Mozan/Urkesh, excavations in Area AA, June–October 1999", *MDOG* 132: 133–183.
Buccellati, G. and Kelly-Buccellati, M. (2002), "Tar'am Agade, daughter of Naram-Sin, at Urkesh", in al-Gailani Werr et al., eds., 11–31.
Buccellati, G. and Kelly-Buccellati, M. (2004), "Der monumentale Palasthof von Tall Mozan/Urkesh und die stratigraphische Geschichte des *abi*", *MDOG* 136: 13–39.
Buchwald, H. (1981), "The Church of St John the Theologian in Alaşehir (Philadelphia)", *Jahrbuch der Österreichischen Byzantinistik* 30: 301–318.
Buhl, F. and Bosworth, C.E. (1999), "Taymā", *Encyclopaedia of Islam* 10: 430–431.
Buitenhuis, H. (1997), "Aşikli Höyük: a 'protodomestication' site", *Anthropozoologica* 25–26: 655–662.
Buitenhuis, H. (2004), "The importance of Yumuktepe in the origin and spread of animal domestication", in Caneva and Sevin, eds., 163–168.
Buitenhuis, H. (2008), "Ilipinar: the faunal remains from the late Neolithic and early Chalcolithic periods", in Vila et al., eds., 299–322.
Buitenhuis, H., Bartosiewicz, L. and Choyke, A.M., eds. (1998), *Archaeozoology of the Near East III*. Groningen.
Buitenhuis, H. and Caneva, I. (1998), "Early animal breeding in south-eastern Anatolia: Mersin-Yumuktepe", in Anreiter et al., eds., 122–130.
Buitenhuis, H., Choyke, A.M., Martin, L., Bartosiewicz, L. and Mashkour, M., eds. (2005), *Archaeozoology of the Near East VI*. Groningen.
Buitenhuis, H., Choyke, A.M., Mashkour, M. and Al-Shiyab, A.H., eds. (2002), *Archaeozoology of the Near East V*. Groningen.

Buitenhuis, H. and Clason, A.T., eds. (1993), *Archaeozoology of the Near East: Proceedings of the first international symposium on the archaeozoology of southwestern Asia and adjacent areas*. Leiden.

Bukharin, M. (2007), "Der zentralarabische Zweig der Weihrauchstraße", *AAE* 18: 80–85.

Bulgarelli, G.M. (1981), "Turquoise working in the Helmand civilisation", in Härtel, ed., 65–70.

Bunnens, G., ed. (1990), *Tell Ahmar: 1988 season*. Melbourne.

Bunnens, G., ed. (2000a), *Essays on Syria in the Iron Age*. Louvain.

Bunnens, G. (2000b), "Syria in the Iron Age: problems of definition", in Bunnens ed., 3–19.

Bunnens, G. (2006), *A New Luwian Stele and the Cult of the Storm-God at Til Barsib-Masuwari*. Louvain.

Burdajewicz, M. and Młynarczyk, J. (2006), "Elements of the liturgical furniture in an 8th century church (NWC) in Hippos (Sussita) Israel", *Series Byzantina* 4: 9–37.

Burdon, D.J. (1977), "Flow of fossil groundwater", *Quarterly Journal of Engineering Geology & Hydrogeology* 10/2: 97–124.

Buringh, P. (1960), *Soils and Soil Conditions in Iraq*. Baghdad.

Burke, A.A. (2008), *"Walled up to Heaven": The Evolution of Middle Bronze Age Fortification Strategies in the Levant*. Winona Lake.

Burke, B. (2005), "Textile production at Gordion and the Phrygian economy", in Kealhofer, ed., 69–81.

Burkett, M.E. (1977), "An early date for the origin of felt", *AnSt* 27: 111–115.

Burkett, M.E. (1979), *The Art of the Felt Maker*. Kendal.

Burkholder G. (1984), *An Arabian Collection: Artifacts from the Eastern Province*. Boulder City.

Burmeister, S. and Müller-Scheeßel, N., eds. (2011), *Fluchtpunkt Geschichte. Archäologie und Geschichtswissenschaften im Dialog*. Münster.

Burn, A.R. (1984), *Persia and the Greeks: The defence of the west, c. 546–478 BC*. London.

Burney, C.A. (1957), "Urartian fortresses and towns in the Van region", *AnSt* 7: 37–53.

Burney, C.A. (1975), "Excavations at Haftavan Tepe 1973: fourth preliminary report", *Iran* 8: 157–171.

Burney, C.A. (2004), *Historical Dictionary of the Hittites*. Toronto and Oxford.

Burney, C.A. and Lang, D.M. (1971), *The Peoples of the Hills: Ancient Ararat and Caucasus*. London.

Burnouf, J., Bravard, J.-P. and Chouquer, G., eds. (1997), *La Dynamique des paysages protohistoriques, antiques, médiévaux et modernes*. Sophia Antipolis.

Burns, T.S., and Eadie, J.W., eds. (2001), *Urban Centers and Rural Contexts in Late Antiquity*. East Lansing.

Burstein, S.M. (1996), "Ivory and Ptolemaic exploration of the Red Sea: the missing factor", *Topoi* 6/2: 799–807.

Burstein, S.M. (2008), "Trogodytes = Blemmyes = Beja? The misuse of ancient ethnography", in Barnard and Wendrich, eds., 250–263.

Buschmann, K. (1991), "Motiv und Ziel des Aelius-Gallus-Zuges nach Südarabien", *WO* 22: 85–93.

Butcher, K. (2003), *Roman Syria and the Near East*. London.

Butcher, K. and Gill, D.W.J. (1993), "The director, the dealer, the goddess and her champions: the acquisition of the Fitzwilliam goddess", *AJA* 97: 383–491.
Butler, H.C. (1929), *Early Churches in Syria, Fourth to Seventh Century*. Princeton.
Butterlin, P., ed. (2009), *A propos de Tepe Gawra: Le monde proto-urbain de Mésopotamie*. Turnhout.
Butterlin, P., Lebeau, M. and Pierre, B., eds. (2006), *Les Espaces syro-mésopotamiens: Dimensions de l'expérience humaine au Proche-Orient ancien, volume d'hommage offert à Jean-Claude Margueron*. Turnhout.
Butz, K. (1978–79), "Fischabgabe und Feldabgabe in Fischen und Vögeln an den Nanna-Tempel in Ur in altbabylonischer Zeit? Ein Versuch", *AfO* 26: 30–44.
Butzer K.W. (1958), "Quaternary stratigraphy and climate in the Near East", *Bonner Geographische Abhandlungen* 24: 1–157.
Butzer, K.W. (1971), *Environment and Archeology: An Ecological Approach to Prehistory*. Chicago.
Butzer, K.W. (1978), "The late prehistoric environmental history of the Near East", in Brice, ed., 5–12.
Butzer K.W. (1995), "Environmental change in the Near East and human impact on the land", in Sasson, ed., 123–151.
Butzer K.W. (1997), "Environmental archaeology", in Meyers, ed., 244–252.
Byrd, B.F (1989), "The Natufian: settlement variability and economic adaptations in the Levant at the end of the Pleistocene", *JWP* 3: 159–197.
Byrd, B.F. (1994), "Public and private, domestic and corporate: the emergence of the Southwest Asian village", *AA* 59: 639–666.
Byrd, B.F. (2000), "Households in transition: Neolithic social organization within Southwest Asia", in Kuijt, ed., 63–98.
Byrd, B.F. (2005a), *Early Village Life at Beidha, Jordan: Neolithic Spatial Organization and Vernacular Architecture. The Excavations of Mrs Diana Kirkbride-Helbæk*. Oxford.
Byrd, B.F. (2005b), "Reassessing the emergence of village life in the Near East", *JAR* 13/3: 231–290.
Byrd, B.F. and Banning, E.B. (1988), "Southern Levantine pier houses: intersite architectural patterning during the Pre-Pottery Neolithic B", *Paléorient* 14/1: 65–72.
Byrd, B.F. and Monahan, C.M. (1995), "Death, mortuary ritual, and Natufian social structure", *Journal of Anthropological Archaeology* 14: 251–287.
Cagni, L., ed. (1981), *La Lingua di Ebla*. Naples.
Cahill, N.D. (1988), "Taş Kule: a Persian-period tomb near Phokaia", *AJA* 92: 481–501.
Cahill, N.D. (2002), "Lydian houses, domestic assemblages, and household size", in Hopkins, ed., 173–185.
Cahill, N.D., ed. (2010a), *The Lydians and Their World. Catalogue of an Exhibit at the Yapi Kredi Vedat Nedim Tör Museum, Istanbul*. Istanbul.
Cahill, N.D. (2010b), "The city of Sardis", in Cahill, ed., 75–105.
Cahill, N.D. and Kroll, J.H. (2005), "New Archaic coin find at Sardis", *AJA* 109: 589–617.
Caldwell, J.R., ed. (1967), *Investigations at Tal-i Iblis*. Springfield.
Caldwell, J.R. (1968a), "Pottery and cultural history on the Iranian Plateau", *JNES* 28: 178–183.

Caldwell, J.R. (1968b), "Tell-i Ghazir", *RlA* 3: 348–355.

Callataÿ, F. de (1994), *Les tétradrachmes d'Orodès II et de Phraate IV: Étude du rythme de leur production monétaire à la lumière d'une grande trouvaille*. Paris.

Callaway, J. (1972), *The Early Bronze Age Sanctuary at Ai (et-Tell)*. London.

Callaway, J. (1978), "New perspectives on Early Bronze III in Canaan", in Moorey and Parr, eds., 46–58.

Calley, S. (1986), *Technologie du débitage à Mureybet, Syrie, 9e–8e millenaire*. Oxford.

Callieri, P. (1995), "Une borne routière grecque de la région de Persépolis", *CRAIBL* 1995: 65–73.

Callieri, P. (2003), "At the roots of the Sasanian royal imagery: the Persepolis graffiti", in Comparetti et al., eds.

Callieri, P., ed. (2006), *Architetti, capomastri, crtigiani: l'organizzazione dei cantieri e delle produzione artistica nell'Asia ellenistica. Studi offerti a Domenico Faccenna nel suo ottantesimo compleanno*. Roma.

Callieri, P. (2007), *L'Archéologie du Fārs à l'époque hellénistique*. Paris.

Callot, O. (1991), "La forteresse hellénistique de Failaka", in Schippmann et al., eds., 121–132.

Callot, O. (2010), "A new chronology for the Arabian Alexanders", in Huth and van Alfen, eds., 383–402.

Calmard, J. (2001), "Flandin and Coste", *EnIr* 10: 35–39.

Calmeyer, P. (1973), "Zur Genese altiranischer Motive", *AMI* 6: 135–152.

Calmeyer, P. (1974), "Zur Genese altiranischer Motive II. Der leere Wagen", *AMI* 7: 49–77.

Calmeyer, P. (1981), "Figürliche Fragmente aus Pasargadae nach Zeichnungen E. Herzfelds", *AMI* 14: 27–44.

Calmeyer, P. (1982), "Zur Genese altiranischer Motive, VIII. Die 'Statistische Landcharte des Perserreiches' – I", *AMI* 15: 105–187.

Calmeyer, P. (1983), "Zur Genese altiranischer Motive, VIII. Die 'Statistische Landcharte des Perserreiches' – II", *AMI* 15: 141–222.

Calmeyer, P. (1987a), "Zur Genese altiranischer Motive, VIII. Die 'Statistische Landcharte des Perserreiches' – Nachträge und Korrekturen", *AMI* 20: 129–146.

Calmeyer, P. (1987b), "Art in Iran, III: Achaemenian Art and Architecture", *EnIr* 2: 569–580.

Calmeyer, P. (1988), "Aufreihung–Duplik–Kopie–Umbildung", in Kuhrt and Sancisi-Weerdenburg, eds., 101–119.

Calmeyer, P. (1990a), "Madjdabad", *AMI* 23: 185–190.

Calmeyer, P. (1990b), "Das Persepolis der Spätzeit", in Sancisi-Weerdenburg and Kuhrt, eds., 7–36.

Calmeyer, P. (1991), "Ägyptischer Stil und reichsachaimenidische Inhalte auf dem Sockel der Dareios-Statue aus Susa/Heliopolis", in Sancisi-Weerdenburg and Kuhrt, eds., 285–303.

Calmeyer, P. (1994a), "Metamorphosen iranischer Denkmäler", *AMI* 27: 1–27.

Calmeyer, P. (1994b), "Babylonische und assyrische Elemente in der achaimenidische Kunst", in Sancisi-Weerdenburg et al., eds., 131–147.

Calmeyer, P. (1995–6), "Drei Arten persepolitanischer Rundplastik", *AMI* 28: 295–303.

Calmeyer, P. (2009), *Die Reliefs der Gräber V und VI in Persepolis*. Mainz.

Calmeyer, P. and Kleiss, W. (1975), "Das unvollendete achaemenidische Felsgrab bei Persepolis", *AMI* 8: 81–98.

Calmeyer, P. and Seidl, U. (1983), "Eine frühurartäische Siegeldarstellung", *AnSt* 33: 103–114.

Calvet, Y. (1996), "Maisons privées paléo-babyloniennes à Larsa, remarques d'architecture", in Veenhof, ed., 197–209.

Calvet, Y. and Gachet, J., eds. (1990), *Failaka fouilles françaises 1986–1988*. Lyon.

Calvet, Y. and Jamous, B. (2004), "Un royaume levantin de l'âge du bronze", in Galliano and Calvet, eds., 25–27.

Calvet, Y. and Pic, M., eds. (2008), *Failaka fouilles françaises 1984–1988. Matériel céramique du temple-tour et épigraphie*. Lyon.

Çambel, H. (1999), *Corpus of hieroglyphic Luwian inscriptions*. Vol. II: *Karatepe-Aslantaş. The Inscriptions: Facsimile Edition*. Berlin.

Çambel, H. and Braidwood, R.J. (1980), *İstanbul ve Chicago Üniversiteleri karma projesi güneydoğu anadolu tarihöncesi araştırmaları – The Joint Istanbul – Chicago Universities Prehistoric Research in Southeastern Anatolia*. Istanbul.

Çambel, H. and Özyar, A. (2003), *Karatepe/Aslantaş. Azatiwataya: Die Bildwerke*. Mainz.

Cambon, P., ed. (2007a), *Afghanistan: les trésors retrouvés. Collections du Musée National de Kaboul*. Paris.

Cambon, P. (2007b), "Begram, ancienne Alexandrie du Caucase ou capitale kouchane", in Cambon, ed., 81–112.

Cameron, A. (1993), *The Later Roman Empire, AD 284–430*. London.

Cameron, A. ed. (2005), *Eastern Christian Art in its Late Antique and Islamic Context*. Leuven.

Cameron, C.M., and Tomka, S.A., eds. (1993), *Abandonment of Settlements and Regions: Ethnoarchaeological and Archaeological Approaches*. Cambridge.

Cameron, G.G. (1936), *History of Early Iran*. Chicago.

Campbell, S. (1998), "Problems of definition: the origins of the Halaf in North Iraq", in Lebeau, ed., 39–52.

Campbell, S. (2000), "The Burnt House at Arpachiyah: a reexamination", *BASOR* 318: 1–40.

Campbell, S. (2007), "Rethinking Halaf chronologies", *Paléorient* 33/1: 101–134.

Campbell, S. (2007–8), "The dead and the living in Late Neolithic Mesopotamia", in Bartoloni and Benedettini, eds., 125–140.

Campbell, S., Carter, E., Healey, E., Anderson, S., Kennedy, A. and Whitcher, S. (1999), "Emerging complexity on the Kahramanmaraş Plain, Turkey: the Domuztepe Project 1995–1997", *AJA* 103: 395–418.

Campbell, S. and Fletcher, A. (2010), "Questioning the Halaf-Ubaid transition", in Carter and Philip, eds., 69–83.

Campbell, S. and Green, A., eds. (1995), *The Archaeology of Death in the Ancient Near East*. Oxford.

Campbell Thompson, R. (1929), "The excavation on the temple of Nabu at Nineveh", *Archaeologia* 79: 103–148.

Campbell Thompson, R. and Hutchinson, R.W. (1931), "The site of the palace of Ashurnasirpal at Nineveh, excavated in 1929–30 on behalf of the British Museum", *AAA* 18: 79–112.

Campbell Thompson, R. and Hutchinson, R.W. (1932), "The British Museum excavations on the Temple of Ishtar at Nineveh, 1930–31", *AAA* 19: 55–116.

Campbell Thompson, R. and Mallowan, M.E.L. (1933), "The British Museum excavations at Nineveh, 1931–32", *AAA* 20: 71–186.

Canal, D. (1976), "Note sur un fragment de carreau décoré", *DAFI* 6: 83–91.

Canal, D. (1978a), "La terrasse de l'Acropole de Susa", *DAFI* 9: 11–15.

Canal, D. (1978b), "La haute terrasse de l'Acropole de Suse", *Paléorient* 4: 169–76.

Canby, J., Porada, E., Ridgway, B.S. and Stech, T., eds. (1986), *Ancient Anatolia, Aspects of Change and Cultural Development: Essays in Honor of Machteld Mellink*. Madison.

Caner, D.F., Brock, S., Price, R.M. and van Bladel, K. (2010), *History and Hagiography from the Late Antique Sinai, Including Translations of Pseudo-Nilus' Narrations, Ammonius' Report on the Slaughter of the Monks of Sinai and Rhaithou, and Anastasius of Sinai's Tales of the Sinai Fathers*. Liverpool.

Caner, E. (1983), *Fibeln in Anatolien I*. Stuttgart.

Canepa, M. (2010), "Technologies of memory in early Sasanian Iran: Achaemenid sites and Sasanian memory", *AJA* 114/4: 563–596.

Caneva, I. (2004), "The citadel tradition (5000–4200 BC)", in Caneva and Sevin eds., 57–72.

Caneva, I., Lemorini, C., Zampetti, D. and Biagi, P., eds. (2001), *Beyond Tools: Redefining the PPN Lithic Assemblages of the Levant*. Berlin.

Caneva, I. and Sevin, V., eds. (2004), *Mersin-Yumuktepe, A Reappraisal*. Lecce.

Canivet, P. and Rey-Coquais, J., eds. (1992), *La Syrie de Byzance à l'Islam*. Damascus.

Canti, M.G. (2003), "Aspects of the chemical and microscopic characteristics of plant ashes found in archaeological soils", *Caten* 54: 339–361.

Cappers, R. and Bottema, S., eds. (2002), *The Dawn of Farming in the Near East*. Berlin.

Cardew, M. (1969), *Pioneer Pottery*. New York.

Cardona, G., Hoenigswald, H.M. and Senn, A., eds. (1970), *Indo-European and Indo-Europeans*. Philadelphia.

Carlsen, J., Due, B., Due, O.S. and Poulsen, B., eds. (1993), *Alexander the Great: Reality and Myth*. Roma.

Carruthers, D. (2003), *Hunting and Herding in Anatolian Prehistory: The 9th and 7th Millennium Site at Pınarbaşı*. Edinburgh.

Carsten, J. and Hugh-Jones, S., eds. (1995), *About the House: Lévi-Strauss and Beyond*. Cambridge.

Carswell, J. (1991), "The port of Mantai, Sri Lanka", in Begley and de Puma, eds., 197–203.

Carter, E. (1971), *Elam in the Second Millennium BC: The Archaeological Evidence*. Chicago.

Carter, E. (1989–90), "A surface survey of Lagash, Al-Hiba, 1984", *Sumer* 46: 60–63.

Carter, E. (1994), "Bridging the gap between the Elamites and the Persians in southeastern Khuzistan", in Sancisi-Weerdenburg et al., eds., 65–95.

Carter, E. (1998), "Elam ii. The archeology of Elam", *EnIr* 8: 313–25.

Carter, E., Campbell, S. and Gauld, S. (2003), "Elusive complexity: new data from late Halaf Domuztepe in south central Turkey", *Paléorient* 29/2: 117–133.

Carter, E. and Stolper, M.W. (1984), *Elam: Surveys of Political History and Archaeology*. Berkeley/Los Angeles/London.

Carter, E. and Wright, H.T., Jr. (2003), "Archaeological survey on the western Ram Hormuz Plain, 1969", in Miller and Abdi, eds., 60–82.

Carter, R.A. (2001), "Saar and its external relations: new evidence for interaction between Bahrain and Gujarat during the early second millennium BC", *AAE* 12: 183–201.

Carter, R.A. (2006), "Boat remains and maritime trade in the Persian Gulf during the 6th and 5th millennia BC", *Antiquity* 80: 52–63.

Carter, R.A. (2008), "Christianity in the Gulf during the first centuries of Islam", *AAE* 19: 71–108.

Carter, R.A. (2010), "The social and environmental context of Neolithic seafaring in the Persian Gulf", in Anderson, Barrett and Boyle, eds., 191–202.

Carter, R.A., Challis, K., Priestman, S.M.N. and Tofighian, H. (2006), "The Bushehr hinterland: results of the first season of the Iranian-British archaeological survey of Bushehr Province, November-December 2004", *Iran* 44: 63–103.

Carter, R.A. and Crawford, H.E.W., eds. (2010), *Maritime Interactions in the Arabian Neolithic: The Evidence from H3, As-Sabiyah, an Ubaid-Related Site in Kuwait*. Boston/Leiden.

Carter, R.A. and Philip, G., eds. (2010a), *Beyond the Ubaid: Transformation and Integration in the Late Prehistoric Societies of the Middle East*. Chicago.

Carter, R.A. and Philip, G. (2010b), "Deconstructing the Ubaid", in Carter and Philip, eds., 1–22.

Casabonne, O. (2006), "Buffles et zebus au Proche-Orient", *Colloquium Anatolicum* 5: 71–84.

Casana, J.J. (2008), "Mediterranean valleys revisited: linking soil erosion, land use and climate variability in the Northern Levant", *Geomorphology* 101: 429–442.

Casana, J.J. (2009), "Alalakh and the archaeological landscape of Mukish: the political geography and population of a Late Bronze Age kingdom", *BASOR* 353: 7–37.

Casana, J.J. and Herrmann, J.T. (2010), "Settlement history and urban planning at Zincirli Höyük, southern Turkey", *JMA* 23: 55–80.

Casana J.J. and Wilkinson T.J. (2005), "Settlement and landscapes in the Amuq Region", in Yener, ed., 25–65.

Casanova, M. (1992), "The sources of the lapis-lazuli found in Iran", in Jarrige, ed., 49–56.

Casanova, M. (1994), "Lapis lazuli beads in Susa and Central Asia: a preliminary study", in Parpola and Koskikallio, eds., 137–145.

Casanova, M. (1998), *Le Lapis-lazuli dans l'Orient ancien: gisements, production, des origines au début du second millénaire avant J.-C.* Paris.

Casanova, M. (2008), "Shahr-i Sokhta, Sector 7, Craftsmen's Zone", *Iran* 56: 328–333.

Cassis, M. (2002), "The bema in the East Syriac church in light of new archaeological evidence", *Hugoye: Journal of Syriac Studies* 5/2 (on-line, 19 pages).

Casson, L. (1989), *The Periplus Maris Erythraei: Text with Introduction, Translation and Commentary*. Princeton.

Casson, L. (1993), "Ptolemy II and the hunting of African elephants", *Transactions of the American Philological Association* 123: 247–260.

Casson, L. (1995), *Ships and Seamanship in the Ancient World*. Baltimore.

Castel, C. (2000), "Le quartier dit 'Hyksos' dans la ville basse orientale d'Ougarit", in Matthiae et al., eds., 185–198.

Castel, C. (2007), "Stratégies de subsistence et modes d'occupation de l'espace dans la micro-région d'Al-Rawda au Bronze Ancien final (Shamiyeh)", in Morandi Bonacossi, ed., 283–294.

Castelfranchi, M. (1981), "Il battistero della chiesa di San Giovanni ad Efeso (Ayasoluk)", in Anonymous, ed., 129–142.

Castiglioni A., Castiglioni, A. and Vercoutter, J. (1998), *Das Goldland der Pharaonen: Die Entdeckung von Berenike Pancrisia*. Mainz.

Catagnoti, A. and Bonechi, M. (1992), "Le volcan Kawkab, Nagar et problèmes connexes", *N.A.B.U.* 1992/2: 50–53.

Cattani, M. (2004), "Margiana at the end of Bronze Age and beginning of Iron Age", in Kosarev et al., eds., 303–315.

Cattani, M. (2008a), "Excavations at sites no. 1211 and no. 1219 (Final Bronze Age)", in Salvatori et al., eds., 119–132.

Cattani, M. (2008b), "The final phase of the Bronze Age and the 'Andronovo Question' in Margiana", in Salvatori et al., eds., 133–151.

Cattani, M. and Genito, B. (1998), "The pottery chronological seriation of the Murghab Delta from the end of the Bronze Age to the Achaemenid period: a preliminary note", in Gubaev, Koshelenko and Tosi, eds., 75–87.

Caubet, A. (1991), "Répertoire de la vaisselle de Pierre: Ougarit 1929–1988", in Yon, ed., 205–264.

Caubet, A. (1992), "The reoccupation of the Syrian coast after the destruction of the 'crisis years'", in Ward and Joukowsky, eds., 123–131.

Caubet, A. (1995), *Khorsabad, le palais de Sargon II, roi d'Assyrie*. Paris.

Caubet, A. (1998), "The International Style: a point of view from the Levant and Syria", in Cline and Harris-Cline, eds., 105–113.

Caubet, A., ed. (1999), *Cornaline et pierres précieuses: La Méditerranée de l'antiquité à l'Islam*. Paris.

Caubet, A. (2002), "Animals in Syro-Palestinian art", in Collins, ed., 211–234.

Caubet, A. (2007), *Faïences et matières vitreuses de l'Orient ancien*. Paris.

Caubet, A. (2010), "From Susa to Egypt: Vitreous materials from the Achaemenid period", in Curtis and Simpson, eds., 409–416.

Caubet, A. and Daucé, N. (2010), "Les arts du feu", in Perrot, ed., 322–347.

Caubet, A. and Muscarella, O. (1992), "Achaemenid brick decoration", in Harper, Aruz and Tallon, eds., 223–241.

Cauvin, J. (1968), *Fouilles de Byblos IV: Les outillages néolithiques de Byblos et du litoral libanais*. Paris.

Cauvin, J. (1979), "Les fouilles de Mureybet (1971–1974) et leur signification pour les origines de la sédentarisation au Proche-Orient", in Freedman, ed., 19–48.

Cauvin, J. (1980), "Le Moyen Euphrate au VIIIe millénaire d'après Mureybet et Cheikh Hasan", in Margueron, ed., 21–34.

Cauvin, J. (1994), *Naissance des divinités. Naissance de l'agriculture*. Paris.

Cauvin, J. (2000), *The birth of the gods and the origins of agriculture*. Cambridge.

Cauvin, J., Aurenche, O., Cauvin, M-C. and Balkan-Atli, N. (1999), "The Pre-Pottery site of Çafer Höyük", in Özdoğan and Başgelen, eds., 87–14.

Cauvin, J. and Sanlaville, P., eds. (1981), *Préhistoire du Levant*. Paris.

Cauvin, M-C. (1973), "Une station de tradition natoufienne dans le Hauran (Syrie): Taibé, près de Deraa", *AAAS* 22: 105–110.

Cauvin, M-C. (1974), "Outillage lithique et chronologie a Tell Aswad (Damascene, Syrie)", *Paléorient* 2: 429–436.

Cauvin, M-C. (1979), "Étude comparative d'apres l'outillage lithique", *Paléorient* 5: 157–160.

Cauvin,, M-C. (1983), "Les faucilles préhistorique du Proche Oriente: données morphologique et functionelles", *Paléorient* 9: 63–79.

Cauvin, M-C. and Abbés, F. (2008), "Analyse du mobilier retouché", in Ibáñez, ed., 281–361.

Cauvin, M-C. and Chataigner, C. (1998), "Distribution de l'obsidienne dans les sites archeologiques du Proche et du Moyen Orient (par phase chronologique)", in Cauvin, Gourgaud, Gratuze, Arnaud, Poupeau, Poidevin and Chataigner eds., 325–350.

Cauvin, M-C., Coqueugniot, E., Le Mière, M., Muhesen, S. and Nierlé, M-C. (1982), "Prospéctions préhistorique à Mallaha-Jayroud (Qalamoun), Syrie", *AAAS* 32: 273–281.

Cauvin, M-C., Gourgaud, A., Gratuze, B., Arnaud, N., Poupeau, G., Poidevin, J,-L. and Chataigner, C., eds. (1998), *L'obsidienne au Proche et Moyen Orient: Du volcan à l'outil*. Oxford.

Cavigneaux, A. and Khalil Ismail, B. (1990), "Die Statthalter von Suhu und Mari im 8. Jh. v. Chr.", *BaM* 21: 231–456.

CDLI (2010), *Cuneiform Digital Library Initiative* (http://cdli.ucla.edu/).

Cecchini, S.M. and Mazzoni, S., eds. (1998), *Tell Afis (Siria). Scavi sull'acropoli 1988–1992/ The 1988–1992 excavations on the Acropolis*. Pisa.

Cecchini, S.M., Mazzoni, S. and Scigliuzzo, E., eds. (2009), *Syrian and Phoenician ivories of the early first millennium BCE: Chronology, regional styles and iconographic repertories, patterns of inter-regional distribution*. Pisa.

Cerasetti, B. (1998), "Preliminary report on ornamental elements of 'incised coarse ware'", in Gubaev et al., eds., 67–74.

Cessford, C. and Near, J. (2006), "Fire, burning, and pyrotechnology at Çatalhöyük", in Hodder, ed., 171–182.

Çevik, Ö. (2007), "The emergence of different social systems in Early Bronze Age Anatolia: urbanisation versus centralisation", in Greaves and Fletcher, eds., 131–140.

Chabot, J. (2002), *Tell 'Atij, Tell Gudeda, industrie lithique*. Quebec.

Chakrabarti, D.K. (1978), "Lapis lazuli in early India", *Man & Environment* 2: 51–58.

Chakrabarti, D.K. and Moghadam, P. (1977), "Some unpublished Indus beads from Iran", *Iran* 15: 192–194.

Chan, A. (in press), "A historical perspective on the 'Midianite' question of Qurayyah Painted Ware", in Eichmann and Hausleiter, eds.

Chaniotis, A. (2005), *War in the Hellenistic world*. Oxford.

Charaf-Mullins, H. (2006), "Les céramiques importées de l'Ouest", in Thalmann, ed., 173–192.

Charles, J.A. (1967), "Early arsenical bronzes: a metallurgical view", *AJA* 71: 21–26.

Charles, J.A. (1980), "The coming of copper and copper-base alloys and iron: a metallurgical sequence", in Wertime and Muhly, eds., 151–182.

Charles, J.A. (1985), "Determinative mineralogy and the origins of metallurgy", in Craddock and Hughes, eds., 21–28.

Charpentier, V. (1996), "Archaeology of the Erythraean Sea: craft specialization and resources optimization as part of the coastal economy on the eastern coastlands of Oman during the 4th and 3rd millennia BC", in Afanas'ev et al., eds., 181–192.

Charpentier, V. (2003), "From the Gulf to the Hadramawt: fluting and plunging processes in Arabia", in Potts et al., eds., 66–71.

Charpentier, V., Blin, O. and Tosi, M. (1998), "Un village de pêcheurs néolithiques de la péninsule d'Oman: Suwayh 2 (SWY–2), première campagne de fouille", *PSAS* 28: 21–38.

Charpentier, V., Marquis, P. and Pellé, E. (2003), "La nécropole et les derniers horizons Ve millénaire du site du Gorbat al-Mahar (Suwayah, SWY–1, Sultanat d'Oman). Premier résultats", *PSAS* 33: 11–19.

Charpentier, V. and Méry, S. (1997), "Hameçons en nacre et limes en pierre d'Océanie et de l'Océan indien: analyse d'une tendance", *Journal de la Société des Océanistes* 2: 147–156.

Charpentier, V. and Méry, S. (2008), "A Neolithic settlement near the Strait of Hormuz: Akab Island, United Arab Emirates", *PSAS* 38: 117–136.

Charpin, D. (1986), *Le Clergé d'Ur au siècle d'Hammurabi (XIXe-XVIIIe siècles av. J.-C.)*. Geneva.

Charpin, D. (1996), "Maisons et maisonnés en Babylonie ancienne de Sippar à Ur: remarques sur les grandes demeures des notables paléo-babyloniens", in Veenhof, ed., 221–228.

Charpin, D. (2002 [app. 2004]), "Chroniques bibliographiques 2. La commémoration d'actes juridiques: à propos des Kudurrus babyloniens", *RA* 96: 169–191.

Charpin, D. (2003), "La politique immobilière des marchands de Larsa à la lumière des découvertes épigraphiques de 1987 et 1989", in Huot, ed., 311–320.

Charpin, D. (2004), "Histoire politique du proche-orient Amorrite (2002–1595)", in Charpin et al., 25–480.

Charpin, D. and Durand, J-M. (1991), "La suzeraineté de l'emperor (sukkalmah) d'Élam sur la Mésopotamie et le 'nationalisme' Amorrite", in De Meyer and Gasche, eds., 59–66.

Charpin, D., Edzard, D.O. and Stol, M. (2004), *Mesopotamien: Die altbabylonische Zeit*. Fribourg and Göttingen.

Charpin, D. and Joannès, F., eds. (1991), *Marchands, diplomates et empereurs. Études sur la civilisation mésopotamienne offertes à Paul Garelli*. Paris.

Charvát, P. (2002), *Mesopotamia Before History*. London.

Chay, J. and Ross, T., eds. (1986), *Buffer States in World Politics*. Boulder.

Chazan, M. and Lehner, M. (1990), "An ancient analogy: pot-baked bread in ancient Egypt and Mesopotamia", *Paléorient* 16: 21–35.

Chen, K-T. and Hiebert, F.T. (1995), "The late prehistory of Xinjiang and its relationship to its neighbors", *JWP* 9/2: 243–300.

Chen, S., Lin, B-Z., Baig, M., Mitra, B., Lopes, R.J., Santos, A.M., Magee, D.A., Azevedo, M., Tarroso, P., Sasazaki, S., Ostrowski, S., Mahgoub, O., Chaudhuri, T.K., Zhang, Y-P., Costa, V., Royo, L.J., Goyache, F., Luikart, G., Boivin, N., Fuller, D.Q., Mannen, H., Bradley, D.G. and Beja-Pereira, A. (2010), "Zebu cattle are an exclusive legacy of the South Asia Neolithic", *Molecular Biology and Evolution* 27: 1–6.

Cheng, J. and Feldman, M.H., eds. (2007), *Ancient Near Eastern Art in Context: Studies in Honor of Irene J. Winter by her Students*. Leiden.

Cheng, T. (1960), *Archaeology in China*. Vol. 2: *Shang China*. Cambridge.
Cherian, P.J., Selvakumar, V. and Shajan, K.P. (2007), "The Muziris Heritage Project: excavations at Pattanam – 2007", *Journal of Indian Ocean Archaeology* 4: 1–10.
Chernykh, E.N. (1992), *Ancient Metallurgy in the USSR: The Early Metal Age*. Cambridge.
Chernykh, E.N. (2009), "Formation of the Eurasian Steppe Belt cultures: viewed through the lens of archaeometallurgy and radiocarbon dating", in in Hanks and Linduff, eds., 115–145.
Chernykh, E.N., Avilova, L.I. and Orlovskaya, L.B. (2002), "Metallurgy of the Circumpontic area: from unity to disintegration", in Yalçin, ed., 83–100.
Cherry, J. (1990), "The first colonization of the Mediterranean islands: a review of recent research", *JMA* 3: 145–221.
Chessa, B., Pereira, F., Arnaud, F., Amorim, A., Goyache, F., Mainland, I., Kao, R.R., Pemberton, J.M., Beraldi, D., Stear, M.J., Alberti, A., Pittau, M., Iannuzzi, L., Banabazi, M.H., Kazwala, R.R., Zhang, Y-P., Arranz, J.J., Ali, B.A., Wang, Z., Uzun, M., Dione, M.M., Olsaker, I., Holm, L-E., Saarma, U., Ahmad, S., Arzanov, N., Eythorsdottir, E., Holland, M.J., Ajmone-Marsan, P., Bruford, M.W., Kantanen, J., Spencer, T.E. and Palmarini, M. (2009), "Revealing the history of sheep domestication using retrovirus integrations", *Science* 324: 532–536.
Chesson, M.S. and Philip, G. (2003), "Tales of the city? 'Urbanism' in the Early Bronze Age Levant from Mediterranean and Levantine perspectives", *JMA* 16: 3–16.
Chevalier, N., ed. (1997), *Une Mission en Perse: 1897–1912*. Paris.
Chevalier, N. (2010), "Les découvreurs du palais de Suse", in Perrot, ed., 74–115.
Childe, V.G. (1936), *Man Makes Himself*. London.
Childe, V.G. (1942), "Prehistory in the USSR. II. The Copper Age in south Russia", *Man* 42: 130–136.
Childe, V.G. (1950), "The urban revolution", *Town Planning Review* 21: 3–17.
Childe, V.G. (1952), *New Light on the Most Ancient East: The Oriental Prelude to European Prehistory*, rev. edn. New York.
Childs, W.P. (1981), "Lycian relations with Persians and Greeks in the fifth and fourth centuries re-examined", *AnSt* 31: 55–80.
Chiocchetti, L. (2007), "The children's burials of the Ubaid period: Tell Abu Husaini, the Hamrin area and beyond", *Mesopotamia* 42: 117–142.
Cholidis, N. (2002), *Der Tell Halaf und sein Ausgräber Max Freiherr von Oppenheim*. Mainz.
Christian, D. (1998), *A History of Russia, Central Asia and Mongolia*. Vol. 1: *Inner Eurasia from Prehistory to the Mongol Empire*. Oxford and Malden.
Christie, N. and Loseby, S.T., eds. (1996), *Towns in Transition: Urban Evolution in Late Antiquity and the Early Middle Ages*. Aldershot.
Ciasca, A. (1988), "Phoenicia", in Moscati, ed., 168–184.
Çilingiroğlu, A. (2002), "The reign of Rusa II: towards the end of Urartian kingdom", in Aslan et al., eds., 483–489.
Çilingiroğlu, A. and Çilingiroğlu, C. (2007), "Ulucak", in Özdoğan and Başgelen, eds., 361–372.
Çilingiroğlu, A. and Darbyshire, G., eds. (2005), *Anatolian Iron Ages 5*. London.
Çilingiroğlu, A. and French, D., eds. (1994), *Anatolian Iron Ages 3*. London.

Çinaroğlu, A. and Genç, E. (2003), "Alaca Höyük ve Alaca Höyük hittit baraji kazilari, 2002", *Kazi Sonuçlari Toplantisi* 25/1: 279–288.

Çilingiroğlu, A. and Sagona, A., eds. (2007), *Anatolian Iron Ages 6*. Louvain.

Cilingiroğlu, A. and Salvini, M., eds. (2001), *Ayanis I: Ten Years Excavations at Rusahi-nili Eiduru-kai 1989–1998*. Rome.

Civil, M. (1987), "Ur III bureaucracy: quantitative aspects", in Gibson and Biggs, eds., 43–53.

Civil, M. (1994), *The Farmer's Instructions: A Sumerian Agricultural Manual*. Barcelona.

Civil, M. (1995), "Ancient Mesopotamian lexicography", in Sasson, ed., 2305–2314.

Clamer, C. (1997), *Fouilles archéologiques de 'Aïn ez-Zâra/Callirrhoé, villégiature hérodi-enne*. Beirut.

Clark, J.D. (1975-7), "Interpretation of prehistoric technology from ancient Egypt and other sources. Part 2: Prehistoric arrow forms in Africa as shown by surviving examples of traditional arrows from ancient Egypt and other sources", *Paléorient* 3: 127–150.

Clarke, G.W. (2003), *Excavating and Interpreting the Governor's Palace, Acropolis, Jebel Khalid*. Canberra.

Clarke, G.W. (2005), "Jebel Khalid, Area B: the Jebel Khalid temple", *MeditArch* 18: 128–135.

Clarke, G.W., Connor, P.J., Crewe, L., Frohlich, B., Jackson, H., Littleton, J., Nixon, C.E.V., O'Hea, M. and Steele, D. (2002), *Jebel Khalid on the Euphrates*. Vol. 1. *Report on Excavations 1986–1996*. Sydney.

Clason, A., Payne, S. and Uerpmann, H.-P., eds. (1993), *Skeletons in her Cupboard: Festschrift for Juliet Clutton-Brock*. Oxford.

Clason, A.T. (1978), "Late Bronze Age-Iron Age zebu cattle in Jordan?", *JAS* 5: 91–93.

Clason, A.T., ed. (1975), *Archaeozoological Studies*. Amsterdam.

Clauss-Balty, P., ed. (2008a), *Hauran III. L'Habitat dans les campagnes de Syrie du Sud aux époques classiques et médiévales*. Beirut.

Clauss-Balty, P. (2008b), "Maisons romano-byzantines dans les villages de Batanée: missions 2002–2004", in Clauss-Balty, ed., 41–104.

Clay, A.T. (1915), *Miscelleneous Inscriptions in the Yale Babylonian Collection*. New Haven.

Clayton, P. and Price, M., eds. (1988), *The Seven Wonders of the Ancient World*. London.

Clermont-Ganneau, C. (1919), "Les Nabatéens en Égypte", *Revue de l'Histoire de Religions* 80: 1–29.

Cleuziou, S. (1980), "Three seasons at Hili: toward a chronology and culture history of the Oman Peninsula in the 3rd millennium BC", *PSAS* 10: 19–32.

Cleuziou, S. (1982), "Hili and the beginnings of oasis life in Eastern Arabia", *PSAS* 12: 15–22.

Cleuziou, S. (1984), "Oman Peninsula and its relations eastward during the third millennium", in Lal and Gupta, eds., 371–394.

Cleuziou, S. (1986), "Tureng Tepe and burnished grey ware: a question of 'frontier'?", *Oriens Antiquus* 25: 221–256.

Cleuziou, S. (1989), "Excavations at Hili 8: a preliminary report on the 4th to 7th campaigns", *AUAE* 5: 61–87.

Cleuziou, S. (1996), "The emergence of oases and towns in eastern and southern Arabia", in Afanas'ev et al., eds., 159–165.

Cleuziou, S. (1997), "Construire et protéger son terroir: les oasis d'Oman à l'Âge du Bronze", in Burnouf et al., eds., 389–412.

Cleuziou, S. and Tosi, M. (1994), "Black boats of Magan: some thoughts on Bronze Age water transport in Oman and beyond, from the impressed bitumen slabs of Ra's al-Junayz", in Parpola and Koskikallio, eds., 745–761.

Cleuziou, S. and Tosi, M. (2000), "Ra's al-Jinz and the prehistoric coastal cultures of the Ja'alan", *JOS* 11: 19–74.

Cleuziou, S. and Tosi, M. (2007), *In the Shadow of the Ancestors: The Protohistoric Foundations of the Early Arabian Civilization in Oman*. Muscat.

Cleuziou, S., Tosi, M. and Zarins, J., eds. (2002), *Essays on the Late Prehistory of the Arabian Peninsula*. Rome.

Clifford, J. (1988), *The Predicament of Culture: Twentieth-Century Ethnography, Literature, and Art*. Cambridge.

Cline, E.H. and Harris-Cline, D., eds. (1998), *The Aegean and the Orient in the Second Millennium*. Liège.

Cline, E.H. and O'Connor, D. (2003), "The mystery of the 'sea peoples' ", in O'Connor and Quirke, eds., 108–138.

Cline, E.H. and O'Connor, D., eds. (2005), *Thutmosis III: A New Biography*. Ann Arbor.

Clutton-Brock, J. (1989a), "A reconsideration of the fossil fauna from C-spring, Azraq", in Copeland and Hours, eds., 391–397.

Clutton-Brock, J., ed. (1989b), *The Walking Larder*. London.

Clutton-Brock, J. (1992a), *Horse Power: A History of the Horse and Donkey in Human Societies*. Cambridge.

Clutton-Brock, J. (1992b), "The process of domestication", *Mammal Review* 22: 79–85.

Clutton-Brock, J. and Grigson, C., eds. (1984), *Animals and Archaeology 3. Early Herders and their Flocks*. Oxford.

Clutton-Brock, J., Vishnu-Mittre and Gulati, A.N., eds. (1961), *Technical Reports on Archaeological Remains III*. Poona.

Cochavi-Rainey, Z. (1999), *Royal Gifts in the Late Bronze Age: Fourteenth to Thirteenth Centuries BC*. Jerusalem.

Cocquerillat, D. (1968), *Palmeraies et cultures de l'Éanna d'Uruk (558–520)*. Berlin.

Cogan, M. and Tadmor, H. (1977), "Gyges and Assurbanipal", *Or* 46: 65–85.

Coghlan, H.H. (1975), *Notes on the Prehistoric Metallurgy of Copper and Bronze in the Old World*. Oxford.

Cohen, A. (2005), *Death Rituals, Ideology, and the Development of Early Mesopotamian kingship: Toward a new Understanding of Iraq's Royal Cemetery of Ur*. Leiden.

Cohen, G.M. (2006), *The Hellenistic Settlements in Syria, the Red Sea Basin, and North Africa*. Berkeley/Los Angeles/London.

Cohen, M., Snell, D. and Weisberg, D., eds. (1993), *The Tablet and the Scroll: Near Eastern Studies in Honor of William W. Hallo*. Bethesda.

Cohen, R. and Westbrook, R., eds.(2000), *Amarna Diplomacy: The Beginnings of International Relations*. Baltimore/London.

Cohen, R. and Westbrook, R., eds. (2008), *Isaiah's Vision of Peace in Biblical and Modern International Relations: Swords into Plowshares*. New York.

Cohen, S.L. (2001), *Canaanites, Chronologies, and Connections: The Relationship of Middle Bronze IIa Canaan to Middle Kingdom Egypt*. Winona Lake.

Colbow, G. (1995), *Die spätaltbabylonische Glyptik Südbabyloniens*. Munich/Vienna.

Cole, S.W. (1994), "Marsh formation in the Borsippa region and the course of the lower Euphrates", *JNES* 53: 81–109.

Cole, S.W. and De Meyer, L. (1999), "Tepti-ahar, king of Susa, and Kadašman-^{d}KUR.GAL", *Akkadica* 112: 44–45.

Cole, S.W. and Gasche, H. (1998), "Second and first millennium BC rivers in northern Babylonia", in Gasche and Tanret, eds., 1–64.

Colinart, S. and Menu, M., eds. (1998), *La Couleur dans la peinture at l'émaillage de l'Egypte ancienne*. Bari.

Colledge, S. (1998), "Identifying pre-domestic cultivation using multivariate analysis", in Damania et al., eds., 121–131.

Colledge, S. (2001), *Plant Exploitation on Epipaleolithic and Early Neolithic Sites in the Levant*. Oxford.

Colledge, S. and Conolly, J., eds. (2007), *The Origins and Spread of Domestic Plants in Southwest Asia and Europe*. Walnut Creek.

Collins, B.J. (1990), *The Hittites and Their World*. Atlanta.

Collins, B.J., ed. (2002a), *A History of the Animal World in the Ancient Near East*. Leiden.

Collins, B.J. (2002b), "Animals in Hittite literature", in Collins, ed., 237–250.

Collins, B.J. (2004), "The politics of Hittite religious iconography", in Hutter and Hutter-Braunsar, eds., 83–115.

Collins, B.J. (2007), *The Hittites and Their World*. Atlanta.

Collins, B.J., Bachvarova, M.R. and Rutherford, I.C. (2008), *Anatolian Interfaces: Hittites, Greeks and their Neighbours*. Oxford.

Collins, P. (2009), *Assyrian Palace Sculptures*. Austin.

Collon, D. (1975), *The Seal Impressions from Tell Atchana/Alalakh*. Kevelaer.

Collon, D. (1986), *Catalogue of the Western Asiatic seals in the British Museum. Cylinder Seals III: Isin-Larsa and Old Babylonian Periods*. London.

Collon, D. (1987), *First Impressions: Cylinder Seals in the Ancient Near East*. London.

Collon, D. (1996), "A hoard of sealings from Ur", in Boussac and Invernizzi, eds., 65–84.

Collon, D. (2001), *Catalogue of the Western Asiatic Seals in the British Museum. Cylinder Seals V: Neo-Assyrian and Neo-Babylonian Periods*. London.

Collon, D. and George, A., eds. (2004), "Nineveh: Papers of the XLIXe Rencontre Assyriologique 2003, Part One", *Iraq* 66: 1–264.

Collon, D., Otte, C., Otte, M. and Zaqzuq, A. (1975), *Sondages au flanc sud du Tell de Qal'at el-Mudiq*. Brussels.

Compagnoni, B. (1980), "On the probable presence of the urial (*Ovis vignei* Blyth) at the protohistoric site of Shahr-i Sokhta (Sistan, Iran)", *EW* 30: 9–15.

Compagnoni, B. and Tosi, M. (1978), "The camel: its distribution and state of domestication in the Middle East during the third millennium BC in light of finds from Shahr-i Sokhta", in Meadow and Zeder, eds., 91–104.

Comparetti, M., Raffetta, P. and Scarcia, G., eds. (2003), *Ērān ud Anērān, Webfestschrift Marshak*. http://www.transoxiana.org/Eran/.
Conard, N.J., ed. (2006a), *Tübingen-Damascus Excavation and Survey Project 1999–2005*. Tübingen.
Conard, N.J. (2006b), "An overview of the recent excavations at Baaz Rockshelter, Damascus Province, Syria", in Conard, ed., 5–23.
Conard, N., Drechsler, P. and Morales, A., eds. (2011), *Between Sand and Sea: The Archaeology and Human Ecology of southwestern Asia*. Tübingen.
Conard, N.J., Kandel, A.W., Dodonov, A.E. and Abdulrahman, A. (2006), "The 2000 Ma'aloula Paleolithic Survey", in Conard, ed., 297–304.
Conermann, S., ed. (1998), *Der Indische Ozean in historischer Perspektiv*. Hamburg.
Coningham, R.A.E. and Allchin, F.R. (1995), "The rise of cities in Sri Lanka", in Allchin, ed., 152–183.
Coningham, R.A.E., Fazeli, H., Young, R.L. and Donahue, R.E. (2004), "Location, location, location: a pilot survey of the Tehran Plain in 2003", *Iran* 42: 1–12.
Conkey, M., Soffer, O., Stratmann, D. and Jablonski, N.G., eds. (1997), *Beyond Art: Pleistocene Image and Symbol*. San Francisco.
Connan, J. and Carter, R.A. (2007), "A geochemical study of bituminous mixtures from Failaka and Umm an-Namel (Kuwait), from the Early Dilmun to the Early Islamic period", *AAE* 18: 139–181.
Connan, J., Carter, R.A., Crawford, H.E.W., Tobey, M., Charrié-Duhaut, A., Jarvie, D., Albrecht, P. and Norman, K. (2005), A comparative geochemical study of bituminous boat remains from H3, As-Sabiyah (Kuwait), and RJ-2, Ra's al-Jinz (Oman). *AAE* 15: 1–46.
Connan, J., Zumberge, J., Imbus, K. and Moghaddam, A. (2008), "The bituminous mixtures of Tall-e Abu Chizan: a Vth millennium BC settlement in southwestern Iran", *Organic Geochemistry* 39: 1772–1789.
Conner, S. and Sagona, A. (2007), "Environment and society in the late prehistory of southern Georgia, Caucasus", in Lyonnet, ed., 21–36.
Conolly, J. (1999), *The Çatalhöyük Obsidian Industry*. Oxford.
Contenau, G. and Girshman, R. (1935), *Fouilles de Tépé Giyan, près du Néhavend, 1931 et 1932*. Paris.
Contenson, H. de (1992), *Ras Shamra – Ougarit VIII: Préhistoire de Ras Shamra. Les Sondages stratigraphiques de 1955 à 1976*. Paris.
Contenson, H. de (2000), *Ramad: Site néolithique en Damascène (Syrie) aux VIIIe et VIIe millénaires avant l'ère chrétienne*. Beirut.
Contenson, H. de, Anderson, A., Cauvin, M-C., Clere, J., Ducos, P., Dupeyron, M., Maréchal, C. and Stordeur, D. (1995), *Aswad et Ghoraifé: Sites néolithiques en Damascène (Syrie) aux IXème et VIIème millénaires avant l'ère chrétienne*. Beirut.
Contenson, H. de, Blot, J., Courtois, L., Dupeyron, M. and Leroi-Gourhan, A. (1992), *Préhistoire de Ras Shamra: Les Sondages stratigraphiques de 1955 à 1976*. Paris.
Cook, B. (1995), "The trade in antiquities: a curator's view", in Tubb, ed., 181–192.
Coon, C.S. (1957), *The Seven Caves: Archaeological Exploration in the Middle East*. New York.
Coombes, P. and Barber, K. (2005), "Environmental determinism in Holocene research: causality of coincidence?", *Area* 37/3: 303–311.

Cooper, J.P. (2005), *The Nile–Red Sea Canal in Antiquity: A Consideration of the Evidence for its Existence, Duration and Route*. Southampton.

Cooper, J.P. (2009), "Nile-Red Sea canals: chronology, location, seasonality and function", in Blue et al., 195–209.

Cooper, J.S. (1973), "Sumerian and Akkadian in Sumer and Akkad", *Or* 42: 239–246.

Cooper, J.S. (1983a), *Reconstructing History From Ancient Inscriptions: The Lagash-Umma Border Conflict*. Malibu.

Cooper, J.S. (1983b), *The Curse of Agade*. Baltimore.

Cooper, J.S. (1990), "Mesopotamian historical consciousness and the production of monumental art in the third millennium BC", in Gunter, ed., 39–52.

Cooper, J.S. (1993), "Paradigm and propaganda: the dynasty of Akkade in the 21st century", in Liverani, ed., 11–23.

Cooper, J.S. and Schwartz, G.M., eds. (1996), *The Study of the Ancient Near East in the Twenty-First Century*. Winona Lake.

Cooper, L. (2006a), "The pottery from Tell 'Asharneh. Part I: Typological considerations and dating according to excavated areas in the Upper and Lower Towns. 1998–2002", in Fortin, ed., 140–190.

Cooper, L. (2006b), *Early Urbanism on the Syrian Euphrates*. New York and London.

Cope, C. (1991), "Gazelle hunting strategies in the southern Levant", in Bar-Yosef and Valla, eds., 341–358.

Copeland, L. (1996), "The flint and obsidian industries", in Akkermans, ed., 285–338.

Copeland, L. and Hours, F., eds. (1989), *The Hammer on the Rock: Studies in the Early Palaeolithic of Azraq, Jordan*. Oxford.

Copeland, L. and Wescombe, P.J. (1965), "Inventory of Stone-Age sites in Lebanon", *MUSJ* 41: 31–147.

Copeland, L. and Wescombe, P.J. (1966), "Inventory of Stone-Age sites in Lebanon", *MUSJ* 42: 1–174.

Coqueugniot, E. (1991), "Outillage de pierre taillée au Bronze récent, Ras Shamra 1978–1988", in Yon, ed., 127–204.

Coqueugniot, E. (1998), "L'obsidienne en Méditerranée orientale aux époques post-néolithiques", in Cauvin et al., eds., 351–362.

Coqueugniot, E. (1999), "Tell Dja'de el-Mughara", in del Olmo Lete and Montero Fenollós, eds., 41–55.

Coqueugniot, E. (2000), "Dja'de, Syrie: un village à la veille de la domestication (seconde moitié du IXe millénaire av. J.-C.)", in Guilaine, ed., 63–79.

Corbo, V. (1955), *Gli Scavi di Kh. Siyar el-Ghanam (Campo dei pastori) e i monasteri dei dintorni*. Jerusalem.

Córdoba, J.M., Molist, M., Pérez, C.M., Rubio, I. and Martínez, S., eds. (2008), *Proceedings of the 5th International Congress on the Archaeology of the Ancient Near East, Madrid, April 3–8 2006*, vol. 3. Madrid.

Cordova, C. (2000), "Geomorphological evidence of intense prehistoric soil erosion in the highlands of central Jordan", *Physical Geography* 21: 538–567.

Cordova, C. (2007), "The degradation of the Near Eastern environment", in Snell, ed., 125–141.

Cordova, C. (2008), "Floodplain degradation and settlement history in Wadi al-Wala and Wadi ash-Shallalah, Jordan", *Geomorphology* 101: 443–457.

Corfù, N.A. (2006), "Die Wasseraufbereitungsanlage von Čogā Zanbil, Iran", *AMIT* 38: 137–140.
Cornelius, I. and Niehr, H. (2004), *Götter und Kulte in Ugarit. Kultur und Religion einer nordsyrischen Königsstadt in der Spätbronzezeit*. Mainz.
Cornwall, I.W. (1981), "Appendix A. The Pre-Pottery Neolithic burials", in Kenyon, 395–406.
Coskunsu, G. and Lemorini, C. (2001), "The function of Pre-Pottery Neolithic projectile points: the limits of morphological analogy", in Caneva et al., eds., 145–159.
Costa, P.M. (1977), "A Latin-Greek inscription from the Jawf of Yemen", *PSAS* 7: 69–72.
Costa, P.M. (1988), "Fishing stations of the coast of Oman: a theme of ethno-archaeological research", *PSAS* 18: 3–13.
Costa, P.M. and Tosi, M., eds. (1989), *Oman Studies*. Rome.
Costantini, L. (1977), "Le piante", in Tucci, ed., 159–171.
Costantini, L. (1984), "The beginning of agriculture in the Kachi Plain: the evidence of Mehrgarh", in Allchin, ed., 29–33.
Costantini, L. (1985), "Considerazioni su alcuni reperti di palma da dattero e sul centro di origine e l'area di coltivazione della *Phoenix dactylifera* L.", in Gnoli and Lanciotti, eds., 209–218.
Costantini, L. and Dyson, R.H., Jr. (1990), "The ancient agriculture of the Damghan plain: the archaeobotanical evidence from Tepe Hissar", in Miller, ed., 46–64.
Costello, S. (2010), "The Mesopotamian 'nude hero': context and interpretations", in Counts and Arnold, eds., 25–35.
Costin, C.L. (1991), "Craft specialization: issues in defining, documenting, and explaining the organisation of production", in Schiffer, ed., 1–56.
Costin, C.L. (2001), "Craft production systems", in Feinman and Price, eds., 273–328.
Cosyns, P. and Hurt, V. (2007), "Les perles en verre de Neufchâteau Le-Sart", *Arduinna* 62: 1–5.
Cotterrell, B. and Kamminga, J. (1987), "The formation of flakes", *AmAnt* 52: 675–708.
Cotton, H., Lernau, O. and Goren, Y. (1996), "Fish sauces from Herodian Masada", *JRA* 9: 223–238.
Counts, D. and Arnold, B., eds. (2010), *The Master of Animals in Old World Iconography*. Budapest.
Coupland, G. and Banning, E.B., eds. (1996), *People Who Lived in Large Houses*. Madison.
Courtils, J. des and Moretti, J-C. (1993), *Les Grands Ateliers d'architecture dans le monde égéen du VIe siècle av. J.-C.* Istanbul.
Courtois, J-C. (1973), "Prospection archéologique dans la moyenne vallée de l'Oronte (El Ghab et Er Roujd – Syrie du nord-ouest)", *Syria* 50: 53–99.
Courty, A. and Roux, V. (1995), "Identification of wheel throwing on the basis of ceramic surface features and microfabrics", *JAS* 22: 17–50.
Crabtree, P.J., Campana, D. and Ryan, K., eds. (1989), *Early Animal Domestication and Its Cultural Context*. Philadelphia.
Crabtree, P.J. and Monge, J.M. (1986), "Faunal analysis", in Joukowsky, ed., 180–190.

Craddock, P.T. (1978), "The composition of the copper alloys used by the Greek, Etruscan and Roman civilizations 3. The origins and early use of brass", *JAS* 5: 1–16.
Craddock, P.T., ed. (1980), *Scientific Studies in Early Mining and Extractive Metallurgy*. London.
Craddock, P.T. (1995), *Early Metal Mining and Production*. Washington, DC.
Craddock, P.T. (2000), "From hearth to furnace: evidences for the earliest metal smelting technologies in the eastern Mediterranean", *Paléorient* 26: 151–165.
Craddock, P.T., Cowell, M.R. and Guerra, M-F. (2005), "Controlling the composition of gold and the invention of gold refining in Lydian Anatolia", in Yalçin, ed., 67–78.
Craddock, P.T. and Eckstein, K. (2003), "Production of brass in Antiquity by direct reduction", in Craddock and Lang, eds., 216–230.
Craddock, P.T. and Hughes, M.J. (1985), *Furnaces and Smelting Technology in Antiquity*. London.
Craddock. P.T. and Lang, J., eds. (2003), *Mining and Metal Production Through the Ages*. London.
Craddock, P.T., La Niece, S. and Hook, D.R. (2003), "Evidences for the production, trading and refining of copper in the Gulf of Oman during the third millennium BC", in Stöllner et al., eds., 103–112.
Crawford, H.E.W. (1973), "Mesopotamia's invisible exports in the third millennium BC", *WA* 5/2: 232–241.
Crawford, H.E.W. (1998), *Dilmun and her Gulf Neighbours*. Cambridge.
Crawford, H.E.W. (2004), *Sumer and the Sumerians*, 2nd edn. Cambridge.
Crawford, H.E.W., Killick, R. and Moon, J., eds. (1997), *The Dilmun Temple at Saar*. London and New York.
Crawford, H.E.W., McMahon, A. and Postgate, J.N., eds. (in press), *Preludes to Urbanism: Studies in the Late Chalcolithic of Mesopotamia in Honour of Joan Oates*. Oxford.
Crawford, S.W., ed. (2007), *Up to the Gates of Ekron: Essays on the Archaeology and History of the Eastern Mediterranean in Honor of Seymour Gitin*. Jerusalem.
Crespin, A.-S. (1999), "Between Phrygia and Cilicia: the Porsuk area at the beginning of the Iron Age", *AnSt* 49: 61–71.
Cresswell, R. (1972), "Les trois sources d'une technologie nouvelle", in Thomas and Bernot, eds., 21–27.
Cribb, J. and Herrmann, G., eds. (2007), *After Alexander: Central Asia Before Islam*. Oxford and New York.
Crockford, S., ed. (2000), *Dogs Through Time: An Archaeological Perspective*. Oxford.
Crone, P. (1987), *Meccan Trade and the Rise of Islam*. Princeton.
Croucher, K. (2006), "Death, display and performance: a discussion of the mortuary remains at Çayönü Tepesi", in Georgiadis and Gallou, eds., 11–44.
Croucher, K. (2010), "Figuring out identity: the body and identity in the Ubaid", in Carter and Philip eds., 113–124.
Crowfoot, J. (1935), "Notes on the flint implements from Jericho 1935", *AAA* 22: 174–184.
Crowfoot, J. (1937), "Notes on the flint implements of Jericho 1936", *AAA* 24: 35–52.
Crowfoot, J.W. (1941), *Early Churches in Palestine*. London.
Cruells, W. and Nieuwenhuyse, O. (2004), "The Proto-Halaf period in Syria: new sites, new data", *Paléorient* 30/1: 47–68.

Crüsemann, N. (2000), *Vom Zweistromland zum Kupfergraben: Vorgeschichte und Entstehungsjahre (1899–1918) der Vorderasiatischen Abteilung der Berliner Museen vor fach- und kulturpolitischen Hintergründen*. Berlin.

Cucchi, T., Vigne, J.D. and Auffray, J.C. (2005), "First occurrence of the house mouse (*Mus musculus domesticus* Schwarz & Schwarz, 1943) in the Western Mediterranean: a zooarchaeological revision of subfossil occurrences", *Biological Journal of the Linnaean Society* 84: 429–45.

Cullen, H.M. and deMenocal, P.B. (2000), "North Atlantic influence on Tigris-Euphrates streamflow", *International Journal of Climatology* 20: 853–863.

Cullen, H.M., deMenocal, P.B., Hemming, S., Hemming, G., Brown, F.H., Guilderson,T. and Sirocko, F. (2000), "Climate change and the collapse of the Akkadian Empire: evidence from the deep sea", *Geology* 28: 379–82.

Cumont, F. (1926), *Fouilles de Doura-Europos 1922–23*. Paris.

Cuno, J. (2008), *Who Owns Antiquity?* Princeton.

Cunningham, A. (1961), *Corpus Inscriptionum Indicarum I. Inscriptions of Asoka*. Varanasi.

Cureton, W. (1861), *History of the Martyrs in Palestine, by Eusebius, Bishop of Caesarea, Discovered in a Very Ancient Syriac Manuscript*. London.

Curry, A. (2006), "Anasazi in the backyard", in Vitelli and Colwell-Chanthaphonh, eds., 64–70.

Curtis, J.E., ed. (1982a), *Fifty Years of Mesopotamian Discovery*. London.

Curtis, J.E. (1982b), "Chagar Bazar", in Curtis, ed., 79–85.

Curtis, J.E. (1989a), "Case of the missing column", *British Museum Society Bulletin* 60: 7–9.

Curtis, J.E. (1989b), *Excavations at Qasrij Cliff and Khirbet Qasrij*. London.

Curtis, J.E. (1993), "William Kennett Loftus and his excavations at Susa", *IrAnt* 28: 1–55.

Curtis, J.E., ed. (1997), *Mesopotamia and Iran in the Persian Period: Conquest and Imperialism, 529–331 BC*. London.

Curtis, J.E., ed. (2000), *Mesopotamia and Iran in the Parthian and Sasanian periods*. London.

Curtis, J.E. (2003), "The Assyrian heartland in the period 612–539 BC", in Lanfranchi et al., eds., 157–167.

Curtis, J.E. (2005a), "The archaeology of the Achaemenid period", in Curtis and Tallis, eds., 30–49.

Curtis, J.E. (2005b), "The Achaemenid period in Northern Iraq", in Briant and Boucharlat, eds., 175–196.

Curtis, J.E. (2005c), "Iron Age Iran and the transition to the Achaemenid period", in Curtis and Stewart, eds., 112–131.

Curtis, J.E. (2009), "Relations between archaeologists and the military in the case of Iraq", *Papers from the Institute of Archaeology (London)* 19: 2–8.

Curtis, J.E., Collon, D., Green, A.R. and Searight, A. (1993), "British Museum excavations at Nimrud and Balawat in 1989", *Iraq* 55: 1–37.

Curtis, J.E. and Green, A. (1997), *Excavations at Khirbet Khatuniyeh*. London.

Curtis, J.E., McCall, H., Collon, D. and al-Gailani Werr, L., eds. (2008), *New light on Nimrud*. London.

Curtis, J.E. and Reade, J.E. (1995), *Art and Empire*. London.

Curtis, J.E. and Simpson, St.J., eds. (2010), *The World of Achaemenid Persia: History, Art and Society in Iran and the Ancient Near East.* London.

Curtis, J.E. and Tallis, N., eds. (2005), *Forgotten Empire: The World of Ancient Persia.* London.

Curtis, J.E. and Tallis, N. (2008), *The Balawat Gates of Assurnasirpal II.* London.

Curtis, J.E., Wheeler, T.S., Muhly J.D. and Maddin R. (1979), "Neo-Assyrian ironworking technology", *Proceedings of the American Philosophical Society* 123/6: 369–390.

Curtis, J.E. et al., ed. (in press), *Proceedings of the 7th International Congress of the Archaeology of the Ancient Near East, London 2010.* Wiesbaden.

Curtis, V.S., Hillenbrand, R. and Rogers, M.J., eds. (1998), *The Art and Archaeology of Ancient Persia: New Light on the Parthian and Sasanian Empires.* London.

Curtis, V.S. and Stewart, S., eds. (2005), *Birth of the Persian Empire*, vol. 1. London and New York.

Curtis, V.S. and Stewart, S., eds. (2008), *The Idea of Iran III: The Sasanian Era.* London.

Curvers, H. and Stuart, B. (2004), "Beirut Central District Archaeology Project 1994–2003", in Doumet-Serhal, ed., 248–265.

Curwen, E.C. (1935), "Agriculture and the flint sickle in Palestine", *Antiquity* 9: 61–66.

Curzon, G.N. (1882), *Persia and Persian Question*, vol. 2. London.

Cuvigny, H., ed. (2003a), *La Route de Myos Hormos. L'Armée romaine dans le désert Oriental d'Égypte. Praesidia du désert de Bérénice* I. Cairo.

Cuvigny, H. (2003b), "Introduction", in Cuvigny, ed., 1–35.

Czichon, R. (1998–2001), "Nebukadnezar II. B. Archäologisch", *RlA* 9: 201–206.

Czichon, R.M. (2000), "Das Hattuša/Boğazköy Surveyprojekt", in Matthiae et al., eds., 269–278.

Dabrowski, B., LaBianca, O.S. and Dubis, E. (1994), "Megalithic tomb at Tell El-'Umeiri, Jordan", *BA* 57: 241–242.

Daems, A. (2010), "A snake in the grass: reassessing the ever-intriguing ophidian figurines", in Carter and Philip, eds., 149–161.

Dagron, G. (1974), *Naissance d'une capitale. Constantinople et ses institutiones de 330 à 451.* Paris.

Dagron, G. (1979), "Entre village et cité: la bourgade rurale des IVe-VIIe siècles en Orient", *Koinonia* 3: 29–52.

Dagron, G. (1995), "Poissons, pêcheurs et poissonniers de Constantinople", in Mango and Dagron, eds., 57–73.

Dahari, U. (2000), *Monastic Settlements in South Sinai in the Byzantine Period: The Archaeological Remains.* Jerusalem.

Dahl, J. (2002), "Proto-Elamite sign frequencies", *Cuneiform Digital Library Bulletin* 2002/1: 1–3.

Dahl, J. (2009), "Early writing in Iran, a reappraisal", *Iran* 47: 23–31.

Daim, F. and Drauschke, J., eds. (2010), *Byzanz – Das Römerreich im Mittelalter*, vol. 2/1. Mainz.

Dales, G.F. (1960), *Mesopotamian and Related Female Figurines: Their Chronology, Diffusion and Cultural Functions.* Philadelphia.

Dales, G.F. (1968), "Of dice and men", *JAOS* 88: 14–23.

Dalfes, H.N., Kukla, G. and Weiss, H., eds. (1997), *Third Millennium BC Climate Change and Old World Collapse.* Berlin.

Dalley, S. (1985), "Foreign chariotry and cavalry in the armies of Tiglath-Pileser III and Sargon II", *Iraq* 47: 31–48.
Dalley, S. (1991), "Ancient Assyrian textiles and the origins of carpet design", *Iran* 29: 117–136.
Dalley, S. (1994), "Nineveh, Babylon and the Hanging Gardens: cuneiform and Classical sources reconciled", *Iraq* 56: 45–58.
Dalley, S. (2002), *Mari and Karana: Two Old Babylonian Cities*, 2nd edn. Piscataway.
Dalley, S. and Goguel, A. (1997), "The Sela sculpture: a Neo-Babylonian rock relief in southern Jordan", *ADAJ* 41: 169–176.
Dalley, S., Walker, C.B.F. and Hawkins, J.D. (1976), *The Old Babylonian Tablets from Tell al Rimah*. London.
Dalton, G., ed. (1971), *Primitive, Archaic, and Modern Economies: Essays of Karl Polanyi*. Boston.
D'Altroy, T.N. and Hastorf, C.A. (2001), *Empire and Domestic Economy*. New York/Boston/Dordrecht/London/Moscow.
Damania, A., Valkoun, J., Willcox, G. and Qualset C., eds., (1998), *The Origins of Agriculture and Crop Domestication*. Aleppo.
Damerji, M. (1999), *Gräber assyrischer Königinnen aus Nimrud*. Mainz.
Dana, E.S. (1949), *A Textbook of Mineralogy: With an Extended Treatise on Crystallography and Physical Mineralogy*, 4th edn., rev. and enlarged by W.E. Ford. New York.
Dandamayev, M. (1998–2001), "Nabonid (Nabû-nā'id). A.", *RlA* 9: 6–11.
Dani, A.H. and Masson, V.M., eds. (1992), *History of Civilizations of Central Asia*, vol. 1. Paris.
Danti, M.D. and Zettler, R.L. (2007), "The Early Bronze Age in the Syrian north-west Jazireh: the Tell es-Sweyhat region", in Peltenburg, ed., 164–183.
Dar, S. (1993), *Settlements and Cult Sites on Mount Hermon, Israel: Iturean Culture in the Hellenistic and Roman Periods*. Oxford.
Dark, K. (2007), "Roman architecture in the Great Palace of the Byzantine emperors at Costantinople during the sixth to the ninth century", *Byzantion* 77: 87–105.
Daryaee, T. (2002), *Šahrestānīhā ī Ērānšahr: A Middle Persian Text of Geography, Epic and History*. Costa Mesa.
Daryaee, T. (2003), "The Persian Gulf trade in Late Antiquity", *Journal of World History* 14/1: 1–16.
Daryaee, T. (2008), *Sasanian Iran: Portrait of a Late Antique Empire*. Costa Mesa.
Daryaee, T. (2009), *Sasanian Persia: The Rise and Fall of an Empire*. London/New York.
Dauphin, C. (1995), "Pélerinage ghassanide au sanctuaire byzantin de saint Jean-Baptiste à Er-Ramthaniyye en Gaulanitide", *Jahrbuch für Antike und Christentum Supplement* 20: 667–673.
Dauphin, C. (1998), *La Palestine byzantine: Peuplement et population*, 3 vols. Oxford.
Dauphin, C., Brock, S., Gregg, R.C. and Beeston, A.F.L. (1996), "Païens, Juifs, Judéo-Chrétiens, Chrétiens et Musulmans en Gaulanitide: les inscriptions de Na'aran, Kafr Naffakh, Farj et Er-Ramthaniyye", *Proche-Orient Chrétien* 46: 305–340.
Davidde, B. (1997a), "I porti dell'Arabia Felix: un nuovo campo di indagine per la ricerca dell'archeologia subacquea", in Anonymous, ed., 351–355.
Davidde, B. (1997b), "Qanà: alla ricerca del porto perduto", *Archeologia viva* 63: 86–87.

Davidde, B. (1998), "Progetto Qanà", *L'archeologo subacqueo* 2: 8.

Davidde, B., Petriaggi, R. and Williams, D. (2004), "New data on the commercial trade of the harbour of Kanē through the typological and petrographic study of the pottery", *PSAS* 34: 85–100.

Davidson, D.A. and Shackley, M.L., eds. (1976), *Geoarchaeology: Earth Science and the Past*. London.

Davidzon, A. and Gilead, I. (2009), "The Chalcolithic workshop at Beit Eshel: preliminary refitting studies and possible socio-economic implications", in Rosen and Roux, eds., 25–40.

Davidzon, A. and Goring-Morris, A.N. (2007), "Knapping in the graveyard: a refitted naviform sequence from Kfar HaHoresh, Lower Galilee, Israel", in Astruc et al., eds., 295–309.

Davies, C.P. (2006), "Holocene paleoclimates of southern Arabia from lacustrine deposits of the Dhamar highlands,Yemen", *QR* 66: 454–464.

Davies, N. de G. (1933), *Tomb of Nefer-hotep at Thebes*, vol. 1. New York.

Davies, N. de G. (1944), *The Tomb of Rekh-mi-re at Thebes*. New York.

Davies, W.V., ed. (1991), *Egypt and Africa: Nubia from Prehistory to Islam*. London.

Davis, S.J.M. (1984), "The advent of milk and wool production in Western Iran: some speculations", in Clutton-Brock and Grigson, eds., 265–278.

Davis, S.J.M. and Valla, F.R. (1978), "Evidence for the domestication of the dog 12,000 years ago in the Natufian of Israel", *Nature* 276: 608–610.

Day, P. (2002), "Dies Diem Docet: the decipherment of Ugaritic", *SEL* 19: 37–57.

Dayan, T. (1994), "Early domesticated dogs of the Near East", *JAS* 21: 633–640.

Dayan, T. and Simberloff, D. (1995), "Natufian gazelles: proto-domestication reconsidered", *JAS* 22: 671–675.

Debaine-Francfort, C. and Idriss, A. (2000), *Keriya, mémoire d'un fleuve: Archéologie et civilisation des oasis du Taklamakan*. Paris.

Debevoise, N.C. (1934), *Parthian Pottery from Seleucia on the Tigris*. Ann Arbor.

Debevoise, N.C. (1938), *A Political History of Parthia*. Chicago.

De Bode, C.A. (1845), *Travels in Luristan and Arabistan*, vol. 2, London.

Deckers, K., Doll, M., Pfälzner, P. and Riehl, S. (2010), *Development of the Environment, Subsistence and Settlement of the city of Urkeš and its Region*. Wiesbaden.

Deckers, K. and Pessin, H. (2010), "Vegetation development in the Middle Euphrates and Upper Jazireh (Syria/Turkey) during the Bronze Age", *QR* 74: 216–226.

Deckers K. and Riehl S. (2007), "Fluvial environmental contexts for archaeological sites in the Upper Khabur basin (northeastern Syria)", *QR* 67: 337–348.

Deckers, K. and Riehl, S. (2008), "Resource exploitation of the Upper Khabur Basin (NE Syria) during the 3rd millennium BC", *Paléorient* 34/2: 173–189.

De Graef, K. and Tavernier, J., eds. (in press), *Susa and Elam*. Gent.

De Graeve, M.-C. (1981), *The Ships of the Ancient Near East (c.2000–500 BC)*. Leuven.

De Grossi Mazzorin, J. and Minniti, C. (2000), "The Northern Palace of Tell Mardikh-Ebla (Syria): archaeozoological analysis of the refuse pit F.5861/F.5701", in Matthiae et al., eds., 311–322.

Degryse, P., Boyce, A., Erb-Satullo, N., Eremin, K., Kirk, S., Scott, R., Shortland, A.J., Schneider, J. and Walton, M. (2010), "Isotopic discriminants between Late Bronze Age glasses from Egypt and the Near East", *Archaeometry* 52/3: 380–388.

Degryse, P., Freestone, I.C., Schneider, J. and Jennings, S. (2010), "Technology and provenance of Levantine plant ash glass using Sr-Nd isotope analysis", in Drauschke and Keller, eds., 83–90.

Degryse, P., Henderson, J. and Hodgins, G., eds. (2009), *Isotopes in Vitreous Materials*. Leuven.

Degryse, P. and Schneider, J. (2008), "Pliny the Elder and Sr-Nd isotopes: tracing the provenance of raw materials for Roman glass production", *JAS* 35: 1993–2000.

Degryse, P., Schneider, J., Poblome, J., Waelkens, M., Haack, U. and Muchez, P. (2005), "A geochemical study of Roman to early Byzantine glass from Sagalassos, south-west Turkey", *JAS* 32: 287–299.

Delage, C., ed., (2004), *The Last Hunter-Gatherer Societies in the Near East*. Oxford.

Delaporte, L. (1940), *Malatya: Fouilles de la mission archéologique française*. Paris.

Delaunay, J.A. (1974), "À propos des 'Aramaic Ritual Texts from Persepolis' de R.A. Bowman", in Duchesne-Guillemin, ed., 193–217.

Deleman, I., ed. (2007), *The Achaemenid Impact on Local Populations and Cultures in Anatolia (Sixth–Fourth Centuries BC)*. Istanbul.

De Lillis-Forrest, F., Milano, L. and Mori, L. (2007), "The Akkadian occupation in the Northwest Area of the Tell Leilan acropolis", *Kaskal* 4: 43–64.

Deller, K. (1984), "Ausgewählte neuassyrische Briefe betreffend Urartu zur Zeit Sargons II", in Pecorella and Salvini, eds., 97–122.

Deller, K. (1999), "The Assyrian eunuchs and their predecessors", in Watanabe, ed., 303–311.

Delmas, A.B. and Casanova, M. (1990), "The lapis lazuli sources in the ancient east", in Taddei, ed., 493–505.

del Olmo Lete, G. and Montero Fenollós, J-L., eds. (1999), *Archaeology of the Upper Syrian Euphrates: The Tishrin Dam Area*. Barcelona.

Delougaz, P. (1940), *The Temple Oval at Khafājah*. Chicago.

Delougaz, P. (1952), *Pottery from the Diyala Region*. Chicago.

Delougaz, P., Hill, H.D. and Lloyd, S. (1967), *Private Houses and Graves in the Diyala Region*. Chicago.

Delougaz, P. and Kantor, H.J., eds. (1996), *Chogha Mish Volume 1: The First Five Seasons of Excavations 1961–1971*. Chicago.

Delougaz, P. and Lloyd, S. (1942), *Pre-Sargonid Temples in the Diyala Region*. Chicago.

Demarée, R.J. and Veenhof, K.R., eds. (2003), *Zij schreven Geschiedenis. Historische documenten uit het Oude Nabije Oosten (2500–100 v.Chr.)*. Leiden/Leuven.

DeMarrais, E., Gosden, C. and Renfrew, C., eds. (2004), *Rethinking Materiality: The Engagement of Mind with the Material World*. Cambridge.

Demerji, M.S., ed. (1987), *Researches on the Antiquities of Saddam Dam Basin Salvage and Other Researches*. Baghdad.

De Meyer, L., ed. (1980), *Tell ed-Der III. Sounding at Abu Habbah (Sippar)*. Leuven.

De Meyer, L., ed. (1984), *Tell ed-Der IV*. Leuven.

De Meyer, L. and Gasche, H., eds. (1991), *Mésopotamie et Elam*. Gent.

De Meyer, L., Gasche, H. and Vallat, F., eds. (1986), *Fragmenta Historiae Elamicae: Mélanges offerts à M.J. Steve*. Paris.

De Meyer, L. and Haerinck, E., eds. (1989), *Archaeologia Iranica et Orientalis: Miscellanea in Honorem Louis Vanden Berghe*. Gent.

deMenocal, P.B. (2001), "Cultural responses to climate change during the Late Holocene", *Science* 292: 667–673.

Demir, T., Westaway, R., Bridgland, D.R. and Seyrek, A. (2007), "Terrace staircases of the River Euphrates in southeast Turkey, northern Syria and western Iraq: evidence for regional surface uplift", *QSR* 26: 2844–2863.

Denel, E. (2007), "Ceremony and kingship at Carchemish", in Cheng and Feldman, eds., 177–204.

Denham, T. (2007), "Early fig domestication, or gathering of wild parthenocarpic figs?", *Antiquity* 81: 457–461.

Deniz, E. (1975), "Neolithic, Chalcolithic and Early Bronze Age faunal remains from Pulur Höyük (Keban Dam region), Turkey", in Clason, ed., 284–294.

Dentzer, J.-M., ed. (1985), *Hauran I. Recherches archéologiques sur la Syrie du Sud à l'époque hellénistique et romaine*. Paris.

Dentzer, J.-M. (1989), "Fouilles franco-syrienne à l'est de l'arc nabatéen (1985–1987): une nouvelle cathédral à Bosra?", in Farioli Campanati, ed., 13–34.

Dentzer, J.-M. and Orthmann, W., eds. (1989), *Archéologie et histoire de la Syrie*. Saarbrücken.

Dentzer-Feydy, J., Vallerin, M., Fournet, T., Mukdad, R. and Mukdad, A. (2007), *Bosra aux portes de l'Arabie*. Beirut/Damascus/Amman.

Dercksen, J.G. (1996), *The Old Assyrian Copper Trade in Anatolia*. Istanbul.

Dercksen, J.G., ed. (2004a), *Assyria and Beyond: Studies Presented to Mogens Trolle Larsen*. Leiden.

Dercksen, J.G. (2004b), *Old Assyrian Institutions*. Leiden.

Dercksen, J.G. (2005), "Metals according to documents from Kültepe-Kanish dating to the Old Assyrian Colony Period", in Yalçin, ed., 17–34.

Derks, H. (2003), "Kalkriese – oder wie man eine Schlacht ausstellt", *Archäologische Informationen* 26/1: 127–132.

De Romanis, F. (1988), "Romanukharaṭṭha e Taprobane: sui rapporti Roma-Ceylon nel 1 sec. d.C.", *Helikon* 28: 5–58.

De Romanis, F. (1993), "Puteoli e l'Oriente", in Zevi, ed., 61–72.

De Ryck, I., Adriaens, A. and Adams, F. (2005), "An overview of Mesopotamian bronze metallurgy during the 3rd millennium BC", *Journal of Cultural Heritage* 6: 261–268.

Desanges, J. (1978), *Recherches sur l'activité des Méditerranéens aux confins de l'Afrique (VIe siècle avant J.-C. – IVe siècle après J.-C.)*. Rome.

Deshayes, J. (1960), *Les Outils de bronze l'Indus au Danube, IVe au IIe Millenaire*. Paris.

Deshayes, J. (1968), "Tureng tepe and the plain of Gorgan in the Bronze Age", *Archaeologia Viva* 1: 35–38.

Deshayes, J. (1969), "New evidence for the Indo-Europeans from Tureng Tepe, Iran", *Archaeology* 22/1: 10–17.

Deshayes, J. (1975), "Tessons de céramique peinte de Tappeh Hesar", in Bagherzadeh, ed., 103–120.

Deshayes, J. (1977), "A propos des terrasses hautes de la fin du IIIe millénaire en Iran et en Asie centrale", in Deshayes, ed., 95–111.

Deshayes, J., ed. (1977), *Le Plateau iranien et l'Asie Centrale des origines à la conquête islamique*. Paris.

Desreumaux, A., Gaborit, J. and Caillou, J-S. (1999), "Nouvelles découvertes à Apamée d'Osrhoène", *CRAIBL* 1999: 78–105.

Desse, J. (1983), "Les faunes de gisement Obeidien Final de Tell El'Oueli", in Huot, ed., 193–199.

Desse, J. (1988), "Khor 'P', Khor 'F.B.' et 'Shagra' les faunes. Le rôle de la pêche", in Inizan, 157–165.

Desse, J. and Desse-Berset, N. (1990), "La faune: Les mammifères et les poissons", in Calvet and Gachet, eds., 51–70.

Devedjian, S.G. (1981), *Lori-Berd I*. Erevan.

Develle, A.-L., Herreros, J., Vidal, L., Sursock, A. and Gasse, F. (2010), "Controlling factors on a paleo-lake oxygen isotope record (Yammouneh, Lebanon) since the last glacial maximum", *QSR* 29: 865–886.

Dever, W.G. (1980), "New vistas on the EB IV ('MB I') horizon in Syria-Palestine", *BASOR* 237: 35–64.

Dever, W.G., ed. (1986), *Gezer IV*. Jerusalem.

Dever, W.G. (1989), "The collapse of the urban Early Bronze Age in Palestine", in de Miroschedji, ed., 225–246.

Dever, W.G. (1992), "The chronology of Syria-Palestine in the second millennium BCE: a review of current issues", *BASOR* 288: 1–25.

Dever, W.G. (1995), "Social structure in the Early Bronze IV period in Palestine", in Levy, ed., 282–296.

Devreesse, R. (1945), *Le Patriarcat d'Antioche depuis la paix de l'église jusqu'à la conquête arabe*. Paris.

DeVries, K., ed. (1980), *From Athens to Gordion: The Papers of a Memorial Symposium for Rodney S. Young*. Philadelphia.

DeVries, K. (2007), "The date of the destruction level at Gordion: imports and the local sequence", in Çilingiroğlu and Sagona, eds., 79–101.

DeVries, K. (2008), "The age of Midas at Gordion and beyond", *ANES* 45: 30–64.

De Waele, E. (1973), "Une page d'art iranien: les reliefs rupestres d'Īzeh Mālamīr", *Archeologia* 60: 31–46.

Diakonoff, I.M. (1971), *Hurrisch und Urartäisch*. Munich.

Dietl, H. (2009), *Analyse der paläolithischen Siedlungsdynamik an Freilandfundplätzen in der levantinischen Steppenzone*. Rahden.

Dietl, H. and Conard, N.J. (in press), "Survey im Gebiet des mittleren Orontes zwischen ar-Rastan und Qal'at Shayzar – Analyse und Interpretation des paläolithischen Fundmaterials", *ZOA*.

Dietler, M. and Hayden, B., eds. (2001), *Feasts: Archaeological and Ethnographic Perspectives on Food, Politics, and Power*. Washington, DC.

Dietrich, M., and Loretz, O., eds. (1994), *Beschreiben und Deuten in der Archäologie des Alten Orients: Festschrift für Ruth Mayer-Opificius*. Münster.

Dietrich, M. and Loretz, O. (1997), "Der Vertrag zwischen Ir-Addu von Tunip und Niqmepa von Mukiš", in Young, Chavalas and Averbeck, eds., 211–242.

Dietrich, M. and Loretz, O. (2003), "Der Untergang am 21.1.1192 v. Chr. von Ugarit", *UF* 34: 53–74.

Dieulafoy, J. (1887), *La Perse, la Chaldée et la Susiane: Relation de voyage*. Paris.

Dieulafoy, J. (1888), *À Suse. Journal des fouilles 1884–1886*. Paris.

Dieulafoy, M. (1884–9), *L'Art antique de la Perse. Achéménides, Parthes, Sassanides*, 3 vols. Paris.

Dieulafoy, M. (1890–2), *L'Acropole de Suse d'après les fouilles exécutées en 1884, 1885, 1886 sous les auspices du Musée du Louvre*, 4 vols. Paris.

Dight, R.J.W. (2002), "The construction and use of canal regulators in ancient Sumer", *Aula Orientalis* 20: 115–122.

Dillon, M., ed. (1996), *Religion in the Ancient World: New themes and approaches*. Amsterdam.

Dimand, M.S. (1933), "An early cut-pile rug from Egypt", *Metropolitan Museum Studies* 4/2: 151–162.

Dimand, M.S. and Mailey, J. (1973), *Oriental Rugs in the Metropolitan Museum of Art*. New York.

Di Mario, F. (1989), "The Western al-Rub'al Khali 'Neolithic': new data from the Ramlat Sab'atayn", *AIUON* 49: 109–148.

Dirven, L.A. (1999), *The Palmyrenes of Dura-Europos: A Study of Religious Interaction in Roman Syria*. Leiden.

Dirven, L.A. (2008), "Aspects of Hatrene religion: a note on the statues of kings and nobles from Hatra", in Kaizer, ed., 209–246.

Dirven, L.A. (forthcoming), *Catalogue of Sculptures from Hatra*.

Di Segni, L. (1999), "Epigraphic documentation on building in the provinces of Palaestina and Arabia 4th–7th century", in Humphrey, ed., 149–178.

Dittenberger, W., ed. (1903–5), *Orientis Graecae Inscriptiones Selectae*. Leipzig.

Dittmann, R. (1984), *Eine Randebene des Zagros in der Frühzeit: Ergebnisse des Behbehan – Zuhreh Surveys*. Berlin.

Dittmann, R. (1986), *Betrachtungen zur Frühzeit des Südwest-Iran: Regionale Entwicklungen vom 6. bis zum frühen 3. vorchristlichen Jahrtausend*. Berlin.

Dittmann, R. (1990), "Eisenzeit I und II in West- und Nordwest-Iran zeitgleich zum Karum-Zeit Anatoliens?", *AMI* 23: 105–138.

Dittmann, R. (1992), "Assur and Kar Tukulti Ninurta", *AJA* 96: 307–312.

Dittmann, R. (2001), "Kontinuitäten und Diskontinuitäten im archäologischen Befund: reflexionen von Migrationen?", in Eichmann and Parzinger, eds., 291–299.

Dittmann, R., Eickhoff, T., Stengele, R., Schmitt, R. and Thürwächter, S. (1988), "Untersuchungen in Kar-Tukulti-Ninurta (Tulul al-'Aqar) 1986", *MDOG* 120: 97–138.

Dittmann, R., Eickhoff, T., Stengele, R., Schmitt, R. and Thürwächter, S. (1989–90), "Kar Tukulti Ninurta/Telul al-'Aqar 1986", *Sumer* 46: 86–97.

Dittmann, R., Hrouda, B., Löw, U., Matthiae, P., Mayer-Opificius, R. and Thürwächter, S., eds. (2000), *Variatio Delectat. Iran und der Westen. Gedenkschrift für Peter Calmeyer*. Münster.

Dittmann, R. et al. (in press), *Ausgrabungen der Deutschen Orient-Gesellschaft in Kar Tukulti-Ninurta*. Berlin.

Djamali, M., de Beaulieu, J-L., Andrieu-Ponel, V., Berberian, M., Miller, N., Gandouin, E., Lahijani, H., Shah-Hosseini, M., Ponel, P., Salimian M. and Guiter F. (2009), "A late Holocene pollen record from Lake Almalou in NW Iran: evidence for changing land-use in relation to some historical events during the last 3700 years", *JAS* 36: 1364–1375.

Djamali, M., de Beaulieu, J-L., Miller, N.F., Andrieu-Ponel, V., Ponel, P., Lak, R., Sadeddin, N., Akhani, H. and Fazeli, H. (2009), "Vegetation history of the SE section of the Zagros Mountains during the last five millennia; a pollen record from the Maharlou Lake, Fars Province, Iran", *VHA* 18: 123–136.

Dobres, M.-A. (2000), *Technology and Social Agency: Outlining an Anthropological Framework for Archaeology*. Oxford.

Dobres, M.-A. and Hoffman, C.R., eds. (1999), *The Social Dynamics of Technology: Practice, Politics, and World Views*. Washington, DC.

Dobres, M.-A. and Robb, J.E. (2000a), "Agency in archaeology, paradigm or platitude?", in Dobres and Robb, eds., 3–17.

Dobres, M.-A. and Robb, J.E., eds. (2000b), *Agency in Archaeology*. London/New York.

Dodd, L.S. (2003), "Chronology and continuity in the Early Iron Age: the northeastern side of the Amanus", in Fischer et al., eds., 127–136.

Dodd, L.S. (2005a), "Legitimacy, identity and history in Iron Age Gurgum", in Çilingiroğlu and Darbyshire, eds., 47–64.

Dodd, L.S. (2005b), "Territory, legitimacy, and wealth in Iron Age Anatolia", in Parker and Rodseth, eds., 238–60.

Dodd, L.S. (2007), "Strategies for future success: remembering the Hittites during the Iron Age", *AnSt* 57: 203–16.

Dodge, T. (2003), *Inventing Iraq: The Failure of Nation Building and a History Denied*. New York.

Dodinet, M., Leblanc, J., Vallat, J-P. and Villeneuve, F. (1990), "Le paysage antique en Syrie: l'example de Damas", *Syria* 67: 339–355.

Doe, D.B. (1971), *Southern Arabia*. New York/St. Louis/San Francisco.

Doe, D.B. (1992), *Socotra: Island of Tranquillity*. London.

Dohmann-Pfälzner, H. and Pfälzner, P. et al. (2006), "Ausgrabungen und Forschungen in Tell Mišrife/Qatna 2004 und 2005: Vorbericht der deutschen Komponente des internationalen Kooperationsprojektes", *MDOG* 138: 57–107.

Dohmann-Pfälzner, H. and Pfälzner, P. et al. (2007), "Ausgrabungen und Forschungen 2006 im Königspalast von Qatna: Vorbericht des syrisch-deutschen Kooperationsprojektes in Tall Mišrife/Qatna", *MDOG* 139: 131–172.

Dohmann-Pfälzner, H. and Pfälzner, P. (2008), "Die Ausgrabungen 2007 und 2008 im Königspalast von Qatna: Vorbericht des syrisch-deutschen Kooperationsprojektes in Tall Mišrife/Qatna", *MDOG* 140: 17–74.

Dohmann-Pfälzner, H. and Pfälzner, P. (2009), "Siegel und Siegelringe als königliche Beigabe", in al-Maqdissi, Morandi Bonacossi and Pfälzner, eds., 234–235.

Dohmann-Pfälzner, H. and Pfälzner, P. (2010), "Die Ausgrabungen 2009 und 2010 im Königspalast von Qatna: Vorbericht des syrisch-deutschen Kooperationsprojektes in Tall Mišrife/Qatna", *MDOG* 142.

Dolce, R. (2002), "Ebla after the 'fall': some preliminary considerations on the EB IVB city", *DaM* 13: 11–28.

Doll, M. (2003), "Animals and men in mines: the bone assemblages from Karnab and Mušiston", in Stöllner et al., eds., 113–126.

Dollfus, G. (1975), "Les fouilles à Djaffarabad de 1972 à 1974, Djaffarabad, périodes I et II", *DAFI* 5: 11–62.

Dollfus, G. (1978), "Djaffarabad, Djowi, Bandebal: contributions a l'étude de la Susiane au Ve millénaire et au début du IVe millénaire", *Paléorient* 4: 141–167.

Dollfus, G. (1983a), "Tépé Bendebal, travaux 1977, 1978", *DAFI* 13: 133–275.

Dollfus, G. (1983b), "Tépé Djowi: contrôle stratigraphique, 1975", *DAFI* 13: 17–131.

Dollfus, G. (1985), "L'occupation de la Susiane au Ve millénaire et au début IVe millénaire: Réflexions et comparisons", *Paléorient* 8: 107–115.

Donceel-Voûte, P. (1988), *Les Pavements des églises byzantines de Syrie et du Liban. Décor, archéologie et liturgie*. Louvain-la-Neuve.

Dönmez, Ş. (2007), "The Achaemenid impact on the central Black Sea region", in Deleman, ed., 107–116.

Döpper, S. (2010), *Fundamente und Fundamentierungstechniken öffentlicher Gebäude der Mittelbronzezeit in Syrien und Mesopotamien*. Tübingen.

Dorna Metzger, F. (2000), "I vetri di Hatra", *Topoi* 10: 253–265.

Dornemann, R.H. (1977), "Tell Hadidi: a millennium of Bronze Age city occupation", in Freedman, ed., 113–151.

Dornemann, R.H. (2007), "The pottery of the Middle Bronze Age in the Euphrates River Valley, in the areas affected by the basins of the Tabqa and the Tishrin Dams", in al-Maqdissi et al., eds., 43–52.

Dossin, G. (1974), "Le site de Tuttul-sur-Balikh", *RA* 68: 25–34.

Dothan, T. (1995), "The Sea Peoples and the Philistines of ancient Palestine", in Sasson, ed., 1267–1279.

Doty, L.T. (1988), "Nikarchos and Kephalon", in Leichty and Ellis, eds., 96–117.

Doumet-Serhal, C., ed., (2004), *A Decade of Archaeology and History in Lebanon*. Beirut.

Doumet-Serhal, C. (2006), *The Early Bronze Age in Sidon: "College Site" Excavations (1998–2000–2001)*. Beirut.

Doumet-Serhal, C. (2010), "Sidon during the Bronze Age: burials, rituals and feasting grounds at the 'College Site'", *NEA* 73/2–3: 114–129.

Downey, G. (1961), *A history of Antioch in Syria*. Princeton.

Downey, S.B. (1969), *The Excavations at Dura: Europos Final Report 3, Pt.1, Fasc.1: The Heracles sculpture*. New Haven.

Downey, S.B. (1988), *Mesopotamian Religious Architecture. Alexander Through the Parthians*. Princeton.

Downing, T.E. and Gibson, McG., eds. (1974), *Irrigation's Impact on Society*. Tucson.

Doyle, M.W. (1986), *Empires*. Ithaca.

Drahor, M.G. and Kaya, M.A. (2000), "A large-scale geophysical prospection in Açemhöyük, the site of the Assyrian trade colony period", *Türkiye Bilimler Akademisi Arkeoloji Dergisi* 3: 85–107.

Drauschke, J. and Keller, D., eds. (2010), *Glass in Byzantium: Production, Usage, Analyses*. Mainz.

Draycott, C.M. (2007), "Dynastic definitions. Differentiating status claims in the archaic pillar tomb reliefs of Lycia", in Sagona and Çilingiroğlu, eds., 103–134.

Draycott, C.M. and Summers, G.D. (2008), *Sculpture and Inscriptions from the Monumental Entrance to the Palatial Complex at Kerkenes Dağ, Turkey*. Chicago.

Drechsler, P. (2007), "Spreading the Neolithic over the Arabian Peninsula", *PSAS* 37: 93–109.

Drechsler, P. (2009), *The Dispersal of the Neolithic over the Arabian Peninsula*. Oxford.

Drechsler, P. (2010), "Life at the end of the Holocene moist phase in south-east Arabia: the Late Neolithic site of Jebel Thanais 1 (JTH1)", *AAE* 21: 1–15.

Drechsler, P. (2011), "Places of contact, spheres of interaction. The 'Ubaid phenomenon in the Central Gulf area as seen from a first season of re-investigations at Dosariyah, Eastern Province, Saudi Arabia", *PSAS* 41: 69–82.

Drews, R. (1993), *The End of the Bronze Age: Changes in Warfare and the Catastrophe ca.1200 BC.* Princeton.

Dreyer, G. (1992), "Recent discoveries at Abydos Cemetery U", in van den Brink, ed., 293–299.

Dreyer, G. (1998), *Umm el-Qaab 1: Das prädynastische Königsgrab U-j und seine frühen Schriftzeugnisse.* Mainz.

Dridi, H. (2002), "Indiens et Proche-Orientaux dans une grotte de Suquṭrā (Yémen)", *JA* 290/2: 565–610.

Dridi, H. and Gorea, M. (2003), "Le voyage d'Abgar à Suqutra", *Archaeologia* 396: 48–57.

Driessen, J. (1989–90), "The proliferation of Minoan Palatial architectural style: (1) Crete", *Acta Archaeologica Lovaniensia* 28–29: 3–23.

Driessen, J. (1999), "The dismantling of a Minoan Hall at Palaikastro (Knossians go home?)", in Betancourt et al., eds., 227–236.

Drijvers, J.W., de Hond, J. and Sancisi-Weerdenburg, H., eds. (1997), *"Ik hadde de nieusgierigheid": De reizen door het Nabije Oosten van Cornelis de Bruijn (ca.1652–1727).* Leiden/Leuven.

Drijvers, J.W. and MacDonald, A.A., eds. (1995), *Centres of Learning: Learning and Location in pre-Modern Europe and the Near East.* Leiden.

Driscoll, C.A., MacDonald, D.W. and O'Brien, S.J. (2009), "From wild animals to domestic pets: an evolutionary view of domestication", *PNAS* 106: 9971–9978.

Drooker, P. and Webster, L. (2000), *Beyond Cloth and Cordage: Current Approaches to Archaeological Textile Research in the Americas.* Salt Lake City.

Drüppel, K and Lehmann, C. (2009), "Fire bombing of the Tell Halaf museum in Berlin during World War II: reconstruction of the succession of events based on mineralogical investigations", *European Journal of Mineralogy* 21: 443–456.

Drysdale, R., Zanchetta, G., Hellstrom, J., Maas, R., Fallick, A., Pickett, M., Cartwright, I. and Piccini, L. (2006), "Late Holocene drought responsible for the collapse of Old World civilizations is recorded in an Italian cave flowstone", *Geology* 34/2: 101–104.

Dubovský, P. (2006), *Hezekiah and the Assyrian spies.* Rome.

Dubreuil, L. (2004), "Long-term trends in Natufian subsistence: a use–wear analysis of ground stone tools", *JAS* 31: 1613–1629.

Duchesne-Guillemin, J. ed. (1974), *Commémoration Cyrus. Actes du Congrès de Shiraz 1971 et autres études rédigées à l'occasion du 2500e anniversaire de la fondation de l'empire perse*, vol. 2. Tehran/Liège/Leiden.

Duchesne-Guillemin, J., ed. (1975), *Monumentum H.S. Nyberg*, 3 vols. Leiden.

Ducos, P. (1969), "Methodology and results of the study of the earliest domesticated animals in the Near East (Palestine)", in Ucko and Dimbleby, eds., 266–275.

Ducos, P. (1993), "Proto-élevage et élevage au Levant sud au VIIe millénaire BC. Les données de la Damascène", *Paléorient* 19/1: 153–173.

Duistermaat, K. (1996), "Seals and sealings", in Akkermans, ed., 399–402.

Du Mesnil du Buisson, R. (1928), "L'ancienne Qaṭna ou les Ruines d'el-Mishrifé au N.-E. de Homs (Émèse). Deuxième campagne de fouilles (1927). 2e article", *Syria* 9: 1–24.

Du Mesnil du Buisson, R. (1930), "Compte rendu de la mission de Khan Sheikhoun et de Souran, au nord de Hama (Syrie)", *CRAIBL* 1930: 320–331.
Du Mesnil du Buisson, R. (1932), "Une campagne de fouilles à Khan Sheikhoun", *Syria* 13: 171–188.
Du Mesnil du Buisson, R. (1935), *Le Site archéologique de Mishrifé-Qatna*. Paris.
Dunand, M. (1928), *Byblos et l'Égypte: Quatre campagnes de fouilles à Gebeil 1921–1924*. Paris.
Dunand, M. (1937), *Fouilles de Byblos I, Atlas*. Paris.
Dunand, M. (1939), *Fouilles de Byblos I, 1926–1932, Texte*. Paris.
Dunand, M. (1950), *Fouilles de Byblos II, 1933–38, Atlas*. Paris.
Dunand, M. (1954/1958), *Fouilles de Byblos II, 1933–1938, Texte*. Paris.
Dunand, M. (1972), *Byblos: Geschichte, Ruinen, Legenden*. Beirut.
Dunand, M. (1973), *Fouilles de Byblos tome V. L'architecture, les tombes, le matériel domestique, des origines néolithiques a l'avènement urbain*. Paris.
Dunand, M. (1978), "Nouvelles inscriptions pseudo-hiéroglyphiques découvertes à Byblos", *Bulletin du Musée de Beyrouth* 30: 51–59.
Dunning, F.W., Garrard, P., Haslam, H.W. and Ixer, R.A., eds. (1989), *Mineral Deposits of Europe 4/5: Southwest and Eastern Europe, with Iceland*. London.
du Plat Taylor, J., Seton Williams, M.V. and Waechter, J. (1950), "The excavations at Sakçe Gözü", *Iraq* 12/2: 53–138.
Dupré, S. (1983), *Porsuk I. La Céramique de l'Âge du Bronze et de l'Âge du Fer*. Paris.
Duprée, L. (1964), "Prehistoric archaeological surveys and excavations in Afghanistan: 1959–1960 and 1961–1963", *Science* 146: 638–640.
Dural, S. with Hodder, I. (2007), *Protecting Çatalhöyük: Memoir of an Archaeological Site Guard*. Walnut Creek.
Durand, J.-M. (1990), "Problèmes d'eau et d'irrigation au royaume de Mari: L'apport des textes anciens", in Geyer, ed. 101–142.
Durand, J.-M. (1994), "Fourmis blanches et fourmis noires", in Vallat, ed., 101–108.
Durand, J.-M. (1998), *Documents épistolaires du palais de Mari* II. Paris.
Durand, J.-M. (2002), *Le Culte d'Addu d'Alep et l'affaire d'Alahtum*. Paris.
Durand, J.-M. (2009), *La Nomenclature des habits et des textiles dans les textes de Mari*. Paris.
Durand, J.-M. and Kupper, J.-R., eds., (1985), *Miscellanea Babyloniaca: Mélanges offerts à Maurice Birot*. Paris.
Durante, S. and Tosi, M. (1977), "The aceramic shell middens of Ra's al-Hamra: a preliminary note", *JOS* 3: 137–162.
Duri, R. (2002), "Aus den irakischen Ausgrabungen in Assur 2001: Spätneuassyrische Wohnbebauung, parthische Grabbauten und der Ostpalast", *MDOG* 134: 87–102.
Düring, B. (2002), "Cultural dynamics of the central Anatolian Neolithic: the early Ceramic Neolithic to the Late Ceramic Neolithic transition", in Gérard and Thissen eds., 219–236.
Düring, B. (2003), "Burials in context: the 1960s inhumations of Çatalhöyük East", *AnSt* 53: 1–15.
Düring, B. (2008), "The Early Holocene occupation of North-Central Anatolia between 10,000 and 6000 BC cal: investigating an archaeological terra incognita", *AnSt* 58: 15–46.

Düring, B. (2010), *The Prehistory of Asia Minor: From Complex Hunter-Gatherers to Early Urban Societies.* Cambridge.

During Caspers, E.C.L. (1972), *Etched Carnelian Beads.* London.

Duru, R. (2008), *From 8000 BC to 2000 BC: Six Thousand Years of the Burdur-Antalya Region.* Istanbul.

Dusinberre, E.R.M. (2003), *Aspects of Empire in Achaemenid Sardis.* Cambridge and New York.

Dusinberre, E.R.M. (2005a), *Gordion Special Studies III: Gordion Seals and Sealings. Individuals and Society.* Philadelphia.

Dusinberre, E.R.M. (2005b), "Herzfeld in Persepolis", in Gunter and Hauser, eds., 137–180.

Dusinberre, E.R.M. (2008), "Seal impressions on the Persepolis Fortification Aramaic tablets: preliminary observations", in Briant, Henkelman and Stolper, eds., 239–252.

Dussaud, R. (1951), *L'Oeuvre scientifique d'Ernest Renan.* Paris.

Dussaud, R., Deschamps, P. and Seyrig. H. (1931), *La Syrie antique et médiévale illustrée.* Paris.

Duval, N. (1994), "L'architecture chrétienne et les pratiques liturgiques en Jordanie en rapport avec la Palestine: recherches nouvelles", in Painter, ed., 149–212.

Duval, N., Baritel, F. and Pergola, P., eds. (1989), *Actes du XIe Congrès international d'archéologie chrétienne.* Vatican City.

Dyson, R.H., Jr. (1964), "Sciences meet in ancient Hasanlu", *Natural History* 73/8: 16–25.

Dyson, R.H., Jr. (1965), "Problems in the relative chronology of Iran, 6000–2000 BC", in Ehrich, ed., 215–256.

Dyson, R.H., Jr. (1966), *Excavations on the Acropolis at Susa and problems of Susa A, B, and C.* Cambridge.

Dyson, R.H., Jr. (1992), "Ceramics i. Neolithic period through Bronze Age in northeastern and north-central Persia", *EnIr* 5: 266–275.

Dyson, R.H., Jr. (1999), "Triangle-Festoon Ware reconsidered", *IrAnt* 34: 115–144.

Dyson, R.H., Jr. and Howard, S.M., eds. (1989), *Tappeh Hesār: Reports of the Restudy Project, 1976.* Florence.

Earl, B. and Özbal, H. (1996), "Early Bronze Age tin processing at Kestel/Göltepe, Anatolia", *Archaeometry* 38: 289–303.

Earle, T., ed. (1984), *On the Evolution of Complex Societies: Essays in Honor of Harry Hoijer.* Malibu.

Easton, D.F. (1997), "The excavation of the Trojan treasures, and their history up to the death of Schliemann in 1890", in Simpson, ed., 194–199.

Eastwood, W.J., Roberts, N. and Lamb, H.F. (1998), "Palaeoecological and archaeological evidence for human occupance in SW Turkey: the Beyshahir occupation phase", *AnSt* 48: 69–86.

Eaton, E.R. (1980), "Early metallurgy in Italy", in Oddy, ed., 159–167.

Eaton, E.R. and McKerrell, H. (1976), "Near Eastern alloying and some textual evidence for the early use of arsenical copper", *WA* 8: 169–191.

Edel, E. (1983), "Zwei Steinschalen mit ägyptischen Inschriften aus dem Palast von Kâmid el-Lôz", in Hachmann, ed., 38–39.

Edens, C. (1982), "Towards a definition of the western Rub' al Khali 'Neolithic'", *Atlal* 6: 109–124.

Edens, C. (1988), "The Rub al Khali 'Neolithic' revisited: the view from Nadqan", in Potts, ed., 15–43.

Edens, C. (1995), "Transcaucasia at the end of the Early Bronze Age", *BASOR* 299/300: 53–64.

Edens, C. (1999), "The chipped stone industry at Haçinebi: technological styles and social identity", *Paléorient* 25/1: 23–33.

Edens, C. and Bawden, G. (1989), "History of Tayma and Hejazi trade during the first millennium BC", *JESHO* 32: 48–103.

Edens, C. and Wilkinson, T.J. (1998), "Southwest Arabia during the Holocene: recent archaeological developments", *JWP* 12/1: 55–119.

Edens, C., Wilkinson, T.J. and Barratt, G. (2000), "Hammat al-Qa and the roots of urbanism in southwestern Arabia", *Antiquity* 74: 854–62.

Eder, W. and Renger, J., eds. (2006), *Chronologies of the Ancient World: Names, Dates and Dynasties*. Leiden.

Edgar, C.C., ed. (1925–1931), *Zenon Papyri*. Cairo.

Edwards, I. and Jacobs, L. (1987), "Experiments with stone 'pottery wheel' bearings – notes on the use of rotation in the production of ancient pottery", *Newsletter: Department of Pottery technology, University of Leiden* 4: 49–55.

Edwards, P.C., Meadows, J., Sayej, G.J. and Westaway, M. (2004), "From the PPNA to the PPNB: new views from the southern Levant after excavations at Zahrat adh-Dhra' 2 in Jordan", *Paléorient* 30/2: 21–60.

Edzard, D.O. (1970), "Die Keilschriftbriefe der Grabungskampagne 1969", in Edzard et al., eds., 55–62.

Edzard, D.O. (1982), "Ein Brief an den 'Großen' von Kumidi aus Kamid el-Loz", in Hachmann, ed., 131–135.

Edzard, D.O. (1997), *Gudea and his dynasty*. Toronto.

Edzard, D.O., Hachmann, R., Maiberger, P. and Mansfeld, G., eds. (1970), *Kamid el-Loz – Kumidi: Schriftdokumente aus Kamid el-Loz*. Bonn.

Eerkens, J.W. and Bettinger, R.L. (2001), "Techniques for assessing standardization in artifact assemblages: can we scale material variability?", *AmAnt* 66: 493–504.

Efstratiou, N., McCartney, C., Karkanas, P. and Kyriakou, D. (2010), "An upland early site in the Troodos Mountains", RDAC.

Egami, N. and Sono, T. (1962), *Marv-Dasht II. The excavation at Tall-i Gap 1959*. Tokyo.

Egberts, A. (2001), "Wenamun", in Redford, ed., vol. 3, 495–496.

Eger, A. (2008), *The Spaces Between the Teeth: Environment, Settlement and Interaction on the Islamic-Byzantine Frontier*. Chicago.

Ehrenberg, E. ed. (2002), *Leaving No Stones Unturned: Essays on the Ancient Near East and Egypt in Honor of Donald P. Hansen*. Winona Lake.

Ehrich, R.W., ed. (1965), *Chronologies in Old World Archaeology*, 2nd edn. Chicago.

Ehrich, R.W., ed., (1992), *Chronologies in Old World Archaeology*, 3rd edn. Chicago.

Eichler, E. (1993), *Untersuchungen zum Expeditionswesen des ägyptischen Alten Reiches*. Wiesbaden.

Eichler, S. and Wäfler, M. (1989–1990), "Tall al-Hamidiya", *AfO* 36–37: 246–251.

Eichmann, R., ed. (2002), *Ausgrabungen und Surveys im Vorderen Orient I*. Rahden.

Eichmann, R. (2007), *Uruk Architektur I: Von den Anfängen bis zur frühdynastischen Zeit*. Rahden.

Eichmann, R. (2009), "Archaeological evidence of the pre-Islamic (4th to 6th cent. AD) period at Taymā", in Schiettecatte and Robin, eds., 55–69.

Eichmann, R. and Hausleiter, A. eds. (in press), *Tayma*, vol. 1.

Eichmann, R., Hausleiter, A., al-Najem, M. and al-Said, S.F. (2006), "Tayma – Spring 2004, Report on the Joint Saudi Arabian-German Archaeological Project", *Atlal* 19: 91–116.

Eichmann, R., Hausleiter, A., al-Najem, M. and al-Said, S.F. (2010), "Tayma – Autumn 2004 and Spring 2005, 2nd Report on the Joint Saudi Arabian-German Archaeological Project", *Atlal* 20: 101–147.

Eichmann, R., Hausleiter, A., al-Najem, M. and al-Said, S.F. (in press a), "Tayma – Autumn 2005 and 2006 (Spring and Autumn), 3rd Report on the Joint Saudi Arabian-German Archaeological Project", *Atlal*.

Eichmann, R., Hausleiter, A., al-Najem, M. and al-Said, S.F. (in press b), "Tayma 2007, 4th Report on the Joint Saudi Arabian-German Archaeological Project", *Atlal*.

Eichmann, R., Müller-Neuhoff, B. and Shakir, S.N. (2001), "A short note on burin sites in Wadi Hauran (Iraq)", *Neo-Lithics* 1/10: 5–8.

Eichmann, R. and Parzinger, H., eds.(2001), *Migration und Kulturtransfer: Der Wandel vorder- und zentralasiatischer Kulturen im Umbruch von 2. zum 1. vorchristlichen Jahrtausend*. Bonn.

Eichmann, R., Schaudig, H. and Hausleiter, A. (2006), "Archaeology and epigraphy at Tayma (Saudi Arabia)", *AAE* 17: 163–176.

Eickhoff, T. (1985), *Kar-Tukulti-Ninurta: Eine mittelassyrische Kult- und Residenzstadt*. Berlin.

Eide, T., Hägg, T., Pierce, R.H. and Török, L. (1998), *Fontes Historiae Nubiorum: Textual Sources for the History of the Middle Nile Region Between the Eighth Century BC and the Sixth Century AD III. From the First to the Sixth Century AD*. Bergen.

Eidem, J., Finkel, I. and Bonechi, M. (2001), "The third millennium inscriptions", in Oates et al., eds., 99–120.

Eiland, M.L. (1998), "Parthians and Romans at Nineveh", *Electrum* 2: 55–68.

Einwag, B. and Otto, A. (2001-3), "Bazi 1998/1999 – Die letzten Untersuchungen in der Weststadt", *DaM* 13: 65–88.

Eisenberg, E., Gopher, A. and Greenberg, R. (2001), *Tel Te'o, a Neolithic, Chalcolithic, and Early Bronze Age Site in the Hula Valley*. Jerusalem.

Eiwanger, J. (1984), *Merimde-Benisalâme. Die Funde der Urschicht*. Mainz.

Ekholm, K., and Friedman, J. (1979), "'Capital' imperialism and exploitation in ancient world systems", in Larsen, ed., 41–58.

El Amin, M. and Mallowan, M.E.L. (1949), "Soundings in the Makhmur Plain, I", *Sumer* 5: 145–153.

El Amin, M. and Mallowan, M.E.L. (1950), "Soundings in the Makhmur Plain, II", *Sumer* 6: 55–68.

Elayi, J. and Elayi, A.G. (1992), "Nouvelle datation d'une tombe achéménide de Suse", *StIr* 21: 265–270.

Elders, J. (2003), "The Nestorians in the Gulf: just passing through? Recent discoveries on the island of Sir Bani Yas, Abu Dhabi Emirate, UAE", in Potts, Al Naboodah & Hellyer, eds., 230–236.

Elia, R.J. (1994), "The world cannot afford many more collectors with a passion for antiquities", *The Art Newspaper* 41 (Oct): 19–20.

Elia, R.J. (1995), "Conservators and unprovenanced objects: preserving the cultural heritage or servicing the antiquities trade", in Tubb, ed., 244–255.

Elia, R.J. (1997), "Looting, collecting, and the destruction of archaeological resources", *Nonrenewable Resources* 6/2: 85–98.

Elia, R.J. (2000), "A comment", in Lynott and Wylie, eds., 84–86.

Eliyahu-Behar, A., Shilstein, S., Raban-Gerstel, N., Goren, Y., Gilboa, A., Sharon, I. and Weiner, S. (2008), "An integrated approach to reconstructing primary activities from pit deposits: iron smithing and other activities at Tel Dor under Neo-Assyrian domination", *JAS* 35: 2895–2908.

Ellis, M.deJ., ed. (1992), *Nippur at the Centennial: Papers read at the 35e Rencontre Assyriologique Internationale, Philadelphia, 1988*. Philadelphia.

Ellis, R. (1968), *Foundation Deposits in Ancient Mesopotamia*. New Haven.

Ellison, R., Renfrew, D., Brothwell, D. and Seeley, N. (1978), "Some food offerings from Ur, excavated by Sir Leonard Woolley, and previously unpublished", *JAS* 5: 167–177.

Elsner, J. (2003), "Archaeologies and agendas: reflections on late ancient Jewish art and early Christian art", *JRS* 93: 114–128.

Elsner, J. and Cardinal, R., eds. (1994), *The Cultures of Collecting*. Cambridge.

Elston, R.G. and Kuhn, S.L., eds. (2002), *Thinking Small: Global Perspectives on Microlithicization*. Arlington.

Elter, R. and Hassoune, A. (2005), "Le monastère de saint Hilarion: les vestiges archéologiques du site de Umm el-'Amr", in Saliou, ed., 13–40.

El-Wailly, F. and Abu es-Soof, B. (1965), "The excavations at Tell es-Sawwan: first preliminary report, 1964", *Sumer* 21: 17–32.

Emberling, G. (1997), "Ethnicity in complex societies: archaeological perspectives", *JAR* 5: 295–344.

Emberling, G. (2002), "Political control in an early state: the Eye Temple and the Uruk expansion in northern Mesopotamia", in al-Gailani Werr et al., eds., 82–90.

Emberling, G. (2008), "Archaeologists and the military in Iraq, 2003–2008: Compromise or contribution?", *Archaeologies* 4/3: 445–459.

Emberling, G. and Hanson, K., eds. (2008), *Catastrophe! The Looting and Destruction of Iraq's past*. Oakville.

Emory, I. (1980), *The Primary Structures of Fabrics. An Illustrated Classification*. Washington, DC.

Emre, K. (2002), "Felsreliefs, Stelen, Orthostaten: Großplastik als monumentale Form staatlicher und religiöser Repräsentation", in Özgüç et al., eds., 218–247.

Emre, K., Mellink, M., Hrouda, B. and Özgüç, N., eds. (1989), *Anatolia and the Ancient Near East: Studies in Honor of Tahsin Özgüç*. Ankara.

Engel, M., Klasen, N., Ginau, A., Patzke, M., Pint, A., Frenzel, P. and Brückner, H. (in press), "Palaeoenvironmental change at Tayma as inferred from sabkha infill", in Eichmann and Hausleiter, eds.

Englund, R.K. (1990), *Organisation und Verwaltung der Ur III-Fischerei*. Berlin.
Englund, R.K. (1998), "Texts from the Late Uruk period", in Attinger and Wäfler, eds., 15–233.
Englund, R.K. (2003), "Worcester slaughterhouse account", *CDLI Bulletin* 2003/1.
Engstrom, C.M.A. 2004. "The Neo-Assyrians at Tell el-Hesi: a petrographic study of imitation Assyrian Palace Ware", *BASOR* 333: 69–81.
Enzel, Y., Bookman, R., Sharon, D., Gvirtzman, H., Dayan, U., Ziv, B. and Stein, M. (2003), "Late Holocene climates of the Near East deduced from Dead Sea level variations and modern regional winter rainfall", *QR* 60/3: 263–273.
Eph'al, I. (1982), *The Ancient Arabs. Nomads on the Border of the Fertile Crescent, 9th–5th Centuries BC*. Jerusalem and Leiden.
Eph'al, I., Ben-Tor, A. and Machinist, P., eds. (2003), *Hayim and Miriam Tadmor Volume*. Jerusalem.
Epimakhov, A.V. (2009), "Settlements and cemeteries of the Bronze Age of the Urals: the potential for reconstructing early social dynamics", in Hanks and Linduff, eds., 74–90.
Eppihimer, M. (2010), "Assembling king and state: the statues of Manishtushu and the consolidation of Akkadian kingship", *AJA* 114/3: 365–380.
Epstein, C. (1985), "Laden animal figurines from the Chalcolithic period in Palestine", *BASOR* 258: 53–62.
Epstein, C. (1998), *The Chalcolithic Culture of the Golan*. Jerusalem.
Epstein, C. and Noy, T. (1988), "Observations concerning perforated tools from Chalcolithic Palestine", *Paléorient* 14: 133–144.
Eqbal, H. (1979), "The Seleucid, Parthian, and Sasanian periods on the Izeh Plain", in Wright, ed., 114–123.
Erdoğan, A. (2007), "Beobachtungen zur achämenidishen Architektur Daskyleions", in Deleman, ed., 177–193.
Erek, C.M. (2009), "2007 Direkli Mağarasi kazilari", in Anonymous (2009c), ed., 323–346.
Ergenzinger, P. and Kühne, H. (1991), "Ein regionales Bewässerungssystem am Ḫābūr", in Kühne, ed., 163–190.
Erikson, B., ed. (2010), *Lithic Technology in Metal Using Societies*. Højbjerg.
Eriksson, K.O., Bourke, S.J. and Hennessy, J.B. (2000), "A Middle Cypriot sherd from Trench I, Tell Nebi Mend, Syria", *ÄL* 10: 205–210.
Erkanal, H. (1977), *Die Äxte und Beile des 2. Jahrtausends in Zentralanatolien*. Stuttgart.
Erskine, A., ed. (2003), *A Companion to the Hellenistic World*. Oxford.
Ervynck, A., De Cupere, B. and Van Neer, W. (1993), "Consumption refuse from the Byzantine castle at Pessinus, central Anatolia, Turkey", in Buitenhuis and Clason, eds., 119–129.
Ervynck, A., Dobney, K., Hongo, H. and Meadow, R.H. (2001), "Born free! New evidence for the status of pigs from Çayonu Tepesi, Eastern Anatolia", *Paléorient* 27: 47–73.
Eshed, V., Gopher, A., Gage, T.B. and Hershkovitz, I. (2004a), "Has the transition to agriculture reshaped the demographic structure of prehistoric populations? New evidence from the Levant", *AJPA* 124: 315–329.

Eshed, V., Gopher, A., Galili, E. and Hershkovitz, I. (2004b), "Musculoskeletal stress markers in Natufian hunter-gatherers and Neolithic farmers in the Levant: the upper limb", *AJPA* 123: 303–315.

Eshed, V., Gopher, A. and Hershkovitz, I. (2006), "Tooth wear and dental pathology at the advent of agriculture: new evidence from the Levant", *AJPA* 130: 145–159.

Esin, U. (1999), "Copper objects from the Pre-Pottery Neolithic site of Aşikli (Kizilkaya village, Province of Aksaray, Turkey)", in Hauptmann et al., eds., 23–30.

Esin, U. and Harmankaya, S. (1999), "Aşikli", in Özdoğan and Başgelen, eds., 115–132.

Eskander, S. (2004), "The tale of Iraq's 'Cemetery of Books'" (http://www.infotoday.com/it/dec04/eskander.shtml). Accessed 12/17/2010.

Esse, D. (1989), "Secondary state formation in Early Bronze Age Palestine", in de Miroschedji, ed., 81–96.

Esse, D. (1991), *Subsistence, Trade, and Social Change in Early Bronze Age Palestine*. Chicago.

Euting, J. (1914), *Tagebuch einer Reise nach Inner-Arabien, Zweiter Theil*. Leipzig.

Evershed, R.P., Payne, S., Sherratt, A.G., Copley, M.S., Coolidge, J., Urem-Kotsu, D., Kotsakis, K., Özdoğan, M., Özdoğan, A.E., Nieuwenhuyse, O., Akkermans, P.M.M.G., Bailey, D., Andeescu, R-R., Campbell, S., Farid, S., Hodder, I., Yalman, N., Özbaşaran, M., Biçakci, E., Garfinkel, Y., Levy, T. and Burton, M.M. (2008), "Earliest date for milk use in the Near East and southeastern Europe linked to cattle herding", *Nature* 455: 528–531.

Evett, D. (1967), "Artifacts and architecture of the Iblis I period: Areas D, F, and G", in Caldwell, ed, 202–271.

Fabian, J. (1983), *Time and the Other: How Anthropology Makes Its Object*. New York.

Fadhil, A. and Alsamarraee, Z.R.A. (2005), "Ausgrabungen in Sippar (Tell Abu Habbah). Vorbericht über die Grabungsergebnisse der 24. Kampagne 2002", *BaM* 36: 157–224.

Fagan, B. (1996), "The arrogant archaeologist", in Vitelli, ed., 238–242.

Fagan, B. (2007), *People of the Earth: An Introduction to World Prehistory*, 12th edn. Upper Saddle River.

Fahd, T., ed. (1981), *La Géographie administrative et politique d'Alexandre à Mahomet*. Leiden.

Fairbairn, A. and Omura, S. (2005), "Archaeological identification and significance of ÉSAG (agricultural storage pits) at Kaman-Kalehöyük, central Anatolia", *AnSt* 55: 15–23.

Fairservis, W.A. (1961), *Archaeological Studies in the Seistan Basin of Southwestern Afghanistan and Eastern Iran*. New York.

Faist, B. (2005), *Neuassyrische Rechtsurkunden*, vol. 3. Saarbrücken.

Faist, B. (2007), *Alltagstexte aus neuassyrischen Archiven und Bibliotheken der Stadt Assur*. Wiesbaden.

Faist, B. (in press), *Neuassyrische Rechtsurkunden*, vol. 4. Wiesbaden.

Faist, B. and Finkbeiner, U. (2002), "Emar. Eine syrische Stadt unter hethitischer Herrschaft", in Anonymous (2002b), ed., 190–195.

Falconer, S.E. (1994), "The development and decline of Bronze Age civilization in the southern Levant: a reassessment of urbanism and ruralism", in Mathers and Stoddart, eds., 305–33.

Falconer, S.E. and Savage, S.H. (1995), "Heartlands and hinterlands: alternative trajectories of early urbanization in Mesopotamia and the Southern Levant", *AA* 60: 37–58.
Fales, F.M., ed. (1981), *Assyrian Royal Inscriptions: New Horizons in Literary, Ideological and Historical Analysis*. Rome.
Fales, F.M. (2003), "Reflections on Neo-Assyrian archives", in Brosius, ed., 195–229.
Fales, F.M. (2004a), *Saccheggio in Mesopotamia. Il museo di Baghdad dalla nascita dell'Iraq a oggi*. Udine.
Fales, F.M. (2004b), "Rileggendo gli inventari di Qatna", *Kaskal* 1: 83–127. [ch. 41?]
Fales, F.M. (2008), "On Pax Assyriaca in the eighth-seventh centuries BCE and its implications", in Cohen and Westbrook, eds., 17–35.
Fales, F.M. and Hickey, B.J., eds. (1987), *Austen Henry Layard tra l'Oriente e Venezia*. Rome.
Falk, H., ed. (2005), *Wege zur Stadt – Entwicklung und Formen urbanen Lebens in der alten Welt*. Bremen.
Falkenstein, A. (1936), *Archaische Texte aus Uruk*. Berlin.
Falkenstein, A. (1941), *Topographie von Uruk, 1. Teil: Uruk zur Seleukidenzeit*. Leipzig.
Faller, S. (2000), *Taprobane im Wandel der Zeit: Das Śrî-Laṅkâ-Bild in griechischen und lateinischen Quellen zwischen Alexanderzug und Spätantike*. Stuttgart.
Falsone, G. (1998), "Tell Shiyukh Tahtani on the Euphrates. The University of Palermo salvage excavations in North Syria (1993–1994)", *Akkadica* 109–110: 22–64.
Falsone, G. (1999), "Tell Shiyukh Tahtani", in del Olmo Lete and Montero Fenollós, eds., 137–142.
Faltings, D. (2002), "The chronological frame and social structure of Buto in the fourth millennium BCE", in van den Brink and Levy, eds., 165–170.
Fanon, F. (1963), *The Wretched of the Earth*. New York.
Fantalkin, A. and Tal, O. (2006), "Redating Lachish level I: identifying Achaemenid imperial policy at the southern frontier of the Fifth Satrapy", in Lipschits and Oeming, eds., 167–197.
Fantini Terzi, L., ed. (2000), *Il giubileo prima del giubileo. Tempo e spazio nelle civiltà mesopotamiche e dell'antico Egitto*. Milan.
Farès-Drappeau, S. (2005), *Dédan et Lihyan. Histoire des Arabes aux confins des pouvoirs perse et hellénistique (IVe-IIe s. avant l'ère chrétienne)*. Lyon.
Farioli Campanati, R., ed. (1989), *La Siria araba da Roma a Bisanzio*. Ravenna.
Farioli Campanati, R. (1992), "Bosra chiesa dei SS. Sergio, Bacco e Leonzio: i nuovi ritrovamenti (1988–1989)", in Canivet and Rey-Coquais, eds., 173–178.
Farmer, P.E. (2004), "An anthropology of structural violence", *CA* 45/3: 305–326.
Farnsworth, M. and Ritchie, P.D. (1938), "Spectrographic studies on ancient glass. Egyptian glass, mainly of the eighteenth dynasty, with special reference to its cobalt content", *Technical Studies in the Field of Fine Arts* 6: 155–173.
Farr, H. (2010), "Island colonization and trade in the Mediterranean", in Anderson et al., eds., 179–189.
Fathy, H. (1986), *Vernacular Architecture: Principles and Examples with Reference to Hot Arid Climates*. Chicago.
Fattovich, R. (2007), "Marsa Gawasis: a Pharaonic coastal settlement by the Red Sea in Egypt", in Starkey et al., eds., 15–22.

Fauvelle-Aymar, F.X. (2009), "Les inscriptions d'Adoulis (Érythrée): fragments d'un royaume d'influence hellénistique et gréco-romaine sur le côte africaine de la mer Rouge", *BIFAO* 109: 135–160.

Fazeli, H., Coningham, R.A.E., Young, R.L., Gillmore, G.K., Maghsoudi, M. and Raza, H. (2007a), "Preliminary report of excavations at Tepe Pardis", *Archaeological Reports* 7: 35–57.

Fazeli, H., Coningham, R.A.E., Young, R.S., Gillmore, G.K., Maghsoudi, M. and Raza, H. (2007b), "Socio-economic transformations in the Tehran Plain: final season of settlement survey and excavations at Tepe Pardis". *Iran* 45: 267–286.

Fazeli, H., Wong, E.H. and Potts, D.T. (2005), "The Qazvin Plain revisited: a reappraisal of the chronology of the northwestern Central Plateau, Iran, in the 6th to 4th millennium BC", *ANES* 42: 3–82.

Fazeli [Nashli], H. (2009), "The Achaemenid/Post Achaemenid remains in Tang-i Bulaghi near Pasargadae: a report on the salvage excavations conducted by five joint teams in 2004–2007", *ARTA* 2009.001.

Fazeli [Nashli], H., Beshkani, A., Markosian, A., Ilkani, H. and Young, R. (2009), "The Neolithic to Chalcolithic transition in the Qazvin Plain, Iran: chronology and subsistence strategies", *AMIT* 41: 1–22.

Fedele, F.G. (2008), "Wadi al-Tayyilah 3, a Neolithic and Pre-Neolithic occupation on the eastern Yemen Plateau, and its archaeofaunal information", *PSAS* 38: 153–172.

Fedele, F.G. and Zaccara, D. (2005), "Wadi al-Tayyila 3: a mid-Holocene site on the Yemen Plateau and its lithic collection", in Sholan, Antonini and Arbach, eds., 213–245.

Feinman G.M. and Manzanilla, L., eds. (2000), *Cultural Evolution: Contemporary Viewpoints*. New York.

Feinman, G.M. and Marcus, J., eds. (1998), *Archaic States*. Santa Fe.

Feinman, G.M. and Price, T.D., eds. (2001), *Archaeology at the Millennium: A Source Book*. New York.

Feldman, M.H. (2006), *Diplomacy by design: Luxury Arts and an "International Style" in the Ancient Near East, 1400–1200 BCE*. Chicago.

Feldman, M.H. (2007), "Frescoes, exotica, and the reinvention of the Northern Levantine kingdoms during the second millennium BCE", in Heinz and Feldman, eds., 39–65.

Feldt, L. (2005), "Fishy monsters: updating the iconographic references of V. Scheil, 'La déesse Nina et ses poissons (1918)'", in Artzi et al., eds., 116–126.

Feller, B. (in press), *Mittelassyrische Siegelabrollungen aus Assur*. Berlin.

Ferrara, A.J. (1973), *Nanna-Suen's journey to Nippur*. Rome.

Ferrara, A.J. (1975), "An inscribed stone slab of Nebuchadrezzar II", *JCS* 27: 231–232.

Festuccia, S. (2000), "The moulds of Ebla: morphology and archaeological contexts", in Matthiae et al., eds., 421–435.

Feynman, J. and Ruzmaikin, A. (2007), "Climate stability and the development of agricultural societies", *Climate Change* 84: 295–311.

Field, J. and Banning, E.B. (1998), "Hillslope processes and archaeology in Wadi Ziqlab, Northern Jordan", *Geoarchaeology* 13: 595–616.

Fielding, D. and Shortland, A. (2010), "An eye for an eye, a tooth for a tooth': political violence and counter-insurgency in Egypt", *Journal of Peace Research* 47/4: 433–447.

Fiema, Z.T. (2001), "Byzantine Petra: a reassessment", in Burns and Eadie, eds., 111–131.

Fiema, Z.T. (2002), "Late Antique Petra and its hinterland: recent research and new interpretations", in Humphrey, ed., 191–252.

Fiema, Z.T. and Frösén, J. (2008), *Petra: The Mountain of Aaron I. The Church and the Chapel*. Helsinki.

Fiema, Z.T. and Frösén, J. (2009), "News from Jabal Haroun", *NEA* 72/1: 62–63.

Fiema, Z.T. and Jones, R.N. (1990), "The Nabataean king-list revised: further observations on the second Nabataean inscription from Tell Esh-Shuqafiya, Egypt", *ADAJ* 34: 239–248.

Fiema, Z.T., Kanellopoulos, C., Waliszewski, T. and Schick, R. (2001), *The Petra Church*. Amman.

Fiey, J.-M. (1958), "Identification of Qasr Serej", *Sumer* 14: 125–7.

Fiey, J.-M. (1959), *Mossoul chrétienne*. Beirut.

Fiey, J.-M. (1967), "Topography of al-Mada'in", *Sumer* 23: 3–38.

Fiey, J.-M. (1968), *Assyrie Chrétienne. Contribution à l'étude de l'histoire et de la géographie ecclésiastique et monastique du nord de l'Iraq*, 3 vols. Beirut.

Figueras, P. (1995), "Monks and monasteries in the Negev Desert", *LA* 45: 401–447.

Fincke, J.S. (2004), "The British Museum's Ashurbanipal Library Project", *Iraq* 66: 55–60.

Fink, A. (2007), "Where was the statue of Idrimi actually found? The later temples of Tell Atchana (Alalakh) revisited", *UF* 39: 161–246.

Finkbeiner, U. (1991), *Uruk: Kampagne 35–37, 1982–1984. Die archäologische Oberflächenuntersuchung (Survey)*. Mainz.

Finkbeiner, U., ed. (1993a), *Materialen zur Archäologie der Seleukiden- und Partherzeit im südlichen Babylonien und im Golfgebiet*. Tubingen.

Finkbeiner, U. (1993b), "Fundstellen der Keramik der Seleukiden- und Partherzeit", in Finkbeiner, ed., 3–16.

Finkbeiner, U. (2001), "Emar 1999 – Bericht über die 3. Kampagne der syrisch-deutschen Ausgrabungen", *BaM* 32: 41–120.

Finkbeiner, U. (2002), "Emar 2001 – Bericht über die 4. Kampagne der syrisch-deutschen Ausgrabungen", *BaM* 33: 109–154.

Finkbeiner, U., Dittmann, R. and Hauptmann, H., eds. (1995), *Beiträge zur Kulturgeschichte Vorderasiens: Festschrift für Rainer Michael Boehmer*. Mainz.

Finkbeiner, U. and Röllig, W., eds. (1986), *Ğamdat Naṣr: Period or regional Style?* Wiesbaden.

Finkbeiner, U. and Sakal, F. (2003), "Emar 2002 – Bericht über die 5. Kampagne der syrisch-deutschen Ausgrabungen", *BaM* 34: 9–118.

Finkel, I.L. (1988), "The Hanging Gardens of Babylon", in Clayton and Price, eds., 38–58.

Finkel, I.L. and Seymour, M.J. (2008), *Babylon: Myth and Reality*. Oxford.

Finkelstein, I. (1995), "Two notes on Early Bronze Age urbanization and urbanism", *Tel Aviv* 22: 47–69.

Finkelstein, I. (1996), "The territorial-political system of Canaan in the Late Bronze Age", *UF* 28: 221–255.

Finkelstein, I., and Gophna, R. (1993), "Settlement, demographic, and economic patterns in the highlands of Palestine in the Chalcolithic and Early Bronze periods and the beginning of urbanism", *BASOR* 289: 1–22.

Finkelstein, I. and Ovadiah, A. (1985), "Byzantine monastic remains in the southern Sinai", *DOP* 39: 39–79. [ch. 58?]

Finkelstein, I. and Silberman, N.A. (2002), *The Bible Unearthed: Archaeology's New Vision of Ancient Israel and the Origin of its Sacred Texts*. New York.

Finlayson, B., Mithen, S., Najjar, M., Smith, S., Maricevic, D., Pankhurst, N. and Yeomans, L. (2011), "Architecture, sedentism and social complexity. Communal building in Pre-Pottery Neolithic A settlements: new evidence form WF16", *PNAS* 108/20: 8183–8188.

Finlayson B. and Warren, G., eds. (2010), *Landscapes in Transition*. Oxford.

Finster, B. and Schmidt, J. (1976), "Sasanidische und frühislamiche Ruine im Iraq", *BaM* 8: 7–168.

Fiorina, P. (1987), "Tell Hassan: les couches Halafiennes et Obeidiennes et la relation entre les deux cultures", in Huot, ed., 243–255.

Fiorina, P. (1997), "Khirbet Hatara – la stratigrafia", *Mesopotamia* 32: 7–62.

Fischer, B., Genz, H., Jean, E. and Köroğlu, K., eds. (2003), *Identifying Changes: The Transition from Bronze to Iron Ages in Anatolia and its Neighbouring Regions*. Istanbul.

Fischer-Genz, B. (2008), "Rock-cut pressing installations in the territory of ancient Heliopolis/Baalbek", in van Ess, ed., 65–76.

Fischer-Genz, B. and Ehrig, H. (2005), "First results of the archaeological survey project in the territory of ancient Heliopolis-Baalbek", in van Ess and Rheidt, 135–138.

Fish, S.K. and Kowalewski, S.A., eds. (1990), *The Archaeology of Regions. A Case for Full-Coverage Survey*. London.

Fisher, W.B. ed. (1968), *The Cambridge History of Iran*. Vol. I: *The Land of Iran*. Cambridge.

Fisher, W.B. (1978), *The Middle East: A Physical, Social and Regional Geography*. London.

Fitzhugh, B. and Habu, J., eds., (2002), *Beyond Foraging and Collecting: Evolutionary Change in Hunter-Gatherer Settlement Systems*. New York.

Flad, R., Li, S., Wu, X., and Zhao, Z. (2010), "Early wheat in China: results from new studies at Donghuishan in the Hexi corridor", *The Holocene* 17: 555–560.

Flandin, E. (1861), "Voyage en Mésopotamie, 1840–42", *Le Tour du Monde: Nouveau journal des voyages* 1861/2: 49–80.

Flandin, E. and Coste, P. (1843–54), *Voyage en Perse*, 6 vols. Paris.

Flannery, K.V. (1965), "The ecology of early food production in Mesopotamia", *Science* 147: 1247–1256.

Flannery, K.V. (1967), "Culture history vs. culture process: a debate in American archaeology", *Scientific American* 217: 119–122.

Flannery, K.V. (1969), "Origins and ecological effects of early domestication in Iran and the Near East", in Ucko and Dimbleby, eds., 73–100.

Flannery, K.V. (1972), "The origins of the village as a settlement type in Mesoamerica and the Near East: a comparative study", in Ucko, Tringham and Dimbleby, eds., 23–53.

Flannery, K.V. (1973), "The origins of agriculture", *ARA* 2: 271–310.

Flannery, K.V. (1993), "Will the real model please stand up: comments on Saidel's 'Round house or square?'", *JMA* 6: 109–117.

Flannery, K.V. (1999), "Chiefdoms in the Early Near East: why it is so hard to identify them?", in Alizadeh et al., eds., 44–63.

Flavin, K. and Sheperd, E. (1994), "Fishing in the Gulf: preliminary investigations at an Ubaid site, Dalma (UAE)", *PSAS* 24: 115–134.

Fleitmann, D., Burns, S.J., Mundelsee, A., Neff, U., Kramers, J., Mangini, A. and Matter, A. (2003), "Holocene forcing of the Indian monsoon recorded in a stalagmite from southern Oman", *Science* 300: 1737–1739.

Fleming, D.E. (1992), "A limited kingship: Late Bronze Age Emar in ancient Syria", *UF* 24: 59–71.

Fontan, E. and Chevalier, N., eds. (1994), *De Khorsabad à Paris, la découverte des Assyriens*. Paris.

Fontugne, M., Kuzucuoğlu, C., Karabiyikoğlu, M., Hatté, C. and Pastre, J-F. (1999), "From Pleniglacial to Holocene: a 14C chronostratigraphy of environmental changes in the Konya Basin", *QSR* 18: 573–592.

Forbes, R.J. (1964), *Studies in Ancient Technology*. Leiden.

Forest, J.-D. (1983a), "Aux origines de l'architecture obeidienne: les plans de type Samarra", *Akkadica* 34: 1–47.

Forest, J.-D. (1983b), *Les Pratiques funéraires en Mésopotamie du cinquieme millénaire au début du troisième*. Paris.

Forest, J.-D. (1987), "Les bevelled rim bowls: nouvelle tentative d'interprétation", *Akkadica* 53: 1–24.

Forest, J.-D. (1996), *Mésopotamie: L'apparition de l'état, VIIe–IIIe millénaires*. Paris.

Forest, J.-D. (2005), "The state: the process of state formation as seen from Mesopotamia", in Pollock and Bernbeck, eds., 184–206.

Forlan, I. (1995), "Cisterne a Dara", in Iacobini and Zanini, eds., 51–65.

Foro, P and Rey, S. (2008), "Archaeology without identity? Antiquity and French archaeological research around the Mediterranean", *Fragmenta* 2: 95–107.

Forstner-Müller, I. and Kopetzky, K. (2009), "Egypt and Lebanon: new evidence for cultural exchanges in the first half of the 2nd millennium BC", in Anonymous (2009e), ed., 143–402.

Forte, M. and Williams, P.R., eds. (2003), *The Reconstruction of Archaeological Landscapes Through Digital Technologies*. Oxford.

Fortin, M., ed. (2006), *Tell 'Acharneh 1998–2004*. Turnhout.

Foss, C. (1977), "Archaeology and the twenty cities of Byzantine Asia", *AJA* 81: 469–486.

Foss, C. (1979), *Ephesus after Antiquity: A Late Antique, Byzantine and Turkish city*. Cambridge.

Foss, C. (1990), *History and Archaeology of Byzantine Asia Minor*. Aldershot.

Foss, C. (1994), "The Lycian coast in the Byzantine Age", *DOP* 48: 1–52.

Foss, C. (1996), *Cities, Fortresses and Villages of Byzantine Asia Minor*. Aldershot.

Foss, C. (1997), "Syria in transition AD 550–750: an archaeological approach", *DOP* 51: 189–269.

Foss, C. (2002), "Pilgrimage in Medieval Asia Minor", *DOP* 56: 129–151.

Foss, C. and Winfield, D. (1986), *Byzantine Fortifications: An Introduction*. Pretoria.

Fossing, P. (1940), *Glass Vessels Before Glass-Blowing*. Copenhagen.

Foster, B.R. and Foster, K.P. (2009), *Civilizations of Ancient Iraq*. Princeton.
Foster, B.R. (1981), "A new look at the Sumerian temple state", *JESHO* 24: 225–241.
Foster, B.R. (1982a), *Administration and Use of Institutional Land in Sargonic Sumer*. Copenhagen.
Foster, B.R. (1982b), *Umma in the Sargonic Period*. Hamden.
Foster, B.R. (1993), "Management and administration in the Sargonic period", in Liverani, ed., 25–39.
Foster, B.R. (2002), "Animals in Mesopotamian literature", in Collins, ed., 271–288.
Foster K.P. (2004), "The Hanging Gardens of Nineveh", *Iraq* 66: 207–220.
Fouache, E., Garçon, D., Rousset, D., Sénéchal, G. and Madjidzadeh, Y. (2005), "La vallée de l'Halil Roud (région de Jiroft, Iran): étude géoarchéologique, méthodologie et résultats préliminaires", *Paléorient* 31/2: 107–122.
Foucault, M. (1980), *Power/Knowledge: Selected Interviews and Other Writings 1972–1977*. New York.
Fourdrin, J-P. and Feissel, D. (1994), "Une porte urbaine construite à Chalcis de Syrie par Isidore de Milet le Jeune (550/551)", *Travaux et mémoires* 12: 299–307.
Fournet, J-L. (2003), "Langues, écritures et culture dans les praesidia", in Cuvigny, ed., 427–500.
Fowden, E.K. (1999), *The Barbarian Plain: Saint Sergius Between Rome and Iran*. Berkeley.
Foxvog, A.A. (2007), "Abgals and carp actors", *N.A.B.U.* 2007/4: 80–81.
Foy, D. and Nenna, M-D., eds. (2003), *Échanges et commerce du verre dans le Monde antique*. Montagnac.
Foy Vaillant, J. (1728), *Arsacidarum imperium, sive regum Parthorum historia. Ad fidem numismatum accommodata*, Tomus Primus. Paris.
Frachetti, M.D. (2008), *Pastoralist Landscapes and Social Interaction in Bronze Age Eurasia*. Berkeley.
Frachetti, M.D. (2009), "Differentiated landscapes and non-uniform complexity among Bronze Age societies of the Eurasian steppe", in Hanks and Linduff, eds., 19–46.
Frachetti, M.D. (in press), "Multi-regional emergence of mobile pastoralism and the growth of non-uniform institutional complexity across Eurasia", *CA*.
Frachetti, M.D. and Benecke, N. (2009), "From sheep to (some) horses: 4500 years of herd structure at the pastoralist settlement of Begash (southeastern Kazakhstan", *Antiquity* 83: 1023–1037.
Frachetti, M.D. and Mar'yashev, A.N. (2007), "Long-term occupation and seasonal settlement of eastern Eurasian pastoralists at Begash, Kazakhstan", *JFA* 32/3: 221–242.
Frachetti, M.D., Spengler, R.S., Fritz, G.J. and Mar'yashev, A.N. (2010), "Earliest evidence of broomcorn millet and wheat in the central Eurasian steppe region", *Antiquity* 84: 1–18.
Frahm, E. (2004), "Royal hermeneutics: Observations on the commentaries from Ashurbanipal's libraries at Nineveh", *Iraq* 66: 45–54.
Frahm, E. (2009), *Keilschrifttexte aus Assur literarischen Inhalts*, vol. 3. Wiesbaden.
Frame, G. (1995), *Rulers of Babylonia from the Second Dynasty of Isin to the End of the Assyrian Domination (1157–612 BC)*. Toronto.
Frame, G. and George, A. (2005), "The royal libraries of Nineveh: new evidence for King Ashurbanipal's tablet collecting", *Iraq* 67: 265–284.

Frame, L.D. (2004), *Investigations at Tal-i Iblis: Evidence for Copper Smelting During the Chalcolithic Period*. Cambridge.

Frame, L.D. and Lechtman, H. (in press), "Early Chalcolithic crucible smelting of copper ores at Tal-i Iblis, Iran", *JFA*.

Francfort, H.-P. (1984), *Fouilles d'Aï Khanoum III. Le sanctuaire du temple à niches indentées*. Paris.

Francfort, H.-P. (1994), "The Central Asian dimension of the symbolic system in Bactria and Margiana", *Antiquity* 68: 406–418.

Francfort, H.-P. (2005a), "Asie centrale", in Briant and Boucharlat, eds., 313–352.

Francfort, H.-P. (2005b), "Observations sur la toreutique de la civilisation de l'Oxus", in Bopearachi and Boussac, eds., 21–64.

Francfort, H.-P. (2009), "Le vin en Asie centrale à la Protohistoire, du IIIe millénaire aux Achéménides", *Cahier des thèmes transversaux ArScAn* 9 (*2007–2008*): 393–404.

Franck, G. (2005), *Mentaler Kapitalismus*. Munich.

Frangipane, M. (2001), "Centralization processes in greater Mesopotamia: Uruk 'expansion' as the climax of systematic interaction among areas of the Greater Mesopotamian region", in Rothman, ed., 307–348.

Frangipane, M. (2002), "'Non-Uruk' developments and Uruk-linked features on the northern borders of greater Mesopotamia", in Postgate, ed., 123–148.

Frangipane, M., ed. (2007a), *Arslantepe Cretulae: An Early Centralized Administrative System Before Writing*. Rome.

Frangipane, M. (2007b), "Different types of egalitarian societies and the development of inequality in early Mesopotamia", *WA* 39/2: 151–76. [ch. 22?]

Frangipane, M., Andersson Strand, E., Laurito, R., Möller-Wiering, S., Nosch, M.L., Rast-Eicher, A. and Wisti Lassen, A. (2009), "Arslantepe, Malatya (Turkey): textiles, tools and imprints of fabrics from the 4th to the 2nd millennium BCE", *Paléorient* 35: 5–29.

Frangipane, M., Hauptmann, H., Liverani, M., Matthiae, P. and Mellink, M., eds. (1993), *Between the Rivers and Over the Mountains: Archaeologica Anatolica et Mesopotamica Alba Palmieri Dedicata*. Rome.

Frangipane, M., Nocera, G.M.D., Hauptmann, A., Morbidelli, P., Palmieri, A., Sadori, L., Schultz, M. and Schmidt-Schultz, T. (2001), "New symbols of the new power in a 'royal' tomb from 3000 BC Arslantepe, Malatya (Turkey)", *Paléorient* 27/2: 105–139.

Frangipane, M. and Palumbi, G. (2007), "Red-Black Ware, pastoralism, trade, and Anatolian-Transcaucasian interactions in the 4th–3rd millennium BC", in Lyonnet, ed., 233–256.

Frank, C. (2010), "La tombe d'Acropole", in Perrot, ed., 364–337.

Franke, S. (1995), "Kings of Akkad: Sargon and Naram-Sin", in Sasson, ed., 831–841.

Franke-Vogt, U. and Weisshaar, H.-J., eds. (2005), *South Asian Archaeology 2003*. Bonn.

Frankel, R., Avitsur, S. and Ayalon, E. (1994), *History and Technology of Olive Oil in the Holy Land*. Arlington.

Franken, H.J. (1974), *In Search of the Jericho Potters: Ceramics from the Iron Age and from the Neolithicum*. New York.

Frankfort, H. (1939a), *Cylinder Seals*. London.

Frankfort, H. (1939b), *Sculpture of the Third Millennium BC from Tell Asmar and Khafajah*. Chicago.

Frankfort, H. (1954), *The Art and Architecture of the Ancient Orient*. London.
Fraser, P.M. (1972), *Ptolemaic Alexandria*, 2 vols. Oxford.
Frayne, D. (1990), *Old Babylonian Period (2003–1595 BC)*. Toronto.
Frayne, D. (1993), *Sargonic and Gutian Periods (2334–2113 BC)*. Toronto.
Freedman, D.N., ed. (1979), *Archaeological Reports from the Tabqa Dam Project, Euphrates Valley, Syria*. Cambridge.
Freeman, P. (2001), "Roman Jordan", in MacDonald, Adams and Bienkowski, eds., 427–459.
Freestone, I.C. (1987), "Composition and microstructure of early opaque red glass", in Bimson and Freestone, eds., 173–191.
Freestone, I.C. (2006), "Glass production in Late Antiquity and the Early Islamic period: a geochemical perspective", in Maggetti and Messiga, eds., 201–216.
Freestone, I.C. and Gorin-Rosen, Y. (1999), "The great glass slab at Bet She'arim, Israel: an early Islamic glassmaking experiment?", *JGS* 41: 105–116.
Freestone, I.C., Gorin-Rosen, Y. and Hughes, M.J. (2000), "Primary glass from Israel and the production of glass in late antiquity and the early Islamic period", in Nenna, ed., 65–82.
Freestone, I.C., Leslie, K.A., Thirwall, M. and Gorin-Rosen, Y. (2003), "Strontium isotopes in the investigation of early glass production: Byzantine and early Islamic glass from the Near East", *Archaeometry* 45: 19–32.
French, D.H. (1962), "Excavations at Çan Hasan: First preliminary report, 1961", *AnSt* 12: 27–40.
French, D.H., ed. (1994), *Studies in the History and Topography of Lycia and Pisidia: In Memoriam A.S. Hall*. London.
French, D.H. (2005), *Çanhasan I: The Pottery*. London.
French, D.H. and Lightfoot, C.S., eds. (1989), *The Eastern Frontier of the Roman Empire*. Oxford.
Frend, W.H.C. (1996), *The Archaeology of Early Christianity: A History*. London.
Frenez, D. and Tosi, M. (2005), "The Lothal sealings: Records from an Indus Civilization town at the eastern end of the maritime trade circuits across the Arabian Sea", in Perna, ed., 65–103.
Freyberger, K.S. (2004), "The use of ponds and cisterns in the Hauran during the Roman period", in Bienert and Häser, eds., 337–344.
Freyberger, K.S. and Joukowsky, M.S. (1997), "Blattranken, Greifen und Elefanten: Sakrale Architektur in Petra", in Weber and Wenning, eds., 71–86.
Freydank, H. (2006), *Mittelassyrische Rechtsurkunden und Verwaltungstexte*, vol. 7. Saarwellingen.
Freydank, H. and Feller, B. (2004), *Mittelassyrische Rechtsurkunden und Verwaltungstexte*, vol. 5. Saarbrücken.
Freydank, H. and Feller, B. (2005), *Mittelassyrische Rechtsurkunden und Verwaltungstexte*, vol. 6. Saarbrücken.
Freydank, H. and Feller, B. (2008), *Mittelassyrische Rechtsurkunden und Verwaltungstexte*, vol. 8. Wiesbaden.
Frézouls, E., ed. (1987), *Sociétés urbaines, sociétés rurales dans l'Asie Mineure et la Syrie hellénistiques et romaines*. Strasbourg.
Friedman, R., ed. (2002), *Egypt and Nubia: Gifts of the desert*. London.

Frierman, J.D. (1971), "Lime firing as the precursor of fired ceramics", *IEJ* 21: 212–216.
Frifelt, K. (1975), "A possible link between the Jemdet Nasr and the Umm an-Nar graves of Oman", *JOS* 1: 57–80.
Frifelt, K. (1976), "Evidence of a third millennium BC town in Oman", *JOS* 2: 57–74.
Frifelt, K. (1995), *The Island of Umm an-Nar. The Third Millennium Settlement.* Aarhus.
Frifelt, K. and Sørensen, P., eds. (1989), *South Asian Archaeology 1985.* London.
Frumkin, A. (2009), "Stable isotopes of a subfossil tamarix tree from the Dead Sea region, Israel, and their implications for the Intermediate Bronze Age environmental crisis", *QR* 71: 319–328.
Frye, R.N. (1970a), "Sassanian clay sealings in the Baghdad Museum", *Sumer* 26: 237–240.
Frye, R.N. (1970b), "Sasanian seal inscriptions", in Stiehl and Stiehl, eds., 77–84.
Frye, R.N. (1974a), "Methodology in Iranian history", in Frye, ed., 57–69.
Frye, R.N., ed. (1974b), *Neue Methodologie in der Iranistik.* Wiesbaden.
Frye, R.N. (1982), "The 'Aramaic' inscription on the tomb of Darius", *IrAnt* 17: 85–90.
Frye, R.N. (1983), "The political history of Iran under the Sasanians", *CHI* 3/1: 116–180.
Frye, R.N. (1991), "Commerce iii. In the Parthian and Sasanian periods", *EnIr* 6: 61–64.
Fugmann, E. (1958), *Hama. Fouilles et recherches 1931–1938. 1. L'architecture des périodes préhellénistiques.* Copenhagen.
Fujii, H., ed. (1981), "Preliminary report of excavations at Gubba and Songor", *Al-Rāfidān* 2: 131–241.
Fujii, H. (1987), "Working report on second season of Japanese archaeological excavation in Saddam Dam Salvage Project (Tell Jigan)", in Anonymous, ed., 62–67.
Fujii, H., Ohnuma, K., Shibata, H., Okada, Y., Matsumoto, K. and Numoto, H. (1989), "Excavations at Ain Sha'ia ruins and Dukakin caves", *Al-Rāfidān* 10: 27–88.
Fujii, S. (2006), "Wadi Abu Tulayha: a preliminary report of the 2005 spring and summer excavation seasons of the al-Jafr Basin Prehistoric Project, Phase 2", *ADAJ* 50: 9–32.
Fujii, S. and Abe, M. (2008), "PPNB frontier in southern Jordan: a preliminary report on the archaeological surveys and soundings in the Jafr Basin, 1995–2005", *Al-Rāfidān* 29: 1–32.
Fukai, S., Horiuchi, K. and Matsutani, T. (1973), *Marv-Dasht III: The Excavation at Tall-i-Mushki 1965.* Tokyo.
Fukuda, K., Kashima, K, Tsumura, H., Momohara, N., Shiraishi, K., Nakai, I. and Omura, S. (2004), "Geophysical survey on the Karum of 'Kültepe Kaniš': city wall of the Karum", in Omura, ed., 147–52.
Fuller D.Q. (2001), "Responses: Harappan seeds and agriculture, some considerations", *Antiquity* 75: 410–414.
Fuller, D.Q. (2007), "Contrasting patterns in crop domestication and domestication rates: Recent archaeobotanical insights from the Old World", *Annals of Botany* 100/5: 903–924.
Gabriel, A. (1940), *Voyages archéologiques dans la Turquie orientale.* Paris.

Gachet, J. (1998), "Akkaz (Kuwait), a site of the Partho-Sasanid period: a preliminary report on three campaigns of excavation (1993–1996)", *PSAS* 28: 69–79.
Gachet, J. and Salles, J.-F. (1993), "Failaka, Koweit", in Finkbeiner, ed., 59–85.
Gadd, C.J. (1932), "Seals of ancient Indian style found at Ur", *PBA* 18: 191–210.
Gadd, C.J. (1956), *Teachers and Students in the Oldest Schools*. London.
Gadd, C.J. (1958), "The Harran inscriptions of Nabonidus", *AnSt* 8: 35–92.
Gadjiev, M.S. (2007), "The writing of Caucasian Albania: Facts and falsifications", in Kohl, Kozelsky and Ben-Yehuda, eds., 99–126.
Gadzhiev, M.G. and Korenevskii, S.N. (1984), "Metall velinentskoi katakomby", *Drevnie Promysly, Remeslo i Torgovyla v Dagestane*: 7–27.
Gagošidze, J. and Kipiani, G. (2000), "Neue Beobachtungen zur achaimenidischen Baukunst in Kartli", *AMIT* 32: 59–65.
Gaibov, V. (1996), "Bullae from Göbekly-depe (Margiana): Bronze Age traditions in Parthian sphragistics", in Boussac and Invernizzi, eds., 385–393.
Gaibov, V. (2007), "The Bullae of Gobekly-depe", in Cribb and Herrmann, eds., 285–294.
Gaibov, V. and Koshelenko, G.A. (2002), "La Margiane: Asie centrale", *DA* 271: 46–53.
Gail, A.J., Mevissen, G.J.R., and Zehmke, B., eds. (1993), *South Asian Archaeology 1991*. Stuttgart.
Gal, Z., Smithline, H. and Shalem, D. (1999), "New iconographic aspects of Chalcolithic art: preliminary observations on finds from the Peqi'in Cave", *'Atiqot* 37: 1–16.
Gale, N.H., ed. (1991), *Bronze Age Trade in the Mediterranean*. Jonsered.
Galili, E., Eshed, V., Rosen, B., Kislev, M.E., Simchoni, O., Hershkovitz, I. and Gopher, A. (2009), "Evidence for a separate burial ground at the submerged Pottery Neolithic site of Neve-Yam, Israel", *Paléorient* 35/1: 31–46.
Galili, E. and Rosen, B. (2008), "Fishing gear from a 7th-century shipwreck off Dor, Israel", *IJNA* 37/1: 67–76.
Galili, E., Rosen, B. and Sharvit, J. (2002), "Fishing gear sinkers recovered from an underwater wreckage site, off the Carmel coast, Israel", *IJNA* 31/2: 182–201.
Galili, E., Stanley, D.J., Sharvit, J. and Weinstein-Evron, M. (1997), "Evidence for the earliest olive-oil production in submerged settlements off the Carmel Coast, Israel", *JAS* 24: 1141–1150.
Galili, E., Weinstein-Evron, M., Hershkovitz, I., Gopher, A., Kislev, M., Lernau, O., Kolska-Horwitz, L. and Lernau, H. (1993), "Atlil-Yam: a prehistoric site on the sea floor off the Israeli coast", *JFA* 20: 133–57.
Galliano, G. and Calvet, Y., eds. (2004), *Le Royaume d'Ougarit. Aux origines de l'alphabet*. Paris/Lyon.
Galliazzo, V. (1994), *I ponti romani*. Treviso.
Galtung, J. (1969), "Violence, peace, and peace research", *Journal of Peace Research* 6/3: 167–191.
Ganji, M.H. (1968), "Climate", *CHI* 1: 212–249.
Garbrecht, G. (2004), "Historische Wasserbauten in Ost-Anatolien", in Ohlig, ed., 1–103.
Gardiner, A.H., Peet, T.E. and Černy, J. (1952), *The inscriptions of Sinai*, vol. 1. Oxford.
Gardiner, A.H., Peet, T.E. and Černy, J. (1955), *The inscriptions of Sinai*, vol. 2. Oxford.
Garelli, P., ed. (1974), *Le Palais et la royauté: Archéologie et civilisation*. Paris.

Garfinkel, Y. (1993), "The Yarmukian Culture in Israel", *Paléorient* 19/1: 115–134.

Garfinkel, Y. (2002), "The stone tools", in Garfinkel and Miller, eds., 182–186.

Garfinkel, Y. (2003), *Dancing at the Dawn of Agriculture*. Austin.

Garfinkel, Y. (2006), "The social organization at Neolithic Sha'ar Hagolan: the nuclear family, the extended family and the community", in Banning and Chazan, eds., 103–111.

Garfinkel, Y. and Ben-Shlomo, D. (2009), *Sha'ar Hagolan, vol. 2. The rise of urban concepts in the ancient Near East*. Jerusalem.

Garfinkel, Y., Ben-Shlomo, D. and Kuperman, T. (2009), "Large-scale storage of grain surplus in the sixth millennium BC: The silos of Tel Tsaf", *Antiquity* 83: 309–25.

Garfinkel, Y., Korn, N. and Miller, M.A. (2002), "Art from Sha'ar Hagolan: visions of a Neolithic village in the Levant", in Garfinkel and Miller, eds., 188–208.

Garfinkel, Y. and Miller, M. (2002), *Sha'ar Hagolan, vol 1. Neolithic art in context*. Oxford.

Garner, H. (1956a), "The use of imported and native cobalt in Chinese blue and white", *Oriental Art* 2: 48–50.

Garner, H. (1956b), "An early piece of glass from Eridu", *Iraq* 18: 147–149.

Garrison, M.B. (1991), "Seals and the elite at Persepolis: some observations on early Achaemenid Persian art", *AO* 21: 1–29.

Garrison, M.B. (1996), "A Persepolis fortification seal on the tablet MDP 11 308 (Louvre Sb 13078)", *JNES* 55: 15–35.

Garrison, M.B. (1999), "Fire Altars", *EnIr* online.

Garrison, M.B. (2000), "Achaemenid iconography as evidenced by glyptic art: subject matter, social function, audience and diffusion", in Uehlinger, ed., 115–163.

Garrison, M.B. (2008), "The uninscribed tablets from the Fortification archive: a preliminary analysis", in Briant, Henkelman and Stolper, eds., 149–238.

Garrison, M.B. (2009), "Visual representation of deities and demons in early Achaemenid Iran: old problems, new directions" (www.religionswissenschaft.uzh.ch/idd/prepublication.php).

Garrison, M.B. (2010), "The heroic encounter in the visual arts of Ancient Iraq and Iran c. 1000–500 BC", in Counts and Arnold, eds., 151–174.

Garrison, M.B. (2011), "The seal of 'Kuraš the Anzanite, son of Šešpes' (Teispes), PFS 93*: Susa – Anšan – Persepolis", in Álvarez-Mon and Garrison, eds., 375–405.

Garrison, M.B. and Root, M.C. (1998), *Persepolis Seal Studies: An Introduction with Provisional Concordances of Seal Numbers and Associated Documents on Fortification Tablets 1–2087*. Leiden (updates on www.achemenet.com).

Garrison., M.B. and Root, M.C. (2001), *Seals on the Persepolis Fortification Tablets, vol. I. Images of Heroic Encounter*. Chicago.

Garrison, M.B. and Root, M.C. (in press a), *Seals on the Persepolis Fortification Tablets, Part 2: Images of Human Activity*. Chicago.

Garrison, M.B. and Root, M.C. (in press b), *Seals on the Persepolis Fortification Tablets, Part 3: Images of Animals, Geometric and Abstract Designs*. Chicago.

Garrod, D. (1957), "The Natufian culture: the life and economy of a Mesolithic people in the Near East", *PBA* 43: 211–227.

Garstang, J. (1910), *The Land of the Hittites: An Account of Recent Explorations and Discoveries in Asia Minor, with Descriptions of the Hittite monuments*. London.

Gasche, H. (1989), *La Babylonie au 17e siècle avant nôtre ère: Approche archéologique, problèmes et perspectives.* Gent.

Gasche, H., ed. (2004), "The Persian Gulf shorelines and the Karkheh, Karun and Jarrahi Rivers: a geo-archaeological approach. A joint Belgo-Iranian project. First progress report", *Akkadica* 125: 141–215.

Gasche, H., ed. (2005), "The Persian Gulf shorelines and the Karkeh, Karun and Jarrahi Rivers: a geo-archaeological approach. A joint Belgo-Iranian project. First progress report, part 2", *Akkadica* 126: 5–43.

Gasche, H., ed. (2007), "The Persian Gulf Shorelines and the Karkheh, Karun, and Jarrahi Rivers: a Geo-Archaeological Approach (3)", *Akkadica* 128: 1–72.

Gasche, H. (2009), "Susa, I. Excavations", *EnIr* online.

Gasche, H. (2010), "Les palais achéménides de Babylone", in Perrot, ed., 446–463.

Gasche, H., Armstrong, J.A., Cole, S.W. and Gurzadyan, V.G. (1998), *Dating the Fall of Babylon: A Reappraisal of Second-Millennium Chronology.* Gent/Chicago.

Gasche, H. and De Meyer, L. (1980), "Ébauches d'une géographie historique de la région d'Abū Ḥabbah/Tell ed-Dēr", in De Meyer, ed., 1–13.

Gasche, H. and Hrouda, B., eds. (1996), *Collectanea Orientalia. Histoire, arts de l'espace et industrie de la terre. Études offertes en hommage à Agnès Spycket.* Neuchâtel/Paris.

Gasche, H. and Tanret, M., eds. (1998), *Changing Watercourses in Babylonia: Towards a Reconstruction of the Ancient Environment in Lower Mesopotamia.* Gent/Chicago.

Gasche, H., Tanret, M., Cole, S.W. and Verhoeven, K. (2002), "Fleuves du temps et de la vie: Permanence et instabilité du réseau fluviatile babylonien entre 2500 et 1500 avant notre ère", *Annales* 57/3: 531–544.

Gasche, H., Tanret, M., Janssen, C. and Degraeve, A., eds. (1994), *Cinquante-deux reflexions sur le Proche-Orient ancien offertes en hommages à Léon de Meyer.* Leuven.

Gates, C. (2005), "The place of the Achaemenid Persian period in archaeological research in Cilicia and Hatay (Turkey)", in Briant and Boucharlat, eds., 49–69.

Gates, C., Morin, J. and Zimmermann, T., eds. (2009), *Sacred Landscapes in Anatolia and Neighboring Regions.* Oxford.

Gates, J.E. (2005), *Traveling the Desert Edge: The Ptolemaic Roadways and Regional Economy of Egypt's Eastern Desert in the Fourth through First Centuries BCE.* Ann Arbor.

Gates, M.-H. (2001), "Potmarks at Kinet Höyük and the Hittite ceramic industry", in Jean et al., eds., 137–157.

Gates, M.-H. (2010), "Potters and consumers in Cilicia and the Amuq during the 'Age of Transformations' (13th–10th Centuries BC)", in Venturi, ed., 103–110.

Gates, M.-H. (in press), "From Late Bronze to Iron Age on Syria's northwest frontier: Cilicia and the Amuq".

Gatier, P.-L. (1985), "Nouvelles inscriptions de Gerasa", *Syria* 62: 297–308.

Gatier, P.-L. (2005), "Les villages du Proche-Orient protobyzantin: Nouvelles perspectives (1994–2004)", in Lefort et al., eds., 101–119.

Gatier, P.-L. and Salles, J.-F. (1988), "Appendice. L'emplacement de Leuké Komé", in Salles, ed., 186–187.

Gaultier, M., Guy, H., Munoz, O., Tosi, M. and Usai, D. (2005), "Settlement structures and cemetery at Wadi Shab-GAS1, Sultanate of Oman: report on the 2002 and 2003 field seasons", *AAE* 16: 1–20.

Gautier, J.E. and Lampre, G. (1905), "Fouilles de Moussian", *MDP* 8: 59–149.

Gawlikowski, M. (1987), "The Roman frontier on the Euphrates", *Mesopotamia* 22: 77–80.
Gawlikowski, M. (1997), "The Syrian desert under the Romans", in Alcock, ed., 37–54.
Gazit, D. (1986), "Polish on flint axes: the result of mining?", *Michmanim* 3: 37–39 (in Hebrew).
Gebel, H.-G. (2001–2), *Subsistenzformen, Siedlungsweisen und Prozesse des sozialen Wandels vom akeramischen bis zum keramischen Neolithikum*, vol. 2. Freiburg im Breisgau.
Gebel, H.-G., Hermansen, B.D. and Hoffmann-Jensen, C., eds. (2002), *Magic practices and ritual in the Near Eastern Neolithic*. Berlin.
Gebel, H.-G., Kafafi, Z. and al-Ghul, O., eds. (2009), *Modesty and patience: Archaeological studies and memories in honour of Nabil Qadi "Abu Salim"*. Berlin.
Gebel, H.-G., Kafafi, Z. and Rollefson, G.O., eds. (1997), *The Prehistory of Jordan II: Perspectives from 1997*. Berlin.
Gebel, H.-G. and Kozlowski, S.K., eds. (1994), *Neolithic Chipped Stone Industries of the Fertile Crescent: Studies in Early Near Eastern Production, Subsistence, and Environment I*. Berlin.
Gebel, H.-G., Nissen, H.J. and Zaid, Z. (2006), *Basta II. The Architecture and Stratigraphy*. Berlin.
Geijer, A. (1979), *A History of Textile Art*. New York.
Gelb, I.J. (1935), *Inscriptions from Alishar and Vicinity*. Chicago.
Gelb, I.J. (1949), "The date of the Cruciform Monument of Manishtushu", *JNES* 8: 346–348.
Gelb, I.J. (1968), "The word for dragoman in the ancient Near East", *Glossa* 2: 93–104.
Gelb, I.J. (1979), "Household and family in early Mesopotamia", in Lipiński, ed., 1–99.
Gelb, I.J. and Kienast, B. (1990), *Die altakkadischen Königsinschriften des dritten Jahrtausends v. Chr.* Stuttgart.
Genç, E. and Çelik, D., eds. (2009), *Studies in Honor of Altan Cilingiroğlu*. Istanbul.
Gening, V.F., Zdanovich, G.V. and Gening, V.V. (1992), *Sintashta*. Chelyabinsk.
Genito, B. (1996), "The Iranian empires and Central Asia: an archaeological perspective", in Anonymous (1996b), ed., 401–421.
Genito, B. (2010), "The Achaemenid Empire as seen as from its eastern periphery: the case of Dahan-i Ghulaman in Sistan forty years later, a preliminary revision of data", in Matthiae et al., eds., vol. 1, 77–92.
Genz, H. (2000) "The organisation of Early Bronze Age metalworking in the Southern Levant", *Paléorient* 26/1: 55–65.
Genz, H. (2003), "The Early Iron Age in central Anatolia", in Fischer et al., eds., 179–191.
Genz, H. (2004), *Büyükkaya I. Die Keramik der Eisenzeit*. Mainz.
Genz, H. (2005), "Thoughts on the origin of the Iron Age pottery traditions in central Anatolia", in Çilingiroğlu and Darbyshire, eds., 75–84.
Genz, H. (2006), "Imports and their methodological implications for dating Hittite material culture", in Mielke et al., eds., 185–96.

Genz, H. (2007), "Late Iron Age cccupation on the northwest slope at Boğazköy", in Çilingiroğlu and Sagona, eds., 135–151.

Genz, H. (2010), "Recent excavations at Tell Fadous-Kfarabida", *NEA* 73/2–3: 102–113.

Genz, H. (in press), "The Early Bronze Age in Lebanon", in Steiner and Killebrew, eds.

Genz, H. (2011), "Restoring the balance: An Early Bronze Age scale beam from Tell Fadous-Kfarabida, Lebanon", *Antiquity* 85: 838–850.

Genz, H., Çakirlar, C., Damick, A., Jastrzębska, E., Riehl, S., Deckers, K. and Donkin, A. (2009), "Excavations at Tell Fadous-Kfarabida: preliminary report on the 2009 season of excavations", *BAAL* 13: 71–123.

Genz, H. and Hauptmann, A. (2002), "Chalcolithic and EBA metallurgy in the Southern Levant", in Yalçin, ed., 149–158.

Genz, H. and Mielke, D.P., eds. (2011), *Insights into Hittite History and Archaeology*. Leuven, Paris and Walpole.

Genz, H. and Sader, H. (2008), "Tell Hizzin: digging up new material from an Old Excavation", *BAAL* 12: 183–201.

George, A.R. (1993), *House Most High: The Temples of Ancient Mesopotamia*. Winona Lake.

Georghiu, D., ed. (2003), *Chalcolithic and Early Bronze Age Hydrostrategies*. Oxford.

Georgiadis, M. and Gallou, C., eds. (2006), *Archaeology of Cult and Death*. Budapest.

Gérard, F. and Thissen, L., eds. (2002), *The Neolithic of Central Anatolia: Internal Developments and External Relations During the 9th–6th Millennia cal BC*. Istanbul.

Gerlach, I. (2005), "Sirwah: new research at the Sabaean city and oasis", in Gunter, ed., 34–41.

Gernez, G. (2006), "À propos de quelques rares haches de l'âge du Bronze à Byblos", *BAAL* 10: 183–193.

Gernez, G. (2008), "Le métal de Tell Arqa à l'âge du Bronze", *BAAL* 12: 221–264.

Gerschevitch, I., ed. (1985), *The Cambridge History of Iran*. Vol. 2: *The Medianand Achaemenian Periods*. Cambridge.

Gershuny, L. (1985), *Bronze Vessels from Israel and Jordan*. Stuttgart.

Gerstenblith, P. (2006), "Recent developments in the legal protection of cultural heritage", in Brodie et al., eds., 68–92.

Gervers, M. and Gervers, V. (1974), "Felt-making craftsmen of the Anatolian and Iranian Plateaux", *The Textile Museum Journal* 4/1: 14–29.

Gervers, V. (1973), "Methods of traditional felt-making in Anatolia and Iran", *Bulletin de Liaison du Centre International d'Étude des Textiles Anciens* 38/2: 152–163.

Gervers, V., ed. (1977), *Studies in Textile History*. Toronto.

Gervers-Molnár, V. (1973), *The Hungarian Szur: An Archaic Mantle of Eurasian Origin*. Toronto.

Geyer, B., ed. (1990a), *Techniques et pratiques hydro-agricoles traditionnelles en domaine irrigué*. Paris.

Geyer, B. (1990b), "Aménagements hydrauliques et terroir agricole dans la moyenne vallée de l'Euphrate", in Geyer, ed., 63–84.

Geyer, B. and Monchambert, J.-Y. (1987), "Prospection de la moyenne vallée de l'Euphrate: Rapport préliminaire (1982–1985)", *MARI* 5: 293–344.

Geyer, B. and Monchambert J-Y. (2003), *La Basse Vallée de L'Euphrate Syrien: Du Néolithique à l'avènement de l'Islam*. Beirut.

Geyer, B. and Sanlaville, P. (1996), "Nouvelle contribution à l'étude géomorphologique de la région de Larsa-Oueili (Iraq)", in Huot, ed., 391–408.

Gezgin, I. (2001), "Defensive systems in Aiolis and Ionia regions in the Achaemenid period", in Bakir, ed., 181–188.

Ghanimati, S. (2000), "New perspectives on the chronological and functional horizons of Kuh-e Khwaja in Sistan", *Iran* 36: 137–150.

Ghazal. R.O, Kouchoukos, N., Speakman, R.J., Glascock M.D., and Descantes, C. (2008), "Production zone sourcing and intraregional exchange of ceramics in the fourth-millennium BC Susiana plain: a case study", in Alizadeh, ed., 93–152.

Ghirshman, R. (1938), *Fouilles de Sialk, près de Kashan 1933, 1934, 1937*. Paris.

Ghirshman, R. (1946), *Bégram. Recherches archéologiques et historiques sur les Kouchans*. Cairo.

Ghirshman R. (1947), "Une saison de fouilles à Suse", *CRAIBL* 1947: 444–449.

Ghirshman, R. (1951), "Campagne de fouilles à Suse en 1950–1951", *CRAIBL* 1951: 293–301.

Ghirshman, R. (1952), "Cinq campagne de fouilles à Suse, 1946–1951", *RA* 46: 1–18.

Ghirshman, R. (1953), "Mission archéologique en Susiane en hiver, 1952–1953", *Syria* 30: 222–33.

Ghirshman, R. (1954), *Village Perse-Achéménide*. Paris [= MDP 34].

Ghirshman, R. (1962), *Persian Art: The Parthian and Sassanian Dynasties, 249 BC–AD 651*. London.

Ghirshman, R. (1963), *Perse: Proto-Iraniens, Mèdes, Achéménides*. Paris.

Ghirshman, R. (1964a), *The Art of Ancient Iran*. New York.

Ghirshman, R. (1964b), "Suse, campagne de fouilles 1962–1963, Rapport préliminaire", *Arts Asiatiques* 10: 3–10.

Ghirshman, R. (1965a), "Suse du temps des *sukkalmah*. Campagne de Fouilles 1963–1964", *Arts Asiatiques* 11: 3–7.

Ghirshman, R. (1965b), "L'architecture élamite et ses traditions", *IrAnt* 5: 93–102.

Ghirshman, R. (1966), *Tchoga Zanbil (Dur-Untash), Vol. I, La Ziggurat*. Paris.

Ghirshman, R. (1968a), *Tchoga Zanbil (Dur-Untash). Vol II. Temenos, temples, palais, tombes*. Paris.

Ghirshman, R. (1968b), "Suse au tournant du IIIe au IIe millénaire avant notre ère. Travaux de la Délégation Archéologique en Iran – hiver 1966–1967, rapport préliminaire", *Arts Asiatiques* 17: 3–44.

Ghirshman, R. (1971a), *The Island of Kharg*. Tehran.

Ghirshman, R. (1971b), *Bichapour*, vol. 1. Paris.

Ghirshman, R. (1976), *Terrasses sacrées de Bard-è Néchandeh et Masjid-e Solaiman*. Paris.

Ghirshman, R., Minorsky, V. and Sanghvi, R. (1971), *Persia: The Immortal Kingdom*. London.

Gholami, A. (in press), "The pottery of Konar Sandal North: a preliminary study", in Majidzadeh and Pittman, eds.

Gibson, McG. (1972), *The City and Area of Kish*. Coconut Grove.

Gibson, McG. (1973), "Population shift and the rise of Mesopotamian civilization", in Renfrew, ed., 447–463.

Gibson, McG. (1974), "Violation of fallow and engineered disaster in Mesopotamian civilization", in Downing and Gibson, eds., 7–19.

Gibson, McG. (1977), "An Indus Valley stamp seal from Nippur, Iraq", *Man & Environment* 1: 67.
Gibson, McG. (1982), "A re-evaluation of the Akkad period in the Diyala region on the basis of recent excavations at Nippur and in the Hamrin", *AJA* 86: 531–538.
Gibson, McG. (1992), "Patterns of occupation at Nippur", in Ellis, ed., 33–54.
Gibson, McG., ed. (1993a), *Nippur III. Kassite buildings in Area WC-1*. Chicago.
Gibson, McG. (1993b), "Introduction", in Zettler, 1–10.
Gibson, McG. (2008), "The acquisition of antiquities in Iraq, 19th century to 2003, legal and illegal", in Stone and Bajjaly, eds., 31–40.
Gibson, McG. (2010), "The dead hand of Deimel", in Carter and Philip, eds., 85–92.
Gibson, McG., Armstrong, J.A., and McMahon, A. (1998), "The city walls of Nippur and an Islamic site beyond: Oriental Institute excavations, 17th Season, 1987", *Iraq* 60: 11–44.
Gibson, McG. and Biggs, R.D., eds. (1977), *Seals and Sealing in the Ancient Near East*. Malibu.
Gibson, McG. and Biggs, R.D., eds. (1987), *The Organization of Power: Aspects of Bureaucracy in the Ancient Near East*. Chicago.
Gibson, McG., Franke, J.A., Civil, M., Bates, M.L., Boessneck, J., Butzer, K.W., Rathbun, T.A. and Mallin, E.F. (1978), *Excavations at Nippur, Twelfth Season*. Chicago.
Gibson, McG. and McMahon, A. (1995), "An investigation of the Early Dynastic-Akkadian transition: report of the 18th and 19th seasons of excavation in Area WF, Nippur", *Iraq* 57: 1–44.
Gibson, McG. and McMahon, A. (1997), "The Early Dynastic-Akkadian transition, part 2: the authors' response", *Iraq* 59: 9–14.
Gibson, M., Zettler, R.L. and Armstrong, J.A. (1983), "The southern corner of Nippur: excavations during the 14th and 15th seasons", *Sumer* 39: 170–190.
Giddens, A. (1995), *Politics, Sociology and Social Theory: Encounters with Classical and Contemporary Social Thought*. Cambridge.
Gignoux, P. (1980), "Sceaux chrétiens d'époque sasanide", *IrAnt* 15: 299–314.
Gignoux, P. (1998), "Les inscriptions en moyen-perse de Bandiān", *StIr* 27/2: 251–258.
Gignoux, P. and Gyselen. R. (1982), *Sceaux sassanides de diverses collections privées*. Leuven.
Gignoux, P. and Gyselen. R. (1987), *Bulles et sceaux sassanides de diverses collections*. Paris.
Gilan, A. (2008), "Hittite ethnicity? Constructions of identity in Hittite literature", in Collins et al., eds., 107–116.
Gilbert, A.S. (1991), "Equid remains from Godin Tepe, Western Iran: an interim summary and interpretation, with notes on the introduction of horse into Southwest Asia", in Meadow and Uerpmann, eds., 75–122.
Gilead, I. (1984), "The Micro-endscraper: a new tool type of the Chalcolithic Period", *Tel Aviv* 11: 3–10.
Gilead, I. (1990), "The Neolithic-Chalcolithic transition and the Qatifian of the Northern Negev and Sinai", *Levant* 27: 47–63.
Gilead, I., ed. (1995), *Grar, a Chalcolithic Site in the Northern Negev*. Beersheva.
Gilead, I., Hershman, D. and Marder, O. (1995), "The flint assemblages from Grar", in Gilead, ed., 223–280.

Gilead, I., Marder, O., Khalaily, H., Fabian, P., Abadi, Y. and Israel, Y. (2004), "The Beit Eshel Chalcolithic flint workshop in Beer Sheva: a preliminary report", *JIPS* 34: 245–263.
Gillis, C. and Nosch, M.-L., eds. (2007), *Ancient Textiles: Production, Craft and Society*. Oxford.
Gimbutas, M. (1970), "Proto-Indo-European culture", in Cardona et al., eds., 155–197.
Giorgieri, M., Salvini, M., Trémouille, M.-C. and Vannicelli, P., eds. (2003), *Licia e Lidia prima dell' Ellenizzazione*. Rome.
Gitin, S., Mazar, A. and Stern, E., eds. (1998), *Mediterranean Peoples in Transition, Thirteenth to Early Tenth Centuries BCE in Honor of Trude Dothan*. Jerusalem.
Giusfredi, F. (2010), *Sources for a Socio-Economic History of the Neo-Hittite states*. Heidelberg.
Glassner, J.-J. (1986), *La Chute d'Akkadé, L'évènement et sa mémoire*. Berlin.
Glassner, J.-J. (2008), "Textes cunéiformes", in Calvet and Pic, eds., 171–205.
Glatz, C. (2007), *Contact, Interaction, Control: The Archaeology of Inter-Regional Relations in Late Bronze Age Anatolia*. London.
Glatz, C. (2009), "Empire as network: spheres of material interaction in Late Bronze Age Anatolia", *JAA* 28/2: 127–141.
Glatz, C., Matthews, R. and Schachner, A. (2009), "A landscape of conflict and control: Paphlagonia during the second millennium BC", in Matthews and Glatz, eds., 107–148.
Gnoli, G. (1985), "The quadripartition of the Sassanian empire", *EW* 35: 265–270.
Gnoli, G. (1989), *The idea of Irān: An essay on its origin*. Rome.
Gnoli, G. (1993), "Dahan-e Golāmān", *EnIr* Online.
Gnoli, G. and Lanciotti, L., eds. (1985), *Orientalia Josephi Tucci Memoriae Dicata*. Rome.
Gnoli, G. and Vernant, J.-P., eds. (1982), *La Mort, les morts dans les sociétés anciennes*. Paris.
Göbl, R. (1973), *Der Sāsānidische Siegelkanon*. Braunschweig.
Göbl, R. (1983), "Sasanian numismatics", *CHI* 3/2: 322–342.
Godard, A. (1937), "Les statues parthes de Shami", *Athār-é Īrān* 2: 285–305.
Godard, A. (1938), "Les monuments du feu", *Athār-é Īrān* 3: 7–80.
Godard, A. (1965), *The Art of Iran*. London.
Goetze, A. (1969), "Hittite instructions", in Pritchard, ed., 207–211.
Gogadze, E.M. (1972), *Periodizatsiya i Genezis Kurgannoy Kultury Trialeti*. Tbilisi.
Gogte, V.D. (2000), "Indo-Arabian maritime contacts during the Bronze Age: study of pottery from Ra's al-Junayz (Oman)", *Adumatu* 2: 7–14.
Gogte, V.D. (2002), "Ancient maritime trade in the Indian Ocean: evaluation by scientific studies of pottery", *Man & Environment* 27/1: 57–67.
Gohl, E.P.G. and Vilensky, L.D., (1983), *Textile Science: An Explanation of Fibre Properties*, 2nd edn. Melbourne.
Gokhale, B.G. (1966), *Aśoka Maurya*. New York.
Goldberg, J. (2004), "The Berlin letter, Middle Elamite chronology and Šutruk-Nahhunte I's genealogy", *IrAnt* 39: 33–42.
Goldberg, P. (1998), "The changing landscape", in Levy, ed., 40–57.

Golden, J. (2009), "New light on the development of Chalcolithic metal technology in the Southern Levant", *JWP* 22: 283–300.

Goldmann, K. (1997), "The Trojan treasures in Berlin: the disappearance and search for the objects after World War II", in Simpson, ed., 200–203.

Gong, Y. and Chen, Y., eds. (2006), *Special Issue of Oriental Studies. A Collection of papers on Ancient Civilizations of Western Asia, Asia Minor and North Africa.* Beijing.

Gonnella, J., Khayyata, W. and Kohlmeyer, K. (2005), *Die Zitadelle von Aleppo und der Tempel des Wettergottes: Neue Forschungen und Entdeckungen.* Münster.

González, R.J. (2010), *Militarizing Culture: Essays on the Warfare State.* Walnut Creek.

Good, I. (1995), "Notes on a Bronze Age textile fragment from Hami, Xinjiang, with comments on the significance of twill", *JIES* 23/3–4: 319–345.

Good, I. (1998), "Bronze Age cloth and clothing of the Tarim Basin: the Chärchän evidence", in Mair, ed., 656–658.

Good, I. (1999), *The Ecology of Exchange: Textiles from Shahr-i Sokhta, Eastern Iran.* Philadelphia.

Good, I. (2001), "Archaeological textiles: a review of current research", *ARA* 30: 209–226.

Good, I. (2006), "Textiles as a medium of exchange in third millennium BCE Western Asia", in Mair, ed., 191–214.

Good, I. (2007), "Cloth in the Babylonian world", in Leick, ed., 141–154.

Good, I. (2011), *Cloth and Carpet in Early Inner Asia.* Leiden.

Goodchild, R.G. (1949), "The coast road of Phoenicia and its milestones", *Berytus* 9: 91–127.

Goossens, G. (1948), "Les recherches historiques à l'époque néo-babylonienne", *RA* 42: 149–159.

Gopher, A. (1989), *The Flint Assemblages of Munhata. Final Report.* Paris.

Gopher, A. (1994), *Arrowheads of the Neolithic Levant.* Winona Lake.

Gopher, A. and Barkai, R. (1997), "Here are the microliths: a reply to 'Where are the Microliths?'", *Neo-Lithics* 7: 16–18.

Gopher, A. and Gophna, R. (1993), "Cultures of the eighth and seventh millennia BP in the Southern Levant: a review for the 1990s", *JWP* 7/3: 297–353.

Gopher, A. and Rosen, S.A. (2001), "Lithics of Strata XIII–III, the Pre-Pottery Neolithic-Early Bronze Age", in Eisenberg et al., 49–82.

Gopher, A. and Tsuk, T. (1996), *The Nahal Qanah Cave: Earliest Gold in the Southern Levant.* Tel Aviv.

Gopher, A., Tsuk, T., Shalev, S. and Gophna, R. (1990), "Earliest gold artifacts in the Levant", *CA* 31/4: 436–443.

Gophna, R. (1995), "Early Bronze Age Canaan: some spatial and demographic observations", in Levy, ed., 269–280.

Gopnik, H. (2010), "Why columned halls?", in Curtis and Simpson, eds., 195–206.

Goren, A. (2000), "Les Nabatéens et la route de l'encens", in Lemaire, ed., 107–115.

Goren, Y. (2008), "The location of specialized copper production by the lost wax technique in the Chalcolithic southern Levant", *Geoarchaeology* 23/3: 374–397.

Goren, Y., Finkelstein, I. and Na'aman, N. (2003), "The expansion of Amurru according to the petrographic investigation of the Amarna tablets", *BASOR* 329: 1–11.

Goren, Y., Goring-Morris, A.N. and Segal, I. (2001), "The technology of skull modelling in the Pre-Pottery Neolithic B (PPNB): regional variability, the relation of technology and iconography and their archaeological implications", *JAS* 28: 671–690.

Goren-Inbar, N., Sharon G., Melamed, Y. and Kislev, M. (2002), "Nuts, nut cracking, and pitted stones at Gesher Benot Ya'aqov, Israel", *PNAS* 99/4: 2455–2460.

Goring-Rosen, Y. (2000), "The ancient glass industry in Israel: summary of the finds and new discoveries", in Nenna, ed., 49–63.

Goring-Morris, A.N. (1987), *At the Edge: Terminal Pleistocene Hunter-Gatherers in the Negev and Sinai*. Oxford.

Goring-Morris, A.N. (1998), "Complex hunter/gatherers at the end of the Paleolithic (20,000–10,000 BP)", in Levy, ed., 141–168.

Goring-Morris, A.N. and Belfer-Cohen, A., eds. (2003), *More Than Meets the Eye: Studies on Upper Palaeolithic Diversity in the Near East*. Oxford.

Goring-Morris, A.N., Gopher, A. and Rosen, S.A. (1994), "The Tuwailan cortical knife industry of the Negev, Israel", in Gebel and Kozlowski, eds. 511–524.

Gorny, R.L. (1995), "Viticulture and Ancient Anatolia", in McGovern et al., eds., 133–174.

Gorz, A. (2003), *Wissen, Wert und Kapital. Zur Kritik der Wissensökonomie*. Zürich.

Göttlicher, A. (1978), *Materialien für ein Corpus der Schiffsmodelle im Altertum*. Mainz.

Goudie, A.S., Colls, A., Stokes, S., Parker, A.G., White, K. and Al-Farraj, A. (2000), "Latest Pleistocene dune construction at the north-eastern edge of the Rub al Khali, United Arab Emirates", *Sedimentology* 47: 1011–1021.

Goulder, J. (2010), "Administrators' bread: an experiment-based reassessment of the functional and cultural role of Uruk bevel-rim bowls", *Antiquity* 84: 351–362.

Gourdin, W.H. and Kingery, W.D. (1975), "The beginning of pyro-technology: Neolithic and Egyptian lime plaster", *JFA* 2: 133–150.

Gourichon, L. and Helmer, D. (2003), "Preliminary analysis of the faunal remains from Tell Kosak Shamali (Syria): Squares AD5, AE5, BD6 and BE6", in Nishiaki and Matsutani, eds., 273–282.

Graadt van Roggen, D.L. (1905), "Notice sur anciens travaux hydrauliques en Susiane", *MDP* 7: 166–207.

Grabar, A. (1947), "Le témoignage d'une hymne syriaque sur l'architecture de la cathédrale d'Edesse au VIe siécle et sur la symbolique de l'édifice chrétien", *Cahier Archéologique* 2: 41–67.

Grabar, A. (1958), *Ampoules de Terre Sainte (Monza, Bobbio)*. Paris.

Graepler, D. (2004), "Archäologie und illegaler Antikenhandel: die Rolle der Universitätssamlungen", in Heilmeyer and Eule, eds., 116–130.

Graepler, D. and Mazzei, M., eds. (1994), *Fundort: unbekannt. Raubgrabungen zerstören das archäologische Erbe, eine Dokumentation*. Munich.

Graf, D.F. (1990), "Arabia during Achaemenid times", in Sancisi-Weerdenburg and Kuhrt, eds., 131–148.

Graf, D.F. and Sidebotham, S.E. (2003), "Nabataean trade", in Markoe, ed., 65–73.

Grajetzki, W. (2006), *The Middle Kingdom of Ancient Egypt: History, Archaeology and Society*. London.

Gramsci, A. (1971), *Selections from the Prison Notebooks*. London.

Gran-Aymerich, È. (1999), "Archéologie et politique française en Iran: convergences et contradictions (1881–1947)", *JA* 287/1: 357–374.

Grann, D. (2010), "The mark of a masterpiece", *The New Yorker* (July 12 and 16): 50–71.

Gräslund, B., Knutsson, H., Knutsson, K. and Taffinder, J., eds. (1990), *The Interpretative Possibilities of Microwear Studies*. Uppsala.

Gratuze, B. (1999), *Étude des perles protohistoriques en verre de l'inhumation de Marmilhat (Lempdes 63)*. Orléans.

Gratuze, B. (2000), *Étude des perles protohistoriques en verre des dolmens de la Planaise de Sampzon (07) conservées au Museum d'Histoire Naturelle de Lyon*. Orléans.

Gratuze, B. (2001a), *Étude des perles protohistoriques en verre des domens d'Eyne – les Pascarets et la Borda – et d'Enveitg – Bragnoli (Pyrenées Orientales)*. Orléans.

Gratuze, B. (2001b), *Étude des perles protohistoriques en verre de tumulus de Mons (Saint-Georges, 15)*. Orléans.

Gratuze, B. (2002), *Étude d'éléments de parure provenant du site protohistorique de Mez-Notariou (Ouessant, 29)*. Orléans.

Gratuze, B. (2005), *Les perles protohistoriques en verre du Puech de Mus (Sainte-Eulalie-de-Cernon, Aveyron)*. Orléans.

Gratuze, B. (in press a), *Étude des perles protohistoriques en verre conservées au Musée de Chambéry*. Orléans.

Gratuze, B. (in press b), *Étude des perles protohistoriques en verre conservées au Musée d'archéologie de Lons-le-Saunier: – Grotte des Planches (Arbois) – Champ-de-Mont (Quitigny)*. Orléans.

Gratuze, B. (in press c), *Étude des perles protohistoriques en verre de la nécropole de Ventavon (tumulus 7 des Mollards)*. Orléans.

Gratuze, B. (in press d), *Étude des perles protohistoriques de l'Aveyron*. Orléans.

Gratuze, B. and Cosyns, P. (2007), "La composition chimique des perles en verre de la tombe à char de la nécropole latenienne de Neufchâteau-Le Sart par LA-ICP-MS", *Arduinna* 63: 1–7.

Gratuze, B. and Picon, M. (2005), "Utilisation par l'industrie verrière des sels d'aluns des oases égyptiennnes au début du premier millénaire avant notre ère", in Borgard et al., eds., 269–276.

Grave, P., Kealhofer, L. and Marsh, B. (2005), "Ceramic compositional analysis and the Phrygian sanctuary at Dümrek", in Kealhofer, ed., 149–160.

Grayson, A.K. (1982), "Assyria: Ashur-dan II to Ashur-Nirari V (934–745 BC)", *CAH* 3/1: 238–281.

Grayson, A.K. (1991a), *Assyrian Rulers of the Early First Millennium BC (1114–859)*. Toronto.

Grayson, A.K. (1991b), "Assyria, *CAH* 3/2: 71–162.

Grayson, A.K. (1993), "Assyrian officials and power in the ninth and eighth centuries", *State Archives of Assyria Bulletin* 7: 19–52.

Grayson, A.K. (1996), *Assyrian Rulers of the Early First Millennium BC II (858–745 BC)*. Toronto.

Greaves, A. and Fletcher, A., eds. (2007), "Transanatolia: proceedings of the conference held at the British Museum, 31 March–April 1, 2006", *AnSt* 57: 1–204.

Green, A. (1986), "A note on the Assyrian 'goat-fish', 'fish-man' and 'fish-woman'", *Iraq* 48: 25–30.

Green, A. (1999), "The Ninevite countryside: pots and places of the Eski-Mosul-region in the Neo-Assyrian and post-Assyrian periods", in Hausleiter and Reiche, eds., 91–126.

Green, E.L., ed. (1984), *Ethics and Values in Archaeology.* New York.

Green, M.W. (1980), "Animal husbandry at Uruk in the Archaic period", *JNES* 39: 1–35.

Green, M.W. and Nissen, H.J. (1987), *Zeichenliste der archaischen Texte aus Uruk.* Berlin.

Greenberg, R. (2001), "Early Bronze Age II–III Palestinian cylinder seal impressions and the north Canaanite Metallic Ware jar", in Wolff, ed., 189–197.

Greenberg, R. (2002), *Early Urbanization in the Levant: A Regional Narrative.* New York.

Greenewalt, C.H., Jr. (1978), *Ritual Dinners in Early Historic Sardis.* Berkeley.

Greenfield, H.J. (1988), "The origins of milk and wool production in the Old World", *CA* 29/4: 573–594.

Greenfield, H.J. (2010), "The secondary products revolution: the past, the present and the future", *WA* 42: 29–54.

Greenfield, J. (2007), *The Return of Cultural Property.* Cambridge.

Greiss, E. (1955), "Anatomical identification of plant remains and other materials from 1. El Omari excavations at Helwan from the Neolithic period; 2. The excavations at Helwan from the 1st Dynasty", *Bulletin de l'Institut d'Égypte* 36: 227–235.

Grekyan, Y. (2006), "The will of Menua and the gods of Urartu", *Aramazd* 1: 150–195.

Gremliza, F.G.L. (1962), *Economy and Endemic Diseases in the Dez Irrigation Pilot Area: A Report to the Khuzestan Water and Power Authority and Plan Organization of Iran.* New York.

Gremmen, W.H.E. and Bottema, S. (1991), "Palynological investigations in the Syrian Ǧazira", in Kühne, ed., 105–116.

Grenet, F. (2005), "Découverte d'un relief sassanide dans le nord de l'Afghanistan", *CRAIBL* 2005: 115–134.

Gricina, A. and Genito, B. (2010), "The Achaemenid period in the Samarkand area (Sogdiana): trial trenches at Koj tepa 2009 campaign", *Newsletter di Archeologia CISA* 1: 113–161.

Griffin, G.G. (1989), "Collecting pre-Columbian art", in Messenger, ed., 103–115.

Griggo, C. (2004), "Mousterian fauna from Dederiyeh Cave and comparisons with fauna from Umm El Tlel and Douara Cave", *Paléorient* 30: 149–162.

Grigson, C. (1989), "Size and sex: evidence for the domestication of cattle in the Near East", in Milles et al., eds., 77–109.

Grillot, F. (1987), *Éléments de grammaire élamite.* Paris.

Grillot, F. (1990), "Les textes de fondation du palais de Suse", *JA* 278: 213–222.

Groddek, D. and Zorman, M., eds. (2007), *Tabularia Hethaeorum: Hethitologische Beiträge Silvin Košak zum 65. Geburtstag.* Wiesbaden.

Groom, N. (1981), *Frankincense and Myrrh: A Study of the Arabian Incense Trade.* London and New York.

Groom, N. (2005), "Trade, incense, and perfume", in Gunter, ed., 104–113.

Grose, D.F. (1989), *Early Ancient Glass.* New York.

Grosman, L. and Belfer-Cohen, A. (2002), "Zooming onto the 'Younger Dryas'", in Cappers and Bottema, eds., 49–54.

Gross, M. (2010), *Rogues' Gallery: The Secret Story of the Lust, Lies, Greed, and Betrayals that Made the Metropolitan Museum of Art.* New York: Broadway.

Grove, A.T. and Rackham, O. (2001), *The Nature of Mediterranean Europe.* New Haven.

Grupe, G. and Schutkowski, H. (1989), "Dietary shift during the 2nd millennium BC in prehistoric Shimal, Oman Peninsula", *Paléorient* 15/2: 77–84.

Gschwind, M. and Hasan, H. (2008), "Das römische Kastell Qreiye-Ayyash, Provinz Deir ez-Zor, Syrien. Ergebnisse des syrisch-deutschen Kooperationsprojektes", *ZOA* 1: 316–334.

Gubaev, A., Koshelenko, G. and Tosi, M., eds. (1998), *The Archaeological Map of the Murghab Delta: Preliminary Reports 1990–95*. Rome.

Guerrero, E., Molist, M., Kuijt, I. and Anfruns, J. (2009), "Seated memory: new insights into Near Eastern Neolithic mortuary variability from Tell Halula, Syria", *CA* 50/3: 379–391.

Guidetti, M. (2009), "The Byzantine heritage in Dar Al-Islam: churches and mosques in Al-Ruha between the sixth and the twelfth centuries", *Muqarnas* 26: 1–36.

Guilaine, J., ed. (2000), *Premiers Paysans du monde: Naissances des agricultures*. Paris.

Guilaine, J., ed. (2001), *Communautés villageoises du Proche-Orient à l'Atlantique (8000–2000 avant notre ère)*. Paris.

Guilaine, J. and Le Brun, A., eds. (2003), *Le Néolithique de Chypre*. Paris.

Gulati, A.N. (1961), "A note on the early history of silk in India", in Clutton-Brock et al., eds., 53–59.

Gulliksen, S., Birks, H.H., Possnert, G. and Mangerud, J. (1998), "A calendar age estimate of the Younger Dryas-Holocene boundary at Krakenes, western Norway", *The Holocene* 8: 249–259.

Gullini, G. (1964), *Architettura iranica dagli Achemenidi ai Sasanidi. Il "Palazzo" di Kuh-i Khwagia (Seistan)*. Turin.

Gullini, G. (1966), "Problems of an excavation in northern Babylonia", *Mesopotamia* 1: 7–38.

Gumperz, J. and Wilson, R. (1971), "Linguistic hybridization and the 'special case' of pidgins and creoles", in Hymes, ed., 151–167.

Gunbatti, C. (2004), "Two treaty texts found at Kültepe", in Dercksen, 249–268.

Gündem, C.Y. (2009), *Animal Based Economy in Troia and the Troas During the Maritime Troy Culture (c.3000–2200 BC) and a General Summary for West Anatolia*. Tübingen.

Gundlach, R. and Vogel, C., eds. (2008), *Militärgeschichte des pharaonischen Ägypten. Altägypten und seine Nachbarkulturen im Spiegel der aktuellen Forschung*. Paderborn, Munich, Vienna and Zürich.

Gunter, A.C. (1982), "Representations of Urartian and western Iranian fortress architecture in the Assyrian reliefs", *Iran* 20: 103–112.

Gunter, A.C., ed. (1990), *Investigating Artistic Environments in the Ancient Near East*. Washington, DC.

Gunter, A.C., ed. (2005), *Caravan Kingdoms: Yemen and the Ancient Incense Trade*. Washington, DC.

Gunter, A.C. (2006), "Issues in Hittite ceramic production: a view from the western frontier", in Mielke, Schoop and Seeher, eds., 349–63.

Gunter, A.C. and Hauser, S.R. (2005), *Ernst Herzfeld and the Development of Near Eastern Studies, 1900–1950*. Leiden.

Gupta, A.K., Anderson, D. and Overpeck, T. (2003), "Abrupt changes in the Asian southwest monsoon during the Holocene and their links to the North Atlantic Ocean", *Nature* 421: 354–357.

Gupta, S.P. (1979), *Archaeology of Soviet Central Asia and the Indian Borderlands*. Delhi.
Guralnick, E., ed. (1987), *Sardis: Twenty-Seven Years of Discovery*. Chicago.
Gurdil, B. (2010), "Exploring social organizational aspects of the Ubaid communities: a case study of Değirmentepe in eastern Turkey", in Carter and Philip, eds., 361–376.
Gurnet, F. (1994), "Deux notes à propos du monnayage de Xusrō II", *Revue belge de Numismatique* 140: 36–37.
Gurney, O.R. (1977), *Some Aspects of Hittite Religion*. Oxford.
Gurney, O.R. (1990[1952]), *The Hittites*. Harmondsworth.
Gustavson-Gaube C. (1981), "Shams ed-Din Tannira: the Halfian pottery of Area A", *Berytus* 29: 9–182.
Gyselen, R. (1989), *La Géographie administrative de l'empire sassanide, les témoignages sigillographiques*. Paris.
Gyselen, R. (2001), *The Four Generals of the Sasanian Empire: Some Sigillographic Evidence*. Rome.
Gyselen, R. (2006a), *Chrétiens en terre d'Iran: Implantation et acculturation*. Paris.
Gyselen, R. (2006b), "Les témoinages sigillographiques sur la présence chrétienne dans l'Empire sassanide", in Gyselen, ed., 17–78.
Gyselen, R (2007), *Sasanian Seals and Sealings in the A. Saeedi Collection*. Leuven.
Gyselen, R. and Gasche, H. (1994), "Suse et Ivān-e Kerkha, capitale provinciale d'Ērānxwarrah – Šāpūr. Note de géographie historique sassanide", *StIr* 23/1: 19–35.
Haas, V. (1994), *Geschichte der hethitischen Religion*. Leiden.
Habas, L. (2000), "The bema and chancel screen in synagogues and their origin", in Levine and Weiss, eds., 111–130.
Haber, A. and Dayan, T. (2004), "Analyzing the process of domestication: Hagoshrim as a case study", *JAS* 31: 1587–1601.
Hachmann R. (1982), "Der Palast eines syrischen Kleinkönigs der späten Bronzezeit in Kāmid el-Lōz", in Papenfuss and Strocka, eds., 21–41.
Hachmann, R., ed. (1982), *Kamid el-Loz 1971–74*. Bonn.
Hachmann, R., ed. (1983), *Frühe Phönikier im Libanon*. Mainz.
Hachmann, R. ed. (1996), *Kamid el-Loz 16. „Schatzhaus"-Studien*. Bonn.
Hackin, J. (1939), *Recherches archéologiques à Begram, chantier no. 2 (1937)*. Paris.
Hackl, U., Jacobs, B. and Weber, D., eds. (2010), *Quellen zur Geschichte des Partherreiches. Textsammlung mit Übersetzungen und Kommentaren*, 3 vols. Göttingen.
Hadidi, A., ed. (1982), *Studies in the history and archaeology of Jordan*, vol. I. Amman.
Hadidi, A., ed. (1987), *Studies in the history and archaeology of Jordan*, vol. 3. London.
Haerinck, E. (1973), "Le palais achéménide de Babylone", *IrAnt* 10: 108–132.
Haerinck, E. (1983), *La Céramique en Iran pendant la période parthe (ca. 250 av. J.C. à ca. 225 après J.C.): Typologie, chronologie et distribution*. Gent.
Haerinck, E. (1984), "L'Iran méridional, des Achéménides jusqu'à l'avènement de l'Islam. Bilan des recherches", in Boucharlat and Salles, eds., 299–306.
Haerinck, E. (1995), "Babylonia under Achaemenid rule", in Curtis, ed., 26–34.
Haerinck, E. (1999), "L'art des bas-reliefs rupestres", *DA* 243: 54–61.
Haerinck, E. (in press), "Recent discoveries at Ram Hormuz (SW-Iran)", in De Graef and Tavernier, eds.
Haerinck E. and Overlaet, B. (1996), *Hakalan and Dum Gar Parchinah. The Chalcolithic Period*. Brussels.

Haerinck, E. and Overlaet, B. (2003), "Soundings at Tall-i Qaleh (Hasanabad), Fars Province, Iran", in Miller and Abdi, eds., 192–200.

Haerinck, E. and Stevens, K.G. (1996), *Bibliographie analytique de l'archéologie de l'Iran ancien: supplément 3 (1986–1995)*. Leuven.

Haerinck, E. and Stevens, K.G. (2005), *Bibliographie analytique de l'archéologie de l'Iran ancien: supplément 4 (1996–2003)*. Leuven.

Haex, O.M.C., Curvers, H.H. and Akkermans, P.M.M.G., eds. (1989), *To the Euphrates and Beyond: Archaeological Studies in e of Maurits N. van Loon*. Rotterdam.

Hagedorn, A. and Shalem, A., eds. (2007), *Facts and artefacts: Festschrift for Jens Kröger on his 65th Birthday*. Leiden.

Haïdar-Boustani, M. (2001–2), "Le Néolithique du Liban dans le contexte proche-oriental: États des connaissances", *Tempora* 12–13: 1–39.

Haïdar-Boustani, M., Ibáñez, J.J., al-Maqdissi, M., Armendariz, A., Gonzalez Urquijo, J.E. and Teira, L. (2007), "New data on the Epipalaeolithic and Neolithic of the Homs Gap: Three campaigns of archaeological survey (2004–2006)", *Neo-Lithics* 01/07: 3–9.

Haïdar-Boustani, M., Ibáñez, J.J., al-Maqdissi, M., Armendariz, A., Gonzalez Urquijo, J.E. and Teira, L. (2008), "Prospections archéologiques à l'ouest de la ville de Homs: rapport préliminaire campagne 2005", *Tempora* 16–17: 9–38.

Haider, P.W. (2008), "Tradition and change in the beliefs at Assur, Nineveh and Nisibis between 300 BC and 300 AD", in Kaizer, ed., 193–207.

Haines, R.C. (1971), *Exacavations in the Plain of Antioch*, vol. 2. Chicago.

Hajar, L., Haïdar-Boustani, M., Khater, C. and Cheddadi, R. (2010), "Environmental changes in Lebanon during the Holocene: man vs. climate impacts", *JAE* 74: 746–755.

Hakemi, A. (1990), "The excavations at Khurha", *EW* 40: 1–40.

Hald, M. (2010), "Distribution of crops at late Early Bronze Age Titriş Höyük, southeast Anatolia: towards a model for the identification of consumers of centrally organised food distribution", *VHA* 19/1: 69–77.

Haldon, J. (1999), "The idea of town in the Byzantine Empire", in Brogiolo and Ward-Perkins, eds., 1–23.

Haldon, J. (2006), "Social transformation in the 6th–9th c. East", in Bowden, Gotteridge and Machado, eds., 603–647.

Hall, H.R. and Woolley, C.L. (1927), *Ur Excavations 1. Al-'Ubaid*. Oxford.

Hallo, W.W., ed. (1997), *The Context of Scripture*. Vol. I: *Canonical Compositions from the Biblical World*. London.

Hallo, W.W. and Younger, K.L., eds. (2003), *The Context of Scripture*. Leiden.

Halloran, J.A. (2006), *Sumerian Lexicon: A Dictionary Guide to the Ancient Sumerian Language*. Los Angeles.

Halstead, P. (2001), "Mycenaean wheat, flax and sheep: palatial intervention in farming and its implications for rural society", in Voutsaki and Killen, eds., 38–50.

Halstead, P. and Isaakidou, V. (in press), "Revolutionary secondary products: The development and significance of milking, animal-traction and wool-gathering in later prehistoric Europe and the Near East", in Wilkinson et al., eds.

Halstead, P. and O'Shea, J., eds. (1989), *Bad Year Economics: Cultural Responses to Risk and Uncertainty*. Cambridge.

Hamarneh, B. (1996), "Evergetismo ecclesiastico e laico nella Giordania bizantina ed omayyade nel V–VIII secolo. Testimonianze epigrafiche", *Vetera Christianorum* 33: 57–75.

Hamarneh, B. (2003), *Topografia cristiana ed insediamenti rurali nella Giordania bizantina ed islamica V–IX secolo*. Vatican City.

Hamarneh, B. and Roncalli, A. (2009), "Wadi al-Kharrar – Sapsaphas. Gli scavi archeologici nel luogo del battesimo", in Sonzogni, ed., 194–212.

Hamid, A.A. (1988), "Archaeological remains of the Arabic Hira city", *Bayn al Nahrayn* 17/67–68: 3–13 (in Arabic).

Hamilakis, Y. (1999), "Stories from exile: fragments from the cultural biography of the Parthenon (or 'Elgin') Marbles", *WA* 31/2: 303–321.

Hamilakis, Y. (2003), "The sacred geography of hunting: wild animals, social power and gender in early farming societies", in Kotjabopoulou et al., eds., 239–247.

Hamilakis, Y. (2009), "The 'War on Terror' and the military-archaeology complex: Iraq, ethics, and neo-colonialism", *Archaeologies* 5/1: 39–65.

Hamilakis, Y. and Duke, P., eds. (2007), *Archaeology and Capitalism: From Ethics to Politics*. Walnut Creek.

Hammade, H. and Yamazake, Y. (2006), *Tell al-'Abr (Syria): Ubaid and Uruk Periods*. Paris.

Hammond, P.C. (1979), "Nabataean epigraphy", in Whitcomb and Johnson, eds., 245–247.

Hammond, W.M. (1977), *The Raw and the Chipped: An Analysis of Correlations Between Raw Materials and Tools of a Lithic Industry from Tell el Hesi, Israel*. Ann Arbor.

Hamzehpour, B., Paul, D., and Wiesner, E. (1999), "Views on the structural development of the Zagros simply folded belt in Khuzestan Province, Iran", *Zeitschrift der Deutschen Geologischen Gesellschaft* 150: 167–188.

Hanfmann, G.M.A., ed. (1983), *Sardis from Prehistoric to Roman Times*. Cambridge.

Hanks, B.K. and Linduff, K., eds. (2009), *Social Complexity in Prehistoric Eurasia: Monuments, Metals and Mobility*. Cambridge.

Hannestad, L. (1983), *The Hellenistic Pottery from Failaka with a Survey of Hellenistic Pottery in the Near East*. Aarhus.

Hannestad, L. (1994), "The chronology of the Hellenistic fortress (F5) on Failaka", *Topoi* 4/2: 587–595.

Hannestad, L. (2004), "Seleukos Nikator and Syria", in von Folsach et al., eds., 165–184.

Hannestad, L. (in press a), "A comparative study of the cultural dynamics in two cities of the eastern Seleukid kingdom: Uruk and Ai Khanoum", in Hansen and Lindström, eds.

Hannestad, L. (in press b), "A royal signature landscape: new light on the transformation of Northern Syria after the conquest of Alexander", in Ivantchik, ed.

Hannestad, L. and Potts, D.T. (1990), "Temple architecture in the Seleucid Kingdom", in Bilde et al., eds., 91–124.

Hannibal-Deraniyagala, A.S. (2000), "Beads from Tissamaharama, Sri Lanka", in Taddei and de Marco, eds. 647–651.

Hansen, D.P. (1965), "The relative chronology of Mesopotamia. Part 2. The pottery sequence at Nippur from the Middle Uruk to the end of the Old Babylonian period (3400–1600 BC)", in Ehrich, ed., 201–214.

Hansen, D.P. (1969), "Some remarks on the chronology and style of objects from Byblos", *AJA* 73/3: 281–284.

Hansen, D.P. (2003), "Art of the Akkadian Dynasty", in Aruz, ed., 189–198.

Hansen, M.H.. ed. (2002), *A Comparative Study of Six City-State Cultures: An Investigation Conducted by the Copenhagen Polis Centre*. Copenhagen.

Hansen, S., ed. (2009), *Azerbaijan: Land Between East and West*. Berlin.

Hansen, S., ed. (2010), *Leben auf dem Tell als soziale Praxis*. Bonn.

Hansen, S. and Lindström, G., eds., (in press), *Zwischen Ost und West – neue Forschungen zum antiken Zentralasien*. Mainz.

Hansman, J. (1967), "Charax and the Karkheh", *IrAnt* 7: 21–58.

Hansman, J. (1968), "The problems of Qūmis", *Journal of the Royal Asiatic Society*: 111–39.

Hansman, J. (1975), "An Achaemenian stronghold", in Duchesne-Guillemin, ed., vol. 3, 289–309.

Hansman, J. (1978), "Seleucia and the three Dauraks", *Iran* 16: 154–161.

Hansman, J. (1999), "Fasā II. Tall-e Żaḥḥāk", *EnIr* 9: 389–391.

Hansman, J. (2006), "Isfahan IV, Pre-Islamic period, *EnIr* 13: 635–638.

Hansman, J. and Stronach, D. (1974), "Excavations at Shahr-i Qūmis, 1971", *JRAS*: 8–22.

Hanson, K.C. (1997), "The Galilean fishing economy and the Jesus tradition", *Biblical Theology Bulletin* 27: 99–111.

Harden, D.B. (1956), "Glass and glazes", in Singer, ed., 319.

Harden, D.B. (1968), "Ancient glass, I: Pre-Roman", *Archaeological Journal* 125: 46–72.

Harding, D., Olsen, S. and Jones Bley, K. (2000), "Reviving their fragile technologies: reconstructing perishables from pottery impressions from Botai, Kazakhstan". Unpublished ms.

Hardt, M. and Negri, A. (2004), *Multitude: War and Democracy in the Age of Empire*. New York.

Harlan, J., (1967), "A wild wheat Harvest in Turkey", *Archaeology*, 20/3: 197–201.

Harlan, J. (1995), *The Living Fields: Our Agricultural Heritage*. Cambridge.

Harmankaya, S. (1983), "Pendik Kazisi 1981", *Kazi Sonuçlari Toplantisi* 4: 25–30.

Harmanşah, Ö. (2007), "Upright stones and building narratives: formation of a shared architectural practice in the Ancient Near East", in Cheng and Feldman, eds., 69–99.

Harmanşah, Ö. (2011), "Monuments and memory: Architecture and visual culture in ancient Anatolian history", in Steadman and McMahon, eds., 623–656.

Harmatta, J., ed. (1994), *History of Civilizations of Central Asia*. Vol. II: *The Development of Sedentary and Nomadic Civilizations: 700 BC to AD 250*. Paris.

Harper, P.O. (1978), *The Royal Hunter: Art of the Sasanian Empire*. New York.

Harper, P.O, Aruz, J. and Tallon F., eds. (1992), *The Royal City of Susa: Ancient Near Eastern Treasures in the Louvre*. New York.

Harper, P.O., Klengel-Brandt, E., Aruz, J. and Benzel, K., eds. (1995), *Discoveries at Ashur on the Tigris: Assyrian Origins*. New York.

Harper, P.O. and Pittman, H., eds. (1983), *Art and Archaeology in Honor of Charles Kyrle Wilkinson*. New York.

Harper, R.P., ed. (1995), *Upper Zohar, an Early Byzantine Fort in Palaestina Tertia: Final Report of Excavations in 1985–1986*. Oxford.

Harrak, A. (2001a), "Recent archaeological excavations in Takrit and the discovery of Syriac inscriptions", *Journal of the Canadian Society for Syriac Studies* 1: 11–40.

Harrak, A. (2001b), "Recent archaeological excavations in Takrit and the discovery of Syriac inscriptions", *Hugoye* 4/1: 1–5.

Harris, D.R. (1977), "Alternative pathways toward agriculture", in Reed, ed., 179–243.

Harris, D.R., ed. (1996), *The Origins and Spread of Agriculture and Pastoralism in Eurasia*. Washington, DC.

Harrison, D. (2000), "Recent Australian and New Zealand field work in the Mediterranean region, Jebel Khalid on the Euphrates, excavations", *MeditArch* 13: 123–159.

Harrison, R.M. (1985), *Excavations at Saraçahane in Istanbul I. The Excavations, Structures, Architectoral Decoration, Small Finds, Coins, Bones and Molluscs*. Princeton.

Harrison, T.P. (1993), "Economics with an entrepreneurial spirit: Early Bronze trade with late Predynastic Egypt", *BA* 56: 81–93.

Harrison, T.P. (1995), *Life on the Edge: Human Adaptation and Resilience in the Semi-Arid Highlands of Central Jordan During the Early Bronze Age*. Chicago.

Harrison, T.P. (1997), "Shifting patterns of settlement in the highlands of central Jordan during the Early Bronze Age", *BASOR* 306: 1–37.

Harrison, T.P. (2009a), "Lifting the veil on a 'Dark Age': Ta'yinat and the north Orontes Valley during the Iron Age", in Schloen, ed., 171–184.

Harrison, T.P. (2009b), "Neo-Hittites in the 'Land of Palistin': Renewed investigations at Tell Ta'yinat on the Plain of Antioch", *NEA* 72: 174–89.

Harrison, T.P. (2010), "The Late Bronze/Early Iron Age transition in the north Orontes Valley", in Venturi, ed., 83–102.

Härtel, H., ed. (1981), *South Asian Archaeology 1979*. Berlin.

Hartenberger, B. (2003), *A Study of Craft Specialization and the Organization of Chipped Stone Production at Early Bronze Age Titriş Höyük, Southeastern Turkey*. Boston.

Hartenberger, B., Rosen, S. and Matney, T. (2000), "The Early Bronze Age blade workshop at Titriş Höyük: lithic specialization in an urban context", *NEA* 63/1: 51–58.

Hartmann, U. (2001), *Das palmyrenische Teilreich*. Stuttgart.

Hartnell, T. (2010), "Persepolis in regional context", *The Oriental Institute News and Notes* 205: 15–19.

Hartnell, T. and Asadi, A. (2010), "An archaeological survey of water management in the hinterland of Persepolis", in Matthiae et al., eds., vol. 2, 219–232.

Hartung, U. (2001), *Umm el-Qaab II. Importkeramik aus dem Friedhof U in Abydos (Umm el-Qaab) und die Beziehungen Agyptens zu Vorderasien im 4. Jahrtausend v. Chr.* Mainz.

Hartung, U. (2002), "Imported jars from Cemetery U at Abydos and the relations between Egypt and Canaan in Predynastic times", in van den Brink and Levy, eds., 437–449.

Hartung, U. (2004), "Rescue excavation in the Predynastic Settlement of Maadi", in Hendrickx et al., eds., 337–356.

Harvey, S.A. and Hunter, D.G., eds. (2008), *The Oxford Handbook of Early Christian Studies*. Oxford.

Hashim, S.A. (2007), *Pre-Islamic Ceramics in Saudi Arabia: The Chronological and Typological Study of the Ceramics Technology and Craft Production Discovered in Saudi Arabia, from the Neolithic Period until the Dawn of Islam.* Riyadh.

Haspels, C.H.E. (1971), *The Highlands of Phrygia: Sites and Monuments,* 2 vols. Princeton.

Hassan, F.A. (1998), "Memorabilia, archaeological materiality and national identity in Egypt", in Meskell, ed., 200–216.

Hassig, R. (1985), *Trade, Tribute, and Transportation: The Sixteenth-Century Political Economy of the Valley of Mexico.* Norman.

Hauptmann, A. (1985), *5000 Jahre Kupfer in Oman. Band 1: Die Entwicklung der Kupfermetallurgie vom 3. Jahrtausend bis zur Neuzeit.* Bochum.

Hauptmann, A. (2007), *The Archaeometallurgy of Copper: Evidence from Faynan, Jordan.* Heidelberg/Berlin/New York.

Hauptmann, A., Begemann, F., Schmitt-Strecker, S. and Palmieri, A. (2002), "Chemical composition and lead isotopy of metal objects from the 'Royal' tomb and other related finds at Arslantepe, eastern Anatolia", *Paléorient* 28/2: 43–69.

Hauptmann, A., Busz, R., Klein, S., Vettel, A. and Werthmann, R. (2001), "The roots of glazing techniques: copper metallurgy?", *Paléorient* 26/2: 113–129.

Hauptmann, A., Pernicka, E., Rehren, T. and Yalçin, Ü., eds. (1999), *The Beginnings of Metallurgy.* Bochum.

Hauptmann, H. (1991–2), "Nevali Çori: Eine Siedlung des akeramischen Neolithikums am mittleren Euphrat", *Nürnberger Blätter zur Archäologie* 8: 15–33.

Hauptmann, H. (1993), "Ein Kultgebäude in Nevali Çori", in Frangipane et al., eds., 37–69.

Hauptmann, H. (2000), "Ein frühneolithisches Kultbild aus Kommagene", in Wagner, ed., 5–9.

Hauptmann, H. and Pernicka, E. (2004), *Die Metallindustrie Mesopotamiens von den Anfängen bis zum 2. Jahrtausend v. Chr.* Rahden.

Hauser, S.R. (1994), *Chronologische und historisch-politische Untersuchungen zur östlichen Ǧazira in vorislamischer Zeit.* Berlin.

Hauser, S.R. (1998), "Hatra und das Königreich der Araber", in Wiesehöfer, ed., 493–528.

Hauser, S.R. (1999), "Babylon in arsakidischer Zeit", in Renger, ed., 207–239.

Hauser, S.R. (2000), "Ecological borders and political frontiers: the eastern Jazirah in the later Preislamic period", in Milano et al., eds., 187–201.

Hauser, S.R. (2001), "'Greek in subject and style, but a little distorted': Zum Verhältnis von Orient und Okzident in der Altertumswissenschaft", in Altekamp et al., eds., 83–104.

Hauser, S.R. (2005), "Die ewigen Nomaden? Bemerkungen zu Herkunft, Militär, Staatsaufbau und nomadischen Traditionen der Arsakiden", in Meissner et al., eds., 163–208.

Hauser, S.R., ed. (2006a), *Die Sichtbarkeit von Nomaden und saisonaler Besiedlung in der Archäologie: Multidisziplinäre Annäherungen an ein methodisches Problem.* Halle.

Hauser, S.R. (2006b), "Was there no paid standing army? A fresh look on military and political institutions in the Arsacid Empire", in Mode and Tubach, eds., 295–319.

Hauser, S.R. (2007a), "Veh Ardashīr and the identification of the ruins at al-Madāin", in Hagedorn and Shalem, eds., 461–489.

Hauser, S.R. (2007b), "Tempel für den palmyrenischen Bel", in Rollinger et al., eds., 228–255.
Hauser, S.R. (2011), "Assur und sein Umland in der Arsakidenzeit", in Renger, ed., 114–148.
Hauser, S.R. and Tucker, D.J. (2009), "The final onslaught: the Sasanian siege of Hatra", *ZOA* 2: 106–139.
Hausleiter, A. (2010a), "The oasis of Tayma", in al-Ghabban et al., eds., 218–239.
Hausleiter, A. (2010b), "Early Iron Age pottery", in al-Ghabban et al., eds., 240.
Hausleiter, A. (2010c), "Late Iron Age pottery", in al-Ghabban et al., eds., 242.
Hausleiter, A. (2010d), "106. Head of a royal statue of the Lihyanite dynasty", in al-Ghabban et al., eds., 258–259.
Hausleiter, A. (2010e), "107. Fragment of a statue", in al-Ghabban et al., eds., 260.
Hausleiter, A. (2010f), *Neuassyrische Keramik im Kerngebiet Assyriens*. Wiesbaden.
Hausleiter, A. (in press), "Divine representations at Tayma", in Sachet and Robin, eds.
Hausleiter, A., Kerner, S. and Müller-Neuhof, B., eds. (2002), *Material Culture and Mental Spheres*. Münster.
Hausleiter, A. and Reiche, A., eds. (1999), *Iron Age Pottery in Northern Mesopotamia, Northern Syria and South-Eastern Anatolia*. Münster.
Hausleiter, A. and Schaudig, H. (2010a), "100. Stele of Nabonidus, king of Babylon", in al-Ghabban et al., eds., 252–3.
Hausleiter, A. and Schaudig, H. (2010b), "101. Disc-shaped object with inscription of King Nabonidus", in al-Ghabban et al., eds., 253.
Haussperger, M. (1991), *Die Einführungsszene: Entwicklung eines mesopotamischen Motivs von der altakkadischen bis zum Ende der altbabylonischen Zeit*. Munich/Vienna.
Hawkins, J.D. (1976–80a), "Irqata", *RlA* 5: 165–166.
Hawkins, J.D. (1976–80b), "Karkamiš", *RlA* 5: 426–446.
Hawkins, J.D. (1986), "Writing in Anatolia: imported and indigenous systems", *WA* 17/3: 363–367.
Hawkins, J.D. (1988), "Kuzi-Tešub and the 'Great Kings' of Karkamiš", *AnSt* 38: 99–108.
Hawkins, J.D. (1995), *The Hieroglyphic Inscription of the Sacred Pool Complex at Hattuša (Südburg)*. Wiesbaden.
Hawkins, J.D. (1998), "Tarkasnawa king of Mira: 'Tarkondemos' Boğazköy sealings and Karabel", *AnSt* 48: 1–31.
Hawkins, J.D. (2000), *Corpus of Luwian Hieroglyphic Inscriptions*, vol. 1. Berlin.
Hawkins, J.D. (2002), "Anatolia: the end of the Hittite Empire and after", in Braun-Holzinger and Matthäus, eds., 143–51.
Hawkins, J.D. (2003), "Scripts and texts", in Melchert, ed., 128–169.
Hawkins, J.D. (2009), "Cilicia, the Amuq, and Aleppo: new light in a Dark Age", *NEA* 72: 174–173.
Hayden, B., ed. (1979), *Lithic Use-Wear Analysis*. New York.
Hazbun, W. (2008), *Beaches, Ruins, Resorts: The Politics of Tourism in the Arab World*. Minneapolis.
Hazenbos, J. (2003), *The Organization of the Anatolian Local Cults During the Thirteenth Century BC: An Appraisal of the Hittite Cult Inventories*. Leiden.
Hayes, J.W. (1992), *Excavations at Saraçahane in Istanbul II. The Pottery*. Princeton.
Healey, E. (2006), "Lithics", *Anatolica* 32: 94–99.

Healey, E. (2010), "Ubaid lithics revisited: their significance for the interpretation of Ubaid society", in Carter and Philip, eds., 181–200.
Hecker, H. (1975), *The Faunal Analysis of the Primary Food Animals from Pre-Pottery Neolithic Beidha (Jordan)*. New York.
Hedges, R.E.M. (1982), "Early glazed pottery and faience in Mesopotamia", in Wertime and Wertime, eds., 93–103.
Heidorn, L.A. (1991), "The Saite and Persian period forts at Dorginarti", in Davies, ed., 205–219.
Heilmeyer, W.-D. and Eule, J.C., eds. (2004), *Illegale Archäologie? Internationale Konferenz über zukünftige Probleme bei unerlaubtem Antikentransfer*. Berlin.
Heim, S. (1992), "Royal and religious structures and their decoration", in Harper et al., eds., 123–127.
Heimpel, W. (2009), *Workers and Construction Work at Garšana*. Bethesda.
Heimpel, W. (n.d.), "Records of counts of trees in Garshana and Zabala".
Heinrich, E. (1982), *Die Tempel und Heiligtümer im alten Mesopotamien*. Berlin.
Heinrich, E. (1984), *Die Paläste im alten Mesopotamien*. Berlin.
Heinz, M. and Feldman, M.H., eds. (2007), *Representations of Political Power: Case Histories from Times of Change and Dissolving Order in the Ancient Near East*. Winona Lake.
Helbaek, H. (1959), "Notes on the evolution and history of Linum", *Kuml 1959*: 103–120.
Helbaek, H. (1969), "Plant collecting, dry farming and irrigation in prehistoric Deh Luran", in Hole et al., eds., 383–426.
Helbaek, H. (1972), "Samarran irrigation agriculture at Choga Mami", *Iraq* 34: 35–48.
Helck, W. (1971), *Die Beziehungen Ägyptens zu Vorderasien*. Wiesbaden.
Helck, W. (1973), "Die Lage der Stadt Tunip", *UF* 5: 286–288.
Hellyer, P. and Ziolkowski, M.C., eds. (2005), *Proceedings of the 1st Annual Symposium on Recent Palaeontological & Archaeological Discoveries in the Emirates, Al Ain 2003*. Al Ain.
Helmer, D. (1992), *La Domestication des animaux par les hommes préhistoriques*. Paris.
Helmer, D. (2008), "Révision de la faune de Çafer Höyük (Malatya, Turquie): apports des méthodes de l'analyse des mélanges et de l'analyse de Kernel à la mise en évidence de la domestication", in Vila et al., eds., 169–196.
Helmer, D. and Gourichon, L. (2008), "Premières données sur les modalités de subsistance à Tell Aswad (Syrie, PPNB Moyen et Récent, Néolithique Céramique Ancien). Fouilles 2001–2005", in Vila et al., eds., 119–151.
Helmer, D., Gourichon, L., Monchot, H., Peters, J. and Sana Segui, M. (2005), "Identifying early domestic cattle from Pre-Pottery Neolithic sites on the Euphrates using sexual dimorphism", in Vigne et al., eds., 86–95.
Helmer, D., Gourichon, L. and Stordeur, D. (2004), "À l'aube de la domestication animale: imaginaire et symbolisme animal dans les premièrs sociétés néolithiques du nord du Proche-Orient", *Anthropozoologica* 39/1: 143–163.
Helmer, D., Gourichon, L. and Vila, E. (2007), "The development of the exploitation of products from Capra and Ovis (meat, milk and fleeces) from the PPNB to the Early Bronze in the northern Near East (8700 to 2000 BC cal.)", *Anthropozoologica* 42: 41–69.

Helms, S.W. (1981), *Jawa: Lost City of the Black Desert*. Ithaca.
Helms, S.W. (1982), "Paleo-Bedouin and transmigrant urbanism", in Hadidi, ed., 97–113.
Helms, S.W. (1997), *Excavations at Old Kandahar in Afghanistan 1976–1978*. Oxford.
Heltzer, M. (1978), *Goods, Prices and the Organization of Trade in Ugarit: Marketing and Transportation in the Eastern Mediterranean in the Second Half of the II Millennium BCE*. Wiesbaden.
Heltzer, M. (1979), "Royal economy in ancient Ugarit", in Lipiński, ed., 459–496.
Helwing, B. (2004), "Tracking the Proto-Elamite on the central Iranian Plateau", in Malek Shahmirzadi, ed., 45–58.
Helwing, B. (2011), "Conclusions: The Arisman copper production in a wider context", in Vatandoust et al., eds., 523–531.
Helwing, B. (in press), "Some thoughts on the mode of culture change in the 4th millennium BC Iranian highlands", in Petrie, ed.
Helwing, B. and Chegini, N.N. (2011), "Archaeological survey in the hinterland of Arismān and Kāšān", in Vatandoust et al., eds., 421–483.
Helwing, B., Makki, M. and Seyedin, M. (2010), "Prehistoric settlement patterns in Darre-ye Bolaghi, Fars, Iran: Results of archaeological and geoarchaeological fieldwork", in Matthiae et al., eds., 233–247.
Helwing, B. and Seyedin, M. (2009), "The Achaemenid period occupation at Tang-i Bulaghi site 73", *ARTA* 2009.0006.
Henderson, J. (1985), "The raw materials of early glass production", *OJA* 4: 267–291.
Henderson, J. (1997), "Scientific analysis of glass and glaze from Tell Brak and its archaeological implications", in Oates, Oates and McDonald, eds., 94–100.
Henderson, J. (2000), *The Science and Archaeology of Materials: An Investigation of Inorganic Materials*. London.
Hendrickx, S. and Bavay, L. (2002), "The relative chronological position of Predynastic and Early Dynastic tombs with objects imported from the Near East and the nature of interregional contacts", in van den Brink and Levy, eds., 58–80.
Hendrickx, S., Friedman, R.F., Ciałowicz, K.M. and Chłodnicki, M., eds. (2004), *Egypt at its Origin: Studies in Memory of Barbara Adams*. Leuven/Paris/Dudley.
Henkelman, W.F.M. (1995–6), "The royal Achaemenid crown", *AMI* 28: 275–293.
Henkelman, W.F.M. (2003a), "Persians, Medes and Elamites: acculturation in the Neo-Elamite period", in Lanfranchi et al., eds., 181–231.
Henkelman, W.F.M. (2003b), "Defining 'Neo-Elamite history'", *BiOr* 60: 251–263.
Henkelman, W.F.M. (2003c), "An Elamite memorial: the šumar of Cambyses and Hystaspes", in Henkelman and Kuhrt, eds., 101–172.
Henkelman, W.F.M. (2003d), "'Dit paleis dat ik in Susa bouwde.' Bouwinscriptie(s) van koning Dareios I (DSf, DSz, DSaa)", in Demarée and Veenhof, eds., 373–386.
Henkelman, W.F.M. (2007), "Ruhurater", *RlA* 11/5–6: 449.
Henkelman, W.F.M. (2008a), *The Other Gods Who are: Studies in Elamite-Iranian Acculturation Based on the Persepolis Fortification Texts*. Leiden. [ch. 39? 50??]
Henkelman, W.F.M. (2008b), "From Gabae to Taoce: the geography of the central administrative province", in Briant et al., eds., 303–316.
Henkelman, W.F.M. (2010), "'Consumed before the King.' The table of Darius, that of Irdabama and Irtaštuna, and that of his satrap, Karkiš", in Jacobs and Rollinger, eds., 667–775.

Henkelman, W.F.M. (2011), "Parnakka's feast: šip in Pārsa and Elam", in Álvarez-Mon and Garrison, eds., 89–166.

Henkelman, W.F.M. (in press a), "Cyrus the Persian and Darius the Elamite, a case of mistaken identity", in Rollinger and Truschnegg, eds.

Henkelman, W.F.M. (in press b), "Tāravā", RlA.

Henkelman, W.F.M. (in press c), "Tirazziš", RlA.

Henkelman, W.F.M. (in press d), "Irdabama's Perspective: Šullaggi between Elam and Persia".

Henkelman, W.F.M. (in press e), "Takht-e Rustam", RlA.

Henkelman, W.F.M., Jones, C.E. and Stolper, M.W. (2006), "Achaemenid Elamite administrative tablets, 2: the Qaṣr-i Abu Naṣr Tablet", ARTA 2006.003.

Henkelman, W.F.M. and Kuhrt, A. (2003), *Achaemenid History XIII: A Persian Perspective: Essays in Memory of Heleen Sancisi-Weerdenburg*. Leiden.

Hennessy, B. (1967), *The Foreign Relations of Palestine During the Early Bronze Age*. London.

Henrickson, E.F. (1981), "Non-religious residential settlement patterning in the late Early Dynastic of the Diyala region", *Mesopotamia* 16: 43–140.

Henrickson, E.F. (1982), "Functional analysis of elite residences in the late Early Dynastic of the Diyala region", *Mesopotamia* 17: 5–34.

Henrickson, E.F. (1994), "The outer limits: settlements and economic strategies in the central Zagros highlands during the Uruk era", in Stein and Rothman, eds., 85–102.

Henrickson, E.F. and Thuesen, I., eds. (1989), *Upon This Foundation: The 'Ubaid Reconsidered*. Copenhagen.

Henrickson, R.C. (1994), "Continuity and discontinuity in the ceramic tradition at Gordion during the Iron Age", in Çilingiroğlu and French, eds., 95–129.

Henrickson, R.C. (2005), "The local potter's craft at Phrygian Gordion", in Kealhofer, ed., 124–135.

Henrickson, R.C. and Voigt, M.M. (1998), "The Early Iron Age at Gordion: the evidence from the Yassihöyük stratigraphic sequence", in Tuna et al., eds., 79–106.

Henry, D.O. (1974), "The utilization of the microburin technique in the Levant", *Paléorient* 2: 389–398.

Henry, D.O. (1989), *From Foraging to Agriculture: The Levant at the End of the Ice Age*. Philadelphia.

Henry, D.O. (1995), *Prehistoric Cultural Ecology and Evolution: Insights from Southern Jordan*. New York.

Henry, D.O., Cordova, C., White, J.J., Dean, R.M., Beaver, J.E., Ekstrom, H., Kadowaki, S., McCorriston, J., Nowell, A. and Scott-Cummings, L. (2003), "The Early Neolithic site of Ayn Abû Nukhayla, southern Jordan", *BASOR* 330: 1–30.

Henton, E. (2010), *Herd Management and the Social Role of Herding at Neolithic Çatalhöyük: An Investigation Using Oxygen Isotope and Dental Microwear Evidence in Sheep*. London.

Herling, A. and Salles, J.-F. (1993), "Hellenistic cemeteries in Bahrain", in Finkbeiner, ed., 161–182.

Hermon, S. (2008), *Socio-Economic Aspects of Chalcolithic (4500–3500 BC) Societies in the Southern Levant: A Lithic Perspective*. Oxford.

Herrmann, G. (1968), "Lapis lazuli: the early phases of its trade", *Iraq* 30/2: 1–54.

Herrmann, G. (1977), *The Iranian Revival*. Oxford.

Herrmann, G. (1983), *The Sasanian Rock Reliefs at Bishapur, vol. 3. Bishapur I, The Investiture/Triumph of Shapur I and Sarab-i Bahram, Bahram II Enthroned; The Rock Relief at Tang-i Qandil*. Berlin.

Herrmann, G., ed. (1996), *The Furniture of Western Asia Ancient and Traditional*. Mainz.

Herrmann, G., ed. (1999), *Monuments of Merv: Traditional Buildings of the Karakum*. London.

Herrmann, G. (2000), "Ivory carving of first millennium workshops, traditions and diffusion", in Uehlinger, ed., 267–282.

Herrmann, G. (2005), "Naming, defining, explaining: A view from Nimrud", in Suter and Uehlinger, eds., 11–21.

Herrmann, G. (2008), "The ivories from Nimrud", in Curtis et al., eds. 225–232.

Herrmann, G. and Curtis, J. (2002), "Sasanian rock reliefs", *EnIr* online.

Herrmann, G. and Moorey, P.R.S. (1980–3), "Lapis lazuli", *RlA* 6: 489–492.

Hershkovitz, I., ed. (1989), *People and culture in change*. Oxford.

Herveux, L. (2007), *Le Phénomène agricole à l'âge du Bronze au Proche-Orient (3000–1200 av. J.C.)*. Paris.

Herzfeld, E.E. (1926), "Reisebericht", *ZDMG* 80: 225–284.

Herzfeld, E.E. (1929), "Prehistoric Persia I. A Neolithic settlement at Persepolis. Remarkable new discoveries", *ILN* 174: 892–893.

Herzfeld, E.E. (1929–30a), "Bericht über die Ausgrabungen von Pasargadae 1928", *AMI* 1: 4–16.

Herzfeld, E.E. (1929–30b), "Rapport sur l'état actuel des ruines de Persépolis et propositions pour leur conservation", *AMI* 1: 17–40.

Herzfeld, E.E. (1930), *Die Ausgrabungen von Samarra V: Die vorgeschichtlichen Töpfereien von Samarra*. Berlin.

Herzfeld, E.E. (1934), "Recent discoveries at Persepolis", *JRAS*: 226–232.

Herzfeld, E.E. (1936), *Archaeological History of Iran*. Oxford.

Herzfeld, E.E. (1941), *Iran in the Ancient East*. London and New York.

Hess, K., Hauptmann, A., Wright, H.T. and Whallon, R. (1998), "Evidence of fourth millennium BC silver production at Fatmali-Kalecik, East Anatolia", in Rehren, Hauptmann & Muhly, eds., 57–68.

Hessari, M. (2005), *Culture Around Halil Roud and Jiroft: The Catalogue of Exhibition of Select Restituted Objects*. Tehran.

Hesse, A. (1979), "Reconnaissance d'ensemble du Palais du Chaour par la méthode des résistivités électriques", *DAFI* 10: 137–144.

Hesse, A. (2010), "La prospection électrique des radiers achéménides", in Perrot, ed., 146–159.

Hesse, B. and Wapnish, P. (1998), "Pig use and abuse in the ancient Levant: ethnoreligious boundary-building with swine", in Nelson, ed., 123–136.

Hesse, B. and Wapnish, P. (2002), "An archaeozoological perspective on the cultural use of mammals in the Levant", in Collins, ed., 457–491.

Heun, M., Schäfer-Pregl, R., Klawan, D., Castagna, R., Accerbi, M., Borghi, B. and Salamini, F. (1997), "Site of einkorn wheat domestication identified by DNA fingerprinting", *Science* 278: 1312–1314.

Heyvaert, V.M.A. and Baeteman. C. (2007), "Holocene sedimentary evolution and palaeocoastlines of the lower Khuzestan plain (SW-Iran)", *Marine Geology* 242/1: 83–108.

Heyvaert, V.M.A. and Baeteman, C. (2008), "A middle to late Holocene avulsion history of the Euphrates River: a case study from Tell ed-Der, southern Mesopotamia", *QSR* 27: 2401–2410.

Hiebert, F.T. (1994a), *Origins of the Bronze Age Oasis Civilization in Central Asia*. Cambridge.

Hiebert, F.T. (1994b), "Production evidence for the origins of the Oxus Civilization", *Antiquity* 68: 372–387.

Hiebert, F.T. (1998), "Central Asians on the Iranian Plateau: a model for Indo-Iranian expansionism", in Mair, ed., 148–161.

Hiebert, F.T. and Cambon, P., eds. (2008), *Afghanistan: Hidden Treasures from the National Museum, Kabul*. Washington, DC.

Hiebert, F.T., Kurbansakhatov, K. and Schmidt, H. (2003), *A Central Asian Village at the Dawn of Civilization: Excavations at Anau, Turkmenistan*. Philadelphia.

Hiebert, F.T. and Lamberg-Karlovsky, C.C. (1992), "Central Asia and the Indo-Iranian borderlands", *Iran* 30: 1–15.

Hiebert, F.T. and Moore, K.M. (2004), "A small steppe site near Gonur", in Kosarev et al., eds., 294–302.

Hijara, I. (1978), "Three new graves at Arpachiyah", *WA* 10: 125–128.

Hikade, T. (1998), "Economic aspects of the New Kingdom: the expeditions to the copper mines of the Sinai", *Bulletin of the Australian Centre for Egyptology* 9: 43–52.

Hikade, T. (2001), *Das Expeditionswesen im ägyptischen Neuen Reich: Ein Beitrag zu Rohstoffversorgung und Außenhandel*. Heidelberg.

Hikade, T. (2007), "Crossing the frontier into the desert: Egyptian expeditions to the Sinai Peninsula", *AWE* 6: 1–22.

Hikade, T. (2009), "The lithic industry at Tall Hujayrat al-Ghuzlan", in Khalil and Schmidt, eds., 233–245.

Hill, J.A. (2004), *Cylinder Seal Glyptic in Predynastic Egypt and Neighboring Regions*. Oxford.

Hill, J.B. (2004), "Time, scale and interpretation: 10,000 years of land use on the Transjordan plateau amid multiple contexts of change", in Athanassopoulis and Wandsnider, eds., 125–142.

Hill, J.N., ed. (1977), *Explanation of Prehistoric Change*. Albuquerque.

Hillman, G.C. (2000), "The plant food economy of Abu Hureyra 1 and 2", in Moore et al., eds., 327–398.

Hillman, G.C. and Davies, M.S. (1990), "Measured domestication rates in wild wheats and barley under primitive cultivation, and their archaeological implications", *JWP* 4: 157–222.

Hillman, G.C., Hedges, R., Moore, A., Colledge, S. and Pettitt, P. (2001), "New evidence of Late Glacial cereal cultivation at Abu Hureyra on the Euphrates", *The Holocene* 11/4: 383–393.

Hilprecht, H.V. (1903), *Explorations in Bible Lands During the 19th Century*. Edinburgh.

Hintze, A. (1998), "The Avesta in the Parthian period", in Wiesehöfer, ed., 147–161.

Hinz, W. (1967), "Elams Vertrag mit Narām-Sîn von Agade", *ZA* 58: 66–96.

Hinz, W. (1971), "Persia, c.2400–1800 BC", *CAH* 1/2: 644–680.

Hinz, W. (1973), *The Lost World of Elam*. New York.

Hinz, W. (1975), "Zu den Mörsern und Stösseln aus Persepolis", in Duchesne-Guillemin, ed., vol. 1, 371–385.

Hirsch, H. (1963), "Die Inschriften der Könige von Agade", *AfO* 20: 1–82.

Hirsch, H., ed. (1982), *Vorträge gehalten auf der 28. Rencontre Assyriologique Internationale in Wien*. Horn.

Hirsch, U. (1992), "The fabric of deities and kings", *Hali* 58: 104–111.

Hirschfeld, Y. (1990), "List of Byzantine monasteries in the Judean Desert", in Bottini et al., eds., 1–90.

Hirschfeld, Y. (1992), *The Judean Desert Monasteries in the Byzantine Period*. New Haven.

Hirschfeld, Y. (1997), "Farms and villages in Byzantine Palestine", *DOP* 51: 33–71.

Hirschfeld, Y. (2004), "The monasteries of Gaza: an archaeological review", in Bitton-Ashkelony and Kofsky, eds., 61–88.

Hirschfeld, Y. (2006), "The monasteries of Palestine in the Byzantine period", in Limor and Stroumsa, eds., 401–419.

Hmayakian, C.G. (1990), *Gosudarstvenaya Religiya Vanskovo Tsarstva*. Yerevan.

Hobsbawm, E. (1983), "Introduction: inventing traditions", in Hobsbawm and Ranger, eds., 1–14.

Hobsbawm, E. and Ranger, T., eds. (1983), *The Invention of Traditions*. Cambridge.

Hoch, J.E. (1995), "Egyptian hieratic writing in the Byblos pseudo-hieroglyphic stele L1", *JARCE* 32: 59–65.

Hockmann, D. (2010), *Gräber und Grüfte in Assur I. Von der zweiten Hälfte des 3. bis zur Mitte des 2. Jahrtausends*. Wiesbaden.

Hodder, I. (1990), *The Domestication of Europe: Structure and Contingency in Neolithic Societies*. Oxford.

Hodder, I. (2001a), "Symbolism and the origins of agriculture in the Near East", *CAJ* 11: 107–111.

Hodder, I., ed. (2001b), *Archaeological Theory Today*. Cambridge.

Hodder, I., ed. (2004), *Inhabiting Çatalhöyük: Reports from the 1995–1999 Seasons*. Cambridge.

Hodder, I., ed. (2005), *Changing Materialities at Çatalhöyük: Reports from the 1995–99 Seasons*. Cambridge and London.

Hodder, I. (2006a), *The Leopard's Tale: Revealing the Mysteries of Çatalhöyük*. London.

Hodder, I., ed. (2006b), *Çatalhöyük Perspectives*. Cambridge.

Hodder, I., ed. (2010), *Religion in the Emergence of Civilisation*. Cambridge.

Hodder, I., Isaac, G. and Hammond, N., eds. (1981), *Pattern of the Past: Studies in Honour of David Clarke*. Cambridge.

Hodder, I., and Meskell, L., (2010), "The symbolism of Çatalhöyük in its regional context", in Hodder ed., 32–72.

Hodder, I. and Meskell, L. (2011), "A 'curious and sometimes a trifle macabre artistry': some aspects of the symbolism in Neolithic Turkey", *CA* 52/2: 235–264.

Hodder, I. and Pels, P. (2010), "History houses: a new interpretation of architectural elaboration at Çatalhöyük", in Hodder ed., 163–186.

Hoepfner, W., ed. (1999a), *Geschichte des Wohnens, 5000 v.Chr.–500 n.Chr. Vorgeschichte – Frühgeschichte – Antike*. Stuttgart.

Hoepfner, W. (1999b), "Antiochia die Grosse und Epiphaneia", in Hoepfner, ed., 472–491.
Hofenk de Graaff, J. (2004), *The Colourful Past: Origins, Chemistry and Identification of Natural Dyestuffs*. London.
Hoffner, H.A. (1990), *Hittite Myths*. Atlanta.
Hoffner, H.A. (1974), *Alimenta Hethaeorum: Food Production in Hittite Asia Minor*. New Haven.
Hoffner, H.A. (1997a), *The Laws of the Hittites: A Critical Edition*, Leiden, New York and Cologne.
Hoffner, H.A. (1997b), "Hittite laws", in Roth, ed., 213–247.
Hoffner, H.A. (1998), *Hittite Myths*, 2nd edn. Atlanta.
Hoffner, H.A. (2009), *Letters from the Hittite Kingdom*. Atlanta.
Hoffner, H.A. and Beckman, G.A., eds. (1986), *Kanissuwar: A Tribute to Hans G. Güterbock*. Chicago.
Hogarth, D.G. (1904), *The Penetration of Arabia*. London.
Hogarth, D.G. (1914), *Carchemish: Report on the Excavations at Djerablus on Behalf of the British Museum. Part 1, Introductory*. London.
Højlund, F. (1990), "Date honey production in the mid 2nd millennium BC: steps in the technological evolution of the *madbasa*", *Paléorient* 16/1: 77–86.
Højlund, F. and Andersen, H.H. (1994), *Qala'at al-Bahrain, vol. 1. The Northern City Wall and the Islamic Fortress*. Aarhus.
Højlund, F. and Andersen, H.H. (2004), *The Barbar Temples*, vol. 1. Aarhus.
Højte, J.M. (2005), "The archaeological evidence for fish processing in the Black Sea region", in Bekker-Nielsen, ed., 133–160.
Hole, F. (1962), "Archaeological survey and excavation in Iran, 1961", *Science* 137: 524–526.
Hole, F., ed. (1969), *Preliminary Reports of the Rice University Project in Iran 1968–1969*. Houston.
Hole, F., ed. (1977), *Studies in the Archaeological History of the Deh Luran Plain: The Excavation of Chagha Sefid*. Ann Arbor.
Hole, F. (1980), "Archaeological surveys in Southwest Asia", *Paléorient* 6: 21–44.
Hole, F. (1983), "Symbols of religion and social organization at Susa", in Young et al., eds., 315–333.
Hole, F. (1984), "Analysis of structure and design in prehistoric ceramics", *WA* 15: 326–347.
Hole, F. (1985), "The organization of Susiana society: periodization of site distributions", *Paléorient* 11/2: 21–24.
Hole, F., ed., (1987a), *The Archaeology of Western Iran: Settlement and Society from Prehistory to the Islamic Conquest*. Washington, DC.
Hole, F. (1987b), "Archaeology of the Village Period", in Hole, ed., 29–78.
Hole, F. (1987c), "Settlement and society in the Village Period", in Hole, ed., 79–105.
Hole, F. (1989), "Patterns of burial in the fifth millennium", in Henrickson and Thuesen, eds., 149–180.
Hole, F. (1990), "Cemetery or mass grave? Reflections on Susa I", in Vallat, ed., pp. 1–14.

Hole, F. (2000), "Is size important? Function and hierarchy in Neolithic settlements", in Kuijt, ed., 191–209.

Hole, F. and Flannery, K.V. (1968), "The prehistory of southwestern Iran: a preliminary report", *PPS* 22: 147–206.

Hole, F., Flannery, K.V. and Neely, J.A., eds. (1969), *Prehistory and Human Ecology of the Deh Luran Plain: An Early Village Sequence from Khuzistan, Iran*. Ann Arbor.

Holmes, D.L. (1989), *The Predynastic Lithic Industries of Upper Egypt*. Oxford.

Holum, K.G. and Hohfelder, R.L. (1988), *King Herod's Dream: Caesarea on the Sea*. New York.

Honeychurch, W. and Amartuvshin, C. (2007), "Hinterlands, urban centers, and mobile settings: the 'New' Old World archaeology from the Eurasian Steppe", *Asian Perspectives* 46: 36–64.

Hongo, H. (1996), *Patterns of Animal Husbandry in Central Anatolia from the Second Millennium BC through the Middle Ages: Faunal Remains from Kaman-kalehöyük, Turkey*. Cambridge.

Hongo, H. (1997), "Patterns of animal husbandry, environment, and ethnicity in Central Anatolia in the Ottoman Empire period: faunal remains from Islamic layers at Kaman-kalehöyük", *Japan Review* 8: 275–307.

Hongo, H. (1998), "Patterns of animal husbandry in central Anatolia in the second and first millennia BC: faunal remains from Kaman-kalehöyük, Turkey", in Buitenhuis et al., eds., 255–275.

Hongo, H., Meadow, R.H., Öksüz, B. and Gülçin, I. (2004), "Animal exploitation at Çayönü Tepesi, southeastern Anatolia/Güneydogu Anadolu, Çayönü Tepesi'nde hayvanlardan yararlanılması", *TÜBA-AR* 7: 107–119.

Hongo, H., Meadow, R.H., Öksuz, B. and Ilgezdi, G. (2002), "The process of ungulate domestication in Prepottery Neolithic Çayönü, southeastern Turkey", in Buitenhuis et al., eds., 153–165.

Hopkins, C. (1972), *Topography and Architecture of Seleucia on the Tigris*. Ann Arbor.

Hopkins, C. (1979), *The Discovery of Dura-Europos*. New Haven and London.

Hopkins, D.C., ed. (1996), *Across the Anatolian Plateau: Readings in the Archaeology of Ancient Turkey*. Boston.

Hopkins, D.C., ed. (2002), *Across the Anatolian Plateau*. Boston.

Hoppe, L.J. (1994), *The Synagogues and Churches of Ancient Palestine*. Collegeville.

Horn, C.B. (2003), "Peter the Iberian and Palestinian anti-Chalcedonian monasticism in fifth- and early sixth-century Gaza", *ARAM* 15: 109–128.

Horn, C.B. (2006), *Asceticism and Christological Controversy in Fifth-Century Palestine: The Career of Peter the Iberian*. Oxford.

Horn, C.B. and Phenix, R.R., Jr. (2008), *John Rufus: The Lives of Peter the Iberian, Theodosius of Jerusalem, and the Monk Romanus*. Atlanta.

Horwitz, L.K. and Ducos, P. (1998), "An investigation into the origins of domestic sheep in the southern Levant", in Buitenhuis et al., eds., 80–94.

Horwitz, L.K. and Ducos, P. (2005), "Counting cattle: trends in Neolithic Bos frequencies from the southern Levant", *Revue de Paléobiologie* 10: 209–224.

Horwitz, L.K., Tchernov, E., Ducos, P., Becker, C., von den Driesch, A., Martin, L. and Garrard, A. (1999), "Animal domestication in the southern Levant", *Paléorient* 25: 63–80.

Hötzl, H. and Zötl, J.G. (1984), "Hydrogeology", in Jado and Zötl, eds., 246–274.
Houghton, A. and Lorber, C. (2002), *Seleucid Coins. A Comprehensive Catalogue, Part I. Seleucus I through Antiochus III*. Lancaster/London.
Houlihan, P.F. (2002), "Animals in Egyptian art and hieroglyphs", in Collins, ed., 97–143.
Hours, F., Aurenche, O., Cauvin, J., Cauvin, M.-C., Copeland, L. and Sanlaville, P. (1994), *Atlas des sites du Proche-Orient (14000–5700 BP)*. Lyon/Paris.
Houtkamp, J. (1992), "Some remarks on fire altars of the Achaemenid period", in Kellens, ed., 23–48.
Hovers, E., Ilani, S., Bar-Yosef, O. and Vandermeersch, B. (2003), "An early case of color symbolism: ochre use by modern humans in Qafzeh Cave", *CA* 44/4: 491–522.
Howland, H. (1958), *The Athenian Agora: Results of Excavations Conducted by the American School of Classical Studies at Athens, vol. 4: Greek Lamps and their Survival*. Princeton.
Hoyland, R. (2009), "Late Roman Provincia Arabia, Monophysite monks and Arab tribes: a problem of centre and periphery", *Semitica et Classica* 2: 117–139.
Hritz, C. (2004), "The hidden landscape of southern Mesopotamia", *Akkadica* 125: 93–106.
Hritz, C. and Wilkinson, T.J. (2006), "Using shuttle radar topography to map ancient water channels in Mesopotamia", *Antiquity* 80: 415–424.
Hrouda, B. (1971), *Vorderasien I. Mesopotamien, Babylonien, Iran und Anatolien*. Munich.
Hrouda, B. (1977), *Isin – Išān Baḥrīyāt I. Die Ergebnisse der Ausgrabungen 1973–1974*. Munich.
Hrouda, B. (1981), *Isin – Išān Baḥrīyāt II. Die Ergebnisse der Ausgrabungen 1975–1978*. Munich.
Hrouda, B. (1987), *Isin – Išān Baḥrīyāt III. Die Ergebnisse der Ausgrabungen 1983–1984*. Munich.
Hrouda, B., ed. (1991), *Der alte Orient: Geschichte und Kultur des alten Vorderasien*. Gütersloh.
Hrouda, B. (1998–2001), "Neu– und spätbabylonische Kunstperiode", *RlA* 9: 277–283.
Hu, D., ed. (1982), *Explorations in the History of Science and Technology in China*. Shanghai.
Hudson, M. and Levine, B., eds. (1999), *Urbanization and Land Ownership in the Ancient Near East*. Cambridge.
Huff, D. (1971), "Qal'a-ye Dukhtar bei Firuzabad: ein Beitrag zur sasanidischen Palastarchitektur", *AMI* 4: 127–171.
Huff, D. (1972), "Der Takht-i Nishin in Firuzabad", *AAnz 1972*: 517–540.
Huff, D. (1974), "An archaeological survey in the area of Firuzabad, Fars, 1972", in Bagherzadeh, ed., 155–179.
Huff, D. (1978a), "Ausgrabungen auf Qal'a-ye Dukhtar bei Firuzabad 1976", *AMI* 11: 117–148.
Huff, D. (1978b), "Recherches archéologiques à Takht-i Suleiman (Iran), centre religieux royal sassanide", *CRAIBL* 1978: 774–789.
Huff, D. (1986), "Archaeology iv. Sasanian", *EnIr* 2: 302–308.

Huff, D. (1988), "Zum Problem zoroastrischer Grabanlagen in Fars, I. Gräber", *AMI* 21: 145–176.
Huff, D. (1990), "Fertigteile im iranischen Gewölbebau", *AMI* 23: 145–160.
Huff, D. (1991), "Observations at minor monuments in the Persepolis Area", in De Meyer and Gasche, eds., 197–200.
Huff, D. (1993), "Architecture sassanide", in Vanden Berghe, ed., 45–61.
Huff, D. (1998), "Fire altars and astodans", in Curtis et al., eds., 74–83.
Huff, D. (1999), "Fīrūzābād", *EnIr* 9: 633–636.
Huff, D. (2004), "Takht-i Suleiman: Sasanian fire sanctuary and Mongolian palace", in Stöllner et al., eds., 462–471.
Huff, D. (2008), "The formation and ideology of the Sasanian state in the context of archaeological evidence", in Curtis and Stewart, eds., 31–59.
Huff, D. (2009), "Fürsten, Festungen und Feuertempel: das sassanidische Imperium (224–651 n. Chr.)", in Stronach and Mousavi, eds., 76–109.
Huff, D. (2010), "Überlegungen zu Funktion, Genese und Nachfolge des Apadana", in Jacobs and Rollinger, eds., 311–374.
Humphrey, J.H., ed. (1999), *The Roman and Byzantine Near East: Some Recent Archaeological Research*. Portsmouth.
Humphrey, J.H., ed. (2002), *The Roman and Byzantine Near East*, vol. 3. Portsmouth.
Humphries, M. (2008), "Material evidence (1): Archaeology", in Harvey and Hunter, eds., 87–103.
Hundt, H.-J. (1971), "On prehistoric textile finds", *JRGZM* 16: 59–71.
Hunger H. and Restle, M., eds. (1972), *Festschrift für Otto Demus zum 70. Geburtstag*. Vienna.
Hunt, E.D. (1982), *Holy Land Pilgrimage in the Later Roman Empire, AD 312–460*. Oxford.
Hunt, N.B. (2004), *Historical Atlas of Ancient Mesopotamia*. New York.
Hunter, E.C.D. (1989a), "Report and catalogue of inscribed fragments: Ain Sha'ia and Dukakin caves near Najaf, Iraq", *Al-Rāfidān* 10: 89–108.
Hunter, E.C.D. (1989b), "Syriac inscriptions from a Melkite monastery on the Middle Euphrates", *BSOAS* 52/1: 1–17.
Hunter, E.C.D. (1991), "An inscribed reliquary from the Middle Euphrates", *Oriens Christianus* 75: 147–165.
Hunter, E.C.D. (1993), "The cult of saints in Syria during the fifth century AD", in Livingstone, ed., 308–312.
Hunter, E.C.D. (1996), "Syriac inscriptions from al-Hira", *Oriens Christianus* 80: 66–81.
Hunter, E.C.D. (1997), "A Syriac ostracon from Ctesiphon", *Al-Rāfidān* 18: 361–367.
Hunter, E.C.D. (1997–8), "Aramaic-speaking communities of Sasanid Mesopotamia", *ARAM* 9/1: 323–340.
Hunter, E.C.D. (1998), "Syriac ostraca from Mesopotamia", *Oriens Christianus Analecta* 256: 617–639.
Hunter, E.C.D. (2008), "The Christian matrix of al-Hira", in Jullien and Jullien, eds., 41–56.
Hunter, E.C.D. (2009), *The Christian Heritage of Iraq*. Piscataway.

Huntington, E. (1907), *The Pulse of Asia*. Boston.
Huot, J., ed. (1983), *Larsa et 'Oueili: Travaux de 1978–1981*. Paris.
Huot, J.-L. (1985), "L'É.babbar de Larsa durant le Ier millénaire (travaux de 1983)", *Akkadica* 44: 14–17.
Huot, J.-L., ed. (1987a), *La Préhistoire de la Mésopotamie*. Paris.
Huot, J.-L., ed. (1987b), *Larsa (10e campagne, 1983) et 'Oueili (4e campagne, 1983): Rapport préliminaire*. Paris.
Huot, J.-L., ed. (1989), *Larsa: Travaux de 1985*. Paris.
Huot, J.-L., ed. (1991), *'Oueili: Travaux de 1985*. Paris.
Huot, J.-L. (1994), *Les Premiers Villageois de Mésopotamie*. Paris.
Huot, J.-L., ed. (1996), *'Ouelli: Travaux de 1987 et 1989*. Paris.
Huot, J.-L., ed. (2003), *Larsa: Travaux de 1987 et 1989*. Beirut.
Huot, J.-L., Bachelot, L., Kepinski, C., Lecomte, O. and Suire, J. (1987), "Rapport préliminaire sur la dixième campagne à Larsa (1983)", in Huot, ed., 169–211.
Huot, J.-L., Rougeulle, A. and Suire, J. (1989), "La structure urbaine de Larsa", in Huot, ed., 19–52.
Huot, J.-L., Yon, M. and Calvet, Y., eds. (1985), *De l'Indus aux Balkans: Recueil à la mémoire de Jean Deshayes*. Paris.
Hussein, M.M. and Suleiman, A. (2000), *Nimrud: A City of Golden Treasures*. Baghdad.
Huth, M. and van Alfen, P.G., eds. (2010), *Coinage of the Caravan Kingdoms: Studies in Ancient Arabian Monetization*. New York.
Hutter, M. (2003), "Aspects of Luwian religion", in Melchert, ed., 211–280.
Hutter, M. and Hutter-Braunsar, S., eds. (2004), *Offizielle Religion, lokale Kulte und individuelle Religiosität*. Münster.
Hutter, M. and Hutter-Braunsar, S., eds. (2006), *Pluralismus und Wandel in den Religionen im vorhellenistichen Anatolien*. Münster.
Hymes, D., ed. (1971), *Pidginization and Creolization of languages*. Cambridge.
Iacobini, A. and Zanini, E., eds. (1995), *Arte profana e arte sacra a Bisanzio*. Roma.
Ibáñez, J.J., ed. (2008), *Le Site Néolithique de Tell Mureybet (Syrie due Nord)*. Oxford.
Ibáñez, J.J., González Urquijo, J.E. and Rodríguez, A. (2008), "Analyse fonctionnelle de l'outillage lithique de Mureybet", in Ibáñez, ed., 363–406.
Ibáñez, J.J., Haïdar-Boustani, M., Al Maqdissi, M., González Urquijo, J., Armendáriz, Á., Balbo, A., Boix, J., Himi, M., Iriarte, E., Lagüera, M., Lazuén, T., Rodríguez, A., Sabren, E., Santana, J., Tapia, J., Teira, L., Terradas, X. and Zapata, L. (2008), *Rapport de terrain 2008. Mission syro-libano-espagnole à l'ouest de Homs* (http://biblioteca.universia.net/html_bura/ficha/params/id/38510541.html).
Ibrahim, J.K. (1986), *Pre-Islamic Settlement in the Jazirah*. Baghdad.
Ibrahim, J.K. and Amin Agha, A. (1983), "The Humaidat tombs", *Sumer* 39: 157–171.
Ibrahim, M. (1982), *Excavations of the Arab Expedition at Sar al-Jisr, 1978–1979*. Manama.
Ikram, S. (2003), "A preliminary study of zooarchaeological changes between the Bronze and Iron ages at Kinet Höyük, Hatay", in Fischer et al., eds., 283–294.
Ikram, S. and Dodson, A., eds. (2010), *Beyond the Horizon: Studies in Egyptian Art, Archaeology and History in Honour of Barry J. Kemp*. Cairo.
Ingholt, H. (1942), "The Danish excavations at Hama on the Orontes", *AJA* 46/4: 469–476.

Ingold, T. (1990), "Society, nature and the concept of technology", *Archaeological Review from Cambridge* 9/1: 5–17.
Ingraham, M.L., Johnson, T.D., Rihani, B. and Shatla, I. (1981), "Saudi Arabian Comprehensive Survey Program: preliminary report on a reconnaissance survey of the Northwestern Province", *Atlal* 5: 59–84.
Inizan, M-L., ed. (1988), *Préhistoire à Qatar*. Paris.
Inizan, M.-L., Reduron-Ballinger, M., Roche, H. and Tixier, J. (1999), *Technology and Terminology of Knapped Stone*. Nanterre.
Invernizzi, A. (1989), "Héraclès à Séleucie du Tigre", *Revue Archéologique*: 65–113.
Invernizzi, A. (1993), "Seleucia on the Tigris: centre and periphery in Seleucid Asia", in Bilde et al., eds., 230–250.
Invernizzi, A. (1994), "Hellenism in Mesopotamia: a view from Seleucia on the Tigris", *Al-Rāfidān* 15: 1–24.
Invernizzi, A. (1999), *Sculture di metallo da Nisa*. Louvain.
Invernizzi, A. (2000), "The Square House at Nisa", *Parthica* 2: 13–53.
Invernizzi, A. (2001), "Arsacid dynastic art", *Parthica*, 3: 133–157.
Invernizzi, A. (2004), *Seleucia al Tigri: Le impronte si sigillo dagli archive 1–3*. Alessandria.
Invernizzi, A. (2005), *Il Genio Vagante: Babilonia, Ctesifonte, Persepoli in racconti di viaggio e testimonianze dei secoli XII-XVIII*. Alessandria.
Invernizzi, A. (2007), "The culture of Nisa, between steppes and empire", in Cribb and Herrmann, eds., 163–177.
Invernizzi, A., ed. (2007), *Sulla via di Alessandro da Seleucia al Gandhara*. Turin.
Invernizzi, A. and Lippolis, C., eds. (2007), *Nisa Partica. Ricerche nel complesso monumentale arsacide 1990–2006*. Florence.
Invernizzi, A. and Salles, J.-F., eds. (1993), *Arabia Antiqua: Hellenistic centres around Arabia*. Rome.
Invernizzi, A. and Venco Ricciardi, R. (1999), "Séleucie et Ctésiphon, centres parthe et sassanide", *DA* 243: 40–43.
Ionides, M.G. (1937), *The Regime of the Rivers Euphrates and Tigris*. London.
Irsheid, C. (1997), "The protection of cultural property in the Arab world", *International Journal of Cultural Property* 6: 11–46.
Isaac, B.H. (1991), "Tax collection in Roman Arabia: a new interpretation of the evidence from the Babatha archive", *JRA* 4: 336–344.
Isaac, B.H. (1992), *The Limits of Empire: The Roman Army in the East*. Oxford.
Isaakidou, V. (2006), "Ploughing with cows: Knossos and the secondary products revolution", in Serjeantson and Field, eds., 95–112.
Isager, J., ed. (1994), *Hekatomnid Caria and the Ionian renaissance*. Odense.
Işik, F. (1996), "Zur Ursprung lykischer Felsheiligtümer", in Blakolmer et al., eds., 51–64.
Işik, F. and Yilmaz, H.I. (1996), "Likya'da konut ve gömüt arasindaki yapisal ilişkiler", in Sey, ed., 171–181.
Ivanov, V.G., Samoylov, V.S., Petrov, L.L. and Yaroshenko, S.K. (1976), "Geochemical features of the genesis of lazurite-bearing metasomatites in the south Baikal region", *Doklady Earth Science Section* 222: 200–202.
Ivantchik, A.I., ed. (in press), *The World of Antiquity: In Memory of G. Bongard-Levin*.

Ivantchik, A.I. and Licheli, V., eds. (2007), *Achaemenid Culture and Local Traditions in Anatolia, Southern Caucasus and Iran: New Discoveries*. Leiden.

Iwasaki, T., Nishino, H. and Tsuneki, A. (1995), "The prehistory of the Rouj Basin, Northwest Syria: a preliminary report", *Anatolica* 21: 143–187.

Iwasaki, T. and Tsuneki, A. (2003), *Archaeology of the Rouj Basin: A Regional Study of the Transition from Village to City in Northwest Syria*, vol. 1. Tsukuba.

Jackson, C.M., Baxter, M.J. and Cool, H.E.M. (2003), "Identifying group and meaning: an investigation of Roman colourless glass", in Foy and Nenna, eds., 33–39.

Jackson, C.M., Booth, C.A. and Smedley, J.W. (2005), "Glass by design? Raw materials, recipes and compositional data", *Archaeometry* 47: 781–795.

Jackson, C.M. and Nicholson, P.T. (2007), "Compositional analysis of the vitreous materials found at Amarna", in Nicholson, ed., 101–116.

Jackson, C.M. and Nicholson, P.T. (2010), "The provenance of some glass ingots from the Ulu Burun shipwreck", *JAS* 37: 295–301.

Jackson, C.M., Nicholson, P.T. and Gneisinger, W. (1998), "Glassmaking at Tell el-Amarna: an integrated approach", *JGS* 40: 11–23.

Jackson, C.M. and Smedley, J.W. (2008), "Medieval and post-medieval glass technology: seasonal changes in the composition of bracken ashes from different habitats through a growing season", *Glass Technology* 49: 240–245.

Jackson, C.M. and Wager, E.C.W., eds. (2008), *Vitreous Materials in the Late Bronze Age Aegean*. Oxford.

Jackson, H. (2003), "The Housing Insula", *MeditArch* 16: 175–181.

Jackson, H. (2005), "Jebel Khalid, the 2004 and 2005 Seasons: the Housing Insula", *MeditArch* 18: 119–160.

Jackson, H. (2009), "Erotes on the Euphrates: a figured frieze in a private house at Hellenistic Jebel Khalid on the Euphrates", *AJA* 113/2: 231–253.

Jacobs, B. (1997), "Eine Planänderung an den Apadāna-Treppen und ihre Konsequenzen für die Datierung der Planungs- und Bebauungsphasen von Persepolis", *AMI* 29: 281–302.

Jacobs, B. (2002), "Achämenidische Kunst – Kunst im Achämenidenreich. Zur Rolle der achämenidsichen Großplastik als Mittel der herrscherlichen Selbstdarstellung und der Verbreitung politischer Botschaften im Reich", *AMI* 34: 345–395.

Jacobs, B. (2010), "From gabled hut to rock-cut tomb: a religious and cultural break between Cyrus and Darius?", in Curtis and Simpson, eds., 91–101.

Jacobs, B. and Macdonald, M.C.A. (2009), "Ritzzeichnung eines Reiters aus der Umgebung von Taymā", *ZOA* 2: 364–376.

Jacobs, B. and Rollinger, R., eds. (2010), *Der Achämenidenhof/The Achaemenid Court*. Wiesbaden.

Jacobs, L.K. (1994), "Darvāza Tepe", *EnIr* 7: 71–2.

Jacobsen, A.L.L. (2005), "The reliability of fishing statistics as a source for catches and fish stocks in antiquity", in Bekker-Nielsen, ed., 97–104.

Jacobsen, T. (1939), *The Sumerian King List*. Chicago.

Jacobsen, T. (1943), "Primitive democracy in Ancient Mesopotamia", *JNES* 2: 159–172.

Jacobsen, T. (1957), "Early political development in Mesopotamia", *ZA* 18: 91–140.

Jacobsen, T. (1970), "On the textile industry at Ur under Ibbi Sîn", in Moran, ed., 216–229.

Jacobsen, T. (1982), *Salinity and Irrigation Agriculture in Antiquity*. Malibu.

Jacobsen, T. and Adams, R.McC. (1958), "Salt and silt in ancient Mesopotamian agriculture", *Science* 128: 1251–1258.

Jacobsen, T. and Lloyd, S. (1935), *Sennacherib's Aqueduct at Jerwan*. Chicago.

Jacquat, C. and Martinoli, D. (1999), "*Vitis vinifera* L.: wild or cultivated? Study of the grape pips found at Petra, Jordan; 150 BC–AD 40", *VHA* 8: 25–30.

Jado, A.R. and Zötl, J.G., eds. (1984), *Quaternary period in Saudi Arabia*, vol. 2. New York.

Jakob-Rost, L. (1989), "Borsippa", *Forschungen und Berichte* 27: 65–88.

Jakob-Rost, L. and Fales, M. (1996), *Neuassyrische Rechtsurkunden*, vol. 1. Saarbrücken.

Jakob-Rost, L., Radner, K. and Donbaz, V. (2000), *Neuassyrische Rechtsurkunden*, vol. 2. Saarbrücken.

James, F. and McGovern, P.E. (1993), *The Late Bronze Egyptian Garrison at Beth Shan: A Study of Levels VII and VIII*. Philadelphia.

James, S. (2006), "The impact of steppe peoples and the Partho-Sasanian world on the development of Roman military equipment and dress, 1st to 3rd Centuries AD", in Mode and Tubach, eds., 357–392.

Jameson, S. (1968), "Chronology of the campaigns of Aelius Gallus and C. Petronius", *JRS* 58: 71–84.

Jammous, B. and Stordeur, D. (1999), "Jerf el-Ahmar: un site Mureybetien du Moyen Euphrate Syrien. Horizon PPNA – Xe millenaire avant JC", in del Olmo Lete and Montero Fenollós, eds., 57–69.

Jansen, M., Mulloy, M. and Urban, G., eds. (1991), *Forgotten Cities on the Indus: Early Civilization in Pakistan from the 8th to the 2nd Millennium BC*. Mainz.

Janssen, J.J. (1975), *Commodity Prices from the Ramessid Period*. Leiden.

Jarrige, C., ed. (1992), *South Asian Archaeology 1989*. Madison.

Jarrige, C., Jarrige, J.-F., Meadow, R.H. and Quivron, G., eds. (1995), *The Production Technology of Early Pottery at Mehrgarh*. Karachi.

Jarrige, C. and Lefèvre, V., eds. (2005), *South Asian Archaeology 2001*. Paris.

Jarrige, C. and Tosi, M. (1981), "The natural resources of Mundigak: Some observations on the location of the site in relation to its economic space", in Härtel, ed., 115–142.

Jarrige, J.-F. (2000), "Mehrgarh Neolithic: new excavations", in Taddei and de Marco, eds., 259–283.

Jarrige, J.-F. (2008), "The treasure of Tepe Fullol", in Hiebert and Cambon, eds., 67–79.

Jarvis, H. (2010), *The "Looting Question" Bibliography* (http://wings.buffalo.edu/anthropology/Documents/lootbib.shtml).

Jas, R.M., ed. (2000), *Rainfall and Agriculture in Northern Mesopotamia*. Leiden.

Jasim, A.K., Hamza, H.A. and Altaweel, M.R. (2006), "Tell Abu Shijar, near 'Aqar Quf: Summary of excavations", *Akkadica* 127: 155–166.

Jasim, S.A. (1985), *The Ubaid Period in Iraq: Recent Excavations in the Hamrin Region*. Oxford.

Jasim, S.A. (1989), "Structure and function in an 'Ubaid Village", in Henrickson and Thuesen, eds., 79–90.

Jasim, S.A. and Oates, J. (1986), "Early tokens and tablets in Mesopotamia", *WA* 17: 348–362.

Jasim, S.A., Uerpmann, H.-P. and Uerpmann, M. (2005), "Neolithic life and death in the desert: 8 seasons of excavations at Jebel al-Buhais", in Hellyer and Ziolkowski, eds., 29–36.

Jasink, A.M. and Marino, M. (2007), "The West-Anatolian origins of the Que Kingdom dynasty", *SMEA* 49: 407–26.

Jasmin, M. (2005), "Les conditions d'émergence de la route de l'encens à la fin du IIe millénaire avant notre ère", *Syria* 82: 49–62.

Jaussen, A. and Savignac, R. (1909), *Mission archéologique en Arabie*. Vol I: *De Jérusalem au Hedjaz Médaine-Saleh (mars-mai 1907)*, Paris.

Jaussen, A. and Savignac, R. (1914), *Mission archéologique en Arabie*. Vol. II: *El-ʿEla, d'Hegra à Teima, Harrah de Tebouk. Atlas*. Paris.

Jawad, L. (2006), "Fishing gear and methods of the lower Mesopotamian plain with reference to fishing management", *Marina Mesopotamica Online* 1/1: 1–37.

Jean, É., Dinçol, A. and Durugönül, S., eds. (2001), *La Cilicie: Espaces et pouvoirs locaux (2e millénaire av. J.-C. – 4e siècle ap. J.-C.)*. Istanbul.

Jenkins, N. (1980), *The Boat Beneath the Pyramid: King Cheops' Royal Ship*. London.

Jennings, J. (2003), "Inca imperialism, ritual change, and cosmological continuity in the Cotahuasi Valley of Peru", *JAA* 59: 433–462.

Jensen, C.H., Hermansen, B.D., Bille Petersen, M., Kinzel, M., Hald, M.M., Bangsgaard, P., Lynnerup, N. and Thuesen, I. (2005), "Preliminary report on the excavations at Shakârat al-Musay'îd, 1999–2004", *ADAJ* 49: 115–134.

Jensen, R. (2008), "Material evidence (2): visual culture", in Harvey and Hunter, eds., 104–119.

Jeppesen, K. (1960), "Et kongebud til Ikaros", *Kuml 1960*: 153–198 (in Danish with English summary).

Jeppesen, K. (1989), *Ikaros, The Hellenistic Settlements*. Vol. 3: *The Sacred Enclosure in the Early Hellenistic Period*. Aarhus.

Jerphanion, G. de (1926), *Le Calice d'Antioche. Les théories du docteur Eisen et la date probable du calice*. Rome.

Jesus, P.S. de (1980), *The Development of Prehistoric Mining and Metallurgy in Anatolia*. Oxford.

Jigoulov, V.S. (2010), *The Social History of Achaemenid Phoenicia: Being a Phoenician, Negotiating Empires*. London.

Joannès, F. (1990), "Textes babyloniens de Suse d'époque achéménide", in Vallat, ed., 173–180.

Joannès, F. (2001), *Dictionnaire de la civilisation mésopotamienne*. Paris.

Joannès, F. (2004), *The Age of Empires: Mesopotamia in the First Millennium BC*. Edinburgh.

Joannès, J. (2005), "Les relations entre Babylonie et Iran au début de la période achéménide: quelques remarques", in Baker and Jursa, eds., 183–196.

Jockenhövel, A., ed. (2009), *Grundlagen der globalen Welt. Vom Beginn bis 1200 v. Chr.* Darmstadt.

Joffe, A.H. (1991), "Early Bronze I and the evolution of social complexity in the southern Levant", *JMA* 4: 3–58.

Joffe, A.H. (1993), *Settlement and Society in the Early Bronze Age I and II Southern Levant: Complementarity and Contradiction in a Small-Scale Complex Society*. Sheffield.

Joffe, A.H. (2001), "Early Bronze Age seal impressions from the Jezreel Valley and the problem of sealing in the southern Levant", in Wolff, ed., 355–375.

Joffe, A.H., Dessel, J.P. and Hallote, R.S. (2001), "The 'Gilat woman': female iconography, Chalcolithic cult, and the end of Southern Levantine prehistory", *NEA* 64/1–2: 8–23.

Johnson, G.A. (1973), *Local Exchange and Early State Development in Southwestern Iran*. Ann Arbor.

Johnson, G.A. (1987), "Nine thousand years of social change in western Iran", in Hole, ed., 283–291.

Johnson, P. (2010), *Landscapes of Achaemenid Paphlagonia*. Philadelphia.

Joint Italian-Turkmen Archaeological Mission to the Murghab Alluvial Fan (2006), *Preliminary Report: Site 1211*. Ashgabat.

Jomier, J. (1954), "Les graffiti 'sinaïtiques' du Wadi Abou Daradj", *RB* 61: 419–424.

Jones, A.H.M. (1964), *The Later Roman Empire*, vol. 1. Oxford.

Jones, A.H.M. (1971), *The Cities of the Eastern Roman Provinces*. Oxford.

Jones, A.H.M. (1974), *The Roman Economy*. Oxford.

Jones, C.E. and Stolper, M.W. (1986), "Two late Elamite tablets at Yale", in De Meyer et al., eds., 243–254.

Jones, M.D. and Roberts, C.N. (2008), "Interpreting lake isotope records of Holocene environmental change in the Eastern Mediterranean", *QI* 181: 32–38.

Jones, M.D., Roberts, C.N., Leng, M. and Turkes, M. (2006), "A high-resolution late Holocene lake isotope record from Turkey and links to North Atlantic and monsoon climate", *Geology* 34/5: 361–364.

Jones-Bley, K. and Zdanovich, D.G., eds. (2002), *Complex Societies of Central Eurasia from the 3rd to the 1st Millennium BC: Regional Specifics in Light of Global Models*. Washington, DC.

Joukowsky, M.S., ed. (1986), *Prehistoric Aphrodisias: An Account of the Excavations and Artifact Studies*, vol. 1. Providence/Louvain.

Judkins, G., Smith, M. and Keys, E. (2008), "Determinism within human-environment research and the rediscovery of environmental causation", *GJ* 174: 17–29.

Jullien, C. and Jullien, F. (2002), *Apôtres des confins. Processus missionaires chrétiens dans l'Empire iranien*. Bures-sur-Yvette.

Jullien, C. and Jullien, F., eds. (2008), *Les Controverses des Chrétiens dans l'Iran sassanide*. Leuven.

Jurriaans-Helle, G., ed. (1998), *Cornelis de Bruijn: Reizen van Rome naar Jeruzalem en van Moskou naar Batavia/Voyages from Rome to Jerusalem and from Moscow to Batavia*. Amsterdam.

Jursa, M. (1995), *Die Landwirtschaft in Sippar in neubabylonischer Zeit*. Vienna.

Jursa, M. (2004a), "Palast. A.IV.b. Neubabylonisch", *RlA* 10: 209–212.

Jursa, M. (2004b), "Grundzüge der Wirtschaftsformen Babyloniens im ersten Jahrtausend v.Chr.", in Rollinger and Ulf, eds., 115–136.

Jursa, M. (2005), *Neo-Babylonian Legal and Administrative Documents: Typology, Contents and Archives*. Münster.

Kaboli, M.-A. (2000), "The Apadana gateway at Susa", *Iran* 38: 161–162.

Kaczmarczyk, A. (1986), "The source of cobalt in ancient Egyptian pigments", in Olin and Blackman, eds., 369–376.

Kaczmarczyk, A. and Hedges, R.E.M. (1983), *Ancient Egyptian Faience*. Warminster.

Kadowaki, S. (2006), "Ground-stone tools and implications for the use of space and social relations at 'Ain Abu Nukhayla, a PPNB settlement in Southern Jordan", in Banning and Chazan, eds., 53–64.

Kadowaki, S., Gibbs, K. and Banning, E.B. (2009), "Late Neolithic settlement in Wadi Ziqlab, Jordan: al-Basatîn", *Paléorient* 341: 105–129.

Kafafi, Z.A. (1986), "White objects from 'Ain Ghazāl, near Amman", *BASOR* 261: 51–56.

Kafafi, Z.A. (1993), "The Yarmoukians in Jordan", *Paléorient* 19/1: 101–114.

Kafafi, Z.A. (2006), "Domestic activities at the Neolithic Site, 'Ain Ghazal'", in Banning and Chazan, 81–89.

Kaim, B. (2004), "Ancient fire temples in the light of the discovery at Mele Hairam", *IrAnt* 39: 323–337.

Kaim, B. (2006), "Où adorer les dieux? Un spectaculaire temple du feu d'époque sassanide", *DA* 317: 66–71.

Kaizer, T. (2000), "The 'Heracles figure' at Hatra and Palmyra: problems of interpretation", *Iraq* 62: 219–232.

Kaizer, T., ed. (2008), *The Variety of Local Religious Life in the Near East in the Hellenistic and Roman Periods*. Leiden.

Kalantarian, A., ed. (1996), *10th Scientific Session Devoted to the Results of Archaeological Investigations in the Republic of Armenia (1993–1995)*. Yerevan.

Kallweit, H. (2003), "Remarks on the Late Stone Age in the UAE", in Potts, Al Naboodah and Hellyer, eds., 56–63.

Kampen, N. and Bergmann, B., eds. (1996), *Sexuality in Ancient Art: Near East, Egypt, Greece, and Italy*. Cambridge.

Kaniewski, D., Paulissen, E., De Laet, V. and Waelkens, M. (2008), "Late Holocene fire impact and post-fire regeneration from the Bereket basin, Taurus Mountains, southwest Turkey", *QR* 70: 228–239.

Kaniewski, D., Paulissen, E., Van Campo, A., al-Maqdissi, M., Bretschneider, J. and van Lerberghe, K. (2008), "Middle East coastal ecosystem response to Middle-to-Late Holocene abrupt climate changes", *PNAS* 105: 13941–13946.

Kansa, S.W., Gauld, S.C., Campbell, S. and Carter, E. (2009), "Whose bones are those? Preliminary comparative analysis of fragmented human and animal bones in the 'death pit' at Domuztepe, a Late Neolithic settlement in southeastern Turkey", *Anthropozoologia* 44/1: 159–172.

Kantor, H.J. (1974), "The Čoqa Miš excavations 1972–73", in Bagherzadeh, ed., 15–22.

Kantor, H.J. (1976), "The excavations at Čoqa Miš, 1974–1975", in Bagherzadeh, ed., 23–41.

Kantor, H.J. (1992), "The relative chronology of Egypt and its foreign correlations before the First Intermediate Period", in Ehrich, ed., 3–21.

Kantor, H.J. and Delougaz, P. (1996), *Choga Mish Vol. 1: The First Five Seasons, 1961–1971*. Chicago.

Kapel, H., (1967), *Atlas of the Stone-Age Cultures of Qatar: Reports of the Danish Archeological Expedition to the Arabian Gulf.* Aarhus.

Kaper, O.E., ed. (1998), *Life on the Fringe: Living in the Southern Egyptian Deserts During the Roman and Early Byzantine Periods.* Leiden.

Kaplan, M. (1992), *Les Hommes et la terre à Byzance du Ve au Xe siècle.* Paris.

Kaptan, D. (2003), "A glance at northwestern Asia Minor during the Achaemenid period", in Henkelman and Kuhrt, eds., 189–202.

Kaptijn, E. and Petit, L.P., eds. (2009), *A Timeless Vale: Archaeology and Related Studies of the Jordan Valley.* Leiden.

Karageorghis, V., ed. (2001), *The White Slip Ware of Late Bronze Age Cyprus.* Vienna.

Karnapp, W. (1976), *Die Stadtmauer von Rasafa in Syrien.* Berlin.

Karsgaard, P. (2010), "The Halaf-Ubaid transition", in Carter and Philip, eds., 51–67.

Karsgaard, P. (in press), "On the Brak chalice: prestige and consumption at early urban Brak", in Crawford et al., eds.

Karvonen-Kannas, K. (1995), *The Seleucid and Parthian Terracotta Figurines from Babylon in the Iraq Museum, the British Museum, and the Louvre.* Florence.

Kassian, A., Korolëv, A. and Sidel'steve, A. (2002), *Hittite Funerary Ritual: Šalliš Waštaiš.* Münster.

Kataja, L. and Whiting, R. (1995), *Grants, Decrees and Gifts of the Neo-Assyrian Period.* Helsinki.

Katzenstein, H.J. (1997), *The History of Tyre: From the Beginning of the Second Millennium BCE. until the Fall of the Neo-Babylonian Empire in 538 BCE.* Jerusalem.

Kaulicke, P. and Dillehay, T.D., eds. (2009), *Procesos y expresiones de poder, identidad y orden tempranos en Sudamérica. Segunda parte [Early Processes and Expressions of Power, Identity and Order in South America. Part II].* Lima.

Kavtaradze, G.L. (1983), *K Khronologii Epokhi Eneolita i Bronzy Gruzii.* Tbilisi.

Kavtaradze, G.L. (1999), "The importance of metallurgical data for the formation of central Transcaucasian chronology", in Hauptmann et al., eds., 67–103.

Kawami, T.S. (1972), "A possible source for the sculptures of the Audience Hall, Pasargadae", *Iran* 10: 146–148.

Kawami, T.S. (1987), *Monumental Art of the Parthian Period in Iran.* Leiden.

Kawami, T.S. (1992), "Archaeological evidence for textiles in pre-Islamic Iran", *Iranian Studies* 25/1–2: 7–18.

Kawanabe, H., Coulter, G.W. and Roosevelt, A.C., eds. (1999), *Ancient Lakes: Their Cultural and Biological Diversity.* Belgium.

Kaye, L.M. and Main, C.T. (1995), "The sage of the Lydian hoard antiquities: from Uşak to New York and back and some related observations on the law of cultural repatriation", in Tubb, ed., 150–162.

Kazanski, M. (2003), *Qal'at Sem'an. Volume IV: Rapport final. Fascicule 3: Les objets métalliques.* Beirut.

Kazansky, N.N., ed. (2008), *Colloquia Classica et Indogermanica IV. Studies in Classical Philology and Indo-European Languages.* St. Petersburg.

Kealhofer, L., ed. (2005), *The Archaeology of Midas and the Phrygians: Recent Work at Gordion.* Philadelphia.

Kealhofer, L., Grave, P., Genz, H. and Marsh, B. (2009), "Post-collapse: the re-emergence of polity in Iron Age Boğazköy, Central Anatolia", *OJA* 28: 275–300.

Keall, E.J. (1970), *The Significance of Late Parthian Nippur*. Ann Arbor.
Keall, E.J. (1982), "Qal'eh-i Yazdigird: an overview of the monumental architecture", *Iran* 20: 51–72.
Keall, E.J. (1986), "Ayvān (or Tāq)-e Kesrā", *EnIr* 3: 155–159.
Keall, E.J. (1994), "How many kings did the Parthian king of kings rule?", *IrAnt* 29: 253–272.
Keall, E.J. (2002), "Qal'eh-i Yazdigird", *DA* 271: 64–71.
Keall, E.J., Leveque, M.A. and Willson, N. (1980), "Qal'eh-i Yazdigird: its architectural decorations", *Iran* 18: 1–41.
Kedar, B.Z. and Werblowsky, R.J.Z., ed. (1998), *Sacred Space: Shrine, City, Land*. London.
Keeley, L.H. (1980), *Experimental Determination of Stone Tool Uses*. Chicago.
Keen, A.G. (1995), "The tombs of Lycia: evidence for social stratification?", in Campbell and Green, eds., 221–225.
Keen, A.G. (1998), *Dynastic Lycia: A Political History of the Lycians and Their Relations with Foreign Powers, c.545–362 BC*. Leiden.
Keen, A.G. (2002), "The 'kings' of Lycia in the Achaemenid period", in Brock and Hodkinson, eds., 267–279.
Keenan, D.J. (2004), "Radiocarbon dates from Gordion are confounded", *AWE* 3: 100–103.
Kehl, M., Frechen, M. and Skowronek, A. (2009), "Nature and age of Late Quaternary basin fill deposits in the Basin of Persepolis, Southern Iran", *QI* 196: 57–70.
Keith, K. (1998), "Spindle whorls, gender, and ethnicity at Late Chalcolithic Haçinebi Tepe", *JFA* 25: 497–515.
Keith, K. (2003), "The spatial patterns of everyday life in Old Babylonian neighborhoods", in Smith, ed., 56–80.
Kelker, N.L. and Bruhns, K.O. (2010), *Faking Ancient Mesoamerica*. Walnut Creek.
Kellens, J. (1992), *La Religion iranienne à l'époque achéménide*. Gent.
Kellner, H.J., ed. (1976), *Urartu: Ein wiederentdeckter Rivale Assyriens*. Munich.
Kellner, H.J. (1991), *Gürtelbleche aus Urartu*. Stuttgart.
Kelp, U. (2004), "Der Einfluss des späthethitischen Kulturraumes auf Orthostaten in Gordion", in Novák et al., eds., 285–305.
Kelterborn, P. (1984), "Towards replicating Egyptian Predynastic flint knives", *JAS* 11: 433–53.
Kempinski, A. (1978), *The Rise of an Urban Culture*. Jerusalem.
Kempinski, A. (1983), "Early Bronze Age urbanization of Palestine: some topics in a debate", *IEJ* 33: 235–241.
Kempinski, A. (1989), "Urbanization and metallurgy in southern Canaan", in Miroschedji, ed., 163–168.
Kennedy, D. (2006), "Demography, the population of Syria and the census of Q. Aemilius Secundus", *Levant* 38: 109–124.
Kennedy, H. (1992), "Antioch: from Byzantium to Islam and back again", in Rich, ed., 181–198.
Kennedy, J. (1898), "The early commerce of Babylon with India", *JRAS*: 241–288.
Kennet, D. (2002), "Sasanian pottery in southern Iran and eastern Arabia", *Iran* 40: 153–162.

Kennet, D. (2007), "The decline of eastern Arabia in the Sasanian period", *AAE* 18: 86–122.

Kennett, D.J. and Kennett, J.P. (2007), "Influence of Holocene marine transgression and climate change on cultural evolution in southern Mesopotamia", in Anderson et al., eds., 229–264.

Kenoyer, J.M., ed. (1994), *From Sumer to Meluhha: Contributions to the Archaeology of South and West Asia in Memory of George F. Dales, Jr.* Madison.

Kenoyer, J.M. (1997), "Trade and technology of the Indus Valley: new insights from Harappa, Pakistan", *WA* 29: 262–280.

Kenoyer, J.M. (2004), "Chronology and interrelations between Harappa and Central Asia", *Journal of the Japanese Society for West Asian Archaeology* 5/3: 8–45.

Kenoyer, J.M. (2009), "Carts and wheeled vehicles of the Indus Civilizaton: new evidence from Harappa, Pakistan", in Osada and Uesugi, eds., 1–34.

Kent, R.G. (1953), *Old Persian. Grammar, Texts, Lexicon*, 2nd edn. New Haven.

Kenyon, K.M. (1957), *Digging up Jericho*. London.

Kenyon, K.M. (1960), *Archaeology of the Holy Land*. London.

Kenyon, K.M. (1979), *Archaeology of the Holy Land*, 4th edn. New York.

Kenyon, K.M. (1981), *Excavations at Jericho III. The Architecture and Stratigraphy of the Tell*. London.

Kenyon, K.M. and Holland, T.A., eds. (1983), *Excavations at Jericho V: The Pottery Phases of the Tell and Other Finds*. London.

Kepinski-Lecomte, C. (1996), "Spatial occupation of a new town: Haradum (Iraqi Middle Euphrates, 18th–17th centuries BC)", in Veenhof, ed., 191–196.

Kepinski-Lecomte, C. (2009), "Grai Resh et la haute-Mésopotamie de 4200 à 3600 av. J.-C.: de contacts lointains aux strategies territoriales", in Butterlin, ed., 121–128.

Kerber, J.E., ed. 2006. *Cross-Cultural Collaboration: Native Peoples and Archaeology in the Northeastern United States*. Lincoln.

Kerner, S. (1993), *Vakilabad-Keramik*. Berlin.

Kerner, S., Dann, R. and Bangsgaard Jensen, P., eds. (in press), *Ancient Society and Climate*. Copenhagen.

Ker Porter, R. (1822), *Travels in Georgia, Persia, Armenia, Ancient Babylonia, &c. &c. During the Years 1817, 1818, 1819, and 1820*, vol. 2. London.

Kerr, R.A. (1998), "Sea-floor dust shows drought felled Akkadian Empire", *Science* 279: 325–326.

Kerschner, M. (2010), "The Lydians and their Ionian and Aiolian neighbours", in Cahill, ed., 247–265.

Kersel, M. (2006), "From the ground to the buyer: a market analysis of the trade in illegal antiquities", in Brodie et al., eds., 188–205.

Kersten, A.M.P. (1987), "Age and sex composition of Epipaleolithic fallow deer and wild goat from Ksar 'Akil", *Palaeohistoria* 29: 119–131.

Kervran, M. (1972), "Une statue de Darius découverte à Suse: Le contexte archéologique", *JA* 260: 235–239.

Kervran, M., Stronach, D., Vallat, F. and Yoyotte, J. (1972), "Une statue de Darius découverte à Suse", *Journal Asiatique* 260: 235–266.

Khačikyan, M.L. (1995), "Sur la characteristique typologique de l'Hourrite et l'Ourartéen", in Owen and Lacheman, eds., 21–27.

Khalaily, H. (2009), "The 'Ghazalian Culture', a transitional phase from Pre-Pottery to the Early Pottery Neolithic Periods: technological innovation and economic adaptation", in Rosen and Roux, eds., 179–191.

Khalidi, L. (2007), "The formation of a southern Red Seascape in the late prehistoric period", in Starkey et al., eds., 35–43.

Khalidi, L. (2009), "Holocene obsidian exchange in the Red Sea region", in Petraglia and Rose, eds., 279–291.

Khalidi, L., Gratuze, B. and Boucetta, S. (2009), "Provenance of obsidian excavated from late Chalcolithic levels at the sites of Tell Hamoukar and Tell Brak, Syria", *Archaeometry* 51/6: 879–893.

Khalidi, T., ed. (1984), *Land Tenure and Social Transformation in the Middle East*. Beirut.

Khalil, L. and Schmidt, K., eds. (2009), *Prehistoric Aqaba* I. Rahden.

Khatchadourian, L. (2007), "Unforgettable landscapes: attachments to the past in Hellenistic Armenia", in Yoffee, ed., 43–75.

Khatchadourian, L. (2008), *Social Logics Under Empire: The Armenian "Highland Satrapy" and Achaemenid Rule, ca.600–300 BC*. Ann Arbor.

Khatchadourian, L. (in press), "An archaeology of hegemony: the Achaemenid Empire and the remaking of the fortress in the Armenian highlands", in Areshian, ed.

Khlopin, I.N. (1982), "The manufacture of pile carpets in Bronze Age Central Asia", *Hali* 5/2: 116–119.

Khosrowzadeh, A. (2010), "Preliminary results of the 1st season of archaeological survey of Farsan, Bakhtiari Region, Iran", in Matthiae et al., eds., vol. 2, 317–337.

Khozhaniyazov, G. (2006), *The Military Architecture of Ancient Chorasmia*. Paris.

Kiani, M.Y., ed. (1976), *The Memorial Volume of the VIth International Congress of Iranian Art & Archaeology, Oxford, September 11–16th 1972*. Tehran.

Kiani, M.Y. (1982), *Parthian Sites in Hyrcania: The Gurgan Plain*. Berlin.

Kidner, F.L. (2001), "Christianizing the Syrian countryside: an archaeological and architectural approach", in Burns and Eadie, eds., 349–379.

Kiesewetter, H. (2006), "Analyses of the human remains from the Neolithic cemetery at al-Buhais 18 (Excavations 1996–2000)", in Uerpmann et al., eds., 103–380.

Kiguradze, T. and Sagona, A. (2003), "Origins of the Kura-Araxes cultural complex", in Smith and Rubinson, eds., 38–94.

Killebrew, A.E. (2007), "The Canaanite storage jar revisited", in Crawford, ed., 166–188.

Killen, J.T. (1984), "The textile industries at Pylos and Knossos", in Palaima and Shelmerdine, eds., 49–63.

Killick, R. and Moon, J., eds. (2005), *The Early Dilmun Settlement at Saar*. Ludlow.

Kimball, F. (1964), "The Sasanian building at Damghan (Tepe Hissar)", in Pope, ed., 579–583.

King, G.R.D. (1997), "A Nestorian monastic settlement on the island of Sīr Banī Yās, Abu Dhabi: a preliminary report", *BSOAS* 60: 221–235.

King, G.R.D. (1998), *Abu Dhabi Islands Archaeological Survey. Season 1: An Archaeological Survey of Sir Bani Yas, Dalma and Marawah*. London.

King, G.R.D. and Cameron, A., eds. (1994), *The Byzantine and Early Islamic Near East II. Land Use and Settlement Patterns*. Princeton.

Kinoshita, H. (2009), "Foreign glass excavated in China, from the 4th to 12th centuries", in Mango, ed., 253–261.

Kirch, P.V. (1980), "The archaeological study of adaptation: theoretical and methodological issues", in Schiffer, ed., 101–156.

Kircho, L.B., Salvatori, S. and Vidale, M. (2008), "A topographic and stratigraphic map of Altyn-depe: new evidence on craft activities from surface analysis", in Raven, ed., 15–30.

Kirkbride, D. (1969), "Early Byblos and the Beqa'a", *MUSJ* 45/3: 45–60.

Kirkbride, D. (1973), "Umm Dabaghiyah 1972", *Iraq* 35: 1–11.

Kirkbride, D. (1974), "Umm Dabaghiyah: a trading outpost? *Iraq* 36: 85–92.

Kirkbride, D. (1975), "Umm Dabaghiyah 1974: a fourth preliminary report", *Iraq* 37: 3–100.

Kirkbride, D. (1982), "Umm Dabaghiyah", in Curtis, ed., 11–21.

Kirkby, A.V.T. (1973), *The Use of Land and Water Resources in the Past and Present in the Valley of Oaxaca, Mexico*. Ann Arbor.

Kirkby A.V.T. and Kirkby, M.J. (1976), "Geomorphic processes and surface survey of archaeological sites in semiarid areas", in Davidson and Shackley, eds., 229–253.

Kirkby, M.J. (1977), "Land and water resources of the Deh Luran and Khuzestan Plain", in Hole, ed., 251–288.

Kislev, M.E. (1995), "Wild olive endocarp at submerged Chalcolithic Kfar Samir, Haifa, Israel", *JIPS* 26: 134–145.

Kislev, M.E. (1997), "Early agriculture and paleoecology of Netiv Hagdud", in Bar-Yosef and Gopher, eds., 209–236.

Kislev, M.E., Hartmann, A. and Bar-Yosef, O. (2006), "Early domesticated fig in the Jordan Valley", *Science* 312: 1372–1374.

Kislev, M.E., Hartmann, A. and Galili, E. (2004), "Archaeobotanical and archaeoentomological evidence from a well at Atlit-Yam indicates colder, more humid climate on the Israeli coast during the PPNC period", *JAS* 31: 1301–1310.

Kislev, M.E., Nadel, D. and Carmi, I. (1992), "Epipalaeolithic (19,000 BP) cereal and fruit diet at Ohalo II, Sea of Galilee, Israel", *Review of Palaeobotany and Palynology* 73: 161–166.

Kitchen, K.A. (1996), *The Third Intermediate Period in Egypt (1100–650 BC)*, 2nd edn. Warminster.

Kitchen, K. (2001), "Economics in Ancient Arabia From Alexander to the Augustans", in Archibald et al., eds., 157–173.

Kjærum, P. (1983), *Failaka/Dilmun: The Second Millennium Settlements. The Stamp and Cylinder Seals*. Aarhus.

Kjeldsen, K. and Zahle, J. (1975), "Lykische Gräber, ein vorläufiger Bericht", *AAnz 1975*: 313–350.

Kleber, K. (2004), "Die Fischerei in der spätbabylonischen Zeit", *Wiener Zeitschrift für die Kunde des Morgenlandes* 94: 133–165.

Klein, J. (1990), "Šulgi and Išmedagan: originality and dependence in Sumerian royal hymnology", in Klein and Skaist, eds., 64–136.

Klein, J. and Skaist, A., eds. (1990), *Bar-Ilan studies in Assyriology dedicated to Pinhas Artzi*. Ramat-Gan.

Klein, J.J. (1974), "Urartian hieroglyphic inscriptions from Altintepe", *AnSt* 24: 77–94.

Klein, S. and Hauptmann, A. (1999), "Iron Age leaded tin bronzes from Khirbet Edh-Darih, Jordan", *JAS* 26: 1075–1082.

Kleinerman, A. and Owen, D.I. (2009), *Analytical Concordance to the Garšana Archives*. Bethesda.

Kleiss, W. (1971), "Der Takht-i Rustam bei Persepolis und das Kyros-Grab in Pasargadae", *AAnz 1971*: 157–162.

Kleiss, W. (1973), "Qal'eh Zohak in Azerbaijan", *AMI* 6: 163–188.

Kleiss, W. (1975), "Fundnotizen zu einigen Säulenbasen aus West-Iran", *AMI* 8: 75–79.

Kleiss, W. (1976), "Beobachtungen in der Umgebung von Persepolis und Naqš-i Rustam", *AMI* 9: 131–150.

Kleiss, W. (1978), "Felsgräber südostlich Behbahan", *AMI* 11: 87–89.

Kleiss, W., ed. (1979a), *Bastam I: Ausgrabungen in den urartäische Anlagen 1972–1975*. Berlin.

Kleiss, W. (1979b), "Madar-e Suleiman. Das Grab des Kyros als islamisches Heiligtum", *AMI* 12: 281–287.

Kleiss, W. (1980), "Zur Entwicklung der achaemenidischen Palastarchitektur", *IrAnt* 15: 199–211.

Kleiss, W. (1981), "Ein Abschnitt der achaemenidischen Königsstrasse von Pasargadae und Persepolis nach Susa, bei Naqsh-i Rustam", *AMI* 14: 45–53.

Kleiss, W. (1983), "Brückenkonstruktionen in Iran", *Architectura* 13: 105–112.

Kleiss, W., ed. (1988), *Bastam II: Ausgrabungen in den urartäische Anlagen 1977–1978*. Berlin.

Kleiss, W. (1991), "Wasserschutzdämme und Kanalbauten in der Umgebung von Pasargadae", *AMI* 24: 23–30.

Kleiss, W. (1992a), "Dammbauten aus achaemenidischer und aus sasanidischer Zeit in der Provinz Fars", *AMI* 25: 131–145.

Kleiss, W. (1992b), "Beobachtungen auf dem Burgberg von Persepolis", *AMI* 25: 155–167.

Kleiss, W. (1993a), "Flächensteinbrüche und Einzelsteinbrüche in der Umgebung von Persepolis und Naqsh-i Rustam", *AMI* 26: 91–103.

Kleiss, W. (1993b), "Bermerkungen zur Felsanlage Qadamgah am Kuh-i Rahmat südöstlich von Persepolis", *AMI* 26: 161–164.

Kleiss, W. (1993c), "Achaemenidische Befestigungen und Anlagen in der westlichen Umgebung von Persepolis am Kuh-e Ayub", *IstMitt* 43: 331–338.

Kleiss, W. (1994), "Istakhr und Umgebung – archäologische Beobachtungen und Befunde", *AMI* 27: 165–189.

Kleiss, W. (2000), "Zur Planung von Persepolis", in Dittmann et al., eds., 355–368.

Klemm, D.D., Klemm, R. and Murr, A. (2001), "Gold of the Pharaohs: 6000 years of gold mining in Egypt and Nubia", *Journal of African Earth Sciences* 33/3–4: 643–659.

Klemm, D.D., Klemm, R. and Murr, A. (2002), "Ancient gold mining in the Eastern Desert of Egypt and the Nubian Desert of Sudan", in Friedman, ed., 113–130.

Klengel, H. (1965), *Geschichte Syriens im 2. Jahrtausend v. u. Z. Teil 1 – Nordsyrien*. Berlin.

Klengel, H. (1969), *Geschichte Syriens im 2. Jahrtausend v. u. Z. Teil 2 – Mittel- und Südsyrien*. Berlin.

Klengel, H. (1970), *Geschichte Syriens im 2. Jahrtausend v. u. Z. Teil 3 – Historische Geographie und allgemeine Darstellung*. Berlin.

Klengel, H. (1974), "Königtum und Palast nach den Alalah-Texten", in Garelli, ed., 273–282.

Klengel, H. (1979a), "Handel and Kaufleute im hethitischen Reich", *AoF* 6: 69–80.

Klengel, H. (1979b), "Die Palastwirtschaft in Alalah", in Lipiński, ed., 435–458.

Klengel, H. (1984), "Sumur/Simyra und die Eleutheros-Ebene in der Geschichte Syriens", *Klio* 66: 5–18.

Klengel, H, ed. (1989), *Kulturgeschichte des alten Vorderasien*. Berlin.

Klengel, H. (1992), *Syria: 3000 to 300 BC. A Handbook of Political History*. Berlin.

Klengel, H. (1995), "Tunip und andere Probleme der historischen Geographie Mittelsyriens", in van Lerberghe and Schoors, eds., 125–134.

Klengel, H. (1999), *Geschichte des hethitischen Reiches*. Leiden.

Klengel, H. (1999–2001), "Nuhašše", *RlA* 9: 610–611.

Klengel, H. (2000), "Qatna – ein historischer Überblick", *MDOG* 132: 239–252.

Klengel, H. (2002), "Die Geschichte des hethitischen Reiches", in Anonymous (2002b), ed., 62–73.

Klengel, H. and Renger, J., eds. (1999), *Landwirtschaft im alten Orient: Ausgewählte Vorträge der XLI Recontre Assyriologique Internationale, Berlin, 1994*. Berlin.

Klengel-Brandt, E. (1968), *Die Terrakotten aus Assur im Vorderasiatischen Museum Berlin*. Berlin.

Klengel-Brandt, E. (1990), "Gab es ein Museum in der Hauptburg Nebukadnezars II. in Babylon?", *Forschungen und Berichte* 28: 41–46.

Klengel-Brandt, E. and Böhme, S. (in press), *Neuassyrische Siegel aus Assur*. Wiesbaden.

Klengel-Brandt, E. and Cholidis, N. (2006), *Die Terrakotten von Babylon im Vörderasiatischen Museum in Berlin. Teil 1. Die anthropomorphen Figuren*, 2 vols. Saarwelligen.

Klengel-Brandt, E. and Onasch, H.-U. (in press), *Terrakotten aus Assur im Vorderasiatischen Museum Berlin*. Wiesbaden.

Kletter, R. (2003), "A very general archaeologist: Moshe Dayan and Israeli archaeology", *The Journal of Hebrew Scriptures* 4: article 5.

Klinkott, H. (2005), *Der Satrap: Ein achaimenidischer Amtsträger und seine Handlungsspielräume*. Frankfurt.

Klinkott, H. and Kubisch, S., eds. (2007), *Geschenke und Steuern, Zölle und Tribute. Antike Abgabenformen*. Leiden.

Knapp, A.B., ed. (1992), *Archaeology, Annales, and Ethnohistory*. Cambridge.

Knapp, A.B. (1993), *Society and Polity at Bronze Age Pella: An Annales Perspective*. Sheffield.

Knapp, A.B. (2010), "Cyprus' earliest prehistory: seafarers, foragers and settlers", *JWP* 23: 79–120.

Knapp, A.B. and van Dommelen, P., eds. (in press), *Cambridge Handbook of the Mediterranean World in the Bronze and Iron Ages*. Cambridge.

Knauf, E.A. (1990), "The Persian administration in Arabia", *Transeuphratène* 2: 201–217.

Knauss, F. (2005), "Caucasus", in Briant and Boucharlat, eds., 197–220.

Knauss, F. (2006), "Ancient Persia and the Caucasus", *IrAnt* 41: 80–118.

Knauss, F., Gagošidze, J. and Babaev, I.A. (2010), "A Persian propyleion in Azerbaijan: excavations at Karačamirli", in Nieling and Rehm, eds., 111–122.

Kobishchanov, Y.M. (1979), *Axum*. University Park/London.

Kocabaş, U. and Özasait-Kocabaş, I. (2010), "Le port de Théodose: trésors de l'archéologie marine", in Anonymous, ed., 143–147.

Koch, H. and Mackenzie, D.N., eds. (1983), *Kunst, Kultur und Geschichte der Achämenidenzeit und ihr Fortleben*. Berlin.

Koczka, C.S. (1989), "The need for enforcing regulations on the international art trade", in Messenger, ed., 185–208.

Kohl, P.L. (1975), *Seeds of Upheaval: The Production of Chlorite at Tepe Yahya and an Analysis of Commodity Production and Trade in Southwest Asia in the mid-Third Millennium*. Cambridge.

Kohl, P.L. (1978), "The balance of trade in southwest Asia in the mid-third millennium BC", *CA* 19/3: 463–492.

Kohl, P.L., ed. (1981), *The Bronze Age Civilization of Central Asia: Recent Soviet Discoveries*. Armonk.

Kohl, P.L. (1984), *Central Asia: Palaeolithic Beginnings to the Iron Age*. Paris.

Kohl, P.L. (1992), "The Transcaucasian periphery in the Bronze Age", in Urban and Schortman, eds., 117–137.

Kohl, P.L. (2001), "Reflections on the production of chlorite at Tepe Yahya: 35 years later", in Potts, 209–230.

Kohl, P.L. (2002), "Archaeological transformations: crossing the pastoral/agricultural bridge", *IrAnt* 37: 151–190.

Kohl, P.L. (2007), *The Making of Bronze Age Eurasia*. Cambridge.

Kohl, P.L. and Fawcett, C., eds. (1995), *Nationalism, Politics and the Practice of Archaeology*. Cambridge.

Kohl, P.L., Gadzhiev, M. and Magomedov, R.G. (2002), "Between the steppe and the sown: cultural developments on the Caspian littoral plain of southern Daghestan, Russia, c.3600–1900 BC", in Boyle et al., eds., 113–130.

Kohl, P.L., Kozelsky, M. and Ben-Yehuda, N., eds. (2007), *Selective Remembrances: Archaeology in the Construction, Commemoration, and Consecration of National Pasts*. Chicago.

Köhler, E.C. (1998), *Tell el-Faraʿin – Buto. Die Keramik von der späten Naqada-Kultur bis zum frühen Alten Reich (Schichten III bis VI)*. Mainz.

Kohler, E.L. (1980), "Cremations of the Middle Phrygian period at Gordion", in DeVries, ed., 65–89.

Kohler, E.L. (1995), *The Gordion Excavations (1950–1973): Final Reports Volume II: The lesser Phrygian Tumuli*. Philadelphia.

Köhler-Rollefson, I. (1989), "Changes in goat exploitation at 'Ain Ghazal between the Early and Late Neolithic: a metrical analysis", *Paléorient* 15/1: 141–146.

Köhler-Rollefson, I. (1996), "The one-humped camel in Asia: origin, utilization, and mechanisms of dispersal", in Harris, ed., 282–294.

Kohlmeyer, K. (1994), "Zur frühen Geschichte von Blei und Silber", in Wartke, ed., 41–48.

Kohlmeyer, K. (1996), "Houses in Habuba Kabira-South: spatial organization and planning of Late Uruk residential architecture", in Veenhof, ed., 89–103.

Kohlmeyer, K. (2000), *Der Tempel des Wettergottes von Aleppo*. Münster.

Kohlmeyer, K. (2008), "Zur Datierung der Skulpturen von 'Ain Dara", in Bonatz et al., eds., 119–130.

Kohlmeyer, K. (2009), "The temple of the storm god in Aleppo during the Late Bronze and Early Iron Ages", *NEA* 72/4: 190–202.

Kohlmeyer, K. and Strommenger, E. (1995), "Die Ausgrabungen in Tall Bi'a 1994 und 1995", *MDOG* 127: 43–55.

Köksal-Schmidt, Ç. and Schmidt, K. (2007), "Perlen, Steingefäße, Zeichentäfelchen. Handwerkliche Spezialisierung und steinzeitliches Symbolsystem", in Anonymous (2007a), ed., 97–109.

Köksal-Schmidt, Ç. and Schmidt, K. (2010), "The Göbekli Tepe 'totem pole': a first discussion of an Autumn 2010 discovery (PPN, Southeastern Turkey)", *Neo-Lithics* 1/10: 74–76.

Kökten, I.K. (1960), "Anadolu Maraş vilayetinde tarihten dip tarihe gidiş", *Türk Arkeolji Dergisi* 10/1: 42–52.

Koldewey, R. (1911), *Die Tempel von Babylon und Borsippa*. Leipzig (repr. Osnabrück 1972).

Koldewey, R. (1990), *Das wiedererstehende Babylon* (rev. B. Hrouda). Munich.

Koliński, R. (2007), "The Upper Khabur region in the second part of the third millennium BC", *AoF* 34: 342–369.

König, F.W. (1965), *Die elamischen Königsinschriften*. Graz.

Konrad, M. (2001), *Resafa 5. Der spätrömische Limes in Syrien. Archäologische Untersuchungen an den Grenzkastellen von Sura, Tetrapyrgium, Cholle und in Resafa*. Mainz.

Kooyman, B.P. (2000), *Understanding Stone Tools and Archaeological Sites*. Albuquerque.

Kopcke, G. and Moore, M.B., eds. (1979), *Studies in Classical Art and Archaeology: A Tribute to Peter Heinrich von Blanckenhagen*. Locust Valley.

Korenevskii, S.N. (2004), *Drevneishie Zemledel'tsy i Skotovody Predkavkaz'ya: Maikopsko-Novosvobodnenskaya Obshchnost'*. Moscow.

Körte, G. and Körte, A. (1904), *Gordion. Ergebnisse der Ausgrabung im Jahre 1900*. Berlin.

Koryakova, L. and Epimakhov, A. (2007), *The Urals and Western Siberia in the Bronze and Iron Ages*. Cambridge.

Košak, S. (1986), "The gospel of Iron", in Hoffner and Beckman, eds., 125–135.

Kosarev, M.F., Kozhin, P.M. and Dubova, N.A., eds. (2004), *U istokov tsivilizatsii: Sbornik statej k 75-letiyu Viktora Ivanovicha Sarianidi* [*Near the Sources of Civilizations: The Issue in Honor of the 75th anniversary of Victor Sarianidi*]. Moscow.

Kose, A. (1998), *Uruk. Architektur IV. Von der Seleukiden- bis zur Sasanidenzeit*. Mainz.

Koshelenko, G.A. (2007), "The fortifications at Gobekly-depe", in Cribb and Herrmann, eds., 269–283.

Koshelenko, G.A. and Pilipko, V.N. (1994), "Parthia", in Harmatta, ed., 131–150.

Kotjabopoulou, E., Hamilakis, I., Halstead, Gamble, C. and Elefanti, P., eds. (2003), *Zooarchaeology in Greece: Recent Advances*. London.

Kottek, M., Grieser, J., Beck, C., Rudolf, B. and Rubel, F. (2006), "World map of the Köppen-Geiger climate classification updated", *Meteorologische Zeitschrift* 15: 259–263.

Kouchoukos, N. (1998), *Landscape and Social Change in Late Prehistoric Mesopotamia*. New Haven.

Kouchoukos, N. and Hole, F. (2003), "Changing estimates of Susiana's prehistoric settlement", in Miller and Abdi, eds., 53–59.

Kouchoukos, N. and Wilkinson, T.J. (2007), "Landscape archaeology in Mesopotamia: past, present, and future", in Stone, ed., 1–18.

Kozłowoski, S.K. (1987), "The chipped stone industry of the Ubaid site Tell el-Saadiya in Iraq (Hamrin)", in Huot, ed., 277–291.

Kozłowski, S.K. (1997), "The gods from Nemrik", *Al-Rāfidān* 18: 33–44.

Kozłowski, S.K. (1998), "M'lefaat: Early Neolithic site in northern Irak", *Cahiers de l'Euphrate* 8: 179–273.

Kozłowoski, S.K. (1999), "The Big Arrowhead Industries (BAI) in the Near East", *Neo-Lithics* 2/99: 8–10.

Kozłowoski, S.K. (2002), *Nemrik: An Aceramic Village in Northern Iraq*. Warsaw.

Kozłowoski, S.K. and Aurenche, O. (2005), *Territories, Boundaries and Cultures in the Neolithic Near East*. Oxford.

Kozłowoski, S.K. and Gebel, H.-G., eds. (1996), *Neolithic Chipped Stone Industries of the Fertile Crescent, and Their Contemporaries in Adjacent Regions*. Berlin.

Krader, L. (1955), "Ecology of Central Asian pastoralism", *SWJA* 11/4: 301–326.

Kraeling, C.H. (1938), *Gerasa: City of the Decapolis*. New Haven.

Kraeling, C.H. (1967), *The Excavations at Dura-Europos. Final Report VIII.2: The Christian Building*. New Haven.

Kraemer, C.J. (1958), *Excavations at Nessana, Vol. 3. Non-literary papyri*. Princeton.

Kramer, C. (1977), "Pots and peoples", in Levine and Young, eds., 91–112.

Kramer, N. (2004), *Gindaros: Geschichte und Archäologie einer Siedlung im nordwestlichen Syrien von hellenistischer bis in frühbyzantinischer Zeit*. Rahden.

Kramer, S.N. (1963), *The Sumerians: Their History, Culture, and Character*. Chicago.

Krämer, W. and Buchner, E., eds. (1981), *150 Jahre Deutsches Archäologisches Institut 1829–1979*. Mainz.

Kramers, J.H. and Bosworth, C.E. (1996), "Shushtar", *Encyclopaedia of Islam* 9: 512–513.

Kraus, C.S., ed., (1999), *The Limits of Historiography: Genre and Narrative in Ancient Historical Texts*. Leiden.

Kraus, F.R. (1968), *Briefe aus dem Archive des Šamaš-ḫāzir in Paris und Oxford*. Leiden.

Krautheimer, R. (1986), *Early Christian and Byzantine Architecture*. New Haven.

Krefter, F. (1968), "Achaemenidische Palast- und Grabtüren", *AMI* 1: 99–113.

Krefter, F. (1971), *Persepolis Rekonstruktionen*. Berlin.

Krefter, F. (1979), "Mit Ernst Herzfeld in Pasargadae und Persepolis, 1928 und 1931–1934", *AMI* 12: 13–25.

Krefter, F. (1989), "Persepolis in Farbe", *AMI* 22: 131–132.

Krencker, D. (1939), *Die Wahlfahrtskirche des Simeon Stylites in Kal'at Sim'ân. I. Bericht über Untersuchungen und Grabungen im Frühjahr 1938, ausgeführt im Auftrag des Deutschen Archäologischen Instituts*. Berlin.

Kreppner, F.J. (2008), "The collapse of the Assyrian Empire and the continuity of ceramic culture: the case of the Red House at Tall Sheikh Hamad", *ANES* 45: 147–165.

Kreps, C.F. (2003), *Liberating Culture: Cross-Cultural Perspectives on Museums, Curation, and Heritage Preservation*. London.

Krishnamurthy, R. (2000), *Non-Roman Ancient Foreign Coins from Karur in India*. Chennai.

Kröger, J. (1982), *Sasanidisches Stuckdekor*. Mainz.

Kröger, J. (1993), "Ctesiphon", *EnIr* 6: 446–448.

Krogulska, M. (1992), "Bijan Island: Polish excavations on the Middle Euphrates", *Études et Travaux* 16: 353–362.

Kroll, S. (1976a), "Urartäische Architektur", in Kellner, ed., 28–44.

Kroll, S. (1976b), *Keramik urartäischer Festungen in Iran*. Berlin.

Kroll, S. (1984), "Urartus Untergang in anderer Sicht", *IstMitt* 34: 151–170.

Kron, G. (2008), "Animal husbandry, hunting, fishing, and fish production", in Oleson, ed., 175–222.

Kubba, S.A.A. (1987), *Mesopotamian Architecture and Town Planning from the Mesolithic to the End of the Proto-Historic Period, ca.10,000–3500 BC*. Oxford.

Kuftin, B.A. (1940), "K Voprosu O Rannykh Stadiyakh Bronzovoy Kultury na Territorii Kavkaza", *Kratkiye Soobshcheniya O Dokladakh i Polevykh Issledovaniyakh Instituta Istorii* 8: 5–35.

Kuhn, D. (1982), "The silk workshops of the Shang Dynasty (16th–11th century BC)", in Hu, ed., 367–408.

Kuhn, S.L. (2002), "Paleolithic archeology in Turkey", *Evolutionary Anthropology* 11: 198–210.

Kuhn, S.L. (2004), "From initial Upper Paleolithic to Ahmarian at Üçağizli Cave, Turkey", *Anthropolgie* 42/3: 249–262.

Kuhn, S.L., Stiner, M.C. and Güleç, E. (1999), "Initial Upper Palaeolithic in south-central Turkey and its regional context: a preliminary report", *Antiquity* 73: 505–517.

Kuhn, S.L., Stiner, M.C., Güleç, E., Özer, I., Yilmaz, H., Baykara, I., Açikkol, A., Goldberg, P., Molist, K.M., Ünay, E. and Suata-Alpaslan, F. (2009), "The early Upper Paleolithic occupations at Üçağizli Cave (Hatay, Turkey)", *Journal of Human Evolution* 56: 87–113.

Kuhn, S.L., Stiner, M.C., Kerry, K.W. and Güleç, E. (2003), "The Early Upper Palaeolithic at Üçağizli Cave (Hatay, Turkey)", in Goring-Morris and Belfer-Cohen, eds., 106–117.

Kühne, C. (1982), "Politische Szenerie und internationale Beziehungen Vorderasiens um die Mitte des 2. Jahrtausends vor Chr. (zugleich ein Konzept der Kurzchronologie)", in Nissen and Renger, eds., 203–267.

Kühne, H., ed. (1991), *Die rezente Umwelt von Tall Šēḫ Ḥamad und Daten zur Umweltrekonstruktion der assyrischen Stadt Dūr-Katlimmu*. Berlin.

Kuhrt, A. (1995), *The Ancient Near East, c.3000–330 BC*. London.

Kuhrt, A. (2001a), "The palace(s) of Babylon", in Nielsen, ed., 77–93.

Kuhrt, A. (2001b), "The Achaemenid Persian Empire (c.550–330 BCE): continuities, adaptations, transformations", in Alcock et al., eds., 93–123.

Kuhrt, A. (2007), *The Persian Empire: A Corpus of Sources from the Achaemenid Period*, 2 vols. London.

Kuhrt, A. (2010), "Achaemenid images of royalty and empire", in Lanfranchi and Rollinger, eds., 87–106.

Kuhrt, A. and Sancisi-Weerdenburg, H.W.A.M., eds. (1988), *Method and Theory. Proceedings of the London 1985 Achaemenid History Workshop*. Leiden.

Kuhrt, A. and Sancisi-Weerdenburg, H.W.A.M., eds. (1990), *Achaemenid History IV*. Leiden.

Kuijt, I. (1994), "Pre-Pottery Neolithic A period settlement variability: evidence for sociopolitical developments in the Southern Levant", *JMA* 7: 165–192.

Kuijt, I. (1996a), "Negotiating equality through ritual: a consideration of Late Natufian and Prepottery Neolithic A period mortuary practices", *JAA* 15: 313–336.
Kuijt, I. (1996b), "Where are the microliths? Lithic technology and Neolithic chronology as seen from the PPNA cccupations at Dhra', Jordan", *Neo-Lithics* 2/96: 7–8.
Kuijt, I. (2000a), "People and space in early agricultural villages: exploring daily lives, community size, and architecture in the Late Pre-Pottery Neolithic", *JAA* 19: 75–102.
Kuijt, I. (2000b), "Keeping the peace: ritual, skull caching, and community integration in the Levantine Neolithic", in Kuijt, ed., 2000, 137–164.
Kuijt, I., ed. (2000c), *Life in Neolithic Farming Communities: Social Organization, Identity, and Differentiation*. New York.
Kuijt, I. (2001a), "Lithic inter-assemblage variability and cultural-historical sequences: a consideration of the Pre-Pottery Neolithic A occupation of Dhra', Jordan", *Paléorient* 27: 107–25.
Kuijt, I. (2001b), "Place, death, and the transmission of social memory in early agricultural communities of the Near Eastern Pre-Pottery Neolithic", *Archaeological Papers of the American Anthropological Association* 10/1: 80–99.
Kuijt, I. (2004), "Pre-Pottery Neolithic A and Late Natufian at 'Iraq ed-Dubb, Jordan", *JFA* 29: 291–308.
Kuijt, I. and Finlayson, B. (2009), "Evidence for food storage and predomestication granaries 11,000 years ago in the Jordan Valley", *PNAS*, 106/27: 10966–10970.
Kuijt, I. and Goring-Morris, A.N. (2002), "Foraging, farming, and social complexity in the Pre-Pottery Neolithic of the Southern Levant: a review and synthesis", *JWP* 16: 361–440.
Kulakoğlu, F. (2008–10), "Kültepe-Kaniş", papers presented in the 30–32nd meetings of *Uluslararasi Kazi, Araştirma ve Arkeometri Sempozyumu*. Istanbul.
Kushnareva, K.K. (1997), *The Southern Caucasus in Prehistory: Stages of Cultural and Socioeconomic Development from the Eighth to the Second Millennium BC*. Philadelphia.
Kutzbach, J.E. and Liu, Z. (1997), "Response of the African monsoon to orbital forcing and ocean feedbacks in the Middle Holocene", *Science* 278: 440–443.
Kuz'mina, E.E. (1986), *Drevneishie Skotovody ot Urala do Tian'-Shania*. Frunze.
Kuz'mina, E.E. (2007), *The Origin of the Indo-Iranians*. Leiden.
Kuzucuoğlu, K. (2007), "Climatic and environmental trends during the third millennium BC in Upper Mesopotamia", in Kuzucuoğlu and Marro, eds., 459–480.
Kuzucuoğlu, K. and Marro, C., eds. (2007), *Sociétés humaines et changement climatique à la fin du troisième millénaire: Une crise a-t-elle eu lieu en Haute Mésopotamie?* Paris.
Labat, R. (1975a), "Elam c.1600–1200 BC", *CAH* 2/2: 379–416.
Labat, R. (1975b), "Elam and western Persia, c.1200–1100 BC", *CAH* 2/2: 482–506.
Labrousse, A. and Boucharlat, R. (1972), "La fouille du Palais du Chaour à Suse en 1970 et 1971", *DAFI* 2: 61–167.
Ladiray, D. (2010), "Les données archéologiques", in Perrot, ed., 160–221.
Laffineur, R. and Basch, L., eds. (1991), *THALASSA. L'Egée préhistorique et la mer*. Liège.
Lafont, B. (2000), "Irrigation agriculture in Mari", in Jas, ed., 129–146.
Laiou, A.E., ed. (2002), *The Economic History of Byzantium: From the Seventh through the Fifteenth Century*. Washington, DC.

Lal, B.B. and Gupta, S.P., eds. (1984), *Frontiers of the Indus Civilization*. New Delhi.
Lamb, H.H. (1977), *Climate Past, Present and Future*. London.
Lamberg-Karlovsky, C.C. (1978), "The Proto-Elamites on the Iranian Plateau", *Antiquity* 52: 114–120.
Lamberg-Karlovsky, C.C., ed. (1989), *Archaeological Thought in America*. Cambridge.
Lamberg-Karlovsky, C.C. (1996), *Beyond the Tigris and Euphrates: Bronze Age Civilization*. Beer-Sheva.
Lamberg-Karlovsky, C.C. (2002), "Archaeology and language: the Indo-Iranians", *CA* 43: 63–88.
Lamberg-Karlovsky, C.C. (2003), "Civilization, state, or tribes? Bactria and Margiana in the Bronze Age", *The Review of Archaeology* 24: 11–19.
Lamberg-Karlovsky, C.C. and Magee, P. (1999), "The Iron Age platforms at Tepe Yahya (Iran)", *IrAnt* 34: 41–52.
Lamberg-Karlovsky, C.C. and Tosi, M. (1973), "Shahr-i Sokhta and Tepe Yahya: Tracks on the earliest history of the Iranian Plateau", *EW* 23: 21–53.
Lambert, W.G. (1957), "Ancestors, authors, and canonicity", *JCS* 11: 1–14.
Lambert, W.G. (1960a), "The domesticated camel in the second millennium: evidence from Alalakh and Ugarit", *BASOR* 160: 42–43.
Lambert, W.G. (1960b), *Babylonian Wisdom Literature*. Oxford.
Lambert, W.G. (1987), "A vocabulary of an unknown language", *MARI* 5: 409–413.
Lamprichs, R. (1997), "Assur", in Meyers, ed., 225–228.
Landesmuseum Württemberg, ed. (2009), *Schätze des Alten Syrien: Die Entdeckung des Königreichs Qatna*. Stuttgart.
Landsberger, B. (1957), *The Series Ḫa-ra = ḫubullu. Tablets I–IV*. Berlin.
Landsberger, B. (1962), *The Fauna of Ancient Mesopotamia. The Series Ḫa-ra = ḫubullu. Tablets XIV–XVIII*. Rome.
Landsberger, B. (1967), *The Date Palm and its By-Products According to the Cuneiform Sources*. Graz.
Laneri, N., ed. (2007), *Performing Death: Social Analyses of Funerary Traditions in the Ancient Near East and Mediterranean*. Chicago.
Lanfranchi, G. (1983), "Some new texts about a revolt against the Urartian king Rusa I", *Oriens Antiquus* 22: 123–135.
Lanfranchi, G. (1998), "The library at Nineveh", in Westenholz, ed., 147–156.
Lanfranchi, G.B. and Parpola, S. (1990), *The Correspondence of Sargon II, Part II: Letters from the Northern and Northeastern Provinces*. Helsinki.
Lanfranchi, G.B., Roaf, M. and Rollinger, R., eds. (2003), *Continuity of Empire (?) Assyria, Media, Persia*. Padua.
Lanfranchi, G.B. and Rollinger, R., eds. (2010), *Concepts of Kingship in Antiquity*. Padua.
Langdon, S. (1912), *Die neubabylonischen Königsinschriften*. Leipzig.
Langdon, S. (1915), "New inscriptions of Nabuna'id," *American Journal of Semitic Languages and Literature* 32: 102–117.
Lange, S. (in press), "The funerary banquet in Ugarit", in Niehr et al., eds.
Langfeldt, J.A. (1994), "Recently discovered early Christian monuments in northeastern Arabia", *AAE* 5: 32–60.
Langsdorff, A. and McCown, D.E. (1942), *Tall-i Bakun A: Season of 1932*. Chicago.
La Niece, S. (1995), "Depletion gilding from third millennium BC Ur", *Iraq* 57: 41–47.

La Niece, S., Hook, D. and Craddock, P. (2007), *Metals and Mines: Studies in Archaeometallurgy*. London.

Lapatin, K.D.S. (2000a), "Boy gods, bull leapers, and mother goddesses", *Source* 20/1: 18–28.

Lapatin, K.D.S. (2000b), "Proof? The case of the Getty kouros", *Source* 20/1: 43–53.

Lapp, P. (1970), "Palestine in the Early Bronze Age", in Sanders, ed., 101–131.

La Rocca, E. (1992), "La fondazione di Costantinopoli", in Bonamente and Fusco, eds., 553–583.

Larsen, C.E (1983), *Life and Land Use on the Bahrain Islands*. Chicago.

Larsen, C.E. and Evans, G. (1978), "The Holocene geological history of the Tigris-Euphrates-Karun delta", in Brice, ed., 227–244.

Larsen, M.T., ed. (1979), *Power and Propaganda: A Symposium on Ancient Empires*. Copenhagen.

Larsen, M.T. (1996), *The Conquest of Assyria: Excavations in an Antique Land 1840–1860*. London/New York.

Larsen, M.T. (2008), "The Old Assyrian Merchant Colonies", in Aruz et al., eds., 70–81.

Larson, G., Albarella, U., Dobney, K., Rowley-Conwy, P., Schibler, J., Tresset, A., Vigne, J.-D., Edwards, C.J., Schlumbaum, A., Dinu, A., Balacsescu, A., Dolman, G., Tagliacozza, A., Manaseryan, N., Miracle, P., van Wijngaarden-Bakker, L., Masseti, M., Bradley, D.G. and Cooper, A. (2007), "Ancient DNA, pig domestication and the spread of the Neolithic into Europe", *PNAS* 104: 15276–15281.

Lassus, J. (1947), *Sanctuaires chrétiens de Syrie. Essai sur la genèse, la forme et l'usage liturgique des édifices du culte chrétien, en Syrie, du IIIe siècle à la conquête musulmane*. Paris.

Lassus, J. (1972a), review of Napoleone-Lemaire, J. and Balty, J.C., *L'Église à atrium de la Grande Colonnade. Fouilles d'Apamée de Syrie I, Syria* 49/1: 261–267.

Lassus, J. (1972b), *Antioch-on-the-Orontes V. Les portiques d'Antioche*. Princeton.

Last, J. (2005), "Pottery from the East Mound", in Hodder, ed. 101–138.

Latour, B. (2005), *Reassembling the Social: An Introduction to Actor-Network Theory*. Oxford.

Laufer, B. (1930), "The early history of felt", *AA* 32: 1–18.

Laufer, B. (1937), *The Early History of Felt*. Chicago.

Lauffray, J. (1991), *Halabiya-Zenobia, place forte du limes oriental de la Haute-Mesopotamie au VIe siècle*, vol. 2. Paris.

Lauffray, J. (2008), *Fouilles de Byblos VI. L'urbanisme et l'architecture. Collationements et complément des dessins originaux par Yasmine Makaroun-Bou Assaf*. Beirut.

Lauren, P.G. (2003), *The Evolution of International Human Rights: Visions Seen*. Philadelphia.

Laurito, R. and Pers, M. (2002), "Attestations of canals in the royal sources from the Sumerian to the Paleobabylonian period", *Egitto e Vicino Oriente* 25: 275–325.

Law, R. (2006), "Moving mountains: the trade and transport of rocks and minerals within the greater Indus Valley region", in Robertson et al., eds., 301–313.

Lawergren, B. (2000), "A 'Cycladic' harpist in the Metropolitan Museum of Art", *Source* 20/1: 3–9.

Lawler, A. (2004), "Rocking the cradle", *Smithsonian* May: 40–48.

Layard, A.H. (1849a), *The Monuments of Nineveh*. London.

Layard, A.H. (1849b), *Nineveh and its Remains*. London.
Layard, A.H. (1853a), *A Second Series of the Monuments of Nineveh*. London.
Layard, A.H. (1853b), *Discoveries Among the Ruins of Nineveh and Babylon; with Travels in Armenia, Kurdistan, and the Desert*. London.
Leahy, A. and Tait, J., eds. (1999), *Studies on Ancient Egypt in Honour of H.S. Smith*. London.
Lebeau, M., ed. (1998), *À Propos de Subartu: Études consacrées à la Haute Mésopotamie*, 2 vols. Turnhout.
Lebeau, M. (2000), "Stratified archaeological evidence and compared periodizations in the Syrian Jazirah during the third millennium BC", in Marro and Hauptmann, eds., 167–192.
Lebeau, M. and Suleiman, A., eds. (2003), *Tell Beydar, The 1995–1999 Seasons of Excavations. A Preliminary Report*. Turnhout.
Lebeau, M. and Suleiman, A., eds. (2008), *Beydar Studies 1*. Turnhout.
Leblanc, J. and Poccardi, G. (1999), "Étude de la permanence des tracés urbains et ruraux antiques à Antioche-sur l'Oronte", *Syria* 76: 91–126.
LeBlanc, S.A. (2010), "Early Neolithic warfare in the Near East and its broader implications", *Neo-Lithics* 1/10: 40–49.
Le Breton, L. (1957), "The early periods at Susa: Mesopotamian relations", *Iraq* 19: 79–124.
Le Brun, A. (1971), "Recherches stratigraphiques à l'Acropole de Suse", *DAFI* 1: 163–216.
Lechevallier, M. and Ronen, A., eds. (1994), *Le Gisement de Hatoula en Judée occidentale, Israel*. Paris.
Lechtman, H. (1996), "Arsenic bronze: dirty copper or chosen alloy? A view from the Americas", *JFA* 23: 477–514.
Lechtman, H. and Klein, S. (1999), "The production of copper-arsenic alloys (arsenic bronze) by cosmelting: modern experiment, ancient practice", *JAS* 26: 497–526.
Lecoq, P. (1997), *Les Inscriptions de la Perse achéménide*. Paris.
Lecuyot, G. (1993), "Résidences hellénistiques en Bactriane, résidences parthes en Iran et en Mésopotamie: diffusion ou communauté d'origine", *NAPR* 8: 31–45.
Leemans, W.F. (1960), *Foreign Trade in the Old Babylonian Period as Revealed by Texts from Southern Mesopotamia*. Leiden.
Lees, G.M. and Falcon, N.L. (1952), "The geographical history of the Mesopotamian plains", *GJ* 118: 24–39.
Lees, S.H. and Bates, D.G. (1974), "The origins of specialized nomadic pastoralism: a systemic model", *AmAnt* 39/2: 187–193.
Lefort, J., Morrisson, C. and Sodini, J.P., eds. (2005), *Les Villages dans l'empire byzantin IVe–XVe siécle*. Lethielleux.
Legge, A.J. (1996), "The beginning of caprine domestication in Southwest Asia", in Harris, ed., 238–262.
Legge, A.J. and Rowley-Conwy, P.A. (2000), "The exploitation of animals", in Moore et al., eds., 423–471.
Legrain, L. (1951), *Ur Excavations X. Seal cylinders*. New York.
Le Guen-Pollet, B. and Pelon, O., eds. (1991), *La Cappadoce méridionale jusqu'à la fin de l'époque romaine*. Paris.
Lehmann-Haupt, C. (1926), *Armenien Einst und Jetzt*. Berlin/Leipzig.

Leichty, E. (2011), *The Royal Inscriptions of Esarhaddon, King of Assyria (687–669 BC)*. Winona Lake.

Leichty, E. and Ellis, M.DeJ., eds. (1988), *A Scientific Humanist: Studies in Memory of Abraham Sachs*. Philadelphia.

Leick, G., ed. (2007), *The Babylonian World*. London.

Lehmann, G. (2002), *Bibliographie der archäologischen Fundstellen und Surveys in Syrien und Libanon*. Rahden.

Le Long, J., Andreose, A. and Ménard, P. (2010), *Le Voyage en Asie d'Odoric de Pordenone: Iteneraire de la Peregrinacion et du voyaige (1351)*. Geneva.

Lemaire, A., ed. (2000), *Les Routes du Proche-Orient: Des séjours d'Abraham aux caravanes de l'encens*. Paris.

Lemcke, G. and Sturm, M. (1997), "^{18}O and trace element measurements as proxy for the reconstruction of climate changes at Lake Van (Turkey): preliminary results", in Dalfes et al., eds., 653–678.

Le Mière, M. (1989), "Les débuts de la céramique sur le Moyen-Euphrate (6500–5500 BC)", in Haex et al., eds., 53–64.

Le Mière, M. (2000), "L'occupation Proto-Hassuna du Haut-Khabur Occidental d'après la céramique", in Lyonnet, ed., 127–149.

Le Mière, M. (2009), "Early Neolithic pottery from the Near East: the question of temper and its implications", in Astruc, Gaulon and Salanova, eds., 73–80.

Le Mière, M. and Nieuwenhuyse, O. (1996), "The prehistoric pottery", in Akkermans, ed., 119–284.

Le Mière, M. and Nishiaki Y. (2005), "The oldest pottery Neolithic of Upper Mesopotamia : new evidence from Tell Seker al-Aheimar, the Khabur, northeast Syria", *Paléorient* 31/2: 55–68.

Le Mière, M. and Picon, M (1987), "Productions locales et circulation des céramiques au VIe millénaire, au Proche-Orient", *Paléorient* 13/2: 133–147.

Le Mière, M. and Picon, M. (1998), "Les débuts de la céramique au Proche-Orient", *Paléorient* 24/2: 27–48.

Lemonnier, P., ed. (1993), *Technological Choices: Transformation in Material Cultures Since the Neolithic*. London.

Lentini, M.C., ed. (2009), *Mosaici mediterranei*. Caltanissetta.

Lenzen, H.J. (1960), *UVB* 16. Berlin.

Lenzen, H.J. (1961), *UVB* 17. Berlin.

Lenzen, H.J. (1968), *UVB* 24. Berlin.

Lenzen, H.J. (1974), "Die Architektur in Eanna in der Uruk IV Periode", *Iraq* 36: 111–128.

Leonard, J.A., Wayne, R.K., Wheeler, J., Valadez, R., Guillen, S. and Vilà, C. (2002), "Ancient DNA evidence for Old World origin of New World dogs", *Science* 298: 1613–1616.

Leriche, P. (1987), "Urbanisme défensif et occupation du territoire en Syrie héllenistique", in Frézouls, ed., 57–79.

Leriche, P. (2003), "Doura-Europos hellénistique: les témoignages archéologiques", in Sartre et al., eds., 171–191.

Leriche, P. (2004), "La rue principale et l'urbanisme d'Europos-Doura, étude préliminaire", *Parthica* 6: 145–159.

Leriche, P. (2007), "Le città dell'Oriente ellenistico", in Invernizzi, ed., 83–92.

Leriche, P. and Gelin, M., eds. (1997), *Doura-Europos, Études IV, 1991–1993*. Beirut.

Leriche, P., Gélin, M., Gharbi, M. and Yon, J-B. (1997), "Le palais du stratège à Doura-Europos", in Leriche and Gelin, eds., 55–80.

Leriche, P. and Mahmoud, A. (1994), "Doura-Europos. Bilan des recherches récentes", *CRAIBL* 1994: 395–420.

Le Rider, G. (1965), *Suse sous les Séleucides et les Parthes. Trouvallies monétaire et l'histoire de la ville*. Paris.

Lernau, H. (1986), "Fishbones excavated in two late Roman-Byzantine castella in the southern desert of Israel", in Brinkhuizen and Clason, eds., 85–102.

Lernau, H. and Lernau, O. (1994), "The fish remains", in Lechevallier and Ronen, eds., 111–121.

Lernau, O. (1995), "The fish remains of Upper Zohar", in Harper, ed., 99–111.

Lerner, J. (1977), *Christian Seals of the Sasanian Period*. Istanbul.

Lerner, J. (1991), "Some so-called Achaemenid objects from Pazyryk", *Source* 10/4: 8–15.

Lerner, J. (1992), "Christianity ii. In Pre-Islamic Persia: material remains", *EnIr* 5: 528–530.

Lerner, J.D. (1999), *The Impact of Seleucid Decline on the Eastern Iranian Plateau: The Foundations of Arsacid Parthia and Graeco-Bactria*. Stuttgart.

Leroi-Gourhan, A. (1964), *Le Geste et la parole I: Technique et langage*. Paris.

Leroi-Gourhan, A. (1965), *Le Geste et la parole II: La Mémoire et les rythmes*. Paris.

Leroux, G., Véron, A., Scholz, C. and Doumet-Serhal, C. (2003), "Chemical and isotopical analysis on weapons from the Middle Bronze Age in Sidon", *Archaeology and History in the Lebanon* 18: 58–61.

Leroy, S. (2010), "Pollen analysis of core DS7 15C (Dead Sea) showing interwoven effects of climatic change and human activities in the late Holocene", *JAS* 37: 306–316.

Leslie, K.A., Freestone, I.C., Lowry, D. and Thirwall, M. (2006), "The provenance and technology of Near Eastern glass: oxygen isotopes by laser fluorination as a complement to strontium", *Archaeometry* 48: 253–270.

Le Strange, G. (1890), *Palestine Under the Moslems*. London.

Le Strange, G. (1905), *The Lands of the Eastern Caliphate*. Cambridge.

Le Strange, G. and Nicholson, R., eds. (1921), *The Fársnáma of Ibnu'l-Balkhí*. Cambridge.

Lévêque, R. (2002), "Découvertes lors du tournage d'un documentaire sur Socotra", *Regards, Spéléo Info* 42: 8–10.

Levey, M., ed. (1967), *Archaeological Chemistry: A Symposium*. Philadelphia.

Levi, D. (1947), *Antioch Mosaic Pavements*. Princeton.

Levine, L.D. (1977a), "Notes on felt-making and the production of other textiles at Seh Gabi, a Kurdish village", in Gervers, ed., 202–213.

Levine, L.D. (1977b), "Sargon's eighth campaign", in Levine and Young, eds., 135–151.

Levine, L.D. and Young, T.C., Jr., eds. (1977), *Mountains and Lowlands: Essays in the Archaeology of Greater Mesopotamia*. Malibu.

Levine, L.I. and Weiss, Z., eds. (2000), *From Dura to Sepphoris: Studies in Jewish Art and Society in Late Antiquity*. Portsmouth.

Levine, M.A. (1999), "The origins of horse husbandry on the Eurasian steppe", in Levine et al., eds., 5–58.

Levine, M.A, Renfrew, A.C. and Boyle, K., eds. (2003), *Prehistoric Steppe Adaptation and the Horse*. Cambridge.

Levine, M.A., Rassamakin, Y.Y., Kislenko, A.M. and Tatarintseva, N.S., eds. (1999), *Late Prehistoric Exploitation of the Eurasian Steppe*. Cambridge.

Lévi-Strauss, C. (1995), *Myth and Meaning: Cracking the Code of Culture*. New York.

Levy, T.E., ed. (1995), *The Archaeology of Society in the Holy Land*, 1st edn. New York.

Levy, T.E. (1986), "The Chalcolithic period", *BA* 49/2: 82–108.

Levy, T.E., ed. (1987), *Shiqmim I*. Oxford.

Levy, T.E., ed. (1998a), *The Archaeology of Society in the Holy Land*, 2nd edn. Leicester.

Levy, T.E. (1998b), "Cult, metallurgy and rank societies: Chalcolithic Period (ca.4500–3500 BCE)", in Levy, ed., 226–244.

Levy, T.E., ed. (2003), *The Archaeology of Society in the Holy Land*, 3rd edn. London/New York.

Levy, T.E. (2006), *Archaeology, Anthropology and Cult: The Sanctuary at Gilat, Israel*. London.

Levy, T.E., Adams, R.B., Hauptmann, A., Prange, M., Schmitt-Strecker, S. and Najjar, M. (2002), "Early Bronze Age metallurgy: a newly discovered copper manufactory in southern Jordan", *Antiquity* 76: 425–437.

Levy, T.E., Burton, M. and Rowan, Y. (2006), "Chalcolithic hamlet excavations near Shiqmim, Negev Desert, Israel", *JFA* 31: 41–60.

Levy, T.E., Daviau, P.M.M., Younker, R.W. and Shaer, M., eds. (2007), *Crossing Jordan: North American Contributions to the Archaeology of Jordan*. London/Oakville.

Levy, T.E. and Najjar, M. (2007), "Ancient metal production and social change in southern Jordan: the Edom Lowlands Regional Archaeology Project and hope for a UNESCO World Heritage site in Faynan", in Levy et al., eds., 97–105.

Levy, T.E. and Rosen, S.A. (1987), "The chipped stone industry at Shiqmim: Typological considerations", in Levy, ed., 281–294, 564–610.

Levy, T.E. and Shalev, S. (1989), "Prehistoric metalworking in the southern Levant: archaeometallurgical and social perspectives", *WA* 20: 352–372.

Lev-Yadun, S., Gopher, A. and Abbo, S. (2000), "The cradle of agriculture", *Science* 288: 1602–1603.

Lewin, R. (1987), "Africa: Cradle of modern humans", *Science* 237: 1292–1295.

Lewis, B. (1980), *The Sargon Legend: A Study of the Akkadian Text and the Tale of the Hero who was Exposed at Birth*. Cambridge.

Lewis-Williams, D. and Pearce, D. (2005), *Inside the Neolithic Mind: Consciousness, Cosmos, and the Realm of the Gods*. London.

Lézine, A.-M., Saliège, J.-F., Robert, C., Wertz, R. and Inizan, M.-L. (1998), "Holocene lakes from Ramlat as-Sab'atayn (Yemen) illustrate the impact of monsoon activity in Southern Arabia", *QR* 50: 290–299.

Lézine, A.-M., Tiercelin, J.-J., Robert, C., Saliège, J.-F., Cleuziou, S., Inizan, M.-L. and Braemer, F. (2007), "Centennial to millennial-scale variability of the Indian monsoon during the early Holocene from a sediment, pollen and isotope record from the desert of Yemen", *Palaeogeography, Paleoclimatology, and Paleoecology* 243: 235–249.

Lichtheim, M. (1975), *Ancient Egyptian Literature*. Vol. I: *The Old and Middle Kingdom*. Berkeley/Los Angeles/London.

Lichtheim, M. (1976), *Ancient Egyptian Literature*. Vol. II: *The New Kingdom*. Berkeley, Los Angeles and London.
Lieberman, S. ed. (1975), *Sumerological Studies in Honor of Thorkild Jacobsen*. Chicago.
Lieberman, S. (1990), "Canonical and official cuneiform texts: towards an understanding of Ashurbanipal's personal tablet collection", in Abusch et al., eds., 305–336.
Liebeschuetz, W. (1997), *The Rise of the Bishop in the Christian Roman Empire and the Successor Kingdoms*. Krakow.
Liebman, M. and Rizvi, U.Z., eds. (2008), *Archaeology and the Postcolonial Critique*. Lanham.
Lilyquist, C. and Brill, R.H. (1996), "A collaborative study of early glassmaking in Egypt c.1500 BC", in Anonymous (1996a), ed., 1–9.
Lilyquist, C., Brill, R.H. with Wypyski, M.T. (1993), *Studies in Early Egyptian Glass*. New York.
Limet, H. (1960), *Le Travail du métal au pays de Sumer au temps de la IIIe dynastie d'Ur*. Paris.
Limet, H. (1972), "Les métaux à l'époque d'Agadé (2370–2250 av. J.-C.)", *JESHO* 15: 3–34.
Limet, H. (1985), "La technique du bronze dans les archives de Mari", in Durand and Kupper, eds., 201–210.
Limet. H. (1993), "Metalle und Metallurgie. A.I. In Mesopotamien", *RlA* 8/1: 96–112.
Limor, O. and Stroumsa, G.G., eds. (2006), *Christians and Christianity in the Holy Land: From the Origin to the Latin Kingdom*. Turnhout.
Lincoln, B. (2007), *Religion, Empire and Torture: The Case of Achaemenian Persia, with a Postscript on Abu Ghraib*. Chicago.
Lindström, G. (2003), *Uruk. Siegelabdrücke auf hellenistischen Tonbullen und Tontafeln*. Mainz.
Linduff, K. (2003), "A walk on the wild side: late Shang appropriation of horses in China", in Levine et al., eds., 139–162.
Linduff, K. (2004), *Silk Road Exchange in China*. Philadelphia.
Lipiński, E., ed. (1979), *State and Temple Economy in the Ancient Near East*. Leuven.
Lipiński, E. (2000), *The Aramaeans: Their Ancient History, Culture, Religion*. Leuven.
Liphschitz, N., Gophna, R., Bonani, G. and Feldstein, A. (1996), "Wild olive (Olea europaea) stones from a Chalcolithic cave at Shoham, Israel, and their implications", *Tel Aviv* 23: 135–142.
Liphschitz, N., Gophna, R., Hartman, M. and Biger, G. (1991), "The beginning of olive (Olea europea) cultivation in the Old World: A reassessment", *JAS* 18: 441–453.
Lipschits, O. and Blenkinsopp, J., eds. (2003), *Judah and the Judeans in the Neo-Babylonian Period*. Winona Lake.
Lipschits, O. and Oeming, M., eds. (2006), *Judah and the Judeans in the Persian Period*. Winona Lake.
Littauer, M.A. and Crouwel, J.H. (1979), *Wheeled Vehicles and Ridden Animals in the Ancient Near East*. Leiden.
Littleton, J. and Frohlich, B. (1993), "Fish-eaters and farmers: dental pathology in the Arabian Gulf", *AJPA* 92: 427–447.
Littmann, E. and Meredith, D. (1953), "Nabataean inscriptions from Egypt", *BSOAS* 15: 1–28.

Littmann, E. and Meredith, D. (1954), "Nabataean inscriptions from Egypt-II", *BSOAS* 16: 211–246.

Liverani, M. (1974), "La royauté syrienne de l'Age du Bronze récent", in Garelli, ed., 329–356.

Liverani, M. (1975), "Communautés de village et palais royale dans la Syrie à IIème mill.", *JESHO* 18: 146–164.

Liverani, M. (1981), "Critique of variants and the titulary of Sennacherib", in Fales, ed., 225–257.

Liverani, M. (1987), "The collapse of the Near Eastern regional system at the end of the Bronze Age: the case of Syria", in Rowlands et al., eds., 66–73.

Liverani, M. (1988), "The growth of the Assyrian Empire in the Habur/Middle Euphrates area: a new paradigm", *State Archives of Assyria Bulletin* 2: 81–98.

Liverani, M. (1989), "Economy of Ugaritic royal farms", in Zaccagnini, ed., 127–168.

Liverani, M. (1990), *Prestige and Interest: International Relations in the Near East ca.1600–1100 BC*. Padua.

Liverani, M. (1992), "Early caravan trade between South Arabia and Mesopotamia", *Yemen* 1: 111–115.

Liverani, M., ed. (1993a), *Akkad, the First World Empire: Structure, Ideology, Traditions*. Padua.

Liverani, M. (1993b), "Akkad: An introduction", in Liverani, ed., 1–10.

Liverani, M. (1993c), "Model and actualization. The kings of Akkad in the historical tradition", in Liverani, ed., 41–67.

Liverani, M., ed. (1995), *Neo-Assyrian Geography*. Rome.

Liverani, M. (2004), "Toward a definition of private economic activity in third millennium Babylonia", in Rollinger and Ulf, eds., 91–111.

Liverani, M. (2005), "Imperialism", in Pollock and Bernbeck, eds., 223–243.

Liverani, M. (2006), *Uruk: The First City*. London/Oakville.

Liverani, M. (2007), "City and countryside in third-millennium southern Babylonian", in Stone, ed., 185–211.

Liverani, M. (2008), "The Late Bronze Age: materials and mechanisms of trade and cultural exchange", in Aruz et al., eds., 160–168.

Livingstone, A. (1988), "The Isin 'Dog House' revisited", *JCS* 40: 54–60.

Livingstone, E.A., ed. (1993), *Studia Patristica XXV. Papers presented at the Eleventh International Conference on Patristic Studies held in Oxford 1991. Biblica et Apocrypha, Orientalia, Ascetica*. Leuven.

Lloyd, A.B. (2000), "The Late Period (664–332 BC)", in Shaw, ed., 364–387.

Lloyd, S. (1938), "Some ancient sites in the Sinjar District", *Iraq* 5: 123–142.

Lloyd, S. (1978), *The Archaeology of Mesopotamia: From the Old Stone Age to the Persian Conquest*. London.

Lloyd, S. (1980), *Foundations in the Dust: The Story of Mesopotamian Exploration*. London.

Lloyd, S. and Safar, F. (1943), "Tell Uqair: Excavations by the Iraq Government Directorate of Antiquities in 1940 and 1941", *JNES* 2: 131–189.

Lloyd, S. and Safar, F. (1945), "Tell Hassuna: excavations by the Iraq Government Directorate General of Antiquities in 1943 and 1944, *JNES* 4: 255–289.

Lloyd, S. and Safar, F. (1947), "Eridu: a preliminary communication on the first season's excavations: January–March 1947", *Sumer* 3: 84–111.

Lloyd, S. and Safar, F. (1948), "Eridu: a preliminary communications [sic] on the second season's excavations: 1947–1948", *Sumer* 4: 115–125.

Loffreda, S. (1990), "The Greek inscriptions on the Byzantine lamps from the Holy Land", in Bottini et al., eds., 475–500.

Loftus, R.T., MacHugh, D.E., Bradley, D., Sharp, P.M. and Cunningham, P. (1994), "Evidence for two independent domestications of cattle", *PNAS* 91: 2757–2761.

Loftus, W.K. (1856), "On the excavations undertaken at the ruins of Susa in 1851-2", *Transactions of the Royal Society of Literature* 5: 422–453.

Loftus, W.K. (1857), *Travels and Researches in Chaldaea and Susiana with an Account of Excavations at Warka, the "Erech" of Nimrod, and Shush, "Shushan the Palace" of Esther, in 1849–52*. London.

Lombard, P. and Kervran, M. (1993), "Les niveaux 'Hellénistique' du Tell de Qal'at al-Bahrain. Donnés préliminaires", in Finkbeiner, ed., 127–160.

Longacre, W.A. (1999), "Standardization and specialization: what's the link?", in Skibo and Feinman, eds., 44–58.

Longacre, W.A., Kvamme, K. and Kobayashi, M. (1988), "Southwestern pottery standardisation: an ethno-archaeological view from the Philippines", *Kiva* 53: 101–112.

Longman, T. (1991), *Fictional Akkadian Autobiography: A Generic and Comparative Study*. Winona Lake.

Longo, O. (1987), "A trip among fish eaters", *Newsletter of Baluchistan Studies* 4: 11–17.

Loosley, E. (2003), *The Architecture and Liturgy of the Bema in Fourth- to Sixth-Century Syrian Churches*. Kaslik.

Lora, S., Petiti, E. and Hausleiter, A. (2010), "Burial contexts at Tayma, NW-Arabia – Archaeological and anthropological data", in Weeks, ed., 237–247.

Lorentz, K.O. (2010), "Ubaid headshaping: negotiations of identity through physical appearance?", in Carter and Philip, eds., 125–148.

Lorey, I. (2008), "Virtuosinnen der Freiheit. Zur Implosion von politischer Virtuosität und produktiver Arbeit", in Altenhain et al., eds., 153–164.

Losch, S., Grupe, G. and Peters, J. (2006), "Stable isotopes and dietary adaptations in humans and animals at Pre-Pottery Neolithic Nevali Çori, Southeast Turkey", *AJPA* 131: 181–193.

Loseva, I.M. (1962), "Nekotoryeurartskie juvelirnye isdelija s izobraženiem ritual'nych scen (K voprosy ob ikonografii boga Chaldi i bogini Arubani)", in Pigulevskaja., ed., 300–311.

Loud, G. and Altman, C.B. (1938), *Khorsabad*, vol. 2. Chicago.

Loud, G., Frankfort, H. and Jacobsen, T. (1936), *Khorsabad*, vol. 1. Chicago.

Lovell, J. and Rowan, Y.M., eds. (2011), *Culture, Chronology, and the Chalcolithic: Theory and Transition*. London.

Löw, U. (1993), "Kunsthandel und Fälschungsproblamatik", *Mitteilungen des Deutschen Archäologen-Verbandes* 24: 36–41.

Löw. U. (1998), *Figürlich verzierte Metallgefäße aus Nord- und Nordwestiran*. Münster.

Löw, U. (2003), "Die Plünderung der kulturellen Einrichtungen im Irak unter besonderer Berücksichtigung des Nationalmuseums in Bagdad", *MDOG* 135: 13–56.

Lucas, A. and Harris, J.R. (1989), *Ancient Egyptian Materials and Industries*. London.

Lucassen, J., Lucassen, L. and Manning, P., eds. (2010), *Migration History in World History: Multidisciplinary Approaches*. Leiden.

Luciani, M. (2000), "Iron Age graves in northern Syria: the Tell Shiukh Fawqani evidence", in Matthiae et al., eds., 803–811.

Luciani, M. (2003), "The Lower City of Qatna in the Late Bronze and Iron Ages: Operation K", *Akkadica* 124: 144–163.

Lucke, B., Schmidt, M., al-Saad, Z., Bens, O. and Hüttl, R.F. (2005), "The abandonment of the Decapolis region in northern Jordan: forced by environmental change?", *Quaternary International* 135: 65–81.

Luckenbill, D.D. (1924), *Annals of Sennacherib*. Chicago.

Luckenbill, D.D. (1927), *Ancient Records of Assyria and Babylonia*, Vol. 2. New York.

Ludwig, A., Pruvost, M., Reissmann, M., Benecke, N., Brockmann, G.A., Castanos, P., Cieslak, M., Lippold, S., Llorente, L., Malaspinas, A-S., Slatkin, M. and Hofreiter, M. (2009), "Coat color variation at the beginning of horse domestication", *Science* 324: 485.

Luedtke, B.E. (1992), *An Archaeologist's Guide to Chert and Flint*. Los Angeles.

Luff, R. and Rowley-Conwey, P. eds.(1994), *Whither Environmental Archaeology?* Oxford.

Luft, U. (2010), *Bi'r Minayh: Reprt on the Survey 1998–2004*. Budapest.

Luke, C. and Kersel, M. (2006), "Mysterious shepherds and hidden treasure: the culture of looting in Lydia, Western Turkey", *JFA* 31: 185–198.

Luke, C. and Roosevelt, C.H. (2009), "The Central Lydia Archaeological Survey: documenting the prehistoric through Iron Age periods", in Manning and Bruce, eds., 199–218.

Lumsden, S. (2004), "The production of space at Nineveh", *Iraq* 66: 187–197.

Lund, J. (2004), "The Iron Age and the Graeco-Roman period", in Riis et al., 38–84.

Lundström, S. (2009), *Die Königsgrüfte im Alten Palast von Assur*. Wiesbaden.

Lundström, S. (in press), *Die Fragmente von Torleibungsfiguren aus dem Alten Palast von Assur*. Wiesbaden.

Lupton, A. (1996), *Stability and Change: Socio-Political Development in North Mesopotamia and South-East Anatolia 4000–2700 BC*. Oxford.

Luschey, H. (1983), "Die Darius-Statuen aus Susa und ihre Rekonstruktion", in Koch and MacKenzie, eds., 191–206.

Luther, A. (1999), "Medo nectis catenas? Die Expedition des Aelius Gallus im Rahmen der augusteischen Parther politik", *Orbis Terrarum* 5: 157–182.

L'vov-Basirov, O.P.C. (2001), "Achaemenian funerary practices in western Asia Minor", in Bakir, ed., 101–107.

Lynott, M.J. and Wylie, A. (2000), *Ethics in American Archeology*. Washington, DC.

Lyonnet, B. (1996), *Sarazm (Tadjikistan), céramiques: (Chalcolithique et Bronze ancien)*. Paris.

Lyonnet, B., ed. (2000), *Prospection archéologique du Haut-Khabur occidental (Syrie du N.E.)*, vol. 1. Beirut.

Lyonnet, B., ed. (2007), *Les Cultures du Caucase (VIe–IIIe millénaires avant notre ère): Leurs relations avec le Proche-Orient*. Paris.

Maas, M. (1992), *John Lydus and the Roman Past: Antiquarianism and Politics in the Age of Justinian*. London.

MacAdam, H.I. (1984), "Some aspects of land tenure and social development in the Roman Near East: Arabia, Phonicia and Syria", in Khalidi, ed., 45–62.

Macalister, R.A.S. (1912), *The Excavation of Gezer: 1902–1905 and 1907–1909*, vol. 2. London.

Macchiarelli, R. (1989), "Prehistoric 'fish-eaters' along the eastern Arabian coasts: dental variation, morphology, and oral health in the Ra's al-Hamra community (Qurum, Sultanate of Oman, 5th–4th millennia BC)", *AJPA* 78: 575–594.

MacDonald, B. (2001), "The Bible, archaeology and Jordan", in MacDonald, Adams and Bienkowski, eds., 663–669.

MacDonald, B. (2009), *Pilgrimage in Early Christian Jordan: A Literary and Archaeological Guide*. Oakville.

MacDonald, B., Adams, R. and Bienkowski, R., eds. (2001), *The Archaeology of Jordan*. Sheffield.

Macdonald, M.C.A. (1994), "A dated Nabataean inscription from Southern Arabia", in Nebes, ed., 132–141.

Macdonald, M.C.A. (1995), "North Arabia in the first millennium BCE", in Sasson, ed., 1351–1369.

Macdonald, M.C.A. (1997), "Trade routes and trade goods at the northern end of the 'incense road' in the first millennium BC", in Avanzini, ed., 333–349.

Macdonald, M.C.A. (2004), "Ancient North Arabian", in Woodard, ed., 488–533.

Macdonald, M.C.A. and Phillips, C.S., eds. (2005), *A.F.L. Beeston and the Arabian Seminar and Other Papers Including a Personal Reminiscence by W.W. Müller*. Oxford.

Machinist, P. (1983), "Assyria and its image in the First Isaiah", *JAOS* 103: 719–737.

Machule, D., Benter, M., Czichon, R.M. and Werner, P. (1996), "Tall Munbaqa/Ekalte 1994", *MDOG* 128: 11–32.

Mackay, E.J.H. (1929), *A Sumerian Palace and the "A" Cemetery at Kish, Mesopotamia, Part II*. Chicago.

Mackay, E.J.H. (1937–8), *Further Excavations at Mohenjo-Daro, Being an Official Account of Archaeological Excavations at Mohenjo-daro carried out by the Government of India between the years 1927 and 1931*. New Delhi.

Mackay, E.J.H. (1943), *Chanhu-Daro Excavations 1935–36*. New Haven.

Mackenzie, S.R.M. (2005), *Going, Going, Gone: Regulating the Market in Illicit Antiquities*. Leicester.

Macklin, M.G. and Lewin, J. (1993), "Holocene river alluviation in Britain", *Zeitschrift für Geomorphologie* (suppl.) 88: 109–122.

Mączyńska, A. (2004), "Pottery from Tell el-Farkha", in Hendrickx et al., eds., 421–442.

Maddin, R. (1982), "Early iron technology in Cyprus", in Muhly et al., eds., 303–314.

Maddin, R. (2003), "The beginning of the use of iron", in Stöllner et al., eds., 309–318.

Maddin, R., Muhly, J.D. and Stech, T. (1999), "Early metalworking at Çayönü", in Hauptmann et al., eds., 37–44.

Maffei, F. de' (1985), "Le fortificazioni sul limes orientale ai tempi di Giustiniano", *Corsi di Cultura sull'Arte ravvenate e Bizantina* 32: 109–150.

Maffei, F. de', Barsanti, C. and Guiglia, A., eds. (1990), *Costantinopoli e l'arte delle province orientali*. Rome.

Magee, P. (2003), "Columned halls, power and legitimation in the Southeast Arabian Iron Age", in Potts et al., eds., 181–191.

Magee, P. (2004), *Excavations at Tepe Yahya, Iran, 1967–1975: The Iron Age Settlement*. Cambridge.

Magee, P. (2008), "Perceptions on the morphology and style of artefacts *vs* the carbon cycle: a response to O.W. Muscarella's dating of Muweilah", *AWE* 7: 203–217.

Magee, P., Thompson, E., MacKay, A., Kottaras, P. and Weeks, L. (2002), "Further evidence of desert settlement complexity: report on the 2001 excavations at the Iron Age site of Muweilah, Emirate of Sharjah, United Arab Emirates", *AAE* 13: 133–156.

Maggetti, M. and Messiga, B., eds. (2006), *Geomaterials in Cultural Heritage*. London.

Magnussen, B., Renzetti, S., Vian, P. and Voicu, S.J., eds. (1997), *Ultra Terminum Vagari. Scritti in onore di Carl Nylander*. Roma.

Magny, M., Vannière, B., Zanchetta, G., Fouache, E., Touchais, G., Petrika, L., Coussot, C., Walter-Simonnet, A.-V. and Arnaud, F. (2009), "Possible complexity of the climatic event around 4300–3800 cal. BP in the central and western Mediterranean", *The Holocene* 19: 823–833.

Maher, L., Banning, E. and Chazan, M. (2011), "Oasis or mirage? Assessing the role of abrupt climate change in the prehistory of the southern Levant", *CAJ* 21/1: 1–30.

Maier, F.G. (1996), "History from the earth: the Kingdom of Paphos in the Achaemenid period (XI–XX)", *Transeuphratène* 12: 121–137.

Maigret, A. de (1996), *Arabia Felix. Un Viaggio nell'Archeologia dello Yemen*. Milan.

Maigret, A. de (1997), "The frankincense road from Najran to Ma'an: a hypothetical itinerary", in Avanzini, ed., 315–331.

Maigret, A. de (1999), "The Arab nomadic people and the cultural interference between the 'Fertile Crescent' and 'Arabia Felix'", *AAE* 10: 220–224.

Maigret, A. de (2004), "La route caravanière de l'encens dans l'Arabie préislamique: éléments d'information sur son itinéraire et sa chronologie", *CY* 11: 36–46.

Maiocchi, M. (2009), *Classical Sargonic Tablets Chiefly from Adab in the Cornell University Collections*. Bethesda.

Mair, V.H. (1995), "Mummies of the Tarim Basin", *Archaeology* 48/2: 28–35.

Mair, V.H., ed. (1998), *The Bronze Age and Early Iron Age People of Eastern Central Asia*. Washington, DC.

Mair, V.H., ed. (2006), *Contact and Exchange in the Ancient World*. Honolulu.

Majd, M.G. (2003), *The Great American Plunder of Persia's Antiquities, 1925–1941*. Lanham.

Majidzadeh, Y. (1981), "Sialk III and the pottery sequence at Tepe Ghabristan: the coherence of the cultures of the Iranian Plateau", *Iran* 19: 141–146.

Majidzadeh, Y. (1982), "Lapis lazuli and the Great Khorasan road", *Paléorient* 8/1: 59–70.

Majidzadeh, Y. (2003), *Jiroft: The Earliest Oriental Civilization*. Tehran.

Majidzadeh, Y. (2008a), "Excavations at Konar Sandal in the region of Jiroft in the Halil Basin: first preliminary report (2002–2008)", *Iran* 46: 69–104.

Majidzadeh, Y. (2008b), *Excavations at Tepe Ghabristan, Iran*. Rome.

Majidzadeh, Y. (in press), "Halil Rud Archaeological Project: a fabulous discovery", in Majidzadeh and Pittman, eds.

Majidzadeh, Y. and Pittman, H. (in press), *Jiroft: Archaeology of the Bronze Age in the Halil River Basin, Southeast Iran*. Philadelphia.

Majumdar, N.G. (1934), *Exploration in Sind*. New Delhi.

Makarewicz, C. (2005), "Pastoral production in a corporate system: the Early Bronze Age at Khirbet El-Minsahlat, Jordan", in Buitenhuis et al., eds., 167–181.

Makarewicz, C. (2007), *Evolution of Foddering Practices in the Southern Levantine Pre-Pottery Neolithic*. Cambridge.

Malbran-Labat, F. (1995), *Les Inscriptions royales de Suse: Briques de l'époque paléo-élamite à l'Empire néo-élamite*. Paris.

Malek Shahmirzadi, S. (1986), "A review of the development of archaeology in Iran", *Asar* 12–14: 133–160 (in Persian).

Malek Shahmirzadi, S. (1987), "History of the archaeological research in Iran", *Iranian Journal of Archaeology and History (Majalle-ye Bāstān Šenāsī va Tarikh)* 2: 57–73 (in Persian).

Malek Shahmirzadi, S. (1990), Development of archaeological research in Iran, in Mousavi Garmarudi, ed., 373–447 (in Persian).

Malek Shahmirzadi, S. (1997), "Pishnahadi baraye tadvin-e jadaval-e gahnegari-ye Khuzestan [A proposal for the chronology of the Khuzestan]", in Mousavi, ed., 395–419 (in Persian).

Malek Shahmirzadi, S., ed., (2004), *The Potters of Sialk*. Tehran.

Mallampati, H. (2005), "Archaeology and collecting: law, ethics, politics", in Root, ed., 109–125.

Mallet, M. (2000), *Woven Structures: A Guide to Oriental Rug and Textile Analysis*. Atlanta.

Mallon, A., Koeppel, R. and Neuville, R. (1934), *Teleilat Ghassul I: Compte rendu des fouilles de l'Institut Biblique Pontifical, 1929–1932*. Rome.

Mallory, J.P. and Mair, V. (2000), *The Tarim mummies*. London.

Mallowan, M.E.L. (1936), "The bronze head of the Akkadian period from Nineveh", *Iraq* 3: 104–110.

Mallowan, M.E.L. (1947), "Excavations at Brak and Chagar Bazar", *Iraq* 9: 1–259.

Mallowan, M.E.L., ed. (1966), *Nimrud and its Remains*, vol. 2. London.

Mallowan, M.E.L. and Rose, J.C. (1935), "Excavations at Tell Arpachiyah, 1933", *Iraq* 2: 1–178.

Mangafa, M. and Kotsakis, K. (1996), "A new method for the identification of wild and cultivated charred grape seeds", *JAS* 23: 409–418.

Mango, C.A. (1959), *The Brazen House: A Study on the Vestibule of the Imperial Palace of Constantinople*. Copenhagen.

Mango, C.A. (1972), "The Church of Saints Sergius and Bacchus at Constantinople and the alleged tradition of octagonal Palatine churches", in Hunger and Restle, eds., 189–193.

Mango, C.A. (1980), *Byzantium: The Empire of New Rome*. London.

Mango, C.A. (1985), *Le Développement urbain de Costantinople (IV–VII siècles)*. Paris.

Mango, C.A. (1986), *Byzantine Architecture*. London.

Mango, C.A. and Dagron, G., eds. (1995), *Constantinople and its Hinterland*. Aldershot.

Mango, M.M. (1982), "Catalogue of sites and monuments", in Bell, ed., 97–173.

Mango, M.M. (1986), *Silver from Early Byzantium: The Kapr Karaon and Related Treasures*. Baltimore.

Mango, M.M. (1996), "Byzantine maritime trade with the East (4th–7th centuries)", *ARAM* 8: 139–163.

Mango, M.M., ed. (2009), *Byzantine Trade, 4th–12th Centuries: The Archaeology of Local, Regional and International Exchange*. Farnham.

Maniyattu, P. (1995), *Heaven on Earth: The Theology of Liturgical Spacetime in the East Syrian Qurbana*. Rome.

Manning, S.W. and Bruce, M.J., eds. (2009), *Tree-Rings, Kings, and Old World Archaeology and Environment: Papers Presented in Honor of Peter Ian Kuniholm*. Oxford.

Many, B., ed. (2003), *The Seventy Great Mysteries of ancient Egypt*. London.

Manzoor, S. (1989), *Tradition and Development: An Approach to Vernacular Architectural Patterns in Iran*. Gothenburg.

Maraqten, M. (1996), "The Aramaic pantheon of Tayma", *AAE* 7: 17–31.

Maras, S. (2010), "A reassessment of brick motifs and brick-building techniques at Achaemenid Susa", in Curtis and Simpson, eds., 207–219.

Marchand, S.L. (1996), *Down from Olympus: Archaeology and Philhellenism in Germany, 1750–1970*. Princeton.

Marchegay, S. (2008), "Les pratiques funéraires à Ougarit au IIe millénaire. Bilan et perspectives des recherches", in Yon and Calvet, eds., 97–118.

Marchesi, G. (2006), *LUMMA in the Onomasticon and Literature of Ancient Mesopotamia*. Padua.

Marchetti, N. and Nigro, L. (1995–6), "Handicraft production, secondary food transformation and storage in the public building P4 at EB IVA Ebla", *Berytus* 42: 9–36.

Marcus, E.S. (2002), "Early seafaring and maritime activity in the southern Levant from prehistory through the third millennium BCE", in van den Brink and Levy, eds., 137–190.

Marcus, E.S. (2007), "Amenemhet II and the sea: maritime aspects of the Mit Rahina (Memphis) inscription", *ÄL* 17: 137–190.

Marcus, J. and Sabloff, J.A., eds. (2008), *The Ancient City: New Perspectives on Urbanism in the Old and New World*. Sante Fe.

Marek, C. (1993), "Die Expedition des Aelius Gallus nach Arabien Jahre 25 v. Chr.", *Chiron* 23: 121–156.

Marek, C. (1994), "Der römische Inschriftenstein von Barāqiš", in Nebes, ed., 178–190.

Marfoe, L. (1979), "The integrative transformation: patterns of sociopolitical organization in southern Syria", *BASOR* 234: 1–42.

Marfoe, L. (1980), review of Kempinski, *The Rise of an Urban Culture* and Amiran, Early Arad, *JNES* 39: 315–322.

Marfoe, L. (1982), "Empire and ethnicity in Syrian society: 'From archaeology to historical sociology' revisited", in Yon et al., eds., 463–479.

Marfoe, L. (1987), "Cedar forest to silver mountain: social change and the development of long distance trade in early Near Eastern societies", in Rowlands et al., eds., 25–35.

Marfoe, L. (1995), *Kamid el-Loz 13. The Prehistoric and Early Historic Context of the Site*. Saarbrücken.

Marfoe, L. (1998), *Kamid el-Loz. 14. Settlement History of the Biqa' up to the Iron Age*. Saarbrücken.

Margalit, S. (1987), "The north church of Shivta: the discovery of the first church", *PEQ* 119: 106–121.

Margueron, J.-C., ed. (1980), *Le Moyen Euphrate: Zone des contacts et d'échanges*. Strasbourg.
Margueron J.-C. (1982), "Architecture et urbanisme", in Beyer, ed., 23–39.
Margueron, J.-C. (1987a), "Du nouveau sur la cour du Palmier", *MARI* 5: 463–469.
Margueron, J.-C. (1987b), "État présent des recherches sur l'urbanisme de Mari I", *MARI* 5: 483–498.
Margueron, J.-C. (1991), "Fondations et refondations au Proche Orient au Bronze Recent", in Mazzoni, ed., 3–27.
Margueron, J.-C. (1992), "Les bois dans l'architecture", *BSA* 6: 79–96.
Margueron, J.-C. (1995), "Emar, capital of Aštata in the fourteenth century BC", *BA* 58: 126–138.
Margueron, J.-C. (2000), *Mari, métropole de l'Euphrate*. Paris.
Margueron, J.-C. (2004), "Le palais royal d'Ougarit", in Galliano and Calvet, eds., 143–149.
Margueron, J.-C. (2008), "Mari", in Aruz et al., eds., 27–33.
Mark, S. (1997), *From Egypt to Mesopotamia*. London.
Markoe, G., ed. (2003), *Petra Rediscovered: Lost city of the Nabataeans*. New York/Cincinnati.
Marks, A.E., ed. (1977), *Prehistory and Paleoenvironments of the Central Negev, Israel*, vol. 2. Dallas.
Marksteiner, T. (2002a), "Städtische Strukturen im vorhellenistischen Lykien", in Hansen, ed., 57–72.
Marksteiner, T. (2002b), *Trysa, Eine zentrallykische Niederlassung im Wandel der Zeit*. Vienna.
Marksteiner, T. (2005), "Das achämenidenzeitliche Lykien", in Briant and Boucharlat, eds., 27–48.
Markwart, J. (1931), *A Catalogue of the Provincial Capitals of Ērānšahr (Pahlavi text, version and commentary)*. Rome.
Marro, C. (2007), "Upper-Mesopotamia and Transcaucasia in the Late Chalcolithic Period (4000–3500 BC)", in Lyonnet, ed., 77–94.
Marro, C. and Hauptmann, H., eds. (2000), *Chronologie des pays du Caucase et de l'Euphrate aux IVe-IIIe millénaires*. Istanbul.
Marshack, A. (1997), "Paleolithic image making and symboling in Europe and the Middle East: A comparative review", in Conkey et al., eds., 53–91.
Marshall, J. (1931), *Mohenjo-Daro and the Indus Civilization*. London.
Martin, H.P. (1983), "Settlement patterns at Shurruppak", *Iraq* 45: 24–31.
Martin, L., McCorriston, J. and Crassard, R. (2009), "Early Arabian pastoralism at Manayzah in Wadi Sana, Hadramawt", *PSAS* 39: 271–282.
Martin, L., Russell, N. and Carruthers, D. (2002), "Animal remains from the Central Anatolian Neolithic", in Gérard and Thissen, eds., 193–216.
Martinez-Sève, L. (1996), "Une statuette romaine trouvée à Suse et la chronologie du Donjon", in Gasche and Hrouda, eds., 171–80.
Martinez-Sève, L (2002), *Les Figurines de Suse. De l'époque néo-élamite à l'époque sassanide*. Paris.
Martinon-Torres, M. and Rehren, T., eds. (2008), *Archaeology, History and Science: Integrating Approaches to Ancient Materials*. London.

Marx, K. and Engels, F. (1958), *Die Deutsche Ideologie*. Berlin.

Mar'yashev, A.N. and Goryachev, A.A. (1998), *Naskal'nye Izobrazheniya Semirech'ya*. Almaty.

Marzahn, J., ed. (2008), *Babylon: Wahrheit*. Berlin.

Marzahn, J. and Salje, B., ed. (2003), *Wiedererstehendes Assur. 100 Jahre deutsche Ausgrabungen in Assyrien*. Mainz.

Mashkour, M. (1998), "The subsistence economy in the rural community of Geoktchik Depe in southern Turkmenistan: preliminary results of the faunal analysis", in Buitenhuis et al., eds., 200–220.

Mashkour, M. (2002), "Chasse et élevage au nord du plateau central Iranien entre le Neolithique et l'âge du fer", *Paléorient* 28: 27–42.

Mashkour, M., ed. (2006a), *Equids in Time and Space*. Oxford.

Mashkour, M. (2006b), "Towards a specialized subsistence economy in the Marv Dasht Plain: Preliminary zooarchaeological analysis of Tall-E Mushki, Tall-E Jari a and B, and Tall-E Bakun A and B", in Alizadeh, ed., 101–105.

Mashkour, M., Choyke, A.M., Buitenhuis, H. and Poplin, F., eds. (2000), *Archaeozoology of the Near East IVB*. Groningen.

Masimov, I.S. (1981), "The study of Bronze Age sites in the Lower Murghab", in Kohl, ed., 194–220.

Masry, A.H. (1997[1974]), *Prehistory in Northeastern Arabia: The Problem of Interregional Interaction*. Miami.

Mass, J.L., Wypyski, M.T. and Stone, R.E. (2001), "Evidence for the metallurgical origins of glass at two ancient Egyptian glass factories", *Materials Research Society Bulletin* (January): 38–43.

Mass, J.L., Wypyski, M.T. and Stone, R.E. (2002), "Malkata and Lisht glassmaking technologies: towards a specific link between second millennium BC metallurgists and glassmakers", *Archaeometry* 44: 67–82.

Masson, M.E. and Pugachenkova, G.A. (1982), *The Parthian Rhytons of Nisa*. Florence.

Masson, V.M. (1968), "The urban revolution in South Turkmenia", *Antiquity* 42: 178–187.

Masson, V.M. (1988), *Altyn-Depe*. Philadelphia.

Masson, V.M. (1992), "The decline of the Bronze Age civilization and movements of the tribes", in Dani and Masson, eds., 337–356.

Masson, V.M. (2002), "Cultures of the Steppe Bronze Age and urban civilizations in the south of Central Asia", in Jones-Bley and Zdanovich, eds., 547–557.

Masuda, S. (1984), "The excavations at Tappeh Sang-e Caxmaq", *AfO* 31: 209–212.

Masuda S. and Shaath, S. (1983), Qminas, the Neolithic site near Tell Deinit, Idlib (preliminary report), *AAAS* 33: 199–231.

Mathers, C. and Stoddart, S., eds. (1994), *Development and Decline in the Mediterranean Bronze Age*. Sheffield.

Matheson, S.B. (1982), *Dura Europos: The Ancient City and the Yale Collection*. New Haven.

Mathiesen, H.E. (1992), *Sculpture in the Parthian Empire: A Study in Chronology*, 2 vols. Aarhus.

Mathieu, J.R. and Meyer, D.A. (1997), "Comparing axe heads of stone, bronze, and steel: studies in experimental archaeology", *JFA* 24: 333–352.

Matney, T. (1996), "Urban planning and the archaeology of society at Early Bronze Age Titriş Höyük", in Hopkins, ed., 19–34.
Matney, T. and Algaze, G. (1995), "Urban development at mid-late Early Bronze Age Titriş Höyük in southeastern Anatolia", *BASOR* 299/300: 33–52.
Matney, T., Roaf, M., MacGinnis, J. and McDonald, H. (2002), "Archaeological excavations at Ziyaret Tepe, 2000 and 2001", *Anatolica* 28: 47–89.
Matoïan, V. (1999), "L'art des objets en matériaux vitreux", *Le Monde de la Bible* 120: 56–57.
Matoïan, V. (2000a), "Données nouvelles sur le verre en Syrie au IIe millénaire av. J.-C.: Le cas de Ras Shamra-Ougarit", in Nenna, ed., 23–47.
Matoïan, V. (2000b), "Matières premières – matériaux vitreux: données récentes", *Orient-Express* 2: 41–42.
Matson, F.R. (1951), "The composition and working properties of ancient glass", *Journal of Chemical Education* 28: 82–87.
Matson, F.R. (1953), "A study of wall plaster, flooring, and bitumen", in Schmidt, 285–288.
Matson, F.R. and Rindone, G.E., eds. (1963), *Advances in Glass Technology, Part 2. History Papers and Discussions of the Technical Papers of the VI International Congress on Glass*. New York.
Matsumoto, K. (1981), "Tells Songor B and C", *Al-Rāfidān* 2: 182–193.
Matsumoto, K. (1987), "The Samarra period at Tell Songor A", in Huot, ed., 189–198.
Matsumoto, K. (1991), "Preliminary report on the excavations at Kish/Hursagkalamma, 1988–1989", *Al-Rāfidān* 12: 261–297.
Matthäus, H. (1985), *Metallgefäße und Gefäßuntersätze der Bronzezeit, der geometrischen und archaischen Periode auf Cypern mit einem Anhang der bronzezeitlichen Schwertfunde auf Cypern*. Stuttgart.
Matthers, J., ed. (1981), *The River Qoueiq, Northern Syria, and its Catchment*. Oxford.
Matthews, D.M. (1997a), "The Early Dynastic–Akkadian transition, Part 1. When did the Akkadian period begin?", *Iraq* 59: 1–8.
Matthews, D.M. (1997b), *The Early Glyptic of Tell Brak: Cylinder Seals of Third Millennium Syria*. Fribourg.
Matthews, D.M. (1997c), "Seal impressions on sherds from Hama", *EVO* 19: 121–155.
Matthews, D.M. and Eidem, J. (1993), "Tell Brak and Nagar", *Iraq* 55: 201–207.
Matthews, J.F. (1984), "The tax law of Palmyra", *JRS* 74: 157–180.
Matthews, R.J. (1993), *Cities, Seals and Writing: Archaic Seal Impressions from Jemdet Nasr and Ur*. Berlin.
Matthews, R.J. (1994), "Imperial catastrophe or local incident? An Akkadian hoard from Tell Brak, Syria", *CAJ* 4/2: 290–302.
Matthews, R.J. (2000), *The Early Prehistory of Mesopotamia, 500,000 to 4,500 BC*. Turnhout.
Matthews, R.J. (2002a), "Zebu: Harbingers of doom in Bronze Age Western Asia?", *Antiquity* 76: 438–446.
Matthews, R.J. (2002b), *Secrets of the Dark Mound: Jemdet Nasr 1926–1928*. Warminster.
Matthews, R.J. (2003a), *Excavations at Tell Brak*. Vol. 4. *Exploring an Upper Mesopotamian Regional Centre, 1994–1996*. Cambridge.

Matthews, R.J. (2003b), *The Archaeology of Mesopotamia: Theories and Approaches*. London and New York.

Matthews, R.J. and Fazeli, H. (2004), "Copper and complexity: Iran and Mesopotamia in the fourth millennium BC", *Iran* 42: 61–75.

Matthews, R.J. and Glatz, C., eds. (2009), *At Empires' Edge: Project Paphlagonia, Regional Survey in North-Central Turkey*. Ankara.

Matthews, R.J., Mohammadifar, Y., Matthews, W. and Motarjem, A. (2010), "Investigating the Early Neolithic of Western Iran: the Central Zagros Archaeological Project (CZAP)", *Antiquity* 84, Project Gallery.

Matthews, R.J. and Postgate, J.N. (1987), "Excavations at Abu Salabikh, 1985–86", *Iraq* 49: 91–119.

Matthews, W. and Postgate, J.N. (1994), "The imprint of living in an early Mesopotamian city: questions and answers", in Luff and Rowley-Conwy, eds., 171–212.

Matthiae, P. (1981), *Ebla: An Empire Rediscovered*. New York.

Matthiae, P. (1997a), "Where were the Early Syrian kings of Ebla buried?", *AoF* 24: 268–276.

Matthiae, P. (1997b), "Ebla and Syria in the Middle Bronze Age", in Oren, ed., 379–414.

Matthiae, P. (1998), *Ninive*. Munich.

Matthiae, P. (2002), "A preliminary note on the MB I-II fortification system at Ebla", *DaM* 13: 29–51.

Matthiae, P. (2006), "Old Syrian statuary and carved basins from Ebla: new documents and interpretations", in Butterlin et al., eds., 423–438.

Matthiae, P. (2010), "Recent excavations at Ebla, 2006–2007", in Matthiae et al., eds., 3–26.

Matthiae, P., Enea, A., Peyronel, L., and Pinnock, F., eds. (2000), *Proceedings of the First International Congress on the Archaeology of the Ancient Near East 1998*. Rome.

Matthiae, P., Pinnock, F., Nigro, L., Marchetti, N. and Romano, L., eds. (2010), *Proceedings of the 6th International Congress on the Archaeology of the Ancient Near East. May 5th–10th, 2008, "Sapienza" – Università di Roma*. Wiesbaden.

Mattila, R. (2000), *The King's Magnates: A Study of the Highest Officials of the Neo-Assyrian Empire*. Helsinki.

Mattli, K. and Gasser, J. (2008), "A neutral, impartial and independent approach: Key to ICRC's acceptance in Iraq", *International Review of the Red Cross* 90 (869): 153–168.

Maul, S.M. (2010), "Die Tontafelbibliothek aus dem sogenannten 'Haus des Beschwörungspriesters'", in Maul and Heeßel, eds., 189–228.

Maul, S.M. and Heeßel, N.P., eds. (2010), *Assur-Forschungen*. Wiesbaden.

Maupoix, M., and Coulon, G., eds. (1998), *Regards sur la Perse antique*. Paris.

Maurer-Trinkaus, K. (1983), "Pre-Islamic settlement and land use in Damghan", *IrAnt* 18: 119–144.

Maurer-Trinkaus, K. (1989), "Archaeological survey of the Damghan plain, northeastern Iran, 1976–1977", in Dyson and Howard, eds., 135–141.

Maxwell-Hyslop, K.R. (1971), *Western Asiatic Jewellery, c.3000–612 BC*. London.

Maxwell-Hyslop, K.R. (1972), "The metals *amūtu* and *aši'u* in the Kültepe texts", *AnSt* 22: 159–162.

Mayer, W. (2001), *Tall Munbaqa – Ekalte II: Die Texte*. Saarbrücken.
Mayerson, P., ed. (1994a), *Monks, Martyrs, Soldiers and Saracens: Papers on the Near East in Late Antiquity (1962–1993)*. Jerusalem.
Mayerson, P. (1994b), "The island of Iotabê in the Byzantine sources: A reprise", in Mayerson, ed., 352–355.
Mazar, A. (1992), *Archaeology of the Land of the Bible, 10,000–596 BCE*. New York.
Mazar, A. (2003), "Beth Shean in the second millenium BCE: from Canaanite town to Egyptian stronghold", in Bietak, ed., 323–339.
Mazurowski, R.F. (2004), "Tell Qaramel: Excavations, 2003", *Polish Archaeology in the Mediterranean* 15: 355–370.
Mazurowski, R.F. (2007), "Tell Qaramel: Excavations 2006", *Polish Archaeology in the Mediterranean* 18: 571–586.
Mazzoni, S. (1990), "La période perse à Tell Mardikh dans le cadre de l'évolution de l'âge du Fer en Syrie", *Transeuphratèane* 2: 187–199.
Mazzoni, S., ed. (1991), *Nuove Fondazioni nel Vicino Oriente antico: Realtà e ideologia*. Pisa.
Mazzoni, S. (1992), *Le Impronte su Giara Eblaite e Siriane nel Bronzo Antico*. Rome.
Mazzoni, S. (1997), "The gate and the city: change and continuity in Syro-Hittite urban ideology", in Wilhelm, ed., 307–338.
Mazzoni, S. (1998), "The Late Iron I and Early Iron II levels", in Cecchini and Mazzoni, eds., 163–171.
Mazzoni, S. (2000), "Syria and the periodization of the Iron Age: a cross-cultural perspective", in Bunnens, ed., 31–59.
Mazzoni, S. (2002), "The ancient Bronze Age pottery tradition in northwestern central Syria", in al-Maqdissi, Matoïan & Nicolle, eds., 69–96.
Mazzoni, S. (2003), "Ebla: crafts and power in an emergent state of third millennium BC Syria", *JMA* 16/2: 173–191.
McAnany, P. and Yoffee, N. (2010a), "Why we question collapse and study human resilience, ecological vulnerability and the aftermath of empire", in McAnany and Yoffee, eds., 1–17.
McAnany, P.A. and Yoffee, N. (eds) (2010b), *Questioning Collapse: Human Resilience, Ecological Vulnerability and the Aftermath of Empire*. Cambridge.
McCall, B.K. (2009), *The Mamasani Archaeological Survey: Epipalaeolithic to Elamite Settlement Patterns in the Mamasani District of the Zagros Mountains, Fars Province, Iran*. Sydney.
McCartney, C. (1999), "Opposed platform technology and the Cypriot Aceramic Neolithic", *Neo-Lithics* 1/99: 7–10.
McClure, H.A. (1976), "Radiocarbon chronology of late Quaternary lakes in the Arabian desert", *Nature* 263: 755–756.
McClure, H.A. (1978), "Ar-Rub' Al Khali", in Al-Sayari and Zötl, eds., 252–263.
McConaughy, M.A. (1980), "F. Chipped stone tools", *BASOR* 240: 53–58.
McConchie, M. (2004), *Archaeology at the North-East Anatolian Frontier V. Iron Technology and Iron-Making Communities of the First Millennium BC*. Leuven.
McCorriston, J. (1992), "The Halaf environment and human activities in the Khabur drainage, Syria", *JFA* 19: 315–333.
McCorriston, J. (1994), "Acorn eating and agricultural origins: California ethnographies as analogies for the ancient Near East", *Antiquity* 68: 97–107.

McCorriston, J. (1997), "The fiber revolution: textile extensification, alientation, and social stratification in ancient Mesopotamia", *CA* 38: 517–549.

McCorriston, J. (2002), "Spatial and temporal variation in Mesopotamian agricultural practices in the Khabur Basin, Syrian Jazira", *JAS* 29: 485–498.

McCown, D.E. (1942), *The Comparative Stratigraphy of Early Iran*. Chicago.

McCown, D. and Haines, R.C. (1967), *Nippur I: Temple of Enlil, Scribal Quarter and Soundings*. Chicago.

McCracken, C.D. (1986), "Clothing as language: an object lesson in the study of the expressive properties of material culture", in Reynolds and Stott, eds., 103–128.

McCray, P. and Kingery, W.D., eds. (1998), *The Prehistory and History of Glassmaking Technology*. Westerville.

McCrindle, J.W. (1882), *Ancient India as Described by Ktesias the Knidian*. Calcutta.

McCrindle, J.W. (1897), *The Christian Topography of Cosmas, an Egyptian Monk*. London.

McCrindle, J.W. (1926), *Ancient India as Described by Megasthenes and Arrian: Being a Translation of the Fragments of the Indika of Megasthenes Collected by Dr. Schwanbeck, and of the First Part of the Indika of Arrian*. Calcutta.

McEvilley, T. (2002), *The Shape of Ancient Thought: Comparative Studies in Greek and Indian Philosophies*. New York.

McEwan, C.W., Braidwood, L.S., Frankfort, H., Güterbock, H.G., Haines, R.C., Kantor, H.J. and Kraeling, C.H. (1957), *Soundings at Tell Fakhariyah*. Chicago.

McGovern, P.E. (1980), *Ornamental and Amuletic Jewelry Pendants of Late Bronze Age Palestine: An Archaeological Study*. Ann Arbor.

McGovern, P.E. (1985), *Late Bronze Palestinian Pendants: Innovation in a Cosmopolitan Age*. Sheffield.

McGovern, P.E. (1986), *The Late Bronze and Early Iron Ages of Central Transjordan: The Baq'ah Valley Project, 1977–1981*. Philadelphia.

McGovern, P.E. (1987a), "Central Transjordan in the Late Bronze and Early Iron Ages: an alternative hypothesis of socio-economic transformation and collapse", in Hadidi, ed., 267–273.

McGovern, P.E. (1987b), "Silicate industries of Late Bronze-Early Iron Palestine: technological interaction between Egypt and the Levant", in Bimson and Freestone, eds., 91–114.

McGovern, P.E. (1995), "Technological innovation and artistic achievement in the Late Bronze and Iron Ages of Central Transjordan", in Amr et al., eds., 29–37.

McGovern, P.E. (2007), *Ancient Wine: The Search for the Origins of Viniculture*, 4th edn. Princeton/Oxford.

McGovern, P.E. (2009), *Uncorking the Past: The Quest for Wine, Beer and Other Alcoholic Beverages*. Berkeley/Los Angeles/London.

McGovern, P.E., Fleming, S.J. and Katz, S.H., eds. (1995), *The origins and ancient history of wine*. Luxembourg.

McGovern, P.E., Fleming, S.J. and Swann, C.P. (1991), "The beads from Tomb B10a B27 at Dinkha Tepe and the beginnings of glassmaking in the ancient Near East", *AJA* 95: 395–402.

McGovern, P.E., Fleming, S.J. and Swann, C.P. (1993), "The Late Bronze Egyptian garrison at Beth Shan: glass and faience production and importation in the Late New Kingdom", *BASOR* 290/291: 1–27.

McGovern, P.E., Voigt, M.M., Glusker, D.L. and Exner, L.J. (1986), "Neolithic resinated wine", *Nature* 381 (June 6): 480–481.

McGrail, S. (2001), *Boats of the World*. Oxford.

McKeon, J.F.X. (1970), "An Akkadian victory stele", *Boston Museum Bulletin* 68: 226–243.

McLaughlin, R. (2010), *Rome and the Distant East: Trade Routes to the Ancient Lands of Arabia, India and China*. London and New York.

McMahon, A. (2006), *Nippur V: The Early Dynastic to Akkadian Transition. The Area WF Sounding at Nippur*. Chicago.

McMahon, A. (2009a), "The lion, the king and the cage : Late Chalcolithic iconography and ideology in northern Mesopotamia", *Iraq* 71: 115–124.

McMahon, A. (2009b), *Once There Was a Place: Settlement Archaeology at Chagar Bazar, 1999–2002*. London.

McMahon, A. and Oates, J. (2007), "Excavations at Tell Brak 2006–2007", *Iraq* 69: 145–171.

McMahon, A., Tunca, Ö. and Bagdo, A.-M. (2001), "New excavations at Chagar Bazar, 1999–2000", *Iraq* 63: 201–222.

McMahon, G. (1991), *The Hittite State Cult of the Tutelary Deities*. Chicago.

McNicoll, A.W. (1997), *Hellenistic Fortifications*. Oxford.

Meadow, R.H. (1984a), "Notes on the faunal remains from Mehrgarh, Pakistan, with a focus on cattle (Bos)", in Allchin, ed., 34–40.

Meadow, R.H. (1984b), "Animal domestication in the Middle East: a view from the eastern margin", in Clutton-Brock and Grigson, eds., 309–337.

Meadow, R.H. (1986a), "Some equid remains from Çayönü, southeastern Turkey", in Meadow and Uerpmann, eds., 266–301.

Meadow, R.H. (1986b), "The geographical and palaeoenvironmental setting of Tepe Yahya", in Beale, 21–38.

Meadow, R.H. (1986c), *Animal Exploitation in Prehistoric Southeastern Iran: Faunal Remains from Tepe Yahya and Tepe Gaz Tavila-R37, 5500–3000 BC*. Cambridge.

Meadow, R.H. (1989), "Osteological evidence for the process of animal domestication", in Clutton-Brock, ed., 80–96.

Meadow, R.H. and Uerpmann, H.-P., eds. (1986), *Equids in the Ancient World*, vol. 1. Wiesbaden.

Meadow, R.H. and Uerpmann, H.-P., eds. (1991), *Equids in the Ancient World*, vol. 2. Wiesbaden.

Meadow, R.H. and Zeder, M.A., eds. (1978), *Approaches to Faunal Analysis in the Middle East*. Cambridge.

Meadows, J.R.S., Cemal, I., Karaca, O., Gootwine, E. and Kijas, J.W. (2007), "Five ovine mitochondrial lineages identified from sheep breeds of the Near East", *Genetics* 175: 1371–1379.

Mecquenem, R. de (1911), "Constructions élamites du Tell de l'Acropole de Suse", *MDP* 12: 65–78.

Mecquenem, R. de (1928), "Notes sur la céramique peinte archaïque en Perse", *MDP* 20: 99–132.

Mecquenem, R. de (1930), "Les derniers résultats des fouilles de Suse", *Revue des Arts Asiatiques* 6: 73–88.

Mecquenem, R. de (1934), "Fouilles de Suse 1929–1933", *MDP* 25: 177–188.

Mecquenem, R. de (1938), "Achaemenid Architecture, B: the Achaemenid and later remains at Susa", in Pope, ed., 321–329.

Mecquenem, R. de (1943), "Fouilles de Suse 1933–1939", *MDP* 29: 3–161.

Mecquenem, R. de (1947), "Contribution à l'étude du palais achéménide de Suse", in Mecquenem, Le Breton and Rutten, eds., 3–119.

Mecquenem, R. de (1980), "Les fouilleurs de Suse", *IrAnt* 15: 1–48.

Mecquenem, R. de, Contenau, G., Pfister, R. and Belaiew, N. (1943), *Archéologie Susienne*. Paris.

Mecquenem, R. de, Le Breton, L. and Rutten, M., eds. (1947), *Archéologie Susienne*. Paris.

Mehendale, S. (2005), *Begram: New Perspectives on the Ivory and Bone Carvings*. Los Angeles (http://ecai.org/begramweb/).

Mehryar, M. (2000), "Sima-ye shahr-e Bishāpur dar dowrān-e eslamī", in Anonymous, ed., 11–138.

Mei, J. (2003), "Qijia and Seima-Turbino: the question of early contacts between Northwest China and the Eurasian steppe", *Bulletin of the Museum of Far Eastern Antiquities* 75: 31–54.

Mei, J. and Rehren, T. (2009), *Metallurgy and Civilisation: Eurasia and Beyond*. London.

Meier, D. (1986), *A Survey in Northeastern Syria*. Istanbul.

Meier, S.A. (2000), "Diplomacy and international marriages", in Cohen and Westbrook, eds., 165–173.

Meinhold, W. (2009), *Ištar in Aššur*. Münster.

Meissner, B., Schmitt, O. and Sommer, M., eds. (2005), *Krieg – Gesellschaft – Institutionen, Beiträge zu einer vergleichenden Kriegsgeschichte*. Berlin.

Melchert, H.C. (2002), "Tarhuntašša in the SÜDBURG hieroglyphic inscription", in Yener and Hoffner, eds., 137–43.

Melchert, H.C., ed. (2003), *The Luwians*. Leiden.

Melchert, H.C. (2010), "Lydian language and inscriptions", in Cahill, ed., 267–272.

Meldgaard, J., Mortensen, P. and Thrane, H. (1963), "Excavations at Tepe Guran, Luristan: preliminary report of the Danish Archaeological Expedition to Iran 1963", *Acta Archaeologica* 34: 97–133.

Melikishvili, G.A. (1960), *Urartskiie Klinoobrazniie Nadpisi (UKN)*. Moscow.

Melikishvili, G.A. (1971), *Die Urartäische Sprache*. Rome.

Melka, R.L. (1973), "Max Freiherr von Oppenheim: sixty years of scholarship and political intrigue in the Middle East", *Middle Eastern Studies* 9: 81–93.

Mellaart, J. (1964), "Excavations at Çatal Hüyük, 1963, Third Preliminary Report", *AnSt* 14: 39–119.

Mellaart, J. (1966), "Excavations at Çatal Hüyük, 1965, Fourth Preliminary Report", *AnSt* 16: 165–191.

Mellaart, J. (1967), *Çatal Hüyük: A Neolithic Town in Anatolia*. London.

Mellaart, J. (1970), *Excavations at Haçilar*. Edinburgh.

Mellaart, J. (1975), *The Neolithic of the Near East*. London.

Mellink, M.J., ed. (1971), "Archaeology in Asia Minor", *AJA* 75: 161–181.

Mellink, M.J. (1974), "Hittite friezes and gate sculptures", in Bittel et al., eds., 201–214.

Mellink, M.J., ed. (1982), "Archaeology in Asia Minor", *AJA* 86: 557–576.

Mellink, M.J. (1991), "Native kingdoms of Anatolia", *CAH2* 3/2: 619–665.

Mellink, M.J. (1998), "Bilinguals and the alphabet in Cilicia, Tabal and Phrygia", in Arsebük et al., eds., 495–498.

Menant, J.D. (1887), "The French expedition to Susiana", *AJA* 3: 87–93.

Merpert, N.I. and Munchaev, R.M. (1993), "Burial practices of the Halaf culture", in Yoffee and Clark, eds., 207–224.

Merrillees, P.H. (2005), *Catalogue of the Western Asiatic Seals in the British Museum. Cylinder Seals VI. Pre-Achaemenid and Achaemenid Periods.* London.

Merrillees, R.S. (1983), "Late Cypriote pottery from Byblos 'Necropole K'", *RDAC 1983*: 188–192.

Merrillees, R.S. (2003), "The first appearances of Kamares Ware in the Levant", *ÄL* 13: 127–142.

Merryman, J.H., ed. (2006), *Imperialism, Art and Restitution.* Cambridge.

Méry, S. and Tengberg, M. (2009), "Food for eternity? The analysis of a date offering from a 3rd millennium BC grave at Hili North, Abu Dhabi (United Arab Emirates)", *JAS* 36/9: 2012–2017.

Meshel, Z. (2000), *Sinai: Excavations and Studies.* Oxford.

Meskell, L. ed. (1998), *Archaeology Under Fire: Nationalism, Politics and Heritage in the Eastern Mediterranean and Middle East.* London.

Meskell, L. (1999), *Archaeologies of Social Life.* Oxford.

Meskell, L. (2002), "Negative heritage and past mastering in archaeology", *Anthropological Quarterly* 75/3: 557–574.

Meskell, L. (2004), *Object Worlds in Ancient Egypt.* New York.

Meskell, L. and Preucel, R.W., eds. (2004), *A Companion to Social Archaeology.* Oxford.

Messenger, M. ed. (1989), *The Ethics of Collecting Cultural Property: Whose Culture? Whose Property?* Albuquerque.

Messina, V. (2007), "Seleucia al Tigri", in Invernizzi, ed., 107–115.

Metropolitan Museum of Art (October 2006), "The Antioch Chalice, [Byzantine] (50.4)" (http://www.metmuseum.org/toah/works-of-art/50.4).

Metzger, M. (1991), *Kamid el-Loz 7. Die spätbronzezeitlichen Tempelanlagen. Stratigraphie, Architektur und Installationen.* Bonn.

Metzger, M. (1993), *Kamid el-Loz 8. Die spätbronzezeitlichen Tempelanlagen. Die Kleinfunde.* Bonn.

Meuszynski, J. (1981), *Die Rekonstruktion der Reliefdarstellungen und ihrer Anordnung im Nordwestpalast von Kalḫu (Nimrud).* Mainz.

Meyer, E. (1929), "Seleukia und Ktesiphon", *MDOG* 67: 1–26.

Meyer, K.E. (1973), *The Plundered Past.* New York.

Meyer-Plath, G. and Schneider, A.M. (1943), *Die Landmauer von Konstantinopel.* Berlin.

Meyers, E.M., ed. (1997), *The Oxford Encyclopedia of Archaeology in the Near East.* New York.

Meyers, E.M., ed. (1999), *Galilee Through the Centuries: Confluence of Cultures.* Winona Lake.

Meyers, P. (2000), "The casting process of the statue of Queen Napir-Asu in the Louvre", *JRA Supplementary Series* 39: 11–18.

Mgaloblishvili, T. (2007), "An unknown Georgian monastery in the Holy Land", *ARAM* 19: 527–539.

Michalowski, P. (1987), "Charisma and control: on continuity and change in early Mesopotamian bureaucratic systems", in Gibson and Biggs, eds., 55–68.

Michalowski, P. (1993), "Memory and deed: the historiography of the political expansion of the Akkad state", in Liverani, ed., 69–90.

Michalowski, P. (1995), "Sumerian literature: an overview", in Sasson, ed., 2279–2291.

Michel, A. (2001), *Les Églises d'époque byzantine et umayyade de la Jordanie (provinces d'Arabie et de Palestine), Ve–VIIIe siècle: Typologie architecturale et aménagements liturgiques*. Turnhout.

Michel, C. (2008), "The Alāhum and Aššur-taklāku archives found in 1993 at Kültepe Kaniš", *AoF* 35: 53–67.

Micklin, P. (2007), "The Aral Sea disaster", *Annual Review of Earth and Planetary Sciences* 35: 47–72.

Mielczarek, M. (1993), *Cataphracti and Clibanarii: Studies on the Heavy Armoured Cavalry of the Ancient World*. Lodz.

Mielke, D.P. (2001), "Die Grabungen an der Südspitze", in Müller-Karpe, 237–243.

Mielke, D.P. 2011a), "Hittite cities: looking for a concept", in Genz and Mielke, eds., 153–194.

Mielke, D.P. (2011b), "Key sites of the Hittite Empire", in Steadman and McMahon, eds., 1031–1054.

Mielke, D.P., Schoop, U.-D. and Seeher, J., eds. (2006), *Strukturung und Datierung in der hethitischen Archäologie/Structuring and dating in Hittite archaeology: Requirements, problems and new approaches*. Istanbul.

Miglus, P. (1985), "Zur Großen Zikkurat in Assur", *MDOG* 117: 21–45.

Miglus, P. (1989), "Untersuchungen zum Alten Palast in Assur", *MDOG* 121: 93–133.

Miglus, P. (1996), *Das Wohngebiet von Assur*. Berlin.

Miglus, P. (1999), *Städtische Wohnarchitektur in Babylonien und Assyrien*. Berlin.

Miglus, P. (2004), "Palast. B. Archäologisch", *RlA* 10: 233–276.

Miglus, P. (2006), "Prozession(sstraße). B. Archäologisch", *RlA* 11/1–2: 103–105.

Miglus, P. (2010), "Festungswerke von Assur im 2. Jahrtausend v. Chr.", in Maul and Heeßel, eds., 229–243.

Migne, J.-P. (1865), *Patrologia Graeca*, vol. 86b. Paris.

Migowski, C., Stein, M., Prasad, S., Negenendank, J. and Agnon, A. (2006), "Holocene climate variability and cultural evolution in the Near East from the Dead Sea record", *QR* 66: 421–31.

Mikesell, M. (1969), "The deforestation of Mount Lebanon", *Geographical Review* 59: 1–28.

Milano, L., de Martino, S., Fales, F.M. and Lanfranchi, G.B., eds. (1999), *Landscapes: Territories, Frontiers and Horizons in the Ancient Near East*, vol 1. Padua.

Milano, L., de Martino, S., Fales, F.M. and Lanfranchi, G.B., eds. (2000), *Landscapes: Territories, Frontiers and Horizons in the Ancient Near East*, vol. 2. Padua.

Milburn, R. (1988), *Early Christian Art and Architecture*. Berkeley/Los Angeles.

Mildenberg, L. (1995), "Petra on the Frankincense Road?", *Transeuphratène* 10: 69–72.

Mildenberg, L. (1996), "Petra on the Frankincense Road – Again?", *ARAM* 8: 55–65.

Miles, R. and Zavala, L., eds. (1994), *Towards the Museum of the Future: New European Perspectives*. London.

Milevski, I. (1996–7), "Settlement patterns in northern Judah during the Achaemenid period, according to the Hill Country of Benjamin and Jerusalem surveys", *Bulletin of the Ango-Israel Archaeological Society* 15: 7–29.

Milevski, I.M., Fabian, P. and Marder, O. (2011), "Canaanean blades in Chalcolithic contexts in the southern Levant", in Lovell and Rowan, eds. 149–159.

Millar, F. (1981), *The Roman Empire and its Neighbours*, 2nd edn. London/New York.

Millar, F. (1990), "The Roman coloniae of the Near East: a study of cultural relations", in Solin and Kajava, eds., 7–58.

Millar, F. (1993), *The Roman Near East, 31 BC–AD 337*. Cambridge/London.

Millar, F. (1998), "Caravan cities: the Roman Near East and long-distance trade by land", in Austin et al., eds., 119–137.

Millard, A.R. (1988), "The bevelled-rim bowls: their purpose and significance", *Iraq* 50: 49–57.

Millard, A.R. (2010), "The cuneiform tablets from Tell Nebi Mend", *Levant* 42/2: 226–236.

Mille, B., Besenval, R. and Bourgarit, D. (2004), "Early 'lost-wax casting' in Baluchistan (Pakistan): the 'leopards weight' from Shahi-Tump", in Stöllner et al., eds., 274–281.

Miller, D. (1987), *Material Culture and Mass Consumption*. Oxford.

Miller, J.M. and Hayes, J.H. (1986), *A History of Ancient Israel and Judah*. Philadelphia.

Miller, M. (1991), *Archaeological Survey of the Kerak Plateau*. Atlanta.

Miller, N.F. (1977), "Preliminary report on the botanical remains from Tepe Jaffarabad, 1969–1974 campaigns", *DAFI* 7: 49–53.

Miller, N.F. (1981), "The plant remains", in Wright, ed., 227–232.

Miller, N.F. (1984), "Vegetation and plant use at Kurban Höyük", *Anatolica* 13: 85–89, 119–120.

Miller, N.F., ed. (1990), *Economy and Settlement in the Near East*. Philadelphia.

Miller, N.F. (1997), "Farming and herding along the Euphrates: environmental constraint and cultural choice (fourth to second millennia BC)", in Zettler, 123–132.

Miller, N.F. (1998), "The macrobotanical evidence for vegetation in the Near East, c.18000/16000 BC to 4000 BC", *Paléorient* 23/2: 197–207.

Miller, N.F. (1999), "Agricultural development in western Central Asia in the Chalcolithic and Bronze Ages", *VHA* 8: 13–19.

Miller, N.F. (2000), "Plant forms in jewellery from the Royal Cemetery at Ur", *Iraq* 62: 149–155.

Miller, N.F. (2003), "Archaeobotany in Iran, past and future", in Miller and Abdi, eds., 9–16.

Miller, N.F. (2008), "Sweeter than wine? The use of the grape in early Western Asia", *Antiquity* 82: 937–946.

Miller, N.F. and Abdi, K., eds., (2003), *Yeki Bud, Yeki Nabud: Essays on the Archaeology of Iran in Honor of William M. Sumner*. Los Angeles.

Miller, N.F. and Sumner, W.M. (2004), "The Banesh-Kaftari interface: the view from Operation H5, Malyan (corrected)", *Iran* 42: 77–89.

Miller, R. (1985), *Flint Knapping and Arrowhead Manufacture at Tell Hadidi, Syria*. Milwaukee.

Milles, A., Williams, D. and Gardner, N. eds. (1989), *The Beginnings of Agriculture.* Oxford.

Milson, D. (2007), *Art and Architecture of the Synagogue in Late Antique Palestine: In the Shadow of the Church.* Leiden/Boston.

Minchin, C.F. (1907), *Jhalawan District.* Bombay.

Minorsky, V. (1944), "Roman and Byzantine campaigns in Atropatene", *BSOAS* 11: 243–265.

Minzoni-Déroche, A. (1992), "Üçağizli magara, un site aurignacien dans le Hatay (Anatolie). Premiers résultats", *Paléorient* 18/1: 89–96.

Minzoni-Déroche, A. (1993), "Middle and Upper Paleolithic in the Taurus-Zagros region", in Olszewski and Dibble, eds., 147–158.

Miranda, S. (1983), "Etudes sur le Palais de Sacré Constantinople. The Walker Trust et le Palais de Daphné", *Byzantinoslavica* 44: 41–49, 196–204.

Miron, E. (1992), *Axes and Adzes from Canaan.* Stuttgart.

Miron, R. (1982), "Die 'mittelbronzezeitlichen' Gräber am Nordhang des Tells", in Hachmann, ed., 101–121.

Miron, R. (1990), *Kamid el-Loz 10. Das Schatzhaus im Palastbereich. Die Funde.* Bonn.

Miroschedji, P. de (1971), *L'Époque pré-urbaine en Palestine.* Paris.

Miroschedji, P. de (1972), "Prospections dans les vallées de Fasa et de Darab (rapport préliminaire)", in Bagherzadeh, ed., 1–13.

Miroschedji, P. (1974), "Tépé Jalyan, une nécropole du IIIe millnaire av. J.-C. au Fars oriental (Iran)", *Arts Asiatiques* 30: 19–64.

Miroschedji, P. de (1981a), "Fouilles du chantier Ville Royale II à Suse (1975–1977)", *DAFI* 12: 9–136.

Miroschedji, P. de (1981b), "Observations dans les couches néo-élamites au nord-ouest du tell de la Ville Royale à Suse", *DAFI* 12: 143–167.

Miroschedji, P. de (1981c), "Prospections archéologiques au Khuzistan en 1977", *DAFI* 12: 169–192.

Miroschedji, P. de (1981d), "Le dieu élamite au serpent et aux eaux jaillissantes", *IrAnt* 16: 1–25.

Miroschedji, P. de (1985), "La fin du royaume d'Anšan et de Suse et la naissance de l'Empire perse", *ZA* 75: 265–306.

Miroschedji, P. de (1986), "La localisation de Madaktu et l'organisation politique de l'Élam à l'époque néo-élamite", in De Meyer, Gasche, and Vallat, eds., 209–225.

Miroschedji, P. de (1987a), "Fouilles du chantier Ville Royale II à Suse (1975–1977), II. Niveaux d'époques achéménide, séleucide, parthe et islamique", *DAFI* 15: 11–136.

Miroschedji, P. de (1987b), "Observations dans les couches néo-élamites au nord-ouest du Tell de la Ville Royale à Suse", *DAFI* 15: 143–167.

Miroschedji, P. de (1989a), "Le processus d'urbanisation en Palestine au Bronze Ancien: Chronologie et rythmes", in de Miroschedji, ed., 63–79.

Miroschedji, P. de, ed. (1989b), *L'Urbanisation de la Palestine à l'Âge du bronze ancien.* Oxford.

Miroschedji, P. de (1990), "La fin de l'Élam: essai d'analyse et d'interprétation", *IrAnt* 25: 47–95.

Miroschedji, P. de (2002), "The socio-political dynamics of Egyptian-Canaanite interaction in the Early Bronze Age", in van den Brink and Levy, eds., 39–57.

Miroschedji, P. de (2003), "Susa and the highlands: major trends in the history of Elamite civilization", in Miller and Abdi, eds., 17–38.

Miroschedji, P. de (2009), "Rise and collapse in the southern Levant in the Early Bronze Age", *Scienze dell'Antichità* 15: 101–129.

Misra, M.K., Ragland, K.W. and Baker, A.J. (1993), "Wood ash composition as a function of furnace temperature", *Biomass and Bioenergy* 4: 103–116.

Mitchell, T.C. (2000), "The Persepolis sculptures in the British Museum", *Iran* 38: 49–56.

Mitchell T.C. and Searight, A. (2008), *Catalogue of the Western Asiatic Seals in the British Museum. Stamp Seals III. Impressions of Stamp Seals on Cuneiform Tablets, Clay Bullae, and Jar Handles*. Leiden.

Mithen, S.J. (2003), *After the Ice: A Global Human History, 20,000–5000 BC*. London.

Mittmann, S. (1970), *Beiträge zur Siedlungs- und Territorialgeschichte des nördlichen Ostjordanlandes*. Wiesbaden.

Miyake, Y. and Tsuneki, A. (1996), "The earliest pottery sequence of the Levant: new data from Tell El-Kerkh 2, northern Syria", *Paléorient* 22/1: 109–123.

Młynarczyk, J. and Burdajewicz, M. (2005), "North-West Church in Hippos (Sussita), Israel: five years of archaeological research (2000–2004)", in Cameron, ed., 39–57.

Mode, M. and Tubach, J., eds. (2006), *Arms and Armour as Indicators of Cultural Transfer: The Steppes and the Ancient World from Hellenistic Times to the Early Middle Ages*. Wiesbaden.

Mofidi Nasrabadi, B. (2005), "Eine Steininschrift des Amar-Suena aus Tappeh Bormi (Iran)", *ZA* 95: 161–171.

Mofidi Nasrabadi, B. (2007), *Archäologische Ausgrabungen und Untersuchungen in Čogā Zanbil*. Münster.

Moghaddam, A. (2008), *Later Village Period Settlement Development in the Karun River Basin, Greater Susiana, Southwestern Iran*. Sydney.

Moghaddam A. and Miri, N. (2003), "Archaeological research in the Mianab Plain of lowland Susiana, southwestern Iran", *Iran* 41: 99–137.

Moghaddam, A. and Miri, N. (2007), "Archaeological surveys in the 'eastern corridor', south-western Iran", *Iran* 45: 23–55.

Moghaddam, A., Tengberg, M., Mashkour, M., Mohaseb, A. and Naderi, R. (2008), "Tall-e Abu Chizan (Tol-e Borchizun), Dar Bastare Bastanshenakhtiye Avakhere *Dowrane Rousta Neshini Shushan* e Bozorg (Tall-e Abuchizan, in the Later Village Period context of the Greater Susiana)", *Nāme-ye Pazhuheshgāh-e Mirās-e Farhangi* 20–21: 35–58 (in Persian).

Molenaar, A. (1956), *Water Lifting Devices for Irrigation*. Rome.

Molist, M., ed. (1996), *Tell Halula (Siria): Un yacimiento Neolitico del valle medio del Éufrates. Campañas de 1991–1992*. Madrid.

Molist, M. (1998), "Des représentations humaines peintes au IXe millénaire BP sur le site de Tell Halula (Vallée de l'Euphrate, Syrie)", *Paléorient*, 24/1: 81–87.

Molist, M. (2001), "Halula, village néolithique en Syrie du nord", in Guilaine, ed., 35–52.

Molist, M. and Faura, J.M. (1999), "Tell Halula: un village des premiers agriculteurs-éleveurs dans la vallée de l'Euphrate", in del Olmo Lete and Montero Fenollós, eds., 27–40.

Molleson, T. (2000), "The people of Abu Hureyra", in Moore et al., eds., 301–324.

Molleson, T. and Campbell, S. (1995), "Deformed skulls at Tell Arpachiyah: the social context", in Campbell and Green, eds., 45–55.

Molleson, T., Jones, K. and Jones, S. (1993), "Dietary change and the effects of food preparation on microwear patterns in the Late Neolithic of Abu Hureyra, northern Syria", *Journal of Human Evolution* 24/6: 455.

Momigliano, A. (1950), "Ancient history and the antiquarian", *Journal of the Warburg and Courtauld Institutes* 13: 285–315.

Monahan, B.H. (2000), *The Organization of Domestication at Gritille, a Pre-Pottery Neolithic B Site in Southeastern Turkey*. Chicago.

Monchambert, J.-Y. (1987), "Réflexions à propos de la datation des canaux: le cas de la basse vallée de l'Euphrate syrien", in Geyer, ed., 87–99.

Montero Fenollós, J.-L. (1997), "L'activité métallurgique dans la vallée du Haut Euphrate Syrien (IIIe et IIe millénaires av. J.C.)", *Akkadica* 103: 6–28.

Montet, P. (1928), *Byblos et l'Égypte: Quatre campagnes des fouilles à Gebeil 1921–24, Text.* Paris.

Montet, P. (1929), *Byblos et l'Égypte: Quatre campagnes des fouilles à Gebeil 1921–24, Atlas.* Paris.

Montgomery, J. (1913), *Aramaic Incantation Texts from Nippur*. Philadelphia.

Moon, J. (2005), "Tools, weapons, utensils and ornaments", in Killick and Moon, eds., 163–233.

Moon, J. and Irving, B. (1997), "Faunal remains", in Crawford et al., eds., 81–83.

Moore, A.M.T. (2000), "Stone and other artifacts", in Moore et al., eds., 165–186.

Moore, A.M.T. and Hillman, G.C. (1992), "The Pleistocene to Holocene transition and human economy in Southwest Asia: the impact of the Younger Dryas", *AmAnt* 57: 482–494.

Moore, A.M.T., Hillman, G.C. and Legge, A.J., eds. (2000), *Village on the Euphrates: From Foraging to Farming at Abu Hureyra*. Oxford.

Moore, C.B., ed. (1974), *Reconstructing Complex Societies*. Cambridge.

Moore, K.M., Miller, N.F., Hiebert, F.T. and Meadow, R.H. (1994), "Agriculture and herding in the early oasis settlements of the Oxus Civilization", *Antiquity* 68: 418–427.

Mooren, L. (1972), "The date of *SB* V 8036 and the development of the Ptolemaic maritime trade with India", *Ancient Society* 3: 127–133.

Moorey, P.R.S. (1978), *Kish Excavations 1923–1933*. Oxford.

Moorey, P.R.S. (1980), *Cemeteries of the First Millennium BC at Deve Hüyük, near Carchemish, salvaged by T.E. Lawrence and C.L. Woolley in 1913*. Oxford.

Moorey, P.R.S. (1985), *Materials and Manufacture in Ancient Mesopotamia: The Evidence of Archaeology and Art. Metals and Metalwork, Glazed Materials and Glass*. Oxford.

Moorey, P.R.S. (1989), "The Hurrians, the Mitanni and technological innovation", in De Meyer and Haerinck, eds., 273–286.

Moorey, P.R.S. (1991a), "The decorated iron work of the early Iron Age attributed to Luristan in western Iran", *Iran* 29: 1–12.

Moorey, P.R.S. (1991b), *A Century of Biblical Archaeology*. Oxford.

Moorey, P.R.S. (1994), *Ancient Mesopotamian Materials and Industries: The Archaeological Evidence*. Oxford.

Moorey, P.R.S. (2003), *Idols of the People: Miniature Images of Clay in the Ancient Near East*. Oxford.

Moorey, P.R.S. and Parr, P.J., eds. (1978), *Archaeology in the Levant: Essays for Kathleen Kenyon*. Warminster.

Moradi, Y. (2003), "Preliminary report on the first season of the third campaign of archaeological excavations at Takht-e Suleiman", *Nāme-ye Pazhuheshgāh-e Mirās-e Farhangi* 1/2: 12.

Moran, W.L., ed. (1970), *Toward the Image of Tammuz and Other Essays on Mesopotamian History and Culture, Thorkild Jacobsen*. Cambridge.

Moran, W.L. (1992), *The Amarna Letters*. Baltimore.

Moran, W. (1995), "The Gilgamesh Epic: a masterpiece from Ancient Mesopotamia", in Sasson, ed., 2327–2336.

Morandi Bonacossi, D. (1996), *Tra el fiume e la steppa*. Padua.

Morandi Bonacossi, D., ed. (2007a), *Urban and Natural Landscapes of an Ancient Syrian Capital: Settlement and Environment at Tell Mishrifeh/Qatna and in Central-Western Syria*. Udine.

Morandi Bonacossi, D. (2007b), "Qatna and its hinterland during the Bronze and Iron Ages: a preliminary reconstruction of urbanism and settlement in the Mishrife region", in Morandi Bonacossi, ed., 65–90.

Morandi Bonacossi, D. (2007c), "The chronology of the Royal Palace of Qatna revisited: a reply to a paper by Mirko Novák", *ÄL* 17: 221–239.

Morandi Bonacossi, D. (2009a), "Stadtmauer und Akropolis – Das Stadtbild im 2. Jahrtausend v. Chr.", in al-Maqdissi et al., eds., 130–133.

Morandi Bonacossi, D. (2009b), "Der Unterstadtpalast", in al-Maqdissi et al., eds., 156–159.

Morandi Bonacossi, D., Da Ros, M., Garna, G., Iamoni, M. and Merlino, M. (2009), "The 'Eastern Palace' and the residential architecture of Area T at Mishrifeh/Qatna", *Mesopotamia* 44: 61–112.

Moreland, J. (2001), *Archaeology and Text*. London.

Morenz, L.D. and Schmidt, K. (2009), "Große Reliefpfeiler und kleine Zeichentäfelchen, ein frühneolithisches Zeichensystem in Obermesopotamien", in Andrássy et al., eds., 13–31.

Morgan, E.D., ed. (1893), *Transactions of the Ninth International Congress of Orientalists*, 2 vols. London.

Morgan, J. de (1889), *Mission scientifique au Caucase: Études archéologiques et historiques*. Paris.

Morgan, J. de (1894–1905), *Mission scientifique en Perse*. Paris.

Morgan, J. de (1898), *Compte rendu sommaire des travaux archéologiques exécutés du 3 novembre 1897 au 1er juin 1898*. Paris.

Morgan, J. de, ed. (1900a), *Recherches archéologiques, première série: Fouilles à Suse en 1897–1898 et 1898–1899*. Paris.

Morgan, J. de (1900b), "Étude géographique sur la Susiane", *MDP* 1: 4–32.

Morgan, J. de (1900c), "Travaux en tranchées", *MDP* 1: 88–99.

Morgan, J. de (1902), *La Délégation en Perse du Ministère de l'Instruction publique 1897–1902*. Paris.

Morgan, J. de, ed. (1905a), *Recherches archéologiques, troisième série*. Paris.

Morgan, J. de (1905b), "Découverte d'une sépulture achéménide à Suse", in Morgan, ed., 29–58.
Morgan, J. de (1905c), "Constructions élamites", in Morgan, ed., 196–198.
Morgan, J. de (1912), "Observations sur les couches profondes de l'Acropole se Suse", *MDP* 13: 1–25.
Morgan, J. de, Lampre, G. and Jéquier, G. (1900), "Travaux de l'hiver 1897–1898", *MDP* 1: 55–110.
Morgan, P.H. (2003), "Some remarks on a preliminary survey in eastern Fars", *Iran* 41: 323–338.
Mørkholm, O. (1991), *Early Hellenistic Coinage: From the Accession of Alexander to the Peace of Apamea (336–188 BC)*. Cambridge.
Morony, M. (1994), "Land use and settlement patterns in Late Sasanian and early Islamic Iraq", in King and Cameron, eds., 221–229.
Morony, M. (2009), "Madā'en", *EnIr* online.
Morozova, G.S. (2005), "A review of Holocene avulsions of the Tigris and Euphrates rivers and possible effects on the evolution of civilizations in Lower Mesopotamia", *Geoarchaeology* 20: 401–423.
Morris, C. (1998), "Inka strategies of incorporation and governance", in Feinman and Marcus, eds., 293–309.
Morrisson, C. and Sodini, J.P. (2002), "The sixth century economy", in Laiou, ed., 171–220.
Morsch, M.G.F. (2002), "Magic figurines? Some remarks about the clay objects of Nevali Çori", in Gebel et al., eds., 145–162.
Mortensen, P. (1970), "A preliminary study of the chipped stone industry from Beidha", *Acta Archaeologica* 41: 1–54.
Mortensen, P. (2002), "A note on the chipped stone industry of Tamerkhan", *IrAnt* 37: 219–227.
Moscati, S., ed. (1988a), *The Phoenicians*. New York.
Moscati, S. (1988b), "Sarcophagi", in Moscati, ed., 355–359.
Moser, S. (2007), "On disciplinary culture: archaeology as fieldwork and its gendered associations", *JAMT* 14/3: 235–263.
Mostafavi, M.T. (1967), "The Achaemenid Royal Road. Post stations between Susa and Persepolis", in Pope, ed., 3008–3010.
Mostafavi, M.T. (1978), *The Land of Pārs*. Chippenham.
Moulherat, C., Tengberg, M., Haquet, J.-F. and Mille, B. (2002), "First evidence of cotton at Neolithic Mehrgarh, Pakistan: analysis of mineralized fibres from a copper bead", *JAS* 29: 1393–1401.
Mountjoy, P.A. (2005), "The Mycenaean pottery from the 1931–1939 excavations at Tarsus", in Özyar, ed., 83–134.
Mourad, T.O. (2007), "An ethical archaeology of the Near East: confronting empire, war and colonisation", in Hamilakis and Duke, eds., 151–168.
Mousavi, A. (1990), "Obituary: Professor Ali Sāmi (1910–1989)", *IrAnt* 25: 189–193.
Mousavi, A. (1992), "Parsa, a stronghold for Darius: a preliminary study of the defense system of Persepolis", *EW* 42: 203–226.
Mousavi, A. (1996), "Early archaeological adventures and methodological problems in Iranian archaeology: the evidence from Susa", *IrAnt* 31: 1–17.

Mousavi, M. (1999a), "Kuh-e Khadjeh, un complexe religieux de l'est iranien", *DA* 243: 81–84.
Mousavi, A. (1999b), "La ville de Parsa: quelques remarques sur la topographie et le système défensif de Persépolis", *IrAnt* 34: 145–155.
Mousavi, A. (2002), "Persepolis in retrospect: histories of discovery and archaeological exploration at the ruins of ancient Parseh", *AO* 32: 209–251.
Mousavi, S.M., ed., (1997), *Proceedings of the 1st Archeological Symposium after the Islamic Revolution, Susa, 1373*. Tehran (in Persian).
Mousavi Garmarudi, A. (1990), *Proceedings of the 1st Symposium of Iranian Studies*. Tehran (in Persian).
Mouterde, R. and Poidebard, A. (1945), *Le Limes de Chalcis: Organisation de la steppe en haute Syrie romaine*. Paris.
Mouton, M., Sanlaville, P. and Suire, J. (2006), "La port sudarabique de Qâni': paléogéographie et organisation urbaine", *CRAIBL* 2006: 777–808.
Mudar, K. (1982), "Early Dynastic III animal utilization in Lagash: a report on the fauna of Tell al-Hiba", *JNES* 41: 23–34.
Muhle, B. (in press), *Die Keulenköpfe aus Assur*. Wiesbaden.
Muhly, J.D. (1973), *Copper and Tin*. Hamden.
Muhly, J.D. (1993), "Early Bronze Age tin and the Taurus", *AJA* 97: 239–253.
Muhly, J.D. (1995), "Mining and metalwork in ancient Western Asia", in Sasson, ed., 1501–1521.
Muhly, J.D., Begemann, F., Öztunali, Ö., Pernicka, E., Schmitt-Strecker, S. and Wagner, G.A. (1991), "The Bronze Age metallurgy of Anatolia and the question of local tin sources", in Pernicka and Wagner, eds., 209–220.
Muhly, J.D., Maddin, R. and Karageorghis, V., eds. (1982), *Early Metallurgy in Cyprus, 4000–500 BC*. Nicosia.
Muhly, J.D., Maddin, R., Stech, T. and Özgen, E. (1985), "Iron in Anatolia and the nature of the Hittite iron industry", *AnSt* 35: 67–84.
Mukherjee, A.J., Roßberger, E., James, M.A., Higgitt, C., White, R., Peggie, D., Azar, D., Evershed, R.P. and Pfälzner, P. (2008), "The Qatna lion: scientific confirmation of Baltic amber in Late Bronze Age Syria", *Antiquity* 82: 49–59.
Müller, H. (2004), "Militär, Rüstungsdynamik und Frieden", *Leviathan* 32/1: 46–63.
Müller, U. (1999a), "Die eisenzeitliche Keramik des Lidar Höyük", in Hausleiter and Reiche, eds., 403–434.
Müller, U. (1999b), "Die eisenzeitliche Stratigraphie von Lidar Höyük", *AnSt* 49: 123–131.
Müller, U. (2003), "A change to continuity: Bronze Age traditions in Early Iron Age", in Fischer et al., eds., 137–143.
Müller, U. (2005), "Norşun Tepe and Lidar Höyük: two examples for cultural change during the early Iron Age", in Çilingiroğlu and Darbyshire, eds., 107–114.
Müller, W.W. and al-Said, S.F. (2002), "Der babylonische König Nabonid in taymanitischen Inschriften", in Nebes, ed., 105–122.
Müller-Beck, H.-J. (1960), "Neufunde aus dem Paläolithikum Anatoliens", *Prähistorische Zeitschrift* 38: 111–118.
Müller-Karpe, A. (1999), "Untersuchungen in Kuşakli 1998", *MDOG* 131: 57–131.
Müller-Karpe, A., (2001), "Untersuchungen in Kuşakli 2000", *MDOG* 133: 225–250.

Müller-Karpe, A. (2002), "Kuşakli-Sarissa", in Willinghöfer, ed., 176–188.
Müller-Karpe, M. (1991), "Aspects of early metallurgy in Mesopotamia", in Pernicka and Wagner, eds., 105–116.
Müller-Karpe, M. (1993), *Metallgefäße im Iraq I (Von den Anfängen bis zur Akkad-Zeit)*. Stuttgart.
Müller-Kessler, C. and Kessler, K.-H. (1999), "Spätbabylonische Gottheiten in spätantiken mandäischen Texten", *ZA* 89: 65–87.
Mumford, L. (1961), *The City in History: Its Origins, its Transformations, and its Prospects.* New York.
Mulville, J. and Outram, A., eds. (2005), *The Zooarchaeology of Fats, Oils, Milks and Dairying.* Oxford.
Munro, N.D. (2003), "Small game, the younger dryas, and the transition to agriculture in the southern Levant", *Mitteilungen der Gesellschaft für Urgeschichte* 12: 47–71.
Munro-Hay, S.C.H. (1982), "The foreign trade of the Aksumite port of Adulis", *Azania* 17: 107–125.
Munro-Hay, S.C.H. (1996), "Aksumite overseas interests", in Reade, ed., 403–416.
Muscarella, O.W. (1973), "Antiquities and collections: a curator's viewpoint", *Association for Field Archaeology Newsletter* 1/2: 2–5.
Muscarella, O.W. (1974), "The antiquities market: a colloquium", *JFA* 1: 221–222.
Muscarella, O.W. (1976), "Antiquities legislation pending in Congress", *Archaeology* 29/4: 275–276.
Muscarella, O.W. (1977a), "'Ziwiye' and Ziwiye: the forgery of a provenience", *JFA* 4: 197–219.
Muscarella, O.W. (1977b), "Unexcavated objects and ancient Near Eastern art", in Levine and Young, eds., 153–205.
Muscarella, O.W. (1977c), review of P. Calmeyer, *Reliefbronzen in babylonischen Stil* (1973), *JAOS* 97/1: 76–80.
Muscarella, O.W. (1980), "Die gefälschte Kunstgeschichte – ein Hausputz in der Vorderasiatischen Altertumskunde: a reply", *Acta Praehistorica et Archaeologica* 11–12: 117–120.
Muscarella, O.W. (1988), *Bronze and Iron: Ancient Metal Artifacts in the Metropolitan Museum of Art.* New York.
Muscarella, O.W. (1992), "Achaemenid art and architecture at Susa", in Harper, Aruz and Tallon, eds., 216–222.
Muscarella, O.W. (1995), "Bazaar archaeology", in Finkbeiner et al., eds., 449–453.
Muscarella, O.W. (1999), "The Pope and the bitter fanatic," in Alizadeh et al., eds., 5–12.
Muscarella, O.W. (2000a), *The Lie Became Great.* Groningen.
Muscarella, O.W. (2000b), "Excavated in the bazaar: Ashurbanipal's beaker", *Source* 20/1: 29–37.
Muscarella, O.W. (2000c), review of Löw, U., *Figürlich verzierte Metallgefäße aus Nord- und Nordwestiran. BiOr* 57: 188–195.
Muscarella, O.W. (2001), "Jroft and 'Jiroft'-Aratta", *BAI* 15: 173–198.
Muscarella, O.W. (2003a), "Museum constructions of the Oxus Treasure: forgeries of provenience and ancient culture", *ACSS* 9: 259–275.
Muscarella, O.W. (2003b), "The date of the destruction of the early Phrygian period at Gordion", *AWE* 2: 225–252.

Muscarella, O.W. (2005a), review of Gunter, A. and Hauser, S., eds., *Ernst Herzfeld and the development of Near Eastern studies, 1900–1959, JAOS* 125: 431–432.

Muscarella, O.W. (2005b), "Some thoughts on fakes, addendum", *N.A.B.U.* 2005/4: 97–98.

Muscarella. O.W. (2006), "Urartian metal artifacts: an archaeological review", *ACSS* 12: 147–175.

Muscarella, O.W. (2007), "Archaeology and the plunder culture", *International Journal of the Classical Tradition* 14: 602–618.

Muscarella, O.W. (2008a), "The veracity of 'scientific' testing by conservators", in Pernicka and von Berswordt-Wallrabe, eds., 9–18.

Muscarella, O.W. (2008b), "The Iranian Iron III chronology at Muweilah in the Emirate of Sharjah", *AWE* 7: 189–202.

Muscarella, O.W. (2009a), "The Fifth Column in the archaeological realm: the great divide", in Genç and Çelik, eds., 395–406.

Muscarella, O.W. (2009b), "A review and addenda: Michael Gross' *Rogues' Gallery*", September 16 (http://www.scoop.co.nz/stories/HL0909/S00139.htm).

Muscarella, O.W. (2010), "Shelby White's Foundation expansion", *SAFE* Corner, June 1 (http://safecorner.savingantiquities.org/2010/06/shelby-whites-foundation-expansion.htm).

Muscarella, O.W. (in press a), "Archaeologists and acquisitionists", *International Journal of the Classical Tradition*.

Muscarella, O.W. (in press b), "An unholy quartet: museum trustees, antiquity dealers, scientific experts, and government".

Museibli, N. (2009), "Ethnocultural connections between the regions of the Near East and the Caucasus in the IVth millennium BC", in Hansen, ed., 52–54.

Na'aman, N. (1980), "The historical introduction of the Aleppo treaty reconsidered", *JCS* 32/1: 34–42.

Na'aman, N (1997), "The network of Canaanite Late Bronze kingdoms and the city of Ashdod", *UF* 29: 599–626.

Na'aman, N. (2000), "The Egyptian-Canaanite correspondence", in Cohen and Westbrook, eds., 125–138.

Nadali, D. (2006), *Percezione dello spazio e scansione del tempo. Studio della composizione narrativa del rilievo assiro di VII secolo A.C.* Rome.

Nadali, D. and Verderame, L. (2008), "The Akkadian 'Bello Stile'", in Biggs et al., eds., 309–320.

Nadel, D. (1989), "Flint heat treatment at the beginning of the Neolithic period in the Levant", *JIPS* 22: 61–67.

Nadel, D. (1997), "The chipped stone industry from Netiv Hagdud", in Bar-Yosef and Gopher, eds., 71–149.

Naderi, S., Rezaei, H.-R., Pompanon, F., Blum, M.G.B., Negrini, R., Naghash, H.-R., Balkiz, O., Mashkour, M., Gaggiotti, O.E., Ajmone-Marsan, P., Kence, A., Vigne, J.-D. and Taberlet, P. (2008), "The goat domestication process inferred from large-scale mitochondrial DNA analysis of wild and domestic individuals", *PNAS* 105: 17659–17664.

Nagel, A. (2010), *Colors, Gilding and Painted Motifs in Persepolis: Approaching the Polychromy of Achaemenid Persian Architectural Sculpture, c.520–330 BCE.* Ann Arbor.

Nagin, C. (1986), "Patrons of plunder", *Boston Review* (August 5–6): 23–25.

Nappo, D. (2010), "On the location of Leuke Kome", *JRA* 23: 335–348.

Narimanov, I.G. (1985), "Obejdskie Plemena Mesopotamii v Azerbajdzhane", in Anonymous (1985b), ed., 271–272.

Nasif, A.A. (1988), *Al-ʿUlā: An Historical and Archaeological Survey with Special Reference to its Irrigation System*. Riyadh.

Nau, F. (1909), *Patrologia Orientalis 3/1. Histoires d'Ahoudemmeh et de Marouta, métropolitains jacobites de Tagrit et de l'Orient (Vie et VIIe siècles) suivies du Traité d'Ahoudemmeh sur l'homme*. Paris.

Naumann, R. (1965), "A fire-temple of the Magians in NW Persia", *ILN* January 16: 23–25.

Naumann, R. (1977), *Die Ruinen von Tacht-e Suleiman und Zendan-e Suleiman und Umgebung*. Berlin.

Naumkin, V.V. and Sedov, A.V. (1993), "Monuments of Socotra", *Topoi* 3/2: 569–623.

Naveh, J. and Shaked, S. (1973), "Ritual texts or treasury documents?", *Or* 42: 445–457.

Nebes, N., ed. (1994), *Arabia Felix: Beiträge zur Sprache und Kultur des vorislamischen Arabien. Festschrift Walter W. Müller zum 60. Geburtstag*. Wiesbaden.

Nebes, N., ed. (2002), *Neue Beiträge zur Semitistik. Erste Arbeitstreffen der Arbeitsgemeinschaft Semitistik in der Deutschen Morgenländischen Gesellschaft vom 11. bis 13. September 2000 an der Friedrich-Schiller-Universität Jena*. Wiesbaden.

Needham, J. (1965), *Science and Civilization in China*, vol. 4. Cambridge.

Neef, R. (1989), "Plant remains from archaeological sites in lowland Iraq: Hellenistic and Neobabylonian Larsa", in Huot, ed., 321–329.

Neef, R. (1990), "Introduction, development and environmental implications of olive culture: the evidence from Jordan", in Bottema et al., eds., 295–306.

Neef, R. (1991), "Plant remains from archaeological sites in lowland Iraq: Tell el'Oueili", in Huot, ed., 322–329.

Neely, J.A. (1969), "Preliminary report on the archaeological survey of Deh Luran", in Hole, ed., 9–24.

Neely, J.A. (1970), "The Deh Luran region", *Iran* 8: 202–203.

Neely, J.A. (1974), "Sasanian and early Islamic water-control and irrigations systems on the Deh Luran plain, Iran", in Downing and Gibson, eds., 21–42.

Neely, J.A. and Wright, H.T., Jr. (1994), *Early Settlement and Irrigation on the Deh Luran Plain, Iran*. Ann Arbor.

Neely, J.A., and Wright, H.T., Jr. eds. (2010), *Elamite and Achaemenid Settlement on the Deh Lurān Plain: Towns and Villages of the Early Empires in Southwestern Iran*. Ann Arbor.

Neff, U., Burns, S.J., Mangini, A., Mudelsee, M., Fleitmann, D. and Matter, A. (2001), "Strong coherence between solar variability and the monsoon in Oman between 9 and 6 kyr ago", *Nature* 411: 290–293.

Negahban, E.O. (1983), *Metal Vessels from Marlik*. Stuttgart.

Negahban, E.O. (1991), *Excavations at Haft Tepe, Iran*. Philadelphia.

Negbi, O. and Moskowitz, S. (1966), "The 'foundation deposits' or 'offering deposits' of Byblos", *BASOR* 184: 21–26.

Negev, A. (1974), "The churches of the central Negev: an architectural survey", *RB* 81: 416–421.

Negev, A. (1989), "The cathedral of Elusa and the new typology and chronology of the Byzantine churches in the Negev", *LA* 39: 129–142.
Negro, F. (1997), "Hatra Livello 8", *Mesopotamia* 32: 163–187.
Negro Ponzi, M. (1968–9), "Sasanian glassware from Tell Mahuz", *Mesopotamia* 3–4: 293–384.
Negro Ponzi, M. (1972), "Glassware from Abu Shair (Central Iraq)", *Mesopotamia* 7: 215–237.
Negro Ponzi, M. (2002), "The glassware from Seleucia (Central Iraq)", *Parthica* 4: 63–156.
Negro Ponzi, M. (2005), "Al-Madāin: problemi di Topografia", *Mesopotamia* 40: 145–169.
Nehmé, L. (2009), "Central and secondary places in north-western Arabia during the Nabataean period", unpublished ms.
Nehru, L. (1999–2000), "Khalchayan revisited", *SRAA* 6: 217–239.
Nelson, S.M., ed. (1998), *Ancestors for the Pigs: Pigs in Prehistory*. Philadelphia.
Nenna, M.-D., ed. (2000), *La Route du verre. Ateliers primaires et secondaires de verriers du second millénaire av. J.-C. au Moyen-Âge*. Lyon.
Nenna, M.-D., Picon, M. and Vichy, M. (2000), "Ateliers primaires et secondaires en Égypte à l'époque greco-romaine", in Nenna, ed., 97–112.
Nesbitt, M. (1993), "Archaeobotanical evidence for early Dilmun diet at Saar, Bahrain", *AAE* 4/1: 20–47.
Nesbitt, M. (2002), "When and where did domesticated cereals first occur in Southwest Asia?", in Cappers and Bottema, eds., 113–132.
Neu, E. and Rüster, C., ed. (1988), *Documentum Asiae Minoris Antiquae: Festschrift für Heinrich Otten zum 75. Geburtstag*. Wiesbaden.
Neumann, K., Butler, A. and Kahlheber, S., eds. (2003), *Food, Fuel and Fields: Progress in African Archaeobotany*. Cologne.
Neumann, F.H., Kagan, E.J., Leroy, S., and Barach, U. (2010), "Vegetation history and climatic fluctuations on a transect along the Dead Sea west shore and their impact on past societies over the last 3500 years", *JAE* 74: 756–764.
Neuville, R. (1933), "Statuette érotique du désert de Judée", *L'Anthropologie* 43: 558–560.
Neuville, R. (1934), "Le préhistoire de Palestine", *RB* 43: 237–259.
Neuville, R. (1934–5), "Les débuts de l'agriculture et la faucille préhistorique en Palestine", *Bulletin of the Jewish Palestine Exploration Society* 3: 17–42.
Neve, P. (1969), "Der Große Tempel und die Magazine", in Bittel, ed., 9–19.
Neve, P. (1992), *Hattuša: Stadt der Götter und Tempel: neue Ausgrabungen in der Hauptstadt der Hethiter*. Mainz.
Neve, P. (1995), "Kammer 2 und der 'Heilige Teich'", in Hawkins, 9–12.
Neve, P. (2002), "The Great Temple in Boğazköy-Hattuša", in Hopkins, ed., 77–97.
Newberry, P.E. (1893), *Beni Hasan* I. London.
Newfield, C. (2009), "Structure et silence du cognitariat", *Multitudes* 39: 68–78.
Newson, P., Abdulkarim, M., McPhillips, S., Mills, P., Reynolds, P. and Philip, G. (2008–9), "Landscape study of Dar es-Salaam and the basalt region north-west of Homs, Syria: report on work undertaken 2005–2007", *Berytus* 51–52: 9–35.
Newton, R.G. and Davison, S. (1989), *Conservation of Glass*. London.

Nezafati, N., Pernicka, E. and Momenzadeh, M. (2006), "Ancient tin: old question and a new answer", *Antiquity* 80/308: Project Gallery.

Nezafati, N., Pernicka, E. and Momenzadeh, M. (2009a), "Iranian ore deposits and their role in the development of the ancient cultures", in Yalçin, ed., 77–90.

Nezafati, N., Pernicka, E. and Momenzadeh, M. (2009b), "Introduction of the Deh Hosein ancient tin-copper mine, western Iran: evidence from geology, archaeology, geochemistry and lead isotope data", *TÜBA-AR* 12: 223–236.

Nickerson, J.W. (1977), "Malyan wall paintings", *Expedition* 19: 2–6.

Nichols, D.L. and Charlton, T.H., eds. (1997), *The Archaeology of City-States: Cross Cultural Approaches*. Washington, DC.

Nicholson, P.T. (1993), *Egyptian Faience and Glass*. Princes Risborough.

Nicholson, P.T. (1995a), "Glass making/working at Amarna: some new work", *JGS* 37: 11–19.

Nicholson, P.T. (1995b), "Recent excavations at an ancient Egyptian glassworks: Tell el-Amarna 1993", *Glass Technology* 36: 125–128.

Nicholson, P.T. (1996), "New evidence for glass and glazing at Tell el-Amarna (Egypt)", in Anonymous (1996a), ed., 11–19.

Nicholson, P.T. ed. (2007), *Brilliant Things for Akhenaten: The Production of Glass, Vitreous Materials and Pottery at Amarna Site 045*. London.

Nicholson, P.T. and Henderson, J. (2000), "Glass", in Nicholson and Shaw, eds., 195–224.

Nicholson, P.T. and Jackson, C.M. (2000), "Tell el-Amarna and the glassmakers' workshop of the second millennium BC", in Nenna, ed., 12–21.

Nicholson, P.T., Jackson, C.M. and Trott, K.M. (1997), "The Ulu Burun glass ingots, cylindrical vessels and Egyptian glass", *JEA* 83: 143–153.

Nicholson, P.T. and Shaw, I., eds. (2000), *Ancient Egyptian Materials and Technology*. Cambridge.

Nickerson, J.W. (1977), "Malyan wall paintings", *Expedition* 19: 2–6.

Nicol, M.B. (1970), "Rescue excavations at Dorūdzan", *EW* 20: 245–284.

Nicolotti, M. and Guerin, C. (1992), "Le zebu (*Bos indicus*) dans l'Égypte ancienne", *Archaeozoologia* 5: 87–108.

Niebuhr, C. (1772), *Beschreibung von Arabien aus eigenen Beobachtungen und im Lande selbst gesammelten Nachrichten*, vol. 1. Kopenhagen (repr. Graz 1968).

Niehr, H. (2006a), "Ein König wird zum Gott: Bestattung und Nachleben der Herrscher von Ugarit (Syrien)", *Antike Welt* 37: 47–52.

Niehr, H. (2006b), "The royal funeral in ancient Syria: a comparative view on the tombs in the palaces of Qatna, Kumidi and Ugarit", *Journal of Northwest Semitic Languages* 32: 1–24.

Niehr, H., Pernicka, E. and Pfälzner, P., eds. (in press), *(Re-)constructing Funerary Rituals in the Ancient Near East*. Wiesbaden.

Nieling, J. and Rehm, E., eds. (2010), *Achaemenid Impact in the Black Sea: Communication of Powers*. Aarhus.

Nielsen, I., ed. (2001), *The Royal Palace Institution in the First Millennium BC: Regional Development and Cultural Interchange Between East and West*. Aarhus.

Niemeier, W.-D. (1991), "Minoan artisans travelling overseas. The Alalakh frescoes and the painted plaster floor at Tel Kabri (Western Galilee)", in Laffineur and Basch, eds., 189–201.

Niemeier W.-D. and Niemeier, B. (1998), "Minoan frescoes in the Eastern Mediterranean", in Cline and Harris-Cline, eds., 69–98.

Niemeier W.-D. and Niemeier, B. (2000), "Aegean frescoes in Syria-Palestine: Alalakh and Tel Kabri", in Sherratt, ed., 763–802.

Nieuwenhuyse, O.P. (2008), *Plain and Painted Pottery: The Rise of Late Neolithic Ceramic Styles on the Syrian Plains*. Brussels.

Nieuwenhuyse O.P. (2009a), "The Late Neolithic ceramics from Shir: a first assessment", *ZOA* 2: 310–356.

Nieuwenhuyse, O.P. (2009b), "The 'painted pottery revolution': emulation, ceramic innovation and the Early Halaf in northern Syria", in Astruc et al., eds., 81–91.

Nieuwenhuyse, O.P., Akkermans, P.M.M.G. and van der Plicht, J. (2010), "Not so coarse, nor always plain: the earliest pottery of Syria", *Antiquity* 84: 71–85.

Nieuwenhuyse, O.P., Russell, A., Bernbeck, R. and Akkermans, P.P.M.G. (in press), *Interpreting the Late Neolithic of Upper Mesopotamia*. Turnhout.

Nigro, L. (1998), "The two steles of Sargon: iconology and visual propaganda at the beginning of royal Akkadian relief", *Iraq* 60: 85–102.

Nigro, L. (2000), "Coordinating the MB I pottery horizon of Syria and Palestine", in Matthiae et al., eds., 1187–1212.

Nigro, L. (2002), "The Middle Bronze Age pottery horizon of northern inner Syria on the basis of the stratified assemblages of Tell Mardikh and Hama", in al-Maqdissi, Matoïan & Nicolle, eds., 97–128.

Nigro, L. (2003), "The smith and the king of Ebla: Tell el-Yahudiyeh Ware, Metallic Wares and the ceramic chronology of Middle Bronze Age Syria", in Bietak, ed., 345–363.

Nilakanta Sastri, K.A. (1939), *Foreign Notices of South India, from Megasthenes to Ma Huan*. Madras.

Nimchuk, C.L. (2010), "Empire encapsulated: the Persepolis Apadana foundation deposits", in Curtis and Simpson, eds., 221–229.

Nishiaki, Y. (2000), *Lithic Technology of Neolithic Syria*. Oxford.

Nishiaki, Y. (2003), "Chronological developments of the Chalcolithic flaked stone industries at Tell Kosak Shamali", in Nishiaki and Masutani, eds., 115–112.

Nishiaki, Y. and Le Mière, M. (2005), "The oldest pottery Neolithic of Upper Mesopotamia: new evidence from Tell Seker al-Aheimar, the Khabur, northeast Syria", *Paléorient* 31/2: 55–68.

Nishiaki, Y. and Matsutani, T., ed. (2001), *Tell Kosak Shamali, vol. 1. The Archaeological Investigations on the Upper Euphrates, Syria. Chalcolithic Architecture and the Earlier Prehistoric Remains*. Tokyo.

Nishiaki, Y. and Masutani, T., eds. (2003), *Tell Kosak Shamali*. Vol. 2: *The Archaeological Investigations of the Upper Euphrates, Syria. Chalcolithic Technology and Subsistence*. Tokyo.

Nissen, H.J. (1970), "Grabung in den Planquadraten K/L XII in Uruk-Warka", *BaM* 5: 101–191.

Nissen, H.J. (1976), "The Behbehan plain in the fifth millennium BC", in Kiani, ed., 273–279.

Nissen, H.J. (1986), "The occurrence of Dilmun in the oldest texts of Mesopotamia", in al-Khalifa and Rice, eds., 335–339.

Nissen, H.J. (1988), *The Early History of the Ancient Near East 9000–2000 BC*. Chicago.

Nissen, H.J. (1993a), "Settlement patterns and material culture of the Akkadian period: continuity and discontinuity", in Liverani, ed., 91–106.

Nissen, H.J. (1993b), "The early Uruk period: a sketch", in Frangipane et al., eds., 123–132.

Nissen, H.J. (1993c), "The PPNC, the sheep and the 'Hiatus palestinien'", *Paléorient* 19/1: 177–183.

Nissen, H.J. (1998), *The Early History of the Ancient Near East*. Chicago.

Nissen, H.J. (2002), "Uruk: key site of the period and key site of the problem", in Postgate, ed., 1–16.

Nissen, H.J. (2004), "Proto-urbanism: an Early Neolithic feature? – in lieu of an introductory remark", in Bienert et al., 41–44.

Nissen, H.J., Damerow, P. and Englund, R.K. (1993), *Archaic Bookkeeping: Early Writing and Techniques of Economic Administration in the Ancient Near East*. Chicago.

Nissen, H.J. and Redman, C.L. (1970–1), "Preliminary notes on an archaeological surface survey in the plain of Behbehan and the Lower Zuhreh Valley", *Bāstān Šenāsī va Honar-e Īrān* 6: 48–50.

Nissen, H.J. and Renger, J. (1982), *Mesopotamien und seine Nachbarn: Politische und Kulturelle Wechselbeziehungen im Alten Vorderasien vom 4. bis 1. Jahrtausend v. Chr.* Berlin.

Nixon, C.E.V. (2002), "The coins", in Clarke et al., 291–335.

Nokandeh, J. (2010a), *Neue Untersuchungen zur Sialk III-Periode im zentraliranischen Hochland: Auf der Grundlage der Ergebnisse des "Sialk Reconsideration Project"*. Berlin.

Nokandeh, J. (2010b), "Archaeological survey in the Mehran Plain, south western Iran", in Matthiae et al., eds., 483–509.

Nokandeh, J., Sauer, E.W., Omrani Rekavandi, H., Wilkinson, T., Ali Abbasi, G., Schwenninger, J.-L., Mahmoudi, M., Parker, D., Fattahi, M., Usher-Wilson, L.S., Ershadi, M., Ratcliffe, J. and Gale, R. (2006), "Linear barriers of northern Iran: the Great Wall of Gorgan and the wall of Tammishe", *Iran* 44: 121–173.

Northedge, A, Bamber, A. and Roaf, M. (1988), *Excavations at 'Ana, Qal'a Island*. Warminster.

Novák, M. (2004), "The chronology of the Royal Palace of Qatna", *ÄL* 14: 299–317.

Novák, M. and Pfälzner P. (2000), "Ausgrabungen in Tall Mišrife/Qatna 1999: Vorbericht der deutschen Komponente des internationalen Kooperationsprojektes", *MDOG* 132: 253–295.

Novák, M. and Pfälzner P. (2001), "Ausgrabungen in Tall Mišrife-Qatna 2000: Vorbericht der deutschen Komponente des internationalen Kooperationsprojektes", *MDOG* 133: 157–198.

Novák, M. and Pfälzner P. (2002a), "Ausgrabungen in Tall Mišrife-Qatna 2001. Vorbericht der deutschen Komponente des internationalen Kooperationsprojektes", *MDOG* 134: 207–246.

Novák, M. and Pfälzner P. (2002b), "Excavations in the western part of the Bronze Age palace (Operation G)", in al-Maqdissi, Luciani et al., 63–110.

Novák, M. and Pfälzner P. (2003), "Ausgrabungen im bronzezeitlichen Palast von Tall Mishrife – Qatna 2002: Vorbericht der deutschen Komponente des internationalen Kooperationsprojektes", *MDOG* 135: 131–166.

Novák, M. and Pfälzner, P. (2005), "Ausgrabungen in Tall Mišrife-Qatna 2003: Vorbericht der deutschen Komponente des internationalen Kooperationsprojektes", *MDOG* 137: 57–78.

Novák, M., Prayon, F. and Wittke, A-M., eds. (2004), *Die Aussenwirkung des späthethitischen Kulturraumes: Güteraustausch, Kulturkontakt, Kulturtransfer*. Münster.

Noy, T. (1987), "Small truncated notched tools from Gilgal III", *JIPS* 20: 158–160.

Nunome, J. (1992), *The Archaeology of Fiber Before Your Eyes: A Compilation of Photographs of Fiber Artifacts*. Kyoto.

Nylander, C. (1966a), "Clamps and chronology (Achaemenid Problems II)", *IrAnt* 6: 130–146.

Nylander, C. (1966b), "The toothed chisel in Pasargadae: further notes on Old Persian stonecutting", *AJA* 70: 373–376.

Nylander, C. (1970), *Ionians in Pasargadae: Studies in Old Persian Architecture*. Uppsala.

Nylander, C. (1975), "Anatolians in Susa and Persepolis", in Duchesne-Guillemin, ed., vol. 3, 317–323.

Nylander, C. (1979), "Achaemenid imperial art", in Larsen, ed., 345–359.

Nylander, C. (1991), "The toothed chisel", *Archeologia Classica* 43: 1037–1052.

Nylander, C. (2006), "Stones for kings: stone-working in Ancient Iran", in Callieri, ed., 121–136.

Nunn, A. (2006), *Knaufplatten und Knäufe aus Assur*. Saarwellingen.

Nunn, A., ed. (2009), *Mauern als Grenzen*. Mainz.

O'Connor, D. (2000), "The Sea Peoples and the Egyptian sources", in Oren, ed., 85–102.

Oates, D. (1968), *Studies in the Ancient History of Northern Iraq*. London.

Oates, D. (1982), "Tell Brak", in Curtis, ed., 86–98.

Oates, D. and Oates, J. (1976a), "Early irrigation in Mesopotamia", in Sieveking et al., eds., 109–135.

Oates, D. and Oates, J. (1976b), *The Rise of Civilization*. Oxford.

Oates, D. and Oates, J. (1993), "Excavations at Tell Brak 1992–93", *Iraq* 55: 155–199.

Oates, D., Oates, J. and McDonald, H. (1997), *Excavations at Tell Brak, vol. 1. The Mitanni and Old Babylonian Periods*. Iraq.

Oates, D., Oates, J. and McDonald, H. (2001), *Excavations at Tell Brak, vol. 2. Nagar in the Third Millennium BC*. Cambridge.

Oates, J. (1959), "Late Assyrian pottery from Fort Shalmaneser", *Iraq* 21: 130–146.

Oates, J. (1960), "Ur and Eridu, the prehistory", *Iraq* 22: 32–50.

Oates, J. (1966a), "Survey in the region of Mandali and Badra", *Sumer* 22: 51–60.

Oates, J. (1966b), "The baked clay figurines from Tell es-Sawwan", *Iraq* 28/2: 146–153.

Oates, J. (1969), "Choga Mami 1967–68", *Iraq* 30: 115–152.

Oates, J. (1982), "Choga Mami", in Curtis, ed., 22–29.

Oates, J. (1983), "Ubaid Mesopotamia reconsidered", in Young et al., eds., 251–281.

Oates, J. (1986), *Babylon*. London.

Oates, J. (1987a), "Ubaid Chronology", in Aurenche et al., eds., 473–482.

Oates, J. (1987b), "A note on 'Ubaid and Mitanni pottery from Tell Brak", *Iraq* 49: 193–198.

Oates, J. (1988), *Babylon*, rev. edn. London.

Oates, J. (1993), "Trade and power in the fifth and fourth millennium BC: new evidence from northern Mesopotamia", *WA* 24: 403–422.

Oates, J. (1996), "A prehistoric communication revolution", *CAJ* 6: 165–176.

Oates, J. (1997), "An open gate: cities of the 4th millennium BC (Tell Brak)", *CAJ* 7/2: 287–297.

Oates, J. (2001a), "The evidence of the sealings", in Oates et al., eds., 121–150.

Oates, J. (2001b), "A prehistoric communication revolution", *CAJ* 6/1: 165–76.

Oates, J. (2004), "Ubaid Mesopotamia revisited", in von Folsach et al., eds., 87–104.

Oates, J. (2010), "More thoughts on the Ubaid period", in Carter and Philip, eds., 45–49.

Oates, J. (in press), "Samarran issues", in Niewenhuyse et al., eds.

Oates, J., Calvet, Y., Velde, B., Courtois, L., Dollfus, G. and Matsumoto, K. (1987), "Le Choga Mami Transitional et l'Obeid", in Huot, ed., 129–206.

Oates, J., Davidson, T.E., Kamilli, D. and McKerrell, H. (1977), "Seafaring merchants of Ur?", *Antiquity* 51: 221–234.

Oates, J., McMahon, A., Karsgaard, P., al-Quntar, S. and Ur, J. (2007), "Early Mesopotamian urbanism: a new view from the north", *Antiquity* 81: 585–600.

Oates, J. and Oates, D. (1994), "Tell Brak: a stratigraphic summary, 1976–1993", *Iraq* 56: 167–176.

Oates, J. and Oates, D. (2001), *Nimrud: An Assyrian Imperial City Revealed*. London.

Ochsenschlager, E.L. (1992), "Ethnographic evidence for wood, boats, bitumen and reeds in southern Iraq: ethnoarchaeology at al-Hiba", *BSA* 6: 47–78.

Ochsenschlager, E.L. (2004), *Iraq's Marsh Arabs in the Garden of Eden*. Philadelphia.

O'Connor, D. and Quirke, S. eds. (2003), *Mysterious Lands: Encounters with Ancient Egypt*. London.

Oddy, W.A., ed. (1980), *Aspects of early metallurgy*. London.

Oded, B. (1979), *Mass Deportation and Deportees in the Neo-Assyrian Empire*. Wiesbaden.

Odell, G.O. (2004), *Lithic Analysis*. New York.

Oelsner, J. (1986), *Materialien zur babylonischen Gesellschaft und Kultur*. Budapest.

Oguchi, T. and Oguchi, C.T. (1998), "Mid-Holocene floods of the Syrian Euphrates inferred from 'tell sediments'", in Benitom et al., eds., 307–315.

Öğün, B. (1978), "Die urartäischen Bestattungsgebräuche", in Şahin et al., eds., 639–678.

Ohlig, C., ed. (2003), *Wasserhistorische Forschungen: Schwerpunkt Antike*. Siegburg.

Ohlig, C., ed. (2004), *Wasserbauten im Königreich Urartu und weitere Beiträge zur Hydrotechnik in der Antike*. Siegburg.

Okada, Y. (1990), "Reconsideration of plaque-type crosses from Ain Sha'ia near Najaf", *al-Rāfidān* 10: 103–112 .

Okada, Y. (1991), "Early Christian architecture in the Iraqi south-western desert", *al-Rāfidān* 11: 71–83.

Okada, Y. (1992), "Ain Sha'ia and the early Gulf churches: an architectural analogy", *al-Rāfidān* 12: 87–93.

Olbrycht, M.J. (2003), "Parthia and nomads of Central Asia: elements of steppe origin in the social and military developments of Arsacid Iran", in Schneider, ed., 69–109.

Oldenburg, E. and Rohweder, J. (1981), *The Excavations at Tell Daruk (Usnu?) and 'Arab al-Mulk (Paltos)*. Copenhagen.

Oldenburg, E. (1991), *Sukas IX. The Chalcolithic and Early Bronze Age Periods*. Copenhagen.
Oleson, J.P., ed. (2008), *The Oxford Handbook of Engineering and Technology in the Classical World*. New York.
Olijdam, E. and Spoor, R., eds. (2008), *Intercultural Relations Between South and Southwest Asia: Studies in Commemoration of E.C.L. During Caspers (1934–1996)*. Oxford.
Olin, J.S. and Blackman, M.J., eds. (1986), *Proceedings of the 24th International Archaeometry Symposium*. Washington, DC.
Olivier-Utard, F. (1997), *Politique et archéologie. Histoire de la Délégation archéologique française en Afghanistan (1922–1982)*. Paris.
Olsen, S.L., Grant, S., Choyke, A.M. and Bartosiewicz, L., eds. (2006), *Horses and Humans: The Evolution of the human–equine Relationship*. Oxford.
Olshausen, E. and Sonnabend, H., eds. (2002), *Stuttgarter Kolloquium zur historischen Geographie des Altertums 7, 1999. Zu Wasser und zu Land. Verkehrswege in der antiken Welt*. Stuttgart.
Olszewski, D. (1993a), "Subsistence ecology in the Mediterranean forest: implications for the origins of cultivation in the Epipaleolithic southern Levant", *AA* 95: 420–435.
Olszewski, D. (1993b), "Zarzian microliths from Warwasi rockshelter, Iran: Scalene triangles as arrow components", in Peterkin, Bricker and Mellars, eds., 199–205.
Olszewski, D. and Dibble, H.L., eds. (1993), *The Paleolithic Prehistory of the Zagros-Taurus*. Philadelphia.
Omrani Rekavandi, H., Sauer, E., Wilkinson, T., Abbasi, G.A., Priestman, S., Safari Tamak, E., Ainslie, R., Mahmoudi, M., Galiatsatos, N., Roustai, K., Jansen Van Rensburg, J., Ershadi, M., MacDonald, E., Fattahi, M., Oatley, C., Shabani, B., Ratcliffe, J. and Usher-Wilson, L.S. (2008), "Sasanian walls, hinterland fortresses and abandoned ancient irrigated landscapes: the 2007 season on the Great Wall of Gorgan and the Wall of Tammishe", *Iran* 46: 151–178.
Omrani Rekavandi, H., Sauer, E.W., Wilkinson, T., Safari Tamak, E., Mahmoudi, M., Griffiths, S., Ershadi, M., Van Rensburg, J.J., Fattahi, M., Ratcliffe, J., Nokandeh, J., Nazifi, A., Thomas, R., Gale, R. and Hoffmann, B. (2007), "An imperial frontier of the Sasanian empire: further fieldwork at the Great Wall of Gorgan", *Iran* 45: 95–136.
Omura, S. (2004), "Preliminary report on the 18th excavation at Kaman-Kalehöyük (2004)", *AAS* 13: 1–36.
Omura, S. (2005), "Preliminary report on the 19th excavation at Kaman-Kalehöyük (2005)", *AAS* 14: 1–36.
Omura, S. (2006), "Preliminary report on the 20th Excavation at Kaman-Kalehöyük (2006)", *AAS* 15: 1–36.
Omura, S. (2007), "Preliminary report on the 21st Excavation at Kaman-Kalehöyük (2007)", *AAS* 16: 1–36.
Onasch, H-U. (2010), *Ägyptische und assyrische Alabastergefäße aus Assur*. Wiesbaden.
O'Neale, L. (1936), "A survey of woolen textiles from the Sir Aurel Stein Collections", *AA* 38: 414–432.
Oppenheim, A.L. (1954), "The seafaring merchants of Ur", *JAOS* 74: 6–17.
Oppenheim, A.L. (1960), "The city of Assur in 714 BC", *JNES* 19: 133–147.
Oppenheim, A.L. (1964), *Mesopotamia: Portrait of a Dead Civilization*. Chicago.

Oppenheim, A.L. (1973), "Towards a history of glass in the ancient Near East", *JAOS* 93: 259–266.
Oppenheim, A.L. (1977), *Ancient Mesopotamia: Portrait of a Dead Civilization*, rev. edn. Chicago.
Oppenheim, A.L., Brill, R.H., Barag, D. and Von Saldern, A. (1970), *Glass and Glass-making in Ancient Mesopotamia*. Corning.
Oppenheimer, A. (1983), *Babylonia Judaica in the Talmudic Period*. Wiesbaden.
Orchard, J.J. and Brill, R.H. (1978), "Some miniature painted glass plaques from Fort Shalmaneser, Nimrud. Part I: Description and a restoration", *Iraq* 40: 1–22.
Oren, E. (1973), *The Northern Cemetery at Beth Shean*. Leiden.
Oren, E., ed. (1997), *The Hyksos: New Historical and Archaeological Perspectives*. Philadelphia.
Oren, E., ed. (2000), *The Sea Peoples and Their World: A Reassessment*. Philadelphia.
Orlamünde, J. (2011), *Die Obeliskenfragmente aus Assur*. Wiesbaden.
Orlamünde, J. and Lundström, S. (2011), *Die Orthostaten Tiglat-Pilesers I. und Assurnasirpals II. aus dem Alten Palast in Assur*. Wiesbaden.
Orthmann, W. (1971), *Untersuchungen zur späthethitischen Kunst*. Bonn.
Orthmann, W. (2002), "Die Bildkunst im Übergang von der Großreichszeit zur späthethitischen Periode", in Braun-Holzinger and Matthäus, eds., 153–159.
Ortner, S. (2005), "Subjectivity and cultural critique", *Anthropological Theory* 5/1: 31–52.
Osada, T. and Uesugi, A., eds. (2009), *Linguistics, Archaeology, and the Human Past*. Kyoto.
Osiek, C., MacDonald, M. and Tulloch. J.H. (2006), *A Woman's Place: House Churches in Earliest Christianity*. Philadelphia.
Ottaway, B.S. and Wang, Q. (2004), *Casting Experiments and Microstructure of Archaeologically Relevant Bronzes*. Oxford.
Otte, M., ed. (1998), *Préhistoire d'Anatolie. Genèse de deux mondes/ Anatolian Prehistory. At the crossroads of two worlds*. Liège.
Otte, M., Pelegrin, J. and Colin, F. (1990), "Towards an integrated approach: the use of the Canaanean blades", in Gräslund et al., eds., 135–145.
Otte, M., Yalçinkaya, I., Leotard, J.-M., Kartal, M., Bar-Yosef, O., Kozlowski, J., Lopez-Bayon, I. and Marshack, A. (1995), "The epi-palaeolithic of Öküzini cave (SW Anatolia) and its mobilary art", *Antiquity* 69: 931–944.
Otten, H. (1957), *Keilschrifttexte aus Boghazköi. 9. Heft, vorwiegend Texte der Grabungen 1955 und 1956*. Berlin.
Otto, A. (2006a), "Qal'at al-Mudiq", *RlA* 11: 145–146.
Otto, A. (2006b), *Alltag und Gesellschaft zur Spätbronzezeit: Eine Fallstudie aus Tall Bazi (Syrien)*. Turnhout.
Otto, A. (2008), "Organization of Late Bronze Age cities in the upper Syrian Euphrates Valley", in Córdoba et al., eds., 715–731.
Otto, A. and Einwag, B. (2005), "Ein Tempel für den Ältestenrat", *Alter Orient Aktuell* 6: 27–29.
Otto, A. and Einwag, B. (2007), "Ein Tempel hoch über dem Euphrattal", *Antike Welt* 4/2007: 39–46.
Otto, W. and Bengtson, H. (1938), *Zur Geschichte des Niedergangs des Ptolemäerreiches. Ein Beitrag zur Regierungszeit des 8. und des 9. Ptolemäers*. Munich.

Ouseley, W. (1823), *Travels in Various Countries of the East*, vol. 3. London.
Ousterhout, R.R., ed. (1990), *The Blessings of Pilgrimage*. Champaign.
Ousterhout, R.R. (2010), "Archaeologists and travellers in Ottoman lands", *Expedition* 52: 10–20.
Outram, A.K., Stear, N.A., Bendrey, R., Olsen, S., Kasparov, A., Zaibert, V., Thorpe, N. and Evershed, R.P. (2009), "The earliest horse harnessing and milking", *Science* 323: 1332–1335.
Ovadiah, A. (1970), *Corpus of the Byzantine Churches in the Holy Land*. Bonn.
Ovadiah, A. and de Silva, C.G. (1981), "Supplement to the corpus of churches in the Holy Land", *Levant* 13: 200–261.
Ovadiah, A. and de Silva, C.G. (1982), "Supplement to the corpus of churches in the Holy Land", *Levant* 14: 122–170.
Ovadiah, A. and de Silva, C.G. (1984), "Supplement to the corpus of churches in the Holy Land", *Levant* 16: 129–165.
Overlaet, B. (1997), "A report on the 1952 and 1954/55 soundings at Tall-i Taimuran (Fars), Iran: a file-excavation at the Royal Museums of Art and History, Brussels", *IrAnt* 32: 1–51.
Overlaet, B. (2007), "Soundings at Tall-Kamin (Kur River Basin), Fars, Iran", *IrAnt* 42: 61–103.
Owen, D.I. and Lacheman, E.R., eds. (1995), *General Studies and Excavations at Nuzi*, vol. 9/3. Winona Lake.
Özbal R., Gerritsen, F., Diebold, B., Healey, E., Aydin, N., Loyette, M., Nardulli, F., Reese, D., Ekstrom, H., Sholts, S., Mekel-Brobov, N. and Lahn, B. (2004), "Tell Kurdu Excavations 2001", *Anatolica* 30: 37–107.
Özbaşaran, M. (1999), "Musular: a general assessment on a new Neolithic site in central Anatolia", in Özdoğan and Başgelen eds., 147–155.
Özbaşaran, M. and Molist, M. (2007), "Akarçay Tepe: Orta Firat'ta Neolitik Döneme Ait Yeni Bir Yerleşme", in Özdoğan and Başgelen, ed., 179–187.
Özbek, M. (2009), "Remodelled human skulls in Köşk Höyük (Neolithic age, Anatolia): a new appraisal in view of recent discoveries", *JAS* 36: 379–386.
Özdoğan, A. (1999), "Çayönü", in Özdoğan and Başgelen, eds., 35–63.
Özdoğan, M. (2003), "Mezraa Teleilat: un site néolithique en bordure de l'Euphrate", *DA* 281: 36–41.
Özdoğan, M. (2010), "Westward expansion of the Neolithic way of life: sorting the Neolithic package into distinct packages", in Matthiae et al., eds., 883–896.
Özdoğan, M. and Başgelen, N., eds. (1999), *Neolithic in Turkey, the Cradle of Civilization: New Discoveries*. Istanbul.
Özdoğan, M. and Başgelen, N., eds. (2007), *Türkiye'de Neolitik Dönem. Yeni kazilar, yeni bulgular*. Istanbul.
Özdoğan, M. and Başgelen, N., eds. (in press), *Neolithic in Turkey: New Excavations, and New Research*. Istanbul.
Özdoğan, M., Hauptmann, H. and Başgelen, N., eds. (2003), *From Primary Villages to Cities: Studies Presented to Ufuk Esin*. Istanbul.
Özdoğan, M. and Özdoğan, A. (1999), "Archaeological evidence for early metallurgy at Çayönü Tepesi", in Hauptmann et al., eds., 13–22.
Özfirat, A. (2001), *Dogu Anadolu: Yayla Kültürleri*. Istanbul.

Özfirat, A. (2006), "The Middle Bronze Age settlement pattern of the eastern Anatolian high plateau in light of new evidence", in Peterson et al., eds., 160–171.

Özfirat, A. (2008), "The highland plateau of eastern Anatolia in the second millennium BCE: Middle/Late Bronze Ages", in Rubinson and Sagona, eds., 101–122.

Özgen, I. and Öztürk, J. (1996), *Heritage Recovered: The Lydian Treasure*. Ankara.

Özgüç, N. (1966), "Açemhöyük Kazilari/Excavations at Açemhöyük", *Anadolu (Anatolia)* 10: 1–52.

Özgüç, N. (1969), *Altıntepe II. Mezarlar, Depo Binası ve Fildişi Eserler*. Ankara.

Özgüç, N. (1980), "Seal Impressions from the Palaces at Acemhöyük", in Porada, ed., 61–100.

Özgüç, T. (1971), "Kültepe", in Mellink, ed., 164.

Özgüç, T. (1982), "Kültepe", in Mellink, ed., 559–560.

Özgüç, T. (1986a). *Kültepe-Kaniş II: New Researches at the Trading Center of the Ancient Near East*. Ankara.

Özgüç, T. (1986b). "New observations on the relationship of Kültepe with southeast Anatolia and North Syria during the third millennium BC", in Canby et. al., eds., 31–47.

Özgüç, T. (1999), *The Palaces and Temples of Kültepe-Kaniš/Neša*. Ankara.

Özgüç, T. (2002), "Maşathöyük", in Willinghöfer, ed., 168–171.

Özgüç, T. (2003), *Kültepe. Kaniş/Neşa: The Earliest International Trade Center and the Oldest Capital City of the Hittites*. Ankara.

Özgüç, T., Frings, J., Willinghöfer, H., Hasekamp, U. and Baykal-Seeher, A., eds. (2002), *Die Hethiter und ihr Reich: Das Volk der 1000 Götter*. Stuttgart.

Özkan, H., Willcox, G., Graner, A., Salamini, F. and Kilian, B. (2010), "Geographic distribution and domestication of wild emmer wheat (*Triticum dicoccoides*)", *Genetic Resources and Crop Evolution*. DOI 10.1007/s10722-010-9581-5.

Özkaya, V. and Coskun, A. (2008), "Anadolu'nun erken kültür tarihinde Körtik Tepe'nin yeri ve önemi", *Arkeoloji ve Sanat – Journal of Archaeology and Art* 129: 1–18.

Özkaya, V. and San, O. (2004), "2001 Körtik Tepe kazilari. Excavations at Körtik Tepe 2001", in Tuna and Velibeyoğlu, eds., 669–693.

Özyar, A. (1998), "On the use and abuse of re-use at Karkemish", in Arsebük et al., eds., 633–640.

Özyar, A. (2000), "Noch einmal zu den Standartenaufsätzen aus Alaçahöyük", in Yalçin, ed., 101–112.

Özyar, A., ed. (2005), *Tarsus-Gözlükule I. Field Seasons 2001–2003 of the Tarsus-Gözlükule Interdisciplinary Research Program*. Istanbul.

Painter, K.S., ed. (1994), *Churches Built in Ancient Times: Recent Studies in Early Christian Archaeology*. London.

Palaima, T.G. and Shelmerdine, C.W., ed. (1984), *Pylos Comes Alive: Industry and Administration in a Mycenaean Palace*. New York.

Paley, S.M. and Sobolewski, R.P. (1987), *The Reconstruction of the Relief Presentations and their Positions in the Northwest-Palace at Kalḫu (Nimrud) II*. Mainz.

Paley, S.M. and Sobolewski, R.P. (1992), *The Reconstruction of the Relief Presentations and their Positions in the Northwest-Palace at Kalḫu (Nimrud) III*. Mainz.

Palmer, J.A.B. (1951), "*Periplus Maris Erythraei* ἐμπτοριον νόμιμον and other expressions", *CQ* 1: 156–158.

Palmieri, A. and Hauptmann, A. (2000), "Metals from Ebla: chemical analyses of metal artefacts from the Bronze and Iron Ages", in Matthiae et al., eds., 1259–1281.

Palumbi, G. (2003), "Red-Black Pottery: Eastern Anatolian and Transcaucasian relationships around the mid-fourth millennium BC", *ANES* 40: 80–134.

Palumbi, G. (2008), *The Red and the Black: Social and Cultural Interaction Between the Upper Euphrates and Southern Caucasus Communities in the Fourth and Third Millennium BC*. Rome.

Palumbo, G. (1991), *The Early Bronze Age IV in the Southern Levant: Settlement Patterns, Economy, and Material Culture of a "Dark Age"*. Rome.

Palumbo-Liu, D. and Gumbrecht, H.U., eds. (1997), *Streams of Cultural Capital: Transnational Cultural Studies*. Stanford.

Pang, J.-F., Kluetsch, C., Zou, X.-J., Zhang, A.-B., Luo, L.-Y., Angleby, H., Ardalan, A., Ekstrom, C., Skollermo, A., Lundeberg, J., Matsumura, S., Leitner, T., Zhang, Y.-P. and Savolainen, P. (2009), "mtDNA data indicate a single origin for dogs south of the Yangtze River, less than 16,300 years ago, from numerous wolves", *Molecular Biolology and Evolution* 26: 2849–2864.

Papenfuss, D. and Strocka, V.M., eds. (1982), *Palast und Hütte: Beiträge zum Bauen und Wohnen im Altertum von Archäologen, Vor- und Frühgeschichtlern*. Mainz.

Paper, H. (1954), "Note préliminaire sur la date des trois tablettes élamites de Suse", in Ghirshman, 79–82.

Parker, A.G. (2009), "Pleistocene climatic change in Arabia: developing a framework for Hominin dispersal over the last 350 ka", in Petraglia and Rose, eds., 39–50.

Parker, A.G., Davies, C. and Wilkinson, T.J. (2006), "The early to mid-Holocene moist period in Arabia: some recent evidence from lacustrine sequences in eastern and southwestern Arabia", *PSAS* 36: 243–255.

Parker, A.G., Eckersley, L., Smith, M.M., Goudie, A.S., Stokes, S., White, K. and Hodson, M.J. (2004), "Holocene vegetation dynamics in the northeastern Rub' al-Khali desert, Arabian Peninsula: a pollen, phytolith and carbon isotope study", *JQS* 19: 665–676.

Parker, A.G. and Goudie, A., (2008), "Geomorphological and palaeoenvironmental investigations in the southeastern Arabian Gulf region and the implication for the archaeology of the region", *Geomorphology* 101: 458–470.

Parker, A.G., Goudie, A.S., Strokes, S., White, K., Hodson, M.J., Manning, M. and Kennet, D. (2006), "A record of Holocene climate change from lake geochemical analyses in southeastern Arabia", *QR* 66: 465–476.

Parker, A.G., Preston, G., Walkington, H. and Hodson, M.J. (2006), "Developing a framework of Holocene climatic change and landscape archaeology for the lower Gulf region, southeastern Arabia", *AAE* 17: 125–130.

Parker, B.J. (1997), "Garrisoning the empire: aspects of the construction and maintenance of forts on the Assyrian frontier", *Iraq* 59: 77–87.

Parker, B.J. (2001), *The Mechanics of Empire: The Northern Frontier of Assyria as a Case Study in Imperial Dynamics*. Helsinki.

Parker, B.J. (2003), "Archaeological manifestations of empire: Assyria's imprint on southeastern Anatolia", *AJA* 107: 525–557.

Parker, B.J. and Rodseth, L., eds. (2005), *Untaming the Frontier in Anthropology, Archaeology, and History*. Tucson.

Parker, S.T. (1996), "The Roman 'Aqaba Project: The 1994 campaign", *ADAJ* 40: 231–257.
Parker, S.T. (1997), "Preliminary report on the 1994 season of the Roman 'Aqaba Project", *BASOR* 305: 19–44.
Parker, S.T. (1998a), "The Roman 'Aqaba Project: the 1996 campaign", *ADAJ* 42: 375–394.
Parker, S.T. (1998b), "An early church, perhaps the oldest in the world, found at 'Aqaba", *NEA* 61/4: 254.
Parker, S.T. (1999a), "An empire's new Holy Land: the Byzantine period", *NEA* 62/3: 134–180.
Parker, S.T. (1999b), "Brief notice on a possible early 4th-c. church at 'Aqaba, Jordan", *JRA* 12: 372–376.
Parker, S.T. (2000), "The Roman Aqaba Project: the 1997 and 1998 campaigns", *ADAJ* 44: 373–394.
Parker, S.T. (2002), "The Roman 'Aqaba Project: the 2000 campaign", *ADAJ* 46: 409–428.
Parker, S.T. (2006), "Roman Aila and the Wadi Arabah: an economic relationship", in Bienkowski and Galor, eds., 223–230.
Parker, S.T. (2007), "Rome's Arabian frontier east of the Dead Sea", in Levy et al., eds., 349–357.
Parpola, A. and Koskikalio, P., eds. (1994), *South Asian Archaeology 1993*. Helsinki.
Parpola, S. (1970), *Letters from Assyrian scholars to the Kings Esarhaddon and Assurbanipal*. Neukirchen-Vluyn.
Parpola, S. (1981), "Assyrian royal inscriptions and Neo-Assyrian letters", in Fales, ed., 117–142.
Parpola, S. (1986), "The royal archives of Nineveh", in Veenhof, ed. 223–236.
Parpola, S. (1987), *The Correspondence of Sargon II, Part I. Letters from Assyria and the West*. Helsinki.
Parpola, S., Parpola, A. and Brunswig, R.H. (1977), "The Meluhha village: evidence of acculturation of Harappan traders in the late third millennium", *JESHO* 20/2: 129–165.
Parpola, S. and Whiting, R.M., ed. (1997), *Assyria 1995: Proceedings of the 10th Anniversary Symposium of the Neo-Assyrian Text Corpus Project*. Helsinki.
Parr, P.J. (1983), "The Tell Nebi Mend Project", *AAAS* 33: 99–117.
Parr, P.J. (1988), "The pottery of the late second millennium BC from north west Arabia and its historical implications", in Potts, ed., 73–90.
Parr, P.J. (1991), "The Tell Nebi Mend Project", *Journal of the Ancient Chronology Forum* 4: 78–85.
Parr, P.J., ed. (2003), *Excavations at Arjoune, Syria*. Oxford.
Parr, P.J., Harding, G.L. and Dayton, J.E. (1970), "Preliminary survey of north-west Arabia 1968 (1)", *Bulletin of the Institute of Archaeology* 8–9: 139–242.
Parr, P.J., Harding, G.L. and Dayton, J.E. (1972), "Preliminary survey of north-west Arabia 1968", *Bulletin of the Institute of Archaeology* 10: 23–61.
Parrot, A. (1946), *Archéologie mésopotamienne*, vol. 1. Paris.
Parrot, A. (1948), *Tello. Vingt campagnes de fouilles* (1877–1933). Paris.
Parzinger, H. and Boroffka, N., eds. (2003), *Das Zinn der Bonzezeit in Mittelasien I: Die siedlungsarchäologischen Forschungen im Umfeld der Zinnlagerstätten*. Mainz.

Patrich, J. (1994), *Sabas, Leader of Palestinian Monasticism: A Comparative Study in Eastern Monasticism, Fourth to Seventh Centuries*. Washington, DC.

Patrich, J. (1995), "Church, state and the transformation of Palestine: the Byzantine period (324–640 CE)", in Levy, ed., 470–487.

Patrich, J. (2003), "Early Christian churches in Israel", in Richard, ed., 479–486.

Patrich, J. (2004), "Monastic landscape", in Bowden et al., eds., 413–445.

Patrich, J. (2006), "Early Christian churches in the Holy Land", in Limor and Stroumsa, 355–399.

Patrich, J. (2011), *Studies in the Archaeology and History of Caesarea Maritima, Caput Judaeae, Metropolis Palaestina*. Leiden.

Paul, S.M. (1978), "Fishing imagery in Amos 4:2", *Journal of Biblical Literature* 97/2: 183–190.

Payne, J.C. (1960), "Flint implements from Tell al Judaidah", in Braidwood and Braidwood, eds., 525–529.

Payne, J.C. (1983), "The flint industries of Jericho", in Kenyon and Holland, eds., 622–757.

Payne, S. (1983), *The Animal Bones from the 1974 Excavations at Douara Cave*. Tokyo.

Peacock, D. and Blue, L. (2006), *Myos Hormos – Quseir al-Qadim. Roman and Islamic Ports on the Red Sea. Volume 1: Survey and Excavations 1999–2003*. Oxford.

Peacock, D. and Blue, L., eds. (2007), *The Ancient Red Sea Port of Adulis, Eritrea. Results of the Eritro-British Expedition, 2004–5*. Oxford.

Peacock, D. and Williams, D., eds. (2007), *Food for the Gods: New Light on the Ancient Incense Trade*. Oxford.

Pearce, L.E. (1995), "The scribes and scholars of Ancient Mesopotamia", in Sasson, ed., 2265–2278.

Pearce, S., ed. (1994), *Interpreting Objects and Collections*. London.

Pearce, S., ed. (1995), *On Collecting: An Investigation into Collecting in the European Tradition*. London.

Pearce, S. and Bounia, A., eds. (2000), *The Collector's Voice: Critical Readings in the Practice of Collecting, Vol. 1. Ancient Voices*. Aldershot.

Pearson, M. (2003), *The Indian Ocean*. London.

Peasnall, B. and Algaze, G. (2010), "The survey of Pir Hüseyin, 2004", *Anatolica* 36: 165–195.

Pecorella, P.E. and Salvini, M., eds. (1984), *Tra lo Zagros e l'Urmia: Ricerche storiche ed archeologiche nell'Azerbaigian iraniano*. Rome.

Pedde, F. (2000), *Vorderasiatische Fibeln. Von der Levante bis Iran*. Saarbrücken.

Pedde, F. (2010), "The Assur-Project: a new analysis of the Middle- and Neo-Assyrian graves and tombs", in Matthiae et al., eds., vol. 1, 913–923.

Pedde, F. (in press a), *Gräber und Grüfte in Assur. Die mittel- und neuassyrische Zeit*. Wiesbaden.

Pedde, F. (in press b), "The Assur Project: The Middle and Neo-Assyrian graves and tombs", in Curtis et al., eds.

Pedde, F. and Lundström, S. (2008), *Der Alte Palast in Assur*. Wiesbaden.

Pedersen, C.H. (1995), *Natufian Chipped Lithic Assemblage from Sunakh near Petra, Southern Jordan*. Copenhagen.

Pedersén, O. (1985), *Archives and Libraries in the City of Assur*, Pt. I. Uppsala.

Pedersén, O. (1986), *Archives and Libraries in the City of Assur*, Pt. II. Uppsala.

Pedersén, O. (1997), *Katalog der beschrifteten Objekte aus Assur*. Saarbrücken.

Pedersén, O. (1998), *Archives and Libraries in the Ancient Near East 1500–300 BC*. Bethesda.

Pedersen, R.K. (2000), "Under the Erythraean Sea: an ancient shipwreck in Eritrea", *Quarterly of the Institute of Nautical Archaeology* 27/2–3: 3–12.

Pedersen, R.K. (2004), "Traditional Arabian watercraft and the ark of the Gilgamesh epic: interpretations and realizations", *PSAS* 34: 231–238.

Pedrosa, S., Uzun, M., Arranz, J.J., Gutierrezz-Gil, B. and San Primitivo, F. (2005), "Evidence of three maternal lineages in Near Eastern sheep supporting multiple domestication events", *Proceedings of the Royal Society B: Biological Sciences* 272: 2211–2217.

Peet, T.E. (1930), *The Great Tomb-Robberies of the Twentieth Egyptian Dynasty*. London.

Pelegrin, J. and Otte, M. (1991), "Einige Bemerkungen zur Präparations- und Ausbeuttechnik der Kernsteine aus Raum 29", in Behm-Blancke, ed., 219–224.

Peli, A. (2006), "Les mines de la Péninsule arabique d'après les auteurs arabes (VIIe–XIIe siècles)", *CY* 13: 29–57.

Peli, A. and Téreygeol, F. (2007), "Al-Radrad (al-Jabali): a Yemeni silver mine, first results of the French Mission (2006)", *PSAS* 37: 187–200.

Peltenburg, E.J. (1999a), "Tell Jerablus Tahtani 1992–1996: a summary", in del Olmo Lete and Montero Fenollós, eds., 97–105.

Peltenburg, E.J. (1999b), "The living and the ancestors: Early Bronze Age mortuary practices at Jerablus Tahtani", in del Olmo Lete and Montero Fenollós, eds., 427–442.

Peltenburg, E.J., ed. (2007), *Euphrates River Valley Settlement: The Carchemish Sector in the Third Millennium BC*. Oxford.

Peltenburg, E.J. and Wasse, A., eds. (2004), *Neolithic Revolution: New Perspectives on Southwest Asia in Light of Recent Discoveries on Cyprus*. Oxford.

Pelzel, S.M. (1977), "Dating the Early Dynastic votive plaques from Susa", *JNES* 36: 1–15.

Pembroke, S. (1965), "Last of the matriarchs: a study in the inscriptions of Lycia", *JESHO* 8/3: 217–247.

Peña, I., Castellana, P. and Fernández, R. (1980), *Les Reclus syriens: Recherches sur les anciennes formes de vie solitaire en Syrie*. Jerusalem.

Peña, I., Castellana, P. and Fernández, R. (1983), *Les Cénobites Syriens*. Jerusalem.

Peña, I., Castellana, P. and Fernández, R. (1987), *Inventaire du Jébel Baricha. Recherches archéologiques dans la région des villes mortes de la Syrie du Nord*. Jerusalem.

Peña, I., Castellana, P. and Fernández, R. (1990), *Inventaire du Jebel el-A'la: Recherches archéologiques dans la région des villes mortes de la Syrie du Nord*. Milan.

Peña, I., Castellana, P. and Fernández, R. (2003), *Inventaire du Jébel Doueili. Recherches archéologiques dans la région des villes mortes de la Syrie du Nord*. Milan.

Peña-Chocarro, L. and Rottoli, M. (2007), "Crop husbandry practices during the Bronze and Iron Ages in Tell Mishrifeh (central-western Syria)", in Morandi Bonacossi, ed., 123–143.

Périnet, G. and Courtois, L. (1983), "Évaluation des températures de cuisson de céramiques et de vaisselles blanches néolithiques de Syrie", *Bulletin de la Société Préhistorique Française* 80: 157–160.

Perkins, A. (1949), "Archaeological news", *AJA* 53/1: 36–57.

Perkins, D. (1966), "Appendix B: The fauna from Madamagh and Beidha, a preliminary report", *PEQ* 98: 66–67.
Perlès, C. (2001), *The Early Neolithic in Greece*. Cambridge.
Perlman, I. and Yellin, J. (1980), "The provenance of obsidian from Neolithic sites in Israel", *IEJ* 30: 83–88.
Perna, M., ed. (2005), *Studi in onore di Enrica Fiandra*. Paris.
Pernicka, E. (2004), "Copper and silver in Arisman and Tappeh Sialk and the early metallurgy in Iran", in Stöllner et al., eds., 232–239.
Pernicka, E., Begemann, F., Schmitt-Strecker, S. and Grimianis, A.P. (1990), "On the composition and provenance of metal objects from Poliochni on Lemnos", *OJA* 9: 263–298.
Pernicka, E. and Hauptmann A. (1989), "Chemische und mineralogische Analyse einiger Erz- und Kupferfunde von Maadi", in Rizkana and Seeher, 137–141.
Pernicka, E. and von Berswordt-Wallrabe, S., eds. (2008), *Original–Copy–Fake? Examining the Authenticity of Ancient Works Of Art, Focusing on Asian and African Bronzes and Terracottas*. Mainz.
Pernicka, E., Rehren, T. and Schmitt-Strecker, S. (1998), "Late Uruk silver production by cupellation at Habuba Kabira, Syria", in Rehren, Hauptmann & Muhly, eds., 123–134.
Pernicka, E., Seeliger, T.C., Wagner, G.A., Begemann, F., Schmitt-Strecker, S., Eibner, C., Oztunali, O. and Baranyi. I. (1984), "Archäometallurgische Untersuchungen in Nordwestanatolien", *JRGZM* 31: 533–599.
Pernicka, E. and Wagner, G.A., eds. (1991), *Archaeometry '90*. Basel.
Perrot, J. (1955), "The excavations at Tell Abu Matar, near Beersheba", *IEJ* 5: 17–40, 73–84, 167–189.
Perrot, J. (1966), "Le gisement natoufien de Mallaha (Eynan), Israel", *L'Anthropologie* 70/5–6: 437–484.
Perrot, J. (1968), "La préhistorie palestinienne", *SDB* 43: 286–446.
Perrot, J. (1978), "Introduction aux Actes de la rencontre internationale de Suse (Iran) du 23 au 28 octobre 1977", *Paléorient* 4: 133–140.
Perrot, J. (1981), "L'architecture militaire et palatiale des Achéménides à Suse", in Krämer and Buchner, eds., 79–94.
Perrot, J. (1984), "Structures d'habitat, mode de vie et environnement: les villages souterrains des pasteurs de Beershéva, dans le sud d'Israël, au IVe millénaire avant l'Ère chrétienne", *Paléorient* 10/1: 75–96.
Perrot, J. (2010a), "Convention relative à la concession des antiquités de la Perse", in Perrot, ed., 72–73.
Perrot, J., ed. (2010b), *Le Palais de Darius à Suse, une résidence royale sur la route de Persépolis à Babylone*. Paris.
Perrot, J. (2010c), "Le programme franco-iranien (1969–1979)", in Perrot, ed., 120–145.
Perrot, J. (2010d), "Restauration, reconstitution", in Perrot, ed., 224–255.
Perrot, J. and Ladiray, D. (1974), "La porte de Darius à Suse", *DAFI* 4: 43–56.
Perrot, J., Ladiray, D. and Vallat, F. (1999), "The propylaeum of the palace of Darius at Susa", in Alizadeh et al., eds., 158–177, 220.
Perrot, J. and Madjidzadeh, Y. (2005), "L'iconographie des vases et des objets en chlorite de Jiroft (Iran)", *Paléorient* 32/1: 123–152.

Peterkin, G., Bricker, H. and Mellars, P., eds. (1993), *Hunting and Animal Exploitation in the Later Palaeolithic and Mesolithic of Eurasia*. Washington, DC.

Peterman, G. and Schick, R. (1996), "The monastery of Saint Aaron", *ADAJ* 40: 473–480.

Peters, F.E. (1985), *Jerusalem: The Holy City in the Eyes of Chroniclers, Visitors, Pilgrims, and Prophets from the Days of Abraham to the Beginnings of Modern Times*. Princeton.

Peters, J. (1997), "The dromedary: ancestry, history of domestication and medical treatment in early historic times", *Tierärztliche Praxis. Ausgabe G, Grosstiere/Nutztiere* 25/6: 559–565.

Peters, J., Helmer, D., von den Driesch, A. and Sana Segui, M. (1999), "Early animal husbandry in the northern Levant", *Paléorient* 25: 27–47.

Peters, J. and Schmidt, K. (2004), "Animals in the symbolic world of Pre-Pottery Neolithic Göbekli Tepe, south-eastern Turkey: a preliminary assessment", *Anthropozoologica* 29: 179–218.

Peters, J. and von den Driesch, A. (1997), "The two-humped camel (Camelus bactrianus): new light on its distribution, management, and medical treatment in the past", *Journal of Zoology* 242: 651–679.

Peters, J., von den Driesch, A. and Helmer, D. (2005), "The upper Ephrates-Tigris basin: cradle of agro-pastoralism?", in Vigne et al., eds., 96–124.

Peters, J.P. (1921), "The tower of Babel at Borsippa", *JAOS* 41: 157–159.

Peterson, D.L. (2007), *Changing Technologies and Transformation of Value in the Middle Volga and Northeastern Caucasus, circa 3000–1500 BCE*. Chicago.

Peterson, D.L., Popova, L.M. and Smith, A.T., eds. (2006), *Beyond the Steppe and the Sown*. Leiden.

Peterson, J. (2002), *Sexual Revolutions: Gender and Labor at the Dawn of Agriculture*. Lanham.

Peterson, J. (2010), "Domesticating gender: Neolithic patterns from the Southern Levant", *JAA* 29: 249–264.

Petraglia, M.D. and Rose, J., eds. (2009), *The Evolution of Human Populations in Arabia: Paleoenvironments, Prehistory and Genetics*. Dordrecht.

Petrie, C.A., ed. (2010), *Sheri Khan Tarakai and Early Village Life in the Borderlands of North-West Pakistan*. Oxford.

Petrie, C.A. (2011), "'Culture', innovation and interaction across southern Iran from the Neolithic to the Bronze Age (6500–3000 BC)", in Roberts and Vander Linden, eds., 151–182.

Petrie, C.A., ed. (in press), *Ancient Iran and Its Neighbours*. London.

Petrie, C.A., Asgari Chaverdi, A. and Seyedin, M. (2005), "From Anshan to Dilmun and Magan: the spatial and temporal distribution of Kaftari and Kaftari-related ceramic vessels", *Iran* 43: 49–86.

Petrie, C.A., Asgari Chaverdi, A. and Seyedin, M. (2006), "Excavations at Tol-e Spid", in Potts and Roustaei, eds., 89–134.

Petrie, C.A., Knox, J.R., Khan, F., Thomas, K.D., Morris, J.C. and Joyner, L. (2010), "Ceramic vessels from Sheri Khan Tarakai", in Petrie, ed., 71–193.

Petrie, C.A., Sardari Zarchi, A., Alamdari, K. and Javanmard Zadeh, A. (2007), "Transformations in fourth millennium BC Fars: further excavations at Tol-e Spid", *Iran* 45: 1–9.

Petrie, C.A., Weeks, L.R., Potts, D.T. and Roustaei, K. (2006), "Perspectives on the cultural sequence of Mamasani", in Potts et al., eds., 169–192.
Petrie, W.M.F. (1895), *Egyptian Tales, Translated from the Papyri*. London.
Petrie, W.M.F. (1917), *Tools and weapons*. London.
Petrie, W.M.F. (1926), "Glass in the early ages", *JSGT* 10: 229–234.
Pettinato, G. (1981), *Testi Lessicali Monolingui della Biblioteca L. 2769*. Naples.
Pézard, M. (1914), *Mission à Bender-Bouchir*. Paris.
Pézard, M. (1931), *Qadesh: Mission archéologique à Tell Nebi Mend, 1921–1922*. Paris.
Pfälzner, P. (1995), *Mitannische und mittelassyrische Keramik: Eine Chronologie, functionale und produktionsökonomische Analyse*. Berlin.
Pfälzner, P. (1997), "Wandel und Kontinuität im Urbanisierungsprozess des 3. Jtsds. in Nordmesopotamien", in Wilhelm, ed., 239–265.
Pfälzner, P. (1998), "Eine Modifikation der Periodisierung Nordmesopotamiens im 3. Jtsd. v. Chr.", *MDOG* 130: 69–71.
Pfälzner, P. (2002/3), "Die Politik und der Tod im Königtum von Qatna", *Nürnberger Blätter zur Archäologie* 19: 85–102.
Pfälzner, P. (2005), "Syrien: Qatna. Ahnenkult im 2. Jahrtausend v. Chr.", *Welt und Umwelt der Bibel* 2/2005: 56–59.
Pfälzner, P. (2006), "Qatna. B. Archäologisch", *RlA* 11/1–2: 161–170.
Pfälzner, P. (2007a), "Das System des 'kommerzialisierten Geschenkaustausches' im 2. Jahrtausend v. Chr. in Syrien", in Klinkott and Kubisch, eds., 117–131.
Pfälzner, P. (2007b), "Archaeological Investigations in the Royal Palace of Qatna", in Morandi Bonacossi, ed., 29–64.
Pfälzner, P. (2008a), "The Royal Palace at Qatna: power and prestige in the Late Bronze Age", in Aruz, Benzel and Evans, eds., 218–221.
Pfälzner, P. (2008b), "Inlaid rosette", in Aruz et al., eds., 223.
Pfälzner, P. (2009a), "Macht und Reichtum in der Königsresidenz", in al-Maqdissi et al., eds., 164–171.
Pfälzner, P. (2009b), "Das Königtum von Qatna", in al-Maqdissi et al., eds., 134–137.
Pfälzner, P. (2009c), "Elefantenjagd in Syrien", *Damals* 11/2009: 47–48.
Pfälzner, P. (2009d), "Die Wasserversorgung der Herrscher", in al-Maqdissi et al., eds., 174–175.
Pfälzner, P. (2009e), "Zederholz aus Qatna", *Damals* 11/2009: 48.
Pfälzner, P. (2009f), "Die Bestattungsrituale der Könige von Qatna", in al-Maqdissi et al., eds., 240–243.
Pfälzner, P. (2009g), "Die Verehrung der Vorfahren – Ahnenkult im Alten Syrien", in al-Maqdissi et al., eds., 84–87.
Pfälzner, P. (2009h), "Meisterwerke der Plastik – Die Ahnenstatuen aus dem Hypogäum", in al-Maqdissi et al., eds., 204–207.
Pfälzner, P. (2009i), "Residenz der toten Herrscher – Die Königsgruft", in al-Maqdissi et al., eds., 200–203.
Pfälzner, P. (2010), "Introduction and synthesis: urban development and ecology at Tell Mozan", in Deckers et al., 1–12.
Pfälzner, P., ed. (2011a), *Interdisziplinäre Studien zur Königsgruft von Qatna*. Wiesbaden.
Pfälzner, P. (2011b), "Das systemische und das archäologische Inventar der Königsgruft von Qatna und seine Interpretationsmöglichkeiten", in Pfälzner, ed., 39–62.

Pfälzner, P. (2011c), "Die Königsgruft von Qatna als architektonisches Ensemble", in Pfälzner, ed., 69–84.
Pfälzner, P. (in press a), "How did they bury the kings of Qatna?", in Niehr et al., eds.
Pfälzner, P. (in press b), "The art of Qatna and the question of the 'International Style'", in Pfälzner, ed.
Pfälzner, P., ed. (in press c), *Qatna and the Networks of Bronze Age Globalism*. Wiesbaden.
Pfälzner, P. and Dohmann-Pfälzner, H. (2010), "Elefantenknochen und über 50 Schädel", *Antike Welt* 4/2010: 75–78.
Pfälzner, P. and Dohmann-Pfälzner, H. (2011), "Die Rollsiegel, Siegelungen und Skarabäen aus der Königsgruft", in Pfälzner, ed., 332–362.
Pfälzner, P. and Rossberger, E. (2009), "Das Gold des Nordens – Die Bernsteinobjekte", in al-Maqdissi, Morandi Bonacossi and Pfälzner, eds., 212–215.
Pfälzner, P. and von Rüden, C. (2008a), "Wall painting fragments", in Aruz, Benzel and Evans, eds., 126–127.
Pfälzner, P. and von Rüden, C. (2008b), "Between the Aegean and Syria: the wall paintings from the Royal Palace of Qatna", in Bonatz et al., eds., 95–118.
Pfannenstiel, M. (1941), *Die altsteinzeitlichen Kulturen Anatoliens*. Berlin.
Pfrommer, M. (1993), *Metalwork from the Hellenized East*. Malibu.
Philby, H.St.J.B. (1959), "The eastern marshes of Mesopotamia", *GJ* 125/1: 65–69.
Philip, G. (1989), *Metal Weapons of the Early and Middle Bronze Ages in Syria-Palestine*. Oxford.
Philip, G. (1991), "Tin, arsenic, lead: alloying practices in Syria-Palestine around 2000 BC", *Levant* 23: 93–104.
Philip, G. (1995), "Warrior burials in the Ancient Near Eastern Bronze Age: the evidence from Mesopotamia, western Iran and Syria-Palestine", in Campbell and Green, eds., 140–154.
Philip, G. (1999), "Complexity and diversity in the Southern Levant during the third millennium BC: the evidence of Khirbet Kerak Ware", *JMA* 12/1: 26–57.
Philip, G. (2007), "The metalwork of the Carchemish region and the development of grave repertories during the third millennium BC", in Peltenburg, ed., 187–197.
Philip, G., Abdulkarim, A., Newson, P., Beck, A., Bridgeland, D., Bshesh, M., Shaw, A., Westaway, R. and Wilkinson, K. (2005), "Settlement and landscape development in the Homs Region, Syria: report on work undertaken during 2001–2003", *Levant* 37: 21–42.
Philip, G. and Bradbury, J. (2010), "Pre-Classical activity in the basalt landscape of the Homs Region, Syria: implications for the development of 'sub-optimal' zones in the Levant during the Chalcolithic-Early Bronze Age", *Levant* 42: 136–169.
Philip, G. and Williams-Thorpe, O. (1993), "A provenance study of Jordanian basalt vessels of the Chalcolithic and Early Bronze Age I periods", *Paléorient* 19/2: 51–63.
Phillips, C.S. (2002), "Prehistoric middens and a cemetery from the southern Arabian Gulf", in Cleuziou, Tosi and Zarins, eds., 169–186.
Phillipson, D.W. (2009), "Aksum, the entrepot, and highland Ethiopia, 3rd–12th centuries", in Mango, ed., 353–368.
Photos, E. (1989), "The question of meteoritic versus smelted nickel-rich iron: archaeological evidence and experimental results", *WA* 20/3: 403–421.

Piaskowski, J. (1982), "A study of the origin of the ancient high-nickel iron generally regarded as meteoritic", in Wertime and Wertime, eds., 237–243.
Piccirillo, M. (1981), *Chiese e mosaici della Giordania Settentrionale*. Jerusalem.
Piccirillo, M. (1989a), *Chiese e mosaici di Madaba*. Jerusalem.
Piccirillo, M. (1989b), "Gruppi episcopali nelle tre Palestine e in Arabia?", in Duval et al., eds., 459–501.
Piccirillo, M. (1992), "Monks and monasteries in Jordan from the Byzantine to the Abbasid period", *Al-Liqa'* 1: 17–30.
Piccirillo, M.T. (1993), *The Mosaics of Jordan*. Amman.
Piccirillo, M. (1998), "The churches on Mount Nebo: new discoveries", in Piccirillo and Alliata, eds., 221–263.
Piccirillo, M., ed. (1999), *The Madaba Map Centenary 1897–1997: Travelling Through the Byzantine-Umayyad Period*. Jerusalem.
Piccirillo, M. (2000), "Sui luoghi delle tracce di Gesù, dei suoi discepoli e dei profeti", in Fantini Terzi, ed., 73–89.
Piccirillo, M.T. (2001), "The mosaics of Jordan", in MacDonald et al., eds., 671–676.
Piccirillo, M. (2002), *L'Arabia cristiana. Dalla provincia imperiale al primo periodo islamico*. Milan.
Piccirillo, M.T. (2003), "The mosaics of Jordan", in Richard, ed., 205–209.
Piccirillo, M. (2005), "Aggiornamento delle liste episcopali delle diocesi in territorio transgiordanico", *LA* 55: 377–394.
Piccirillo, M. (2007a), "La chiesa cattedrale di Hama-Epifania in Siria", *LA* 57: 597–621.
Piccirillo, M. (2007b), "Dall'archeologia alla storia. Nuove evidenze per una rettifica di luoghi comuni riguardanti le province di Palestina e di Arabia nei secolo IV–VIII d.C.", in Quintavalle, ed., 95–111.
Piccirillo, M. (2008), *La Palestina cristiana*. Bologna.
Piccirillo, M. and Alliata, E. (1994), *Umm al-Rasas – Mayfa'ah I: Gli scavi del complesso di Santo Stefano*. Jerusalem.
Piccirillo M. and Alliata, E., eds. (1998), *Mount Nebo: New Archaeological Excavations 1967–1997*. Jerusalem.
Piccirillo, M. and Alliata, E., eds. (1999), *The Madaba Map Centenary 1897–1997: Travelling Through the Byzantine-Umayyad Period*. Jerusalem.
Pidaev S.R., ed. (2008), *Kul'tura nomadov Tsentral'noĭ Azii: materialy mezhdunarodnoĭ konferentsii, Samarkand, 22–24, 2007g*. Samarkand.
Pierrat-Bonnefois, G. (1999), "Les objets en lapis-lazuli dans le trésor de Tôd", in Caubet, ed., 285–302.
Piesinger, C.M. (1983), *Legacy of Dilmun. The Roots of Ancient Maritime Trade in Eastern Coastal Arabia in the 4th/3rd millenniums BC*. Madison.
Pigott, V.C. (1985), "Āhan", *EnIr* 1: 624–633.
Pigott, V.C. (1989a), "Archaeo-metallurgical investigations at Bronze Age Tappeh Hesar, 1976", in Dyson and Howard, eds., 25–34.
Pigott, V.C. (1989b), "The emergence of iron use at Hasanlu", *Expedition* 31: 67–79.
Pigott, V.C. (1996), "Near Eastern archaeometallurgy", in Cooper and Schwartz, eds., 139–176.
Pigott, V.C. (1999a), "The development of metal production on the Iranian Plateau: an archaeometallurgical perspective", in Pigott, ed., 73–106.

Pigott, V.C. (1999b), "A heartland of metallurgy: Neolithic/Chalcolithic metallurgical origins on the Iranian Plateau", in Hauptmann et al., eds., 107–120.

Pigott, V.C., ed. (1999c), *The Archaeometallurgy of the Asian Old World*. Philadelphia.

Pigott, V.C. and Lechtman, H. (2003), "Chalcolithic copper-base metallurgy on the Iranian Plateau: a new look at old evidence", in Potts, Roaf & Stein, eds., 291–312.

Pigulevskaja, N.V., ed. (1962), *Drevnij mir: Sbornik statej Akademiku Vasiliju Vasil'jeviču Struve*. Moscow.

Pilipko, V.N. (2008), "The central ensemble of the fortress Mihrdatkirt: layout and chronology", *Parthica* 10: 33–51.

Pillet, M.L. (1914), *Le Palais de Darius Ier à Suse, Ve siècle av. J.C.*. Paris.

Piltz, E. (2007), *From Constantine the Great to Kandinsky: Studies in Byzantine and Post-Byzantine Art and Architecture*. Oxford.

Pinnock, F. (2006), "The raw lapis lazuli in the Royal Palace G of Ebla: new evidence from the annexes of the throne room", in Alberti et al., eds., 347–357.

Pintaud, J.-C. Zehdi, S., Couvreur, T., Barrow, S., Henderson, S., Aberlenc-Bertossi, F., Tregear, J. and Billotte, N. (2010), "Species delimitation in the genus *Phoenix* (Arecaceae) based on SSR markers, with emphasis on the identity of the date palm (*Phoenix dactylifera* L.)", in Seberg et al., eds., 267–286.

Pintore, F. (1978), *Il matrimonio interdinastico nel Vicino Oriente durante i secoli XV-XIII*. Rome.

Piotrovskii, B. (1959), *Vanskoe Tsarstvo (Urartu)*. Moscow.

Piotrovskii, B. (1967), *The Kingdom of Van and its Art*. New York.

Piotrovskii, B. (1969), *The Ancient Civilization of Urartu*. New York.

Piotrovsky, B. (1973), "Early cultures of the lands of the Scythians", *The Metropolitan Museum of Art Bulletin* 32/5: 12–25.

Piperno, D.R., Weiss, E., Holst, I. and Nadel, D. (2004), "Processing of wild cereal grains in the Upper Paleolithic revealed by starch grain analysis", *Nature* 430: 670–673.

Piperno, M. and Salvatori, S. (2007), *The Shahr-i Sokhta Graveyard (Sistan, Iran): Excavation Campaigns 1972–1978*. Rome.

Piperno, M. and Tosi, M. (1973), "Lithic technology behind the ancient lapis lazuli trade", *Expedition* 16: 15–23.

Piran, S. (in press), "The pottery of Konar Sandal South: a preliminary study", in Majidzadeh and Pittman, eds.

Pittman, H. (1984), *Art of the Bronze Age*. New York.

Pittman, H. (2001), "Mesopotamian intraregional relations reflected through glyptic evidence in the Late Chalcolithic 1–5 periods", in Rothman, ed., 403–443.

Pittman, H. (2002), "The 'Jeweler's seal from Susa and the art of Awan", in Ehrenberg, ed., 211–235.

Pittman, H. (in press), "The glyptic art of Konar Sandal South: gods, chiefs and the marriage union", in Majidzadeh and Pittman, eds.

Pizchelauri, K.N. (2003), "Drevnyaya Tsivilizatsiya na Kholmakh Udabno-David Garedzhi", *Drevhejshaya Kul'tura Armenii* 3: 61–66.

Pizchelauri, K. and Pizchelauri, K. (2002), "Übersicht metallurgischer Entwicklungen von der Bronze- bis zur Eisenzeit in Ostgeorgien", in Yalçin, ed., 101–114.

Place, V. (1867–1870), *Ninive et l'Assyrie*, 3 vols. Paris.

Planhol, X. de (2000), "Garmsīr and sardsīr", *EnIr* 10: 316–317.

Planhol, X. de (2006), "Isfahan ii. Historical geography: an overview since Ancient times", *EnIr* 13: 617–622.

Plu, A. (1985), "Bois et graines", in Balout and Roubet, eds., 166–175.

Poetto, M. (1993), *L'iscrizione luvio-geroglifica di Yalburt. Nuove acquisizioni relative alla geografia dell'anatolia sud-occidentale*. Pavia.

Pohanka, R. (1983), "Zu einigen Architekturstücken von Tell-e Zohak bei Fasa, Südiran", *Anzeiger der Österreichischen Akademie der Wissenschaften (philosophisch-historische Klasse)* 120: 255–265.

Poidebard, A. (1934), *La Trace de Rome dans le désert de Syrie*. Paris.

Polanyi, K. (1957), "Marketless trading in Hammurabi's time", in Polanyi, Arensberg and Pearson, eds., 12–26.

Polanyi, K. (1971a), "Ports of trade in early societies", in Dalton, ed., 238–260.

Polanyi, K. (1971b), "Societies and economic systems", in Dalton, ed., 3–25.

Polanyi, K. (1971c), "On the comparative treatment of economic institutions in Antiquity with illustrations from Athens, Mycenae, and Alalakh", in Dalton, ed., 306–334.

Polanyi, K. (1971d), "Redistribution: the state sphere in eighteenth-century Dahomey", in Dalton, ed., 207–237.

Polanyi, K. (1975), "Traders and trade", in Sabloff and Lamberg-Karlovsky, eds., 133–154.

Polanyi, K., Arensberg, C.M. and Pearson, H.W., eds. (1957), *Trade and Market in the Early Empires: Economies in History and Theory*. New York.

Politis, K.D. (2010), "The Monastery of Agios Lot at Deir 'Ain 'Abata in Jordan", in Daim and Drauschke, eds., 1–23.

Pollock, S. (1983), "Style and information: an analysis of Susiana ceramics", *JAA* 2: 354–390.

Pollock, S. (1989), "Power politics in the Susa A Period", in Henrickson and Thuesen, eds., 281–292.

Pollock, S. (1991), "Of priestesses, princes and poor relations: the dead in the Royal Cemetery of Ur", *CAJ* 1: 171–189.

Pollock, S. (1999), *Ancient Mesopotamia: The Eden That Never Was*. Cambridge.

Pollock, S. (2003), "The looting of the Iraq Museum: thoughts on archaeology in a time of crisis", *Public Archaeology* 3: 117–124.

Pollock, S. (2005), "Archaeology goes to war at the newsstand", in Pollock and Bernbeck, eds., 78–96.

Pollock, S. (2007), "The Royal Cemetery of Ur: ritual, tradition, and the creation of subjects", in Heinz and Feldman, eds., 89–110.

Pollock, S. (2010), "Decolonizing archaeology: political economy and archaeological practice in the Middle East", in Boytner et al., eds., 196–216.

Pollock, S. (2011), "Making a difference: mortuary practices in Halaf times", in Baadsgaard et al., eds.

Pollock, S. and Bernbeck, R., eds. (2005), *Archaeologies of the Middle East: Critical Perspectives*. Oxford.

Pollock, S., Bernbeck, R. and Abdi, K., eds. (2010), *The 2003 Excavations at Tol-e Baši, Iran: Social Life in a Neolithic Village*. Mainz.

Pollock, S. and Lutz, C. (1994), "Archaeology deployed for the Gulf War", *Critique of Anthropology* 14: 263–284.

Pollock, S., Pope, M. and Coursey, C. (1996), "Household production at the Uruk Mound, Abu Salabikh, Iraq", *AJA* 100: 683–698.

Pomper, P. (2005), "The history and theory of empires", *History and Theory* 44: 1–27.

Pope, A.U., ed. (1938), *A Survey of Persian Art from Prehistoric Times to the Present*, vol. 1. London/New York.

Pope, A.U., ed. (1964), *A Survey of Persian art from Prehistoric Times to the Present*, vol. 2, 2nd ed. Tokyo.

Pope, A.U., ed. (1967), *A Survey of Persian Art from Prehistoric Times to the Present*. Vol. 14: *New Studies: Proceedings, the IVth International Congress of Iranian Art and Archaeology, April 24–May 3, 1960, Part A*. Tehran.

Pope, A.U., ed. (1977), *A Survey of Persian Art from Prehistoric Times to the Present*, 3rd edn. Tehran/New York/London/Ashiya.

Pope, A.U., Crane, M. and Wilber, D.N. (1937), "The Institute's survey of Persian architecture, preliminary report on Takht-e Suleiman", *Bulletin of the American Institute for Iranian Art and Archaeology* 5: 71–105.

Pope, M. and Pollock, S. (1995), "Trade, tools, and tasks: a study of Uruk chipped stone industries", *Research in Economic Anthropology* 16: 227–265.

Porada, E. (1962), *The Art of Ancient Iran*. New York.

Porada, E. (1979), "Some thoughts on the audience reliefs of Persepolis", in Kopcke and Moore, eds., 37–43.

Porada, E., ed. (1980), *Ancient Art in Seals*. Princeton.

Porada, E. (1984), "The cylinder seal from Tell el-Dabʿa", *AJA* 88: 485–488.

Porter, A. (2007), "The ceramic assemblages of the third millennium in the Euphrates region", in al-Maqdissi, Matoïan & Nicolle, eds., 3–21.

Portillo, M., Albert, R.M. and Henry, D.O. (2009), "Domestic activities and spatial distribution in Ain Abū Nukhayla (Wadi Rum, southern Jordan): the use of phytoliths and spherulites studies", *QI* 193/1–2: 174–183.

Portugali, J. and Gophna, R. (1993), "Crisis, progress and urbanization: the transition from Early Bronze I to Early Bronze II in Palestine", *Tel Aviv* 20: 164–186.

Posener, G. (1940), *Princes et pays d'Asie et de Nubie: Textes hiératiques sur les figurines d'envoûtement du Moyen Empire*. Brussels.

Possehl, G.L. (1979), "Pastoral nomadism in the Indus Civilization: An hypothesis", in Taddei, ed., 537–551.

Possehl, G.L. (1981), "Cambay bead making: an ancient craft in modern India", *Expedition* 23/4: 39–46.

Possehl, G.L., ed. (1993), *Harappan Civilization: A Recent Perspective*. New Delhi/Bombay/Calcutta.

Possehl, G.L. (1994), "Of men", in Kenoyer, ed., 179–186.

Possehl, G.L. (1996), "Meluhha", in Reade, ed., 133–208.

Possehl, G.L. (1997), "The transformation of the Indus Civilization", *JWP* 11/4: 425–472.

Possehl, G.L. (1999), *Indus Age: The Beginnings*. Philadelphia.

Possehl, G.L. (2002a), *The Indus Civilization: A Contemporary Perspective*. Walnut Creek.

Possehl, G.L. (2002b), "Indus-Mesopotamia trade: the record in the Indus", *IrAnt* 37: 322–340.

Possehl, G.L. (2004), "The Middle Asian Interaction Sphere: trade and contact in the 3rd millennium BC", *Expedition* 49/1: 40–42.

Possehl, G.L. (2006), "Shu-ilishu's cylinder seal", *Expedition* 48/1: 42–43.
Possehl, G.L. (2007), "The Middle Asian Interaction Sphere", *Expedition* 49/1: 40–42.
Postgate, C., Oates, D. and Oates, J. (1997), *The Excavations at Tell al Rimah: The Pottery*. Warminster.
Postgate, J.N. (1974), *Taxation and Conscription in the Assyrian Empire*. Rome.
Postgate, J.N. (1986), "The equids of Sumer, again", in Meadow and Uerpmann, ed., 194–206.
Postgate, J.N. (1987), "Notes on fruits in the cuneiform sources", *BSA* 3: 115–144.
Postgate, J.N. (1992), *Early Mesopotamia: Society and Economy at the Dawn of history*. London.
Postgate, J.N. (1994), "How many Sumerians per hectare? Probing the anatomy of an early city", *CAJ* 4: 47–65.
Postgate, J.N. (1995), "Assyria: the home provinces", in Liverani, ed., 1–17.
Postgate, J.N., ed. (2002), *Artefacts of Complexity: Tracking the Uruk in the Near East*. Warminster.
Postgate, J.N. (2007), "The ceramics of centralisation and dissolution: a case study from Rough Cilicia", *AnSt* 57: 141–150.
Postgate, J.N. (2008), "The chronology of the Iron Age seen from Kilise Tepe", *ANES* 45: 166–187.
Postgate, J.N. and Moon, J.A. (1982), "Excavations at Abu Salabikh", *Iraq* 44: 103–136.
Postgate, J.N. and Payne, S. (1975), "Some Old Babylonian shepherds and their flocks", *JSS* 20: 1–21.
Postgate, J.N. and Thomas, D., eds. (2007), *Excavations at Kilise Tepe, 1994–98: From Bronze Age to Byzantine in Western Cilicia*. London.
Potemkina, T.M. (1995), "Problemy Svyzzei i smeny kul'tur naseleniya Zaural'ya v Epokhu Bronzy (rannii i srednii Etapy)", *Rosskaya Arkheologiya* 1: 14–27.
Potter, L., ed. (2009), *The Persian Gulf in History*. New York.
Potts, D.T. (1984), "On salt and salt gathering in Ancient Mesopotamia", *JESHO* 27: 225–271.
Potts, D.T. (1985), "Reflections on the archaeology and history of Bahrain", *JAOS* 105: 675–710.
Potts, D.T. (1986), "Eastern Arabia and the Oman peninsula during the late fourth and early third millennium BC", in Finkbeiner and Röllig, eds., 121–170.
Potts, D.T., ed. (1988a), *Araby the Blest: Studies in Arabian Archaeology*. Copenhagen.
Potts, D.T. (1988b), "Trans-Arabian routes of the pre-Islamic period", in Salles, ed., 129–162.
Potts, D.T. (1990), *The Arabian Gulf in Antiquity*, vol. 1, Oxford.
Potts, D.T. (1991a), *The pre-Islamic coinage of eastern Arabia*. Copenhagen.
Potts, D.T. (1991b), "Tayma and the Assyrian Empire", *AAE* 2: 10–23.
Potts, D.T. (1993a), "A new Bactrian find from southeastern Arabia", *Antiquity* 67: 591–596.
Potts, D.T. (1993b), "The sequence and chronology of Thaj", in Finkbeiner, ed., 87–110.
Potts, D.T. (1993c), "Tell Abraq and the Harappan tradition in southeastern Arabia", in Possehl, ed., 323–333.

Potts, D.T. (1994), "Nestorian crosses from Jabal Berri", *AAE* 5: 61–5.

Potts, D.T. (1995), "Watercraft of the Lower Sea", in Finkbeiner et al., eds., 559–571.

Potts, D.T. (1996), "The Parthian presence in the Arabian Gulf", in Reade, ed., 269–285.

Potts, D.T. (1997a), *Mesopotamian Civilization: The Material Foundations*. London/Ithaca.

Potts, D.T. (1997b), "The Roman relationship with the *Persicus sinus* from the rise of Spasinou Charax (127 BC) to the reign of Shapur II (AD 309–379)", in Alcock, ed., 89–107.

Potts, D.T. (1998), "The Gulf Arab states and their archaeology", in Meskell, ed., 189–199.

Potts, D.T. (1999), *The Archaeology of Elam: Formation and Transformation of an Ancient Iranian State*. Cambridge.

Potts, D.T. (2000), *Ancient Magan: The Secrets of Tell Abraq*. London.

Potts, D.T., ed. (2001a), *Excavations at Tepe Yahya, Iran, 1967–1975: The Third Millennium.Bulletin*. Cambridge.

Potts, D.T. (2001b), "Before the Emirates: an archaeological and historical account of developments in the region c.5000 BC to 676 AD", in Al Abed and Hellyer, eds., 28–69.

Potts, D.T. (2001c), "Madaktu and Badace", *Isimu* 2: 13–28.

Potts, D.T. (2004a), "Camel hybridization and the role of *Camelus bactrianus* in the Ancient Near East", *JESHO* 47: 143–165.

Potts, D.T. (2004b), "The numinous and the immanent: some thoughts on Kūrangūn and the Rudkhaneh-e Fahliyān", in von Folsach et al., eds., 143–56.

Potts, D.T. (2005), "In the beginning: Marhashi and the origins of Magan's ceramic industry in the third millennium BC", *AAE* 16: 67–78.

Potts, D.T. (2007), "Foundation houses, fire altars and the *frataraka*: interpreting the iconography of some post-Achaemenid Persian coins", *IrAnt* 42: 271–300.

Potts, D.T. (2008a), "An Umm an-Nar-type compartmented soft-stone vessel from Gonur Depe, Turkmenistan", *AAE* 19: 168–181.

Potts, D.T. (2008b), "Puzur-Inšušinak and the Oxus Civilization (BMAC): reflections on Šimaški and the geo-political landscape of Iran and Central Asia in the Ur III period", *ZA* 98: 165–194.

Potts, D.T. (2008c), "The Persepolis Fortification texts and the Royal Road: Another look at the Fahliyan area", in Briant, Henkelman and Stolper, eds., 275–301. [ch. 39? 50??]

Potts, D.T. (2009a), "Bevel-rim bowls and bakeries: Evidence from Iran and the Indo-Iranian Borderlands", *JCS* 61: 1–23.

Potts, D.T. (2009b), "The archaeology and history of the Persian Gulf", in Potter, ed., 27–56.

Potts, D.T. (2010), "Achaemenid interests in the Persian Gulf", in Curtis and Simpson, eds., 523–533.

Potts, D.T. (2011), "*Equus asinus* in highland Iran: evidence old and new", in Conard et al., eds., 167–176.

Potts, D.T., Al Naboodah, H. and Hellyer, P., eds. (2003), *Archaeology of the United Arab Emirates*. London.

Potts, D.T., Askari Chaverdi, A., McRae, I.K., Alamdari, K., Dusting, A., Jaffari, J., Ellicott, T.M., Setoudeh, A., Lashkari, A., Ameli Rad, Sh. and Yazdani, A. (2009), "Further excavations at Qaleh Kali (MS 46) by the Joint ICAR-University of Sydney Mamasani Expedition. Results of the 2008 season", *IrAnt* 44: 207–282.

Potts, D.T., Askari Chaverdi, A., Petrie, C.A., Dusting, A., Farhadi, F., McRae, I.K., Shikhi, S., Wong, E.H., Lashkari, A. and Javanmard Zadeh, A. (2007), "The Mamasani Archaeological Project, Stage Two: excavations at Qaleh Kali (Tappeh Servan/Jinjun [MS 46])", *Iran* 45: 287–300.

Potts, D.T. and Pittman, H. (2009), "The earliest cylinder seal in the Arabian peninsula", *AAE* 20: 109–121.

Potts, D.T. and Roustaei, K., eds. (2006), *The Mamasani Archaeological Project, Stage One: A report on the first two seasons of the ICAR – University of Sydney expedition to the Mamasani District, Fars Province, Iran*. Tehran.

Potts, D.T., Roustaei, K., Petrie, C.A. and Weeks, L.R., eds. (2009), *The Mamasani Archaeological Project Stage One*. Oxford.

Potts, D.T., Roustaei, K., Weeks, L.R. and Petrie, C.A. (2006), "The Mamasani District and the Archaeology of Southwestern Iran", in Potts and Roustaei, eds., 1–16.

Potts, T.F. (1993), "Patterns of trade in third millennium BC Mesopotamia and Iran", *WA* 24/3: 379–402.

Potts, T.F., Roaf, M. and Stein, D., eds. (2003), *Culture Through Objects: Ancient Near Eastern Studies in Honour of P.R.S. Moorey*. Oxford.

Pournelle, J.R. (2003a), "The littoral foundations of the Uruk state: using satellite photography toward a new understanding of 5th/4th millennium BCE landscapes in the Warka survey area, Iraq", in Georghiu, ed., 5–23.

Pournelle, J.R. (2003b), *Marshland of Cities: Deltaic Landscapes and the Evolution of Early Mesopotamian Civilization*. San Diego.

Pournelle, J.R. (2007), "KLM to CORONA: A bird's eye view of cultural ecology and early Mesopotamian urbanization", in Stone, ed., 29–62.

Powell, M.A. (1985), "Salt, seeds and yields in Sumerian agriculture. A critique of the theory of progressive salinization", *ZA* 75: 7–38.

Powell, M.A. (1987), "The tree section of ur$_5$ (= HAR)-RA = *hubullu*", *BSA* 3: 145–151.

Powell, M.A. (1992), "Timber production in Presargonic Lagaš", *BSA* 6: 99–122.

Powell, M.A. (1995), "Wine and the vine in Ancient Mesopotamia: the cuneiform evidence", in McGovern et al., eds., 97–122.

Prag, K. (1978), "Silver in the Levant in the fourth millennium BC", in Moorey and Parr, eds., 36–45.

Prange, M.K. (2001), "5000 Jahre Kupfer in Oman Band II. Vergleichende Untersuchungen zur Charakterisierung des omanischen Kupfers mittels chemische und isotopische Analysenmethoden", *Metalla* 8: 1–126.

Prange, M.K., Götze, H.-J., Hauptmann, A. and Weisgerber, G. (1999), "Is Oman the ancient Magan? Analytical studies of copper from Oman", in Young et al., eds., 187–192.

Préaux, C. (1978), *Le Monde hellénistique. La Grèce et l'Orient (323–146 av. J.-C.)*. Paris.

Préaux, C. (1979), *L'économie royale des Lagides*. New York.

Preisigke, F. and Bilabel, F., eds. (1913–1934), *Sammelbuch griechischer Urkunden aus Ägypten*. Strassburg/Berlin/Leipzig/Heidelberg.

Preucel, R. and Bauer, A. (2001), "Archaeological pragmatics", *Norwegian Archaeological Review* 34/2: 85–96.

Preusser, C. (1954), *Die Wohnhäuser in Assur*. Berlin.

Preusser, C. (1955), *Die Paläste in Assur*. Berlin.

Preziosi, D. and Hitchcock, L.A. (1999), *Aegean Art and Architecture*. Oxford.

Price, R.M. (1985), *A History of the Monks of Syria, by Theodoret of Cyrrhus*. Kalamazoo.

Price, T.D. and Gebauer, A., eds. (1995), *Last hunters, First Farmers: New Perspectives on the Prehistoric Transition to Agriculture*. Santa Fe.

Priestman, S.M.N. (2003), "The Williamson Collection Project: Sasanian and Islamic survey ceramics from southern Iran, current research", *Iran* 41: 345–348.

Pritchard, J.B., ed. (1969), *Ancient Near Eastern Texts Relating to the Old Testament*. Princeton.

Pritchard, J.B. (1978), *Recovering Sarepta, a Phoenician City*. Princeton.

Privat, K., O'Connell, T. and Hedges, R.M. (2006), "The distinction between freshwater- und terrestrial-based diets: methodological concerns and archaeological applications of sulphur stable isotope analysis", *JAS* 34/8: 1197–1204.

Prott, L.V. (2006), "Protecting cultural heritage in conflict", in Brodie et al., eds., 25–35.

Pruß, A. (2004), "Remarks on the chronological periods", in Anastasio et al., eds., 7–21.

Pucci, M. (2008), *Functional Analysis of Space in Syro-Hittite Architecture*. Oxford.

Pugachenkova, G.A. (1967), *Isskustvo Turkmenistana. Ocherk s drevneishikh vremen do 1917*. Moscow.

Pugachenkova, G.A. (1971), *Skulp'tura Khalchayana*. Moscow.

Pugachenkova, G.A. (1988), *The Art of Central Asia*. Leningrad.

Pugliese Carratelli, G. (1966), "Greek Inscriptions of the Middle East", *EW* 16: 31–36.

Pulak, C. (1988), "The Bronze Age shipwreck at Ulu Burun, Turkey: 1985 campaign", *AJA* 92: 1–37.

Pulak, C. (1998), "The Uluburun shipwreck: an overview", *International Journal of Nautical Archaeology* 27/3: 188–224.

Pulak, C. (2000), "The copper and tin ingots from the Late Bronze Age shipwreck at Uluburun", in Yalçin, ed., 137–157.

Pulak, C. (2001), "The cargo of the Uluburun ship and evidence for trade with the Aegean and beyond", in Bonfante and Karageorghis, eds., 13–60.

Pulak, C. (2005), "Das Schiffswrack von Uluburun", in Yalçin et al., eds., 55–102.

Pulak, C. (2008), "The Uluburun shipwreck and the Late Bronze Age trade", in Aruz et al., eds., 289–310.

Pusch, E. and Rehren, T., eds. (2007), *Hochtemperatur-Technologie in der Ramses-Stadt – Rubinglas für den Pharao*. Hildesheim.

Puschnigg, G. (1999), "Kharoba Koshuk: An early church?", in Herrmann, ed., 103–105.

Puschnigg, G. (2006), *Ceramics of the Merv Oasis: Recycling the city*. Walnut Creek.

Pustovoytov, K., Schmidt, K. and Taubald, H. (2007), "Evidence for Holocene environmental changes in the northern Fertile Crescent provided by pedogenic carbonate coatings", *QR* 67: 315–327.

Pyankova, L.T. (1994), "Central Asia in the Bronze Age: sedentary and nomadic cultures", *Antiquity* 68: 355–372.

Pyankova, L.T. (2002), "South Tajikistan: synthesis of settled and steppe cultures at the end of the Bronze Age", in Jones-Bley and Zdanovich, eds., 558–573.

Qandgar, J., Esmaili, H. and Rahmatpour, M. (2004), "Kavoshhāye-e bāstānshenākhtiy-e qal'eh Azhdahāk, Hashtrud", in Azarnoush, ed., 193–228.

Qualls, C. (1981), *Boats of Mesopotamia Before 2000 BC*. Columbia.

Quibell, J.E. and Green, F.W. (1902), *Hierakonpolis, Part II*. London.

Quintavalle, A.C., ed. (2007), *Medioevo mediterraneo: l'Occidente, Bisanzio e l'Islam*. Parma.

Quintero, L.A. and Köhler-Rollefson, I. (1997), "The 'Ain Ghazal dog: a case for the Neolithic origin of *Canis familiaris* in the Near East", in Gebel et al., eds., 567–574.

Quintero, L.A. and Wilke, P. (1995), "Evolution and economic significance of naviform core-and-blade technology in the Southern Levant", *Paléorient* 21: 17–33.

Quirke, S. (1990), *The Administration of Egypt in the Late Middle Kingdom*. New Malden.

Radies, D., Hasiotis, S.T., Preusser, F., Neubert, E. and Matter, A. (2005), "Paleoclimatic significance of Early Holocene faunal assemblages in wet interdune deposits of the Wahiba Sand Sea, Sultanate of Oman", *JAE* 62: 109–125.

Radner, K. (1999), *Ein neuassyrisches Privatarchiv der Tempelgoldschmiede von Assur*. Saarbrücken.

Radner, K. and Robson, E., eds. (2011), *The Oxford Handbook of Cuneiform Culture*. Oxford.

Raedler, C. (2008), "Zur Prosopographie von altägyptischen Militärangehörigen", in Gundlach and Vogel, eds., 309–343.

Rahbar, M. (1997), "Excavations at Bandiyān, Darreh Gaz, Khorāsān", *Archaeological Reports of Iran* 1: 9–32 (in Persian with English abstract).

Rahbar, M. (1998), "Découverte d'un monument d'époque sassanide à Bandian, Dargaz (Nord Khorassan). Fouilles 1994 et 1995", *StIr* 27/2: 213–250.

Rahbar, M. (1999a), "Khorheh, une résidence d'époque parthe sur le Plateau iranien", *DA* 243: 44–6.

Rahbar, M. (1999b), "À Dargaz (Khorassan): découvertes de panneaux de stucs sassanides", *DA* 243: 62–65.

Rahbar, M. (1999c), "A Greek marble statue from Borazjan, Fars", in Alizadeh et al., eds., 192–207 (in Persian), 228 (English summary).

Rahimifar, M. (2005), "Mo'arafi-ye barkhī az barčasbhā-ye geli-ye Takht-e Ğamšīd", *Bāstān Šenāsī* 1: 72–77, 10.

Rahmstorf, L. (2006), "In search of the earliest balance weights: scales and weighing systems from the East Mediterranean, the Near and Middle East", in Alberti et al., eds., 9–45.

Raikes, R.L. (1967), *Water, Weather and Prehistory*. London.

Rakic, Y. (2003), *The Contest Scene in Akkadian Glyptic: A Study of its Imagery and Function within the Akkadian Empire*. Philadelphia.

Ramage, A. (1987), "Lydian Sardis", in Guralnick, ed., 6–15.

Ramage, A. (1994), "Early Iron Age Sardis and its neighbors", in Çilingiroğlu and French, eds., 6–12.

Ramage, A. and Craddock, P.T. (2000), *King Croesus' Gold: Excavations at Sardis and the History of Gold Refining*. Cambridge.

Raman, K.V. (1991), "Further evidence of Roman trade from coastal sites in Tamil Nadu", in Begley and de Puma, eds., 125–133.

Ranov, V.A. and Karimova G.R. (2005), *Kamennyĭ vek Afgano-Tadzhikskoĭ depressii*. Dushanbe.

Rao, S.R. (1963), "A 'Persian Gulf' seal from Lothal", *Antiquity* 37: 96–99.

Rao, S.R. (1985), *Lothal: A Harappan Port Town, 1955–62*. Delhi.

Rapin, C. (1983), "Les inscriptions économiques de la trésorie hellénistique d'Aï Khanoum (Afghanistan)", *Bulletin de correspondence hellénique* 108: 315–371.

Raschke, M.G. (1975), "Papyrological evidence for Ptolemaic and Roman trade with India", in Anonymous, ed., 241–246.

Raschke, M.G. (1978), "New studies in Roman commerce with the East", *ANRW* 2/9/2: 604–1378.

Rashid, M. (1978), "Excavations at Tell Haidar", *Sumer* 34: 75–118 (in Arabic).

Rashid, S.A. (1983), *Gründungsfiguren im Iraq*. Stuttgart.

Rasmussen, S.O., Andersen, K.K., Svensson, A.M., Steffensen, J.P., Vinther, B.M., Clausen, H.B., Siggaard-Andersen, M.-L., Johnsen, S.J., Larsen, L.B., Dahl-Jensen, D., Bigler, M., Röthlisberger, R., Fischer, H., Goto-Azuma, K., Hansson, M.E. and Ruth, U. (2006), "A new Greenland ice core chronology for the last glacial termination", *Journal of Geophysical Research* 111. D06102, doi:10.1029/2005JD006079.

Rassam, H. (1897), *Asshur and the Land of Nimrod*. Cincinnati/New York.

Ratnagar, S. (1981), *Encounters: The Westerly Trade of the Harappa Civilization*. Delhi.

Ratnagar, S. (2004), *Trading Encounters: From the Euphrates to the Indus in the Bronze Age*. New Delhi.

Ratté, C. (1992), "The "Pyramid Tomb" at Sardis", *IstMitt* 42: 135–161.

Ratté, C. (1993), "Lydian contributions to archaic East Greek architecture", in Courtils and Moretti, eds., 1–12.

Raven, E.M., ed. (2008), *South Asian Archaeology 1999*. Groningen.

Rawlinson, H.C. (1839), "Notes on a March from Zohab, at the foot of the Zagros, along the Mountains to Khuzistan (Susianan)", *JRGS* 9: 26–116.

Rawlinson, H.C. (1840), "Notes on a Journey from Tabriz, through Persian Kurdistan, to the ruins of Takhti- Soleiman, and from thence by Zenjan and Tarom, to Gilan, in October and November, 1838. With a memoir on the site of the Atropatenian Ecbatana", *JRGS* 10: 1–64.

Rawson, E. (1985), *Intellectual Life in the Late Roman Republic*. Baltimore.

Rawson, P.S. (1954), "Palace Wares from Nimrud: technical observations on selected examples", *Iraq* 16/2: 168–172.

Ray, H.P. (1986), *Monastery and Guild: Commerce under the Sātavāhanas*. Delhi.

Ray, H.P. and Salles, J.-F., eds. (1996), *Tradition and Archaeology: Early Maritime Contacts in the Indian Ocean*. New Delhi and Lyon.

Razmjou, S. (2002), "Assessing the damage: notes on the life and demise of the statue of Darius from Susa", *AO* 32: 81–104.

Razmjou, S. (2005a), "Notes on a forgotten Achaemenid site at Farmeshgan, Iran", in Briant and Boucharlat, eds., 293–312.

Razmjou, S. (2005b), "Religion and burial customs", in Curtis and Tallis, eds., 150–180.

Razmjou, S. (2005c), "Ernst Herzfeld and the study of graffiti at Persepolis", in Gunter and Hauser, eds., 315–341.

Razmjou, S. (2010), "Persepolis: a reinterpretation of palaces and their function", in Curtis and Simpson, eds., 231–245.

Reade, J.E. (1978), "Studies in Assyrian geography", *RA* 72: 47–72, 175–180.

Reade, J.E. (1979a), "Ideology and propaganda in Assyrian art", in Larsen, ed. 329–345.

Reade, J.E. (1979b), "Narrative composition in Assyrian sculpture", *BaM* 10: 52–110.

Reade, J.E. (1982), "Nimrud", in Curtis, ed., 99–112.

Reade, J. (1986a), "Archaeology and the Kuyunjik archives", in Veenhof, ed., 213–222.

Reade, J.E. (1986b), "Rassam's excavations at Borsippa and Kutha, 1879–82", *Iraq* 48: 105–116.

Reade, J.E., ed. (1996), *The Indian Ocean in Antiquity*. London.

Reade, J.E. (2000), "Alexander the Great and the Hanging Gardens of Babylon", *Iraq* 62: 195–217.

Reade, J.E. (2010), "How many miles to Babylon?", in Baker et al., eds., 281–290.

Reade, W.J., Freestone, I.C. and Bourke, S. (2009), "Innovation and continuity in Bronze and Iron Age glass from Pella in Jordan", in Anonymous (2009a), ed.

Reade, W.J., Freestone, I.C. and Simpson, S.J. (2005), "Innovation or continuity? Early first millennium BCE glass in the Near East: the cobalt blue glasses from Assyrian Nimrud", in Anonymous, ed., 23–27.

Reade, W.J. and Potts, D.T. (1993), "New evidence for late third millennium linen from Tell Abraq, Umm al-Qaiwain, UAE", *Paléorient* 19/2: 99–106.

Reddé, M. and Brun, J-P. (2003), "L'architecture des *praesidia* et la genèse des dépotoirs", in Cuvigny, ed., 73–185.

Redding, R. (1981), "The faunal remains", in Wright, ed., 233–261.

Redding, R. (1985), "The role of faunal remains in the explanation of the development of complex societies in south-west Iran: potential, problems and the future", *Paléorient* 11/2: 121–124.

Redford, D.B. (1985), "Sais and the Kushite invasions of the eighth century BC", *JARCE* 22: 5–15.

Redford, D.B. (1992), *Egypt, Canaan, and Israel in Ancient Times*. Princeton.

Redford, D.B., ed. (2001), *The Oxford Encyclopedia of Ancient Egypt*, 3 vols. New York.

Redford, D.B. (2003), *The Wars in Syria and Palestine of Thutmosis III*. Leiden and Boston.

Redford, D.B. (2005), "The northern wars of Thutmosis III", in Cline and O'Connor, eds., 325–343.

Redman, C., Berman, M.J., Curtin, E.V., Langhorne, W.T., Versaggi, N.M. and Wanser, J.C., eds. (1978), *Social Archaeology: Beyond Subsistence and Dating*. New York.

Redmount, C.A. and Friedman, R.F. (1997), "Tales of a Delta site: the 1995 field season at Tell el-Muqdam", *JARCE* 34: 57–83.

Reed, C.A., ed. (1977), *The Origins of Agriculture*. The Hague.

Rehder, J.E. (1991), "The decorated iron swords from Luristan: their material and manufacture", *Iran* 29: 13–20.

Rehder, J.E. (1992), "Iron versus bronze for edge tools and weapons", *Journal of the Minerals, Metals and Materials Society* 44/2: 42–46.

Rehren, T. (2000), "Rationales in Old World base glass compositions", *JAS* 27: 1225–1234.

Rehren, T. (2001), "Aspects of the production of cobalt-blue glass in Egypt", *Archaeometry* 43: 483–489.

Rehren, T. (2008), "A review of factors affecting the composition of early Egyptian glasses and faience: alkali and alkali earth oxides", *JAS* 35: 1345–1354.

Rehren, T., Hauptmann, A. and Muhly, J.D. (1998), *Metallurgica Antiqua: In Honour of Hans-Gert Bachmann and Robert Maddin*. Bochum.

Rehren, T. and Pusch, E. (1997), "New Kingdom glass-melting crucibles from Qantir-Piramesses", *JEA* 83: 127–141.

Rehren, T. and Pusch, E. (1999), "Glass and glass making at Qantir-Piramesses and beyond", *ÄL* 9: 171–179.

Rehren, T. and Pusch, E. (2005), "Late Bronze Age glass production at Qantir-Piramesses, Egypt", *Science* 308: 1756–1758.

Rehren, T. and Pusch, E. (2007), "Glas für den Pharao – Glasherstellung in der Spätbronzezeit des Nahen Ostens", in Wagner, ed., 215–235.

Rehren, T. and Pusch, E. (2008), "Crushed rock and molten salt? Some aspects of the primary glass production at Qantir/Pi-Ramesse", in Jackson and Wager, eds., 14–33.

Rehren, T., Pusch, E. and Herold, A. (1998), "Glass coloring works within a copper-centered industrial complex in Late Bronze Age Egypt", in McCray and Kingery, eds., 227–250.

Rehren, T., Pusch, E. and Herold, A. (2001), "Qantir-Piramesses and the organisation of the Egyptian glass industry", in Shortland, ed., 223–238.

Reid, D.M. (2002), *Whose Pharaohs? Archaeology, Museums and Egyptian Identity from Napoleon to World War I*. Berkeley.

Reider, C. (1996), "Legend variations of the coins of Ardashir the Great", *Oriental Numismatic Society* 147: 10–11.

Reiner, E., (1985), *Your Thwarts in Pieces, Your Mooring Rope Cut: Poetry from Babylonian and Assyria*. Ann Arbor.

Reitlinger, G. (1938), "Medieval antiquities west of Mosul", *Iraq* 5: 143–156.

Renfrew, C. (1972), *The Emergence of Civilisation: The Cyclades and the Aegean in the Third Millennium BC*. London.

Renfrew, C. ed., (1973), *The Explanation of Culture Change: Models in Prehistory*. London.

Renfrew, C. (1977), "The later obsidian of Deh Luran: the evidence of Chogha Sefid", in Hole, ed., 289–311.

Renfrew, C. (1984a), "Culture systems and the multiplier effect", in Renfrew, ed., 258–282.

Renfrew, C., ed. (1984b), *Approaches to Social Archaeology*. Cambridge.

Renfrew, C. (2000), *Loot, Legitimacy and Ownership: The Ethical Crises in Archaeology*. London.

Renfrew, C. (2001), "Symbol before concept: material engagement and the early development of society", in Hodder, ed. 122–140.

Renfrew, C. (2004), "Towards a theory of material engagement", in DeMarrais et al., eds., 23–31.

Renfrew, C. (2006), "Museum acquisitions: responsibilities for the illicit traffic in antiquities", in Brodie et al., eds., 245–257.

Renfrew C. and Bahn, P. (2000), *Archaeology: Theories, Methods and Practice*. London.
Renfrew, C., Dixon, J.E. and Cann, J.R. (1966), "Obsidian and early cultural contact in the Near East", *PPS* 32: 30–72.
Renger, J. (1990), "Rivers, watercourses and irrigation", *BSA* 5: 161–172.
Renger, J., ed. (1999), *Babylon: Focus mesopotamischer Geschichte, Wiege früher Gelehrsamkeit, Mythos in der Moderne. 2. Internationales Colloquium der Deutschen Orient-Gesellschaft 24.–26. Marz 1998 in Berlin*. Saarbrücken.
Renger, J., ed. (in press), *Assur – Gott, Stadt und Land*. Wiesbaden.
Renhart, E. (1995), *Das syrische Bema. Liturgisch-archäologische Untersuchungen*. Graz.
Republic of Iraq (1975), *Antiquities Law No. 59 of 1936 and the two Amendments? No. 120 of 1974 and No. 164 of 1975*. Baghdad.
Retsö, J. (2003), *The Arabs in Antiquity: Their History from the Assyrians to the Umayyads*. Milton Park and New York.
Reuther, O. (1929a), *Die Ausgrabungen der Deutschen Ktesiphon-Expedition im Winter 1928/9*. Berlin.
Reuther, O. (1929b), "The German excavations at Ctesiphon", *Antiquity* 3: 434–451.
Reuther, O. (1964), "Sasanian architecture", in Pope, ed., 493–577.
Reuther, O. (1977), "Sāsānian Christian churches", in Pope, ed., 560–566.
Rey-Coquais, J.-P. (1978), "Syrie Romaine, de Pompée à Dioclétien", *JRS* 68: 44–73.
Reynolds, B. and Stott, M., eds. (1986), *Material Anthropology: Contemporary Approaches to Material Culture*. New York.
Reynolds, F. (2007), "Food and drink in Babylonia", in Leick, ed., 171–184.
Rice, M. (1984), *Dilmun Discovered*. New York.
Rice, P.M. (1987), *Pottery Analysis: A Sourcebook*. Chicago.
Rice, P.M. (1991), "Specialization, standardization and diversity: a retrospective", in Bishop and Lange, eds., 257–279.
Rich, C.J. (1836), *Narrative of a Residence in Koordistan, and on the Site of Ancient Nineveh*. London.
Rich, J., ed. (1992), *The City in Late Antiquity*. London/New York.
Richard, S. (1980), "Toward a consensus of opinion on the end of the Early Bronze Age in Palestine-Transjordan", *BASOR* 237: 5–34.
Richard, S. (1987), "The Early Bronze Age: the rise and collapse of urbanism", *BA* 50/1: 22–43.
Richard, S. (1990), "The 1987 expedition to Khirbet Iskander and its vicinity: Fourth Preliminary report", *BASOR Supplement* 26: 33–58.
Richard, S., ed. (2003), *Near Eastern Archaeology: A Reader*. Winona Lake.
Richerson, P., Boyd, R. and Bettinger, R.L. (2001), "Was agriculture impossible during the Pleistocene but mandatory during the Holocene? A climate change hypothesis", *AmAnt* 66: 387–411.
Richmond, J. (2006), "Textile production in prehistoric Anatolia: a study of three Bronze Age sites", *ANES* 43: 203–238.
Richter, G.M. (1929), "Silk in Greece", *AJA* 33: 27–33.
Richter, H. (in press), *Gräber und Grüfte in Assur. Die parthische Zeit*. Wiesbaden.
Richter, T (2003a), "Zu einigen Tontafelfunden der Grabungskampagne 2002 in Mišrife/Qatna", *UF* 34: 603–618.
Richter, T (2003b), "Das 'Archiv des Idanda': Bericht über Inschriftenfunde der Grabungskampagne 2002 in Mišrife/Qatna", *MDOG* 135: 167–188.

Richter, T (2005), "Qatna in the Late Bronze Age: Preliminary remarks", *SCCNH* 15: 109–126.

Richter, T. and Lange, S. (in press), *Das Archiv des Idadda. Die Keilschrifttexte aus den syrisch-deutschen Ausgrabungen (1999–2003) im Königspalast von Qatna*. Wiesbaden.

Riehl, S. (2008), "Climate and agriculture in the ancient Near East: a synthesis of the archaeobotanical and stable carbon isotope evidence", *VHA* 17, Supplement 1: 43–51.

Riggins, S.H., ed. (1994), *The Socialness of Things: Essays on the Socio-Semiotics of Objects*. Berlin.

Riis, P.J. (1948), *Hama, fouilles et recherches 1931–1938, 2:3. Les cimetières à crémation*. Copenhagen.

Riis, P.J. and Thrane, H. (1974), *Sukas III. The Neolithic Period*. Copenhagen.

Riis, P.J, Thuesen. I., Lund, J. and Riis, T. (2004), *Topographical Studies and Investigations in the Ğabla Plain*. Copenhagen.

Rindos, D. (1984), *The Origins of Agriculture*. New York.

Ristvet, L. (2008), "Legal and archaeological territories of the second millennium BC in northern Mesopotamia", *Antiquity* 82: 585–599.

Ristvet, L., Guilderson, T. and Weiss, H. (2004), "The dynamics of state development and imperialization at third millennium Tell Leilan, Syria", *Orient-Express* 21/2: 94–99.

Ritchie, I. (1994), "An architect's view of recent developments in European museums", in Miles and Zavala, eds., 7–30.

Rivaroli, M (2004), "Nineveh: from ideology to topography", *Iraq* 66: 199–205.

Rizkana, I. and Seeher, J. (1985), "The chipped stones at Maadi: preliminary reassessment of a predynastic industry and its long distance relations", *Mitteilingen des Deutschen Archäologischen Instituts Kairo* 41/2: 35–36.

Rizkana, I. and Seeher, J. (1987), *Maadi I. The Pottery of the Predynastic Settlement*. Mainz.

Rizkana, I. and Seeher, J. (1988), *Maadi II. The Lithic Industries of the Predynastic Settlement*. Mainz.

Rizkana, I. and Seeher, J. (1989), *Maadi III. The Non-Lithic Small Finds and the Structural Remains of the Predynastic Settlement*. Mainz.

Rizkana, I. and Seeher, J. (1990), *Maadi IV. The Predynastic Cemeteries of Maadi and Wadi Digla*. Mainz.

Roaf, M. (1973), "The diffusion of the *Salles à Quatre Saillants*", *Iraq* 35: 83–91.

Roaf, M. (1974), "The subject peoples on the base of the statue of Darius", *DAFI* 4: 73–160.

Roaf, M. (1976), "Excavations at Al Markh, Bahrain", *PSAS* 6: 144–160.

Roaf, M. (1980), "Texts about the sculptures and sculptors at Persepolis", *Iran* 18: 65–74.

Roaf, M. (1983), *Sculptures and Sculptors at Persepolis*. London.

Roaf, M. (1987), "Checklist of Persepolis reliefs not at the site", *Iran* 25: 155–158.

Roaf, M. (1989), "Social organization and social activities at Tell Madhhur", in Henrickson and Thuesen, eds., 91–146.

Roaf, M. (1990a), *Cultural Atlas of Mesopotamia and the Ancient Near East*. Oxford.

Roaf, M. (1990b), "Sculptors and designers at Persepolis", in Gunter, ed., 105–114.

Roaf, M. (1998), "Multiple rabbets on doors in Iron Age Assyria and western Iran", *IrAnt* 33: 57–80.
Roaf, M. (2001), "Doubts about the two-lobed burial and the survival of Early Dynastic to Akkadian transitional building levels in Area WF at Nippur", *Iraq* 63: 55–66.
Roaf, M. (2004), "Persepolis", *RlA* 10: 393–412.
Roaf, M. and Galbraith, J. (1994), "Pottery and p-values: 'seafaring merchants of Ur?' re-examined", *Antiquity* 68: 770–783.
Roaf, S. (1982), "Wind-catchers", in Beazley and Harverson, eds., 57–70.
Robert, L. (1968), "De Delphes à l'Oxus: inscriptions grecques nouvelles de la Bactriane", *CRAIBL* 1968: 416–457.
Roberts, B.W., Thornton, C.P. and Pigott, V.C. (2009), "Development of metallurgy in Eurasia", *Antiquity* 36: 1012–1022.
Roberts, B.W. and Vander Linden, M., eds. (2011), *Investigating Archaeological Cultures: Material Culture, Variability and Transmission*. Berlin.
Roberts, C.N. (1998), *The Holocene*. Oxford.
Roberts, C.N. (2002), "Did prehistoric landscape management retard the post-glacial spread of woodland in SW Asia?", *Antiquity* 76: 1002–1010.
Roberts, C.N., Eastwood, W.J., Kuzucuoğlu, C., Fiorentino, G. and Caracuta V. (2011), "Climatic, vegetation and cultural change in the eastern Mediterranean during the mid-Holocene environmental transition", *The Holocene* 21/1: 147–162.
Roberts, C.N., Meadows, M. and Dodson, J.R. (2001), "The history of Mediterranean-type environments: Climate, culture and landscape", *The Holocene* 11/6: 631–634.
Roberts, C.N., Reed, J.M., Leng, M.J., Kuzucuoğlu, C., Fontugne, M., Bertaux, J., Woldring, H., Bottema, S., Black, S., Hunt, E. and Karabiyikoğlu, M. (2001), "The tempo of Holocene climatic change in the eastern Mediterranean region: new high-resolution crater-lake sediment data from central Turkey", *The Holocene* 11/6: 721–736.
Roberts, C.N. and Rosen, A. (2009), "Diversity and complexity in early farming communities of SW Asia: new insights into the economic and environmental basis of Çatalhöyük", *CA* 50/3: 393–402.
Robertson, E.C., Seibert, J.D., Fernandez, D. and Zender, M.U. (2006), *Space and Spatial Analysis in Archaeology*. Calgary.
Robin, C.J. (2005), "Saba and the Sabaeans", in Gunter, ed., 8–19.
Robin, C.J. (2008), "La lecture et l'interprétation de l'abécédaire Ra's Shamra 88.2215. La preuver par l'Arabie?", in Roche, ed., 233–244.
Robin, C.J. and Gorea, M. (2002), "Les vestiges antiques de la grotte de Hôq (Suquṭra, Yémen)", *CRAIBL* 2002: 409–445.
Robinson, S.A., Black, S., Sellwood, B.W. and Valdes, P. (2006), "A review of palaeoclimates and palaeoenvironments in the Levant and Eastern Mediterranean from 25,000 to 5000 years BP: setting the environmental background for the evolution of human civilisation", *QSR* 25: 1517–1541.
Robson, E. (2001), "Society and technology in the Late Bronze Age: a guided tour of the cuneiform sources", in Shortland, ed., 39–57.
Rochberg-Halton, F. (1984), "Canonicity in cuneiform texts", *JCS* 36: 127–144.
Roche, C., ed. (2008), *D'Ougarit à Jérusalem. Recueil d'études épigraphiques et archéologiques en l'honneur de Pierre Bordreuil*, Paris.

Roche, M.-J. (1996), "Remarques sur les Nabatéens en Méditerranée", *Semitica* 45: 73–99.
Roll, I. (1999), "The roads in Roman-Byzantine Palaestina and Arabia", in Piccirillo, ed., 109–113.
Rolle, R. (1989), *The World of the Scythians*. Berkeley.
Rollefson, G.O. (1993), "The origins of the Yarmoukian at 'Ain Ghazal", *Paléorient* 19/1: 91–100.
Rollefson, G.O. (1997), "Changes in architecture and social organization at 'Ain Ghazal", in Gebel et al., eds., 287–307.
Rollefson, G.O. (2000), "Ritual and social structure at Neolithic 'Ain Ghazal", in Kuijt, ed., 165–190.
Rollefson, G.O. (2009), "Slippery slope: the Late Neolithic rubble layer in the southern Levant", *Neo-Lithics* 1/09: 12–18.
Rollefson, G.O. and Kafafi, Z. (1994), "The 1993 season at 'Ain Ghazal: preliminary report", *ADAJ* 38: 11–32.
Rollefson, G.O. and Köhler-Rollefson, I. (1989), "The collapse of Early Neolithic settlements in the southern Levant", in Hershkovitz, ed., 73–89.
Rollefson, G.O. and Köhler-Rollefson, I. (1993), "PPNC adaptations in the first half of the 6th millenium BC", *Paléorient* 19/1: 33–42.
Roller, L.E. (1983), "The legend of Midas", *Classical Antiquity* 2: 299–313.
Roller, L.E. (1987), *Gordion Special Studies I: Nonverbal Graffiti, Dipinti and Stamps*. Philadelphia.
Roller, L.E. (1999), *In Search of God the Mother: The Cult of Anatolian Cybele*. Berkeley.
Roller, L.E. (2006), "Midas and Phrygian cult practice", in Hutter and Hutter-Braunsar, eds., 123–135.
Roller, L.E. (2007), "Towards the formation of a Phrygian iconography in the Iron Age", in Çilingiroğlu and Sagona, eds., 207–223.
Roller, L.E. (2009a), *Gordion Special Studies IV: The Early Phrygian Incised Drawings*. Philadelphia.
Roller, L.E. (2009b), "Sacred landscapes of Matar: continuity and change from the Iron Age through the Roman Period", in Gates et al., eds., 1–10.
Röllig, W. (1999), "Nihi, Ni'i, Nija", *RlA* 9/3–4: 313–314.
Rollinger, R., Luther, A. and Wiesehöfer, J., eds. (2007), *Getrennte Wege? Kommunikation, Raum und Wahrnehmung in der Alten Welt*. Frankfurt.
Rollinger, R. and Truschnegg, B., eds. (in press), *Herodot und das Perserreich*.
Rollinger, R. and Ulf, C., eds. (2004), *Commerce and Monetary Systems in the Ancient World: Means of Transmission and Cultural Interaction*. Stuttgart.
Romer, J. and Romer, E. (1995), *The Seven Wonders of the World: A History of the Modern Imagination*. New York.
Ronen, A. and Adler, D. (2001), "The walls of Jericho were magical", *Archaeology, Ethnology and Anthropology of Eurasia* 2: 97–103.
Roodenberg, J.J. (1979), "An Epipalaeolithic industry on the Nahr el-Homr", in Freedman, ed., 9–17.
Roodenberg, J.J. (1986), *Le Mobilier en pierre de Bouqras*. Istanbul.
Roodenberg, J.J. (1995), *The Ilipinar Excavations I*. Istanbul.

Roodenberg, J.J. and Alpaslan-Roodenberg, S., (2008), *Life and Death in a Prehsitoric Settlement in Northwest Anatolia: The Ilipinar Excavations III, with Contributions on Hacilartepe and Menteşe.* Leiden.

Rooksby, H.P. (1959), "An investigation of ancient opal glasses with special reference to the Portland vase", *JSGT* 43: 285T–288T.

Rooksby, H.P. (1962), "Opacifiers in opal glasses", *Journal of Science and Technology* 29: 20–26.

Roos, P. (1970), "An Achaemenian sketch slab and the ornaments of the royal dress at Persepolis", *EW* 20: 51–59.

Roosevelt, C.H. (2006), "Tumulus survey and museum research in Lydia, western Turkey: determining Lydian- and Persian-period settlement patterns", *JFA* 31/1: 61–76.

Roosevelt, C.H. (2009), *The Archaeology of Lydia, from Gyges to Alexander.* Cambridge.

Roosevelt, C.H. (2010), "Lydia before the Lydians", in Cahill, ed., 37–73.

Roosevelt, C.H. and Luke, C. (2006), "Looting Lydia: the destruction of an archaeological landscape in western Turkey", in Brodie et al., eds., 173–187.

Root, M.C. (1979), *The King and Kingship in Achaemenid Art: Essays on the Creation of an Iconography of Empire.* Leiden.

Root, M.C. (1985), "The Parthenon frieze and the Apadana reliefs at Persepolis: reassessing a programmatic relationship", *AJA* 89: 103–120.

Root, M.C. (1986), review of M. Roaf, *Sculptures and Sculptors at Persepolis, AJA* 90: 113–114.

Root, M.C. (1988), "Evidence from Persepolis for the dating of Persian and Archaic Greek coinage", *The Numismatic Chronicle* 148: 1–12.

Root, M.C. (1990), "Circles of artistic programming: strategies for studying creative process at Persepolis", in Gunter, ed., 115–139.

Root, M.C. (1991), "From the heart: powerful Persianisms in the art of the western empire", in Sancisi-Weerdenburg and Kuhrt, eds., 1–29.

Root, M.C. (1996), "The Persepolis Fortification Tablets: archival issues and the problem of stamp versus cylinder seals", in Boussac and Invernizzi, eds., 3–27.

Root, M.C. (1997), "Cultural pluralisms on the Persepolis Fortification Tablets", in Boussac, ed., 229–252.

Root, M.C. (1999), "The cylinder seal from Pasargadae: of wings and wheels, date and fate", *IrAnt* 34: 157–190.

Root, M.C., ed. (2005), *This Fertile Land: Signs and Symbols in the Early Arts of Iran and Iraq.* Ann Arbor.

Root, M.C. (2008), "The legible image: how did seals and sealing matter in Persepolis?", in Briant et al., eds., 87–147.

Root, M.C. (2011), "Elam in the imperial imagination: from Nineveh to Persepolis", in Álvarez-Mon and Garrison, eds., 419–474.

Root, M.C., and Abdi, K. (in preparation), *Harmonious Hegemony: Visual Valences of Persian Kingship and Empire, The Iranian Excavations of Persepolis by Akbar Tadjvidi: An Annotated Translation, Expanded Documentation.* Leiden.

Rorimer, J. (1954), *The Authenticity of the Chalice of Antioch.* Princeton.

Rose, C.B. (2007), "The tombs of the Granicus Valley", in Deleman, ed., 247–264.

Rose, J.I. (2010), "New light on human prehistory in the Perso-Arabian Gulf oasis", *CA* 51: 849–883.

Rose, J.I. and Petraglia, M.D. (2009), "Tracking the origin and evolution of human populations in Arabia", in Petraglia and Rose, eds., 1–12.

Rose, M. and Acar, Ö. (1996), "Turkey's war on the illicit antiquities trade", in Vitelli, ed., 71–89.

Roselló-Izquierdo, E., Morales-Muñiz, A. and Popov, S.V. (2005), "Gihayu: a Late Stone Age fishing station in the coast of Yemen", *Paléorient* 31: 116–125.

Rosen, A.M. (1986), *Cities of Clay: The Geoarchaeology of Tells*. Chicago.

Rosen, A.M. (1989), "Environmental change at the end of Early Bronze Age Palestine", in Miroschedji, ed., 247–255.

Rosen, A.M. (1995), "The social response to environmental change in Early Bronze Age Canaan", *JAA* 14: 26–44.

Rosen, A.M. (2007), *Civilizing Climate: Social Responses to Climate Change in the Ancient Near East*. Lanham.

Rosen, S.A. (1983), "Tabular scraper trade: a model of material culture dispersion", *BASOR* 249: 79–86.

Rosen, S.A. (1986), "The Gezer flint caches 1970–71", in Dever, ed., 259–263.

Rosen, S.A. (1987), "The potentials of lithic analysis in the Chalcolithic of the Northern Negev", in Levy, ed., 295–312.

Rosen, S.A. (1988), "A preliminary note on the Egyptian component of the chipped stone assemblage from Tel 'Erani", *IEJ* 38: 105–116.

Rosen, S.A. (1997), *Lithics After the Stone Age: A Handbook of Stone Tools from the Levant*. Walnut Creek.

Rosen, S.A. (2004), "The chipped stone assemblages", in Ussishkin, ed., 2197–2225.

Rosen, S.A. (2010), "The desert and the sown: a lithic perspective", in Erikson, ed., 189–205.

Rosen, S.A. and Roux, V., eds. (2009), *Techniques and People: Anthropological Perspectives on Technology in the Archaeology of the Proto-Historic and Early Historic Periods in the Southern Levant*. Paris.

Rosen-Ayalon, M., ed. (1977), *Studies in Memory of Gaston Wiet*. Jerusalem.

Rosenberg, D. (2010a), "Early maceheads in the Southern Levant: a 'Chalcolithic' hallmark in Neolithic context", *JFA* 35/2: 204–216.

Rosenberg, D. (2010b), "Flying stones: the slingstones of the Wadi Rabah Culture in the Southern Levant", *Paléorient* 35/2: 99–112.

Rosenberg, D., Shimelmitz, R. and Nativ, A. (2007), "Basalt bifacial tool production in the Southern Levant: a glance at the quarry and workshop site of Giv'at Kipod, Israel", *Antiquity* 82: 367–376.

Rosenberg, M. (1999), "Hallan Çemi and the beginnings of settled life in eastern Anatolia", in Anonymous, ed., 359–371.

Rosenberg, M. (2003), "The strength of numbers: from villages to towns in the Aceramic Neolithic of southwestern Asia", in Özdoğan, Hauptmann and Başgelen, eds., 91–102.

Rosenberg, M. and Peasnall, B.L. (1998), "A report on soundings at Demirköy Höyük: an aceramic Neolithic site in eastern Anatolia", *Anatolica* 24: 195–207.

Rosenberger, V. (1996), "Taprobane – Trauminsel oder der Beginn einer neuen Welt?", *Laverna* 7: 1–16.

Rosenfeld, A., Ilani, S. and Dvorachek, M. (1997), "Bronze alloys from Canaan during the Middle Bronze Age", *JAS* 24: 857–864.

Rosenthal-Heginbottom, R. (1982), *Die Kirchen von Sobota und die Dreiapsidenkirchen des Nahen Ostens*. Wiesbaden.

Roshwalb, A. (1981), *Protohistory in the Wadi Ghazzeh: A Typological and Technological Study Based on the Macdonald Excavations*. London.

Ross, J. (1839), "Notes on two journeys from Baghdad to the ruins of Al Hadhr, in Mesopotamia, in 1836 and 1837", *JRGS* 9: 443–475.

Rossberger, E. (2009), "Schmuck für Könige und Götter – Funde aus der Königsgruft", in al-Maqdissi et al., eds., 228–233.

Rossberger, E. (in press), *Schmuck für Lebende und Tote: Form und Funktion des Schmuckinventars der Königsgruft von Qatna in seinem soziokulturellen Umfeld*. Tübingen.

Rossel, S., Marshall, F., Peters, J., Pilgram, T., Adams, M.D. and O'Connor, D. (2008), "Domestication of the donkey: timing, processes, and indicators", *PNAS* 105: 3715–3720.

Rostoker, W. and Bronson, B. (1990), *Pre-Industrial Iron: Its Technology and Ethnology*. Philadelphia.

Rostoker, W. and Dvorak, J.R. (1991), "Some experiments with co-smelting to copper alloys", *Archaeomaterials* 5: 5–20.

Rostovtzeff, M.I. (1922), *Iranians and Greeks in South Russia*. Oxford.

Rostovtzeff, M.I. (1932), "Foreign commerce of Ptolemaic Egypt", *Journal of Economic and Business History* 4: 728–769.

Rostovtzeff, M.I. (1934), *The Excavations at Dura-Europos. Conducted by Yale University and the French Academy of Inscriptions and Letters. Preliminary Report of Fifth Season of Work, October 1931–March 1932*. New Haven.

Rostovtzeff, M.I. (1938), *Dura Europos and Its Art*. Oxford.

Roth, M.T., ed., (1995), *Law Collections from Mesopotamia and Asia Minor*. Atlanta.

Rothenberg, B. (1972), *Timna: Valley of the Biblical Copper Mines*. London.

Rothenberg, B. (1990), *The Ancient Metallurgy of Copper*. London.

Rothenberg, B. (1999), "Archaeo-metallurgical researches in the southern Arabah 1959–1990 Part I. Late Pottery Neolithic to Early Bronze IV", *PEQ* 131: 68–83.

Rothfield, L., ed., (2008), *Antiquities Under Siege*. Lanham.

Rothfield, L. (2009), *The Rape of Mesopotamia: Behind the Looting of the Iraq Museum*. Chicago.

Rothman, M.S., ed. (2001), *Uruk Mesopotamia and its Neighbors: Cross Cultural Interactions in the Era of State Formation*. Santa Fe.

Rothman, M.S. (2002), *Tepe Gawra: The Evolution of a Small, Prehistoric Center in Northern Iraq*. Philadelphia.

Rothman, M.S. (2003), "Ripples in the stream: Transcaucasia–Anatolian interaction in the Murat/Euphrates Basin at the beginning of the third millennium BC", in Smith and Rubinson, eds., 95–110.

Rothman, M.S. (2004), "Studying the development of complex society: Mesopotamia in the late fifth and fourth millennia BC", *JAR* 12: 75–119.

Rouault, O. and Wäfler, M., eds. (2000), *La Djéziré et l'Euphrate syriens de la protohistoire à la fin du second millénaire av. J.C.* Turnhout.

Rougeulle, A. (1982), "Des étuves à dates à Bahreïn et en Oman: le problème de l'apparition des techniques de transformation de la date", *Paléorient* 8/2: 67–77.

Roux, G., ed., (1984), *Temples et sanctuaires: séminaire de recherche 1981–1983*. Lyon.

Roux, V. (2003), "A dynamic systems framework for studying technological change: application to the emergence of the potter's wheel in the Southern Levant", *JAMT* 10: 1–30.

Roux, V. and Corbetta, D. (1990), *The Potter's Wheel: Craft Specialisation and Technical Competence*. New Delhi.

Roux, V. and Courty, M.A. (1998), "Identification of wheel-fashioning methods: technological analysis of 4th–3rd millennium BC oriental ceramics", *JAS* 25: 747–763.

Roux, V. and de Miroschedji, P. (2009), "Revisiting the history of the potter's wheel in the southern Levant", *Levant* 41: 155–173.

Rowan, Y. and Golden, J. (2009), "The Chalcolithic period of the Southern Levant: a synthetic review", *JWP* 22/1: 1–92.

Rowan, Y. and Levy, T.E. (1991), "Use wear analysis of a Chalcolithic scraper assemblage from Shiqmim", *JIPS* 24: 112–134.

Rowlands, M., Larsen, M. and Kristiansen, K., eds. (1987), *Centre and Periphery in the Ancient World*. Cambridge.

Rowton, M.B. (1967), "The woodlands of ancient Western Asia", *JNES* 26: 261–277.

Ruas, M.-P., Boissinot, P., Bouby, L., Durand, A., Mane, P., Pradat, B., Puig, C. and Terral, J.-F. eds. (in press), *Histoire des fruits. Savoirs en pratique, pratiques des savoirs*. Paris.

Rubin, Z. (1989), "Byzantium and Southern Arabia. The policy of Anastasius", in French and Lightfoot, eds., 383–420.

Rubinson, K. (1990), "The textiles from Pazyryk: a study in transfer and transformation of artistic motifs", *Expedition* 32/1: 49–61.

Rubinson, K. and Sagona, A., eds. (2008), *Ceramics in Transition: Chalcolithic Through Iron Age in the Highlands of the Southern Caucasus and Anatolia*. Leuven.

Rudenko, S. (1970), *Frozen Tombs of Siberia*. Berkeley.

Ruffing, K. (2002), "Wege in den Osten: Die Routen des römischen Süd- und Osthandels (1. bis 2. Jahrhundert n. Chr.)", in Olshausen and Sonnabend, eds., 360–378.

Runciman, W., ed. (2001), *The origin of human social institutions*. Oxford.

Rush, L. (2008), review of Rothfield, L., ed. *Antiquities Under Siege: Cultural Heritage Protection After the War*, *Heritage Management* 1/2: 261–263.

Russell, J.M. (1991), *Sennacherib's Palace Without Rival at Nineveh*. Chicago.

Russell, K.W. (1986), "Transformations in early Byzantine urban life: the contribution and limitations of archaeological evidence", in Anonymous, ed., 137–154.

Russell, N. (2010), "Navigating the human-animal boundary", *Reviews in Anthropology* 39: 3–24.

Russell, N. and Martin, L. (2005), "The Çatalhöyük mammal remains", in Hodder, ed., 33–98.

Russell, N., Martin, L. and Buitenhuis, H. (2005), "Cattle domestication at Çatalhöyük revisited", *CA* 46 *Supplement*: S101–108.

Rust, A. (1950), *Die Höhlenfunde von Jabrud (Syrien)*. Neumünster.

Rutten, K. (2007), "The Roman fine wares of ed-Dur (Umm al-Qaiwain, U.A.E.) and their distribution in the Persian Gulf and Indian Ocean", *AAE* 18: 8–24.

Rutten, M. (1954), "Tablette no 4", in Ghirshman, 83–85.

Ryan, W.B.F., Pitman, W.C., Major, C.O., Shimkus, K., Moskalenko, V., Jones, G.A., Dimitrov, P., Görür, N., Sakinç, M., and Yüce, H. (1997), "An abrupt drowning of the Black Sea shelf", *Marine Geology* 138: 119–126.

Ryder, M.L. (1960), "A study of the coat of the mouflon *Ovis musimon* with special reference to seasonal change", *Proceedings of the Zoological Society of London* 135: 387–408.

Ryder, M.L. (1964), "Fleece evolution in domesticated sheep", *Nature* 4958: 555–558.

Ryder, M.L. (1983), "A re-assessment of Bronze Age wool", *JAS* 10: 327–331.

Ryder, M.L. (1987), "The evolution of fleece", *Scientific American* 257: 112–119.

Rye, O.S. (1981), *Pottery Technology: Principles and Reconstruction*. Washington, DC.

Rye, O.S. and Evans, C. (1976), *Traditional Pottery Techniques of Pakistan: Field and Laboratory Studies*. Washington, DC.

Saadé, G. (1990), "Note sur les tells archéologiques du royaume ougaritien", *Syria* 67: 195–199.

Sabloff, J.A. and Lamberg-Karlovsky, C.C., eds. (1975), *Ancient Civilization and Trade*. Albuquerque.

Sachet, I. and Robin C., eds. (in press), *Actes du colloque "Images et representations des dieux et deesses en Arabie"*, Collège de France, Site d'Ulm, 1–2 octobre 2007. Paris.

Sadeq, M.M. (1999), "Mosaic pavements recently found in the Gaza Strip", in Piccirillo and Alliata, eds., 214–215.

Sadeq, M.M., Abu Hassuneh, Y.M. and Humbert, J.-P., OP (1999), "Gaza", *DA* 240: 46–67.

Sader, H. (2000), "The Aramaean kingdoms of Syria: Origin and formation processes", in Bunnens, ed., 61–76.

Sader, H. and Kamlah, J. (2010), "Tell el-Burak: a new Middle Bronze Age site from Lebanon", *NEA* 73/2–3: 130–141.

Safar, F. (1949), "Soundings at Tell al-Lahm", *Sumer* 5/2: 154–172.

Safar, F. and Mustafa, M.A. (1974), *Hatra, the City of the Sun God*. Baghdad.

Safar, F., Mustafa, M.A. and Lloyd, S. (1981), *Eridu*. Baghdad.

Saggs, H.W.F. (1963), "Assyrian warfare in the Sargonid period", *Iraq* 25: 167–170.

Saggs, H.W.F. (1969), "Neo-Babylonian fragments from Harran", *Iraq* 31/2: 166–169.

Saggs, H.W.F. (1984), *The Might that was Assyria*. London.

Saghieh, M. (1983), *Byblos in the Third Millennium BC: A Reconstruction of the Stratigraphy and a Study of the Cultural Connections*. Warminster.

Sagona, A.G. (1984), *The Caucasian Region in the Early Bronze Age*. Oxford.

Sagona, A.G., ed. (2004), *A View from the Highlands: Archaeological Studies in Honour of Charles Burney*. Leuven.

Sagona, A.G. and Çilingiroğlu, A., eds. (2007), *Anatolian Iron Ages 6*. Louvain.

Sagona, A.G., Sagona, C., Newton, J.C., Pemberton, E.G. and McPhee, I. (2004), *Archaeology at the North-East Anatolian Frontier*. Louvain.

Sagona, A.G. and Zimansky, P. (2009), *Ancient Turkey*. Abingdon/New York.

Şahin, S., Schwertheim, E. and Wagner, J., eds. (1978), *Studien zur Religion und Kultur Kleinasiens: Festschrift für Friedrich Karl Dörner zum 65. Geburtstag am 28. Februar 1978*. Leiden.

Sahrhage, D. (1999), *Fischfang und Fischkult im alten Mesopotamien*. Frankfurt-am-Main.

Sahrhage, D. and Lundbeck, J. (1992), *A History of Fishing*. Berlin/Heidelberg/New York.

Saidah, R. (1979), "Fouilles de Sidon-Dakerman: l'aggomération chalcolithique", *Berytus* 27: 29–55.

Saidel, B. (1993), "Round house or square? Architectural form and socio-economic organization in the PPNB", *JMA* 6: 65–108.

Sajjadi, S.M.S. (2003), "Excavations at Shahr-i Sokhta: first preliminary report on the excavations of the graveyard 1997–2000", *Iran* 41: 21–98.

Sajjadi, S.M.S. (2007), "Wall painting from Dahaneh-ye Gholaman", in Ivantchik and Licheli, eds., 129–154.

Salah, A.S., Chmyriov, V.M., Shareq, A., Stazhilo-Alekseev, K.F., Dronov, V.I., Azimi, N.A., Gannon, P.J., Lubemov, B.K., Kafarskiy, A.K. and Malyarov, E.P. (1977), *Mineral resources of Afghanistan*. Kabul.

Salamini, F., Özkan, H., Schäfer-Pregl, R. and Martin, W. (2002), "Genetics and geography of wild cereal domestication in the Near East", *Nature Reviews Genetics* 3: 429–441.

Salavert, A. (2008), "Olive cultivation and oil production in Palestine during the early Bronze Age (3500–2000 BC): the case of Tell Yarmouth, Israel", *VHA* 17: 53–61.

Saliou, C., ed. (2005), *Gaza dans l'Antiquité tardive. Archéologie, rhétorique et histoire*. Salerno.

Sallaberger, W. (1996), *Der babylonische Töpfer und seine Gefäße nach Urkunden altsumerischer bis altbabylonischer Zeit sowie lexikalischen und literarischen Zeugnissen*. Gent.

Sallaberger, W., Einwag, B. and Otto, A. (2006), "Schenkungen von Mittani-Königen an die Einwohner von Basiru. Die zwei Urkunden aus Tall Bazi am Mittleren Euphrat", *ZA* 96: 69–104.

Sallaberger, W., Volk, K. and Zgoll, A., eds. (2003), *Literatur, Politik und Recht in Mesopotamien: Festschrift für Claus Wilcke*. Wiesbaden.

Salles, J.-F. (1980), *La Nécropole "K" de Byblos*. Lyon.

Salles, J.-F., ed. (1988), *L'Arabie et ses bordières* I. *Itinéraires et Voisinages*. Lyon.

Salles, J.-F. (1992), "Découvertes du Golfe Arabo-Persique aux époques grecque et romaine", *Revue des Études Anciennes* 94/1–2: 79–97.

Salles, J.-F. (1993), "Hellénisme et traditions orientales à Failaka", in Invernizzi and Salles, eds., 223–255.

Salles, J.-F. (1995), "Rituel mortuaire et rituel social à Ras Shamra-Ougarit", in Campbell and Green, eds., 171–184.

Salles, J.-F. (1996), "Achaemenid and Hellenistic trade in the Indian Ocean", in Reade, ed., 251–267.

Salles, J.-F. (2005), "The Periplus of the Erythraean Sea and the Arab-Persian Gulf", in Boussac and Salles, eds., 115–146.

Salles, J.-F. and Sedov, A.V. (2010), *Qāni': Le Port antique du Hadramawt entre le Méditerranée, l'Afrique et l'Inde. Fouilles russes 1972, 1985–1989, 1991, 1993–1994*. Turnhout.

Salomon, R. (1991), "Epigraphic remains of Indian traders in Egypt", *JAOS* 111: 731–736.

Salomon, R. (1993), "Addenda to 'Epigraphic Remains of Indian traders in Egypt'", *JAOS* 113: 593.
Salonen, A. (1939), *Die Wasserfahrzeuge in Babylonien*. Helsinki.
Salonen, A. (1970), *Die Fischerei im alten Mesopotamien*. Helsinki.
Salvatori, S. (1996), "Death and ritual in a population of coastal food foragers in Oman", in Afanasev et al., eds., 205–222.
Salvatori, S. (2008a), "Cultural variability in the Bronze Age Oxus Civilisation and its relations with the surrounding regions of Central Asia and Iran", in Salvatori et al., eds., 75–98.
Salvatori, S. (2008b), "The Margiana settlement pattern from the Middle Bronze Age to the Parthian-Sasanian: a contribution to the study of complexity", in Salvatori et al., eds., 57–74.
Salvatori, S. (2008c). "A new cylinder seal from ancient Margiana: cultural exchange and syncretism in a 'world wide trade system' at the end of the 3rd millennium BC", in Salvatori et al., eds., 111–118.
Salvatori, S. and Tosi, M. (2005), "Shahr-i Sokhta revised sequence", in Jarrige and Lefèvre, eds., 281–292.
Salvatori, S., Tosi, M. and Cerasetti, B., eds. (2008), *The Bronze Age and Early Iron Age in the Margiana Lowlands: Facts and Methodological Proposals for a Redefinition of the Research Strategies*. Oxford.
Salvatori, S. and Vidale, M. (1997), *Shahr-i Sokhta 1975–1978: Central Quarters Excavations*. Rome.
Salvatori, S., Vidale, M., Guida, G. and Masioli, E. (2009), "Ilgynly-Depe (Turkmenistan) and the 4th millennium BC metallurgy of Central Asia", *Paléorient* 35: 47–67.
Salvini, M. (1989), "Le pantheon de l'Urartu et le fondement de l'état", *SEL* 6: 79–91.
Salvini, M. (1994), "The historical background of the Urartian monument of Meher Kapisi", in Çilingiroğlu and French, eds., 205–210.
Salvini, M. (1995), "Some historic-geographical problems concerning Assyria and Urartu", in Liverani, ed., 43–53.
Salvini, M. (1996), *The Habiru prism of King Tunip-Teššup of Tikunani*. Rome.
Salvini, M. (2001), "Pas de qanāts en Urartu!" in Briant, ed., 143–155.
Salvini, M., Parmegiani, N. and Dan, R. (2008), *Corpus dei testi urartei*. Rome/Paris.
Sami, A. (1956), *Pasargadae: The Oldest Imperial Capital of Iran*. Shiraz.
Sami, A. (1967), *Persepolis (Takht-i-Jamshid)*, 5th ed. Shiraz.
Sams, G.K. (1974), "Phrygian painted snimals: Anatolian Orientalizing art", *AnSt* 24: 169–196.
Sams, G.K. (1989), "Sculpted orthostates at Gordion", in Emre et al., eds., 447–454.
Sams, G.K. (1994), *The Gordion Excavations (1950–1973): Final Reports Volume IV. The Early Phrygian Pottery*, 2 vols. Philadelphia.
Sams, G.K. (2005), "Gordion: exploration over a century", in Kealhofer, ed., 10–21.
Sana, M. and Tornero, C. (2008), "Consumption of animal resources at the site of Akarçay Tepe and Tell Halula (Middle Euphrates Valley, 8th–6th millennia cal. BC)", in Vila et al., eds., 153–168.
Sana Segui, M. (2000), "Animal resource management and the process of animal domestication at Tell Halula (Euphrates valley-Syria) from 8800 BP to 7800 BP", in Mashkour et al., eds., 241–256.

Sánchez Priego, J.A. (2008), "Analyse technologique et fonctionelle des herminettes de Mureybet", in Ibáñez, ed., 407–434.
Sancisi-Weerdenburg, H.W.A.M. (1983), "The Zendan and the Ka'bah", in Koch and Mackenzie, eds., 145–151.
Sancisi-Weerdenburg, H.W.A.M. (1987), "The Fifth Oriental Monarchy and Hellenocentrism", in Sancisi-Weerdenburg and Kuhrt, eds., 117–131.
Sancisi-Weerdenburg, H.W.A.M. (1989), "The personality of Xerxes, King of Kings", in De Meyer and Haerinck, eds., 549–561 (repr. 2002 in Bakker et al., eds., 579–590).
Sancisi-Weerdenburg, H.W.A.M. (1991), "Nowruz in Persepolis", in Sancisi-Weerdenburg and Drijvers, eds., 173–201.
Sancisi-Weerdenburg, H.W.A.M. (1992), review M. Roaf, *Sculptures and Sculptors at Persepolis*, *BiOr* 49: 244–251.
Sancisi-Weerdenburg, H.W.A.M. (1993), "Alexander and Persepolis", in Carlsen et al., eds., 177–188.
Sancisi-Weerdenburg, H.W.A.M. (1999), "The Persian king and history", in Kraus, ed., 91–112.
Sancisi-Weerdenburg, H.W.A.M. and Drijvers, J.W., eds. (1991), *Achaemenid History VII: Through Travellers' Eyes. European Travellers on the Iranian Monuments*. Leiden.
Sancisi-Weerdenburg, H.W.A.M. and Kuhrt, A., eds. (1987), *Achaemenid History II: The Greek Sources*. Leiden.
Sancisi-Weerdenburg, H.W.A.M. and Kuhrt, A., eds. (1990), *Achaemenid History IV: Centre and Periphery*. Leiden.
Sancisi-Weerdenburg, H.W.A.M. and Kuhrt, A., eds. (1991), *Achaemenid History VI: Asia Minor and Egypt. Old Cultures in a New Empire*. Leiden.
Sancisi-Weerdenburg, H.W.A.M., Kuhrt, A. and Root, M.C., eds. (1994), *Achaemenid History VIII: Continuity and Change*. Leiden.
Sandars, N.K. (1985), *The Sea Peoples: Warriors of the Ancient Mediteranean*. London.
Sanders, J., ed. (1970), *Near Eastern Archaeology in the Twentieth Century: Essays in Honor of Nelson Glueck*. Garden City.
Sanders, S.L., ed. (2007), *Margins of Writing, Origins of Cultures*, 2nd edn. Chicago.
Sanderson, D.C.W. and Hunter, J.R. (1981), "Composition variability in vegetable ash", *Science and Archaeology* 23: 27–30.
Sandford, M.K., ed. (1993), *Investigations of Ancient Human Tissue*. Langhorne.
Sanlaville, P. (1989), "Considérations sur l'évolution de la basse Mesopotamie au cours des derniers millénaires", *Paléorient* 15/2: 5–27.
Sanlaville, P. (1996), "Changements climatiques dans la région levantine à la fin du Pléistocène supérieur et au début de l'Holocène: leurs relations avec l'évolution des sociétés humaines", *Paléorient* 22/1: 7–30.
Sanlaville, P. (1998), "Les changements dans l'environnement au Moyen-Orient de 20,000 BP au 6000 BP", *Paléorient* 23/2: 249–262.
Sanlaville, P. (2000), *Le Moyen-Orient arabe: Le milieu et l'homme*. Paris.
Saradi, H.G. (2006), *The Byzantine City in the Sixth Century: Literary Images and Historical Reality*. Athens.
Sardari Zarchi, A. and Razai, A. (2008), *Gozaresh-e moghadamati-ye kawosh-haye bastanshenasi, nejat bakhshi, Tappe Mehr 'Ali (Eqlid, Fars)*. Tehran.
Sarfaraz, A.A. (1970), "Bishāpūr", *Iran* 8: 178.

Sarfaraz, A.A. (1971), "Un pavillon de l'époque de Cyrus le Grand à Borazdjan", *Bāstān-Šenāsī va Honar-e Īrān* 7–8: 22–25.

Sarianidi, V.I. (1971), "The lapis lazuli route in the ancient Near East", *Archaeology* 24: 12–15.

Sarianidi, V.I. (1975), "Stepnye plemena epokhi bronzy v Margiane", *Sovietskaya Arkheologia* 2: 20–29.

Sarianidi, V.I (1977), "Bactrian centre of ancient art", *Mesopotamia* 12: 97–110.

Sarianidi, V.I. (1984), "Southern Turkmenia and Margiane in the Bronze Age", *Information Bulletin* 7: 5–16.

Sarianidi, V.I. (2002), *Margush: Ancient Oriental kingdom in the Old Delta of the Murghab River*. Ashgabat.

Sarianidi, V.I. (2007), *Necropolis of Gonur*. Athens.

Sarianidi, V.I. (2008), "Ancient Bactria's golden hoard", in Hiebert and Cambon, eds., 211–217.

Sarraf, M.R. (2003), "Archaeological excavations in Tepe Ekbatana (Hamadan) by the Iranian Archaeological Mission between 1983 and 1993", in Lanfranchi et al, eds., 269–279.

Sartre, M. (1981), "La frontière méridionale de l'Arabie romaine", in Fahd, ed., 77–92.

Sartre, M. (1987), "Le Hawran byzantin à la veille de la conquête musulmane", in Bakhit, ed., 155–167.

Sartre, M. (1991), *L'Orient romain: Provinces et sociétés provinciales en Méditerranée orientale d'Auguste aux Sévères (31 avant J.-C.–235 après J.-C.)*. Paris.

Sartre, M. (2001), *D'Alexandre à Zénobie: Histoire du Levant antique, IVe siècle avant J.-C.-IIIe siècle après J.-C.* Paris.

Sartre, M., ed. (2003), *La Syrie hellénistique*. Lyon.

Sartre, M. (2005), *The Middle East under Rome*. Cambridge/London.

Sartre, M., Bousdroukis, A., Duyrat, F. and Salles, J.-F., eds. (2003), *La Syrie hellénistique*. Lyon.

Sarzec, E. de (1884–1912), *Découvertes en Chaldée*, 2 vols. Paris.

Sasson, J., ed. (1995a), *Civilizations of the Ancient Near East*. New York.

Sasson, J. (1995b), "King Hammurabi of Babylon", in Sasson, ed., 901–915.

Sauer, E.W., Omrani-Rekavandi, O., Nokandeh, J. and Wilkinson, T.J. (2009), "Die sasanidischen Grenzwälle im Nord-Iran", in Nunn, ed., 126–143, 212–215.

Sauren, H. (1966), *Topographie der Provinz Umma nach den Urkunden der Zeit der III. Dynastie von Ur. Teil I: Kanäle und Bewässerungsanlagen*. Heidelberg.

Savage, S.H., Falconer, S.E. and Harrison, T.P. (2007), "The Early Bronze Age city states of the southern Levant: neither cities nor states", in Levy et al., eds., 285–297.

Sayed, A.M.A.H. (1984), "Reconsideration of the Minaean inscription of Zayd'il bin Zayd", *PSAS* 14: 93–99.

Sayre, E.V. (1963), "The intentional use of antimony and manganese in ancient glasses", in Matson and Rindone, eds., 263–282.

Sayre, E.V. (1964), *Some Ancient Glass Specimens with Compositions of Particular Archaeological Significance*. New York.

Sayre, E.V. (1965), "Summary of the Brookhaven program of analysis of ancient glass", in Young, ed., 145–154.

Sayre, E.V. and Smith, R.H. (1967), "Some materials of glass manufacturing in antiquity", in Levey, ed., 279–311.

Sayre, E.V. and Smith, R.W. (1974), "Analytical studies of ancient Egyptian glass", in Bishay, ed., 47–70.

Scandone Matthiae, G. (1988), "Les relations entre Ebla et l'Égypte au IIIème and IIème millénaire av. J.-Chr.", in Waetzoldt and Hauptmann, eds., 67–73.

Scandone Matthiae, G. (1997), "The relations between Ebla and Egypt", in Oren, ed., 415–427.

Scarborough, J. (1982), "Roman pharmacy and the eastern drug trade: Some problems as illustrated by the example of aloe", *Pharmacy in History* 24/4: 135–143.

Scerrato, U. (1966), "Excavations at Dahan-i Ghulman (Seistan-Iran): first preliminary report", *EW* 16: 9–30.

Scerrato, U. (1979), "Evidence of religious life at Dahan-e Ghulaman, Sistan", in Taddei, ed., 709–735.

Schachner, A. (1999), *Von der Rundhütte zum Kaufmannshaus: Kulturhistorische Untersuchungen zur Entwicklung prähistorischer Wohnhäuser in Zentral-, Ost- und Südostanatolien*. Oxford.

Schachner, A. (2006), "Auf welchen Fundamenten? Überlegungen zum Stand der Erforschung der hethitischen Architektur", in Mielke et al., eds., 149–166.

Schachner, A. (2007), *Bilder eines Weltreichs*. Turnhout.

Schacht, R.M. (1987), "Early historic cultures", in Hole, ed., 171–203.

Schaeffer, C.F.A. (1939), "Aperçu de l'histoire d'Ugarit", *Ugaritica* 1: 3–52.

Schaeffer, C.F.A. (1962), *Ugaritica IV*. Paris.

Schaub, T. (1982), "The origins of the Early Bronze Age walled town culture of Jordan", in Hadidi, ed., 67–75.

Schaudig, H. (2001), *Die Inschriften Nabonids von Babylon und Kyros' des Großen samt den in ihrem Umfeld enstandenen Tendenzschriften. Textausgabe und Grammatik*. Münster.

Scheftelowitz, N. and Oren, R. (2004), *Giv'at Ha-Oranim, a Chalcolithic site*. Tel Aviv.

Scheil, V. (1905), *Textes élamites-sémitiques, troisième série*. Paris.

Scheil, V. (1911), *Textes élamites-anzanites, quatrième série*. Paris.

Scheil, V. (1939), *Mélanges épigraphiques*. Paris.

Schenk, H. (2000), "Rouletted ware and other imports of Tissamaharama: observations on the pottery sequence from southern Sri Lanka", in Taddei and de Marco, G., eds., 653–677.

Sherwin-White, S. and Kuhrt, A. (1993), *From Samarkhand to Sardis: A New Approach to the Seleucid Empire*. London.

Schick, R. (1995), *The Christian Communities of Palestine from Byzantine to Islamic rule: A Historical and Archaeological Study*, 2 vols. Princeton.

Schiestl, R. (2008), "Tomb types and layout of a Middle Bronze IIA cemetery at Tell el-Dab'a, Area F/I. Egyptian and non-Egyptian features", in Bietak and Czerny, eds., 243–256.

Schiestl, R. (2009), *Tell el-Dab'a 18: Die Palastnekropole von Tell el-Dab'a. Die Gräber des Areals F/I der Straten d/2 und d/1*. Vienna.

Schiettecatte, J. (2010), "The Arabian Iron Age funerary stelae and the issue of cross-cultural contacts", in Weeks, ed., 191–203.

Schiettecatte, J. and Robin, C.J., eds. (2009), *L'Arabie à la veille de l'Islam. Bilan clinique*. Paris.
Schiffer, M.B., ed. (1980), *Advances in Archaeological Method and Theory*, vol. 3. New York.
Schiffer, M.B., ed. (1982), *Advances in Archaeological Method and Theory*, vol. 5. New York.
Schiffer, M.B., ed. (1991), *Archaeological Method and Theory*, vol. 3. New York.
Schilman, B., Ayalon, A., Bar-Matthews, M., Kagan, J., and Almogi-Labin, A., (2002), "Sea-land palaeoclimate correlation in the eastern Mediterranean region during the late Holocene", *Israel Journal of Earth Sciences* 51: 181–190.
Schiltz, V. (2008), "Tilya Tepe, the Hill of Gold: a nomad necropolis", in Hiebert and Cambon, eds., 219–293.
Schipper, B.U. (2005), *Die Erzählung des Wenamun: Ein Literaturwerk im Spannungsfeld von Politik, Geschichte und Religion*. Fribourg/Göttingen.
Schippmann, K. (1967), "Archäologische Unterschungen in Aserbaidschan im Jahre 1964", *IrAnt* 7: 77–81.
Schippmann, K. (1971), *Die iranische Feuerheiligtümer*. Berlin.
Schippmann, K. (1980), *Grundzüge der parthischen Geschichte*. Darmstadt.
Schippmann, K. (1987), "Arsacids ii. The Arsacid dynasty", *EnIr* 2: 525–536.
Schippmann, K. (1988), "Bard-e Nešānda", *EnIr* 3: 761–762.
Schippmann, K. (1990), *Grundzüge der Geschichte des sasanidischen Reiches*. Darmstadt.
Schippmann, K., Herling, A. and Salles, J.-F., eds. (1991), *Golf-Archäologie. Mesopotamien, Iran, Kuwait, Bahrain, Vereinigte Arabische Emirate und Oman*. Buch am Erlbach.
Schirmer, W. (1990), "Some aspects of building at the 'aceramic-neolithic' settlement of Çayönü Tepesi", *WA* 21: 363–387.
Schirmer, W. (2002), "Stadt, Palast, Tempel: Charakteristika hethitischer Architektur im 2. und 1. Jahrtausend v. Chr.", in Özgüç et al., eds., 204–17.
Schlereth, T., ed. (1982), *Material Culture Studies in America: An Anthology*. Madison.
Schlick-Nolte, B. and Lierke, R. (2002), "From silica to glass: on the track of the ancient glass artisans", in Bianchi et al., eds., 11–40.
Schlick-Nolte, B. and Werthmann, R. (2003), "Glass vessels from the burial of Nesikhons", *JGS* 45: 11–34.
Schloen, J.D. (2001), *The House of the Father as Fact and Symbol: Patrimonialism in Ugarit and the Ancient Near East*. Winona Lake.
Schloen, J.D., ed. (2009), *Exploring the Longue Durée: Essays in Honor of Lawrence E. Stager*. Winona Lake.
Schloen, J.D. and Fink, A.S. (2009a), "New excavations at Zincirli Höyük (ancient Sam'al) and the discovery of an inscribed mortuary stele", *BASOR* 356: 1–13.
Schloen, J.D. and Fink, A.S. (2009b), "Searching for ancient Sam'al: new excavations at Zincirli in Turkey", *NEA* 72: 203–219.
Schmandt-Besserat, D. (1980), "Ochre in prehistory: 300,000 years of the use of iron ores as pigments", in Wertime and Muhly, eds., 127–150.
Schmandt-Besserat, D. (1992), *Before Writing*. Austin.
Schmandt-Besserat, D. (1998), "Ain Ghazal 'monumental figures'", *BASOR* 310: 1–17.

Schmid, S.G. (2007), "La distribution de la céramique nabatéenne et l'organisation du commerce nabatéen de longue distance", *Topoi supplément* 8: 61–91.

Schmidt, A. and Fazeli, H. (2007), "Tepe Ghabristan: a Chalcolithic tell buried in alluvium", *Archaeological Prospection* 14: 38–46.

Schmidt, E.F. (1933), "Tepe Hissar Excavations, 1931", *The Museum Journal* 23/4: 323–483.

Schmidt, E.F. (1937), *Exacavations at Tepe Hissar (Damghan)*. Philadelphia.

Schmidt, E.F. (1939), *The Treasury of Persepolis and Other Discoveries in the Homeland of the Achaemenians*. Chicago.

Schmidt, E.F. (1940), *Flights over Ancient Cities of Iran*. Chicago.

Schmidt, E.F. (1953), *Persepolis I. Structures, Reliefs, Inscriptions*. Chicago.

Schmidt, E.F. (1957), *Persepolis II. Contents of the Treasury and Other Discoveries*. Chicago.

Schmidt, E.F. (1970), *Persepolis III. The Royal Tombs and Other Monuments*. Chicago.

Schmidt, J. (1974), "Zwei Tempel der Obed-Zeit in Uruk", *BaM* 7: 173–187.

Schmidt, J. (2010), "Fritz Rudolph Kraus in Istanbul (1937–1949) and the development of ancient Near Eastern studies in Turkey", *BiOr* 67: 5–22.

Schmidt, K. (1982), "Zur Verwendung der mesopotamischen 'Glockentöpfe'", *Archäologisches Korrespondenzblatt* 12: 317–319.

Schmidt, K. (1992), "Tell El-Fara'in/Buto and el-Tell el-Iswid (South): the lithic industries from the Chalcolithic to the Early Old Kingdom", in van Den Brink, ed., 31–41.

Schmidt, K. (1995), "Investigations in the Upper Mesopotamian Early Neolithic: Göbekli Tepe and Gürcütepe", *Neo-Lithics* 2/95: 9–10.

Schmidt, K. (1996), "Helwan in Egypt: a PPN Site?", in Kozłowoski and Gebel, eds., 127–135.

Schmidt, K. (2000), "'Zuerst kam der Tempel, dann die Stadt': Vorläufiger Bericht zu den Grabungen am Göbekli Tepe und am Gürcütepe 1995-1999", *IstMitt* 50: 5–41.

Schmidt, K. (2005a), "Die 'Stadt' der Steinzeit", in Falk, ed., 25–38.

Schmidt, K. (2005b), "Ritual centres and the Neolithisation of Upper Mesopotamia", *Neo-Lithics* 2/05: 13–21.

Schmidt, K. (2006), *Sie bauten die ersten Tempel. Das rätselhafte Heiligtum der Steinzeitjäger. Die archäologische Entdeckung am Göbekli Tepe*. München.

Schmidt, K. (2007a), "Die Steinkreise und die Reliefs des Göbekli Tepe", in Anonymous (2007a), ed., 83–96.

Schmidt, K. (2007b), "Göbekli Tepe", in Özdoğan and Başgelen eds., 115–129.

Schmidt, K. (2009a), "Göbekli Tepe. Eine Beschreibung der wichtigsten Befunde erstellt nach den Arbeiten der Grabungsteams der Jahre 1995–2007", in ArchaeNova, ed., 187–223.

Schmidt, K. (2009b), "Von den ersten Dörfern zu frühurbanen Strukturen", in Jockenhövel, ed., 128–144.

Schmidt, K. (2009c), "Göbekli Tepe: Santuarios de la Edad de Piedra en la Alta Mesopotamia", in Kaulicke and Dillehay, eds., 263–288.

Schmidt, M., Lucke, B., Baumlerb, R., al-Saad, Z., al-Qudah, B. and Hutcheon, A. (2006), "The Decapolis region (Northern Jordan) as historical example of desertification? Evidence from soil development and distribution", *QI* 151: 74–86.

Schmitt, A. (in press), *Die jüngeren Ischtar-Tempel in Assur*. Wiesbaden.

Schmitt, R. (1987), "Apadāna, i. Term", *EnIr* 2: 145–146.
Schmitt, R. (1998), "Parthische Sprach- und Namenüberlieferung aus arsakidischer Zeit", in Wiesehöfer, ed., 163–204.
Schmitt, R. (1999), *Beiträge zu altpersischen Inschriften*. Wiesbaden.
Schmitt, R. (2000a), *The Old Persian Inscriptions of Naqsh-i Rustam and Persepolis*. London.
Schmitt, R. (2000b), "Gabae", *EnIr* 10: 235.
Schmitt, R. (2009), *Die Altpersischen Inschriften der Achaimeniden. Editio minor mit deutscher Übersetzung*. Wiesbaden.
Schneider, I., ed. (2003), *Militär und Staatlichkeit*. Halle.
Schneider, T. (2003), *Ausländer in Ägypten während des Mittleren Reiches und der Hyksoszeit. Teil 2: Die ausländische Bevölkerung*. Mainz.
Schoer, B. and Rehren, T. (2007), "The composition of glass and associated ceramics from Qantir", in Pusch and Rehren, eds., 171–199.
Schoop, U.-D. (1999), "Aspects of early metal use in Neolithic Mesopotamia", in Hauptmann et al., eds., 31–36.
Schoop, U.-D. and Seeher, J. (2006), "Absolute Chronologie in Boğazköy-Ḫattuša: Das Potential der Radiokarbondaten", in Mielke et al., eds. 53–75.
Schotsmans, J. and Taddei, M., eds., (1985), *South Asian Archaeology 1983*. Naples.
Schreiber, K. (2001), "The Wari empire of Middle Horizon Peru: the epistemological challenge of documenting an empire without documentary evidence", in Alcock et al., eds., 70–92.
Schreurs, J.W.H. and Brill, R.H. (1984), "Iron and sulfur related colours in ancient glasses", *Archaeometry* 26: 199–209.
Schroeder, B. (1970), "A prehistoric survey in the northern Bekaa Valley", *Bulletin du Musée de Beyrouth* 23: 193–204.
Schulz, E. and Whitney, J.W. (1986), "Upper Pleistocene and Holocene lakes in the An-Nafud, Saudi Arabia", *Hydrobiologia* 143: 175–190.
Schulz, R. (2002), "Der Sturm auf die Festung: Gedanken zu einigen Aspekten des Kampfbildes im Alten Ägypten vor dem Neuen Reich", in Bietak and Schwarz, eds., 19–41.
Schuol, M. (2000), *Die Charakene: Ein mesopotamisches Königreich in hellenistisch-parthischer Zeit*. Stuttgart.
Schwab, M.J., Neumann, F., Litt, T., Negendank, J.F.W. and Stein, M. (2004), "Holocene palaeoecology of the Golan Heights (Near East): investigation of lacustrine sediments from Birkat Ram crater lake", *QSR* 23: 1723–1731.
Schwartz, G.M. (1987), "The Ninevite V period and the development of complex society in Northern Mesopotamia", *Paléorient* 13/2: 93–100.
Schwartz, G.M. (2007a), "Taking the long view on collapse: a Syrian perspective", in Kuzucuoğlu and Marro, eds., 45–67.
Schwartz, G.M. (2007b), "Status, ideology, and memory in third-millennium Syria: 'Royal' tombs at Umm el-Marra", in Laneri, ed., 39–68.
Schwartz, G.M. (2008), "Problems of chronology: Mesopotamia, Anatolia, and the Syro-Levantine region", in Aruz et al., eds., 450–452.
Schwartz, G.M., Curvers, H.H., Gerritsen, F.A., MacCormack, J.A., Miller, N.F. and Weber, J.A. (2000), "Excavation and survey in the Jabbul Plain, Western Syria: the Umm el-Marra Project 1996–1997", *AJA* 104: 419–462.

Schwartz, G.M. and Weiss, H. (1992), "Syria, ca. 10,000–2000 BC", in Ehrich, ed., 221–243.
Schwartz, M. (2002), "Early evidence of reed boats from southeast Anatolia", *Antiquity* 76: 617–618.
Schwartz, M., Hollander, D. and Stein, G. (1999), "Reconstructing Mesopotamian exchange networks in the 4th millennium BC: geochemical and archaeological analyses of bitumen artifacts from Haçinebi Tepe, Turkey", *Paléorient* 25/1: 67–82.
Schweingruber, F.H. (1990), *Anatomie europäischer Hölzer. Ein Atlas zur Bestimmung europäischer Baum-, Strauch- und Zwergtrauchhölzer*. Bern/Stuttgart.
Scott, D.A. (1991), *Metallography and Microstructure of Ancient and Historic Metals*. Santa Monica.
Scott, M.L. and Macginnis, J. (1990), "Notes on Nineveh", *Iraq* 52: 63–73.
Scott, T.R. (1977), "The Harifian of the central Negev", in Marks, ed., 271–322.
Scullard, H.H. (1974), *The Elephant in the Greek and Roman World*. Ithaca.
Seaman, G., ed. (1987), *Foundations of Empire*, vol. 3. Berkeley.
Seberg, O., Petersen, G., Barfod, A.S. and Davis, J.I., eds. (2010), *Diversity, Phylogeny, and Evolution in the Monocotyledons*. Aarhus.
Secretary of Defense (2003), "DoD News Briefing – Secretary Rumsfeld and Gen. Myers. April 11, 2003" (http://www.defense.gov/transcripts/transcript.aspx?transcriptid=2367).
Sedov, A.V. (1992), "New archaeological and epigraphical material from Qana (South Arabia)", *AAE* 3: 110–137.
Sedov, A.V. (1996), "Qana' (Yemen) and the Indian Ocean: the archaeological evidence", in Ray and Salles, eds., 11–35.
Sedov, A.V. (1997), "Sea-trade of the Hadramawt Kingdom from the 1st to the 6th Century AD", in Avanzini, ed., 365–383.
Sedov, A.V. (2005), *Temples of Ancient Hadramawt*. Pisa.
Sedov, A.V. (2007), "The port of Qana' and the incense trade", in Peacock and Williams, eds., 71–111.
Seeden, H. (1980), *The Standing Armed Figurines in the Levant*. Stuttgart.
Seeger, J.A. (2001), "A preliminary report on the 1999 field season at Marsa Nakari", *JARCE* 38: 77–88.
Seeger, J.A. and Sidebotham, S.E. (2005), "Marsa Nakari: an ancient port on the Red Sea", *Egyptian Archaeology* 26: 18–20.
Seeher, J. (2000), "Getreidelagerung in unterirdischen Großspeichern: zur Methode und ihrer Anwendung im 2. Jahrtausend v. Chr. am Beispiel der Befunde in Hattuša", *SMEA* 42: 261–301.
Seeher, J. (2001), "Die Zerstörung der Stadt Hattuša", in Wilhelm, ed., 623–634.
Seeher, J. (2002), *Hattusha Guide*, 2nd edn. Istanbul.
Seeher, J. (2005), *Hattuscha Führer: Ein Tag in der hethitischen Hauptstadt*. Istanbul.
Seeher, J. (2006), "Chronology in Hattuša: new approaches to an old problem", in Mielke et al., eds., 197–214.
Segal, J.B. (1970), *Edessa "The Blessed City"*. Oxford.
Seidl, U. (1976), "Urartäische Glyptik", in Kellner, ed., 61.
Seidl, U. (1979), "Die Siegelbilder", in Kleiss, ed., 137–149.
Seidl, U. (1986), *Die elamischen Felsreliefs von Kūrāngūn und Naqš-e Rustam*. Berlin.
Seidl, U. (1988), "Die Siegelbilder", in Kleiss, ed., 145–163.

Seidl, U. (1994), "Achaimenidische Entlehnungen aus der urartäischen Kultur", in Sancisi-Weerdenburg et al., eds., 107–129.

Seidl, U. (1999), "Naqš-i Rustam", *RlA* 9: 165–168.

Seidl, U. (2003), "Wie waren die achaimenidischen Doppelprotomen-Kapitelle ausgerichtet?", in Henkelman and Kuhrt, eds., 67–77.

Seipel, W., ed. (1998), *Jemen. Kunst und Archäologie im Land der Königen von Saba*. Vienna.

Seipel, W., ed. (2000), *7000 Jahre persische Kunst. Meisterwerke aus dem Iranischen Nationalmuseum in Teheran*. Milan.

Seland, E.H. (2005), "Ancient South Arabia: trade and strategies of state control as seen in the *Periplus Maris Erythraei*", *PSAS* 35: 271–280.

Seland, E.H., ed. (2007), *The Indian Ocean in the Ancient Period: Definite Places, Translocal Exchange*. Oxford.

Sellin, G. and Watzinger, C. (1913), *Jericho: Die Ergebnisse der Ausgrabungen*. Leipzig.

Sellwood, D. (1980), *An Introduction to the Coinage of Parthia*. London.

Senior, L. and Weiss, H. (1992), "Tell Leilan 'sila bowls' and the Akkadian reorganization of Subarian agricultural production", *Orient-Express* 1992/2: 16–24.

Serjeantson, D. and Field, D., eds. (2006), *Animals in the Neolithic of Britain and Europe*. Oxford.

Severinghaus, J.P. and Brook, E.J. (1999), "Abrupt climate change at the end of the last glacial period inferred from trapped air in polar ice", *Science* 286: 930–934.

Sevin, V. and Belli, O. (1976–77), "Yeşilaliç Urartu Kutsal Alanı ve Kalesi/ Urartian sacred area and fortress at Yeşilaliç", *Anadolu Araştırmaları/Jahrbuch für kleinasiatische Forschungen* 4–5: 367–409.

Sey, Y., ed. (1996), *Tarihten günümüze Anadolu'da konut ve yerleşme / Housing and Settlement in Anatolia: A Historical Perspective*. Istanbul.

Shaffer, J.G. (1986), "The archaeology of Baluchistan: a review", *Newsletter of Baluchistan Studies* 3: 63–111.

Shaffer, J.G. (1992), "The Indus Valley, Baluchistan and Helmand Traditions: Neolithic through Bronze Age", in Ehrich, ed., 441–464.

Shahbazi, A.S. (1977), "From Pārsa to Taxt-e Jamšīd", *AMI* 10: 197–207.

Shahbazi, A.S. (1985), *Old Persian Inscriptions of the Persepolis platform*. London.

Shahbazi, A.S. (2002), "Gondēšāpur i. the city", *EnIr* online.

Shahbazi, A.S. (2004), *The Authoritative Guide to Persepolis*. Tehran.

Shahbazi, A.S. (2009), "Persepolis", *EnIr* online.

Shahid, I. (1989), *Byzantium and the Arabs in the Fifth Century*. Washington, DC.

Shaked, S. (1977), "Jewish and Christian seals of the Sasanian period", in Rosen-Ayalon, ed., 17–31.

Shakir, B. (2005–6), "The excavation results in Tell Assidr and Hoogna, the 1st season 1999", *Sumer* 53: 171–206.

Shalev, S. (2004), *Swords and Daggers in Late Bronze Age Canaan*. Stuttgart.

Shalev, S. and Northover, J.P. (1993), "Metallurgy of the Nahal Mishmar hoard reconsidered", *Archaeometry* 35: 35–47.

Sharjah Museums Department (2008), *Athar Sharjah: Highlights from the Collection of the Sharjah Archaeology Museum*. Sharjah.

Shaw, I., ed. (2000), *The Oxford History of Ancient Egypt*. Oxford.

Shaw, W.M.K. (2003), *Possessors and Possessed: Museums, Archaeology and the Visualization of History in the late Ottoman Empire*. Berkeley.

Shea, J.J., Davis, Z. and Brown, K. (2001), "Experimental tests of Middle Palaeolithic spear points using a calibrated crossbow", *JAS* 28: 807–816.

Sheehan, P. (2010), *Babylon of Egypt: The Archaeology of Old Cairo and the Origins of the City*. Cairo/New York.

Shelestiuk, H.V. (2003), "The semantics of symbol", *Semiotica* 144: 233–259.

Sherratt, A.G. (1981), "Plough and pastoralism: aspects of the secondary products revolution", in Hodder et al., eds., 261–305.

Sherratt, A.G. (1983), "The secondary exploitation of animals in the Old World", *WA* 15: 90–104.

Sherratt, A.G. (1997), *Economy and Society in Prehistoric Europe*. Edinburgh.

Sherratt, A.G. and Sherratt, E.S. (1991), "From luxuries to commodities: the nature of Mediterranean Bronze Age trading systems", in Gale ed., 351–386.

Sherratt, E.S. (1998), "'Sea Peoples' and the economic structure of the late second millennium in the eastern Mediterranean", in Gitin et al., eds., 292–313.

Sherratt, E.S., ed. (2000), *Proceedings of the First International Symposium "The Wall Paintings of Thera"*. Athens.

Sherwin-White, S. and Kuhrt, A. (1993), *From Samarkhand to Sardis: A New Approach to the Seleucid Empire*. London.

Shimelmitz, R. (2009), "Variability in specialized Canaanean blade production of the Early Bronze Age Levant", in Rosen and Roux, eds., 133–154.

Shinnie, P.L. (1960), "Socotra", *Antiquity* 34: 100–110.

Shipley, G. (2000), *The Greek World After Alexander 323–30 BC*. London/New York.

Shirai, N. (2010), *The Archaeology of the First Farmer-Herders in Egypt: New Insights into the Fayum Epipalaeolithic and Neolithic*. Leiden.

Shishlina, N.I. (1999), *Textiles of the Bronze Age Eurasian Steppe*. Moscow.

Shishlina, N.I. (2008), *Reconstruction of the Bronze Age of the Caspian Steppes: Life Styles and Life Ways of Pastoral Nomads*. Oxford.

Shishlina, N.I., Golikov, V. and Orfinskaya, O. (2000), *Bronze Age Textiles of the Caspian Sea Maritime Steppes*. Oxford.

Shishlina, N.I., Orfinskaya, O.V. and Golikov, V.P. (2003), "Bronze Age textiles from the North Caucasus: new evidence of fourth millennium BC fibres and fabrics", *OJA* 22: 331–344.

Sholan, A.M., Antonini, S. and Arbach, M., eds. (2005), *Sabaean Studies: Archaeological, Epigraphical and Historical Studies in Honour of Yusuf M. 'Abdallah, Alessandro de Maigret, Christian J. Robin on the Occasion of their Sixtieth Birthdays*. Naples/Sana'a.

Shortland, A.J. (2000a), "The number, extent and distribution of the vitreous materials workshops at Amarna", *OJA* 19: 115–134.

Shortland, A.J. (2000b), *Vitreous Materials at Amarna: The Production of Glass and Faience in 18th Dynasty Egypt*. Oxford.

Shortland, A.J. (2000c), "Depictions of glass vessels in two Theban tombs and their role in the dating of early glass", *JEA* 86: 159–161.

Shortland, A.J., ed. (2001), *The Social Context of Technological Change: Egypt and the Near East 1650–1550 BC*. Oxford.

Shortland, A.J. (2002), "The use and origin of antimonate colorants in early Egyptian glass", *Archaeometry* 44: 517–530.

Shortland, A.J. (2004), "Evaporites of the Wadi Natrun: seasonal and annual variation and its implication for ancient exploitation", *Archaeometry* 46: 497–516.

Shortland, A.J. (2005), "The raw materials of early glasses: the implications of new LA-ICPMS analyses", in Anonymous, ed., 1–5.

Shortland, A.J. (2007), "Who were the glassmakers? Status, theory and method in mid-second millennium glass production", *OJA* 26: 261–274.

Shortland, A.J. (2008), "Cuneiform glass texts: a question of meaning", in Martinon-Torres and Rehren, eds., 61–75.

Shortland, A.J. and Eremin, K. (2006), "The analysis of second millennium glass from Egypt and Mesopotamia, part 1: new WDS analyses", *Archaeometry* 48: 581–603.

Shortland, A.J., Rogers, N. and Eremin, K. (2007), "Trace element discriminants between Egyptian and Mesopotamian Late Bronze Age glasses", *JAS* 34: 781–789.

Shortland, A.J., Schachner, L., Freestone, I.C. and Tite, M.S. (2006), "Natron as a flux in the early vitreous materials industry: sources, beginnings and reasons for decline", *JAS* 33: 521–530.

Shortland, A.J. and Tite, M.S. (1998), "The interdependence of glass and vitreous faience production at Amarna", in McCray and Kingery, eds., 251–268.

Shortland, A.J. and Tite, M.S. (2000), "Raw materials of glass from Amarna and implications for the origins of Egyptian glass", *Archaeometry* 42: 141–151.

Shugar, A. and Rehren, T. (2002), "Formation and composition of glass as a function of firing temperature", in Anonymous (2002a), ed., 145–150.

Sidebotham, S.E. (1986), *Roman Economic Policy in the Erythra Thalassa 30 BC–AD 217*. Leiden.

Sidebotham, S.E. (1993), "University of Delaware Archaeological Project at 'Abu Sha'ar: the 1992 season", *Newsletter of the American Research Center in Egypt* 161–162: 1–9.

Sidebotham, S.E. (1994a), "Preliminary report on the 1990–1991 seasons of fieldwork at 'Abu Sha'ar (Red Sea Coast)", *JARCE* 31: 133–158.

Sidebotham, S.E. (1994b), "University of Delaware fieldwork in the Eastern Desert of Egypt, 1993", *DOP* 48: 263–275.

Sidebotham, S.E. (1997), "Caravans across the Eastern Desert of Egypt: recent discoveries on the Berenike-Apollinopolis Magna-Coptos roads", in Avanzini, ed., 385–393.

Sidebotham, S.E. (1999), "Survey of the hinterland", in Sidebotham and Wendrich, eds., 349–369.

Sidebotham, S.E. (2011), *Berenike and the Ancient Maritime Spice Route*. Berkeley.

Sidebotham, S.E., Hense, M. and Nouwens, H.M. (2008), *The Red Land: The Illustrated Archaeology of Egypt's Eastern Desert*. Cairo/New York.

Sidebotham, S.E., Riley, J.A., Hamroush, H.A. and Barakat, H. (1989), "Fieldwork on the Red Sea coast: the 1987 season", *JARCE* 26: 127–166.

Sidebotham, S.E. and Wendrich, W.Z., eds. (1999), *Berenike 1997: Report of the 1997 Excavations at Berenike and the Survey of the Egyptian Eastern Desert including Excavations at Shenshef*. Leiden.

Siegelová, J. (2005), "Metalle in hethitischen Texten", in Yalçin, ed., 35–40.

Siehr, K.G. (2006), "The beautiful one has come – to return: The return of the bust of Nefertiti from Berlin to Cairo", in Merryman, ed., 114–134.

Sieveking, G. de G., Longworth, I.H. and Wilson, K.E., ed. (1976), *Problems in Economic and Social Archaeology*. London.

Sievertsen, U. (2004), "Der späthethitische Kulturraum und die eisenzeitliche Keramik Zentralanatoliens", in Novák et al., eds.. 237–257.

Silberman, N.A. (1982), *Digging for God and Country: Exploration, Archaeology and the Secret Struggle for the Holy Land, 1799–1917*. New York.

Silberman, N.A. (1989), *Between Past and Present: Archaeology, Ideology, and Nationalism in the Modern Middle East*. New York.

Silberman, N.A. and Goren, Y. (2006), "Faking biblical history", in Vitelli and Colwell-Chanthaphonh, eds., 49–62.

Sillar, B. and Tite, M.S. (2000), "The challenge of 'technological choices' for materials science approaches to archaeology", *Archaeometry* 42: 2–20.

Sillen, A. and Lee-Thorp, J. (1991), "Dietary change in the Late Natufian", in Bar-Yosef and Valla, eds., 399–410.

Silva, R. (1985), "Mantai: a second Arikamedu?", *Antiquity* 59: 46–47.

Silver, M. (1983), "Karl Polanyi and markets in the Ancient Near East: the challenge of the evidence", *The Journal of Economic History* 53: 795–829.

Silver, V. (2006), "The role of museum trustees", *Bloomberg News* (February 25): 1–13.

Simmons, A. (1999), *Faunal Extinctions in an Island Society: Pygmy Hippopotamus Hunters of Cyprus*. New York.

Simmons, A. (2007), *The Neolithic Revolution in the Near East: Transforming the Human Landscape*. Tucson.

Simmons, A. (2008), "American researchers and the earliest Cypriots", *NEA* 71: 21–29.

Simmons, A. and Mandel, R. (2007), "Not such a new light: a response to Ammerman and Noller", *WA* 39: 475–482.

Simmons, A., Neely, J.A. and Reese, D.S. (1999), "Additional archaeological investigations on the Akrotiri Peninsula", in Simmons, 239–258.

Simonyan, A.E. (1984), "Dva Pogrebeniya Epokhi Sredney Bronzy Mogil'nika Verin Naver", *Sovetskaya Arkheologiya* 3: 122–135.

Simpson, E. (1996), "Phrygian furniture from Gordion", in Herrmann, ed., 187–209.

Simpson, E. (1997a), "Schliemann's 'treasures' from the Second City of Troy", in Simpson, ed., 191–193.

Simpson, E., ed. (1997b), *The Spoils of War*. New York.

Simpson, E. (2005), "Tall tales: Celts, connoisseurs, and the fabrication of archaeological context", *Source* 24/2: 28–41.

Simpson, E. (2010), *The Gordion Wooden Objects*. Vol. 1: *The Furniture from Tumulus MM*. Leiden.

Simpson, E. and Spirydowicz, K. (1999), *Gordion Ahşap Eserler/Gordion Wooden Furniture*. Ankara.

Simpson, St.J. (1996), "From Tekrit to the Jaghjagh: Sasanian sites, settlement patterns and material cultures in northern Mesopotamia", in Bartl and Hauser, eds., 87–126.

Simpson, St.J. (2000), "Mesopotamia in the Sasanian period: settlement patterns, arts and crafts", in Curtis, ed., 57–66.

Simpson, St.J. (2005), "Making their mark: foreign travellers at Persepolis", *ARTA* 2005.001.

Simpson, W.K. (1960), "Papyrus Lythgoe: a fragment of a literary text of the Middle Kingdom from El-Lisht", *JEA* 46: 65–70.

Singer, C., ed. (1956), *A History of Technology*, vol. 2. Oxford.
Singer, I. (1984), "The AGRIG in the Hittite Texts", *AnSt* 34: 97–127.
Singer, I. (1998), "A city of many temples: Hattuša, capital of the Hittites", in Kedar and Werblowsky, eds., 32–44.
Singer, I. (2000), "New evidence on the end of the Hittite Empire", in Oren, ed., 21–33.
Singh, P. (1974), *Neolithic Cultures of Western Asia*. London/New York.
Sinopoli, C.M. (1988), "The organization of craft production at Vijayanagara, South India", *AA* 90: 580–597.
Sinopoli, C.M. (1994), "The archaeology of empires", *ARA* 23: 159–181.
Sinopoli, C.M. (1999), "Levels of complexity: ceramic variability at Vijayanagra", in Skibo and Feinman, eds., 115–136.
Sinopoli, C.M. (2001a), "Imperial integration and imperial subjects", in Alcock et al., eds., 195–200.
Sinopoli, C.M. (2001b), "Empires", in Feinman and Price, eds., 439–471.
Sivan, H. (2008), *Palestine in Late Antiquity*. Oxford.
Sivas, H. and Tüfekçi Sivas, T., eds. (2007), *Friglerin Gizemli Uygarliği/The Mysterious Civilization of the Phrygians*. Istanbul.
Skjærvø, P.O. (n.d.), "Weaving a world of thought: the myth of the *fravashis* and Old Iranian ritual".
Sjöberg, A.W. (1975), "The Old Babylonian edubba," in Lieberman, ed., 159–179.
Skibo, J.M. and Feinman, G.M., eds. (1999), *Pottery and People: A Dynamic Interaction*. Salt Lake City.
Slanski, K.E. (2003), *The Babylonian Entitlement Narûs (Kudurrus): A Study in their Form and Function*. Boston.
Smedley, J.W. and Jackson, C.M. (2006), "Medieval and post-medieval glass technology: bracken as a sustainable resource for glassmaking", *Glass Technology* 47: 39–47.
Smedley, J.W., Jackson, C.M. and Booth, C.A. (1998), "Back to the roots: the raw materials, glass recipes and glassmaking practices of Theophilus", in McCray and Kingery, eds., 145–165.
Smirnov, V.I. (1989), "Ore deposits in the European part of the USSR", in Dunning et al., eds., 279–407.
Smith, A.T. (2001), "The limitations of doxa: agency and subjectivity from an archaeological point of view", *Journal of Social Archaeology* 1/2: 155–171.
Smith, A.T. (2003), *The Political Landscape: Constellations of Authority in Early Complex Polities*. Berkeley.
Smith, A.T. (2006), "Prometheus unbound: southern Caucasia in prehistory", *JWP* 19/4: 229–279.
Smith, A.T., Badalyan, R.S. and Avetisyan, P. (2009), *The Archaeology and Geography of Ancient Transcaucasian Societies I: The Foundations of Research and Regional Survey in the Tsaghkahovit Plain, Armenia*. Chicago.
Smith, A.T. and Rubinson, K., eds. (2003), *Archaeology in the Borderlands: Investigations in Caucasia and Beyond*. Los Angeles.
Smith, C. (2007), "Visa stories: Human rights, structural violence and ethical globalisation", *Archaeologies* 3/2: 179–185.
Smith, C.S. (1969), "Analysis of the copper bead from Ali Kosh", in Hole et al., eds., 427–428.

Smith, C.S. (1971), "The techniques of the Luristan smith", in Brill, ed., 32–54.

Smith, C.S. (1965), "An examination of the arsenic-rich coating on a bronze bull from Horoztepe", in Young, ed., 96–102.

Smith, C.S. (1981), *A Search for Structure: Selected Essays on Science, Art, and History*. Cambridge.

Smith, H. and Jones, G. (1990), "Experiments on the effects of charring on cultivated grapes", *JAS* 17: 317–327.

Smith, J., Risk, M., Schwarcz, H.P. and McConnaughey, T.A. (1997), "Rapid climate change in the North Atlantic during the Younger Dryas recorded by deep-sea corals", *Nature* 386: 818–820.

Smith, M.E. (1992), "Braudel's temporal rhythms and chronology theory in archaeology", in Knapp, ed., 23–34.

Smith, M.E. (2001), "The Aztec empire and the Mesoamerican world system", in Alcock et al., eds., 128–154.

Smith, M.L., ed. (2003), *The Social Construction of Ancient Cities*. Washington/London.

Smith, M.L. (2005), "Networks, territories, and the cartography of ancient states", *Annals of the Association of American Geographers* 95: 832–839.

Smith, P. (1991), "The dental evidence for nutritional status in the Natufians", in Bar-Yosef and Valla, eds., 425–432.

Smith, P.E.L. (1968), "Prehistoric excavations at Ganj Dareh Tepe in 1967", in Anonymous, ed., 183–191.

Smith, P.E.L. (1970), "Ganj Dareh Tepe", *Iran* 8: 174–176.

Smith, P.E.L. (1972), "Survey of excavations in Iran during 1970–1971: Ganj Dareh Tepe", *Iran* 10: 165–168.

Smith, P.E.L. (1975), "Survey of excavations in Iran during 1974", *Iran* 13: 1–6.

Smith, P.E.L. (1990), "Architectural Innovation and Experimentation at Ganj Dareh, Iran", *WA* 21: 323–335.

Smith, P.E.L. and Crépeau, R. (1983), "Fabrication expérimentale de répliques d'un vase néolithique du site de Ganj Dareh, Iran: recherche technologique", *Paléorient* 9/2: 55–62.

Smith, R.H., Maddin, R., Muhly, J.D. and Stech, T. (1984), "Bronze Age steel from Pella", *CA* 25: 234–236.

Smith, R.W. (1963), "Archaeological evaluation of analyses of ancient glass", in Matson and Rindone, eds., 283–290.

Smith, S. (1949), *The Statue of Idri-mi*. London.

Snead, J.E., Erickson, C. and Darling, W.A., eds. (2009), *Landscapes of Movement: Paths, Trails, and Roads in Anthropological Perspective*. Philadelphia.

Snell, D.C., ed. (2007), *A Companion to the Ancient Near East*. Oxford.

Snyder, G.F. (2003), *Ante Pacem: Archaeological Evidence of Church Life Before Constantine*, 2nd edn. Macon.

Snyder, J.A., Wasylik, K., Fritz, S.C. and Wright, H.E., Jr. (2001), "Diatom-based conductivity reconstruction and palaeoclimatic interpretation of a 40-ka record from Lake Zeribar, Iran", *The Holocene* 11/6: 737–745.

Sodini, J.-P., Tate, G., Bavant, B., Bavant, S., Biscop, J.-L. and Orssaud, D. (1980), "Déhès (Syrie du Nord), Campagnes I–III (1976–1978)", *Syria* 57: 1–304.

Sokal, M.P. (2006), "The US legal response to the protection of the World Cultural Heritage", in Brodie et al., eds., 36–67.

Sokolov, L.I. and Tsepkin, E.A. (1996), "Sturgeons from the Azov-Black Seas and Caspian Basins: a historical review", *Journal of Ichthyology* 36: 11–23.
Solecki, R.S. (1969), "A copper mineral pendant from northern Iraq", *Antiquity* 43: 311–314.
Solecki, R.S. and Solecki, R.L. (1987–8), "Archaeological researches at Yabroud, Syria and vicinity, summer 1987", *AAAS* 38–39: 9–49.
Solecki, R.S., Solecki, R.L. and Agelarakis, A.P. (2004), *The Proto-Neolithic Cemetery in Shanidar Cave*. College Station.
Solin, H. and Kajava, M., eds. (1990), *Roman Eastern Policy and Other Studies in Roman History*. Helsinki.
Sommerfeld, W. (1995), "The Kassites of ancient Mesopotamia: origins, politics, and culture", in Sasson, ed., 917–930.
Sommerfeld, W. (2005), "Die Vernichtung der Vergangenheit. Raubgrabungen im Irak", *Spektrum der Wissenschaft* (March): 70–75.
Sonnabend, H. (1986), *Fremdenbild und Politik. Vorstellungen der Römer von Ägypten und dem Partherreich in der späten Republik und frühen Kaiserzeit*. Frankfurt.
Sonzogni, V., ed. (2009), *Giordania. Terrasanta di meditazione. Progetto del parco del battesimo*. Bergamo.
Southworth, F.C. (1971), "Detecting prior creolization: an analysis of the historical origins of Marathi", in Hymes, ed., 255–273.
Soutzo, M.-C., Pézard, G., Bondoux, G., de Mecquenem, R., Pézard, M., Gautier, J.-E. and Toscanne, P. (1911), *Recherches archéologiques, quatrième série*. Paris [= MDP 12].
Sowada, K. (2009), *Egypt in the Eastern Mediterranean During the Old Kingdom: An Archaeological Perspective*. Göttingen.
Spalinger, A.J. (1978), "The date of Gyges and its historical implications", *JAOS* 98: 400–409.
Spalinger, A.J. (2005), *War in Ancient Egypt: The New Kingdom*. Oxford/Malden.
Spar, I. (2008), "The Amarna letters", in Aruz et al., eds., 168–169.
Sperber, D. (1968), "Some observations of fish and fisheries in Roman Palestine", *ZDMG* 118: 265–269.
Sperveslage, G. (in press a), "Ägypten und Arabien", in Eichmann and Hausleiter, eds.
Sperveslage, G. (in press b), "Ägyptische und ägyptisierende Objekte aus Tayma", in Eichmann and Hausleiter, eds.
Spoor, R. (1997), "Human population groups and the distribution of lithic arrowheads in Arabian Gulf", *AAE* 8: 143–160.
Spriggs, M., ed. (1984), *Marxist Perspectives in Archaeology*. Cambridge.
Spurrell, F.C.J. (1898), "Analysis of flint implements", in Bliss, 190–195.
Stager, L.E. (1985), "The first fruits of civilization", in Tubb, ed., 172–188.
Stammers, M. (2009), *The Elite Late Period Egyptian Tombs of Memphis*. Oxford.
Stampfli, H.R. (1983), "The fauna of Jarmo with notes on animals bones from Matarrah, the 'Amuq, and Karim Shahir", in Braidwood et al., eds., 431–483.
Stanish, C. (2008), "Forging ahead", *Archaeology* (May/June): 18, 58–66.
Stapleton, C.P. and Swanson, S.E. (2002a), "Chemical analysis of glass artifacts from Iron Age levels at Hasanlu, Northwestern Iran", *Journal of Glass Technology* 43C: 151–157.
Stapleton, C., P. and Swanson, S.E. (2002b), "Batch material processing and glassmaking technology of 9th century BC artifacts excavated from the site of Hasanlu, Northwest Iran", in Vandiver et al., eds., 315–321.

Starkey, J., ed. (2005), *People of the Red Sea: Proceedings of Red Sea Project II*. Oxford.
Starkey, J., Starkey, P. and Wilkinson, T., eds. (2007), *Natural Resources and Cultural Connections of the Red Sea*. Oxford.
Starkovich, B.M. and Stiner, M.C. (2009), "Hallan Çemi Tepesi: high-ranked game exploitation alongisde intensive seed processing at the Epipaleolithic-Neolithic transition in southeastern Turkey", *Anthropozoologica* 44: 41–62.
Starr, R.F.S. (1938), *Nuzi; Report on the Excavation at Yorgan Tepa near Kirkuk, Iraq, Conducted by Harvard University in Conjunction with the American Schools of Oriental Research and the University Museum of Philadelphia, 1927–1931*. Cambridge.
Starzmann, M.T. (2008), "Cultural imperialism and heritage politics in the event of armed conflict: prospects for an 'activist archaeology'", *Archaeologies* 4/3: 368–389.
Staubwasser, M., Sirocko, F., Grootes, P.M. and Segl, M. (2003), "Climate change at the 4.2 ka BP termination of the Indus valley civilization and Holocene South Asian monsoon variability", *Geophysical Research Letters* 30/8: 1425–1428.
Staubwasser, M. and Weiss, H., eds. (2006), "Holocene climate and cultural evolution in later prehistoric–early historic West Asia", *QR* 66/3: 371–504.
St Clair, W. (1998), *Lord Elgin and the Marbles*. Oxford.
Steadman, S. and McMahon, G. (2011), *The Oxford Handbook of Ancient Anatolia*. Oxford.
Stech-Wheeler, T., Muhly, J.D. and Maxwell-Hyslop, K.R. (1981), "Iron at Taanach and early iron metallurgy in the eastern Mediterranean", *AJA* 85/3: 245–268.
Stech, T. (1999), "Aspects of early metallurgy in Mesopotamia and Anatolia", in Pigott, ed., 59–71.
Stech, T. and Pigott, V.C. (1986), "The metals trade in Southwest Asia in the third millennium BC", *Iraq* 48: 39–64.
Steele, C.S. (1990), "Early Bronze Age socio-political organization in southwestern Jordan", *ZDPV* 106: 1–33.
Steele, D. (2002), "Faunal remains", in Clarke et al., 125–145.
Steensberg, A. (1943), *Ancient Harvesting Implements*. Copenhagen.
Steensberg, A. (1986), *Man the Manipulator*. Copenhagen.
Stein, G.J. (1989), "Strategies of risk reduction in herding and hunting systems of Neolithic southeast Anatolia", in Crabtree et al., eds., 87–97.
Stein, G.J. (1994), "Economy, ritual and power", in Stein and Rothman, eds., 35–46.
Stein, G.J. (1999), *Rethinking World-Systems: Diaspora, Colonies, and Interaction in Uruk Mesopotamia*. Tucson.
Stein, G.J. (2001), "Indigenous social complexity at Haçinebi (Turkey) and the organization of Uruk colonial contact", in Rothman, ed., 265–306.
Stein, G.J. (2009), "Tell Zeidan", *Oriental Institute Annual Report*: 126–37.
Stein, G.J. (2010), "Local identities and interaction spheres", in Carter and Philip, eds., 23–44.
Stein, G.J., Boden, K., Edens, C., Pearce, J., Keith, K., McMahon, A. and Özbal, H. (1997), "Excavations at Haçinebi, Turkey – 1996", *Anatolica* 23: 111–171.
Stein, G.J. and Özbal, R. (2007), "A tale of two oikumenai: variation in the expansionary dynamics of 'Ubaid and Uruk Mesopotamia", in Stone, ed., 356–370.
Stein, G.J. and Rothman, M.S., eds. (1994), *Chiefdoms and Early States in the Near East*. Madison.

Stein, G.J. and Wattenmaker, P. (1990), "The 1987 Tell Leilan Regional Survey: preliminary report", in Miller, ed., 8–18.
Stein, M.A. (1916), "A third journey of exploration in Central Asia, 1913–16", GJ 48: 193–225.
Stein, M.A. (1928), "Alexander's campaign on the North-West Frontier", The Indian Antiquary 58: 15–7.
Stein, M.A. (1929), On Alexander's track to the Indus: Personal Narrative of Explorations on the North-west Frontier of India Carried Out Under the Orders of H.M. Indian Government. London.
Stein, M.A. (1934), "Archaeological reconnaissances in southern Persia", GJ 83: 119–134.
Stein, M.A. (1936), "An archaeological tour in the ancient Persis", Iraq 3: 111–225.
Stein, M.A. (1937), Archaeological Reconnaissances in North-Western India and South-Eastern Iran. London.
Stein, M.A. (1940), Old Routes of Western Īrān. London.
Stein, M.A. (1943), "On Alexander's route into Gedrosia: an archaeological tour in Las Bela", GJ 102/5–6: 193–227.
Stein, P. (in press), "Die reichsaramäischen Inschriften der Kampagnen 2005–2009 aus Taymā", in Eichmann and Hausleiter, eds.
Stein, R.L. (2008), Itineraries in Conflict: Israelis, Palestinians and the Political Lives of Tourism. Durham.
Steiner, M.L. and Killebrew, A.E., eds. (in press), The Oxford Handbook of the Archaeology of the Levant (ca.8000–332 BCE). Oxford.
Steinkeller, P. (1980), "Mattresses and felt in early Mesopotamia", Oriens Antiquus 19: 79–100.
Steinkeller, P. (1988), "On the identity of the toponym LÚ.SU(.A)", JAOS 108: 197–202.
Steinkeller, P. (1993), "Early political development in Mesopotamia and the origins of the Sargonic empire", in Liverani, ed., 107–129.
Steinkeller, P. (1995), "Sheep and goat terminology in Ur III sources from Drehem", BSA 8: 49–56.
Steinkeller, P. (1998), "The historical background of Urkesh and the Hurrian beginnings in Northern Mesopotamia", in Buccellati and Buccellati, eds., 75–98.
Steinkeller, P. (2001), "New light on the hydrology and topography of Southern Babylonia in the third millennium", ZA 91: 22–84.
Steinkeller, P. (2003), "An Ur III manuscript of the Sumerian King List", in Sallaberger et al., eds., 267–292.
Steinkeller, P. (2004), "Toward a definition of private economic activity in third millennium Babylonia", in Rollinger and Ulf, eds., 91–111.
Steinkeller, P. (2007), "City and countryside in third-millennium southern Babylonia", in Stone, ed., 185–211.
Stekelis, M. (1972), The Yarmukian Culture of the Neolithic Period. Jerusalem.
Stellmacher, T. (1991), Lower-Habur. Archaeological Settlement Map 10000 BC–1350 AD. Berlin.
Stern, E. (1990), "The Dor province in the Persian period in the light of the recent excavations at Dor", Transeuphratène 2: 147–155.

Stern, E., ed. (1994), *The New Encyclopedia of Archaeological Excavations in the Holy Land*. New York.

Stern, E. (2001), *Archaeology of the Land of the Bible, vol. II. The Assyrian, Babylonian, and Persian Periods, 732–332 BCE*. New Haven and London.

Stern, M.E. and Schlick-Nolte, B. (1994), *Early Glass of the Ancient World 1600 BC – AD 50*. Ostfildern.

Steve, M.-J. (1986), "La fin de l'Élam: à propos d'une empreinte de sceau-cylindre", *StIr* 15: 7–21.

Steve, M.-J. (1987), *Ville Royale de Suse 7, Nouveaux Mélanges Épigraphiques, Inscriptions Royales de Suse et de la Susiane*. Nice [= MDP 53].

Steve, M.-J. (2003), *L'Île de Kharg: Une Page de l'histoire du Golfe persique et du monachisme oriental*. Neuchâtel.

Steve, M.-J., and Gasche, H. (1971), *l'Acropole de Suse*. Paris and Leiden [= MDP 46].

Steve, M.-J., and Gasche, H. (1990), "Le tell de l'Apadana avant les Achéménides: contribution à la topographie de Suse", in Vallat, ed., 15–60.

Steve, M.-J., Vallat, F., Gasche, H. and Jullien, F. (2002/3), "Suse", *SDB* 73: 360–512 (bibliog. in *SDB* 74: 620–52).

Stevens, L.R., Ito, E., Schwalb, A. and Wright, H.E., Jr. (2006), "Timing of atmospheric precipitation in the Zagros Mountains inferred from a multi-proxy record from Lake Mirabad, Iran", *QR* 66: 494–500.

Stevenson, D.W.W. (1992), "A proposal for the irrigation of the Hanging Gardens of Babylon", *Iraq* 54: 35–55.

Stewart, S.T. and Rupp, D.W. (2004), "Tools and toys or traces of trade: the problem of the enigmatic incised objects from Cyprus and the Levant", in Peltenberg and Wasse, eds., 163–174.

Stiehl, R. and H.E., eds. (1970), *Beiträge zur Alten Geschichte und deren Nachleben: Festschrift für Franz Altheim zum 6.10.1968*, vol. 2. Berlin.

Stiner, M. and Munro, N. (2002), "Approaches to prehistoric diet breadth, demography, and prey ranking systems in time and space", *JAMT* 9: 175–208.

Stocking, G.W., Jr. (1985), *Objects and Others: Essays on Museums and Material Culture*. Madison.

Stol, M. (1976–80), "Kanal(isation): A. Philologisch", *RlA* 5: 355–365.

Stol, M. (1988), "Old Babylonian fields", *BSA* 4: 173–188.

Stöllner, T. (2004), "Prehistoric and ancient ore-mining in Iran", in Stöllner et al., eds., 44–63.

Stöllner, T. (2005), "Early mining and metallurgy on the Iranian Plateau", in Yalçin, ed., 191–208.

Stöllner, T., Korlin, G., Steffens, G. and Cierny, J., eds. (2003), *Man and Mining – Mensch und Bergbau*. Bochum.

Stöllner, T., Slotta, R. and Vatandoust, A., eds. (2004), *Persiens antike Pracht*. Bochum.

Stolper, M. (1985), *Entrepreneurs and Empire: The Murašû Archive, the Murašû Firm and Persian Rule in Babylonia*. Leiden.

Stolper, M.W. (1992), "The Murašû texts from Susa", *RA* 86: 69–77.

Stolper, M.W. (2001), "Ganzabara", *EnIr* 10: 286–289.

Stolper, M.W. (2004), "Hidali", *EnIr* 12: 308–309.

Stolper, M.W. and André-Salvini, B. (1992), "Cuneiform texts from Susa", in Harper et al., eds., 253–278.

Stolze, F. and Andreas, F.C. (1882), *Die achaemenidischen und sasanidischen Denkmäler und Inschriften von Persepolis, Istakhr, Pasargadae, Shâhpúr*, 2 vols. Berlin.
Stone, E.C. (1981), "Texts, architecture and ethnographic analogy: patterns of residence in Old Babylonian Nippur", *Iraq* 43: 19–33.
Stone, E.C. (1987), *Nippur Neighborhoods*. Chicago.
Stone, E.C. (1997), "City-states and their centers: the Mesopotamian example", in Nichols and Charlton, eds., 15–26.
Stone, E.C. (1999), "The constraints on state and urban form in Ancient Mesopotamia", in Hudson and Levine, eds., 203–228.
Stone, E.C. (2003), "Remote sensing and the location of the ancient Tigris", in Forte and Williams, eds., 157–162.
Stone, E.C. (2007a), "The Mesopotamian urban experience", in Stone, ed., 213–234.
Stone, E.C., ed. (2007b), *Settlement and Society: Essays Dedicated to Robert McCormick Adams*. Los Angeles.
Stone, E.C. (2008), "Patterns of looting in southern Iraq", *Antiquity* 82: 125–138.
Stone, E.C. and Zimansky, P.E. (1999), *The Iron Age Settlement at 'Ain Dara, Syria. Survey and soundings*. Oxford.
Stone, E.C. and Zimansky, P. (2004), *The Anatomy of a Mesopotamian city: Survey and Soundings at Mashkan-shapir*. Winona Lake.
Stone, M.E. (1982a), *The Armenian Inscriptions from the Sinai. With Appendices on the Georgian and Latin Inscriptions by Michel van Esbroeck and William Adler*. Cambridge.
Stone, M.E. (1982b), "Sinai Armenian inscriptions", *Biblical Archaeology* 45: 27–31.
Stone, P.G. and Bajjaly, J.F, eds. (2008), *The Destruction of Cultural Heritage in Iraq*. Woodbridge.
Stordeur, D., ed. (1987), *La Main et l'outil. Manches et emmanchements préhistoriques*. Lyon.
Stordeur, D. (1998), "Jerf el Ahmar et l'horizon P.P.N.A en Haute Mésopotamie: Xe–IXe millénaire avant J.C.", in Lebeau, ed., 13–27.
Stordeur, D. (1999), "Organisation de l'espace construit et organisation sociale dans la Néolithique de Jerf el Ahmar (Syrie) (Syrie, Xe-IXe millénaires av. JC)", in Braemer et al., eds., 131–149.
Stordeur, D. (2000), "New discoveries in architecture and symbolism at Jerf el Ahmar (Syria), 1997–1999", *Neo-Lithics* 1: 1–4.
Stordeur, D., (2003), "Tell Aswad. Résultats préliminaires des campagnes 2001 et 2002", *Neo-Lithics* 1/03: 7–15.
Stordeur, D., Brenet, M., Der Aprahmian, G. and Roux, J.-Cl. (2000), "Les bâtiments communautaires de Jerf el Ahmar et Mureybet. Horizon PPNA. Syrie", *Palèorient* 26: 29–44.
Stordeur, D. and Khawam, R. (2008), "Une place pour les morts dans les maisons de Tell Aswad (Syrie) (Horizon PPNB ancien et PPNB moyen)", in Córdoba et al., eds., 561–589.
Stordeur, D. and Willcox, G. (2009), "Indices de culture et d'utilisation des céréales à Jerf el Ahmar", in Anonymous (2009b), ed., 693–710.
Stos-Gale, Z.A. (1992), "The origin of metal objects from the Early Bronze Age site of Thermi on the island of Lesbos", *OJA* 11/2: 155–177.
Stos-Gale, Z.A., Gale, N.H. and Gilmore, G.R. (1984), "Early Bronze Age Trojan metal sources and Anatolians in the Cyclades", *OJA* 3/3: 23–37.

Strasser, T.F. (1996), "The boat models from Eridu: sailing or spinning during the 'Ubaid Period?", *Antiquity* 70: 920–925.
Strasser, T.F., Panagopoulou, E., Runnels, C.N., Murray, P.M., Thompson, N., Karkanas, P., McCoy, F.W. and Wegmann, K.W. (2010), "Stone Age seafaring in the Mediterranean: evidence from the Plakias region for Lower Palaeolithic and Mesolithic habitation of Crete", *Hesperia* 79: 145–190.
Strauch, I. and Bukharin, M.D. (2004), "Indian Inscriptions from the Cave Hoq on Suquṭrā (Yemen)", *AIUON* 64: 121–138.
Strawn, B.A. (2005), *What Is Stronger than a Lion? Leonine Image and Metaphor in the Hebrew Bible and the Ancient Near East*. Fribourg.
Streck, M. (1916), *Assurbanipal und die letzten assyrischen Könige bis zum Untergange Nineveh's*. Leipzig.
Streck, M. (1917), *Seleucia und Ktesiphon*. Leipzig.
Streily, A.H. (2000), "Early pottery kilns in the Middle East", *Paléorient* 26: 69–82.
Stride, S., Rondelli, B. and Mantellini, S. (2009), "Canals versus horses: political power in the oasis of Samarkand", *WA* 41: 73–87.
Strommenger, E. (1964), *The Art of Mesopotamia*. London.
Strommenger, E. (1980), *Habuba Kabira: Eine Stadt vor 5000 Jahren*. Mainz.
Strommenger, E. (1986), "Early metal figures from Assur and the technology of metal casting", *Sumer* 42: 114–115.
Strommenger, E. (1994), "Die Ausgrabungen in Tall Bi'a 1993", *MDOG* 126: 11–31.
Stronach, D. (1961), "The excavations at Ras al 'Amiya", *Iraq* 23: 95–137.
Stronach, D. (1963), "Excavations at Pasargadae: first preliminary report", *Iran* 1: 19–42.
Stronach, D. (1964), "Excavations at Pasargadae: second preliminary report", *Iran* 2: 21–39.
Stronach, D. (1965), "Excavations at Pasargadae: third preliminary report", *Iran* 3: 9–40.
Stronach, D. (1967), "Urartian and Achaemenid tower temples", *JNES* 26: 278–288.
Stronach, D. (1971), "A circular symbol on the tomb of Cyrus", *Iran* 9: 155–158.
Stronach, D. (1974a), "La statue de Darius le Grand découverte à Suse", *DAFI* 4: 61–72.
Stronach, D. (1974b), "Achaemenid Village I at Susa and the Persian migration to Fars", *Iraq* 36: 239–248.
Stronach, D. (1978), *Pasargadae: A Report on the Excavations Conducted by the British Institute of Persian Studies from 1961 to 1963*. Oxford.
Stronach, D. (1985a), "Pasargadae", in Gershevitch, ed., 838–855.
Stronach, D. (1985b), "On the evolution of the early Iranian fire temple", in Bailey et al., eds., vol. 2, 605–627.
Stronach, D. (1987a), "Apadāna, ii. Building", *EnIr* 2: 146–148.
Stronach, D. (1987b), "Archeology, ii. Median and Achaemenid", *EnIr* 2: 288–296.
Stronach, D. (1989), "The royal garden at Pasargadae: evolution and legacy", in De Meyer and Haerinck, eds., 475–502.
Stronach, D. (1990), "The garden as a political statement: some case studies from the Near East in the first millennium BC", *BAI* 4: 171–180.

Stronach, D. (1994), "Parterres and stone watercourses at Pasargadae: notes on the Achaemenid contribution to garden design", *Journal of Garden History* 14: 3–12.
Stronach, D. (1997a), "Anshan and Persia: early Achaemenid history, art and architecture on the Iranian Plateau", in Curtis, ed., 35–53.
Stronach, D. (1997b), "Darius at Pasargadae: a neglected source for the history of Achaemenid Persia", in Boussac, ed., 351–363.
Stronach, D. (2000), "Of Cyrus, Darius and Alexander: a new look at the 'epigraphs' of Cyrus the Great", in Dittmann et al., eds., 681–702.
Stronach, D. (2005), "Ernst Herzfeld and Pasargadae", in Gunter and Hauser, eds., 103–135.
Stronach, D. and Gopnik, H. (2009), "Pasargadae", *EnIr* online.
Stronach, D. and Mousavi, A., eds. (2009), *Irans Erbe*. Mainz.
Stronach, D. and Roaf, M. (2007), *Nush-i Jan, vol. 1. The Major Buildings of the Median Settlement*. Leuven/Paris/Dudley.
Strube, C. (1973), *Die westliche Eingangsseite der Kirchen von Konstantinopel in justinianischer Zeit*. Weisbaden.
Struble, E.J. and Herrmann, V.R. (2009), "An eternal feast at Sam'al: the new Iron Age mortuary stele from Zincirli in context", *BASOR* 356: 15–49.
Strzygowski, J., Millet, G. and Sénéchal, C. (1936), *L'Ancien Art Chrétien de Syrie, son caractère et son évolution d'après les découvertes de Vogüé et de l'expédition de Princeton. La façade de Mschatta et le calice d'Antioche*. Paris.
Studer, J. (1994), "Roman fish sauce in Petra, Jordan", in Van Neer, ed., 191–196.
Stummer, A. (1911), "Zum Urgeschichte der Rebe und des Weinbaus", *Mitteilungen der Anthropologischen Gesellschaft in Wien* 41: 283–296.
Sudo, H. (2010), "The development of wool exploitation in Ubaid-period settlements of northern Mesopotamia", in Carter and Philip, eds., 169–179.
Süel, A. (2002), "Ortaköy-Shapinuwa", in Yener and Hoffner, eds., 157–165.
Summerer, L. and von Kienlin, A. (2010), "Achaemenid impact in Paphlagonia: rupestral tombs in the Amnias Valley", in Nieling and Rehm, eds., 195–221.
Summers, G.D. (2006), "Aspects of material culture at the Iron Age capital on the Kerkenes Dağ", *ANES* 43: 164–202.
Summers, G.D. (2007), "Public spaces and large halls at Kerkenes", in Çilingiroğlu and Sagona, eds., 245–263.
Summers, G.D. (2008), "Periodization and terminology in the Central Anatolian Iron Age: archaeology, history and audiences", *ANES* 45: 202–217.
Sumner, W.M. (1972), *Cultural Development in the Kur River Basin, Iran: An Archaeological Analysis of Settlement Patterns*. Philadelphia.
Sumner, W.M. (1977), "Early settlements in Fars Province", in Levine and Young, eds., 291–305.
Sumner, W.M. (1985), "The Proto-Elamite city wall at Tal-e Malyan", *Iran* 23: 153–161.
Sumner, W.M. (1986a), "Proto-Elamite civilization in Fars", in Finkbeiner and Röllig, eds., 199–211.
Sumner, W.M. (1986b), "Achaemenid settlement in the Persepolis Plain", *AJA* 90: 3–31.
Sumner, W.M. (1988), "Maljan, Tall-e (Anšan)", *RlA* 7: 306–320.

Sumner, W.M. (1989), "Anshan in the Kaftari phase: patterns of settlement and land use", in De Meyer and Haerinck, eds., 135–161.

Sumner, W.M. (1990a), "An archaeological estimate of population trends since 6000 BC in the Kur River Basin, Fars Province, Iran", in Taddei, ed., 3–16.

Sumner, W.M. (1990b), "Full-coverage regional archaeological survey in the Near East: An example from Iran", in Fish and Kowalewski, eds., 87–115.

Sumner, W.M. (1994), "Archaeological measures of cultural continuity and the arrival of the Persians in Fars", Sancisi-Weerdenburg et al., eds., 97–105.

Sumner, W.M. (1997), "Malyan", in Meyers, ed., 406–409.

Sumner, W.M. (2003), *Early Urban Life in the Land of Anshan: Excavations at Tal-e Malyan in the Highlands of Iran*. Philadelphia.

Sürenhagen, D. (2002), "Death in Mesopotamia: the 'Royal Tombs' of Ur revisited", in al-Gailani Werr et al., eds., 324–338.

Suter, C.E. (2000), *Gudea's Temple Building: The Representation of an Early Mesopotamian Ruler in Text and Image*. Groningen.

Suter, C.E. and Uehlinger, C., eds. (2005), *Crafts and Images in Contact: Studies on Eastern Mediterranean Art of the First Millennium BCE*. Fribourg.

Swann, C.P., McGovern, P.E. and Fleming, S.J. (1989), "Colorants in glasses from ancient Syro-Palestine: specialized studies using PIXE spectrometry", *Nuclear Instruments and Methods in Physics Research* B40/41: 615–619.

Swift, G.S. (1958), *The Pottery of the Amuq Phases K to O, and its Historical Relationships*. Chicago.

Sylwan, V. (1941), "A survey of woolen textiles from the Sir Aurel Stein Collections", *AA* 38: 414–432.

Symington, D.S. (1996), "Hittite and Neo-Hittite furniture", in Herrmann, ed., 111–138.

Szarzynska, K. (2002), *Sheep Husbandry and Production of Wool, Garments and Cloths in Archaic Sumer*. Warsaw.

Taddei, M., ed. (1979), *South Asian Archaeology 1977*. Naples.

Taddei, M., ed. (1990), *South Asian Archaeology 1987*. Naples.

Taddei, M. and de Marco, G., eds. (2000), *South Asian Archaeology 1997*. Rome.

Tadjvidi, A. (1970), "Persepolis", *Iran* 8: 186–187.

Tadjvidi, A. (1973), "Persepolis", *Iran* 11: 200–201.

Tadjvidi, A. (1976), *Dānestanīhā-ye novīn darbāreh-ye honar va bāstānšenāsi-ye aṣr-e hakhāmaneši bar bonyād-e kāvoshā-ye panǧ sāleh-ye Takht-e Ǵamšīd* [New Knowledge about Achaemenid Art and Archaeology Based on Five Years of Excavations at Persepolis]. Tehran.

Tadmor, H. (1997), "Propaganda, literature, historiography: cracking the code of the Assyrian royal inscriptions", in Parpola and Whiting, eds., 325–338.

Tadmor, M., Kedem, D., Begemann, F., Hauptmann, A., Pernicka, E. and Schmitt-Strecker, S. (1995), "The Nahal Mishmar hoard from the Judean Desert: technology, composition, and provenance", *'Atiqot* 27: 95–148.

Taft, R.F. (1968), "Some notes on the Bema in the East and West Syrian traditions", *OCP* 34: 326–59.

Tal, O. (2000), "Some notes on the settlement patterns of the Persian period southern Sharon Plain in light of recent excavations at Apollonia-Arsuf", *Transeuphratène* 19: 115–125.

Tal, O. (2005), "Some remarks on the coastal plain of Palestine under Achaemenid rule: An archaeological synopsis", in Briant and Boucharlat, eds., 71–96.

Talbot-Rice, D. (1932a), "The Oxford Excavations at Ḥīra", *Ars Islamica* 1: 51–73.

Talbot-Rice, D. (1932b), "The Oxford Excavations at Ḥīra", *Journal of the Royal Central Asian Society 1932*: 254–68.

Talbot-Rice, D. (1932c), "The Oxford Excavations at Hira, 1931", *Antiquity* 6: 276–291.

Talbot Rice, D. (1956), "Excavations by the Walker Trust (St. Andrews) on the site of the Great Palace, Costantinople: Preliminary report on the work done in 1952 and 1953", *Türk Arkeoloji Dergisi* 6: 11–16.

Talebian, M.H. (2010), "A review of research and restoration activities at Parsa-Pasargadae: Analysis, evaluation and future perspectives", in Curtis and Simpson, eds., 299–307.

Talgam, R. (2000), "Similarities and differences between synagogue and church mosaics in Palestine during the Byzantine and Umayyad periods", in Levine and Weiss, eds., 93–110.

Tallgren, Å.M. (1933), "Dolmens of North Caucasia", *Antiquity* 7/26: 190–202.

Tallon, F. (1987), *Métallurgie Susienne I: De la fondation de Suse au XVIIIe avant J.-C.*, 2 vols. Paris.

Tallon, F. (1992), "The Achaemenid tomb on the Acropole", in Harper et al., eds., 242–252.

Talon, P. (1986), "Le coton et la soie en Mesopotamie?", *Akkadica* 47: 75–78.

Tanimoto, S. and Rehren, T. (2008), "Interactions between silicate and salt melts in LBA glassmaking", *JAS* 35: 2566–2573.

Tanno, K. and Willcox, G. (2006), "How fast was wild wheat domesticated?", *Science* 311: 1886.

Tarhan, M.T. (1983), "The structure of the Urartian state", *Anadolu Araştırmaları/ Jahrbuch für kleinasiatische Forschungen* 9: 295–310.

Tarhan, M.T. and Sevin, V. (1975), "The relation between Urartian temple gates and monumental rock niches", *Belleten* 39: 389–412.

Tarhan, T. (2007), "Median and Achaemenid periods at Tušpa", in Deleman, ed., 117–130.

Tarn, W.W. (1929), "Ptolemy II and Arabia", *JEA* 15: 9–25.

Tashbaeva, K. and Gritsina, A., eds. (2005), *Civilizations of Nomadic and Sedentary Peoples of Central Asia*. Samarkand.

Tate, G. (1992), *Les Campagnes de la Syrie du nord du IIe au VIIe siécle: Un exemple d'expansion démographique et économique à la fin de l'antiquité*. Paris.

Tate, G. (1997), "The Syrian countryside during the Roman era", in Alcock, ed., 55–71.

Tavernier, J. (2004), "Some thoughts on Neo-Elamite chronology", *ARTA* 2004.003.

Tavernier, J. (2006), "Elam: Neo-Elamite Period (ca.1000–530 BC)", in Eder and Renger, eds., 22–24.

Tavernier, J. (2007), *Iranica in the Achaemenid Period (ca.550–330 BC). Lexicon of Old Iranian Proper Names and Loanwords, Attested in non-Iranian Texts*. Leuven/Paris/ Dudley.

Taylor, J. (2000), "The Third Intermediate Period", in Shaw, ed., 324–363.

Tchalenko, G. (1953-8), *Villages antiques de la Syrie du Nord. Le massif du Bélus à l'époque romaine*, 3 vols. Paris.

Tchalenko, G. (1990), *Églises syriennes à bêma. Texte*. Paris.

Tchalenko, G. and Baccache, E. (1979), *Églises de village de la Syrie du nord. Planches*. Paris.

Tchernov, E. (1993), "From sedentism to domestication: a preliminary review for the southern Levant", in Clason et al., eds., 189–233.

Tchernov, E. and Valla, F. (1997), "Two new dogs, and other Natufian dogs, from the southern Levant", *JAS* 24: 65–95.

Teixidor, J. (1973), "The Nabataean Presence at Palmyra", *Journal of the Ancient Near Eastern Society of Columbia University* 5: 405–409.

Teixidor, J. (1984), *Un Port romain du désert: Palmyre et son commerce d'Auguste à Caracalla*. Paris.

Tekoğlu, R. and Lemaire, A. (2000), "La bilingue royale louvito-phénicienne de Çineköy", *CRAIBL* 2000: 961–1007.

Teller, J.T., Glennie, K.W., Lancaster, N. and Singhvi, A.K. (2000), "Calcareous dunes of the United Arab Emirates and Noah's flood: the postglacial reflooding of the Persian (Arabian) Gulf", *QI* 68–71: 297–308.

Tengberg, M. (2003), "Archaeobotany in the Oman Peninsula and the role of Eastern Arabia in the spread of African crops", in Neumann et al., eds., 229–237.

Tengberg, M., and Lombard, P. (2002), "Paléoenvironnement et économie végétale à Qal'at al-Bahreïn aux périodes Dilmoun et Tylos: Premiers éléments d'archéobotanique", *Paléorient* 27/1: 167–181.

Tengberg, M., Shirazi, Z., Vahdati, A. and Francfort, H.-P. (in press), "A preliminary report on archaeobotanical studies in Tepe Damghani, Sabzevar, spring 2008", *Bāstān Šenāsī va Honar-e Īrān* 3/6 (in Persian).

Tennant, N. (1999), *The Conservation of Glass and Ceramics: Research, Practice and Training*. London.

Tenu, A., and Bachelot, L. (2005), "Tell Shiukh Fawqani (Syrie): la campagne de sondages 2003 dans le nécropole à incinération", *Akkadica* 126: 159–168.

Tenu, A., Bachelot, L. and Le Goff, I. (2005), "La nécropole de Tell Shiukh Fawqani", *Ktema* 30: 11–15.

Ter-Martirosov, F.I. (2009), "Stamps and images on the ceramics of the Urartian period from Erebuni", *Aramazd* 4/2: 127–145.

Terral, J.-F., Alonso, N., Buxo, R., Chatti, N., Fabre, L., Fiorentino, G., Marinval, P., Perez, G., Pradat, B. and Alibert, P. (2004), "Historical biogeography of olive domestication (*Olea europaea* L.) as revealed by geometrical morphometry applied to biological and archaeological material", *Journal of Biogeography* 31: 63–77.

Terral, J.-F., Tabard, E., Bouby, L., Ivorra, S., Pastor, T., Figueiral, I., Picq, S., Chevance, J.-B., Jung, C., Fabre, L., Tardy, C., Compan, M., Bacilieri, R., Lacombe, T. and This, P. (2010), "Evolution and history of grapevine (*Vitis vinifera*) under domestication: New morphometric perspectives to understand seed domestication syndrome and reveal origins of ancient European cultivars", *Annals of Botany* 105/3: 443–455.

Terral, J.-F., Newton, C., Gros-Balthazard, M., Tito De Morais, C., Picq, S., Tengberg, M. and Pintaud, J.-C. (in press), "First insights into the complex structure of date palm agrobiodiversity (*Phoenix dactylifera* L.) and history of ancient Egyptian cultivated forms assessed by geometric morphometrical analysis of modern and archaeological seeds", *Journal of Biogeography*.

Testart, A. (2008), "Des crânes et des vautours ou la guerre oubliée", *Paléorient* 34/1: 35–58.

Thalmann, J.-P., ed. (2006), *Tell Arqa – I. Les Niveaux de l'âge du bronze*. Beirut.

Thalmann, J.-P. (2007), "Settlement patterns and agriculture in the Akkar Plain during the late Early and early Middle Bronze Ages", in Morandi Bonacossi, ed., 219–232.

Thalmann, J.-P. (2008), "Tell Arqa et Byblos: essai de corrélation", in Bietak and Czerny, eds., 61–78.

Thalmann, J.-P. (2010), "Tell Arqa: a prosperous city during the Bronze Age", *NEA* 73/2-3: 86–101.

Thapar, R. (1997), *Aśoka and the Decline of the Mauryas*. Delhi and New York.

Thapar, R. (2002), *Early India from the Origins to AD 1300*. London/New York.

Thesiger, W. (1964), *The Marsh Arabs*. London.

Thiébault, S. (1989), "A note on the ancient vegetation of Baluchistan based on charcoal analysis of the latest periods from Mehrgarh, Pakistan", in Frifelt and Sørensen, eds., 186–188.

Thjis, A. (2005), "In search of king Herihor and the penultimate ruler of the 20th Dynasty", *Zeitschrift für Ägyptische Sprache und Altertumskunde* 132: 73–91.

Thomas, J.D. (1975), *The Epistrategos in Ptolemaic and Roman Egypt. The Ptolemaic Epistrategos*. Opladen.

Thomas, J.M.C. and Bernot, L., eds. (1972), *Langues et techniques, nature et société II. Approche ethnologique, approche naturaliste*. Paris.

Thomas, R.I. (2007), "The Arabaegypti Ichthyophagi: cultural connections with Egypt and the maintenance of identity", in Starkey et al., eds., 149–160.

Thomason, A.K. (1999), *Capturing the Exotic: Royal Ivory Collecting and the Neo-Assyrian imaging of North Syria*. New York.

Thomason, A.K. (2001), "Representations of the North Syrian landscape in Neo-Assyrian art", *BASOR* 323: 63–96.

Thomason, A.K. (2005), *Luxury and Legitimation: Royal Collecting in Ancient Mesopotamia*. Aldershot.

Thompson, J. (1988), *Oriental Carpets from the Tents, Cottages and Workshops of Asia*. New York.

Thomsen, M.-L. (1975), "'The Home of the Fish': a new interpretation", *JCS* 27/4: 197–200.

Thornton, C.P. (2007), "Of brass and bronze in prehistoric southwest Asia", in La Niece et al, eds., 123–135.

Thornton, C.P. (2009), *The Chalcolithic and Early Bronze Age Metallurgy of Tepe Hissar, Northeast Iran: A Challenge to the "Levantine Paradigm"*. Philadelphia.

Thornton, C.P. (2010), "The rise of arsenical copper in southeastern Iran", *IrAnt* 45: 31–50.

Thornton, C.P. and Ehlers, C. (2003), "Early brass in the ancient Near East", *Institute for Archaeo-Metallurgical Studies Journal* 23: 3–8.

Thornton, C.P., Gürsan-Salzmann, A. and Dyson, R.H., Jr. (in press), "Tepe Hissar and the fourth millennium of northeastern Iran", in Petrie, ed.

Thornton, C.P. and Lamberg-Karlovsky, C.C. (2004), "A new look at the prehistoric metallurgy of southeastern Iran", *Iran* 42: 61–76.

Thornton, C.P., Lamberg-Karlovsky, C.C., Liezers, M. and Young, S.M.M. (2002), "On pins and needles: tracing the evolution of copper-base alloying at Tepe Yahya, Iran, via ICP-MS analysis of common-place items", *JAS* 29/12: 1451–1460.

Thornton, C.P., Rehren, T. and Pigott, V.C. (2009), "The production of speiss (iron arsenide) during the Early Bronze Age in Iran", *JAS* 36/2: 308–316.

Thuesen, I. (1988), *Hama 1. The Pre- and Protohistoric Periods. Fouilles et Recherches 1931–1938.* Copenhagen.

Thuesen, I. (2000), "Ubaid Expansion in the Khabur. New Evidence from Tell Mashnaqa", in Rouault and Wäfler, eds., 71–79.

Thureau-Dangin, F. and Dunand, M. (1936), *Til-Barsip.* Paris.

Tibbetts, G.R. (1981), *Arab Navigation in the Indian Ocean Before the Coming of the Portuguese: Being a Translation of Kitāb al-Fawā'id fi uṣūl al-baḥr wa'l-qawā'id of Aḥmad b. Mājid al'Najdī.* London.

Tigay, J.H. (1982), *The Evolution of the Gilgamesh Epic.* Philadelphia.

Tilia, A.B. (1968), "A study of the methods of working and restoring stone and on the parts left unfinished in Achaemenian architecture and sculpture", *EW* 18: 67–95.

Tilia, A.B. (1969), "Reconstruction of the parapet on the terrace wall at Persepolis, south and west of Palace H", *EW* 19: 9–43.

Tilia, A.B. (1972), *Studies and Restorations at Persepolis and Other Sites of Fārs*, vol. 1. Rome.

Tilia, A.B. (1974), "Discovery of an Achaemenian palace near Takht-i Rustam to the north of the terrace of Persepolis", *Iran* 12: 200–204.

Tilia, A.B. (1978), *Studies and Restorations at Persepolis and Other Sites of Fārs*, vol. 2. Rome.

Tilia, G. (1997), "Ponte-Diga sul Fiume Kor – Fārs Iran", in Magnusson et al., eds., 331–338.

Tilley, C. (1999), *Metaphor and material culture.* Oxford.

Tinney, S. (1995), "A new look at Naram-Sin and the 'Great Rebellion'", *JCS* 47: 1–14.

Tite, M.S. (1999), "Pottery production, distribution and consumption: the contribution of the physical sciences", *JAMT* 6: 181–233.

Tite, M.S. and Maniatis, Y. (1975), "Examination of ancient pottery using the scanning electron microscope", *Nature* 257: 122–123.

Tite, M.S., Shortland, A.J., Maniatis, Y., Kavoussanaki, D. and Harris, S.A. (2006), "The composition of the soda-rich and mixed alkali plant ashes used in the production of glass", *JAS* 33: 1284–1292.

Tite, M.S., Shortland, A.J., Nicholson, P.T. and Jackson, C.M. (1998), "The use of copper and cobalt colorants in vitreous materials in ancient Egypt", in Colinart and Menu, eds., 111–120.

Tite, M.S., Shortland, A.J. and Paynter, S. (2002), "The beginnings of vitreous materials in the Near East and Egypt", *Accounts of Chemical Research* 35: 585–593.

Todd, I. (1976), *Çatal Hüyük in Perspective.* Menlo Park.

Toll, C. (1994), "Two Nabataean ostraca from Egypt", *BIFAO* 94: 381–382.

Tomber, R. (2005), "Troglodites and Trogodites: exploring interaction on the Red Sea during the Roman period", in Starkey, ed., 41–49.

Tomber, R. (2008), *Indo-Roman Trade: From Pots to Pepper.* London.

Toplyn, M.R. (1994), *Meat for Mars: Livestock, Limitanei, and Pastoral Provisioning for the Roman Army on the Arabian Frontier*. Cambridge.

Tosi, M. (1970), "On the route for lapis lazuli", *ILN* (January 24): 24–25 and (February 7): 24–25.

Tosi, M. (1974), "The lapis lazuli trade across the Iranian Plateau in the 3rd millennium BC", in Anonymous (1974b), ed., 3–22.

Tosi, M. (1980), "Karneol", *RlA* 5: 448–452.

Tosi, M., ed. (1983), *Prehistoric Sistan 1*. Rome.

Tosi, M. (1984), "The notion of craft specialization and its representation in the archaeological record of early states in the Turanian Basin", in Spriggs, ed., 22–52.

Tosi, M. (1989), "The distribution of industrial debris on the surface of Tappeh Hesār as an indication of activity areas", in Dyson and Howard, eds., 13–24.

Tosi, M. (1991), "The Indus Civilization beyond the Indian Subcontinent", in Jansen et al., eds., 111–128.

Tosi, M. and Lamberg-Karlovsky, C.C. (2003), "Pathways across Eurasia", in Aruz, ed., 347–375.

Tosi, M. and Piperno, M. (1973), "Lithic technology behind the ancient lapis lazuli trade", *Expedition* 16/1: 15–23.

Tosi, M. and Wardak, R. (1972), "The Fullol hoard: a new find from Bronze Age Afghanistan", *EW* 22/1–2: 9–17.

Traill, D.A. (1995), *Schliemann of Troy: Treasure and Deceit*. New York.

Tregenza, L.A. and Walker, J. (1949), "Nabataean inscriptions from the E. Desert of Egypt", *Univ. of Egypt Bulletin of the Faculty of Arts* 11/2: 151–160.

Trenkwalder, H. (1997–8), "Preliminary report on the 14th season work in Borsippa (autumn 1997)", *Sumer* 49: 97–103.

Trenkwalder, H. (1999–2000), "Austrian archaeological expedition to Iraq: preliminary report on the 17th campaign in Borsippa, autumn 2000", *Sumer* 50: 11–20.

Trenkwalder-Piesl, H. (1981), "Report about the excavations in Borsippa (second season 1981)", *Sumer* 41: 101–105.

Trichet, J. and Vallat, F. (1990), "L'origine égyptienne de la statue de Darius", in Vallat, ed., 205–208.

Trigger, B. (1989), *A History of Archaeological Thought*. Cambridge.

Trilling, J. (1982), *The Roman Heritage: Textiles from Egypt and the Eastern Mediterranean, 300–600 AD*. Washington, DC.

Trinkaus, K.M. (1986), "Pottery from the Damghan plain, Iran: chronology and variability from the Parthian to the early Islamic periods", *StIr* 15: 23–88.

Trinkaus, K.M. (1989), "Survey of the Damghan Plain", in Dyson and Howard, eds., 135–141.

Trümpelmann, L. (1983), "Zu den Gebäuden von Persepolis und ihrer Funktion", in Koch and MacKenzie, eds., 225–237.

Trümpelmann, L. (1988), *Persepolis. Ein Weltwunder der Antike*. Mainz.

Trümpler, C., ed. (2008), *Das große Spiel: Archäologie und Politik zur Zeit des Kolonialismus (1860–1940)*. Cologne.

Tsafrir, Y., ed. (1993), *Ancient Churches Revealed*. Jerusalem.

Tsafrir, Y. and Foerester G. (1997), "Urbanism at Scythopolis-Bet Shean in the fourth to seventh centuries", *DOP* 51: 85–146.

Tsahar, E., Izhaki, I., Lev-Yadun, S. and Bar-Oz, G. (2009), "Distribution and extinction of ungulates during the Holocene of the southern Levant", *PLoS One* 4/4: e5316.

Tsangadas, B.C.P. (1980), *The Fortifications and Defence of Constantinople*. New York.

Tsetskhladze, G.R. (2007), "Thracians versus Phrygians: about the origin of the Phrygians once again", in Çilingiroğlu and Sagona, eds., 283–310.

Tsuneki, A. and Hydar, J. (2007), *A Decade of Excavation at Tell el-Kerkh, 1997–2006*. Tsukuba.

Tsuneki, A., Hydar, J., Miyake, Y., Maeda, O., Odaka, T., Tannos, K.-I. and Hasegawa, A. (2000), "Fourth preliminary report of the excavations at Tell el Kerkh (2000), northwestern Syria", *Bulletin of the Ancient Orient Museum* 21: 1–36.

Tsuneki, A. and Miyake, Y. (1996), "The earliest pottery sequence of the Levant: New data from Tell el-Kerkh 2, Northern Syria", *Paléorient* 22/1: 109–123.

Tsuneki, A., Zeidi, M. and Ohnuma, K. (2007), "Proto-Neolithic caves in the Bolaghi Valley, South Iran", *Iran* 45: 1–22.

Tubach, J. (1986), *Im Schatten des Sonnengottes. Der Sonnenkult in Edessa, Harran und Hatra am Vorabend der christlichen Mission*. Wiesbaden.

Tubb, J.N., ed. (1985), *Palestine in the Bronze and Iron Ages: Papers in Honour of Olga Tufnell*. London.

Tubb, J.N. (1998), *Canaanites*. London.

Tubb, J.N. and Chapman R.L. (1990), *Archaeology and the Bible*. London.

Tubb, K.W. (1995a), "The antiquities trade: an archaeological conservator's perspective", in Tubb, ed., 256–263.

Tubb, K.W., ed. (1995b), *Antiquities Trade or Betrayed Legal, Ethical and Conservation Issues*. London.

Tubb, K.W. (2002), "Point, counterpoint", in Brodie and Tubb, eds., 286–292.

Tucci, G., ed. (1977), *La Città bruciata del Deserto Salato*. Venice.

Tucker, D.J. (1994), "Representations of Imgur-Enlil on the Balawat Gates", *Iraq* 56: 107–116.

Tufnell, O. and Ward, W.A. (1966), "Relations between Byblos, Egypt, and Mesopotamia at the end of the third millennium BC", *Syria* 43: 165–241.

Tuna, N., Aktüre, Z. and Lynch, M., eds. (1998), *Thracians and Phrygians: Problems of parallelism*. Ankara.

Tuna, N. and Velibeyoğlu, J., eds. (2004), *Ilisu ve Karkamiş Baraj Gölleri Altinda Kalacak Arkeolojik ve Kültür Varliklarini Kurtarma Projesi 2001 Yili Çalişmalari – Salvage Project of the Archaeological Heritage of the Ilisu and Charchemish Dam Reservoirs Activities in 2001*. Ankara.

Tunca, Ö., McMahon, A. and Baghdo, A.-M. (2007), *Chagar Bazar (Syrie) II. Les vestiges "post-Akkadiens" du Chantier D et études diverses*. Leuven.

Tunca, Ö. and Molist, M., eds. (2004), *Tell Amarna (Syrie) I. La période de Halaf*. Louvain/ Paris/Dudley.

Tuplin, C. (2007a), "The Achaemenid impact in Anatolia: a summary", in Deleman, ed., 291–298.

Tuplin, C., ed. (2007b), *Persian Responses*. Swansea.

Turner, G. (1970), "The state apartments of Late Assyrian palaces", *Iraq* 32: 177–213.

Turner, P.J. (1989), *Roman Coins from India*. London.

Turner, P.J. and Cribb, J. (1996), "Numismatic evidence for the Roman trade with ancient India", in Reade, ed., 309–319.

Turner, W.E.S. (1954), "Studies of ancient glasses and glass-making processes. Part II. The composition, weathering characteristics and historical significance of some Assyrian glasses of the eighth to sixth centuries BC from Nimrud", *JSGT* 38: 445T–456T.

Turner, W.E.S. (1955), "Glass fragments from Nimrud of the eighth to the sixth century BC, *Iraq* 17: 57–68.

Turner, W.E.S. (1956a), "Studies in ancient glasses and glassmaking processes. Part III. The chronology of the glassmaking constituents", *JSGT* 40: 39T–52T.

Turner, W.E.S. (1956b), "Studies in ancient glasses and glassmaking processes. Part IV. The chemical composition of ancient glasses", *JSGT* 40: 162T–186T.

Turner, W.E.S. (1956c), "Studies in ancient glasses and glassmaking processes. Part V. Raw materials and melting processes", *JSGT* 40: 277T–300T.

Turner, W.E.S. and Rooksby, H.P. (1959), "A study of opalizing agents in ancient glasses throughout three thousand four hundred years, part 1", *Glastechnische Berichte* 32 K 17: 17–28.

Turner, W.E.S. and Rooksby, H.P. (1961), "Further historical studies based on x-ray diffraction methods of the reagents employed in making opal and opaque glasses", *JRGZM* 8: 1–16.

Turner, W.E.S. and Rooksby, H.P. (1963), "A study of the opalizing agents in ancient glasses throughout 3400 years, Part II", in Matson and Rindone, eds., 306–307.

Twigger, E. (2009), *The Question, Nature and Significance of Neolithic Craft Specialization in Anatolia*. Liverpool.

Ucko, P.J. and Dimbleby, G.W., eds. (1969), *The Domestication of Plants and Animals*. London.

Ucko, P., Tringham, R. and Dimbleby, D.W., eds. (1972), *Man, Settlement and Urbanism*. London.

Uehlinger, C., ed. (2000), *Images As Media: Sources for the Cultural History of the Near East and the Eastern Mediterranean (1st Millennium BCE)*. Fribourg.

Uehlinger, C. and Graf, F., eds. (forthcoming), *Iconography of Ancient Near Eastern Religions, vol. 1: Pre-Hellenistic Periods, Introductory Essays*. Leiden.

Uerpmann, H.-P. (1979), *Probleme der Neolithisierung des Mittelmeeraums*. Wiesbaden.

Uerpmann, H.-P. (1986), "Halafian equid remains from Shams ed-Din Tannira in Northern Syria", in Meadow and Uerpmann, eds., 246–265.

Uerpmann, H.-P. (1987), *The Ancient Distribution of Ungulate Mammals in the Middle East*. Wiesbaden.

Uerpmann, H.-P. (1989), "Problems of archaeo-zoological research in Eastern Arabia", in Costa and Tosi, eds., 163–168.

Uerpmann, H.-P. (1991), "Equus africanus in Arabia", in Meadow and Uerpmann, eds., 12–33.

Uerpmann, H.-P. (1999), "Camel and horse skeletons from protohistoric graves at Mleiha in the Emirate of Sharjah (UAE)", *AAE* 10: 102–118.

Uerpmann, H.-P., Potts, D.T. and Uerpmann, M. (2009), "Holocene (re-)occupation of Eastern Arabia", in Petraglia and Rose, eds., 205–214.

Uerpmann, H.-P. and Uerpmann, M. (2002), "The appearance of the domestic camel in SE-Arabia", *JOS* 12: 235–260.

Uerpmann, H.-P. and Uerpmann, M. (2003), *Stone Age Sites and their Natural Environment: The Capital Area of Northern Oman*, Pt. III. Wiesbaden.

Uerpmann, H.-P., Uerpmann, M. and Jasim, S.A., eds. (2006), *Funeral Monuments and Human Remains from Jebel al-Buhais, vol. 1. The Archaeology of Jebel al-Buhais*. Sharjah, United Arab Emirates. Tübingen/Sharjah.

Uerpmann, H.-P., Uerpmann, M. and Jasim, S.A., eds. (2008), *Archaeological Sites and their Natural Environment: The Archaeology of Jebel al-Buhais*, vol. 2. Tübingen.

Uerpmann, M. (2003), "The dark millennium: remarks on the final Stone Age in the Emirates and Oman", in Potts et al., eds., 74–81.

Uerpmann, M. (2011), "The Holocene Stone Age in Southeast Arabia: a reconsideration", in Conard et al., eds., 113–130.

Uerpmann, M. and Uerpmann, H.-P. (1996), "Ubaid pottery in the eastern Gulf: new evidence from Umm al-Qawain (U.A.E.)", *AAE* 7: 125–139.

Uerpmann, M. and Uerpmann, H.-P. (2005a), "Animal bone finds and their relevance to the ecology and economy of Saar", in Killick and Moon, eds., 293–308.

Uerpmann, M. and Uerpmann, H.-P. (2005b), "Fish exploitation at Bronze Age harbour sites in the Arabian Gulf area", *Paléorient* 31/1: 108–115.

Uerpmann, M. and Uerpmann, H.-P. (2008a), "Neolithic faunal remains from al-Buhais 18 (Sharjah, UAE)", in Uerpmann et al., eds., 97–132.

Uerpmann, M. and Uerpmann, H.-P. (2008b), "Animal economy during the Early Bronze Age in South-East Arabia", in Vila et al., ed., 465–486.

Uerpmann, M., Uerpmann, H.-P. and Jasim, S.A. (2006), "Früher Wüstennomadismus auf der arabischen Halbinsel", in Hauser, ed., 87–103.

Uhlmann, G. (n.d.), Çatal Höyük (http://www.gabriele-uhlmann.de/catal_hoeyuek.htm). Accessed 12/10/2010.

Ulbert, T. (1986), *Die Basilika des Heiligen Kreuzes in Resafa-Sergiupolis*. Mainz.

Ulbert, T. (1989), "Villes et fortifications de l'Euphrate à l'époque paléochrétienne", in Dentzer and Orthmann, eds., 283–296.

Unger, E. (1931), *Babylon, die heilige Stadt*. Berlin and Leipzig.

Ünlü, E. (2005), "Locally produced and painted Late Bronze to Iron Age transitional pottery of Tarsus-Gözlükule", in Özyar, ed., 145–168.

Ur, J.A. (2003), "CORONA satellite photography and ancient road networks: a Northern Mesopotamian case study", *Antiquity* 77: 102–115.

Ur, J. (2005), "Sennacherib's northern Assyrian canals: new insights from satellite imagery and aerial photography", *Iraq* 67/1: 317–345.

Ur, J.A. (2009), "Emergent landscapes of movement in Early Bronze Age Northern Mesopotamia", in Snead et al., eds., 180–203.

Ur, J. (2010a), "Cycles of civilization in northern Mesopotamia, 4400–2000 BC", *JAR* 18: 387–431.

Ur, J.A. (2010b), *Urbanism and Cultural Landscapes in Northeastern Syria: The Tell Hamoukar Survey, 1999–2001*. Chicago.

Ur, J.A. (in press a), "Urban adaptations to climate change in Northern Mesopotamia", in Kerner et al., eds.

Ur, J.A. (in press b), "Urban form at Tell Brak across three millennia", in Crawford et al., eds.

Ur, J.A., Karsgaard, P. and Oates, J. (2007), "Urban development in the ancient Near East", *Science* 317: 1188.

Ur, J.A. and Wilkinson, T.J. (2008), "Settlement and economic landscapes of Tell Beydar and its hinterland", in Lebeau and Suleiman, eds., 305–327.

Urban, P.A. and Schortman, E., eds. (1992), *Resource Power and Regional Interaction*. London.

Urice, S.K. (1997), "Claims to ownership of the Trojan treasures", in Simpson, ed., 204–206.

Urman, D. (2006), *Rafid on the Golan: A Profile of a Late Roman and Byzantine Village*. Oxford.

Ussishkin, D. (1980), "The Ghassulian shrine at En-Gedi", *Tel Aviv* 7/1–2: 1–44.

Ussishkin, D., ed. (2004), *The Renewed Archaeological Excavations at Lachish*, vol. 5. Tel Aviv.

Valbelle, D. and Deferenz, C. (1994), "Les sites de la frontière égypto-palestinienne à l'époque perse", *Transeuphratène* 7: 94–100.

Valla, F.R. (1984), *Les Industries de silex de Mallaha (Eynan) et du Natoufien dans le Levant*. Paris.

Valla, F.R. (1987), "Les Natoufiens connaissaient-ils l'arc?", in Stordeur, ed., 165–174.

Valla, F.R. (1991), "Les Natoufiens de Mallaha et l'espace", in Bar-Yosef and Valla, ed., 111–122.

Valla, F.R. (1995), "The first settled societies – Natufian (12,500–10,200 bp)", in Levy, ed. 169–187.

Valla, F.R. (1998), "The first settled societies – Natufian (12,500–10,200 BP)", in Levy, ed., 169–187.

Vallat, F. (1974), "La triple inscription cunéiforme de la statue de Darius Ier (DSab)", *RA* 68: 157–166.

Vallat, F., ed. (1990), *Mélanges Jean Perrot*. Paris.

Vallat, F. (1994a), "Succession royale en Elam au IIème millenaire", in Gasche et al., eds., 1–14.

Vallat, F., ed. (1994b), *Contributions à l'histoire de l'Iran, Mélanges offerts à Jean Perrot*. Paris.

Vallat, F. (1996), "Nouvelle analyse des inscriptions néo-élamites", Gasche and Hrouda, eds., 385–395.

Vallat, F. (1998), "Elam i. The history of Elam", *EnIr* 8: 301–313.

Vallat, F. (1999a), "L'hommage de l'élamite Untash-Napirisha au Cassite Burnaburiash", *Akkadica* 114–115: 109–117.

Vallat, F. (1999b), "Le palais élamite de Suse", *Akkadica* 112: 34–43.

Vallat, F. (2002), "Suse", *DB* 73–74: 361–651.

Vallat, F. (2006a), "La chronologie méso-élamite et la lettre de Berlin", *Akkadica* 127: 123–135.

Vallat, F. (2006b), "Atta-hamiti-Inšušinak, Šutur-Nahhunte et la chronologie néo-élamite", *Akkadica* 127: 59–62.

Vallat, F. (2010), "Les principales inscriptions achéménides à Suse", in Perrot, ed., 300–317.

Vallet, R. (1996), "Habuba Kebira, ou la naissance de l'urbanisme", *Paléorient* 22: 45–76.

Vallet, R. (1998), "L'urbanisme colonial urukien: l'exemple de Djebel Aruda", in Lebeau, ed., 53–87.

Valtz, E. (1984), "Pottery from Seleucia on the Tigris", in Boucharlat and Salles, eds., 41–48.

Valtz, E. (1991), "New observations on the Hellenistic pottery from Seleucia-on-the-Tigris", in Schippmann et al., eds., 45–56.
van Alfen, P.G. (2011), "A die study of the 'Abiel' coinage of eastern Arabia", in Huth and van Alfen, eds., 549–594.
Van Berchem, D. (1954), "Recherches sur la chronologie des enceintes de Syrie et de Mésopotamie", *Syria* 31: 254–270.
van Buren, E.D. (1939), *The Fauna of Ancient Mesopotmia as Represented in Art*. Rome.
van Buren, E.D. (1948), "Fish-offerings in Ancient Mesopotamia", *Iraq* 10/2: 101–121.
Van de Mieroop, M. (1992a), *Society and Enterprise in Old Babylonian Ur*. Berlin.
Van de Mieroop, M. (1992b), "Reed in the Old Babylonian texts from Ur", *BSA* 6: 147–153.
Van de Mieroop, M. (1992c), "Wood in the Old Babylonian texts from Southern Mesopotamia", *BSA* 6: 155–161.
Van de Mieroop, M. (1997), *The Ancient Mesopotamian City*. Oxford.
Van de Mieroop, M. (1999), *Cuneiform Texts and the Writing of History*. London.
Van de Mieroop, M. (2000), "Sargon of Agade and his successors in Anatolia", *SMEA* 42/1: 133–159.
Van de Mieroop, M. (2003), "Reading Babylon", *AJA* 107/2: 257–275.
Van de Mieroop, M. (2007), *A History of the Ancient Near East ca.2000–323 BC*, 2nd edn. Oxford.
Vanden Berghe, L. (1952), "Archaeologische opzoekingen in de Marv Dasht vlakte (Irān)", *JEOL* 12: 211–220.
Vanden Berghe, L. (1953), "Monuments récemment découverts en Iran méridional", *BiOr* 10: 5–8.
Vanden Berghe, L. (1954), "Archaeologische navorsingen in de omstreken Van Persepolis", *JEOL* 13: 394–408.
Vanden Berghe, L. (1959), *Archéologie de l'Irān ancien*. Leiden.
Vanden Berghe, L. (1961), "Récentes découvertes de monuments sassanides dans le Fars", *IrAnt* 1: 161–198.
Vanden Berghe, L. (1963), "Les reliefs élamites de Mālamir", *IrAnt* 3: 22–39.
Vanden Berghe, L. (1965), "Nouvelles découvertes de monuments du feu d'époque sassanide", *IrAnt* 5: 128–147.
Vanden Berghe, L. (1970), "La nécropole de Kalleh Nisar", *Archeologia* 32: 64–73.
Vanden Berghe, L. (1979), *Bibliographie analytique de l'archeologie de l'Iran ancien*. Leiden.
Vanden Berghe, L. (1983), *Reliefs rupestres de l'Iran ancien*. Brussels.
Vanden Berghe, L. (1984), "Le Chahār Tāq de Qanāt-i Bāgh (Fārs) et l'inventaire des Chahār Tāqs en Irān", *IrAnt* 19: 201–225.
Vanden Berghe, L. (1986), "Données nouvelles concernant le relief rupestre élamite de Kūrangūn", in De Meyer et al., eds., 157–167.
Vanden Berghe, L. (1990), "Bozpār", *EnIr* 4: 429–430.
Vanden Berghe, L., ed. (1993), *Splendeur des Sassanides*. Brussels.
Vanden Berghe, L. and Haerinck, E. (1981), *Bibliographie analytique de l'archeologie de l'Iran ancien: Supplément 1 (1978–1980)*. Leiden.
Vanden Berghe, L. and Haerinck, E. (1987), *Bibliographie analytique de l'archeologie de l'Iran ancien: Supplément 2 (1981–1985)*. Leuven.

Vanden Berghe, L. and Schippmann, K. (1985), *Les Reliefs rupestres d'Elymaïde (Iran) de l'époque parthe*. Gent.

van den Brink, E.C.M. and Levy, T.E., eds. (2002), *Egypt and the Levant: Interrelations from the 4th through the Early 3rd Millennium BCE*. London/New York.

van den Brink, E.C.M., ed. (1992), *The Nile Delta in Transition: 4th–3rd Millennia BC*. Jerusalem.

van den Hout, T. (2001), "Zur Geschichte des jüngeren hethitischen Reiches", in Wilhelm, ed., 213–223.

van den Hout, T. (2003), "Maeonien und Maddunašša: Zur Frühgeschichte des Lydischen", in Giorgieri et al., eds., 301–10.

van den Hout, T. (2006), "Institutions, vernaculars, publics: the case of second millennium Anatolia", in Sanders, ed., 217–56.

Vanderhooft, D. (2003), "Babylonian strategies of imperial control in the West: royal practice and rhetoric", in Lipschits and Blenkinsopp, eds., 235–262.

van der Spek, R.J. (1997–8), "New evidence from the Babylonian astronomical diaries concerning Seleucid and Arsacid history", *AfO* 44–45: 167–175.

van der Spek, R.J. (1998), "Cuneiform documents on Parthian history: the Raḥimesu Archive", in Wiesehöfer, ed., 205–258.

van der Spek, R.J. (2007), "Commodity prices in Babylon 385–61 BC". www.iisg.nl/hwp/babylon.phd.

van Dijk, J. (1978), "Išbi'erra, Kindattu, l'homme d'Elam, et la chute de la ville d'Ur", *JCS* 30/4: 189–208.

van Dijk, J. (1986), "Die dynastichen Heiraten zwischen Kassiten und Elamern: eine verhängnisvolle Politik", *Or* 55: 159–70.

Vandiver, P.B. (1982), "Second millennium soda-lime-silicate technology at Nuzi (Iraq)", in Wertime and Wertime, eds., 73–92.

Vandiver, P.B. (1983), "Glass technology at the mid-second-millennium BC Hurrian site of Nuzi", *JGS* 25: 239–247.

Vandiver, P.B. (1987), "Sequential slab construction: s conservative southwest Asiatic ceramic tradition, ca.7000–3000 BC", *Paléorient* 13: 9–35.

Vandiver, P.B. (1995), "The production technology of early pottery from Mehrgarh", in Jarrige et al., eds., 648–661.

Vandiver, P.B., Druzik, J.R., Wheeler, G.S. and Freestone, I.C., eds. (1993), *Materials Issues in Art and Archaeology III*. Pittsburgh.

Vandiver, P., Goodway, M. and Mass, J.L., eds. (2002), *Materials Issues in Art and Archaeology VI*. Warrendale.

van Driel, G. (1988), "Neo-Babylonian agriculture", *BSA* 4: 121–159.

van Driel, G. (1993), "Neo-Babylonian sheep and goats", *BSA* 7: 219–258.

van Driel, G. (2002), "Jebel Aruda: variation on a Late Uruk domestic theme", in Postgate, ed., 191–206.

van Driel, G. and van Driel-Murray, C. (1983), "Jebel Aruda: the 1982 season of excavation, interim report", *Akkadica* 33: 1–26.

van Ess, M., ed. (2008a), *Baalbek/Heliopolis: Results of Archaeological and Architectural Research in Baalbek*. Beirut.

van Ess, M. (2008b), "First results of the archaeological cleaning of the Deep Trench in the Great Courtyard of the Jupiter Sanctuary", in van Ess, ed., 99–120.

van Ess, M. and Pedde, F. (1992), *Uruk Kleinfunde II*. Mainz.

van Ess, M. and Petersen, L. (2003), "Excavation of a Late Roman Necropolis in Baalbek – Douris", *BAAL* 7: 83–108.

van Ess, M. and Rheidt, K. (2005), "Archaeological research in Baalbek: a preliminary report of the 2004 and 2005 seasons", *BAAL* 9: 117–146.

van Ingen, W. (1939), *Figurines from Seleucia on the Tigris*. Ann Arbor.

van Lerberghe, K. and Schoors, A., eds. (1995), *Immigration and Emigration Within the Ancient Near East*. Leuven.

van Loon, M.N. (1966), *Urartian Art: Its Distinctive Traits in the Light of New Excavations*. Istanbul.

van Loon M.N. (1968), "The Oriental Institute excavations at Mureybit, Syria: preliminary report on the 1965 campaign", *JNES* 27: 265–290.

van Loon, M.N., ed. (1988), *Hammam et-Turkman*, vol. 1. Istanbul.

Van Neer, W., ed. (1994), *Fish Exploitation in the Past: Proceedings of the 7th Meeting of the ICAZ Fish Remains Working Group*. Tervuren.

Van Neer, W. and Gautier, A. (1993), "Preliminary report on the faunal remains from the coastal site of ed-Dur, 1st–4th century AD, Umm al-Quwain, United Arab Emirates", in Buitenhuis and Clason, eds., 110–118.

Van Neer, W. and Uerpmann, M. (1994), "Fish remains from excavation 520 at Qal'at al-Bahrain", in Højlund and Andersen, 445–454.

Van Neer, W., Zohar, I. and Lernau, O. (2005), "The emergence of fishing communities in the eastern Mediterranean region: a survey of evidence from pre- and protohistoric periods", *Paléorient* 31/1: 131–157.

Van Soldt, W.H. (1995), "Ugarit: a second-millennium kingdom on the Mediterranean coast", in Sasson, ed., 1255–1266.

Van Soldt, W.H. (1997), "Studies in the topography of Ugarit (2): the borders of Ugarit", *UF* 29: 683–705.

Van Soldt, W.H. (1998), "Studies in the topography of Ugarit (3): groups of towns and their locations", *UF* 30: 703–744.

Van Soldt, W.H. (2005), *The Topography of the City-State of Ugarit*. Münster.

Vanstiphout, H.L.J. (1995), "On the Old Babylonian Eduba curriculum", in Drijvers and MacDonald, eds., 3–16.

Vanstipout, H.L.J. (1997), "Sumerian canonical compositions, C. Individual focus, 6. School dialogues", in Hallo, ed., 588–593.

van't Haaff, P.A. (2007), *Catalogue of Elymaean coinage, ca.147 BC-AD 228*. Lancaster.

van't Hooft, P.P.M., Raven, M.J., van Rooij, E.H.C. and Vogelsang-Eastwood, G.M. (1994), *Pharaonic and Early Medieval Egyptian Textiles*. Leiden.

Van Wijngaarden, G.J. (2002), *Use and Appreciation of Mycenean Pottery in the Levant, Cyprus and Italy (ca. 1600–1200 BC)*. Amsterdam.

Van Zeist, W. (1967), "Late quaternary vegetation history of western Iran", *Revue of Palaeobotany and Palynology* 2: 301–311.

Van Zeist, W. and Bakker-Heeres, J.A. (1984), "Archaeobotanical studies in the Levant 3. Late Palaeolithic Mureybet", *Palaeohistoria* 26: 171–199.

Van Zeist, W. and Bottema, S. (1991), *Late Quaternary Vegetation of the Near East*. Wiesbaden.

Van Zeist, W. and de Roller, G.J. (1994), "Plant husbandry of Aceramic Çayönü, SE Turkey", *Palaeohistoria* 33–34: 65–96.

Van Zeist, W. and de Roller, G.J. (1995), "Plant remains from Aşikli Höyük, a Pre-Pottery Neolithic site in central Anatolia", *VHA* 4: 179–185.

Van Zeist, W. and Vynckier, J. (1984), "Palaeobotanical investigations of Tell ed-Der", in De Meyer, ed., 119–133.

Vartavan, C. de and Asensi Amorós, V. (1997), *Codex of Ancient Egyptian Plant Remains*. London.

Vasiliev, A.A. (1950), *Justin the First: An Introduction to the Epoch of Justinian the Great*. Cambridge.

Vassileva, M. (2008), "King Midas in southeastern Anatolia", in Collins et al., eds., 165–171.

Vatandoust, A., Parzinger, H. and Helwing, B., eds. (2011), *Early Mining and Metallurgy on the Western Central Iranian Plateau: The First Five Years of Work*. Mainz.

Vats, M.S. (1940), *Excavations at Harappa*. Delhi.

Vaux, R. de (1971), "Palestine in the Early Bronze Age", *CAH* 1/1: 208–237.

Veenenbos, J. (1958), *Unified Report on the Soil and Land Classification Survey of Dezful Project, Khuzestan Iran*. Tehran.

Veenhof, K.R. (1972), *Aspects of Old Assyrian Trade and its Terminology*. Leiden.

Veenhof, K.R. (1982), "The Old Assyrian merchants and their relations with the native population of Anatolia", in Nissen and Renger, eds., 147–155.

Veenhof, K.R., ed. (1986), *Cuneiform Archives and Libraries*. Leiden.

Veenhof, K.R. (1995), "Kanesh: An Assyrian colony in Anatolia", in Sasson, ed., vol. 2, 859–871.

Veenhof, K.R., ed. (1996), *Houses and Households in Ancient Mesopotamia*. Leiden.

Veenhof, K.R. (2008), "The Old Assyrian period", in Wäfler, ed., 13–266.

Veenhof, K.R. (2010), "Ancient Assur: the city, its traders, and its commercial network", *JESHO* 53: 39–82.

Veldhuijzen, H.A. (2009), "Of slag and scales, micro-stratigraphy and micro-magnetic material at metallurgical excavations", in Kaptijn and Petit, eds., 163–174.

Veldhuijzen, H.A. and Rehren, T. (2007), "Slags and the city: early iron production at Tell Hammeh, Jordan and Tel Beth-Shemesh, Israel", in La Niece et al., eds., 189–201.

Veldhuis, N. (2004), *Religion, Literature, and Scholarship: The Sumerian Composition "Nanše and the Birds"*. Leiden and Boston.

Venco Ricciardi, R. (1967), "Pottery from Choche", *Mesopotamia* 2: 93–104.

Venco Ricciardi, R. (1968–69), "The excavations at Choche", *Mesopotamia* 3–4: 57–68.

Venco Ricciardi, R. (1980), "Archaeological survey in the Upper Atrek Valley (Khorasan, Iran). Preliminary report", *Mesopotamia* 15: 51–72.

Venturi, F. (2007), *La Siria nell'età delle trasformazioni (XIII-X sec. a.C.). Nuovi contributi dallo scavo di Tell Afis*. Bologna.

Venturi, F., ed. (2010), *Societies in Transition: Evolutionary Processes in the Northern Levant Between Late Bronze Age II and Early Iron Age*. Bologna.

Verginelli, F., Capelli, C., Coia, V., Musiani, M., Falchetti, M., Ottini, L., Palmirotta, R., Tagliacozzo, A., De Grossi Mazzorin, I. and Mariani-Costantini, R. (2005), "Mitochondrial DNA from prehistoric canids highlights relationships between dogs and South-East European wolves", *Molecular Biology and Evolution* 22: 2541–2551.

Verheyden, S., Nader, F.H., Cheng, H.J., Edwards, L.R., and Swennen, R. (2008), "Paleoclimate reconstruction in the Levant region from the geochemistry of a Holocene stalagmite from the Jeita Cave, Lebanon", *QR* 70: 368–381.

Verhoeven, K. (1998), "Geomorphological research in the Mesopotamian floodplain", in Gasche and Tanret, eds., 159–245.

Verhoeven, M. (1999), *An Archaeological Ethnography of a Neolithic Community*. Leiden.

Verhoeven, M. (2000), "Death, fire and abandonment: ritual practice at later Neolithic Tell Sabi Abyad, Syria", *Archaeological Dialogues* 7/1: 46–83.

Verhoeven, M. (2002), "Ritual and ideology in the Pre-Pottery Neolithic B of the Levant and southeast Anatolia", *CAJ* 12/2: 233–258.

Verhoeven, M. (2006), "Megasites in the Jordanian Pre-Pottery Neolithic B: Evidence for 'Proto-Urbanism'?", in Banning and Chazan, eds., 75–79.

Verhoeven, M. (2010), "Igniting transformations: on the social impact of fire with special reference to the Neolithic of the Near East", in Hansen, ed., 25–43.

Verhoeven, M. and Akkermans, P.M.M.G., ed. (2000), *Tell Sabi Abyad II: The Pre-Pottery Neolithic B Settlement*. Leiden/Istanbul.

Verzone, P. (1982), "Le fasi costruttive della basilica di S. Giovanni di Efeso", *Rendiconti Pontificia Accademia Romana di Archeologia* 51–52: 213–232.

Veuve, S. (1987), *Fouilles d'Aï Khanoum VI. Le gymnase. Architecture, céramique, sculpture*. Paris.

Vidale, M. (2005), "The short-horned bull on the Indus seals: a symbol of the families in the western trade?", in Franke-Vogt and Weisshaar, eds., 146–158.

Vigne, J.-D. and Helmer, D. (2007), "Was milk a 'secondary product' in the Old World Neolithisation process? Its role in the domestication of cattle, sheep, and goats", *Anthropozoologica* 42: 9–40.

Vigne, J.-D., Carrère, I. and Guilaine, J. (2003), "Unstable status of early domestic ungulates in the Near East: the example of Shillourokambos (Cyprus, IX-VIIIth millennia cal. BC)", in Guilaine and Le Brun, eds., 239–251.

Vigne, J.-D., Carrère, I., Saliège, J.-F., Person, A., Bocherens, H., Guilaine, J. and Briois, J.-F. (2000), "Predomestic cattle, sheep, goat, and pig during the late 9th and the 8th millennium cal. BC on Cyprus: preliminary results of Shillourokambos (Parakklisha, Limassol)", in Mashkour et al., eds., 83–106.

Vigne, J.-D., Guilaine, J., Debue, K., Haye, L. and Gérard, P. (2004), "Early taming of the cat in Cyprus", *Science* 304: 259.

Vigne, J.-D., Peters, J. and Helmer, D., eds. (2005), *The First Steps of Animal Domestication: New Archaeological Approaches*. Oxford.

Vigne, J.-D., Zazzo, A., Saliège, J-F., Poplin, F., Guilaine, J. and Simmons, A. (2009), "Pre-Neolithic wild boar management and introduction to Cyprus more than 11,400 years ago", *PNAS* 106: 16135–16138.

Vikan, G. (1982), *Byzantine Pilgrimage Art*. Washington, DC.

Vilà, C., Savolainen, P., Maldonado, J.E., Amorim, I.R., Rivce, J.E., Honeycut, R.L., Crandall, K.A., Lundeberg, J. and Wayne, R.K. (1997), "Multiple and ancient origins of the domestic dog", *Science* 276: 1687–1689.

Vila, E. (2006), "Data on equids from late fourth and third millennium sites in Northern Syria", in Mashkour, ed.,102–123.

Vila, E. and Gourichon, L. (2007), "Apport de l'étude de la faune mammalienne et de l'avifaune à la réflexion sur l'environnement de Qatna à l'Age du Bronze et à l'Age du Fer", in Morandi Bonacossi, ed., 161–168.

Vila, E., Gourichon, L., Choyke, A.M. and Buitenhuis, H., eds. (2008), *Archaeozoology of the Near East VIII*. Lyon.

Vila, E., Leonard, J.A., Götherstrom, A., Marklund, S., Sandberg, K., Liden, K., Wayne, R.K. and Ellegren, H. (2001), "Widespread origins of domestic horse lineages", *Science* 291: 474–477.

Villard, P. (1995), "Shamshi-Adad and sons: the rise and fall of an Upper Mesopotamian empire", in Sasson, ed., 873–883.

Villeneuve, E. (2002), "Océan Indien, île de Socotra. Bénis soient Abgar et les spéléologues!", *Le Monde de la Bible* 145: 58.

Villeneuve, E. (2003), "Indischer Ozean Insel Sokotra: Gesegnet seien Abgar und die Höhlenforscher", *Welt und Umwelt der Bibel* 1: 72.

Villeneuve, F. (1985), "L'économie rurale et la vie des campagnes dans le Hauran antique (1er siècle av. J.-C.–VIIe siècle ap. J.-C.). Une approche", in Dentzer, ed., 63–136.

Villeneuve, F., Phillips, C. and Facey, W. (2004a), "Une inscription latine sur l'archipel Farasân, Arabie Séoudite, sud de la mer Rouge", *CRAIBL* 2004: 419–429.

Villeneuve, F., Phillips, C. and Facey, W. (2004b), "Une inscription latine de l'archipel Farasān (sud de la mer Rouge) et son contexte archéologique et historique", *Arabia* 2: 143–190.

Vinogradova, N.M. (1993), "Interrelation between farming and 'steppe' tribes in the Bronze Age South Tadjikistan", in Gail et al., eds., 289–301.

Vinogradova, N.M. (1994), "The farming settlement of Kangurttut (South Tadjikistan) in the Late Bronze Age", *AMI* 27: 29–47.

Virno, P. (2004), *A Grammar of the Multitude*. Los Angeles (also available at http://www.generation-online.org/c/fcmultitude3.htm).

Visicato, G. (2000), *The Power and the Writing: The Early Scribes of Mesopotamia*. Bethesda.

Vita-Finzi, C. (1969), *The Mediterranean Valleys: Geological Changes in Historical Times*. Cambridge.

Vita-Finzi, C. (1978), "Recent alluvial history in the catchment of the Arabo-Persian Gulf", in Brice, ed., 255–261.

Vitelli, K.D. (1984), "The international traffic in antiquities: archaeological ethics and the archaeologist's responsibility", in Green, ed., 143–155.

Vitelli, K.D., ed. (1996), *Archaeological Ethics*. Lanham.

Vitelli, K.D. and Colwell-Chanthaphonh, C., eds. (2006), *Archaeological Ethics*, 2nd edn. Lanham.

Vogel, C. (2004), *Ägyptische Festungen und Garnisonen bis zum Ende des Mittleren Reiches*. Hildesheim.

Vogel, C. (2008), "Das ägyptische Festungssystem bis zum Ende des Neuen Reiches", in Gundlach and Vogel, eds., 165–185.

Vogel, C. (2010), *The Fortifications of Ancient Egypt 3000–1780 BC*. Colchester.

Vogelsang, W.J. (1992), *The Rise and Organisation of the Achaemenid Empire: The Eastern Iranian Evidence*. Leiden.

Vogelsgang-Eastwood, G. (1993), "Unearthing history: Archaeological textiles in Egypt", *Hali* 67: 85–89.

Vogler, U. (1997), *Faunenhistorische Untersuchungen am Sirkeli Höyük/Adana, Türkei (4.-1. Jahrtausend v. Chr.)*. Munich.

Vogt, B. (1994), "In search for coastal sites in prehistoric Makkan: Mid-Holocene 'shell eaters' in the coastal desert of Ras al-Khaimah, UAE", in Kenoyer, ed., 113–128.

Vogt, B. and Franke-Vogt, U., eds. (1987), *Shimal 1985/86: Excavations of the German Archaeological Mission in Ras Al-Khaimah, UAE. A Preliminary Report.* Berlin.

Voigt, M.M. (1983), *Hajji Firuz Tepe, Iran: The Neolithic Settlement.* Philadelphia.

Voigt, M.M. (2005), "Old problems and new solutions: recent excavations at Gordion", in Kealhofer, ed., 22–35.

Voigt, M.M. (2007), "The Middle Phrygian occupation at Gordion", in Çilingiroğlu and Sagona, eds., 311–333.

Voigt, M.M. and Dyson, R.H., Jr. (1992), "The chronology of Iran, 8000 to 2000 BC", in Ehrich, ed., 122–178.

Voigt, M.M. and Henrickson, R.C. (2000a), "The Early Iron Age at Gordion: the evidence from the Yassihöyük stratigraphic sequence", in Oren, ed., 327–360.

Voigt, M.M. and Henrickson, R.C. (2000b), "Formation of the Phrygian state: the Early Iron Age at Gordion", *AnSt* 50: 37–54.

Voigt, M.M. and Young, T.C., Jr. (1999), "From Phrygian capital to Achaemenid entropot: Middle and Late Phrygian Gordion", *IrAnt* 34: 191–241.

Volk, K. (2009), "Schöpfwerk", *RlA* 12: 246–248.

Von Dassow, E. (2008), *State and Society in the Late Bronze Age: Alalaḫ under the Mittani Empire.* Bethesda.

von den Driesch, A. (1986), "Fischknochen aus Abu Salabikh/Iraq", *Iraq* 48: 31–38.

von den Driesch, A. (1993), "Faunal remains from Habuba Kabira in Syria", in Buitenhuis and Clason, eds., 52–59.

von den Driesch, A. and Boessneck, J. (1981), *Reste von Haus- und Jagdtieren aus der Unterstadt von Boğazköy-Hattuša: Grabungen 1958–1977.* Berlin.

von den Driesch, A., Bruckner, H., Obermaier, H. and Zander, A. (2008), "The hunt for wild dromedaries at the United Arab Emirates coast during the 3rd and 2nd millennium BC: Camel bones from the excavations at Al Sufouh 2, Dubai, UAE", in Vila et al., eds., 487–498.

von den Driesch, A. and Manhart, H. (2000), "Fish bones from Al Markh, Bahrain", in Mashkour et al., eds., 50–67.

von den Driesch, A. and Vagedes, K. (2010), "Archaeozoological investigations at Qāni", in Salles and Sedov, eds., 307–325.

von den Driesch, A. and Wodtke, U. (1997), "The fauna of 'Ain Ghazal, a major PPN and early PN settlement in central Jordan", in Gebel et al., eds., 511–556.

von der Osten, H.H. (1934), *Ancient Oriental Seals in the Collection of Mr. Edward T. Newell.* Chicago.

von Folsach, K., Thrane, H. and Thuesen, I., eds. (2004), *From Handaxe to khan: Essays Presented to Peder Mortensen on the Occasion of his 70th birthday.* Aarhus.

von Gall, H. (1974), "Beobachtungen zu den sogenannten medischen Felsgräbern", in Bagherzadeh, ed., 139–154.

von Gall, H. (1979), "Bermerkungen zum Kyrosgrab in Pasargadae und zu verwandten Denkmälern", *AMI* 12: 271–279.

von Gall, H. (1993), "Dā o Doktar", *EnIr* 6: 529–530.
von Haller, A. (1954), *Die Gräber und Grüfte von Assur*. Berlin.
von Haller, A. (1955), *Die Heiligtümer des Gottes Assur und der Sin-Šamaš-Tempel*. Berlin.
von Haller, A.V. (1961), "Der Sinkašid-Palast", *UVB* 17: 20–23.
von Rüden, C. (2009), "Ägäisierende Wandmalerei—Ein Hauch von westlichem Luxus", in al-Maqdissi et al., eds., 176–181.
von Rüden, C. et al. (2011), *Die Wandmalereien von Tall Mischrife/Qatna im Kontext überregionaler Kommunikation*. Wiesbaden.
von Saldern, A. (1959), "Glass finds at Gordion", *JGS* 1: 23–50.
von Saldern, A. (1965), "Recent excavations at Nimrud, Iraq, and their importance for the history of glass of the first millennium BC", in Anonymous, ed., paper 241.
von Saldern, A. (1966a), "Glass", in Mallowan, ed., 623–634.
von Saldern, A. (1966b), "Mosaic glass from Hasanlu, Marlik, and Tell Al-Rimah", *JGS* 8: 9–25.
von Saldern, A. (1970), "Other Mesopotamian glass vessels (1500–600 BC)", in Oppenheim et al., eds., 203–228.
von Saldern, A. (2004), *Antikes Glas*. Munich.
von Wickede, A. (1990), *Prähistorische Stempelglyptik in Vorderasien*. Munich.
von Wissmann, H. (1978), "Die Geschichte des Sabäerreichs und der Feldzug des Aelius Gallus", *ANRW* 2/9/1: 308–544.
Vosmer, T. (1996), "Watercraft and navigation in the Indian Ocean: An evolutionary perspective", in Afanas'ev et al., eds., 223–242.
Vosmer, T. (2000), "Ships in the ancient Arabian Sea: the development of a hypothetical reed boat model", *PSAS* 30: 235–242.
Vosmer, T. (2003a), "The Magan Boat Project: a process of discovery, a discovery of process", *PSAS* 33: 49–58.
Vosmer, T. (2003b), "The naval architecture of Early Bronze Age reed-built boats of the Arabian Sea", in Potts et al., eds., 152–7.
Vosmer, T. (2008), "Shipping in the Bronze Age: how large was a 60-gur ship?", in Olijdam and Spoor, eds., 230–235.
Voss, B. (2008), "Domesticating imperialism: sexual politics and the archaeology of empire", *AA* 110: 191–203.
Vryonis, S. (1971), *The Decline of Medieval Hellenism in Asia Minor*. Berkeley.
Wachsmann, S. (1998), *Seagoing Ships and Seamanship in the Bronze Age Levant*. London.
Waerzeggers, C. (2010), "Babylonians in Susa: the travels of Babylonian businessmen to Susa reconsidered", in Jacobs and Rollinger, eds., 777–813.
Waetzoldt, H. (1972), *Untersuchungen zur neusumerischen Textilindustrie*. Rome.
Waetzoldt, H. (1981), "Zur Terminologie der Metall in den Texten aus Ebla", in Cagni, ed., 363–378.
Waetzoldt, H. (1990), "Zu den Bewässerungseinrichtungen in der Provinz Umma", *BSA* 5: 1–29.
Waetzoldt, H. (1992), "'Rohr' und dessen Verwendungsweisen anhand der neusumerischen Texte aus Umma", *BSA* 6: 125–146.
Waetzoldt, H. and Hauptmann, H., eds. (1988), *Wirtschaft und Gesellschaft von Ebla*. Heidelberg.
Wäfler, M., ed., (2008), *Mesopotamia: The Old Assyrian Period*. Fribourg.

Wagensonner, K. (2008), "Nin-Isina(k)s journey to Nippur reconsidered", *Wiener Zeitschrift für die Kunde des Morgenlandes* 98: 277–294.

Wagner, G.A., ed. (2007), *Eihführung in die Archäometrie*. Berlin.

Wagner, G.A. and Öztunali, Ö. (2000), "Prehistoric copper sources in Turkey", in Yalçin, ed., 31–68.

Wagner, G.A., Wagner, I., Öztunali, Ö., Schmitt-Strecker, S. and Begemann, F. (2003), "Archäometallurgischer Bericht über Feldforschung in Anatolien und bleiisotopische Studien an Erzen und Schlacken", in Stöllner et al., eds. 475–494.

Wagner, J., ed. (2000), *Gottkönige am Euphrat: Neue Ausgrabungen und Forschungen in Kommagene*. Mainz.

Wahida, G. (1967), "Excavations at Tell es-Sawwan", *Sumer* 23: 167–78.

Wald, M.L. (2008), "Tax scheme is blamed for damage to artifacts", *The New York Times*, February 4.

Waldbaum, J.C. (1980), "The first archaeological appearance of iron and the transition to the Iron Age", in Wertime and Muhly, eds., 69–98.

Waldbaum, J.C. (1999), "The coming of iron in the eastern Mediterranean: thirty years of archaeological and technological research", in Pigott, ed., 27–58.

Waliszewski, T. and Ortali Tarazi, R. (2002), *Chhim. 2000 ans d'histoire au coeur d'un village antique du Liban*. Warsaw/Beirut.

Walker, C.B.F. (1987a), *Cuneiform*. Berkeley.

Walker, C.B.F. (1987b), "The Kuyunjik collection of cuneiform texts: formation, problems, and prospects", in Fales and Hickey, eds., 183–201.

Walker, C.B.F. and Collon, D. (1980), "Hormuzd Rassam's excavations for the British Museum at Sippar in 1881–1882", in De Meyer, ed., 93–114.

Walker, P.W.L. (1990), *Holy City, Holy Places? Christian Attitudes to Jerusalem and the Holy Land in the Fourth Century*. Oxford.

Wall-Romana, C. (1990), "An areal location of Agade", *JNES* 49: 205–246.

Walmsley, A. (1996), "Byzantine Palestine and Arabia: urban prosperity in Late Antiquity", in Christie and Loseby, eds., 126–158.

Walmsley, A. (2005), "The village ascendant in Byzantine and Early Islamic Jordan: socio-economic forces and cultural responses", in Lefort, Morrisson and Sodini, eds., 511–522.

Walser, G. (1966), *Die Völkerschaften auf den Reliefs von Persepolis: Historische Studien über den sogenannten Tributzug an der Apadanatreppe*. Berlin.

Walters, S.D. (1970), *Water for Larsa: An Old Babylonian Archive Dealing with Irrigation*. New Haven.

Walton, M.S., Shortland, A., Kirk, S. and Degryse, P. (2009), "Evidence for the trade of Mesopotamian and Egyptian glass to Mycenaean Greece", *JAS* 36: 1496–1503.

Wapnish, P. and Hesse, B. (1988), "Urbanization and the organization of animal production at Tell Jemmeh in the Middle Bronze Age Levant", *JNES* 47: 81–94.

Ward, W.A. and Joukowsky, M.S. (1992), *The Crisis Years: The 12th Century BC, From Beyond the Danube to the Tigris*. Dubuque.

Ward, W.H. (1910), *The Seal Cylinders of Western Asia*. Washington, DC.

Warmington, E.H. (1974), *The Commerce Between the Roman Empire and India*, 2nd ed. London.

Wartke, R.B., ed. (1994), *Handwerk und Technologie im Alten Orient*. Mainz.

Wartke, R.B. (2005), *Sam'al. Ein aramäischer Stadtstaat des 10. bis 8. Jhs. v. Chr. und die Geschichte seiner Erforschung*. Mainz.

Wasse, A. (2001), "The wild goats of Lebanon: evidence for early domestication?", *Levant* 33: 21–33.

Watanabe, K., ed. (1999), *Priests and Officials in the Ancient Near East*. Heidelberg.

Watelin, C.L. (1964), "The Sasanian buildings near Kish", in Pope, ed., 584–592.

Waters, M. (1999), "The earliest Persians in southwestern Iran: the textual evidence", *Iranian Studies* 32/1: 99–107.

Waters, M. (2000), *A Survey of Neo-Elamite history*. Helsinki.

Watkins, T. (1990), "The origins of house and home?", *WA* 21: 336–347.

Watkins, T. (1995), *Qermez Dere, Tell Afar; Interim Report No. 3*. Edinburgh.

Watkins, T. (2004), "Building houses, framing concepts, constructing worlds", *Paléorient* 30: 5–23.

Watkins, T. (2008), "Supra-regional networks in the Neolithic of southwest Asia", *JWP* 21: 139–171.

Watkins, T. (2010a), "Changing people, changing environments: how hunter-gatherers became communities that changed the world", in Finlayson and Warren, eds., 106–114.

Watkins, T. (2010b), "New light on the Neolithic Revolution in South-West Asia", *Antiquity* 84: 1–14.

Watson, C.M. (1915), *Fifty Years' Work in the Holy Land: A Record and Summary 1865–1915*. London.

Watson, P. (2001), "The Byzantine period", in MacDonald et al., eds., 461–502.

Watson, P. and Todeschini, C. (2006), *The Medici Conspiracy*. New York.

Wattenmaker, P. (1998), *Household and State in Upper Mesopotamia: Specialized Economy and the Social Uses of Goods in an Early Complex Society*. Washington, DC.

Waxman, S. (2008), *Loot: The Battle over the Stolen Treasures of the Ancient World*. New York.

Webb, V.E.S. (1987), "Aegean glass: continuity or discontinuity?", in Bimson and Freestone, eds., 145–150.

Weber, A. (1995), "The Neolithic and Early Bronze Age of the Lake Baikal region: a review of recent research", *JWP* 9/1: 99–165.

Weber, J.A. (2008), "Elite equids: redefining equid burials of the mid to late 3rd millennium BC from Umm el-Marra, Syria", in Vila et al., ed., 499–520.

Weber, M. (1978), *Economy and Society*, vol. 2. Berkeley.

Weber, T. and Wenning, R., eds.(1997), *Petra. Antike Felsstadt zwischen arabischer Tradition und griechischer Norm*. Mainz.

Weber, U. and Wiesehöfer, J. (1996), *Das Reich der Achaimeniden: Eine Bibliographie*. Berlin.

Wedepohl, K.H. (1997), "Chemical composition of medieval glass from excavations in West Germany", *Glastechnische Berichte/ Glass Science and Technology* 70: 246–255.

Weedon, M. (2011), *Hittite logograms and Hittite scholarship*. Wiesbaden.

Weeks, L.R. (1999), "Lead isotope analyses from Tell Abraq, United Arab Emirates: new data regarding the 'tin problem' in Western Asia", *Antiquity* 73: 49–64.

Weeks, L.R. (2003), *Early Metallurgy of the Persian Gulf: Technology, Trade and the Bronze Age world*. Boston.

Weeks, L.R. (2008), "The 2007 Early Iranian Metallurgy Workshop at the University of Nottingham", *Iran* 46: 335–345.

Weeks, L.R., ed. (2010), *Death and Burial in Arabia and Beyond: Multidisciplinary Perspectives*. Oxford.

Weeks, L.R., Alizadeh, K., Niakan, L., Alamdari, K., Khosrowzadeh, A. and Zeidi, M. (2006a), "Excavations at Tol-e Nurabad", in Potts and Roustaei, eds., 31–88.

Weeks, L.R., Alizadeh, K., Niakan, L., Alamdari, K., Zeidi, M., Khosrowzadeh, A. and McCall, B. (2006b), "The Neolithic settlement of highland SW Iran: new evidence from the Mamasani District", *Iran* 44: 1–31.

Weeks, L.R., Keall, E., Pashley, V., Evans, J. and Stock, S. (2009), "Lead isotope analyses of Bronze Age copper-base artefacts from Al-Midamman, Yemen: towards the identification of an indigenous metal production and exchange system in the southern Red Sea region", *Archaeometry* 51/4: 576–597.

Weeks, L.R., Morris, M., McCall, B. and al-Zubairy, K. (2002), "A recent archaeological survey on Soqotra: report on the preliminary expedition season January 5th-February 2nd 2001", *AAE* 13: 95–125.

Weeks, L.R., Petrie, C.A. and Potts, D.T. (2010), "Ubaid-related-related? contextualising the 'black-on-buff' ceramic traditions of highland southwest Iran", in Carter and Philip, eds., 245–276.

Weimann, R. (1997), "Value, representation and the discourse of modernization: toward a political economy of postindustrial culture", in Palumbo-Liu and Gumbrecht, eds., 221–248.

Weinberg, S.S., ed. (1956), *The Aegean and the Near East: Studies Presented to Hetty Goldman on the Occasion of her Seventy-Fifth Birthday*. Locust Valley.

Weinstein, J.M. (1989), "The gold scarab of Nefertiti from Ulu Burun: its implications for Egyptian history and Egyptian-Aegean relations", *AJA* 93: 17–29.

Weisberg, D.B. (1998), "The 'antiquarian' interests of the Neo-Babylonian kings", in Westenholz, ed. 177–186.

Weisgerber, G. (1981), "Mehr als Kupfer in Oman – Ergebnisse der Expedition 1981", *Der Anschnitt* 33: 174–263.

Weisgerber, G. (2006), "The mineral wealth of ancient Arabia and its use I. Copper mining and smelting at Feinan and Timna – comparison and evaluation of techniques, production, and strategies", *AAE* 17: 1–30.

Weisgerber, G. and Cierny, J. (2002), "Tin for ancient Anatolia", in Yalçin, ed., 179–187.

Weisgerber, G. and Willies, L. (2000), "The use of fire in prehistoric and ancient mining – firesetting", *Paléorient* 26/2: 131–149.

Weiss, E., Kislev, M.E. and Hartmann, A. (2006), "Autonomous cultivation before domestication", *Science* 312: 1608–1610.

Weiss, E., Wetterstrom, W., Nadel, D. and Bar-Yosef, O. (2004), "The broad spectrum revisited: evidence from plant remains". *PNAS* 101/26: 9551–9555.

Weiss, H. (1976), *Ceramics for Chronology: Discrimination and Cluster Analysis of Fifth Millennium Ceramic Assemblages from Qabr Sheykheyn, Khuzestan*. Philadelphia.

Weiss, H. (1983), "Excavations at Tell Leilan and the origins of North Mesopotamian cities in the third millennium BC", *Paléorient* 9/2: 39–52.

Weiss, H., ed. (1986), *The Origins of Cities in Dry-Farming Syria and Mesopotamia in the Third Millennium BC*. Guilford.

Weiss, H. (1990), "Tell Leilan 1989: new data for mid-third millennium urbanization and state formation", *MDOG* 122: 193–218.

Weiss, H. (2000), "Beyond the Younger Dryas: collapse as adaptation to abrupt climate change in ancient West Asia and the Eastern Mediterranean", in Bawden and Reycraft, eds., 75–98.

Weiss, H. and Bradley, R. (2001), "What drives societal collapse?", *Science* 291: 609–610.

Weiss, H. and Courty, M.-A. (1993), "The genesis and collapse of the Akkadian Empire: the accidental refraction of historical law", in Liverani, ed., 131–155.

Weiss, H., Courty, M.-A., Wetterstrom, W., Guichard, F., Senior, L., Meadow, R. and Curnow, A. (1993), "The genesis and collapse of third millennium north Mesopotamian civilization", *Science* 261: 995–1004.

Weiss, H., De Lillis, F., deMoulins, D., Eidem, J., Guilderson, T., Kasten, U., Larsen, T., Mori, L., Ristvet, L., Rova, E. and Wetterstrom, W. (2002), "Revising the contours of history at Leilan", *AAAS* 45: 59–74. Also available at http://research.yale.edu/leilan/.

Weiss, H. and Schwartz, G. (1987), "The Ninevite V period and the development of complex society in northern Mesopotamia", *Paléorient* 13: 93–100.

Weiss, H. and Young, T.C., Jr. (1975), "The merchants of Susa: Godin V and plateau–lowland relations in the late fourth millennium BC", *Iran* 13: 1–17.

Weisshaar, H-J. and Wijeyapala, W. (2000), "Tissamaharama Project (Sri Lanka): excavations in the Citadel Area", in Taddei and de Marco, eds., 633–645.

Weld Blundell, H. (1893), "Persepolis", in Morgan, ed., vol. 2, 537–559.

Welsby, D.A. and Anderson., J.R., eds. (2004), *Sudan: Ancient Treasures*. London.

Welter, J.-M. (2003), "The zinc content of brass: a chronological indicator?", *Technè* 18: 27–36.

Wengrow, D. (2001), "The evolution of simplicity: aesthetic labour and social change in the Neolithic Near East", *WA* 33/2: 168–188.

Weninger, B. (2009), "Yarmoukian rubble slide: evidence for early Holocene rapid climate change in southern Jordan", *Neo-Lithics* 1/09: 5–11.

Weninger, B., Alram-Stern, E., Bauer, E., Clare, L., Danzeglocke, U., Jöris, O., Kubatzki, C., Rollefson, G., Todorova, H. and van Andel, T. (2006), "Climate forcing due to the 8200 cal yr BP event observed at Early Neolithic sites in the eastern Mediterranean", *QR* 66: 401–420.

Wenke, R.J. (1975–6), "Imperial investments and agricultural developments in Parthian and Sasanian Khuzestan: 150 BC to AD 160", *Mesopotamia* 10–11: 31–157.

Wenke, R.J. (1987), "Western Iran in the Partho-Sasanian period: the imperial transformation", in Hole, ed., 251–282.

Wensinck, A. (1923), *The Mystic Treatises by Isaac of Nineveh*. Amsterdam.

Werner, P. (1994), *Die Entwicklung der Sakralarchitektur in Nordsyrien und Südostkleinasien vom Neolithikum bis in das 1. Jt. v. Chr.* Munich.

Werner, P. (2009), *Der Sîn-Šamaš-Tempel in Assur*. Wiesbaden.

Werner, P. (in press), *Der Anu-Adad-Tempel in Assur*. Wiesbaden.

Werner, P. and Busch, R. (1998), *Tall Munbaqa. Bronzezeit in Syrien*. Neumünster.

Wernick, A. (2003), "The new Tarde: sociology after the end of the social", *Theory, Culture & Society* 20: 81–98.

Wernke, S.A. (2007), "Analogy of erasure? Dialectics of religious transformation in the early *Doctrinas* of the Colca Valley, Peru", *International Journal of Historical Archaeology* 11: 152–182.

Wertime, J.T. (1998), "Back to basics – 'primitive' pile rugs of West and Central Asia", *Hali* 100: 86–97.

Wertime, T.A. and Muhly, J.D., eds. (1980), *The Coming of the Age of Iron*. New Haven.

Wertime, T.A. and Wertime, S., eds. (1982), *Early pyrotechnology: The Evolution of the First Fire-Using Industries*. Washington, DC.

Westenholz, A. (1987), *Old Sumerian and Old Akkadian texts in Philadelphia, part two: The "Akkadian" texts, the Enlilemaba texts, and the Onion Archive*. Copenhagen.

Westenholz, A. (1999), "The Old Akkadian period: history and culture", in Attinger and Wäfler, eds., 17–117.

Westenholz, J.G. (1997), *Legends of the Kings of Akkade*. Winona Lake.

Westenholz, J.G., ed. (1998), *Capital Cities: Urban Planning and Spiritual Dimensions*. Jerusalem.

Weszeli, M. (2009), "Schiff und Boot. B. In mesopotamischen Quellen des 2. und 1. Jahrtausends", *RlA* 12: 160–171.

Wetzel, F., Schmidt, E. and Mallwitz, A. (1957), *Das Babylon der Spätzeit*. Berlin.

Wharton, A.J. (1995), *Refiguring the Post-Classical city: Dura Europos, Jerash, Jerusalem and Ravenna*. Cambridge.

Wheatley, P. (1971), *The Pivot of the Four Quarters: A Preliminary Enquiry into the Origins and Character of the Ancient Chinese City*. Chicago.

Wheeler, R.E.M., Ghosh, A. and Krishna Deva (1946), "Arikamedu: an Indo-Roman trading-station on the east coast of India", *Ancient India* 2: 17–124.

Wheeler, T.S., and Maddin, R. (1980), "Metallurgy and ancient man", in Wertime and Muhly, eds., 99–126.

Whitcomb, D. (1971), *The Proto-Elamite Period at Tal-i-Ghazir, Iran*. Atlanta.

Whitcomb, D. (1979), "The city of Istakhr and the Marvdasht plain", in Anonymous, ed., 363–370.

Whitcomb, D. (1985), *Before the Roses and Nightingales: Excavations at Qasr-i Abu Nasr, Old Shiraz*. New York.

Whitcomb, D. (1989a), "Coptic glazed ceramics from the excavations at Aqaba, Jordan", *JARCE* 26: 167–182.

Whitcomb, D. (1989b), "Evidence of the Umayyad period from the Aqaba excavations", in Bakhit and Schick, eds., 164–184.

Whitcomb, D. (1990), "Diocletian's *miṣr* at 'Aqaba'", *ZDPV* 106: 156–161.

Whitcomb, D. (1994), *Ayla: Art and Industry in the Islamic port of Aqaba*. Chicago.

Whitcomb, D. (1995), "A street and the beach at Ayla: the fall season of excavations at 'Aqaba, 1992", *ADAJ* 39: 499–507.

Whitcomb, D.S. and Johnson, J.H., eds. (1979), *Quseir al-Qadim 1978. Preliminary Report*. Cairo.

Whitcomb, D.S. and Johnson, J.H., eds. (1982), *Quseir al-Qadim 1980: Preliminary Report*. Malibu.

White, C. and Makarewicz, C. (in press), "Harvesting practices and early Neolithic barley cultivation at el-Hemmeh, Jordan", *VHA*.

White, L.M. (1996), *The Social Origins of Christian Architecture*, 2 vols. Valley Forge.
Whitehouse, D. (1991), "Epilogue: Roman trade in perspective", in Begley and de Puma, eds., 216–220.
Whitehouse, D. (1996), "Sasanian maritime activity", in Reade, ed., 339–349.
Whitehouse, H. (2004), *Modes of Religiosity: A Cognitive Theory of Religious Transmission*. Walnut Creek.
Whitehouse, H. and Hodder, I. (2010), "Modes of religiosity at Çatalhöyük", in Hodder, ed., 122–145.
Whittaker, J.C. (1996), "Athkiajas: a Cypriot flintknapper and the threshing sledge industry", *Lithic Technology* 21: 108–120.
Whittaker, J.C. (1998), *Flintknapping: Making and Understanding Stone Tools*. Austin.
Whittow, P. (1990), "Ruling the Late Roman and early Byzantine city: a continuous history", *Past and Present* 129: 3–29.
Wick, L., Lemcke, G. and Sturm, M. (2003), "Evidence of late glacial and Holocene climatic change and human impact in eastern Anatolia: high-resolution pollen, charcoal, isotopic and geochemical records from the laminated sediments of Lake Van, Turkey", *The Holocene* 13/5: 665–675.
Wicke, D. (2010), *Die Kleinfunde aus Elfenbein und Knochen aus Assur*. Wiesbaden.
Wieczorek, A. and Lind, C. (2007), *Ursprünge der Seidenstrasse*. Stuttgart.
Wiesehöfer, J. (1994), *Die "dunklen Jahrhunderte" der Persis: Untersuchungen zu Geschichte und Kultur von Fārs in frühhellenistischer Zeit (330–140 v.Chr.)*. München.
Wiesehöfer, J. (1996), *Ancient Persia, from 550 BC to 650 AD*. London.
Wiesehöfer, J. (1998), "Mare Erythraeum, Sinus Persicus und Fines Indiae: Der Indische Ozean in hellenistischer und römischer Zeit", in Conermann, ed., 9–36.
Wiesehöfer, J., ed., (1998), *Das Partherreich und seine Zeugnisse*. Stuttgart.
Wiesehöfer, J. (2009), "Persis, kings of", *EnIr* online.
Widell, M. (2003), *The Administrative and Economic Ur III Texts from the City of Ur*. Piscataway.
Widell, M. (2007), "Historical evidence for climate instability and environmental catastrophes in Northern Syria and the Jazira: the Chronicle of Michael the Syrian", *Environment and History* 13/1: 47–70.
Widell, M. (2009), "Schiff und Boot. A. In sumerischen Quellen", *RlA* 12: 158–160.
Wiessner, P. (1983), "Style and social information in Kalahari projectile points", *AmAnt* 48: 253–276.
Wiggermann, F.A.M. (1992), *Mesopotamian Protective Spirits: The Ritual Texts*. Groningen.
Wilcken, U. (1963), *Grundzüge und Chrestomathie der Papyruskunde. Erster Band: Historischer Teil zweite Hälfte: Chrestomathie*. Hildesheim.
Wilhelm, A. (1937), "Papyrus Tebtunis 33", *JRS* 27/1: 145–151.
Wilhelm, G. (1982), *Grundzüge der Geschichte und Kultur der Hurriter*. Darmstadt.
Wilhelm, G. (1991), "Hethiter und Hurriter", in Hrouda, ed., 85–112.
Wilhelm, G. (1997a), *Kuşakli-Šarišša, Band 1: Keilschrifttexte aus Gebäude A*. Rahden.
Wilhelm, G., ed. (1997b), *Die orientalische Stadt: Kontinuität, Wandel, Bruch*. Saarbrücken.
Wilhelm, G., ed. (2001), *Akten des IV. Internationalen Kongresses für Hethitologie, Würzburg, 4.–8 Oktober 1999*. Wiesbaden.

Wilk, R. (2004), "Miss Universe, the Olmec and the Valley of Oaxaca", *Journal of Social Archaeology* 4: 81–98.

Wilkens, B. (2002), "The consumption of animal products at Sumhuram", in Avanzini, ed., 271–322.

Wilkens, B. (2005), Fishing in the Arabian Sea: a short note on the prehistoric sites RH6 and R'as al-Jinz 1 in Oman", *Paléorient* 31/1: 126–130.

Wilkinson, J. (1977), *Jerusalem Pilgrims Before the Crusades*. Warminster.

Wilkinson, T. (2003), "Did the Egyptians invent writing?", in Many, ed., 24–27.

Wilkinson, T. (2010), "Cones, nails, and pegs: enigmatic clay objects from Buto and their implications for contacts between Egypt and Western Asia in the fourth millennium BC", in Ikram and Dodson, eds., 601–610.

Wilkinson, T., Sherratt, E.S. and Bennet, J, eds. (2011), *Interweaving Worlds: Systemic Interactions in Eurasia, 7th to 1st Millennia bc*. Oxford.

Wilkinson, T.J. (1990), *Town and Country in SE Anatolia. Vol.1: Settlement and Land Use at Kurban Höyük and Other Sites in the Lower Karababa Basin*. Chicago.

Wilkinson, T.J. (1993), "Linear hollows in the Jazira, Upper Mesopotamia", *Antiquity* 67: 548–562.

Wilkinson, T.J. (1994), "The structure and dynamics of dry farming states in Upper Mesopotamia", *CA* 351: 483–520.

Wilkinson, T.J. (1995), "Late-Assyrian settlement geography in Upper Mesopotamia", in Liverani, ed., 139–159.

Wilkinson, T.J. (1997), "Holocene environments of the high plateau, Yemen: recent geoarchaeological investigations", *Geoarchaeology* 12/8: 833–864.

Wilkinson, T.J. (1998a), "Water and human settlement in the Balikh Valley, Syria: Investigations from 1992 to 1995", *JFA* 25: 63–87.

Wilkinson, T.J. (1998b), "Akkadian Empire: where to look?", *Science* 279: 1283.

Wilkinson, T.J. (2000), "Regional approaches to Mesopotamian archaeology: the contribution of archaeological surveys", *JAR* 8: 219–267.

Wilkinson, T.J. (2002), "Physical and cultural landscapes of the Hamoukar area", *Akkadica* 123: 89–105.

Wilkinson, T.J. (2003a), *Archaeological Landscapes of the Near East*. Tucson.

Wilkinson, T.J. (2003b), "The organization of settlement in highland Yemen during the Bronze and Iron Ages", *PSAS* 33: 157–168.

Wilkinson, T.J. (2005), "Soil erosion and valley fills in the Yemen highlands and southern Turkey: integrating settlement, geoarchaeology and climate change", *Geoarchaeology* 20/2: 169–192.

Wilkinson, T.J., Christiansen, J.H., Ur, J.A., Widell, M. and Altaweel, M. (2007), "Urbanization with a dynamic environment: modeling Bronze Age communities in Upper Mesopotamia", *AA* 109/1: 52–68.

Wilkinson, T.J., Edens, C. and Gibson, McG. (1997), "The archaeology of the Yemen high plains: a preliminary chronology", *AAE* 8: 99–142.

Wilkinson, T.J. and Moore, A.T.M. (1978), "A prehistoric site near Dibsi Faraj in Syria", *Levant* 10: 26–36.

Wilkinson, T.J., Peltenburg, E., McCarthy, A., Wilkinson, E.B. and Brown, B. (2007), "Archaeology in the land of Carchemish: landscape surveys in the area of Jerablus Tahtani, 2006", *Levant* 39: 213–247.

Wilkinson T.J. and Tucker, D. (1995), *Settlement Development in the North Jazira, Iraq: A Study of the Archaeological Landscape*. London.

Wilkinson, T.J., Ur, J., Wilkinson, E.B. and Altaweel, M. (2005), "Landscape and settlement in the Neo-Assyrian Empire", *BASOR* 340: 23–56.

Will, E. (1979/82), *Histoire politique du monde hellénistique*, 2 vols. Nancy.

Willcox, G. (2002a), "Geographical variation in major cereal components and evidence for independent domestication", in Cappers and Bottema, eds., 133–140.

Willcox, G. (2002b), "Charred plant remains from a 10th millennium B.P. kitchen at Jerf el Ahmar (Syria)", *VHA* 11: 55–60.

Willcox, G. (2004), "Measuring grain size and identifying Near Eastern cereal domestication: evidence from the Euphrates valley", *JAS* 31: 145–50.

Willcox, G. (2005), "The distribution, natural habitats and the availability of wild cereals in relation to their domestication in the Near East: multiple events, multiple centres", *VHA* 14: 534–541.

Willcox, G. (in press), "Utilisation des fruits au Proche-Orient. Un premier bilan du Paléolithique au Néolithique", in Ruas et al., eds.

Willcox, G., Buxo, R. and Herveux, L.H. (2009), "Late Pleistocene and Early Holocene climate and the beginnings of cultivation in northern Syria", *The Holocene* 19/1: 151–158.

Willcox, G., and Fornite, S. (1999), "Impressions of wild cereal chaff in pisé from the tenth millennium at Jerf el Ahmar and Mureybet: Northern Syria", *VHA* 8/1–2: 14–21.

Willcox, G., Fornite, S. and Herveux, L.H. (2008), "Early Holocene cultivation before domestication in northern Syria", *VHA* 17: 313–25.

Williams Jackson, A.V. (1906), *Persia Past and Present*. New York.

Willies, L. (1993), "Appendix: Early Bronze Age tin working at Kestel", *AJA* 97: 262–264.

Willinghöfer, H., ed. (2002), *Die Hethiter und ihr Reich. Das Volk der 1000 Götter*. Stuttgart.

Winkelmann, S. (1997), "Southeast Iranian and Indo-Iranian elements on Bactrian and Murghab style seals", in Allchin and Allchin, eds., 265–277.

Winkler, H.A. (1938), *Archaeological Survey of Egypt. Rock-Drawings of Southern Upper Egypt*. I. *Sir Robert Mond Desert Expedition. Season 1936–1937 Preliminary Report*. London.

Winlock, H.E. (1941), *The Temple of Hibis in El Khargeh Oasis*. New York.

Winnett, F.V. and Reed, W.L. (1970), *Ancient Records from North Arabia*. Toronto/Buffalo.

Winnicki, J.K. (2009), *Late Egypt and Her Neighbours: Foreign Population in Egypt in the First Millennium BC*. Warsaw.

Winter, I. (1983), "The program of the throneroom of Assurnasirpal II", in Harper and Pittman, eds., 15–31.

Winter, I. (1996), "Sex, rhetoric and the public monument: the alluring body of Naram-Sin of Agade", in Kampen and Bergmann, eds., 11–26.

Winter, I. (1999), "Tree(s) on the mountain: landscape and territory on the victory stele of Naram-Sin of Agade", in Milano et al., eds., 63–72.

Winter, I. (2000), "Babylonian archaeologists of the(ir) Mesopotamian past", in Matthiae et al., eds., 1785–1800.

Winter, I. (2005), "Establishing group boundaries: toward methodological refinement in the determination of sets as a prior condition to the analysis of cultural contact and/or innovation in first millennium BCE ivory carving", in Suter and Uehlinger, eds., 23–42.
Wirth, E. (1962), *Agrargeographie des Irak*. Hamburg.
Wirth, E. (1971), *Syrien, eine Geographische Landeskunde*. Darmstadt.
Wittfogel, K.A. (1957), *Oriental Despotism: A Comparative Study of Total Power*. New Haven.
Wittke, A.-M. (2007), "Remarks on the early history of Phrygia (twelfth to eighth century BC)", in Çilingiroğlu and Sagona, eds., 335–347.
Wolff, S.R., ed. (2001), *Studies in the Archaeology of Israel and Neighboring Lands in Memory of Douglas L. Esse*. Chicago.
Wolff, S.R. (2002), "Mortuary practices in the Persian period of the Levant", *NEA* 65: 131–137.
Wolska-Conus, W., ed. (1968), *Cosmas Indicopleustès Topographie Chrétienne*, vol. 1. Paris.
Wolska-Conus, W., ed. (1973), *Cosmas Indicopleustès Topographie Chrétienne*, vol. 3. Paris.
Wolski, J. (1981), "L'aristocratie et l'organisationde l'armée parthe", *Klio* 63: 105–122.
Wolski, J. (1993), *L'Émpire des Arsacides*. Leuven.
Woodard, R.D., ed. (2004), *The Cambridge Encyclopaedia of the World's Ancient Languages*. Cambridge.
Woods, C. (2005), "On the Euphrates", *ZA* 95: 7–45.
Woods, C. (2006), "Bilingualism, scribal learning, and the death of Sumerian", in Sanders, eds., 95–124.
Woolley, C.L. (1921), *Carchemish. Report on the Excavations at Jerablus on Behalf of the British Museum. Part 2: The Town Defences*. London.
Woolley, C.L. (1928), "Excavations at Ur, 1926–27, Part II", *The Antiquaries Journal* 8/1: 1–29.
Woolley, C.L. (1934), *Ur Excavations 2. The Royal Cemetery*. London.
Woolley, C.L. (1935), "Antiquities Law, Iraq", *Antiquity* 33: 84–88.
Woolley, C.L. (1939), *Ur Excavations 5. The Ziggurat and its Surroundings*. London.
Woolley, C.L. (1939–40), "The Iron-Age graves of Carchemish", *AAA* 26: 11–137.
Woolley, C.L. (1955a), *Ur Excavations 4. The Early Periods*. London and Philadelphia.
Woolley, C.L. (1955b), *Alalakh, an Account of the Excavations of Tell Atchana in the Hatay, 1937–1949*. London.
Woolley, C.L. (1962), *Ur Excavations 9. The Neo-Babylonian and Persian Periods*. London.
Woolley, C.L. (1965), *Ur Excavations 8. The Kassite Period and the Period of the Assyrian kings*. London.
Woolley, C.L. (1974), *Ur Excavations 6. The Buildings of the Third Dynasty*. London.
Woolley, C.L. and Barnett, R.D. (1952), *Carchemish. Report on the Excavations at Jerablus on behalf of the British Museum. Part 3: The Excavations in the Inner Town and the Hittite inscriptions*. London.
Woolley, C.L. and Hall, H.R. (1927), *Ur Excavations 1. al-'Ubaid*. Oxford.

Woolley, L., and Mallowan, M.E.L. (1962), *Ur Excavations 9. The Neo-Babylonian and Persian Periods.* London.

Woolley, C.L. and Mallowan, M.E.L. (1976), *Ur Excavations 7. The Old Babylonian Period.* London.

Wossink, A. (2009), *Challenging Climate Change: Competition and Cooperation Among Pastoralists and Agriculturalists in Northern Mesopotamia (c.3000–1600 BC).* Leiden.

Wright, G. (1978), "Social differentiation in the Early Natufian", in Redman et al., eds., 201–233.

Wright, G.E. (1971), "The archaeology of Palestine from the Neolithic through the Middle Bronze Age", *JAOS* 91: 276–293.

Wright, G.R.H. (1991), "Abu Qubur: The 'Parthian Building' and its affinities", *NAPR* 7: 75–91.

Wright, H.T. (1969), *Archeological Survey in the Areas of Ram Hormoz, Shushtar and Gotwand.* Ann Arbor.

Wright, H.T. (1977a), "Recent research on the origin of the state", *ARA* 6: 379–397.

Wright, H.T. (1977b), "Toward an explanation of the origin of the state", in Hill, ed., 215–230.

Wright, H.T., ed. (1979), *Archaeological Investigations in Northeastern Xuzestan, 1976.* Ann Arbor.

Wright, H.T. (1981a), "The southern margins of Sumer: archaeological survey of the area of Eridu and Ur", in Adams, 295–345.

Wright, H.T., ed (1981b), *An Early Town in the Deh Luran Plain: Excavations at Tepe Farukhabad.* Ann Arbor.

Wright, H.T. (1984), "Prestate political formations", in Earle, ed. 41–77.

Wright, H.T. (1987), "The Susiana hinterland during the era of primary state formation", in Hole, ed., 141–155.

Wright, H.T. (1994), "Pre-state political formations", in Stein and Rothman, eds., 67–84.

Wright, H.T. (1998), "Uruk states in southwestern Iran", in Feinman and Marcus, eds., 173–197.

Wright, H.T. (2000), "Modeling tributary economies and hierarchical polities", in Feinman and Manzanilla, eds., 197–213.

Wright, H.T. (2001), "Cultural action in the Uruk world", in Rothman, ed., 123–147.

Wright, H.T. and Carter, E. (2003), "Archaeological survey on the western Ram Hormuz plain, 1969", in Miller and Abdi, eds., 60–82.

Wright, H.T. and Johnson, G.A. (1975), "Population, exchange, and early state formation in southwestern Iran", *AA* 77: 267–289.

Wright, H.T., Miller, N., Neely J.A., and Redding, R.W. (1999), "A Late Susiana society in southwestern Iran", in Alizadeh et al., eds., 64–79.

Wright H.T., Neely, J.A., Johnson, G.A., and Speth, J.D. (1975), "Early fourth millennium developments in southwestern Iran", *Iran* 13: 129–147.

Wright, H.T. and Rupley, E.S.A. (2001), "Radiocarbon age determinations of Uruk-related assemblages", in Rothman, ed., 85–122.

Wright, K.E. (1994), "Ground stone tools and hunter-gatherer subsistence in Southwest Asia: Implications for the transition to farming", *AA* 59: 238–263.

Wright, K.E. (2000), "The social origins of cooking and dining in early villages of western Asia", *PPS* 66: 89–121.

Wright, K.E. and Garrard, A.N. (2003), "Social identities and the expansion of stone bead making in Neolithic Western Asia: new evidence from Jordan", *Antiquity* 77: 267–284.

Wright, M. (1988), "Contacts between Egypt and Syro-Palestine during the Old Kingdom", *BA* 51: 143–162.

Wright, R.P. (1989), "New tracks on ancient frontiers: Ceramic technology in the Indo-Iranian borderlands", in Lamberg-Karlovsky, ed., 268–279.

Wu, Y. (1994), *A Political History of Eshnunna, Mari and Assyria During the Early Old Babylonian Period*. Changchun.

Wunsch, C. (2000), *Das Egibi-Archiv I. Die Felder und Gärten*. Groningen.

Wurster, W.W. (1974), "Die Burg von Limyra", *AAnz* 89: 259–273.

Wushiki, H. (1997), "Some hydro-scientific aspects of Arabia", *Al-Rāfidān* 18: 3–24.

Wuttmann, M., et al. (1996), "Premier rapport préliminaire des travaux sur le site de 'Ayn Manāwīr (oasis de Kharga)", *BIFAO* 96: 385–451.

Wyart, J.P.B., Bariand, P. and Filippi, J. (1981), "Lapis lazuli from Sar-i Sang, Badakhshan, Afghanistan", *Gems and Gemology* 17/4: 184–190.

Wylie, A. (2000), "Ethical dilemmas in archaeological practice: looting, repatriation, stewardship and the (trans)formation of disciplinary identity", in Lynott and Wylie, eds., 138–157.

Yağci, R. (2003), "The stratigraphy of Cyprus WS II and Mycenaean cups in Soli Höyük excavations", in Fischer et al., eds., 93–106.

Yaghmaee, E. (2006), "Čand manzelgāh-e rāh-e šāhī-ye hakhāmanešī: az Nūrābād-e Mamasanī tā Arǧān-e Behbahān", *Bāstānpazhuhi* 2: 32–49.

Yaghmaee, E. (2010), "Excavations in Dashtesan (Borazjan, Iran)", in Curtis and Simpson, eds., 317.

Yakar, J. (2002), "East Anatolian metallurgy in the fourth and third millennia BC: some remarks", in Yalçin, ed., 15–26.

Yakubovich, I. (2008a), *Sociolinguistics of the Luvian Language*. Chicago.

Yakubovich, I. (2008b), "Hittite-Luvian bilingualism and the development of Anatolian hieroglyphs", in Kazansky, ed., 9–36.

Yalçin, Ü. (1998), "Der Keulenkopf von Çan Hasan (TR): Naturwissenschaftliche Untersuchung und neue Interpretation", in Rehren, Hauptmann & Muhly, eds., 279–290.

Yalçin, Ü. (2000a), "Anfänge der Metallverwendung in Anatolien", in Yalçin, ed., 17–30.

Yalçin, Ü., ed. (2000b), *Anatolian Metal I*. Bochum.

Yalçin, Ü., ed. (2002), *Anatolian Metal II*. Bochum.

Yalçin, Ü. (2003), "Metallurgie in Anatolien", in Stöllner et al., eds., 527–536.

Yalçin, Ü., ed. (2005), *Anatolian Metal III*. Bochum.

Yalçin, Ü., ed. (2009), *Anatolian Metal IV*. Bochum.

Yalçin, Ü. and Pernicka, E. (1999), "Frühneolithische Metallurgie von Aşikli Höyük", in Hauptmann et al., eds., 45–54.

Yalçin, Ü., Pulak, C. and Slotta, R., eds. (2005), *Das Schiff von Uluburun: Welthandel vor 3000 Jahren*. Bochum.

Yalçinkaya, I. (1998), "La grotte Karain: généralités dans le contexte Anatolien", in Otte, ed., 453–462.

Yamada, S. (2000), *Development of the Neolithic: Lithic Use-Wear Analysis of Major Tool Types in the Southern Levant.* Cambridge.

Yamazaki, Y. (1999), "Excavations at Tell al-'Abr", in del Olmo Lete and Montero Fenollós, eds., 83–96.

Yardimci, N. (2004), *Harran Ovasi Yüzey Araştirmasi/Archaeological Survey in the Harran Plain.* Istanbul.

Yaroshevich, A., Kaufman D., Nuzhnyy D., Bar-Yosef, O. and Weinstein-Evron, M. (2010), "Design and performance of microlith implemented projectiles during the Middle and the Late Epipaleolithic of the Levant: experimental and archaeological evidence", *JAS* 37: 368–388.

Yartah, T. (2004), "Tell 'Abr 3, un village du Néolithique précéramique (PPNA) sur le Moyen Euphrate. Première approche", *Paléorient* 30/2: 141–158.

Yartah, T. (2005), "Les bâtiments communautaires de Tell 'Abr 3 (PPNA, Syrie)", *Neo-Lithics* 1/05: 3–9.

Yasin, W. (1970), "Excavation at Tell es-Sawwan (1969)", *Sumer* 26: 3–20.

Yasuda, Y., Kitagawa, H. and Nakagawa, T. (2000), "The earliest record of major anthropogenic deforestation in the Ghab Valley, northwest Syria: a palynological study", *QI* 73-74: 127–36.

Yasur-Landau, A. (2010), *The Philistines and Aegean Migration at the End of the Late Bronze Age.* Cambridge.

Yelon, A., Saucier, A., Larocque, J.-P., Smith, P.E.L. and Vandiver, P. (1993), "Thermal analysis of early Neolithic pottery from Tepe Ganj Dareh, Iran", in Vandiver et al., eds., 591–608.

Yener, K.A. (2000), *The Domestication of Metals: The Rise of Complex Metal Industries in Anatolia.* Boston.

Yener, K.A., ed. (2005), *The Amuq Valley Regional Projects.* Vol. 1. *Surveys in the Plain of Antioch and Orontes Delta, Turkey, 1995–2002.* Chicago.

Yener, K.A. and Edens, C. (2000), "Tell Kurdu Excavations 1999", *Anatolica* 26: 31–117.

Yener, K.A. and Hoffner, H.A., eds. (2002), *Recent Developments in Hittite Archaeology and History: Papers in Memory of Hans G. Güterbock.* Winona Lake.

Yener, K.A. and Vandiver, P. (1993a), "Tin processing at Göltepe, an Early Bronze Age site in Anatolia", *AJA* 97: 207–238.

Yener, K.A. and Vandiver, P. (1993b), "Reply to J.D. Muhly, 'Early Bronze Age tin and the Taurus'", *AJA* 97: 255–262.

Yerkes, R.W., Barkai, R. and Gopher, A. (2003), "Microwear analyses of Early Neolithic (PPNA) axes and bifacial tools from Netiv Hagdud in the Jordan Valley, Israel", *JAS* 30: 1051–1066.

Yoffee, N. (1995), "Political economy in early Mesopotamian states", *ARA* 24: 281–311.

Yoffee, N., ed. (2007), *Negotiating the Past in the Past: Identity, Memory, and Landscape in Archaeological Research.* Tucson.

Yoffee, N. and Clark, J.J., ed. (1993), *Early Stages in the Evolution of Mesopotamian Civilization: Soviet Excavations in the Sinjar Plain, Northern Iraq.* Tucson.

Yon, J.-B. (2003), "Les villes de Haute-Mésopotamie et de l'Euphrate", in Sartre et al., eds., 193–210.

Yon, M., ed. (1991), *Ras Shamra-Ougarit VI: Arts et Industries de la Pierre.* Paris.

Yon, M. (1997), *La Cité d'Ougarit sur le tell de Ras Shamra*. Paris.

Yon, M. (2001), "White Slip Ware in the northern Levant", in Karageorghis, ed., 117–126.

Yon, M. (2006), *The City of Ugarit at Tell Ras Shamra*. Winona Lake.

Yon M., Aurenche, O., Calvet, Y. and Marcillet-Jaubert, J., eds. (1982), *Archéologie du Levant: Recueil à la mémoire de Roger Saidah*. Lyon/Paris.

Yon, M. and Calvet, Y., eds. (2008), *Ougarit au Bronze Moyen et au Bronze Récent*. Lyon.

Yon, M., Calvet, Y. and Huot, J.-L., eds. (1985), *De l'Indus aux Balkans: Recueil à la mémoire de Jean Deshayes*. Paris.

Yon, M., Karageorghis, V. and Hirschfeld, N. (2000), *Céramiques mycéniennes d'Ougarit*. Paris.

Youkana, D.G. (1997), *Tell es-Sawwan: The Architecture of the Sixth Millennium BC*. London.

Young, G.D., Chavalas, M.W. and Averbeck, R.E., eds. (1997), *Crossing Boundaries and Linking Horizons: Studies in Honor of Michael C. Astour on his 80th birthday*. Bethesda.

Young, G.K. (2001), *Rome's Eastern Trade: International Commerce and Imperial Policy, 31 BC-AD 305*. London and New York.

Young, R.S., DeVries, K., Kohler, E.L., McClellan, J.F., Mellink, M.J. and Sams, G.K. (1981), *The Gordion Excavations (1950–1973): Final Reports Volume I. Three Great Early Tumuli*. Philadelphia.

Young, S.M.M., Pollard, A.M., Budd, P. and Ixer, R.A., eds. (1999), *Metals in Antiquity*. Oxford.

Young, T.C., Jr. (1985), "Early Iron Age Iran revisited: preliminary suggestions for the re-analysis of old constucts", in Huot et al., eds., 61–78.

Young, T.C., Jr. (1988), The early history of the Medes and the Persians and the Achaemenid empire to the death of Cyrus, *CAH* 4: 1–52.

Young, T.C., Jr. (2003), "Parsua, Parsa, and potsherds", in Miller and Abdi, eds., 242–248.

Young, T.C., Jr., Smith, P.E.L. and Mortensen, P., eds. (1983), *The Hilly Flanks and Beyond: Essays in the Prehistory of Southwestern Asia Presented to Robert J. Braidwood*. Chicago.

Young, W.J., ed. (1965), *The Application of Science in Examination of Works of Art*. Boston.

Yoyotte, J. (1972), "Les inscriptions hiéroglyphiques: Darius et l'Égypte", *JA* 260: 253–266.

Yoyotte, J. (2010), "La statue égyptienne de Darius", in Perrot, ed., 256–299.

Yule, P. and Weisgerber, G. (2001), *The Metal Hoard from Ibri/Selme, Sultanate of Oman*. Stuttgart.

Zaccagnini, C. (1983), "Patterns of mobility among ancient Near Eastern craftsmen", *JNES* 42: 245–264.

Zaccagnini, C. (1987), "Aspects of Ceremonial Exchange in the Near East during the Late Second Millennium BC", in Rowlands et al., eds., 57–65.

Zaccagnini, C., ed. (1989), *Production and Consumption in the Ancient Near East*. Budapest.

Zadok, R. (1985), *Geographical Names According to New- and Late-Babylonian Texts*. Wiesbaden.

Zagarell, A. (1982), "The first millennium in the Bakhtiari Mountains", *AMI* 15: 31–52.
Zah, A. (2003), "Lo sviluppo degli insediamenti costieri bizantini nell'Asia Minore sud occidentale", *Quaderni Friulani di Archeologia* 12: 175–233.
Zahle, J. (1983), *Arkæologiske studiere i lykiske klippgrave og ders reliefer fra c. 550–300 f.Kr. Sociale og religiøse aspekter*. Copenhagen.
Zahle, J. (1991), "Achaemenid influences in Lycia (coinage, sculpture, architecture). Evidence for political changes during the 5th century BC", in Sancisi-Weerdenburg and Kuhrt, eds., 145–160.
Zahle, J. (1994), "Hekatomnid Caria, a province in Achaemenid Asia Minor", in Isager, ed., 85–87.
Zander, G., ed. (1968), *Travaux de restauration de monuments historiques en Iran*. Rome.
Zanini, E. (1990), "La cinta muraria di Dara: materiali per un'analisi stratigrafica", in Maffei et al., eds., 229–264.
Zaqzuq, A. and Piccirillo, M. (1999), "The mosaic floor of the Church of the Holy Martyrs at Tayyibat al-Imam, Hamah, in central Syria", *LA* 49: 443–464.
Zarins, J. (1978), "The domesticated equidae of third millennium BC Mesopotamia", *JCS* 30: 3–17.
Zarins, J. (1986), "Equids associated with human burials in third millennium BC Mesopotamia: two complementary facets", in Meadow and Uerpmann, eds., 164–193.
Zarins, J. (2008), "Magan shipbuilders at the Ur III Lagash state dockyards (2062–2025 BC)", in Olijdam and Spoor, eds., 209–229.
Zayadine, F. (1971), "Deux inscriptions grecques de Rabbat Moab (Areopolis)", *ADAJ* 16: 71–76.
Zayadine, F. (1990), "The pantheon of the Nabataean inscriptions in Egypt and the Sinai", *ARAM* 2/1-2: 151–174.
Zayadine, F. (1996), "Palmyre, Pétra, la mer erythrée et les routes de la soie", *AAAS* 42: 167–178.
Zeder, M.A. (1986), "The equid remains from Tal-e Malyan, southern Iran", in Meadow and Uerpmann, eds., 366–412.
Zeder, M.A. (1994), "After the revolution: post-Neolithic subsistence in northern Mesopotamia", *AA* 96: 97–126.
Zeder, M.A. (1998), "Pigs and emergent complexity in the ancient Near East", in Nelson, ed., 109–122.
Zeder, M.A. (2000), "Animal domestication in the Zagros: a review of past and present research", *Paléorient* 25: 11–25.
Zeder, M.A. (2005), "A view from the Zagros: new perspectives on livestock domestication in the Fertile Crescent", in Vigne et al., eds., 125–146.
Zeder, M.A. (2008a), "Domestication and early agriculture in the Mediterranean basin: origins, diffusion, and impact", *PNAS* 105: 11597–11604.
Zeder, M.A. (2008b), "Animal domestication in the Zagros: an update and directions for future research", in Vila et al., eds., 243–278.
Zeder, M.A., Bradley, D., Emshwiller, E. and Smith, B.D., eds. (2006), *Documenting Domestication: New Genetic and Archaeological Paradigms*. Berkeley/Los Angeles.
Zeder, M.A. and Hesse, B. (2000), "The initial domestication of goats (*Capra hircus*) in the Zagros mountains 10,000 years ago", *Science* 287: 2254–2257.

Zeidi, M., McCall, B. and Khosrowzadeh, A. (2009), "Survey of Dasht-e Rostam-e Yek and Dasht-e Rostam-e Do", in Potts and Roustaei, eds., 147–168.

Zertal, A. (1990), "The Pahwah of Samaria (Northern Israel) during the Persian period: types of settlement, economy, history and new discoveries", *Transeuphratène* 3: 9–30.

Zettler, R.L. (1977), "The Sargonic royal seal: a consideration of sealing in Mesopotamia", in Gibson and Biggs, eds., 33–38.

Zettler, R.L. (1979), "On the chronological range of Neo-Babylonian and Achaemenid seals", *JNES* 38: 257–270.

Zettler, R.L. (1987), "Administration of the temple of Inanna at Nippur under the Third Dynasty of Ur: Archaeological and documentary evidence", in Gibson and Biggs, eds., 117–131.

Zettler, R.L. (1993), *Nippur III. Kassite Buildings in Area WC-1*. Chicago.

Zettler, R.L. (1997), *Subsistence and Settlement in a Marginal Environment: Tell es-Sweyhat, 1989–1995 Preliminary Report*. Philadelphia.

Zettler, R.L. (2003), "Reconstructing the world of ancient Mesopotamia: divided beginnings and holistic history", *JESHO* 46: 3–45.

Zettler, R.L. and Horne, L., eds. (1998), *Treasures from the Royal Tombs of Ur*. Philadelphia.

Zevi, F., ed. (1993), *Puteoli*. Naples.

Zhang, X., Good, I. and Laursen, R. (2008), "Characterization of dyestuffs in ancient textiles from Xinjiang", *JAS* 35: 1095–1103.

Ziegler, C. (1953), *Die Keramik von der Qal'a des Haǧǧi Mohammed*. Berlin.

Ziegler, K.-H. (1964), *Die Beziehungen zwischen Rom und dem Partherreich: Ein Beitrag zur Geschichte des Völkerrechts*. Wiesbaden.

Zimansky, P.E. (1985), *Ecology and Empire: The Structure of the Urartian State*. Chicago.

Zimansky, P.E. (1995a), "Urartian material culture as state assemblage: an anomaly in the archaeology of empire", *BASOR* 299–300: 103–115.

Zimansky, P.E. (1995b), "An Urartian Ozymandias", *BA* 58/2: 94–100.

Zimansky, P.E. (1998), *Ancient Ararat: A Handbook of Urartian Studies*. New York.

Zimansky, P. (2002), "The 'Hittites' at 'Ain Dara", in Yener and Hoffner, eds., 177–191.

Zimmerman, M. (1992), *Untersuchungen zur Historischen Landeskunde Zentrallykien*. Bonn.

Zivie, A. (1990), *Découverte à Saqqarah: Le vizier oublié*. Paris.

Zivotovsky A.Z. and Amar, Z. (2006), "Identifying the ancient shibuta fish", *Environmental Biology of Fishes* 75: 361–363.

Zohar, I., Belmaker, M., Nadel, D., Gafny, S., Goren, M., Hershkovitz, I. and Dayan, T. (2008), "The living and the dead: How do taphonomic processes modify relative abundance and skeletal completeness of freshwater fish?", *Palaeogeography, Palaeoclimatology, Palaeoecology* 258: 292–316.

Zohar, I., Dayan, T., Galili, E. and Spanier, E. (2001), "Fish processing during the early Holocene: a taphonomic case study from coastal Israel", *JAS* 28: 1041–1053.

Zohar, M. (1992), "Megalithic cemeteries in the Levant", in Bar-Yosef and Khazanov, eds., 43–63.

Zohary, D. (1969), "The progenitors of wheat and barley in relation to domestication and agricultural dispersals in the Old World", in Ucko and Dimbleby, eds., 47–66.

Zohary, D. and Hopf, M. (1988), *Domestication of Plants in the Old World: The Origins and Spread of Cultivated Plants in West Asia, Europe and the Nile Valley*, 1st edn. Oxford.

Zohary, D. and Hopf, M. (2000), *Domestication of Plants in the Old World: The Origins and Spread of Cultivated Plants in West Asia, Europe and the Nile Valley*, 3rd edn. Oxford.

Zournatzi, A. (2003), "The palace of Vouni (Cyprus): an Achaemenid perspective", http://www.achemenet.com.

Zournatzi, A. (2011), "Cyprus in the Achaemenid period", *EnIr* online.

Zvelebil, M. (2009), "Choice and necessity: a view from the Old World on the origins and dispersal of agriculture", *CA* 50/5: 699–702.

Zwicker, U. (1980), "Investigations on the extractive metallurgy of Cu/Sb/As ore and excavated smelting products from Norşuntepe (Keban) on the Upper Euphrates (3500–2800 BC)", in Oddy, ed., 13–26.

Index

Aaron, St 1075
Abaqa 1087
Abarnia 344
abarnium 344
Abdi-Ashirta 844
Abila 1073
Abir'ilu 822
Abi-Shemu 839
Abiyate 822
Abraham, Church of 1099
Abu, temple at Tell Asmar 34, 542
   see also Eshnunna; Tell Asmar
Abu Dalaf 1086
Abu Dhabi 229, 491, 499
Abu Habbah 60
Abu Hatab 59, 61
Abu Hjeira 665
Abu Khamis 492, 493
Abu Matar 302
Abu Qubur 1017
Abu Salabikh, *see* Tell Abu Salabikh
Abu Salem 142

Abu Sarbut 1102
Abu Sha'ar 1050ff.
Abu Skheir 1017
Abusir 836, 976
Abydos 188, 834, 835, 836
abzu 362
Açemhöyük 109, 579ff., 583, 587
Achaeans 731
Achaemenid empire 755
   pottery 934ff.
Achaemenids 855, 911, 931ff., 963ff.
   in Arabia 824
Achet-Aten 772
Acheulian 221
Achzib 981
Acigöl, lake 176
acorns 182
Actium 1023, 1029
Adab 59, 540, 658, 666
Adad 853, 861, 862
Adad-apla-iddina 915
Adad-nadin-ahi 43

A Companion to the Archaeology of the Ancient Near East, First Edition.
Edited by D.T. Potts.
© 2012 Blackwell Publishing Ltd. Published 2012 by Blackwell Publishing Ltd.

Adad-nirari I 571, 854
Adad-nirari III 857, 858, 859, 864
Adad-nirari, of Nukhashe 779–80
Adad-shuma-usur 718
Adad-sululi 585
Adams, Robert McC. 94, 515, 519, 520, 536, 635, 655, 1084
Adana 802
Adda-guppi 928
Aden 56
  Gulf of 1047
Adiabene 1004, 1010, 1016
Adir, Mount 312
Adiyaman 148, 808
Adiyamanian 146
Adramytteion 901
Adulis 1049, 1051ff.
Adummatu 822, 823, 826
Adygea 669
adze 249, 252, 257, 308, 314
Aegean influence 624
Aegean pottery 802
Aegean Sea 608
Aelia Capitolina 1031
Aemilius Secundus 1024
Aetokremnos, *see* Akrotiri *Aetokremnos*
Afamia 986
Afanas'evo culture 703
Afghanistan 341, 599, 762, 985, 994
Afyon 109
Agade, *see* Akkad
Aganzana 1007
agate 657, 762
aggradation 21
Agora 310
agora 993
Ağri Dağ, *see* Ararat, Mount
AGRIG 580, 582
Agriophagoi 1052
Agrippa I, II 1030
Agum II 716–17, 719
Ägyptisches Museum Berlin 70
Ahhiyawa 731

Ahlatlibel 309
Ahmarian 146, 147
Ahudemmeh, hagiography of 1105
Ahuramazda 980
  see also Zoroastrianism
Ahwaz 931
Ai Khanoum 985ff., 987, 994ff., 1006
Aila 1021, 1049, 1051, 1053, 1102ff.
  Gulf of 1030
Ailun 563
Ain Abu Kukhayla 403
Ain al-Kanisah 1074
Ain al-Tamr 1108
Ain Dara 790, 804, 806ff.
Ain el-Kerkh 282
Ain Ghazal 175, 281, 402ff.
Ain Jammam 402, 404
Ain Mallaha 132, 137, 380ff., 435
Ainon-Saphsaphas 1075
Ain Qannas 487ff., 491ff.
Ain Sakhri 132
Ain Sha'ia 1109ff.
Aiolis 968
Aitakama 780
Ajanta, caves 1057
Ajlun 62, 1074
Akab 225, 495–6
Akarçay Tepe 204, 205, 283, 386
Akhaioi 731
Akhenaten 570, 752, 772, 844
Akhtala 668
Akhur-e Rustam 956
Akhziv 977
akitu
  festival 1015
  house, see *bīt akitu*
Akkad 366, 651, 707, 762
Akkadian
  language 650, 718, 732, 778, 894
  period 544, 649ff.
Akkadians 545

Akkar, plain 610, 617, 777
Akkaz 1110
Akko 231, 773, 970, 973, 1024
Aknashen 675
Akrotiri *Aetokremnos* 140, 141, 370
Akywash 845
alabaster 468, 470, 600, 602, 603, 795, 953
Alaça Höyük 63, 107, 309, 314, 582, 593, 736, 799
al-Ain 197, 499
Alakul, culture 695
Alalakh 191, 226, 319, 570, 612, 622, 624, 724, 771, 772, 774, 791, 789, 791, 806
Alans 1005
al-'Aqr 855
Alaşehir 1067
al-'Atïqa 1009
Alaverdi 668
al-Awamleh, Adeeb bek al-Kayed 85
al-Batra 1024
Alburz, mountains 4, 1007
Albus Portus 1048
Alcelaphus buselaphus 216–17
alcohol 463
al-Dreijat 970
Aleppo 25, 610, 622, 724, 728, 729, 730, 748, 771, 778, 780, 781ff., 790ff., 800, 806, 807, 1071, 1072
Alexander Balas 989
Alexander, of Corinth 1056
Alexander the Great 224, 849, 984ff., 966, 986
Alexander's Wall 1089
Alexandria (Egypt) 1014
al-Hammam 1074
al-Hamra, stele 825
al-Hasa 487, 488, 491
al-Hawa (Yemen) 15
al-Hawiza, marshes 932

al-Hayit 823
al-Hiba, *see* Tell al-Hiba
al-Hinnah 1110
al-Hira 1104ff., 1106ff., 1109ff.
al-Huda, Tawfiq Abu 85
al-Husri 76, 77, 78
al-Huwayit 823
Ali Kosh, *see* Tepe Ali Kosh
Alişar Höyük 583, 584, 799
alkali 324, 326
al-Khuraybah 819ff., 826ff.
Allahad 748
al-Lajjun 1028
Allerød-Bølling 129
alloy 306ff.
alloying 620
alluvium 22
Al-Mada'in 1081
Almalou lake 13, 18
Alman 716
Al Markh 222
al-Milah, Wadi 276
al-Mocha 1053
almond 169, 176, 182, 199, 435
Alniunu 879
aloe 1054, 1055
al-Pachachi, Abdul Qadir 75
al-Qatif 491
al-Qura, Wadi 826
al-Quweismeh 1074
al-Rabba 1103
al-Rawda 617
Al-Sur 1081
Altai 704
altar, fire 979ff., 1010, 1088
al-Tayyila, Wadi 490
Altin Tepe (Iran) 893ff.
Altintepe (Anatolia) 333, 969
Altyn-depe 695; 10 979
al-'Ula 56, 826, 1046
alum 329, 330, 927
alumelu 742
alumina 324

aluminum 325, 329
Al Untash-Napirisha 37
    see also Choga Zanbil
Alyattes 901, 902ff., 904, 905
Amanus mountains 4, 803
Amarah 20
Amaravati 1057
Amarna, see Tell el-Amarna
Amar-Suena 708, 746
Amathus 312
ambar (marshlands) 361
amber 793, 794, 891
Amenemhet I 837, 838
Amenemhet II 609, 839, 840
Amenemhet III 840
Amenemhet IV 840
Amenhotep II 843
Amenhotep III 570, 772, 843, 845
Amenhotep IV 843
    see also Akhenaten
American Institute of Archaeology 118
American Oriental Society 58
American Palestine Exploration Society 84
American Schools of Oriental Research 84
Amida 1067, 1069
Amiranis Gora 678
Amkuwa 584
Amman 1074, 1101
Ammon 824
Amorite, language 29
Amorites 642, 653, 666, 711, 713, 748
Ampelome 1048
Amphiaraion 902
Amphiaraus 906
amphiblêstron 227
ampullae 1099
Amrit 54, 980
Amu Darya 690, 692
Amun 846, 981

Amuq cultures 675, 675
    plain 4, 21, 378, 391, 610, 611, 613, 781, 804, 1034
    points 467
Amurru 731, 773
    kingdom of 777, 844
    see also Amorites
Amygdalus 169, 177
Amygdalus communis 199
An 8, 716
Anahita 980, 1006, 1009, 1088
Anarak 297
    see also Talmessi
Anastasius I 1066, 1068, 1070
Anau 507
Anaxarchos 996
Anazarba 1067
ancestors 399, 789
anchors 368
anchovies 226
Ancyra 1067
Andrae, Walter 61, 94, 855
Andragoras 1003
Andreas, Friedrich Carl 66, 943
    metropolitan 1063
Andrew, St 1065
Andronovo 304, 695
Ani 681
Anitta 217, 722ff.
Ankara 64, 813, 814, 1067ff.
anše BARxAN (kunga) 214
Anshan 37, 597, 741ff., 746, 747, 958
    see also Tal-e Malyan
AN.TAH.ŠUM 733
Antakya 986, 988, 1023, 1067
Antalya 148, 907
    caves 434
antefixes 1009
anti-Chalcedonian 1100
Antigonus Gonatas of Macedonia 1056
Antigonus the One-Eyed (Monopthalmus) 984

Anti-Lebanon 381, 383, 608, 780, 1021, 1034
antimony 307, 308, 328, 330
Antioch-on-the-Orontes 25, 986ff., 988, 1023, 1029, 1030, 1037ff., 1061, 1069, 1070ff., 1081
Antiochia-in-Pieria 1028ff.
Antiochus I 991, 993
Antiochus II 1056
Antiochus III 984, 990, 992ff.
Antiochus IV 988, 1003
Antiochus VII 1004
Antiochus VII Sidetes 992–3
Antiochus XIII 985
Antipatris 1030
Antiphellus 908
antiquarianism 42–3
antler 238
Antum 997, 1007
Anu 853, 861, 923, 997, 1007, 1015
   ziggurat 481
   see also Uruk
Anuradhapura 1058
Anu-uballit Kephalon 997
   Nikarchos 997
Anyang 704
Anzaf 880, 887, 889
apadana 65, 66, 742, 944, 950ff., 1009
Apamea (Syria) 231, 778, 986, 988ff., 1024ff., 1028ff., 1031ff., 1036ff., 1039, 1070ff.
Apamea-on-the-Euphrates 989ff.
Apasa 898
Aper-al 845
Aphrodite 904, 910, 1006, 1010, 1039
Apkallatu 821, 822
apkallu 234, 822
Apollo 904, 906, 910, 986, 1015, 1069
Apollo-Nabu 993
Apollonia 911
Apollonopolis Magna 1051
apple 18, 198, 230
   crab 198
apsû 234
Apum, kings of 568
Aqaba 834, 1021, 1049
   Gulf of 1102
Aqar Quf 49, 550, 719
aqarqi 894
Aq Kupruk 341
Aq Tepe 1092
aqueducts 1067
Arabah, Wadi 834
Arabia 485ff., 816ff.
   Provincia 1027, 1044, 1049, 1073
Arabian Bifacial Tradition 249, 487
Arabian Sea 759
Arabic 1104
Arabs 816ff., 865
   conquest 1067, 1082
Arad 198, 633, 636
Arados 1028ff.
Aragats, Mount 882
Arahtu 918
Araks river 684, 879, 880
Aral Sea 692
Aramaean, deities 804
Aramaeans 798, 818, 846ff.
Aramaic 798, 808, 816, 949, 956, 997, 1013
   inscriptions 829, 830
   Jewish Babylonian 1104
   papyri 973
Aramu 878
Ararat, Mount 682, 684, 881
Aratashen 675
Arbela 866, 1010
   see also Erbil
Arca-Caesarea 1030, 1032, 1037
Arcadius 1069
Archaic texts, *see* Uruk, Archaic texts
Archibald, Dickie 62
archives 270, 584–5, 620, 737, 774

Ardashir I 1005, 1011, 1027, 1079ff.
Ardashir-Khurrah 1078ff.
Ardini 879
Ardjesh 884
Ard Tlaili 380, 389
Ardys 901
Areni 675, 676
Areni-1 186
Aretas IV 830
Arethusa 1026
argentite 303
Argishti I 880ff., 884, 888, 889, 893
Argishti II 893, 884
Argistihinili 881, 882
aridity 13, 528, 665
Arindela 1074
Arinna 733, 736
Arisman 301, 303, 509, 510, 511
Aristotle 228
Arjan 529, 755ff., 957
  burial 933
Arjoune 390
Arkadiana 1068
Armenia 11, 186, 668ff., 878, 884, 886, 965, 969, 973
Armina 886
armor 889
army 734
  Babylonian 716
Arnaud, Thomas Joseph 55
Arnuwanda 729
aromatics 820ff., 824, 927, 1042
Arpa, valley 674
Arpachiyah 302, 417, 425, 426, 427, 460, 475
Arqa 1030
ar-Raqqa 1027, 1070, 1097
arrowheads 241, 245, 247, 248, 254, 488, 492, 676
  blade 487
  Scythian 885–6
  transverse 252
Arsaces 1003

Arsacids 1001ff.
arsenic 307, 308, 309, 659
Arsinoë 1050
Arslan Tash 81, 813
Arslantepe 107, 303, 308, 311, 429, 562, 676, 677, 678
Artabanus IV 1005, 1079
Artashshu-marra 570
Artatama I 570, 771
Artatama II 571
Artaxerxes I 946, 948, 952
Artaxerxes II 65, 825, 951, 954
Artaxerxes III 849, 944, 947ff., 954, 956
Artemis 910, 981, 1006, 1015, 1068
  Coloëne 904
  of Sardis 903
Artemisia 16, 974
Artsruni 884
Arttumpara 912
Arubaini 887
Aruch 682
Aruna Pass 843
Arvandrood river 515
Arwad 793, 1028
Aryenis 902
Arzawa 728, 729
Ascalon 1032, 1063
  see also Ashkelon
ash, plant 326–7, 330
Ashdod 772, 967, 970
Ashima 830
Ashkelon 643, 773, 970, 1032, 1063
Ashtata 774, 782ff.
Aşikli Höyük 175, 204, 207, 297, 433, 440, 441, 448, 449, 451, 453–4, 457, 461
Aśoka 1042, 1056ff.
Aspros 141
ass 152, 496, 511, 991
  African 213
As-Sabiyah 195, 196, 349, 350, 351, 493–5

as-Sana'iye, pottery 829
assemblages, flint 242
Assessos 902
as-Sifiya 402, 404
Assur 52, 54, 61, 94, 274, 322, 344, 567, 568, 572, 584, 586, 658, 662, 712, 717, 851ff., 853ff., 883, 889, 928, 1002, 1005, 1010ff., 1015ff.
Assur, god 1015
Assurbanipal 30, 38, 39, 41, 43, 54, 188, 189, 277, 755, 818, 821, 826, 854, 860, 885, 899, 901, 916, 921, 922
  library of 39–40, 321
Assur-bel-kala 854, 864
Assur-etel-ilani 916
Assur-nadin-ahhe II 853–4
Assurnasirpal II 217, 266, 274, 275, 852, 854, 857, 858, 860
Assur-nirari I 853
Assur-resh-ishi I 864
Assur-resuwa 874
Assur-Sherua 855
Assur-uballit I 717, 864
Assur-uballit II 848
Assuwan, Confederacy 728
Assyria 732, 851ff.
Assyrian, language 29, 586; texts 584
Assyrians 586, 720, 809, 821, 851ff., 867ff., 933
Astarte 791, 826, 980, 1039
Aştepe 675
astōdān 957
Astyages 902, 906
Atamrum 748
Atargatis 1039
Atarquruma 822
Atarsamayin 822
Atatürk Dam Lake 149
Athar-e Iran 83
Athena 902, 910, 1006

Athens 1044
Athtar 826
Atiya 821
Atlit 977
Atlit-Yam 224
Atra-hasis 370
Atrek, valley 1013
Atrush 273
attribute analysis 241
Atum 849
Atur Gushnasp 1086
Atyad, Dynasty 899
Atys 899
Augustaeum 1064ff.
Aurelian 1037ff., 1048
  see also Octavian
Aurignacian 146, 147
aurochs 208, 444
Avaris 644, 840, 841, 842
Avdat 1064, 1098
Avena sp. 499
Aventicum 1044
Avesta 1016
Avidius Cassius, C. 1005
Avşar Tepesi 911
avulsion 8
Awafi, lake 12, 15
Awan 662, 744ff., 746
Awariku, *see* Warika
Awayli, *see* Tell Oueili
'Awaz'i 1072
awl 245, 249, 251, 252
axe 241, 247, 249, 251, 254, 257, 308, 314, 407, 585
  battle 683
  fenestrated 841
Axum 1046, 1048, 1051ff.
Axumites 1045
āyadana 955, 957
Ayanis 884, 888
Ayn az-Zara 1102
Ayn Manawir 973. 981
Ayn Musa 1102

Ayn Sokhna 1041
Aynunah 1048
Ayyas 1027
(a)zamru 183
Azatiwataya 803, 808
Azekah 62
Azerbaijan 1085
Aziru 844

Baal 791
Ba'alat 847
Baalbek 384, 608, 1031ff., 1072
Baalshamin 827, 1039
Baal Zephon 841
Ba'ar 1102
Baarou 1102
Baaz 381
Baba Jan 952
bābanu 854
Babatha, archive 1024
Babel, tower of 919
Bab el-Mandeb 1047, 1053
Babila, St 1069
Babylon 37, 41, 49, 60, 74, 270, 546, 549, 550, 712, 714, 717, 719, 724, 748, 752, 824, 844, 916, 917ff., 922, 936, 939, 924ff., 966, 984, 1002, 1007, 1013, 1016ff., 1085
   First Dynasty of 270, 713ff., 716
Babylonian 949
   Exploration Fund 59
Babylonians 852, 865
Bacchus, St 1066, 1071
Bachmann, W. 855
Bactria 689, 695, 749, 969, 979, 984ff., 995, 1003, 1006
Bactria-Margiana 597
Badakhshan 510, 762ff., 794
Badarian 284
Bademağaci 433, 450, 453, 456, 459
Bad-tibira 540
Bag-e Firuzi 949

Baghdad 21, 1082
   Museum 110
   railway 64
Baghouz 472
Bahandawaya, Wadi 276
bahar 292
Bahrain 56–7, 222, 226, 233, 761ff., 767, 768, 929, 1015, 1110
Bahram II 1082
   Kushanshah 1088
Bakhtiari, mountains 937
Baki 904
Bakir river 898
Balaat Gebal 624
Balawat 60, 854, 860, 888ff.
   gates 859, 862, 878
Balikh
   river 283, 423, 427, 472, 558, 564, 572
   valley 24
Balikligöl 155
Balkans 844
Balkash, Lake 693
Baluchistan 186, 224, 282, 291, 296, 313, 600, 762, 1015
Bandar Abbas 936
Bandar Bushehr 68
Band-e Dokhtar 959
Band-e Mizan 1083
Band-e Qaysar 1083
Band-e Qir 1083
Band-e Valerian 1083
Bandian 1087
Banesh, period 598, 743ff.
Banks, Edgar J. 59, 74
banquet, scene 188, 620
Baq'ah, valley 332
Baraqish 1048
Barbalissos 1070
Barbar temple 234, 368
Barbaricum/Barbarikon 1055, 1058
barbel 228
Barbus grypus 223

Barcin 433
Bardak-e Siah 940, 958
Bard Burideh 959
Bard-e Neshanda 957, 1016
Barga 773
Bar Kokhba, revolt 1026, 1031
barley 9, 19, 166, 168, 169, 170, 171, 173, 174, 177, 196, 197, 400, 408, 418, 499, 525, 528, 557, 621
Barm-Delak 1090
barracks, military 591
Barrois, Abel 81
Barygaza 1054
basalt 237
Bash-Adar 339
Bashar, Mount 653
Bashime 746, 747
Basiru 783
basketry 194
Baslu 821
Bassetki, statue 659
Basta 402
Bastam 884
Bastura, Wadi 273
Bat 500, 767
bath 995, 1065ff., 1082
Batman 558
Batrakataš 940
Batrun 1072
Bau 229, 230
Bauer, Hans 82
Bayindir 814, 907
Bazu 822
beads 296, 297, 411, 462, 492, 496, 661, 762
   etched carnelian 764
   Harappan 768
bears 217
Bedri Bey 74
beer 188, 280, 292, 463
Beer Sheba, culture 397, 411
Begash 703, 704

Begram 1014
Behbehan 756, 932, 936, 956; plain 519, 527, 528, 529
Beidha 206, 402, 403–4
Beirut 625, 773, 774ff., 840, 1044
   see also Beruta, Berytus
Beisamoun 281
Beit Mirsim 772
Bel 1008, 1015, 1039
Belbaşi 145
Beldibi 145
Belemounta 1074
Belet-Ekallim 792
Belisarius 1066
Belkis 1021
Bell, Gertrude 75–6, 77, 78
bellows 300, 585
Bel-shalti-Nannar 924
belt 888
Belus river 321, 326
bema 1098, 1107
Beniamin 970
Beni Hasan 838, 841
Benjamin of Tudela 863
Benjaminites 234
Bent, Theodore 57
Beqaa, valley 12, 322, 377, 380, 381, 384, 386, 389, 393, 608, 610, 635–6, 781, 844, 1026, 1034, 1039, 1072
Berekat basin 18
Berenike 1042, 1049, 1051, 1053
Berikldeebi 675
Berne 383
Beroea 1071
Beruta 773, 774ff., 840
   see also Beirut, Berytus
Berytus 1024, 1030ff., 1036ff., 1072
   see also Beirut, Beruta
Besorian 397
Bethany 1063
Bethlehem 1063, 1099

Beth Mazunaye 1110
Beth Qatraye 1110
Beth Shean 332, 772, 846, 1037, 1063
Beth Yerah 639
bēt kārim 585
Bet She'arim 326
Betthorus 1028
bevel rim bowl 291, 393, 482, 529, 538
Beyçesultan 343
bezoar 205, 206, 207
Biainili 878, 879
bilingual inscriptions
  Greek-Latin 1048
  Lycian-Greek 909
  Phoenician-hieroglyphic Luwian 803
  Sabaean-Nabataean 1043
  texts 737
  Urartian-Assyrian 879, 894
bilingualism 650
Bingöl 420
Bin Tepe 905
Bir 'Ali 1054
bird-man 892
birds 130, 892
Bireçik 678, 989
Biris Mezarliği 149
Birkat Ram 16, 17, Fig. 1.3
Birs Nimrud 49, 60, 61, 763
  see also Borsippa
Biruti 776
Bishapur 1078ff., 1082, 1085, 1090
bishoprics 1110
Bismaya 59, 61
  head 658
Bisotun 65, 886, 957, 960, 1012, 1019
bīt akitu 923
bītanu 854
bīt-ḫilāni 41, 787, 807, 908
Bithynia 63, 232, 1067

Bit Resh 997, 1007
bits, horse 683
bīt ṭuppi 28
bītum 545
bitumen 245, 269, 285, 349, 350, 355, 357, 362, 363, 364, 365, 366, 367, 370, 495, 506, 515, 527, 751
Black Sea 19, 692, 723, 968
blacksmith 314–15
blade 237, 239, 247, 254, 441
  backed 244
  Canaanean 242, 251, 253, 256, 257, 834
  sickle 676
bladelet 129–30, 132, 148, 237, 239, 249, 257
blanks 239, 255
Blastophaga psenes 192
Bliss, Frederick Jones 61
bloom 305, 311
Blundell, Herbert Weld 943
BMAC 694ff., 704
  see also Bactria-Margiana
boar 133, 208, 217, 401, 444
boats 347ff., 495
  Harappan 761ff.
  Magan 767
  models 348
boatyards 365ff.
Boğazköy 63, 109, 216, 218, 306, 575ff., 735ff., 799, 801, 813, 814
Bogdanos, Col. Matthew 97
Bohtan 558
Bolkardağ mountains 304
Boncuklu 433, 440, 441, 443, 444, 449, 452, 453, 459, 461, 462
bone 238
Borazjan 939ff., 958ff., 961
Borchardt, Ludwig 113
borders 875
borers 245, 247, 251

Borsippa 49, 61, 763, 915, 916, 918, 919, 926, 1015
Bos indicus 215
Bosra 1030, 1070ff., 1074
  see also Bostra
Bos taurus 215
Boston Museum of Fine Art 123
Bostra 1030, 1032ff., 1037ff., 1071
Botta, Paul-Émile 48–52, 73, 77, 861, 863
boule 1030
Bouqras 271, 425, 460, 467, 470
Boutcher, William 54
bovines 904
bow 888
box (tree) 18
Boz Daği 898
Bozpar 955
Brahmi, script 1057
Braidwood, Robert J. 149, 391, 503, 611
brass 307, 310
brazing 314
bread 230
Breasted, James Henry 77, 113, 117
bricks 269
  cigar-shaped 473, 477
  glazed 944, 948, 949, 950, 951, 952, 953ff., 955, 997
  plano-convex 654, 920
bridges 1067, 1082ff.
Brissa, Wadi 928
British Museum 70, 75, 76, 100, 107, 112
British School of Archaeology, Jerusalem 84
Broach 1054
broad bean 166
bronze 308, 659, 676, 684, 753, 756, 888ff., 891
  casting 696
Bruijn, Cornelis de 943

Bubalus bubalis 215
bucrania 455, 456
Buddhism 1016
Bulgaria 23
bull 941
  winged 953
  -man 32
bullae 392, 579, 655, 726, 742, 949, 985, 993, 998, 1017, 1092ff.
bulrush 361, 367
Bünyan 980
burials 387, 408, 409, 426, 428, 479, 480, 496, 497, 505, 509, 604, 613, 614–615, 618, 624–5, 641, 654, 665, 668, 684, 703, 736, 787ff. 808, 812, 854, 857, 893, 905, 929, 953, 955ff., 974, 977ff., 998
  inscriptions 909
  Lydian 955
  Natufian 136–7
  Phrygian 955
  pithos 615, 619
burin 132, 245, 247, 251, 254
Burnaburiash II 717, 752
Burqush 1070
Burunkaya 800
Buseirah 929, 970
Bushehr 931, 934, 936ff., 939ff.
butnu 199
Buto 834, 835
butter 583
buttresses 893
Büyük Menderes river 898
Büyükkale 590, 592, 724, 735ff.
Byblos 54, 80, 223, 371, 378, 380, 385, 389, 391, 392, 393, 433, 609, 610, 613, 614, 617, 619, 621, 622, 624, 625, 626, 772, 774, 795, 836, 837, 839, 840, 841, 846, 847, 1029, 1037, 1072
Byzantium 1060ff.

Caesarea 231, 1030
  of Cappadocia 1067
  Maritima 1030ff., 1036, 1063ff.
Cafer Höyük 174, 440
čahārbāġ 942
Caicus river 898
cairns 956
Calah, *see* Nimrud
calamine 310
calcite 281
calcium 329
calendars 577, 582, 586
Callinicum 1027, 1070
Callirhoe 1102
Calotropis 226
Cambay, Gulf of 1055
Çambel, Halet 149
Cambyses 45, 824, 848ff., 955, 957, 966
camel 211, 214, 820, 822, 991
Camelus bactrianus 214
Camelus dromedarius 214
Campbell Thompson, R. 60, 64
Çan 976
Cana 1101
Canaan 844
Canaanite, culture 774
Canaanites 844
canals 21, 265, 267, 268, 269, 270, 272, 276, 548, 551, 573, 917, 920, 923, 926, 959
Canatha 1035
Candaules 901
candelabrum 890
Çan Hasan 296, 433, 435, 443, 444, 451, 453, 456, 457, 458, 461, 462
Canis domesticus 210
Canis lupus 210
Canning, Sir Stratford 52
canoe 350
Cape Gelidonya 318, 371
Capernaum 1064

capitalism 90
Capitolium 1062
Cappadocia 420, 433, 435, 443, 445, 461, 463, 885
Capra aegagrus 204
  see also goat
Capra nubiana 216
  see also ibex
caravans 584, 1025, 1038, 1046, 1097
  donkey 214
caravanserai 600, 604
carbon 307
Carbone, Cesare 944
cardo maximus 1062
cargo 361
Caria 901, 907, 974ff., 981, 1067
Carians 906
caries 232, 401
Carmania 35
Carmel, Mount 131, 135
carnelian 367, 597, 600, 762
  etched 768
Carnuntum 1044
carp 221, 228
carpenters 366, 590
carpet 339, 342
Carrhae 1004, 1067
Çarsamba river 227
carts 214, 680, 687, 703
Caspian Gray Ware 603
Caspian Sea 19, 67, 232, 504, 1001
cassiterite 301, 303, 304
castellae 1027ff.
castimoniarum 232
casting 659
cat 210, 762
Catacomb horizon 679
Çatal Höyük 21, 94–5, 121, 146, 148, 149, 165, 227, 281, 282, 296, 301, 433, 435, 440, 443, 444, 445, 446–7, 448, 449, 451, 452, 453, 454, 456, 457, 458, 459, 460, 461, 462, 464

catch-per-unit-effort (CPUE) 225
catfish 225, 231
Catherine, Monastery of St 1063, 1103
cattle 196, 207, 208, 215, 216, 217, 232, 407, 411, 418, 444, 486, 487, 490, 495, 496, 558, 583, 881
  wild 152
  see also aurochs, bovines
Caucasus 311, 668ff., 970ff.
cauldron 890
Cauvin, Jacques 458
cavalry 872
Çavuştepe 884
Çayönü Tepesi 146, 149, 150, 157, 171, 203, 204, 205, 206, 208, 281, 296, 297, 420, 422
Cayster valley 898
cedar 362, 608, 837, 846, 1036
  Indian (*Cedrus deodara*) 763
Cedar Forest 661
cementation 310
cemeteries, see burials
census 1024
Center for Environmental Management of Military Lands 99
centers
  primate 597ff.
  symbiotic 597ff., 602
Central Asia 600, 620, 687ff., 701, 745, 965, 1014
Central Asians 604
ceramics 280ff.
cerargyrite 303
cereals 904
  see also barley; wheat; millet, broomcorn
cerussite 303
Cesnola, Luigi Palma di 107
Çevlik 986, 1029
Chagai Hills 763

Chagar Bazar 563, 565, 566, 569, 665, 666
chahar taq 1080, 1085
chaîne opératoire 242, 249, 287, 288, 290
chalcedony 762
Chalcidice 1034
Chalcis-ad-Belum 25, 1034, 1070ff.
Chaldaeans 848, 859
Chalke 1065
Chal-Tarkhan 1088
chamfer technique 247
Chanhu-daro 762, 766
channels, irrigation 267
Chantre, Ernest 63
Charax, see Spasinou Charax
Chärchän 345
charcoal 16, 168, 305, 696, 703, 744, 858, 889
chariots 214, 704
chasing 314
Checheno-Ingushetiya 894
Chechnya 669
Chehab, M. 610
Chehel Minar 943
Chelonia mydas 216, 496
  see also turtle
Chenopodiaceae 470
chenopods 16
Cheops 836
Cheras 1057
chert 237
Cheshmeh-Ali 509
Chhim 1036
chicken 763
chickpea 166, 407, 418
chiefdom 392, 411
Chiera, Edward 77
Childe, V. Gordon 164, 631
China 703, 1014
chineh 282, 505
chisels 249, 308
  toothed 941

chiton 345
chlorite 603, 605;
  see also steatite
Choga Mami 268, 471, 473, 475, 479
  Transitional (pottery) 477
Choga Zanbil 332
Chogha Bonut 503, 520
Chogha Dosar 527
Chogha Mish 292, 520, 521, 523, 524, 526, 527, 529, 601, 934ff., 960
Chogha Sefid 281, 477, 527
Chogha Zanbil 752
Cholas 1057
Chorasmia 35, 969, 1005
Choricius 1063
Chosroes 1069
  see also Khosrow II Parviz
Christianity 234, 1016, 1095ff.
Christians 1052
  at Najran 1046
  Nestorian 1085
chronology 558, 612, 621, 626, 650, 693, 771, 811, 936
Church of the East 1100, 1110
Cibyratis 907
Cicer arietinum 166
Cicer reticulatum 166
Cilicia 218, 228, 291, 301, 771, 802ff., 902, 969, 1026, 1038
  Rough 803, 806
Cilicians 917
Cimmerians 811, 882, 901
Cimon 911
Çineköy 802
cire perdue 308, 313
  see also lost-wax, casting technique
cisterns 1035
citadels 587–8
city 560ff.
  walls 540
clamps, dovetail 941

Clarias cf. *anguillaris* 225
Clarias gariepinus 231
Claudius 1031
clay 284
  sources 288
Clazomenae 902
Cleopatra VII 1026
Cleopatris 1050
Clermont-Ganneau, Charles 61, 62
Cleveland Museum of Art 123
climate 262, 664ff.
  change 10
clones 183
cloth 429
  see also textiles
clover 400
Clysma 1050
Coba Höyük 291, 479
  bowls 291, 479
cobalt 328ff.
coffins, slipper 1008
coinage 905, 910ff., 912, 944, 953, 986, 989, 1092ff.
  Axumite 1049
  Byzantine 1075
  Parthian 1012
  Satavahana and Andhra 1056ff.
Colchis 881
collapse
  environmental 564
  societal 23, 397, 405, 641, 664ff., 686, 712, 738
collecting 34
Coloë, Lake 904
Colonia Iulia Augusta Felix Heliopolis 1031
Colonia Iulia Felix Berytus 1031
colonies 392, 428, 483, 613–14
  Assyrian 567
Colophon 802, 901
colophons 30–1
color 947ff.
colorant 324, 328

Çolpan 675
columns 948
combs, ivory 767
Commagene 803, 1023, 1028
Common Anatolian 898, 909
Conder, C.R. 62
cones, mosaic 536
  see also Uruk
conflict, see warfare
Constans II 1066, 1069, 1070, 1073
Constantine 1022, 1060, 1062ff., 1069
Constantine II 1067
Constantinople 1060ff., 1064ff., 1068
Contenau, Georges 55, 80
contracts 270
Contrapollonopolis Magna 1051
Cooke, R.S. 76
cooking 231
copper 231, 286, 329, 366, 367, 420, 462, 506, 509, 659, 668, 762, 834, 835, 881, 883
  Cypriot 927
  ingots 844
  ox-hide ingots 793
Coptus 1051
core 237, 239, 245, 247, 252, 464
cores, ice 664
coriander 197
Corinthian, order 994
Coromandel coast 1049ff., 1058
cortex 238, 239
Cosmas Indicopleustes 1049, 1052ff.
Cosmas, St 1063
Coste, Pascal 65, 940, 943
cotton 197, 756, 769, 1054
couch, funerary 905
court 952
courts 783ff.
  Babylonian 716
Courtship of Inanna and Dumuzi 337
crab 496

craft production 280ff., 659, 783ff.
Crassus 1004
cremation 703, 808
Crete 141, 212, 908
Crimean War 54
crocus 733
Croesus 848, 901ff., 906
Cro-Magnon man 146
Cros, Capt. Gaston 58, 60
Cross, Holy 1063, 1071, 1105, 1107
crossbreeding 213
crucibles 310, 585, 603
crustaceans 234
crystal, rock 320, 657
Ctesiphon 1004, 1005, 1009, 1013, 1016, 1076, 1080, 1105, 1109ff.
Cucumis sp. 499
cults, ancestor 618
Culture Without Context 118
cuneiform 726
cupbearers 590
cupellation 303
curators 1030
curiales 1061
Curse of Agade, The 30, 653, 666
Curzon, Lord 940
Cuthean Legend, see Naram-Sin
Cyaxares 854, 902
Cybele 813, 903ff., 980, 1039
Cyclades 370
cyma 1009
Cyperaceae 170
cypress 276, 362
Cyprus 140–1, 174, 175, 204, 207, 208, 210, 258, 312, 370, 371, 409, 462, 589, 608, 794, 838, 844ff., 906, 914, 967, 970, 1044
Cyrrhus 1028ff.
Cyrus, the Great 45, 756, 824, 855, 932, 941ff., 957, 965, 967, 975
  tomb of 940
Cyrus Cylinder 96

Dadanu 823, 827
Dadishoʻ, of Qatar 1111
Dagan 234, 791
Dagestan 894
dagger 841
 Elamite 849
 shaft-hole 683
Daghestan 669
Dahan-e Golaman 957, 970, 973, 979ff.
daiālu 874
dairy products 211
Dakerman 380, 389, 391, 613
Dakhla Oasis 329
dakhma 957, 1085
Dalma Island 195, 196, 224, 492
 wares 509
daluwatum 271
dam 959
Damascus 731, 773, 781, 844, 987, 1032, 1072
 basin 384
Dam Dam Cheshme 504
Damghan 506, 603, 1078
Damian, St 1063
dams 270, 276
Danan 827
dang 1093
Danuna 845
Da o Dokhtar 956
Daphne, in Syria 1069
 Palace of 1065
Dara 1067, 1070
Darab 936, 938, 960, 1085, 1088, 1092
Darabgird 938, 958, 1077, 1079, 1090
Darb Ghaza 1103
Dardians 36
Darius I 33, 35, 36, 65, 742, 849, 911, 931, 941ff., 944ff., 951ff., 954, 956, 959, 966, 979
 statue of 952
 Susa Charter 954

Darius II 954
Darius III 956
Dark Age 569
dark-faced burnished ware 283, 388, 506
dar-me-luh-ha-mušen 763
Dar Qita 1096
Darvazeh Tepe 754
Dasher 938
Dasht-e Gohar 949
Dasht-e Kavir 501, 509
Dasht-e Lut 501, 600
Dasht-e Mehran 516
Dasht-e Murghab 940
Dashti Kozy 695
Daskyleion 970
date 183, 191, 198, 230, 499, 932
 honey 193
 palm 192–3, 196, 197, 485
 bark 227
Daya 822
Dayan, Moshe 117
Dead Cities 1034ff.
Dead Sea 12–14, 664, 1101ff.
Decapolis 1024, 1026, 1029, 1101
decision-making 242
decolorants 328, 330
Dedan 819, 821, 823ff., 827, 1046
Dederiyeh Cave 169, 381
deer 133, 217, 991
 fallow 401
 red 152
defensor civitatis 1061
deforestation 16
Değirmentepe 301, 426, 480, 674
Deh-e Now 751, 752
Deh Hosein 298, 299, 305
Deh Luran 67, 514ff., 516, 519, 525, 526, 527, 528, 744, 755, 932, 935ff., 1077
deification 711–12
Deir Ain Abbata 1075

Deir Allaj 1109
Délégation Scientifique Française en Iran 67
Délégation Scientifique Française en Perse 950
Della Valle, Pietro 1081
Delos 827, 1044, 1046
Delphi 901ff., 906
Demeter 904
Demetrius, St 1065
Demirköy 158
denar 1093
denarius 1093
dentalium 132
denticulates 249
deportation 870, 1078
Der 60
Deshasheh 836
Déthier, Anton Philip 73
Deutsche Orient-Gesellschaft 61, 62, 735, 835, 1105
Deutsche Verein zur Erforschung Palästinas 84
Deutsches Palästina Verein 62
Deve Höyük 808, 977
devitrification 330
Dexandros 1038
Dezful 1083
Dhamar lake 12
Dharanikota 1057
Dhashur 609
Dhiban 1074
Dhofar 224, 1046ff., 1054
Dhorme, Paul 82
Dhra' 171, 399, 401
Dhu Ghabat 827
Dhu Nuwas 1052
diaries, astronomical 1002
Diauehi 880ff.
Dibba 1054
Dibsi Faraj 381, 1070
Didyma 902
Dieulafoy, Jane 66

Dieulafoy, Marcel 940, 950, 1081, 1084;
Dilbat 916
Dilmun 57, 360, 361, 364, 367, 368, 652, 761ff., 767ff., 929
dimtu 570
Dindymus, Mount 898
Dinkha Tepe 107, 332
dioceses, episcopal 1073
Diocletian 1027ff.
  reforms of 1025
Diodotus 1003
Dionysus 1006, 1010
  Lydian 904
Diophysites 1111
diorite 653, 658, 661, 836
Dioscorides 1054
Dioscurida 1047
Diqdiqah 290, 357
Direkli Cave 146, 148
Divar-e Gorgan 1089
  see also Gorgan Wall
Diyala
  region 713, 718
  river 227, 916ff., 1013
Diyarbakir 565, 572, 1067, 1069
Diz river 752, 936, 1083
Dja'de al-Mughara 171, 174, 177, 281, 384, 422, 453
Djarkutan 199
Djehuti 843
Djeitun 507
DNA 177–8, 202, 833
dockyards 366
dog 133, 210, 211, 496, 591, 762, 892, 921
dolmens 638
  see also burials; *kurgans*; tumuli
Dolni Vestonice 147
domestication 133
Domuztepe 420, 424, 425, 808
Donjon 742, 744, 950, 953
donkey 211, 214, 411, 665, 841, 820

Dor, *see* Tel Dor
Dora 1036
Dorak 121
Dorginarti 968
Doric, order 990ff.
Dorudzan 959
Dosariyah 492, 493
Do Toluene 528
Doughty, Charles Montagu 56
drachma 1093
drahm 1093
Drangiana 970
Dravidian languages 933
Drehem 338, 609
drill 247, 249; bow 251, 254
drupes 190
Du-ashaga 362
Dudu 661
dugong (*Dugong dugon*) 216
Dukakin, caves 1109
Duma 819, 823, 826
Dumat al-Jandal 819, 826
Du Mesnil du Buisson, Robert 81
Dümrek 813
Dunand, Maurice 80
dung 289
dunnu 572
Dura Europos 271, 472, 990, 991ff., 1005, 1016, 1021, 1024, 1029, 1031ff., 1037, 1044, 1096
Durand, Capt. E.L. 57
Duri-Assur 873
Dur-katlimmu, *see* Tell Sheikh Hamad
Dur-Kurigalzu 342, 550, 719
Durnali 1013
Dur-Sharrukin, *see* Khorsabad
Dursunlu 145
Dussaud, René 81
Duthoit, Edmond 55
Dvin 1092
dye 927
dykes 272
Dzhungar mountains 689, 692ff., 702

é 545
Ea 716, 862, 916
eagle 1006
Eanna 270, 481, 916, 923
  see also Uruk
Eannatum 657, 661
  Vulture Stele 657, 661
Early Dynastic period, Mesopotamia 654, 744, 853
Early Trans-Caucasian Culture 596
  see also Kura-Araxes, culture
earthquakes 1067, 1070, 1102ff.
Eastern Province (Saudi Arabia) 491, 492
Eastern Sigillata A 990ff., 1038, 1055
Ebabbar 44, 270, 916, 920, 921, 922
Ebarat 747, 751
Ebla 24, 191, 222, 309, 362, 564, 565, 609, 612, 617–18, 620, 621, 622, 624, 625, 626, 653, 789, 840, 970
ebony 793, 844
Ecbatana 986, 1004, 1012, 1086
École biblique 62, 84
ed-Dur 222, 1015, 1017, 1054
Edessa 1067ff.
Edfu 1051
Edom 824, 827, 929
É.DUB.BA.A 28
egalitarianism 405
Egeria 1069, 1099
Egibi 270
Egipar 45, 922
Egypt 70, 191, 231, 256, 297, 305, 314, 320, 322, 329, 331, 332, 334, 337, 345, 355, 609, 620, 626, 640, 642, 644, 731ff., 771ff., 778, 780, 824, 833ff., 927, 952, 966, 968, 976, 1041ff.
  Exploration Fund 71
Egyptian, objects 795

Faynan 16, Wadi 453
Feast of the Barley(-eating) 229
Feast of the Malt(-eating) 229
feasts and feasting 159, 456, 458, 583, 905
Fedorovo culture 695
Feinan 100, 298, 299, 300, 302, 834, 1037
Felis silvestris lybica 210
felt 212, 339, 341, 343, 344
fertilization 195
fibrillum 194
festivals 583, 586, 591, 733
Fethiye 907
Ficus carica 181, 191, 192, 400
 see also figs
Ficus sycomorus 181
 see also figs
Fidan 4 302
figs 181, 182, 183, 184, 191, 195, 198, 400, 621
 sycamore 192
figurines
 anthropomorphic 132, 408, 468, 599, 626, 766, 927
 bird 762
 bronze 839
 female 155, 473, 1019
 male 154, 155
 molded 1019
 ophidian 479–80
 zoomorphic 132, 399
Fikirtepe 433, 443, 444, 445
filigree 314
fir trees 362
fire-setting 299, 304
firing, temperatures 289
First Jewish Revolt 232
Firuzabad 938, 958, 1077, 1079ff., 1082, 1090
fish 220ff., 366, 581, 661, 750
 -goat 234, 892
 nets, traps, spears, hooks 221, 225

 offerings 233
 sauce 232, 1037
Fisher, Clarence Stanley 62
fisheries 229
fishermen 225, 229
fishing 220ff., 615
flake 238, 239, 247, 248, 249
Flandin, Eugène 65, 861, 889, 940, 943
flax 18, 166, 227, 336, 337, 525
fleece 337, 338
Flinders Petrie, William Matthew 61, 71, 84
flint
 sources 242
 tabular 393
flintknappers 407, 441, 462
flintknapping 237, 502, 573
flood 920
 Noah's 20
flux 286, 324, 325, 326
fodder 19, 203
foraminifera 664
forests 361, 377
Fort Shalmaneser, see Shalmaneser
fortifications 617, 622, 869, 892ff., 903, 960, 967ff., 1013, 1027, 1051, 1067ff., 1069
Fossey, Charles 68
fountains 1066
fowl 904
fox 130
fracture, conchoidal 238
Franchthi Cave 141
francolin 763
Francolinus francolinus henrici 763
Frankfort, Henri 77, 513
frankincense 823, 1046ff., 1050, 1054
 road 819
fratarakā 948
Frehat en-Nufegi 998
fresco 1084

Fresnel, Fulgence 51–2
frit 891
frontality 1018
frontiers 635, 875
fuel 289
Furg 960
furnace, smelting 301
furniture 809, 859
Fustat 339

Gabae 939
Gabaza 1052
Gachsaran 515
Gadara 1032ff., 1073
Gaillardot, Charles 54
Galatia 63, 463
galena 303
Galilee 54, 135, 227, 380, 1099, 1101
  Sea of 130, 190, 228, 232, 639, 845, 1063ff.
gallinule, purple 225
Gallus gallus murghi 763
GAL SUḪUR 229
gaming pieces 828
Gandara 35
Gangir river 268
gangue 301
Ganj Dareh 207, 282, 503, 504, 505
Ganzak 1086
Gardan Reg 599
Gardane, General 65
gardens 40, 942
  botanical 40–1
  zoological 40
Gareus, temple 1007
Gargar river 1083
garlic 904
garmsir 932
garrigue 17
Garrod, Dorothy 131
Garshana 18, 230
Garstang, John 64, 84

garum 232
Garzan 558
Gasur 570
  see also Nuzi
gathering 167
  see also hunter-gatherers
Gaul 1051, 1055
Gautier, Joseph-Étienne 67
Gawasis, Wadi 1042
Gaza 84, 188, 821, 824, 844, 1032, 1036, 1043ff., 1061, 1063ff., 1100
gazelle 133, 142, 152, 195, 217, 381, 399, 401, 496, 626, 865, 892, 991
  Dorcas 130
gazi 232
Gaziantep, province 144
Gebel el-Arak 834
Gediz river 897
Gedrosia 224, 940
Gegharot 684, 685
Gelilot 1064
gender, Natufian 139
Genouillac, H. de 919, 920
Geoksur oasis 692
Geoktchik Tepe 232
Geoponica 232
George, St 1101
Georgia 675, 681, 683, 881, 894
Geoy Tepe 682
Gerasa 1030, 1032ff., 1073, 1100ff.
German Archaeological Institute 735
germination 167
Gerrha 1046
Gesher Bennot Ya'aqov 168, 221, 225
geš-keš-du 269
geštin 183
geštin duru$_5$ 188
geštin had$_2$ 188
Gethsemane 1063

Getty Museum 114, 123
Gezer 62, 772ff.
Ghab
　lake 176
　river 4, 12, 17
　valley 377, 777
Gharandal 1074
Ghassanids 1070
Ghassulian culture 249, 252, 256, 393, 411
ghee 292
Ghirshman, Roman 108, 116, 117, 118, 119, 950, 1083ff.
Ghoraife 384
Ghwair I 402
Gibala 776
Gihayu 224
Gilat 412
gilding, depletion 310, 314
Gilgal 171, 399, 400
Gilgamesh 30, 707
　Epic of 365
gimra, Hitt. 577
Gindaros 987
Gindibu 820
Giricano Tepe 572
Girnavaz 563
Girsu 36, 57, 229, 230, 234, 264, 269, 361, 363, 365, 366, 652, 746
giš-ab-ba-me-luḫ-ḫa 763
gi-sa-kilib 361
^(giš)**gag** 365
giš-kiri 198
giš-lam-gal 199
Giyimly 890
Giza 620, 976
gi-zi 361
glacial maximum 176
Glaser, Eduard 56
glass 317ff.
　bottles 1096
　goblets 1096

HMHK 324–5, 328, 330, 333, 334
ingots 793, 844
lamps 1096
LMLK 324–5, 327, 330, 1014ff., 1017, 1037, 1054, 1104ff.
slag 1082
Glaucus 908
glaze 286
globalization 89
glyptic 31–2, 352ff., 356ff., 368, 540, 580, 604, 615
　see also seal
Gnuni 884
goat 133, 204, 205, 208, 212, 232, 407, 411, 418, 486, 487, 496, 525, 528, 557, 615, 626; hair 212, 338, 343, 362, 702, 904, 991
goat-fish, *see* fish-goat
Gobayra 1078
Göbekli Tepe 14, 94, 102, 146, 150ff., 179, 180, 203, 205, 206, 222, 382, 422, 453, 458
Göbekly-Depe 1018
Godard, André 83, 101, 108, 117
Godin Tepe 83, 186, 596, 744, 952
goethite 305
Golan 16, 62, 412, 1063
gold 297, 305, 314, 567, 618, 625, 661, 756, 762, 793ff., 840ff., 845, 881, 883, 898, 904, 953
Golgotha 1062
Göllüdağ 441, 807
Gölpinar 808
Göltepe 304
Gomal river 276
Gonbad-e Qabus 1089
Gonur 340, 697, 704
　necropolis 604
Gordion 109, 123, 798ff., 801, 810ff., 814, 901, 966ff., 973
Gorgan plains 4, 8, 602
Gorgan Wall 19, 1013, 1089

Gotarzes II 1012
Grai Resh 428, 480
granaries 472, 736
granite 795, 1038
grape 18, 181, 182, 185, 187, 191, 197, 198, 276, 582, 615, 621, 640, 904, 932, 1034
  vine 188
grass 170, 400
  C3 486, 497
  C4 497
  halfa 362, 363, 371
graves 468
  see also burials
Gravettian 147
graveyard, *see* burials
gray wares, burnished 603
great goddess 154
Great Revolt, *see* Naram-Sin
Greece 23
  Minoan 795
  Mycenaean 321, 332, 731, 793, 795, 802
Greek 997
  inscriptions 961
Greeks 906, 994
greenstone 132
greywacke 849
griffins 752, 953, 1006
grill-plan 149, 391
Gritille 204, 205
gromwells 400
groundstone 132, 172, 254, 390, 401, 408
groundwater 266, 491
groupers 223
Guabba 230
Guardafui, Cape 1047
Gubla 772, 774
Gudea of Lagash 36, 43, 360
Gu'edena 269
Gugu 899
Gujarat 760, 762, 767

Gula 550, 916, 921
Gulaym Shahrum 825
Gullini, Giorgio 1088
Gumbati 970
Gungunum 747
Gupta, empire 1058
gur 360, 361
Gürcütepe 205
Güre 905
Gur-e Dokhtar 955
Gurgum 803, 806
Guti 653, 666
  Dynasty 666
Gutium 716, 748
Guyum 1090
Guzana 64, 928
Gygaean Lake 898, 904
Gyges 899, 901ff.
gymnasium 994ff., 1006
gypsum 751

H3, *see* As-Sabiyah
Habuba Kabira 221, 226, 303, 392, 429, 537, 614
Haçilar 121, 433, 434, 435, 442, 443, 448, 449, 450, 452, 458
Haçinebi Tepe 227, 355, 429, 978
hackberries 182
Hadad, of Aleppo 591
hadiš 946
Haditha 1074
Hadramaut 55, 1046, 1046ff., 1053ff.
Hadrian 1026, 1036, 1038, 1062
Haftavan Tepe 682
hafting 244, 247, 253, 254
Haft Tepe 751ff., 955
Hagmatana 1086
  see also Ecbatana; Hamadan
Hagoshrim 409
Hahhum 724
Hajar mountains 4, 488
Hajiabad 1088
Hajji Bahram Cave 504

Hajji Firuz Tepe 186, 282
Hajji Muhammad 467, 478
Halab 771, 778, 781ff.
Halaf
 culture 389, 475, 857
 period 379, 389, 391, 393, 408, 424ff.
Halawa A 617
Halawa B 614
Haldi 879ff., 883, 886ff., 888ff.
Halévy, Joseph 56
Halicarnassus 913, 981
 Mausoleum of 974
Halieutika 228
Halil Bey 82
Halil Rud 196, 604
Hallan Çemi 158, 203, 296
halmarraš 960
Halula 175, 204, 205, 386
Halys river 722, 800, 901, 906
Hama 378, 380, 386, 389, 391, 392, 393, 612, 613, 614, 615, 620, 624, 804, 808, 812, 1071
Hamadan 108, 986, 1004
Hamadani, Ibn Faqih 1081
Hamath, *see* Hama
Hamdi Bey, Osman 49, 55, 74
Hammamat, Wadi 355
Hammam et-Turkman 427
Hammeh, Wadi 169
hammer 308
hammerscale 315
Hammurabi 36, 68, 195, 270, 568, 569, 609, 713ff., 724, 734, 747, 753
 Codex Hammurabi 713, 718
Hamoukar, *see* Tell Hamoukar
Hamun, lake 1088
Hanago 675
Han-'Aktab 827
Han-'Aws 825
Hansen, Donald P. 1084
Hantili II 735

Han-'Uzza 827
ḫappiriya, Hitt. 577, 583, 589
Haradum 548, 553
Harappa 766
Harappan civilization 704, 758ff.
 see also Indus Valley
Harappans 604
harbors 792ff.
hare 130, 217, 401
Harif phase 130
Harifian industry 135
Harifian points 141
Harlan, Jack 166
Harminuia 886
Harpagid, Dynasty 912
Harpagus 906ff., 910
Harpy Tomb 912
ḫAR-ra = *ḫubullu* 360
Harran 46, 218, 928, 1004, 1015, 1067
 stele 827
Hartapu 800
hartebeest 216
Hasanlu 83, 107, 108, 111, 314, 315, 320, 325, 333, 335, 340, 507, 952
hašhûru 198
hašhur 198, 199
Hasmonean, kingdom 1026
Hassuna 284, 467
 culture 423
 period 379, 863
Hatarikka 804
Hatay, province 144
Hatip 800
Hatipler, building 579
Hatoula 231
Hatra 1002, 1005, 1010ff., 1015ff.
Hatshepsut 371, 843
Hatti 594, 722, 725, 728ff., 738
Hattian 725ff., 797, 804
Hattians 578
Hattush, *see* Hattusha

Hattusha 575ff., 722, 724, 725, 727ff., 732, 735ff., 738, 774, 797, 800, 805
Hattushili I 610, 621, 723ff., 845
Hattushili III 732, 734
Hauran 62, 1026, 1028ff., 1034ff., 1070, 1101
haute terrasse 521, 602, 742
Hawa lake 12
Hawagir 498
Haynes, John H. 59
Hayonim B 174
Hayonim Cave 133, 169, 391
Hayonim Terrace 137
Haza'il 821ff.
Hazor 643, 772ff., 787, 792, 967
Hecatomnid Dynasty 913, 981
Hecatompylos 1007
hedgehog 401, 892
Helbaek, Hans 165, 526
Helen, mother of Emperor Constantine 1062
Heliopolis 845, 849, 952, 976, 1031ff., 1035ff., 1039, 1069
Hellenistic period 860
Hellenocentrism 963
Helmand
  lake (Hamun-e Helmand) 225
  river 600
helmet 889
Helwan 244, 834
  phase 130
hematite 305, 308, 658
hemiones 213
  see also onager
Henderson, Patrick 64
Hephthalites 1090
Hera 904
Heracles 904, 995, 1018, 1101
Heracles-Nergal 1011, 1016
Heraclid, Dynasty 899, 901
Heraclius 1060, 1069
Herihor 846

Hermes 995, 1018
Hermione, St 1068
Hermus river 897, 903
Herod, the Great 1030, 1036, 1063
Herodians 1026
heroes, nude 657
herrings 226
Herzfeld, Ernst 61, 68, 116, 117, 940, 943, 1088ff.
Hetepibre 840
Heuzey, Léon 57
Hexi corridor 703
hiatus palestinien 385
Hibis 979, 981
Hibra 823
Hidali/u 755, 938ff.
hides 366, 370, 470
Hierakonpolis 834
Hierapolis 25, 1067
hieroglyphs,
  Egyptian 834
  Luwian 592–3, 727
Hijaz 823, 825, 831, 1101
Hilakku 803, 806
Hili 8 197, 499
  North 193
Hillah 78, 479
Hillman, Gordon 165
Hilprecht, Hermann V. 57, 58, 59, 74
Himyar 1046ff., 1052ff.
Himyarites 1047
Hindanu 823
Hindian 741
Hindu Kush 689, 692, 702, 762
hippopotamus
  ivory 793
  pygmy 140
history houses 455–6
Hit 21, 362
Hita 662
Hittite 62, 306, 345, 610, 621, 725ff., 797, 894, 898
  period 790

Hittites 717, 719, 722ff., 771ff., 774, 784, 806, 845, 881, 896, 898, 908
hiyan 952
Hiyawa 802
hoe 249
hollow cities 622
Holocene 7, 10, 13–14, 15, 16, 19, 20, 24, 128, 172, 175, 176, 241, 435, 438, 486
Holy Sepulcher 1062ff.
Home of the Fish, The 229, 234
Homer 731
Homeritae 1047
Homo erectus 833
Homo sapiens 146, 147, 164
Homs 1023, 1069ff., 1072;
Homs Gap 380, 381, 384, 391, 608, 777, 1022
honey 292
honorati 1061
Honorius 1065
Hopf, Maria 165
Hoq 1053
Hordeum distichon 166, 499
Hordeum murinum 400
Hordeum spontaneum 166, 169
Hordeum vulgare 499
Horhor 893
  inscription 881
Hormuz, Straits of 19
horns 946
Horom 676
Horoztepe 109, 307, 309
horse 211, 213, 626, 702, 881, 888, 892, 941, 1055
  see also equids
Horsfield, George 84
Horus, Way of 838
Horvat Migdal 1064
Horvat Zikhrin 1064
Hotu Cave 504

"House with the roof" 230
  see also storage
house societies 452
households 405, 545, 546, 554
Höyücek 433, 450, 453, 456, 459
Hrozný, Bedřich 726
Huana 1074
Huber, Charles Auguste 56, 829
Hudra 1109
Huhnur 937ff.
Hula Basin 377
Hula Lake 168, 176, 221, 380
Humaima 1074
Humann, Carl 63
Humban-nikash II 755
Humban-numena 752
Humban-shimti 747
Hung-e Nauruzi 1012, 1019
Huns, White 1090
hunt, royal 217
hunter-gatherers 167, 398, 834
hunting 402, 407, 408
Hurrian 570, 571, 584, 589, 733, 737, 778, 797, 804, 887, 894
Hurrians 322, 570, 586, 590, 724
Hursagkalamma 920
husking, trays 388
Hussein, Saddam 96, 110
Hutelutush-Inshushinak 753
Hutuini 887
huwar 407
hybrids 215
hydraulic hypothesis 268
hydreumata 1051
hydrology 11
Hyksos 644, 841ff.
hymn 711, 715
Hyrcania 1003
Hystaspes 957

Iadihu 823
Iatribu, *see* Yathrib
Ibbi-Suen 365, 708, 712, 746

ibex 130, 133, 142, 216, 401
   Nubian 206
Ibn Balkhi 1080
Ibn Battuta 863
Ibni-Sharrum 657
Ichthyophagi/oi 224, 227, 1051
Idadda 778, 780
Idalion 312
Iddin-Dagan 747
Idrimi 781, 789
Idumaea 967
Ierapolis 1070
Iğdir plain 675
Igihalki 751, 752
Igihalkid Dynasty 750
Ignatius, Church of St 1070
Ikadion 996
Ikaros 996
   see also Failaka
Ilam 502, 515
Ilgynly-Depe 303
Iliad 899, 908
Ilipinar 433, 444, 449, 451, 459
Illustrated London News 119, 121
Imazu 747
Imgur-Enlil 854, 860ff., 878
Immeya 840
imperialism 659ff., 868ff.
   see also empire
impurities 306ff.
Imsefnu 1108
Inanna 342, 343, 550, 747, 921, 1008, 1015
Inanna and Enki 30
Inanna's descent to the netherworld 30
incest 748
Incised Coarse Ware 696ff.
India 758ff., 1014
Indian Ocean 142, 1041
Indians 1053
indigo 345
Indo-European 722–3, 727, 754
Indo-Iranians 933ff.

Indus civilization 758ff.
Indus Valley 652, 662, 700
ingots 304, 322, 585, 603
   glass 321
Ingushetia 669
Initial Upper Paleolithic 146, 147, 148
Inner Asian Mountain Corridor 702ff
inscriptions
   Armenian 1103
   Georgian 1103
   Greek 996ff., 1006, 1103
   Latin 1031, 1103
   royal 715
   Tamil 1057
Inshushinak 37, 749ff.
insulae, housing 408, 991ff.
Inter-Tropical Convergence Zone 15
Inti 836
Inushpua 880
investiture 940
Ionia 907, 966, 968, 981
Ionians 903
   masons 941
Ionic, order 1007
Ip-shemu-abi 839
iqdu/uqdu 199
Iran Bastan Museum 83, 101
Iranian plateau 596ff.
Iranians 754, 912
'Iraq ad-Dubb 400
Iraq Museum 75, 76, 80, 97
Irdabama 959
Irene, St 1066
Irigal 997
Irnina 8
iron 258, 297–8, 305, 314, 325, 329
   Cilician 927
   slag 1082
   wrought 311
Irqata 609, 777
irrigation 25, 261ff., 959, 1013
Irtashtuna 959

Irtysh river 692
Isaac, of Nineveh 1111
Isfahan 939
Ishbi-Erra 365, 712, 746
Ishhara 925
Ishim-Yahdun-Lim canal 271, 272
Ishme-Dagan 748
Ishpuini 878ff., 886ff., 889
Ishtar 270, 624, 653, 719, 826, 853, 863ff., 916, 920
 temple of at Nineveh, 39
Ishtar-of-Akkad 919
Ishtar-of-Babylon 916
Ishtar-of-Nineveh 591, 659
Ishtar-Shaushka 808
Isin 546, 549, 550, 712, 746, 918, 921
isotopes
 stable 232
 carbon 18
Israel 847
 Antiquities Authority 85
 Stele 845
Istakhri 1080
Istanbul 1066
iš-te-na-ma 344
It'amra 821
itlebi 909
Ituraeans 1029
Iufaa 976
ius italicum 1031ff.
ivory 38–9, 308, 320, 367, 793, 809, 828, 840, 927, 1014
Ivriz 808
iwan 1008ff., 1011, 1015, 1017, 1079, 1082, 1084, 1087ff.
Iwan-e Karkheh, *see* Eyvan-e Karkheh
Izeh 754, 936ff.
 valley 932
Izmir, *see* Smyrna

Ja'alan 490
Jabal Ala 1071
Jabal al-Luweibdeh 1101
Jabal Aruda 392, 429
Jabal Bashiqa 275
Jabal Berisha 1071
Jabal Berri 1110
Jabal Dueili 1071
Jabal Halaqa 1071
Jabal Hamrin 352, 426, 473
Jabal Makhul 274
Jabal Samn 1071
Jabal Sinjar 419, 420, 421, 480
Jabal Umm Daraj 827
Jabal Wastani 1071
Jabal Zawiye 1071
Jableh plain 664
Jagjag, Wadi 272
Jamdat Nasr 226
 period 510
Jarmo 149, 204, 471, 505
Jarrahi 741
Jarvis 118
jasper 657, 891
Jaussen, Antonin 56, 825
Java 1051
javelin 841
Jawa 631
Jaxartes 690
Jayrud 381
Jazirah 377, 470, 546, 557, 570, 607, 656
Jbeil 378
 see also Byblos
Jebel al-Arab 1028
Jebel Ansariyeh 608, 777, 1021, 1024
Jebel Arak 355
Jebel Bishri 653
Jebel Buhais 233, 487
Jebel el-Aqra 776
Jebel Haroun 1103
Jebel Khalid 987, 990ff.
Jebel Qusair 1105
Jebel Zawiyah 608, 1021

Jeftelik 381
Jenah 1072
Jerablus Tahtani 64, 393, 429, 618, 621
Jerash 1032, 1100
Jerf el-Ahmar 158, 169, 171, 172, 173, 174, 177, 180, 207, 281, 382, 416, 422, 453
Jericho 148, 179, 198, 281, 283, 378, 382, 383, 396, 399–400, 402, 403, 409, 630, 1100
Jerusalem 62, 231, 773, 847, 870, 1031, 1062ff., 1072, 1099, 1100
Jerwan, aqueduct 277
Jesus Christ 1062
jewelry 314, 585, 953
Jewish Palestine Exploration Fund 85
Jezreel Valley 639
Jiddah 56
Jiroft 111, 120, 196, 511, 604
  see also Halil Rud; Konar Sandal
Jisr esh-Shoghur 377
Jiza 1074
John the Baptist
  Church of St 1069
  Monastery of 1075
John the Evangelist, St 1068
John Studios, St 1066
joints, anathyrosis 941
Jokha 61
Jones, Indiana 118
Joppe 843
Jordan, Julius 61, 76
Josiah 848
Jouannin, André 57
Journal of Field Archaeology 118
Jubayl 1110
Judah 54, 62, 824, 847
  see also Judea
Judaism 1016, 1096
Judea 1024, 1026, 1038, 1064, 1099
Judean Desert 1099ff.
Judeans 232, 917

jujube 197, 496, 499
Julian (360–363 AD) 25
Jundishapur 1077, 1083ff.
juniper 362, 435, 1036
Junnar 1057
Juno 1062
Jupiter 1062
Jupiter Dolichenus 1038
Jupiter Heliopolitanus 1038ff.
  sanctuary at Heliopolis 1033
Justin I 1045
Justin II 1065
Justinian I 1045, 1053, 1061, 1063, 1066ff., 1070ff., 1081, 1097, 1099
Justinianopolis 1070

Kabardino-Balkaria 669
Kabar'il 827
Kabash 939
Kaʻba-ye Zardošt 949
Kabnak 751ff.
  see also Haft Tepe
Kabul Museum 110
Kadashman-Enlil II 717
Kadashman-Harbe I 751
Kadim 383
Kaf 823
Kaftari 598
Kahramanmaraş, valley 806
Kainepolis 1050
Kakzu 1011
ka-lá 370
kalakku 370
Kala'li-gi'ir 969ff.
Kale Köyü 893
Kaletepe 441, 462, 464
Kalhu, see Nimrud
Kalleh Nisar 768
Kalmakarra, hoard 109, 120, 933
Ka-lu-lim/si 766
Kalydon 995
Kamal, Ahmed 72

Kaman-Kalehöyük 216, 580, 584, 587, 799, 814
Kamarband Cave 504
Kamid el-Loz 386, 610, 773, 781, 787, 789, 839, 844, 977
kamidu 341
Kamil, Mustafa 72
Kamose 842
Kandahar, Old 933, 969ff.
Kané, *see* Qani'
Kanesh 298, 304, 306, 338, 344, 370, 567–8, 575ff., 722
  see also Kültepe
Kangavar, valley 509, 744
Kangurt-tut 695
Kapannu 823
Kaper Koraon 1072, 1096
Karaçada 134
Karacamirli 970
Karachy-Cherkessia 669
Karadağ 800
Karahardash 717
Kara Höyük 63
Karahöyük-Konya 583
Karain 145, 146
Karain B 146, 148
Karaindash I 717, 719
Kara Koyun river 1068
Karakul Valley 339
Karakum 690
Karana 569
karânu 184
Karashamb 680, 682
Karatepe 727, 803, 808
Karaz ware 615
Karduniash 717
Karib'il 822
Karimnagar 1057
Karkamish 64, 188, 563, 565, 610, 622, 678, 729ff., 738, 782ff., 800, 803, 806ff., 808ff., 811ff., 848
Karkheh 226, 525, 741, 936, 1083

Karmir-Berd 681, 682, 683
Karmir Blur 884ff., 889ff.
Karmir-Vank 681, 682, 683
Karnab 299, 304
Karnak 843, 845, 847
Karnamak-e Ardashir-e Babakan 1080
Kar-Tukulti-Ninurta 274, 572, 852, 855–6
karum 567, 579, 584–5
Karun river 528, 741, 1083
Kashka 731, 801
Kashkashok III 563
Kashtiliashu IV 717, 718
kasiru 341
Kassite, empire 706ff.
Kassites 342, 369, 549ff., 750, 752, 842, 915
Kastron Ammatha 1074
Kastron Zadakathon 1074
Kaula Kandal 866
kaunakes 339, 340, 341, 345
Kavad I 1084, 1091
Kawkab, volcano 663
Kaymakçi 898ff.
Kaynarca 814
Kayseri 1067
Kazakhstan 689, 692, 704
Kazane Höyük 424, 563
Kebaran 129, 130, 146, 149, 379, 390
Kef Kalesi 884
Kel Dağ 968
kelek 370
Kelermes 890
Kelishin 879
Kenyon, Dame Kathleen 283, 632
Kenyon, Sir Frederic 75
Kerak Plateau 642
Kerala 1050, 1054, 1058
Kerbala 1108
  escarpment 1109
Kerkenes Dağ 107, 799, 813, 814

Kerma 562, 838
Kerman 938, 1078
Kermanshah 337, 505
Ker Porter, Sir Robert 940, 1086
Kestel 298, 299, 304
Khabur river 4, 16, 218, 263, 271, 272, 283, 556, 558, 563, 564, 565, 566, 570, 572, 573, 656, 663, 708, 771, 928
Khafajah 227, 354, 538, 543
Khalchyan 1006
khamsin 271
Khan Khalde 1072
Kharg 1110
Kharga Oasis 329, 849, 879
Kharoba Koshuk 1108
Khasekhemwy 836
Khaybar 823
Khebded 837
Kheir, Hisham 85
Khiamian 142, 168
  see also points, Khiam
Khilda 1074
Khinis 276
Khirbat al-Fakhar 427, 562
Khirbet al-Mukhayyat 1102
Khirbat al-Mureigha 1074
Khirbet Daria 1074
Khirbet Deir Situn 1092
Khirbet esh-Shennef 389
Khirbet es-Samra 1074
Khirbet Faynan 1101
  see also Feinan
Khirbet Garsour 417
Khirbet Hamra Ifdan 302
Khirbet Hatara 866
Khirbet Iskander 641, 642
Khirbet Karhasan 866
Khirbet Khatuniya 866
Khirbet Nahas 1074
Khirbet Qasrij 866
Khirbet Shireena 866
Khnumhotep 609, 838, 841

Khor 224
Khor Milkh 1 225
Khor Rori 224, 1046, 1054ff.
Khorasan, road 745, 882
Khorkhe 1017, 1090
Khorsabad 33, 51, 52, 56, 57, 77, 266, 275, 306, 851ff., 857, 859, 861ff., 889
Khosr river 273, 275, 276
Khosrow I Anushirvan 1081, 1091
Khosrow II Parviz 1085, 1087, 1091, 1093, 1110
Khoy 880
Khu-Sobek 838
Khufu 836
Khuraybah 825, 1048
Khurbet Ajlan 84
Khuzestan 4, 7, 20, 195, 511, 598, 740ff., 755, 931ff., 933, 936, 938, 960, 1013, 1083
Khuziyan 515
Kiddin-Hutran II 752
Kidinu 751
Kidinuids 750
KI.LAM 733
Kili Gul Mohammad 284
Kilise Tepe 231, 802
Kilisik 156
Kilizu 1011, 1017
kiln 287, 289, 391, 479
kiln, pottery 775
Kindattu 746
Kineas 995
Kinet Höyük 218, 802
King, L.W. 60
King of Battle, see Sargon of Akkad
kingship 659
Kinza 780
Kiöldün 976
Kirkuk 570
kirš 198
Kirwashir 751

Kish 60, 107, 226, 303, 309, 357, 540, 542, 549, 650, 652, 654, 744, 764, 918ff., 925ff., 1085
Kisiri 276
kispu 788
kiššatu 652
Kissik 922
Kissura 59
Kitchener, Lord H.H. 62
Kiuzeli-gi'ir 969
Kizildağ 800
Kizilirmak river 447, 722, 800, 803, 901
Kizil Vank 681, 684
Kizzuwatna 725, 771
Klady-Novsvobodnaya 678
kleroi 987
kline 905, 998
knife 248, 249, 254, 407, 487
  pile 340
knob-plaques 752
knotting, carpet 338–9
Koj Tepa 969
Koldewey, Robert 60–1, 63, 64, 74
Konar Sandal 196, 604–5
Konya 8, 64
  basin 433, 438, 448
  lake 12
  plain 4, 433, 435, 442, 443, 445, 452
Konya-Karahöyük 584
Kopet Dagh 507, 689, 693
Koptos 1051
Kore 904
Körte, Alfred and Gustav 810
Körtik Tepe 158, 203
Kos 1044, 1055
Kosak Shimali 381, 389, 391
Köşk 435, 451, 456, 459, 461
Kostienki 147
Kotilingala 1057
Kouklia-Skales 312
Kourion 1044

Kranzhügel 6, 564
Krasnodar 669
Krefter, Friedrich 944, 946
ku$_6$ 223
Kubaba 813
Kuban 673
kubileya 813
Küçük Çatma 681
Küçük Menderes 898
Kudur-Nahhunte 36, 718, 753
kudurru 718, 720, 915
Kufa 1106
Kuftin, Boris 676
Kug-nuna 362
Kuh-e Ayyub 956, 957, 960
Kuh-e Khajeh 1088ff.
Kuh-e Pataweh 750
Kuh-e Rahmat 948
kukunnum 752
Kul-e Farah 754
kuliltu 234
Kültepe (Turkey) 212, 298, 304, 306, 338, 344, 567, 575ff., 625
Kül Tepe I and II (Nakhichevan) 679, 684
kulullû 234
Kululu 803
Kumidi 773, 781, 839, 844
Kumme 874
Kummuh 738, 803, 806
kunga 214
Kunulua 802
Kuprlli 912
Kur river (Fars) 22, 508, 741, 931, 934
  basin 509, 598ff.
Kura-Araxes, culture 596, 675ff.
Kurangun 233, 749–50
Kurban Höyük 187
Kurdistan 11
kurgans 669, 679ff., 682, 683, 684, 704
Kurigalzu I 717, 751ff.

Kurigalzu II 717
Kurnub 1064
Kuruçay 433, 434, 448, 449, 451, 461
Kurunta 726
Kuruntiya 800
Kuşakli 737
Kuşakli-Sharishsha 580, 592, 593
Kush 847ff.
Kushan, empire 341, 1004, 1058
Kushans 1005
Kushites 842
Kusshara 723
Kut 8
Kutch 760
Kutha 926
Kuvava 903
  see also Cybele
Kuwait 195, 222, 350, 367, 493, 996
Küyünjik, see Nineveh
Kvatskhelebi 678
Kyaneani 1067
Kybernis 912
Kyrrhos 987
Kyzylkum 690

Labarna 723, 724, 727
labor, corvée 874
Labweh 380, 384
Lachish 188, 231, 772ff., 968, 970
Lagash 43, 221, 229, 269, 544, 661, 666, 701, 764
  1st Dynasty of 269, 366
Lake District, Turkey 433, 449
Lakipum 585
lamashtu 359
lamassu 857, 858, 860, 962, 865
Lamentation over the destruction of Sumer and Ur, The 30, 712, 746
Lamerd 938, 959
Lampre, Georges 67
lamps 1099
lance 888

land, sale 652
Landberg, Carlo de 56
Langenegger, Felix 64
Langi 362
Langraumtempel 572
Lankester Harding, Gerald 85
Laodikeia 986, 989, 994, 1028ff., 1032, 1036ff., 1055, 1070
lapis lazuli 303, 320, 367, 509, 510ff., 586, 588, 597, 599, 602ff., 618, 620, 657, 689, 762, 794, 835, 839, 891
Lapithos 312
lard 292
Laristan 938
Larsa 7, 8, 58, 61, 196, 267, 365, 540, 546, 548, 550, 552, 553, 712, 747ff., 918, 929
lasurite 762
Latakia 986, 1028
Late Glacial Maximum 13, 19, 128
law 576, 711, 713, 734, 1037, 1073
  Hittite 726
  Roman 1034
Lawdhan I 825
Lawrence, Thomas Edward 64, 65, 75, 98
Layard, Austen Henry 51, 53, 65, 73, 77, 853, 856, 860, 863
lazulite 762
Lchashen-Metsamor or Lchashen-Tsitelgori 683, 684
lead 302, 303, 883
lead-isotope analysis 302, 304
leatherworkers 590
Lebanon 12, 361
  Mount 16, 377, 607, 608, 1026, 1036
Le Breton, Louis 513
Lefkadia 995
Legio III Gallica 1028
Legio IV Scythica 1028
Legio V Macedonica 1031

Legio VI Ferrata 1028
Legio VIII Gallica 1028
Legio X Fretensis 1028
Legio XV Apollinaris 1028
Legio XVI Flavia Firma 1028
legumes 400, 408
Leiladepe 675
Le Lasseur, Denyse 80
Lens culinaris 166
Lens orientalis 166
lentil 18, 166, 170, 408, 418, 557
Leonidas of Byzantium 228
Leontius, St 1071
Leontopolis 1070
leopard 217, 218
Lesbos 303
Lethrinidae 223
Leto 910
Letoön 907, 910
Leuke Kome 1043, 1048ff.
Leus 904
Levallois 145
Levantine Painted Ware 625
levees 263, 267, 269
levers, pressure 251
Libona 1074
library 30–1, 859, 865
Libur-nirum 746
Libyans 848
Licinius 1064
Lidar Höyük 806
Lihyan 825
Lihyanite, dynasty 825ff., 829
Lim Dynasty 568
lime 324, 325, 326
  plaster 385
limes 1027, 1035, 1050, 1067, 1073, 1089
limestone 132, 237
Limestone Temple 484
  see also Uruk
limonite 305
Limyra 908, 911ff., 980

Limyrikê 1054
linen 337, 341, 1037
Linum bienne 166
Linum usitatissimum 166, 336
lion 41, 217, 218, 592, 790, 794, 808, 834, 865, 892, 941
Lisan, Lake 13
Lisht 329
Litani river 377
literature, Akkadian 653
litharge 303
lithics 236ff.
Little Mesopotamia 520
Livias 1102
Liyan 940
lizards 130
Lloyd, Seton 77
Lodian 249
loess 22
Loftus, W.K. 51, 53, 54, 58, 65, 856, 859, 863, 865, 950
logistai 1030
loincloth 154
loom 338
  weight 338
Looting Matters 118
Lori Berd 680
Lostalot, Félix de 56
lost-wax, casting technique 308, 313, 411, 683, 753
Lot, Sanctuary of 1075
Lothal 764, 767
Loud, G. 861
loutron 995
Louvre 52, 57, 70, 73, 81, 83, 100, 111, 123, 512, 950
Lovett, Beresford 1088
Lower Sea 650
Lucas, St 1065
Lucius Verus 1026ff.
Luddi 899
Lu-Enlilla 366
Lugalbanda 30, 360

LUGAL *kibratim arba'im* 653
LUGAL.KIŠ 652
Lugalzagesi 650, 652
Lukka Lands 896, 908
Lukki 845
Lullubi 658
lú-mar-sa 366
lunate 148, 244, 254
lunate, Helwan 834
Luristan 108, 111, 120, 305, 509, 514, 744, 933
  bronze 915
LÚ*ša bet kudini* 873
Luschan, Felix von 63
luster, edge 241
LÚ.SU[ki] 746ff.
Lutipri 878ff.
Luwian 592–3, 727ff., 733, 738, 804, 899
  hieroglyphic 797, 798, 801ff., 885
Lycia 896ff., 907, 975, 977, 980, 1067
Lycian League 913
Lyconia 1067
Lydia 109, 848, 886, 896ff., 965, 968, 975ff., 980
Lydian, masons 941
Lydus 899
Lykos river 1066
Lyon, David Gordon 62
Lysippus 1018

ma$_2$ 354
Ma'ad 1072
Maadi 834, 835
Macalister, Robert Alexander Stewart 61
macehead 411, 448, 683
Macridi Bey, Theodor 55, 63
Mada'in Saleh 56, 830
Madaba 1073ff.
  map mosaic 1102
  plain 641, 642

Madaktu 936
Madamagh 206
madbasa 193
Maeander river 898
Maeonia 899
Magan 344, 360, 363, 364, 365, 366, 367, 652, 761ff., 766ff.
Magas 1056
Magdalenian 147
Maghzaliyah 421
Magna Mater 154
Magnesia 1067
magnesia 324, 326, 328
magnesium 329
magnetite 305
magur boat 360, 362
Maharashtra 1057
Maharlu, Lake 932, 938
Mahkmur 274, 852
Mahmatlar 309
Maikop 669ff.
Ma'in (South Arabia) 827, 1046ff., 1053
Ma'in/Belemounta 1074, 1102
Makran 224, 227
Malabar 1050, 1057ff.
malachite 132, 296, 301
má-lah$_4$ 366
Malamir 754
Malatya 562, 738, 800, 803, 807, 812, 880, 1067
Malazgirt 880
Malgium 748
Maliya 910
Malkata 329
Mallowan, M.E.L. 856, 857, 861, 863
Maltai 276
Malus sylvestris 198
Maly Pergit 681
Mamasani, region 4, 508, 750, 936ff., 958, 961, 1079
Mami-sharrat canal 270

Mampsis 1064
Mamre 1099
Mamshit 1098
Mamu 860
Mandaic 1104
Mandali 268
Mandilion 1069
manganese 328, 330
mangrove 489, 496
Manishtushu 36, 37, 649, 651, 652, 864
  Cruciform Monument of 652
  Obelisk 652
Mannea 883
Mantai 1059, 1092
maps
  ancient 551–2
  Kassite 921
maquis 17
Marad 546
Maraş 808
  province 144
Marassantiya 722, 723
Marawah 491–2
marble 1038, 1081
Marc Antony 1026
Marcus Aurelius 1029
Marduk 36, 44, 715ff., 753, 916, 918, 922, 925, 1008
Marduk-apla-iddin II 916
Marduk-zakir-shumi I 44, 859
Mareshah 62
Margiana 340, 662, 695, 704, 746, 748, 969, 1004, 1013, 1018
Mari 21, 24, 188, 194, 234, 271, 272, 563, 564, 567, 568, 608, 609, 610, 625, 653, 708, 712ff., 747ff., 821
Marib 55, 56, 1047, 1053
Mariette, Auguste 71
Mark Pethion 1106
Marlik Tepe 107, 109, 120, 123, 314, 333, 768

Mar Liyas, Monastery of 1074
Marmara, Gölü (Lake) 898; Sea of 1065
Mar Narkhos 1106
Marneion 1063
Marqas 803
marriage
  diplomatic 746
  inter-dynastic 662, 752
Marsa Gawasis 371
Marsa Nakari 1050ff.
marshes 20, 361
MAR.TU 711, 712, 713
Martyrius, Monastery of 1100
Martyropolis 1067
martyrs 1097
Marun 741
Marv Dasht 528, 529, 743, 931, 936ff., 949, 1079
Marx, Karl 164
Masada 232
Maşat Höyük 593, 737
Masǧed-e Soleymān 932, 957, 1009, 1012, 1016
Mashkan-Shapir 290, 548, 573
mason's marks 941
Maspero, Gaston 71
mašqitum 271
Massa 818, 821
massif funéraire 521, 742
mass-production 291
Massuh 1102
mast 350
master of animals 524, 834
mastic 199
Masuwari 803
Matar 813
māt aribi 820
Matarrah 472
Mati''il 827
Matum-niattum 747
Mauryan, empire 1042
Mauryans 1056ff.

mausoleum 994
Maussollos 974
Maximianopolis 1050
Maysar 1 302, 499
Mazgert 893
McCown, Donald E. 513, 519
Meander river 1067
measurement 360–1
meat 583
Mebaragesi, see Enmebaragesi
Mecca 1101
Mecquenem, Roland de 68, 950
Medes 36, 848, 852, 854, 886, 906, 1004, 1007
Media 824, 965
  Atropatene 1007
Medina 819, 823
Mefaa 1074
megaliths 638
megaron 810–11
mega-sites 175
Megasthenes 1056
Megiddo 62, 226, 231, 371, 639, 643, 772ff., 845, 848, 967ff., 973
  battle of 771, 780, 843
Meherdates 1012
Meher Kapisi 886
Mehran 514
Mehrgarh 186, 282, 283, 284, 296
mekku 321
Mekubi 747
Melanopsis praemorsa 401
Melardi 887
Melas 902
Melebiya 563
Mele Hairam 1088
Melgunov 890
Melid 800, 803
Meli-Shipak 752
Melitene 1067
Mellaart, James 121, 149, 454
melons 499

Melos 141, 370
Melqart-Heracles 980
Meluhha 360, 366, 367, 652, 761ff.
memory, historical 660
Memphis 848, 966, 976
Menbij 1070
Menteşe 433, 444
Mentuhotep II 837
Menua 878ff., 886ff.,
Menuahinili 881
Meredates, king of Mesene 1004
Merenptah 845
Merikare 836
Merimde-Benisalâme 834
Merkes 918ff.
Mermnad, Dynasty 899ff., 906
Merneptah 908
Merodach-baladan II 923
Mersin 444, 448–9, 451, 457, 462, 462
Merv 1005, 1092, 1108
Mese 1065
Mesene 1004, 1012, 1014, 1018
Meskani 299
mesocarp 190
metallurgists 590
metallurgy 295ff., 452, 603
metrology 620, 650
metropolis 1038
Metropolitan Museum of Art 100, 107, 109, 115, 116, 123
Metsamor 679
Meydancikkale 969ff.
Mezraa Teleilat 205, 283, 386
Mheri Dur 886ff.
Mian Ab 936
  canal 1083
  plain 934
microblade 237
microburin 239, 244
microhabitat 172
microlith 244, 254

Midas 109, 799, 809, 811
   City 799, 813
   Mound 812
midden, shell 489, 492, 493, 1036
Middle Asian Interaction Sphere 700ff., 758ff.
Middle Persian, inscriptions 1091
Mikhmoret 967
Milawanda 731
Milawata 731
milestones 1035
Miletus 731, 901ff., 904, 1044, 1048, 1067
Milion 1065
military 868ff.
milk 209, 292, 444, 583
millet, broomcorn 703
Milyas 907
Minaean, inscriptions 1046
Minaeans 824, 828
Minerva 1062
mines, silver 1094
Minet el-Beidha 793
mining 298ff., 304
Minoan, pottery 625
Minorsky, Vladimir 1086
minti 909
mints 989, 992, 1093
   marks 1093
Minusinsk 344
Mira 896, 898
Mirabad, Lake 13, 932
Misis 1067
Mission Scientifique au Caucase 668
Mita 809
Mitanni 319, 570, 571, 610, 728ff., 732, 751, 771ff., 778, 781ff., 842ff., 853
   Common Style 685
   texts 783
Mithra 980, 1009
Mithradatkert 1006

Mithrapata 912
Mithridates I 1004
Mithridates II 1004, 1012, 1019, 1089
Mithridates of the Omani 1015
Mit Rahina, inscription 609
Mittelsaalhaus 392, 787
Mizpe Yammim 981
M'lefaat 205, 421
Mleiha 198
moʿtadel 932
Moab 823
mobility 130
   see also nomadism
models, boat 354ff., 357ff.
Modestus 1063
Modurgi emporium 1059
Modutti 1059
Mohenjo-daro 766, 767
Mohl, Jules 50
Mohs scale 237
mold 603
mollusks 401, 494, 496
monasteries 234, 1050, 1064, 1100, 1109
Mongolia 692, 695, 699
Mongols 1087
monkeys 41
Monophysites 1100, 1105, 1108ff., 1110ff.
Mons Admirabilis 1070
monsoon 11, 13, 224, 486, 495, 497, 665, 1045
Montet, Pierre 80
Montet Jar 626, 840
montmorillonite 284
Mopsos 802
mordant 927
Morgan, Jacques de 60, 66, 67, 68, 668–9, 936, 950
Moritz, Bruno 60
morphology, lithic 242
mortar 390, 949

mosaics 1071, 1074, 1081, 1101ff.
Moscha Limen 1046ff., 1054ff.
Moschophagoi 1052
Moses 370
Moses of Khoren 884
Mosul 851, 856
mother-of-pearl 225
Motza 402
mouflon 205, 211
Mount Eiduru 884
mouse 174
Mousterian 146
Mouterde, René 1034
Mouza 1053ff.
Mozzaffer ed-Din, Shah 67
Muballitat-Sherua 717
Mugharet el-Wad 131
Muhammad Ali 71
Mukish 771
Muksas 802
mule 214
Müller, David Heinrich 56
Müller, Karl 64
multiplier effect 637
Munbaqa, *see* Tell Munbaqa
Munhata 409
Murashu 270
Murat Daği 898
Murat river 879
murex 345, 1036
Mureybet 134, 169, 172, 173, 174, 176, 203, 205, 281, 380, 381, 382
Murghab river 692, 694, 696, 697, 698, 701
Murmuriga 782
Murshili I 610, 621, 724, 800; II 729, 730, 733ff., 776
Musasir 879, 883, 887, 889
muscular stress 136
musculature 139
Museion 1068
Mushabian 130

Mushiston 299, 300, 304, 305
Mushki 809
Musil, Alois 56
Mus musculus domesticus 174
Musri, Mount 276
Mustafa, Mohammed Ali 476
mustard seed 232
Musular 433, 445
mutation 167
muthummu 183
Muwattalli II 731, 735, 771, 845
Muweilah 197, 952
Muziris 1058
Mycenaeans 844
Mylasa 913
Myos Hormos 1050ff., 1053
myrrh 1046ff., 1050
Mysians 906
myth 651, 657, 660
mythology 152

Nabada 663
Nabataea 1049
Nabataean
  inscriptions 829
  period 826
  pottery 1038
Nabataeans 830, 1026, 1030, 1042ff., 1048, 1053
Nablus 1032
Nabonidus 44–6, 56, 823ff., 826ff., 914, 920, 922ff., 928ff.
Nabopolassar 43, 44, 914, 920, 924, 926
Nabu 827, 853, 859, 861, 864, 916, 1015
  temple of, at Nineveh 39
Nabu-nasir 915
Nabu-sharru-usur 869
Nabu-shuma-ishkun 915
Nabutum 366
Nabu-zuqup-kenu 30
Nachcharini cave 381, 383, 384

Nad al-Thamam 487
Nafud, desert 488
Nagar 565, 570, 662
Nagorno-Karabakh 669, 681
Nagub tunnel 275
Nahal Hemar 281, 461
Nahal Mishmar 308, 313, 345, 411
Nahal Oren 137, 399
Nahal Qaneh 297
Nahal Tut 967
Nahr al-'Asi 377
Nahr Daurin 272
Nahr el-Homr 381
Nahr el-Kelb 928
Nahr Ham'a 272
Nahrin 842
Nahr Sa'id 272
nails, wall 742
Nairi 877ff.
Najaf 1109
Najran 1046
nakharar 886
Nakhichevan 674, 679
Nakhlak 303
Nalaini 887
Nalchik *kurgans* 678
Namazga 599, 603
  sequence 693
Nanaya 1015
Nanna 543, 548, 709, 711, 746ff., 981
Nanna-Ningal, temple at Ur 230
Nanna-Suen 363
Nanna-Suen's Journey to Nippur 362
Nanshe 229, 367
Napir-Asu 313, 753
Napirisha 750
Napoleon I 65
Napoleon III 71
Naqsh-e Rajab 1090ff.
Naqsh-e Rustam 749, 942, 949, 956ff., 960, 966, 1082, 1090

Naram-Sin 36, 37, 45, 565, 609, 650ff., 711ff., 718, 745, 864
  Cuthean Legend of 653
  Great Revolt 653
  Victory Stele 652, 657–8
Nar Gölü 11
Narundi 746
Nasiriyah 20, 658
Naširma 960
Nasr ed-Din Shah 66
Nahal Tut 967
Natir-Il 825
Nativity, Church of the 1063, 1099
natron 324, 326, 327, 330
Natrun, Wadi 328
Natufian 129, 131, 146, 168, 169, 179, 190, 231, 244, 245, 254, 379, 380, 398, 399, 434, 435
Nazi-Bugash 717
Nea Ekklesia 1063
Neanderthals 145, 146
Neapolis 1032
Nebayot 818, 1043
Nebi Huri 1028
Nebi Yunus 52, 60, 865, 967
Nebo, Mount 1075, 1102
Nebuchadnezzar I 37, 753
Nebuchadnezzar II 37, 44, 45, 823, 848, 918ff., 921ff., 924ff., 928ff.
Nechesia 1050ff.
Nefertiti 70, 102, 113, 845
Negahban, Ezat 117, 123
Negev 13, 130, 137, 141, 412, 1063ff., 1098, 1103
neighborhoods 547
Neirab 81
Nekau II 848
Nelkynda 1058
Nemrik 158, 205, 421, 422, 473
Nemrut Dağ 419
Neo-Assyrian, *see* Assyria
Neo-Babylonian, empire 914ff.
Neocaesaria 1070
Neo-Elamite, period 754ff., 935ff.

Neo-Hittite, kingdoms 797ff.
Neolithic 486ff.
 Rub al-Khali 487
Neolithization 149, 382
Nereid Monument 912
Nerkin Godedzor 674
Nesa 217, 722
Nesikhons 325, 328
Nesite 586, 723, 797, 804, 898
Nessana 1064, 1098, 1103
net, fishing 227
net-sinker 226
Netiv Hagdud 169, 171, 174, 399, 400
neutron activation analysis 526
Nevali Çori 146, 149, 150, 155, 156, 157, 174, 203, 205, 206, 422
Neve Yam 409, 410
Nicaea 1067
nickel 298, 329
Nicomedia 1067
Niebuhr, Carsten 50, 55, 943
Niffar, *see* Nippur
níg-sa-(h)a 183
Niha 1031
Nike 1012
Nile 231, 355, 1050
 Delta 834, 838, 840, 847, 968, 973
NIM 740
Nimrud 30, 38, 41, 52, 73, 100, 107, 234, 266, 274, 297, 314, 320, 321, 322, 324, 325, 331, 333, 334, 335, 342, 572, 809, 821, 854, 856ff., 873, 882
Nineveh 30, 38, 41, 43, 48, 50, 188, 265, 266, 275, 276, 277, 321, 322, 424, 427, 562, 563, 569, 572, 651, 658ff., 662ff., 713, 822, 851ff., 856, 863ff., 866, 1005, 1011, 1015, 1018
Ninevite V, pottery 562, 563, 564

Ningal 709, 862, 922
Ningirsu 36, 229, 657
Ningizzida 916
Ninhursag 746, 753
Nin Isina(k)'s Journey to Nippur 363
Ninlil 920
Ninmah 916
Ninurta 862, 925
Ninurta-kudurri-usur 821
Nippur 41, 43, 57, 59, 74, 194, 196, 221, 222, 226, 230, 270, 290, 322, 325, 481, 524, 538, 540, 547, 549, 550, 551, 552, 651ff., 654, 660, 666, 707, 709, 712, 719, 766, 916, 918, 921ff., 1002, 1005ff., 1007ff., 1013, 1015, 1017, 1104
Niqmaddu 780
Niqmepa 787
Nisa 1002ff., 1005ff., 1016
Nisaba 548
Nişantaş 727
Nişantepe 592
Nisibis 1037
Nissi Bay 141
Nitl 1074
Niya 777ff., 842
Nizzana 1064
Noah 184, 370
nomad 341, 523
nomadism 407, 598
nomadization 641
North Atlantic Oscillation 11
No Ruz 950
Novosvodobnaya 673
Nubia 842
nude hero 32
Nuhaya 822
Nukhashe 773, 779ff.
numerical system, sexagesimal 483
nuntarriyashas 733

nurma 198
nurmš 184, 198
Nurrugum 569
Nusaybin 1037
Nush-e Jan 952
Nusku 752
nuts 176
nu-úr-ma 184
Nuzi 76, 317, 321, 322, 324, 329, 332, 570, 571, 666

oak 16, 17, 176, 377, 434, 1036
oases 818ff., 826
oat 499
obelisk 71, 858, 859, 861, 864
Obelisks, Temple of the 624, 626, 839, 841
Oboda 1064
obsidian 132, 237, 247, 248, 249, 370, 385, 397, 420, 441, 462, 463, 506, 579, 676, 680, 684, 840
Ocelis 1053
ocher 296, 951
Octavian 1023, 1029
offerings, votive 652
Ohalo II 130, 169, 171, 190, 228
oil 190, 292, 463
  fish 220, 229, 231, 233, 362
  olive 411, 621, 1034, 1072
  pistachio 199
  sesame 366
Öküzini 145, 146, 148
Old Babylonian, period 569, 706ff.
Old Iranian 933
Old Phrygian 810
Olea europaea 181, 189
oleaster 189
olive 16, 18, 181, 182, 189, 198, 411, 615, 621, 640, 1034, 1036ff.
  oil 411, 621, 1034, 1072

Olives, Mount of 1063, 1099, 1100
olivine gabbro 653, 658, 661
Oman 224, 226, 299, 302, 355, 360, 367, 496, 604
  Gulf of 489, 490, 498, 659, 664, 761ff., 766ff.
omen 28
onager 152, 470, 626, 865, 991
onyx 891
opacifier 328
Ophel 62
Oppenheim, Baron Max von 64, 65, 74, 80, 82
Oppert, Jules 51, 57
Oppian 228
opus sectile 1081
orchard 198
Ordu 109
Oriens 1025
Oriental Institute 77
Orientalism 91
Orontes
  river 6, 147, 377, 381, 570, 609, 731, 772, 777, 781, 804, 842, 847, 987, 1036
  valley 612
Ortaköy 593, 736
oryx, Arabian (*Oryx leucoryx*) 216
Osiris 981
Osorkon I 847
Osorkon II 847
Osrhoene 1005, 1011, 1013, 1026
Ossetia 669
ossuaries 1085
Ostia 1044
ostraca 973, 1002, 1106, 1109
ostrich 41
Ottoman Imperial Museum 55, 60
Ovis aries 203
Ovis orientalis 203
Ovis vignei 338
oxen 211
oxide, iron 296, 324, 325

Oxus
  civilization 694ff.
  river 692
  treasure 107
  see also BMAC
oxygen isotopes 11, 15
oyster 493
  see also pearl; *Pinctada margaritifera*

Pab Hills 762
Pactolus river 898, 903ff.
Padakku 823
Padan 716
pagus Augustus 1031
Pahir-ishshan 752
Pahlavas 1057
Pahlavi 1088, 1104
Pahlavi, Reza Shah 83
painting, wall 624, 795, 1096
Paišiyāuvādā 960
Paithan 1057
palace 590, 617, 623, 783ff.
Palaestina
  Prima 1026, 1062ff.
  Secunda 1026, 1062ff.
  Tertia 1026, 1044, 1062ff., 1072, 1102
Palaic 723, 898
Palaipaphos 967
Palanli 148
Palastini 808
  see also Palistin
Palermo Stone 609
Palestine 824
Palestine Archaeological Museum 85
Palestine Exploration Fund 61, 83–4
Palestinian hiatus 385
palette 408, 412
Palistin 802, 808
palm
  fronds 194
  rope/fiber 362
palmette 756, 1009

Palmyra 194, 1024ff., 1029, 1032ff., 1035, 1037, 1039, 1044
Palmyrene, inscription 1053
Palmyrenes 1014
palynology 11
Pamir mountains 698, 702ff., 763
Pammukale 1067
Pamphylia 907
Panagia 1067
Panayr-Dağ 1068
Pandayas 1057
pandemic 1071
Panjikent 1087
Panjshir 1094
panku 725
Panthera leo 218
Panthera pardus 218
Paphlagonia 723, 975ff.
papyri 997, 1074
paradise 955
parchment 997
Parga 961
park 865
Parkai 340
Parnaka 33
Parnakka 959
Paropamisus 692
Parrot, André 64
Parsa 931, 935
Parthia 1001, 1056
Parthian period 855
Parthians 1001ff., 1057
Parthyene 1001, 1003
partridge, Persian black 763
Pasargadae 66, 68, 935, 937, 939ff., 949, 957, 960ff., 975, 979
pashiz 1093
pastoralism 598, 687ff., 695
pastoralists 566, 695, 698ff., 702
  see also nomads
Pataliputra 1058
Patara 907
Patina 804

Patriarchate, of Antioch and
    Jerusalem 1072
Pattanam 1058
Paul, Bishop 1073
Paul, St 1066
pavilions 957ff.
Pavo cristatus 763
Pazyryk 107, 339–40, 342
pea (*Pisum sativum*) 18, 166, 171,
    197, 408, 525
peafowl 763
pear 182
pearl 481, 493, 762, 1059
    oyster 225
Peleset 845
Pella (Jordan) 312, 317, 329, 333,
    334, 335, 1073
Pelusium 231
pendant 158
Pendik 443, 444
Pentapolis 845
Peqi'in 413
percussion 238, 253
    indirect 251
perforator 132
Pergamon Museum 100
Pergamum 1067
Perge 123
Pericles 912
Periplus Maris Erythraei 1047
Peroz I 1085, 1089
Perrot, Georges 63
Persepolis 37, 66, 96, 116, 325, 345,
    931ff., 935, 939ff., 944ff., 950,
    955ff., 958, 1010
    Fortification archive 33, 936,
        939ff., 948, 950, 957, 960
    plain 936
    West 949
Persian Gulf 20, 351, 650, 699, 700,
    713, 718, 741, 749, 751, 759,
    932, 996, 1014, 1042, 1044,
    1046, 1056, 1078, 1110

Persis 1012
Peruwa 585
peš 184, 191
Pescennius Niger 1032
pestle 390, 949
petasos 995
Peter, the Iberian 1099
Peter, St 1066, 1072
Petra 102, 232, 1024, 1030,
    1032ff., 1037ff., 1043,
    1049,1102ff.
    church 1074
    papyri 1074, 1103
petroglyphs 355
Petrovka culture 695
Peucestes 961
Pevrebi 681
Pézard, Maurice 68, 81
Phaeno 1101
Phellus 907, 911
Philadelphia 1101
Philip the Arab 1032
Philippopolis 1032
Philistia 802, 967
Philistines 845
philoi 987
Philoteras 1050
Phoenicia 54, 320, 774, 965, 976ff.,
    980–1, 984, 1026, 1028, 1029,
    1072
    Libanensis 1070
    Prima 1070
Phoenician 798, 802, 803
Phoenix dactylifera 181, 192, 194,
    196, 485, 499
    see also date
Phokaia 975
photography, aerial 536
Phraaspa 1086
Phraates II 1004, 1017
Phragmites australis 361
    see also reeds
Phrygia 814, 885, 966, 976, 1067

Phrygian, kingdom 797
Phrygians 798ff., 801, 809, 906
pick 132
pickling 230
pig 196, 207, 208, 216, 407, 411, 418, 558, 591, 904, 991
  wild 152
  see also boar
pile 340
pilgrimage 412, 1067, 1071, 1075, 1097, 1099, 1102ff.
pillars, T-shaped 152ff.
Pinara 907
Pinarbaşi 206, 433, 436, 438, 440, 447, 449, 460, 463
Pinctada margaritifera 225
pine 361
pins, double spiral-headed 603
Pinus brutia 361
Piotrovskii, Boris 673
piquants trièdres 244
Pi-Ramesse 732
Pir-Hussein, relief 565, 658
piscina 234
Pishkamar 1089
pistachio 168, 182, 186, 199, 381, 507
Pistacia 16, 177
  atlantica 168, 176, 199
  terebinthus 186
  vera 199
Pisum humile 166
Pisum sativum 166
Pit-Grave culture, *see* Yamnaya culture
Pithana 722ff.
Pithiae 1067
pithoi 579, 582, 613, 890
pits 390
Piyassili 729
Piyusti 722
Place, Victor 51, 861
plague 1061

planning, Hippodamian 973
plaster 492, 944
Pleiades 887
plough 578
ploughshares 314
Poduca emporium 1058
Poduke 1058
Poidebard, Antoine 1023, 1034
points 464
  Amuq 433
  Byblos 467
  Helwan 255
  Khiam 245, 255, 401
  transverse 248, 252
polchromy 286
Poliochni 304
polis 1022, 1030
pollen 11, 16, 436, 664
pollination 192, 195
Polyeuctos, St 1074
  Church of 1066
Polygonum 170
  tinctorium 345
pomegranate 184, 197, 198
Pompeian First Style 990
Pompey 1025, 1029
Pontus 1067
pools, sacred 591, 592
Pope, Arthur Upham 117, 1086
Pordenone, Odoric de 943
Porphyrio porphyrio 225
Porsuk 803
ports-of-trade 792
possessores 1061
postholes 496, 497
potash 324, 328, 330
potters 280, 287, 288, 292
Pottery Neolithic 148
praesidia 1051
Prathisthan 1057
Preboreal 399

Pre-Pottery Neolithic
   A (PPNA) 138, 141, 146, 148, 151, 155, 160, 168, 170, 171, 172, 174, 179, 202, 206, 207, 208, 209, 217, 222, 231, 244, 254, 378, 379, 382, 383, 393, 399, 401, 402, 433, 435
   B (PPNB) 138, 141, 146, 148, 151, 168, 174, 175, 177, 180, 202, 204, 206, 207, 208, 211, 216, 217, 225, 241, 248, 249, 254, 255, 281, 378, 379, 383–6, 393, 396, 397. 398, 401, 402, 404, 405, 409, 433, 440, 467, 486, 487
   C (PPNC) 146, 148, 255, 396, 406–7
Prideaux, Francis Beville 57
Priene 901, 1044, 1067
Princeton Art Museum 123
prisoners, Roman 1082ff.
processual archaeology 92
Project ArAGATS 683
propaganda 714, 716, 870ff.
protein 223, 232
proto-cuneiform 483
   see also Uruk, Archaic texts
Proto-Elamite 596, 598, 743ff.
   seals 354
Proto-Hassuna 284, 467, 470
Proto-Urban cultures 632–3
Prunus dulcis 199
Psametik I, *see* Psammetichus I
Psammetichus I 848, 901
PSGW, of Lihyan 825
Pteria 906
Ptolemais 1024, 1029, 1031
Ptolemies 984, 1042ff., 1048
Ptolemy II Philadelphus 1048, 1050, 1056
Ptolemy III Euergetes 1050
Pu-abum 193, 198, 764
Puduhepa 734

pulses 904
Pulvar river 741, 942
Pune 1057
Punica granatum 198
Punt 371, 1041
Pura 940
Purattum 8
purple 823
purulli 733
Pusht-e Kuh 502, 744
Puteoli 1044
Puzrish-Dagan 338
Puzur-Inshushinak 745ff.

Qabr-e Madar-e Soleyman 942
Qabr-e Sheykheyn 521
Qabr Hiram 1072
Qadamgah 956
Qadesh 731, 734ff., 771, 773, 780ff., 843, 845
Qalamun region 381
Qalat al-Bahrain 193, 197, 198, 223, 367, 368, 970
Qalat es-Salihiye, *see* Dura Europos
Qalat Mudiq 391, 778, 1024
Qalat Sherqat, *see* Assur
Qalat Siman 1097
Qaleh 934
Qaleh Dokhtar 1079, 1082
Qaleh Yazdigird 1010, 1017
Qaleh-ye Kali 936, 957ff., 959
Qaleh Zohak 1010, 1090
qanat 266, 936, 960, 1035, 1109
Qanawat 1035
Qani' 55, 224, 1046ff., 1054ff.
Qantir-Piramesses 321
Qaousiyah 1069
Qaplantu 108
Qara Quzaq, *see* Tell Qara Quzaq
Qarnaw 827, 1046, 1053
Qarqar 847
Qasr al-Hamra 829–30
Qasr bint al-Qadi 1105

Qasr-e Abu Nasr 939, 1078, 1092
Qasr-e Shirin 1077
Qasrij Cliff 866
Qasr Serej 1105, 1108ff., 1110ff.
Qasr Shamamuk 866
Qataban 824, 1046ff., 1053
Qatar 224, 492
  B industry 487
Qatifian 397
Qatna 24, 81, 100, 610, 612, 617, 622, 623, 625, 626, 748, 770ff., 778ff., 818ff., 821ff., 826
Qazvin 4
Qedar 818, 822, 824, 826, 827
Qena 1050
Qermez Dere 205, 416, 421, 422
Qeshm 938
Qidru, *see* Qedar
Qilbanu, Mount 884
Qinnesrin 1034
Qldans 904
Qminas 384
Qornet Rharra 381
Qos 827
Qreiye 1027
quartz 325, 326
quartzite 325
Que 802, 809
Quera 887
Quercus 168
  see also oak
quern 172, 408
Quetta Ware 599, 701
quffa 370
Qulha 881
Qunf Cave 10, 12, 13, 14, 15, 665
quppu 370
Qurayyah 820
  pottery 820, 829
Qurna 52
Qusair 1108, 1110
Qusair as-Saila 1027

Quseir al-Qadim 339, 1050ff.
Quwair 275

Ra 845
Rabah, Wadi 389, 396, 409–10, 632
rab alani 873
rabbit 211
Rabel II 1037
rabisu 844
rafts 370
Rag-e Bibi 1090
Rahaliya 1107ff., 1109ff.
rainfall 11, 12, 262, 273, 608, 690
raisins 188
Raithou 1103
Ramesses II 731ff., 771, 845
Ramesses III 820, 829, 846
Ramesses XI 846
Ram Hormuz 519, 527, 528, 755, 932, 936, 957
Ramlat al-Sabatayn 488
Ramsay, William Mitchell 63
rann 760
Raphanaea 1028
rapid climate change 388
Raqa'i 562
Ras al-'Amiya 467, 476, 478
Ra's al-Hadd 767
  (5) 225
  (6) 224, 226, 489
Ra's al-Hamra 489
  (5) 224, 226, 232, 496
Ra's al-Jins
  (1) 226
  (2) 225, 362, 364, 367, 498–9, 767
  (40) 225
Ra's al-Khabbah (1) 225
Ra's al-Khaimah 492
Ra's az-Zor 493
Ras el-Bassit 772
Ras Fartak 1047
Ras Ibn Hani 772, 776

Rassam, Hormuzd 52, 54, 59, 853, 856, 859ff., 863, 865, 919
Ras Shamra 212, 222, 282, 283, 322, 378, 384, 385, 386, 391, 570, 612, 772, 800
rations 229–30, 483
Rawlinson, Henry Creswicke 51, 53, 65
Rayy 1007, 1088, 1090
Rayyan, Wadi 400
reaping 245
reciprocity 793
Red-Black Burnished Ware 615
Red Sea 20, 142, 664, 1037, 1041ff.
reduction, lithic 238
reeds 349, 361, 362, 365, 370
Rehkmire 843
Rehovot-in-the-Negev 1098
Reisner, George Andrew 62
reliefs 153, 656, 736, 750, 782, 803, 807ff., 811, 837, 856, 859, 953, 1019
  Neo-Assyrian 234
  rock 593, 754
  Sasanian rock 1090ff.
Renan, Ernest 54, 55
repoussé 314
reptiles 130
reservoirs 267, 269, 270, 959, 1035
Reshahr 940
Resheph 624
resin 844
Retenu, Upper 837
retouch 247, 248, 249, 254
Reuther, Oscar 1104
Revolt, Great Satraps 913
Rhagae 1007
Rhambeans 1029
Rhene Island 1044
Rhodes 1044
rhyton 1006
Rib-Addu 773, 844
rice 1013, 1054

Rich, Claudius James 49, 856, 863
Riemchen 510
Rift valley 608
Rihab 1074
Rim-Sin 270
Rimush 649, 655, 657, 662
rituals, funerary 788ff.
roads 590, 960
  Roman 1035
  Royal Achaemenid 936ff., 960, 966
rock-art 704
Rockefeller Museum 85
rodents 173–4
Rohoba 1064
Romans 1021ff.
Rome 1044
Roodias 141
Rosetta Stone 70, 112
Rosh Zin 137
Ross, Henry James 52
Rostovtzeff, Mikhail 673
Rouj basin 384, 389, 391, 392
Royal Ontario Museum 113
Ruad 54
Rub al-Khali 486
Rubar Dahuk 276
ruderals 171
Ruheibe 1064
ruhushak 748
Rulda'u 822
Rumeilah 952
Rumex 170
Runtiya 808
Rusa I 882ff.
Rusa II 878, 884, 893
Rusa III 885
Rusa IV 885
Rusa, son of Argishti 889
Rusa, son of Erimena 889
Rusafa 1070, 1097, 1105
Rusahinili 884

rushes 361
rye 170, 172

Saar 222, 226, 233, 368
Saba 55, 821–2, 1046, 1046ff., 1053
Saba'a, *see* Saba
Sabaeans 824, 1047
Sabarmati, delta 767
Sabas, St 1099
   Great Lavra of 1099
Sabatier, Raymond 71
sabkha (salt flat) 20, 493, 828
Sachau, Eduard 60
sacrifice
   animal 841
   horse 680
   ox 680
Sadaqa 1074
Sadd-e Eskandar 1089
Sadyattes 901
Safadi 302
Safar, Fuad 476
SAFE *Corner* 118
Sagalassos 231
sagênê 227
Saggaratum 271
Şahankaya 968
Sahara 11
Sahure 836
Saida 744, 1032
Sa'ida II 384
Sais 848
šakkanaku 565, 745
Salamis 1044
Salat Cami Yani 283
salinity 9, 263–4, 664
salinization 269
Salm 830
   HGM 830
   Mahram 830
Salmas 1090
salt 230, 232, 985
Sam'al 63, 803

Samaria 62, 1064, 1099
Samaria-Sebaste 1030, 1032
Samarra 8, 61, 194, 284, 466, 470
Samarran period 268, 379, 408, 470, 471–2, 477
Sami, Ali 940, 943
Samosata 1028
Sampsigeramos 1026
Samsat 1028
Samsi 821
Samsu-iluna 715, 716
Sandas 904
SANGA SUḪUR 229
Sang-e Siah 940, 958
Şanlıurfa 155
Saphon, Mount 776
Saqqara 836, 849, 976
Sarab-e Bahram 1090
Sarab-e Qandil 1082
Sarab, *see* Tepe Sarab
Sarafand 775
   see also Sarepta
Sarakhs 1088
Sarazm 702–3
sardines 226
   see also fish
Sardis 109, 310, 897, 899ff., 902ff., 936, 966ff., 968, 970, 974, 981, 986, 1067ff.
sardsir 932
Sarduri I 878ff., 894
Sarduri II 881ff., 884, 889
Sarduri III 885
Sarepta 775, 981
Sargon of Akkad 35, 36, 366, 370, 586, 609
   King of Battle 653; II 30, 33, 51, 275, 650ff., 762, 821, 852, 857ff., 861ff., 882ff., 889, 916, 923
Sarikaya, palace 579
Sar-i Sangh 762
Šarišša 580
Sarissa 736ff.

Sari Tepe 970
Sar-Mashad 1090
Sarpedon 908
Sart river 898
Sarvestan 938
Sarzec, Ernest Chocquin de 57
Sasan 1005
Sasanians 855, 1005, 1056, 1076ff.
Satavahana 1057
Satchkere 678
satellite imagery 536
Satiyaputras 1057
satraps 985
satrapy 966, 985
Saudi Arabia 491, 1110
Saurashtra 762
Savignac, Raphaël 56, 825
Sayce, Archibald Henry 63
Sayin 1055
scales 615
scarab, Egyptian 626, 840ff.
scepter 157, 158
Schaeffer, Claude 81
Schechem 62, 975
Scheil, Vincent 60, 68, 743
Schliemann, Heinrich 102, 113, 116
Schmidt, Erich F. 936, 943
Schotterhofbau 853
Schumacher, Gottlieb 62
scorpion 152, 158
scorpion-man 891
scraper 132, 241, 245, 247, 249, 252, 254, 487, 676
  fan 251
  tabular 249, 251, 252, 257, 834
screw, Archimedean 264
scribes 28, 30–1, 590
sculpture 910
  monumental 626
Scythians 906
Scythopolis 1037, 1063
seafaring 141

seal
  Arsacid 1017
  Christian 1104
  cylinder 228, 233, 264, 580, 604, 615, 626, 655ff., 665, 685, 701, 710, 720, 750, 765, 794, 835, 839, 841, 891, 915, 949, 960
  Dilmun 368
  Harappan 767
  impressions 392, 429, 604, 620, 892, 992
  Indus or Harappan 701
  stamp 695, 726, 765, 891, 949
  stamp impressions 993, 1008
  use 544–5
  see also glyptic
Sealand 717
sea-level 19–20
Sea Peoples 738, 772, 776, 845, 908
Sebaste 62
Sebastiya 1030
secondary
  products 210
  states 633–4
sedentarization 438
sedentism 135, 137
sedimentation 12
sediments, lake 664
Seetzen, Ulrich Jasper 55
Sé Girdan 107
Seha River Land 896, 899
Seker al-Aheimer 422
Sekhemkhet 836
Sela' 929
Selene 1015
Selenkahiye 618
Seleucia-in-Pieria 1029, 1036, 986ff.
Seleucia-on-the-Tigris 985ff., 992ff., 1004ff., 1007, 1008ff., 1012ff., 1016ff.
Seleucia-Zeugma 1021, 1026, 1028ff., 1032
Seleucids 961, 984ff.

Seleucus I 984, 986ff., 989ff., 993
Seleucus II 993
Seleucus III 993
Sellin, Ernest 62
Semirech'ye 693
Senkereh 58
  see also Larsa
sen-murw 1010
Sennacherib 30, 38, 39, 43, 44, 52, 188, 265, 266, 276, 277, 821ff., 848, 852, 854, 857, 863, 884, 916, 925
Senwosret I 837
Senwosret III 609, 838, 839
Septimius Severus, L. 1005, 1026, 1031
Seqenenra 842
sequential slab construction 284
Sergiopolis 1070, 1097, 1105
Sergius, St 1063, 1066, 1071, 1072, 1074, 1096ff., 1105
serpentine 158, 657, 795
Serranidae 223
sesame 197, 292
Sesostris 837
Seti I 845
settlement patterns 638ff., 655–6, 917, 1077ff.
Sevan, Lake 683, 878, 880, 882
Sevan-Artsakh 681
Sevan-Uzerlik 681
Seyrig, Henri 82
Sha'ar Hagolan 406, 407, 408
Sha-Assur-dubbu 874
Shab, Wadi 496, 497
Shabwa 56, 1053
Shadorvan, weir 1083
shaduf 264, 265, 266
Shaduppum 548, 553
Shagarakti-Shuriash 44
shahanshah 1093
Shahba 1032
Shahdad 604

Shahr-e Qumis 1007, 1018, 1078
Shahrestaniha-ye Iranshahr 1078
Shahr-i Sokhta 186–7, 196, 225, 338, 340, 342, 343, 344, 511, 599ff., 604, 689, 743
Shah Tepe 602ff., 768
Šāhūr river 954
Shakarat al-Musay'id 403
Shalmaneser, Fort 858, 860
Shalmaneser I 571, 857, 864, 877
Shalmaneser III 820, 847, 854, 857, 858–9, 860ff., 878, 888
Shalmaneser IV 880
Shalmaneser V 857
shaman 411
Shamash 45, 270, 624, 715ff., 853, 861ff., 920, 922, 929, 1015
Shamash-shum-ukin 822, 916, 921
Shamsabad 507, 508
Shams ed-Din 389
Shamshi-Adad I 546, 568, 569, 656, 747, 748, 853, 864
Shamshi-Adad V 854, 857, 864
Shamshi-Addu, *see* Shamshi-Adad I
Shang, period 704
Shanidar Cave 136, 296
Shapinuwa 593, 736ff.
Shapur I 855, 1078, 1082ff., 1091
Shapur II 1084, 1088, 1091
Shapur III 1091
Shaqurri, Mount 821
Sharif-Khan 276
Sharjah 233, 487
Shar-kali-sharri 651, 657, 661, 666
Sharon, plain 967
Sharrat-niphi 572
Sharri-Kushukh 729
Sharrishsha 593
Sharrumma 733
Sharrupshe 780
shasha 352, 370
Shatt al-Arab 194, 515
Shatuppu 782

Shebitu 887
Shechem 643, 838
sheep 203, 204, 206, 208, 212, 230, 232, 338, 407, 411, 418, 429, 440, 486, 487, 496, 525, 528, 557, 583, 615, 626, 702, 904, 991
Shehna 568, 662, 663
Sheikh Abad 505
Shekaft-e Salman 754
Shekelesh 845
shell 506
shellfish 233, 234, 489, 494
   see also mollusks
Sherden 845
Sherratt, Andrew 674
Sheshonq I 847
shibuta 223
shields 889
Shilhaha 747
Shilhak-Inshushinak 753
Shimal 232, 768
Shimashki 745ff.
   dynasty of 598
Shimbishhuk-Inshushinak 745
Shingalla 830
shipwright 366
shipyard 365ff.
Shiqmim 302, 411
Shiqmona 973
Shir 386, 387, 388
Shiraz 939
Shiruk-tuh 748
Shiru Malikta 276
Shishak 847
Shivta 1064, 1098
Shiwini 880, 886ff., 888
Shoga 934
   see also Tal-e Teimuran
Shomutepe 507
Shortugai 689, 701
shrine 405
   see also temple

Shubat-Enlil 546, 568, 569
Shu-Durul 666
Shugu 745
Shu-ilishu 747, 765
Shukbah Cave 131
Shuksu, see Souksi
Shulaveris 507
Shulgi 338, 707ff., 711, 746
Shullaggi 936, 938
Shumaliya 717
Shupi-ahshu 585
Shuppiluliuma I 728, 729ff., 752ff., 771, 778ff., 782, 800
Shuppiluliuma II 727
Shuqamuna 717
Shuruppak 544; see also Fara
Shushtar 936, 1077, 1083
Shu-Suen 708, 712, 746
Shuteit 1083
Shutrukids 750, 752ff.
Shutruk-Nahhunte I 36, 37, 718, 752ff.
Shuttarna II 570
Sia 1039
Siberia 692
sickle 132, 241, 248, 251, 252, 253, 254, 255, 257, 258, 314, 443
   blade 174
šid 361
Sidon 54, 80, 380, 610, 613, 621, 622, 625, 773ff., 824, 848, 980, 1032, 1036, 1044, 1072
Siduna 774
silica 324, 325
silk 1037
   tree 226
Silk Road 687, 1014, 1058
silos 173, 410–11, 579, 580, 967
silt 263, 270
silver 303, 367, 567, 618, 625, 680, 840, 845, 883, 898, 904, 953, 1094
   coils 657
   ingots 657, 839

Silver Mountain 661
Simeon, St
  the Elder 1070
  the Younger 1070
Simyra 777
Sin 45, 46, 716, 853, 862, 922, 1015
  temple of at Khafajah 354
Sinai 836ff., 968, 1064, 1103ff.
  Mount 1103
  peninsula 225
Sin-balassu-iqbi 916, 922
sindhu 769
singer 590
Sin-iddinam 8, 270
Sinkashid, palace of 196
  see also Uruk
Sin-leqe-unninni 30
Sintashta 704
Sinuhe, Tale of 837
Sippar 8, 21, 37, 43, 45, 60, 270, 549, 652, 713, 753, 916, 918, 920
šiqqum 232
Siraf 1078
Sir Bani Yas 1110
Sirçan Tepe 445
Sirhan, Wadi 826
Sirkeli Höyük 218, 231
Sirwah 55
Sistan 599, 957, 973
Sivand 941
Siyanu 776ff.
skins, *see* hides
Skirtos river 1068
skolepoi 1051
skull, curation 401, 426, 422, 437, 442
  plastered 281, 384
slag 301, 302, 305, 308, 315, 585
slaves 906, 985, 1054
slingstones 409, 449

smelting 299, 300ff., 305, 310, 311, 509
Smendes I 846
Smith, George 54
Smith, Sydney 76
smiths 590
Smyrna 901, 902
snakes 158, 892
Sneferu 609
Society for American Archaeology 118
soda 324
  mineral 327
software 283, 506
Sogdiana 35, 969
Soghun, valley 1078
Sohr Damb 186
soil 5
soldering 314
Soli Höyük 802
Solomon 847
Solutrean 147
Sophia, Church of St 1065
Soqotra 1047, 1053ff.
Sorath 767
Soreq Cave 12, 14, 388
sorghum (*Sorghum bicolor*) 499
Sos Höyük 676, 677, 681
Soteira 996
Soter Megas 341
Souksi 776
soumak, technique 342, 343
South Arabia 1043, 1046, 1052
sowing 263
spahbed 1093
Spain 1051, 1055
Sparta 902
Spasinou Charax 1014
spear 234, 248
  fishing 228
spearhead 314
specialization, craft 258, 292, 615
speiss 308

speleothems 664
sphinx 592, 790, 808, 953
spices 276, 1037
spiders 152
spies 874
spindle whorl 24
Spondylus 496
springs 736, 1102
spruce 1036
Sri Lanka 1044, 1058ff.
standardization 287
stannite 303
Starr, R.F.S. 76
statuary 154, 651–2, 656, 658, 789ff., 841, 849, 1106
status 412
Stavropol 669
steatite 603, 765
  see also chlorite
steel 307, 312
Stein, Sir Marc Aurel 936, 1088
Steingebäude 479
  see also Uruk
stelae 626, 657, 808, 854, 884, 887
Stephen, Church of St 1074, 1102
stibnite 330
Stipa 170
stoa 993
Stolze, Franz 66, 943
storage 230, 429, 563, 578, 579, 582, 641, 858, 894, 918, 959, 967
  cereal 173
strata Diocletiana 1028, 1035
Straton 995
strigil 998
stucco 1009ff., 1017, 1081, 1087ff., 1104, 1106ff.
Subaita 1064
Subartu 565, 748
Suberde 204, 205, 433
Sudan 1042
Suez 1050
Suhu 821, 823
  canal of 273
SUḪUR 222
suḫurmāšu 234
sukkal 748
sukkalmaḫ 746ff.
  dynasty 598, 601
Šulgi and Ninlil's Boat 362
Sulpicius Quirinius, P. 1024
Sultanhan 803
Sultanian 142
sulupp̂ 183
Sumbar Valley 340
Sumer 707
Sumerian
  King list 652, 666, 744
  language 650, 718
Sumerians 540, 545
Sumhuram 224, 1046ff., 1054ff.
Sumuabum 713
Sumu'il 822
Sumur 777, 844
Su-people, *see* LÚ.SU^{ki}
Suppiluliuma 592
Sur 774, 1032
Sura 911, 1027
Surb Sahak 882
Surghul 60
Sur Jar´a 821
Surkh Dum (-e Luri) 108
surplus 578, 583, 635
  food 580
Surri 774
Susa 36, 37, 38, 67, 83, 107, 233, 297, 311, 313, 354, 357, 512ff., 520, 521, 523, 525, 527, 597, 598, 600ff., 652, 662, 687, 701, 718, 741ff., 768, 849, 935ff., 938ff., 950ff., 955, 959ff., 966, 1002, 1006, 1009, 1013, 1015, 1018, 1076ff., 1084
  Acropole 952, 956
  Ville Royale 744, 745, 749, 950, 952ff., 954, 956, 1009, 1084

Susiana 65, 66, 512ff., 528, 740ff., 755
Suwayh (1) 490
Suwayh (2) 225
Suwayh (4) 225
sword, sickle 839
symbols 153, 234, 399
symposium 998
synagogue 1055, 1096, 1102
Syr Darya 690
Syria
   Coele 1026, 1028, 1038
   Palaestina 1026, 1038
   Phoenicia 1026
   Prima 1070
   Salutaris 1070
Syriac 1104, 1106, 1109

Ta'anach 772
Tabal 800, 803, 807ff.
Tabaqat al-Buma 408
Tabari 1081
Tabarna 737
Tabqa Dam 570, 612
Tabu'a 821ff.
Tabula Peutingeriana 1008
tačara 944, 956
Tadjvidi, Akbar 943
Tadmur 1024
Taharqa 848
Taita 802, 808
Tajikistan 304, 339, 690, 702
Takht-e Belqeys 1087
Takht-e Jamshid 943
Takht-e Rustam 955, 957
Takht-e Suleiman 1085ff., 1092
Takht-e Taqdis 1087
Takht Neshin 1079
Takuwa 778
Tal'a 829
Tal-e Bakun 507, 508, 526
Tal-e Gap 508
Tal-e Ghazir 743

Tal-e Iblis 506, 510
Tal-e Malyan 37, 187, 510, 596, 597, 598–9, 743, 753, 958, 1078
Talesh 67
Tal-e Shoga 754
Tal-e Teimuran 754
Tal-e Zohak 938
Tal-i Iblis 301
Talin 676
Tall al-'Umayri 638, 640, 641
Tall al-Khalayfi 929
Tall al-Mazar 973
Tall-e Abu Chizan 529
Tall-e Ghazir 934, 936
Tall-e Hakavan 958
Tall-e Kandaq 940
Tall-e Pol-e Bizdan 938
Tall-e Takht 940ff., 961
Tall-e Tendi 936
Tall-e Zohak 936, 958, 960
Tallgren, Årne 673
Tall-i Ghazir 519
   see also Tol Geser
Tall-i Jari 296, 507, 508
Tall-i Mushki 296, 507
Tall Jalul 970
Talmessi 297, 299
Talmud 231
   Babylonian 1016
Talpush-atili 570
tamarisk 18, 193
Tamerkhan 471
Tammaritu I 755
Tamukkan 939, 959
Tangab 1079, 1090ff.
Tang-e Bolaghi 937, 940, 943, 956, 957ff., 959ff., 961, 1010
Tang-e Chowgan 1090
Tang-e Qandil 1090
Tang-e Sarvak 1010, 1012
Tanit-Astarte 981
Tan-Ruhuratir 747

Tanwentamun 848
Taoce 939, 959
Tapikka 736ff.
Tappe Mehrali 509
Tappeh Pahnu 958
Tappeh Sabzabad 940
Tappe Sang-e Chaxmagh 504, 506
Taq-e Bustan 1090ff.
Taq-e Kesra 1081
Taram-Agade 663
Tarava 961
Tarbisu 276
Tarhuntassa 726, 800
Tarhunza 808
Taricheae 232
Tarsus 309, 802, 1067
Tartus 54
Tarum 960
Tashmetum 859, 1015
Tasian 284
Taş Kule 975
Taurus mountains 4, 144, 148, 207
Tawannana 733
Tawfiq, Rida 85
Tawilan 929
Tawwag 939
Tawwaz 939
tax 579, 650, 655, 968, 1024ff., 1037, 1044, 1061, 1074
  salt 985
Taylor, John George 53, 58
Tayma 56, 819ff., 823ff., 828, 929
Taymanite, inscriptions 825
tayyibat al-Imam 1071
Tazakend 681
Tbeik, Wadi 225
teak 763
Tectonis grandis 763
Tedjen river 692
Te'elhunu 821ff.
Tehran 4
Teimuran (Taymuran) 934
Teisheba 880, 886ff.

Teishebaini 884ff., 889
Teispes 756
Tekrit 1111
Tel Ali 410
Tel al-Wawayat 231
Tel Aphek 1030
Tel Dan 643, 981
Tel Dor 227, 228, 315, 967ff., 970, 973, 1036, 1064
Teleilat Ghassul 190, 411, 412, 413
Tel Halif 967
Tel Harassim 231
Tel Haror 968
Telipinu 724ff.
  decree 580
Tel Iztaba 1063
Tel Masos 1100
Tel Megadim 973
Tel Michal 967, 970, 973, 977, 981
Tell Abada 289, 349, 352, 426, 478, 479, 480
Tell Abd el-Aziz 389, 391, 392
Tell Abila 1100
Tell Abr 3 158, 171, 173, 391, 393
Tell Abraq 226, 303, 304, 768
Tell Abu Chizan 520
Tell Abu Dhahir 866
Tell Abu Habbah 270
Tell Abu Hamid 410, 411, 412
Tell Abu Hureyra 131, 133, 134, 136, 138, 165, 169, 170, 171, 175, 176, 177, 179, 204, 205, 206, 281, 282, 380, 386, 421, 435
Tell Abu Salabikh 222, 285, 290, 538, 542, 543
Tell Afar 416, 468
Tell Afis 391, 804
Tell Ahmar 81, 612, 618, 803, 808
Tell Ain el-Kerkh 384, 385, 389
Tell al-Fakhar 322
Tell al-Haidiya 563
Tell al-Hamidiya 570, 571, 572
Tell al-Hawa 425, 427, 562, 563

Tell al-Hiba 20, 60, 221, 290, 357
Tell al-Katheeb 829
Tell al-Lahm 918, 922
Tell al-Mazar 975, 977
Tell al-Muqqayar, *see* Ur
Tell al-Rimah 322, 332, 570, 866
Tell al-Ubaid 78, 194, 349
   see also Ubaid, period, etc.
Tell Al Uhaimir 49
   see also Kish
Tell Amarna (Syria) 389
Tell Arbid 665, 666
Tell Arqa 610, 614, 622, 617, 619, 620, 62, 625, 626, 777
Tell Ashara 716
   see also Terqa
Tell Asmar 34, 77, 226, 290, 654, 712, 747
   Abu Temple at 34, 542
   see also Eshnunna
Tell as-Sidr 866
Tell Aswad 175, 206, 383, 384
Tell Atchana 771, 781, 806
Tell 'Atij 562
Tell Balatah 62
Tell Banat 617, 618, 619, 621
Tell Barri 563
Tell Bazi 570, 783
Tell Bderi 563, 571
Tell Beth Shemesh 315
Tell Beydar 563, 564, 565, 566, 663, 665
Tell Bi'a 563, 567
Tell Billa 352
Tell Brak 215, 291, 319, 321, 322, 332, 420, 424, 427, 428, 429, 479, 480, 481, 536, 562, 563, 565, 566, 570, 654ff., 660, 662, 665, 677, 708
Tell Chuera 563, 564, 565, 571, 572
Tell Daillam 60
Tell ed-Daim 970
Tell ed-Der 8, 41, 196, 199

Tell el-Amarna (Egypt) 321, 570
   letters 321
Tell el-Amarna 772; letters 843
Tell el-Burak 610, 623, 624
Tell el-Dab'a 644, 840
Tell el-Far'ah South 967
Tell el-Farkha 835
Tell el-Herr 968
Tell el-Hesi 61, 84, 967
Tell el-Judeideh 62, 393, 615
Tell el-Katheeb 827
Tell el-Kerkh 283, 384, 385, 386, 387, 388, 424
Tell el-Mashkuta 968
Tell el-Muqdam 973
Tell el-Mutesellim 62
Tell el-Safi 62
Tell el-'Umeri 970, 973
Tell el-Yahudiya 841
   ware 625
Tell esh-Sheikh 389
Tell es-Sa'idiyeh 970, 977
Tell es-Sakan 188
Tell es-Sawwan 425, 467, 468, 472–3
Tell es-Sultan, *see* Jericho
Tell es-Sweyhat 24, 565, 617, 620, 622
Tell Ezou 384
Tell Fadous-Kfarabida 610, 614, 615, 622
Tell Fakhariyah 82, 570, 572
Tell Frach 386
Tell Hadidi 617, 618, 622
Tell Halaf 64, 65, 80, 82, 789, 928
   Museum 82
Tell Halawa A 624
Tell Halula 207, 283, 384, 385, 422
Tell Hammeh 306
Tell Hamoukar 420, 556, 562, 565, 566, 661, 677
Tell Hariri, *see* Mari

Tell Hassan 475
Tell Hassuna 388, 471
Tell Hazna 563
Tell Hizzin 610, 626
Tell Ibrahim 60
Tell Ibrahim Awad 836
Tell Ingharra 920
Tell Iris 776
Tell Jemmeh 967
Tell Jenin 231
Tell Jigan 866
Tell Jokha, see Umma
Tell Judaidah 309, 389, 392
Tell Kabir 617
Tell Kazel 777, 792, 795
Tell Kedoua 968
Tell Kesaran 290
Tell Khan Sheykhun 780
Tell Khoshi 563
Tell Kroum 386
Tell Kurdu 389, 391
Tell Leilan 562, 563, 566, 568, 569, 655, 660, 662, 665
Tell Madhhur 539
Tell Maghzaliyah 296
Tell Majnuna 428
Tell Mardikh, see Ebla
Tell Marj 386
Tell Mashnaqa 349, 352
Tell Meskene 782, 800, 1070
  see also Emar
Tell Mishrife, see Qatna
Tell Mohammed Diyab 571
Tell Mozan 24, 563, 565, 570, 571, 662, 663, 677
Tell Munbaqa 570, 783, 791
Tell Museifneh 1108, 1111
Tell Nebi Mend 81, 625, 780
Tell Oueili 7, 21, 196, 212, 349, 466, 467, 471, 476, 481
Tell Qaramel 158, 383
Tell Qara Quzaq 309, 614, 615, 617, 624

Tell Qasile 970
Tell Ramad 281, 384
Tell Rijm 866
Tell Sabi Abyad 23, 281, 283, 387, 389, 390, 423, 424, 426, 460, 472, 475, 572
Tell Sakka 624
Tell Sandahanna 62
Tell Sekar Foqani 566
Tell Seker al-Aheimar 283, 284
Tell Sheikh Hamad 218, 272–3, 572, 928
Tell Sheikh Hasan 382, 393
Tell Shiyukh Fawqani 614, 782, 808, 977
Tell Sianu 776
Tell Songor
  A 471, 473, 475
  B 475
Tell Sotto 284, 419
Tell Sukas 385, 386, 389, 624, 776, 981
Tell Tannek 62
Tell Taya 563, 866
Tell Tayinat 802, 804, 806ff.
Tell Tsaf 410
Tell Tweini 776
Tell Umar 993, 1008
Tell Uqair 349, 352, 479, 481
Tell Yarmuth 285
Tell Yelkhi 290
Tell Zakariya 62
Tell Zeidan 478, 480, 481
Telloh 20, 43, 57, 58, 60, 226, 229, 269, 357, 359, 361, 366, 369, 657ff., 746
Telmessus 911, 913
Tel Qatif 967ff.
Tel Sera' 967
Telul eth-Thalathat 284
Tema 819, 821ff.
temper (ceramic) 282, 284
temperature 12

temple 405, 413, 481, 536, 541, 545, 547, 548, 550, 553, 554, 591, 614, 617, 624
  broad-room 412
  fire 1079, 1082, 1085ff.
Temple of the Obelisks 624, 626, 839, 841
Temple of the Storm God 727, 735, 781–2, 790, 802, 804, 807–8
Temti-Wartash 749
Tennes Revolt 967
Teos 849
Tepe Abdul Hosein 504
Tepe Ali Kosh 92, 207, 282, 296, 503
Tepe Asiab 207, 504
Tepe Atashi 504
Tepe Bandebal 520, 521
Tepe Bormi 934, 936ff.
Tepeçik 301, 676
Tepeçik-Çiftlik 301, 435, 461
Tepe Damghani 187
Tepe Farukhabad 92, 524, 527
Tepe Fullol, hoard 694
Tepe Garan 936
Tepe Gawra 291, 297, 428, 526, 674
Tepe Gaz Tavila 196, 283
Tepe Ghabristan 510, 596
Tepe Giyan 502
Tepe Guran 204, 282
Tepe Hissar 187, 303, 308, 342, 502, 509, 511, 596, 602, 768, 1078, 1088
Tepe Jaffarabad 520, 521
Tepe Jalyan 598
Tepe Jowi 520, 521
Tepe Musiyan 67, 528
Tepe Özbaki 596, 743
Tepe Pardis 285, 289, 509
Tepe Patak 935ff.
Tepe Rahmatabad 504
Tepe Sabz 526
Tepe Sarab 204, 337, 471, 504, 506
Tepe Sialk 296, 502, 507, 509, 510, 596, 763
Tepe Sofalin 743
Tepe Sohz 519, 527, 528
Tepe Suruvan 936
Tepe Yahya 83, 186, 196, 283, 296, 510, 604, 701, 743, 768, 938, 1078
Tepti-Ahar 751
terebinth 186, 435
Terebralia palustris 489
Terek river 669
Terekty 704
Teresh 845
Termilae 908ff.
Terqa 271, 272, 716
terracottas 1019
terusi 894
Teseti 910
Teshub 887
Tetrapolis 986, 988
Tetrapyrgium 1027
Tetrastoos 1064
Teumman 188
Texier, Charles 63, 65
textiles 24, 211, 212, 336ff., 586, 588, 783, 809, 823, 927, 1037
Thaj 1015, 1110
Tharthar, Wadi 270, 470
theater 994, 1006, 1008, 1016
Thebes 846, 902
Theodorias 1070
Theodoros 1074
Theodosianus, Codex 1034
Theodosiopolis 1067
Theodosius
  pilgrim 1075
  St 1065, 1069
  Monastery of St 1063
Theodosius I 1068
Theodosius II 1065, 1066, 1069
Theopolis 1070
Theotokos Chalkoprateia 1066

Thermi 303
Thiloua 1015
tholos 390, 391
Thomas, Félix 51, 861
threshing 241, 252
throne, serpent 750
Thunnus albacares 224
Thureau-Dangin, François 81
Thutmose I 848
Thutmose III 329, 848, 717, 728, 771, 777ff., 843
Thutmose IV 570, 771
Tiberius I 1065
Tidu 572
Tien Shan 692, 698, 702ff.
Tiglath-pileser I 218, 275, 798, 820, 823, 879
Tiglath-pileser III 38, 342, 821, 823, 847, 857, 859, 882
Tigris river 19, 262, 263, 270, 273, 275, 276, 515, 557, 558, 565, 567, 571, 572, 651, 663, 854, 856, 863, 866, 881, 925, 932, 1081
Tihama 367
Tikunani 724
Til Barsip 612, 803
Tilbeşar 563
tiles 1009
Tilia, Giuseppe and Ann Brit 944
Tille Höyük 803, 970, 973
Tillya Tepe 107
timber 198, 608
Timna (Israel) 298, 299ff., 302, 834, 846
Timna (South Arabia) 1047, 1053
Timnian 249
Timothy, St 1065, 1068
tin 298, 303, 304–5, 307, 308, 329, 620, 659, 704, 748, 844
  ingots 793
Tinos 1044
tir 361

Tirazzish 939
Tishrin Dam 570, 612, 990
Tissamaharama 1059
Titles and Professions List, Archaic texts 482
titles, Akkadian 652–3
Titriş Höyük 563, 565, 573
  plain 4
tittu 184
Tlos 908
Tmolus 898
toads 152
Tobol
  river 692
  valley 344
Tod, Treasure 839
Togolok 701
tokens 479, 483
Tol-e Bashi 507
Tol-e Gachgaran-e Ka Khodada 958
Tol-e Nurabad 296, 509, 755, 934ff.
Tol-e Pir 938
Tol-e Spid 509, 755, 935, 937
Tol Geser 519, 527
tolls 1037, 1044
Tomb-e Bot 938, 959
tombs, *see* burials
Toprak Kale 884, 885, 889
  ware 890
Toprak-Kale (Chorasmia) 1013
tortoise 130, 401
  shell 1054
Touqan, Ala al-Din bek 85
tournette 285, 391
towers of silence 1085
Trablus 1036
trace elements 318
traction, animal 211
Trajan 1008, 1026, 1028, 1037, 1044
Tranchard, G. 861
Transbaikal 344

Transcaucasian style 677
transhumance 390, 598, 679
Trapa natans 168
traps, fish 228
treaties 732
    vassal 730
Trebizond 1067
Treli 681
Treligorebi 683
Trialeti 680
    "Trialeti–Vanadzor" assemblages 680, 681
triangle 132, 148
Triballos 995
tributum capitis 1024
tributum soli 1024
trilingual inscriptions
    Achaemenid 948
    Lydian-Greek-Aramaic 909
tripartite building 392, 539
Tripoli 1029
Tripolis 1036ff.
Triticum boeoticum 166
Triticum dicoccoides 166, 169
Triticum dicoccum 166, 499
Triticum monococcum 166
Triticum urartu 166
Trmmili 909
Trog(l)odytes 1051ff.
Trojan War 908
trona 327, 328
Troodos Mountains 141
Troy 309, 338
Trqqas 910
Trysa 911
Tsaghkahovit 969, 973ff.
    fortress 684
    plain 683, 685
Tsalka plateau 677
Tudhaliya I/II 725, 728
Tudhaliya III 728, 735, 737
Tudhaliya IV 591, 726, 733, 736, 908

Tudhaliya the Younger 729
túg-du$_8$-a 343
Tukulti-Ninurta I 44, 274, 572, 572, 717, 852, 854ff
Tukulti-Ninurta II 272, 882, 854
Tülintepe 301
Tulmay 825
Tulul Al 'Aqar, *see* Kar-Tukulti-Ninurta
Tulul al-Ukhaidir 1104
Tummal 362
tumuli 905, 976ff.
    see also kurgan
tuna 224, 228, 496
Tunb-e Karam 941
Tunip 773, 777ff.
Tunip-Teshub 724
Tuniya 724
tunnels 276
Tur Abdin 1067
Tureng Tepe 342, 602ff., 1078
Turkmenistan 504, 689, 692ff., 1003, 1005, 1087, 1108
turntable 285
turquoise 320, 600, 835
    mines 836
turtle
    green 496
    sea 216
    see also Chelonia mydas
turtlebacks 7, 467
Tushhan 572
Tushpa 878, 978
Tushpuea 890
Tushratta 570, 571, 729
Tutankhamun 107, 314
Tuwana 803, 809, 814
Tyana 803, 809, 814
Tychaion 1069
tyche 1018, 1069
Typha sp. 361, 367
Tyre 54, 321, 609, 773ff., 824, 848, 1032, 1036ff., 1072

Ua 887
Uaush 883
ubadinnum 578
Ubaid
 period 233, 249, 252, 268, 348, 379, 391, 392, 408, 426, 476ff., 491, 496, 508, 539, 674ff., 860
 pottery 492, 493, 494, 495
Ubeidiya 833
Üçağizli Cave 146, 147
Üçtepe 572
Udabno 683
Udjahorresnet 976
udu-gukkal 338
Ugarit 80, 81, 82, 191, 314, 321, 378, 570, 612, 624, 625, 626, 734, 771ff., 776ff., 780ff., 785ff., 792ff., 795, 800, 838, 840
Ugulzat 780
Ujaini 1058
Ulai 226
 see also Eulaios, Karkheh
Ulam-buriash 717
'Ulaym Shahru 825
uligi 338
Ullaza 609, 838ff.
Uluburun 227, 318, 304, 321, 332, 371, 793
Ulucak 433, 443
Ulug Depe 187
Umayyads 1074
 fortress at Ukhaidir 1108
Ume er-Rasas 1074
Umm al-Hafriyat 290
Umm al-Jimal 1101
Umm al-Qaiwain 226, 495
Umm an-Nar 367, 499
Umm an-Nussi 355, 500
Umm ar-Ramadh 355, 500
Umm ar-Rasas 1102
Umm Dabaghiyah 281, 284, 387, 419, 421, 467, 468, 470
Umm el-Amad 54

Umm el-Jimal 1073
Umm el-Marra 107, 617, 620, 626
Umm el-Quttein 1073
Umm Lakis 84
Umm Leisan 1100
Umm Qeis 1032
Umm Qseir 420
Umma 61, 267, 269, 292, 361, 363, 365, 366, 540, 544, 554, 652ff., 658, 666
Unas 836
UNESCO 102, 944, 1083
 Convention of 1970 86, 110
Unger, E. 118
United Arab Emirates 12, 766ff.
University Museum, Philadelphia 76
Unqi 802, 804
Untash-Napirisha 752ff.
Upe 844
Uperi 57
Upper Sea 650
Ur 981
Ur 20, 41, 42, 45, 58, 107, 222, 226, 230, 267, 285, 290, 297, 314, 338, 357, 365, 366, 480, 540, 541, 543, 547, 548, 549, 550, 552, 652ff., 701, 707, 709, 712ff., 744, 746ff., 916, 918, 922ff., 924, 926ff., 981
 Royal Cemetery 34, 76, 193, 198, 309, 345, 359, 544, 600, 604, 654, 659, 764
 Standard of 212, 214, 687, 704
 Third Dynasty of 544ff., 706ff.
Ura 838, 887
Ural
 mountains 344, 763
 river 692
Urartian
 fortresses 971
 inscriptions 879, 885
 language 893ff.
Urartians 874, 877ff.

Urartu 109–10, 682ff., 874, 877ff.
Urash 916
Urashtu 886
urbanism 558ff., 597
urbanization 632, 1078
Urfa 155, 1067
urial 338
Urkesh 565, 571, 662, 663, 665
Urmia, Lake 878ff., 883
Ur-Nammu 658, 707ff.
   Codex 711
Ur-Nanshe 366
Ur-Schatt river 19
uruatri 877, 893
Uruinimgina 269
Uruk 41, 58, 61, 196, 222, 226,
   229, 230, 267, 270, 285, 290,
   291, 297, 349, 352, 355, 429,
   467, 479, 481, 484, 524, 536ff.,
   539, 540, 541, 542, 546, 550,
   562, 613, 650, 659, 666, 676,
   678, 707, 709, 712, 719, 744,
   768, 915ff., 918, 923, 926ff.,
   985ff., 997ff., 1002, 1007, 1013,
   1017, 1019, 1085
   Archaic texts 212, 222, 229, 483,
     538, 539
   Expansion 537
   period 268, 392, 393, 510, 523,
     529, 860
Urzana 883
Uşak 109, 115
ù-suh_5 361
Utu-hegal 707
Uzbekistan 304, 690, 692, 1005ff.
Uzerlik Tepe 679

Valens 1066, 1070
Valerian 1082
Van
   Lake 10, 12ff., 17, 684, 877, 879ff.
   Rock of 878, 882
Vanadzor 680

Vanden Berghe, Louis 108, 111, 936
van Zeist, Willem 165
Vase à la Cachette 601
   see also Susa
vassaldom 872ff.
vassals 859
Vaux, Roland de 630
Vavilov, N.I. 186
Veh-Ardashir 1081
Veh-Shapur 1082
Velikent 309, 311
Venus 1018
Verethragna 1016
Verin Naver 681
Veselovskii, Nikolai 669
Veshnoveh 298, 299
Vespasian 1031, 1036
vetch 18, 166, 525
vetchling 525
veterans, Roman 1028
via nova Hadriana 1050
via nova Traiana 1024, 1027
Vicia ervilia 166
   V. faba 166
Ville des Artisans 950
Ville Royale, *see* Susa, Ville Royale
vines 276
vineyards 582
Virolleaud, Charles 80, 81, 82
viticulture 187
Vitis vinifera 181, 185, 186
vitrification 330
Vogüé, Melchior de 55
Volga river 692
Vologases I 1005, 1013, 1016
Vologases IV 1004
Vologases VI 1005
Vorderasiatisches Museum 113, 855
   see also Pergamon Museum
Vouni 970

Wad Valley 762
Wadd 828

Waddington, William Henry 55, 57
wagons 680
Wala, Wadi 641
Walistin 802
Wallis Budge, Ernest A. 59
warehouses 1066
warfare 397, 405, 448, 523, 661, 868ff.
Warika 802
Warka, *see* Uruk
Washosh 845
Washukanni 570, 729
wasters 287
watchtowers 1051
water 292, 736, 750
water buffalo 215
water chestnut 168
watercraft 347ff.
water lily 168
water-wheel 264
Watzinger, Carl 62
Way of the Sea 608
weaving 337, 339
weeds 400
Weh-Andiog-Shapur 1078
Weh-Ardashir 1078
weights and measures 615
  bronze 793
  Harappan 764, 768
wells 1035, 1051
Wellsted, James Raymond 55
Wenamun, Story of 846
Weni 836
wetlands 21, 444
wheat 9, 168, 177, 197, 408, 525, 528, 557, 703
  bread 499
  free-threshing 18
wheel, potter's 285–6, 294
Wheeler, Sir Mortimer 149
wheels, chariot 744
White Temple 536
White-Spunner, Gen. B. 98

wildcat 210
Williams Jackson, A.V. 1086
Williams, Col. W.F. 65
Wilson, John 82
Winckler, Hugo 63
winds 271
wine 188, 292, 463, 583, 640, 927, 989, 1075
wolf 210
Wolfe, Catherine 58
wood 193, 361
  mesu 762
woodlands 361
wool 211, 212, 337, 338, 343, 344, 366, 367, 823
Woolley, C. Leonard 64, 76, 78, 113, 612, 781
workshops 258, 292, 509, 573, 585, 591, 604, 625, 659, 783f., 858, 904, 918
  glass 322
Wright, William B.A. 63

Xanthus 897, 907ff., 911ff.
Xerxes 886, 911, 919, 942, 944, 946ff., 948, 952
Xinjiang 345, 1014
xwarrah 1078

Yabis, Wadi 400
Yabrin oasis 500
Yabrud 381
Yakto 1070
Yalburt, inscription 908
Yamkhad 569, 610, 724, 781ff.
  see also Aleppo
Yamnaya culture 704
Yapa' 821
Yarim Tepe 281, 302, 387, 420, 426, 471
Yarimburgaz Cave 145
Yarmoukian 249, 388, 396, 406, 407, 408, 409

Yarmut 639
Yassihöyük 798, 801
Yathi'e 821
Yathil 1048
Yathrib 819, 823
Yautha' 822
Yazd-e Khast 1085
Yazilikaya 63, 592, 733
Yellibelen 445
Yemen 4, 12, 224, 376, 488ff., 497ff., 827
Yenikapi 1066
Yerevan 881
Yerkapi Postern 591
Yeşilaliç 887
Yorgan Tepe 570
Young, R.S. 810
Younger Dryas 13, 129, 134, 140, 170, 202, 434–5, 486
Yüechi 1004, 1006

Zab
  Greater 273, 274, 275, 558, 856
  Lesser or Lower 274, 558, 748, 851
Zababa 920
Zabalam 18, 540
Zabibe 821
Zafar 55, 56, 1047
Zaghloul, Saad 72–3
Zagros mountains 4, 504, 514, 882, 952
Zahrani 1072
Zahrat adh-Dhra 171, 172
Zaker-Baal 846
Zalaja 781
zamru 183
Zand 1016
Zanjan 1007
Zardcha Khalifa 695

Zargaran 957
Zarzian 148
Zawi Çemi 203
zebu 215
Zendan-e Soleman 942
Zenobia 1027, 1037
Zerafshan 702, 703, 704
Zeraqon 639
Zeribar, lake 13
Zeus 910, 986, 994, 1069, 1072
  Akraius 1063
  Labryanda 981
  Lydian 904
  Megistos 992
Zeuxippus 1065
Zeyve Höyük 803
ziggurat 359, 541, 709ff., 714, 752, 853, 856, 858, 862, 863, 864, 919, 922ff., 925, 955, 981, 997, 2008
Zimri-Lim 271, 568, 748
zinc 307, 310, 329
Zincirli Höyük 60, 63, 64, 80, 803, 806ff., 808, 811
Ziqlab, Wadi 408, 409
Ziwiye 83, 108, 120, 890
ziyan 957
Ziyaret Tepe 572
Zizia 1074
Zizium 1074
Zizyphus spina Christi 496, 499
  see also jujube
Zodocatha 1074
Zohary, Daniel 166
Zoroastrianism 957, 975, 979, 1016, 1086
Zuhreh
  river 528, 529, 741, 937
  plain 516, 519, 527
zú-lum 183